Let's Review Regents:

U.S. History and Government

Revised Edition

John McGeehan, B.A., M.A., J.D.

Former American History/Constitutional Law Teacher,
Hampton Bays Secondary School, New York
Writer and Consultant for Curriculum Revision
in United States History and Government for
State of New York

Morris Gall, J.D., Ph.D.

Former Professor of Education and Assistant Dean,
Yeshiva University Graduate School of Education,
New York

Eugene V. Resnick, B.A., M.A.

Social Studies Teacher
Midwood High School
Brooklyn, New York

ACKNOWLEDGMENTS

p. 20   Copyright William H. Sadlier, Inc. with permission of publisher. All rights reserved.

p. 47   Reprinted from *Gavel to Gavel, A Guide To The Televised Proceedings of Congress* with permission from the Benton Foundation, Washington, D.C.

p. 75, 109, 262   Mary Beth Norton, David M. Katzman, Paul D. Escott, Howard P. Chudacoff, Thomas G. Patterson, William M. Tuttle, Jr. *A People And A Nation*, Fourth Edition © 1994 by Houghton Mifflin Company. Reprinted with permission.

p. 104   From The Americans 4E/1-VOL Ed., A Brief History 4th Ed. by Bedford 1985. Reprinted with permission of Wadsworth a division of Thomson Learning. *www.thomsonrights.com*

p. 194   From ETHNIC AMERICANS: A HISTORY OF IMMIGRATION AND ASSIMILATION by Leonard Dinnerstein and David Reimers. Copyright © 1975. Reprinted with permission.

p. 259   "The American Empire" from THE AMERICAN PAST: A SURVEY OF AMERICAN HISTORY by Joseph Conlin, Copyright © 1984 by Harcourt Brace Jovanovich, Inc., reprinted by permission of the publisher.

Published by Kaplan, Inc., d/b/a Barron's Educational Series
750 Third Avenue
New York, NY 10017
www.barronseduc.com

ISBN: 978-1-5062-6482-0

10 9 8 7 6 5 4 3 2 1

Kaplan, Inc., d/b/a Barron's Educational Series print books are available at special quantity discounts to use for sales promotions, employee premiums, or educational purposes. For more information or to purchase books, please call the Simon & Schuster special sales department at 866-506-1949.

TABLE OF CONTENTS

PREFACE

This edition is designed as a review of the New York State Regents Course in United States History and Government. The material follows the last major revision in the syllabus in Regents Social Studies: United States History and Government, which is used throughout New York State as the basis of a course of study in history on the secondary level. The curriculum incorporates the following Thirteen Enduring Constitutional Issues:

- National Power—limits and potential
- Federalism: the balance between nation and state
- The Judiciary: interpreter of the Constitution or shaper of public policy
- Civil Liberties: the balance between government and the individual
- Criminal Penalties—rights of the accused and protection of the community
- Equality: its definition as a Constitutional value
- The Rights of Women under the Constitution
- The Rights of Ethnic and Racial Groups under the Constitution
- Presidential Power in Wartime and in Foreign Affairs
- The Separation of Powers and the Capacity to Govern
- Avenues of Representation
- Property Rights and Economic Policy
- Constitutional Change and Flexibility

The following concepts and themes in United States history are also emphasized in the curriculum:

- Change
- Citizenship
- Civic Values
- Constitutional Principles
- Culture and Intellectual Life
- Diversity
- Economic Systems
- Environment
- Factors of Production
- Foreign Policy
- Government
- Human Systems
- Immigration and Migration
- Individuals, Groups, Institutions
- Interdependence
- Physical Systems
- Places and Regions

- Presidential Decisions and Actions
- Reform Movements
- Science and Technology

Although the material has been prepared to meet the needs of New York State students, this book can help students in any secondary-level U.S. History and Government course.

What Are the Special Features of This Book?

The arrangement of topical information parallels, for the most part, that of the New York State Regents syllabus in United States History and Government. Each of the seven major units begins with a brief explanation of the key ideas in the unit followed by a list of **connections** emphasized by the state syllabus. Each unit is broken down into several chapters that are consistent with the major divisions in the United States History and Government syllabus.

The format of the Regents Examination is as follows:

- **50 Multiple-Choice Questions**   **50 Minutes**   **55% of grade**
- **One Thematic Essay***   **45 Minutes**   **15% of grade**
- **One Document-Based Question***   **60 Minutes**   **30% of grade**

At the end of each chapter are multiple-choice questions and essays that coincide with the style of questions in Parts I, II, and III of the New York State Regents Examination. Each unit ends with **thematic** and **document-based essays**. In some cases, past Regents Examination questions have been included. The questions range from recall-drill to complex stimulus-based questions.

Stimulus-Based Questions

In future Regents Exams, there will be greater use of stimulus-based multiple-choice questions. This type of question asks you to respond to stimulus material: a primary or secondary source, images, charts, graphs, maps, etc. It is important that you note the date and source of the stimuli (chart, map, quote, political cartoon, etc.). You must take a moment to "read" the stimuli and be comfortable with the information presented. The multiple-choice question will test your ability to understand the stimulus material and apply that understanding to the historical issue at hand. The following is an example of a stimulus-based multiple-choice question.

*There will be no choice in the two essay sections.

1. The changes shown in the graph below support the recent concerns of Americans about the

**Percent Distribution of
United States Population
By Age, 1900 and 2000**

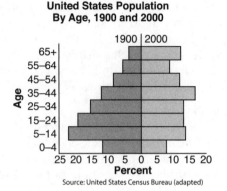

Source: United States Census Bureau (adapted)

A. future of Social Security and Medicare.
B. return to an agrarian society.
C. surplus of health care workers.
D. shortage of schools and colleges.

In this question, you should take note of the dates presented (1900 and 2000), the source (United States Census Bureau, primary source), and the data provided in each axis (age and percent). Once you understand the information presented, you should be able to conclude that Social Security and Medicare are age-based entitlements and, therefore, the best answer would be choice A.

Because of the intimidating amount and complexity of the information presented in a course on United States History and Government, you should find the **Chronology of Events in American History** at the end of the book helpful. It shows the cause and effect pattern of our nation's story. This edition also contains a **Glossary of Terms**, short biographies of **Notable Americans**, a list of **Historical Documents**, and a collection of significant **Quotations**, organized chronologically. These materials are intended both as reference aids and guides for study and review. Key United States Supreme Court decisions appear at the beginning of the book.

Complementing the text are graphs, political cartoons, maps, and charts to help portray necessary information, express points of view, and allow you to apply interpretive skills.

Historiography

Historians aim to reconstruct a record of human events into what we refer to as history. You must understand that history does not present us with absolute answers, but often requires us to make judgments based on evidence that may require thoughtful interpretation. Historiography is actually the history of history. You must be able to distinguish between primary and secondary sources. As you take on any course in history, you must learn to think like historians and ask the following questions as you read historical accounts:

- Who is writing the history?
- Does the nature of the account have an agenda (as most do)?
- How might the historian's gender, age, and affiliations (national, ideological, religious, economic) affect the agenda?
- Is there a selection (or lack of selection) of facts and use of sources that may promote a certain outcome of the historian's work?

The New York City Department of Education has set forth "Thinking and Process Skills for Social Studies." Among these are the following:

- Comparing and contrasting
- Identifying cause and effect
- Drawing inferences and making conclusions
- Evaluating
- Distinguishing fact *vs.* opinion
- Handling diversity of interpretations

As you study history and develop an understanding of the actual events being discussed, apply the questions and skills listed above. Many times a grasp of historiography can be the very point of the assignment at hand, including test questions.

The Regents Examination

The edition of **Let's Review: United States History and Government** follows the syllabus of the New York State Regents curriculum in United States History and Government and is designed to prepare students for the Regents Exam. Here are some key tips to consider at test time:

- Preparation for the Regents Exam begins the first day of class. Good study habits, effective note-taking, completion of all assignments, and a positive attitude throughout the year will make success on any exam easier at the completion of the course.
- Follow directions closely on the test itself. Many students are not successful because they do not provide requested information, or they leave sections of the question unanswered.

- **Part I: 50 Multiple-Choice Questions, 50 minutes, 55% of score.** Answer all questions. Budget your time. Watch out for the answer that is correct in itself, but does not answer the question. Do easy questions first, then go back to more difficult questions. Use the process of elimination when necessary.
- **Part II: One Thematic Essay, 45 minutes, 15% of score.** Write a well-organized essay that includes an introduction, several paragraphs that address the task, and a conclusion. Be aware of key terms in the question, for example, **show**, **discuss**, **compare**. The thematic essay does not ask for only a recollection of facts, but rather asks the student to focus on themes and to demonstrate critical thinking. Those scoring the essay will use the following generic scoring rubric:

**Generic Scoring Rubric
Thematic Essay**

5

- Shows a thorough understanding of the theme
- Addresses all aspects of the task
- Shows an ability to analyze, evaluate, compare, and/or contrast issues and events
- Richly supports essay with relevant facts, examples, and details
- Writes a well-developed essay, consistently demonstrating a logical and clear plan of organization
- Includes a strong introduction and conclusion
- Is more analytical than descriptive

4

- Shows a good understanding of the theme
- Addresses all aspects of the task
- Shows an ability to analyze, evaluate, compare, and/or contrast issues and events
- Includes relevant facts, examples, and details, but may not support all aspects of the task evenly
- Writes a well-developed essay, demonstrating a logical and clear plan of organization
- Includes a good introduction and conclusion
- Is analytical and descriptive

3

- Presents a satisfactory understanding of the theme
- Addresses most aspects of the task or addresses all aspects in a limited way
- Is able to analyze or evaluate issues and events, but not in any depth

- Writes a satisfactorily developed essay, demonstrating a general plan of organization
- Uses some facts, examples, and details
- Restates the theme in the introduction and concludes with a simple restatement of the theme
- Is more descriptive than analytical

2

- Attempts to address the theme, but uses vague and/or inaccurate information
- Develops a faulty analysis or evaluation of theme
- Writes a poorly organized essay, lacking focus and using few facts, examples, and details
- Has vague or is missing introduction and/or conclusion

1

- Shows limited understanding of the theme; omits concrete examples; details are weak or nonexistent
- Lacks an analysis or evaluation of the issues and events beyond stating vague and/or inaccurate facts
- Attempts to complete the task, but essay demonstrates a major weakness in organization
- Uses little or no accurate or relevant facts, details, or examples
- Has no introduction or conclusion

0

- Fails to address the theme
- Is illegible
- Blank paper

- **Part III: One Document-Based Question, 60 minutes, 30% of score.** The Document-Based Question is divided into two parts: Part A short-answer section (15%) and Part B essay (15%). Following the questions, approximately eight short documents are provided. Each Part A question will address a specific document. Answer the question using the document and the author's point of view, and incorporate information about the time period from which the document has been selected. The Part B essay requires that the student state their position (thesis) in an introductory paragraph, then develop their argument in the body of the essay using information from most of the documents to support their position. Using outside information from the student's knowledge of the time period will enhance the essay. The student should include a brief conclusion restating his or her position. As with the multiple-choice section, budget your time. Those scoring the essay will use the following generic scoring rubric:

Generic Scoring Rubric
Document-Based Question

5

- Thoroughly addresses all aspects of the task by accurately analyzing and interpreting most of the documents
- Incorporates relevant outside information
- Richly supports essay with relevant facts, examples, and details
- Writes a well-developed essay, consistently demonstrating a logical and clear plan of organization
- Uses information from the documents in the body of the essay
- Includes a strong introduction and conclusion
- Is more analytical than descriptive

4

- Addresses all aspects of the task by accurately analyzing and interpreting most of the documents
- Incorporates relevant outside information
- Includes relevant facts, examples, and details, but may not support all aspects of the task evenly
- Writes a well-developed essay, demonstrating a logical and clear plan of organization
- Includes a good introduction and conclusion
- Is both analytical and descriptive

3

- Addresses most aspects of the task or addresses all aspects in a limited way; uses some of the documents
- Incorporates limited or no relevant outside information
- Uses some facts, examples, and details, but discussion is more descriptive than analytical
- Writes a satisfactorily developed essay, demonstrating a general plan of organization
- States the theme in the introduction and concludes with a simple restatement of the theme or topic

2

- Attempts to address some aspects of the task, making limited use of the documents
- Presents little or no relevant outside information
- Uses few facts, examples, and details; discussion simply restates contents of the documents
- Writes a poorly organized essay, lacking focus
- Has vague or is missing introduction and/or conclusion

- Shows limited understanding of the task with vague, unclear references to the documents
- Presents no relevant outside information
- Attempts to complete the task, but essay demonstrates a major weakness in organization
- Uses little or no accurate or relevant facts, details, or examples
- Has no introduction or conclusion

0

- Fails to address the task
- Is illegible
- Blank paper

Tips for Regents Essay Writing

To help explain some of the following essay-writing tips, refer to the following Thematic Essay Question from the June 2013 U.S. History and Government Regents Examination.

Theme:

Throughout the history of the United States, the primary goal of its foreign policy has been to protect the nation's interests. The United States has taken military and economic foreign policy actions to achieve this goal. These actions have resulted in varying degrees of success.

Task:

Select *two* military *and/or* economic foreign policy actions taken by the United States to protect its national interests and for *each*

- Describe the historical circumstances that led to the action.
- Discuss the extent to which this action was successful in protecting the national interests.

You may use any military and/or economic foreign policy action taken by the United States to protect its national interests. Some suggestions you might wish to consider include fighting the Mexican-American War (1846–1848), declaring war on Spain (1898), implementing the Open Door Policy (1899), building the Panama Canal (1904–1914), carrying out the Marshall Plan (1947–1952), engaging in the Cuban Missile Crisis (1962), fighting the Vietnam War (1964–1973), and fighting the Persian Gulf War (1990–1991).

1. For the question posed above, first read the theme and make sure you understand the question presented. Take a moment to make sure you understand the terms *foreign policy*, *military*, and *economic*.
2. Pay attention to key instructions. The writers of the exam place words such as **two**, **and/or**, and **each** in boldface for a reason. For example, if you know two military actions well, do not feel that you have to use an economic action.
3. Pay attention to words directing your task; *Describe historical circumstances* and *Discuss the extent of success*.
4. Answer the question, the whole question, and nothing but the question. A helpful hint is to go back and re-read the question multiple times while writing your essay.
5. Take time to think about your response before you start writing. Use the scrap paper provided. You may find that you list 4–5 foreign policy actions. Take a few moments of thought to decide which actions you know best.
6. Try to write your sentences in the following format: Term + identification + interpretive comment. Example: The Mexican-American War, a conflict between the United States and Mexico between 1846 and 1848, resulted in the territorial expansion of the United States and the establishment of the Rio Grande as the border between Mexico and the United States.
7. In your introductory paragraph, demonstrate that you understand the task at hand. Perhaps start by defining the term "foreign policy" (e.g., a government's strategy in dealing with foreign nations). Follow by identifying the two foreign policy actions you plan to address in your response (e.g., Mexican-American War, Cuban Missile Crisis).
8. Your middle paragraphs (two) are your direct responses to the task presented. In other words, the first middle paragraph will identify the foreign policy action, **describe** circumstances that led to putting that action in place, **and discuss** the extent of its success. Remember, *extent* also allows for a discussion of lack of success! With regards to the Mexican War, success can be argued with the settlement of the Texas boundary with Mexico and the gaining of the Mexican Cession (New Mexico Territory and California). The "A+" response will mention that another result was the aggravation of the slavery extension question.
9. In your final paragraph, summarize what has been presented above. Remember, your final paragraph is not the place to be introducing new examples.

10. With regards to the Document-Based Questions (DBQ), the preceding writing tips are also applicable. Keep in mind that the DBQ is actually the easier of the test essays.
11. Once you have read the question presented, brainstorm and jot down all the facts you recall before reading the documents.
12. Read the documents and underline the main points of each document. As you read the document, write down one or more facts about the document that come to mind.
13. Now that you know what you have to work with, develop your thesis.

    Example: *The precedents that George Washington set as America's first president greatly benefited the American political system.*

    Place your thesis at the end of the introductory paragraph.
14. Categorize your facts and documents into 2–3 subtopics and give support to your thesis.
15. Finish with a concluding paragraph.

SUPREME COURT CASES

SUPREME COURT CASES (continued)

Date	Cases	Concepts	Page
1957	*Watkins* v. *United States*	Un-American Activities/ Self-Incrimination	417
1961	*Mapp* v. *Ohio*	Warrantless Search/Privacy versus Police Powers	536
1962	*Baker* v. *Carr*	Reapportion/Equal Protection Voter's Rights	483
1962	*Engle* v. *Vitale*	School Prayer/Establishment	536
1963	*Gideon* v. *Wainwright*	Rights of the Accused/Counsel	536
1964	*Heart of Atlanta Motel* v. *United States*	Commerce Clause/Property Rights/Discrimination	483
1966	*Miranda* v. *Arizona*	Rights of Accused Self-Incrimination	536
1969	*Tinker* v. *Des Moines*	Student Symbolic Speech	514
1971	*New York Times Co.* v. *United States*	Free Press/Executive Power	510
1973	*Roe* v. *Wade*	Privacy/Abortion	485
1974	*United States* v. *Nixon*	Impeachment Separation of Powers	539
1978	*Regents of the University of California* v. *Bakke*	Affirmative Action	486
1985	*New Jersey* v. *T.L.O.*	Student Search/Due Process	553
1986	*Bowers* v. *Hadwick*	Privacy and Anti-Sodomy Law	666
1990	*Cruzan* v. *Director, Missouri Department of Health*	Right to Die/Police Power	566
1992	*Planned Parenthood of Southeastern Pennsylvania* v. *Casey*	Privacy, Abortion	566
1995	*Vernonia School District* v. *Acton*	Student Search	553
1997	*Reno* v. *A.C.L.U.*	Speech and the Internet	585
1998	*Clinton* v. *City of New York*	Line Item Veto	585
2000	*Bush* v. *Gore*	2000 Presidential Election	595
2001	*U.S.* v. *Oakland Cannabis Buyers Cooperative*	Medicinal Marijuana	664
2004	*Elk Grove* v. *Newdow*	Pledge/Establishment Clause	670
2005	*Kelo* v. *City of New London*	Eminent Domain	672
2006	*Hamdan* v. *Rumsfeld*	Separation of Powers	646
2007	*Ledbetter* v. *Goodyear Tire and Rubber Co.*	Fair Pay Act	671

SUPREME COURT CASES (continued)

Date	Cases	Concepts	Page
2008	*District of Columbia* v. *Heller*	Right to Bear Arms	663
2010	*Citizens United* v. *Federal Election Commission*	Speech and Political Contributions	625
2010	*McDonald* v. *Chicago*	Right to Bear Arms	663
2013	*United States* v. *Windsor*	Marriage Rights	667
2013	*Shelby County* v. *Holder*	Voting Rights	638
2014	*Burwell* v. *Hobby Lobby*	Religious Rights	670
2014	*Riley* v. *California*	Arrest and Search	672
2015	*Obergefell* v. *Hodges*	Marriage Rights	667
2016	*Whole Women's Health* v. *Hellerstedt*	Abortion Rights	669
2016	*United States* v. *Texas*	Immigration, Executive Powers	640

UNITED STATES HISTORY DOCUMENTS*

UNITED STATES HISTORY DOCUMENTS* (continued)

UNITED STATES HISTORY DOCUMENTS* (continued)

Date	Document	Page
1987	Iran-Contra Report	559–560
1990	Americans with Disabilities Act	565
1993	North American Free Trade Agreement	584
1994	Brady Law	583
1998	Kyoto Protocols	673
1998	International Criminal Court	645
1998–99	Clinton Impeachment Proceedings	592–593
1999	Senate Rejection of Comprehensive Test Ban Treaty	593
2001	USA PATRIOT Act	613–614
2002	State of the Union Address	615
2004	9/11 Commission Report	615
2005	Central American Free Trade Agreement	696
2009	The American Recovery and Reinvestment Act of 2009	632
2010	Dodd-Frank Wall Street Reform and Consumer Protection Act	633
2010	Don't Ask, Don't Tell Repeal Act	666–667
2010	Patient Protection and Affordable Care Act	634–635

*Currently cited in the 11th Grade United States History and Government Scope and Sequence as notable documents.

UNIT ONE ────────────────────────

Constitutional Foundations of the United States

> **KEY IDEAS** Unit One explores both the formative stage of the Constitution and its implementation through the Civil War period. Chapters 1 and 2 illustrate the origins of the document, the actual structure and functions of its components, and the tests our constitutional system faced in its early development.

UNIT CONNECTIONS: By the end of the unit you should understand the following points.

- Development of American political institutions
- Reasons for the American Revolution
- Strengths and weaknesses of the Articles of Confederation
- Necessity of Constitutional Convention
- Constitution: Structure, federalism, and basic principles
- Bill of Rights: Balance between government and the individual
- Hamilton and Jefferson; rise of political parties
- Maturing of the Supreme Court, the Marshall Court
- Early foreign policy, Monroe Doctrine, Manifest Destiny
- National unity versus developing sectionalism
- Geographic and economic growth of the new nation
- Early immigrant experience
- The Age of Jackson and reform movements
- Constitutional Crisis: the American Civil War

THE CONSTITUTION: THE FOUNDATION OF AMERICAN SOCIETY

FOUNDATIONS, REVOLUTION, AND CONFEDERATION

> Let Americans disdain to be the instruments of European greatness. Let the thirteen states, bound together in a strict and indissoluble Union, concur in erecting one great American system, superior to the control of all transatlantic force or influence, and able to dictate the terms of the connection between the old and the new world!
>
> Alexander Hamilton, *The Federalist* (1787–1788), No. 11

Before the founding of the American republic, there were few examples in history of a successful republic that included more than a single city or a small confederation of a few cities and territories. The ancient city-state of Athens and the republic of Rome contributed many important concepts to the Western tradition of government, including direct and representative democracy, jury systems, and the development of legal systems. However, when Athens and Rome began to expand and took over new territories, their democratic governments eventually came to an end. They first became tyrannical empires and then either collapsed into anarchy or fell under the rule of military or oligarchic despotism.

Although the U.S. Constitution was not the first one in history, it is the oldest written constitution still in effect. The word **constitution** means the entire legal framework of a nation, or the nation's plan of government. A written constitution that specifically set forth a plan of government, established its institutions, and outlined the rights of citizens as the American Constitution does, is a relatively new development in history.

Foundations

Democratic Roots in the English Experience

During the colonial period (1607–1763) many of the political institutions of England were transmitted to the English colonies in America. Four major landmarks in English history provided a foundation for American constitutional government:

3

- *Magna Carta (1215).* Although this document was originally designed to protect the feudal nobles from the absolute rule of the king, it later came to apply to all English subjects and provided that (1) the king was subject to the rule of law; (2) Parliament was responsible for the levying of taxes; and (3) all accused persons were guaranteed a trial by jury of peers, or equals.

- *English Bill of Rights (1689).* This document was truly revolutionary because, at a time when absolute monarchs ruled, it established the idea that there were limits on the powers of kings and queens. The English Bill of Rights, much of which was later incorporated into our own, provided that (1) the king could not interfere with parliamentary elections and debates; (2) the king could not suspend laws, levy taxes, or maintain an army without the consent of Parliament; and (3) the people were guaranteed basic rights to **petition the government**, to an **impartial and speedy trial**, to protection against **excessive fines and bails**, and to protection from **cruel and unusual punishment**.

- *Common Law.* In England, the verdicts of judges were written down, collected, and became the basis for future legal decisions. These common practices and legal decisions formed a body of law known as **common law**. Certain **fundamental rights** that developed from the English common law and later became part of statute law were designed to protect the citizen from tyrannical government.

- *A Bicameral Legislature.* By the 14th century, Parliament, the legislative body of English government, had divided into two houses or chambers: (1) the **House of Lords**, consisting of higher clergy and nobility; and (2) the **House of Commons**, representing the wealthy middle class.

Constitutional Development in Colonial America

Many of the democratic characteristics of American constitutional government can be traced back to the colonial experience. Two important precedents that influenced the development of government in the colonies concerned (1) the structure of government (primarily the distribution of power among its parts); and (2) the relationship of the individual to government. By the time the colonies were being settled, English subjects had already developed a theory of **limited government**, or the idea that government did not have absolute power, but was restricted by certain laws and procedures.

- *Colonial Charters.* During the early period of English settlement, the colonies in America were largely self-governing. This was due to the privileges granted by the colonial charters and because geographical distance and other conditions made it difficult for the Crown to tightly control the colonies during the 17th century. Each colony had a charter, or grant, of privileges from the king. There were three basic types of colonial government, the major difference being in the way the governor was chosen. In the **self-governing** colonies, such as Connecticut and Rhode Island, the governor was chosen by the colonists. In the **proprietary** colonies, such as Pennsylvania, Maryland, and Delaware, the governor was selected by the proprietor. In the **royal** colonies, such as New York, Virginia, and Georgia, the governor and other high officials were selected by the king. Later in the colonial period, most of the colonies were made royal colonies in order to bring them under direct control of the Crown.

• *Colonial Governing Instruments.* England did not send a governor and a council to each settlement in North America (as was the practice of the Spanish and the French). As a result, other methods of government were used in some of the English settlements in the early colonial period. Among these were the joint-stock corporation, the concept of government by compact, and the proprietorship.

Joint-Stock Principle. Some colonies were settled by a joint-stock company, a form of business organization. The company received a charter from the English Crown granting it a monopoly over trade and colonization for a period of years within a specific area. In return, the company was to give the Crown a share of profits earned and precious metals such as gold or silver that it acquired.

Virginia, the earliest successful English colony, was founded in 1607 by the Virginia Company of London under a grant from the Crown. In 1619 the governor allowed the eligible voters in the colony to elect a local representative assembly. This lawmaking body, called the **Virginia House of Burgesses**, was the first elected legislature in the colonies and marked the first step toward representative government in the colonies.

The Massachusetts Bay Colony, which was also established by a jointstock company, was founded by middle-class Puritans who wanted to establish a refuge for their religious beliefs in North America.

Government by Compact. Although the settlements of Plymouth, Rhode Island, Connecticut, and New Haven were never as politically important as Virginia and Massachusetts Bay, they were significant in that their governments were based on a **social contract**. In 1620, before they landed at Plymouth, the settlers on board the *Mayflower* realized that they had no recognized authoritative body and made plans for self-government. The adult males drew up and signed an agreement that later became known as the **Mayflower Compact**, in which they agreed to obey the laws that they would adopt. They agreed to consult each other about matters affecting the community and to abide by majority rule.

In 1636, after his banishment from Massachusetts Bay for advocating **separation of church and state**, **Roger Williams** and his followers founded the town of Providence in Rhode Island. They entered into a compact agreement very similar to that of the Plymouth settlers. In 1644 Williams obtained a charter for the colony of Rhode Island that did not require voters to be church members.

The settlements of New Haven and those along the Connecticut River were also settled by Puritan dissenters moving southward. Perhaps the most significant of all the early covenants was the **Fundamental Orders of Connecticut**, adopted in 1639, the first written constitution in America. The Fundamental Orders implied that government rested upon the **consent of the governed** and that it should express the will of the majority.

Proprietorship. The proprietary colonies were established by a feudal patent or a royal grant of land in the New World given by the Crown, usually to friends or relatives. Under this grant, the proprietor, or owner, was given the right to establish a colony and to rule it.

Such a royal grant was used in the founding of Maryland by George Calvert, the first Lord Baltimore, in 1632. James, the Duke of York, the younger brother of King Charles II, became the proprietor of New York after the Dutch surrendered what had been their colony of New Netherland to a British fleet stationed in the Hudson River in 1664.

Signs of Colonial Unity

Colonial unity, within the colonies and among them, evolved slowly. Although each colony maintained independent ties with England and in many ways acted independently, early attempts at achieving colonial union were made both by the colonies themselves and by England in order to gain greater control over its colonies.

• *The New England Confederation (1643–1684).* Massachusetts Bay, Plymouth, Connecticut, and New Haven made up the membership of this Puritan confederacy.

• *Dominion of New England (1684–1688).* In 1686 King James II created the Dominion of New England, which joined the colonies of New York, New Jersey, and the New England colonies of Massachusetts Bay, Plymouth, New Hampshire, Maine, Rhode Island, and Connecticut under one government. **Town meetings**, the basic form of local government in New England, were restricted. James took these actions because the colonists refused to comply with the Navigation Acts, which were designed to regulate the trade of the colonies. As a storm of opposition rose from the colonists, the **Glorious Revolution** of 1688 in England brought about the overthrow of James II and confirmed the supremacy of Parliament over the king. As a result, the Dominion of New England collapsed.

• *The Albany Congress (1754).* In 1754 England called the Albany Congress to establish intercolonial cooperation in dealing with the growing French influence in the Ohio Valley and in lower Canada and to attempt to keep the Iroquois Indians loyal to the British. The **Albany Plan of Union**, drafted by **Benjamin Franklin**, who proposed that the colonies unite in a permanent union for defense. Although the Albany Plan failed, it introduced the concept of a **federal** plan of representative government, with specific powers given to a central authority, which later served as a model for the United States Constitution.

- *The Iroquois Confederation.* The **Iroquois Confederation** included the Six Nations—the Mohawk, Tuscarora, Cayuga, Seneca, Onondaga, and Oneida nations. Its purpose was to keep peace among the tribes and to provide for mutual defense. Based on a federal system, the individual nations maintained their independence while granting some powers to the Confederation. It is likely that the union served as a model for colonial union and influenced the Albany Plan of Union and, later, the Articles of Confederation.

Benjamin Franklin drafted a plan for a colonial union in 1754.

Problems of Control

By the middle of the 18th century, there were thirteen British colonies in North America. By 1750 most of the colonies had been made royal colonies, with governing structures reflecting those of the British government. A governor's council, made up mainly of conservative, wealthy colonists, sat as an upper house of the legislature. It could amend or reject legislation passed by the popularly elected assembly. This lower house of the legislature was chosen by the colonists who met the property qualifications for voting. The assembly could initiate tax bills, exercise administrative oversight concerning the expenditure of funds, and fix qualifications for their own membership. The governor, appointed by the Crown, had the power to veto legislation passed by the colonial assembly and to call or dissolve the assembly.

Frequent conflicts between the popularly elected assemblies and the royally appointed governors symbolized the struggle for colonial self-rule during the 18th century. An early example of this conflict was **Bacon's Rebellion** in Virginia. **Nathaniel Bacon**, a member of the Virginia House of Burgesses, led an uprising against the royal governor Berkeley that resulted in the burning of Jamestown in 1676. The governors gradually lost power to the colonial assemblies largely because the assemblies' control of finances allowed them to deny appropriations of money to governors who defied the popular will. The bulleted factors on page 9 allowed the colonial legislatures to expand their powers and control over colonial government.

Figure 1.1 The English Colonies in North America

- *Expansion of Colonial Suffrage.* Although property ownership was a requirement for voting in the colonies, the abundance of inexpensive land made it possible for many colonists to own property and therefore to vote. By the time of the Revolution, about 75 percent of the adult white males in the colonies were able to vote.

- *Actual Representation* v. *Virtual Representation.* **Virtual representation** was the belief that all English subjects were represented in Parliament simply by virtue of their status as citizens. However, the colonists came to believe in the concept of **actual representation**, the idea that to be properly represented in a legislature, citizens had to vote directly for delegates who represented their interests. By the time of the American Revolution, the American colonists formally rejected the British argument that they were "virtually represented" in Parliament.

- *Separation of Powers.* Rather than the overlapping of many powers between the executive and the legislature, such as existed between the British Crown and Parliament, the colonists believed that the powers of their legislatures ought to be free from executive (governor) control.

- *England's "Salutary Neglect."* Because of England's own problems— such as the Glorious Revolution of 1688 and wars with Holland, France, and Spain during the 17th century—the local governing bodies of the colonies were allowed to expand their powers and activities. During this period of so-called salutary neglect, the British allowed the colonies a great amount of self-government and economic freedom.

Revolution and Independence

Importance of Locke's Ideas

> The natural liberty of man is to be free from any superior power on earth, and not to be under the will or legislative authority of man, but to have only the law of nature as his rule. The liberty of man in society is to be under no other legislative power but that established in the commonwealth; nor under the dominion of any will or restraint of any law but what that legislative shall enact according to the trust put in it.
> John Locke, *The Second Treatise of Government* (1690)

In this quote the English philosopher and political thinker **John Locke** (1632–1704) refers to the law of nature. **Thomas Jefferson** later stated this idea in the Declaration of Independence:

> We hold these truths to be self-evident, that all men are created equal, that they are endowed by their Creator with certain inalienable rights, that among these are **life, liberty, and the pursuit of happiness**.
> Declaration of Independence (1776)

9

The second half of Locke's quote stresses the importance of self-rule and the responsibility of a government to those whom it governs. Again, Jefferson's reliance upon the thoughts of Locke becomes apparent when one examines the Declaration of Independence:

> That to secure these rights, governments are instituted among men, deriving their just powers from the consent of the governed. That whenever any form of government becomes destructive to these ends, it is the right of the people to alter or to abolish it, and to institute a new government . . .
>
> Declaration of Independence (1776)

Natural law, as referred to in Locke's *The Second Treatise of Government,* includes those rights essential to the natural existence of humankind. Among these are the rights to life, liberty, and property and the belief that all people are equal in the possession of these rights.

The Fifth Amendment to the United States Constitution was prepared by **James Madison** as a necessary addition to the Constitution (along with the rest of the **Bill of Rights**) to place restrictions upon both the federal and state governments. The Fifth Amendment reads in part:

> No person shall . . . be deprived of life, liberty, or property, without due process of law.
>
> Fifth Amendment to the United States Constitution (1791)

Theory of Limited Government (Locke, Montesquieu, and Rousseau)

The period of English colonization came at a time when European political thinkers were setting forth the idea that governments should be structured on a foundation of law and that a contract existed between the government and the governed. It was not too great a step from that idea to the belief that revolution against those who abused the existing contract was justified. The makers of the American revolution and later the founders of the constitutional system of government were guided in their actions and beliefs by the theory of natural rights and the idea of representative government, as advocated by Locke; the idea of separation of the powers of government by dividing it into **executive**, **legislative**, and **judicial** branches, as outlined by **Montesquieu**; and finally, by the idea of **popular sovereignty**, as championed by **Rousseau**.

Although the common sentiment among the colonists on the eve of the Revolution was that the law of England prevailed, a transformation was taking place. The strong tendency toward political involvement among the colonists, combined with the evolution of a uniquely American form of representative government, made it difficult for the American colonists to find their place in the English parliamentary system.

British Mercantilism and American Capitalism

By the end of the French and Indian War in 1763, the American colonies had grown to be a strong and thriving part of the British Empire. This was a result of lax British regulation under the policy of salutary neglect, which allowed a considerable amount of manufacturing to develop within the colonies. It was also due to the "triangular trade" that involved Africa, the West Indies, and the colonies.

• *Mercantilism.* During the 17th and 18th centuries, England, as did most European countries, believed that power depended upon monetary wealth and that the colonies were a source of wealth in that they would (1) provide raw materials for the mother country; (2) import manufactured products of higher values from England; and (3) not compete with the mother country in economic activities.

After 1763 Britain decided to tighten its control over both the political and economic affairs of the colonies. To carry this out, Britain ended the policy of salutary neglect and began to enforce the mercantilist system, a policy that aroused strong colonial opposition.

Because of the debts incurred from fighting the French and Indian War (1754–1763) and the need to protect the new territory acquired from France after the war, Britain found it necessary to create new sources of revenue. Since the British felt that the colonists should help pay for their defense, Britain decided to raise money by taxing the colonists. In addition, it tried to place restrictions on westward expansion. After the French and Indian War, many colonists began to migrate westward. This invasion of Indian land by white settlers resulted in Pontiac's Rebellion (May 1763), an uprising in which several Indian tribes joined together and attacked settlements and forts on the frontier. The British, who could not protect the frontier, and who wished to avoid further conflicts, issued the **Proclamation of 1763**. This forbade settlement west of the Appalachian Mountains. Encouraged by an adventurous and growing population, which had grown from a quarter of a million in 1700 to over two million in 1770, the colonists continued to settle in western Pennsylvania, Tennessee, and Kentucky.

The New Colonial System and the Formation of the American Resistance Movement

In its attempt to more closely supervise the colonies, Britain's "new" colonial policy had four main objectives: (1) to regulate western expansion and Indian affairs; (2) to keep a standing army in America; (3) to enforce the Navigation Acts; and (4) to raise money in the colonies through taxes including, for the first time, direct taxation of the colonists for the purpose of raising revenue rather than obtaining revenue through the regulation of trade.

• *The Grenville Ministry (1763–1765).* At the urging of George Grenville, the British Prime Minister from 1763 to 1765, Parliament set out to raise money to balance Britain's budget by strictly enforcing the existing mercantile laws and by passing new taxes for the colonies.

The Sugar Act (1764). Designed to replace the Molasses Act of 1733, the Sugar Act lowered the duty on imported molasses in an attempt to stop colonial smuggling.

Currency Reform (1764). The Currency Act of 1764 forbade the colonies from issuing paper money.

The Stamp Act (1765). Passed in February 1765, the Stamp Act was the second measure in Grenville's program that attempted to raise revenue to pay for Britain's costs in defending the colonies. It required that certain documents be written or printed on paper carrying a stamp from the British treasury office.

The tax, a constant reminder of Parliament's authority, affected nearly every aspect of commercial and industrial life in the colonies. Especially hard hit by the new tax were lawyers, merchants, and editors—those with the greatest ability to voice their objections to the revenue-raising measure. Those accused of violating its provisions could be tried in an admiralty court—without a jury.

When news of the passage of the Stamp Act reached the colonies in March 1765, opposition exploded. Following a fiery speech by **Patrick Henry**, the Virginia House of Burgesses adopted the Virginia Resolves, which denied that Parliament had the right to tax the colonies without their consent, claiming that only the House of Burgesses could tax the Virginia colonists.

With Massachusetts in the lead, delegates from nine colonies met in New York in October 1765 to voice their opposition to the Stamp Act. The resolutions drafted by the **Stamp Act Congress** rejected the concept of "virtual representation" in the House of Commons and they agreed to resist all taxes not consented to by the colonial legislatures.

Colonial opposition to the Stamp Act resulted in numerous nonimportation agreements, in which the colonists promised not to buy British goods. Early in 1766 Parliament repealed the Stamp Act, causing much celebration in the colonies.

The Declaratory Act. Early in 1766 Parliament also passed the Declaratory Act, which stated that Parliament had absolute authority over the colonies "in all cases whatsoever." This meant that Parliament had the authority to tax the colonies, in spite of colonial protests over the Stamp Act.

The Stamp Act crisis was significant in several ways. The Stamp Act Congress and the effectiveness of the widespread nonimportation agreements showed that the colonies could unite and work together. Resistance groups, such as the **Sons of Liberty**, coordinated opposition throughout the colonies. Secondly, the crisis helped bring into focus the primary issues that existed between Britain and the American colonies: the status of the colonists in the British Empire, and the taxation powers of Parliament over the American colonies.

• *The Townshend Acts (1767–1770).* Following the repeal of the Stamp Act, King George III appointed William Pitt as Prime Minister and **Charles Townshend** as Chancellor of the Exchequer. The Townshend Acts included new taxes and stricter enforcement of the existing mercantile laws.

Import Duties on Glass, Lead, Paint, Paper, and Tea. These were passed to regulate trade and therefore were within the right of Parliament to create and enforce. However, their stated purpose was for "the support of civil government, in such provinces as it shall be found necessary." That is, they were to raise money to defend the colonies. Therefore, the colonists objected to the import duties because they were a tax measure to raise revenue, not a commercial regulation.

Board of Commissioners and Writs of Assistance. Under the Townshend Acts, Parliament established a special Board of Commissioners within the colonies to enforce the Navigation Acts and to make sure the duties were collected. The use of writs of assistance, or search warrants, by British customs officials to search colonists' businesses, homes, and ships for smuggled goods was approved. Opposition to the writs of assistance was best expressed by **James Otis**, a Boston attorney. Using the principles of natural law, which included the freedom of one's "house" from unauthorized searches and seizures without **probable cause**, Otis argued that an act of Parliament against natural rights was void.

Opposition to the Townshend Acts. Opposition to the Townshend Acts in the colonies was strong. As colonial discontent and resistance grew, the difficulty of maintaining order increased. As a result, more British troops were sent to America. A period of greater disorder followed as customs agents were mobbed and tarred and feathered, and troops were harassed.

• *The Boston Massacre.* On March 5, 1770, ironically the same day the Townshend duties (except the tax on tea) were repealed, a

The Boston Massacre, in an engraving by Paul Revere.

few British soldiers in Boston fired upon a hostile Boston crowd, killing five persons. The event was publicized in newspapers throughout the colonies as a "massacre" against the defenseless colonists. With the help of engravings created by **Paul Revere** and pamphlets of anti-British propaganda written by **Samuel Adams**, the leader of the Sons of Liberty, the American colonists became further inflamed in their resentment of British rule.

• *The Tea Act (1773).* To help the struggling **British East India Company**, Parliament decided to allow the direct shipment of tea from India to the colonies without having the tea go through London, thereby reducing the price of tea sold in the colonies. The Tea Act meant that British tea could now be purchased in the colonies for about half the price of smuggled tea.

The colonists who smuggled and sold the tea took the lead in opposing the Tea Act. On the evening of December 16, 1773, approximately 60 men, thinly disguised as Mohawk Indians, boarded three ships in Boston harbor and threw 342 chests of tea worth approximately £10,000 ($15,000) into the sea.

• *The Coercive, or "Intolerable," Acts (1774).* In March 1774, in response to the Boston Tea Party, Britain retaliated with five acts that the colonies called the "Intolerable" Acts.

The Boston Port Act closed the port of Boston until the colonists paid the British East India Company for the destroyed tea.

The Massachusetts Government Act altered the Massachusetts charter of 1691, giving Britain greater control over the colony and severely limiting self-government.

The Administration of Justice Act provided that, in the cases of crimes committed by officials of the Crown while enforcing British laws, the trial could be moved to Great Britain.

The Quartering Act, passed June 2, 1774, gave British officials within the colonies broad authority to quarter, or house, troops wherever they chose in a town, rather than in barracks provided by the colonies.

The Quebec Act was passed in an effort to maintain the allegiance of the French. It allowed Catholicism and French civil law in Canada and established the boundaries of Quebec as the Ohio River on the south, the Mississippi River on the west, and the Proclamation Line of 1763 on the east. The Quebec Act, though not passed to punish the colonists, outraged them for several reasons. First, it appeared to violate several colonial charters by destroying the claims of three colonies to lands west of the Appalachians. Second, it allowed religious freedom to the Roman Catholics, a religion strongly disliked by Protestant colonists.

Declaration and Revolution (1774–1783)

Most colonists strongly opposed the Intolerable Acts, and some came close to outright rebellion. On a call from Virginia, all the colonies except Georgia sent delegates to a **Continental Congress**.

• *The First Continental Congress (1774).* It met at Carpenters Hall in Philadelphia on September 5, 1774. The delegates at the Congress were narrowly divided between those who favored resistance and those who advocated conciliation. Although illness kept **Thomas Jefferson** of Virginia away from the meeting, his *Summary View of the Rights of British America,* claiming Parliament to be only the "legislature of one part of the empire," was used as supportive argument by the more radical members at the Congress.

Declaration of Rights and Grievances. Adopted by Congress on October 14, 1774, the Declaration of Rights and Grievances held that: (1) obedience would be paid only to the king; (2) Parliament did not have the right to tax the colonies; and (3) the following rights were guaranteed to the colonists by the laws of nature, principles of the English constitution, and the several charters or compacts: "life, liberty, and property"; "all rights, liberties, and immunities of free and natural-born subjects within the realm of England"; the right to assemble peacefully, petition the king, list their grievances, and to be free from a "standing army" in the colonies at a time of peace; and the right to popularly selected colonial councils.

The Continental Association. This measure called for an intercolonial effort to prohibit the importation of British goods after December 1774, and exportation of colonial goods to England after September 1775, unless the Coercive Acts were repealed by Parliament.

War in Massachusetts (1775). Nonimportation was enforced so effectively that trade between Britain and the colonies was almost at a standstill. As a result, colonial manufacturing was encouraged and "homespun" garments became symbols of patriotism. Patrick Henry urged that the colonies prepare for war in a famous speech before the Virginia legislature that ended with the words, "Give me liberty or give me death."

Resistance to British measures spread through the colonies in 1775.

- *Lexington and Concord.* **General Thomas Gage**, the British commander in Boston, took the offensive against the rebellious colonists and sent British troops to Concord to seize colonial military supplies. Warned by Paul Revere, William Dawes, and Samuel Prescott, an undermanned and underarmed group of colonial minutemen were waiting for the British at Lexington on the morning of April 19th. Shots were fired, and the American Revolution began. After leaving eight Americans dead, the British troops moved to Concord, five miles away. The British were then driven out of Concord and retreated to Boston under heavy colonial fire.

- *The Second Continental Congress (1775).* The Congress met on May 10, 1775, shortly after the outbreak of war in Massachusetts.

Declaration of the Causes and Necessity of Taking Up Arms (1775).
On July 6, 1775, deciding on continued resistance, the Congress issued the Declaration of the Causes and Necessity of Taking Up Arms. Prepared by Thomas Jefferson and John Dickinson, it promised armed resistance until the end of unconstitutional imperial control by England and the acknowledgement of the colonials' rights as British subjects.

- *Common Sense (January 1776).* **Thomas Paine**, a 39-year-old political agitator and writer who had only one year earlier moved to the colonies from England, wrote a pamphlet entitled *Common Sense* that had tremendous influence. His 47-page document advocated the establishment of an independent American republic. Written in an emotional style in the language of the common people, it sold 120,000 copies in just three months and caused many colonists to favor independence.

Paine attacked the balance of monarchy, aristocracy, and democracy in the English system. Suggesting the abolition of the Crown and nobility, Thomas Paine advocated a republic that would derive its powers exclusively from the governed. Paine's advice would be remembered in one of the restrictions on Congress included in Article II, Section 9, Paragraph 8 of the United States Constitution, which prohibits the granting of titles of nobility.

- *The Declaration of Independence (July 4, 1776).* By the late spring of 1776, independence had clearly become inevitable. The Second Continental Congress formally recommended to the colonies that they individually form governments of their own.

The Drafting.
On June 7, 1776, **Richard Henry Lee**, representing the colony of Virginia, introduced into the Continental Congress the following resolution: "That these United Colonies are, and of right ought to be, free and independent states."

On June 11 the Congress referred the resolutions to an appointed committee consisting of Benjamin Franklin, John Adams, Robert R. Livingston, Roger Sherman, and Thomas Jefferson, and asked that they draft a "declaration of independence." The committee delegated the actual writing of the document to Jefferson, who submitted the draft to the Congress on June 28.

The resolution offered by Lee was adopted by the Congress on July 2 with the approval of twelve of the colonies (New York abstained). On July 4, 1776, the **Declaration of Independence** was formally adopted by all the colonies except New York, which finally granted approval on July 15. Congress ordered it printed and distributed to colonial officials, military units, and the press.

The Content. The Declaration of Independence had a profound effect on the political life of the United States. Following are explanations of the four sections and why they were included.

The **Preamble**, an opening statement or introduction, explains that separation has become necessary to preserve natural law and natural rights.

The paragraph following the Preamble contains a theory of democratic government and sets forth four fundamental political ideas: (1) the doctrine of "certain **unalienable Rights**," among them "Life, Liberty, and the pursuit of Happiness"; (2) the compact theory of government; (3) the doctrine of popular sovereignty in the form of governments "instituted among Men deriving their just powers from the consent of the governed"; and (4) the right of revolution to "throw off such Government" that is guilty of "a long train of abuses and usurpations."

The longest section of the Declaration is the list of complaints against King George III that are the reasons for separation. It should be noted that the entire Declaration of Independence is directed toward the king and not Parliament, because Americans claimed that Parliament had no authority over them and they did not want to alienate those members of Parliament who supported them.

The final section of the document is the actual declaration of independence and separation from England, resulting in "Free and Independent States." It is also a formal declaration of war.

The Effects. The Declaration of Independence's immediate effect was a revolution and the establishment of a new nation. However, its longer-lasting effect was to commit the new American nation to carry out the highest political ideals of the age. In Jefferson's own words, the document was "an expression of the American mind."

• *War and Peace (1776–1783).* About one third of the colonists who were called **Tories**, **Loyalists**, or sometimes Friends of the King remained loyal to Britain.

Those Americans who supported the Revolution were called **Patriots**, **Yanks**, or even **Whigs**, a term used in the colonies since the early 1700s to refer to those who opposed various measures of the royal governors. Poorly trained and inadequately equipped, the Patriot army never numbered more than 18,000 soldiers at any one time.

British Advantages and Disadvantages. Among the advantages of the British were a unified effort, greater financial resources, better trained and disciplined troops, and, for most of the war, control of the seas. Disadvantages included the problems of supplying an army fighting 3,000 miles away from home, subduing an enemy that was thinly scattered over a vast area, adjusting to the "guerilla-type" warfare used by the colonists, fighting several enemies, including France, Holland, and Spain after 1778, and cutting off the flow of aid to the colonists from their European allies.

Colonial Advantages and Disadvantages. Colonial advantages included patriotic spirit spurred by defending their towns, homes, and families; superior officers, both native and foreign, including Lafayette of France, von Steuben of Prussia, and Kosciusko and Pulaski of Poland; and the extensive aid in money, supplies, troops, and naval support they received through a treaty of alliance with France in 1778. Major disadvantages of the colonists were problems associated with the lack of central governmental authority as the Continental Congress had little real authority, had not established a sound financial system, and did not have the power to tax; the Tories, who were hostile to independence and aided the British through subversive acts; and the constant struggle to raise and maintain the **Continental Army**.

• *Turning Point and the French Alliance.* The **Battle of Saratoga** (October 1777) was the turning point of the American Revolution. France, eager to avenge its defeat in the French and Indian War, saw an opportunity to split the British Empire apart by allying itself with the American colonies. The alliance provided that if war broke out between France and Great Britain, the two allies (France and the United States) would fight the war together and neither would make peace with the enemy without the consent of the other.

• *British Surrender at Yorktown.* In 1781 the Americans began to win battles against the British in the South. General Cornwallis withdrew his troops to Virginia, near the coast, where the British navy could support him. The British now held only New York City and a few Southern ports. Trapped by the French fleet behind him and a superior combined force of American and French troops before him, Cornwallis was forced to surrender on October 19, 1781. Peace negotiations soon began in Paris.

• *Treaty of Paris (September 3, 1783).* Problems developed between the United States and France because of the Treaty of Alliance signed by the two nations in 1778. According to the terms of the treaty, the United States was obligated to continue fighting Britain until France stopped. France was obligated to Spain to continue fighting until Gibraltar was retrieved from the British.

Although the American diplomats **John Jay**, **John Adams**, and **Benjamin Franklin** were instructed by Congress not to enter into any separate peace agreements with Britain, and to be guided by France in the negotiations, they ignored these instructions. Negotiations were held with the British and a preliminary treaty with very favorable terms was signed in September 1782.

On January 30, 1783, France and Spain signed their own provisional treaties of peace with Britain. The final treaties were signed on September 3, 1783, and the United States Congress proclaimed the treaty of peace and independence, January 14, 1784.

The Revolution in Retrospect

Many historians have offered different interpretations about the American Revolution and its causes. Among them are

- a struggle between the tyrannical control of England and the liberty-loving Americans who saw an opportunity to carry out the beliefs of the Enlightenment thinkers;
- the impossibility of England's maintaining colonies 3,000 miles away as part of its empire;
- a struggle between the growing American free enterprise system and the English mercantile system;
- a conflict of religions—between the dissenting sects that settled America and the Church of England, the dominant religion of English officials and aristocrats;
- the development of a new class structure in the colonies primarily due to the ending of heredity, birthright status, and primogeniture, and the availability of land and the expansion of the franchise (vote) as leveling factors;
- the internal problems of English politics and the inconsistencies of English policy toward the colonies; and
- the fact that the revolution was actually no revolution at all, but a struggle to preserve a social and economic order rather than to change it.

When America freed itself from British control, it also eliminated a system of law and order that had to be replaced if the new republic was to have any chance of survival. The **Articles of Confederation**, the nation's first constitution, was a natural outcome of the revolutionary movement within the American colonies—a constitutional expression of the philosophy of the Declaration of Independence.

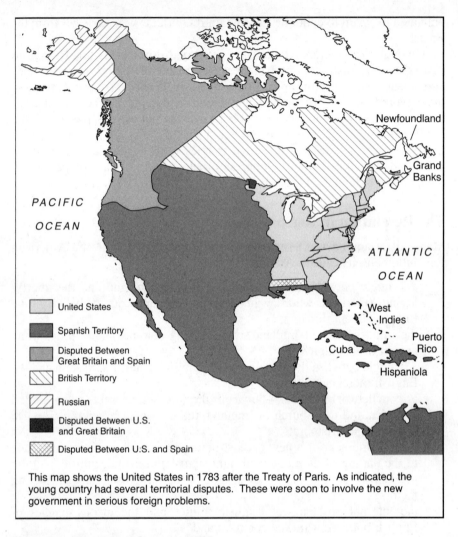

PACIFIC

OCEAN

Newfoundland

Grand
Banks

ATLANTIC

OCEAN

West
Indies

Puerto
Rico

Cuba

Hispaniola

☐ United States

■ Spanish Territory

▨ Disputed Between
Great Britain and Spain

▧ British Territory

▨ Russian

■ Disputed Between U.S.
and Great Britain

▨ Disputed Between U.S. and Spain

This map shows the United States in 1783 after the Treaty of Paris. As indicated, the young country had several territorial disputes. These were soon to involve the new government in serious foreign problems.

Figure 1.2 The United States in 1783

Problems of Confederation

> It has long been a grave question whether any government, not too strong for the liberties of its people, can be strong enough to maintain its existence in great emergencies.
>
> Abraham Lincoln, November 10, 1864

The winning of independence made necessary the establishment of a new government to replace British rule. How would the Americans meet the unprecedented task of establishing a government that was strong enough to govern and protect the nation, but restrained enough to preserve individual liberties?

The British surrender at Yorktown on October 19, 1781, and the Treaty of Paris in 1783 resulted in the establishment of the sovereign state known as the United States. The first years of the new nation under the Articles of Confederation from 1781 to 1789 are called the "critical period." Eventually, this first constitution was replaced by the one written at the **Constitutional Convention of 1787**.

State Constitutions

Between May 1776—when the Continental Congress instructed the colonies to form local governments—and 1780, most of the colonies, which were now states, had written new state constitutions and established governments.

• *Characteristics.* A common characteristic of all these state governments was constitutional republicanism; that is, the source of political authority rested with the people. Another similarity was concern to control the abuses of political power; all of the states developed written constitutions that placed restraints upon the powers of government. All these documents provided for regular and frequent elections to keep the government close and accountable to its constituency. Some of the early constitutions included a list of principles that the government could not violate. Specific guarantees of civil liberties, including freedom of speech and press, protection from arbitrary arrest, the right to jury trial, liberty of conscience, and due process rights were also included in many of them.

Perhaps the most significant feature of these state constitutions was their treatment of the executive and legislative branches of government. The most feared branch, the **executive**, was kept comparatively weak. Most governors were elected for one-year terms by the legislature, stripped of veto power, and usually had only ceremonial functions. The legislature, the branch closest to the people, retained most of the governing power.

• *Separation of Powers.* During the colonial period the belief had developed that good government required the separation of powers between the three branches of government. The 1776 Virginia state constitution specified:

> The *legislative, executive,* and *judiciary* departments shall be separate and distinct, so that neither exercises the powers properly belonging to the other; nor shall any person exercise the powers of more than one of them at the same time.

The constitutions adopted by the American states used the idea of separation of powers as an organizing principle of government.

Figure 1.3 shows how the state constitutions established systems of government that used the concept of separation of powers.

Movement Toward Confederation

The need for a central government was recognized early in the Revolutionary War. The **Articles of Confederation** were accepted by the Continental Congress in 1777, but disputes over western land claims postponed their ratification by the thirteen states until March 1781. At this time, the new league of states came into being.

• *A "League of Friendship."* The most perplexing issue facing Americans during the Confederation Period may have been trying to define the term "United States."

The wording of the Articles of Confederation, especially Article 2, made it clear that state sovereignty was to be maintained. If the states reserved for themselves such a high degree of independence from the central government, what then was the function of the national Congress?

• *Form of Government under the Articles.* The central government, consisting of a **unicameral** (one-house) Congress, acted as an administrative agency for the states. Although Congress was expressly granted the powers to control war and foreign affairs, regulate trade with the Indians, regulate the value of its coinage, maintain a post office, and standardize weights and measures, it could not infringe upon the right of a state to legislate upon matters within its own limits.

Powers of Congress. In the Congress established under the Confederation, each state had one vote. The votes of two-thirds of the states were required to pass legislation, and an amendment to the Articles required a unanimous vote by the states.

Powers of the States. Consistent with Article 2, the states retained all the powers (reserved powers) that were not expressly delegated to the central government. This left the states with such critical powers as (1) authority over commerce with other states and, in part, with other nations; and (2) the power to tax.

Contributions of the Articles of Confederation

The ratification of the Articles of Confederation in 1781 legalized the measures carried out by the Continental Congress since 1775. Despite the severe limitations on its power, the Congress under the Articles of Confederation did make lasting contributions to the nation's well-being.

• *War and Diplomacy.* Under the leadership of the Continental Congress, and the Confederation Congress, the American Revolution was fought and won and a peace treaty concluded.

EXECUTIVE

Powers: Limited administrative appointments, enforcement of laws, limited veto power (New York and Massachusetts) usually reversible by simple majority of legislature.

LEGISLATIVE

Powers: Supreme lawmaker, election of governor in most states, impeachment powers, powers to establish own rules such as meeting frequency, procedures, and membership requirements.

JUDICIAL

Powers: Interpretation of laws (including bills of rights limiting government's authority over the people), life tenure during good behavior, beginning of judicial review (the right to declare acts of the legislature unconstitutional).

THE PEOPLE

Powers: Actual representation through the vote. Although restrictions on suffrage rights still existed (property qualifications, religious exclusions, lack of voting power among women, slaves, Indians), there were movements toward universal manhood suffrage. For example, limited substitution of a taxpayer qualification for property holding took place in Pennsylvania, New Hampshire, New Jersey, Georgia, and Maryland.

Figure 1.3 State Constitutions: Separation of Powers

- ***Establishment of a Federal System.*** Federalism is the doctrine that advocates the division of powers between the national and state governments. Although the division of powers between the national government—the Congress—and the state governments under the Articles lacked the proper balance, the Articles did outline a federal system that provided a basis for establishment of a government at the Constitutional Convention of 1787.

- ***Western Lands.*** Perhaps the greatest contribution of the Articles of Confederation was the establishment of a policy for the settlement of western lands and the establishment of government in these new lands. These principles of settlement were used as Americans expanded across the continent throughout the 1800s.

Cessation of Western Land Claims. The United States had acquired the **Northwest Territory**, the land north of the Ohio River and west of the Appalachians, as a result of the Treaty of Paris of 1783 with Great Britain. Maryland refused to ratify the Articles of Confederation until Virginia turned over its claims to much of this territory to Congress, which it finally did, with conditions, in 1781. Formal adoption of the Articles of Confederation came in March 1781 with Maryland's ratification.

Ordinance of 1785. With the passage of the Land Ordinance of 1785, the Congress established a pattern for the orderly division and settlement of the land north of the Ohio River. The Ordinance provided that (1) townships of six miles square would be divided into 36 subdivisions of 640 acres each (the minimal amount to be sold); (2) each section would be sold at auction for at least one dollar an acre with the revenue to be used to pay off the national debt; and (3) the revenue from the sale of one section from each township would be used to support public education—this provided a precedent for federal aid to education. Although some changes in the policy were made in later years, the Ordinance of 1785 remained the basis of public land policy until the **Homestead Act of 1862**.

The Northwest Ordinance of 1787. The Northwest Ordinance combined the concepts of **federalism**, **republicanism**, and **regard for civil liberties** in a plan of national development that ranks in significance with the Declaration of Independence and the Constitution. The Ordinance of 1787, passed by the Confederation Congress and later reaffirmed as federal law by the new United States Congress under the Constitution in 1789, provided for the government of the Northwest Territory, an area of more than 265,000 square miles.

Between 1803 and 1848, Ohio (1803), Indiana (1816), Illinois (1818), Michigan (1837), and Wisconsin (1848) were admitted as states from the Northwest Territory.

Weaknesses of the Articles of Confederation—Foreign Affairs

• *Foreign Occupation of the West.* Great Britain continued to occupy posts in the Northwest Territory, even though the Treaty of Paris of 1783 had provided that the British would leave this area "with all convenient speed."

American problems with Spain included disputes over the boundaries established by the Treaty of Paris of 1783 and the navigation of the lower Mississippi River. Spain's decision to close the Mississippi to American shipping in 1784 led to negotiations between Secretary of Foreign Affairs John Jay and the Spanish minister.

• *Foreign Debts.* Between 1778 and 1783 the United States borrowed several million dollars from the French and the Dutch governments. Because of its failure to meet even the interest payments on these loans, the United States lost the respect of its former allies.

• *Barbary Pirates.* Commerce in the Mediterranean Sea had long been subject to attacks by coastal pirates unless financial tributes, or bribes, were paid. Since the United States was no longer protected by the British navy, and had no navy of its own, it could do little to prevent violations of its commercial rights by the Barbary pirates.

Weaknesses of Articles—Domestic Affairs

• *Problems of Commerce.* Under the Confederation, Congress lacked the power to control and regulate both domestic and foreign trade. As jealousies over trade developed between the states, they started to levy tariffs on each other's goods. This brought domestic trade almost to a standstill.

• *Need of Revenue.* Most of Congress's difficulties between 1776 and 1787 were related to its inability to raise money. Congressional income was dependent on the whims of the states, since Congress had no power to raise money on its own.

• *Currency Problems.* A postwar depression led to a wide demand for the issuance of paper money by the state legislatures.

During the fall of 1786, an incident in western Massachusetts helped to convince many Americans that changes in the national government were necessary. In Massachusetts, farmers who were crushed by demands for payment of debts and taxes joined together. They took matters into their own hands after the courts ordered that their homes and land be sold to pay their debts. Led by **Daniel Shays**, a captain during the Revolutionary War, some 1,200

Specie, or hard money, was scarce in the new nation.

armed followers gathered to attack the federal arsenal at Springfield. This attack was unsuccessful. A militia was raised and sent by the governor to put down the rebellion. It was completely suppressed by February 1787.

Shays' rebellion caused much fear among Americans and was used by conservative forces to bolster their demand for a stronger central government.

• *Political Structure.* It was with Shays' Rebellion and the weaknesses of the Confederation government in mind that the framers of the Constitution included Section 4 of Article IV:

> The United States shall guarantee to every State in this Union a Republican Form of Government, and shall protect each of them against Invasion; and on Application of the Legislature, or of the Executive (when the Legislature cannot be convened) against domestic violence.
>
> Article IV, Sec. 4, United States Constitution

Movement Toward a Constitutional Convention

The weaknesses of the Articles of Confederation, combined with the political, social, and economic difficulties faced by the nation at this time, led the states to consider revisions in the Confederation government.

• *The Annapolis Conference (1786).* Although eight states named representatives to the September meeting, delegates from only five states arrived in time for the Annapolis Conference. At the suggestion of **James Madison** and **Alexander Hamilton**, a convention was called to meet in Philadelphia in May of the following year to discuss revising the Articles of Confederation.

From Radicalism to Conservatism

There is evidence to support the idea that the American Revolution, although a concerted effort for independence, was fought by a population with distinct class lines. A conservative group, composed primarily of Northern lawyers, merchants, bankers,

Alexander Hamilton encouraged the rewriting of the Articles of Confederation.

speculators, and wealthy Southern planters and merchants, sought independence from Britain's trade regulations and restrictions on capitalist growth. They had no desire to see the Revolution upset their positions in society, and were firm believers in a government that was controlled by the wellborn who were capable of maintaining the class structure. On the other hand, the small business owners, artisans, and farmers fought the Revolution in order to break America's political ties with England and to destroy the economic and social privileges of the colonial aristocracy. They regarded the principles of the Declaration of Independence as the guidelines for a new social order, as well as the political transformation of power to local representative bodies. The central issue between the conservative and the radical groups in America in the period of the 1780s was still the question of where supreme authority was to be located.

The Articles of Confederation represented the attempt to deny authority to any government superior to the legislative bodies of the states. A change in the balance of political power took place between 1776 and 1787. The movement to centralize power, which was assisted by the problems of the Confederation period, engineered a conservative counterrevolution and created a nationalistic government. Although this protected the interests of the conservative, propertied classes, it also preserved the system of republican government, the primary concern of all groups in the United States.

Exercise Set 1.1

1. In framing a government which is to be administered by men over men, the great difficulty lies in this; you must first enable the government to control the governed, and next, oblige it to control itself.

   James Madison, *The Federalist,* No. 51

   Which concept of government is being referred to in the quotation?
   A. Unicameral legislature
   B. Cabinet system
   C. Popularly elected assemblies
   D. System of checks and balances

2. In most of the thirteen original colonies, the settlers gained experience in self-government by
   A. choosing governors to administer colonial affairs.
   B. electing members of colonial assemblies.
   C. regulating trade with England.
   D. sending representatives to vote in Parliament.

3. Which of the following democratic practices of the American heritage cannot be found in English history?
   A. A written constitution
   B. Common law
   C. Representative government
   D. The concept of limited government

4. As a result of the Albany Congress of 1754
   A. the Dominion of New England was eliminated.
   B. an experiment in intercolonial union was proposed.
   C. the colonies were granted limited tax power.
   D. an intercolonial legislature was established.

5. The most significant step toward intercolonial union was
   A. the New England Confederation.
   B. the use of the town meeting in the New England colonies.
   C. the drafting of the Mayflower Compact.
   D. the formation of the Virginia Company of London.

6. Colonial legislatures were often able to control royal governors by
   A. threatening impeachment.
   B. controlling finances, including the governor's salary.
   C. overruling the governor with authority granted by Parliament.
   D. using the colonial militia.

Base your answers to questions 7 and 8 on the following excerpt from the Declaration of Independence and your knowledge of social studies:

> We hold these truths to be self-evident, that all men are created equal, that they are endowed by their creator with certain unalienable rights, that among these are life, liberty, and the pursuit of happiness. That to secure these rights, governments are instituted among men, deriving their just powers from the consent of the governed.

7. According to Jefferson's Declaration of Independence, governments receive their authority and power from
   A. only men.
   B. military strength.
   C. the people.
   D. God.

8. The ideas expressed in the preceding excerpt from the Declaration of Independence are consistent with the writings of which pair of Enlightenment thinkers?
   A. John Locke and Baron de Montesquieu
   B. Jean-Jacques Rousseau and John Locke
   C. Sir William Blackstone and Jean-Jacques Rousseau
   D. John Locke and Sir Henry Clinton

9. A review of the events that came before the American Revolution indicates that
   A. the Boston Massacre marked a point of no return toward independence.
   B. after 1763 most Americans wanted nothing less than complete independence from England.
   C. as late as February 1775, reconciliation was probably possible.
   D. Parliament clearly welcomed the armed conflict in hopes of bringing the colonies back under control.

10. According to the Declaration of Independence, the purpose of government is to
    A. equalize opportunities for all citizens.
    B. provide for the common defense.
    C. secure the people in their natural rights.
    D. suppress the dangers of "raw democracy."

11. The original reason for adding bills of rights to early state constitutions was to
    A. prohibit state governments from depriving individuals of certain basic rights.
    B. deprive the national government of any regulation of natural rights.
    C. ensure the supremacy of the legislature over the executive in state governments.
    D. provide an example for the eventual Bill of Rights added to the Constitution in 1791.

12. The colonial branch of government that Americans had grown to suspect most during the period before the Revolution was the
    A. judicial branch.
    B. executive branch.
    C. legislative branch.
    D. Continental Congress.

13. Among the weaknesses of the Articles of Confederation was
    A. the need for a unanimous vote to amend the Articles.
    B. the failure to establish a peace treaty at the conclusion of the American Revolution.
    C. the abandonment of the principle of federalism.
    D. the inability to deal with the western land problem.

14. Which of the following best describes the "United States" under the Articles of Confederation?
    A. A confederation of colonies existing within an empire
    B. One nation, consisting of thirteen subordinate components
    C. Free and independent states loosely held together by a Confederation Congress
    D. Sovereign states with no cohesive element whatsoever

15. The Declaration of Independence
    A. contained a list of grievances against Parliament.
    B. was written by Jefferson and adopted without change.
    C. contained Jefferson's objections to slavery.
    D. directed the grievances of the colonists against George III.

CONSTITUTIONAL CONVENTION, RATIFICATION, AND A BILL OF RIGHTS

> The whole people declared the colonies in their united condition, of right, free and independent States . . . . But there still remained the last and Crowning act, by which the People of the Union alone were competent to perform the institution of civil government, for that compound nation, the United States of America.
>
> John Quincy Adams, *The Jubilee of the Constitution* (1839)

In 1786 James Madison described the Articles of Confederation as "nothing more than a treaty of amity and of alliance between independent and sovereign states." As attempts to amend the Articles failed, and the nation's problems, which stemmed from the lack of a central authority, increased, steps toward forming a new government began.

Constitutional Convention

The Delegates

The Convention met in Philadelphia on May 25, 1787 with 55 delegates from seven states in attendance. By July, twelve states were represented, Rhode Island choosing not to participate.

The delegates at the Constitutional Convention were as brilliant an assembly of statesmen as ever had met in America. The group included **George Washington**, who was selected as presiding officer of the Convention, **James Madison**, who kept a journal of the debates, **Benjamin Franklin**, George Mason, Gouverneur Morris, James Wilson, Roger Sherman, and Elbridge Gerry. Notable absences included the more radical leaders of the Confederation period: **Samuel Adams**, **Patrick Henry**, and **Thomas Paine**. Also absent were **Thomas Jefferson** and **John Adams**, who were serving as ambassadors in Europe.

James Madison (1751–1836), 4th President of the United States. Madison was a key participant in the Constitutional Convention.

Most of the delgates to the Constitutional Convention were men of property, representing primarily the upper classes of American society. Their class status was reflected in their interest in a strong central government. Their goal was to form a government that would avoid the polar extremes of despotism and uncontrolled popular rule. Congress had authorized the Convention only for "the sole and express purpose of revising the Articles of Confederation." Few of them realized at the outset that their efforts would result in a new "constitution," rather than changes in the Articles of Confederation. In order to allow the delegates to debate freely without public pressure, sessions were secret and very little news leaked.

The Virginia, or "Large States," Plan

Primarily the work of James Madison and Virginia Governor Edmund Randolph, the plan called for drafting a new document to organize a new form of government rather than for amending the Articles of Confederation. Introduced on May 29 by Edmund Randolph, the Virginia Plan proposed **a bicameral legislature** representing the states proportionately (based on population), with the lower house elected by the people and the upper house to be chosen by the lower house.

The New Jersey, or "Small States," Plan

Presented to the Convention on June 15 by William Paterson of New Jersey, it called for changes in the Articles of Confederation rather than the drafting of a new document. The smaller states claimed that representation in Congress based upon population would allow the larger states to constantly outvote the smaller states. The New Jersey Plan proposed **a unicameral legislature** similar to that under the Articles with each state having one vote.

The Great, or Connecticut, Compromise

On June 19 the convention decided to scrap the Articles of Confederation and write a new plan of government. The major area of debate concerned the method by which the states would be represented in the national Congress. On July 12, Roger Sherman of Connecticut offered a compromise plan, which provided for a Congress with two houses—a **Senate** and a **House of Representatives**. The lower house of Congress, the House, would be filled according to **proportional representation** (by population) with one member for every 40,000 residents. The upper house, the Senate, would be filled by **equal representation** of the states, each state having two members elected by the legislature of the individual states.

The Three-Fifths Compromise

Three suggestions were made concerning how the population should be counted in order to determine the number of representatives each state was to have in the lower house. Each plan showed strong sectional biases. The first, supported primarily by the slave states, wanted all people (free and slave) counted for purposes of representation, but not for taxation. In the second, the nonslave-holding states of the North wanted only the free population counted. The third proposal, the method which was adopted by the members of the Convention, was to count three-fifths of the slave population for both representation and taxation. (Article I, Section 2, Clause 3. Overruled by Amendments 13 [1865] and 14 [1868].) It was also decided that the method for counting the population would be a census taken every ten years. (Article I, Section 2, Clause 3, Amendment 17.)

Prohibition on Banning of Slave Trade

Linked to the Three-Fifths Compromise, this provided that Congress would pass no law prohibiting the importation of slaves for twenty years. The importation of slaves became illegal after 1808. (Article I, Section 9, Clause 1.)

Fugitive Slave Clause

To placate the Southern states, this clause declared that slaves ("persons held to service or labor under the laws of a state") who escaped to a free state would be returned to their rightful owners. (Article IV, Section 2, Clause 3. Overruled in 1865 by Amendment 13.)

Tariffs

Again, geographic differences surfaced over the question of duties on trade. Southerners who exported agricultural products disapproved of granting power to the national government to impose taxes on exports. Northern business groups, however, wanted tariffs on imports to protect their interests from foreign competition. A compromise was reached and the delegates to the Convention granted Congress the authority to tax imports, but not exports. (Article I, Section 8, Clause 1 and Article I, Section 9, Clause 5.)

The Presidency

The small states desired a weak executive, chosen by and responsible to the legislature. The larger states supported a strong executive selected through direct election by the people. James Wilson's compromise proposal, that the people of the states should choose presidential electors through their own methods who then should meet and choose the executive, was accepted as the method of election. (Article II, Sections 2 and 3, Amendment 12.)

Principles of the Document

Separation of Powers

The arrangement of Articles I, II, and III—the first devoted to the Congress, the second to the President, and the third to the federal judiciary—made it clear that Montesquieu's thoughts, and the experiences of the state governments, were well studied by the members of the Convention. The delegates established a government based on the idea of the separation of powers.

Checks and Balances

The framers of the Constitution were concerned that the government should not act in a hasty or arbitrary manner. The system of checks and balances within our system requires an interaction between the three branches that prevents the abuse of power by any one of them. Figure 1.4 helps demonstrate some of the checks and balances among the three branches of government.

Federalism

This concept of distributing powers of government between one central or national government (usually called the "federal government") and the governments of the several states into which a country is divided was adopted by those at the Constitutional Convention.

Structure of the Document

The final document consisted of a preamble setting forth the reasons the Constitution was adopted and a main body of seven articles divided into sections and clauses. Shortly after ratification, an appendix of amendments to the Constitution was added.

Preamble

This opening paragraph of the Constitution establishes the people as the source of authority for the Constitution and sets forth six goals: (1) to set up a stronger government than had existed under the Articles of Confederation; (2) to improve the judicial system; (3) to guarantee peace within and among the states; (4) to provide protection for the country; (5) to provide for the general welfare; and (6) to maintain liberty for citizens, present and future.

EXECUTIVE
President

The **President** may:
• veto laws
• call special sessions of Congress
• propose laws

The **President**:
• grants pardons and reprieves
• appoints Supreme Court justices and other federal judges

Congress:
• may impeach and remove President from office
• may override President's veto
• Senate can refuse to ratify treaties and confirm appointments

Supreme Court:
• may declare executive acts unconstitutional
• Supreme Court justices are appointed for life and thus are free from executive control

Congress may:
• impeach and remove judges
• refuse judicial appointments
• propose constitutional amendments
• create lower courts
• regulate Supreme Court's jurisdiction

LEGISLATIVE
Congress

JUDICIAL
Supreme Court

Supreme Court may:
• declare laws of Congress unconstitutional

Figure 1.4 Checks and Balances

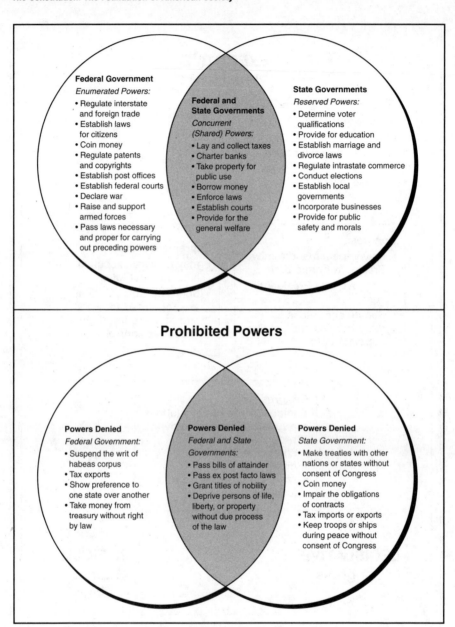

Figure 1.5   The Federal System

Articles I through VII

The first three articles of the Constitution describe the organization and functions of the three branches of the federal government: the **legislative**, **executive**, and **judicial**. Articles IV through VII set forth how the powers of the government are to be shared by the federal government, the states, and the people.

Article I:	Legislative Branch
Article II:	Executive Branch
Article III:	Judicial Branch
Article IV:	Relations among the states
Article V:	Amending the Constitution
Article VI:	Supremacy Clause
Article VII:	Ratification Procedures

Amendments

Article V of the Constitution provides that the document may be changed when the need arises. Although there have been many attempts at amending the Constitution, there have been only 27 amendments added to the Constitution since 1789.

Ratification

Article VII provided that state conventions would be called and that, upon the approval of only nine states, the Constitution would go into effect. On September 28, 1787, Congress directed the state legislatures to call ratification conventions in each state.

The ratification of the Constitution led to the formation of **political factions** and the nation's first organized political battle between the **Federalists** and the **antifederalists**.

Federalists

Those who supported the ratification of the Constitution called themselves **Federalists**. In favor of a stronger Union, the Federalists felt that anarchy could result without a stronger national government. Many of the Federalists came from the business and propertied classes and therefore had a personal economic interest in the establishment of a strong stable government. Alexander Hamilton and John Adams were early Federalist leaders.

Antifederalists

The **antifederalists** did not fear strong government as much as they feared a strong centralized government at the expense of local state governments. Another major concern of the antifederalists was the potential danger to individual liberties posed by the lack of a bill of rights.

While the antifederalists wanted the states to maintain a large degree of sovereignty, they also wanted Congress to act for the states in areas where the states could not act for themselves—notably foreign policy, western settlement, commerce, and disputes between the states. Among the early leaders of the antifederalists were Richard Henry Lee of Virginia, and **Thomas Jefferson**.

State Conventions

The debate over ratification took place in conventions within the individual states. By the time New Hampshire ratified in June 1788, the requirement of ratification by nine states had been satisfied. However, New York and Virginia had not yet voted, and most realized that the chances of the Constitution's succeeding without the support of those states were slim.

The Federalist Papers

The most serious criticism of the Constitution by the antifederalists was its lack of a bill of rights. In New York, Governor George Clinton expressed this and other fears in several published newspaper essays, while **Patrick Henry** and **James Monroe** led the opposition in Virginia. Between October 1787 and August 1788, **James Madison** of Virginia, and **Alexander Hamilton** and **John Jay**, both of New York, published 85 essays in New York newspapers above the signature "Publius" to answer the fears of the antifederalists. Madison's leading role in the drafting of the Constitution has made *The Federalist* the most authoritative source for interpreting the Constitution.

A Bill of Rights

The first Congress under the new constitutional government met in April 1789. One of its first tasks was to respond to the calls of the state ratification conventions for amendments to the Constitution in the form of a bill of rights. Of the twelve proposals sent to the states, ten were accepted and officially became part of the Constitution on December 15, 1791, when three-quarters of the states had ratified them. Article V of the Constitution provides for the amending process.

The following cases involving the Bill of Rights will be addressed throughout the text and will demonstrate how the Constitution, in particular the Bill of Rights, has proven to be a "living document" over time:

- *Tinker* v. *Des Moines*, 1969 (First Amendment)—p. 514
- *Engle* v. *Vitale*, 1962 (First Amendment)—p. 536
- *New York Times* v. *United States*, 1971 (First Amendment)—p. 510
- *Mapp* v. *Ohio*, 1961 (Fourth Amendment)—p. 536
- *Vernonia School District* v. *Acton*, 1995 (Fourth Amendment)—p. 553
- *Scott* v. *Sanford*, 1857 (Fifth Amendment)—p. 224
- *Miranda* v. *Arizona*, 1966 (Fifth and Sixth Amendments)—p. 536

Throughout our nation's history, only Congress has proposed amendments for consideration by the states. The procedure allowing for two-thirds of the states to petition Congress to call a constitutional convention has never been used. The scope and authority of such a convention are not defined or limited by the Constitution and therefore the method has prompted much debate.

The only amendment to be ratified by popularly elected state constitutional conventions was the Twenty-First Amendment (1933) repealing Prohibition. All other amendments have been ratified by the state legislatures.

By studying the over 80 proposals from the state conventions for ratifying the Constitution, Madison was able to incorporate those he considered most important into his nineteen original proposals.

The **first ten amendments** to the United States Constitution gave formal recognition to certain traditionally accepted natural rights that had been included in the English tradition, colonial charters, and states' bills of rights. The wording of the first ten amendments makes it clear that those powers that are granted or denied to the federal government are powers that come directly from free people. Contrary to our provisions for individual liberties are those systems in which the government grants rights. For example: The First Amendment to the United States Constitution reads in part: *"Congress shall make no law* respecting the establishment of religion . . . or abridging the freedom of speech." Article 125 of the former Soviet Union's Fundamental Rights and Duties of Citizens reads in part: "In conformity with the interests of the working people, and in order to strengthen the socialist system, *the citizens are guaranteed* by law: freedom of speech, freedom of press . . ."

The important distinction is the source of authority in the two different systems of government, the first being the people, the second being the government.

PROPOSAL	RATIFICATION
Amendments to the Constitution may be proposed by a two-thirds vote of Congress in both the House of Representatives and the Senate	The amendment must be ratified by at least three-fourths of the state legislatures
or	or
when two-thirds of the state legislatures request Congress to call a Constitutional Convention, which then proposes an amendment.	be ratified by a majority vote in three-fourths of the state conventions called to vote on the amendment.

Figure 1.6 The Amending Process

Amendments	Provisions
I	1. The establishment clause of Amendment I states that Congress shall make no law that establishes religion in any manner. This has been referred to as the "wall of separation between church and state." 2. The second part of Amendment I prevents Congress from restricting the free practice of religion, freedom of speech, press, the right to assemble peacefully, or to petition the government.
II	Amendment II was designed to prevent Congress from denying states the right to have a militia of armed citizens. It is currently argued that the amendment guarantees people the right to own weapons, although states do have the right to restrict such ownership.
III	In peacetime, no citizen may be forced to quarter (house and feed) soldiers. In time of war, Congress may pass legislation allowing for such quartering. The quartering of troops in the colonists' homes by the British government was well remembered by the residents of the states.
IV	Remembering the writs of assistance, supporters of the Fourth Amendment required that search warrants could be issued only under the following conditions: (a) the warrant must be issued by a judge; (b) there must be probable cause (good reason) for its issuance; and (c) the warrant must describe the place to be searched and the items to be seized.
V	1. Grand Juries: A person accused of a serious crime and tried in a federal court must first be indicted (charged) by a grand jury (jury of 12 to 23 persons). 2. Double Jeopardy: A person may not be tried twice for the same crime. 3. Self-Incrimination: A person may not be forced to say anything that would help convict himself or herself. This provision finds its origins in confessions that were obtained through forceful measure, i.e., torture. 4. Due Process: A person may not be deprived of life, liberty, or property (natural rights) except according to law. The Fourteenth Amendment applies this clause to the states as well as the federal government. 5. Eminent Domain: Congress may not (without paying a fair price) take private property for the benefit of the public, e.g., roads, hospitals, and airports.
VI	Amendment VI continues the rights of the accused started in Amendment V. The person accused of a crime must be given a prompt trial in public, and guilt or innocence must be decided by a jury chosen from the state and district where the crime was committed. The accused must be informed of the charges, be present when witnesses testify against him or her, and be provided with a lawyer if he or she cannot provide one. The Fourteenth Amendment has also applied these provisions to state courts.
VII	Amendment VII provides for a jury trial in federal civil cases (trials where one person sues another, usually for damages). The second part of the amendment limits the power of judges to interfere with a jury's decision.

Figure 1.7 The Bill of Rights

Amendments	Provisions
VIII	If a person is accused of a crime and must await trial, he or she may be released from prison on bail—an amount of money that is put up to guarantee the accused will appear for trial; bail is forfeited if he or she fails to appear. Amendment VIII guarantees that a fine should be calculated according to the wrong done and that "cruel and unusual punishment" may not be inflicted on those convicted. The death penalty continues to be debated on the "cruel and unusual" punishment argument.
IX	Amendment IX was added out of fear that it might be dangerous to make only a partial listing of the basic rights guaranteed in the Constitution. This amendment makes it clear that the federal government may still do only what is authorized by the Constitution.
X	This amendment was added to reserve "all other powers" to the states and the people. The powers of the federal government are listed in Article I, Section 8. The powers denied to the states are listed in Article I, Section 10. All others are reserved to the states.
XIV*	Section 1 of Amendment XIV denied to the states the power to deprive any person of life, liberty, or property without due process of law. This due process clause protects individuals from unfair actions by state government, whereas, Amendment V protected individuals from unfair actions by the federal government.

*Note: The Bill of Rights was added to protect the people from the federal government. The Fourteenth Amendment, ratified in 1868, extended some of the original provisions of the Bill of Rights and applied them to the state governments. It protected individuals from actions by state governments.

Figure 1.7 continued The Bill of Rights

Exercise Set 1.2

1. Arrested persons claiming they have already been acquitted of the charge for which they are now being tried are claiming the defense of
   A. ex post facto.
   B. unreasonable search and seizure.
   C. double jeopardy.
   D. right to trial by jury.

2. The right of government to take private property for public use, providing just compensation is made, is known as
   A. habeas corpus.
   B. self-incrimination.
   C. Federalism.
   D. eminent domain.

3. When a judge tells the accused person what he or she is charged with and that he or she may have legal counsel and a jury trial, the accused is being
   A. indicted by a grand jury.
   B. denied due process of law.
   C. informed of constitutional rights.
   D. protected from cruel and unusual punishment.

4. The principle of Federalism as established by the United States Constitution provides for the
   A. separation of powers of the three branches of government.
   B. placement of ultimate sovereignty in the hands of the state governments.
   C. division of power between the state governments and the national government.
   D. creation of a republican form of government.

5. The Great Compromise of the Constitutional Convention of 1787 concerned the
   A. issue of slavery.
   B. representation of the states in Congress.
   C. election of the President.
   D. allocation of judicial power in the federal government.

6. Which of the following compromises made at the Constitutional Convention was later changed by a constitutional amendment?
   A. The establishment of a bicameral legislature
   B. The Three-Fifths Compromise
   C. The tariff-commerce compromise
   D. Representation in the House of Representatives

7. The Constitution differed most from the Articles of Confederation in that the Constitution
   A. gave greater power to the federal government.
   B. gave greater power to the state governments.
   C. made the amending process more difficult.
   D. changed the method of admitting new states to the union.

8. Which of the following is an illustration of the system of checks and balances?
   A. An individual pays income tax to both the federal government and the state government.
   B. New York State requires at least 180 days of school per year.
   C. The Senate must approve an appointment by the President to the Supreme Court.
   D. Congress may pass no law establishing a state religion.

9. The powers of Congress were limited by the Constitution, chiefly because
   A. representatives of the states feared too powerful a central government.
   B. the Federalists desired strong, independent state governments.
   C. the new government lacked a judiciary to check Congressional power.
   D. supporters of a strong central government planned to carry out legislative powers through the executive branch.

10. Within the first ten amendments to the United States Constitution is one providing
    A. that under no conditions shall soldiers be housed and fed by citizens at the request of the government.
    B. that slavery will be banned.
    C. for the right of the people to petition the government.
    D. for women's suffrage.

CONSTITUTIONAL STRUCTURE, FUNCTION, AND THIRTEEN ENDURING ISSUES

> Our Constitution is in actual operation; everything appears to promise
> that it will last, but in this world nothing is certain but death and taxes.
> Benjamin Franklin, letter to M. Leroy, 1789

Structure and Function

Article I, Congress

• *The Structure.* Congress is organized according to provisions in Article I of the Constitution.

• *Sessions of Congress.* Beginning with the first Congress of 1789–1790, each Congress serves for a two-year term. Each Congress meets in two sessions, each session convening, in accordance with the Twentieth Amendment, on or soon after January 3.

• *Powers of Congress.* The first 17 clauses of Article I, Section 8, detail the power of Congress. Some of the major delegated or enumerated powers of Congress include: the levying and collection of taxes, borrowing money, coining money and regulating its value, regulating interstate and foreign trade, granting patents and copyrights, declaring war, raising and supporting an army and navy, creating courts below the Supreme Court, using state militias to execute the laws of the nation, establishing post offices, controlling naturalization of aliens, and controlling federal property within the states. Powers shared by Congress and the states are referred to as concurrent powers.

• *Necessary and Proper Clause.* Clause 18 of Article I, Section 8 provides that Congress may "Make all laws necessary and proper for carrying into execution the foregoing powers . . ." This is commonly referred to as the **elastic clause**. The Supreme Court case of *McCulloch* v. *Maryland* (1819) provided one of the earliest opportunities to test the use of the powers implied through the "necessary and proper clause." In this case the issue was whether Congress had the right to establish a national bank, even though the Constitution did not specifically grant it that power. Two groups with opposing views on how to interpret the Constitution developed as a result of the dispute:

Strict Constructionists. Those who felt that the Constitution should be read literally and that the elastic clause should be used only for expanding the powers of Congress in cases where the expansion is absolutely necessary.

Loose Constructionists. Those who held the belief that the Constitution, and specifically the elastic clause, should be read broadly and that the framers

	SENATE	HOUSE
Qualifications	• At least 30 years of age • U.S. citizen for nine years • Resident of state represented (Art. I, Section 3, Clause 3)	• At least 25 years of age • U.S. citizen for seven years • Resident of state represented (Art. I, Section 2, Clause 2)
Term of Office	• Six years • One-third of members elected every two years (Art. I, Section 3, Clauses 1 and 2)	• Two years • Full House is elected every two years (Art. I, Section 2, Clause 1)
Method of Election	• Originally by state legislatures (Art. I, Section 3, Clause 1) • Today, directly by voters of state (Amendment 17, 1913)	• Directly by voters of state and, district (Art. I, Section 2, Clause 1)
Membership	• Two Senators from each state (100) (Art. I, Section 3, Clause 1)	• Now set at 435 by law (1910). Determined by population of a state. Census taken every ten years. As of the 1990 census, each member of the House represented approximately 573,563 persons. (Art. I, Section 2, Clause 3)
Filling Vacancies	• Originally by Governor and state legislature. Today, Governor may appoint until a popular election within the state takes place (Amendment 17, 1913)	• Governor of state calls an election to fill vacancy (Art. I, Section 2, Clause 4)
Presiding Officer	• Vice President of the United States; Majority vote in case of tie vote. (Art. I, Section 3, Clause 4) • President Pro Tempore chosen by Senate as presiding officer to preside when Vice President is absent (Art. I, Section 3, Clause 5)	• Chosen by members, usually represents majority party (Art. I, Section 2, Clause 5)
Special Powers	• Chooses Vice President if no majority in electoral vote (Amendment 12, 1913) • Sits as jury in impeachment trial (Art. I, Section 3, Clause 6) • Ratifies treaties with foreign nations by two-thirds vote (Art. II, Section 2, Clause 2) • Approves presidential appointments (Art. II, section 2, Clause 2)	• Chooses President if no majority in electoral vote (Amendment 12, 1913) • Brings impeachment charges (Art. I, Section 2, Clause 5) • All bills for raising revenue originate in the House of Representatives (Art. I, Section 7, Clause 1)

Figure 1.8   Structure of House and Senate

had intended the clause to mean that Congress should have the "proper" powers resulting from its other powers.

Taking a broad view of the elastic clause, the Supreme Court in *McCulloch* v. *Maryland,* in an opinion written by **Chief Justice John Marshall**, held that the national bank was necessary and proper for carrying out Congress's powers of collecting taxes and coining and borrowing money.

The trend throughout our history has been toward loose construction. Examples include Congress's broadened definition of "commerce," increased government control over business practices, labor unions, minimum wages, and the establishment of a Social Security system and Medicare.

John Marshall (1755–1835). As Chief Justice of the Supreme Court, Marshall expanded federal power over the states.

• *How a Bill Becomes a Law.* The primary function of Congress is legislative—to make the laws that govern our nation. Article I, Section 7, provides for the lawmaking procedures of Congress. Except for money bills, which must originate in the House of Representatives, any bill may be introduced by any member of Congress. Of the thousands of bills introduced each year, only a small percentage actually become law.

Article II, The Executive

Perhaps the most powerful political office in the world, the presidency of the United States combines the roles of chief of state, chief diplomat, Commander-in-Chief of the armed forces, chief executive, chief legislator, and head of his or her political party.

• *Structure.* The office of the President and the executive branch are outlined in Article II, Sections 1 through 4, and in Amendments 12, 20, 22, 23, and 25.

• *Election of the President.* The election of the President actually involves two races: the first to be nominated by his or her political party and the second to win the national election for the office of the President.

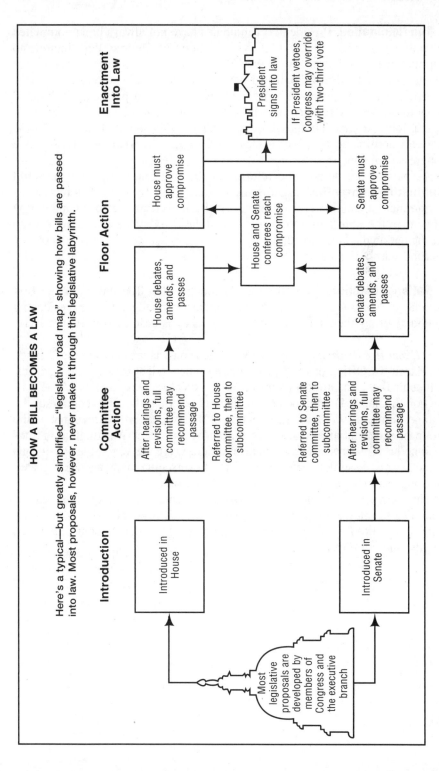

HOW A BILL BECOMES A LAW

Here's a typical—but greatly simplified—"legislative road map" showing how bills are passed into law. Most proposals, however, never make it through this legislative labyrinth.

Introduction

Introduced in House

Introduced in Senate

Most legislative proposals are developed by members of Congress and the executive branch

Committee Action

After hearings and revisions, full committee may recommend passage

Referred to House committee, then to subcommittee

Referred to Senate committee, then to subcommittee

After hearings and revisions, full committee may recommend passage

Floor Action

House debates, amends, and passes

House and Senate conferees reach compromise

Senate debates, amends, and passes

House must approve compromise

Senate must approve compromise

Enactment Into Law

President signs into law

If President vetoes, Congress may override with two-third vote

Figure 1.9

Unit One **CONSTITUTIONAL FOUNDATIONS OF THE UNITED STATES**

47

The Nomination. Presidential candidates have not always been nominated by political parties. In the first two elections of George Washington, no nominations were necessary as Washington was unanimously chosen by the Electoral College. But as political parties formed and became better established, groups composed of individuals with common political, social, and economic interests competed to have their choice nominated for the presidency. John Adams, Thomas Jefferson, James Madison, and James Monroe were all nominated by party leaders in Congress in what was known as a congressional caucus.

As part of the democratic reforms of the Jacksonian Era, the **national nominating convention**, a gathering of delegates from the different states to nominate a candidate, was developed. It allowed greater participation by citizens in the nomination of a party candidate. Today, delegates are chosen for the national convention either through the caucus method, or the **primary method** within the states.

National Election. Every four years, on the first Tuesday after the first Monday in November, Americans vote for electors pledged to one presidential candidate or another. The road to the presidency is described in Figure 1.11.

• *Executive Branch.* The executive branch consists primarily of the Cabinet, the Executive Office of the President, and independent offices and agencies. Although the Constitution mentions only executive departments (Article II, Section 2, Clause 1) and does not mention a Cabinet (the first mention of the Cabinet came in 1967 with the adoption of the Twenty-Fifth Amendment), the group of presidential advisers was started by President Washington and has become an American governmental tradition. Over the years, the President's office has also assumed the responsibility of overseeing many agencies created by Congress to deal with domestic and world problems.

The entire executive branch has expanded greatly, especially in the past 50 years as the role of government has widened. A President today is aided by some 2.6 million civilian employees working within departments, agencies, boards, and commissions.

Article II, Section 1	Executive power shall be vested in the President, four-year term, electoral system (changed by Amendment 12), date of elections, qualifications for President, succession to the presidency, salary, and oath of office.
Article II, Section 2	Powers of the President: Military, treaties, appointments, powers over executive departments, pardon and reprieve, filling vacancies.
Article II, Section 3	State of the Union Address, calling special sessions of Congress, veto power, receiving ambassadors, execution of the laws.
Article II, Section 4	Impeachment and removal from office for treason, bribery, or other high crimes and misdemeanors.
Amendment 12 (1804)	Amendment 12 alters Article 2, Section 1, Clause 3. Prior to this amendment electors voted for two persons without designating who would become President and who would become Vice President. Now, electors cast separate ballots for President and Vice President.
Amendment 20 (1933)	Known as the "lame duck" amendment. Changed office-taking date for the presidency from March 4 to January 20 to shorten length of period a "lame duck" President would stay in office. Also provided that newly-elected members of Congress would take office January 3.
Amendment 22 (1951)	Although Presidents Washington and Jefferson set the two-term tradition, nothing in the Constitution limited a President to only two terms. After President Franklin Delano Roosevelt was elected to a third term in 1940 and then a fourth in 1944, the 22nd Amendment became law limiting a President to two terms or a maximum of ten years.
Amendment 23 (1961)	Gave the District of Columbia three electoral votes and enabled residents to vote for the President and Vice President.
Amendment 25 (1967)	In an attempt to clarify Article 2, Section 1, Clause 6 dealing with disability and succession of the presidency, Amendment 25 became law.

Figure 1.10 The Presidency

Article III, The Judicial Branch

> Watergate has taught us that our system is not invulnerable to the
> arrogance of power . . . (and) that our system of law is the most valu-
> able asset in this land.
>
> Judge John J. Sirica, 1974

The Supreme Court is the only federal court specifically mentioned in the
Constitution. Article III, Section I provides for a Supreme Court and gives
Congress the power to establish inferior (lower) courts. Congress made use
of this power with the passage of the **Judiciary Act of 1789**, which estab-
lished thirteen **district courts** in principal cities, three **circuit courts**, and
one **Supreme Court** with a **Chief Justice** and five **Associates**. Because the
Constitution does not state the number of Justices to be appointed to the
Supreme Court, Congress decides the number by law. Today the Supreme
Court has nine Justices.

• *Structure.* The Constitutional provisions for the judicial branch are set
out in Article III.

• *Judicial Review.* The Court reviews the constitutionality of legislative
acts. Like Federalism and separation of powers, the concept of judicial review
is rooted in the principles of **limited government**. Although the framers of
the Constitution refrained from specifically spelling out judicial review, they
did state in Article III that "the judicial power of the United States, shall be
vested in one Supreme Court . . ." Moreover, Hamilton supported the concept
of judicial review in *Federalist No. 78* when he said that when the legislatures
are in conflict with the Constitution, "the judges should be governed by the
latter rather than the former."

The opinion of Chief Justice John Marshall in the Supreme Court case of
Marbury v. Madison in 1803 established the precedent for judicial review. In
this case, the Court held part of the Judiciary Act of 1789, an act of Congress, to
be unconstitutional. The Marbury case marked the first time the Supreme Court
ruled an act of Congress to be contrary to the Constitution.

There have been efforts to curb judicial review by those who feel that the
Supreme Court has abused its interpretive powers. This occurred after the
desegregation decision in **Brown v. Board of Education** (1954), when cries
for the impeachment of the Chief Justice and other members of the Court
were heard. One of the more recent movements for restriction of the Court's
jurisdiction has been in the area of religion in schools.

Primary Elections

In states not using caucuses or state conventions, primary elections are held in which voters pick either a candidate by name or delegates to the national convention who will support the particular candidate.

Caucuses and State Conventions

In states not having primaries, party members hold caucuses to pick delegates who then attend state conventions where the state's delegates to the national convention are chosen.

National Conventions

The delegates who have been selected in the state primaries and the state conventions attend the national convention of the party during the summer before the national election. At the convention the delegates vote for their choice for President and Vice President and adopt a platform on which they run. The individuals selected become the candidates for the national election in November.

Election Day

After intense campaigning by the candidates of the major parties during the late summer and fall, American voters cast their ballots on the first Tuesday after the first Monday in November for electors pledged to one of the candidates. This is the popular vote.

Electoral Vote

In each state the electors of the party that won the greatest popular vote assemble in December and vote for the Presidential and Vice Presidential candidates, usually of their own parties. Certified copies of these votes are sent to the President of the United States Senate. (Amendment 12)

Counting and Inauguration

The President of the Senate counts the electoral votes (538, the total number of members of Congress, plus 3 for the District of Columbia) in the presence of the House of Representatives and the Senate. The candidates with the majority of the electoral vote are elected and are sworn into office on January 20. (Amendment 20)

Figure 1.11   Election of the President

EXECUTIVE BRANCH

President's Cabinet
(In order of creation)
Department of State (1789)
Department of Treasury (1789)
Department of Justice (1789)
Department of the Interior (1849)
Department of Agriculture (1889)
Department of Commerce (1903)
Department of Labor (1913)
Department of Defense (1947)
Department of Health and
  Human Services (1953)
Department of Housing and
  Urban Development (1965)
Department of Transportation (1966)
Department of Energy (1977)
Department of Education (1979)
Department of Veterans Affairs (1988)
Department of Homeland Security
  (2003)

The Executive Office
(Partial Listing)
The White House Staff
Office of Management and Budget
Council of Economic Advisers
Council on Environmental Quality
Domestic Policy Staff
National Security Council
Central Intelligence Agency
Office of Administration

INDEPENDENT FEDERAL AGENCIES

(Partial Listing)

Federal Reserve System
Environmental Protection Agency
Equal Employment Opportunity
  Commission
Farm Credit Administration
Federal Communications
  Commission
Federal Deposit Insurance
  Corporation
Federal Election Commission
Federal Trade Commission

Interstate Commerce Commission
National Academy of Sciences
National Aeronautics and Space
  Administration (NASA)
National Foundation on the Arts
  and Humanities
National Labor Relations Board
Nuclear Regulatory Commission
Securities and Exchange
  Commission
Small Business Administration
Smithsonian Institution
Tennessee Valley Authority
United States Postal Service
Veterans Administration

Figure 1.12 The Executive Branch

Article III, Section 1	Establishment of the Supreme Court and the provision for Congress to establish inferior courts. Judges appointed for life assuming good behavior. Justices are appointed by the President and approved by the Senate (Article II, Section 2).
Article III, Section 2	The power of the federal courts extends to two types of cases: (1) those involving the interpretation of the Constitution, federal laws, treaties, and (2) those involving the United States government itself, foreign diplomatic officials, two or more state governments, citizens of different states, and states or citizens involved in disputes with foreign states. The Supreme Court has *original* jurisdiction in cases affecting ambassadors, public ministers, and in cases in which a state is a party. In all other cases, the jurisdiction of the Supreme Court is *appellate* with such exceptions as Congress shall make.
Article III, Section 3	Treason is the only crime to be defined in the Constitution. Article III, Section 3 provides for the definition and punishment of treason.

Figure 1.13   The Judicial Branch

THE MARSHALL COURT
EARLY SUPREME COURT CASES 1803–1824

CASE	ISSUE	DECISION
1803 *Marbury* v. *Madison*	Can the Supreme Court declare a federal law unconstitutional?	Declared the right of the Supreme Court to annul a law of Congress.
1810 *Fletcher* v. *Peck*	Can a state pass a law breaking a contract? Can the Supreme Court review a state law?	Established the right of the Supreme Court to declare state laws unconstitutional and protected private property.
1816 *Martin* v. *Hunters Lessee*	Can the Supreme Court review and reverse the decisions of the state courts?	Set the appellate jurisdiction of the Supreme Court over the state courts.
1819 *McCulloch* v. *Maryland*	Has Congress power to create a bank? Can the states tax such a structure?	Accepted broad "implied" powers of Congress and sovereign power of the federal government.
1819 *Dartmouth College* v. *Woodward*	Is a charter to a corporation a contract, and is this beyond control of the state?	The Supreme Court limited state powers over individuals and companies and protected contracts.
1824 *Gibbons* v. *Ogden*	What is "commerce" and what is the extent of Congress's power to regulate "commerce"?	Enlarged rights of Congress to control commerce.

Figure 1.14

• *Federal Court System and Routes to the Supreme Court.* The United States is served by 12 regional federal judicial circuits. Each has its own court of appeals and a varying number of district, or trial, courts—94 in all. Each state has its own judicial structure with trial courts, courts of appeals, and a highest court of final state appeal. Cases reach the Supreme Court either through the federal court system or on appeal from the highest court within a state. Of the thousands of cases that seek Supreme Court review each year, only a small percentage are accepted by the Court.

Figure 1.15 Route to the Supreme Court

Comparison to New York State Government

Each of the 50 state governments has political structures similar to the federal government, including republican forms of representative government, division of powers, and a system of federalism between state and local governments. Figure 1.18 shows the similarities between the New York State governmental structure and that of the federal government.

Thirteen Enduring Issues

National Power—limits and potential
Federalism—the balance between nation and state
The Judiciary—interpreter of the Constitution or shaper of public policy
Civil Liberties—the balance between government and the individual
Criminal Penalties—rights of the accused and protection of the community
Equality—its definition as a constitutional value
The Rights of Women under the Constitution
The Rights of Ethnic and Racial Groups under the Constitution
Presidential Power in Wartime and in Foreign Affairs
The Separation of Powers and the Capacity to Govern
Avenues of Representation
Property Rights and Economic Policy
Constitutional Change and Flexibility

National Power—Limits and Potential

The framers of the Constitution carefully limited the power of the federal government by enumerating the delegated powers and, in the Bill of Rights, reserving all other powers to the states and people. Yet, over the years, as the society has become more complex, legislation, executive acts, and decisions by the courts have increased the power of the federal government enormously.

Federalism—the Balance Between Nation and State

The Constitution balances the powers between the federal government and the states by specifically delegating certain powers to the national government and reserving all others to the states or the people. Throughout the history of the nation, however, the flow of power has gone from the states to the national government.

EXECUTIVE BRANCH
Governor, elected by the people of New York for a four-year term
LEGISLATIVE BRANCH
Bicameral legislature consisting of a 50-member Senate and a 150-member Assembly
JUDICIAL BRANCH
Court of Appeals: the highest appellate court in the state Appellate Divisions Supreme Courts: the lowest trial courts of the state system

Figure 1.16 New York State Government

The Judiciary—Interpreter of the Constitution or Shaper of Public Policy

Although the Supreme Court has been granted the judicial power of the United States by Article III of the Constitution, has it also become a second legislative body, establishing policy when Congress fails to do so?

Civil Liberties—the Balance Between Government and the Individual

In the famous Supreme Court case of *Schenck* v. *United States* (1919) involving civil liberties during wartime, Justice Holmes wrote, "Free speech would not protect a man in falsely shouting fire in a theatre, and causing a panic." On a larger scale, when does national security require the restriction of civil liberties? How should the Court go about balancing the two forces?

Criminal Penalties—Rights of the Accused and Protection of the Community

How can the government protect the citizens of this country and yet uphold the rights of those who have been accused of committing crimes? If Amendments 4, 5, 6, and 8 protect the accused, what protects the victim of a crime?

Equality—Its Definition as a Constitutional Value

Are all men and women created equal as the Declation of Independence sug-gests? If the Constitution guarantees equality before the law, does it guaran-tee equality of opportunities for people, or equality of results?

56

The Rights of Women Under the Constitution

Although the Constitution does not mention "women," it does make reference to "persons." Yet, the document prohibits only one form of sex-based discrimination, that no state may deny women the right to vote (Amendment 19). The proposed **Equal Rights Amendment**, which has not been approved, would prohibit discrimination on account of sex.

The Rights of Ethnic and Racial Groups
Under the Constitution

The trend during the 20th century has been toward much stronger guarantees of minority rights. However, can this go too far and begin to discriminate against the majority? Is it the obligation of society today to make up for the wrongs done to minorities in the past, as affirmative action suggests?

Presidential Power in Wartime

History shows that the President has exercised extraordinary powers during wartime both in restricting civil liberties at home and in sending troops into hostile environments without a declaration of war from Congress. Does the existence of the power of Congress to declare war and the President's power as Commander-in-Chief present an irreconcilable conflict that will be a continuing struggle between the executive and legislative branches?

The Separation of Powers and the Capacity to Govern

Through the system of checks and balances, combined with separation of powers, the framers of the Constitution tried to assure that no one branch would gain oppressive power over either of the other two. As a result, the federal government is often accused of being ineffective, too slow, or pitted against itself to the point of getting nothing done.

Avenues of Representation

Is the American system truly a republic, government by the people representing the majority will, or have political parties, special interest groups, and political action committees helped create a government that may be for sale?

Property Rights and Economic Policy

Congress is delegated the power to provide for the general welfare of the United States. Through the enumerated powers and the "necessary and proper" clause, the federal government has assumed economic responsibilities in the areas of trade, taxation, and contracts, and has helped perpetuate a system of free enterprise. However, as Congress uses its powers to promote

American business, it is also responsible for protecting Americans from abuses by businesses.

Constitutional Change and Flexibility

Although the Constitution has been amended only sixteen times since the addition of the Bill of Rights in 1791, in the last decade there have been numerous proposals for amending the document. How many times may the original document be amended without diluting its effectiveness? What are the assurances against insignificant changes to the document? Although the states have never made use of their constitutional power to call a constitutional convention, what would be the limits of such an exercise of power?

Exercise Set 1.3

1. Much of the authority of the United States Supreme Court is based on its power to
   A. propose legislation to Congress.
   B. change the distribution of powers as outlined in the federal Constitution.
   C. amend state and federal constitutions.
   D. interpret the federal Constitution.

2. The most serious threat to democracy resulting from high election campaign costs is that, once elected, candidates frequently
   A. owe money to friends and relatives.
   B. plan to use public funds to pay their debts.
   C. owe loyalty to a few major contributors.
   D. have little of their own savings left.

3. Base your answer to question 3 on the following headline and your knowledge of social studies.

THOMAS CONFIRMATION FIGHT
CONTINUES FOR HIGH COURT

The confirmation fight referred to in the headline is one that would take place among
A. Supreme Court Justices.
B. Senators.
C. Cabinet members.
D. members of the House Judiciary Committee.

4. When Congress makes laws "necessary and proper for carrying into execution the foregoing powers," it is using
A. enumerated powers.
B. implied powers.
C. concurrent powers.
D. general welfare powers.

5. Which headline would be an example of judicial review?
A. "Impeachment Charges Brought Against President"
B. "Attorney General Advises Presidential Veto"
C. "Judiciary Rules Law Unconstitutional"
D. "Senate Rejects Nomination of Federal Judge"

6. "The Supreme Court is not so much a court of justice as America's ultimate lawmaking body."
This statement is most concerned with the power of the U.S. Supreme Court to
A. exercise judicial review.
B. propose Constitutional amendments.
C. exercise original jurisdiction.
D. sit as a jury in impeachment proceedings.

7. Which headline is the best example of the application of the system of checks and balances?
A. "President Truman Fires General MacArthur"
B. "Senate to Debate Abortion Funding Bill"
C. "Supreme Court Nominee Rejected by Senate"
D. "House of Representatives Votes to Discipline Its Own Member"

8. Base your answer to question 8 on the following headline and your knowledge of social studies.

President Bush Refuses to Finish
Term as a "Lame Duck"

An assumption that may be drawn from the headline is that the President has
A. had numerous bills defeated by Congress.
B. approached the end of his term of office.
C. appointed ineffective staff members to the executive office.
D. dismissed some of his Cabinet directors.

DOCUMENT-BASED QUESTION

This question is based on the accompanying documents (1–7). The question is designed to test your ability to work with historical documents. Some of these documents have been edited for the purposes of this exercise. As you analyze the documents, take into account both the source of each document and any point of view that may be presented in the document.

Historical Context:

The United States Constitution divides the power to govern among the executive, legislative, and judicial branches of the national government. The Constitution provides for a system of checks and balances to prevent one branch from dominating the other two.

Task:

Using information from the documents and your knowledge of United States history, answer the questions that follow each document in Part A. Your answers to the questions will help you write the Part B essay, in which you will be asked to:

- Describe how the system of checks and balances functions.
- Show how this system has been applied in specific circumstances in United States history.

Part A
Short-Answer Questions

Analyze the documents and answer the short-answer questions that follow each document in the space provided.

DOCUMENT 1

The House of Representatives . . . shall have the sole power of impeachment. . . . The Senate shall have the sole power to try all impeachments.

—United States Constitution, Article 1

1. Which branch of the United States government is responsible for the impeachment process?

DOCUMENT 2

> He shall have power, by and with the advice and consent of the Senate, to make treaties, provided two thirds of the senators present concur; and he shall nominate, and by and with the advice and consent of the Senate, shall appoint ambassadors, other public ministers and consuls, judges of the Supreme Court, and all other officers of the United States. . . .

—United States Constitution, Article 2, Section 2, Clause 2

2*a*. To whom does "He" refer?

_____

2*b*. Under Article 2, Section 2, Clause 2, what role does the Senate play in the appointment of ambassadors or the appointment of judges to the Supreme Court?

_____

_____

_____

DOCUMENT 3

Presidential Vetoes, 1901–1990

President	Regular Vetoes	Pocket Vetoes	Total Vetoes	Vetoes Overridden
T. Roosevelt	42	40	82	1
Taft	30	9	39	1
Wilson	33	11	44	6
Harding	5	1	6	—
Coolidge	20	30	50	4
Hoover	21	16	37	3
F. Roosevelt	372	263	635	9
Truman	180	70	250	12
Eisenhower	73	108	181	2
Kennedy	12	9	21	—
L. Johnson	16	14	30	—
Nixon	24	18	42	6
Ford	53	19	72	12
Carter	13	18	31	2
Reagan	39	39	78	9
G. Bush	14	6	20	0

3*a*. What does this chart indicate about how the President can check the power of Congress?

_____

_____

_____

3*b*. What does this chart indicate about how Congress can check the power of the President?

_____

_____

_____

DOCUMENT 4

4. In this cartoon, why is the Treaty of Versailles in the wastebasket?

_____

_____

_____

DOCUMENT 5

The Ingenious Quarterback

(adapted)

5. In this cartoon, which branch of the government is President Franklin D. Roosevelt trying to change?

_____

_____

_____

DOCUMENT 6

So if a law be in opposition to the Constitution, if both the law and the Constitution apply to a particular case, so that the Court must either decide that case conformably to the law, disregarding the Constitution or conformably to the Constitution, disregarding the law, the Court must determine which of these conflicting rules governs the case. This is of the very essence of judicial duty. . . .

—Chief Justice John Marshall

6. According to this quotation by Chief Justice John Marshall, what "power" does the Supreme Court have?

_____

_____

_____

DOCUMENT 7

Yesterday, December 7, 1941—a date which will live in infamy—the United States of America was suddenly and deliberately attacked by naval and air forces of the empire of Japan. . . . I ask that the Congress declare that since the unprovoked and dastardly attack by Japan on Sunday, December 7, 1941, a state of war has existed between the United States and the Japanese Empire.

—President Franklin D. Roosevelt, to Congress

The Congress shall have the power . . . to declare war.

—United States Constitution, Article 1, Section 8, Clause 11

7. Why was it necessary for President Franklin D. Roosevelt to ask Congress for a declaration of war against Japan in December 1941?

_____

_____

_____

Part B
Essay

Write a well-organized essay that includes an introduction, several para-graphs, and a conclusion. Use evidence from *at least four* documents in the body of the essay. Support your response with relevant facts, examples, and details. Include additional outside information.

Historical Context:

> The United States Constitution divides the power to govern among the executive, legislative, and judicial branches of the national government. The Constitution provides for a system of checks and balances to prevent one branch from dominating the other two.

Task:

> Using information from the documents and your knowledge of United States history, write an essay in which you:
>
> - Describe how the system of checks and balances functions.
> - Show how this system has been applied in specific circumstances in United States history.

Guidelines:

In your essay, be sure to
- Address all aspects of the *Task* by accurately analyzing and interpreting *at least four* documents.
- Incorporate information from the documents in the body of the essay.
- Incorporate relevant outside information.
- Support the theme with relevant facts, examples, and details.
- Use a logical and clear plan of organization.
- Introduce the theme by establishing a framework that is beyond a simple restatement of the *Task* or *Historical Context* and conclude with a summa-tion of the theme.

LAUNCHING A NEW GOVERNMENT

> All communities divide themselves into the few and the many. The
> first are the rich and the wellborn; the other, the mass of the people
> . . . Give therefore to the first class a distinct permanent share in
> the government. They will check the unsteadiness of the second . . .
>
> Alexander Hamilton, 1787

> Men . . . are naturally divided into two parties. Those who fear and
> distrust the people . . . and . . . those who identify themselves with
> the people.
> I am not among those who fear the people. They, and not the rich,
> are our dependence for continued freedom.
>
> Thomas Jefferson, 1824, 1816

On March 4, 1789, the first Congress under the new Constitution assembled
in New York City. The members of Congress were supporters of the new
Constitution and many of them had served as delegates in Philadelphia during the summer of 1787. Their primary intention was to carry out the purposes of the nationalists; to make the federal government a lasting institution
and to create respect for the republic among the older nations of the world.

George Washington, who had been unanimously elected President,
was inaugurated in New York City on April 30th, 1789. **John Adams** had
been chosen Vice President. Congress created three executive departments
to which Washington appointed **Thomas Jefferson** as Secretary of State,
Alexander Hamilton as Secretary of the Treasury, and Henry Knox as
Secretary of War. The office of Attorney General was created by Congress
as the government's chief law officer.

The Hamiltonian Program: Steps Toward Domestic Stability

Alexander Hamilton, as the first Secretary of the Treasury, formulated an
economic program aimed at building the political support and respect necessary to assure the legitimacy of the new government. Hamilton proposed the
following financial plan:

Repayment of the Foreign Debt

The national government should repay approximately $12 million to foreign
governments and investors, mostly to France.

Federal Assumption of the State Debts

Amounting to $25 million, this repayment was opposed primarily by
Southern states such as Virginia, which had partially paid some of their debts.
To win their support, Hamilton made a deal with Jefferson to give Northern

support for a bill to locate the future national capital on the Potomac River, i.e., Washington, D.C.

Excise Taxes

To raise revenue to help repay both the foreign and domestic debt that Congress incurred during the Revolution and confederation period, a tax was placed on whiskey. Resentment to the tax on whiskey came to a head during the summer of 1794 with the "**Whiskey Rebellion**." President Washington called out 13,000 militiamen to put down the uprising, demonstrating that the new government possessed the power to enforce its authority—a power that had been absent under the Articles of Confederation.

Establishment of a National Bank

Hamilton asked Congress to establish a Bank of the United States that would be a depository of federal funds and able to issue sound paper money on the basis of the securities it held.

• *Jefferson's arguments against the bank:* Using the "strict constructionist" view, Jefferson declared the proposed United States bank unconstitutional. He claimed that the power to create the bank was not listed in the enumerated powers (Article I, Section 8), nor could the power be implied from any other power through the use of the elastic clause.

• *Hamilton's arguments for the bank:* Using the "loose" or "broad constructionist" view, Hamilton held the bank to be constitutional. He claimed that the power to create the bank could be implied from the enumerated powers to coin money, borrow money, and raise money through taxation.

Passage of Hamilton's Program

After listening to the arguments of Jefferson and Hamilton, Washington was convinced that the Bank of the United States was constitutional and advisable. The bank proved to be a sound financial institution and the funding and assumption of the state's debts helped to put the new nation on a solid economic footing.

The Unwritten Constitution (1789–1808)

The reason the United States Constitution has lasted for such a long time is that the document was written so that it could be changed and adapted to future conditions. The provisions that have allowed for adaptation include the elastic clause, the doctrine of implied powers, judicial interpretation, and the amendment process. The flexibility of our Constitution has also been made possible by the practice of custom and tradition, or what is sometimes referred to as the unwritten Constitution.

During the young nation's first three administrations, growth, experimentation, and necessity led to unwritten developments in our constitutional form of government. These included the development of a Cabinet, the formation of political parties, the establishment of judicial review, and a **two-term tradition** for the President. Later developments were the growth of the committee system within Congress, lobbying, and the practice of presidential electors pledging their votes for specific candidates. These elements were not provided for in the Constitution but developed over time through practice.

The Cabinet System

Article II, Section 2, Clause 1 of the Constitution provides that the President may "require the Opinion in writing, of the principal Officer in each of the executive Departments . . ." Functioning at the pleasure of the President, the purpose of the Cabinet is to advise the President on any matter. The evolution of the Cabinet is shown in Figure 1.17.

Political Parties

American political parties began as early as 1796 and the election of John Adams. The followers of Hamilton came to be known as **Federalists** and the supporters of Jefferson as **Republicans**. By 1796 presidential candidates were assuming political party identification.

ORIGINAL CABINET	ADDED, 1798–1913	ADDED, 1947–2006
State Dept., 1789 Treasury Dept., 1789 War Dept., 1789–1946 Attorney General, 1789 (Not head of Justice Dept. until 1870)	Navy Dept., 1798–1946 Postmaster General, 1829–1970 Interior Dept., 1849 Agriculture Dept., 1889 Commerce and Labor, 1903 (divided in 1913) Commerce, 1913 Labor, 1913	Defense Dept., 1947 (combined War and Navy) Health, Education and Welfare, 1953 (divided in 1979) Housing and Urban Development Dept., 1965 Transportation Dept., 1966 Energy Dept., 1977 Health and Human Services, 1979 Education Dept., 1979 Veterans Affairs Dept., 1988 Homeland Security, 2003

Figure 1.17 Evolution of the Cabinet

The two major political parties in the United States today are the **Republicans** and the **Democrats**. Although third parties have existed in our political structure many times, they have never won real political power. These parties were usually formed because of a single issue. Some of these third parties have included: the **Free Soil Party**, which opposed the extension of slavery; the **Greenback Labor Party** of the 1870s, which supported farmers and workers; the **Progressive Party** in the early 20th century that worked for political and social reform; the **Socialist Party** that advocated government ownership of the means of production in American industry; the States Rights Party (Dixiecrats) of the 1940s, composed of Southern Democrats who opposed the more liberal wing of the Democratic Party; the **Right to Life Party** of the 1970s, 1980s, and 1990s that opposed abortion; and Ross Perot's United We Stand Party in the election of 1992. Third parties have often had their proposals adopted by the major parties and some have been passed into law.

In the United States, political parties perform the following functions: (1) provide qualified and responsible candidates; (2) establish public policy; (3) educate the electorate; (4) encourage voter participation; and (5) finance political campaigns.

Judicial Review

The practice of judicial review by the Supreme Court, a power not specifically delegated in Article III of the Constitution, but implied by the Constitution and assumed by the Supreme Court itself, has broadened the authority of the national government. The primary basis of the judicial power in our system of government has been the practice of judicial review, that is, the practice by which courts can determine whether legislative acts, both federal and state, are constitutional.

Two-Term Tradition

Although Article II, Section 1, Clause 1 states that the President shall "hold his office during the Term of four Years," it does not say how many terms a President may serve. George Washington chose to leave office after two terms, and all Presidents followed that precedent until Franklin Delano Roosevelt was elected to four terms (1932–1945; dying during his fourth term). The two-term (or ten-year limit) custom became part of the written Constitution through the Twenty-Second Amendment (1951).

Committee System of Congress

Because of the many complex issues that must be considered by the legislative branch, the Senate and the House of Representatives are divided into small legislative bodies called committees. The committee system, which is part of the unwritten Constitution, grew out of necessity and became custom.

Lobbying

The term describes attempts to influence elected representatives during the passage of legislation through Congress. Lobbyists present to legislators the opinion of various groups. They also provide legislators with information concerning issues and bills before Congress. Recently, much criticism has been directed against lobbyists' efforts to influence members of Congress and to purchase the First Amendment "right to petition" with large funds from special interest groups. Deriving somewhat from the concept of lobbying are **Political Action Committees** (PACS), special interest groups who contribute money to political candidates for their election campaigns. PACS now supply more than a third of funds raised by the House candidates and close to a fifth for the Senate.

Pledging of Electoral Votes

Although the Electoral College was designed because of the founders' distrust of the common citizen's capability to select a President, this undemocratic intent has been overcome. Today, political parties name the electors who are pledged in advance to vote for the party's presidential candidate. However, only some states legally bind electors to honor their pledges and, although it is uncommon, electors sometimes do break their pledges and change their vote.

The Birth of American Foreign Policy (1789–1824)

The Administration of George Washington (1789–1797)

- *The French Revolution (1789–1793).* Most Americans supported the French Revolution, until the executions under the Reign of Terror increased. After this and the entrance of Great Britain and Spain into the war against the Revolutionists, opinion in the United States was mixed. It was divided along political lines, with the Federalists supporting England and the Republicans supporting the French.

- *Proclamation of Neutrality (1793).* The French Revolution proved to be one of the most important events in the diplomatic history of the United States, because it established the principles of American neutrality concerning European affairs. Although President Washington recognized the French Republic, he issued a proclamation of neutrality that never used the word "neutral," but stated that the United States would adopt "a conduct friendly and impartial toward the belligerent powers."

- *Problems with England and Jay's Treaty (1794).* Although the United States tried to remain neutral as British hostilities with France continued, its economic ties and trade with both sides placed the nation in danger. The United States and Britain came close to war because of Britain's refusal to abide by rules of international law (primarily the right of neutral shipping), the impressment of American sailors by the British navy, and the failure of the British to evacuate forts in the American Northwest according to the provisions of the Treaty of Paris (1783). President Washington sent Chief Justice John Jay to England to settle differences between the two nations. Jay negotiated a treaty with the following provisions: (1) the British would evacuate the Northwest forts by June 1, 1796; (2) commissions would be set up to establish the amount due to American shippers for loss of goods and other controversies; (3) England's contention that food was contraband was accepted; and (4) direct commerce between the United States and the British East Indies was provided for.

The treaty was a success because it avoided war with Britain at a time when the United States was weak and not ready to fight its former mother country.

• *Washington's Farewell Address (1796).* Before leaving office to be succeeded by Federalist **John Adams**, President Washington conveyed through the press on September 19 his "Farewell Address." Written mostly by Hamilton, Washington advised in the address that the United States should maintain commercial, but not political, ties to other nations, and not enter into any "**entangling**," or **permanent alliances**. While not advocating isolationism, Washington laid out principles that would be followed in the making of American foreign policy until the 1940s and 1950s.

The Administration of John Adams (1797–1801)

• *Failure of Attempts at Neutrality.* Relations between France and the United States grew steadily worse after 1793. Hostile toward the treaties of the United States with England and Spain (the Jay and Pinckney treaties), and unhappy with the fact that the United States had abandoned the 1778 Franco-American Treaty, France ordered its vessels to start seizing American ships carrying British goods. Attempts by the United States to negotiate its differences with France were frustrated by the **XYZ Affair** of 1797 (request of bribes in exchange for negotiations by France) and by an undeclared naval war from 1798 to 1800. In 1800 **Napoleon**, who now ruled France and wanted to avoid war with the United States, agreed to the **Convention of 1800**, which established peace between the two nations and finally recognized an end to the Treaty of 1778.

The Administrations of Thomas Jefferson (1801–1809)

• *Tripolitan War (1801).* The problems of raids on American shipping by the Barbary pirates continued. In 1801 President Jefferson refused the demand of the Tripoli government for payments of "tribute," a form of extortion. Instead of payment, Jefferson sent a naval squadron to protect American shipping. One of the Barbary states, Tripoli, declared war on the United States in 1801, causing hostilities until 1805 when Tripoli was subdued.

• **Problems with England.** After a brief interlude, Britain and France were at war again in 1803. The neutrality of the American shipping was again threatened, as both England and France issued decrees ordering the seizure of ships carrying goods to the other. The British navy resumed its practice of impressing sailors aboard American vessels, claiming they were deserters from the British fleet.

• **The Louisiana Purchase (1803).** During Jefferson's first term, thousands of American farmers had moved west to the lands between the Appalachian Mountains and the Mississippi River. They used the port of New Orleans at the base of the Mississippi River to export much of their produce.

The Louisiana Territory had been given to Spain by France at the end of the French and Indian War. Americans became alarmed when it was learned that Spain had transferred the area back to France by the Treaty of San Ildefonso (1800) and that Spanish officials left in control of New Orleans had ended the right of American farmers to use the port (suspension of the "**right of deposit**"). Jefferson, fearful of a strong and aggressive France as a neighbor and concerned over conflicts concerning the use of New Orleans, sent **James Monroe** and **Robert Livingston** to France to try to buy New Orleans. Napoleon, burdened with problems in Europe, decided to sell the entire Louisiana Territory to the United States for $15,000,000.

Problems arose when the strict constructionist Jefferson realized that the Constitution did not authorize Congress to purchase territory. Jefferson was forced to modify his constitutional theories because of the importance of the purchase, and in 1803 the treaty was ratified authorizing the purchase, which nearly doubled the size of the United States.

• **The Embargo Act (1807).** Seeking to force England to respect American rights while avoiding war, Jefferson pushed through Congress the Embargo Act, which forbade all exports from the United States to any country. Although it caused some harm to England, the act hurt the American economy by causing a depression.

• **The Non-Intercourse Act (1809).** In his last days of office, President Jefferson replaced the disastrous Embargo Act with the Non-Intercourse Act, which opened trade with all nations except France and England.

The Administrations of James Madison (1809–1817)

• **Macon's Bill No. 2.** Congress allowed the Non-Intercourse Act to expire in 1810 and replaced it with Macon's Bill No. 2. This promised both England and France that the United States would resume trade with the first nation that stopped abusing American shipping rights. Macon's Bill No. 2 allowed Madison to resume trade with France and to forbid all trade with England in March 1811.

• **Sectional Politics.** Sentiment for war against England came from land-hungry Southerners and Westerners (**War Hawks**) led by **Henry Clay** of

Kentucky and **John Calhoun** of South Carolina. The commercial interests of the New England states caused them to oppose war because they feared a complete shutdown of trade and continuing depression. Opposition from the New England states increased in 1814 as the British blockade strangled New England commercial interests. At the **Hartford Convention** (December 1814) Federalist representatives declared that a state had the right to oppose congressional action believed to violate the Constitution, thus supporting the doctrine of **states' rights**.

• *War of 1812.* Unable to resist the pressure by the War Hawks in Congress, President Madison recommended that Congress declare war on June 1, 1812. A close vote representing sectional divisions of the country resulted in the declaration of war on June 18, 1812.

• *Treaty of Ghent (December 1814).* For the most part, the peace settlement simply restored the prewar status. Provisions of the treaty included an end to hostilities and British influence in the Northwest Territory, restoration of conquered territory, and arbitration of boundary disputes. Perhaps the longest lasting result of the War of 1812 was the rise of American **nationalism** and the new impulse to expand the nation.

James Monroe (1758–1831), 5th President of the United States. The Monroe Doctrine discouraged European involvement in the Western Hemisphere.

The Administrations of James Monroe (1817–1825)

James Monroe, Madison's Secretary of State, defeated the last Federalist candidate, Rufus King, to become the fifth President. Much of Monroe's success in foreign affairs can be credited to his Secretary of State, **John Quincy Adams**.

John Quincy Adams (1767–1848), 6th President of the United States. As Secretary of State to President Monroe, Adams was the real author of the Monroe Doctrine.

• *Monroe Doctrine (1823)*. As the stability of the Western Hemisphere was threatened by European events, the United States could ally with Great Britain in defending its close-to-home interests, or act independently. Russia was threatening to expand and was establishing trading posts on the West Coast. Moreover, the European alliance of France, Russia, Prussia, and Austria was considering an attempt to reclaim as colonies the Latin American states that had recently gained their independence in their war with Spain. President Monroe addressed Congress on December 2, 1823, with a statement of foreign policy that came to be known as the **Monroe Doctrine**. It declared: (1) the American continent was no longer open to colonization by European nations; (2) the United States would not interfere in European affairs; and (3) an act of intervention by a European power in the affairs of a country in the Western Hemisphere would be considered an act against the United States.

Manifest Destiny (1789–1853)

As nationalism grew, Americans came to believe that westward expansion would spread American freedom and democracy across the continent.

The acquisition of large tracts of territory during the 19th century increased sectional conflict, primarily over the extension of slavery. As the nation expanded rapidly from coast to coast, the American population with its varying social, political, and especially economic interests was able to find harmony only through compromise. However, in time, sectional differences made compromise impossible, and the final result was the Civil War. In the name of manifest destiny, more than 70,000 Native Americans were forced from their homelands and relocated to settlements. Many thousands died.

Sectional Specialization and Improvements in Transportation

As the nation's economy developed, differences between the sections grew. In the North, industry advanced, helped by the decreased trade before and during the War of 1812, and because of the supply of adequate water power, a wealthy class with commercial capital to invest, and a plentiful labor supply. The South had an agricultural economy based on slave labor. After the invention of the **cotton gin** in 1793, the South had a one-crop economy based upon the cultivation of cotton. At the same time, the grains of the West were quickly transforming that area into the "breadbasket" of the nation.

The need to transport raw materials and manufactured goods between the sections and to ship products to their market created a demand for a better transportation system. Between 1800 and 1825 hundreds of turnpikes (privately built toll roads) and roads financed by the federal government were built to help transport people and products. In 1808, Secretary of the Treasury Albert Gallatin proposed a system of internal improvements at federal expense, an issue that would eventually raise debate between states' righters and nationalists.

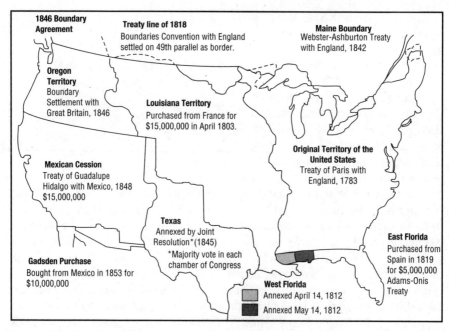

Figure 1.18   Territorial Growth of the United States, 1783–1853

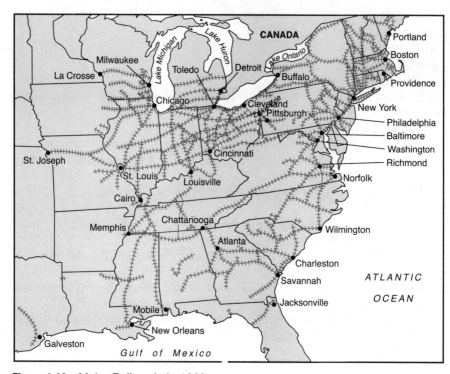

Figure 1.19   Major Railroads in 1860

The years from 1820 to 1850 were the age of the steamboat and canal building to connect interior waterways, which resulted in over 3,300 miles of canals by 1840. In 1828 the first major railroad, the Baltimore and Ohio, was chartered, and by 1840 the nation's total railway mileage equaled that of its canals. At the begin-

ning of the Civil War, railroads overshadowed all other forms of long-distance transportation in the country. Figure 1.19, showing the routes of the major railroads in 1860, helps to demonstrate the economic interdependency between the North and the West, a factor of great importance during the Civil War.

The growth of transportation brought with it legal questions. One of the earliest questions was who would regulate interstate commerce. The Supreme Court addressed this issue in the case of ***Gibbons* v. *Ogden*** (1824), when the Court held that, although Congress did not have the power to control trade within one state, its authority did extend to trade from one state to another and to the navigable rivers on which interstate or foreign commerce could be carried.

Exercise Set 1.4

1. The argument over the creation of the Bank of the United States concerned
   A. its effect on the funds kept in the state banks.
   B. whether or not the country needed a central banking institution.
   C. whether or not the Constitution provided for congressional authority to create a bank.
   D. the creation of the Treasury Department by Congress.

2. The Supreme Court under Chief Justice John Marshall influenced United States history in that the Court
   A. stimulated the states' rights movement by supporting the idea that states could reject acts of Congress.
   B. helped to create a sense of national unity by strengthening the federal government.
   C. weakened the judiciary by refusing to deal with controversial issues.
   D. became heavily involved in foreign affairs.

3. Which of the following practices has changed from custom and tradition to become part of the written Constitution?
   A. The pledging of electoral votes
   B. The existence of political parties
   C. Limiting the number of terms for the presidency
   D. The committee system of Congress

Base your answers to questions 4 and 5 on the following quotation and your knowledge of social studies.

> "Now it appears . . . that this general principle is inherent in the very definition of government, and essential to every step of the progress to be made by that United States, namely: that every power vested in a government is in its nature sovereign, and includes, by force of the term, a right to employ all the means requisite and fairly applicable to the attainment of the ends of such power and which are not precluded by restrictions . . . in the Constitution, or not immoral, or not contrary to the essential ends of political society."

4. The quotation expresses the position on the Constitution advocated by
   A. a strict constructionist.
   B. one in agreement with Thomas Jefferson.
   C. a loose, or broad, constructionist.
   D. a states' righter.

5. The preceding quotation is most likely from
   A. Washington's Farewell Address.
   B. Jefferson's opinions on the constitutionality of the National Bank.
   C. Article III of the United States Constitution.
   D. Hamilton's opinions on the constitutionality of the National Bank.

6. All of the following are characteristic of the Embargo Act of 1807 EXCEPT
   A. it was initially destructive to the American economy.
   B. it was generally recognized as a failure.
   C. it was America's last attempt at economic pressure on warring European nations.
   D. it was beneficial to American industry in the long run.

7. The vote in favor of war in 1812 in the House of Representatives indicated that
   A. almost all Americans wanted war.
   B. the country was divided over going to war with England.
   C. when it came to an issue as serious as the consideration of war, Representatives put aside sectional differences.
   D. most Americans desired war with France as opposed to England.

8. The original Monroe Doctrine was part of
   A. a joint resolution of Congress.
   B. a message to Congress.
   C. a Supreme Court ruling.
   D. an agreement between the United States and Latin America.

9. The significance of the Supreme Court's decision in *Gibbons* v. *Ogden* (1803) was that it affirmed that
   A. intrastate trade fell within the jurisdiction of Congress.
   B. tariffs on imported goods were prohibited by the Constitution.
   C. the Bank of the United States was found to be permissible by the "necessary and proper" clause of the Constitution.
   D. trade involving two or more states on the nation's internal waterways fell under the commerce clause of the Constitution and therefore was subject to congressional control.

CHAPTER REVIEW QUESTIONS

1. Which of the reasons listed below was the most important for social and political mobility in the English colonies of North America during the 17th and 18th centuries?
   A. Early emphasis on rapid industrialization
   B. Existence of a strong cultural heritage
   C. Absence of racial prejudice among the colonists
   D. Availability of land

2. The best evidence that a nation is a democracy is its provisions for
   A. a system of civil and criminal courts.
   B. a limited government responsible to the people.
   C. the holding of periodic elections.
   D. a two-house legislature.

3. Which feature of the current day U.S. government is based upon the principles found in the Magna Carta (1215) and the English Bill of Rights (1689)?
   A. Universal suffrage
   B. Power of Congress to declare war
   C. Power of the House of Representatives to originate all revenue bills
   D. Presidential veto power

4. The Mayflower Compact was
    A. an early example of intercolonial unity.
    B. a landmark in religious toleration.
    C. an agreement to submit to the will of the majority.
    D. an example of a successful proprietorship.

5. The Dominion of New England was designed to
    A. promote self-government among the New England colonists.
    B. enforce the Navigation Acts.
    C. encourage fur trading with the French.
    D. assist in the development of a Puritan confederation.

6. Most English subjects came to America in the colonial period to
    A. enjoy religious freedom.
    B. escape political oppression.
    C. find economic opportunity.
    D. join the forces of slave labor.

7. "Direct democracy" is best illustrated by the
    A. New England town meeting.
    B. British Parliament.
    C. United States Congress.
    D. Virginia House of Burgesses.

8. The most troubling aspect of the Proclamation of 1763 for the colonists was that it
    A. increased the jurisdiction of the admiralty courts.
    B. mandated the quartering of troops in the colonies.
    C. discouraged settlement on western lands.
    D. was another example of a revenue-raising tax.

9. The American victory at Yorktown in 1781
    A. was assisted by French control of the sea.
    B. ended fighting in America.
    C. marked the end of the French Alliance.
    D. convinced the Second Continental Congress to issue the Declaration of Independence.

10. The Articles of Confederation
    A. created a supreme national government with subordinate state governments.
    B. instituted a system of checks and balances between the executive, legislative, and judicial branches of government.
    C. placed control over foreign and domestic trade at the national level.
    D. created a national government that did not have adequate taxation powers.

11. The convention in 1787 at Philadelphia was called for the purpose of
    A. completing the provisions of the Treaty of Paris (1783).
    B. drafting the Bill of Rights.
    C. revising the Articles of Confederation.
    D. writing a new Constitution.

12. Under the original Constitution, the only government officials elected directly by qualified voters were
    A. Supreme Court Justices.
    B. Representatives.
    C. Senators.
    D. the President and Vice President.

13. The provision that all powers not delegated to the national government are reserved to the states is included within
    A. Article I.
    B. the Bill of Rights.
    C. Article III.
    D. the Preamble.

14. In conflicts between the national Constitution and state constitutions, the national Constitution
    A. is silent.
    B. states that it is the supreme law of the land and therefore takes precedence over state constitutions.
    C. defers to the state constitutions.
    D. is restricted by Amendment 10 of the Bill of Rights.

15. Political parties were formed early during the country's history and were one of the earliest examples of
    A. the "necessary and proper" clause.
    B. the unwritten constitution.
    C. the use of the elastic clause.
    D. separation of powers.

16. Hamilton's arguments in support of a national bank included *all* the following EXCEPT
    A. the bank was among the listed, or enumerated, powers of Congress.
    B. the bank would provide a stable currency for the nation.
    C. in the use of the "necessary and proper" clause, the ends justified the means.
    D. a national bank would benefit the commercial interests of the nation.

17. Washington's Farewell Address
   A. favored political parties.
   B. condemned all alliances.
   C. advocated temporary, nonentangling alliances.
   D. promoted economic and military alliance with all major European nations.

18. In general, support for war against England in 1812 came from
   A. commercial interests in the East.
   B. agrarian interests in the West and the South.
   C. the Federalist party.
   D. coastal shippers.

19. The basis for federal control over interstate commerce was affirmed by the Supreme Court in
   A. *Marbury* v. *Madison.*
   B. *Fletcher* v. *Peck.*
   C. *Brown* v. *Board of Education.*
   D. *Gibbons* v. *Ogden.*

20. The Monroe Doctrine was
   A. basically a self-defense measure.
   B. an example of an executive check on Congress.
   C. soon abandoned for active United States involvement in European affairs.
   D. inspired primarily for the defense of European colonies in the Western Hemisphere.

THEMATIC ESSAY

Directions: Write a well-organized essay that includes an introduction, several paragraphs addressing the task below, and a conclusion.

Theme: Government: Power of the Judiciary

Shortly after the formation of the new constitutional government, the Supreme Court established itself as an equal to the legislative and executive branches.

Task:

> From your study of the Supreme Court under the leadership of Chief
> Justice John Marshall, identify *two* cases that strengthened the power of
> the Supreme Court.
>
> For each case identified:
>
> - Discuss the facts of the case.
> - Describe the court's decision.
> - Explain how the decision strengthened the power of the Supreme
>   Court and the federal government.

You may use cases decided during the Marshall Court era. Some
suggestions you might wish to consider are *Marbury* v. *Madison* (1803),
McCulloch v. *Maryland* (1819), and *Gibbons* v. *Ogden* (1824).

You are *not* limited to these suggestions.

DOCUMENT-BASED QUESTION

This question is based on the accompanying documents. The question is
designed to test your ability to work with historical documents. Some of
these documents have been edited for the purposes of this exercise. As you
analyze the documents, take into account the source of each document and
any point of view that may be presented in the document. Keep in mind that
the language used in a document may reflect the historical context of the time
in which it was written.

Historical Context:

> In the early years of the republic, various controversial issues divided
> the American people. Three such issues were *ratification of the
> Constitution*, *purchase of the Louisiana Territory*, and *expansion of
> slavery into the territories*.

Task:

> Using the information from the documents and your knowledge of United States history, answer the questions that follow each document in Part A. Your answers to the questions will help you write the Part B essay in which you will be asked to:
>
> Choose *two* issues mentioned in the historical context and for *each*
>
> - Describe the historical circumstances surrounding the issue.
> - Discuss arguments of those *in favor of* **and** of those *opposed to* the issue. In your discussion, include *at least one* argument on *each* side of the issue.

Part A
Short-Answer Questions

Analyze the documents and answer the short-answer questions that follow each document in the space provided.

DOCUMENT 1

> . . . Almost immediately after the Confederation was created, many Americans, including [James] Madison, came to see that it was much too weak to do what they wanted. By the 1780s the problems were severe and conspicuous [obvious]. The Congress could not tax and pay its bills. It could not feed, clothe, or supply the army. It could not levy tariffs to regulate trade or to retaliate against the mercantilist European empires. It was even having trouble gathering a quorum to conduct business. Attempts to revise the Articles and grant the Congress the power to levy a 5 percent impost [tax] on imported European goods were thwarted by the need to get the unanimous consent of all thirteen states. Internationally the United States were being humiliated. In the Mediterranean the Barbary pirates were seizing American ships and selling their sailors into slavery, and the Confederation was powerless to do anything. It was unable even to guarantee the territorial integrity of the new nation. Great Britain continued to hold posts in the northwestern parts of United States territory in defiance of the peace treaty of 1783. In the southwest Spain was claiming territory that included much of present-day Alabama and Mississippi and plotting with American dissidents to break away from the Union. . . .

Source: Gordon S. Wood, *Revolutionary Characters: What Made the Founders Different*, Penguin Press, 2006

1. According to Gordon S. Wood, what were *two* weaknesses of the national government under the Articles of Confederation that led to the Constitutional Convention?

(1) _____

_____

(2) _____

_____

DOCUMENT 2

John Jay of New York wrote *The Federalist*, Number 4, in support of ratification of the Constitution. This is an excerpt from that publication.

> But whatever may be our situation, whether firmly united under one national government, or split into a number of confederacies, certain it is, that foreign nations will know and view it exactly as it is; and they will act toward us accordingly. If they see that our national government is efficient and well administered, our trade prudently regulated, our militia properly organized and disciplined, our resources and finances discreetly managed, our credit re-established, our people free, contented, and united, they will be much more disposed to cultivate our friendship than provoke our resentment. If, on the other hand, they find us either destitute of [lacking] an effectual government (each State doing right or wrong, as to its rulers may seem convenient), or split into three or four independent and probably discordant [quarreling] republics or confederacies, one inclining to Britain, another to France, and a third to Spain, and perhaps played off against each other by the three, what a poor, pitiful figure will America make in their eyes! How liable would she become not only to their contempt but to their outrage, and how soon would dear-bought experience proclaim that when a people or family so divide, it never fails to be against themselves.

Source: John Jay, *The Federalist*, Number 4, November 7, 1787

2. Based on this excerpt from *The Federalist*, Number 4, state one argument used by John Jay to support ratification of the Constitution.

_____

_____

... The first question that presents itself on the subject is, whether a confederated government be the best for the United States or not? Or in other words, whether the thirteen United States should be reduced to one great republic, governed by one legislature, and under the direction of one executive and judicial; or whether they should continue thirteen confederated republics, under the direction and controul [control] of a supreme federal head for certain defined national purposes only? ...

In a republic of such vast extent as the United–States, the legislature cannot attend to the various concerns and wants of its different parts. It cannot be sufficiently numerous to be acquainted with the local condition and wants of the different districts, and if it could, it is impossible it should have sufficient time to attend to and provide for all the variety of cases of this nature, that would be continually arising. ...

These are some of the reasons by which it appears, that a free republic cannot long subsist [survive] over a country of the great extent of these states. If then this new constitution is calculated to consolidate the thirteen states into one, as it evidently is, it ought not to be adopted. ...

Source: *Antifederalist Papers*, Brutus Number 1, October 18, 1787

3a. Based on this document, state *one* argument the antifederalists used to oppose ratification of the Constitution.

_____

_____

There is no declaration of rights; and the laws of the general government being paramount [superior] to the laws and constitutions of the several states, the declarations of rights in the separate states are no security. Nor are the people secured even in the enjoyment of the benefits of the common law, which stands here upon no other foundation than its having been adopted by the respective acts forming the constitutions of the several states. ...

There is no declaration of any kind for preserving the liberty of the press, the trial by jury in civil cases, nor against the danger of standing armies in time of peace. ...

Source: George Mason, "Objections to the Constitution," October 7, 1787

85

3*b*. According to George Mason, what is *one* argument against ratifying the new Constitution?

_____

_____

DOCUMENT 4a

. . . There is on the globe one single spot, the possessor of which is our natural and habitual enemy. It is New Orleans, through which the produce of three-eighths of our territory must pass to market, and from its fertility it will ere [before] long yield more than half of our whole produce and contain more than half our inhabitants. France, placing herself in that door, assumes to us the attitude of defiance. . . .

Source: President Thomas Jefferson, Letter to Robert Livingston, 1802

DOCUMENT 4b

United States in 1803

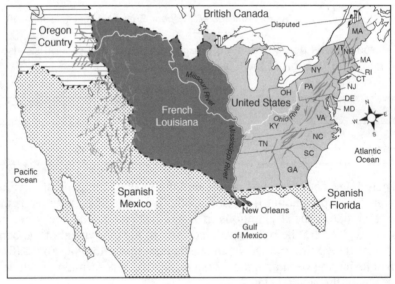

Source: Emma J. Lapsansky-Werner et al., *United States History*,
Pearson Prentice Hall, 2008 (adapted)

4. Based on these documents, why was New Orleans important to the United States?

_____

_____

DOCUMENT 5

. . . To acquire an empire of perhaps half the extent of the one we possessed, from the most powerful and warlike nation on earth, without bloodshed, without the oppression of a single individual, without in the least embarrassing the ordinary operations of your finances, and all this through the peaceful forms of negotiation, and in despite too of the opposition [despite the opposition] of a considerable portion of the community, is an achievement of which the archives of the predecessors, at least, of those now in office, cannot furnish a parallel. . . .

Source: Senator John C. Breckenridge, November 3, 1803

5. According to Senator John C. Breckenridge, what is *one* reason he supports the purchase of the Louisiana Territory?

_____

_____

DOCUMENT 6

. . . When news of the [Louisiana] purchase reached the United States, President [Thomas] Jefferson was surprised. He had authorized the expenditure of $10 million for a port city, and instead received treaties committing the government to spend $15 million on a land package which would double the size of the country. Jefferson's political opponents in the Federalist Party argued that the Louisiana purchase was a worthless desert, and that the Constitution did not provide for the acquisition of new land or negotiating treaties without the consent of the Senate. What really worried the opposition was the new states which would inevitably be carved from the Louisiana territory, strengthening Western and Southern interests in Congress, and further reducing the influence of New England Federalists in national affairs. President Jefferson was an enthusiastic supporter of westward expansion, and held firm in his support for the treaty. Despite Federalist objections, the U.S. Senate ratified the Louisiana treaty in the autumn of 1803. . . .

Source: National Park Service

6. Based on this document, state *two* reasons the Federalist Party opposed the purchase of the Louisiana Territory.

(1) _____

_____

(2) _____

_____

DOCUMENT 7a

The expiring months of the [James K.] Polk Administration in 1848–49 gave a dark augury [sign] of the storms to come. Congress no sooner met in December than the agitation of the slavery question recommenced [began again]; and even when the surface of the political sea for a few days grew calm, beneath it all was commotion and intrigue. Polk in his last annual message dwelt upon the importance of promptly supplying Territorial governments for California and New Mexico. Three modes of settlement, he suggested, were open. One, which he preferred, was to carry the Missouri Compromise line to the Pacific; another, to let the people of the Territories decide the slavery question when they applied for admission; and the third, to lay the issue before the Supreme Court. But Northern free-soilers and Southern extremists could agree on none of the three. . . .

Source: Allan Nevins, *Ordeal of the Union*, Volume 1, Charles Scribner's Sons, 1947

7a. Based on this document, what were *two* ways President Polk proposed to address the issue of slavery in the territories?

(1) _____

_____

(2) _____

_____

DOCUMENT 7b

**Effects of the Compromise of 1850 on the Territory
Gained from the Mexican Cession**

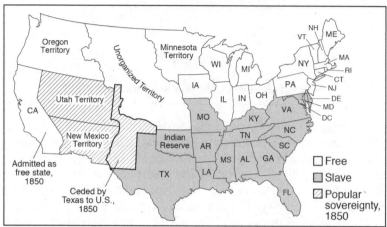

Source: Thomas A. Bailey et al., *The American Pageant: A History of the Republic*,
Houghton Mifflin, 1998 (adapted)

7b. Based on this map, what is *one* way the Compromise of 1850 dealt with the issue of the expansion of slavery into the territory gained from the Mexican Cession?

_____

_____

DOCUMENT 8

. . . It is not for them [the North], nor for the Federal Government to determine, whether our domestic institution [slavery] is good or bad; or whether it should be repressed or preserved. It belongs to us [the South], and us only, to decide such questions. What then we do insist on, is, not to extend slavery, but that we shall not be prohibited from immigrating with our property, into the Territories of the United States, because we are slaveholders; or, in other words, that we shall not on that account be disfranchised [deprived] of a privilege possessed by all others, citizens and foreigners, without discrimination as to character, profession, or color. All, whether savage, barbarian, or civilized, may freely enter and remain, we only being excluded. . . .

Source: Senator John C. Calhoun, "The Southern Address," 1849

89

8. According to Senator John C. Calhoun, what is *one* reason Southerners should be allowed to take their slaves into the new territories?

_____

_____

DOCUMENT 9

Excerpt from Republican Party Platform, 1860

That the normal condition of all the territory of the United States is that of freedom: That, as our Republican fathers, when they had abolished slavery in all our national territory [Northwest Territory], ordained that "no persons should be deprived of life, liberty or property without due process of law," it becomes our duty, by legislation, whenever such legislation is necessary, to maintain this provision of the Constitution against all attempts to violate it; and we deny the authority of Congress, of a territorial legislature, or of any individuals, to give legal existence to slavery in any territory of the United States.

Source: Republican Party Platform, May 17, 1860

9. According to this document, what was the position of the Republican Party in 1860 on the issue of expanding slavery into the territories?

_____

_____

Part B
Essay

Write a well-organized essay that includes an introduction, several paragraphs, and a conclusion. Use evidence from *at least **four*** documents in the body of the essay. Support your response with relevant facts, examples, and details. Include additional outside information.

Historical Context:

In the early years of the republic, various controversial issues divided the American people. Three such issues were ***ratification of the Constitution***, ***purchase of the Louisiana Territory***, and ***expansion of slavery into the territories***.

Task:

Using information from the documents and your knowledge of United States history, write an essay in which you:

Choose *two* issues mentioned in the historical context and for *each*

- Describe the historical circumstances surrounding the issue.
- Discuss arguments of those *in favor of and* of those *opposed to* the issue.

In your discussion, include *at least one* argument on *each* side of the issue.

Guidelines:

In your essay, be sure to
- Develop all aspects of the task.
- Incorporate information from *at least four* documents.
- Incorporate relevant outside information.
- Support the theme with relevant facts, examples, and details.
- Use a logical and clear plan of organization, including an introduction and a conclusion that are beyond a restatement of the theme.

DOCUMENT-BASED QUESTION

The following questions (Part A and Part B) are based on the accompanying documents (1–6). Some of these documents have been edited for the purpose of this exercise. The question is designed to test your ability to work with historical documents and to demonstrate your knowledge of the subject matter being presented. As you analyze the documents, take into account both the source of the document and the author's point of view.

Historical Context:

American political rights and institutions are derived from English political traditions and 18th century Enlightenment thought.

Task:

Using information from the documents and your knowledge of United States history, answer the questions that follow each document in Part A. Your answers to the questions will help you write the Part B essay, in which you will be asked:

Discuss how American political development was not entirely original in nature, but actually an adaptation of English political traditions and 18th century Enlightenment thought.

Part A
Short-Answer Questions

The documents below relate to issues concerning the sources of American political rights and institutions. Examine each document carefully and then answer the questions that follow.

DOCUMENT 1

They also which do not agree in Christ's religion fear no man from it nor Speak against any man that hath received it, . . . For this is one of the ancientest laws Among them, that no man shall be blamed for reasoning in the maintenance of His own religion.

—Sir Thomas More, *Utopia* (1516)

1. How were Sir Thomas More's opinions expressed in *Utopia* adopted by the First Amendment to the United States Constitution?

_____

_____

_____

_____

The liberty of man in society is to be under no other legislative power but that established in the commonwealth; nor under the dominion of any will or restraint of any law but what the legislative shall enact according to the trust put in it.

—John Locke, *The Second Treatise of Government* (1690)

2. Which branch of the federal government embodies the thoughts of John Locke expressed above?

_____

_____

_____

_____

3. How have Americans demonstrated their trust in the legislative bodies of both the federal government and the state governments?

_____

_____

_____

DOCUMENT 3

No free man shall be detained or imprisoned, dispossessed, outlawed, exiled,
Or destroyed in any way, except by the lawful judgment of his peers or by the law of the land.

—Magna Carta (1215)

4. Name three rights provided in the Bill of Rights (1791) that were addressed earlier in the Magna Carta.

_____

_____

_____

_____

DOCUMENT 4

> The constant will of all the members of the state is the greater will;
> By virtue of it they are citizens and free.

—Jean-Jacques Rousseau, *The Social Contract* (1762)

5. How was Rousseau's comment regarding a consensus adopted by the framers of the United States Constitution?

_____

_____

_____

_____

6. How was Rousseau's comment regarding a consensus *not* adopted by the framers of the United States Constitution?

_____

_____

_____

_____

DOCUMENT 5

> Laws are the necessary relations which derive from the nature of things;
> And in this sense, all beings have their laws; the divinity has its laws,
> The material world its laws . . . man has his laws.

—Montesquieu, *The Spirit of the Laws* (1748)

7. Give an example of how the importance of law was adopted in either the American colonial governments or in the constitutional government of the United States.

_____

_____

_____

_____

The Crown cannot tax without the consent of the Parliament.

—Bill of English Rights (1689)

8. Explain how the power to tax operated in many of the English colonies and discuss its reference in the Federal Constitution of the United States.

_____

_____

_____

_____

Part B
Essay

Your essay should be well organized with an introductory paragraph that states your position on the question. Develop your position in the next paragraphs and then write a conclusion. In your essay, include specific historical details and refer to the specific documents you analyzed in Part A. You may include additional information from your knowledge of social studies.

Historical Context:

American political rights and institutions are derived from English political traditions and 18th century Enlightenment thought.

Task:

Discuss how American political development was not entirely original in nature, but actually an adaptation of English political traditions and 18th century Enlightenment thought.

Guidelines:

In your essay, be sure to
• Develop all aspects of the task.
• Incorporate information from *at least five* documents.
• Incorporate relevant outside information.
• Support the theme with many relevant facts, examples, and details.
• Use a logical and clear plan of organization, including an introduction and a conclusion that are beyond a restatement of the theme.

Unit One CONSTITUTIONAL FOUNDATIONS OF THE UNITED STATES

CHAPTER 2

THE CONSTITUTION TESTED: NATIONALISM AND SECTIONALISM

CONSTITUTIONAL STRESS AND CRISIS

> When my eyes shall be turned to behold for the last time the sun in heaven, may I not see him shining on the broken and dishonored fragments of a once glorious Union . . .
> Daniel Webster, Speech on Foote's Resolution
> (January 26, 1830)

> I have heard something said about allegiance to the South. I know no South, no North, no East, no West, to which I owe my allegiance. The Union, sir, is my country.
> Henry Clay (1848)

Growth of Nationalism

With the end of the War of 1812, the United States experienced a period of nationalism, when westward expansion and internal improvements demanded much of the nation's attention.

Judicial Nationalism

The Supreme Court under Chief Justice John Marshall handed down a number of decisions that increased the power of the national government at the expense of the states, including the doctrine of judicial review.

Economic Nationalism

Henry Clay (American statesman and orator, 1777–1852). Clay was a lifelong advocate of economic nationalism.

• *Rechartering of the National Bank (1816).* Under the direction of **John C. Calhoun** of South Carolina, the Second Bank of the United States was established with a twenty-year charter.

- *Tariff of 1816.* Supported by **Henry Clay** of Kentucky and John Calhoun, a 25 percent tariff was placed on imported goods as a protective measure.

Era of Good Feelings

This term, dubbed by a Boston newspaper to describe the period's absence of political strife, was somewhat deceiving. The election of 1816 gave a victory to the Republicans, with Madison winning the electoral vote 183 to 34, painting a picture of national unity, and the Federalists disappeared as a political party. Yet, by 1819, postwar nationalism and economic stability were eroding, and sectionalism was beginning to become increasingly apparent.

Sectionalism

This term was used to describe the varying interests of the "sections" of the country, which were geographically different and had different economic enterprises suited to their environment. By 1824 three sections were emerging, each with its own concerns and therefore demands on the national government: the industrial Northeast, the cotton-producing South, and the agricultural West. Figure 1.20 lists some of the major issues facing the nation in 1828 and how each section stood on the issue.

Federal-State Relations (1798–1835)

Central to many of the standoffs between the federal government and groups of states' righters was the **nullification doctrine**, which claimed that when the national government assumed rights or powers that had not been delegated to it, the states could nullify the act.

Virginia and Kentucky Resolutions (1798)

In response to the **Alien and Sedition Acts of 1798** (acts passed by Federalists that changed naturalization laws and suppressed criticism of the government to weaken political influence of the Republicans), the Republican-controlled legislatures of Virginia and Kentucky passed resolutions endorsing the doctrine that the Constitution was a compact between states and that the states could legitimately object when Congress exceeded the authority delegated to it by the states. The Kentucky Resolution, authored by Thomas Jefferson, went further and claimed that the states could refuse to obey the law, thereby **nullifying** legislation of Congress.

The Hartford Convention (1814)

On October 18, 1814, the Massachusetts legislature called for a convention to discuss constitutional means to protect New England's interests. Some discussion of secession was aired, but the major emphasis was to propose several constitutional amendments to address concerns specific to the New England states.

Issue	Northeast	South	West
Sale of inexpensive federal land (mostly in the West)	Opposed (early)	Favored	Favored
Internal improvement at federal expense	Favored	Opposed	Favored
Protective tariff	Favored	Opposed	Favored
Territorial expansion (new states)	Opposed (early)	Favored	Favored
Second Bank of the United States	Favored	Opposed	Opposed
Extension of slavery into the territories	Opposed	Favored	Opposed
Attitude toward European immigration	Favored	Opposed	Favored
Attitude toward use of implied powers (elastic clause)	Favored	Opposed	Favored

Figure 1.20   Sectionalism (1828)

Webster-Hayne Debate (1830)

The debate in Congress over the limitation of land sales inspired sharp debate. Senator Robert Y. Hayne of South Carolina defended the right of a state to nullify a federal law that "violated the sovereignty and independence of the states." In response to Hayne, Daniel Webster contended that it was the people, and not the states, who created the Constitution and that if the states could defy the laws of Congress at will, the Union would be a mere "rope of sand." President Jackson, despite his sympathies to states' rights, was against nullification.

Daniel Webster (American statesman, lawyer & orator, 1782–1852). Webster believed that the Union took precedence over the states.

The Tariff Controversy (1832)

In 1828 Congress passed the so-called **Tariff of Abominations**, imposing high import duties that were opposed by the South. Although the Tariff of 1832 lowered some duties, South Carolina talked of nullification. Calhoun's **Exposition and Protest (1828)** claimed that state conventions had the power to declare laws passed by Congress unconstitutional and to nullify such laws. Calhoun went so far as to suggest secession as a last resort. South Carolina nullified the tariff in December 1832. The Compromise Tariff of 1833, sponsored by Henry Clay, caused South Carolina to withdraw its nullification and prevented a Jackson-Calhoun showdown on the constitutionality of the nullification doctrine. Although the doctrine of nullification is in direct conflict with the Supremacy Clause of the Constitution (Article VI, Section 2), even in recent times it has been threatened in heated debate. After the *Brown* v. *Board of Education* (1954) decision, Southern politicians threatened nullification of the Supreme Court's decree to end segregation "with all deliberate speed."

The Bank War (1832)

When a bill to recharter the Bank of the United States passed in 1832, Jackson vetoed the measure with an interesting constitutional argument. In addition to his dislike for the political power of the bank, Jackson claimed that, although the Supreme Court had affirmed the bank's constitutionality in *McCulloch v. Maryland* (1819), the separate branches of the federal government were not bound by the judiciary's readings of the Constitution. The bank's charter was allowed to expire, federal deposits were placed in state banks, and control of the nation's banking system returned to the states.

Secessionists

Although actual secession did not take place until shortly after the election of Abraham Lincoln to the presidency in 1860, the theory had been discussed for some time. Those who supported the right of secession claimed that the Union was a league from which member states could withdraw.

A Democratic party emblem from the 1840s.

The Age of Jackson

Historians have long regarded the period that came to be known as that of "**Jacksonian Democracy**" as something unique, and have debated its significance in American history.

The "Revolution of 1828" placed the first westerner in the White House. Although sometimes identified as the representative of the common man, he was truly a frontier aristocrat, owning many slaves and living in the Hermitage, one of the finest mansions in America. Like the antifederalists of the 1790s, he was suspect of the federal government as a body for the privileged.

Although he did not introduce the **spoils system** (rewarding political supporters with public office), he did introduce it into federal government on a larger scale than any of his predecessors. During his eight years in office, he dismissed nearly 2,000 civil servants, replacing them with those loyal to Andrew Jackson.

Extension of the Franchise

Popular participation in politics continued to increase during the first decades of the 19th century, and the right to vote was eventually extended to all white males over 21. Most of the new Western states ended property qualifications for voting, and the older states, concerned about loss of population to the West, followed their example. Whereas less than 4 percent of the population actually voted in 1824, over 14 percent voted by 1840, indicating extension of suffrage rights and participation in politics.

Modern Party Politics

From 1800 through 1820 the congressional **caucus** was the method used to select presidential nominees. However, democratic reforms during the early 1800s led to greater participation by the electorate. By 1824, 18 out of 24 states chose presidential electors by popular vote. The introduction of the convention system of nominating candidates for the presidency by the Anti-Masonic party in 1831 offered a more democratic system that was quickly adopted by the Democrats and the National Republicans. Jackson and his running mate, **Martin Van Buren**, were nominated at the Democratic convention in 1832 and Jackson was re-elected easily.

Reform Movements of the 1830s and 1840s

The reform movements of the 1830s–1840s centered around religion, temperance, health, antislavery, women's rights, education, and abolition.

• *Religion.* The **Second Great Awakening**, starting in the late 1790s and continuing through the 1840s, was a prime motivator of reform. Rapid changes, including industrialization, the growth of urban areas, and expansion, helped spark this religious movement.

• *Temperance.* Because the excessive consumption of alcohol was widespread among all classes of Americans, movements in the 1820s began demanding abstinence from liquor. The formation of the United States Temperance Union in 1833 led to demands for the legal prohibition of alcoholic beverages, and a dozen states passed such laws prior to the Civil War.

• *Health.* The movement to build asylums for the insane rather than housing them in prisons was spurred by the efforts of **Dorothea Dix**. Because of her work, prison reforms were also implemented in some states.

• *Women's Rights.* Among the reform movements of the 1830s was the women's rights movement that sought to overcome the inferior legal status of women. Chief among the issues were women's lack of rights concerning property, voting, and education. In 1848, **Lucretia Mott** and **Elizabeth Cady Stanton** organized the **Women's Rights Convention** at Seneca Falls, New York. Minimal gains were made, and by the 1850s, women were focusing more and more on the issue of suffrage.

Elizabeth Cady Stanton (1815–1902) helped organize the first Women's Rights Convention.

• *Education.* The demand for free public education grew out of the concern that only intelligent voters could support and perpetuate democracy; therefore, the state had the responsibility of financing education. The principal reformer in education was **Horace Mann** of Massachusetts. As Secretary of the State Board of Education, he helped establish public backing for tax-supported schools, lengthened the school year, increased the number of secondary schools, formalized the training of teachers, and broadened educational subjects beyond religious studies.

• *Abolition.* The Quakers led the earliest antislavery movement in the mid-1700s, preaching that it was a sin for Christians to keep people in bondage. By 1800 most states in the North had abandoned slavery. However, as the South became increasingly dependent on cotton

Frederick Douglass (American abolitionist, 1817–1895) escaped from slavery to become a newspaper publisher and political organizer.

production after the invention of the cotton gin in 1793, the South's increased cotton production furthered slavery and exploitation of the African people.

The abolitionist movement of the 1830s differed from earlier movements against slavery by emphasizing that slavery was morally wrong and that black people were not inferior. This came into direct conflict with the beliefs of **white supremacy** in the South. Among the notable abolitionist leaders were **Frederick Douglass**, **Sojourner Truth**, **William Lloyd Garrison**, and **Harriet Tubman**. Garrison, founder of the abolitionist newspaper, *The Liberator* (1831), demanded immediate and complete emancipation, as opposed to the gradual emancipation supported by more moderate abolitionists. Tubman's efforts to assist the escape of Southern slaves to Canada by means of the **underground railroad** continued up to the eve of the Civil War.

The slave rebellion led by **Nat Turner** in Virginia in 1831, which resulted in the deaths of sixty white people, and the flow of radical Northern abolitionist literature into the South, turned Southerners from apologists for slavery into aggressive defenders of the institution.

As the Civil War approached, free labor and slave labor were pitted against each other. The North saw free labor as the key to a successful economy and realized that the free labor economic system had to be extended to the territories of the West if future generations were to prosper. Southerners, having built their fortunes and society on the institution of slavery, found it difficult to accept the moral arguments of abolitionists and felt that slavery was necessary to their way of life.

The Indian Removal Act

The reforms of the Jackson Age did not extend to Native Americans. The attempts of Native Americans to remain on their ancestral lands came into conflict with the government's aim to remove them from settled areas in the East and to resettle them in the West. This aim was facilitated by passage of the **Indian Removal Act of 1830**. When the Cherokees were ordered to leave their lands in Georgia, they refused and took the issue to the Supreme Court. In *Cherokee Nation* v. *Georgia* (1831), the Supreme Court ruled that the Cherokees could stay until they voluntarily ceded their lands to the United States. The Court went further in *Worcester* v. *Georgia* (1832) to state that the Cherokee Nation was a distinct political community in which the laws of Georgia had no force. President Jackson, having little sympathy for the Native Americans, refused to enforce the Court's decision.

The rulings of the Supreme Court had little effect on the destiny of the Indian tribes, and many groups, including the Seminole, Choctaw, Creek, Chickasaw, and Cherokee, were moved west. The so-called "**Trail of Tears**," in which thousands of Cherokees died on the forced journey westward, was repeated many times between 1831 and 1840. By 1840, the forced removal of 60,000 Native Americans had been carried out.

Constitutional Debates (1800–1860)

Although most constitutional debate during the first half of the 19th century involved the extension of slavery, the constant battle of state versus federal authority was involved in most issues. It was inevitable that the Supremacy Clause (Article VI) of the Constitution was going to come into conflict with the reserved powers provided for by the Tenth Amendment.

States' Rights v. Federal Supremacy

The early tests of state versus federal authority involved the battles over the **Sedition Act of 1800**, passed by the Federalists to suppress hostile criticism, the **Virginia and Kentucky Resolutions**, and the **Hartford Convention**.

The decisions of the Marshall Court enforced the sovereignty of the federal government and its right to exercise its constitutional powers. The **Louisiana Purchase**, which went against Jefferson's belief in strict construction of the Constitution, required that Congress use its implied powers to purchase the territory. It also demonstrated the need to shift constitutional positions when circumstances such as Napoleon's demands for quick action demanded such flexibility. This "flexibility" in constitutional positions has been used throughout our political history and has become part of our constitutional system.

Slavery and Struggle

The rising dispute over slavery coincided with the territorial expansion of the United States. Although the issue of extending slavery to the territories was solved by the **Missouri Compromise** in 1820, it was only a temporary solution. The controversy arose again after the acquisition of the **Mexican Cession** (1848) and the rapid growth of California's population. At the center of the slavery controversy was the delicate balance in the Senate, where the South was concerned about losing its equal footing with the North. (The larger population of the North had already given them control of the House of Representatives.)

After the Mexican War (1846–1848), Americans held four different views concerning slavery and the new territories: (1) barring slavery forever from the new territories; (2) extending the Missouri Compromise line to the Pacific Coast; (3) no federal interference with the extension of slavery; and (4) popular sovereignty (allowing the people of the territory to decide whether or not to permit slavery).

California's application to enter the Union as a free state brought up the slavery problem and marked the last of the great debates among **Daniel Webster**, **Henry Clay**, and **John Calhoun**. The result was the **Compromise of 1850**, which temporarily solved the problem and postponed the Civil War for ten years. The **Kansas-Nebraska Act** (1854), which divided the remainder of the Louisiana Territory into the territories of Kansas and Nebraska and provided for the admission of the territories as states according to the principle of popular sovereignty, resulted in the repeal of the Missouri Compromise. It also led antislavery elements among the Democrats and the Whigs to join with the antislavery third party Free Soilers to form the **Republican Party** in 1854.

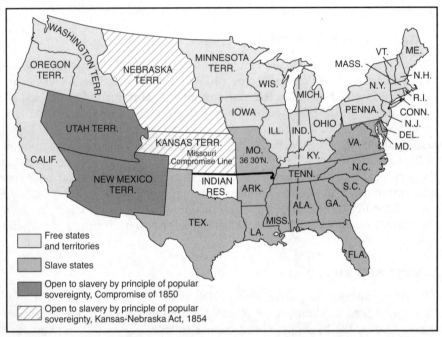

Figure 1.21   Status of Slavery (1854)

Dred Scott Decision (1857)

Dred Scott was a fugitive slave who argued for his freedom based upon the fact that his master had died, and he (Scott) had spent time in the "free" state of Illinois and the Wisconsin Territory. The Supreme Court decided that the Missouri Compromise was unconstitutional by virtue of the fact that a slave was property and that a slave owner who was protected by the Constitution could bring his or her property into a territory of the United States. It set the stage, in the Illinois senatorial campaign of 1858, for the **Lincoln-Douglas debates**, over the question of popular sovereignty. Although Stephen Douglas offered the Freeport Doctrine, stating that the legislature of a territory could still refuse to pass laws supporting slavery, the stand weakened Douglas in the South and cost him the presidential nomination from a united Democratic party in 1860. Instead, it split the Democrats over the slavery issue and allowed the Republicans to elect Lincoln in 1860.

Event	Issue	Solution
Sedition Act of 1800	Freedom of speech and press	Virginia and Kentucky Resolutions suggesting interposition and nullification; election of 1800 and expiration of act.
Supreme Court decisions of the Marshall Court (1801–1835)	Federal-State relations	Expansion of federal power and jurisdiction.
Louisiana Purchase (1803)	Power of Congress to purchase territory	Jefferson reads Constitution with "loose construction."
Embargo Act (1807)	Does commerce clause imply power to restrict commerce?	Yes; power to regulate includes power to control.
Hartford Convention (1814)	States' rights v. federal supremacy	Matter died down with end of War of 1812.
Slavery	Constitutional or unconstitutional?	*Northern Argument:* Though not claiming that slavery was unconstitutional, provisions had been made in the Constitution for its gradual demise. *Southern Argument:* Slavery was recognized within the Constitution concerning representation (Article I, Section 2), and Fugitive Slave Law (Article IV, Section 2), and therefore legal.
Missouri Compromise (1820)	Power of Congress to prohibit slavery in territories and admit states with conditions	Congress could legislate against slavery in territories but not within states. *Compromise:* 1. Missouri admitted as a slave state. 2. Maine admitted as a free state. 3. No slavery in Louisiana Territory north of 36°30' line.
Wilmot Proviso (1846)	Could Congress ban slavery in territory acquired from Mexico?	*Northern Argument:* Congress could legally bar slavery acquired by virtue of Article IV, Section 3: "make all needful rules and regulations respecting the territory of the United States." *Southern Argument:* People had the right to take their property (slaves) into the territories. Debate over the Wilmot Proviso necessitated the Compromise of 1850.

Figure 1.22   Constitutional Debates (1800–1860)

Event	Issue	Solution
Compromise of 1850	Extension of slavery into California, New Mexico Territory, and Utah Territory	*Compromise:* 1. California admitted as a free state. 2. Utah and New Mexico Territories admitted under popular sovereignty provision. 3. Slave trade in District of Columbia abolished. 4. Stricter Fugitive Slave Law enacted.
Kansas-Nebraska Act (1854)	Status of slavery in remainder of Louisiana Territory	Kansas-Nebraska Act: Popular sovereignty in both territories.
Dred Scott Decision (1857)	Could a slave sue in federal court? If a slave resided in free territory, did that end his or her status as a slave?	1. Slaves were not citizens and, therefore, could not sue in federal court. 2. Congress could not prevent citizens from transporting their property (slaves) into a territory (Fifth Amendment protection of property). The Dred Scott decision declared the Missouri Compromise unconstitutional and the territories open to slavery.
Secession	Constitutional instrument?	*Argument of Calhoun and other secessionist theorists:* **Yes.** Union is a mere league from which states may withdraw at their pleasure. Constitution is a compact between states and a self-evident right. *Argument of Lincoln and other antisecessionist theorists:* **No.** Constitution is a compact between the people of the United States, not the states. Constitution is silent on the issue of secession and, finally, the very doing away with the confederation style of government is an argument against the league theory.

Figure 1.22 continued Constitutional Debates (1800–1860)

1. In the *Dred Scott* v. *Sandford* (1857) decision, the Supreme Court held that
   A. slavery could not be prohibited by any state.
   B. the Fugitive Slave Law was unconstitutional.
   C. Congress could not prohibit slavery in the territories.
   D. the Missouri Compromise was valid.

2. Chief Justice John Marshall is remembered most accurately for
   A. being a strict constructionist.
   B. emphasizing states' rights in his decisions.
   C. increasing the power and role of the Supreme Court.
   D. frequently deferring to the opinions of state courts.

3. The election of Andrew Jackson in 1828 indicated that
   A. political power was shifting to the Western states.
   B. the Federalists were making a comeback.
   C. Henry Clay was an incompetent opponent.
   D. the Bank of the United States was a popular issue.

4. All of the following were arguments of Southerners in their defense of slavery EXCEPT
   A. slavery had constitutional support.
   B. the Bible justified slavery.
   C. blacks were inherently inferior to whites.
   D. most European nations still used slave labor.

5. The most critical question facing the nation in the 1850s was
   A. what the status of states would be after secession.
   B. the political balance between the North and South in the House of Representatives.
   C. the extension of slavery into the territories.
   D. the significance of a multiparty system in American politics.

6. The history of the tariff between 1800 and 1860 shows that
   A. economic issues had little influence over political positions.
   B. the North supported low protective tariffs.
   C. the tariff issue contributed to the conflict between the North and South over states' rights.
   D. higher tariff legislation received uniform support from all sections of the nation.

THE CONSTITUTION IN JEOPARDY: THE AMERICAN CIVIL WAR

> My paramount object in this struggle is to save the Union, and is not either to save or to destroy slavery. If I could save the Union without freeing any slave, I would do it; and if I could save it by freeing all the slaves, I would do it; and if I could do it by freeing some and leaving others alone, I would also do that.
>
> Abraham Lincoln, letter to Horace Greeley
> (August 22, 1862)

At the outset, the purpose of the Civil War from the northern point of view was to restore the Union and preserve the Constitution. Lincoln's goal of preserving the Union, even at the cost of tolerating slavery (as expressed in the preceding quote), was paramount. But as Congress became more determined to make emancipation a primary issue of the war, Lincoln drafted his own emancipation proclamation (July 1862) and the South realized that what was at stake was their entire way of life.

Abraham Lincoln opposed slavery, but his first concern was to save the Union.

Just before the outbreak of the Civil War, two issues faced the nation. Slavery in the territories was the first issue. Although the Dred Scott decision had supposedly decided the matter, a new President had been elected (the "Party of the North") and the Supreme Court was in the process of turnover with Chief Justice Taney, the author of the Dred Scott decision, old and ill. Southerners believed that Lincoln's election spelled doom for the property protection reasoning of *Dred Scott* v. *Sandford* (1857).

The second issue was that of secession. As Calhoun had proposed during the 1820s–1830s, supporters of the right of secession held that the United States was merely a league of states, from which member states might withdraw at their pleasure. President Lincoln, among others, argued that secession was not constitutional and that the constitutional system of government was a compact between the people of the United States.

A Nation Divided

Formation of the Confederacy

South Carolina led the way for the formation of the Confederacy when it adopted, through the use of a popularly elected convention, an **"Ordinance of Secession"** in December 1860. Ten additional states eventually followed South Carolina's example and the **Confederate States of**

America was formed in February 1861, with **Jefferson Davis** of Mississippi as President.

In seceding from the Union, the Southern states affirmed the **compact theory** of the Constitution and claimed that it was the Northern states that had broken the compact by obstructing the constitutionally mandated return of fugitive slaves.

Jefferson Davis was U.S. Secretary of War before becoming President of the Confederacy.

Lincoln and Constitutional Issues of the War

The Civil War brought an unprecedented clash between the Executive and the Congress in their war power roles. Although minor differences had occurred during the War of 1812 and the Mexican War, the Civil War was about to spell out a new chapter in constitutional history. A reading of the Constitution shows potential conflict between Article I, Section 8, which grants Congress the power to declare war, raise and support armies, maintain a navy, and provide for the regulation of the land and naval forces, including militia, and Article II, Section 2, which provides that the President is Commander-in-Chief of the army and navy and Article II, Section 1, which states that the President is vested with full executive power of the government.

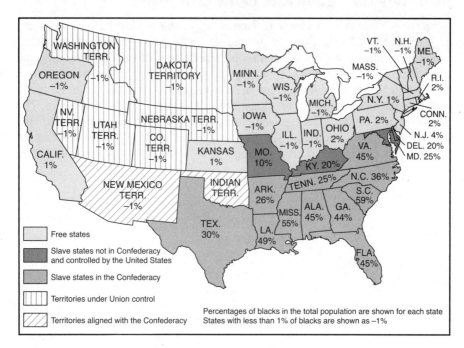

Figure 1.23 A Nation Divided

Lincoln believed that the oath he had taken to "preserve, protect, and defend the Constitution" obligated him to resort to practically any action necessary to maintain the Union.

Emancipation

At the outset of the Civil War, the federal government had been careful to insist that it was fighting to preserve the Union and not to free the slaves. In this way, proslavery forces, primarily in the border states, who were sympathetic to the Union cause were kept with the North. Yet, as the war progressed, Congress moved in the direction of emancipation. The Confiscation Act of 1862 provided that slaves who had escaped from those who were still in rebellion would be "forever free of their servitude." On January 1, 1863, President Lincoln issued the **Emancipation Proclamation** declaring that "all slaves in those regions still in rebellion on that date would be free." Not applying to border states or the regions under Union control, but only to those under Confederate control, the Emancipation Proclamation did not immediately free any slaves. Following the Union victory at Gettysburg, Pennsylvania in July 1863, President Lincoln dedicated the cemetery at the battlefield in his **Gettysburg Address** stating that "government of the people, by the people, and for the people shall not perish from the earth." The actual end of slavery did not come until the passage of the **Thirteenth Amendment** in 1865.

Constitutional Significance of the Civil War

With the surrender by **Robert E. Lee** at Appomattox Court House on April 1, 1865, the Civil War came to an end. Perhaps the most important constitutional result of the Civil War was the repudiation of state sovereignty and the compact theory of union. The concepts of states' rights of secession and the United States as a "league" of states were ended and the nation emerged as a true sovereign entity. The Constitution had survived the war years. The emancipation of the slaves raised numerous issues to be addressed in the following decades, including the rights of states and the role of the federal government in relation to **civil rights**.

Actions by Lincoln	Constitutional Provisions	Justification
Labeled actions by South as "insurrection"	None	South could not legally secede.
Initiation of war by President	Art. I, Sec. 8: "Congress has power to declare war." "Congress has power to suppress insurrections."	President suppressing an insurrection; *Prize Cases* (1863), Art. IV, Sec. 4.
Blockade of South	Art. I, Sec. 8: "Congress has power to declare war."	Approved by Congress (1861).
Increased size of army and navy	Art. I, Sec. 8: "Congress shall raise and support armies."	Approved by Congress (1861).
Appropriated funds from Treasury for war effort	Art. I, Sec. 8: "support armies."	Approved by Congress (1861).
Suspension of writ of habeas corpus; disregard for Supreme Court ruling in *Ex Parte Merryman* (1861)	Art. I, Sec. 9: "The privilege of the Writ of Habeas Corpus shall not be suspended, unless in Cases of Rebellion or Invasion the public Safety may require it."	First, none; Supreme Court rules against Lincoln in *Ex Parte Merryman* (1861); Congress later permits with passage of *Habeas Corpus Act* (1863).
Use of military courts where civil courts still in operation	Amendments V, VI, and VII	Supreme Court in *Ex Parte Vallandigham* (1864) refused to hear case; claimed no jurisdiction; in *Ex Parte Milligan* (1866), Court held Lincoln's actions to be unconstitutional.
Suspension of freedom of speech and press	First Amendment	Permissible to a point during insurrection to prevent prolonged war and additional loss of life

Figure 1.24 Lincoln *v.* the Constitution

Exercise Set 1.6

1. The Dred Scott decision held that a slave
   A. could bring suit in a federal court.
   B. was no longer a slave when he or she entered free territory.
   C. was private property even in free territory.
   D. could purchase his or her freedom when in a free territory.

2. President Lincoln's interpretation and use of the Constitution was
   A. consistently supported by the Supreme Court.
   B. influenced by his war aims.
   C. never supported by Congress.
   D. was typical of Presidents in wartime up to that point.

3. The Emancipation Proclamation
   A. ended slavery in the United States.
   B. freed slaves only in those areas where the North was not in control.
   C. maintained slavery only in those areas that were still in rebellion.
   D. was vetoed by Lincoln after passage in Congress.

4. Many of Lincoln's actions during the Civil War would have been supported by a
   A. believer in the compact doctrine of the national government.
   B. strict constructionist of the Constitution.
   C. proponent of the nullification doctrine.
   D. loose constructionist of the Constitution.

5. The greatest threat to civil liberties during the Civil War was the
   A. suspension of the writ of habeas corpus.
   B. blockade of the South.
   C. use of Treasury funds by the President without initial congressional approval.
   D. identification of the South's actions as an "insurrection."

6. The Emancipation Proclamation was
   A. a law passed by Congress.
   B. the result of a Supreme Court decision.
   C. a use of the elastic clause.
   D. a presidential order.

7. The slaves were finally freed by the
   A. surrender of the Confederacy.
   B. Emancipation Proclamation.
   C. Thirteenth Amendment.
   D. capture of Richmond.

CHAPTER REVIEW QUESTIONS

1. The most serious problem facing the United States in the first half of the 19th century involved
   A. gaining territory for excess population.
   B. the powers of the state governments and the national government.
   C. gaining recognition as a sovereign nation.
   D. unemployment.

2. Sedition can best be described as
   A. preventing aliens from becoming citizens.
   B. the illegal criticism of the government.
   C. ignoring a law of Congress.
   D. obstructing the war effort of a country.

3. The Constitution, treaties made by the United States, and laws of Congress are to predominate when conflict arises with state or local laws. This concept, provided for in the Constitution, is called the
   A. reserved powers amendment.
   B. elastic clause.
   C. supremacy clause.
   D. preamble.

4. An analysis of the history of the presidency during wartime indicates that executive powers
   A. are usually curtailed severely by the judiciary.
   B. operate through a strict construction approach to the Constitution.
   C. are expanded and sometimes come into conflict with other branches of the federal government.
   D. are unchecked.

5. The event that caused the first Southern states to secede from the Union was
   A. the Dred Scott decision.
   B. the Compromise of 1850.
   C. the election of Lincoln as President.
   D. the election of Jefferson Davis as President of the Confederacy.

Unit One CONSTITUTIONAL FOUNDATIONS OF THE UNITED STATES

6. The West supported all of the following EXCEPT
   A. internal improvements at national expense.
   B. sale of inexpensive government lands.
   C. the Second Bank of the United States.
   D. squatters' rights.

7. In which of the following pairs was the second event a result of the first?
   A. The Mexican War—passage of the Missouri Compromise.
   B. Indian land claims in Georgia—*Dred Scott* v. *Sandford*.
   C. The application of California for statehood—Compromise of 1850.
   D. The Thirteenth Amendment—Emancipation Proclamation.

8. The doctrine that indicated that a state could object to a law of Congress if it was felt that Congress had abused its delegated authority was
   A. nullification.
   B. sectionalism.
   C. interposition.
   D. secession.

9. The basic cause of sectionalism in the United States during the first half of the 19th century was
   A. economic differences.
   B. social differences.
   C. political differences.
   D. religious differences.

10. Regarding the Native Americans, President Jackson favored
    A. upholding Cherokee rights.
    B. removal to the trans-Mississippi area.
    C. supporting the Supreme Court decision in the Georgia cases.
    D. allowing Congressional control of the situation.

THEMATIC ESSAYS

Directions: Write a well-organized essay that includes an introduction, several paragraphs addressing the task below, and a conclusion.

Theme: Compromises Necessary for Ratification of the Constitution

> At the Constitutional Convention in 1787 differences between the delegates and the interests they represented made compromise absolutely necessary.

Task:

> Identify *two* compromises necessary for the ratification of the Constitution.
>
> - Discuss the two initial positions that led to compromise.
> - Describe the resulting compromise.
> - From today's perspective, evaluate the compromise reached.

Some suggestions you might wish to consider include: representation, taxation, slave trade, tariffs, and the election of the President.

You are *not* limited to these suggestions.

Directions: Write a well-organized essay that includes an introduction, several paragraphs addressing the task below, and a conclusion.

Theme: Developing Sectionalism and the Need for Compromise

> As the United States became politically, socially, and economically sectionalized during the first half of the 19th century, compromise became necessary to avert crisis.

Task:

> Identify *two* compromises necessary during the first half of the 19th century.
>
> - Discuss the two initial positions that led to compromise.
> - Describe the resulting compromise.
> - Evaluate whether the resulting compromise was successful in averting crisis.

Some suggestions you might wish to consider include: the Missouri Compromise of 1820, the Tariff Compromise of 1833, and the Compromise of 1850.

You are *not* limited to these suggestions.

Document-Based Question

The following questions (Part A and Part B) are based on the accompanying documents (1–6). Some of these documents have been edited for the purpose of this exercise. The question is designed to test your ability to work with historical documents and to demonstrate your knowledge of the subject matter being presented. As you analyze the documents, take into account both the source of the document and the author's point of view.

Historical Context:

> The Bill of Rights was added to the Constitution in 1791 to protect individual liberties against government abuse.

Task:

> Using information from the documents and your knowledge of United States history, answer the questions that follow each document in Part A. Your answers to the questions will help you write the Part B essay, in which you will be asked:
>
> The Bill of Rights was added to the Constitution in 1791 to protect individual liberties against government abuse. Assess the validity of this statement with particular attention to the areas of search, interrogation, and prosecution.

Part A
Short-Answer Questions

The documents below relate to issues concerning the Fourth, Fifth, Sixth, and Eighth Amendments. Examine each document carefully and then answer the questions that follow.

DOCUMENT 1

I have little patience with people who take the Bill of Rights for granted. The Bill of Rights, contained in the first ten amendments to the Constitution, is every American's guarantee of freedom.

—President Harry Truman, *Memoirs*, Vol. II (1955)

1. What did President Truman mean by the statement "the first ten amendments . . . is every American's guarantee of freedom"?

_____

_____

_____

_____

DOCUMENT 2

The right of the people to be secure in their persons, houses, papers and effects, against unreasonable searches and seizures, shall not be violated, and no warrants shall issue but upon probable cause, supported by oath or affirmation, and particularly describing the place to be searched, and the persons or things to be seized.

—Fourth Amendment to the U.S. Constitution

2. The Fourth Amendment mentions "unreasonable searches." Give an example of what has been held to be a "reasonable search."

_____

_____

_____

_____

3. Included in the Fourth Amendment is the provision that a search warrant shall not be issued without "probable cause." Define probable cause. Provide an example if you feel it assists your explanation.

_____

_____

_____

_____

DOCUMENT 3

". . . the ultimate measure of the constitutionality of a governmental search is reasonableness. . . . The reasonableness standard is judged by balancing its intrusion on the individual's Fourth Amendment interests against its promotion of legitimate governmental interests . . ."

—*Vernonia School District* v. *Acton* (1995)

4. What does the Supreme Court mean by "legitimate governmental interests" and what was the government interest in the searches being done in the *Vernonia* case?

_____

_____

_____

_____

DOCUMENT 4

Second, the discovery of the rolling papers then gave rise to *reasonable suspicion* that respondent was carrying marijuana as well as cigarettes in her purse, and this suspicion justified the further exploration . . . .

—*New Jersey* v. *T.L.O.* (1985)

5. In *New Jersey* v. *T.L.O.* the Supreme Court referred to "reasonable suspicion" as justification for further search. How does "reasonable suspicion" compare to the standard of "probable cause" within the Fourth Amendment?

_____

_____

_____

_____

DOCUMENT 5

No person shall . . . be compelled in any criminal case to be witness against himself . . .

—Fifth Amendment to the U.S. Constitution

6. In the case of *Miranda* v. *Arizona* (1966), the Supreme Court held that a list of warnings must be read to a person in police custody before questioning could begin. Which two "Miranda" warnings are based on the section of the Fifth Amendment cited above?

_____

_____

_____

_____

DOCUMENT 6

. . . any person hauled into our court, who is too poor to hire a lawyer cannot be assured a fair trial unless counsel is provided for him.

—*Gideon* v. *Wainwright* (1963)

7. How did the Supreme Court's decision in *Gideon* v. *Wainwright* (1963) affect the interpretation of the Sixth Amendment's provision for an attorney?

_____

_____

_____

Part B
Essay

Your essay should be well organized with an introductory paragraph that states your position on the question. Develop your position in the next paragraphs and then write a conclusion. In your essay, include specific historical details and refer to the specific documents you analyzed in Part A. You may include additional information from your knowledge of social studies.

Historical Context:

> The Bill of Rights was added to the Constitution in 1791 to protect individual liberties against government abuse.

Task:

> The Bill of Rights was added to the Constitution in 1791 to protect individual liberties against government abuse. Assess the validity of this statement with particular attention to the areas of search, interrogation, and prosecution.

Guidelines:

In your essay, be sure to
• Develop all aspects of the task.
• Incorporate information from *at least five* documents.
• Incorporate relevant outside information.
• Support the theme with many relevant facts, examples, and details.
• Use a logical and clear plan of organization, including an introduction and a conclusion that are beyond a restatement of the theme.

UNIT TWO _____

Industrialization of the United States

> **KEY IDEAS** Unit Two first examines the restructuring of the Union following the Civil War, with emphasis on emancipation and the strengthening of the federal system of government. Chapters 2 and 3 review the growing diversity of the American population, the industrialization of the United States, and the new challenges to American society as a result of growth.

UNIT CONNECTIONS: By the end of the unit you should understand the following points.

- An understanding of American society from 1865 to 1920
- Reconstruction, views on secession, and balance of power between Congress and the Executive
- Impeachment of Andrew Johnson
- Adoption of the Thirteenth, Fourteenth, and Fifteenth Amendments
- Economic changes brought about in the years after the Civil War
- Supreme Court rulings: Civil Rights Cases and *Plessy* v. *Ferguson*
- Political party alignments following the Civil War; the "Solid South"
- Expansion and consolidation of American business; corporations
- Robber barons and the "Captains of Industry"
- Laissez-faire and the eventual need for government regulation
- Antitrust legislation and the formation of labor unions
- Problems faced by farmers; the Populist movement
- The shift from rural living to urbanization
- The "New Immigration" period, nativism, and immigration legislation
- The ending of the frontier and effects on Native Americans

CHAPTER 1

THE RECONSTRUCTED NATION

RECONSTRUCTION AND THE NATIONALIZATION OF CIVIL RIGHTS

During the period of Reconstruction, or the restoring of the South to the Union from 1865 to 1877, the nation had to answer two challenging questions: (1) How should the seceding states be dealt with and on what terms should they be readmitted to the Union? (2) What should be done about the newly freed slaves and what should be their political rights?

The political reconstruction of the South (as opposed to the social and physical rebuilding) can be divided into four stages: (1) the plans of President Lincoln; (2) the years 1865 and 1866 when President Andrew Johnson tried to carry out his policy; (3) Congressional Reconstruction between 1866 and 1868; and (4) the period of Southern reaction in the years after 1868.

Three Plans of Reconstruction

Lincoln's Plan

Lincoln's plan, which became the moderate approach to Reconstruction, was based on the belief that the war was a rebellion of individual citizens and that, since secession was not constitutionally permissible, the South had never legally left the Union. This view was endorsed by the Supreme Court in *Texas* v. *White (1869)* when the Court held that "the Constitution, in all its provisions, looks to an indestructible Union, composed of indestructible states." Lincoln also believed that Reconstruction should be lenient and carried out by the President. In his Proclamation of Amnesty and Reconstruction in December 1863, Lincoln set out his plan of Reconstruction: (1) all Southerners (except high-ranking Confederate political and military officials) would be pardoned and regain citizenship when they took an oath to support the Constitution and the emancipation of slaves; and (2) when 10 percent of the voters in a state took this oath they could establish a legal government that would be recognized by the President.

• *Congressional Reaction.* The "Radical" Republicans in Congress did not agree with Lincoln's plan. They looked beyond emancipation to the problem of civil liberties of African Americans and felt that Congress should play a greater role in the assurance of such liberties. In the Wade-Davis bill (July 1864) Congress set its own conditions for readmitting the Southern states. It required that: (1) 50 percent of the voters take the loyalty oath rather than

10 percent; (2) Confederate officials be disenfranchised; and (3) Confederate debts be repudiated.

Lincoln killed the Wade-Davis bill with a **pocket veto** because it would have postponed the readmittance of the Southern states. Lincoln and Congress disagreed over Reconstruction, and hopes of compromise and the acceptance of Lincoln's moderate plan ended with his assassination on April 14, 1865.

Johnson's Plan

In May 1865 Johnson issued his plan of Reconstruction, which was similar to Lincoln's: (1) general pardon of all Southerners willing to take an oath upholding the Constitution, except military leaders and those whose wealth exceeded $20,000; (2) recognition of the governments of Virginia, Tennessee, Arkansas, and Louisiana, which had been established under Lincoln's Reconstruction Plan; and (3) the remaining Southern states could re-enter the Union when they repudiated war debts (bonds sold by the Confederate government to individuals to finance the war), disavowed their ordinances of secession, and ratified the Thirteenth Amendment, thereby abolishing slavery.

By December 1865, when Congress met, all the Southern states except Texas were ready to be readmitted to the Union. The **Thirteenth Amendment**, ending slavery, was ratified in December 1865, giving Congress the power to enforce the amendment with appropriate legislation.

Congressional Plan

The Republicans in Congress believed that the seceding states had reverted to territorial status and therefore required congressional legislation for readmission to the Union. They refused to seat in Congress the representatives and senators who had been elected by the new state governments in the Southern states. Under the influence of Radical Republican Thaddeus Stevens, Congress passed the following laws:

• *The Freedman's Bureau Act (1866).** This law extended the existence of a wartime bureau that had cared for freed slaves. It helped to provide the freed slaves with food, clothing, and shelter; helped them find jobs; and founded schools. Particularly troubling to Congress were the "**black codes**," laws passed by the Southern legislatures after the abolition of slavery, which were designed to keep freed blacks in a slavelike role. President Johnson vetoed the bill, questioning the constitutionality of its provisions, but it was passed over Johnson's veto in July 1866.

• *The Civil Rights Act of 1866.* This forbade states to discriminate against blacks, guaranteed persons of color equal protection of the laws, and

*Note: The term *freedmen* was used in this period to refer to the freed slaves.

placed jurisdiction of violations of the act in federal courts. President Johnson vetoed the bill, claiming unconstitutional violations of states' rights, but Congress overrode his veto.

• *The Fourteenth Amendment.* This amendment (ratified by Congress and the states) made blacks citizens of the United States. It provided for national citizenship, forbade states from depriving citizens of equal protection of the law, provided penalties for not granting black Americans the vote, excluded Confederates from holding office unless pardoned by Congress, and repudiated the Confederate war debt.

Military Reconstruction Act

The Congressional elections of 1866 gave the Radical Republicans the support necessary to put their Reconstruction plan into effect. On March 2, 1867, Congress took over Reconstruction with its passage of the Military Reconstruction Act, which (1) stated that no lawful governments existed in any of the Southern states except for Tennessee (which had accepted the Fourteenth Amendment); (2) divided the South into five military districts, each under a military governor with federal troops; and (3) specified that no state could return to civilian rule and be readmitted to the Union until white and black voters framed a constitution that guaranteed suffrage to African Americans and ratified the Fourteenth Amendment.

Impeachment of Andrew Johnson

The struggle over how to reconstruct the Union provoked a clash between President Johnson and Congress. Johnson, intolerant of opposition and not able to compromise, failed to help his political cause. He wanted to restore the prewar federal system as quickly as possible with one change—that states no longer had the right to legalize slavery. Most Congressional Republicans, on the other hand, believed that sectional conflict would not be resolved until there were guarantees that the old Southern ruling class would not regain power and national influence. After two presidential vetoes and two congressional overrides, the Republicans in Congress took extreme steps to assure that the Military Reconstruction Act was carried out.

Denial of Supreme Court Authority

An act passed on March 7, 1868, denied the Supreme Court jurisdiction over the Reconstruction acts of Congress.

Denial of Presidential Authority

Beginning in March 1867, Congress adopted a series of acts intended to restrict the President's authority.

• *Tenure of Office Act.* Of greatest significance was the Tenure of Office Act (March 1867), which prohibited the President from removing any federal officials without the consent of the Senate. President Johnson vetoed the act, asserting that the President possessed a separate right of removal without the Senate's consent, a right that had been recognized since the first Congress.

Impeachment

The Constitution provides in Article II, Section 4 that "The President . . . shall be removed from Office on Impeachment for and Conviction of, Treason, Bribery, or other high Crimes and Misdemeanors." During the spring of 1867, the House of Representatives (responsible for bringing the initial charges, Article I, Section 2) searched for a possible charge against Johnson. The opportunity was finally found when Johnson violated the Tenure of Office Act in February 1868 by removing Secretary of War Edwin M. Stanton. Two days later, the House voted 128 to 47 to impeach the President. He was tried before the Senate with Chief Justice Salmon Chase presiding (Article I, Section 3) and was acquitted by only one vote short of the votes of two-thirds of the Senate needed for conviction. The incident appeared to indicate that the impeachment power could be used only for indictable crimes, not offenses resulting from political battles between two branches of government. The Tenure of Office Act was eventually repealed by Congress in 1887.

Reconstruction Comes to an End

Fifteenth Amendment (1870)

Suffrage had been indirectly granted to African Americans in the Fourteenth Amendment. The Fifteenth Amendment authorized the federal government to regulate voting in a limited sense. Although it prevented the denial of the vote based upon race, color, or previous condition of servitude, it did not stop the states from using literacy or property tests to restrict the vote.

End of Reconstruction

By 1872, Americans were tired of Reconstruction. Congress passed the **Amnesty Act**, which restored the franchise to almost all Confederates. As a result, white Democrats gradually regained control of the Southern states. Claiming that the Republican Party was the party of corruption, the party of the black man, and responsible for the destruction of the South, the Democratic Party became the majority party of the South until well into the 20th century, a phenomenon later referred to as the "Solid South." The withdrawal of the last federal troops took place following the election of 1876.

The Nationalization of Civil Rights

Perhaps with the sole exception of the New Deal era in the 1930s, the period of Reconstruction marked the greatest expansion of federal power in our country's history. The extension of national power over personal liberty and civil rights through the enactment of the Thirteenth, Fourteenth, and Fifteenth Amendments, the Civil Rights Act of 1866, and the Enforcement Acts of the 1870s was carried out at the expense of states' rights and resulted in a new balance of power in the federal Union. Although the states retained the responsibility of regulating civil rights, they did so under the watchful eye of the national government, which now had the right to step in when necessary. Although federal intervention in the South would all but cease by the 1880s, the federal government with greater powers and responsibilities would once again increase its supervisory role over state affairs during the second half of the 20th century.

Exercise Set 2.1

1. Lincoln's plan for Reconstruction was based on the theory that the Confederacy was
   A. to be considered a conquered nation.
   B. to be divided into five states which would apply for statehood.
   C. to be placed under congressional control.
   D. to be considered as never having left the Union.

2. By the 1890s Reconstruction had the effect of
   A. bringing complete civil rights to Southern blacks.
   B. making the South solidly Democratic.
   C. insuring the vote to all freedmen.
   D. subduing all racist groups.

3. The Reconstruction plan of the Radical Republicans (1867)
   A. established military control in the South.
   B. was essentially the plan proposed by President Johnson.
   C. was prompted by the South's acceptance of the Fourteenth Amendment.
   D. included seating former Confederate military leaders in Congress.

4. The most frequent basis for legislation expanding the role of the federal government in the guarantee of civil rights has been
   A. state court decisions.
   B. the war powers of the President.
   C. the Fourteenth Amendment.
   D. the 18-year-old vote.

5. The impeachment of President Johnson by the House of Representatives was based primarily on his
   A. creation of additional Cabinet positions.
   B. attempts to exclude the South from the Union.
   C. desire to run for a second term.
   D. violation of the Tenure in Office Act.

6. The "black codes" developed by the Southern states were designed to
   A. keep Southern blacks in the Democratic Party.
   B. keep freed slaves subordinate to whites.
   C. help freed slaves adjust to their freedom through education.
   D. divide old plantations and distribute land to former slaves.

POST-CIVIL WAR ECONOMICS

In 1860 the United States was still primarily a producer of food and raw materials. However, in the half century that followed the Civil War, the United States became the world's leading industrial power. The statistics in Figure 2.1 demonstrate the extraordinary growth that took place during the 30 years following the Civil War.

Economic and Technological Stimuli

A number of factors were involved in the rapid transformation of American society in the years during and following the Civil War.

Population

Between 1860 and 1890 the country's population soared from 31.5 million to 62.6 million. Besides the high birthrate during this period, millions of immigrants came to the United States. They joined the large number of Americans moving from the farms to the cities. The population boom provided a source of cheap labor necessary during rapid economic growth.

	1860	1890	% of increase
Population	31,450,000	62,600,000	99
Number of factories	140,500	335,400	139
Value of factories	1,000,000,000	6,500,000,000	555
Value of manufactured goods	1,900,000,000	9,400,000,000	394
Industrial workers	1,300,000	4,200,000	223

Figure 2.1   Industrial Growth (1860–1890)

Raw Materials

The new industrial age was based upon steam power and heavy industry that made use of iron and steel. In addition to having about half the world's coal reserves, which were used for fuel, the United States also had abundant raw materials necessary for industrial growth. Iron ore and coal (the two raw materials used in the manufacture of steel with the use of the **Bessemer process** during the 1880s and afterward) were abundant, as were oil, copper, lead, silver, and gold.

Capital

In this period, capital from Americans and from Europe was abundant. As American industry became a lucrative investment opportunity, foreign capital financed many growing industries. By 1900, foreign investors owned approximately $3 billion in American securities. Domestic investment increased in American industry, especially after the decline of American shipping.

Technology

The demand for industrial goods during the Civil War acted as a catalyst to ingenuity and inventions, as American industry had to compete with foreign industry, which could employ labor at lower wages. However, techniques such as interchangeable parts and later the assembly line allowed cheaper production of goods. Inventions of the age included the typewriter (1868), telephone (1876), incandescent lightbulb (1880), linotype (1886), and the gasoline engine in the 1890s.

Expanding Markets

Both domestic and foreign markets for American goods expanded steadily during the second half of the 19th century. This was the result of increased demand by a growing domestic market with greater capability to consume and of increased demand by the foreign market made more accessible through the use of steam-driven iron ships.

Transportation

Before the Civil War, there were only about 30,000 miles of railroad track in the United States, and railroads barely existed west of the Mississippi River. After the war, railroad consolidation united many competing lines into a few giant systems that connected the many fragmented rail systems throughout the nation. By 1900, the New York Central System, created by **Cornelius Vanderbilt**, connected New York to Boston, Cleveland, Detroit, Chicago, St. Louis, Cincinnati, and Indianapolis. The federal government provided land grants to encourage the building of railroads in the sparsely populated West. Initially spurred by the California gold rush of 1849, Western railroad building increased again after the Civil War. The first **transcontinental railroad** was completed with the connection of the Union Pacific and the Central Pacific lines in Promontory, Utah, on May 10, 1869. By 1900, 200,000 miles of track existed in the United States, permitting the rapid transport of people and products.

The shift from wooden sailing vessels to steam-driven steel vessels made the transportation of goods less expensive and helped to expand the world market for American industrial and agricultural goods.

Labor

Before the Civil War, few Americans were wage earners. Most were self-employed in agriculture or small single-owner crafts. By 1900, however, about two-thirds of working adults were wage earners rather than self-employed. As the lives of workers were increasingly controlled by the employers who could hire and fire them at will, the struggle to combine and unionize became important in American labor history.

The Transformation of the South

The Civil War caused both the physical devastation and economic ruin of the South. The financial system based upon Confederate currency and bonds had collapsed, while the emancipation of enslaved people upended the economic system by which the propertied class had made their fortunes.

Labor and Agriculture

• *The Freedmen.* Although the Civil War had emancipated the slaves, the adjustment for the freedmen proved to be difficult, since they did not have the means to become self-sufficient. Although Representative **Thaddeus Stevens** advocated the breaking up of large Southern plantations and the allocation of "forty acres and a mule" to each freedman, proposals for an effective program of land distribution failed to get through Congress. In most cases the freed slaves were forced to work for wages set by white landowners under the immediate supervision of a white overseer.

• *Sharecropping.* Black farmers and white landowners turned to a land and labor system known as sharecropping. The farmworker, often a freedman, farmed a tract of land belonging to a plantation owner and, in return for farming the land, was allowed to keep a percentage of the crop. Black sharecroppers lived in freedom, but they often became so indebted to the landowner and other creditors through the crop-lien system, where farmers borrowed against their expected harvest, that the system effectively re-enslaved the South's black population.

• *Land.* When Southerners returned to producing cotton after the Civil War, they discovered that the world demand for cotton had decreased. During the war, India, Brazil, and Egypt had supplied the cotton needs of the textile industries. The resulting depression in Southern agriculture affected white and black growers alike.

After the war, many large plantations were broken up. Between 1865 and 1880 the number of farms in the Southern states more than doubled, while the size of the average farm decreased. However, because of the sharecropping system, the number of landowners did not increase. As farmers continued to grow cotton and tobacco, overproduction caused prices to plunge, and constant growing exhausted the soil. In time, the necessity of crop diversification and scientific farming methods, including crop rotation, would be recognized.

Industrialization

One of the lessons of the Southern defeat in the Civil War was the realization that industrialization was necessary in the South. While Southern planters, shippers, and manufacturers depended heavily on capital from Northern banks and entrepreneurs, many Southern industries were mere subsidiaries of

Northern firms. In the 1870s textile mills were built in the cotton states, and the South eventually replaced New England as the textile manufacturing center. The tobacco industry, aided by the invention of a cigarette-making machine in 1880, added to the industrialization of the South. Lumbering and iron and steel production increased, as did coal mining and railroad production.

Exercise Set 2.2

1. By the beginning of the 20th century, New England was being displaced as the leading textile center of the nation by
   A. the Canadian Provinces.
   B. the South.
   C. the Northwest.
   D. the Southwest.

2. Immediately following the Civil War, Southern agriculture
   A. was replaced by industrial output.
   B. changed little from the time prior to the Civil War.
   C. relied less on tobacco and cotton and became diversified.
   D. returned to the plantation-slave labor system.

3. The system whereby sharecroppers would borrow against their expected harvest, agreeing to pay a portion of their crops in return for credit, was called
   A. crop rotation.
   B. homesteading.
   C. nullification.
   D. crop-lien.

4. To encourage the building of railroads, the federal government
   A. provided land grants.
   B. practiced a policy of laissez-faire.
   C. increased tariffs on iron and steel products.
   D. provided cheap immigrant labor for the railroad companies.

Year	Total Value* Millions of Dollars	Cotton Millions of Dollars	Leaf Tobacco Millions of Dollars	Wheat Millions of Dollars
1850	101	72	10	1
1853	124	109	11	4
1855	151	88	15	1
1858	157	131	17	9
1860	270	192	16	4
1863	74	7	20	47
1865	154	7	42	19
1868	206	153	23	30
1870	359	227	21	47

*Selected Exports
SOURCE: U.S. Bureau of the Census, *Historical Statistics of the U.S., Colonial Times to 1957.*

Figure 2.2 Value of Selected Exports from the United States

5. According to the information presented in the table on U.S. exports,
   A. the export of leaf tobacco ceased completely during the Civil War.
   B. by 1870 the export of wheat had fallen to 1865 levels.
   C. the total value of United States exports rapidly recovered from the setback and disruption of the Civil War.
   D. the total value of selected exports from the United States increased at a steady rate from 1850 to 1870.

EMANCIPATION: AN UNSETTLED ISSUE

> The freedmen were not really free in 1865, nor are most of their descendants really free in 1965. Slavery was but one aspect of a race and color problem that is still far from solution here, or anywhere. In America particularly, the grapes of wrath have not yet yielded all their bitter vintage.
>
> Samuel Eliot Morison,
> *The Oxford History of the American People,* 1965

Political

Although the Civil War and the post-war amendments had changed the legal status of the ex-slaves, in reality their social and economic status had changed very little. With the withdrawal of the last federal troops from the South in 1877, elements of white Southern society looked for methods to prevent blacks from voting.

Since the Fifteenth Amendment prohibited the denial of the vote due to "**race, color, or previous condition of servitude**," Southern state legislatures found other methods of denying the vote. **Poll taxes** and **literacy tests** were two methods used to disenfranchise black Americans. In some states, voters were asked to read and interpret the Constitution. By the late 1800s the **grandfather clause** became a widespread method of keeping blacks from the polls. This was a clause added to state constitutions giving the right to vote to all persons whose grandfathers could vote in 1867, even if the person could not pay the poll tax or pass the literacy test. Since blacks had been slaves and not able to vote in 1867, this clause disenfranchised them while giving the vote to poor, illiterate whites. By the early 1900s African Americans had effectively lost their political rights in the South.

Social

The inferior social status of African Americans did not change after the Civil War. Although the Fourteenth Amendment prevented the states from discriminating against individuals, the Supreme Court ruled in 1876, in the case of *United States* v. *Cruikshank,* that the amendment "added nothing to the rights of one citizen against another." In other words, it had to be shown that the state was denying rights for the amendment to apply. The Court went further in the **Civil Rights Cases** (1883) when it invalidated the Civil Rights Act of 1875 that had prohibited **segregation** in public facilities. The Court held that the federal government could not regulate the behavior of private individuals. Later cases, primarily ***Plessy* v. *Ferguson*** (1896), held that blacks could be restricted to "separate but equal" facilities. This opened the door for the **Jim Crow** laws separating white and black Americans in Southern society.

Struggle for Political Control

As the Southern states followed the Reconstruction plan of Congress, they held conventions to draft new constitutions and established new state governments. Black voters exercised their newly acquired right to vote and elected black delegates to participate in these conventions and to the new state legislatures. Although black voters were in the majority in five states, only in South Carolina did they hold a majority in the lower house of the state legislature. Northerners known as **carpetbaggers**, who had recently arrived in the South, dominated the state governments in the early part of the Reconstruction period.

The "Reconstruction governments" passed much admirable legislation and introduced many overdue reforms in the South. The new constitutions were more democratic in that many eliminated property qualifications for voting and officeholding and made some former appointive positions now elective. Provisions for public schools, public works, and general rebuilding of the war-torn South were put through by the new governments.

Unfortunately, the Reconstruction governments under Republican rule were riddled with corruption. White resentment, or backlash, against the Reconstruction governments became widespread, and some secret societies such as the **Ku Klux Klan** were organized and turned to acts of terror. Such groups intimidated African Americans to prevent them from exercising their newly gained right to vote. Some relief came with the passage of federal laws, including the Force Act (1870) and the Ku Klux Klan Act (1871), allowing federal supervision of elections and the use of federal troops to control these white supremacy groups. However, the intimidation, including whippings, brandings, lynchings, and murder by these secret societies had already taken its toll.

The "Solid South" developed when white Democrats regained political control in the South. High taxes, corruption, a rising conservative class, and the tradition of white rule combined to end the temporary role of blacks in Southern politics.

The Supreme Court and the Fourteenth Amendment

The Fourteenth Amendment is perhaps the most important amendment ever added to the Constitution, and questions concerning its interpretation began to surface shortly after its ratification in 1868. Did the framers of the amendment intend to bar **discrimination**? If so, did this include private discrimination as well as public discrimination? Perhaps the most perplexing question to face the courts after its ratification: Did the framers intend to make the Bill of Rights applicable to the states as a result of the Fourteenth Amendment?

The wording of Section 1 of the Fourteenth Amendment is critical in understanding the amendment's history and changing interpretations:

> No **State** shall make or enforce any law which shall abridge the privileges or immunities of citizens of the United States; nor shall any State deprive any person of **life**, **liberty**, **or property**, without **due process of law**; nor deny any person within its jurisdiction the **equal protection** of the laws.

The Slaughter-House Cases

During the late 19th century, almost 600 cases involving the Fourteenth Amendment came to the Supreme Court, of which fewer than 30 dealt with ex-slaves. The first detailed discussion by the Supreme Court of the Fourteenth Amendment came in 1873 with the Slaughter-House Cases. When a group of butchers claimed that a monopoly on the slaughtering of livestock deprived them of equal protection of the laws as provided in Section 1 of the Fourteenth Amendment, the Supreme Court answered that the amendment was designed only to protect newly freed slaves. It also stated that the situation the butchers objected to was in the domain of the relationship between the state and its citizens, not the federal government, thus limiting the application of the amendment.

The Civil Rights Cases

In the Civil Rights Cases (1883), the Supreme Court voided the **Civil Rights Act of 1875**, which had forbidden hotels, restaurants, and public accommodations in general to discriminate based on race, color, or previous condition of servitude. The Court held that the Fourteenth Amendment prohibited discrimination only by state governments, not that in which individuals and private citizens engaged. With the *Plessy* case, the power of the Fourteenth Amendment to protect the civil rights of minority Americans reached its lowest point. As of 1896 the amendment was used to sanction "**separate but equal**" facilities and applied only to state actions.

Application of the Fourteenth Amendment to the States

Although the Fourteenth Amendment did not at first apply the Bill of Rights to the states, in time the Supreme Court, explaining the "due process" clause, made certain provisions of the Bill of Rights applicable to the states. The landmark case was *Gitlow* v. *New York* (1925), when the Supreme Court, in incorporating the First Amendment in the due process clause of the Fourteenth Amendment, declared that:

> For the present purposes, we may and do assume that freedom of speech and of the press—which are protected by the First Amendment from abridgement by Congress—are among the fundamental personal rights and "liberties" protected by the due process clause of the Fourteenth Amendment from impairment by the states.

Since the *Gitlow* case, the following guarantees of the Bill of Rights have been applied to the states:

- prohibition against unreasonable searches and seizures (Fourth Amendment, *Mapp* v. *Ohio*, 1961)
- privilege against self-incrimination (Fifth Amendment, *Malloy* v. *Hogan*, 1964 and later **Miranda v. Arizona**, 1966)
- guarantee against double jeopardy (Fifth Amendment, *Benton* v. *Maryland*, 1969)
- right to assistance of counsel (Sixth Amendment, **Gideon v. Wainwright**, 1963)
- right to a speedy trial (Sixth Amendment, *Klopfer* v. *North Carolina*, 1967)
- right to a jury trial (Sixth Amendment, *Duncan* v. *Louisiana*, 1968)
- right to confront opposing witnesses (Sixth Amendment, *Pointer* v. *Texas*, 1965)
- right to compulsory process for obtaining witnesses (Sixth Amendment, *Washington* v. *Texas*, 1967)
- right to public trial (Sixth Amendment)
- right to notice as to the nature and cause of the accusation (Sixth Amendment)
- prohibition against cruel and unusual punishment (Eighth Amendment, *Robinson* v. *California*, 1962)

Role of Black Americans in Post-Civil War Society

In the postwar decades of Reconstruction and the rebuilding of the "New South," racial segregation in the form of Jim Crow laws, as well as poll taxes, grandfather clauses, literacy tests, lynchings, beatings, and other forms of violence by white supremacist groups were used to keep blacks in their "proper place." Between 1880 and 1930, three leading figures were instrumental in defining the position of blacks in American society: **Booker T. Washington**, **W. E. B. Du Bois**, and **Marcus Garvey**.

Booker T. Washington

Founder of the Normal and Industrial Institute at Tuskegee, Alabama (1881), and author of the autobiography *Up From Slavery*, Booker T. Washington stressed the importance of vocational education in preparing African Americans to earn a living and to gain equality. More militant groups and individuals criticized Washington's "willing to wait" methods as "practically accepting the alleged inferiority of the Negro race."

W. E. B. Du Bois

Du Bois's *The Souls of Black Folk* (1903) presented the black American's life to the white public in a series of essays. His **Niagara Movement** (1905) demanded immediate suffrage and civil rights for blacks. Du Bois believed that a small group of educated, talented blacks, referred to as the "Talented Tenth," would save the race by setting an example to whites and other blacks. Du Bois and his associates, black and white, formed the **National Association for the Advancement of Colored People (NAACP)** in 1909 to pursue legal methods to end racial discrimination.

Marcus Garvey

Jamaican-born Marcus Garvey founded the Universal Negro Improvement Association (1916). Preaching racial pride, Garvey insisted that American blacks must return to Africa and create their own civilization in their homeland. Although Garvey's concept of black pride was hailed by many, few chose to leave America and return to Africa.

Exercise Set 2.3

1. Voting rights protection for ex-slaves was provided by the
   A. literacy tests.
   B. poll taxes.
   C. "grandfather clauses."
   D. Fifteenth Amendment.

2. Laws requiring the separation of the races in public facilities were called
   A. equal protection provisions.
   B. Amnesty Acts.
   C. Jim Crow laws.
   D. sharecropper statutes.

3. The Supreme Court case of *Plessy* v. *Ferguson* (1896)
   A. mandated integration of public facilities.
   B. found the poll tax to be unconstitutional.
   C. gave legal support to segregation.
   D. affirmed *Gitlow* v. *United States* in applying the Bill of Rights to the states.

4. The legislatures established in the Southern states during Reconstruction
   A. excluded blacks.
   B. were free from corruption and graft.
   C. were primarily dominated by blacks.
   D. were instrumental in passing necessary legislation.

THE END OF RECONSTRUCTION

The Grant Era

> Let no guilty man escape, if it can be avoided. No personal considerations should stand in the way of performing a public duty.
>
> President Ulysses S. Grant,
> Endorsement of a letter relating to the **Whiskey Ring**,
> July 29, 1875

The Grant Administration (1869–1877)

Ulysses S. Grant, although a capable military leader, proved a failure at providing strong leadership in the White House. As the nation experienced tremendous economic expansion, incidents of widespread graft and corruption plagued American politics and reflected a low point in public morality.

• *Monetary Policy.* President Grant was not directly involved in the numerous scandals that plagued his administration, but he lacked good judgment concerning those he turned to for advice. During his first term he was influenced by two financial speculators, **Jay Gould** and **James Fisk**. Gould and Fisk helped cause the ruin of many business people, financiers, and workers.

• *Crédit Mobilier.* A scandal involving the construction of the Union Pacific Railroad was revealed during Grant's second administration. The owners of the Union Pacific Railroad created the **Crédit Mobilier**, a construction company, to build the railroad. This company charged the railroad several times the actual amount of construction. To hide the fraud and prevent investigation they gave stock to several members of Congress and the vice president.

• *The Whiskey Ring Fraud.* This scandal involved a ring of liquor dealers in St. Louis who, with the assistance of treasury officials, defrauded the government of millions in unpaid taxes.

Urban Politics

Political corruption also existed at the local level. Led by a political "boss," their main goal—to obtain and keep political power—was achieved through graft and bribery. The infamous **Tweed Ring** of New York City's Tammany Hall stole some $100,000 from the tax-

William Marcy "Boss" Tweed (1823–1878) controlled New York City from behind the scenes.

payers before being exposed by *The New York Times* and by the cartoons of **Thomas Nast** in *Harper's Weekly.*

The Solid South

As a result of Reconstruction and political upheaval in the South following the Civil War, the Democrats were able to convince many white voters that the Republican Party was the party of corruption that had forced black rule on the South. The Democratic Party was dominant in the South from 1876 until the 1970s.

Election of 1876 and the Compromise of 1877

As corruption became more widespread, reform-minded Republicans banded together in 1872 in a new wing of the party known as the "**Liberal Republicans**." They wanted to clean up politics and end military Reconstruction. In 1876, the Republican convention, realizing that the reputation of "Grantism" was hurting the party, nominated a compromise candidate, Governor **Rutherford B. Hayes** of Ohio. The Democratic nominee, Governor **Samuel J. Tilden** of New York, campaigned against Republican scandal and supported reform in the area of federal employment, or "civil service reform."

In the general election to choose the presidential electors who were to cast the Electoral College votes for the President, Tilden won a majority of the popular votes. However, neither candidate had enough undisputed electoral votes to win.

To resolve the unprecedented constitutional crisis, Congress established a fifteen-member electoral commission (Electoral Count Act). After lengthy discussion, the members of the commission agreed to accept the Republican returns, giving Hayes a one-vote electoral victory. In an informal compromise between the parties, the Democrats agreed that Hayes would take office in return for withdrawing troops from the two states where they remained, Louisiana and South Carolina, officially ending military Reconstruction in the South.

The Impact of the Civil War and Reconstruction

Political Alignments

During the Civil War and early Reconstruction era, the political parties exhibited clear-cut differences in ideology, primarily in the areas of race relations and civil rights. After the Civil War, however, sharp policy differences between the two parties faded, although they continued to differ on national issues such as the tariff and currency. The Democrats generally favored low tariffs and the silver standard, while the Republicans favored high tariffs and the gold standard. For the most part, the two major parties failed to develop any clear-cut program to deal with the major social and economic issues that faced the nation.

Nature of Citizenship

The Constitution was silent on the issue of citizenship. The Civil Rights Act of 1866 provided that "all persons born or naturalized in the United States . . . were citizens of the United States." The Fourteenth Amendment to the Constitution (1868) further defined citizenship on both the national and state levels: "All persons born or naturalized in the United States, and subject to the jurisdiction thereof, are citizens of the United States and of the State wherein they reside."

Federal-State Relations

With the nationalization of civil rights by virtue of the Civil Rights Act of 1866, the Thirteenth, Fourteenth, and Fifteenth Amendments, and the Civil Rights Act of 1875, the federal government came to play a far greater role in the preservation of civil rights. The Fourteenth Amendment forbade discriminatory acts by states, not those by private individuals. As white rule returned to the South and attention to the rights of the freed slaves faded, the federal government turned its increased power to national economic issues that were a result of the Industrial Revolution of the late 19th century.

The North as an Industrial Power

While the Civil War marked a dividing point in American history, with the United States turning from an agrarian nation into an industrial power in a matter of decades, this development was sectional. As industrial development spread over the North, the South remained overwhelmingly rural. The second half of the 19th century saw industrial growth assisted by protective tariffs and corporate development nurtured by favorable Supreme Court decisions. The effect of industry and business would soon find its way into the lives of most Americans.

Exercise Set 2.4

1. Before the former Confederate states could be readmitted to the Union, the congressional plan for Reconstruction required them to
   A. ratify the 14th Amendment.
   B. imprison all former Confederate soldiers.
   C. provide 40 acres of land to all freedmen.
   D. help rebuild Northern industries.

2. By the Compromise of 1877,
   A. the 14th Amendment to the Constitution was ratified.
   B. Tilden was selected as President of the United States.
   C. military occupation of the South ended.
   D. the Electoral College system ended.

3. The Crédit Mobilier scandal involved
   A. an increase in the salary of the President and members of Congress.
   B. the transcontinental railroad.
   C. whiskey and tax fraud.
   D. different sets of electoral votes being sent to Congress.

4. The section of the 14th Amendment that had the greatest legal significance for the future dealt with
   A. equal protection of the laws guarantee.
   B. the apportionment of representatives.
   C. the repudiation of the Confederate war debt.
   D. the disability clause.

1. The Fifteenth Amendment to the U.S. Constitution does not prevent the denial of the vote based upon
   A. literacy.
   B. race.
   C. color.
   D. previous condition of servitude.

2. In the decades following the Civil War, the expression "Solid South" was used to refer to the
   A. return of the old plantation system based upon slave labor.
   B. dominance by the Democratic Party.
   C. industrialization of the South.
   D. changed attitude on the part of the Southern states toward black Americans.

3. Which factor was *least* important in the industrialization of the United States in the 19th century?
   A. Abundance of raw materials
   B. Inventions
   C. Supply of cheap labor
   D. Foreign demand for American industrial goods

4. The Fourteenth Amendment is important because, in addition to awarding citizenship to former slaves, it
   A. guarantees women the right to vote.
   B. abolishes the poll tax.
   C. guarantees equal protection under the law.
   D. provides protection against illegal search and seizure.

5. The ability to amend the U.S. Constitution lends support to the belief that the document was designed to
   A. preserve the provisions of the original Constitution.
   B. adapt to changing times and beliefs.
   C. maintain the separation of powers in the national government.
   D. accommodate the political party in power.

6. Which of the following guarantees would today apply to the states through the "due process" and "equal protection" clauses of the Fourteenth Amendment?
   A. Assistance of counsel in criminal prosecutions
   B. Ownership of a gun
   C. Consumption of alcohol at age eighteen
   D. Privilege to drive an automobile at age sixteen

THEMATIC ESSAY

Directions: Write a well-organized essay that includes an introduction, several paragraphs addressing the task below, and a conclusion.

Theme: Geography—Territorial Acquisition

> Throughout the nation's history, the United States has expanded through the acquisition of new territories. These acquisitions have had both positive and negative effects on the United States.

Task:

> Select *two* territories acquired by the United States and for *each*
>
> - Describe the historical circumstances that led the United States to acquire the territory.
> - Discuss *positive **and/or** negative* effects of the acquisition of this territory on the United States.

You may use any territory acquired by the United States since 1776. Some suggestions you might wish to consider include the Ohio River valley (1783), Louisiana Territory (1803), Florida (1819), Texas (1845), Oregon Territory (1846), California (1848), Alaska (1867), Hawaii (1898), and Puerto Rico (1899).

You are *not* limited to these suggestions.

THEMATIC ESSAY

Directions: Write a well-organized essay that includes an introduction, several paragraphs addressing the task below, and a conclusion.

Theme: Separation of Powers

> The balance of the three branches of the federal government has, historically, been in a constant state of flux.

Task:

> From your study of the Reconstruction Period (1863–1876), identify *two* examples of the operation of checks and balances within the federal government.
>
> For each example identified:
>
> - Discuss a specific proposed action by the particular branch of government (executive, legislative, or judicial).
> - Describe the reaction to the action by another branch of government.
> - Finally, explain the settlement or outcome of the debated issue.

You may use any examples from the Reconstruction Period. Some suggestions you might wish to consider are Lincoln's Proclamation of Amnesty and Reconstruction (December 1863) and Congress's Wade-Davis Bill (July 1864), President Johnson's plan of Reconstruction (May 1865) and the reaction of Congress with the passage of the Military Reconstruction Act (March 1867) and the passage by Congress of the Tenure in Office Act (March 1867), President Johnson's veto of the Act (1867), and the subsequent impeachment of President Johnson (1868).

You are *not* limited to these suggestions.

DOCUMENT-BASED QUESTION

The following questions (Part A and Part B) are based on the accompanying documents (1–7). Some of these documents have been edited for the purpose of this exercise. The question is designed to test your ability to work with historical documents and to demonstrate your knowledge of the subject matter being presented. As you analyze the documents, take into account both the source of the document and the author's point of view.

Historical Context:

> The Fourteenth Amendment, ratified in 1868, nationalized civil rights by assuring that no state would deny citizens the equal protection of the laws.

Task:

> Using information from the documents and your knowledge of United States history, answer the questions that follow each document in Part A. Your answers to the questions will help you write the Part B essay, in which you will be asked:
>
> Discuss how the Fourteenth Amendment, and its interpretation by the Supreme Court, nationalized civil rights.

Part A
Short-Answer Questions

The documents provided relate to issues concerning the concept of equal protection of the laws. Examine each document carefully and then answer the questions that follow.

DOCUMENT 1

> *Section 1.* All persons born or naturalized in the United States and subject to the jurisdiction thereof, are citizens of the United States and of the State wherein they reside. No State shall make or enforce any law which shall abridge the privileges or immunities of citizens of the United States; nor shall any State deprive any person of life, liberty, or property, without due process of law; *nor deny to any person within its jurisdiction the equal protection of the laws.*
>
> *Section 5.* The Congress shall have the power to enforce, by appropriate legislation, the provisions of this article.

—Fourteenth Amendment, United States Constitution (1868)

1. According the the Fourteenth Amendment, what body was given the power to make sure the amendment was enforced?

_____

_____

2. Keeping in mind the reasons for the addition of the Fourteenth Amendment to the Constitution, why weren't the states given the power of enforcement of the amendment?

_____

_____

_____

_____

DOCUMENT 2

No woman, infant under twenty-one years of age . . . convict . . . nor any free Negro, mulatto, or Indian . . . shall have a vote.

—Statute, Colony of Virginia (1748)

3. What equal protection of the laws issues are raised by the early colonial Virginia statute?

_____

_____

_____

_____

DOCUMENT 3

4. What rights of citizens does the cartoon show being protected by due process and equal protection?

_____

_____

_____

DOCUMENT 4

. . . all railway companies carrying passengers in their coaches in this State shall provide equal but separate accommodations for the white and colored races by providing two or more passenger coaches for each passenger train, or by dividing the passenger coaches by a partition so as to secure separate accommodations.

—Louisiana Statute, (1890) issue of _Plessy_ v. _Ferguson_ (1896)

5. Do you see an "equal protection of the laws" issue with the 1890 Louisiana statute? Why or why not?

_____

_____

_____

DOCUMENT 5

We consider the underlying fallacy of the plaintiff's argument to consist in the assumption that the enforced separation of the two races stamps the colored race with a badge of inferiority. If this be so, it is not by reason of anything found in the act, but solely because the colored race chooses to put that construction upon it.

—Brown, J., Opinion of the Court, *Plessy* v. *Ferguson* (1896)

6. Justice Brown wrote the opinion for the majority in the *Plessy* v. *Ferguson* case. What were his feelings about having races separated in the railway cars?

_____

_____

_____

DOCUMENT 6

In respect of civil rights common to all citizens, the Constitution of the United States does not, I think, permit any public authority to know the race of those entitled to be protected in the enjoyment of such rights. Every true man has pride of race, and, under appropriate circumstances, when the rights of others, his equals before the law, are not to be affected, it is his privilege to express such pride and to take such action based upon it as to him seems proper. But I deny that any legislative body or judicial tribunal may have regard to the race of citizens when the civil rights of those citizens are involved. Indeed, such legislation as that here in question is inconsistent not only with that equality of rights which pertains to citizenship, National and State, but with the personal liberty enjoyed by everyone within the United States.

—Harlan, J., Dissenting Opinion of the Court, *Plessy* v. *Ferguson* (1896)

7. Explain how Justice Harlan's dissenting opinion differs from Justice Brown's majority opinion in the *Plessy* v. *Ferguson* case.

_____

_____

_____

DOCUMENT 7

We come then to the question presented: Does segregation of children in public schools solely on the basis of race, even though the physical facilities and other "tangible" factors may be equal, deprive the children of the minority group of equal educational opportunities? We believe that it does.

—Warren, C.J., Opinion of the Court, *Brown* v. *Board of Education* (1954)

8. Fifty-eight years after the Supreme Court decided *Plessy* v. *Ferguson* (1896), the issue of equal protection of the laws was decided in *Brown* v. *Board of Education* (1954). How did the Supreme Court differ in its view of "equal protection of the laws" in 1954 compared to 1896?

_____

_____

_____

**Part B
Essay**

Your essay should be well organized with an introductory paragraph that states your position on the question. Develop your position in the next paragraphs and then write a conclusion. In your essay, include specific historical details and refer to the specific documents you analyzed in Part A. You may include additional information from your knowledge of social studies.

Historical Context:

The Fourteenth Amendment, ratified in 1868, nationalized civil rights by assuring that no state would deny citizens the equal protection of the laws.

Task:

Discuss how the Fourteenth Amendment, and its interpretation by the Supreme Court, nationalized civil rights.

Guidelines:

In your essay, be sure to
• Develop all aspects of the task.
• Incorporate information from *at least five* documents.
• Incorporate relevant outside information.
• Support the theme with many relevant facts, examples, and details.
• Use a logical and clear plan of organization, including an introduction and a conclusion that are beyond a restatement of the theme.

CHAPTER 2

THE RISE OF AMERICAN BUSINESS, INDUSTRY, AND LABOR (1865–1920)

TECHNOLOGY AND WORLD INDUSTRIALISM

> The fact is, that civilization requires slaves. The Greeks were quite right there. Unless there are slaves to do the uninteresting work, culture and contemplation become almost impossible. Human slavery is wrong, insecure, and demoralizing. On mechanical slavery, on the slavery of the machine, the future of the world depends.
>
> Oscar Wilde,
> *The Soul of Man Under Socialism* (1895)

The Industrial Revolution

The term "Industrial Revolution" refers to changes in the economic organization of society that include the factory system and machine-made goods. The Industrial Revolution began about 1750 in England with certain inventions in the textile industry and spread to many nations of the Western world, including the United States, during the next century. It involved the replacement on a massive scale of human and animal power with machine power. During the Industrial Revolution there was a shift from manufacturing in the home to the gathering of machines and workers to run them under a single roof (the factory). It also involved improved methods of transportation on land and water, and the growth of modern **capitalism** with the private ownership and control of the means of production.

United States

The Industrial Revolution came to the United States somewhat later than to England. English **mercantilism** had stifled the development of some colonial industry. Moreover, after the Revolution, American capital was used primarily for agricultural development and the shipping industry. The difficulty of importing manufactured goods during the Napoleonic Wars and the War of 1812 provided a stimulus for the development of factories in the United States. The three decades following the Civil War brought economic and social transformation unmatched in the history of the United States. Rich in natural resources, human resources both in labor and scientific development, and capital, the United States approached the coming of the 20th century as a leader in industrial development. Large-scale immigration helped to provide the labor needed in the expanding factory system. By 1894 the United States was turning out more manufactured goods than any other country in the world. Of course, many problems accompanied the Industrial Revolution. Among them were problems between labor and management, uneven distribution of wealth, and harmful business combinations.

Impact of Industrial Development

On the surface, the Industrial Revolution appeared to benefit most Americans. Statistics suggest that the American standard of living improved in the decades following the Civil War, with prices declining, wage rates remaining consistent, and therefore "real income" increasing. Average working hours decreased and average life expectancy increased. Yet the new industrial age also brought many problems. As wage earners became more dependent on others, times of fluctuation in production resulted in prolonged periods of unemployment in the 1870s and again in the 1890s. The relationship between the factory owner and the workers was no longer personal, and there was little concern for injured or unemployed workers.

Collective bargaining made little progress by 1870 and there was no public welfare program to ease the hardships caused by injury, unemployment, or old age. As industrialism increased and capitalism thrived, the contrast between the rich and the poor increased. As the technology and business organizations of the industrial era generated unmatched powers for creating goods and services, a class of Americans was being exploited by the factory system. The words of American social critic Henry Demarest Lloyd in his attack upon monopolies, *Wealth Against Commonwealth* (1894), appeared to be coming true: "Liberty produces wealth, and wealth destroys liberty."

Growth of Capitalism

Capitalism, a form of economic organization characterized by the factory system, private ownership, large-scale production, a free market, and wage labor, became the dominant economic system in the industrial societies in the 19th century. Elements of capitalism include (1) **capital**, or the wealth used in producing more wealth; (2) **capitalists**, those who invest money in an enterprise from which a profit is expected; and (3) **labor**, or the working class employed by capitalists. Profits determine what to produce, and what to produce will be determined by what people will buy at profitable prices.

The leading critic of capitalism and its abuses in the 1800s was the German writer **Karl Marx** (1818–1883). According to Marx, all history involves the struggle between social classes. He saw modern society as divided between the **bourgeoisie** (upper class), which controlled the capital, and the **prole-**

tariat (working class), which sold its labor for wages. Marx supported the organization of workers both as an economic force in **trade unions** and as a political force in a revolutionary movement to overthrow the bourgeoisie.

PRE-CIVIL WAR INDUSTRIAL GROWTH

Although the post-Civil War period has come to be identified with the rapid growth of the Industrial Revolution in the United States, manufacturing and industrial development can be traced back to colonial times. Colonists found that British goods cost nearly twice as much in America as they did in Britain. This situation led the colonists to undertake small-scale manufacturing including the production of textiles (cloth), soap, candles, furniture, and crude tools and utensils. Iron smelteries, some subsidized by colonial legislatures, helped meet the need for farm tools and weapons. Although by 1800 manufacturing was still relatively unimportant to the American economy, soon after the War of 1812 the rise of merchant investors, wholesalers, retailers, and improved transportation marked the early beginnings of industrial transformation.

Textile Industry

Textile manufacturing became an important part of American industry shortly after independence was achieved. The first mill, built in Pawtucket, Rhode Island in 1790, used water-powered spinning machines constructed by Samuel Slater. The **Embargo Act (1807)**, **Non-Intercourse Act (1809)**, and **War of 1812** stimulated manufacturing in the United States, and the number of textile mills increased.

Originally, many industries, including the textile industry, used the "putting-out" or domestic system; workers received supplies at home where they finished the product and then returned it to a merchant who sold it. This system had problems of timing, shipping, and quality control. In 1813 Francis Cabot Lowell and other Boston merchants built the first textile factories in Waltham, Massachusetts, combining all the manufacturing operations at a single location. To satisfy the need for workers, the managers of the textile factories recruited young women from the New England countryside to work in the mills. They offered them appealing wages, boarding houses to live in, and cultural events. This came to be known as the Lowell, or Waltham, System and was used in other mills in New England. The textile industry became the most important industry in the country before the Civil War, employing nearly 115,000 workers in 1860.

Iron Production

The iron industry, like the textile industry, was stimulated by the **embargo** on trade before the War of 1812 and by its interruption during the war. A major breakthrough in the iron industry came with the discovery of how to produce **steel** inexpensively and in large quantities. The United States possessed the necessary elements, iron and coal, to produce steel, a mixture of iron, carbon, and other elements. Immense deposits of iron ore lay near the western shores of Lake Superior, and nearly one half of the world's coal reserves lay within our borders. In the 1850s Henry Bessemer of England and William Kelly of the United States independently discovered a revolutionary process for making large quantities of steel inexpensively by burning out the impurities in molten iron. With the use of the **Bessemer process**, steel production soared.

Exercise Set 2.5

1. The introduction of new textile machines in England at the start of the Industrial Revolution increased the employment of textile workers because
   A. the newly developed machinery was less efficient than the hand labor that it replaced.
   B. the cost of machine-made textiles fell rapidly, leading to greater demand.
   C. the division of labor that developed required more workers to produce the same amount of goods.
   D. imported foreign textiles were superior to domestic textiles.

2. The primary purpose of the colonies acquired by England during the 19th century was to provide
   A. raw materials and overseas markets.
   B. a training ground for military forces.
   C. labor for growing industries.
   D. settlements for growing populations.

3. Which of the following inventions had great influence in the 19th century?
   A. The steam engine
   B. The radio
   C. The automobile
   D. The flying shuttle

4. An important result of the War of 1812 was that it
   A. increased U.S. shipping.
   B. encouraged immigration to the United States.
   C. encouraged manufacturing in the United States.
   D. increased investment in agriculture at the expense of industry.

5. America's most important industry before the Civil War was the
   A. rubber industry.
   B. machine tool industry.
   C. automobile industry.
   D. textile industry.

BUSINESS ORGANIZATION: SIZE AND STRUCTURE

> They (corporations) cannot commit treason, nor be outlawed nor excommunicated, for they have no souls.
>
> Sir Edward Coke (1552–1634),
> *Case of Sutton's Hospital*

Proprietorships and Partnerships

Before the middle of the 19th century, most American businesses were either **single proprietorships**, with one owner, or **partnerships**, small businesses with two or more owners. However, as American industry and business grew, facilitated by greater amounts of **capital**, improved transportation, greater demand for products, and an available working force, small organizations often proved to be inadequate. If a business wanted to expand, it was difficult for one or two persons to raise the necessary capital. If the organization faced financial difficulties, the owners who were financially responsible often lost their personal assets. Finally, the death of a proprietor or partner often meant the end of the business.

Incorporation

Following the Civil War, the **corporation** became the major form of business organization, gradually replacing proprietorships and partnerships. By selling part ownerships of the business to the public through the sale of **stocks** and **bonds**, the corporation was able to raise the necessary capital for operations and expansion. During the 1880s and 1890s, corporations received important judicial protection when the Supreme Court ruled that corporations, like individuals, were protected by the **Fourteenth Amendment**. This extension of the Fourteenth Amendment meant that corporations could not be denied equal protection of the laws and could not be deprived of rights or property without due process of law. (*Chicago, Milwaukee, and St. Paul Railway Co.* v. *Minnesota*, 1890)

Consolidation of Corporations

By 1900 corporations were responsible for nearly two-thirds of all the goods manufactured in the United States. As growth continued, corporate managers searched for ways to expand and increase stability. During the late 1800s, there was a trend toward business combination or consolidation, under new corporate forms such as **trusts** and holding companies that promoted growth and cut down on wasteful competition. Between 1889 and 1903 some 300 business combinations were formed. Perhaps the most spectacular was the **United States Steel Corporation**, the nation's first billion-dollar corporation, which controlled 60 percent of the nation's steel production, created by banker and international financier **J.P. Morgan**.

As investment opportunities increased, greater amounts of capital were necessary. In addition to domestic investments in American industry, foreign investment grew. Between 1870 and 1900 foreign investment in American companies increased from $1.5 billion to $3.5 billion.

TRANSPORTATION, COMMUNICATION, AND RESOURCES

Transportation

Railroads

During the first half of the 19th century, the nation's railroads were anything but a uniform system connecting the different sections of the country. There was little mileage beyond the Mississippi and virtually none beyond the Missouri River. Few tracks were connected; short stretches of lines using different gauges required the unloading and reloading of cargo for transport.

As settlement extended westward, it became apparent that the nation's rail system would have to expand into a uniform system. In 1850 the federal government transferred to promoters several million acres of public land for the purpose of railroad construction. This policy was continued by the government primarily in the construction of Western lines. The nation's first **transcontinental** railroad was completed in 1869 with the joining of the **Central Pacific Railroad** and the **Union Pacific Railroad** at Promontory Point, Utah. Between 1865 and 1890 the total mileage of track in the United

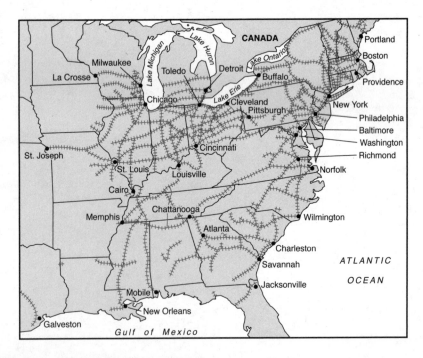

Figure 2.3   Major Railroads in 1860

States grew from 35,000 to 200,000, with the greatest growth taking place west of the Mississippi River. Technological advances, including uniform-gauge tracks, the automatic car coupler, the Pullman Sleeping Car, and the Westinghouse air brake, made rail transportation safer and more efficient. By 1910 the United States had a third of all the railroad track in the world. In the half-century following the Civil War, railroads enabled the growing nation to transport its enormous wealth in natural resources to factories, storehouses, marketplaces, and seaports.

Automobiles

Henry Ford, an electrical engineer with Detroit's Edison Company, developed and introduced the **mass production** of automobiles. Copying the meatpacking industry, Ford set up **assembly lines** to produce automobiles, which greatly reduced the time and expense of manufacturing cars. When the **Ford Motor Company** began production of the **Model T** in 1910, 10,000 cars were sold. By 1914, with the help of assembly-line production, 248,000 Fords, costing as little as $490 each, were sold. The production of automobiles also stimulated the growth of other industries, including steel, road building, service stations, rubber, etc.

Automobile manufacturer Henry Ford (1863–1947) developed the assembly-line method of mass production.

Urban Transportation

The forces of industrialization and urbanization accompanied one another during the second half of the 19th century and into the 20th century. As American cities grew, mass transportation became an area of concern. Horse- and mule-drawn vehicles of the late 1800s were inefficient in urban areas. The first power-driven transportation used in the cities were cable cars. The increased production of electricity enabled electric-powered streetcars to be used by the 1890s. Elevated tracks and subways allowed mass transportation free movement through congested areas. As suburbs spread out from the core of the city, tracks were constructed outward to bring commuters to and from their employment downtown.

Communication

Telegraph

The most revolutionary change in communications before the Civil War was the development of the long-distance telegraph by **Samuel F. B. Morse** in 1844. By 1853, 23,000 miles of telegraph wire spread across the United States, freeing the transport of messages from the human messenger. The first transatlantic cable was laid in 1858, making possible instantaneous communication with other continents.

Telephone

In 1876 **Alexander Graham Bell**, a teacher of the deaf in Boston, received a patent on a telephone he had invented. By 1885 the **American Telephone and Telegraph Company** was organized to put the new invention into widespread use.

Sources of Energy

New sources of energy have coincided with industrial development in the United States. During the late 1700s steam energy produced by wood and coal replaced earlier sources of power—humans, animals, and water power. By the late 1800s two new sources of energy—oil and electricity—came into use.

Oil

In the early 1850s kerosene refined from petroleum was an efficient and inexpensive fuel used primarily in lamps. Discoveries of oil reserves in Pennsylvania, and later in California and Texas, provided a major source of fuel in the 20th century with the invention of the internal combustion engine. By 1920 the United States was producing about 65 percent of the world's petroleum, much of it controlled by **John D. Rockefeller's Standard Oil**.

Electricity

Harvard President Charles W. Eliot pointed out the enormous change electricity brought to American life, saying, "It is the carrier of light and power; devourer of time and space; bearer of human speech over land and sea; greatest servant of man."

In 1878 **Thomas Edison** formed the Edison Electric Light Company and developed the **incandescent lightbulb** which, if not the first, was certainly the most practical lightbulb of the time. Another invention of Edison's laboratories, the **dynamo**, solved some of the problems of power production and distribution, enabling the delivery of electrical power. Edison's work was improved upon by **George Westinghouse**. He used alternating current and transformers to reduce high-voltage power to lower voltage levels and was able to make the transmission of electrical power over long distances less expensive. During the 1890s Henry Villard and J.P. Morgan merged various electric companies to form **General Electric**.

Exercise Set 2.6

1. During the period 1860–1890, big business was characterized by
   A. the use of organizational methods to control prices and do away with competition.
   B. support for union organization among workers.
   C. attempts to curb immigration.
   D. lack of adequate leadership in managerial positions.

2. Business merger movements of the late 1800s and early 1900s were designed, among other reasons, to
   A. increase hourly wages for workers.
   B. control more of the market and reduce wasteful competition.
   C. encourage the growth of unions.
   D. provide for more equitable distribution of wealth.

3. Introduction and improvement of the assembly line and mass production can be largely attributed to
   A. J.P. Morgan.
   B. Thomas Edison.
   C. George Westinghouse.
   D. Henry Ford.

4. Railroad building in the period after 1865 resulted in
   A. the end of industrial tariffs.
   B. greater population growth west of the Mississippi.
   C. a decrease in the growth of towns and cities west of the Mississippi.
   D. a decrease in agricultural output.

REPRESENTATIVE ENTREPRENEURS

> Upon the sacredness of property civilization itself depends—the right
> of the laborer to his hundred dollars in the savings bank, and equally
> the legal right of the millionaire to his millions.
>
> Andrew Carnegie, *Wealth* (1889)

A new group of business owners appeared during the middle of the 19th
century who later became known as the **robber barons**. Through financial
wizardry, stock manipulation, and fierce competition, these men built corporate dynasties that eventually threatened the free enterprise system in the
United States. Yet their management of business and the nation's resources
also lowered the cost of oil, steel, and other goods for America's consumers
and helped create the modern corporation. Moreover, their willingness to
reinvest profits in further business expansion contributed to the economic
growth of the United States during the last half of the 19th century.

Captains of Industry

John Pierpont Morgan (1837–1913)

Born in Hartford, Connecticut, the son of a prominent international banker,
J.P. Morgan built a reputation after the Civil War as a reorganizer of railroads. By the end of the 19th century, he controlled a vast transportation
network. Morgan founded the J.P. Morgan Company in 1895 and in 1901
organized the first billion-dollar corporation, **United States Steel**.

Andrew Carnegie (1835–1919)

Carnegie became rich investing in oil, ironmaking, and bridge building.
The **Carnegie Steel Company** became America's largest steel concern
and was eventually bought by J.P. Morgan in the formation of United States
Steel. Although he was a shrewd businessman, Carnegie's essay "**Gospel of
Wealth**" (1889) demonstrated his belief in philanthropy, setting forth the idea
that the rich are "trustees" of their wealth and should administer it unself-
ishly for the good of the public.

John D. Rockefeller (1839–1937)

Rockefeller's fortune was made in oil, and in 1870 he formed the **Standard
Oil Company** to consolidate his investments. By the 1880s his Standard Oil
Trust controlled almost all the nation's oil refineries, refining 83.7 percent of
all the oil produced in the country. A fierce competitor, Rockefeller explained
his ruthlessness in business by comparing it to the American Beauty rose:

"The American Beauty rose can be produced in all its splendor only by sacrificing the early buds that grow up around it."

The Work Ethic

The American work ethic can be traced back to the Puritan settlements of the 1600s in New England. The Puritans believed that good luck and success during one's life on earth were evidence of the "elect status" necessary to gain entrance into heaven.

Horatio Alger (1834–1899), a 19th-century American writer, dramatized the American dream of success through hard work in over 100 novels based on the idea that virtue is always rewarded. By leading an exemplary life entailing a valiant struggle with poverty and temptation, Alger's heroes all come to wealth and honor.

Public Good *v.* Private Gain

The principle of **laissez-faire** held that the way to obtain the greatest and cheapest productivity was to leave the individual employer and the individual worker to the free market. Those who favored the laissez-faire doctrine believed that interference by unions or government would upset the market and reduce total production. This would have a negative effect on workers, employers, and consumers. After 1870 the doctrine of laissez-faire received additional support from the principle of **Social Darwinism**, the belief that social progress depended upon competition among human beings resulting in the "survival of the fittest."

The industrial age and the growth of business combinations brought many problems to American life, and concern developed over the abuses of industrialism. As Americans saw the suffering of the poor in city slums, the deteriorating working conditions and failing health of America's workers, the monopolistic practices of major businesses, the lack of consumer protection, the exploitation of the nation's resources, and the widening gap in the distribution of the nation's wealth, many realized that some government regulation was necessary. The **Progressive Movement** in the early 1900s was the culmination of a series of responses to the worst abuses of the new industrial age.

Exercise Set 2.7

1. Major industrial leaders contributed to economic growth during the last half of the 19th century by
   A. promoting further competition among businesses.
   B. encouraging government to regulate unfair practices of the nation's businesses.
   C. reinvesting profits in the expansion of business.
   D. supporting the growth of labor organizations.

2. John D. Rockefeller's most significant contribution to the growth of business enterprise in the United States was his
   A. support of labor unions and collective bargaining.
   B. elimination of wasteful competitive practices.
   C. introduction of assembly line techniques.
   D. support of greater government intervention in business and an end to laissez-faire.

3. Which of the following groups would have supported greater government intervention in business during the latter part of the 19th century?
   A. The robber barons
   B. Supporters of laissez-faire and Social Darwinism
   C. Owners of the nation's major railroad lines
   D. The working classes

BUSINESS AND GOVERNMENT

> We accept and welcome . . . the concentration of business, industrial
> and commercial, in the hands of a few, and the law of competition
> between these as being not only beneficial, but essential for the future
> progress of the race.
>
> Andrew Carnegie, *The Gospel of Wealth* (1889)

Capitalism and Laissez-Faire

Capitalism

Capitalism can be defined as an economic system in which the means of
production are privately owned, production and distribution of goods are
determined in a free enterprise system by laws of supply and demand, and
there is little government regulation of the economy. A characteristic of pure
capitalism is the principle of laissez-faire.

Laissez-Faire

The economic policy known as laissez-faire can be traced to **Adam Smith**,
whose *Wealth of Nations*, advocating free international trade, was published in 1776. The concept of laissez-faire was emphasized by Alexander
Hamilton in 1791, when he claimed that "it can hardly ever be wise in a
government to attempt to give a direction to the industry of its citizens . . . .
To leave industry to itself, therefore, is, in almost every case, the soundest as
well as the simplest policy."

• *Principles of Laissez-Faire.* By the middle of the 1800s three characteristics of laissez-faire were obvious in the American economy: (1) Labor
should find its price on the market. In other words, an individual's wages
were dependent on the price he or she could demand in the market. (2) The
value of money should be subject to an automatic mechanism. There should
be a uniform standard for currency among trading nations, such as the gold
standard, that would stabilize currency among nations and allow greater ease
of trade. (3) Goods should be free to flow from country to country without restrictions. Protectionist policies such as tariffs would only hurt trade
among nations.

• *Movement Away from Laissez-Faire.* Beginning in the latter part of the
1800s and continuing through the 1900s, the economic system in the United
States moved away from the laissez-faire doctrine. Labor, represented by
labor unions and protected by federal and state legislation, could no longer
be considered simply a commodity; the country was no longer on a gold standard (ended in 1933), industry was subsidized, and international trade was
not free from protective barriers. Today we have a system known as a mixed

economy. Under this system, the government exercises some control over the nation's business, monetary system, and labor, while at the same time it allows the economy to regulate itself to a considerable extent.

The Supreme Court, Fourteenth Amendment, and Corporations

During the 1880s the Supreme Court began to change its direction concerning involvement in the economic matters within the states. As the social and political pressures of an emerging industrial nation increased, the Court demonstrated a greater willingness to exercise judicial review against state and federal regulation of industry. More specifically, it gave a new economic interpretation to the due process clause of the Fourteenth Amendment.

In the earlier cases testing the application of the due process clause of the Fourteenth Amendment to economic rights, the Supreme Court, demonstrating judicial restraint, upheld state regulations *(Slaughterhouse Cases,* 1873; *Munn* v. *Illinois* 1877*; Granger Cases,* 1877). The Court had accepted the idea in 1886 that the corporation was a person in the sense of the Fourteenth Amendment *(Santa Clara County* v. *Southern Pacific Railway* 1886). But it was the case of *Chicago, Milwaukee and St. Paul Railway Co.* v. *Minnesota* (1890) that marked the first time the Court declared a state law to be in violation of the due process clause of the Fourteenth Amendment, marking greater judicial protection of corporations.

Competition and Absorption: Mergers and Trusts

As competition among businesses during the second half of the 19th century cut prices and profits, business people sought ways to avoid price wars and increase profits. Combinations in business usually took two forms. Some were organized in a horizontal integration so that an organization under one management controlled different producers of the same product. Others were organized in a vertical integration so that an organization under one management controlled the different steps in the production of one commodity. An example of a vertical combination was the Ford Motor Company, which owned mines, shipping lines, railroads, and other businesses necessary for the production of the automobile. A number of business combinations resulted.

Pools

Agreements among business rivals sometimes managed to fix prices or divide profits and markets. During the 1870s and 1880s railroads made use of pooling agreements to fix prices.

Trusts

A trust was a more formal and permanent agreement than the pooling arrangement. Stockholders of competing companies would turn their stocks and voting rights over to a central board of trustees who controlled the member companies to eliminate competition. The result of the trust agreement was a monopoly, or near total control, of an industry. **John D. Rockefeller**, in an attempt to reduce competition in the oil industry, was the first to employ the trust arrangement with the formation of the **Standard Oil Company**.

Merger

A merger joins two or more companies, resulting in a single corporation. When a merger threatens to monopolize a particular industry, the courts may declare it illegal and a restraint on trade.

During the final decades of the 1800s, mergers and consolidations took place in many industries, including sugar, steel, machinery, tobacco, and copper. As combinations began to have an adverse effect on American society, however, the federal government began to consider intervention, moving away from its former laissez-faire policies.

Railroad Abuses and Government Regulation

Practices of the Railroads

The demand for government regulation of business first came from American farmers. Shortly after the Civil War, agricultural profits fell; some causes were overproduction, greater crop production in other nations, and high prices charged by middlemen. Farmers' grievances were directed against operators of grain elevators, manufacturers of farm machinery, bankers, and primarily, the railroads.

Complaints about the railroads included accusation of monopolistic practices. Railroads were absolutely necessary to the nation's farmers to transport their crops. However, in most farming areas there was only one railroad line. Because of the lack of competition, the railroad was able to charge "all that the traffic would bear" on the "short haul." For example, because of high freight rates, Pittsburgh, a large city served by only one railroad, paid 60 percent more for grain from Chicago than did New York, which was twice as far away. Railroads claimed that this was necessary to make up for the low rates charged on busier routes, or the "long hauls," because of fierce competition among the railroads.

Other unfair railroad practices included granting rebates to large shippers, giving free passes to politicians, bribing members of state legislatures, and entering into pooling agreements to control rates. During the 1870s and 1880s, demands for government regulation of the railroads came from farmers, small shippers, retailers, and reform politicians.

State Regulation

Regulation started at the state level with reform groups winning political control over state legislatures and passing legislation to control abuses. The National Grange of the Patrons of Husbandry, organized by Oliver H. Kelley, numbered 1,500,000 by 1874 and dominated the legislatures of Illinois, Wisconsin, Iowa, and Minnesota. Methods of control initiated by the Granger programs were rate regulation legislation, cooperative buying of farm supplies and machinery, and pressure for federal legislation.

State legislation was dealt a blow when the Supreme Court ruled in *Wabash, St. Louis and Pacific Railway* v. *Illinois* (1886) that states had no power to fix rates on shipments passing beyond their borders. **Interstate commerce** is under congressional control.

Federal Regulation

- *Interstate Commerce Act.* Congress responded in 1887 by passing the Interstate Commerce Act and establishing the Interstate Commerce Commission, which had the power to (1) require that railroads post their rates publicly; (2) require rates to be "reasonable and just"; (3) forbid practices such as pooling, rebates, and rate discrimination; (4) prohibit higher charges for short hauls than for longer hauls over the same line; and (5) investigate complaints against railroads and hand down rulings that could be enforced in courts.

- *Munn v. Illinois (1877).* The *Munn* case was one of the several so-called **Granger Cases** that dealt with state regulation of railroads and grain warehouses. The Supreme Court, by allowing the Illinois statute fixing maximum charges for the storage of grain (grain that found its way into **interstate commerce** and was therefore under the control of Congress), held that "when one devotes his property to a use in which the public has an interest, he, in effect, grants to the public an interest in that use, and must submit to be controlled by the public for the common good."

- *Sherman Antitrust Act (1890).* In response to increasing pressure to halt the domination of the market by a small number of powerful corporations, Congress passed the Sherman Antitrust Act in 1890. The provisions of the Act included (1) that every contract, combination, or conspiracy in **restraint of trade** among the states or with foreign countries was illegal; and (2) that persons guilty of monopolizing trade or commerce were subject to fines and/or imprisonment.

The weaknesses of the Sherman Act soon became apparent. Although trusts were prohibited, holding companies soon started to replace them and were able to avoid the reaches of the law. The federal courts were hesitant to enforce the Act and continued to define the word "trade" narrowly. The Supreme Court made the law almost meaningless in the *United States* v. *Knight Company* (1895) case when it held that the sugar refining industry did not involve interstate commerce and therefore the Sherman Act did not apply to an almost complete monopoly that the American Sugar Refining Company had over the sugar industry.

Public Opinion

As the end of the century approached, more and more Americans were becoming concerned about the effects of large business combinations. This new social concern led to a mass of progressive social legislation in the 1900s.

Exercise Set 2.8

1. Of the following, the most important cause of agrarian discontent in the United States during the latter part of the 19th century was
   A. the belief that railroads and middlemen were exploiting the farmers.
   B. the growth of population in the Eastern states.
   C. the rise in prices of agricultural produce.
   D. greater government control over public utilities.

2. A major problem for businesses entering into a pooling agreement was
   A. falling profits.
   B. lawsuits filed against members of pools who went against the agreement.
   C. lack of a legal way to enforce the pooling agreement.
   D. consumers turning to a company that did not participate in the pooling arrangement.

3. Large business combinations of the late 1800s presented a threat to
   A. the currency system.
   B. free enterprise.
   C. the transportation system.
   D. representative democracy.

4. A present-day example of laissez-faire economics would be
   A. deregulation of the airline industry.
   B. minimum wage laws.
   C. farm subsidies.
   D. breakup of American Telephone and Telegraph.

LABOR ORGANIZATION AND STRUGGLE

> To protect the workers in their inalienable rights to a higher and better life; to protect them, not only as equals before the law, but also in their health, their homes, their firesides, their liberties as men, as workers, and as citizens . . . to this workers are entitled . . . . The attainment of these is the glorious mission of the trade unions.
>
> Samuel Gompers, Speech (1898)

> Let us not destroy those wonderful machines that produce efficiently and cheaply. Let us control them. Let us profit by their efficiency and cheapness. Let us run them for ourselves. That, gentlemen, is socialisms . . . .
>
> Jack London, *The Iron Heel* (1906)

National Labor Unions

Organized labor in America can trace its roots to 1792 when the journeymen cordwainers (shoemakers) of Philadelphia organized a local union. Its successor, the Federal Society of Journeyman Cordwainers, operated until 1806 when, after a strike for better wages, the union was found guilty of conspiracy in a court of law. Although the strike and subsequent decision of the courts ended the small union, it marked the beginning of decades of struggle for the **bargaining power** of workers in the workplace. In the case of *Commonwealth* v. *Hunt* (1842), the Massachusetts high court held that labor unions had a right to combine and strike "in such manner as best to subserve their own interests."

The modern labor movement is essentially a product of the Industrial Revolution. The development of the factory system made it impossible for individual workers to bargain on equal terms with a powerful employer. Only by organizing and presenting their demands as a group were the workers able to secure higher wages, shorter working days, improved working conditions, and protection against being discharged without just cause.

National Labor Union

Formed in 1866 under the leadership of **William Sylvis**, the National Labor Union helped to push legislation through Congress for an **8-hour workday** for laborers and mechanics employed by the federal government.

The Knights of Labor

Founded in 1869 by Uriah S. Stephens, the Knights of Labor started as a secret organization whose aim was to unite skilled and unskilled workers into one great national union. They advocated higher wages, 8-hour working days, equal pay for equal work by men and women, abolition of child labor (under 14 years), arbitration of labor disputes, prohibition of foreign contract labor, safety and health laws, workers' cooperative associations, a graduated income tax, and government ownership of railroads and other public utilities. Under the leadership of Terence V. Powderly, the Knights of Labor gained influence, and membership reached 700,000 by 1886. The union declined rapidly after 1886 for several reasons, including the failure of a strike against the Texas and Pacific Railroad and the blame attached to the Knights for the bombing at the **Haymarket Riot** in Chicago.

The American Federation of Labor

Founded in 1881 by **Samuel Gompers**, the AFL was organized as a federation of many separate skilled craft unions rather than a general organization of workers. Each member craft union enjoyed a degree of autonomy in matters affecting its own trade. The goals of the AFL stressed "bread and butter" issues: higher wages, an 8-hour workday, improved working conditions, use of union-made products, and passage of state and federal legislation to benefit labor. The methods used by the AFL to obtain its goals included the **strike** (a work stoppage until goals are met) and the **boycott** (the practice of not purchasing the

Samuel Gompers (1850–1924) founded the AFL in 1881.

product of the employer). By 1900 the AFL claimed 500,000 members and eventually was successful in winning the **closed shop** (plants hiring only union workers) and the abolition of **yellow-dog contracts** (requirement by the employer that a newly hired employee sign an agreement not to join a labor union). Yet, as a union of skilled workers, the AFL excluded 90 percent of the American workers who did not have a craft or the skills to qualify for membership in one of its affiliated unions.

International Ladies Garment Workers Union

Of the 8 million female workers in 1910, only 125,000 were members of unions, primarily because most unions refused to accept women as members. A strike by thousands of women shirtwaist workers in New York in 1909 laid the foundation for the International Ladies Garment Workers Union. The ILGWU was instrumental in bringing relief to the families of the victims of the **Triangle Shirtwaist Factory fire** in New York City in 1911. This tragedy claimed the lives of 146 workers and subsequently brought about a modern factory inspection system and laws to regulate the labor of women and children.

Struggle and Conflict

Between 1881 and 1900 there were over 24,000 strikes in the United States that involved nearly 128,000 establishments. Many tried to blame labor unrest on the infiltration of socialists and anarchists into the work forces. However, the unrest among the American workers who faced great inequities in the late 1800s was typical of the activist undercurrent that flowed throughout American history.

Major Strikes

• *Haymarket Riot (1886)*. Following a nationwide strike for an 8-hour day by the **Knights of Labor**, trouble broke out in Chicago as sympathetic **anarchists** addressed a protest meeting held by the strikers. After police entered the crowd to break up the meeting, a bomb was thrown, killing seven police and wounding sixty more. Because of this incident, the Knights of Labor became identified with anarchism and violence, and this led to the union's decline. It also helped to turn American public opinion against labor unions.

• *Homestead Strike (1892)*. When the **Carnegie Steel Company** threatened to cut wages and crush the **Amalgamated Association of Iron and Steel Workers** in 1892, workers picketed the plant. Management called in Pinkerton guards to protect the plant, but they were attacked by the strikers and run out of town. An appeal to the governor of Pennsylvania brought in the militia. Although the workers struck for nine months, public opinion eventually turned against them and they went back to work, agreeing to the company's terms. The strike crushed the Amalgamated Union and left the steel industry unorganized for 40 years.

Eugene V. Debs (1855–1926) led the American Railway Union in the strike against the Pullman Company.

• *Pullman Strike (1894)*. Workers at the Pullman Palace Car Company struck in protest over policies at the company town near Chicago and cuts in wages. The strike spread, bringing railroad traffic west of Chicago to a standstill when the American Railway Union, under the leadership of **Eugene V. Debs**, aided the strikers by calling a boycott in which union members refused to work on any train with a Pullman car. The railroads appealed to the federal government for protection. President **Cleveland** sent troops to Chicago to "protect the rails," but more probably to crush the strike. The federal government obtained a court **injunction** (order) that forbade the union to strike. Within a month the strike was ended, and Debs was imprisoned for failing to abide by the court injunction to end the strike. The Supreme Court upheld the conviction of Debs in the case of *In Re Debs* (1895) on the grounds that an injunction was valid under the federal government's power to remove obstacles to **interstate commerce** as provided by the Sherman Antitrust Act. The injunction became a powerful weapon of employers to combat strikes.

• *Lawrence Textile Strike (1912).* Unskilled industrial workers ignored by the American Federation of Labor were organized by the **Industrial Workers of the World** (or **Wobblies**) formed in 1905 under the leadership of "**Big Bill**" **Haywood**. They advocated militant agitation, willful obstruction of industry, and damage to businesses. Although the IWW gained few victories, national attention was focused on the union in 1912 when 30,000 textile workers in Lawrence, Massachusetts, struck for better working conditions and higher wages. The American Woolen Company met nearly all of the union's demands. After America's entry into World War I, the federal government prosecuted various IWW leaders for their attempt to obstruct the draft.

Management's Position

Management (owners and managers of means of production) has been at odds with labor throughout modern industrial history. Management's position has usually included (1) conducting production and operations with as little interference from labor unions as possible; (2) increasing productivity and profits through efficiency and laborsaving techniques; (3) being free to increase and decrease work forces according to need; and (4) maintaining an **open shop** (the choice of the employer to hire both union and nonunion labor) as opposed to a **closed shop** (the employment of only union workers).

Tactics Employed in Disputes by Management and Labor

A strike by workers is usually the final means of attempting to gain demands and often hurts both labor and management. Very few disputes end in strikes because of the following techniques:

• *Collective Bargaining.* Representatives of management and labor meet, discuss issues and differences, and settle on a contract acceptable to both sides.

• *Mediation.* The Federal Mediation and Conciliation Service offers the services of mediators, or neutral third parties, who sit in on the negotiations between management and labor, offer suggestions of concessions to both sides, and encourage the two sides to reach an agreeable contract. The mediator's decision is not binding.

• *Arbitration.* Both management and labor agree to a neutral third party. That person hears the dispute and hands down a decision that will be accepted by both sides according to an agreement beforehand. In other words, the arbitrator's decision is binding.

• *Fact-Finding Board.* When a strike affects the welfare of the nation, the President may appoint a board to hear the dispute and hand down a decision.

Weapons Used by Labor and Management

When collective bargaining is not successful in settling labor-management disputes, more drastic means may be used:

• **Labor.** Workers may resort to a **strike**, **picketing** (demonstration by workers usually outside of the workplace), a **boycott**, and **publicity** to convince the public of the legitimacy of their demands and to seek support.

• *Management.* Employers may use **strikebreakers** (sometimes referred to as **scabs**), **lockouts**, in which the employer keeps the workers from their jobs until they accept management's terms, **injunctions** (court orders that say workers must return to work), and **publicity**, or appeal to the public for support.

Attitude and Role of Government

Beginning in the late 1900s government has played a crucial role in affecting the balance between labor and management. Examples of government intervention include:

• *Sherman Antitrust Act (1890).* This was used to restrain activities of unions, finding them to cause "unreasonable restraint of trade."

• *Clayton Antitrust Act (1914).* This act reversed some of the interpretations used under the Sherman Act and declared that legitimate union activities were not subject to antitrust laws. The Clayton Act also restricted the use of injunctions against unions in labor disputes.

• *Norris-LaGuardia Act (1932).* Federal courts were prohibited by this act from granting injunctions against workers who engaged in strikes, boycotts, or peaceful picketing. The Norris-LaGuardia Act also made unenforceable **yellow-dog contracts** (contracts that prevented a worker from joining a union after being employed).

Socialism, Communism, Anarchism

Marxist socialists in America at the end of the 19th century were primarily Germans who brought their political and economic theories with them from Europe. The Marxist Workingmen's Party and the Social Democratic Party attracted some support during the 1870s. In the early 1880s the socialists split into two groups: those who rejected capitalism and those who rejected both capitalism and organized government. The latter group was known as **anarchists**.

In 1900 the **Socialist Party of America**, with **Eugene V. Debs** as its presidential candidate, won about 100,000 votes. In the next decade, after the arrival of many eastern Europeans and continued political interest among American workers, membership in the Socialist Party grew. In 1912 its growth peaked and Debs received nearly one million votes as the Socialist presidential candidate. However, unlike labor in many European countries, American labor never established a major political party in the United States. Instead, it used its influence to seek its goals within the "two-party" system.

"Radicalism" was not restricted to politics and labor movements. The Socialist Party's commitment to democratic gradualism attracted many members of the clergy, writers, and others who believed reform was not possible under the two major parties. Writers in the early 20th century who spoke for socialism and criticized the capitalist system included some of the most notable American literary figures, such as Upton Sinclair, Jack London, Theodore Dreiser, and Frank Norris.

Middle-Class Labor Support

Not all advocates of better working conditions and higher wages came from the "radical fringe" of politics and the labor movement. The Women's Trade Union League combined the forces of the wealthy elite with reformers, like **Jane Addams**, to aid working women in their efforts to organize. The Consumers' Union was a "watchdog" organization formed to promote the purchase of only those goods produced in factories with approved working conditions.

Exercise Set 2.9

1. While the Knights of Labor included both skilled and unskilled workers, the American Federation of Labor consisted of
   A. only industrial workers.
   B. the fringe element of radical labor.
   C. craft unions of skilled workers.
   D. primarily immigrant labor.

2. An important reason for the growth of labor unions in the second half of the 19th century was
   A. the passage of the Clayton Antitrust Act.
   B. a decrease in immigration to the United States.
   C. the growth of a socialist movement in the United States.
   D. the indifference of business to the welfare of employees.

3. The primary reason for support of free compulsory public education by labor unions was to
   A. decrease the number of children in the work force.
   B. educate youth for eventual union leadership.
   C. provide day care for the children of union members.
   D. train youth in different industrial skills.

4. A powerful weapon used by employers to end strikes was
   A. the closed shop.
   B. the injunction.
   C. picketing.
   D. the use of a mediator.

CHAPTER REVIEW QUESTIONS

1. Which is a fundamental idea of laissez-faire capitalism?
   A. Workers should own the means of production.
   B. Employers should provide social benefits for all workers.
   C. Government should control output and wages.
   D. Businesses should gain and lose according to their own efforts.

2. In the United States, economic opportunities for women expanded during the last quarter of the 19th century primarily because of the growth of
   A. opportunities to buy farms in the West.
   B. industry and technology.
   C. big-city political machines.
   D. organized labor.

3. In which way did the joint-stock company help lay the foundation for the modern corporation?
   A. The major reason for forming a company was to produce industrial goods on a large scale.
   B. The company made low-risk investments and thus could guarantee a profit.
   C. The government sponsored and controlled the company.
   D. The company was owned by more than one individual, each of whom received a share of any profits.

4. Urbanization
   A. slowed the industrialization of the United States.
   B. occurred primarily along the West Coast of the United States.
   C. and industrialization stimulated one another.
   D. would have progressed faster if industrialization had grown at a slower pace.

5. In most of the major labor disputes that took place before 1900, the federal government
   A. supported organized labor.
   B. maintained a completely laissez-faire attitude.
   C. supported management.
   D. claimed that strikes did not affect interstate trade and therefore did not become involved.

6. Which was a major obstacle to the formation of labor unions in the United States during the period 1860–1900?
   A. Prohibition of labor organizations by the Constitution
   B. General government support of management
   C. Excellent working conditions in United States factories of the time
   D. Status of factory workers as equal partners with management

7. A major reason for the passage of the Sherman Antitrust Act in 1890 was to
   A. encourage competition in business.
   B. protect the rights and safety of workers.
   C. promote free trade among nations.
   D. raise protective tariffs in the United States.

8. Methods used by management to combat the activities of unions included
   A. general strike.
   B. blacklisting.
   C. antitrust legislation.
   D. the injunction.

9. An event that hurt unions and caused many Americans to associate labor with anarchism and socialism was the
   A. Triangle Shirtwaist fire.
   B. candidacy of Eugene V. Debs for President in 1912.
   C. formation of the National Women's Trade Union.
   D. Haymarket Square incident.

10. During the 20th century, labor unions in the United States were most strengthened by legislation that guaranteed workers
    A. the right to boycott.
    B. the right to bargain collectively.
    C. adequate retirement pensions.
    D. a share of company profits.

THEMATIC ESSAY

Directions: Write a well-organized essay that includes an introduction, several paragraphs addressing the task below, and a conclusion.

Theme: Technology

> Throughout United States history, technological developments have played an important role in transforming American society. These developments have had both positive and negative effects on the United States and on American society.

Task:

> Choose *two* technological developments that have transformed American society and for *each*
>
> - Describe the change brought about by the technological development.
> - Discuss the positive *and/or* negative effects this technological development has had on the United States and/or on American society.

You may use any technological development that has transformed American life. Some suggestions you might wish to consider include:

Cotton gin—plantation economy (1793–1860)
Railroads—local and national markets (1830–1900)
Steel plow—farming on the Great Plains (1860–1940)
Elevators—urbanization (1890–present)
Automobile—population distribution (1920–1980)
Nuclear energy—practical or military applications (1940–present)
Television—political campaigns (1960–present)

You are *not* limited to these suggestions.

DOCUMENT-BASED QUESTION

The following questions (Part A and Part B) are based on the accompanying documents (1–6). Some of these documents have been edited for the purpose of this exercise. The question is designed to test your ability to work with historical documents and to demonstrate your knowledge of the subject matter being presented. As you analyze the documents, take into account both the source of the document and the author's point of view.

Historical Context:

> The rise of American business and industry during the second half of the 18th century.

Task:

> Using information from the documents and your knowledge of United States history, answer the questions that follow each document in Part A. Your answers to the questions will help you write the Part B essay, in which you will be asked:
>
> The second half of the 19th century was one of economic transformation in the American experience. Using the issues identified in the documents (for example, increased government involvement in economics, varying economic theories), discuss why this is an accurate statement.

Part A
Short-Answer Questions

The documents below relate to the rise of American business and industry during the late 1800s. Examine each document carefully and then answer the questions that follow.

DOCUMENT 1

> Let us inquire for a moment what are the proper functions of government, and how far, if at all, it may interfere with the natural laws governing commerce, manufactures, and agriculture . . . . When these general functions are exceeded the result is generally injurious to government. It is better always to leave individual enterprise to do most that is to be done in the country.

—Daniel Knowlton, New York City Merchant, September 27, 1883

1. How are the opinions of the New York City merchant consistent with the concept of laissez-faire?

_____

_____

_____

DOCUMENT 2

The argument is that . . . in the exercise of the power to regulate commerce, Congress may suppress such monopoly directly and set aside the instruments which have created it . . . .

—Chief Justice M.W. Fuller, *United States* v. *E.C. Knight Company* (sugar refining company) (1895)

2. Chief Justice Fuller found that Congress had the power to regulate monopolies. Under what Constitutional provision did Chief Justice Fuller find Congress's power to regulate monopolies?

_____

_____

_____

DOCUMENT 3

The "Gospel of Wealth" but echoes Christ's words. It calls upon the millionaire to sell all that he hath and give it in the highest and best form to the poor, by administering his estate himself for the good of his fellows, before he is called upon to lie down and rest upon the bosom of Mother Earth. So doing, he will approach his end no longer the ignoble hoarder of useless millions, poor, very poor indeed, in money, but rich, very rich, twenty times the millionaire still, in the affection, gratitude, and admiration of his fellow-men . . . .

—Andrew Carnegie, *The Best Fields of Philanthropy*, December 1889

3. Andrew Carnegie was one of 4,047 millionaires in the United States in 1892 who had amassed wealth through industry, trade, and the railroads. According to his thoughts expressed above, what was the best use of the millionaire's fortunes?

_____

_____

_____

DOCUMENT 4

	Growth of Manufacturers in the United States (includes all factories, hand, and neighborhood establishments) (in thousands)			
Year	Number of Establishments	Wage Earners	Value of Products	Amount of Capital Invested
1859	140	1,311	$ 1,886,000	$1,009,000
1869	252	2,054	3,386,000	2,118,000
1879	254	2,733	5,370,000	2,790,000
1889	355	4,252	9,372,000	—
1899	512	5,306	13,014,000	9,835,000

4. According to the chart concerning manufacturing growth between 1859 and 1899, the largest amount of capital invested was during what year?

_____

5. The amount of capital invested increased approximately how many times between 1859 and 1899?

_____

DOCUMENT 5

In the late 19th and early 20th centuries, socialists throughout the world were under the spell of Marx's seemingly impregnable analysis . . . . The United States was undeniably a rising industrial colossus with a pronounced tendency toward industrial monopoly. Marx's theory of capitalistic accumulation and concentration surely applied to the American republic. Yet . . . there had not come into being, for example, a sizable class-conscious proletariat dedicated to the overthrow of capitalism; the economic well-being of American industrial workers was not deteriorating, but improving; . . . the middle class was expanding, and the Socialist Party . . . had not made a significant dent in the traditional party loyalties of American voters.

—Professor Howard H. Quint, University of Massachusetts

6. According to Professor Quint, what were the reasons that Marxist socialism did not become deeply rooted in the American political and economic system in the late 1800s?

_____

_____

DOCUMENT 6

Percentage Distribution of Gainfully Occupied Persons 16 Years of Age and Over, 1870–1900				
Occupation Group	1870	1880	1890	1900
Agriculture and allied occupations	52.8	48.1	41.2	35.9
Mining	1.5	1.6	1.8	2.1
Manufacturing and mechanical industries	22.0	24.8	26.3	27.5
Trade and transportation	9.1	10.7	13.6	16.3
Clerical services	1.7	2.0	2.5	2.8
Domestic and personal service	9.6	8.8	9.7	10.0
Public service not elsewhere classifed	.6	.7	.9	1.0
Professional service	2.7	3.3	4.0	4.4
TOTAL	100.0	100.0	100.0	100.0

7. According to the chart, what was the trend of the percentage of persons employed in agricultural positions compared to the number of persons employed in manufacturing and mechanical industries?

_____

_____

Part B
Essay

Your essay should be well organized with an introductory paragraph that states your position on the question. Develop your position in the next paragraphs and then write a conclusion. In your essay, include specific historical details and refer to the specific documents you analyzed in Part A. You may include additional information from your knowledge of social studies.

Historical Context:

> The rise of American business and industry during the second half of the 18th century.

Task:

> The above-referenced documents address varying aspects of the transformation. Using the issues identified in the documents (for example, increased government involvement in economics, industrial leaders, varying economic theories, statistical information), discuss why this is an accurate statement.
>
> The second half of the 19th century was one of economic transformation in the American experience.

Guidelines:

In your essay, be sure to
• Develop all aspects of the task.
• Incorporate information from *at least five* documents.
• Incorporate relevant outside information.
• Support the theme with many relevant facts, examples, and details.
• Use a logical and clear plan of organization, including an introduction and a conclusion that are beyond a restatement of the theme.

ADJUSTING SOCIETY TO INDUSTRIALISM: AMERICAN PEOPLE AND PLACES

IMPACT OF INDUSTRIALISM

Urbanization and the Quality of Urban Life

Between the Civil War and 1910, the urban population increased dramatically. In addition to the general increase in the number of people living in cities—from about 6.2 million to 42 million—during the period from 1860 to 1910, there was also an extraordinary expansion in the size of large cities such as New York, Philadelphia, and Chicago.

Attractions of the City

People moved to the cities because they offered opportunity. In the urban centers there were jobs in offices and factories, employment for both the skilled and the unskilled. American cities became marketplaces for people, resources, and ideas and centers of transportation, communication, and capital.

Cities also became centers of educational and cultural institutions. In some instances, business leaders accepted the responsibility for using their wealth and resources to improve urban communities. During his lifetime, Andrew Carnegie gave $60 million to help cities establish free public libraries. Wealthy leaders of industry, including John D. Rockefeller, Matthew Vassar, and Cornelius Vanderbilt, founded or endowed colleges and universities. Others, including Andrew Mellon and J.P. Morgan, built extensive art collections, which were eventually opened to the public.

Problems of the Cities

As the American city grew, so did its problems, especially widespread poverty among city residents. Fast-spreading **slums** housed masses of low-income workers. In 1893 there were 702 people per acre in New York's Lower East Side. Poor workers lived in tenements and small apartments that lacked adequate space, safety, or sanitation.

Inadequate **sanitation** and the spread of disease became a by-product of rapid urban growth. By the 1870s few American cities had installed underground sewers, relying instead on cesspools.

Crime, though not exclusively an urban affliction, flourished in the slums of urban areas with their poverty and overcrowding. The fifty percent increase in the prison population between 1880 and 1890 reflected the fact that crime had become a way of life in American cities. Police forces were still at an infant stage and in some cases easily corrupted by various interest groups.

City Architecture

Housing was a pressing problem in most rapidly growing urban centers. With the lack of adequate transportation, workers were forced to live near their jobs no matter how poor and congested the buildings were. The growth of tenements and the terrible sanitary conditions that caused outbreaks of disease eventually forced the passage of Tenement House laws.

The growth of structures in the downtown areas of the city was extraordinary. The concentration of business and professional offices along with the inflation of real estate value made tall buildings inevitable. The development of wrought iron, then steel, and finally the discovery that walls themselves could be supported on steel columns embedded in them allowed **skyscrapers** to grow in height. Finally, the development of the **elevator** allowed architects to overcome the problem of access to higher levels of the building.

Social Darwinism

The publication of *The Origin of Species* in 1859 by the Englishman **Charles Darwin** marked a major step in the **theory of evolution**. It proposed that many more individuals of each species are born than can possibly survive. As a consequence, there is a constant struggle for existence, and only the fittest survive. Social Darwinism affected American political thought by delaying legislation that required factory inspection, the limitation of work hours, and other protective measures.

• *Unequal Distribution of Wealth.* Along with industrial expansion and the growth of American cities came a growing gap between the rich and the poor. As the national wealth increased from $16 billion to $65 billion between 1860 and 1890, the distribution of wealth grew more uneven, with fewer Americans controlling more of the nation's wealth. By 1890 only 9 percent of the population owned 71 percent of the nation's money and 88 percent owned only 14 percent. Yet those who advocated Social Darwinism held that the capable would rise to the top and that eventually the wealth would seep down to the masses in the form of greater employment opportunities.

• **Philanthropy.** The philanthropic activities of the wealthy were consistent with Social Darwinism. Adhering to the laissez-faire beliefs that government should not pass welfare legislation, some of the wealthy believed they had a social responsibility to assist those who were less fortunate.

• **Calls for Reform.** With the unequal balance of wealth and power, it seemed that the rich were growing richer and the poor, poorer. As the growing poverty of America's workers became increasingly apparent, many called for public and private relief that was not forthcoming. Movements for reform were spurred by the humanitarian concerns reflected in literature *(How the Other Half Lives,* Jacob Riis, 1890; *The Bitter Cry of Children,* John Spargo, 1906; *Progress and Poverty,* Henry George, 1879). Early efforts to help included the **Society for the Prevention of Cruelty to Children** (1874), settlement houses such as **Hull House** in Chicago, founded in 1889 by Jane Addams to offer social services, and the establishment of religious institutions such as the **Young Men's Christian Association** (1851), the **Salvation Army** (1879), and city missions.

Work and Workers

Peopling the Cities

Prior to 1870 relatively few Americans were wage earners. The United States was still primarily an agricultural nation, with most Americans owning farms. By 1900, as a result of the Industrial Revolution, the transfer of America's population to the cities and the growing employment in factories, about two-thirds of the working population were selling their labor to employers for a daily or weekly wage.

The flow of workers to the cities came from two sources; first, the movement of large numbers of second-generation Americans from the rural areas and second, the thousands of immigrants from Europe who settled in the cities where they found employment opportunities. The growth of American industry and the absence of restrictions on immigration drew a steady stream of immigrants, which reached its peak in 1907 when 1,285,000 immigrant entries were recorded.

Working Conditions

Gone were the days when workers and employers maintained an intimate and caring relationship. The impersonal relationship between labor and management was a direct result of the urban factory system and led to deteriorating conditions for the average wage earner. Long hours, low wages, child labor, and dangerous working conditions were common during the 19th century when **collective bargaining** was nearly nonexistent and **unions** were looked upon as conspiracies. As the pool of workers increased with the flow of second-generation Americans and immigrants to the cities, the plight of workers grew worse. Although the Thirteenth Amendment (1865) had ended "slavery and involuntary servitude except as punishment for a crime," the employees of the factory system were becoming "wage slaves" of industrial America.

A related problem was that of **child labor**. By 1870 many of the nation's industrial workers were children, under the age of twelve. Working in the factories brought problems for children including lack of education, emotional disruption, family breakdown, and physical abuse. Working from "dark to dark," children toiled six days a week earning little for 12- to 13-hour shifts.

The Working-Class Family

Industrialization also brought changes in the American family. The participation of family members in outside institutions, including schools, political organizations, social clubs, and places of employment replaced some of the companionship that had existed in the rural household. As mother and father each became wage earners, usually out of economic necessity, broken families were sometimes the result. At the turn of the century, the majority of American households consisted of the nuclear family—a married couple with or without children, living with no other relatives. About 15 to 20 percent of households were made up of extended families—households with grandparents, grandchildren, aunts, uncles, cousins, or in-laws.

Ethnic and Racial Impact on Workers

American labor was affected by society's feelings concerning race and ethnic differences. Few labor leaders welcomed blacks into labor unions, the **Industrial Workers of the World** being the exception. Immigration, both early (consisting mostly of northern Europeans), and later (made up primarily of eastern and southern Europeans), provided labor competition that kept wages low and hampered unions' attempts to organize.

Women and the Industrial Age

With the new Industrial Age, the Victorian ideal of women as the pampered and weaker sex quickly disappeared in American society. In early colonial America, women worked as hard as their husbands to build families and homesteads on the frontier. Success in colonial life required a partnership between the sexes. Although life was hard and women did not have equal political rights, they filled many of the same roles as men during these times because of the common goal of survival. As conditions became more settled and life easier, women's roles reverted to homemaking. By the early 1800s most women stayed home to tend to household chores and to raise the family, "protected" from the demands of education, politics, and business.

From Home to Factory

With the arrival of new inventions in the early part of the 19th century, some women began to work away from the home. **Textile mills** in New England provided the earliest industrial opportunities for women to enter the work force. Yet, factory work proved to be a mixed blessing, since women were often exploited and usually hired at wages far below those paid to men doing similar work. Throughout the 19th century the supply of women looking for work increased with the arrival of immigrants from Europe. Employers who had little trouble finding replacements for those women dissatisfied with pay and working conditions were able to impose wage cuts and work speedups. In 1870 women who worked in mills earned $5 to $6 for a 60-hour week, while those who did sewing piecework at home received about 6 cents per shirt and earned little more than $3 per week.

Technology and Women

In the late 1800s, business expansion and new inventions, including the typewriter and telephone, brought about an increasing need for office workers with special skills. Since these jobs were usually filled by women, education became more important; by 1890 twice as many young women were finishing high school as young men.

A profession that welcomed women throughout the 1800s was **teaching**. By the 1890s there were twice as many women teaching as men. Women teachers in city schools earned about $13 a week, while men teachers received two to three times that amount.

Religion in a Diversified Society

As poverty, urban overcrowding, and social disorder increased during this age of government laissez-faire, religious groups joined social reformers in attempting to ease society's problems. Emphasizing social responsibility as a means to salvation and service to fellow human beings as a Christian duty, religious reformers built churches in slum neighborhoods, provided community services, and joined drives to make businesses socially responsible.

The Growing Middle Class

Industrialism helped to create a growing middle class consisting of salaried workers, professionals, salespeople, government workers, and the like. A transformation was taking place in the lives of many Americans, in their homes, work, and leisure time.

Standards of Cultural Values

The buying power of the growing middle class fueled further industrial growth. Goods that had once been available only to a few were becoming available to many. American inventiveness, combined with technology, mass production, and mass marketing, provided goods such as ready-made clothes and home appliances—necessities rather than the luxury they had once been.

Middle-Class Materialism and Morality

As luxuries were being transformed into commonplace articles of everyday life, the difference between those who could afford such goods and services and those who could not became accentuated. As the turn of the century approached, incomes continued to rise. For example, the average yearly pay of a clerical worker rose from $848 a year in 1890 to $1,156 a year in 1910. But as wages increased, the cost of living also rose. For most ordinary workers, it was becoming harder to pay for even the necessities. As the concerns of the working class, middle class, and farmers—the group often referred to as the "common man," "taxpayer," or "man on the street"—began to coincide, they joined to support the Progressive Movement that began in the 1900s.

Leisure Activities

Along with industrialism and the development of labor-saving devices in the factory and at home came a greater amount of leisure time for some

Americans. The average work week for manufacturing workers decreased from 66 hours per week in 1860 to 51 hours per week in 1920. The most popular leisure activities were sports. By 1860 there were at least 50 baseball clubs in the country; football became the most popular collegiate sport; and cycling, tennis, golf, and basketball were also enjoyed. Of course it was the wealthy, with more free time and money to spend on sporting activities, who were able to take the greatest advantage of America's leisure-time revolution.

As they worked fewer hours, Americans had more time for leisure activities.

Art and Literature

Although critics have characterized the post-Civil War era as the "Gilded Age," suggesting crassness and lack of taste in a materialistic society, progress in art and literature was noteworthy.

Literature

As the degree of literacy in America increased, book reading by all levels of society increased. The popular press was reflected in the "dime novels" (low-priced, paperbound adventure novels about the Wild West), detective stories, and science fiction, which became favorites of America's young people. Leading dime novels included stories of The Lone Ranger, Old Cap Collins, and Tom Swift.

"Local-color" writers produced regional literature, which depicted the people and environment of a particular region of the country. Bret Harte wrote about the West *(The Outcasts of Poker Flat)*, **Mark Twain** wrote of the South *(The Adventures of Tom Sawyer, The Adventures of Huckleberry Finn)*, and **Jack London** wrote of the West and Northwest *(The Call of the Wild)*.

Art

The Society of American Artists was formed in 1877 to organize and popularize a new trend in American art: the breaking away from the romanticized works of the earlier generation. Among the new school of American artists were George Inness, a leading landscapist; Winslow Homer, whose art was best demonstrated in his bold paintings of the sea; and James A. McNeill Whistler, painter of realistic portraits. The development of photography helped to free the early American painters from realism and led to impressionism and abstract art.

Music

American music reached its greatest stage of development later in the 20th century. The later 19th century saw the spread of musical appreciation with the formation of the New York Symphony Orchestra in 1878 and the Boston Symphony Orchestra in 1881. A major discovery in the area of music was the reproduction of music by mechanical means. By 1900 over 150,000 American homes had a **phonograph**, an invention of Thomas Edison.

Role of Philanthropists

Cynically described as those who "stole privately and gave publicly," the "**robber barons**," including **John Rockefeller** and **Andrew Carnegie**, gave considerable amounts of money for the development of cultural centers promoting art, music, and education.

1. The trend toward urbanization involved
   A. the growth of rural America due to the unsafe conditions of the city.
   B. the movement of people from rural areas into the cities.
   C. decrease in metropolitan population.
   D. a decrease in immigration.

2. Urban political bosses and machines in the latter part of the 19th century
   A. took advantage of the needs of newly arrived immigrants.
   B. contributed nothing to their cities.
   C. were closely regulated by civil service organizations.
   D. had little influence in urban politics.

3. The belief concerning poverty that was consistent with Social Darwinism was that
   A. the poor were weak individuals.
   B. the federal government had the responsibility of assuring economic equality.
   C. systems of public welfare and relief had to be implemented to ease the hardships of the poor.
   D. the problems of the poor were the fault of the wealthy.

NATION OF IMMIGRANTS

> All of our people all over the country—except the pure-blooded
> Indians—are immigrants, including even those who came over here
> on the *Mayflower*.
>
> Franklin Delano Roosevelt,
> November 4, 1944

The heterogeneous nature of the American population throughout our history has been due to the continual influx of various immigrant groups. The American pluralistic society consists of many subdivisions known as **ethnic groups**, identified by race, religion, places of origin, culture, and history.

Old Immigration (1609–1860)

Motivations

Early immigration to North America came primarily from northern and western Europe. Settlers from the British Isles included English, Irish, Scots, and Welsh. Among the settlers from continental Europe were the Germans, Dutch, Swiss, Swedes, and French.

During the period of "colonial immigration" (1609–1789) most settlers came to the American colonies for one or more of the following reasons: desire for land, political strife at home, religious persecution, or economic opportunities. In the latter part of the old immigration period (1780–1860), motivations for immigration included the availability of land as the United States expanded westward, jobs provided by the early stages of the Industrial Revolution, and opportunities for social mobility that did not exist in Europe. Problems in Europe also encouraged emigration. Political and religious unrest in Germany, France, Austria, Hungary, Ireland, and Denmark during the middle of the 1600s increased rates of emigration. Between 1789 and 1815 Europe was ravaged by the French Revolution and Napoleonic Wars, while in the 1830s revolutions spread through Poland, France, and Belgium. Between 1845 and 1849 Ireland experienced a devastating famine. The European population doubled between 1750 and 1850 and emigration restrictions were relaxed in a number of nations. Improved transportation facilitated the movement of those who wanted to emigrate. Moreover, portions of our diverse population were acquired through conquest and annexation, including the French population of the lower Louisiana Territory and the Spanish population of the Southwest.

Indentured Servants and Forced African Immigration

In the English colonies labor was scarce and most newcomers were unwilling to work for others, because it was easy to acquire land and become independent farmers.

One answer to the labor shortage problem was the use of **indentured servants**. Europeans who lacked the funds to pay for their transportation to America (poor and landless farmers, unemployed and low-paid workers, debtors) were able to sign indentures, or contracts, in which they agreed to work from 4 to 7 years in exchange for their passage to America. Once they had fulfilled the terms of their indentures, they were free to find independent employment. Indentured servants accounted for nearly 80 percent of the 130,000 settlers in the Virginia and Maryland colonies in the 17th century.

Between 1492 and 1770 more **Africans** than Europeans came to the New World, most of them settling in the Caribbean and in South America. However, they were brought in chains against their will. At first, most slaves were brought to the English colonies from the Caribbean islands, but as time passed, they were imported directly from Africa. By the 1660s most blacks in the colonies were legally held as slaves, numbering approximately 400,000 by 1775. The English settlers justified slavery, a tradition that did not exist in England, with the **ethnocentric** belief that fair-skinned people like themselves were superior to dark-skinned races.

Early Nativism

In the early years of settlement, there was little opposition to immigration because labor was needed in the growing country. Moreover, most immigrants to the United States who came from northern and western Europe **assimilated** easily. One group, formed in the 1850s, that supported nativism, or favored native-born Americans and opposed immigration, was the American Party, commonly known as the "**Know-Nothing**" **Party**. Much of their opposition was directed at Irish and German immigrants who, they claimed, threatened native labor by taking jobs, were clannish, and failed to quickly assimilate. But the most important source of conflict between Protestant native-born Americans and immigrants was religion, specifically objections to Irish Catholics. Many feared that if the Catholics "took over" America, the Pope in Rome would rule, and religious and political liberty would be destroyed. Goals of the American party were the limitation of political officeholding to native-born Americans, a 21-year residency requirement for naturalization, and greater restrictions on immigration.

Ethnic Distribution (1820–1930)

Between 1820 and 1930 more than 37 million immigrants came to the United States, mostly from Europe. While most came from northern and western Europe prior to 1880, most came later from southern and eastern Europe. Figure 2.4 illustrates the geographic distribution of immigration to the United States during these years.

Decade	Germany	Ireland	England, Scotland, Wales	Scandinavia	Italy	Austro-Hungary	Russia & Baltic States	Totals
1820	968	3,614	2,410	23	30		14	7,059
1821–30	6,761	50,724	25,079	260	409		75	83,308
1831–40	152,454	207,654	75,810	2,264	2,253		277	440,712
1841–50	434,626	780,719	267,044	13,122	1,970		551	1,498,032
1851–60	951,657	914,119	423,929	24,680	9,231		457	2,324,073
1861–70	827,468	435,697	607,076	126,392	11,725	7,800	2,515	2,018,673
1871–80	718,182	436,871	548,043	242,934	55,795	72,969	39,287	2,114,081
1881–90	1,452,970	655,540	807,357	655,494	307,309	362,719	213,282	4,454,671
1891–1900	505,152	388,416	271,538	371,512	651,873	574,069	505,281	3,267,841
1901–10	341,498	339,065	525,950	505,324	2,045,877	2,145,266	1,597,308	7,500,288
1911–20	143,945	146,199	314,408	123,452	1,209,524	901,656	921,957	3,841,141
1921–30	412,202	220,564	330,168	98,210	455,315	214,806	89,423	1,920,688
Totals	5,947,883	4,579,182	4,198,812	2,343,667	4,751,311	4,279,285	3,370,427	

Figure 2.4 Immigration to America (1820–1930)

New Immigration (1870–1930)

New Sources

Emigration from southern and eastern Europe at the end of the 19th century affected cities worldwide. Although cities like Warsaw, Berlin, Vienna, Naples, and London received new immigrants, the United States, with its higher standard of living and reputation for being a land of opportunity, received the bulk of the new immigrants. Between 1880 and 1930 over 27 million immigrants came to the United States, many to Ellis Island in New York Harbor. The new immigration included Italians, Greeks, Jews, Poles, Romanians, and those emigrating from the Austro-Hungarian Empire and Russia.

Reasons for Immigration

The "new immigrants" sought to escape the same economic problems that had caused many earlier immigrants to leave their homelands in northern and western Europe. Unemployment, high birth rates, overpopulation, and epidemics of malaria and cholera drove many southern Italians abroad, for example. The easing of immigration restrictions and faster, less expensive transportation made immigration into the United States a more viable option for many.

Attractions of the United States

America's greatest attraction was the opportunity for social mobility through economic opportunities not available in Europe and Asia. America's rapidly growing industries continually needed inexpensive labor, and the numerous foreign immigrants provided the necessary hands. As older immigrants were less likely to tolerate the deteriorating working conditions of unregulated industrial expansion, Slavs and Italians replaced British, Irish, and Germans in coal mines, while Portuguese, Greeks, and Italians found employment in New England textile mills. East European Jews took jobs formerly held by the Irish and Germans in New York City's garment factories, and the Japanese on the West Coast replaced many Chinese in agricultural and service tasks.

America's democratic and constitutional form of government, allowing for civil liberties and political freedoms not available in many European countries, was a strong attraction. Those persecuted in other countries, as the Jews were in Russia, were able to combat discrimination in their new home with the formation of constitutionally protected groups such as the **B'nai B'rith Anti-Defamation League**.

Urbanization and the Inner City

As the decades following the Civil War saw increased immigration, many large cities developed a patchwork of ethnic neighborhoods. The new immigrants settled together in neighborhoods called "Little Germany," "Little Italy," and so on, where they clung to their own language and customs. Because immigrants felt more comfortable working and living among friends and relatives, ethnic groups concentrated in particular industries and locations.

Americanization Process

Most new Americans experienced stages of change as the "Americanization process" took place. The first stage, especially with the later immigrants from southern and eastern Europe, usually included discrimination by native-born Americans. Many times, these immigrants were excluded from better residential areas, received little protection in employment, and were belittled.

As immigrants began to adopt the ways of American society—the English language, an understanding of the legal system and government and its customs and traditions—they experienced the stage of acculturation, or the adaptation to the American culture.

A later stage of Americanization occurred when the immigrant was finally absorbed into American society. This is known as the stage of assimilation, which usually does not occur until the second or third generation of immigrant families.

Contributions of Immigrants to American Society

Most immigrants came to the United States seeking political, economic, and social freedom. As a result, they have continued to contribute to the American democratic heritage and its preservation. The rich cultural heritage that came to the United States with different groups of immigrants has continued to add to a heterogeneous society.

Reaction to the "New" Immigration

Cultural Pluralism

The long held concept of the "melting pot" suggested that all immigrants absorb the aspects of a uniform American culture and, as a result, become "Americanized." However, in reality, the patterns of acculturation and assimilation have not produced such homogeneous results. Although American society does have a homogeneous core including a democratic political system and uniform economic institutions, American society is at the same time quite heterogeneous. Although different ethnic groups become Americanized, they also maintain a degree of their cultural heritage. This idea of "cultural pluralism," rather than a pure melting pot, was first expressed in 1915 by the Jewish-American philosopher Horace Kallen in his articles entitled "Democracy Versus the Melting Pot."

Nativist Reactions

Ironically, although the majority of the original settlers and immigrants to the English colonies and early United States came for economic opportunity, political freedom, and religious freedom, they lacked tolerance for anyone who deviated significantly from themselves. Americans of every generation have feared that newcomers would subvert established customs and undermine the traditions of society. Opposition to immigrants began toward the Scotch-Irish and Germans in the middle of the 19th century, followed by discrimination against Italians, Chinese, Jews, Poles, and Japanese at the turn of the century, and Mexicans, Puerto Ricans, Latin Americans, and Vietnamese in the 20th century. Native-born Americans have demonstrated "nativism" toward immigrants of minority groups who have deviated from the dominant culture. Stereotyping, or a fixed conception of groups, became a common form of discrimination.

Nativist groups discriminated against individuals because of race, religion, political beliefs, and economic fears. In 1887 the **American Protective Association** was founded, based on anti-Catholicism. The **Ku Klux Klan** originated as primarily a violent anti-black organization during the Civil War era and resurfaced as an anti-Semitic, anti-Catholic, anti-immigrant group in the 20th century. White workers in 1877 organized the **Workingmen's Party** in California as an anti-Chinese organization based primarily on economic fears and racism. Pressures from nativists helped lead to legislation early in the 1920s designed to keep those with "radical" political beliefs from entering the country.

Nativist discrimination against minority groups, including black Americans, has had numerous effects, perhaps the greatest being economic. Although **affirmative action** legislation has attempted to remedy this trend, minority groups continue to remain at the lower end of the economic scale in the United States.

Immigration Restrictions

On a number of occasions in our history, Congress has responded to nativist sentiments with the passage of restrictive legislation. Figure 2.5 provides a listing of the major restrictive legislation passed by Congress during the 1800s and 1900s.

The immigration restriction acts of the 1920s, combined with the depression of the 1930s, drastically lowered the numbers of foreigners coming to American shores. Only 23,068 came in 1933, 28,470 in 1934, and 34,956 in 1935.

Legislation	Provisions	Causes
Chinese Exclusion Act (1882)	Restricted Chinese immigration for a 10-year period	Racism, economic fears
Gentlemen's Agreement (1907)	Japan persuaded to deny passports to those who wanted to emigrate	"Yellow Peril" racism, economic fears
Literacy Test (1917)	Immigrant required to pass literacy test in either English or another language	To keep out immigrants from eastern and southern Europe; most immigrants from northern and western Europe were literate
Immigration Act of 1921	Quota system set at 3% of total of that nationality in U.S. in 1910; general limit of 350,000 immigrants per year	Fear of Bolshevism (quota reduced immigration from eastern and southern Europe)
Immigration Act of 1924	Lowered quota set in 1921 to 2% and set base year at 1890	As nativism grew, greater cutbacks desired
Immigration Act of 1927	Congress set limit to 150,000 immigrants per year with most from western and northern Europe and virtually no Asians	Continued nativism and desire for racial purity
National Origins System of 1929	No more annually than 150,000 from outside Western Hemisphere; quotas enacted based upon numbers in 1920; no restrictions on immigration from Western Hemisphere; prohibited all immigration from Asian countries	Extreme post-World War I nativism
Refugee and Displaced Persons Acts (1940s–50s)	Provisions to admit immigrants (refugees) from Nazi Germany and later from eastern Europe	Exceptions made by Congress consistent with U.S. foreign policy

Figure 2.5 Immigration Restrictions (1882–1929)

Legislation	Provisions	Causes
McCarran-Walter Act of 1952	Annual total of 156,000 immigrants with quota on those from outside of the Western Hemisphere; 2,000 yearly from Far East; and screening for Communists	"McCarthy Era," fear of Communism
Immigration Act of 1965	Ended quota system; set annual number from outside Western Hemisphere at 170,000; 120,000 from within Western Hemisphere; preference for those with "special talents" and relatives	Improvement on earlier acts claimed to be racist and unfair

Figure 2.5 continued   Immigration Restrictions (1882–1929)

Exercise Set 2.11

1. Which is the main way that ethnic groups in the United States have helped to shape the national identity?
   A. Most of the newer groups have blended in and adopted the ways of earlier immigrants.
   B. Each group kept cultural characteristics that became part of the general culture.
   C. Each group attempted to become the dominant force in society.
   D. Ethnic groups made large financial contributions in support of the arts in the United States.

2. The immigration laws of the 1920s were noteworthy because they
   A. satisfied the Chinese and Japanese governments.
   B. limited immigrants to 25,000 per year.
   C. encouraged immigration from eastern and southern Europe.
   D. established systems of quotas designating specific numbers of immigrants from different countries.

3. Which of the following immigrant groups assimilated with the greatest ease?
   A. The Irish in the 1850s
   B. The Chinese in the 1880s
   C. The English in the 1920s
   D. The Vietnamese in the 1970s

4. Which of the following statements is true about immigration to the United States during the last two decades of the 19th century?
   A. United States immigration laws sharply reduced the number of eligible immigrants.
   B. Nativist objection to immigration drastically reduced the numbers of foreigners coming to the United States.
   C. Quotas were placed on immigrant groups coming from the Western Hemisphere.
   D. Many immigrants of this period faced problems in assimilating into American society.

5. The hostility of the Know-Nothing Party was aimed primarily at
   A. slaveholders.
   B. Protestants from northern Europe.
   C. Irish and German Catholic immigrants.
   D. labor unions.

6. A major reason that no significant restrictions were placed on immigration to the United States before the end of the 19th century was that
   A. the American economy was in need of additional workers.
   B. there were no signs of nativist objections to immigrants before the 20th century.
   C. the numbers of immigrants coming to the United States continued to decrease as the 19th century came to a close.
   D. European and Asian nations halted all emigration.

THE LAST FRONTIER

> The result is that to the frontier the American intellect owes its strik-ing characteristics . . . that restless, nervous energy; that dominant individualism, working for good and evil, and with all that buoyancy and exuberance which comes from freedom—these are the traits of the frontier.
>
> Frederick Jackson Turner,
> *The Significance of the Frontier in American History* (1894)

The Significance of the Frontier in American History, an essay by University of Wisconsin professor **Frederick Jackson Turner**, was read to a conference of historians in connection with the World's Fair in Chicago in 1893 and presented a new theory to the age-old question, "What is the American?" Professor Turner, contemplating the effects of the closing frontier, proposed that one of the major differences between European and American civiliza-tion was that the American was in part the product of the distinctive environ-ment of the New World. The "free land" offered by a continuing westward moving frontier offered hopes of economic gain and adventure, changed the social stratification that typified European society, demanded new political institutions, changed traditional economic practices to meet the demands of self-sufficiency, and gradually produced an "Americanization" of the society that was making up the United States. Although the simplicity of Turner's thesis has been criticized over the years, the operation of the frontier process still remains a well-respected explanation of the development of the Ameri-can character.

Land West of the Mississippi

By the early 1800s the "American West" continued to move as the white frontier advanced beyond the Mississippi River. The nation gained new terri-tory with the purchase of the **Louisiana Territory** (1803), the annexation of Texas (1845), the acquisition of the **Oregon Country** through a treaty with Great Britain (1846), the **Mexican Cession** by treaty with Mexico (1848), and the **Gadsden Purchase** from Mexico (1853), fulfilling the emotional drive for expansion (**Manifest Destiny**). (See Figure 1.18 on page 75, "Territorial Growth of the United States, 1783–1853.")

Native Americans

As the white population continued to press westward, the original settlers, the American Indians, were ruthlessly forced onto poorer lands or onto **reserva-tions**. The newcomers who desired land for railroads, farms, and speculation could not tolerate the nomadic Indian who recognized no individual ownership of land. By 1873, white settlers, with the assistance of federal troops, had subdued most of the native population.

The Homestead Act (1862)

Passed by Congress during the Civil War, the Homestead Act provided 160 acres of federal land for settlers who would inhabit plots of land for at least five years. Problems with the Homestead Act included the inadequacy of the small plots and abuse by mining and timber companies who gained considerable amounts of free federal land by having employees put in claims for homesteads.

The Impact of Industrialization

Transportation

During the 1820s and 1830s trade routes in the United States began to indicate greater **East-West economic interdependenc**y. The transportation improvements of the 19th century helped connect the agricultural interests of the West with the markets of the East, and the industrial centers of the East with the growing need for manufactured goods of the West. The building of canals, the steamboat, the railroad, and the telegraph helped to open up the frontier and brought many farmers into the market economy. Self-sufficient farmers who at one time produced many agricultural products began to specialize in one or two crops.

Immigration

Increased immigration during the 19th century increased the market for agricultural goods in the Eastern cities. Immigrants also contributed to the growing population of Western territories and states. Both public and private interests in the West encouraged the migration of immigrants westward to promote their economies.

Investment Opportunities

Public and private investment and a growing population stimulated economic growth during the 19th century. Lucrative investment opportunities in the nation's growth encouraged investment by banks, insurance companies, corporations, and private individuals.

Development of Urban Centers

As the population of the United States increased, the frontier moved steadily westward and rural settlements became towns and cities. Early cities grew along major river routes (Cincinnati, Louisville, Pittsburgh) and along the shores of the Great Lakes (Cleveland, Chicago, Detroit). With the continued growth of the railroad and telegraph, new cities grew along major lines (Omaha, Kansas City, Denver, Salt Lake City, El Paso, Sacramento, Los Angeles).

Native Americans

Advancing White Settlement

White settlement took its toll on the Native American population almost immediately. The greatest destruction of the American Indian population started long before the infamous wars of the 1800s between Western settlers and the Plains Indians. Diseases carried from Europe killed hundreds of thousands of Native Americans who had no natural immunity to these germs. Most deadly of the diseases was smallpox, which drastically reduced the Indian population in the Caribbean, Central America, the English colonies, and Canada.

Legal Status and Treaties

Early on, the British settlers viewed the American Indian as a type of "savage"—an inferior race, much the same as they viewed the black African. During the colonial period, British policy toward the Indians was to slowly push them westward and avoid conflict. The **Proclamation of 1763** (preventing settlement west of the Appalachians) was passed to prevent friction with the native populations, a problem the financially strained British government could ill afford.

Once independence was gained, the United States government found that conflict with the Indians was "inevitable." The **Northwest Ordinance** of 1787 called for the Indians to be treated in "good faith," and the **Treaty of Greenville** (1795) accepted Indian tribal sovereignty by virtue of their residence in part of the Northwest Territory. However, both provisions were eventually violated.

The Indians, exempted from taxation and not counted in apportionment of representation and taxes, possessed an indefinite status under the Constitution. During the 1820s the federal government urged the removal of the tribes to the West, and several states took independent action to remove the Indians. Congress passed the **Indian Removal Act of 1830**, which appropriated $500,000 for treaties to remove tribes, primarily in the Southeast, west of the Mississippi.

In 1827, following attempts by the state of Georgia to have them removed, the Cherokees of Georgia adopted a written constitution and declared themselves an independent state. In *Cherokee Nation* v. *Georgia* (1831) the Supreme Court held that, although the Cherokee Indians could not bring a suit in federal court, they had a right to their own land until the time they chose to voluntarily cede it to the United States. In ***Worcester v. Georgia*** (1832), the Supreme Court went further in stating that citizens of Georgia had no right to enter Cherokee lands without the consent of the Indians. President **Andrew Jackson**, who, as a general, had led the expedition against the Seminoles in Florida in 1818, had little sympathy for the Indians. Jackson refused to implement the Supreme Court's decisions and, with support from Congress (**Removal Act of 1830**), he ordered the removal of Indians to lands west of the Mississippi, starting with the Choctaw in 1831. In 1835 a minority group of Cherokees signed a treaty agreeing to exchange their land in Georgia for Western land. In 1838, when many Cherokees refused to move, President **Martin Van Buren** sent federal troops to force the Indians from their land and march them to Oklahoma. Nearly one quarter died of disease and exhaustion on this forced move, which has come to be known as the **Trail of Tears**.

Indian Wars (1850–1900)

Although early policy toward the Indians called for their resettlement west of the Mississippi River, by the 1840s the movement of whites to the West forced a change in policy. Government policy now called for the establishment of **Indian reservations**. The legal status of the Indian under the reservation system was that of a ward, or one under the care of the federal government. However, this did not bring peace because whites entered reservation land and the Indians found the reservations too confining after their nomadic lifestyle. Battles continued throughout the 19th century with cruelties and brutalities committed by both sides. The last occurred in 1890 when unarmed Teton Sioux of South Dakota were massacred by federal troops armed with Gatling guns at **Wounded Knee**, South Dakota. The final blow to the American Indian came with the destruction of the buffalo, or bison. Depended upon by the Plains Indians for survival, the buffalo became the white man's source of food, sport (buffalo hunters such as "Buffalo Bill" Cody), and leather, and 9 million bison were killed between 1872 and 1874.

Legislating Indian Life

Reform movements in the late 1800s urged change in federal policy toward the Indians and organizations such as the Indian Rights Association awakened concern. The aim of most reformers was to **assimilate** the Indians into white society. The **Dawes Severalty Laws** of 1887, providing for the division of Indian lands among individual families and citizenship to those Indians who abandoned tribal allegiances, was passed in hopes of accelerating assimilation. Unfortunately, the Dawes Act failed. Attempts at assimilation violated Indian traditions and under the act nearly one half of the Indian lands was lost to white settlement.

Partially in recognition of those Indians who had served in World War I, Congress passed the **Snyder Indian Citizenship Act** in 1924, granting citizenship to all Indians born in the United States. In 1934 Congress passed the **Indian Reorganization Act**, a reform measure designed to stress tribal unity and autonomy. By returning surplus lands to the Indians, authorizing tribes to form corporations, and providing for elected tribal councils, the act attempted to restore the tribe as the center of Indian culture and life. In 1953 Congress began a policy of "**termination**," or the ending of federal responsibility and social services (education, health, welfare) in an attempt to assimilate the Indian into American society. The policy of termination ended in the 1960s and a new militancy surfaced among groups of American Indians in the 1960s and 1970s. The occupation of **Alcatraz Island** in San Francisco Bay in 1969 and the holding of hostages at Wounded Knee in 1973 by the **American Indian Movement** (AIM) are examples of attempts by the American Indians to regain their lands.

The Mining Frontier

The **California Gold Rush** of 1849 brought nearly 100,000 new settlers. After gold was discovered near Denver in 1858, many settlers came to Colorado, and the discovery of the **Comstock Lode** in 1858 increased the population of the **Nevada Territory**, bringing statehood in 1864.

The Cattle Frontier

The grasslands of the Great Plains, east of the Rocky Mountains, were well suited for grazing and quickly became the cattleman's frontier, where large herds of cattle grazed on the "open range." The original market value of the

Discoveries of gold helped draw settlers to the West.

Texas longhorn was for its hide, processed in the tanneries of the Northeast. However, after the Civil War there developed the "**long drive**," or the driving of cattle herds north to the nearest East-running railroad for the Eastern beef market. By the 1880s the long drive became less common as increased numbers of farms closed in the open range and the railroads were located closer to local ranches.

By the 1890s overproduction of cattle caused the prices in the Eastern markets to decline. Prices of steers dropped from $30 apiece to only $8. Over the next few years the "open range" approach to cattle raising ended and, assisted by the invention of **barbed wire** by Joseph Glidden (1874), ranchers turned to smaller herds on fenced land.

The West, sparsely populated and lacking law enforcement officers, lawyers, and judges, developed an unwritten body of customs sometimes known as the Code of the West. Justice on the frontier was carried out by federal district courts and United States marshals, who often employed hired guns to assist them. Some of the more notorious lawmen of the frontier were Wyatt Earp, Bill Tilghman, Texas Ranger Ira Aten, and Judge Isaac C. Parker. At times, when the legal system proved to be incapable of curbing gamblers, gunmen, and desperadoes, groups of self-proclaimed law enforcers formed vigilante committees to cope with lawbreakers.

Much cowboy dress was adopted from the Mexican *vaqueros*.

The Farming Frontier

Farmer versus Nature

The frontier farmer found the turf of the Great Plains hard to manage, for the roots of the grasses extended deep and intermeshed to form sod up to twelve feet thick. Turning this hindrance into an advantage, the ingenious plains farmer used special plows to cut the sod into bricks ("Nebraska Marble"), which was then used to build homes. In an area lacking wood, rock, and brick clay, the **sod house** solved the problem of shelter for the plains farmer.

Perhaps the farmer's greatest foe was nature itself. Drought and wind combined to scorch the crops and lift the dry topsoil, creating swirls of dust that were deposited hundreds of miles away. Prairie fires raced across the plains in the fall when grass became dry. Winter blizzards and subzero weather froze farmers and livestock alike, and plagues of grasshoppers turned millions of acres into a wasteland.

Technology

New farming inventions allowed the plains farmer to cultivate the soil in spite of nature's resistance. **Barbed wire** enabled farmers to enclose the fields, keeping their own livestock in and the rancher's herds out. An improved prairie **plow** made of steel that did not break when it cut through the tough sod was devised in 1868. The **windmill** allowed the farmer to draw spring water from deep underground and cultivate the fields, while improved systems of irrigation made use of limited amounts of water. Laborsaving devices like the horse-drawn **reaper** and later the **combine** helped turn the plains into the "breadbasket" of the nation, and later the world.

Government Policy

The railroads held tremendous amounts of land through federal grants and sold many acres to the farmers. The **Homestead Act** (1862) encouraged further settlement and about 600,000 homesteaders benefited. The **Morrill Land Grant Act** (1862) provided for the sale of federal land to finance agricultural colleges, promoting scientific agricultural development.

Life on the Great Plains Farm

Besides the hostile environment, the isolation and loneliness of the plains farm added to the challenge of survival. It was not uncommon for families to walk many miles to the nearest farm for simple conversation. Medical needs were met by self-proclaimed physicians who, with a mixture of folk remedy, medieval methods, and improvisation, served the needs of the prairie population. Frontier schools, usually an early priority in a prairie settlement, were financed by local districts, and the success of plains education was surprisingly high. By 1900, Nebraska, Kansas, and Iowa boasted the highest literacy rate in the nation.

Agrarian Protest

The Grange Movement

The transition of the American farmers from self-sufficiency to the market economy brought hardships that eventually caused them to form political organizations. During the 19th century, farmers found themselves at the mercy of forces—commodity prices, grain storage charges, interest rates, and shipping costs—that were beyond their control.

The **National Grange of the Patrons of Husbandry** was founded in 1867 to organize farmers into local chapters dedicated to education, culture, and socialization. However, in the 1870s its aims became less social and more political, with membership reaching 1.5 million by 1874. The Grange accused the railroads of discriminatory practices (long haul compared to short haul, rebates, monopolizing practices), the grain-elevator operators of monopoly practices, charging "all that the traffic would bear," and manufacturers of raising prices and the cost of credit so that farmers were unable to make a profit.

Legal Efforts; Court Cases

By the middle of the 1870s the Grangers held the political balance in several of the Midwestern states. In four states **Granger laws** were passed to regulate railroad rates and the practices of the owners of grain elevators. The Supreme Court, in a series of landmark decisions, upheld the principle that government could regulate all those industries "affected with a public interest."

• **Munn v. Illinois (1877).** The Supreme Court upheld state regulation of grain elevators' storage rates, declaring that **"the public has a direct and positive interest"** in private businesses **"clothed with a public interest."** As a consequence, the rates and services of public utilities could be regulated, departing from the tradition of laissez-faire economics.

• **Wabash, St. Louis and Pacific Railway v. Minnesota (1886).** In this case, based on congressional control over interstate commerce, the Supreme Court restricted state control by holding that the states had no power to fix rates on shipments of goods passing beyond their borders.

• **Chicago, Milwaukee and St. Paul Railroad v. Minnesota (1889).** The Supreme Court ruled that corporations could not be denied property rights without being afforded equal protection of the laws and due process.

National Government Response: Interstate Commerce Commission

In response to the Supreme Court's decision in the *Wabash* case, Congress passed the **Interstate Commerce Act** (1887) establishing the Interstate Commerce Commission, which had among its powers the right to require that railroads post rates publicly; demand that rates be "reasonable and just"; forbid pooling, rebates, and rate discrimination; prohibit "long haul vs. short haul discrimination"; and investigate complaints against the railroads.

Populism

• **Farmers' Alliances.** As the agrarian crusade continued into the 1880s, farmers' alliances were formed to demand change concerning a number of issues. In 1887 the Southern Farmers' Alliance had a membership of 3 million. The Northern Farmers' Alliance attracted 2 million members by 1890. In 1889 delegates from both alliances met to discuss a common platform that included demand for free silver; graduated income tax (percent of tax rate increasing with amount earned); government ownership of the railroads; and the direct election of Senators. In the elections of 1890, members of the alliances were elected to many state positions and 53 members of Congress who were sympathetic to the desires of the Farmers' Alliances were sent to Washington, D.C.

• **Populist Party.** The **People's Party**, or **Populist Party**, was formed in 1891 through the efforts of the Farmers' Alliances. **James B. Weaver** ran for president on the Populist ticket in 1892 and received a million popular votes. The Populist platform, known as the **Omaha Platform**, included a graduated income tax, postal savings banks, government ownership of railroads and telegraph lines, the direct election of senators, and the use of initiative (popular introduction of legislation) and referendum (the provision for the popular vote on laws rather than that of the legislatures). The Populist platform also continued to support an increased amount of currency in circulation, an issue endorsed by the **Greenback Party** of the 1870s. Since most farmers were debtors, borrowing and buying on credit, the deflationary trends of the later 1800s proved to be devastating. The Populist platform continued to be pushed by Progressives for a generation. As with many third-party movements in the nation's history, much of the Populist platform was later adopted by the major parties.

• *Election of 1896.* In the election of 1896, **William Jennings Bryan** ran on the Democratic ticket advocating increased coinage of silver. Speaking on the free-silver issue at the 1896 Democratic Convention, Bryan spoke his famous words, "You shall not press down upon the brow of labor this crown of thorns, you shall not crucify mankind upon a cross of gold." The platform of the Democrats was progressive and adopted much of the Populist platform, including reduced tariffs, antitrust legislation, and outlawing the injunction in labor disputes. A vigorous Republican campaign, combined with rising farm prices due to overseas crop failures, resulted in a victory for the Republican candidate, **William McKinley**.

AMERICAN SOCIETY AT THE TURN OF THE CENTURY

In the late 1800s and early 1900s many changes were taking place that helped the nation become a world power. A once predominantly rural nation was becoming a nation of cities. A country whose economy was once based on agriculture was rapidly becoming an industrial giant. From 1860 to 1910 towns and cities developed and grew at a rate unmatched in modern times. While the rural population almost doubled during these years, the urban population multiplied nearly seven times.

Urbanization and Cultural Development

Urbanization stimulated cultural development by the mixing of many different types of people, the establishment of facilities including libraries, schools, museums, orchestras, and theaters, and the concentration of wealth that contributed to cultural growth. While public school systems and colleges received greater support from both government and private sources, curriculums broadened and specialized. The American Library Association was formed in 1876. Daily newspapers increased in number from 700 in 1870 to 2,500 in 1900, while circulation increased from 2.5 million to 15 million and magazines numbered 1,800 by the turn of the century. Museums began display the works of American painters and sculptors. The rise of the city contributed to cultural progress in the United States.

Growth of American Imperialism

American expansionism turned to **imperialism**, or the imposition of control over other peoples. **Manifest Destiny** was completed by the turn of the century and the United States was continentally complete. Imperialism was beginning to play a role in American foreign policy. By 1900 the "American Empire" included Alaska, the Midway Islands, Samoa, the Philippines, Guam, Puerto Rico, Hawaii, and Wake Island.

Problems Caused by Industrialization

America's rise as an industrial power and its race to greatness brought many problems. With the coming of the new century, these problems started to be addressed. With the conquest of the continent had come reckless **abuse of the environment**—the soil, forests, and water. Rapid industrial growth had brought the **exploitation** of women, children, and workers. The belief in "Social Darwinism" had led to disregard for the incompetent and the infirm. Wealth and power was concentrated among only a few, and **poverty** was becoming widespread. Although slavery had ended, **racism** plagued American society. Finally, corruption poisoned the political system. To remedy the nation's problems, it was necessary to cleanse politics and to regulate the business interests that controlled government.

The "**Progressive Era**" was an attempt to solve the many problems caused by an industrial society. In 1906 President Theodore Roosevelt labeled those individuals who were working to uncover corruption "**muck-rakers**." These philosophers, social scientists, and novelists included **Henry George** (*Progress and Poverty,* 1879), **Lester Ward** (*Dynamic Sociology,* 1883), **Edward Bellamy** (*Looking Backward: 2000–1887,* 1887), and **Thorstein Veblen** (*The Theory of the Leisure Class,* 1899). They produced a literature of protest in the late 1800s. The common theme in most of their works was that laissez-faire had not worked and progress was possible only through social planning. The Progressive era was a reaction to laissez-faire and included greater governmental and legal control of big business and greater government accountability.

Exercise Set 2.12

1. The Dawes Severalty Act (1887) changed previous policy toward Native Americans by
   A. abolishing the reservation system.
   B. granting them citizenship.
   C. halting attempts at assimilation of the Indian.
   D. dividing tribal lands among individual families.

2. As the 19th century progressed, farming on the Great Plains became
   A. less threatened by a hostile environment.
   B. further dependent upon the railroad.
   C. less important to the economy of the United States.
   D. primarily a one-crop economy.

3. Which of the following was true of the Grange Movement?
   A. It was primarily a southern agrarian movement.
   B. It started as a social organization and became increasingly political in the 1880s.
   C. It had little effect on future state and federal legislation.
   D. It avoided politics.

4. Cattle raising in the semi-arid lands of the West greatly increased as a result of the
   A. Homestead Act.
   B. invention of the reaper.
   C. extension of the nation's railroad network.
   D. Morrill Land Grant Act.

CHAPTER REVIEW QUESTIONS

1. Between 1890 and 1914 most immigrants to the United States came from
   A. Latin America.
   B. northern and western Europe.
   C. southern and eastern Europe.
   D. Southeast Asia.

2. Which of the following accurately describes the Ku Klux Klan of the 1920s?
   A. Its activities were limited to the South.
   B. It favored immigration restrictions as well as white supremacy.
   C. Many of its members were elected to Congress.
   D. It appeared for the first time during this decade.

3. The destructive impact of white settlement on the Native American population was most strongly felt through
   A. the spread of disease unknown to Native Americans.
   B. immediate elimination of the native population through warfare.
   C. wholesale enslavement of the Indians.
   D. immediate relocation of Indians to lands west of the Mississippi.

4. All but which of the following major transportation developments affecting United States history took place in the period before the 20th century?
   A. The steamboat
   B. The airplane
   C. The stagecoach
   D. The railroad

5. In the 40 years following the Civil War, which of the following areas was affected by only state and local legislation?
   A. Women's suffrage
   B. Interstate commerce
   C. Immigration
   D. Civil rights

6. Which of the following American authors was least concerned with social criticism of America?
   A. Frank Norris
   B. Jacob Riis
   C. Upton Sinclair
   D. Horatio Alger

7. During the second half of the 19th century, an open immigration policy was generally opposed by
A. factory owners.
B. land speculators.
C. sparsely populated Western territories.
D. labor unions.

8. The Populist movement of the 1890s can best be described as a
A. political coalition of farming interests directed against banking and railroad interests.
B. trade union movement located in major Eastern cities.
C. reform movement seeking to eliminate urban poverty and slums.
D. political interest group desiring war with Spain to protect United States interests in Cuba.

THEMATIC ESSAYS

Directions: Write a well-organized essay that includes an introduction, several paragraphs addressing the task below, and a conclusion.

Theme: Government and Economic Systems

During the time period of 1865–1900 the federal government departed from the principles of laissez-faire.

Task:

Identify *two* examples of the federal government's departure from the principles of laissez-faire.

- Discuss the problem that led to the government's change in economic policy in each example.
- Discuss each specific federal government action.
- Evaluate whether the government actions were successful in addressing each problem.

Some suggestions you might wish to consider include: control of interstate commerce, antitrust activities, and railroad land grants.

You are *not* limited to these suggestions.

Directions: Write a well-organized essay that includes an introduction, several paragraphs addressing the task below, and a conclusion.

Theme: Diversity and Government Action

During the time period between 1875 and 1925 the views of the American people changed with regard to immigration, and the federal government responded with changes in immigration laws.

Task:

Identify *two* pieces of immigration legislation passed by the federal government during the 1875–1925 time period.

- For each immigration law identified, discuss changes in the views of the American people that contributed to the change.
- Discuss each specific immigration law.
- Compare each of the 1875–1925 immigration laws used to current immigration legislation.

Some suggestions you might wish to consider include: Chinese Exclusion Act (1882), Gentlemen's Agreement (1907), Literacy Test (1917), Immigration Act of 1921, and Immigration Act of 1924.

You are *not* limited to these suggestions.

THEMATIC ESSAY

Directions: Write a well-organized essay that includes an introduction, several paragraphs addressing the task below, and a conclusion.

Theme: Third Party and Local Political Movements Have Been an Important Factor in the Democratic Process.

Problems faced by farmers in the expanding industrial economy of the late 1800s led to the formation of local political movements and the development of third parties.

Task:

From your study of the period of agrarian protest (1870–1890), identify *two* political movements formed to address problems faced by farmers.

For each movement identified:

- State one issue viewed as a problem by the political movement.
- Discuss what farmers saw as the cause of the problem.
- Describe legislation or court decisions that resulted in addressing the problem.
- Discuss the success or failure of the legislation or court decisions.

You may use any political movements and resulting legislation and/or court decisions. Some suggestions you may wish to consider regarding political movements and third parties include the Greenback party, National Grange of the Patrons of Husbandry, Populist Party, and Farmers' Alliances. Legislation and/or court decisions may include the Interstate Commerce Act (1887), Sherman Silver Purchase Act (1890), *Munn* v. *Illinois* (1877), and *Wabash, St. Louis and Pacific Railway* v. *Minnesota* (1886).

You are *not* limited to these suggestions.

DOCUMENT-BASED QUESTION

The following questions (Part A and Part B) are based on the accompanying documents (1–6). Some of these documents have been edited for the purpose of this exercise. The question is designed to test your ability to work with historical documents and to demonstrate your knowledge of the subject matter being presented. As you analyze the documents, take into account both the source of the document and the author's point of view.

Historical Context:

The industrialization of the United States following the Civil War had a tremendous impact on labor.

Task:

Using information from the documents and your knowledge of United States history, answer the questions that follow each document in Part A. Your answers to the questions will help you write the Part B essay, in which you will be asked:

The organization of American labor into such early unions as the Knights of Labor and the American Federation of Labor was a natural response to the Industrial Revolution during the second half of the 19th century. Assess the validity of this statement.

Part A
Short-Answer Questions

The documents below relate to issues concerning workers in the period of industrialization following the Civil War. Examine each document carefully and then answer the questions that follow.

DOCUMENT 1

—Bibb Mill No. 1, Macon, Georgia

1. Provide two observations of the picture above that were later addressed by labor unions.

_____

_____

_____

DOCUMENT 2

The laboring classes constitute the main part of our population. They should be protected in their efforts peaceably to assert their rights when endangered by aggregated capital, and all statutes on this subject should recognize the care of the State for honest toil, and be framed with a view of improving the condition of the workingman.

—President Grover Cleveland, Albany, N.Y., August 18, 1884

2. How would organized labor use President Cleveland's statement to support their goals?

_____

_____

_____

DOCUMENT 3

1. Accidents and casualties are very numerous, partly owing to the exposed machinery and partly owing to carelessness . . . . It is really painful to go round among the operatives and find hands and fingers mutilated, in consequences of accidents.
2. Unnatural or monotonous working positions . . . in some cases make the worker round-shouldered, in other cases producing curvature of the spine and bow-legs.
3. Work by artificial light. It is very injurious to the eyes.

—Dr. John B. Whitaker, Impact of Factory on Worker Health, 1871

3. Describe how labor could use Dr. Whitaker's report in its demands for improved working conditions.

_____

_____

_____

DOCUMENT 4

An 1889 Payroll Ledger			
Names	Total Hours	Price	Amount
Overseer			
J. W. Doran	60	40	24.00
Sec. Hands			
P. Clifford	60	18	10.80
P. Smith	60	18	10.80
P. King	60	20	12.00
Third Oilers and Roving H'ds			
R. Lathrop	60	12	7.20
A. Blanchard	60	10	6.00
Scrubber			
J. Moriarity	60	5	3.00
Picker Men			
M. Grincovitch	60	10	6.00
M. Goetz	60	10	6.00
J. Chazee	60	10	6.00
A. Icyk	60	10	6.00

—An 1889 Payroll Ledger

4. After studying the payroll ledger, discuss two arguments the workers may have against the employer.

_____

_____

DOCUMENT 5

1. To secure to the toilers a proper share of the wealth that they create.
2. The adopting of measures providing for the health and safety of those engaged in mining and manufacturing.
3. The substitution of arbitration for strikes.
4. The prohibition of the employment of children in workshops, mines, and factories before attaining their fourteenth year.
5. To secure for both sexes equal pay for equal work.

—The Knights of Labor Charter

5. From a reading of the Knights of Labor Charter, discuss what the early labor union saw as major problems of workers in the post-Civil War period.

_____

_____

_____

—Hours and wages, 1860–1900

6. Explain how both management and labor could use the information in the graph to support their position.

_____

_____

_____

7. Since it appears that wages and hours improved for the worker between 1860 and 1900, how do you account for the increasing number of strikes during the time period?

_____

_____

_____

Part B
Essay

Your essay should be well organized with an introductory paragraph that states your position on the question. Develop your position in the next paragraphs and then write a conclusion. In your essay, include specific historical details and refer to the specific documents you analyzed in Part A. You may include additional information from your knowledge of social studies.

Historical Context:

The industrialization of the United States following the Civil War had a tremendous impact on labor.

Task:

The organization of American labor into such early unions as the Knights of Labor and the American Federation of Labor was a natural response to the Industrial Revolution during the second half of the 19th century. Assess the validity of this statement.

Guidelines:

In your essay, be sure to
• Develop all aspects of the task.
• Incorporate information from *at least five* documents.
• Incorporate relevant outside information.
• Support the theme with many relevant facts, examples, and details.
• Use a logical and clear plan of organization, including an introduction and a conclusion that are beyond a restatement of the theme.

UNIT THREE

The Progressive Movement

> **KEY IDEAS** The rapid growth of the United States during the second half of the 19th century, and the problems that accompanied this development, resulted in a period of transition and reform. The age of laissez-faire was coming to an end as social conditions/governmental responsibilities for social conditions increased. As the United States entered the 20th century, expansionist desires, including economic imperialism, became a major component of its foreign policies.

UNIT CONNECTIONS: By the end of the unit you should understand the following points.

- Political, economic, and social problems lead to need for reform
- Muckrakers and the exposure of evils in American society
- Progressivism and the role of the federal government
- Progressivism and farmers, women, labor, African Americans, and Native Americans
- Theodore Roosevelt, Woodrow Wilson, and the power of the presidency
- The spread of Manifest Destiny to Latin America and Asia
- Imperialism versus anti-imperialism
- The failure of Wilsonian attempts at neutrality
- World War I and the restrictions on civil liberties
- The failure of the United States to ratify the Treaty of Versailles
- Isolationism and diplomacy (1920–1933)

REFORM IN AMERICA

THE REFORM TRADITION

The American Republic was founded on the concept of equality. The founders of the nation held it to be a "self-evident truth" that all people are created equal, being endowed with the same basic rights to life, liberty, and the pursuit of happiness. Reform movements were started in various periods as a response to changing social conditions with the belief that the betterment of society was a possibility. Americans believed that in a democracy the people could create a better society through their own efforts.

American Revolution

The American Revolution was the first of a number of conflicts throughout the world that furthered the ideals of the **Enlightenment** thinkers. What distinguished the United States from other 18th century countries was that the American Revolution allowed the political theories of the Enlightenment to be put into practice. The United States based its government upon **Locke's** and **Rousseau's** idea of a "social contract." The purpose of government was to preserve people's natural rights to life, liberty, and property (Locke). The new Constitution, which proved to be an enduring plan of government, included **Montesquieu's** concept of separation of powers and checks and balances.

Abolition Movement

The movement to abolish slavery was a major reform movement during the first half of the 19th century. With the invention of the cotton gin in 1793 cotton exports rose from half a million pounds in that year to 83 million pounds in 1815. Increased demand for cotton intensified the South's justification for the cotton-slave economy, and slavery spread with great speed. The issue of slavery threatened the Union when it became entangled with problems raised by westward expansion.

The earliest reform movements opposing slavery originated with the **Quakers**. Before the American Revolution they freed their slaves, claiming it was a sin for Christians to hold people in bondage. By 1830 there were at least fifty black antislavery societies. However, in the 1840s, the movement became more widespread as many Americans came to realize that slavery was morally wrong. As whites became more involved in the movement, black abolitionists, including Sojourner Truth, Harriet Tubman, and Frederick Douglass, worked with white reformers to end slavery. **William Lloyd Garrison's** newspaper, *The Liberator,* launched a militant abolitionist movement in the North.

By the 1850s the question of slavery was dividing the country. A major setback to the abolitionist movement came with the Supreme Court's decision in *Dred Scott* **v.** *Sandford* (1857). The Court held that slaves were not protected by the Constitution. The Court said that Congress could not prevent citizens from transporting their slaves into a free territory because slaves were property, protected by the due process clause of the Fifth Amendment to the Constitution. Rather than settling the slavery question, however, the Dred Scott decision increased sectional conflict over the issue of slavery, especially over its expansion to western territory.

The end of slavery and the granting of citizenship and civil rights to black Americans did not come until after the Civil War and the passage of the Thirteenth, Fourteenth, and Fifteenth Amendments. Although the slavery question was finally resolved, reform movements for extension of civil rights to African Americans and other marginalized groups continued through the 20th century.

Women's Rights

Women in the 1800s were expected to keep house and raise children. Politics and work were the domains of men; women were the guardians of the home. The laws reinforced these perceptions. For example, married women in many states had no rights over property they inherited or wages they earned. They did not have legal control over their children, could not sue in their own name, and could not be a party to a contract.

Between 1820 and 1860, as other reforms began to sweep America, the women's movement began to develop. Women were active in all the reform movements in this period. Their involvement in these other reform movements made them realize that they were as oppressed as many of the groups they were attempting to assist.

As economic and social conditions changed with increased industrialization, equality slowly came to women. Early industrialization allowed women

Susan Brownell Anthony (1820–1906) was a leader in the women's suffrage movement.

to develop some financial independence and opened new areas of employment. Women's colleges, including Wellesley, Vassar, and Smith, opened between 1865 and 1875. By 1900 about 70 percent of all colleges admitted women. The efforts to gain political equality by reformers such as **Elizabeth Cady Stanton**, **Lucretia Mott**, and **Susan B. Anthony**, and groups such as the **National American Woman Suffrage Association** started to gain results during the second half of the 19th century. By 1895 sixteen states allowed women to vote, and in 1920 the Nineteenth Amendment was ratified, granting women throughout the nation the right to vote.

Civil Service

The movement to appoint people to government jobs based on merit rather than through the **spoils system** aroused great interest following the Civil War. The scandals of the Grant era and later the assassination of President Garfield in 1881 by a "disappointed office seeker" focused attention on the need for civil service reform. The abuse of the spoils system led to the demand that certain offices be filled only by those who had performed adequately on a "civil service" examination. The **Pendleton Act** (1883), adopted during President Arthur's administration, authorized the President to appoint civil service commissioners to administer examinations for "classified" government positions. Today, most government jobs are filled through civil service exams.

Mental Illness

Before the 1840s people with mental illness had been treated either as criminals and placed in jails, or as social misfits placed in poorhouses. A pioneer in the reform movement for those with mental illness was a Massachusetts schoolteacher, **Dorothea Dix**. After reporting to the state legislature the shocking treatment of patients in Massachusetts—"confined . . . in cages, closets, cellars, stalls, pens! Chained, naked, beaten with rods, and lashed into obedience . . ."—legislation was passed to set up a state hospital for those with mental illness Dorothea Dix carried her crusade across the country, resulting in improved care for the mentally ill in many states.

PRESSURE FOR REFORM

> So long as all the increased wealth which modern progress brings goes but to build great fortunes, to increase luxury and make sharper the contrast between the House of Have and the House of Want, progress is not real and cannot be permanent.
>
> Henry George, *Progress and Poverty* (1879)

> In the face of the facts that modern man lives more wretchedly than the caveman, and that his producing power is a thousand times greater than that of the caveman, no other conclusion is possible than that the capitalist class has mismanaged . . . criminally and selfishly mismanaged.
>
> Jack London, *The Iron Heel* (1906)

Struggle for Fair Standards

As industrialization continued to cause poverty for millions and an unequal distribution of the nation's wealth, movements for change gained momentum. Reformers demanded that government begin to regulate industry, finance, working conditions, and agriculture in the interest of the many rather than the few. A new movement known as the **Progressive Movement** resulted in the reform of the worst abuses in government and business. Although Progressives attacked many of the same grievances as **Populists** did in the 1890s, they received wider support from Americans, especially the growing middle class, and from government leaders.

Increasing Inequities of Wealth and Poverty

By 1900 the unequal distribution of the nation's wealth was beginning to threaten political democracy in America. Only 1 percent of the population owned 50 percent of the nation's wealth, while the top 12 percent controlled 90 percent. With so much wealth concentrated in the hands of such a small group, their influence over legislatures and candidates increased. Such class inequities helped to spread **Marxist** thought in the United States. **Karl Marx** predicted that discontent among the proletariat (working class) would result in the overthrow of capitalism and the subsequent end of class struggle. However, change came in the United States through reform legislation passed under the banner of the Progressive Movement rather than through revolution.

Rising Power and Influence of the Middle Class

An important result of industrialization in the United States was the rise of the middle class, which included professionals, technicians, government workers, salespeople, service employees, teachers, social workers, and clerical workers, among others. As the problems caused by business abuses and consolidation began to affect the middle class, they began to support the Progressive Movement and demand reform.

Communication of Progressive Thought

The Progressive Movement in the United States was assisted by a variety of nationwide organizations. Interest groups including the National Consumers League, **National Association for the Advancement of Colored People**, National Child Labor Committee, and **National Housing Administration**, joined with occupational groups such as the **American Bar Association** and the American Health Association, with nationwide membership. Technological improvements in communication—the telephone and telegraph—improved the availability of information and allowed progressivism to become a national movement.

The "Muckrakers" and Reform

> Men with the muckrake are often indispensable to the well-being of society, but only if they know when to stop raking the muck.
> President Theodore Roosevelt, April 14, 1906

The term "**Muckrakers**" was first used by President Theodore Roosevelt in referring to a character in John Bunyan's *Pilgrim's Progress* who rejected a crown for a muckrake (a rake used to gather dung into a pile). The term was applied to writers who investigated and attacked social, political, and economic wrongs. Books and magazine articles in *McClure's, Collier's,* and *Hampton's* exposed the worst abuses of the period and stirred public outcry against them.

The Authors

Magazine articles by **Ida Tarbell** exposed the abuses of the Standard Oil Company. **Lincoln Steffens** published stories of corruption in major American cities. These sensational accounts stirred popular concern. Novelists of the late 19th and early 20th centuries who spoke for socialism and criticized the capitalist system are among the most famous American literary figures. They include **Upton Sinclair, Jack London, Theodore Dreiser**, and **Frank Norris**. Sinclair's novel ***The Jungle*** (1906) brought the conditions in the meat-packing plants of Chicago to the attention of the nation and stimulated demand for laws regulating the meat industry. Jack London, a member of the Socialist Party, wrote *The Iron Heel* (1906), warning of a Fascist America and idealizing a Socialist brotherhood of man. Theodore Dreiser's *The Financier* (1912) and *The Titan* (1914) exposed the ruthlessness of promoters and profiteers. Frank Norris's ***The Octopus*** (1901) showed the control of the railroads and corrupt politicians over California wheat-ranchers.

Legislation

The power to legislate for the health, safety, and welfare of the community belongs principally to the states, but during the early 20th century, Congress began to use its commerce and taxing powers to legislate for the "general welfare." Usually, such legislation followed revelations of corruption and immorality by muckraking publications. The **Pure Food and Drug Act** of 1906 barred adulterated and misbranded foods from interstate commerce. The **Meat Inspection Act** of the same year, passed shortly after the publication of Upton Sinclair's novel *The Jungle,* provided for local inspection services by the Department of Agriculture and banned from interstate commerce uninspected and rejected meat. The **Mann-Elkins Act** of 1910 extended the jurisdiction of the Interstate Commerce Commission over telephone and telegraph lines. The **Keating-Owen Act** of 1916 barred from interstate commerce any products made in factories, canneries, or similar workshops that employed children under fourteen. In *United States* v. *Darby* (1941), the Supreme Court ruled that goods manufactured in violation of the **Fair Labor Standards Act** of 1938 could be barred from interstate commerce.

Contemporary "Muckraking"

Literature designed to make the public aware of problems and abuses in America did not end with the Progressive Era. Societal problems were the subject of many of **John Steinbeck's** novels during the Depression years. The Supreme Court ruled *(New York Times Co.* v. *United States,* 1971) that *The New York Times* could print the "**Pentagon Papers**," a secret document that revealed behind-the-scenes decision making during the Vietnam War. The case provided a classic national security versus First Amendment confrontation, in which the Court ruled that

> paramount among the responsibilities of a free press is the duty to prevent any part of the government from deceiving the people and sending them off to distant lands to die of foreign fevers and foreign shot and shell.
>
> *New York Times* v. *U.S.* (1971)

Finally, investigative reporting by two writers on the *Washington Post* newspaper helped to uncover the **Watergate** scandal during the early 1970s and eventually led to the resignation of President **Richard Nixon**.

Other Areas of Concern

Problems of Poverty

As the imbalance in the distribution of wealth increased during the second half of the 19th century, poverty among the working class grew. The acute housing problems of the poor were described by reformer **Jacob Riis** in *How the Other Half Lives*. He advocated providing housing for low-income families in model tenements. Help for the urban poor also came from individuals like **Jane Addams**, who wanted to improve the lives of working class people by enabling them to obtain an education, better jobs, and better housing. **Hull House**, a settlement house established in Chicago in 1889 by Addams, served the needs of the city's urban poor.

Women's Rights and Efforts for Peace

The movement for women's suffrage rights, which continued throughout the 19th century, culminated in the adoption of the **Nineteenth Amendment** in 1920. The **Fifteenth Amendment** had given the right to vote to black men, but it had ignored women. Prominent women's leaders, such as **Elizabeth Cady Stanton** and **Susan B. Anthony**, led the movements to gain the vote and organized the **National American Woman Suffrage Association**.

The **birth control** movement was led by **Margaret Sanger**, who distributed information about contraceptives in the hopes of preventing unwanted pregnancies among poor women. Although most states still prohibited the sale of contraceptives in 1921, the formation of the American Birth Control League by Sanger enlisted physicians and social workers in the effort to convince the courts to allow the distribution of birth control information.

As the United States approached entry into World War I, **peace movements** developed in the nation. "Peace is a woman's job," Representative Jeannette Rankin believed, "because men have a natural fear of being classed as cowards if they oppose war." Representative Rankin was the first woman ever to be elected to Congress and she voted against the declaration of war in World War I and World War II.

The Black Movement

The **National Association for the Advancement of Colored People**, originally a predominantly white organization, was formed to battle discrimination by **W. E. B. Du Bois** and his supporters in 1909. The 1920s saw the emergence of a revised version of the **Ku Klux Klan**, determined to reach its goal of "native, white, Protestant supremacy." Using violence and political pressure, the Klan terrorized black Americans as well as Catholics, Jews, and immigrants. One response to discrimination was the formation of movements that advocated black independence, such as the Universal Negro Improvement

Association (1914) headed by **Marcus Garvey**. Garvey's movement believed that blacks should separate themselves from the corrupt white society. Advocating the "uniting of all the Negro peoples of the world into one great body to establish a country and government absolutely their own," Garvey led a "**Back to Africa**" movement.

The Temperance Movement

During the Progressive Era the temperance movement made great gains and was supported by several organizations. The **Women's Christian Temperance Union** (1876), with **Frances E. Willard** as its leading spirit, preached that alcohol was the primary factor in crime, poverty, and vice. The Anti-Saloon League carried on a campaign against the evils of alcoholic beverages and saloons. Both organizations worked to outlaw the manufacture and sale of alcoholic beverages. However, they did not approve the methods of **Carrie Nation**, who invaded saloons with her hatchet and smashed bottles and bars. The temperance movement was assisted by the coming of World War I. The **Eighteenth Amendment** was passed in part to conserve grain that was to be used for feeding the armed forces and Europe instead of for alcohol production. It was ratified in 1919; in 1920 **Prohibition** began.

Anti-Defamation League (1913)

Pogroms in Russia brought attention to the plight of **Jewish people** abroad and encouraged the formation of the American Jewish Committee. The Committee pledged itself to protect the civil rights of all Jews throughout the world. In 1913 Jews organized the **B'nai B'rith Anti-Defamation League**, dedicated to combating prejudice in the United States.

1. The Nineteenth Amendment to the U.S. Constitution provided for
   A. the direct election of senators.
   B. voting rights for women.
   C. a national income tax.
   D. the end of slavery.

2. The Progressive Movement, on the whole, did not focus attention on
   A. impure food and harmful medicines.
   B. poor living conditions in urban areas.
   C. the unhealthy results of industrialization.
   D. the plight of African Americans.

3. Of the following pairs, the one that is not correctly matched is
   A. John Steinbeck—*Grapes of Wrath*.
   B. Upton Sinclair—*The Jungle*.
   C. Frank Norris—*Uncle Tom's Cabin*.
   D. Jack London—*The Iron Heel*.

4. Jane Addams worked to help people in city slums by establishing
   A. the American Red Cross.
   B. the National Association for the Advancement of Colored People.
   C. the Salvation Army.
   D. Hull House.

5. The National Association for the Advancement of Colored People
   A. subscribed to the beliefs of Marcus Garvey.
   B. intended to fight discrimination through legal action.
   C. was founded by William Lloyd Garrison.
   D. attracted most of its members from the African American working class.

6. The reform movement which resulted in having a 19th century amendment added to the Constitution was the
   A. women's suffrage movement.
   B. temperance movement.
   C. advocates of better housing conditions.
   D. abolition movement.

PROGRESSIVISM AND GOVERNMENT ACTION

> We demand that big business give the people a square deal; in return
> we must insist that when anyone engaged in big business honestly
> endeavors to do right he shall himself be given a square deal.
>
> President Theodore Roosevelt, *Autobiography* (1913)

Emerging Progressive Movement: Political Reform

The **Progressive Era**, which began about 1900 and came to an end with
the outbreak of World War I, was primarily a response to the industrial and
urban growth of the 1800s. In the late 1800s, labor unions, churches, Populists,
publicists, and utopian novelists called attention to the worst abuses of the
industrial age. Yet, by the turn of the century, class division was even more
obvious, the abuses of business had increased, and the poverty and squalor of
the cities had deepened.

Municipal Reform

A major aim or objective of the Progressive reform movement within the cities was to "clean up" municipal governments. The attack on city "bosses" and
"machines" was led by civic-minded mayors and groups determined to abolish corruption. The concepts of the city manager (a specially trained official in
city government), civil service reform, supervision of public expenditures, and
city commissions (a commission of experts to assist city government) were
introduced. As cities rapidly expanded, pressure was put upon city governments to provide and maintain public utilities. In some of the more progressive
municipalities, there were movements for public ownership of utilities such as
gas, electric, telephone, and transportation systems. Settlement houses, similar
to **Jane Addams' Hull House**, were established in a number of cities. They
provided education, health care, child care, cultural events, and recreation.

State Reform

Reformers began to look to the state governments and the federal government for progressive legislation to address the nation's problems. Governors
became important figures in state reform, including **Woodrow Wilson** of New
Jersey (administrative reforms), **Theodore Roosevelt** of New York (improvement of urban tenements and tax revision), and perhaps most outstanding,
Robert M. La Follette of Wisconsin. La Follette, organizer of the **Progressive American League** in 1911, who was later elected to the Senate and was
instrumental in guiding progressive reform at the national level. With the help
of other reformers, he supported labor legislation, federal aid to farmers, and
the continued government operation of federally owned utilities such as the
hydroelectric dam at **Muscle Shoals**, Alabama.

Many cities and states adopted measures that provided for increased popular control of government. Among these were the **referendum**, which provided for a popular vote on laws rather than, or in addition to, that of the legislatures, **recall**, or popular removal of government officials, and **initiative**, the popular introduction of legislation. **Ballot reform** included the use of the secret ballot. The **Seventeenth Amendment** (1913) eventually provided for the direct election of senators, the **Nineteenth Amendment** (1920) gave the franchise to women, and **direct primaries** allowed more widespread participation in the selection of candidates by registered voters.

Theodore Roosevelt and the Square Deal

Progressivism emerged in full force during the presidency of Theodore Roosevelt between 1901 and 1909. In addition to calling for greater government intervention to protect the welfare of the American people from big business and the social evils of rapid industrialization, the Progressive Movement was marked by a change in the perception of executive leadership. Now reformers looked to the President to be both politically powerful and to demonstrate legislative leadership, while resisting the pressures from powerful business interests.

President **William McKinley** was assassinated in 1901 shortly after his inauguration for his second term. McKinley's successor, Vice President **Theodore Roosevelt**, finished out the term and was re-elected in 1904. Roosevelt's program of domestic reform was called the "**Square Deal**," a term developed from his promise to bring a "square deal" and "opportunity" to every citizen.

The Stewardship Theory of Theodore Roosevelt

Roosevelt looked upon the presidency as a "**stewardship**" in whose care the common welfare and destiny of the American people were entrusted. In this way, he revived the **Hamiltonian** doctrine that the President was not limited in authority by the exact functions listed in Article II. In other words, the President was restricted only by what the Constitution or acts of Congress specifically said he could not do. Roosevelt's use of the office of the President has come to be known as the "**bully pulpit**."

PROGRESSIVE REFORMS

Reform Area	Goals	Accomplishments	Key People
Extension of Democracy	Women's Suffrage Representative government	1895—16 States 1920—19th Amendment 1913—Direct Election of Senators Amendment Referendum, Recall, and Initiative	Susan B. Anthony Robert M. La Follette
Honesty and Efficiency in Government	Appoint people to government based on merit	Pendelton Act (1883) Civil Service Commission (1883) City Manager System	Chester Arthur
Regulation of the Economy—Business	End child labor End abuses of monopolies Regulation of business	Pure Food and Drug Act (1906) Meat Inspection Act (1906) Clayton Antitrust Act (1914) Keating-Owen Act (1916) Fair Labor Standards Act (1938)	Theodore Roosevelt Ida Tarbell Upton Sinclair Frank Norris Woodrow Wilson
Regulation of the Economy—Transportation/ Communication	Reduce discriminatory practices of natural monopolies	Mann-Elkins Act (1910) Hepburn Act (1906) *Northern Securities Co. v. United States* (1904)	Theodore Roosevelt
Social Issues	Municipal reform Equitable distribution of wealth Race relations Prohibition Effective national monetary system	Hull House (1889) Graduated Income Tax (1913) NAACP (1909) Women's Christian Temperance Union National Monetary Commission (1908)	Henry George Francis E. Willard Louis Brandeis Jane Addams Jacob Riis
Conservation	Preservation of natural resources	Desert Land Act (1877) Forest Reserve Act (1891) Newlands Reclamation Act (1902)	Theodore Roosevelt John Muir Gifford Pinchot

Theodore Roosevelt called the office of President a "bully pulpit."

Square Deal Legislation

The legislation passed during Roosevelt's administrations reflected his belief that the modern industrial era demanded government that was powerful enough to guide national affairs. Although Roosevelt has been termed a "**trust buster**," his goal actually was government regulation of uncontrolled competition in order to eliminate unfair practices of bad trusts. Congressional legislation between 1901 and 1909 included (1) establishment of the **Department of Labor and Commerce** (1903) to regulate business and enforce economic regulations; (2) the **Elkins Act** (1903), which added strength to the Interstate Commerce Act by making the granting or acceptance of secret rebates illegal; (3) the **Hepburn Act** (1906), which increased the power of the Interstate Commerce Commission by giving it the power to reduce discriminatory rates of railroads and placing the burden on the railroad to show that the rates were not unreasonable, and forbidding most free passes; and (4) the **Pure Food and Drug Act** and **Meat Inspection Act** (1906), which responded to the efforts of "muckrakers," including Upton Sinclair's *The Jungle,* by giving the government greater power in the protection of the public from inferior and unhealthy foods and drugs.

President **Taft**, who succeeded Roosevelt, was as sympathetic to reform as Roosevelt was. He prosecuted twice as many trust cases in four years as Roosevelt had in eight years.

The Supreme Court and "Trust-Busting"

The regulation of trusts had been inefficient under the administrations of Grover Cleveland and William McKinley. Under Roosevelt and Taft many trusts were broken up. The Roosevelt administration initiated several federal government suits and won notable victories in two cases, *Northern Securities Co.* v. *United States* (1904) and *Swift and Co.* v. *United States* (1905). In *Northern Securities* the United States government brought a suit to break up the Northern Securities Company, a railroad holding company organized by James J. Hill and E. H. Harriman. The Supreme Court held that the company was an "**unlawful combination**" within the meaning of the Sherman Act. In the *Swift* case the Supreme Court affirmed the power of Congress to punish conspiracies in "**restraint of trade**." The Court found that livestock and packing houses were "commerce among the states" and therefore within the Article I, Section 8 powers of Congress.

In *Standard Oil Co.* v. *United States* (1911), the Supreme Court announced its "rule of reason" to be applied to the Sherman Antitrust Act. Ordering the dissolution of the Standard Oil Company of New Jersey, the Court held that the Sherman Act forbade only "**unreasonable combinations**" or "contracts" in restraint of trade. "Reasonable" monopolies, it held, were legal, and size alone was not to be a determinant.

Presidential Mediation

Roosevelt led the way for government's role as an **arbiter** (judge or umpire) in labor disputes affecting the **public interest**. In May 1902 the **United Mine Workers** walked out of the anthracite coal fields of Pennsylvania demanding a shorter work day, better wages, and union recognition. Forcing both sides to accept arbitration, Roosevelt appointed an arbitration board, which decided in favor of a 10 percent increase in wages and a nine-hour work day, but also declared that the owners did not have to recognize the union.

Conservation

President Roosevelt, a lover of the outdoors, was a determined **conservationist**. Roosevelt was effective in pressuring both Congress and the states to pass conservation measures. Roosevelt added nearly 150 million acres to the national forests and was instrumental in protecting natural resources from private exploitation.

The Newlands Reclamation Act (1902) authorized, for irrigation purposes, the use of money obtained from land sales in the arid Western states. In 1908 the President called 44 governors and 500 natural resource experts to a National Conservation Congress, to plan nationwide resource management. Yet, in spite of his efforts, timber and mining companies continued to destroy the environment.

New York State's concern for its environment began in 1885 with the passage of the New York State Forest Preserve Act providing for the protection of much of the Adirondacks and the Catskills. The 1895 **New York State Constitution** provided that the forest preserves would be kept forever wild and not wastefully developed.

The Supreme Court and Labor

Progressive thought entered the legal field and did battle with traditional laissez-faire views. The Supreme Court interpreted the Fourteenth Amendment as protecting the sanctity and freedom of contract at the expense of reforms for workers. In *Lochner* v. *New York* (1905) the Court ruled that a New York law that limited working hours was an infringement upon the **contract rights** between "the master and his employees" and therefore unconstitutional. The Court continued the *Lochner* reasoning in *Adair* v. *United States* (1908) with the Erdman Act of 1898, which made it a crime for an interstate carrier to dismiss an employee for membership in a labor union, an unconstitutional interference with the employer's and employee's liberty of contract.

However, in *Muller* v. *Oregon* (1908) the Supreme Court modified its *Lochner* v. *New York* decision by upholding an Oregon statute that limited the length of the work day for women to ten hours. The Court's conclusion that women were physically inferior and dependent upon men would later work against the continuing equal rights struggle of women.

Woodrow Wilson and the New Freedom

Progressivism was surging as the presidential election of 1912 approached. The victor, Democrat **Woodrow Wilson**, expressed his philosophy of Progressive government when he declared, "Freedom today is something more than being let alone. Without the watchful, resolute interference of the government, there can be no fair play between individuals and such powerful institutions as the trusts."

Election of 1912

The Republican Party found itself split between the conservative followers of incumbent **William Howard Taft** and the Progressives, who themselves were split between **Theodore Roosevelt** and Senator **Robert M. La Follette** of Wisconsin. The Republican convention nominated Taft. Roosevelt and his followers formed the **Progressive Party**, which nominated Roosevelt as the "**Bull Moose**" candidate on a platform embodying **New Nationalism**, the balancing of big business and big government through government's supervision of economic enterprise for the general welfare. The Socialist Party nominated **Eugene V. Debs** as their candidate.

The Democrats, realizing the advantages of a race against the divided Republicans, nominated the Progressive governor of New Jersey, **Woodrow Wilson**. The Democrats' platform included the enforcement of the Sherman Act, better banking and currency laws, and tariff reform. The electoral outcome of the race was 435 votes for Wilson, 88 for Roosevelt, and 8 for Taft. The Socialist Party received its greatest support in the election of 1912 with nearly a million popular votes cast for Debs. The Progressive measures supported by Wilson, Roosevelt, and Debs received the support of three-fourths of the voters, demonstrating the strong national support for Progressivism.

The Underwood Tariff and the Graduated Income Tax

Upon entering office, President Wilson prepared for his attack on what he called the "**triple wall of privilege**": the tariff, the trusts, and the system of banking and currency.

Wilson saw the high rates of 40.8 percent established by the Payne-Aldrich Tariff (1909) as protecting the "special interests" of business while preventing consumers from benefiting from lower prices resulting from international competition. After Wilson's personal delivery of his message to Congress, a practice revived from the times of Washington and Adams, and the revelation of the pressures used by business lobbyists in Washington, the Underwood Tariff was finally approved in 1913. It lowered rates to 27 percent, the first significant tariff reduction since the Civil War.

Reformers during the administrations of Roosevelt and Taft introduced **income tax** legislation, which had been held unconstitutional by the Supreme Court in 1895 (*Pollock* v. *Farmer's Loan and Trust Company, 1895*). As a result, the **Sixteenth Amendment** was proposed and sent to the states for ratification in 1909 and, to the surprise of many, was passed and became part of the Constitution in 1913. Within a short time, the income tax became the principal source of federal revenue. The federal income tax is an example of a **progressive**, or graduated, tax. A person earning a greater income pays taxes at a higher rate. A **regressive** tax, such as a sales tax, is designed so that all people pay the same tax rate, no matter what their income.

Clayton Antitrust Act and the Federal Trade Commission

Wilson's battles against the trusts gained their greatest victories with the passage of the **Federal Trade Commission Act** and the **Clayton Antitrust Act**. Wilson's special message to Congress during January 1914 asking for measures to break up monopolies was answered with the creation of the Federal Trade Commission. It was empowered to issue "**cease and desist**" orders to any business found guilty of unfair methods of competition.

The Clayton Antitrust Act, also passed by Congress in 1914, provided the following: (1) it expanded the definition of "unfair methods of competition" to include interlocking directorates, price discrimination, and purchase of a corporation's stock by a competing corporation; (2) it made officers of corporations liable for illegal acts of the corporation; and (3) it exempted labor unions and agricultural associations from antitrust acts and restricted the use of the labor injunction.

The Federal Reserve System

The third part of the "triple wall of privilege" identified by Wilson was the nation's banking and currency system. A major problem with the existing system, which was a product of the Civil War National Banking Act, was the inability of the amount of currency in circulation to adjust to the needs of the economy. Reform was needed.

The **Federal Reserve Act** was passed in 1913 and it included (1) the division of the country into twelve districts, each having a Federal Reserve bank; (2) the use of the Federal Reserve banks as "bankers' banks" for deposits of cash reserves of national banks and of state banks who wished to join the system; (3) the issuance of Federal Reserve notes (nation's paper currency); (4) the provision for loans from the Federal Reserve banks to member banks in times of need (adding to currency "flexibility"); and (5) the establishment of a Federal Reserve Board.

Direct Election of Senators

The Constitution provided that the state legislatures would elect senators (Article I, Section 3). The Seventeenth Amendment (1913) provided for the direct election of senators by popular vote.

Women's Suffrage Amendment

The women's suffrage movement was part of the reform movement to improve the legal and social status of women in the second half of the 19th century. The franchise was granted to women by the Wyoming Territory in 1869, the state of Wyoming in 1890, and the state of Colorado in 1897. By 1914 twelve states, all of them Western, had granted women the right to vote. The increased role of women in business and industry during World War I finally led Congress to approve the women's suffrage amendment and to send it to the states for ratification. The Nineteenth Amendment was added to the Constitution in 1920.

World War I: Effect on Domestic Reform

The Progressive Era ended when the United States entered World War I. American reform efforts now turned to a "crusading zeal" to make the world "safe for democracy." The war left Americans disillusioned, and after the war they reverted to **conservatism** and **nationalism**, typical of postwar periods.

Exercise Set 3.2

1. Which of the following was not true of the Progressives?
   A. They believed that the age of laissez-faire should come to an end.
   B. Among their members were representatives of the growing middle class.
   C. They did not like the boss-ridden, business-dominated political parties of the day.
   D. They did not believe in a strong, responsible government.

2. Which of the following reforms was not achieved during the Progressive Era, 1901–1914?
   A. Tariff reform
   B. Railroad legislation
   C. Banking reform
   D. A national minimum wage law

3. The public's response to Upton Sinclair's novel *The Jungle* helped bring about
   A. passage of the Clayton Antitrust Act.
   B. the Pure Food and Drug Act.
   C. adoption of the Nineteenth Amendment.
   D. America's entry into World War I.

4. Which of the following functions of the federal government came later than the other three?
   A. Guaranteeing the welfare of the poor and unemployed
   B. The regulation of trusts
   C. Promoting industrial growth by means of a protective tariff
   D. Regulating immigration

1. The name "Boss" Tweed is most closely associated with
   A. civil service reform.
   B. referendum and recall.
   C. increase in city "bossism" politics.
   D. fair and open elections.

2. All of the following were major reforms of President Wilson's "New Freedom" program except
   A. tariff reform.
   B. antitrust legislation.
   C. social security.
   D. banking and currency reforms.

3. A Progressive measure used at the state and local level that permits voters to introduce legislation is referred to as
   A. initiative.
   B. recall.
   C. impeachment.
   D. referendum.

4. The main objective of the Muckrakers was to
   A. establish communism.
   B. cleanse capitalist society.
   C. overthrow the existing form of government in the United States.
   D. end government censorship of American literature.

5. The Federal Trade Commission Act of 1914
   A. made all business combinations that resembled trusts illegal.
   B. established the nation's first income tax.
   C. established an investigatory board with the power to issue "cease and desist" orders.
   D. replaced the Clayton Antitrust Act.

Unit Three

THE PROGRESSIVE MOVEMENT

Base your answer to question 6 on the cartoon below and on your knowledge of social studies.

IF CAPITAL AND LABOR DON'T PULL TOGETHER

Source: John McCutcheon, *Chicago Tribune*, 1919 (adapted)

6. Which statement most accurately describes the main argument made in this 1919 cartoon?
   A. Labor and management have the same economic goals.
   B. The federal government should take ownership of major industries.
   C. Organized workers are more productive than nonunion workers.
   D. Disputes between labor and the leaders of business are hurting the economy.

THEMATIC ESSAY

Directions: Write a well-organized essay that includes an introduction, several paragraphs addressing the task below, and a conclusion.

Theme: Government (Congressional Legislation)

> Throughout United States history, Congress has passed legislation to address important political, social, or economic issues. These laws have often had a significant impact on American society.

Task:

> Select *two* laws passed by the United States Congress and for *each*
>
> • Discuss the historical circumstances that led to the passage of the law.
> • Discuss the impacts of the law on American society.

You may use any federal law that was intended to address an important issue from your study of United States history. Some suggestions you might wish to consider include:

Embargo Act (1807)
Indian Removal Act (1830)
Kansas-Nebraska Act (1854)
Interstate Commerce Act (1887)
Pure Food and Drug Act (1906)
Social Security Act (1935)
GI Bill/Servicemen's Readjustment Act (1944)
Americans with Disabilities Act (1990)

You are *not* limited to these suggestions.

You may *not* discuss constitutional amendments.

DOCUMENT-BASED QUESTION

The following questions (Part A and Part B) are based on the accompanying documents (1–7). Some of these documents have been edited for the purpose of this exercise. The question is designed to test your ability to work with historical documents and to demonstrate your knowledge of the subject matter being presented. As you analyze the documents, take into account both the source of the document and the author's point of view.

Historical Context:

> Although the United States entered the 20th century with the vast material strength that placed it among the great powers of the world, the rich human values of the past were being lost. The Progressive Period was a time for social justice to catch up with industrial capitalism.

Task:

> Using information from the documents and your knowledge of United States history, answer the questions that follow each document in Part A. Your answers to the questions will help you write the Part B essay, in which you will be asked:
>
> In the view of the Progressives, what was wrong with American society? What solutions did the Progressives support to correct these wrongs?

Part A
Short-Answer Questions

The documents below relate to issues concerning the Progressive Period. Examine each document carefully and then answer the questions that follow.

Meat scraps were also found being shoveled into receptacles from dirty floors, where they were left to lie until again shoveled into barrels or into machines for chopping. These floors, it must be noted, were in most cases damp and soggy, in dark, ill-ventilated rooms, and the employees in utter ignorance of cleanliness or danger to health expectorated at will upon them. In a word, we saw meat shoveled from filthy wooden floors, piled on tables rarely washed, pushed from room to room in rotten box carts, in all of which processes it was in the way of gathering dirt, splinters, floor filth, and the expectoration of tuberculosis and other diseased workers. . . . Where comment was made to floor superintendents about these matters, it was always the reply that this meat would afterwards be cooked, and that this sterilization would prevent any danger from its use. . . . In one well-known establishment we came upon fresh meat being shoveled into barrels, and a regular proportion being added of stale scraps that had lain on a dirty floor in the corner of a room for some days previous.

—Upton Sinclair, *The Jungle* (1902)

1. State one reason that reformers wanted to enact regulations of the meatpacking industry.

_____

_____

_____

_____

DOCUMENT 2

> I stand for a square deal. But when I say that I am for the square deal, I mean not merely that I stand for fair play under the present rules of the game, but that I stand for having those rules changed so as to work for a more substantial equality of opportunity and of reward for equally good service . . . now the great special interests too often control and corrupt the men and methods of government for their own profit.

—Theodore Roosevelt, *New Nationalism* (1910)

2. What are the "special interests" referred to by Presidential candidate Theodore Roosevelt?

_____

_____

_____

_____

DOCUMENT 3

> The Senate of the United States shall be composed of two Senators from each State, elected by the people hereof, for six years; and each Senator shall have one vote. The electors in each State shall have the qualifications requisite for electors of [voters for] the most numerous branch of the State legislatures.

—Seventeenth Amendment (1913)

3. Describe how the Seventeenth Amendment could be considered a "progressive amendment."

_____

_____

_____

Sadie is an intelligent, neat, clean girl, who has worked from the time she got her working papers in embroidery factories. She was a stamper and for several years before she was poisoned, earned $10 a week. In her work she was accustomed to use a white powder (chalk or talcum was usual) which was brushed over the perforated designs and thus transferred to the cloth. The design was easily brushed off when made of chalk or of talcum, if the embroiderers were not careful. Her last employer therefore commenced using white lead powder, mixed with rosin, which cheapened the work as the powder could not be rubbed off and necessitate restamping. . . . None of the girls knew of the change in powder, nor of the danger in its use. The workroom was crowded and hot, the stampers' tables were farthest from the windows and the constant use of the powder caused them to breathe it continually and their hands were always covered with it. . . . Sadie was sick in the hospital for six months (losing $10 per week). She said her employer bought off several of her witnesses, but before the case came to trial two years later several of them also became ill and consequently decided to testify for her. The employer appealed to the girl's feelings and induced her, on the day of the trial, to accept $150. He said that he had had business reverses and consequently would be unable to pay in case she won.

—Preliminary Report of the New York State Factory
Investigating Commission (Albany, N.Y.:
The Argus Company, 1912), vol. 1, pp. 488–489

4. Who would use the account provided in the New York State Factory Investigating Commission to promote their interests—labor or management? Why?

_____

_____

_____

_____

DOCUMENT 5

As to the forest reserves, their creation has damaged just one class, that is, the great lumber barons: the managers and owners of those lumber companies which by illegal, fraudulent, or unfair methods have desired to get possession of the valuable timber of the public domain, to skin the land, and to abandon it when impoverished well-nigh to the point of worthlessness.

There are some small men who have wanted to get hold of this lumber land for improper purposes, but they are not powerful or influential, and though they have sometimes been put forward to cause an agitation, the real beneficiaries of the destruction of the forest reserves would be the great lumber companies, which would speedily monopolize them.

If it had not been for the creation of the present system of forest reserves, practically every acre of timberland in the West would now be controlled or be on the point of being controlled by one huge lumber trust. The object of the beneficiaries of this trust would be to exhaust the resources of the country for their own immediate pecuniary benefit, and then when they had rendered it well-nigh worthless to turn it contemptuously over to settlers, who would find too late that those responsible for such conditions had betrayed them and had been false to the public.

—President Theodore Roosevelt Letter (1907)

5. President Theodore Roosevelt has been credited with having been a great conservationist. How does the 1907 letter support this reputation?

_____

_____

_____

_____

6. According to President Roosevelt, what are the objectives of the lumber trusts?

_____

_____

_____

_____

DOCUMENT 6

The right of citizens of the United States to vote shall not be denied or abridged by the United States or by any State on account of sex. Congress shall have power to enforce this article by appropriate legislation.

—Nineteenth Amendment (1920)

7. How did the Nineteenth Amendment expand social justice in the early part of the 20th century?

_____

_____

_____

_____

DOCUMENT 7

Triangle Shirtwaist Factory Fire, "Devil Rising."

8. What message is the cartoon conveying regarding the 1911 Triangle Shirtwaist Factory Fire?

_____

_____

_____

_____

Part B
Essay

Your essay should be well organized with an introductory paragraph that states your position on the question. Develop your position in the next paragraphs and then write a conclusion. In your essay, include specific historical details and refer to the specific documents you analyzed in Part A. You may include additional information from your knowledge of social studies.

Historical Context:

Although the United States entered the 20th century with the vast material strength that placed it among the great powers of the world, the rich human values of the past were being lost. The Progressive Period was a time for social justice to catch up with industrial capitalism.

Task:

In the view of Progressives, what was wrong with American society? What solutions did they put forth to correct those wrongs?

Guidelines:

In your essay, be sure to
• Develop all aspects of the task.
• Incorporate information from *at least five* documents.
• Incorporate relevant outside information.
• Support the theme with many relevant facts, examples, and details.
• Use a logical and clear plan of organization, including an introduction and a conclusion that are beyond a restatement of the theme.

THE RISE OF AMERICAN POWER

THE INDUSTRIAL-COLONIAL CONNECTION

Economic Imperialism

In the 1870s and after, several developments combined to shift America's attention across the oceans. The end of the frontier, announced officially in the census report of 1890, an increase in American agricultural and industrial output, and fluctuations in the American economy fostered the belief that the fixture of the country's growth and prosperity lay outside its own continental borders.

United States Industrial Productivity

By the end of the 19th century, factories and farms in the United States produced more goods than the domestic market could consume. As American industry continued to grow, industrialists looked abroad for new sources of raw materials, additional markets for American goods, and places to invest surplus capital. Both farmers and industrialists were eager to enter new overseas markets, and the growing volume of exports began to change American trade relations. In 1870 United States exports totaled $451 million; in 1880, $853 million; and by 1900, $1.5 billion. In 1898 the United States exported more than it imported, a status known as a favorable balance of trade, beginning a trend that lasted through the 1960s.

Theories of Expansionism

As overseas trade expansion continued to receive more attention, a school of thought developed that held that the only way to save and promote nationalism was through overseas territorial expansion.

President Lincoln's Secretary of State, **William Seward**, had envisioned an American empire that included Canada, Cuba, Central America, Hawaii, Iceland, and Greenland. Although his ambitious designs resulted only in the 1867 purchase from Russia of **Alaska** for $7.2 million, it was an important step toward American territorial expansion. Josiah Strong, a Congregational minister and strong advocate of expansionism, wrote a popular book, *Our Country: Its Possible Future and Its Present Crisis* (1885), that called for overseas missionary work to "civilize the world under the Anglo-Saxon races." A growing popular belief was that Americans, the bearers of civil liberty and Christianity, were members of a God-favored race destined to lead the world.

"As America goes, so goes the world," Strong claimed. Others in America who supported expansion drew on **Charles Darwin's** theories of evolution, applying them to human and social development and calling for the triumph of the fit and the elimination or subjugation of the unfit.

Naval Power

The importance of naval power became increasingly obvious toward the end of the 19th century. The American fleet had fallen into disrepair and by 1880 consisted of only 48 ships that were capable of even firing a gun. Big-navy proponents pointed to the growing fleets of Great Britain, France, and Germany, arguing that the United States needed a stronger fleet to protect its growing overseas interests, and Congress began to authorize new naval construction. One of the main forces behind naval expansion was Captain **Alfred T. Mahan**. After graduating from the Naval Academy in 1859, he devoted a lifetime to studying the influence of sea power in history and for over two decades he headed the Newport Naval War College.

Technological Advances

Technology continued to improve machinery, means of transportation, and methods of communication, as the "need" for expansionism grew. Exports to other countries included the inventions of **Thomas Edison** (electronics, communications) and **Alexander Graham Bell** (communications), **George Westinghouse** (air brakes), **Cyrus McCormick** (farm machinery), and **George Eastman** (photographic equipment). Improvements in transportation and communication accelerated America's involvement in world affairs with the speed and safety provided by **steam-powered ships** and the linking of the United States with other parts of the world through **underwater cables** to transmit **telegraph** communication. Finally, technological improvements in industry increased output and hastened the need for additional foreign markets.

European Imperialism

The last third of the 19th century was characterized by a worldwide scramble for empires. Great Britain, France, and Germany had established colonial claims in Africa and now looked to Asia for further gains. As imperialist expansionism grew throughout the world, Americans considered the acquisition of colonies necessary to attain a position of power in the world.

The Tariff Controversy: Free Trade vs. Protectionism

The tariff question, which was an issue throughout American history, continued to be raised during the expansionist period at the turn of the century.

Through the mid-19th century, tariffs were continually raised to protect American manufacturing and agriculture. Those who advocated protectionism believed that a high tariff was necessary to allow continued economic growth at home. Those who claimed that tariffs were benefiting certain groups and were making prices artificially high for most consumers favored lowering the tariff rates to approach a system of free trade among nations.

The tariff question continues to be an issue today in international economics. Those who favor protectionism claim that the higher standard of living in the United States has resulted in a higher cost of production requiring protection from less expensive foreign goods. Advocates of free trade argue that the American consumer deserves a greater choice of goods at lower prices and that foreign competition would force an increase in the efficiency of American production.

Exercise Set 3.3

1. Which of the following was not a reason for United States expansion between 1880 and 1914?
   A. The desire to extend Christianity
   B. The search for overseas markets
   C. The desire to maintain a position in the international race for power
   D. The search for outlets for surplus population

2. U.S. expansion abroad following the Civil War indicated that
   A. the demand for industrial and agricultural goods within the United States exceeded industry's ability to produce.
   B. advocates of isolationism influenced national foreign policy.
   C. economic expansion, nationalism, and cultural values worked together as reasons for overseas growth.
   D. domestic growth and international growth were unrelated.

3. Before 1898, possessions of the United States beyond its immediate boundaries
   A. included Alaska.
   B. did not exist.
   C. consisted of Alaska, Canada, and Mexico.
   D. included most of Central America.

4. A high protective tariff rate on imports into the United States may reflect
   A. an isolationist view of economic matters.
   B. a desire for free trade.
   C. the need to become more involved in the international market.
   D. the desires of the average American consumer.

AN EMERGING GLOBAL INVOLVEMENT

> Recent events—the navigation of the ocean by steam, the acquisition and rapid settlement by this country of a vast territory on the Pacific—have practically brought the countries of the east in closer proximity to our own. The intercourse between them has already greatly increased and no limits can be assigned to its future extension.
>
> Instructions by Secretary of State Conrad
> to Commodore Matthew Perry, 1852

Manifest Destiny and Expansion into the Pacific

The concept of "**Manifest Destiny**" was first expressed when journalist **John O'Sullivan**, responding to the question of the annexation of Texas, stated that "the fulfillment of our manifest destiny is to overspread the continent by Providence for the free development of our yearly multiplying millions." With the additions of the **Mexican Cession** (1848), the **Oregon Country** (1846), the **Gadsden Purchase** (1853), and **Alaska** (1867), the continental boundaries of the United States were established.

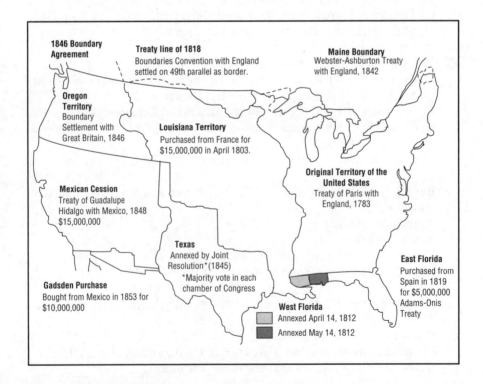

Figure 3.1 Territorial Growth of the United States (1783–1853)

The Opening of Japan

In 1852 President **Millard Fillmore** sent **Commodore Matthew Perry** to end Japan's isolation and to convince the Japanese to open certain ports to American trade. In March 1854 Perry secured a treaty of friendship with Japan that granted some trading concessions. In 1857 Townshend Harris, the first American minister to Japan, negotiated treaties expanding the diplomatic and commercial relations between the two countries.

In the face of American and European imperialism, Japan quickly transformed itself from a medieval feudal state to a modern nation. By establishing a strong central government, creating a powerful army and navy, and encouraging industrialization, Japan soon became a leading trading and manufacturing nation. Japan's need for raw materials and markets for its manufactured goods turned the nation to active imperialism by the end of the 19th century.

Increased Japanese immigration into the United States by the beginning of the 20th century brought about considerable opposition. Newspapers, state and local governments, and labor unions, among others, pressured for immigration restrictions, resulting in the **Gentlemen's Agreement** (1907), which curtailed the flow of Japanese laborers into the United States.

Early Relations with China

The United States had long been involved in trade with China, opening a small, but profitable, exchange of goods in 1784.

During the 1800s many Chinese immigrants came to the United States and settled on the West Coast. Nativists aroused widespread anti-Chinese feelings, claiming that the Chinese worked for low wages and were not able to assimilate into American society. The **Workingmen's Party**, formed in 1877, included in its platform an anti-Chinese stance, and was instrumental in the passage of state and local laws discriminating against Chinese workers and shopkeepers. In 1882 Congress, responding to nativist pressures, passed the **Chinese Exclusion Act**, prohibiting Chinese immigration for ten years. A later law passed in 1902 excluded the Chinese completely. The Supreme Court addressed the treatment of Chinese immigrants in the case of *Yick* v. *Hopkins* (1886). The court ruled that when a law was discriminatorily enforced against a specific group of people, it was a violation of the equal protection of the law clause of the Fourteenth Amendment.

Other Pacific Overtures

The Open Door Policy

Following the **Spanish-American War** (1898–1899) and the **Philippine-American War** (1898–1902), which was a revolt against American rule, the United States annexed the Philippines and increased its Pacific trade. Anticipating increased trade with China, but realizing that the United States had entered the competition late and trade was threatened by the European spheres of influence, President McKinley's Secretary of State, **John Hay**, suggested an **Open Door Policy** in 1898. He proclaimed that "we do not seek advantages in the Orient which are not common to all. Asking only the open door for ourselves, we are ready to accord the open door to others." In 1899 Hay addressed identical diplomatic notes to Germany, England, and Russia, and later to France, Japan, and Italy, asking them to join the United States in respecting the preservation of China's independence and territory. However, the Open Door Policy failed to slow the pace of imperialism in China. The **Russo-Japanese War** (1904–1905) threatened the open door in China by making Japan the dominant power in the Far East. President Theodore Roosevelt persuaded both Japan and Russia to recognize the neutrality of all Chinese territory outside of Manchuria and brought the warring sides to Portsmouth, New Hampshire (September 1905) to draft a peace treaty.

The Boxer Rebellion

As their nation continued to fall into the hands of European and Asian imperialist nations, the **Boxers**, a Chinese society encouraged by Manchu leaders, vowed to drive the "foreign devils" out of China. In June 1900 members of the Boxers attacked the foreign holdings (concessions) in Peiping and killed 300 people. A joint expeditionary force of European, Japanese, and American troops suppressed the rebellion. The Manchu Dynasty was overthrown in 1912 by the Nationalists (Kuomintang) under **Sun Yat-sen**, and China was proclaimed a republic.

The Acquisition of Hawaii

During the early 19th century, American traders, missionaries, and whalers visited the Hawaiian Islands. In 1842 the State Department announced that the Hawaiian Islands would not be open to colonization by any other nation. In 1875 the Reciprocity Treaty granted commercial favors to the islands if the Hawaiian king assured the United States that he would not allow other powers to acquire territory. A treaty in 1887 between Hawaii and the United States provided for the leasing of **Pearl Harbor** as a naval station.

As American interests, represented primarily by sugar plantations and missionaries, grew in Hawaii, the white population of the islands became increasingly influential. When **Queen Liliuokalani** attempted to nationalize the sugar plantations and drive foreign investors out, American planters revolted (January 1893). They overthrew the queen, set up a provisional government establishing the **Republic of Hawaii**, and asked for annexation by the United States. President Cleveland withdrew the annexation treaty from the Senate, and arguments concerning the fate of Hawaii continued through the 1890s. After the victory in the Spanish-American War, annexation of the Philippine

Islands, and emphasis on naval buildup heightened the expansionist excitement in the country, President McKinley obtained a joint resolution from Congress annexing the Hawaiian Islands on July 7, 1898. Hawaii remained a territory until it was admitted as the fiftieth state in 1959.

Samoa and Naval Bases

The Samoan Islands, some 3,000 miles to the southwest of Hawaii, provided strategic locations in the South Pacific shipping lanes. Like Hawaii, the islands had been visited by American sailors and missionaries since the 1830s. In 1872 a United States naval officer negotiated an agreement granting the United States use of the harbor of Pago Pago, the site of a later naval station. Great Britain and Germany also secured treaty rights in Samoa and tensions between the three powers came to a showdown in 1889 when German threats of annexation brought fleets from the three countries face-to-face in the harbor at Pago Pago. A timely hurricane wrecked the fleets and subsequently the three nations established a **tripartite protectorate** over the islands.

Hesitant Colonialism

Review of the Monroe Doctrine (1823–1898)

On December 2, 1823, in a message to Congress, President James Monroe, influenced by Secretary of State John Quincy Adams, put forward an independent American foreign policy that later became known as the **Monroe Doctrine**. Claiming that the Western Hemisphere was no longer open to European colonization, the Doctrine proved to be of great importance to future foreign policy determinations of the United States. But it was not until after the Civil War that the United States was powerful enough to enforce the Monroe Doctrine throughout the Western Hemisphere.

The expansion of American interests led to a need for overseas naval bases.

Mexico's sovereignty was threatened in 1863 when the French took advantage of internal instabilities and created a puppet state under **Archduke Maximilian**. Secretary of State **William Seward** objected to French intervention by **Napoleon III**, emperor of France. In 1865, with the end of the Civil War, American troops were sent to the Mexican border. French troops were withdrawn in 1867, and Maximilian was executed by the Mexicans. The United States saw this as a victory for the Monroe Doctrine and a sign of growing American power in the Western Hemisphere. By the end of the 19th century, the United States had become powerful enough to enforce the Monroe Doctrine.

The Spanish-American War (1898–1899)

American interests in Cuba increased with economic investments totaling over $50 million by 1895 and an annual trade worth $100 million, the strategic importance of the island (especially as plans for a canal across Central America developed), and the growing spirit of manifest destiny. When Cuban Nationalists revolted against Spain in February 1895, American sympathy for an independent Cuba was encouraged by the sensational stories printed in the "**yellow press**"—**Joseph Pulitzer's** *New York World* and **William Randolph Hearst's** *New York Journal*.

Following Cuba's refusal to accept President McKinley's plan for increased self-government under Spanish control, and the sinking of the American battleship *Maine* in Havana Harbor on February 15, 1898, popular support for war resulted in a declaration of war against Spain on April 17. At the same time, Congress adopted the **Teller Amendment**, pledging the United States to acquire no Cuban territory and to turn the island over to the Cuban people as soon as their independence was won.

Spain was defeated in Cuba after the battles of El Caney and San Juan Hill, and the fall of Santiago on July 13, 1898. A bloodless conquest of Spanish Puerto Rico was conducted by General Nelson A. Miles. While the war was being fought in Cuba, American Commodore George Dewey defeated the Spanish fleet in the Philippines and captured Manila on August 13.

Empire Building

The **Treaty of Paris** ending the Spanish-American War was signed December 10, 1898. The treaty provided that American troops would remain in Cuba until 1902 while the Cuban constitution was prepared. Included in the Cuban constitution was the **Platt Amendment**, which required that any treaties involving Cuba would have to be approved first by the United States; Cuba was to grant permission to the United States to intervene, if necessary, to preserve the island's independence, and a naval base at **Guantanamo** was to be leased to the United States. The Platt Amendment governed Cuban-American relations until 1934.

- ***Puerto Rico.*** As a result of the Treaty of Paris (1898), Puerto Rico was ceded to the United States. The **Foraker Act** of 1900 provided that the President of the United States would appoint Puerto Rico's governor and the executive council of its legislature. The **Jones Act** of 1917 granted Puerto Ricans American citizenship and the right to elect both houses of their legislature. In 1948 Puerto Ricans were granted the right to elect their own governor and in 1952 Puerto Rico voted in favor of **commonwealth** status.

- ***Guam.*** After it was annexed to the United States by Spain in 1898, the island of Guam, located east of the Philippines, was governed by the United States Navy. In 1950 Guam received limited self-government, American citizenship for its inhabitants, a governor appointed by the President of the United States, a popularly elected legislature, and a bill of rights.

- ***The Philippines.*** When the Treaty of Paris ending the war between Spain and the United States came before the Senate, the question of the annexation of the Philippines sparked heated debate. Anti-imperialists argued that annexation would violate the sacred concept of self-determination. Imperialists stressed the commercial and strategic advantages of ownership, along with the fact that Germany and Japan would most likely move into the Philippines if the United States were to pull out. The arguments of the imperialists triumphed, and the treaty was ratified on February 6, 1898, by a 57-to-27 vote.

When the Philippines did not receive independence following the Spanish-American War, a rebellion under the leadership of **Emilio Aguinaldo** broke out. This insurrection, known as the **Philippine-American War**, was a war of larger proportions than the Spanish-American War, and resulted in more American casualties. After the rebellion was suppressed, the United States imposed its regime on the Philippines. English was made the official language, public works were introduced, and sedition acts and political imprisonment

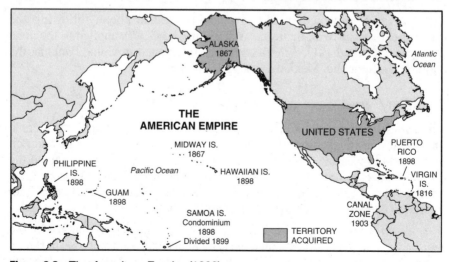

Figure 3.2 The American Empire (1903)

silenced critics. Beginning in 1907 the Filipinos elected the lower house of their legislature. The **Jones Act** of 1916 granted the citizens of the Philippines the right to elect both houses of their legislature and promised eventual independence. During the administration of Franklin Roosevelt, the **Tydings-McDuffie Act** (1934) was passed, providing for eventual independence and allowing the Filipinos to write a constitution. In 1946 the islands formally received independence and the following year granted the United States military bases within their country.

Constitutional Issues

America's new overseas territories raised a constitutional question concerning the status of undocumented immigrants and whether constitutional protections of the United States were extended to them. In the so-called "**insular cases**," particularly *Downes* v. *Bidwell* (1901), the Supreme Court ruled on the question, "Does the Constitution follow the flag?" It concluded that the Constitution protected the basic civil rights of inhabitants of colonial possessions, but did not confer citizenship or political rights on them.

Latin American Affairs

> There is a homely adage which runs, 'Speak softly and carry a big stick; you will go far.' If the American nation will speak softly and yet build and keep at a pitch of the highest training a thoroughly efficient navy, the Monroe Doctrine will go far.
>
> President Theodore Roosevelt, September 2, 1901

West Indies Protectorates

As American influence spread throughout the Caribbean following the Spanish-American War, the term "**American Lake**" was applied to the area. Between 1900 and 1917, American troops intervened in Cuba, Panama, the Dominican Republic, Mexico, Nicaragua, and Haiti.

Panama Canal

Following the acquisition of Oregon and California, the United States became interested in a canal across the isthmus (a narrow strip of land with water on both sides) in Central America. A treaty with Colombia in 1846 granted the United States the right to build either a canal or railroad across Panama (part of Colombia until 1903), and in 1850 the United States and Great Britain agreed to exercise joint control over a future canal.

• *Acquisition and Construction.* America's new possessions in the Caribbean and Pacific underscored the need for a means of faster transportation across Central America. Remembering the seventy-one days required for the battleship *Oregon* to sail from San Francisco around Cape Horn to its battle station in the Pacific at the outset of the Spanish-American War, President Roosevelt pushed for the construction of a canal. The **Hay-Pauncefote Treaty** (1901) with Great Britain gave the United States sole control over a future canal in return for the guarantee that the canal would be open equally to all nations. Colombia, seeking more money, rejected the **Hay-Herran Treaty** (1903), which was to give the United States a ninety-nine-year lease on a canal zone in the Colombian province of Panama. Frustrated by Colombia's lack of cooperation, President Roosevelt hinted at a Panamanian revolt and shortly thereafter (November 1903), Panamanians rose in revolt against Colombia for independence. Panama's independence was recognized immediately by the United States.

The **Hay-Bunau-Varilla Treaty** (1903) with Panama granted the United States perpetual control of a canal zone ten miles wide across the isthmus of Panama in return for a lump sum payment and an annual fee. On August 15, 1914, the first ocean steamer sailed through the completed canal, which had cost $275 million to build.

• *Current Treaty.* During the 1960s and 1970s Panama demonstrated resentment over the presence of the United States and its sole control over the canal. In January 1964 Panama broke off diplomatic relations with the United States resulting in negotiations over the treaty between the two countries. President Lyndon Johnson announced in December 1964 that he would propose a renegotiation of the 1903 treaty. Although a new treaty granting Panama greater control over the canal was concluded, increased tensions between the countries prevented its ratification. In August 1977 the United States and Panama ended years of negotiations when President Carter and General Torrijos Herrara signed two treaties providing for the return of the Panama Canal Zone to Panama in the year 2000. The treaties were ratified by the Senate in 1978 and the return took place on December 31, 1999.

Interpretations of the Monroe Doctrine

As you read, the implementation of the Monroe Doctrine came years after its introduction in 1823. The Monroe Doctrine was tested in 1895 over a boundary dispute between Venezuela and the British colony of British Guiana. The United States demanded that Great Britain accept arbitration concerning the Venezuelan boundary dispute. President Cleveland's Secretary of State **Richard Olney** claimed that the Monroe Doctrine implied that the United States was justified in intervening in Western Hemisphere affairs because "the United States is practically sovereign on the continent." After military force was threatened, Great Britain agreed to arbitration, and Olney's stand became known as the **Olney Interpretation of the Monroe Doctrine**.

President Theodore Roosevelt's interventions in the Venezuela debt dispute (1902) and the Dominican debt default (1904–1905) illustrated his belief that the United States had to assume "international police power" in the Western

261

Hemisphere. This policy of United States intervention in Latin American affairs, excluding intervention by European nations, became known as the **Roosevelt Corollary** to the Monroe Doctrine. Latin American countries soon objected to the paternal and dominating role of the United States.

President Taft and Dollar Diplomacy

United States influence continued to expand in Latin America during the administration of President **Taft** (1909–1913). Under a policy referred to as **"dollar diplomacy,"** United States bankers and businesspeople were encouraged to invest in areas of importance to the United States and were guaranteed full military and diplomatic support. In 1899 two of the largest banana importers merged to form the **United Fruit Company** which, by 1913, owned over one million acres and most of the railroad and steamship lines in Central America. Because of American investments in the countries of Honduras, Nicaragua, and Haiti, the United States felt able to justify military intervention to protect American interests. Intervention came when the United States Marines were ordered into **Nicaragua** in 1912, **Haiti** in 1915, and the **Dominican Republic** in 1916.

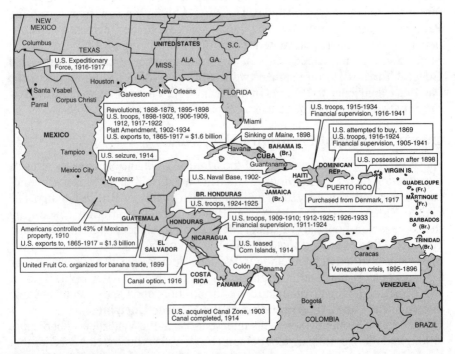

Figure 3.3 The United States and the Caribbean

President Wilson and Mexico

Porfirio Diaz, the dictator of Mexico for 37 years, was overthrown by a revolution in 1911. After a period of constitutional government, General **Victoriano Huerta** seized power in 1913. President Wilson withheld recognition of his government during a time of "watchful waiting," because he considered Huerta a "butcher" whose regime was oppressing the Mexican people. Wilson stationed United States naval units off Mexico and seized the **Port of Vera Cruz** in 1914 to block a German arms shipment. In July 1914 Huerta resigned and Wilson recognized the new government under Venustiano Carranza.

In 1916 **Pancho Villa**, a rival Mexican leader, revolted and led raids into New Mexico, hoping to bring the United States into an action that would help him seize power. American forces under General **John Pershing** were ordered into Mexico to capture Villa. Objections from Carranza, and an elusive Pancho Villa, caused Wilson to recall Pershing. As Mexican objections to **"Yankee Imperialism"** continued, relations between the two countries worsened. As part of the **Good Neighbor** policy in the 1930s, Mexican control of its own resources was recognized, while compensation came to the United States in return for **nationalized oil properties**.

Good Neighbor Policy

The United States changed its policy toward Latin America in the 1930s. In 1933, under the "Good Neighbor" policy of President Franklin Roosevelt, the United States agreed that "no state had the right to intervene in the external or internal affairs of another," thus abandoning the (Theodore) Roosevelt Corollary. Some people feel that the end of the 20th century saw a resurgence of the Roosevelt Corollary to the Monroe Doctrine in the attempts of the United States to curb Communist influence in Nicaragua, El Salvador, and on the island of Grenada.

Exercise Set 3.4

1. Which is the most valid conclusion that can be drawn concerning the territorial acquisitions of the United States?
   A. The use of a show of military force was always necessary.
   B. The "fruits of war" rarely include territorial gains.
   C. The addition of territorial gains increases a country's involvement in international affairs.
   D. The territorial gains of the United States did not extend beyond the Western Hemisphere.

2. The Platt Amendment provided for relations between the United States and
   A. Cuba.
   B. Panama.
   C. Hawaii.
   D. Alaska.

Base your answer to question 3 on the statement below and your knowledge of social studies.

> ... the policy of the government of the United States is to seek a solution which may bring about permanent safety and peace to China, preserve Chinese territorial and administrative entity, protect all rights guaranteed to friendly powers by treaty and international law, and safeguard for the world the principle of equal and impartial trade with all parts of the Chinese Empire ....
>
> Secretary of State John Hay, Circular Letter, July 3, 1900

3. This excerpt from John Hay's Circular Letter became part of the
   A. Open Door Policy.
   B. Roosevelt Corollary to the Monroe Doctrine.
   C. policy of Dollar Diplomacy.
   D. Kellogg-Briand Pact.

4. Which of the following did *not* become a United States possession as a result of the Spanish-American War?
   A. Puerto Rico
   B. Panama
   C. The Philippines
   D. Guam

5. The Roosevelt Corollary to the Monroe Doctrine
   A. was widely accepted by Latin America.
   B. was reinforced by Franklin Roosevelt in the 1930s.
   C. had been used since the introduction of the Monroe Doctrine in 1823.
   D. made the United States the peacekeeper in the Western Hemisphere.

6. The right of American citizens living in China to be tried in American courts was called
   A. "following the flag."
   B. the Open Door Policy.
   C. extraterritoriality.
   D. dollar diplomacy.

RESTRAINT AND INVOLVEMENT (1914–1920)

> The United States must be neutral in fact as well as in name.
> President Wilson, Message to U.S. Senate, 1914

> America cannot be an ostrich with its head in the sand.
> President Wilson, Address to U.S. Senate, 1916

> The world must be made safe for democracy.
> President Wilson, Address to Congress
> asking for declaration of war, April 2, 1917

On July 28, 1914, **Austria-Hungary** declared war on **Serbia** following the assassination of **Archduke Franz Ferdinand**, heir to the Austro-Hungarian throne, by a Serbian nationalist. Germany backed its ally Austria, while Russia mobilized to protect Serbia. Germany in turn declared war on Russia and France, Russia's ally. German troops marched through Belgium to crush France; Britain, honoring its pledge to defend Belgian neutrality, declared war on Germany. The Great War had begun with the Allies (Britain, France, Russia, Serbia, and Belgium) opposing the **Central Powers** (Germany and Austria). Later, the war would engulf most of the nations of the world.

European Background to World War I

Nationalist Rivalries and Alliance System

Following the French Revolution, the nations of Europe had created a "**balance of power.**" However, after the unification of Germany in 1871, **Chancellor Otto von Bismarck** first made an alliance with Austria-Hungary (**Dual Alliance**, 1879); later Italy joined, forming the **Triple Alliance** in 1882.

Seeing the Triple Alliance as a threat, France and Russia ratified a secret alliance in 1894. Although Great Britain did not immediately join the alliance with France and Russia, early in the 20th century an "understanding," which came to be known as the **Triple Entente**, developed between the three nations. Thus, by 1907 the chief European powers had organized themselves into two opposing camps—the Triple Alliance composed of Germany, Austria-Hungary, and Italy, and the Triple Entente, with France, Russia, and Great Britain.

Colonialism and the Spread of War

Underlying reasons for World War I included conflicting **territorial claims**, **imperialistic rivalries**, and **destructive nationalism**. Although the nations of Western Europe had not come into direct conflict, their armies and navies continued to grow in size and the "peace" that existed was an "armed peace," based upon a **"balance of terror."**

Importance of Control of Sea Routes

Great Britain had long followed a policy of keeping its navy superior in strength to any other nation's naval fleet. Germany, realizing that a naval buildup was necessary to compete with Great Britain, began an effort to create a navy second to none. When war broke out in Europe, the fleets of the Allied Powers were effective in forcing German ships to seek the shelter of their home ports. Throughout the war the Allies maintained a **blockade** of Germany and Austria-Hungary that enabled the Allies to import food and raw materials, transport troops, and effectively destroy the commerce of their enemies.

Germany's power on the seas increased with the use of the submarine, or **U-boat**. Although first used to destroy enemy warships, the submarine was eventually used to destroy merchant ships as well. According to international law, a merchant ship was to be warned before attack. However, Germany began a policy of **"unrestricted submarine warfare"** that was so destructive it appeared to spell defeat for the Allies.

United States Involvement

Efforts at Neutrality

When war broke out in Europe in 1914, Americans reacted with horror and wanted to stay out of the hostilities. President Wilson declared American neutrality on August 4, 1914 and, in a message to the Senate, he proclaimed that the United States "must be neutral in fact as well as in name."

Neutrality proved to be a difficult policy as Americans became either pro-Ally, pro-German, or pro-neutral. Those who sympathized with the Allies felt a bond with England and remembered that France had come to the aid of the Americans during their Revolution. The movement to enter the war on the side of the Allies was helped by propaganda describing Germany's militarism and unprovoked invasion of Belgium. A considerable part of the country was either pro-German, pro-neutral, or pacifist (anti-war). Irish-Americans were traditionally anti-British, and approximately 8 million Americans were of German descent. Among Progressives in the United States, war was seen as violating and interrupting the spirit of Progressive reform. In 1915, Progressives, including Jane Addams, Florence Kelley, and Lillian Wald, formed the American Union Against Militarism to stop the "machinery of war." Shortly thereafter, Addams and Carrie Chapman Catt formed the Women's Peace party to organize women against the war. But on the whole American sympathies went out to Britain, France, and the other Allies, and against Germany, Austria, and the

Central Powers. The memory of their Anglo-Saxon background and cultural heritage, along with the gross violations of Belgian neutrality by Germany, gave the Allied cause in the United States the momentum to quiet the dissenting opinions.

Neutrality became difficult to maintain as the United States continued to trade with both the Allies and the Central Powers. Violations of American neutrality came from both the British and the Germans. The British demanded that ships bound for Germany be first inspected in British ports for contraband (smuggled goods). Germany, to compensate for British naval superiority and to blockade Britain, turned to unrestricted submarine attacks in the war zone around the British Isles. The sinking of the British passenger liner *Lusitania* on May 7, 1915, resulting in the deaths of 128 Americans, outraged the American people. The **Sussex Pledge** (1916) by Germany halted unrestricted submarine warfare temporarily, but torpedo attacks began once again in January 1917. Although Woodrow Wilson had been reelected in 1916 on the slogan, "He kept us out of war," the situation in Europe continued to bring the United States closer to entry. After continued strikes against American ships in 1917, President Wilson asked Congress for a declaration of war against Germany. Congress declared war four days later on April 6, 1917.

Causes of United States Entry into War

Although Germany realized that the resumption of unrestricted submarine warfare might force the United States into the war, they felt that United States aid to the Allies would come too late to prevent a German victory. The publication of a telegram ("**Zimmermann Note**"), intercepted by the British in February 1917, turned American opinion against Germany. In the telegram, written by the German foreign minister to Mexico, Germany promised Texas, Arizona, and New Mexico to Mexico in return for its support in the war.

Economic ties with the Allies, including a profitable trade and numerous loans, was an added incentive for Americans to support the Allies. British propaganda, which represented Germany as a threat to democracy, helped convince many Americans that victory for the Allies meant victory for democracy. Finally, when the **Russian Revolution** (1917) resulted in the overthrow of the czar and the establishment of a temporary republican government, the war became more clearly a struggle between democracies and autocracies.

United States Role in the War

Besides American troops, the Allies desperately needed naval power, munitions, industrial goods, and food. The American fleet was primarily responsible for ending the U-boat threat and transporting troops and supplies. The American Expeditionary Force under the leadership of General **John J. Pershing** arrived in France in 1917, and in July 1918, along with French troops, drove the Germans back close to their border. Following major victories by the Allies, Germany agreed to consider a peace plan as provided for by Wilson's **Fourteen Points** (January 1918) and an **armistice** (cease-fire) was signed on November 11, 1918.

Communist Russia

Although the United States was initially pleased to see the overthrow of the czar in Russia, the seizure of power by the **Bolsheviks** and the establishment of communism caused concern. After the war, Europe was ravaged by poverty and chaos—conditions that made the area vulnerable to Communist propaganda and ideology.

Exercise Set 3.5

1. U.S. entry into both the War of 1812 and World War I was caused in part by
   A. foreign troops on American soil.
   B. Presidents who encouraged entry into war.
   C. interference with American shipping.
   D. a foreign nation's threat to Mexico.

2. The factor that was most significant in causing President Wilson to ask Congress for a declaration of War on Germany in April 1917 was
   A. the German invasion of Belgium.
   B. the Russian Revolution of 1917.
   C. the sinking of the *Sussex*.
   D. the resumption of unrestricted submarine warfare by Germany.

3. What was the primary focus of United States foreign policy in the decade after World War I?
   A. To defend the price of freedom of the seas
   B. To reduce United States commitments to other nations
   C. To contain the spread of communism in Eastern Europe
   D. To fulfill collective security agreements with Western European nations.

4. Wilson was re-elected to the presidency in 1916 because of his claim that
   A. entry into World War I was inevitable.
   B. he had kept the United States out of war.
   C. he would immediately bring the United States into the war.
   D. he would begin submarine attacks against the Germans.

THE CONSTITUTION AND WORLD WAR I

> The question in each case is whether the words used are used in such circumstances and are of such nature to create a clear and present danger that they will bring about the substantive evils Congress has the right to prevent.
>
> Majority Opinion, *Schenck* v. *United States* (1919)

> Anarchy stands for the liberation of the human mind from the dominion of religion, the liberation of the human body from the dominion of poverty, liberation from the shackles and restraints of government.
>
> Emma Goldman, *Anarchism* (1910)

War Opposition and Patriotism, the Draft Issue

As America approached entry into war, public opinion was by no means unified. Heated debate continued between those who advocated military support for the Allies, supporters of neutrality, and antiwar critics.

Anti-German Feelings

Anti-German feelings were building before 1917, much the result of submarine warfare. After American entry into the war, preparation was encouraged by groups such as the **National Security League** and the Navy League, while public opinion was mobilized by George Creel's **Committee on Public Information (CPI)**. Recruiting the services of thousands of people in the arts, advertising, and film industries, the CPI effectively publicized the war. Films like *The Prussian Cur* and *The Kaiser, the Beast of Berlin* brought the message to the screen while the Division of Industrial Relations rallied labor around the war effort. As the anti-German sentiment increased, many schools stopped offering instruction in the German language, sauerkraut became "liberty cabbage," and orchestral works by German composers were not performed by American symphony orchestras. Extreme patriotism reached the point of vigilantism in some cases. Radical antiwar leader Frank Little, a member of the **Industrial Workers of the World**, was captured in Butte, Montana and hanged.

Antiwar Sentiment

Antiwar activists claimed that war was repressive to the progressive spirit, needlessly cost the lives of a nation's youth, violated Christian morality, and was a profit-making endeavor of the industrial-military leaders. Leaders in Congress including Senator Robert La Follette and House Majority Leader

Claude Kitchin fought United States preparation for entry. Pacifist Progressives such as **Jane Addams** and Paul Kellogg contributed to the efforts of the American Union Against Militarism. Addams helped found the **Women's Peace Party** and even **Andrew Carnegie** and **Henry Ford** helped to finance the peace movements.

The Draft

In 1917, after entry into the war, Congress passed the **Selective Service Act** establishing a system to **draft**, or **conscript**, men into the armed forces. All males between the ages of 18 and 45 were required to register. By the war's end, 24 million men had been registered by local draft boards, with over 4 million serving in the armed forces. In the *Selective Service Cases,* the Supreme Court decided in January 1918 that the draft was constitutional under Congress's power to "declare war and raise and support armies."

Espionage and Sedition Acts

America's participation in World War I raised again, as it had earlier in the Civil War, the conflict between the Bill of Rights and the needs of war. Two laws passed by Congress in 1917 and 1918, the **Espionage Act** (1917) and the **Sedition Act** (1918), placed certain restrictions and limitations upon the freedoms of the press and speech. The Espionage Act outlawed any obstruction with military registration and enlistment and banned "treasonable and seditious" material from the nation's mails, at the discretion of the postmaster general. Publications seized for violation of the Espionage Act included *The New York Times* and the *Saturday Evening Post*. The Sedition Act, an amendment to the Espionage Act, was passed in reaction to activities of pacifists' groups, certain Labor leaders, and "Bolsheviks and radicals." Extending restrictions on interference with enlistment procedures, the act also made it a felony to "utter, print, or publish disloyal, profane, scurrilous, or abusive language about the form of government, the Constitution, soldiers and sailors, flag or uniform of the armed forces . . . ."

For the most part, the Supreme Court endorsed the repressive measures used against radical political activities during the war years. When Secretary **Schenck** of the **Socialist Party** was convicted under the Espionage Act for distributing antidraft leaflets, the case (*Schenck* v. *United States,* 1919) was appealed to the Supreme Court on the grounds that the act violated the First Amendment and was therefore unconstitutional. **Justice Holmes**, writing for a unanimous court, upheld the constitutionality of the Espionage Act. Explaining that free speech was never an "absolute" right, he held that, during war, civil liberties could be restricted. "Free speech would not protect a man in falsely shouting fire in a theatre, causing a panic," was an example he provided for the court's reasoning that freedom of speech was not absolute. His approach in determining whether speech could be restricted became known as the **"clear and present danger"** rule. According to this, if words presented a "clear and present danger" of causing evils that Congress had the right to prevent, the speech could be curtailed. Holmes, in the later case of *Abrams* v. *United States* (1919), warned in a strong dissent that restriction of speech must be carefully applied so as not to stop the **"free trade in ideas"** so important in a democratic society.

Wartime Convictions

The decision in *Schenck* by the Supreme Court supported the government's prosecution of those who violated wartime security measures. The Espionage Act was upheld again in *Debs* v. *United States* (1919), an appeal from the conviction of Socialist Party leader **Eugene V. Debs**. Debs was found guilty of felonious acts after delivering a speech denouncing capitalism and the war. **"Big Bill" Haywood**, leader of the **Industrial Workers of the World**, joined forces with 75-year-old **Mother Jones** and radical **Elizabeth Gurley Flynn** and appealed mostly to unskilled workers to join in destroying capitalism and stopping the war. Federal prosecutions during the war years sent Haywood and many radicals to prison. American anarchist **Emma Goldman**, imprisoned earlier for advocating birth control and pacifism, was deported to Russia in 1919.

The Red Scare 1918–1920

During the war, the **Bolshevik Revolution** in 1917 brought a Communist government to Russia. After the new Russian government under the leadership of **Lenin** withdrew from the war and made a separate peace with Germany, Americans felt betrayed. They were also frightened by the Bolsheviks' calls for workers everywhere to revolt. A **"Red Scare"** in the United States intensified as communism began to spread in Europe.

American Foreign Policy and Russia

American foreign policy also reflected hostile feelings toward Russia. In June 1918 President **Wilson**, without the consent of Congress, ordered American troops into Siberia to guard allied supplies and to observe Japanese influence in northern Russia. Wilson hoped to smash the Bolshevik government whose Communist influences were felt in short-term uprisings in both Germany and Hungary in early 1919.

Violations of Civil Rights

During the "Red Scare," extreme actions were taken against radicals. The civil liberties of "radicals," including many socialists and communists, were violated when Wilson's Attorney General, A. Mitchell Palmer, ordered the deportation of suspected radicals, raided homes of those suspected of being involved in "subversive" activities, and arrested hundreds whose economic and political views were unorthodox. The political implications of the trial and execution of anarchists **Nicola Sacco** and **Bartolomeo Vanzetti** for murder in 1920 brought worldwide attention to the "blind patriotism" of the Red Scare period.

Exercise Set 3.6

1. Where in the Constitution would you find the "freedom of speech" guarantee?
   A. The Preamble
   B. Article I
   C. The "elastic clause"
   D. The First Amendment

2. The leader of the Industrial Workers of the World who was prosecuted for subversive activities during World War I was
   A. Emma Goldman.
   B. George Creel.
   C. "Big Bill" Haywood.
   D. Eugene V. Debs.

3. A study of the Supreme Court's decision in the case of *Schenck* v. *United States* (1919) indicates that
   A. during times of war civil liberties may be restricted.
   B. the First Amendment is absolute in nature.
   C. all political speech is protected by the First Amendment.
   D. the activities of subversive groups may be restricted without any review by the courts.

4. The case of Sacco and Vanzetti aroused sympathy for them and criticism of government measures because they
   A. were executed immediately.
   B. were found innocent of all charges against them.
   C. probably did not receive a fair trial as a result of unsubstantiated fears.
   D. were imprisoned without a trial.

THE SEARCH FOR PEACE AND ARMS CONTROL (1914–1930)

> A general association of nations must be formed . . . for the purpose of affording mutual guarantees of political independence and territorial integrity to great and small states alike.
>
> President Woodrow Wilson
> Address to Congress, January 8, 1918

The Peace Movement

The movement that had objected to America's entry into World War I gained further support when the United States considered the peace settlement following the war that included membership in an international **League of Nations**. Americans were tired of war and were no longer receptive to President Wilson's justification of America's role in the Great War. Groups including Representative Jeannette Rankin's American Women Opposed to the League of Nations and the Women's International League for Peace and Freedom opposed American membership in the League of Nations. They viewed the League as a vehicle for bringing the United States into future international conflicts. Ironically, later in the 1920s and 1930s, some of these same groups, including the Women's International League for Peace and Freedom, advocated cooperation with the League of Nations and membership in the World Court as preventive measures to avoid war as a solution to international problems.

Wilson's Fourteen Points

President Wilson was able to transform the war, which was a grinding struggle, into a crusade for liberty, democracy, and permanent peace. Wilson's peace aims were developed in a long series of speeches and public papers from 1914 to 1918. His **Fourteen Points** were listed in an address to Congress on January 8, 1918; a list would be circulated among the populations of Europe in millions of leaflets.

President Wilson's Fourteen Points included the following:

- the replacement of secret treaties with **open diplomacy** among nations
- **freedom of the seas**
- **removal of economic/trade barriers** between nations
- **reductions in armaments**
- **adjustment of colonial claims** with respect for native populations

- redrawing of European boundaries with a respect for nationalities and **"self-determination"**
- the formation of an **association of nations**

By the fall of 1918 the Allied Armies, with the assistance of American forces, were advancing toward the German border. Shortly thereafter, the German government opened negotiations with Wilson for peace on the basis of the Fourteen Points.

The Versailles Treaty

Although President Wilson sailed for Paris in December 1918 with the intention of writing his Fourteen Points into the peace treaty, problems for his ambitious plans had already started. Worried about legislative support in the approaching peace negotiations, the President appealed to the American people for Democratic victories in the midterm elections of 1918. However, this appeal backfired. The Republicans captured both houses of Congress and they resented Wilson's partisan tactics. Wilson's second blunder was his failure to take any members of the House or the Senate with him to Paris, instead bringing with him a delegation he expected to dominate in the treaty-writing process.

The **Paris Peace Conference** began its work in January 1919 under the direction of Woodrow Wilson and Prime Ministers **Georges Clemenceau** of France, **David Lloyd George** of Great Britain, and **Vittorio Orlando** of Italy. The final **Treaty of Versailles**, signed by delegates from Germany on June 28, 1919 (separate peace treaties were drawn up with Germany's allies), provided for (1) an admission by Germany of its **war guilt**; (2) stripping Germany of its **colonies**; (3) **adjusting German borders**, taking away Alsace-Lorraine, Posen, the Saar Basin, parts of Schleswig and Silesia; and (4) stripping Germany of most of its military and naval forces.

Reluctantly, President Wilson agreed to a treaty that did not mention freedom of the seas, or reduced tariffs. Negotiations had been secretive and the reparations assigned to Germany were impossible to repay. Wilson's last hope was an effective association of nations in which the United States would have a major role.

The League of Nations and United States Rejection

The **Covenant** for the League of Nations was incorporated into the Versailles Treaty. It provided for an **Assembly** to represent all member nations, a **Secretariat**, permanently located in Geneva, Switzerland, a **Council** controlled by the permanent members (United States, England, France, Italy, and Japan) and four other nations elected by the Assembly, and a separate

Permanent Court of International Justice (known as the **World Court**). Under the Covenant the members of the League were pledged to seek disarmament, to arbitrate differences, and to act together against outside aggressors or covenant breakers in a system of "**collective security.**"

The Struggle over Ratification

The struggle over American ratification of the Treaty of Versailles, including the League of Nations, became a bitter duel between Woodrow Wilson and the Republican Chairman of the Senate Committee on Foreign Relations, **Henry Cabot Lodge**. Much of the objection to the treaty was based on political jealousy, largely due to Wilson's refusal to consult Republican Senators in creating the treaty. However, many feared that participation in the League of Nations might draw the United States into European troubles.

As the Senate carried out its Constitutional role of "Advise and Consent" concerning foreign treaties (Article II, Section 2), three groups developed: Democratic followers of Wilson who favored immediate ratification; hard core "irreconcilables" (including William Borah of Idaho, Robert La Follette of Wisconsin, and Hiram Johnson of California) who opposed American membership in the international organization; and moderates who preferred a watered-down version of the League that would include certain "reservations" to protect American interests. President Wilson decided to appeal directly to the American people, but in the midst of a speaking tour through the Middle West, he suffered a paralytic stroke and remained an invalid during the critical period of debate on the League.

Rejection of the Treaty

On November 19, 1919, Wilson's Democratic supporters and the "irreconcilables" combined to defeat the treaty with the Lodge reservations. The reservationists and the "irreconcilables" then voted down the treaty in its original form. Once again, in March 1920, the treaty failed to receive the necessary two-thirds approval of the Senate, although the vote was 49 to 35 in its favor. Finally, when the Republicans were victorious in the election of 1920, sending **Warren G. Harding** to the White House, they saw their victory as a mandate against the League of Nations. A joint resolution was adopted by Congress on August 25, 1921, declaring the war to be over.

Washington Naval Disarmament Conference

President Harding sponsored the Washington Disarmament Conference of 1921, which led to the limitation of battleship construction among the chief naval powers (Britain, United States, Japan, France, and Italy) and stabilized the balance of power in the Far East. Temporarily, the Conference seemed to be a substantial step toward **arms control** and **economic rehabilitation**.

Kellogg-Briand Pact (1928)

An agreement, eventually signed by 62 nations, and named for United States Secretary of State Frank Kellogg and French Foreign Minister Aristede Briand, was negotiated in 1928 "condemning recourse to war for the solution of international controversies, and renouncing it as an instrument of the national policy." The **Kellogg-Briand Pact** passed the Senate by a vote of 85 to 1, but was looked upon skeptically by many because it provided no means of enforcement.

The World Court

Periodic proposals for U.S. membership in the World Court (the League's judicial agency) were defeated in the Senate during the administrations of Presidents Harding and Coolidge. The Court itself rejected America's admission in 1926 when certain conditions were insisted upon by the United States. Attempts by Presidents Hoover and Franklin Roosevelt to gain America's membership were also frustrated by a Senate that was heavily influenced by isolationist forces and by those who feared that membership in the Court would involve the nation in League affairs and the problems of Europe.

1. The major flaw of the Kellogg-Briand Pact (1928) was that it
   A. was signed by only four nations.
   B. was discouraged by the League of Nations.
   C. had no provisions for enforcement.
   D. violated the provisions of the Washington Naval Disarmament Conference of 1921.

2. The primary reason for the United States Senate's rejection of the Treaty of Versailles was
   A. the forced assumption by Germany of war guilt.
   B. the fact that the war continued in the Western Hemisphere.
   C. the inclusion of the League of Nations Covenant.
   D. the refusal of the Allies to repay their war debts to the United States.

3. At the Paris Peace Conference, President Wilson pushed for
   A. U.S. occupation of Western Europe.
   B. the establishment of a League of Nations.
   C. the immediate repayment of all war debts to the United States.
   D. military occupation of Germany.

4. European nations claimed they were having difficulty paying their war debts to the United States because
   A. the United States failed to join the League of Nations.
   B. Germany had defaulted on its reparations to the Allies.
   C. the United States lowered its tariffs.
   D. American bankers were investing in Germany.

CHAPTER REVIEW QUESTIONS

INTERRUPTING THE CEREMONY

McCUTCHEON, CHICAGO TRIBUNE-NEW YORK NEWS SYNDICATE, INC.

Base your answers to questions 1 and 2 on the cartoon and on your knowledge of social studies.

1. The main purpose of the cartoon is to express opposition to which President's action?
   A. Woodrow Wilson's support of the Treaty of Versailles
   B. Franklin Roosevelt's announcement of the Good Neighbor Policy
   C. Harry Truman's decision to send aid to Europe after World War II
   D. Ronald Reagan's 1985 summit meeting with Chairman Gorbachev of the Soviet Union

2. According to the cartoon, the United States should follow a foreign policy of
   A. collective security.
   B. noninvolvement.
   C. detente.
   D. imperialism.

3. Supreme Court decisions in cases involving the First Amendment to the federal Constitution generally reflect the principle that
   A. if an action is based on a religious belief, it must be allowed.
   B. only demonstrations that support the beliefs of the majority may be held.
   C. freedoms of speech and press are absolute.
   D. individual rights must be balanced against the needs of society at the time.

4. An advantage of the United Nations that has contributed to its success when compared to the League of Nations is
   A. the provision that no armed forces are used to carry out its goals.
   B. the membership of all the world's major powers.
   C. the lack of a judicial body.
   D. its complete prevention of war in the world.

5. The most accurate statement concerning U.S. foreign policy is that the United States has generally
   A. used military confrontation to solve disputes.
   B. reacted forcefully to imperialism around the world.
   C. acted according to national self-interest.
   D. formed entangling alliances with countries in need.

6. The major foreign policy issue facing the Wilson administration between the outbreak of the First World War in 1914 and United States entry in 1917 was
   A. freedom of the seas.
   B. German aggression in the Caribbean.
   C. the future of United States overseas possessions.
   D. tariff controversies with Japan.

7. After the Spanish-American War Cuba was
   A. left completely independent.
   B. restricted by the Platt Amendment.
   C. admitted as a state to the United States.
   D. reoccupied by the Spanish.

THEMATIC ESSAY

Directions: Write a well-organized essay that includes an introduction, several paragraphs addressing the task below, and a conclusion.

Theme: Changing American Society

> The first quarter of the 20th century experienced the testing of civil liberties in a number of ways.

Task:

> Identify *two* events in the first quarter of the 20th century that tested the civil liberties of Americans.
>
> - For each event identified describe its immediate causes.
> - Discuss the specifics of each event.
> - Identify the constitutional issue(s) involved in each event.

Some suggestions you may wish to consider include: the Red Scare of 1919, the Scopes Monkey Trial of 1925, *Schenck* v. *United States* (1919), the trial of Sacco and Vanzetti, and the rise of the Second Ku Klux Klan.

You are *not* limited to these suggestions.

DOCUMENT-BASED QUESTION

The following questions (Part A and Part B) are based on the accompanying documents (1–6). Some of these documents have been edited for the purpose of this exercise. The question is designed to test your ability to work with historical documents and to demonstrate your knowledge of the subject matter being presented. As you analyze the documents, take into account both the source of the document and the author's point of view.

Historical Context:

> Late 19th-century and early 20th-century expansionism by the United States was seen by many as a continuation of earlier 19th-century Manifest Destiny.

Task:

> Using information from the documents and your knowledge of United States history, answer the questions that follow each document in Part A. Your answers to the questions will help you write the Part B essay, in which you will be asked:
>
> Late 19th-century and early 20th-century expansionism by the United States was seen by many as a continuation of earlier 19th-century Manifest Destiny. Using the issues identified in the documents, discuss why this is or is not an accurate statement.

Part A
Short-Answer Questions

The documents below relate to both continental and overseas expansion of the United States during the 1800s and early part of the 1900s. Examine each document carefully and then answer the questions that follow.

DOCUMENT 1

> Our Manifest Destiny is to overspread the continent allotted by Providence for the free development of our yearly multiplying millions.

—John L. Sullivan, *Democratic Review* (1845)

1. Which continent is being referred to by John L. Sullivan?

_____

_____

_____

DOCUMENT 2

Go West, young man, and grow up with the country.

—Horace Greeley, *New York Tribune* (1850)

2. The opinion of John L. Sullivan (see Document 1) and the advice of Horace Greeley in Document 2 both supported westward expansion and settlement by Americans. Which groups of North American inhabitants would have been likely to object to the positions of both of these men?

_____

_____

_____

DOCUMENT 3

We make treaties—that is, we pledge our faith—and then leave swindlers and knaves of all kinds to execute them. We maintain and breed pauper colonies. The savages, who know us, and who will neither be pauperized nor trust our word, we pursue, and slay if we can, at an incredible expense . . . . The fact is that these Indians, with whom we have made a solemn treaty that their territory shall not be invaded, and that they should receive supplies on their reservations, have seen from one thousand to fifteen hundred miners during the present season entering and occupying their territory . . . .

—*Harper's Weekly*, August 5, 1876

3. How does the author of the article in *Harper's Weekly* view the treaties made by the United States government with the various Native American populations?

_____

_____

_____

_____

The Philippines are ours forever . . . . And just beyond the Philippines are China's . . . markets. We will not retreat from either . . . . We will not abandon our opportunity in the Orient. We will not renounce our part in the mission of our race . . . under God, of the civilization of the world . . . . And we will move forward to our *work* . . . with gratitude . . . and thanksgiving to Almighty God that He has marked us his chosen people.

—Senator Albert Beveridge, Speech to 56th Congress,
Congressional Record (1900)

4. What is the "work" that Senator Beveridge believes the United States must move forward with in the Orient?

_____

_____

_____

_____

5. What occurrence had taken place that would lead Senator Beveridge to state in 1900 that "The Philippines are ours forever?"

_____

_____

_____

_____

DOCUMENT 5

Our interests and those of our southern neighbors are in reality identical. They have great natural riches, and if within their borders the reign of law and justice obtains, prosperity is sure to come to them . . . . We would interfere with them only in the last resort, and then only if it became evident that their inability or unwillingness to do justice at home and abroad had violated the rights of the United States or had invited foreign aggression to the detriment of the entire body of American nations.

—President Theodore Roosevelt, Message to Congress, December 6, 1904

6. The segment above is many times referred to as the Roosevelt Corollary to the Monroe Doctrine. What geographic area is being referred to by President Roosevelt?

_____

_____

_____

_____

7. What are President Roosevelt's opinions regarding United States intervention in the "southern neighbors?"

_____

_____

_____

_____

DOCUMENT 6

—Swinging the Big Stick (1905)

8. Who is the President portrayed in the cartoon?

_____

_____

_____

_____

9. The big stick in the cartoon is labeled "The New Diplomacy." What were the new diplomatic policies that were proposed by the President portrayed in the cartoon?

_____

_____

_____

_____

DOCUMENT 7

Alaska and Hawaii

Alaska
1867 purchased from Russia
1912 territorial status granted
1959 admitted as a state

Hawaii
1898 annexed
1900 territorial status granted
1959 admitted as a state

PACIFIC OCEAN

ALASKA

HAWAII

10. Give one advantage to the United States for each of the acquisitions (Alaska and Hawaii) in the map.

_____

_____

_____

_____

Part B
Essay

Your essay should be well organized with an introductory paragraph that states your position on the question. Develop your position in the next paragraphs and then write a conclusion. In your essay, include specific historical details and refer to the specific documents you analyzed in Part A. You may include additional information from your knowledge of social studies.

Historical Context:

> Late 19th-century and early 20th-century expansionism by the United States was seen by many as a continuation of earlier 19th-century Manifest Destiny.

Task:

> Late 19th-century and early 20th-century expansionism by the United States was seen by many as a continuation of earlier 19th-century Manifest Destiny. Using the issues identified in the documents discuss why this is or is not an accurate statement.

Guidelines:

In your essay, be sure to
• Develop all aspects of the task.
• Incorporate information from *at least five* documents.
• Incorporate relevant outside information.
• Support the theme with many relevant facts, examples, and details.
• Use a logical and clear plan of organization, including an introduction and a conclusion that are beyond a restatement of the theme.

DOCUMENT-BASED QUESTION

This question is based on the accompanying documents. The question is designed to test your ability to work with historical documents. Some of these documents have been edited for the purposes of this question. As you analyze the documents, take into account the source of each document and any point of view that may be presented in the document.

Historical Context:

At various times in United States history, the federal government has taken controversial actions that have limited civil liberties. Three such actions were the **passage of the Espionage and Sedition Acts (1917–1918), issuing Executive Order 9066 relocating Japanese Americans (1942)**, and the **passage of the USA PATRIOT Act (2001)**.

Task:

Using the information from the documents and your knowledge of United States history, answer the questions that follow each document in Part A. Your answers to the questions will help you write the Part B essay in which you will be asked to

Select *two* actions taken by the federal government that are mentioned in the historical context and for *each*

- Describe the historical circumstances surrounding the action.
- Discuss an argument used by the government to *support* its action.
- Discuss an argument used by those who *opposed* the government's action.

Part A
Short-Answer Questions

Analyze the documents and answer the short-answer questions that follow each document in the space provided.

DOCUMENT 1

The Espionage Act was passed in 1917. The Sedition Act was passed in 1918.

> . . . Before the war [World War I], the government had had no power to interfere with free speech. During the neutrality years and on into the first months of war, pessimistic rumors, criticism of America's military preparations, and overtly [openly] pro-German propaganda had all gone unchecked. Democrats' moves to introduce press censorship as part of wider antiespionage legislation had been blocked by Republicans claiming that censorship could be used by the President to screen himself from criticism.
>
> But with war fever mounting all the time, a modified Espionage Act (subsequently to be supplemented with the even more stringent [strict] Sedition Act) became law in June 1917. Suddenly, any statement that might interfere with the success of the armed forces, incite disloyalty, or obstruct recruiting to the Army became a punishable offense. A crucial weapon had been added to the government's armory. It now had the legal power to control what its citizens said in public. And rather than simply trusting newspaper editors to be discreet, it had the power to suppress their publications if they spoke out too roughly. In some cases, suppression was temporary; for others, it was permanent. Postmaster General Albert Burleson was given the power to ban offensive material from circulating through the mail. Under postal regulations, if a journal missed one issue, for whatever reason, it automatically lost its second-class mailing privilege—and for a great many publications, this spelled financial death . . . .

Source: Harries and Harries, *The Last Days of Innocence: America at War 1917–1918*, Random House, 1997

1. According to Harries and Harries, what were *two* reasons the Espionage and Sedition Acts were passed?

(1) _____

_____

(2) _____

_____

DOCUMENT 2

William H. Rehnquist was Chief Justice of the Supreme Court from 1986 to 2005.

> . . . Charles T. Schenck was convicted [in 1918] of violating the act [Espionage Act] by printing and distributing to draftees leaflets that urged them to resist the draft. Schenck took his case to the Supreme Court, arguing that his conviction violated the First Amendment's guarantee of freedom of the press. The Supreme Court, in a unanimous opinion authored by Justice Oliver Wendell Holmes, upheld his conviction. It said that "When a nation is at war many things which might be said in time of peace are such a hindrance to its efforts that their utterance will not be endured so long as men fight. . . . No court could regard them as protected by any constitutional right." The Court said that since the leaflet could be found to have been intended to obstruct the recruiting for the armed forces, it was not protected by the First Amendment; its words created "a clear and present danger" of bringing about conduct that Congress had a right to prevent. . . .

Source: William H. Rehnquist, *All the Laws but One: Civil Liberties in Wartime*, Vintage Books, 1998 (adapted)

2. According to William H. Rehnquist, what was *one* argument used by the United States Supreme Court to uphold Charles T. Schenck's conviction under the Espionage Act?

_____

_____

. . . I think all men recognize that in time of war the citizen must surrender some rights for the common good which he is entitled to enjoy in time of peace. But, sir, the right to control their own Government according to constitutional forms is not one of the rights that the citizens of this country are called upon to surrender in time of war.

Rather, in time of war, the citizen must be more alert to the preservation of his right to control his Government. He must be most watchful of the encroachment [intrusion] of the military upon the civil power. He must beware of those precedents in support of arbitrary action by administration officials which, excused on the pleas of necessity in war time, become the fixed rule when the necessity has passed and normal conditions have been restored.

More than all, the citizen and his representative in Congress in time of war must maintain his right of free speech . . . .

Source: Senator Robert M. La Follette, "Free Speech in Wartime," October 6, 1917

3a. What is *one* argument *against* restricting free speech during wartime, according to Senator Robert M. La Follette?

_____

_____

DOCUMENT 3b

The Sedition Act continued to be enforced after World War I.

SWAT THE FLY, BUT USE COMMON SENSE.

Source: Lute Pease, *Newark News*, reprinted in
Literary Digest, March 6, 1920 (adapted)

3*b*. What is the cartoonist's viewpoint of Uncle Sam's use of the Sedition
legislation?

_____

_____

. . . The entire nation was stunned by the Japanese attack on Pearl Harbor, but it seemed much closer to home on the west coast than elsewhere on the mainland. In February 1942, oil installations in the vicinity of Santa Barbara were shelled by a Japanese submarine. The military established a Western Defense Command, which consisted of the coastal portions of California, Oregon, and Washington.

Residents became fearful of ethnic Japanese among them. Japanese immigrants had begun to settle on the west coast shortly before the turn of the century but had not been assimilated into the rest of the population. Those who had emigrated from Japan were not allowed to become citizens; they were prohibited by law from owning land and were socially segregated in many ways. The first generation of Japanese immigrants — the Issei — therefore remained aliens. But their children — the Nisei — being born in the United States, were citizens from birth. Public officials, particularly in California — Governor Culbert Olson, Attorney General Earl Warren, and Los Angeles Mayor Fletcher Bowron — began to call for "relocation" of persons of Japanese ancestry in the interior of the country. There were more than one hundred thousand of these on the west coast if one counted both the Issei and the Nisei. . . .

Source: William H. Rehnquist, *All the Laws but One: Civil Liberties in Wartime*, Vintage Books, 1998

4. According to William H. Rehnquist, what is *one* reason public officials in California called for the relocation of Japanese Americans?

_____

_____

DOCUMENT 5a

The excerpt below is from Executive Order 9066, which resulted in the relocation of Japanese Americans.

Executive Order No. 9066
AUTHORIZING THE SECRETARY OF WAR TO PRESCRIBE MILITARY AREAS

WHEREAS the successful prosecution of the war requires every possible protection against espionage and against sabotage to national-defense material, national-defense premises, and national-defense utilities as defined in Section 4, Act of April 20, 1918, 40 Stat. 533, as amended by the Act of November 30, 1940, 54 Stat. 1220, and the Act of August 21, 1941, 55 Stat. 655 (U.S.C., Title 50, Sec. 104):

Source: President Franklin D. Roosevelt, Executive Order 9066, February 19, 1942

5a. According to President Roosevelt, what is *one* reason for the relocation of Japanese Americans?

_____

_____

DOCUMENT 5b

. . . The policy [relocation and internment of Japanese Americans] stemmed from a myriad of motives, including the insecurity of the army's west coast commander, the racism and hostility of the Pacific states' white population, bureaucratic ambitions, and the political advantages perceived by local, state, and federal officials. The affair involved a variety of officials and institutions, including high ranking military officers, heads and lower officials of the Department of Justice and the War Department, the FBI, the Supreme Court, and the president. Many of these officials knew at the time that the Japanese American community harbored very few disloyal persons; furthermore, knowledgeable parties in key agencies, such as the FBI and the Office of Naval Intelligence, long had been aware of those elements and knew that no military necessity existed to justify so Draconian [harsh] a measure. . . .

Source: Stanley I. Kutler, "Review: At the Bar of History: Japanese Americans versus the United States," *American Bar Foundation Research Journal*, Spring 1985

5b. According to Stanley Kutler, what was *one* motive behind the government's decision to intern Japanese Americans?

_____

_____

DOCUMENT 6

MR. JUSTICE JACKSON, dissenting.

Korematsu was born on our soil, of parents born in Japan. The Constitution makes him a citizen of the United States by nativity, and a citizen of California by residence. No claim is made that he is not loyal to this country. There is no suggestion that, apart from the matter involved here, he is not law-abiding and well disposed. Korematsu, however, has been convicted of an act not commonly a crime. It consists merely of being present in the state whereof he is a citizen, near the place where he was born, and where all his life he has lived.

Even more unusual is the series of military orders which made this conduct a crime. They forbid such a one to remain, and they also forbid him to leave. They were so drawn that the only way Korematsu could avoid violation was to give himself up to the military authority. This meant submission to custody, examination, and transportation out of the territory, to be followed by indeterminate confinement in detention camps.

A citizen's presence in the locality, however, was made a crime only if his parents were of Japanese birth. Had Korematsu been one of four—the others being, say, a German alien enemy, an Italian alien enemy, and a citizen of American-born ancestors, convicted of treason but out on parole—only Korematsu's presence would have violated the order. The difference between their innocence and his crime would result, not from anything he did, said, or thought, different than they, but only in that he was born of different racial stock. . . .

Source: Justice Robert Jackson, Dissenting Opinion,
Korematsu v. United States, December 18, 1944

6. Based on this dissenting opinion in *Korematsu* v. *United States*, state *two* arguments made by Justice Robert Jackson against the conviction of Korematsu.

(1) _____

_____

(2) _____

_____

295aso.Unit Three THE PROGRESSIVE MOVEMENT

295

DOCUMENT 7

... The attacks in New York and Washington [on September 11, 2001], followed closely by the mysterious anthrax mailings and the swift war in Afghanistan, inevitably instigated [prompted] changes in law enforcement, intelligence operations, and security generally. As U.S. Supreme Court Justice Sandra Day O'Connor predicted on September 29, 2001: "We're likely to experience more restrictions on our personal freedom than has ever been the case in our country." The public strongly supported doing whatever was necessary. In fact, one poll showed 55 percent of citizens were worried that the government *would not go far enough* in fighting terrorism in order to protect civil liberties; only 31 percent were worried the government would go too far in fighting terrorism at the expense of civil liberties. . . .

Source: Leone and Anrig, eds., *The War on Our Freedoms: Civil Liberties in an Age of Terrorism*, Century Foundation, 2003

7. According to this document, what was *one* reason for the passage of the USA PATRIOT Act?

_____

_____

This is an excerpt of President George W. Bush's remarks upon signing the USA PATRIOT Act.

. . . For example, this legislation gives law enforcement officials better tools to put an end to financial counterfeiting, smuggling, and money laundering. Secondly, it gives intelligence operations and criminal operations the chance to operate not on separate tracks but to share vital information so necessary to disrupt a terrorist attack before it occurs.

As of today, we're changing the laws governing information-sharing. And as importantly, we're changing the culture of our various agencies that fight terrorism. Countering and investigating terrorist activity is the number one priority for both law enforcement and intelligence agencies.

Surveillance of communications is another essential tool to pursue and stop terrorists. The existing law was written in the era of rotary telephones. This new law that I sign today will allow surveillance of all communications used by terrorists, including emails, the Internet, and cell phones. As of today, we'll be able to better meet the technological challenges posed by this proliferation of communications technology. . . .

Source: President George W. Bush, October 26, 2001

8a. According to President George W. Bush, what is *one* way the USA PATRIOT Act will help law enforcement officials?

_____

_____

8b. According to President George W. Bush, what is the *primary* goal of the USA PATRIOT Act?

_____

_____

DOCUMENT 9a

War on Terrorism

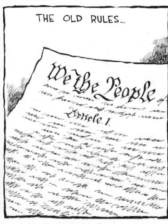

Source: Nick Anderson, *Washington Post Writers Group*,
November 7, 2001 (adapted)

DOCUMENT 9b

. . . The war on terrorism may be launching a legal revolution in America. The changes pose these questions: How necessary are some of the reforms? Have [Attorney General] John Ashcroft and the Justice Department unraveled constitutional protections in trying to ensure our safety? "There is a significant civil-liberties price to be paid as we adopt various national-security initiatives," says Mary Jo White, a former U.S. Attorney in the Southern District of New York, whose office pursued some of the biggest terrorism cases of the 1990s. "For the most part, I think that price is necessary. But what I worry about is government officials who find the answers too easy in this arena. . . ."

Source: Richard Lacayo et al., "Civil Liberties: The War Comes Back Home,"
Time, May 12, 2003

9. Based on these documents, what is *one* criticism of measures taken to fight the war on terrorism?

_____

_____

Part B
Essay

Write a well-organized essay that includes an introduction, several paragraphs, and a conclusion. Use evidence from *at least four* documents in the body of the essay. Support your response with relevant facts, examples, and details. Include additional outside information.

Historical Context:

> At various times in United States history, the federal government has taken controversial actions that have limited civil liberties. Three such actions were the **passage of the Espionage and Sedition Acts (1917–1918)**, **issuing Executive Order 9066 relocating Japanese Americans (1942)**, and the **passage of the USA PATRIOT Act (2001)**.

Task:

> Using information from the documents and your knowledge of United States history, write an essay in which you:
>
> Select *two* actions taken by the federal government that are mentioned in the historical context and for *each*
>
> - Describe the historical circumstances surrounding the action.
> - Discuss an argument used by the government to *support* its action.
> - Discuss an argument used by those who *opposed* the government's action.

Guidelines:

In your essay, be sure to
- Develop all aspects of the task.
- Incorporate information from *at least four* documents.
- Incorporate relevant outside information.
- Support the theme with relevant facts, examples, and details.
- Use a logical and clear plan of organization, including an introduction and a conclusion that are beyond a restatement of the theme.

UNIT FOUR ———————————————

At Home and Abroad: Prosperity and Depression

> **KEY IDEAS** Unit Four details the effect of World War I on the nation and the political, social, and cultural aspects of the decade of the 1920s. The second part of the unit examines the causes and effects of the Great Depression and the changing government role as it dealt with social and economic problems.

UNIT CONNECTIONS: By the end of the unit you should understand the following points.

- Postwar return to peacetime economy
- Fear of Communism and civil liberties at risk
- Warren G. Harding and a scandalous administration
- Henry Ford's automobile and mass production
- Economic problems of the 1920s lead to disaster in the 1930s
- Responses to economic problems by Herbert Hoover and Franklin Delano Roosevelt
- New Deal and Socialism; checks and balances; two-term presidential tradition
- President Roosevelt's "Court Packing"
- Shift of political alliances of African Americans
- The Dust Bowl and Depression Age literature

WAR AND PROSPERITY (1917–1929)

THE FIRST WORLD WAR AT HOME

> We are glad . . . to fight thus for the ultimate peace of the world and for the liberation of its peoples . . . . The world must be made safe for democracy.
>
> Woodrow Wilson, Address to Congress, April 2, 1917

> The highest and best form of efficiency is the spontaneous cooperation of a free people.
>
> Bernard M. Baruch, in *American Industry at War: A Report of the War Industries Board, March 1921*

Selective Service

World War I, like all wars, brought about a dramatic change in people's lives. The **Selective Service Act** of May 28, 1917 required all men 18 to 45 years of age to register for military service. From the nearly 10 million who originally registered, some 700,000 names were drawn by lot for service. By the end of the war, Selective Service had registered 24 million names as a pool from which names could be drawn as needed for the armed services. Of these, close to 5 million were in uniform by the war's end, and more than 2 million were sent overseas. Women served in the Army and Navy Nurses Corps and in the auxiliary forces of the regular Navy.

Mobilizing American Industry

American industry was mobilized for the war. A **War Industries Board** was created, headed by the financier **Bernard M. Baruch**. The Board established priorities for the production of necessary war materiel.

Providing Food and Fuel

Food and fuel were basic to the conduct of the war both for our troops and for our allies. **Herbert Hoover**, a mining engineer with a Quaker background, was put in charge of food distribution. His task was to see that adequate supplies of basic foods were produced and distributed as needed. He instituted "wheatless" Mondays and "meatless" Tuesdays on a voluntary basis as a means of conserving these essential staples. People responded readily to his request that they plant "victory gardens."

Conservation of fuel was achieved under the direction of a fuel administration headed by **Harry A. Garfield**. Daylight savings time was introduced and motorists were urged to observe "gasless" days to aid the war effort.

Financing the War

The war was financed partly by increased taxes but primarily through borrowing from the American people, who bought **government bonds** in four "Liberty Loan" drives and one final "Victory Loan" drive. These drives yielded $22 billion. Another $10 billion, approximately the amount lent to our allies, was raised through income taxes and by special taxes on liquor, tobacco, and theater tickets.

Transportation and Communication

To facilitate the transportation of troops and war supplies by rail, the railroads were placed under the direction of Secretary of the Treasury William G. McAdoo. Government control was later extended to the communication industries—telephone, telegraph, and cable.

Labor and the War

Support of the A.F.L.

Led by Samuel Gompers, the **American Federation of Labor (A.F.L.)**, which had two million members at the outbreak of the war, actively supported the war effort. As millions of men left their jobs to serve in the armed forces, the burgeoning war industries demanded more and more workers and a new labor force had to be formed.

Women in the Labor Force

The labor gap was filled, in part, by women who stepped in to operate the factories, farms, mills, mines, and railroads in place of their brothers, sons, and husbands. The ranks of labor were filled also by a quarter of a million African Americans who moved from the South into the coal mines, steel mills, and railroads of the North.

Mobilizing the Arts for War

The arts, too, proved to be a mighty force in the war effort. Artists created posters to encourage enlistment and to sell war bonds. The classic "I Want You for the U.S. Army" by Samuel Montgomery Flagg and the Liberty Bonds poster by Walter Whitehead provided stirring visual war messages.

Song writers used their talents to support the war effort in music. The nation sang **George M. Cohan's** "Over There" with gusto. Another popular World War I song was **Irving Berlin's** "Oh How I Hate to Get Up in the Morning." With millions of American men in France, the nation sang war-inspired songs such as "Hinky Dinky Parlay Voo" and "How 'Ya Gonna Keep 'em Down on the Farm after They've Seen Paree?"

Propaganda

Propaganda was also a war weapon. The Germans were "Huns" who committed terrible atrocities. The Kaiser was "The Beast of Berlin," and many schools discontinued teaching the German language.

Voices of Dissent

Yet, there were voices of dissent in the country despite the prevailing atmosphere of support for the war. Six members of the United States Senate and 57 members of the House of Representatives voted against Wilson's call for a declaration of war against Germany on April 6, 1917. The dissenting members included the first woman member of Congress, Republican Jeanette Rankin of Montana. In the Middle West, where many areas had large German-American settlements, sentiment against the war was strong. Republican Senator Robert M. La Follette of Wisconsin voted against the war resolution, asserting that "Germany has been patient with us," and Republican Senator George W. Norris of Nebraska charged that the United States was being manipulated into the war by financial and commercial interests that stood to profit from the war. Many parents were singing the popular 1915 antiwar song "I Didn't Raise My Boy to Be a Soldier."

The "Return to Normalcy"

Reconversion and "Normalcy" (1918–1921)

A spirited demand for reconversion to a peacetime economy set in almost immediately after the war. Both the administration under President Wilson, and the Republican opposition, agreed that the dominance of government over industry must be reversed. The **Esch-Cummins Act** of 1920 provided for the return of the railroads to private control. The Jones Merchant Marine Act of the same year authorized the sale of government-built ships to private operators. The Republican campaign slogan in the election of 1920 was "back to normalcy," and the presidential candidate Warren G. Harding of Ohio declared, "We want a period in America with less government in business and more business in government."

The Fordney-McCumber Tariff

A month after his inauguration, Harding called Congress into special session and asked it to pass legislation for higher tariffs, reduction in taxes and spending, and a bonus for the veterans. Congress responded by passing the "protectionist" **Fordney-McCumber Tariff**, whose high rates were designed to keep foreign goods out of the United States. International trade was reduced when European nations retaliated with tariff restrictions of their own.

Tax Reduction

Congress approved Harding's tax proposals by reducing income taxes substantially. "Normalcy" had returned, but a rocky road lay ahead.

Exercise Set 4.1

1. Which action by Germany prompted the United States to enter World War I?
   A. Attacking British shipping
   B. Forming an alliance with Austria-Hungary
   C. Resuming unrestricted submarine warfare
   D. Invading France

2. Which of the following was *not* used during World War I as a means of securing an adequate food supply?
   A. Planting of "victory gardens" by people who were not farmers
   B. Raising the price of wheat to stimulate increased production
   C. Government restriction on the shipment of food to Europe
   D. Encouragement of voluntary reduction in the consumption of food through "wheatless" and "meatless" days during the week

3. Woodrow Wilson's doctrine of "strict accountability" had specific application to
   A. submarine warfare.
   B. loans to belligerents.
   C. investment in foreign countries.
   D. treatment of prisoners of war.

Base your answers to questions 4 through 6 on the cartoon on page 308 and on your knowledge of social studies.

4. Which economic concept is illustrated in the cartoon?
   A. Depression
   B. Protective tariff
   C. Supply and demand
   D. Government price controls

5. Cotton farmers in the South experienced the situation shown in the cartoon because of the region's reliance on
   A. sharecropping.
   B. government subsidies.
   C. subsistence farming.
   D. a single-crop economy.

6. Between 1914 and 1916, which factor helped bring about the change in the financial position of the cotton farmer as shown in the cartoon?
   A. The demand for cotton became high during World War I.
   B. Climatic changes in other cotton-growing nations greatly reduced their cotton crops.
   C. American cotton became more resistant to destructive insect pests.
   D. New styles of clothing required large amounts of cotton.

7. In World War I public opinion
   A. remained strictly neutral until Wilson asked for war.
   B. remained disinterested in the war until the sinking of the *Lusitania*.
   C. preponderantly favored the Allied nations.
   D. was evenly divided between the two opposing sides.

8. During World War I, one method of financing the war effort by the United States was
   A. printing additional greenbacks.
   B. selling bonds.
   C. decreasing taxes.
   D. eliminating all tariffs.

9. The Republicans returned to power with the election of Warren G. Harding in 1920. The new President's call for a "return to normalcy" turned out to mean
   A. low tariffs and high taxes.
   B. active participation in international affairs.
   C. a huge increase in government expenditures.
   D. isolationism and protectionism.

THE TWENTIES: BUSINESS BOOM OR FALSE PROSPERITY?

I have no fear for the future of our country. It is bright with hope.
> Herbert Hoover, Inaugural Address, March 4, 1929

There is little question that in 1929 . . . the economy was fundamentally unsound.
> John Kenneth Galbraith in *The Great Crash*, 1929

The Election of 1920

The country entered a new era with the election of 1920. The Republicans chose Senator **Warren G. Harding** of Ohio as their presidential candidate, and Governor **Calvin Coolidge** of Massachusetts as his running mate. The Democrats nominated Governor **James M. Cox** of Ohio for President and Assistant Secretary of the Navy **Franklin Delano Roosevelt** for Vice President.

Wilson called for a "solemn referendum" on the League of Nations as a key issue in the election. The Republicans accepted the challenge. The war-weary nation supported the Republicans in rejecting the League and the idealism of Woodrow Wilson. The "Red Scare" of 1920, resulting from the Bolshevik revolution in Russia, was another factor contributing to the overwhelming Republican victory—404 to 127 electoral votes and 61 percent of the popular vote—for Warren G. Harding.

The Nineteenth Amendment to the Constitution, granting women the right to vote, was ratified by the required three fourths of the states on August 26, 1920, and, as a result, women were able to vote in a national election for the first time.

Economic Recession (1921–1922)

A severe economic recession, caused in part by the conversion of the industrial war machine to a peace economy, staggered the nation in 1921. The market was glutted with heavy inventories of goods produced during the war. Exports dropped sharply. As 20,000 businesses failed in 1921, unemployment reached 4,750,000 or 11.5 percent of the labor force. As the war demand for food slackened, the American farmers experienced falling prices that resulted in mass bankruptcies and foreclosures. The war's end also brought on serious labor strife. Major strikes occurred in the coal, steel, and railroad industries.

The average work week of steel workers was 68.7 hours. Their demand for an eight-hour day and the right to unions of their own choosing was met

Coal miners struck for better working conditions following World War I.

with outright rejection by powerful corporations. Grievances of the coal miners included extremely dangerous working conditions, a work week often limited to two or three days, and company ownership of the miners' homes and of the markets in which they purchased food, clothing, and other necessities. Railway labor went on strike when wages were reduced by President Harding's Railway Labor Board. The textile industry, which had migrated to the South where labor conditions were more favorable to mill owners, witnessed strikes by employees, many of them young women, whose wages were generally 18 cents an hour for a 56-hour work week.

War Loans and Debts

When the United States entered the war, the Allies had been at war with Germany almost three years. Their financial resources were exhausted. Consequently, loans were extended by the U.S. government to enable them to pay for the food and war materiel supplied by the American farmers and manufacturers. The British war debt, including postwar loans (in money and goods) for rehabilitation, amounted to $4.3 billion; the French $3.5 billion; the Italian $1.6 billion; and smaller amounts were owed by Belgium, Greece, and other Allies. The Allies argued that these debts should be canceled because they had been incurred in a common cause, but the Harding administration insisted they be repaid.

France and Britain presented Germany with a bill for $33 billion in **reparations** for damages caused by the war for which the Versailles Treaty had laid the blame on Germany. To enable Germany to pay, the United States adopted the **Dawes Plan of 1924** proposed by the Illinois financier Charles G. Dawes. Essentially, the plan scaled down reparation payments and provided for American loans to Germany. The entire war debts-reparations issue came to a halt with the **Great Depression** of the 1930s.

Scandal in the Harding Administration

President Harding died suddenly in San Francisco on August 2, 1923, and his Vice President **Calvin Coolidge** was sworn in as President. Shortly before, Harding's death rumors began to circulate about corruption in his administration.

Teapot Dome

A major scandal, but by no means the only one, centered around government oil resources at Teapot Dome in Wyoming and Elk Hills in California. About two months after Harding's death, a Senate committee under Thomas Walsh of Montana was formed to investigate oil leases made to private companies from these government oil reserves. The reserves had been set aside under Presidents Taft and Wilson for the use of the Navy.

Soon after his inauguration, President Harding transferred the Teapot Dome and Elk Hills oil reserves from the Navy Department (Secretary Edwin C. Denby) to the Interior Department (Secretary Albert B. Fall). Denby approved of this transfer. Fall then entered into a secret, illegal, and corrupt deal with two oil men, Harry Sinclair and Edward Doheny. Without competitive bidding and at a bargain price, Teapot Dome was leased to Sinclair, who had made a large contribution to the Republican campaign in 1920, and the Elk Hills reserve was leased to Doheny, a close friend of Fall. In March 1923, Fall resigned from the Cabinet.

The investigation committee discovered that Fall had received a "loan" of $100,000 from Doheny on which he was charged no interest, put up no security, and made no arrangement for repayment. Fall went to jail for accepting a bribe from Doheny. The Supreme Court declared the leases invalid because they were made by a "conspiracy" involving "fraud" and "corruption."

Coolidge Prosperity Not for Everyone

> The Business of America is Business.
>
> Calvin Coolidge

In the election of 1924, the Republicans won an easy victory with President Calvin Coolidge triumphing over the Democratic challenger John W. Davis, a New York corporate lawyer. "Coolidge prosperity" was the keynote of the Republican campaign, which resulted in a popular vote of nearly 2 to 1 and an electoral vote of 382 for Coolidge and 136 for Davis.

Despite the conservative Republican victory, there were disquieting rumblings in their own party, indicating that the Coolidge prosperity was not for everyone. Charging that Coolidge "had literally turned his back on the farmers," Senator **Robert M. La Follette**, Republican of Wisconsin, ran for President on the newly formed **League for Progressive Political Action**. He received support not only from the Farm Belt but also from labor groups and Socialists. The Progressive program called for federal assistance, including low-interest credit to farmers, social legislation for the benefit of labor, and government ownership of railroads and water power. La Follette received almost 5 million votes, about 16 percent of the total cast.

The election of 1924 was marked by a surge of women candidates in state elections. Two women, Miriam A. "Ma" Ferguson of Texas and Nellie T. Ross of Wyoming, were elected Governor of their states. Both were wives of former Governors. And 123 women were elected to state legislatures.

Slump in Agriculture

Agriculture, like other segments of the economy, had enjoyed economic prosperity during the war, heightened by greatly increased demand for food in the European war zone. As prices of wheat, meat, and other farm products rose rapidly, farmers borrowed money to buy farm machinery and to increase their acreage under cultivation. The **gasoline-engine tractor** could sow and cultivate more in an hour than the horse-driven plow could accomplish in a day. As farm hands returned from the war and European farms again entered the market, an overabundance of farm produce caused a severe slump in farm prices. The wholesale price index of farm products (1910–1914 = 100) was at 211 in 1920 and dropped to 121 in 1921. Its high during the 1920s was 149 in 1928. In 1932 it was 68, lowest in 33 years. Farm mortgage debt rose from $7.8 billion in 1920 to $10.8 billion in 1923.

Government support of farm prices was repeatedly vetoed by President Coolidge.

The "Golden Twenties"

"Golden Twenties" was the name given to the period of economic prosperity for many, but not all, segments of the American economy. As we have seen, farmers generally were experiencing hard times. Coal and textiles remained in a slump after the recession of 1921. But most manufacturing, retail trades, transportation, the growing service industries, and other segments of the labor force were earning good wages and spending freely. Business was booming. Few doubted that good times would ever end.

Speculation in the "Big Bull Market"

The stock market offered an almost irresistible temptation to make easy money. People from all walks of life began to "play the market" and watched the paper values of their investments soar. The accelerating boom of the "Big Bull Market" led more and more people to risk their savings in the "get rich quick" frenzy.

Exercise Set 4.2

1. The economic sector that benefited *least* from the Coolidge prosperity was
   A. agriculture.
   B. labor.
   C. large and small business.
   D. banking and finance.

2. Loans made by the United States during World War I to Allied nations
   A. remained largely unrepaid by the debtor nations.
   B. were payable in full under the Dawes Plan.
   C. were repaid in full during the two decades following the war.
   D. were voluntarily canceled during the Coolidge administration.

3. In the 1920s the farmers demanded a change in the government's farm program in order to obtain
   A. a higher tariff barrier on agricultural goods.
   B. a legislative program that would limit farm production and reduce farm indebtedness.
   C. a farm program that included direct farm supports.
   D. agricultural prices designed to give the farmer an equitable share of national income.

4. Which of these was a general characteristic of the period 1920–1930 in the United States?
   A. Strong executive leadership
   B. A retreat from a policy of laissez-faire
   C. Apathy toward reform
   D. Increase in federal tax rates

OPTIMISM AND MATERIALISM

> The good old times were not good old times. Neither master nor servant was as well situated then as today.
>
> Andrew Carnegie, June 1889

Mass Consumption

Rapid Rise of the Automobile

A brief recession in the years between 1921 and 1922 was soon followed by seven years of phenomenal growth in the American economy. The automobile, which was driven by a gasoline engine and was invented as a result of experiments in Europe and America in the late 19th century, played a key role in this economic development. Passenger car registration in the United States reached 8,000 by 1900, jumped to 1.3 million by 1913, rose to 8.1 million by 1920, and catapulted to 26.5 million by 1930—one automobile for every five Americans.

Henry Ford

Industrialist Henry Ford was largely responsible for this phenomenon. Ford, of Dearborn, Michigan, built his first automobile in his shop in 1896. The famous **Model T**, first produced in 1909, began to be turned out on the Ford **assembly line** by **mass production** techniques at the rate of one car every 10 seconds by 1925. In 1914 Ford startled the industrial world by introducing

Ford's assembly line turned out one Model T every ten seconds.

315

the eight-hour day with a minimum daily wage of $5. The rising standard of living, coupled with an increase in leisure time, created a ready market for the sale of automobiles.

Economic and Social Developments Related to the Automobile

The transformation in the American way of life brought about by the automobile was accompanied by other significant economic and social developments. New road construction, required to accommodate the automobile, was also a spur to automobile production. By 1925 there were more than half a million miles of surfaced highways in the United States. Twenty years later the number had tripled. Other industries associated with the automobile came into being or grew to giant proportions—vulcanized rubber for tires, refined petroleum for fuel, steel, glass, batteries, paint, upholstery, and other components of the automobile, as well as gas stations, repair shops, sales agencies, advertising, and insurance. Soon one in every nine American workers was earning a living directly or indirectly from the automobile.

Growth of Suburbia and the Middle Class

In other ways, too, the automobile transformed the character of American life. The movement of the urban middle class from the larger cities to their suburbs was due to automobiles that made it possible to commute to jobs. The growing middle class could afford to move to the suburbs where there was fresh air, space, better homes, and status, and to escape the congestion and the automobile fumes in the cities. This resulted in a real estate boom in suburbia and it accelerated the process of decay in the inner cities.

Decline of the Railroads

The construction of highways and superhighways marked the decline of interurban railroads and trolleys. Railroad mileage, which reached a high of 260,570 miles in 1929, declined to 231,494 thirty years later. Maintenance of the railroads was neglected while expenditures for road building soared.

Impact of Superhighways

Superhighways wrought havoc with planning as they intruded through tree-lined urban neighborhoods and gobbled up parkland. The popular trolley gave way to air-polluting buses. The toll of deaths, injuries, and property damage on the highways mounted steadily.

Life in Suburbia—New Political and Economic Growth

In the suburbs new regional political and economic units developed. Local boards of education, elected town officials, and neighborhood associations assumed added importance with the growth of suburbia. Highways began to be lined with shopping centers, gas stations, and chain restaurants.

Installment (Credit) Buying

Installment buying—buy now and make weekly or monthly payments later—enabled families to purchase durable goods on credit. Sales of automobiles, radios, refrigerators, vacuum cleaners, and other home appliances soared as consumers went deeper and deeper into debt. Chain stores and department stores promoted consumer credit by introducing charge accounts and time payments.

Advertising played a key role in promoting the business boom of the 1920s. **Montgomery Ward** and **Sears Roebuck** issued massive illustrated order catalogs from which buyers nationwide could purchase by mail virtually every consumer item on the market. Ads for soap, cigarettes, and other products in daily use appeared in newspapers, magazines, on outdoor billboards, and over the radio. By 1929, American business was investing $3.5 billion annually to promote its products by advertising.

New Media

Both **radio** and **motion pictures**—destined to have profound influence on American culture—became important media in the 1920s. Regular radio broadcasting began in 1920 with station WWJ in Detroit. The results of the 1920 presidential election were the first to be broadcast over the radio by station KDKA in Pittsburgh. Sales of radio sets and parts, which had already reached $60 million in 1922, skyrocketed to $400 million by 1929. In 1933 President Roosevelt was speaking to the entire nation in his radio "fireside chats."

Motion pictures, which first appeared early in the 20th century, became a major influence in American life during the 1920s. Large motion picture theaters were catering to 100 million viewers, to whom Charlie Chaplin, Mary Pickford, Douglas Fairbanks, Gloria Swanson, Greta Garbo, Harold Lloyd, and Rudolph Valentino became as familiar as their own neighbors. These stars of the silent screen faced a new challenge in 1927 when Al Jolson appeared in the first "talking picture," **The Jazz Singer**, released by Warner Brothers. Color films soon followed and Hollywood, California, became the center of the film industry.

With people all over the country listening to the same radio programs and viewing the same movies, a process of **homogenization** of American culture began. Colorful local speech patterns, dress, music, recreation, manners, and morals tended toward standardization as people took their cues from what they watched and heard on the radio and in the movie theater. This trend was greatly accelerated when television emerged two decades later.

Constitutional and Legal Issues

Attacks on Civil Liberties

In the years after World War I, there was a vigorous drive against Communists, anarchists, and Socialists by the federal government and state governments. The Espionage Act passed during the war remained in effect, and suspected revolutionists were arrested and fined under this law. This postwar concern over radicals in the United States was largely due to the Bolshevik Revolution.

• *The "Big Red Scare."* Toward the end of World War I, the revolutionary **Bolsheviks**, led by **Nikolai Lenin**, overthrew the czarist government of Russia and established a **Communist** regime. A wave of hysteria, the "**Big Red Scare**," swept through the United States. The country had experienced similar periods of fear and hate before. The Alien and Sedition Acts of John Adams's administration, the attacks on life and property of abolitionists in pre-Civil War days, and the rampaging violence of the post-Civil War Ku Klux Klan all had threatened civil liberties guaranteed by the Constitution.

• *The Palmer Raids.* Between 1919 and 1920, during the Big Red Scare, Attorney General A. Mitchell Palmer conducted raids, arresting some 6,000 suspects, 500 of whom were deported as undesirable aliens with little regard for their constitutional rights. It was at this time that the **American Civil Liberties Union** was founded by a group of prominent citizens including Roger Baldwin, its director from 1920 to 1950, attorney **Clarence Darrow**, settlement house founder **Jane Addams**, philosopher **John Dewey**, and Harvard law professor, later Supreme Court Justice, **Felix Frankfurter**.

• *Supreme Court Decisions.* Cases involving the constitutionality of these acts came before the Supreme Court. These cases raised the question of freedom versus order—the need to balance the liberty of the individual with the peace and order of society. Justice **Oliver Wendell Holmes** expressed this balance in two classic opinions. Writing for the Court in *Schenck* v. *United States* (1919), he upheld the conviction of the defendant for distributing leaflets advocating refusal to enlist in the armed services and expressed the "**clear and present danger**" doctrine. Holmes said, "The most stringent protection of free speech would not protect a man in falsely shouting fire in a theatre and causing a panic." (The wartime Espionage Act was found not to have violated the First Amendment.)

In the case of *Abrams* v. *United States* (1919), where the defendant appealed his sentence of twenty years' imprisonment for violating the 1918 Sedition Act by publishing and distributing leaflets alleged to bring the form of government of the United States into contempt, Holmes wrote, in a classic dissenting opinion, "In this case sentences of twenty years' imprisonment have been imposed for the publishing of two leaflets that I believe the defendants have as much right to publish as the government has to publish the Constitution of the United States now vainly invoked by them."

• *The Case of Sacco and Vanzetti (1920–1927).* On May 5, 1920 two Italian aliens, **Bartolomeo Vanzetti**, a fish peddler, and **Nicola Sacco**, a shoe factory employee—both anarchists opposed to all organized government— were arrested and charged with the murder of a payroll official and his guard, at a factory in South Braintree, Massachusetts. The case was tried before Judge Webster Thayer. The defendants were found guilty and sentenced to death, but many believed they were convicted because of their beliefs and their Italian nationality. Harvard law professor **Felix Frankfurter**, in his book *The Case of Sacco and Vanzetti,* wrote of Judge Thayer's opinion, "His twenty-five thousand word document cannot accurately be described otherwise than as a farrago [mixture] of misquotations, misrepresentations, suppressions, and mutilations." Protest meetings were held throughout the world. Appeals to the U.S. Supreme Court were turned down. Protesting their innocence to the end, Sacco and Vanzetti died in the electric chair at Charlestown, Massachusetts, August 23, 1927.

• *The New Ku Klux Klan.* Another attack on civil liberties was mounted by a renewed Ku Klux Klan in the postwar political climate. Targets of the Klan, which was especially strong in the Midwest and the South, were African Americans, Catholics, and Jews. The Klan spread terror by beating and lynching innocent people and by setting fire to homes and houses of worship.

Prohibition—the Eighteenth Amendment

> I believe in liberty . . . . But I have never believed that democracy involved the liberty to guzzle when that liberty to guzzle was a menace . . . to the integrity of that society which constitutes the America we love together.
>
> The Reverend John Haynes Holmes, 1924

The **Eighteenth Amendment**, which went into effect on January 16, 1920, outlawed the "manufacture, sale, or transportation of intoxicating liquors." For decades the **Anti-Saloon League** and the **Women's Christian Temperance Union** (WCTU) had been agitating for Prohibition. Several factors combined to make the period between 1917 and 1920 a favorable time for the adoption of this amendment. During the war many people thought it was wrong to use vast quantities of grain in the production of beer and liquor when food was needed for the Allies and armed forces overseas.

• *The Volstead Act.* The Volstead Act, or the Prohibition Enforcement Act, passed by Congress in 1919 over President Wilson's veto, defined "intoxicating" (as used in the Eighteenth Amendment) as any beverage containing over 1/2 of one percent alcohol. This made even beer and wine illegal. From the beginning, opposition to Prohibition was too strong and widespread to permit effective enforcement. Longtime habits, such as the workingman's pint of beer after a hard day's labor, could not easily be wiped out by law. Making "home brew" became a fad throughout the country. "**Speakeasies**," where patrons had to use passwords before the door was opened, flourished.

• *Repeal of the Eighteenth Amendment—the Twenty-First Amendment.* The movement to repeal the Eighteenth Amendment gained adherents when it became apparent that popular resistance can make a law virtually unenforceable. The Twenty-First Amendment to the Constitution, providing for the repeal of the Eighteenth, was proposed by two-thirds of both houses of Congress on February 20, 1933, and was quickly approved by the necessary three quarters of the state legislatures, so that it was ratified on December 21, 1933.

Science, Religion, and Education

In the summer of 1925, the nation became absorbed in the **Scopes Trial**, or so-called "monkey trial," taking place in Dayton, Tennessee, where John Scopes's job was in jeopardy for teaching evolution to his high school biology class. Laws prohibiting the teaching of Darwin's theory had been passed in three Southern states, including Tennessee, in support of Fundamentalist theology.

The case attracted added attention because of distinguished counsel on both sides: **William Jennings Bryan** for the prosecution, and **Clarence Darrow** for the defense. Bryan, a gifted orator, had run for President three times as the Democratic party candidate. The law under which Scopes was convicted was ultimately repealed, but Fundamentalists continued to demand that "**creationism**" (the Bible account of creation) be taught in the schools on a par with the theory of evolution.

Native Americans

The legal status of Native Americans throughout our history is viewed by many as a test of our adherence to the Constitutional guarantees of civil liberties. From the earliest colonial times, the Indians were driven off their lands and forced to retreat westward by the guns of white settlers and their army units. Treaties with the Indians were repeatedly broken as valuable minerals—gold, silver, copper—were found on their territory or as white farmers and ranchers sought the western lands promised forever to the Indians by the treaties. The Indians were forced to live on reservations located in areas that were usually arid lands of little use to white settlers. Traditional tribal boundaries conflicted with those drawn by the federal government in the interest of white settlers, miners, hunters, and trappers. Government army units often suppressed Indian opposition with wanton cruelty amounting to genocide.

The story is told by Helen Hunt Jackson in her book, published in 1881, aptly entitled *A Century of Dishonor.*

• *The Dawes Act (1887).* In an effort to make the Indians adopt white culture, the Dawes Act was passed in 1887. It attempted to substitute the single-family farm of 160 acres for the traditional Indian tribal way of life. After 25 years of "good behavior," the Indian would get title to the land plus American citizenship. The Dawes Act failed to achieve its purpose because most of the Indians preferred to remain on the reservation and retain their tribal ways. In 1924, citizenship was extended to all Native Americans by an act of Congress. But their plight remained desperate as they continued to have the lowest standard of living of all Americans.

• *Indian Reorganization Act (Wheeler-Howard Act) 1934.* Failure of the policy adopted under the Dawes Act was finally recognized in 1934 by the Indian Reorganization Act, also known as the Wheeler-Howard Act. The former policy was reversed. Native Americans were no longer to be urged to adapt to the "individual" American norm. Traditional tribal life was to be preserved and encouraged. Self-government of the Indian tribes on the reservations was to be protected by law. Education was to receive a high priority. The Indian population began to increase. From a low of less than 250,000 in the 1920s, it rose to 800,000 in 1970.

• *Indian Policy from the 1950s to the 1970s.* In the 1950s the federal government adopted a new Indian policy whose goals were termination and relocation. Its intention was to end all federal responsibility to Indians, transferring responsibility to those states that had large Indian populations. A second goal was to assimilate Indians into the American culture by relocating them to cities. Relocation and termination proved to be a failure, and in 1970, termination was ended. It was replaced by a new policy of "**self-determination**," which encouraged Indians to develop their own tribal life on the reservations. In the 1960s and 1970s, under a new spirit of militancy, Native Americans began to assert their rights, sometimes by direct action. They turned to the courts for redress, as far as possible, for injustices of the past.

Immigration

> Give me your tired, your poor,
> Your huddled masses yearning to breathe free,
> The wretched refuse of your teeming shore,
> Send these, the homeless, tempest-tossed to me,
> I lift my lamp beside the golden door!
>
> Inscription on the Statue of Liberty in New York Harbor
> From "The New Colossus" by Emma Lazarus

The Golden Door, which had beckoned millions of underprivileged and oppressed to seek refuge in America, was almost sealed after World War I.

Prompted by the economic recession of 1920–1921 and the "Red Scare" with its fear of alien ideas, Congress enacted the **Emergency Quota Act of 1921**. This act limited the number of immigrants from any country annually to 3 percent of the number of persons from that country who were living in the United States according to the census of 1910. This was only the beginning. In a calculated decision to limit the number of immigrants from southern and eastern Europe, the immigration laws of 1924 limited the number of immigrants from any country to 2 percent of those living in the United States from that country as determined by the census of 1890 (instead of 1910). Total immigration was reduced to 164,000. The **National Origins Act of 1929** set the annual limit at 150,000 with quotas for each European nation. The Immigration Act of June 25, 1948, authorized the admission of 205,000 European displaced persons. The number was increased to 341,000 by the act of June 16, 1950. The **McCarran-Walter Act of 1952** included new measures designed to keep out "subversives" and gave the Attorney General the power to deport immigrants (even if they had become citizens) for belonging to "Communist or Communist-front" organizations.

The **Immigration Act of 1965** discontinued quotas based on national origin. Race, religion, and color are no longer factors in admission. Occupation and skills of the applicant are key considerations, as is having relatives already living in the United States. The **Immigration and Control Act of 1986** (**Mazzoli-Simpson Act**) provides for legalizing the status of aliens who have been in the United States illegally since before January 1, 1981. Within six months, more than 300,000 aliens sought legal status under this provision. The 1986 law also imposes civil and criminal penalties on employers who knowingly hire, recruit, or refer aliens who are not authorized to work in the United States. The Refugee Act of 1980 provided for granting asylum in the United States to refugees who have good reason to fear persecution in their homeland. Under this act refugees have been admitted from Vietnam, Cambodia, Laos, Afghanistan, Poland, Czechoslovakia, and Central America.

Shifting Cultural Values

A Revolution in Morals and Manners

A revolution in morals and manners that began prior to World War I was greatly accelerated by the war and its aftermath. The psychoanalytic discoveries of **Sigmund Freud**, which opened the hither taboo field of sexual research, was interpreted as a warrant for rejecting the prevailing ethic of premarital chastity for women. The "flapper" of the 1920s "lost generation" took to smoking and drinking, wore short dresses, and found the automobile and movies a way to escape from the scrutiny of a chaperone. Women began to reject the double standard that permitted freedom for men but not for women. The Nineteenth Amendment, adopted in 1920, had finally guaranteed women's suffrage in national elections. By 1923, a **National Women's Party** was campaigning for the adoption of an **Equal Rights Amendment** to the Constitution.

Changing Role of Women

World War I had a dramatic effect on the status of women in American society. During the war, women served in the armed forces. They filled the gap in farms, factories, mills, and mines left by the men who were in military service. The new freedom gained during the war manifested itself in new moral and social behavior. Women were now openly drinking and smoking, and their clothing was more revealing.

The role of women in all aspects of life—economic, political, social, and cultural—was changing rapidly. A majority of women now lived in cities and they increasingly entered the workforce. In 1920, one of every five employed people was a woman. By 1950, 18 million—nearly 30 percent of the workforce—were women. Electric irons, washing machines, refrigerators, vacuum cleaners, canned goods, and ready-made clothing freed women from the relentless pressures traditionally associated with homemaking. Women began playing an active role in politics, civic affairs, the arts, and the pursuit of their individual interests and talents. Women in the workforce began playing an equal role with their husbands in supporting the family. In response to these developments, Congress enacted the 1922 SheppardTowner Act, extending financial aid to the states for the welfare and health of pregnant women and newborn infants. The act authorized the appropriation of $1 million annually for maternity and infant care.

• *The Nineteenth Amendment (1920).* The Nineteenth Amendment, guaranteeing women the right to vote in state and national elections, was proposed by Congress on June 4, 1919, with little opposition. President Wilson urged its adoption, noting the part played by women during World War I. "The services of women during the supreme crisis have been of the most signal usefulness and distinction." The Amendment became the law of the land when it was ratified by the 36th state on August 26, 1920. It declared: "The right of citizens of the United States to vote shall not be denied or abridged by the United States or by any state on account of sex."

Literature and American Life

> And I wish American novelists would give up trying to make business romantically interesting. Nobody wants to read about it unless it's crooked business.
>
> F. Scott Fitzgerald, *This Side of Paradise* (1920)

> He serenely believed that the one purpose of the real-estate business
> was to make money for George F. Babbitt. True, it was a good adver-
> tisement at Boosters Club lunches . . . to speak sonorously of unselfish
> public service . . . and a thing called ethics . . . But they didn't imply
> that you were to be impractical and refuse to take twice the value of
> a house if a buyer was . . . an idiot. . . .
>
> Sinclair Lewis, *Babbitt* (1922)

The 1920s became known as "The Roaring Twenties," "The Gilded Age,"
and "The Jazz Age." Writers of the period, such as **Sinclair Lewis**, **F. Scott
Fitzgerald**, **Theodore Dreiser**, **Ernest Hemingway**, and **John Dos Passos**,
cast doubt on prevailing values and caused the participants in the giddy whirl
to be dubbed "the lost generation."

• *The Search for Heroes.* It is doubtless significant that the period witnessed a frantic search for heroes. As a model, **Charles A. Lindbergh** was
almost too good to be true. A tall, handsome, modest young man, Lindbergh startled the world by his solo, nonstop flight in his single-engine
propeller-driven plane, "**The Spirit of St. Louis**," across the Atlantic from
New York to Paris, May 20–21, 1927. The overnight flight took 33 hours,
39 minutes. On his return to New York, Lindbergh, the "Lone Eagle," was
greeted with a triumphant parade up New York's Broadway. A year later,
Amelia Earhart, a pioneer woman in aviation, made a similar trans-Atlantic
nonstop flight.

In sports, the all-time baseball hero, **Babe Ruth**, came to the New York
Yankees in 1920 as an outfielder after previously winning 24 games as a
pitcher with the Boston Red Sox. He established a lifetime record of 714
home runs and led the great Yankee ball club to seven pennants and four
world championships. Other sports heroes of the period included Jack
Johnson, world heavyweight boxing champion (1910–1915); Jack Dempsey,
who attracted the first million-dollar gate in 1921; Bill Tilden, who was
ranked first in the world in tennis, throughout the 1920s; "Red" Grange, who
scored 31 touchdowns for the University of Illinois; and Gertrude Ederle, the
first woman to swim the English Channel and break the existing men's record
on August 6, 1926.

On the screen, the object of fascination was **Rudolph Valentino**. Born in
Italy, Valentino came to the United States in 1913 and became a national idol
for his performance in two 1921 blockbusters, *The Four Horsemen of the
Apocalypse* and *The Sheik.*

• *The Black Renaissance.* The post-World War I period witnessed a great
black renaissance in Harlem. Poets Langston Hughes and Countee Cullen,
political activist Marcus Garvey, writer Zora Neale Hurston, scholar and
nationalist leader W. E. B. Du Bois, as well as gifted painters and musicians,
gathered in Harlem and made this part of New York, with its wide streets and
classic buildings, an exciting place to live in the 1920s.

Exercise Set 4.3

1. Which of the following was a prime *cause* of the other three?
   A. Imposition of immigration quotas
   B. The Big Red Scare
   C. Raids conducted by Attorney General A. Mitchell Palmer
   D. Rapid growth of the new Ku Klux Klan

2. Federal government policy toward Native Americans may properly be described as
   A. generally one of hostility to their best interest as fellow Americans.
   B. a policy designed to destroy or basically alter their traditional culture patterns.
   C. a series of changes in policy including making treaties with them, attempting to exterminate them, and treating them as wards of the government.
   D. All of the above.

3. Which of the following does *not* apply to the immigration policy of the United States during the 1920s?
   A. It sought to limit the number of immigrants.
   B. It restored the traditional American immigration policy of keeping the Golden Door open.
   C. It established the principle of selective immigration by favoring immigrants from some areas of the world over those from other areas.
   D. It was enacted over the objection of a sizeable minority of public opinion.

4. Between 1920 and 1930 passenger car registration in the United States leaped from 8.1 million to 26.5 million. A direct result of this increase was
   A. less movement of people to the suburbs.
   B. a stimulation of such related industries as advertising, insurance, and finance.
   C. a decrease in road and highway construction.
   D. a decline of the importance of the assembly line.

5. Which was *not* a characteristic of the economic life of the 1920s?
   A. New methods of production
   B. Installment buying and borrowing to finance consumer growth
   C. A government tax policy that retarded accumulation of large personal fortunes
   D. Investment by banks in real estate, mortgages, bonds, and stocks

6. A major effect of the new radio and motion picture industries was
   A. a steady decline in the circulation of newspapers and magazines.
   B. a tendency toward homogenization of American culture.
   C. a shift away from sports as a major source of recreation for both spectators and participants.
   D. a decline in the influence of religion due to falling attendance at religious services.

7. The rapid growth of the automobile industry was made possible by
   A. the introduction by Henry Ford of an eight-hour day and a minimum wage of $5 a day in 1914.
   B. a ready market created by the rising standard of living and the increase of leisure time of the average American.
   C. cooperation of labor and management in the trucking industry.
   D. failure of trolleys and railroads to maintain a high standard in their facilities and operations.

8. Which of the following pairs are associated with the Harlem Renaissance of the 1920s?
   A. Sigmund Freud and Ernest Hemingway
   B. Gertrude Ederle and Rudolph Valentino
   C. Sinclair Lewis and F. Scott Fitzgerald
   D. Langston Hughes and Countee Cullen

9. Which of the following was, at least in part, a cause of the other three?
   A. The changing role of women in economic, social, and cultural affairs
   B. The adoption of the Nineteenth Amendment
   C. The active participation of women in World War I
   D. The emerging emphasis on wife rather than mother

10. The adoption of the Nineteenth Amendment to the Constitution in 1920 was a result of
   A. the fact that many states had already extended suffrage to women before World War I.
   B. the widespread belief that the time had come to stop classifying women with others most commonly denied the ballot: children, illiterates, the "insane," and criminals.
   C. the way women did "men's work" in war industries.
   D. All of the above.

1. During the post-World War I period, civil liberties were under attack. Which of the following is *not* an example of this experience?
A. The conviction of Sacco and Vanzetti
B. The Scopes trial in Dayton, Tennessee
C. The revival of the Ku Klux Klan
D. The novels of Sinclair Lewis

2. An experience of the majority of immigrants to the United States was that they
A. frequently met resentment.
B. settled in rural areas where cheap land was available.
C. were rapidly assimilated into the predominant lifestyle.
D. joined radical parties to bring about economic reform.

3. President Calvin Coolidge once said, "The business of America is business." This slogan is most closely related to
A. a laissez-faire attitude toward the economy.
B. government ownership of heavy industry.
C. the enactment of protective tariffs.
D. legislation benefiting organized labor.

4. At various times throughout history, racial and religious prejudices have been exploited for the purpose of
A. expanding cultural diversity.
B. re-enforcing nationalistic sentiments.
C. expanding international trade.
D. furthering the growth of fine arts.

5. All Native Americans achieved citizenship
A. by the Dawes Act of 1887.
B. in 1968 as part of President Johnson's Great Society.
C. by an act of Congress in 1924.
D. by the Indian Reorganization Act of 1934.

THEMATIC ESSAY

Directions: Write a well-organized essay that includes an introduction, several paragraphs addressing the task below, and a conclusion.

Theme: Changing Cultural Values

The early decades of the 20th century proved to be a time of change in American cultural values.

Task:

From your study of the early decades of the 20th century, identify *two* traditional cultural values that would be tested and subsequently experience considerable change.

For each cultural value identified:

- Identify the subject (women, minorities, children, educational values, music, etc.).
- Discuss circumstances that led to the challenge of the traditional value.
- Discuss one immediate or long-term effect of the challenge and change in the cultural value.

You may use any early 20th-century challenges and changes in American cultural values from your study of United States history. Some suggestions you may wish to consider are Prohibition (1920), women's suffrage (1919), Scopes Trial (1925), Child Labor Act (1919), developments in birth control and divorce, development of jazz, etc.

You are *not* limited to these suggestions.

DOCUMENT-BASED QUESTION

The following questions (Part A and Part B) are based on the accompanying documents (1–6). Some of these documents have been edited for the purpose of this exercise. The question is designed to test your ability to work with historical documents and to demonstrate your knowledge of the subject matter being presented. As you analyze the documents, take into account both the source of the document and the author's point of view.

Historical Context:

> Although the "Golden 1920s" showed early signs of prosperity, a closer examination of the decade reveals that prosperity was not experienced by many.

Task:

> Using information from the documents and your knowledge of United States history, answer the questions that follow each document in Part A. Your answers to the questions will help you write the Part B essay, in which you will be asked:
>
> Although the decade before the Great Depression was called the "Roaring 20s" or the "Golden 20s," a closer examination of the decade reveals that prosperity was not experienced by many. Identify the groups of Americans who were suffering economically and discuss how their conditions may have contributed to the collapse of the American economy in the 1930s.

Part A
Short-Answer Questions

The documents below relate to economic and social issues concerning the 1920s. Examine each document carefully and then answer the questions that follow.

DOCUMENT 1

> By 1929, the richest 1 percent of the American population would own 40 percent of the nation's wealth. The bottom 93 percent would experience a 4 percent drop in real disposable per capita income between 1923 and 1929.

1. Identify one problem that may result when a large part of the population (in this case 93 percent) has less money to spend.

_____

_____

_____

_____

2. How much of the nation's wealth would the remaining 99 percent of the population own by 1929?

_____

_____

_____

_____

DOCUMENT 2

We worked to build this country, mister.
While you enjoyed a life of ease;
You've stolen all that we built, mister;
Now our children starve and freeze.

Think me dumb if you wish mister;
Call me green or blue or red;
This one thing I sure know mister;
My hungry babies must be fed.

I don't want your millions, mister,
I don't want your diamond ring.
All I want is the right to live mister;
Give me back my job again.

—Jim Garland, Coal Miner, Harlan County, Kentucky,
"I Don't Want Your Millions, Mister"

3. According to the author of the song, who was experiencing the benefits and profits of the working classes?

_____

_____

_____

_____

DOCUMENT 3

The present condition of American agriculture constitutes an emergency of the gravest character. The Department of Commerce report shows that during 1923 there was a steady and marked increase in dividends paid by the great industrial corporations. The same is true of the steam and electric railways and practically all other large corporations. On the other hand, the Secretary of Agriculture reports that in the fifteen principal wheat growing states more than 108,000 farmers since 1920 have lost their farms through foreclosure or bankruptcy . . . that more than 122,000 have surrendered their property without legal proceedings . . . .

Almost unlimited prosperity for the great corporations and ruin and bankruptcy for agriculture is the direct and logical result of the policies and legislation which deflated the farmer while extending almost unlimited credit to the great corporations . . .

—Robert La Follette, Progressive Party Platform, 1924

4. According to candidate La Follette, how did American farmers compare with American corporations during the first four years of the 1920s?

_____

_____

_____

_____

DOCUMENT 4

MORTGAGED FARMS IN THE UNITED STATES
IN 1910, 1920, AND 1925

Value of mortgaged farms in 1910

Farmers' equity 72.7%   Debt 27.3%

Inflated values of mortgaged farms in 1920

Farmers' equity 70.9%   Debt 29.1%

Estimated values of mortgaged farms in 1925

Farmers' equity 60%   Debt 40%

5. According to the graph concerning mortgaged farms (1910–1925), what was the trend regarding a farmer's amount of actual ownership of his farm?

_____

_____

_____

_____

DOCUMENT 5

The right of all to the opportunity for self-maintenance; a wider and fairer distribution of wealth; a living wage, as a minimum, and above this a just share for the worker in the product of industry and agriculture.

—*Social Creed of Protestant Churches*, Federal Council
of Churches, December, 1932

6. As the Depression hit following the 1920s, what issues did the Federal Council of Churches identify as in need of change?

_____

_____

_____

_____

DOCUMENT 6

—Two Chickens in Every Garage, 1932

7. How does the author of the political cartoon view President Hoover's promise to the American people of "A chicken in every pot and two cars in every garage?"

_____

_____

_____

_____

Part B
Essay

Your essay should be well organized with an introductory paragraph that states your position on the question. Develop your position in the next paragraphs and then write a conclusion. In your essay, include specific historical details and refer to the specific documents you analyzed in Part A. You may include additional information from your knowledge of social studies.

Historical Context:

Although the "Golden 1920s" showed early signs of prosperity, a closer examination of the decade reveals that prosperity was not experienced by many.

Task:

Although the decade before the Great Depression was called the "Roaring 20s" or the "Golden 1920s," a closer examination of the decade reveals that prosperity was not experienced by many. Identify the groups of Americans who were suffering economically and discuss how their conditions may have contributed to the collapse of the American economy in the 1930s.

Guidelines:

In your essay, be sure to
• Develop all aspects of the task.
• Incorporate information from *at least five* documents.
• Incorporate relevant outside information.
• Support the theme with many relevant facts, examples, and details.
• Use a logical and clear plan of organization, including an introduction and a conclusion that are beyond a restatement of the theme.

CHAPTER 2

THE GREAT DEPRESSION
AND THE NEW DEAL (1933–1940)

FAILURE OF THE OLD ORDER:
HOOVER AND THE CRASH

> Our immediate and paramount task as a people is to rout the forces of economic disruption and pessimism that have swept upon us.
> Herbert Hoover, June 16, 1931

> A glance at the situation today only too clearly indicates that equality of opportunity as we have known it no longer exists . . . . Our task now is . . . distributing wealth and products more equitably, of adapting existing economic organizations to the service of the people.
> Franklin D. Roosevelt, September 23, 1932

Cracks in the Economic Foundation

Overproduction and Maldistribution of Purchasing Power

The short-lived prosperity of the late 1920s was built on a fragile economic base. Technological advances, coupled with overexpansion of credit, brought about a vast increase in industrial production. At the same time the maldistribution of wealth—the concentration of money among wealthy individuals and surpluses in business corporations—meant that farmers and laborers were not able to purchase the goods produced. For a time the gap was made up by installment buying and other forms of credit. But the day of reckoning had to come.

Overexpansion of Credit

Overexpansion of credit was encouraging reckless gambling in the stock market. An investor could purchase shares of stock "on margin," that is, by putting up as little as 10 percent of the cost with the rest of the money on credit. This enabled people to buy much more than they could afford. Stock prices became overinflated.

335

The Stock Market Crash

Many investors went bankrupt in the crash of 1929.

The Crash of 1929

Stock prices began to decline slowly in September 1929, and by October the decline gained momentum. The great crash came on **Black Tuesday**, October 29, 1929, when 16.5 million shares were traded in a precipitous decline that continued for the rest of the year. **U.S. Steel**, which sold for $262 a share in September, was quoted at $22 three months later.

Worldwide Economic Collapse

The economic crash and the resulting **depression** were worldwide. The banking systems of the world were interdependent. American banks had made large loans to their European affiliates. Banks on both sides of the Atlantic failed and caused others to fail. Between October 1, 1929, and August 31, 1932, 4,835 American banks failed. Their total deposits, representing the lifetime savings of millions of Americans, amounted to $3.25 billion. To make matters worse, the **Hawley-Smoot Tariff** of 1930, with its high protectionist rates, served only to dry up the sickly streams of international trade.

Hoover and the Depression

President Hoover did make efforts to revive the economy but he was stopped from taking drastic action by his own economic philosophy. He believed that direct government aid to the needy would destroy "**rugged individualism**" and might even lead to socialism. Moreover, he believed that the depression would soon end and that "prosperity [was] just around the corner."

Moratorium on War Debts

In 1931 Hoover recommended a one-year moratorium (postponement) on the payment of war debts and on reparations owed by Germany to the Allies.

Trickle-down Economics—the Reconstruction Finance Corporation

Hoover also believed in "**trickle-down economics**," the idea that profits of big business would trickle down to average Americans. At Hoover's request, Congress established the **Reconstruction Finance Corporation** (1932). The RFC advanced some $2 billion in loans to state and local governments and to banks, railroads, farm mortgage associations, and large corporations in order to stimulate the economy. But the roots of the depression were too deep to be easily eradicated. Hoover's efforts to stem the tide proved to be inadequate, and the Republican Party was swept out of office in the election of November 1932.

Misery and the Great Depression

Mass Unemployment and Its Effects

Mass unemployment was the hallmark of the Great Depression. Farms were abandoned, factories closed, and men and women stood on breadlines waiting for a handout. Youths rode the railroad lines in empty freight cars. Early in 1932, one fourth of the workforce, some 10 million Americans, were unemployed. Some, like the fictional Joads in Steinbeck's *The Grapes of Wrath*, left their farms and drove West hoping for better times in California. In cities, men peddled apples on street corners. Women and children perhaps suffered most, while marginalized communities were hard hit by this unprecedented economic catastrophe.

Rundown shanty towns, their shacks put together with tin and paper collected in dumps, sprang up all over the country. They were named "Hoovervilles" in derision of an administration that was deemed inept, if not indeed lacking in compassion.

The Bonus Army in Washington

In the spring of 1932, about 15,000 veterans of World War I marched on Washington from all over the country to demand immediate payment of their bonus certificates, which were not due until 1945. They camped in shacks along the Anacostia River near the Capitol. When Congress failed to pass legislation to meet their demand, most of them departed. But some 2,000 remained, refusing the government's offer of funds to pay for their return home. Hoover ordered the Army to drive them out. Led by Chief-of-Staff General **Douglas MacArthur**, army infantry and cavalry units attacked the veterans in force, scattering them with tear-gas bombs, sabers, and tanks, and burned their shacks. MacArthur and Hoover were severely criticized for this tactic, which they claimed was "necessary under the circumstances."

Exercise Set 4.4

1. From 1923 to early 1929 behavior of business cycles
   A. registered sharp fluctuations.
   B. was indiscernible.
   C. created the belief that a serious depression would never return.
   D. created unrest and alarm.

2. A criticism of President Hoover's policies in dealing with the Depression was
   A. he postponed action in the belief that prosperity was just around the corner.
   B. he intervened excessively with businesses and corporations.
   C. the policies of laissez-faire were violated by his administration.
   D. he did less than earlier Presidents had done in similar crises.

3. Which conditions are most characteristic of a depression?
   A. High production and high demand
   B. Few jobs and little demand
   C. Much money in circulation and high stock prices
   D. Supply meeting demand and high unemployment

4. A condition that was for the most part unrelated to the causes of the Great Depression was
   A. the fact that large-scale construction of new highways was undertaken to accommodate the rapid introduction of the automobile.
   B. that increased industrial production was not matched by a corresponding increase in the purchasing power of consumers.
   C. that newly introduced laborsaving devices were causing technological unemployment.
   D. that overextension of credit was encouraging debt as well as speculation in the stock market.

FRANKLIN D. ROOSEVELT: RELIEF, RECOVERY, AND REFORM

> In broad terms I assert that modern society, acting through its government, owes the definite obligation to prevent the starvation or the dire want of any of its fellow men and women who try to maintain themselves but cannot.
>
> Franklin D. Roosevelt, speech in campaign
> for reelection as Governor of New York, 1930

New York Serves as a Prototype for the New Deal

The "Little New Deal"

Soon after his reelection as Governor of New York in 1930, **Franklin D. Roosevelt** called a special session of the legislature to face the problem of mounting economic distress. New York became the first state to appropriate public funds for unemployment relief. The "**New Deal**" was foreshadowed in Roosevelt's governorship. It was, in effect, a "Little New Deal." A State Power Authority was created to control public utilities and establish the principle that the water power of the state belonged to the people. An old-age Pension Law became a forerunner of **Social Security**. Legislation was introduced to end the 54-hour work week, and to require an **8-hour day** and **48-hour week** for women and children. **Minimum-wage legislation** for women was also proposed.

Mayor Fiorello LaGuardia

New York City had its own "Little New Deal," when it elected Fiorello LaGuardia (the "Little Flower") Mayor in 1933. Defeated in his bid for reelection to Congress in 1932, he formed the Fusion Party and was elected Mayor of New York in 1933. He was reelected in 1937 and 1941. On first taking office he declared, "Our theory of municipal government is an experiment to try to show that a nonpartisan, nonpolitical local government is possible."

The LaGuardia administration found a sympathetic reception in Washington. During LaGuardia's first year in office, the federal government made significant commitments to New York City: $20 million for low-cost housing, $1.5 million toward completion of the Triborough Bridge, and $25 million to put 3,000 to work on subway construction. During LaGuardia's tenure, New York built 92 new schools and introduced the first inclusive health insurance plan in the nation for low-income city employees.

The New Deal in Washington

> I pledge you, I pledge myself, to a new deal for the American people.
> Franklin D. Roosevelt, accepting the Democratic
> nomination for the presidency, July 2, 1932

A Strong Cabinet

To help him tackle the problems facing the country and to bring relief, recovery, and reform to the beleaguered nation, Roosevelt surrounded himself with the best people he could find, regardless of their political affiliation. **Harold L. Ickes**, a former Republican, became Secretary of the Interior. **Henry Morgenthau, Jr.**, the President's close friend and Hyde Park neighbor, remained Secretary of the Treasury for twelve years. For Secretary of Labor, Roosevelt appointed **Frances Perkins**, the first woman to serve in a President's cabinet. Perkins, who had worked with Jane Addams at Hull House in Chicago, was to become a key figure in shaping New Deal labor legislation. **Henry A. Wallace**, a former Republican, who was to become Vice President during Roosevelt's third term, was Secretary of Agriculture and later Secretary of Commerce.

A "Brain Trust"

In addition to his Cabinet, Roosevelt brought to Washington a number of brilliant unofficial advisers who came to be known as the "brain trust." Chief among these was **Harry Hopkins**, a former social worker, who had the President's complete confidence and was entrusted with sensitive missions. Also in the "brain trust" were Rexford G. Tugwell, Adolphe A. Berle, Jr., and Raymond Moley, all members of the Columbia University faculty.

Relief of Human Suffering

> Let me assert my firm belief that the only thing we have to fear is
> fear itself.
> Franklin D. Roosevelt, First Inaugural Address,
> March 4, 1933

The first task set for the "New Deal" was relief of human suffering. Loss of people's life savings through bank failures had to be halted. The hungry had to be fed. The unemployed had to be put to work.

The Emergency Banking Relief Act

The day after his inauguration as President, Roosevelt summoned Congress into special session and proclaimed a national bank holiday, closing all the nation's banks for an indefinite period of time. Congress promptly passed the Emergency Banking Relief Act (March 9, 1933) granting extraordinary power to the President. Within a week the solvent banks reopened and deposits exceeded withdrawals. Swift action had restored public confidence in the banking system. Reform, to prevent future catastrophe, was to come later.

The Federal Emergency Relief Act

The Federal Emergency Relief Act (May 12, 1933) established a **Federal Emergency Relief Administration** (**FERA**) and authorized an appropriation of $500 million. The money was to be granted to states and municipalities for emergency relief. Harry L. Hopkins was appointed Administrator of the FERA. Ultimately, some $3 billion was spent under the act. A branch of the FERA was the **Civil Works Administration** (**CWA**), established in November 1933 to provide temporary jobs during the winter emergency. The CWA came under criticism because many of the jobs, such as leaf-raking, hastily created during the emergency, were called "boondoggling," useless or wasteful activities.

Dealing with Unemployment

A **Public Works Administration** (**PWA**) was established in June 1933 under the **National Industrial Recovery Act** (**NIRA**). It was directed by Secretary of the Interior Harold L. Ickes. The object of this legislation was called "pump priming;" that is, the government pumps money into the economy to stimulate the economy. A full-scale attack on unemployment came in the spring of 1935 with the creation of the **Works Progress Administration** (**WPA**). This act, administered by Harry Hopkins, provided 9 million useful jobs during the next eight years. Communities throughout the land were enriched by the construction of 6,000 school buildings, thousands of post-office and courthouse buildings, 128,000 miles of roads, and thousands of bridges. An effort was made to place people in jobs suitable to their education and experience. Unemployed architects designed buildings; engineers built dams; artists painted murals; and authors, musicians, playwrights, and actors were enabled to work at their professions and contribute their talents as government employees during the Depression.

Aid to Youth

Agencies created specifically for the purpose of providing aid to needy youth were the **Civilian Conservation Corps** (**CCC**) and the **National Youth Administration** (**NYA**). The CCC enrolled young men between the ages of 18 and 25 and assigned them to one of the 2,600 work camps throughout the country. There they cleared land for public parks, built dams for flood control, planted trees, and cleared swamps. The CCC ultimately enlisted 2.5 million young men. In addition to food, clothing, and shelter, they received money payments that went in part to their needy families. The **National Youth Administration** (**NYA**), created in 1935, cooperated with schools and colleges in providing an income for needy students who performed tasks useful to their school or college. The NYA gave part-time employment to more than 600,000 college students and 1.5 million high school pupils. Aid was provided also to 2.6 million young Americans who were not in school. Some received vocational training; others were put to work renovating government buildings, repairing equipment, building playgrounds, and upgrading public parks.

Recovery for the American Economy

Besides trying to relieve human suffering caused by the Depression, the New Deal sought to restore the nation's economic health. The New Deal program for recovery set its sights on industry, agriculture, and housing.

Measures to Aid Industry

The **National Industrial Recovery Act** (**NIRA**), which was signed into law June 16, 1933, created the **National Recovery Administration** (**NRA**) under General Hugh S. Johnson. Members of each industry were to establish "codes of fair competition" that, when approved by the President, were to be legally binding on the industry. The code of each industry was to prescribe wages, hours, and prices, provide for a minimum wage, and preserve labor's rights of collective bargaining. A blue eagle was adopted as a symbol that, when displayed, signified compliance with the code of that industry.

Helping Home Owners

The **Home Owners Loan Corporation** (**HOLC**) was established in June 1933 to help home owners save their homes. Every day 1,000 home owners were losing their homes to mortgage holders (banks) for failure to pay the mortgages. The HOLC loaned money at low interest to private home owners to pay off their old mortgages and new long-term mortgages were arranged at low interest rates. Within a year 300,000 loans amounting to almost $1 billion were made. During the three year period 1933–1936 the homes of more than a million families were saved by the HOLC. By insuring building loans made by banks, the **Federal Housing Authority** (**FHA**) created in 1934 encouraged banks to lend money for home repairs and for construction of homes and businesses.

Aid to Agriculture

To halt foreclosures on farms, a **Farm Credit Administration** (**FCA**) was established in June 1933. Farm mortgages were refinanced at low rates of interest for long terms, while farm debts were adjusted on favorable terms. In its first 18 months, the FCA refinanced the mortgages of nearly one fifth of America's family farms. To aid the poorest farmers—the tenant farmers and sharecroppers—a **Farm Security Administration (FSA)** was established in 1937. More than a billion dollars was extended in low-interest, long-term loans to enable tenants to buy farms.

• *The AAA (1933).* Major reform in agriculture was undertaken in two **Agricultural Adjustment Acts (AAA)**. The first AAA of May 1933 was designed to achieve "parity" between agriculture and industry by raising the prices of farm commodities, so that farm income would keep pace with nonfarm income. This was to be attained by curtailing production. Farmers signed agreements to reduce their planting by one fourth to one half, since lower production would help to raise the market price of farm commodities. In return, the government made "benefit payments" to farmers for their crop reduction. The AAA had an immediate effect on production and market prices of farm commodities. For example, with 10 million acres of cotton out of production, cotton prices rose from 5.5 to 9.5 cents per pound in the first year. The Supreme Court, by a 6 to 3 vote in January 1936, declared the AAA unconstitutional.

• *The SCDAA.* Congress then passed the **Soil Conservation and Domestic Allotment Act (SCDAA)** of 1936, which paid farmers for growing soil-conserving crops such as clover and soybeans and not growing soil-exhausting staples like cotton, corn, and tobacco.

• *Second AAA.* A second AAA in 1938 continued the soil conservation program of the 1936 act. With the approval of two thirds of the producers of a specific commodity, the government could decide the amount of corn, wheat, rice, cotton, or tobacco that could be marketed. Surpluses of each commodity were to be stored by the government and released when prices rose to the parity level. Despite all-out efforts at recovery, the level of unemployment and poverty remained above pre-Depression days well into Roosevelt's second term.

Reform Programs

> I see one-third of a nation ill-housed, ill-clad, ill-nourished.
> The test of our progress is not whether we add more to the abundance of those who have much; it is whether we provide enough for those who have too little.
>
> Franklin D. Roosevelt, Second Inaugural Address,
> January 20, 1937

The New Deal search for effective reform programs had a major impact on banking, stock market operations, social security, and labor.

Banking Reform

The **Glass-Steagall Banking Act of 1933** was designed to protect depositors against bank failures. It separated commercial from investment banking and restricted the use of bank credit for financial speculation. Most significant was the provision creating a new agency, the **Federal Deposit Insurance Corporation** (**FDIC**), which insured savings bank deposits up to $2,500. The guarantee was raised to $5,000 the following year and proved a boon to the banks as well as to their depositors. The amount insured—$100,000 in 1994—was steadily increased as the purchasing power of the dollar increased.

Stock Market Reforms

To provide basic protection to investors in the stock markets, the **Securities Act of May 1933** required every new stock offering to contain specific information to enable prospective investors to judge the value of a share and the financial circumstances of the corporation. The **Securities and Exchange Commission** was established the following year to enforce the act.

Social Security

A landmark achievement of the New Deal was the **Social Security Act** of August 14, 1935. The act provided for (1) a fund for **unemployment insurance** to be derived from taxes on payrolls of employers having 8 or more employees. Each state was to administer its own system in conjunction with the federal government; (2) a fund for old-age and survivors insurance to be derived from taxes levied on employers and their employees. This fund was to be administered by the federal government and was to make monthly pension payments to retirees when reaching the age of 65; (3) money grants to states for pensions provided by state law; and (4) grants to states for relief of blind, disabled, and other destitute dependents.

The act was to be administered by a three-member **Social Security Board**. The act, which President Roosevelt described as "a cornerstone in a structure which is being built," had an immediate impact. Two years after the Social Security program was passed into law, 21 million workers were covered by unemployment insurance and 36 million were entitled to old-age pensions.

Labor Legislation

• *The Wagner Act.* Through patient and effective persuasion, Senator **Robert F. Wagner** of New York gained enough support from the business community to make possible the passage of landmark labor legislation. The **National Labor Relations Act** of July 5, 1935, known as the **Wagner Act**, was designed to reduce tension in labor relations and thus avoid strikes and labor disaffection. It provided for an independent **National Labor Relations Board** (**NLRB**) that would conduct plant elections for employees to choose their agents for contract negotiations and grievance resolution. The Board could also issue "cease and desist" orders against "unfair labor practices" such as interference with the union in collective bargaining, refusal to bargain collectively, and discrimination against union members.

• *The Fair Labor Standards Act.* The Fair Labor Standards Act (Wages and Hours Law) of 1938 set minimum wages (40 cents an hour initially) and maximum hours (40 hours per week) and forbade the employment of children under 16 in business establishments engaged in interstate commerce.

• *Formation of the CIO.* In 1935, **John L. Lewis**, president of the **United Mine Workers** and vice president of the **American Federation of Labor** (**AFL**), took his union out of the AFL and started a new organization to be known as the **Congress of Industrial Organization** (**CIO**). Lewis charged that the AFL, whose membership consisted essentially of craft unions, showed little interest in organizing the low-skilled workers in the mass production industries. For the first time, unions organized on an industry basis (automotive, electrical, steel, etc.) were successful in bargaining for all their employees with such industrial giants as General Motors, United States Steel, and General Electric.

Exercise Set 4.5

1. In the early years of the New Deal, Roosevelt
   A. sought advice from very few others.
   B. relied heavily on a "Brain Trust."
   C. consulted primarily business leaders.
   D. sought advice only from politicians in his Cabinet.

2. The policies of Franklin D. Roosevelt revealed
   A. a rejection of the capitalistic system.
   B. a willingness to modify extensively American laissez-faire economic practices.
   C. a Fascist philosophy of economic and political regimentation.
   D. a timidity in dealing with the basic weaknesses of the free enterprise system.

3. Franklin D. Roosevelt first gave his attention to what major problem?
   A. Unemployment
   B. Speculation in securities
   C. Farm relief
   D. Bank failures

4. A major difference between the New Deal and policies followed by earlier administrations was that the New Deal
   A. emphasized and encouraged rugged individualism.
   B. advocated socialism as a solution to the problems of the times.
   C. provided the government with a more active role in the economy.
   D. was able to eliminate discrimination in employment.

5. On the political spectrum Roosevelt's domestic program for relief, recovery, and reform was
   A. at the far left between socialism and communism.
   B. at the far right between conservatism and fascism.
   C. right of center between moderate and conservative.
   D. left of center between moderate and liberal.

CONSTITUTIONAL ISSUES AND THE NEW DEAL

> When an act of Congress is appropriately challenged in the courts
> . . . the judicial branch of government has only one duty—to lay the
> article of the Constitution which is invoked beside the statute which
> is challenged and to decide whether the latter squares with the former.
> Justice Owen J. Roberts, writing for the majority of six in
> *United States* v. *Butler* et al. (1936) invalidating
> the Agricultural Adjustment Act

> A tortured construction of the Constitution is not to be justified by
> recourse to extreme examples . . . .
> Justice Harlan F. Stone, dissenting for the minority of three

The Supreme Court and New Deal Legislation

The Schechter Poultry Case

Opponents of the New Deal were heartened by several key decisions of the
Supreme Court. A major piece of legislation, passed early in the New Deal,
was the **National Industrial Recovery Act** (June 1933), which established
a **National Recovery Administration (NRA)** designed to revitalize industry while protecting labor and consumers. The act was declared unconstitutional by the Supreme Court in the case of *Schechter Poultry Corp.* v.
United States (1935). Chief Justice **Charles Evans Hughes**, writing for a
unanimous court, ruled that the excessive delegation of legislative power to
the executive was unconstitutional.

United States v. *Butler*—the AAA

The following year, the Court invalidated another major piece of New Deal
legislation, the **Agricultural Adjustment Act** of 1933. In a 6 to 3 decision,
the Court, in the case of *United States* v. *Butler,* declared the act unconstitutional on the ground that the processing tax was an abuse of the taxing
power in regulating agricultural output. The action of the Supreme Court
in declaring these and other acts of the New Deal unconstitutional brought
about a storm of resentment. The controversy raised one of the enduring
issues in American history: Is the judiciary the interpreter of the Constitution
or a shaper of public policy?

The Tennessee Valley Authority (TVA)

Purpose and Extent of the Project

One major agency of the New Deal, established by legislation in 1933, survived attacks in the courts. It was the **Tennessee Valley Authority (TVA)**, designed to revitalize one of the most economically depressed regions in the country. This region included parts of seven states—Virginia, North Carolina, Georgia, Alabama, Mississippi, Tennessee, and Kentucky. The TVA constructed 21 large dams on the Tennessee River to provide electric power for the region. Besides supplying cheap power, TVA served the region in many ways. It provided thousands of jobs to residents in the area. Additional benefits included flood control made possible by the newly built dams, prevention of soil erosion by the planting of millions of trees, establishment of public parks, schools, libraries, and hospitals, and improvement in river and road transportation.

The Election of 1936

In 1936, Roosevelt, running for re-election, was pitted against Governor Alfred M. Landon of Kansas. In a campaign speech at Madison Square Garden in New York City, Roosevelt declared:

> I should like to have it said of my first administration that in it the forces of selfishness and of lust for power met their match. I should like to have it said of my second administration that in it these forces met their master.

In 1936 Roosevelt's popular vote was 28 million against 17 million for Landon, but in the electoral college Roosevelt won every state but Maine and Vermont, giving him an electoral victory of 523 to 8. The New Dealers appropriately regarded this as a mandate, since they also won both houses of Congress and all but six governorships.

President Roosevelt and the Supreme Court

The "Court Packing" Proposal

Shortly after his re-election, Roosevelt asked Congress to give him authority to appoint one new Justice (not to exceed six) for every Supreme Court Justice who had reached the age of 70 and failed to retire. Since six of the nine Justices on the Court had reached the age of 70, this meant that, if Congress approved, Roosevelt could increase the Court to a membership of fifteen. This proposal was described by its critics as a **"court packing"** scheme and was seen as a threat to the separation of powers.

Changes in the Court

After Roosevelt's attempt to reform the Court, the Court began to take a more liberal approach, giving rise to a popular saying: "a switch in time saves nine." Moreover, changes in the Court's membership came quickly. Within one term in office President Roosevelt had appointed a majority of the Court's members.

The Election of 1940

The election campaign of 1940 was waged during the dark days when Hitler's forces overran Western Europe and were poised to launch an all-out attack on Britain. The Republicans nominated the charismatic liberal corporation lawyer, **Wendell L. Willkie**, while the Democrats chose Franklin D. Roosevelt to run for a third term.

Third-Term Issue

If Roosevelt won the election, as seemed likely, it would upset the two-term tradition that George Washington had started. No President elected to two consecutive terms had ever sought a third. Despite public misgivings about violation of this tradition, Roosevelt won easily with 449 electoral votes to 82 for the Republicans. Opponents of aid to Britain had no real choice in 1940, for both major party candidates rejected isolationism in favor of opposition to the Nazi challenge. Roosevelt was to win a fourth term in 1944.

The Twenty-Second Amendment

This reversal of the two-term tradition led to a reaction after the death of FDR. In 1951, the Twenty-Second Amendment was added to the Constitution. It specifies: "No person shall be elected to the office of President more than twice . . . ."

Exercise Set 4.6

1. Which of the following New Deal acts or agencies was declared unconstitutional by the Supreme Court in *Schechter Poultry Corp.* v. *United States*?
   A. The Agricultural Adjustment Act
   B. The National Recovery Administration
   C. The Tennessee Valley Authority
   D. The Works Progress Administration

2. Many Americans had misgivings about reelecting Roosevelt to a third term because
   A. it was a violation of precedent.
   B. it was time to give someone else a chance since the problem of the Depression remained unsolved.
   C. Roosevelt was an interventionist while his opponent was an isolationist.
   D. Roosevelt was tampering with the Supreme Court.

3. An argument advanced against the TVA by private power companies was that
   A. its lower rates would be subsidized by the taxpayers.
   B. it would fail to provide cheap electric power for the people of the Tennessee Valley.
   C. its activities would extend over too large an area.
   D. it would eliminate jobs for residents of the area.

4. Roosevelt's attempt to increase the number of Justices on the Supreme Court
   A. was acclaimed by most Americans as a brilliant solution to a Constitutional problem.
   B. received solid support from the majority of both houses of Congress.
   C. was narrowly defeated in the Senate Judiciary Committee.
   D. was ridiculed in a popular book of the time entitled "Nine Old Men."

5. The election of 1936
   A. reflected grudging national support for the New Deal.
   B. saw much debate over the Supreme Court issue.
   C. may not be described as a landslide victory for the New Deal.
   D. overwhelmingly endorsed the New Deal.

6. FDR's attempt to reform the Supreme Court
   A. secured more decisions favorable to the New Deal.
   B. was completely unsuccessful.
   C. was the first attempt to change the number of members of the Supreme Court.
   D. was endorsed by nearly all Democrats.

THE HUMAN FACTOR

Franklin D. Roosevelt as Communicator

Franklin Delano Roosevelt had an extraordinary gift for communicating with the American people. From the very beginning of his first administration, he reached out to them in what he called "fireside chats." Within a week after his inauguration, as the banks reopened under the Emergency Banking Relief Act, he addressed his first nationwide radio audience of 35 million listeners, which included three out of four American families, and told them that it was now safer to keep their money in one of the reopened banks than "under the mattress." This was the first of what were to be some thirty "fireside chats," all calculated to communicate his message directly to the people.

Eleanor Roosevelt, the Eyes and Ears of the President

Eleanor Roosevelt, wife of Franklin D. Roosevelt, played a major, if unofficial, role in his presidential administration, as she had done when he was Governor of New York. By keeping informed of public sentiment on vital issues, Eleanor Roosevelt served as the keen and reliable eyes and ears of the President. From her extensive travels, she brought him extremely useful firsthand information. A humanitarian, she was deeply concerned with the plight of the underdog, victims of the Dust Bowl (the "Okies"), and especially African Americans, who were denied opportunities open to other Americans. On behalf of the underprivileged, Eleanor Roosevelt did not hesitate to speak out to the President.

Ravages of the Dust Bowl

When the plow destroyed the protective grasses of the semiarid plains east of the Rockies, the defenseless soil was ready for catastrophe. It came in the hot drought-ridden spring and summer of 1934. A great dust storm ravaged parts of Oklahoma, Arkansas, Colorado, Kansas, New Mexico, and Texas. Howling winds drove the dust a thousand miles east, covering homes and farms, blackening the sky, disrupting railroad schedules, and spreading despair. In *The Grapes of Wrath* (1939), novelist **John Steinbeck** tells the tragic story of the Joads, a family driven from its Oklahoma farm by the ravages of the Dust Bowl. A quarter of a million farmers, who saw their cattle suffocate, their crops destroyed, and their few possessions menaced by relentless mountains of dust, left their farms and drove west in quest of a better life.

Women During the New Deal Era

The appointment in 1933 of **Frances Perkins** as Secretary of Labor, the first woman to serve as a member of the Cabinet, heralded a new era in the status of women. Perkins remained in the Cabinet during the twelve years of Roosevelt's presidency and then served for seven years under President **Truman** as a member of the **Civil Service Commission**. Outstanding women authors of the period included Ellen Glasgow, literary historian of the South, who won the Pulitzer Prize in 1941 for *In This Our Life,* and **Willa Cather**, whose novels depicted the struggles of pioneer women in frontier Nebraska.

Minorities and the New Deal

African Americans

African Americans found new hope in the relief, recovery, and reform measures of the New Deal. Traditionally Lincoln Republicans—in opposition to the dominant whites who exercised control through the southern Democratic Party—African Americans began switching to the Democratic Party in 1934, and contributed significantly to the New Deal landslide of 1936, especially in the cities of the North.

Native Americans

The Native American minority, too, saw new hope as the **Indian Reorganization Act** of 1934 reversed the antitribal policy of the **Dawes Act** of 1887 and recognized tribal life as the normal and viable Native American mode.

Culture of the Depression

Like wars and other catastrophes, the Great Depression brought forth sympathetic responses in the arts. John Steinbeck's *The Grapes of Wrath* is the quintessential literary portrayal of this disaster, particularly as it affected the poor farmers of the Dust Bowl. **Langston Hughes** depicted the lives of African Americans in his semiautobiographical novel, *Not Without Laughter* (1930) and in his short story, *The Way of White Folks* (1934).

The WPA and the Arts

The New Deal WPA provided funds for unemployed writers, actors, artists, and musicians. A series of WPA books on each of the states created an invaluable record of the period. Plays by Clifford Odets and music dramas like *Pins and Needles* entertained audiences that could not otherwise see a theater production, while it gave writers, actors, and directors a chance to practice their professions. In one WPA project, artists painted murals depicting historic scenes on the walls of public buildings, schools, libraries, and railroad centers.

Music

Music of the period evolved from **ragtime** developed by black orchestras in the South before World War I. A new form called **jazz** came into its own in the 1920s. Great performers and band leaders emerged, including the legendary cornetist **Bix Biederbeck** who died in 1931 at the age of 28, **Louis "Satchmo" Armstrong**, **Duke Ellington**, and the pianist and composer **"Fats" Waller**. **Swing** bands led by Paul Whiteman, Glen Gray, Tommy Dorsey, Glenn Miller, Benny Goodman, and Vincent Lopez played as couples danced to their music on large dance floors, and millions listened on the radio and bought their records. Musicals, too, came into their own with long-run performances of *Oklahoma, Show Boat, Porgy and Bess,* and the music of **Irving Berlin**, **Richard Rodgers**, **George Gershwin**, **Cole Porter**, and **Jerome Kern**.

Opposition to the New Deal

As might be expected, there were those who felt the New Deal had gone too far and others who believed it had not gone far enough to correct the system that had led to the Great Depression.

On the Left

At the far left were the **Communists**, who nominated Earl Browder for President in 1936. He garnered 80,000 votes out of a total of some 46 million cast in the election. The **Socialist Party**, with Norman Thomas again the candidate, polled 187,000.

• *Communist and Socialist Doctrines Differ.* The Communists, influenced by the doctrines of **Karl Marx** and the Russian Bolshevik **Lenin**, believed that justice for the working class (proletariat) would come only through the violent overthrow of capitalism. The Socialists, led by **Eugene V. Debs** and Norman Thomas, believed that democratic methods supported by education and legal agitation would bring about the necessary radical changes in the economic system.

On the Right

Those who attacked the New Deal from the right presented a united front by nominating the former Republican Congressman William Lemke of North Dakota for President. The Union Party was endorsed by most of the major rightist organizations. Lemke received 891,858 votes, about 2 percent of the total cast.

• *Fascists Inspired by Mussolini and Hitler.* At the far right of the political spectrum were the **Fascists**, who drew their inspiration from the systems imposed by force in Italy under Mussolini, in Germany under Hitler, and in Spain under Franco. In the United States, these found their counterparts in the pro-Nazi German-American **Bund** and Italian Fascist "Black Shirts."

Homegrown Demagogues

"Homegrown" demagogues gained a considerable number of converts by denouncing the New Deal and offering their own solutions.

• *Huey P. Long.* A serious challenge was mounted by Senator Huey P. ("Kingfish") Long of Louisiana, who launched a "Share Our Wealth" program with the promise to make "every man a king" and to distribute $5,000 to every family. Long, a skillful rabble-rouser, was planning to take his campaign to New York in a huge parade when he was assassinated in the Louisiana State Capitol in 1935.

• *Father Charles F. Coughlin.* Father Coughlin was from Michigan and gained an army of followers through his weekly radio broadcast, which reached 40 million listeners. His call for "social justice" was accompanied by a steady stream of pro-Fascist, anti-Semitic messages that finally aroused his superiors in the church who in 1942 ordered him to discontinue his broadcasts.

Assessment of the New Deal

A brief assessment of the New Deal program suggests that it introduced at least one major new element in American life, the concept that the national government should assume responsibility for the welfare of the people. As Roosevelt expressed it: ". . . the government has the definite duty to use all its power and resources to meet new social problems with new social controls . . ." Roosevelt maintained that "it was this administration which saved the system of private profit and free enterprise after it had been dragged to the brink of ruin." The New Deal had saved the banking system, promoted the conservation of natural resources, and given new hope to the common people. Yet, on the eve of World War II, millions were still unemployed. It was World War II that finally revitalized the industrial machine and the national economy.

Exercise Set 4.7

1. Which of the following was *not* a factor in bringing about the landslide victory of the Democratic Party in the 1936 election?
   A. The black vote
   B. "Fireside chats"
   C. Solution of the unemployment problem
   D. Press conferences

Base your answer to question 2 on the cartoon below and on your knowledge of social studies.

Source: Carey Orr, *Chicago Tribune*, 1934 (adapted)

2. Which statement most accurately expresses the viewpoint of the cartoonist?
   A. New Deal programs are endangering the country.
   B. Most Americans support New Deal programs.
   C. Supreme Court decisions are overturning New Deal programs.
   D. New Deal programs emphasize health care reforms.

3. Which of the following was a cause of the others?
   A. Departure of thousands of poor farmers from Oklahoma and Arkansas
   B. Publication of the novel *The Grapes of Wrath*
   C. The great dust storm of 1934
   D. Creation of a "dust bowl" in parts of Texas, New Mexico, and Kansas

4. The plight of black Americans during the Depression is depicted in
   A. the novels of Willa Cather.
   B. the works of Langston Hughes.
   C. the photography of Walker Evans.
   D. the movie *Gone With The Wind*.

CHAPTER REVIEW QUESTIONS

1. The major difference between Herbert Hoover and Franklin Roosevelt was
   A. their political philosophy.
   B. their wealth.
   C. the difficulty of the problems they faced.
   D. the cooperation each received from his own party.

2. The election of 1940
   A. showed fundamental foreign policy differences between the two major parties.
   B. was unique in that no minor parties participated.
   C. caused the later adoption of the Twenty-Second Amendment.
   D. helped perpetuate the two-term tradition.

3. Which is a valid conclusion based upon a study of the New Deal?
   A. Labor, but not business, was affected.
   B. It resulted in a government budget surplus.
   C. It forced individuals to accept responsibility for their own economic welfare.
   D. It continued to influence United States economic policy for many years.

4. Although all segments of American society were affected by the Great Depression, those who suffered most severely were
   A. operators of small business.
   B. the lower middle class.
   C. senior citizens.
   D. women and children.

5. The Twenty-Second Amendment to the United States Constitution
   A. eliminated the unproductive "lame duck" Congress.
   B. changed the date of the President's inauguration.
   C. limited Presidents to two terms.
   D. specified that Congress would meet early in January of each year.

6. Private business opposed the Tennessee Valley Authority (TVA) because
   A. it was thought the lakes would soon be filled with silt.
   B. the project did not provide satisfactory protection against floods.
   C. electricity was produced and distributed by a government agency.
   D. it called for regimentation of the farmers of the district.

7. FDR's attempt to reform the Supreme Court
   A. secured more decisions favorable to New Deal laws.
   B. was completely unsuccessful.
   C. was the first attempt to change the number of members of the Court.
   D. was endorsed by nearly all Democrats.

8. As President, Franklin D. Roosevelt did all of the following EXCEPT
   A. continue several of the policies he had put into practice as Governor of New York.
   B. cease relying on his wife Eleanor as his eyes and ears.
   C. demonstrate the same capacity for vote-getting as he had in New York.
   D. bring to Washington a number of key political and personal associates from New York.

THEMATIC ESSAY

Directions: Write a well-organized essay that includes an introduction, several paragraphs addressing the task below, and a conclusion.

Theme: Presidential Powers

During times of crisis throughout our history, the executive branch has assumed, and many times been allowed, greater powers.

Task:

From your study of the early decades of the 20th century, identify *two* presidential administrations that experienced crisis situations and have exercised extraordinary powers.

For each administration:

- Identify the crisis (war, economic, civil rights, etc.).
- Describe the administration's response to the crisis.
- Discuss how the powers of the presidency were expanded during the time of crisis.

You may use any presidential administration from your study of United States history. Some suggestions you may wish to consider are Thomas Jefferson (1801–1809), Abraham Lincoln (1861–1865), Franklin D. Roosevelt (1933–1945), or Lyndon Johnson (1963–1969).

You are *not* limited to these suggestions.

DOCUMENT-BASED QUESTION

The following questions (Part A and Part B) are based on the accompanying documents (1–6). Some of these documents have been edited for the purpose of this exercise. The question is designed to test your ability to work with historical documents and to demonstrate your knowledge of the subject matter being presented. As you analyze the documents, take into account both the source of the document and the author's point of view.

Historical Context:

> *The Great Depression of the 1930s resulted in dramatic* adjustments to the American economic and political system. Some have claimed that the actions of President Franklin Delano Roosevelt and the programs of the New Deal were socialistic threats to capitalism, while others have held that the New Deal was designed to save capitalism.

Task:

> Using information from the documents and your knowledge of United States history, answer the questions that follow each document in Part A. Your answers to the questions will help you write the Part B essay, in which you will be asked:
>
> Franklin Roosevelt's New Deal has been assessed in different ways. Some say it encouraged socialistic change to our form of government, while others say it helped maintain the capitalist system. Using the documents and your knowledge of United States history, answer the following question: Was the New Deal designed to preserve capitalism?

Part A
Short-Answer Question

The documents below relate to the problems of the Great Depression and the tactics utilized by President Roosevelt and the New Deal. Examine each document carefully and then answer the questions that follow.

DOCUMENT 1

Long ago we stated the reason for labor organizations. We said that they were organized out of the necessities of the situation; that a single employee was helpless in dealing with an employer; that he was dependent ordinarily on his daily wage for the maintenance of himself and family; that, if the employer refused to pay him the wages that he thought fair, he was nevertheless unable to leave the employ and resist arbitrary and unfair treatment; that union was essential to give laborers opportunity to deal on an equality with their employer.

—*National Labor Relations Board* v. *Jones and Laughlin Steel Corp.* (1937)

1. The *NLRB* v. *Jones and Laughlin Steel Corp.* case upheld the Wagner Act of 1935, which recognized civil liberties of laborers. Why were many businesses against the Wagner Act and the holding of the Supreme Court?

_____

_____

_____

_____

DOCUMENT 2

UNITED STATES GOVERNMENT FINANCES, 1929–1941 (in billions of dollars)			
Fiscal Year	Expenditures	Surplus or Deficit (–)	Total Public Debt
1929	$3.127	$0.734	$16.9
1930	3.320	0.738	16.2
1931	3.577	–0.462	16.8
1932	4.659	–2.735	19.5
1933	4.598	–2.602	22.5
1934	6.645	–3.630	27.1
1935	6.497	–2.791	28.7
1936	8.422	–4.425	33.8
1937	7.733	–2.777	36.4
1938	6.765	–1.177	37.2
1939	8.841	–3.862	40.4
1940	9.589	–2.710	43.0
1941	13.980	–4.778	44.0

—U.S. Bureau of the Census

2. What is the argument against the increased spending (and therefore larger deficit) of the federal government between 1929 and 1941?

_____

_____

_____

_____

3. What is the argument for the increased spending (and therefore larger deficit) of the federal government between 1929 and 1941?

_____

_____

_____

_____

DOCUMENT 3

. . . . Our greatest primary task is to put people to work. This is no unsolvable problem if we face it wisely and courageously. It can be accomplished in part by direct recruiting by the government itself, treating the problem as we would treat the emergency of war, but at the same time, through this employment, accomplishing greatly needed projects to stimulate and reorganize the use of our natural resources.

—Franklin D. Roosevelt, Inaugural Address, March 4, 1933

4. What is the government's role that President Roosevelt proposed in 1933 to help solve the problem of unemployment?

_____

_____

_____

_____

DOCUMENT 4

Out of the strains and stresses of these years we have come to see that the true conservative is the man who has a real concern for injustices and takes thought against the day of reckoning. The true conservative seeks to protect the system of private property and free enterprise by correcting such injustices and inequalities as arise from it. The most serious threat to our institutions comes from those who refuse to face the need for change . . . .

Wise and prudent men—intelligent conservatives—have long known that in a changing world worthy institutions can be conserved only by adjusting them to the changing time.

—President Franklin D. Roosevelt, Speech, Syracuse, New York,
September 29, 1936

5. According to President Roosevelt in his Syracuse speech, what is the ultimate goal of the changes he and his administration have proposed?

_____

_____

_____

_____

6. Would you say that President Roosevelt's statements are evolutionary or revolutionary? Why?

_____

_____

_____

_____

DOCUMENT 5

No business whose existence depends on paying less than living wages to its workers has any right to continue in this country.

—President Franklin D. Roosevelt, Speech, 1933

7. What legislation resulted from the position put forth by President Roosevelt in the 1933 speech?

_____

_____

_____

_____

DOCUMENT 6

> The following excerpts are from the 1935 Social Security Act. The Act brought the assumption of national responsibility for general social security and constituted a notable chapter in the history of federal centralization in the United States.
>
> *Sec. 1:* . . . for the purpose of enabling each state to furnish financial assistance . . . to aged, needy individuals.
>
> *Sec. 301:* . . . for the purpose of assisting the states in the administration of their unemployment compensation.
>
> *Sec. 401:* . . . for the purpose of enabling each state to furnish financial assistance to needy dependent children.
>
> *Sec. 801:* . . . In addition to other taxes, there shall be levied, collected, and paid upon the income of every individual a (social security) tax . . . .

—Social Security Act, August 14, 1935

8. How does the Social Security Act of 1935 change the federal government's role in caring for the welfare of the American people?

_____

_____

_____

_____

9. In your opinion, does this act encourage socialism or preserve capitalism?

_____

_____

_____

_____

Part B
Essay

Your essay should be well organized with an introductory paragraph that states your position on the question. Develop your position in the next paragraphs and then write a conclusion. In your essay, include specific historical details and refer to the specific documents you analyzed in Part A. You may include additional information from your knowledge of social studies.

Historical Context:

> The Great Depression of the 1930s resulted in dramatic adjustments to the American economic and political system. Some have claimed that the actions of President Franklin Delano Roosevelt and the programs of the New Deal were socialistic threats to capitalism, while others have held that the New Deal was designed to save capitalism.

Task:

> Franklin Roosevelt's New Deal has been assessed in different ways. Some say it encouraged socialistic change to our form of government, while others say it helped maintain the capitalist system. Using the documents above, and your knowledge of United States history, answer the following question: Was the New Deal designed to preserve capitalism?

Guidelines:

In your essay, be sure to
• Develop all aspects of the task.
• Incorporate information from *at least five* documents.
• Incorporate relevant outside information.
• Support the theme with many relevant facts, examples, and details.
• Use a logical and clear plan of organization, including an introduction and a conclusion that are beyond a restatement of the theme.

UNIT FIVE

The United States in an Age of Global Crisis: Responsibility and Cooperation

> **KEY IDEAS** Unit Five explores the American policy of isolation in the 1920s and 1930s and American involvement in World War II. It describes the effects of the war on the United States and America's role in the postwar world, with emphasis on the Cold War.

UNIT CONNECTIONS: By the end of the unit you should understand the following points.

- Isolationism in the 1930s
- United States involvement in World War II prior to congressional declaration in 1941
- The United States home front during World War II
- The role of the United States in World War II compared to World War I
- Wartime moral issues including rights of Japanese Americans, integration of African Americans, the Nazi Holocaust, and nuclear warfare
- War criminals and "crimes against humanity"
- Adjusting to a peacetime economy
- International involvement and the United Nations
- "McCarthyism," the Red Scare, and civil liberties
- The Cold War at home and abroad

PEACE IN PERIL (1933–1950)

ISOLATION AND NEUTRALITY

Neutrality During the 18th and 19th Centuries

> 'Tis our true policy to steer clear of permanent alliances, with any portion of the foreign world.
>
> > George Washington's Farewell Address,
> > September 17, 1796

Washington's admonition against permanent alliances was still in the minds of America's leaders during the **Napoleonic Wars** of the early 19th century. There was pressure both on **Adams'** administration (1797–1801) and on that of his successor, **Jefferson** (1801–1809), to go to war against France as the Federalists urged, or against England as the Republicans demanded. But the sentiment for neutrality prevailed despite provocation by both warring nations. An undeclared naval war with France actually took place during two years of Adams' administration (1798–1800). Ultimately, the policy of non-involvement failed and the United States became involved in the Napoleonic Wars in 1812. The **War of 1812** against Britain was fought to protect "neutral rights" on the high seas.

In the historic **Monroe Doctrine** (1823), President Monroe stated the policy of nonintervention in these words: ". . . our policy in regard to Europe . . . is not to interfere in the internal concerns of any of its powers." These sentiments prevailed and the United States avoided European conflicts for most of the rest of the 19th century, despite the efforts of the hawks during **Polk's** administration, who cried "Fifty-four forty or fight," calling for war with England unless our territory was extended to Russian Alaska (54° 40′ north latitude).

Efforts to Remain Neutral in World War I

When Europe was engaged in World War I, Wilson, echoing the sentiments of the American people, declared, "The United States must be neutral in fact as well as in name . . . We must be impartial in thought as well as in action." This was in 1914, but three years later he called for war, and American troops were sent to Europe. The postwar reaction was dramatic. Popular disillusionment following World War I contributed to the strong sentiment for isolationism that caused the U.S. Senate to reject membership in the League of Nations. It was this sentiment, still strong in the 1930s, that confronted the Roosevelt administration while Hitler moved step by step toward realization of the Nazi boast, "Today we rule Germany; tomorrow the world."

Of course, total isolationism by a great world power is impossible. In the 20th century the United States had territorial possessions in the Pacific Ocean, the Caribbean, and Central America. Moreover, American business interests were engaged in commerce and industry throughout the world, and American capital was a major source of support for worldwide industrial development. It was inevitable that defense of these commitments would make complete isolationism a practical impossibility.

The World Disarmament Conference

When the World Disarmament Conference convened in Geneva, Switzerland, in February 1932, President Hoover, whose Quaker background predisposed him to peace efforts, sent an American delegation. It was understood, however, that prevailing isolationist sentiment in the United States would make any American commitment for participation in international action unlikely. The Conference, sponsored by the League of Nations and attended by representatives of the Soviet Union as well as the United States, adjourned in March 1933 and reconvened in October. It adjourned again when Germany, now led by Hitler, withdrew from the Conference and later, from the League of Nations. Efforts at international disarmament had failed.

Isolationism and the Nye Committee Hearings

In 1934, the U.S. Senate created a special committee to prepare legislation on government control of the munitions industry. The committee, headed by a confirmed isolationist, Senator **Gerald P. Nye** of North Dakota, held widely publicized hearings for the next three years. The hearings disclosed that munitions manufacturers had made huge profits from World War I. They also charged that arms manufacturers had successfully exerted pressure for U.S. involvement in the war. Many who had supported America's participation in World War I now regarded it as a grave error. A spirit of pacifism, dominating college campuses, preached from pulpits, and bolstered on stage and in the cinema, reflected the prevailing national sentiment. The call for preparedness was answered with the phrase "never again."

United States Neutrality Legislation

It was in this atmosphere of isolationism that a series of neutrality laws were passed by Congress in the 1930s. In the summer of 1935, when Mussolini's troops were poised for the invasions of Ethiopia, Congress passed the **Neutrality Act of 1935**. The act required the President to place an **embargo** on arms to nations engaged in war and prohibited travel of U.S. citizens on belligerent vessels. It was designed to prevent any American armaments manufacturer, banker, or merchant from profiting from a foreign war or helping to embroil us in one. This meant that the United States had to remain neutral while Italy invaded and subjugated Ethiopia. Japan and Germany, of course, favored this American policy. Both had already embarked on programs leading to military conquest and expansion. In 1931 the Japanese invaded and occupied **Manchuria**, a large province of China, bordering on Korea, which Japan already controlled. The United States refused to recognize this conquest under the newly declared **Stimson Doctrine**. In 1936 Japan and Germany signed a military agreement called the Anti-Comintern Treaty. In the same year Germany and Italy formed an alliance called the **Rome-Berlin Axis**. With the addition of Japan in 1940, it became known as the **Rome-Berlin-Tokyo Axis**.

Civil War in Spain (1936–1939)

Events moved swiftly on the road to World War II. A "popular front" coalition of Liberals, Socialists, and Communists in Spain ousted the Conservative government in the 1936 national election. Five months later (July 1936) **Generalissimo Francisco Franco** led an uprising to overthrow the **Republican** government of Spain and replace it with a **Fascist** government. The **Spanish Civil War** that followed was a prelude to World War II. Germany and Italy openly aided Franco, while England and France followed policies of nonintervention, and Russia, far from the scene, gave what help it could to the Spanish Republican government. The United States observed its own neutrality laws. Hitler's air force gained experience, valuable in the coming world war, by bombing Spanish cities and strafing their inhabitants. One such raid on Guernica, April 26, 1937, is depicted in a famous painting by the Spanish artist, Pablo Picasso. The war ended in March 1939 with the defeat of the Loyalists (those loyal to the Republic) and the establishment of a Fascist government under Franco.

American Isolationism and Axis Aggression

Meanwhile, in March 1936, Hitler's troops marched into the Rhineland in violation of the Treaty of Versailles. In 1937, Japan invaded China. In a speech in Chicago, President Roosevelt called on the democracies to "quarantine the aggressors," but his hands were tied by neutrality legislation and by the prevailing national sentiment of isolationism or, at least, nonintervention.

Neutrality Legislation of 1936 and 1937

The Neutrality Act of 1935 was due to expire at the end of February 1936. Congress replaced it with the Neutrality Act of 1936, which extended the legislation for another year and added a provision prohibiting loans by Americans to nations engaged in war. A third neutrality law, with no time limit, was passed by Congress in 1937. The legislation banned shipment of munitions to either side in the Spanish Civil War and was particularly disadvantageous to the Republicans, since Franco was receiving supplies from Italy and Germany. In his "quarantine" speech, Roosevelt urged that the United States join the other powers to "quarantine," or check, the aggressor nations. In an opinion poll taken shortly after the speech, only 31 percent of the public favored presidential action to check aggression, whereas the vast majority supported Congressional neutrality legislation.

1. In the years prior to 1939, an isolationist would be in most disagreement with which of the following?
   A. The speech of President Roosevelt urging a "quarantine" of the aggressors
   B. The hearings held in the U.S. Senate committee presided over by Senator Gerald P. Nye
   C. A tradition first expressed by President Washington in his Farewell Address
   D. The Neutrality Acts of 1935 and 1936

2. Neutrality legislation of the 1930s was designed to
   A. prevent aggression by the Rome-Berlin-Tokyo Axis.
   B. give the United States time to prepare for the coming war.
   C. protect American lives and property in Europe and Asia.
   D. keep the United States out of war by avoiding the mistakes of pre-World War I.

3. A major foreign relations problem of the Roosevelt administration after 1935 was to
   A. negotiate a military alliance with Great Britain and the USSR.
   B. persuade the American people of the need to abandon the policy of isolationism.
   C. persuade the Axis powers to rejoin the League of Nations.
   D. persuade the Congress to disband the Nye Committee investigating corrupt practices in the munitions industry.

4. Which of the following was the most important reason for the rise of dictatorships in Europe in the two decades following World War I?
   A. General illiteracy of the working class
   B. Stresses caused by the constant threat of renewed warfare
   C. Destruction of homes and factories during World War I
   D. Widespread economic disorder

FAILURE OF PEACE: TRIUMPH OF AGGRESSION

The Road to World War II (1933–1939)

In retrospect, it is clear that the aggressions of the Axis powers during the 1930s culminated in a world war because the democracies were not willing to go to war to protect the freedom of the nations that the Axis powers invaded. Hitler began rearming Germany in violation of the Treaty of Versailles in 1933 and occupied the Rhineland in 1936. Despite promises to make each demand his last, he annexed **Austria** in 1938, dismembered **Czechoslovakia** in 1938, and demanded the **Polish Corridor** in 1939. Another Axis member, Japan, invaded **Manchuria** in 1931 and the rest of China in 1937. The third Axis member, Italy, invaded **Ethiopia** in 1935 and **Albania** in 1939. With the help of Germany and Italy, the democratic government of **Spain** was overthrown (1936–1939) and replaced with a dictatorship friendly to the Axis. To protect his eastern flank Hitler made a "nonaggression" pact with Stalin on August 23, 1939. On September 1, 1939, Hitler's armies invaded Poland. Two days later France and England declared war on Germany.

The Policy of Appeasement—the Munich Conference (1938)

The policy of appeasement, exemplified in the **Munich Conference** of September 1938, had disastrous consequences. This policy, adopted by British Prime Minister **Neville Chamberlain**, relied on Hitler's Germany becoming a friendly member of the family of nations once Hitler's demands were met. When Hitler insisted that the Sudetenland of Czechoslovakia be turned over to Germany, there was grave concern among opponents of Fascism. Czechoslovakia was a strong democratic country. The Sudetenland was heavily fortified and the Czechs were prepared to resist. However, Chamberlain decided to appease Hitler and he called a conference of four powers—Britain, France, Italy, and Germany—to meet in Munich, Germany. In Munich it was quickly decided to yield to Hitler's demands to occupy the Sudetenland. Hitler promised in return to make no more territorial demands. Chamberlain flew back to England and was greeted with wild acclaim when he said he brought "peace in our time." Six months after the Munich conference Hitler sent his troops to occupy all of Czechoslovakia. **Winston Churchill**, a leading member of Parliament who was opposed to appeasement, called the Munich agreement an unmitigated disaster. Less than a year after the Munich Conference, Britain was at war with Germany.

Changing Public Opinion in the United States

In January 1939 President Roosevelt tried to persuade Congress to revise the neutrality legislation. He saw a war coming between Germany and the democracies of Western Europe—France and Britain. Under the then existing law the United States could not sell war supplies to the democracies. Congress, reflecting public sentiment, refused to change the law. However, after the war started in Europe, public opinion began to shift. On September 21, 1939, three weeks after the beginning of World War II, President Roosevelt addressed a joint session of Congress and urged a change in the neutrality law. He said, ". . . by the repeal of the embargo the United States will more probably remain at peace than if the law remains as it stands today." Congress responded by passing the **Neutrality Act of 1939**, which contained a "cash and carry" provision. Belligerents (that is, Britain or France) could purchase any supplies, including armaments, provided they paid cash and carried the supplies from the United States in their own ships. This would keep American ships out of the war zone and would prevent American banks from making loans that American troops might later have to redeem.

Agreement on Western Hemisphere Defense

One policy on which Americans were in agreement was the defense of the Western Hemisphere against foreign aggression. The achievement of unity in Latin America for support of U.S. foreign policy was attributable in part to the "**good neighbor policy**" that President Roosevelt had proclaimed in his first inaugural address and to which he adhered throughout his presidency.

Victories of the German Armies in Western Europe

The war in Europe took an ominous turn in the spring of 1940 as Germany quickly occupied neutral Norway and Denmark. German troops also overran Holland, Belgium, and Luxembourg. Operating from Belgium, the German army was able to bypass the powerful line of fortifications (**Maginot Line**) on which France relied for its security. German troops poured into France and defeated the British and French defenders. Britain was able to evacuate troops trapped in France at **Dunkirk** on the English Channel by a sea flotilla of civilian ships. Italy invaded southern France, prompting Roosevelt's statement in an address that day at the University of Virginia, "On this tenth day of June 1940 the hand that held the dagger has stuck it in the back of its neighbor."

Moving Toward War

Aid to Britain

Winston Churchill replaced Chamberlain as Prime Minister of Britain after the fall of France. He promised his people only "blood, toil, tears, and sweat." In an appeal to America he said, "Give us the tools and we will finish the job." As Commander-in-Chief of the Armed Forces, Roosevelt took the unprecedented step of making a swap with Britain by transferring to Britain 50 World War I destroyers in exchange for 99-year leases on a number of British air and naval bases in the Atlantic and West Indies. This transfer took place in September 1940.

Peacetime Conscription

Public opinion changed enough in the same month to secure the passage of a peacetime conscription bill of men between the ages of 21 and 35.

Franklin D. Roosevelt's Four Freedoms Message

Shocked by events in Europe, the United States began to see its own defense in a new light. Only the armed forces of Britain stood between the United States and the Nazi military machine. In a fireside chat on December 29, 1940, the month after defeating **Wendell Willkie**, his Republican opponent, for reelection to a third term, Roosevelt told the American people, "We must be the great arsenal of democracy." Public opinion was ready to accept this undertaking.

In his January 6, 1941, State of the Union message to Congress, the President proclaimed the "Four Freedoms":

> In the future days, which we seek to make secure, we look forward to a world founded upon four essential freedoms. The first is freedom of expression—everywhere in the world. The second is freedom of every person to worship God in his own way—everywhere in the world. The third is freedom from want . . . everywhere in the world. The fourth is freedom from fear . . . anywhere in the world.

Lend-Lease (February 1941)

The difficulty of serving as the **arsenal of democracy** was twofold. Britain could no longer pay cash for armaments, and the idea of extending credit raised the specter of old World War I debts that were never repaid. The solution was found in the **Lend-Lease Bill**, passed by Congress on March 11, 1941. Four days earlier, in his State of the Union message, the President had proposed to help Britain and other countries opposing Axis aggression by supplying "in ever-increasing numbers, ships, planes, tanks, guns." The lend-lease measure permitted the President to "sell, transfer, exchange, lease, or otherwise dispose of war equipment to any nation for use in the interests of the United States." The measure met fierce opposition from the **America First Committee** and its friends in Congress.

War Measures

With the passage of the Lend-Lease Act, the adoption of a draft, a vast increase in military appropriations, the repeal of the Neutrality Law of 1939, the use of American naval vessels to convoy supplies bound for Britain as far as Iceland, and the arming of American merchantmen to combat Nazi submarines, the United States was obviously moving toward war late in 1941.

The Atlantic Charter

The moral dimension of the war became the focus of world attention when Roosevelt and Churchill held a conference aboard a warship off the coast of Newfoundland in August 1941 and issued the Atlantic Charter. It declared (1) no territorial gains are sought by the United States or Britain; (2) territorial adjustments must conform to the wishes of the people involved; (3) people have a right to choose their own government; (4) trade barriers should be lowered; (5) there must be disarmament; (6) there must be freedom from fear and want; (7) there must be freedom of the seas; and (8) there must be an association of nations.

The Attack on Pearl Harbor, December 7, 1941

At the very time that the Atlantic Charter was being prepared, the Japanese war department was making plans to attack the United States. A surprise attack was to be made on **Pearl Harbor**, the U.S. naval base in Hawaii. On Sunday morning December 7, 1941, at 7:55 A.M., a wave of 189 Japanese war planes—dive-bombers and torpedo planes—roared over Pearl Harbor meeting little opposition from the completely surprised base. A second wave of attack planes followed. One hundred and seventy American planes were destroyed on the ground. Eight battleships—the pride of the Navy—were sunk or severely damaged. Nineteen fighting ships, including cruisers and destroyers, were incapacitated. Some 2,400 officers and enlisted men were killed, and 1,300 wounded. Japanese losses totaled 29 planes and 6 submarines. It was the greatest disaster in the history of the U.S. armed forces. The next day, December 8, 1941, in his war message to Congress, President Roosevelt said, "Yesterday, December 7, 1941—a date which will live in infamy—the United States of America was suddenly and deliberately attacked by naval and air forces of the Empire of Japan."

With but one dissenting vote, Congress declared war against Japan. On December 11, Italy and Germany declared war on the United States. On the same day, Congress passed a declaration of war on Germany and Italy.

Exercise Set 5.2

1. Which of the following would have been most troubling to the isolation-istic views of the America First Committee?
   A. Passage of the Lend-Lease Act
   B. Assignment of African Americans to integrated army units
   C. Passage of the 1939 Neutrality Law
   D. The Stimson Doctrine

2. The policy of appeasement, pursued by the British government under Prime Minister Neville Chamberlain
   A. achieved the goal of securing "peace in our time."
   B. was disapproved by public opinion in the democracies.
   C. encouraged the Axis powers to engage in aggression.
   D. gained the support of Winston Churchill in England.

3. The first peacetime draft in American history, passed into law September 6, 1940,
   A. showed that the United States was now ready to go to war.
   B. had a significant effect on the national election held two months later.
   C. was approved by both houses of Congress with little dissent.
   D. was reluctantly accepted by the American people as an essential defense measure.

4. Which of the following would have marked a modification of the ideol-ogy of the Monroe Doctrine?
   A. The "lend-lease" law
   B. The exchange of destroyers for lease of bases
   C. The Good Neighbor Policy
   D. The Atlantic Charter

5. Hitler concluded a nonaggression pact with Stalin in August 1939 in order to
   A. protect his eastern flank while he made war on the west.
   B. establish the supremacy of dictatorship over democracy.
   C. carry out the understanding reached with England and France at Munich.
   D. challenge the Atlantic Charter issued by Roosevelt and Churchill.

HOME FRONT: THE HUMAN DIMENSIONS OF THE WAR

> We must be the great arsenal of democracy.
> Franklin Roosevelt, December 29, 1940

The United States, "Arsenal of Democracy"

With America's entry into the war, industry geared up rapidly to meet the challenge and soon performed incredible feats of productivity. By 1942 America's production of war materiel was equal to that of the three Axis powers combined. Two years later it had doubled. Before the war was over the United States had built 300,000 aircraft, 71,000 ships, and over 80,000 tanks. At war's end the fighting power of the Navy had been increased over that of 1941 by 6 more battleships, 21 more aircraft carriers, and 70 more destroyers, and America's merchant marine had become the largest in the world. Despite a decrease in farm labor brought about by military enlistments, agricultural production doubled during the war years. The Depression program of crop limitation gave way to an all-out war effort that produced bumper crops of cotton, corn, hogs, and other foods to supply our own needs as well as those of our allies.

Women, a Major Factor in the War Effort

America's capacity to produce was substantially increased by the addition of three million women—double the number previously employed—to the labor force. Women served in every industry, often performing tasks previously considered the exclusive province of men. More than 250,000 women served in the armed forces wearing uniforms of the Army WACS, Navy WAVES, and Coast Guard SPARS.

Mobilizing the Armed Forces

In 1940, fifteen months before the attack on Pearl Harbor, Congress passed a **conscription** law—the first peacetime draft in American history—designed to secure 1.2 million troops and 800,000 reserves for the armed forces. When the war came, there were 1.6 million in the army. Recruitment and training proceeded rapidly after Pearl Harbor. All men between 18 and 45 were made eligible for military service, though many were rejected for failure to meet standards of physical fitness and intelligence. Over 15 million men and women served in the armed forces during World War II.

Financing the War

Raising Funds for the War

For four years (1941–1945) the United States was not only fighting a global war on land, sea, and in the air, but was serving as the "arsenal of democracy," supplying its allies with planes, tanks, guns, ships, and all the implements of warfare. It is not surprising, therefore, that the war cost $250 million a day. The national debt, which stood at $49 billion in 1941 (most of it incurred during World War I and the Depression of the '30s) zoomed to $258 billion in 1945.

Maintaining this giant enterprise required both taxing and borrowing, since it was impossible to operate on a "pay as you go" basis as President Roosevelt would have preferred. In seven massive **war bond drives**, the government borrowed $100 billion from its citizens.

Preventing Inflation

With full employment and high government expenditures, wages nearly doubled. It became necessary to take steps to prevent runaway inflation. An Office of Price Administration (OPA), headed by Leon Henderson, was established in August 1941. In April 1942 the OPA imposed a general **price freeze** including a freeze on rents. The OPA also distributed **ration booklets**, which limited civilian consumption of gasoline, meat, tires, and other commodities made scarce by the war.

Hollywood Goes to War

The movie industry gave its talents wholeheartedly to the war effort. War films depicted the bravery and skill of America's fighting forces, the cruelty and ineptness of the Axis forces, the sometimes exotic nature of war zones, and ultimately the goals for which we fought. Among outstanding war films were *Casablanca,* which portrayed the Free French in Africa standing firm against the Nazis; *Sahara,* which depicted soldiers of the allied nations gaining control of scarce water resources; *Air Force,* which pictured the exploits of a U.S. bomber "Flying Fortress"; and *A Walk in the Sun*, which presented U.S. Army units establishing a beachhead in Italy. Films that dealt with the war in Asia included *Bataan, Behind the Rising Sun,* and *Dragon Seed*. **Bob Hope**, one of Hollywood's best-known comedians, and many others went overseas to entertain the troops.

The War's Impact on Minorities

Impact on African Americans

World War II had a special impact on African Americans and on Japanese Americans. During the war, half a million African Americans moved from the deep South to seek employment in the defense industries in Northern cities. However, opportunities continued to be denied them despite the great need for labor in defense plants. Membership in the NAACP leaped from 100,000 to half a million in the first three years of the war.

When the **United States Employment Service**, a federal agency, continued to fill defense contracts from employers stipulating "whites only," A. Philip Randolph, president of the Brotherhood of Sleeping Car Porters, proceeded to organize 50,000 people for a protest march on Washington. President Roosevelt met with Randolph at the White House on June 18, 1941. Randolph refused to call off the march until a satisfactory employment directive was issued by the President.

On June 25, 1941, President Roosevelt issued Executive Order 8802, declaring it the policy of the United States "that there shall be no discrimination in the employment of workers in defense industries or government because of race, creed, color, or national origin." The President appointed a **Fair Employment Practices Committee** to "receive and investigate complaints of discrimination" and to take "appropriate steps to redress grievances." Partly as a result of this order the number of black employees in the federal government increased from 40,000 to 300,000.

Impact on Japanese Americans

On the West Coast there was considerable apprehension about the part that Japanese Americans might play in the war. There was also latent prejudice and animosity toward Japanese Americans. On February 19, 1942, two months after the attack on Pearl Harbor, President Roosevelt issued Executive Order 9066, transferring authority for security to the Army. The Army commander of the West Coast, Lt. General John DeWitt, ordered the removal of 127,000 Japanese Americans, more than two thirds of whom were American citizens, from their homes in the western parts of Washington, Oregon, and California, and from southern Arizona. Without any charges or trials, they were forcibly "**relocated**" to internment camps in the Western deserts and the Arkansas swamplands.

A suit to void the order as unconstitutional came to the U.S. Supreme Court and was decided on December 18, 1944. In *Korematsu* v. *United States* the Court was confronted with one of the enduring constitutional issues in American history—the balance between government security and the civil liberties of the individual. By a vote of 6 to 3, the Court upheld the government's action. Writing for the majority, **Justice Hugo Black**, whose overall record marks him as a staunch defender of the Bill of Rights, wrote, "He [Korematsu] was excluded because we are at war with the Japanese Empire, because the properly constituted military authorities feared an invasion of the West Coast, and felt constrained to take proper security measures . . ." In dissent, **Justice Owen J. Roberts** said the facts exhibited "a clear violation of constitutional rights," and **Justice Frank Murphy** said the exclusion went over "the brink of constitutional power" and fell "into the ugly abyss of racism."

On August 10, 1988, the United States finally admitted that the **internment** of Japanese Americans was a "mistake," agreed to issue apologies to each of the surviving internees, and to pay to each $20,000 tax-free over a ten-year period.

Segregation in the Armed Forces

When the draft went into effect in 1940, African American enlistments, proportional to their population, exceeded white enlistments by 60 percent. Yet African Americans were not accepted into the Air Corps or Marine Corps; the Army assigned them to segregated units as laborers and servants, and the Navy placed them as officers' cooks and stewards. African American combat troops served under white officers.

Pressure on the President from the African American community finally resulted in the organization of a few African American combat units, the commissioning of a limited number of African American officers in the Air Force, and the promotion of Colonel Benjamin O. Davis to Brigadier General. The numbers gradually increased during the war and more than 80 African American Air Force officers won the Distinguished Flying Cross. *The Crisis,* journal of the NAACP, contended that "a Jim Crow army cannot fight for a free world," but African Americans fought with distinction in every theater of the war. Complete integration in America's fighting forces did not come until the Korean War in the 1950s.

The Holocaust (1933–1945)

Early in the war, Hitler declared the Nazi policy concerning all the Jews under his control in Germany and the occupied countries. He called it "**the final solution**." It consisted of the systematic murder of the entire Jewish people. The extermination of an ethnic group is called **genocide**. The Nazi "final solution," which resulted in the murder of six million Jews in Europe during the Third Reich (1933–1945), is known in history as the **Holocaust**. Major extermination centers were built at Auschwitz, Buchenwald, Treblinka, Bergen-Belsen, and Majdanek.

When American armed forces entered the death camps in April 1945, they were horrified at what they found—massive starvation, unchecked disease, thousands of unburied corpses. General Eisenhower called the findings "almost unbelievable." Slowly the truth was impressed on the incredulous public. As the cry, "Never again," was raised, Holocaust studies became part of the school curriculum in New York State and throughout the United States.

Failure of the United States to act on the reports of the Holocaust is attributable to a number of causes—disbelief, reluctance of the media to report what they knew, Roosevelt's preoccupation with other war matters, and disinterest of the American public.

In the spring of 1944, President Roosevelt approved a request of the War Refugee Board to admit 1,000 refugees to Fort Ontario at Oswego, New

York. The refugees, at that time in southern Italy, were survivors of the death camps. They were to return to their homelands after the war. During the war, Sweden had welcomed 8,000 Jewish refugees from Denmark. But the admission of 1,000 to the United States under strict "security restrictions" met with bitter resistance from anti-Semites in the United States.

Exercise Set 5.3

1. During World War II the earnings of workers
   A. nearly doubled.
   B. increased by 50 percent.
   C. gained only slightly.
   D. declined in terms of real wages.

2. World War II was financed differently from World War I in that
   A. excess profits taxes were levied.
   B. income taxes were levied.
   C. more of the cost was raised by taxation.
   D. the withholding tax was not used.

3. Which statement best describes an important part of the experience of African Americans in the United States during the period between World War I and World War II?
   A. Many African Americans moved back to the South in an attempt to recapture their roots.
   B. Interracial tensions increased because of the African American migration into Northern cities.
   C. The influence of the Ku Klux Klan declined significantly.
   D. The success of black soldiers in World War I led to equal treatment for African Americans.

4. Agricultural policy during World War II
   A. favored the production of basic raw materials like cotton.
   B. attempted to restrict production in order to enlist farm labor in the war production industries.
   C. fostered bumper crops as a means of exchange for materials needed in defense industries.
   D. was a reversal of New Deal agricultural policy.

Base your answer to question 5 on the posters below and on your knowledge of social studies.

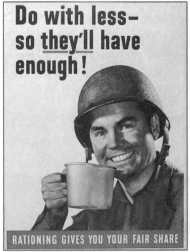

Source: Office of War Information, 1943

Source: Office for Emergency Management, 1942

5. These posters were trying to convince Americans that winning World War II required
   A. wage and price freezes.
   B. the sale of additional war bonds.
   C. higher levels of taxation and spending.
   D. the conservation of scarce resources.

THE UNITED STATES IN WORLD WAR II

> More than any other war in history, this war has been an array of the
> forces of evil against those of righteousness . . . no matter what the
> cost, the war had to be won.
>
> Dwight D. Eisenhower, June 10, 1945

Allied Leadership and Strategy

Allied leadership and strategy were the key factors in attaining victory in
World War II. The United States, under Commander-in-Chief **Franklin
D. Roosevelt**, worked in close and harmonious cooperation with Britain,
under the indomitable Prime Minister **Winston S. Churchill**. The military leaders of both nations, in a secret conference in March 1941, planned
joint strategy. The primary effort was to be directed against Nazi Germany,
because Germany, in control of the seacoast of western Europe, was using its
U-boats to cut communications between Britain and the United States. Also,
Germany had greater military power and resources than Japan, and there
was great apprehension that Germany might develop the atom bomb or some
other fearful weapon if given the time.

Marshall—the Architect of Victory

America's Chief of Staff **General George C. Marshall** was the leading
architect of Allied strategy. Roosevelt turned down his request for a field
command, asserting that Marshall's talents as an overall strategist were
essential to victory.

Planning the Attack on "Fortress Europe"

Leadership of Eisenhower

General Dwight D. Eisenhower was **Supreme Commander of Allied
Expeditionary Forces** in Western Europe. He commanded the successful
Allied invasion of North Africa and was then assigned the task of the invasion of Europe as commander of all Allied forces in Europe with headquarters near London.

From North Africa to Italy

In November 1942 General Eisenhower, in cooperation with the British, made
landings in Africa and took Casablanca, Oran, and Algiers. On February 14,
1943, Eisenhower took command of the Allied forces in North Africa. Aided
by **General George S. Patton** and British **General Bernard Montgomery**,
he forced the surrender on May 13th of 250,000 Axis troops and brought the

African campaign to a close. In September 1943 **General Mark Clark** led an American invasion of Italy at Salerno, south of Naples.

D-Day—June 6, 1944

In June 1944 General Eisenhower was made Supreme Commander of the Allied Expeditionary Forces with Supreme Headquarters, Allied Expeditionary Forces (SHAEF) in London. After months of careful planning, the invasion of Europe, called by the code name "Operation Overlord," was launched on "**D-Day**," **June 6, 1944**. The first few hours of Operation Overlord included heavy air bombardment all along the French coast; 4,000 troop ships crossing the English Channel with 176,000 troops; air cover by 11,000 planes; glider planes with parachute troops being dropped behind enemy lines; and about 600 fighting ships escorting the fighting forces and shelling enemy batteries.

V. E. Day—May 8, 1945

By July 1944 one million troops were in France; by September that number exceeded two million. In September 1944, American troops entered Germany. On **May 8, 1945** (**V. E. Day**), the German General Staff accepted the Allied terms of "unconditional surrender."

Turning Points in the War

At Sea—Midway

In the Pacific, the great air-naval battle of **Midway** (June 3–6, 1942) was a turning point in the war. Japan's attempt to take this strategic American base was repulsed with losses to the enemy of four carriers and about 275 planes.

In the Air—the Battle of Britain

A turning point in the air war in Europe came in the summer of 1940. Hitler's air force (**Luftwaffe**) bombed London and other British cities almost every night for three months. The **Royal Air Force** (**RAF**) downed 2,300 German planes during the **Battle of Britain**. Toward the end of August, the RAF gained control of the skies over Britain. They had won the battle and saved Britain. In the House of Commons on August 20, 1940, Churchill expressed Britain's tribute to the RAF in the classic statement: "Never in the field of human conflict was so much owed by so many to so few."

On Land—Stalingrad

The turning point in the land war between the Nazi army and the Soviet forces came at **Stalingrad** in the fall of 1942, when the Russians broke the back of the German offensive by destroying or capturing more than twenty divisions, containing some 300,000 of Germany's elite troops.

The Atomic Bomb

In 1939, scientists in the field of theoretical physics were aware that **nuclear fission** could be used to make a bomb of incredible destructive power. There was evidence that Germany was working on the **atomic bomb**. In July 1939, **Albert Einstein**, a refugee from Nazi Germany then working at Princeton University, signed a letter to President Roosevelt urging that the U.S. government sponsor a program to harness atomic energy and stating: "This new phenomenon would lead also to the construction of bombs." Roosevelt considered the idea carefully and decided that he must pursue a project that was recommended by Einstein and other leading physicists, including **Enrico Fermi**, a Nobel Prize winner refugee from Italy, and Niels Bohr, another Nobel Laureate refugee from Denmark.

The Manhattan Project

On the morning of July 16, 1945, the first atomic bomb was detonated in the desert south of Los Alamos, New Mexico. Three weeks later, on August 6, 1945, a U.S. Army plane dropped a single atomic bomb over Hiroshima, Japan. The bomb had a force equal to 20,000 tons of TNT (dynamite). A blinding flash was followed by a "mushroom cloud" of debris and atomic radiation that reached skyward and spread over the city and its environs. It killed 260,000 people. When the Japanese refused to surrender, a second bomb was dropped three days later on Nagasaki.

Reason for Truman's Decision to Use the A-Bomb

President Truman's decision to use the bomb was justified in his mind by the need to end the war quickly and save American lives. The war in the Pacific had been bitterly fought with heavy losses. Fighting in the Philippines, Coral Sea, Midway, Guadalcanal, Tarawa, the Marshall Islands, Saipan, and Guam in the Marianas, and the reconquest of the Philippines had contributed substantially to the million American casualties. Now the fighting was on Japanese soil as the main islands of Japan were being approached. Capturing the small island of Iwo Jima took the lives of 5,000 American marines. The conquest of Okinawa, 360 miles from the main islands of Japan, resulted in

11,000 Americans killed and 34,000 wounded. It was estimated that the successful Allied invasion of Japan would result in a million casualties.

The Japanese Surrender

On **August 14, 1945** (**V. J. Day**), five days after the bomb was dropped on Nagasaki, Japan surrendered and World War II ended.

Formal Surrender Ceremonies

Formal ceremonies of surrender and signing of surrender documents took place aboard the battleship *Missouri* in Tokyo Bay, September 2, 1945. The surrender was accepted by General Douglas MacArthur on condition that **Emperor Hirohito** be allowed to remain on the throne as emperor-figurehead. In a brief statement MacArthur concluded: "If we do not devise some . . . more equitable system than war, Armageddon will be at our door."

Occupation of Japan

General MacArthur was virtually the ruler of Japan during most of the period of Allied occupation (1945–1951). The Japanese cooperated in carrying out the reforms he instituted in decrees establishing a democratic, nonmilitary government, redistributing land, restricting the power of the industrial monopolies, establishing labor unions, reforming education, and granting women suffrage. A beginning was made in rebuilding the Japanese economy.

Exercise Set 5.4

1. Which of the following did *not* occur during the Allied occupation of Japan (1945–1951) after World War II?
   A. General MacArthur was not able to participate in the occupation because he was preoccupied with events in the Philippines.
   B. The Japanese cooperated in carrying out the reforms requested by General MacArthur.
   C. A new Japanese Constitution went into effect during the occupation.
   D. The size of Japanese armed forces was substantially reduced.

2. The first atomic bomb was developed in the United States with the help of a number of European scientists who were refugees from the Nazis. Which of the following was included in this group?
   A. Guglielmo Marconi
   B. Enrico Fermi
   C. Alessandro Volta
   D. Cyrus McCormick

3. The most accurate statement concerning U.S. foreign policy is that the United States has generally
   A. acted according to national self-interest.
   B. reacted forcefully to imperialism around the world.
   C. formed alliances with countries in need.
   D. used military confrontation to solve disputes.

4. President Truman's justification for using the atomic bomb on Hiroshima and Nagasaki was
   A. to vindicate the expenditure of $2 billion on solving the problem of nuclear fission.
   B. to avenge the Japanese use of suicide bombing against American ships.
   C. to demonstrate to Stalin that the United States was the strongest military power on earth.
   D. to save perhaps as many as a million American lives.

5. Which group of U.S. residents was subjected to the greatest loss of constitutional rights during a period of U.S. military involvement?
   A. Hispanic Americans during the Spanish-American War
   B. German Americans during World War I
   C. Japanese Americans during World War II
   D. Chinese Americans during the Korean conflict

AFTERMATH OF WORLD WAR II

> The evidence relating to war crimes has been overwhelming in its volume and its detail . . . The truth remains that war crimes were committed on a vast scale, never before seen in the history of war.
> Report of the War Crimes Tribunal of the Nuremberg Trials, 1946

War Crimes Trials

The Nuremberg Trials

At the Nuremberg Trials (1945–1946) six German organizations and 24 top German civil, military, and naval leaders were charged with war crimes. The leaders included **Herman Wilhelm Goering**, the number two Nazi; Joachim von Ribbentrop, Nazi foreign minister; Julius Streicher, editor of *Der Sturmer*; **Rudolph Hess**, the number three Nazi; Generals Wilhelm Keitel and Alfred Jodl; and Admirals Eric Raedler and Karl Doenitz. (Hitler had committed suicide on April 30, 1945.) The charges included the killing of more than 10 million European civilians and captured war prisoners. Eleven of the defendants were sentenced to death by hanging, others to imprisonment for various terms.

War Crimes Trials in Japan

War crimes trials were also held in Japan at the direction of General MacArthur, who ordered the top Japanese war leaders to stand trial. General **Hideki Tojo**, the leading warmonger and former Premier, tried unsuccessfully to commit suicide. He and six of his colleagues were found guilty and hanged on December 23, 1948. The same fate overtook General Tomoyuki Yamashita, the Tiger of the Philippines. Sixteen others were given light sentences. Other trials were held throughout Japan before special courts; 4,200 were convicted, of whom 720 were executed.

The Pursuit of Nazi War Criminals

Many Nazi criminals involved in the slaughter of Jews during the Holocaust escaped from Germany to countries as far away as Argentina.

• *Adolf Eichmann.* A case that stirred worldwide interest was that of Adolf Eichmann, who had been assigned the task of deporting all the Jews from Europe to the extermination camps in Eastern Europe. On March 14, 1945, shortly before the surrender of the Nazis, Eichmann proclaimed, "I'll happily die with the certainty of having killed almost six million Jews." Instead, he fled in disguise to Argentina. Eichmann's capture in Buenos Aires in 1960 by Israeli commandos and his deportation to Israel for trial was made possible by the efforts of one man, Simon Wiesenthal, who spent four and a half years in Nazi concentration camps. In 1947 he founded the Vienna Documentation Center for tracing the whereabouts of war criminals. He helped bring 1,100 criminals, including Eichmann, to justice. He also established the Wiesenthal Center for Holocaust Studies in Los Angeles.

• *Klaus Barbie.* The French Fascist Klaus Barbie was captured in La Paz, Bolivia, in 1983. Barbie, who earned the title "Butcher of Lyons," worked with the Nazis during their occupation of France and was responsible for the murder of thousands of French Jews and resistance fighters.

Conversion to Peace

Demobilization

When the war ended, President Truman wished to demobilize the armed forces slowly in order to have a strong military presence in Europe and Asia in case of emergency. But there was tremendous pressure at home for immediate return of the troops. In less than a year the armed forces were reduced from 12 million to 3 million; the Air Force went from 85,000 to 9,000 planes; and the Navy withdrew hundreds of ships from active service.

End of Price Controls

There was also heavy pressure on the President to remove wartime price controls on consumer goods. When the Democrats lost control of both houses of Congress in the 1946 elections, Truman yielded and withdrew controls on everything but rent.

Postwar Inflation

As might have been expected, runaway inflation was unleashed. People had earned good wages during the war, but consumer goods such as automobiles, refrigerators, and home appliances were not available because industry was engaged in making ships, tanks, and guns. Savings mounted until nearly $50 billion was available for consumer purchases. By the spring of 1947, prices were one third higher than they had been less than two years before.

Labor Unrest

With this surge in prices came a demand by labor for wage increases. A wave of strikes swept across the country. Major industries, including automobiles, steel, and railroads, were hit. The federal courts intervened in a strike of bituminous coal miners, led by **John L. Lewis**, who defied a court injunction in 1946. The strike was broken when a federal district court imposed heavy fines on Lewis and the union.

The Taft-Hartley Act

The Republican-controlled Congress passed the 1947 Taft-Hartley labor law over Truman's veto. The law forbade the "closed shop" and outlawed the "check off," which required employers to deduct union dues from paychecks and turn the money over directly to the union. It authorized the President to seek a court injunction calling for a 60-day "cooling off" period for strikes and authorized an 80-day injunction against strikes affecting public health or safety. The new law was denounced by labor as a "slave labor" law. However, supporters in Congress and among the citizenry felt that it restrained the excessive power that organized labor had gained from the Wagner Act of 1935.

The law also forbade unions from making political contributions and required labor leaders, but not management, to take a non-Communist oath. In the face of a threatened strike of steel unions, President Truman ordered Charles Sawyer, his Secretary of Commerce, to take possession of the steel mills and run them by authority of the federal government. The procedure was declared unconstitutional by a 6 to 3 decision of the Supreme Court in *Youngstown Sheet & Tube Co.* v. *Sawyer* (1952).

Congress Opposes Truman's Reforms

In Social Legislation

Congress and the President were at odds. The President's efforts to expand public housing, Social Security, and federal aid to education were rejected.

In Civil Rights

African Americans continued to find it difficult to obtain a fair deal in housing, employment, and education. When President Truman attempted to put an end to racial injustice, he met even greater resistance. His call for anti-lynching and anti-poll tax laws, stronger civil rights laws, and a permanent Fair Employment Practices Committee was stalled when Southern senators prepared to filibuster against these measures. In December 1946 the President appointed a **Committee on Civil Rights** in response to racial murders in the South. Truman did, however, begin the desegregation of the armed forces. He also appointed African American judges to the federal courts and issued an executive order banning discrimination in federal employment.

The GI Bill of Rights

An important series of laws, called the "**GI Bill of Rights**," was passed by Congress in anticipation of the return of 10 million veterans to civilian life. One of the most far-reaching measures was the law providing subsidies for veterans who wished to continue their education. About 12 million veterans ultimately availed themselves of this opportunity for basic education as well as vocational education and the attainment of advanced professional diplomas and degrees. Other laws favorable to veterans provided reinstatement to their jobs with seniority rights, unemployment pay for up to one year, low-interest government loans for home building and for the purchase of farms or businesses, and provision for medical care.

The Election of 1948

As the election of 1948 approached, it seemed unlikely that President Truman would remain in office. There was even doubt that he would be nominated. The Democratic party split into three factions. Southern Democrats, called "**Dixiecrats**," alarmed by the President's civil rights agenda, organized a **States Rights** Party and nominated Governor **J. Strom Thurmond** of South Carolina for President. Another wing of the Democratic Party, led by former Vice President **Henry A. Wallace**, opposed the President's "cold war" confrontation with the Soviet Union. Wallace was nominated for President by this faction under the name of the Progressive Party.

Meanwhile the Republican Party united behind Governor **Thomas E. Dewey** of New York. Dewey had lost to Roosevelt in 1944, when the war was still being fought. This time he was the strong favorite to win.

But the feisty President went around the country denouncing the "do-nothing, good-for-nothing" Republican-controlled Eightieth Congress. So certain were the Republicans of victory that the *Chicago Daily Tribune* published an early election edition with an eight-column front page headline: "Dewey Defeats Truman." Truman surprised the pollsters by winning 303 electoral votes to 189 for Dewey and 39 for Thurmond. The popular vote was 24.1 million to 21.9 million, with 1.17 million for Thurmond and 1.16 million for Wallace.

Truman's "Fair Deal" Program

In his State of the Union message (January 1949), Truman called for a "**Fair Deal**" for all Americans. The Democrats had gained majorities in both houses of Congress, and the President proposed to extend the social legislation of the New Deal. Most of his proposals met determined opposition by a conservative coalition of Republicans and Southern Democrats in Congress. But Truman did succeed with part of his "Fair Deal" program. Social Security benefits were extended to 10 million additional members; the minimum wage of the Fair Labor Standards Act of 1938 was raised from 40 cents to 75 cents an hour. The **National Housing Act** of 1949 provided for slum clearance and the construction of 810,000 housing units to be built during a six-year period for rental to low-income families. Proposals for strong civil rights measures, for repeal of sections of the Taft-Hartley Act, for a new farm subsidy program, for national health insurance, and for a comprehensive aid to public education program were rejected by Congress.

Exercise Set 5.5

1. An important outcome of the Nuremberg Trials held at the end of World War II was that they
   A. showed that many accounts of Nazi atrocities were exaggerated.
   B. spread the blame for World War II among many nations.
   C. held that moral and ethical considerations do not apply in wartime.
   D. established that individuals are responsible for their actions.

2. The term "open shop" refers to a plant or business where
   A. only unionized workers are hired.
   B. either union or non-union workers are hired.
   C. employees must join a union after six months.
   D. only non-union workers are hired.

3. The Taft-Hartley Act
   A. imposed unusual restrictions on employers.
   B. gave labor greater power than ever.
   C. was opposed by the Republicans.
   D. sought to curb the power of unions.

4. The success of President Truman in the 1948 election was due to
   A. his direct and forthright statement of his position on public issues.
   B. his calls for civil rights legislation.
   C. his conservative position during the period of postwar reaction.
   D. the intellectual quality of his television appearances.

5. The "G.I. Bill of Rights" refers to
   A. an amendment to the Constitution adopted shortly after the end of World War II.
   B. rights of veterans affirmed by the Supreme Court in a series of post-war decisions.
   C. legislation passed by Congress pertaining to education, unemployment compensation, loans for home building, and provisions for medical care of veterans.
   D. guarantees for employment of veterans in federal government departments and agencies.

1. Which statement best describes relations among the major powers during the period between World War I and World War II?
   A. Major powers followed policies of international cooperation in order to ensure peace.
   B. Major powers respected each other's territorial integrity.
   C. The League of Nations was given the power to establish a strong multinational military force.
   D. National interests took priority over international interests.

2. Evidence that the United States generally followed a policy of isolationism during the period 1919–1939 is that the United States
   A. condemned Fascist aggression.
   B. rejected the policy of appeasement.
   C. refused to join the League of Nations.
   D. participated in disarmament conferences.

3. The neutrality legislation of 1935–1937 was based on the contention that one of the chief causes of American involvement in World War I was
   A. economic ties with the belligerents.
   B. Wilson's failure to uphold American rights.
   C. creation by the press of hostile public opinion toward the Central Powers.
   D. failure of the executive and legislative branches of the government to agree on foreign policy.

4. The isolationist policies of the United States in the 1930s were broken down by the danger of
   A. a united Europe under the leadership of Soviet Russia.
   B. a united Asia under the Chinese People's Republic.
   C. a simultaneous two-ocean war against a united Europe and a united Asia.
   D. the growth of British trade in Latin America and Canada.

5. Roosevelt's decision to make the atomic bomb was
   A. more difficult than Truman's decision to use it because there was greater opposition to it.
   B. opposed by the leading scientists on both sides of the Atlantic.
   C. based on reports that Germany was attempting to develop an atomic bomb or other decisive military invention.
   D. not much of a risk since only a few million dollars were invested in the venture.

THEMATIC ESSAY

Directions: Write a well-organized essay that includes an introduction, several paragraphs addressing the task below, and a conclusion.

Theme: Science and Technology

> Science and technology have brought about great changes in many areas of American life.

Task:

> From your study of the 20th century, choose *three* major scientific/technological developments.
>
> For each administration:
>
> - Identify the scientific/technological development.
> - Describe the effects of the scientific/technological development on American life.
> - Discuss the extent to which the development had a positive or a negative effect on American life.

You may use any major scientific/technological developments from your study of 20th-century United States history. Some suggestions you may wish to consider are mass production of the automobile (1900–1930), invention of the airplane and eventual trans-Atlantic flight (1903–1927), television (1945–present), nuclear weapons (1945–present), and home use of the personal computer (1980–present).

You are *not* limited to these suggestions.

DOCUMENT-BASED QUESTION

The following questions (Part A and Part B) are based on the accompanying documents (1–6). Some of these documents have been edited for the purpose of this exercise. The question is designed to test your ability to work with historical documents and to demonstrate your knowledge of the subject matter being presented. As you analyze the documents, take into account both the source of the document and the author's point of view.

Historical Context:

Although post-World War I isolationism ran deep in the United States during the 1930s and early 1940s, many believed that involvement in World War II was inevitable.

Task:

Using information from the documents and your knowledge of United States history, answer the questions that follow each document in Part A. Your answers to the questions will help you write the Part B essay, in which you will be asked:

Discuss the likelihood of U.S. involvement in World War II without the direct attack upon Pearl Harbor in December 1941.

Part A
Short-Answer Questions

The documents below relate to issues concerning United States foreign policy in the 1930s and early 1940s. Examine each document carefully and then answer the questions that follow.

DOCUMENT 1

Sect. 1. (a) Whenever the President shall find that there exists a state of war between, or among, two or more foreign states, the President shall proclaim such fact, and it shall thereafter be unlawful to export, or attempt to export, or cause to be exported, arms, ammunition, or implements of war from any place in the United States to any belligerent state named in such proclamation, or to any neutral state for transshipment to, or for the use of, any belligerent state.

—The Neutrality Act of 1937 (May 1, 1937)

1. How did the Neutrality Act of 1937 distinguish, if at all, between the treatment of Great Britain and Germany?

_____

_____

_____

_____

2. How did the Neutrality Act of 1937 address the issue of shipping arms to neutral countries?

_____

_____

_____

_____

DOCUMENT 2

	Europe (total)		UK		Germany	
Year	Exports to	Imports from	Exports to	Imports from	Exports to	Imports from
1914	1,486	896	594	294	345	190
1915	1,971	614	912	256	29	91
1916	3,813	633	1,887	305	2	6
1917	4,062	551	2,009	280	—	—
1918	3,859	318	2,061	149	—	—
1919	5,188	751	2,279	309	93	11
1920	4,466	1,228	1,825	514	311	89
1921	2,364	765	942	239	372	80
1922	2,083	991	856	357	316	117
1923	2,093	1,157	882	404	317	161
1924	2,445	1,096	983	366	440	139
1925	2,604	1,239	1,034	413	470	164
1926	2,310	1,278	973	383	364	198
1927	2,314	1,265	840	358	482	201
1928	2,375	1,249	847	349	467	222
1929	2,341	1,334	848	330	410	255
1930	1,838	911	678	210	278	177
1931	1,187	641	456	135	166	127
1932	784	390	288	75	134	74
1933	850	463	312	111	140	78
1934	950	490	383	115	109	69
1935	1,029	599	433	155	92	78
1936	1,043	718	440	200	102	80
1937	1,360	843	536	203	126	92
1938	1,326	567	521	118	107	65
1939	1,290	617	505	149	46	52
1940	1,645	390	1,011	155	—	5
1941	1,847	281	1,637	136	—	3
1942	4,009	220	2,529	134	—	—
1943	7,633	240	4,505	105	—	—
1944	9,364	289	5,243	84	—	—
1945	5,515	409	2,193	90	2	1

UNITED STATES IMPORTS and EXPORTS 1914–1945 (in millions of dollars)

—U.S. Bureau of the Census

3. How did import/export activity between the United States and Germany compare with import/export activity with Great Britain (UK) during the 1930–1940 period?

_____

_____

_____

_____

4. What argument could be made using the statistics in the table above for the eventual direction of United States foreign policy that favored protection of Great Britain against Germany?

_____

_____

_____

_____

DOCUMENT 3

It seems to be unfortunately true that the epidemic of world lawlessness is spreading. And mark this well! When an epidemic of physical disease starts to spread, the community approves and joins in a quarantine of the patients in order to protect the community against the spread of the disease.

—Franklin D. Roosevelt, "Quarantine Speech,"
October 5, 1937

5. What problems did the Neutrality Act of 1937 present to Roosevelt's position by October of 1937?

_____

_____

_____

_____

DOCUMENT 4

The Neutrality Act of 1937 made no distinction between aggressor nations (Germany, Japan) and victim nations (France, China). In September 1939 President Roosevelt addressed Congress and urged a repeal of the Act. The following response came from Michigan Senator Arthur Vandenberg.

In the midst of foreign war . . . we are asked to depart from the neutrality which the American Congress has twice told the world would be our role of conduct in such an event. . . . We are asked to depart from international law itself, as we ourselves have officially declared it to exist. Consciously or otherwise, but mostly consciously, we are asked to depart from it on behalf of one belligerent whom our personal sympathies largely favor, and against another belligerent whom our personal feelings largely condemn. In my opinion, this is the road that may lead us to war, and I will not voluntarily take it . . . .

—Senator Arthur Vandenberg, Republican, Michigan,
October 4, 1939

6. Senator Vandenberg refers to two belligerents: one the United States favors and the other the United States condemns. Which country does the United States favor and which does the United States condemn?

_____

_____

_____

_____

7. Would Senator Vandenberg be labeled an isolationist or an interventionist? Why?

_____

_____

_____

_____

It is possible—I will put it that way—for the United States to take over British (war) orders, and, because they are essentially the same kind of munitions that we use ourselves, turn them into American orders . . . . That would be on the general theory that it may still prove true that the best defense of Great Britain is the best defense of the United States, and therefore that these materials would be more useful to the defense of the United States if they were used in Great Britain than if they were kept in storage here.

—President Franklin D. Roosevelt, Speech supporting
Lend-Lease Act, 1940

8. By 1940 it had become quite clear that United States foreign policy was designed to assist what major European warring nation?

_____

_____

_____

_____

DOCUMENT 6

I know I will be severely criticized by the interventionists in America when I say we should not enter a war unless we have a reasonable chance of winning . . . . We have a one-ocean Navy. Our Army is still untrained and inadequately equipped for foreign war. Our air force is deplorably lacking in modern fighting planes because most of them have already been sent to Europe . . . .

There is a policy open to this nation that will lead to success—a policy that leaves us free to follow our own way of life, and to develop our own civilization. It is not a new and untried idea. It was advocated by Washington. It was incorporated in the Monroe Doctrine . . . .

—Charles A. Lindbergh, New York City, August 14, 1935

9. Explain Lindbergh's reference to Washington and Monroe and how the reference supports his argument.

_____

_____

_____

_____

DOCUMENT 7

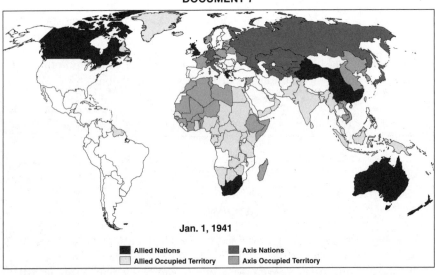

Jan. 1, 1941

■ Allied Nations   ■ Axis Nations
□ Allied Occupied Territory   ▨ Axis Occupied Territory

10. Nearly 11 months before the attack on Pearl Harbor, what concerns might the United States have had for the future of Western Europe?

_____

_____

_____

_____

Your essay should be well organized with an introductory paragraph that states your position on the question. Develop your position in the next paragraphs and then write a conclusion. In your essay, include specific historical details and refer to the specific documents you analyzed in Part A. You may include additional information from your knowledge of social studies.

Historical Context:

> Although post-World War I isolationism ran deep in the United States during the 1930s and early 1940s, many believed that involvement in World War II was inevitable.

Task:

> Do you feel that the involvement of the United States in World War II would have come without the direct attack on Pearl Harbor on December 7, 1941, or do you feel that the proponents of nonintervention would have been successful in keeping the United States out of war?

Guidelines:

In your essay, be sure to
- Develop all aspects of the task.
- Incorporate information from *at least five* documents.
- Incorporate relevant outside information.
- Support the theme with many relevant facts, examples, and details.
- Use a logical and clear plan of organization, including an introduction and a conclusion that are beyond a restatement of the theme.

CHAPTER 2

PEACE WITH PROBLEMS
(1945–1960)

INTERNATIONAL PEACE EFFORTS

> We must cultivate the science of human relationships—the ability of
> all peoples, of all kinds to live together and work together in the same
> world of peace.
>   Franklin D. Roosevelt's last written words, April 11, 1945

Organizing the United Nations

The San Francisco Conference (1945)

Allied leaders met in August 1944 at Dumbarton Oaks, in Washington, D.C.,
where plans were laid for an international organization to be known as the
United Nations. On April 25, 1945, 13 days after the death of President
Roosevelt, delegates from 50 nations met in San Francisco to draft a charter
(constitution) for the United Nations. The United States sent a 5-member del-
egation consisting of Secretary of State Edward Stettinius, two Republicans
(Senator Vandenberg and Representative Eaton) and two Democrats (Senator
Connally and Congressman Bloom).

The UN came into formal existence on October 24, 1945. The charter was
ratified (approved) by the Senate on July 28, 1945, making the United States
a charter member of the UN.

The United Nations Organization

The charter of the United Nations provides for six major organs and numerous
specialized agencies. The **General Assembly** is the major legislative body,
where each member has one vote. The **Security Council** is the peacekeeping authority. It consists of eleven members—five permanent and six others
elected for two-year terms. The five permanent members—the United States,
China, France, Russia, and Great Britain—each has the power to veto any
decision of the Council. The **Secretariat**, headed by a Secretary General, is
the administrative body of the UN. The other three major UN organs are the

Economic and Social Council, the Trusteeship Council (to safeguard the interests of territories that were not self-governing), and the International Court of Justice. Headquarters of the United Nations are in New York City.

The Universal Declaration of Human Rights

Eleanor Roosevelt's Role

The first U.S. delegation to the UN, appointed by President Truman, consisted of five members, one of whom was Mrs. Eleanor Roosevelt. At first she hesitated to accept the appointment, saying she had no experience in foreign affairs. But President Truman insisted and she agreed to serve.

The delegation assigned her to the Human Rights Commission, where it was believed she would engage in trivial activities. She worked with careful attention to every aspect of the task. Delegates from other lands soon came to recognize her leadership qualities, and she was chosen to head the committee drafting the Human Rights Declaration.

Adoption and Contents of the Universal Declaration of Human Rights

It took three years before the Universal Declaration of Human Rights was adopted (December 10, 1948)—a tribute to Eleanor Roosevelt's patient and effective leadership. The vote in the UN General Assembly was 48 in favor and 8 members abstaining. These included six members of the Soviet bloc, Saudi Arabia, and South Africa. The Declaration consists of 30 articles, many with subsections. Included in the Declaration are the following:

Art. 1: All human beings are born free and equal in dignity and rights . . .

Art. 2: Everyone is entitled to all the rights and freedoms set forth in this Declaration without distinction of any kind, such as race, color, sex, language, religion, political or other opinion, national or social origin, property, birth or other status . . .

Art. 3: Everyone has the right to life, liberty, and security of person.

Art. 5: No one shall be subjected to torture or to cruel, inhuman, or degrading treatment or punishment.

Art. 9: No one shall be subjected to arbitrary arrest, detention, or exile.

Art. 11: (I) Everyone charged with a penal offense has the right to be presumed innocent until proven guilty.

Art. 13: (II) Everyone has the right to leave any country, including his own, and to return to his country.

Art. 16: (II) Marriage shall be entered into only with the true and full consent of the intending spouses.

Art. 18: Everyone has the right to freedom of thought, conscience, and religion; the right includes freedom to change his religion or belief . . .

Art. 21: (I) Everyone has the right to take part in the government of his country . . .

Art. 22: Everyone, as a member of society, has the right to social security . . .

Art. 23: (I) Everyone has the right to work, to free choice of employment, to just and favorable conditions of work, and to protection against unemployment.

Art. 23: (II) Everyone, without any discrimination, has the right to equal pay for equal work.

Art. 23: (IV) Everyone has the right to form and to join trade unions for the protection of his interests.

Art. 25: (II) Motherhood and childhood are entitled to special care and assistance. All children, whether born in or out of wedlock, shall enjoy the same social protection.

Attacks on United States Participation in the UN

John Foster Dulles, a prominent international lawyer in Washington, served as a U.S. delegate to the UN (1946–1950). When Eisenhower became President in 1953, he appointed Dulles Secretary of State. A period of reaction was setting in, and attacks were being mounted against U.S. participation in the UN. The cry was heard, "Take the United States out of the UN and the UN out of the United States." In the Senate, the Secretariat of the UN was portrayed by Senator **Joseph R. McCarthy**, Republican of Wisconsin, as a nesting place of Communist spies.

Displaced Persons and Refugees After WW II

The post-World War II problem of displaced persons and refugees was of great magnitude. There were approximately one million such refugees in displaced-person camps, most of them from Eastern Europe. Mrs. Roosevelt observed, "A new type of political refugee is appearing, people who have been against the present governments and if they stay at home or go home will probably be killed." The United Nations established a United Nations High Commission for Refugees (UNHCR) on January 1, 1951. They were to provide "legal protection and, when needed, material assistance to refugees, and to seek permanent solutions to refugee problems on a purely social, humanitarian, and nonpolitical basis."

1. The most representative legislative body of the United Nations is the
   A. Universal Declaration of Human Rights.
   B. General Assembly in which each member nation has one vote.
   C. Security Council in which each of the five permanent members has a veto power.
   D. Trusteeship Council to safeguard the interests of territories that were not self-governing.

2. The appointment of Eleanor Roosevelt as a member of the U.S. delegation to the United Nations
   A. was promptly accepted by Mrs. Roosevelt with great enthusiasm.
   B. was considered by her colleagues as a good appointment from the very beginning.
   C. was largely responsible for the creation of the Universal Declaration of Human Rights.
   D. met with serious opposition in the U.S. Senate.

3. The United Nations Universal Declaration of Human Rights was *not* approved by
   A. several African nations.
   B. six member-states from Latin America.
   C. China, Korea, and Indonesia.
   D. Saudi Arabia, South Africa, and six members of the Soviet bloc.

4. A factor that has strengthened the United Nations as compared with the League of Nations has been the U.S. policy of
   A. imperialism.
   B. isolationism.
   C. expansionism.
   D. internationalism.

5. Which foreign policy approach would advocates of the balance-of-power concept most likely support?
   A. Creation of military alliances
   B. Unilateral disarmament
   C. Abolition of foreign trade
   D. Reliance on world peace organizations

COMMUNIST EXPANSION AND CONTAINMENT IN EUROPE AND ASIA

> I believe that it must be the policy of the United States to support free peoples who are resisting attempted subjugation by armed minorities or by outside pressures.
>
> President Harry S. Truman, Message to Congress
> (The Truman Doctrine), March 12, 1947

Yalta Conference, February 1945

At Yalta, a Black Sea port in southern Russia, the big three—**Roosevelt**, **Churchill**, and **Stalin**—met in February 1945 to plan the final blows against the Axis and to make postwar arrangements. Agreement was reached about the new international organization (the United Nations) that was to be established soon after the end of the war. Stalin agreed to hold free elections in Poland, Bulgaria, and Romania, but these were never carried out. Roosevelt was anxious to have Russia enter the war against Japan, because it was expected there would be heavy casualties before Japan surrendered. Stalin agreed to enter the war against Japan within two or three months after the defeat of Germany. In return, Russia was to get the southern half of Sakhalin Island (which Russia had lost to Japan in the 1905 war) as well as the Kurile Islands. The Soviet Union was also to have special rights in parts of China— the railroads in Manchuria and the ports of Dairen and Port Arthur. Russia entered the war against Japan on August 8, 1945, exactly three months after V. E. Day.

Potsdam Conference, July–August 1945

A final summit conference was held at Potsdam, Germany, from July 17 to August 2, 1945, before the end of the war in Asia. President Truman met there with Churchill and Stalin. Later in the negotiations, **Clement Atlee**, the Labor Prime Minister who had defeated Churchill at the polls, represented Britain. The conference issued a declaration calling for the "unconditional surrender" of Japan. A democratic government was to be set up in Germany, and war criminals were to be tried by an international court. A council of foreign ministers of the victors was to draft treaties with Italy, Austria, Hungary, Bulgaria, Romania, and Finland. Zones of occupation in Germany were established, with East Germany assigned to the USSR, northwest Germany to Britain, southwest to the United States, and two small areas to France. Berlin, though located in the Russian zone, was to be divided into four zones, each to be occupied by one of the four powers.

Origins of the Cold War

The World War II alliance of Western democracies with the Soviet Union was really a "marriage of convenience or necessity." It broke up almost as soon as the war had been won. The hostility that developed, short of actual war, became known as the "**Cold War**." Instead of allowing free elections in neighboring countries, Stalin established Communist regimes in Poland, Romania, Bulgaria, and Albania. The Communists threatened the governments of Greece and Turkey in 1947. Soviet troops were used to install a Communist regime in Hungary (1956). In 1968, the Soviet Union sent 200,000 troops into Czechoslovakia to ensure Communist control of that country.

In a speech at Fulton, Missouri in March 1946, Winston Churchill declared, "From Stettin in the Baltic to Trieste in the Adriatic, an **iron curtain** has descended across the continent." President Truman, who was present during this address, was fully in accord with this statement. The U.S. response to Communist aggression was the policy of **containment**. It sought to "contain" or limit Soviet expansion and prevent the spread of Communism. The first step in this policy was the Truman Doctrine, which was applied to Greece and Turkey.

The Truman Doctrine (March 1947)

In a dramatic appearance before a joint session of Congress on March 12, 1947, President Truman announced a historic new turn in American foreign policy that became known as the Truman Doctrine. "One aspect of the present situation," said the President, ". . . concerns Greece and Turkey." President Truman was gravely concerned because, late in 1946, about 13,000 Communist-led guerrillas entered northern Greece from Albania, Yugoslavia, and Bulgaria. Britain, with a strained economy, was terminating its traditional support, leaving Greece alone to deal with this Communist insurgency.

By 1947, Greek Communists, supported by the Soviet Union, threatened to seize control of the government. In his message, President Truman told Congress: ". . . assistance is imperative if Greece is to survive as a free nation." As for Turkey, it too was under pressure from Russia to give up control of the strategic Dardanelles. Soviet control of Greece and the Dardanelles would enable it to dominate the eastern Mediterranean and the Suez Canal. President Truman told Congress, "As in the case of Greece, if Turkey is to have the assistance it needs, the United States must supply it." The heart of the message, the Truman Doctrine, was stated by President Truman in these words: "I believe it must be the policy of the United States to support free peoples who are resisting attempted subjugation by armed minorities or by outside pressures." Then the President made this request: "I therefore ask Congress to provide authority for assistance to Greece and Turkey in the amount of $400,000,000 for the period ending June 30, 1948." By 1950 the United States had invested nearly $1 billion to preserve the independence of Greece and Turkey.

The Marshall Plan (June 1947)

Europe lay in ruins and economic chaos following the war. The United States responded with a program of economic aid. The program for the rehabilitation of postwar Europe came to be known as the Marshall Plan. The plan was to give aid to 22 European countries including the Soviet Union, but the latter came to regard this plan as an anti-Soviet maneuver and refused to participate. In presenting his plan, Secretary of State **George Marshall** said, "The truth of the matter is that Europe's requirements, for the next 3 or 4 years, of foreign food and other essential products—principally from America—are so much greater than her present ability to pay that she must have substantial additional help, or face economic, social, and political deterioration of a very grave character. It is logical that the U.S. should do whatever it is able to do to assist in the return of normal economic health in the world, without which there can be no political stability and no assured peace." Sixteen European nations answered the call and formulated a four year "**European Recovery Plan**" calling for $16 to $24 billion in aid.

The plan met with mixed reactions in Congress. Opponents called the European Recovery Plan "operation rat-hole." However, after Russia overthrew the government of Czechoslovakia in March 1948 and established a Communist regime, Congress approved the Marshall Plan the following month.

Results of the Plan

Congress appropriated $6.8 billion for the European Recovery Plan for the first 15 months and prepared to extend further support. About $12 billion was spent during a four-year period. Britain, France, and West Germany made a remarkable economic recovery that may well have prevented serious political consequences.

The European Common Market

An outgrowth of the European Recovery Plan was the European Common Market (European Economic Community or EEC), organized in 1957 by France, West Germany, Italy, and the Benelux countries (Belgium, the Netherlands, and Luxembourg). Members reduced tariffs on each other's products and eased travel restrictions among members. Britain's efforts to join the Common Market during the 1960s were vetoed by France. In 1973 Britain, Ireland, and Denmark joined the Common Market. Greece was admitted in 1981. This economic union of 10 European nations stirred talk of political union. In the late 1980s a blueprint was drawn up for a European Parliament with a target date of 1992 for implementation. The nations of the Common Market have made significant progress towards economic cooperation, but political unity still seems far away.

The Berlin Crisis (1948–1949)

A major test of will in the cold war between East and West occurred over Berlin. Deep in the Soviet zone of occupation, Berlin itself had been divided into four zones of occupation among the United States, Britain, France, and the USSR. In the spring of 1948, the Western democracies proposed elections for a new German Federal Republic. In response, the Soviets determined to oust the West from Berlin. On June 24, 1948, they set up a blockade around the city so that no food, fuel, or other supplies could reach the 2 million inhabitants of the western zones of Berlin. Short of trying to break the blockade by force, the Allies had only one means of entry to the city—by air. The Allies undertook an "airlift" to circumvent the blockade and bring food, fuel, and supplies to the 2 million people of Berlin. For almost a year, planes delivered essential supplies to the city. They flew more than 100 million miles and brought more than 2 million tons of food and other necessities to the city. With the face-saving intervention of the United Nations, the crisis was solved and the blockade withdrawn in May 1949.

The North Atlantic Treaty Organization (NATO)

A "hot war" was narrowly averted over Berlin, but steps had to be taken to prepare for future crises. On May 19, 1948, the Senate approved a resolution pledging American support for collective security among the Western democracies. In line with this resolution, President Truman proposed the **North Atlantic Pact**, setting up the **North Atlantic Treaty Organization** (**NATO**), which was signed on April 4, 1949.

The original parties, in addition to the United States and Canada, were Belgium, Denmark, France, Iceland, Italy, Luxembourg, the Netherlands, Norway, Portugal, and the United Kingdom (Great Britain). Article V of the treaty reads: "The parties agree that an armed attack against one or more of them in Europe or North America shall be considered an attack against them all." The treaty, overwhelmingly approved by the public, was ratified in the Senate by a vote of 82 to 13.

Expansion of NATO

In 1951 General Eisenhower took command of all military forces of NATO. Greece and Turkey joined NATO in 1952 and West Germany became a member in 1955. It had become the largest peacetime military alliance in history.

The Warsaw Pact

The Soviet Union countered with a military alliance of its own in 1955—the Warsaw Pact. This Pact united the Soviet Union with six allies in Eastern Europe: Poland, East Germany, Czechoslovakia, Hungary, Romania, and Bulgaria.

The USSR Explodes an A-Bomb (1949)

At the time NATO was organized (April 4, 1949), the Soviet Union did not yet have the atomic bomb, but Soviet scientists had been working frantically toward that end. On September 22, 1949, President Truman announced that the Soviet Union had successfully set off an atomic explosion. A huge buildup of armaments was in progress for NATO. The presence of American servicemen and servicewomen and U.S. armaments again became common throughout Western Europe. Before President Truman left office, $6 billion had been appropriated for NATO.

Truman's "Point Four" Program

In his inaugural address of January 1949, President Truman proposed a program of aid to the economically underdeveloped nations of the "Third World." This came to be known as the **Point Four Aid Program**. He spelled it out in detail in a special message to Congress on June 24, 1949:

> The grinding poverty and the lack of economic opportunity for many millions of people in the economically underdeveloped parts of Africa, the Near and Far East, and certain regions of Central and South America constitute one of the greatest challenges of the world today . . . I recommend the enactment of legislation to authorize an expanded program of technical assistance for such areas . . . To inaugurate such a program, I recommend a first-year appropriation not to exceed $45 million.

Congress approved the program and made an initial appropriation in 1950. This plan for underdeveloped nations was seen as both a means of defeating Communist encroachment in these areas and a spur to foreign trade by creating new markets for American industrial and agricultural products. During the period 1948–1960 the expenditures of the United States in foreign aid amounted to $72 billion.

Containment in Asia

Peace Treaty with Japan

On September 8, 1951, the United States signed a peace treaty with Japan bringing to an end the American occupation. No reparations were to be paid. Japan was to have the limited right to rearm. A security treaty, signed at the same time, gave the United States the right to maintain bases in Japan. In effect the United States was underwriting the security of Japan, a country now seen as an ally.

China Becomes Communist (1949)

China presented a different problem. For many years, the weakness of China was exploited by various powers. In 1927, **Chiang Kai-shek**, leader of the Chinese Nationalist government, sought to destroy the Chinese Communist forces under **Mao Zedong**. The latter fled deep into the interior of China. In 1931, Japanese forces invaded and overran Manchuria. In 1936, the Japanese invaded China. Faced with this crisis, the Chinese **Nationalists** and **Communists** fought the invader separately. But after the defeat of Japan in World War II, the fighting between the Chinese Communists and Nationalists resumed. Mao had built a strong base of support among the Chinese peasants, while Chiang became unpopular with the Chinese people. During 1948 and 1949 Mao's growing armies inflicted one defeat after another on the Nationalists. By December 1949 Chiang Kai-shek and his followers fled by air to the offshore island of Formosa, now called **Taiwan**, and established their government there. The Communist Chinese led by Mao Zedong now controlled all of mainland China.

The "Hot War" in Asia: Korea (1950–1953)

Korea Divided

Korea, formerly controlled by China, came under Japanese domination when Japan defeated China in 1894. At the end of World War II (as agreed at the Potsdam Conference), Russian forces entered Korea from the north, and American from the south. Two Koreas were formed with a dividing line drawn at 38° north latitude, between Communist-dominated North Korea and democratic South Korea. Attempts to reunite the country were unsuccessful. The Republic of (South) Korea was proclaimed in August 1948 and the People's Republic (North) in September. The USSR and the United States withdrew their military forces from Korea by 1949.

North Korea Attacks South Korea

On June 25, 1950, North Korean troops, alleging an attack from the South, suddenly crossed the line in force and launched a full-scale attack on South Korea. President Truman brought the matter at once to the Security Council of the UN, which voted 9 to 0 (the Soviets had been boycotting the UN) for a resolution ordering North Korea to withdraw.

UN and American troops were dispatched to Korea to drive back the invaders in what President Truman characterized as a "police action," since Congress never declared war. General Douglas MacArthur was placed in command of the combined forces, which included troops from 15 UN nations, South Koreans, and American land, naval, and air forces. At first, South Korean armies were driven back, but MacArthur conducted a successful offensive and then invaded North Korea. As MacArthur's troops approached the border with China at the Yalu River, they were caught in a trap by Chinese armies (so-called "volunteers") that had crossed into North Korea in force.

MacArthur Attempts to Make Policy

When UN forces again counterattacked, MacArthur proposed to drive north and invade China. This was contrary to the limited war policy laid down by President Truman. General **Omar Bradley**, chairman of the Joint Chiefs of Staff, testifying before a Senate committee on May 15, 1951, said that MacArthur's proposal would "involve us in the wrong war, at the wrong place, at the wrong time, and with the wrong enemy." The statement implied that a land war in China would leave the way open for Soviet expansion in Europe and the Middle East and could lead to World War III. MacArthur refused to accept Truman's policy decision and appealed to Congress over the President's authority. He continued to press for intensive military operations against the Chinese and proposed to assist Chiang Kai-shek's Nationalist troops to return to the mainland of China.

Truman Removes MacArthur

MacArthur's failure to implement the policy laid down by the President raised the constitutional question of the superiority of the civilian authority over the military. On April 11, 1951, President Truman informed General MacArthur that he was being relieved of his command in the Pacific and replaced by Lt. General Matthew B. Ridgway. President Truman explained his action by saying, "In the simplest terms, what we are doing in Korea is this: We are trying to prevent a third world war . . . By fighting a limited war in Korea we have prevented aggression from succeeding and bringing on a general war." Then he asked, "What would suit the ambitions of the Kremlin better than for our military forces to be committed to a full-scale war with

Red China?" Although there was a roar of outrage in Congress and loud public acclaim for MacArthur, the public supported the President.

Armistice in Korea

On July 10, 1951, General Ridgway began armistice negotiations with the North Koreans and Chinese. The negotiations continued at Panmunjom for two years. On July 27, 1953, North Korea and the UN reached an armistice agreement; an actual peace treaty was never signed. According to the armistice, the ceasefire line was established just north of the **38th parallel**, the previous boundary of the two Koreas. In 1954 the United States and Korea entered into a treaty whereby the United States agreed to come to the aid of South Korea if attacked again. Under the terms of the treaty, American troops have been stationed in Korea continually since 1954.

Exercise Set 5.7

1. The formation of the North Atlantic Treaty Organization (NATO) in 1949 is a significant event in U.S. diplomatic history because it
   A. committed the United States to a peacetime military alliance.
   B. strengthened United States influence in oil-producing nations.
   C. eased tensions with the Soviet Union and its satellites.
   D. created new patterns of international trade.

2. The term "iron curtain" used by Winston Churchill in a speech at Fulton, Missouri in 1946
   A. was a call for the use of the military to put an end to the Soviet dictatorship.
   B. expressed a recognition of the existence of a "Cold War" between the USSR and the Western democracies.
   C. suggested that trade agreements between the United States and Britain could restore the prewar dominance of the West in steel production.
   D. was a first step in restoring diplomatic relations between the Soviet Union and the West.

3. The attempt by the Soviet Union to force the Western Allies out of Berlin (1948–1949) failed because
   A. the United Nations intervened by sending relief supplies to the people of West Berlin.
   B. the blockade did not prevent the British-American airlift from bringing food and fuel to the people of West Berlin.
   C. the Berlin wall had not yet been built.
   D. the people of West Berlin were able to manage on their own despite great hardships.

4. The Truman Doctrine, announced in 1947,
   A. was a reversal of the Monroe Doctrine.
   B. was the first step in the American policy of giving military aid to help nations resist communism.
   C. called for the unification of the occupied zones of West Germany.
   D. required the nations saved from German aggression to adopt democracy.

5. The Marshall Plan and the Point Four Program were similar in that
   A. both were intended to resist Communist aggression in Europe.
   B. both were designed to help economically distressed peoples to help themselves.
   C. both were seen as measures that would help the United States become a creditor nation.
   D. the United States would assume leadership in the United Nations if these plans were implemented.

6. MacArthur was recalled by President Truman because
   A. MacArthur committed acts of insubordination.
   B. MacArthur was a Republican.
   C. American allies demanded his recall.
   D. America was losing the Korean War.

INTERNAL SECURITY AND CONSTITUTIONALISM

Truman and Government Loyalty Checks

The increasingly dangerous international situation and the tension of the Cold War had effects at home. Many Americans became concerned over internal security and Communist subversion within the United States.

Executive Order 9835 (1947)

On March 21, 1947, President Truman issued Executive Order 9835, also known as the Loyalty Order, designed to investigate the loyalty of government employees. Under this executive order some 3,000 persons were investigated, of whom 200 were dismissed. Though this was a small fraction of the 3 million government employees, the atmosphere in government service became poisoned. Many capable people who might otherwise have entered government service became reluctant to do so.

The National Security Act of 1947

In anticipation of the possible heating up of the Cold War, the National Security Act of July 26, 1947 was passed after two years of wrangling between the army and navy. A new **Department of Defense** was established, headed by a **Secretary of Defense** of Cabinet rank. A separate air force was created. Each service—army, navy, and air force—was to have its own secretary below Cabinet rank. To advise the President on security matters, a new agency, the **National Security Council**, was established, along with a new **National Security Adviser**. The Council was to include a new **Central Intelligence Agency** (**CIA**) to gather intelligence and conduct foreign activities associated with national security.

The McCarran Internal Security Act (1950)

The McCarran Internal Security Act required "Communist-front" organizations to register with the Attorney General. It authorized the government to arrest and detain anyone who might endanger the security of the United States by committing acts of espionage or sabotage. President Truman vetoed the act, calling it "a long step toward totalitarianism." But Congress passed it in 1950 over Truman's veto.

Earlier Attempts to Combat "Subversive Activities"

The Smith Act

In 1940, in the anxious days preceding the attack on Pearl Harbor, Congress had enacted the Alien Registration Act, commonly known as the Smith Act after its author, Senator Howard Smith of Virginia. The act made it illegal to advocate the overthrow of any government in the United States by force or violence or to become a member of any organization that adhered to this doctrine.

The House Committee to Investigate Un-American Activities (HUAC)

The House Committee to Investigate Un-American Activities (HUAC) was established in the House of Representatives in 1938, originally under the chairmanship of Congressman Martin Dies, Democrat of Texas. The committee held hearings, examined witnesses, issued reports, and tarnished reputations over the years without ever defining "un-American" or disclosing anything not already known by the Justice Department.

The Supreme Court and Subversive Activities

Dennis v. *United States* (1951)

In 1949, under orders from President Truman, the Justice Department obtained the conviction of eleven high-ranking members of the U.S. Communist party for conspiring to advocate the violent overthrow of the U.S. government. The conviction (and imprisonment), based on the Smith Act of 1940, was appealed to the Supreme Court on the grounds that the act was unconstitutional because it violated the freedom of speech provision of the First Amendment. The conviction was sustained by the Court in a 6 to 2 decision. Writing for the majority, **Chief Justice Frederick M. Vinson** declared that the defendants had conspired to teach and advocate the overthrow of the government of the United States and that this constituted a "clear and present danger" of an attempt to overthrow the government by force and violence.

Yates v. *United States* (1957)

In the *Yates* case, the Supreme Court again considered an appeal from members of the Communist party charged with violating the Smith Act. The Court, speaking through **Justice Harlan**, overruled the conviction of the defendants. In his concurring opinion, **Justice Black** said, "I believe that the First Amendment forbids Congress to punish people for talking about public affairs, whether or not such discussion incites to action legal or illegal.

Watkins v. United States (1957)

John Watkins, a labor union official, was questioned by the House Un-American Activities Committee. He refused to name former Communist party members, stating that this question was not relevant to the work of the Committee. The Court (with only one dissent) reversed his conviction of contempt of Congress, denying the Committee the authority to punish uncooperative witnesses at will. Each of these cases involved the enduring constitutional issue of civil liberties—the balance between government security and individual rights.

The Alger Hiss Case (1948)

This case stirred great public interest because Whitaker Chambers, a former Communist, charged that Alger Hiss, a former official in the State Department, had given him classified government documents. Hiss testified before the House Un-American Activities Committee, denied the charges, and brought a libel suit against Chambers, who then produced microfilm to prove his charges against Hiss. Consequently, Hiss was convicted of perjury (lying under oath) and served a five-year term in prison. His conviction for perjury helped set the stage for the most gruesome aspect of the "national security" drama.

McCarthyism

The Rise of Joseph R. McCarthy

In his quest for a popular cause, Senator McCarthy proposed alerting America to the Red Menace. In a Lincoln's Day address in February 1950 to the Women's Republican Club in Wheeling, West Virginia, McCarthy waved a sheet of paper and declared, "I have in my hand a list of 205 card-carrying members of the Communist party who hold important positions in the State Department." The speech won instant attention throughout the country. McCarthy had found his cause. Thorough investigation later disclosed not one case of a Communist in the State Department and McCarthy never produced the names. McCarthy then charged that General George C. Marshall was a "traitor" and that he and his protégé, General Eisenhower, were involved "in a conspiracy so immense and an infamy so black as to dwarf any previous such venture in the history of man."

By 1952, McCarthy had become the head of a Senate subcommittee on investigations. In this position, he investigated the State Department and other government agencies. Careers of many patriotic Americans in government, colleges, the arts, and the media were ruined by the "witch hunt" unleashed by McCarthy as he investigated and irresponsibly accused many individuals of having Communist affiliations.

The Army Hearings

Although some Americans were critical of McCarthy's unfair methods and accusations, many supported him. In 1954 he began to search for spies and Communists in the Army. Televised hearings were held April 22–June 17, 1954, investigating McCarthy's charges of subversion in the Army Signal Corps at Fort Monmouth, New Jersey.

Censure of McCarthy

After the hearings, Senator **Ralph Flanders**, Republican of Vermont, filed a resolution calling upon the Senate to censure Senator McCarthy. Among the charges were the Senator's contemptuous behavior in refusing to appear before a Senate committee. On December 2, 1954, by a vote of 67 to 22, the United States Senate voted to censure Senator McCarthy. Thereafter, McCarthy was shunned by his colleagues and his statements ceased to be reported in the press.

McCarthyism

McCarthy's tactics added the word "McCarthyism" to the English language. The historian Samuel Eliot Morison called McCarthy "one of the most colossal liars in our history." Eisenhower, in his memoirs, says, "McCarthyism took its toll on many individuals and on the nation." Reckless, unsupported charges of treason and conspiracy destroyed government officials, teachers, scientists, ministers, and scholars. McCarthy's methods are summed up in the word **McCarthyism**.

1. Which of the following internal security measures was adopted prior to World War II?
   A. The McCarran Internal Security Act
   B. President Truman's Executive Order for the investigation of government employees' loyalty
   C. The establishment of the House Un-American Activities Committee
   D. The investigation of Senator Joseph McCarthy's subcommittee

2. The Alger Hiss case stirred great public interest because
   A. Hiss, charged with passing classified information to the Communists, had held high public office.
   B. Whitaker Chambers, who accused Hiss, denied having been a Communist.
   C. Supreme Court Justice Felix Frankfurter testified against Hiss.
   D. Hiss refused to appear before the House Un-American Activities Committee.

3. The Manhattan Project led by Robert Oppenheimer was part of the World War II effort to
   A. develop the atomic bomb.
   B. supply the Allies with more fighter planes.
   C. ban the use of chemical and biological warfare.
   D. coordinate troop movements between New York and Europe.

4. The term "McCarthyism" generally means
   A. efforts to restrict the spread of Communism.
   B. effective use of the media to gain name recognition.
   C. bringing false and reckless charges against people to secure publicity and political advantage for oneself.
   D. the use of negative advertising during a political campaign.

CHAPTER REVIEW QUESTIONS

1. A major reason why a working system of international law has been difficult to achieve is that
   A. the many different languages in the world make communication difficult.
   B. nations are unwilling to give up some of their sovereignty.
   C. no precedent for international law exists.
   D. many nations still lack even an internal system of law.

2. Which was a major cause of tension in Europe during the decade following World War II?
   A. Formation of Soviet-dominated Communist governments in many Eastern European nations
   B. Failure of non-Communist nations to support the United Nations
   C. Cutbacks in fuel supplies by oil-producing nations
   D. Return of United States military forces to pre-World War II levels

3. Totalitarian societies in the 20th century could be most consistently identified by their
   A. unwillingness to allow free elections.
   B. acceptance of a variety of political beliefs.
   C. support for a state-controlled religion.
   D. denial of public education to their citizens.

4. "The parties agree that an attack against one or more of them shall be considered an attack against all."
   This statement most clearly illustrates which foreign policy concept?
   A. Détente
   B. Appeasement
   C. Balance of power
   D. Collective security

5. The relationship between the United States and Western European nations from 1945 to the present has most often been characterized by
   A. cooperation in efforts to gain political control of emerging nations.
   B. division and resentment over competing economic systems.
   C. continuance of military and economic interdependence.
   D. economic conflict and military confrontation.

6. The United States sells manufactured products to Third World nations and purchases raw materials from these nations. This fact illustrates
   A. economic protectionism.
   B. global interdependence.
   C. pooling of resources.
   D. finance capitalism.

7. Evidence that civil liberties in the United States were under attack in the period preceding the Cold War can be traced to
   A. the McCarthy speech at Wheeling, West Virginia.
   B. the "iron curtain" speech of Winston Churchill.
   C. the McCarran Internal Security Act.
   D. the establishment of the House Un-American Activities Committee.

THEMATIC ESSAY

Directions: Write a well-organized essay that includes an introduction, several paragraphs addressing the task below, and a conclusion.

Theme: Human Rights

> As a signatory to the Universal Declaration of Human Rights, the United States became responsible to its civil, political, economic, social, and cultural rights.

Task:

> From your study of U.S. history, choose *three* Articles from the Universal Declaration of Human Rights. (It will be necessary to obtain a copy of this document; see *www.hrusa.org.*)
>
> For each Article chosen:
>
> - Describe the human right provided in the specific Article.
> - Discuss the underlying reasons for the inclusion of the specific Article in the Universal Declaration of Human Rights.
> - Select a topic from U.S. history and discuss how the selected Article would apply to the topic chosen. (The question requires that you use three different Articles and three different topics from U.S. history.)

You may use any major topic from your study of U.S. history. Some suggestions you may wish to consider are: the drafting of the Bill of Rights, forced removal of the Cherokee Nation (1830s), the *Dred Scott* decision (1857), the Pullman Strike (1894), immigration restrictions and quotas, women's suffrage, Social Security Act (1935), Japanese relocation camps (1940s), McCarthy Hearings (1950s), student protests against the Vietnam War (1960s–1970s), and the death penalty.

You are *not* limited to these suggestions.

THEMATIC ESSAY

Directions: Write a well-organized essay that includes an introduction, several paragraphs addressing the task below, and a conclusion.

Theme: Foreign Policy (Cold War)

Following World War II, the threat of communist expansion led the United States to take diplomatic, military, and economic actions to limit the global influence of the Soviet Union and China. These Cold War actions met with varying degrees of success.

Task:

Select *two* specific actions taken by the United States to limit the expansion of communism during the Cold War and for *each*

- Describe the historical circumstances that led to the action.
- Discuss the extent to which the action was successful in limiting the expansion of communism.

You may use any action taken by the United States to limit the expansion of communism during the Cold War. Some suggestions you might wish to consider include the implementation of the Marshall Plan (1947–1952), the establishment of the North Atlantic Treaty Organization [NATO] (1949), intervention in Korea (1950–1953), the blockade of Cuba (1962), the escalation of the Vietnam War (1964–1973), the visit of President Richard Nixon to China (1972), and the pursuit of the Strategic Defense Initiative [SDI] (1983–1989).

You are *not* limited to these suggestions.

DOCUMENT-BASED QUESTION

The following questions (Part A and Part B) are based on the accompanying documents (1–6). Some of these documents have been edited for the purpose of this exercise. The question is designed to test your ability to work with historical documents and to demonstrate your knowledge of the subject matter being presented. As you analyze the documents, take into account both the source of the document and the author's point of view.

Historical Context:

Perhaps the most explosive constitutional issue arising out of the Cold War and the phenomenon of Communism was the tension between internal security requirements and civil liberties guarantees.

Task:

Using information from the documents and your knowledge of United States history, answer the questions that follow each document in Part A. Your answers to the questions will help you write the Part B essay, in which you will be asked:

In the Cold War Era referred to in the documents (1945–1954) did the internal security measures taken by the federal government rise to the level of constitutional infringement of the civil liberties of Americans?

Part A
Short-Answer Questions

The documents below relate to issues concerning the perceived need for internal security measures and the conflicts with civil liberties, in particular, First Amendment rights. Examine each document carefully and then answer the questions that follow.

I feel that this committee could render a great service to the nation through its power of exposure in quickly spotlighting existing front organizations and those which will be created in the future.

The following are questions that Director Hoover proposed to be asked of organizations to determine if they were Communist:

A. Does the organization denounce American and British foreign policy while always lauding (praising) Soviet policy?
B. Does the organization utilize Communist "double-talk" by referring to Soviet-dominated countries as democracies, complaining that the United States is imperialistic and constantly denouncing monopoly-capital?
C. Have outstanding leaders in public life openly renounced affiliation with the organization?
D. Does the organization, if espousing (supporting) liberal progressive causes, attract well-known honest patriotic liberals or does it denounce well-known liberals?
E. Does the organization have a consistent record of supporting the American viewpoint over the years?

As Americans, our most effective defense is a workable democracy that guarantees and preserves our cherished freedoms.

—J. Edgar Hoover, Director of FBI, Testimony to House Committee on Un-American Activities (March 26, 1947)

1. What First Amendment liberties may be in jeopardy if Director Hoover's "test questions" were to be put to use?

_____

_____

_____

_____

2. Identify the glaring contradiction in Director Hoover's testimony to the House Committee on Un-American Activities.

_____

_____

_____

_____

DOCUMENT 2

> My definition of a free society is a society where it is safe to be unpopular.

—Adlai E. Stevenson, Democratic Presidential candidate, 1952

3. Compare and contrast Adlai Stevenson's thoughts on a free society with FBI Director Hoover's concerns with organizations suspected of being Communist (*see* Document 1).

_____

_____

_____

_____

DOCUMENT 3

> I think it is high time for the United States Senate and its Members to do some real soul-searching and to weigh our consciences as to the manner in which we are performing our duty to the people of America, and the manner in which we are using or abusing our individual powers and privileges.
>
> Those of us who shout the loudest about Americanism in making character assassinations are all too frequently those who, by our own words and acts, ignore some of the basic principles of Americanism—
>
> The right to criticize.
> The right to hold unpopular beliefs.
> The right to protest.
> The right of independent thought.
>
> The American people are sick and tired of being afraid to speak their minds lest they be politically smeared as Communists or Fascists by their opponents. Freedom of speech is not what it used to be in America. It has been so abused by some that it is not exercised by others.

—Senator Margaret Chase Smith, Republican (Maine), responding to Senator Joseph McCarthy's allegations of Communist infiltration in government, June 1, 1950

4. In her criticism of Senator Joseph McCarthy's attacks, what does Senator Margaret Chase Smith cite as being contrary to the Constitution and un-American?

_____

_____

_____

_____

DOCUMENT 4

After Russia's explosion of an atomic bomb and China's transition to Communist control in 1949, President Truman directed the State Department and Department of Defense to reexamine American foreign policy and to establish national security objectives. National Security Council Document 68 (NSC 68) was the resulting report.

It is quite clear from Soviet theory and practice that the Kremlin seeks to bring the free world under its dominion by the methods of the Cold War . . . . A comprehensive and decisive program to win peace and frustrate the Kremlin design should be so designed that it can be sustained for as long as necessary to achieve our national objectives. It would probably involve: a substantial increase in expenditures for military purposes . . . development of programs designed . . . to wage overt psychological warfare calculated to encourage mass defections from Soviet allegiance and to frustrate the Kremlin design in other ways . . . development of internal security and civilian defense programs.

—National Security Council Document 68, approved by President Truman, April 1950

5. How did NSC 68 influence the response of the United States to Communist North Korea's invasion of South Korea in June 1950?

_____

_____

_____

_____

DOCUMENT 5

The indictment of eleven high-ranking Communist leaders for allegedly conspiring to teach and advocate the violent overthrow of the government in violation of the Smith Act (1940) reached the Supreme Court of the United States and resulted in the 1951 decision. Below are segments from the majority decision by Chief Justice Vinson and the dissenting decision by Justice Douglas.

C. J. Vinson: . . . We hold that Sec. 2 and Sec. 3 of the Smith Act (*advocating overthrow of government by force and violence and teaching such ideas*) do not . . . violate the First Amendment and other provisions of the Bill of Rights . . . . Petitioners intend to overthrow the government of the United States as speedily as the circumstances would permit. Their conspiracy to organize the Communist party and to teach and advocate the overthrow of the government of the United States by force and violence created a "clear and present danger" . . . . They were properly and constitutionally convicted for violation of the Smith Act.

J. Douglas, dissenting: . . . Free speech has occupied an exalted position because of the high service it has given to our society. Its protection is essential to the very existence of a democracy. The airing of ideas releases pressures which otherwise might become destructive. When ideas compete in the market for acceptance, full and free discussion exposes the false and they gain few adherents . . . .

—*Dennis* v. *United States* (1951)

6. Which Justice is using a specific statute to support restrictions on the freedom of speech provided for by the First Amendment?

_____

_____

_____

_____

7. Does Justice Douglas support the ideas of the Communist party in his dissent? What does he say are the advantages of "airing ideas?"

_____

_____

_____

_____

—The Perils of McCarthyism (1954)

8. What does the author of the cartoon see as being sacrificed with the elimination of the "Communist Pest?"

_____

_____

_____

_____

Part B
Essay

Your essay should be well organized with an introductory paragraph that states your position on the question. Develop your position in the next paragraphs and then write a conclusion. In your essay, include specific historical details and refer to the specific documents you analyzed in Part A. You may include additional information from your knowledge of social studies.

Historical Context:

Perhaps the most explosive constitutional issue arising out of the Cold War and the phenomenon of Communism was the tension between internal security requirements and civil liberties guarantees.

Task:

In the Cold War Era referred to in the documents (1945–1954) did the internal security measures taken by the federal government rise to the level of constitutional infringement of the civil liberties of Americans?

Guidelines:

In your essay, be sure to
• Develop all aspects of the task.
• Incorporate information from *at least five* documents.
• Incorporate relevant outside information.
• Support the theme with many relevant facts, examples, and details.
• Use a logical and clear plan of organization, including an introduction and a conclusion that are beyond a restatement of the theme.

UNIT SIX —————————————————————

A World in Uncertain Times

> **KEY IDEAS** Unit Six explores the global role of the United States in an increasingly interdependent world. It describes the social, political, and economic changes in American society in the period between the 1950s and 1990s as the United States entered the post-industrial era.

UNIT CONNECTIONS: By the end of the unit you should understand the following points.

- Post-World War II presidents; the Cold War; foreign policy of containment
- The continuing struggle for civil rights of African Americans
- Demographic changes in the 1950s and 1960s: the growth of the suburbs
- "New Frontier" policies of the Kennedy administration
- "Great Society" policies of the Johnson administration
- The 1960s and revolutionary change for African Americans, women, Hispanic Americans, Native Americans
- The Warren Court and expansion of rights of the accused
- The Cold War and Southeast Asia: Vietnam War
- Richard Nixon and a departure from the "Great Society"
- The "Reagan Revolution" as a challenge to the New Deal and the "Great Society"
- Recent immigration patterns after 1975
- The Bush and Clinton administrations: Approaching the next century

TOWARD A POST-INDUSTRIAL WORLD: LIVING IN A GLOBAL AGE

> Why does this magnificent applied science which saves work and makes life easier bring us so little happiness? The simple answer runs: Because we have not yet learned to make sensible use of it.
>
> Albert Einstein, in an address at the
> California Institute of Technology, February 1931

UNITED STATES AND POST-INDUSTRIALISM

Changing Energy Sources: Toward Nuclear Power

In the years after World War II, nuclear energy created by fission, or the splitting of atoms, seemed to offer a cheap and unlimited source of power.

The Atomic Energy Commission (AEC)

In 1946, Congress established the Atomic Energy Commission (now called the **Nuclear Regulatory Commission**), a civilian agency with authority to make policy decisions about the use of nuclear power. A program was launched in 1954 whereby private power companies could construct nuclear power plants and operate them under license by the Atomic Energy Commission.

Problems of Nuclear Energy Plants

An accident in March 1979 at the **Three Mile Island** nuclear reactor near Harrisburg, Pennsylvania, caused grave concern about the danger of nuclear radiation escaping into the air and contaminating a wide area with cancer-causing by-products. On April 28, 1986, a major nuclear accident occurred at the Soviet Union's **Chernobyl** power station near the city of Kiev. The resultant cloud of radiation drifted over Europe as far north as Scandinavia. Then there was the March 2011 disaster at the Fukushima Daiichi plant following a devastating earthquake and tsunami that hit Japan. How many future deaths due to radiation exposure are yet to be known.

Changing Technology (Computers)

Advanced technology (hi-tech) is revolutionizing industry so rapidly that it is virtually impossible to keep abreast of developments. Extensive changes are occurring through the use of computers in business and industry, particularly in each of the following fields: missiles, spacecraft and aircraft, scientific instruments, drugs and medicines, electronics and telecommunications, and synthetic materials.

The computer is revolutionizing our lives in the fields of farming, manufacturing, management, business, education, banking, building and construction, entertainment, health, and other daily concerns and activities.

Changing Corporate Structures

The **multinational corporation**—an organization that carries on its business through branches in more than one country—is nothing new in world commerce. But the trend toward multinational corporations has gained momentum since the end of World War II. American corporations open factories, sales offices, mining branches, or other operating units in one or more foreign countries. A percentage of the capital may be raised in the foreign country, making it a joint venture with the percentage of ownership specifically stated. Many American multinationals operate in Africa, Asia, and Latin America, as well as in Europe. Their fields of interest include all types of business and industry, as indicated by names such as Exxon Mobil, General Motors, McDonalds, and Toyota. A major field for American multinationals is oil and petroleum products.

The Changing Nature of Employment

The total labor force in the United States has grown steadily, from 60 million at the end of World War II to 154 million by 2011. At the same time, there has been a dramatic change in the nature of employment.

Agriculture

The percentage of the labor force engaged in agriculture has declined rapidly since the 1930s. Of a total labor force of nearly 49 million in 1930, 10.5 million or 21.4 percent were engaged in farming. By 1970, the labor force had grown to 82 million, but the number of workers in agriculture had declined to 2.5 million or 3.1 percent of the labor force. A further decline continued during the 1970s and 1980s. By 1980, the percentage of workers employed in agriculture was 2.2 percent; in 1985 it was below 2 percent and in 2004, 1.8 percent.

Manufacturing and Service Industries

During the same period (1930–1970), the percentage of workers engaged in manufacturing increased steadily. Among their products were machinery, electrical equipment, textile products, processed foods, transportation equipment, printed materials, metal products, and many others. The percentage in the work force engaged in manufacturing rose from 20 percent in 1930 to 25 percent by 1970. However, the percentage of the work force engaged in manufacturing began to decline after 1970, with the astonishing growth of service occupations including retail sales, office workers, waiters/waitresses, medical services, advertising, and computer programming. By 1986, 75 percent of all employment was in service occupations.

Exercise Set 6.1

1. The potential of nuclear generators to supply America's needs for energy has not been realized because
   A. investors have not been willing to supply the necessary capital.
   B. most of the required resources have been devoted to the production of nuclear weapons.
   C. plans for the construction of new plants ordered after 1973 have been on the increase.
   D. problems of safety, environmental degradation, and plant operation have caused delays in licensing.

2. During the past half century there has been a marked shift in occupations from
   A. agriculture to industry to service occupations.
   B. service to agriculture to industry.
   C. business to industry to professions.
   D. manual to electrical to mechanical.

3. The domestic need for electricity in the United States supplied by nuclear reactors is approximately
   A.   5 percent.
   B. 15 percent.
   C. 25 percent.
   D. 50 percent.

THE WORLD AND POST-INDUSTRIALISM

> It is futile to expect a hungry and squalid population to be anything
> but violent and gross.
>
> Thomas Huxley, 1874

Developed and Developing Nations

Contrasts in a Divided World

The developed nations of the world—those with a strong industrial base—
are primarily located in North America and Europe, plus Japan in Asia. Most
of Africa, the Middle East, Asia, and Latin America are classified as third
world or developing nations. They differ from the developed nations—the
democratic nations of western Europe and North America, and the former
Soviet bloc—in their lower standard of living, lower educational standards,
and lower health standards. The division is sometimes seen as one of
North/South, with the former being developed and the latter developing.
Another point of reference uses the term East/West, with the latter being the
area of development and the former largely developing.

There was for many years an ongoing tension between the Soviet Union
and the Western democracies in an effort to gain influence over or, at least,
allegiance of the developing world. Areas of tension included Latin America
(notably in Central America), in the Middle East, the Persian Gulf, Africa,
and the third world generally. The developing nations, because they are poor
and relatively weak, became a political battleground between the superpowers.

Third-World Debt

Efforts of third-world nations to make economic progress and raise the standard of living of their people have led to extensive borrowing of capital from
banks in the developed world. But the money has not always been properly
used, and living standards have generally not risen. Meanwhile the borrowers
have gone deeper and deeper into debt, reaching a point where it is obvious
to both debtors and creditors that repayment cannot be made. By 1992, the
debt owed to foreign bankers by less developed nations amounted to more
than one trillion (a thousand billion) dollars.

Low Income, Hunger, and Life Expectancy

There is a clear relationship between the per capita income of a nation and
its life expectancy. The developing nations with the lowest average national
income are also at or near the bottom of the scale in life expectancy.

Even developed industrial nations, including the United States, have millions living below the poverty level, and many, especially children, suffering hunger and malnutrition. The poverty level is adjusted each year according to the cost of living. In 1986 in the United States, it was set at an income of $11,203 for a family of four. In that year 13.6 percent of Americans were below the poverty level. Children were the worst off, with 19.8 percent living below the poverty level.

Economic and Social Problems

Agriculture

The developing nations have two thirds of the world's population but produce only one third of the world's agricultural output. The greater output of the developed nations is due to the use of farm machinery, fertilizers and chemicals, irrigation, and other technology applied to production, harvesting, and methods of preservation of agricultural produce. The average American farmer cares for about 15 acres, while the average for a farm worker in the developing world is about 3 acres. The great farm belts of the United States and Canada produce more basic food crops (wheat, rye, barley, oats, and corn) than the entire output of the third world.

• *The Malthusian theory.* The theory propounded by the English economist Thomas Robert Malthus in the late 18th century stated that poverty, hunger, and starvation would soon be the lot of humankind, since the population increases by geometric ratio (2 to 4 to 8 to 16), while the food supply increases by arithmetic ratio (2 to 4 to 6 to 8).

• *The "Green Revolution."* The Malthusian theory, so far as food production is concerned, was challenged by the "Green Revolution," a term first used in the 1960s to describe efforts to produce greater yields from farm acreage. New varieties of rice, wheat, and other grains were developed. These new strains were resistant to plant disease, better able to withstand prolonged drought and cold, and had a greater yield per cultivated acre. Better methods of harvesting, soil conservation, and farm management were introduced. New fertilizers and pesticides were developed. Agricultural output in many parts of the world increased dramatically, causing the term "Green Revolution" to be applied.

World Population Growth

Prior to 1650, the world's population grew slowly. The graph shows the rapid increase in population growth since 1650. In the half-century from 1900 to 1950 the world's population increased by 50 percent. In the years after 1950 it increased by 100 percent. More than half the world's people live in Asia. The continent showing the most rapid population growth is Africa, where

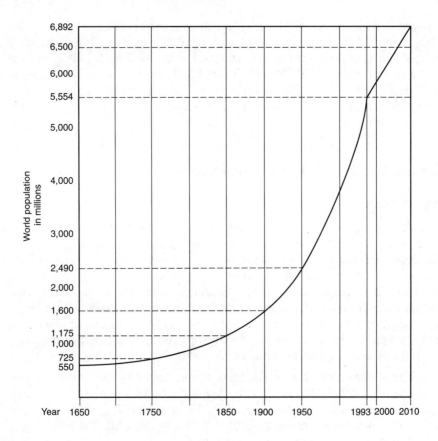

Figure 6.1 World Population (1650–2010)

the population catapulted from 199 million in 1950 to 677 million in 1993. Demographers (people who specialize in population studies) predict that the greatest population increase will be in developing countries. The combined population of Europe, North America (excluding Mexico), and Australia has remained relatively constant since the 1960s. While the population growth of the United States has not kept pace with that of world population, it has nevertheless been increasing steadily. The total population figures for the United States are:

Census Data	U.S. Population
1960	179,323,175
1970	203,302,031
1980	226,545,518
1990	248,709,873
2000	308,745,538

Figure 6.2 United States Population Increase

438

The astonishing momentum of world population growth is placing a heavy strain on the world's natural resources and contributing to grave environmental damage. The very survival of human life is in the balance.

Environmental Concerns

As crude a weapon as the cave man's club, a chemical barrage has been hurled against the fabric of life.
Rachel Carson, *Silent Spring*, 1962

Sooner or later, wittingly or unwittingly, we must pay for every intrusion on the natural environment.
Barry Commoner, *Science and Survival*, 1966

The Greenhouse Effect

The emissions into the atmosphere from the burning of fossil fuels (coal, oil, and natural gas) are causing a relentless global warming that has been named the **greenhouse effect**. The release of gases, especially carbon monoxide, into the atmosphere produces an artificial blanket that prevents heat from the sun from radiating back into space. This is thought to be the cause of a rise in the air temperature throughout the earth.

Air Pollution

The air on which our lives depend has become a receptacle for the discharges from motor vehicles, factories, airplanes, space exploration refuse, nuclear research, electric power plants, cooking and heating chimneys, forest fires, incinerators, and exhausts and dust from construction and demolition projects.

The **Clean Air Act of 1970** set national standards controlling six basic pollutants—notably carbon monoxide gas—but the act has not solved the air pollution problem.

Water Pollution

The first major Federal Clean Water Act was passed in 1965. The Federal Water Pollution Control Act of 1972 was passed over President Nixon's veto. The **Federal Clean Water Act of 1987** was passed by an angry Congress over President Reagan's veto. Despite these laws, our limited supply of clean water is at risk. Not only the nation's rivers and lakes, but also its subterranean groundwater (the sources of our drinking water) are threatened by contamination. There are 5,000 types of wastes that have been released into the nation's ground water from homes, farms, factories, and other sources.

The 20th-century phenomenon of water pollution is worldwide. On one of his exploratory voyages across the Atlantic Ocean, the scientist Thor Heyerdahl reported a 1,400-mile current of chemical contaminants.

Exercise Set 6.2

1. A characteristic of third-world nations is that they
   A. are all located in Asia or Africa.
   B. have a weak industrial base.
   C. are all lacking in natural resources.
   D. have governments controlled by the military.

2. Geographically, the developed nations are chiefly found in the continents of
   A. Europe, North America, and Australia.
   B. Europe, Asia, and North America.
   C. Africa, South America, and Australia.
   D. North America, South America, and Europe.

3. The "Green Revolution" refers to the
   A. fluctuation of the dollar in international finance.
   B. terrorist activities of the Irish Republican Army.
   C. radical program of a West German political group.
   D. dramatic increase in agricultural output.

4. The fact that the agricultural output per acre in developed nations is many times that of developing nations may be explained chiefly by
   A. the difference in soil quality, climate, and other natural advantages.
   B. more advanced agricultural technology.
   C. a higher education and health level.
   D. government support through favorable tariff and tax legislation.

5. World population growth
   A. declined between 1650 and 1850, then began a rapid advance.
   B. grew relatively slowly but steadily between 1650 and 1950 and then picked up momentum rapidly.
   C. shows signs of leveling off at the current figure of about 5 billion people.
   D. is proceeding at approximately the same rate on each of the six major continents.

6. The continent with the highest percentage of population growth is
   A. Africa.
   B. Asia.
   C. Europe.
   D. South America.

CHAPTER 2

CONTAINMENT AND CONSENSUS (1945–1960)

EISENHOWER POLICIES: FOREIGN AFFAIRS

> There is no nook or cranny in all the world into which Communist influence does not penetrate.
>
> John Foster Dulles, 1950

Threat of World Communism

Soviet Expansion In and After World War II

In 1940, while Germany was engaged in fighting France and Britain, the Soviets occupied and annexed the three Baltic States—Estonia, Latvia, and Lithuania. At the end of the war, Russia annexed eastern Poland and established a Communist government in the new Poland and in East Germany. Communist governments were also established in Czechoslovakia, Hungary, Romania, Bulgaria, Albania, and Yugoslavia.

Soviet efforts to overthrow the governments of Greece and Turkey were thwarted by American aid to these countries under the Truman Doctrine. In the Far East, the Soviets took from Japan the southern half of Sakhalin Island and the Kurile Islands. Communists dominated the northern half of Korea.

The Korean War

In 1950 North Korea attacked South Korea. In the ensuing Korean War, American and UN forces defeated Communist efforts to make all of Korea a Communist country. During the presidential campaign of 1952, Eisenhower promised to do all he could to bring the Korean War to an end. In a speech in October 1952, he said, "I shall go to Korea." After the election he kept his promise and in December 1952 went to Korea, where he conferred with American and UN leaders. Peace talks continued between negotiators for North and South Korea at Panmunjom, until finally an armistice agreement ending the war was signed on July 27, 1953. The boundary line between the two was set approximately where it had been before the war. A demilitarized zone was established between North and South Korea.

John Foster Dulles

> You have a row of dominoes set up, you knock over the first one, and
> what will happen to the last one is. . . that it will go over very quickly.
> Dwight D. Eisenhower, on the strategic importance of Indochina,
> in a press conference, April 7, 1954.

John Foster Dulles served as Secretary of State under Eisenhower from 1953
until Dulles died in 1959. During the Truman years, Dulles had contended
that the Truman policy of **containment** of communism should be replaced by
a policy of attempted liberation of Communist-controlled countries. As the
architect of American foreign policy, Dulles adhered to the **domino theory**
described in Eisenhower's statement, believing that if one nation in an area
fell to communism, the rest, like a row of dominoes, would also fall to communism. This doctrine played an important role in the Vietnam War of the
1960s and 1970s.

Massive Retaliation

A Department of State bulletin issued by Secretary of State John Foster
Dulles in January 1954 made two important changes in the nation's military
policy. First, there was to be a cutback in the use of conventional military
weapons. Second, there was to be greater reliance on atomic weapons. In
1952 the nation had successfully tested a new weapon, the **hydrogen** or
H-bomb. This bomb had 500 times the destructive power of the A-bomb that
had destroyed Hiroshima seven years before.

In the 1954 bulletin Dulles declared, "We want, for ourselves and the other
free nations, a maximum deterrent at a bearable cost . . . Local defenses must
be reinforced by the deterrent of massive retaliatory power." This came to be
known as the policy of "**massive retaliation**" dependent on a preponderance
of nuclear weaponry. Under this policy both the Soviet Union and the United
States became involved in an arms race, each trying to build up a stockpile
of nuclear weapons in order to show it could still destroy the other side, even
if attacked first.

Brinkmanship

The Dulles conduct of relations with the Soviets came to be known as
"brinkmanship." Dulles believed that the United States had to show the Communists it was willing to use force and to go to the brink of war in order to
keep the peace. In an address in 1956, Dulles explained his policy in these
words: "You have to take chances for peace just as you take chances in
war . . . the ability to get to the verge without getting into the war is the
necessary art. If you try to run away from it, if you are scared to go to the
brink, you are lost."

The H-Bomb; Atoms for Peace

> The United States pledges... its determination to help solve the fear-
> ful atomic dilemma—to devote its entire heart and mind to find the
> way by which the miraculous inventiveness of man shall not be dedi-
> cated to his death, but consecrated to his life.
>
> Address by President Eisenhower
> to the United Nations General Assembly, December 8, 1953

The explosion of an H-bomb by the United States in 1952 was followed by
the successful explosion of a similar bomb in 1953 by the Soviet Union. In
his address, Eisenhower summarized the developments in atomic weaponry,
predicted the spreading of these weapons of destruction to other nations,
and urged that steps be taken to reverse the trend immediately. He offered to
cooperate toward that end in implementing the UN resolution of November
1953. He proposed that ". . . this fissionable material would be used to serve
the peaceful pursuits of mankind. Experts would be mobilized to apply atomic
energy to the needs of agriculture, medicine, and other peaceful activities."

This atoms-for-peace proposal did not reverse the confrontational trend
that was nourished by the cold-war atmosphere of suspicion and fear.

The Southeast Asia Treaty Organization (SEATO)

On September 8, 1954, a treaty negotiated by Secretary of State John
Foster Dulles was signed in Manila. It had the same purpose and design
for Southeast Asia as NATO did for the North Atlantic, namely, **collective
security** measures against Communist aggression. The nations that signed
the SEATO agreement were: Australia, France, New Zealand, Pakistan, the
Republic of the Philippines, Great Britain, and the United States.

The SEATO agreement specified: "Each Party recognizes that aggression
by means of armed attack against any of the Parties . . . would endanger its
own peace and safety, and that it will in the event act to meet the common
danger in accordance with its constitutional processes."

Aswan Dam and the Suez Canal

In 1956 a crisis developed over the Suez Canal. Egypt, led by **Gamal Abdel
Nasser**, who had led a successful army coup against **King Farouk**, entered
into an arms deal with the Soviets, who agreed to supply Egyptian armies
for their military action against the new state of Israel on Egypt's eastern
border. Afterwards, Nasser approached the United States for help in building
a huge dam at **Aswan** on the Nile River for irrigation and flood control. The
United States turned Nasser down because of Egypt's arms deal with the

Soviets. In response, Nasser seized the Suez Canal, which had been run by a joint Anglo-French company. He declared that the Canal was the property of Egypt and that revenues collected from its use would be applied to the building of the Aswan Dam. Great Britain and France were especially alarmed by Nasser's takeover of the canal, fearing it would interrupt the flow of oil from the Middle East to Europe.

On October 29, 1956, Israel attacked Egypt. Two days later, France and Britain joined Israel, and the three succeeded in gaining control of the Suez Canal. To avoid a military confrontation, both the United States and the Soviet Union supported Egypt and approved a UN resolution ordering a cease-fire and withdrawal from Egyptian territory. Troops of the three occupying powers were withdrawn and replaced by a United Nations peace-keeping force.

Polish and Hungarian Uprisings

In 1956, three years after Stalin's death, the new Soviet premier, **Nikita S. Khrushchev**, denounced Stalin as a tyrant who had committed grave crimes against his own people. This soon led to movements for more freedom in Poland and Hungary, two Communist-dominated Soviet satellite states. Polish workers rioted, demanding better working conditions. A new Polish Premier granted bargaining rights to labor. Khrushchev threatened to intervene but refrained when Poland continued its support of Soviet foreign policy.

In Hungary, the new premier, Imre Nagy, attempted to institute a democratic government and prepared to withdraw Hungary from the Warsaw Pact. An uprising in Hungary in 1956 was suppressed by Soviet troops. Hungary remained under Communist control.

The Eisenhower Doctrine—Intervention in Lebanon

Pressure from the United States resulted in the withdrawal of British, French, and Israeli troops from Egypt after the Suez Canal crisis. But the fear of Soviet infiltration and influence in the Middle East led President Eisenhower in 1957 to request authority from Congress to extend military and financial aid to any country in the Middle East threatened by Communist aggression. Congress responded in March 1957 with legislation that became known as the **Eisenhower Doctrine**. The doctrine applied specifically to "the general area of the Middle East" and authorized economic and military assistance, including the use of "armed force to assist any such nation or group of nations requesting assistance against armed aggression from any country controlled by international communism."

A crisis occurred in the spring of 1958 when Syria and Egypt attempted to overthrow the pro-Western government of Lebanon. When the President of Lebanon asked the United States for help, Eisenhower—in accordance with authority granted by Congress to implement the Eisenhower Doctrine—sent the Sixth Fleet into the Mediterranean and ordered 14,000 United States Marines to Lebanon. U.S. armed forces were withdrawn when Egypt and Syria agreed to refrain from intervention in Lebanon.

China Policy

When the **Nationalist** forces of **Chiang Kai-shek** fled from the mainland of China to the island of **Formosa** (**Taiwan**) in 1948, they also occupied the two offshore islands of Quemoy and Matsu. In the summer of 1958, the Chinese Communists began artillery fire against these islands, seemingly intending to occupy them by force. In a nationwide broadcast, Eisenhower warned that the United States would not "retreat in the face of armed aggression" and deployed the Seventh Fleet in the area as evidence of his determination. Meanwhile, Secretary Dulles flew to Formosa and prevailed on Chiang Kai-shek to give up his idea of invading mainland China. The shelling ceased, but in November the Chinese foreign minister issued this challenge: "The Americans must pull away their hand from the Taiwan Strait . . . We are determined to liberate Formosa and the offshore islands . . ." The issue remained unsettled, and in the 1960 election campaign, Kennedy and Nixon debated as to who would most effectively protect American interests in these islands off the coast of Communist China.

Summits and U-2s

In the fall of 1959, Premier **Nikita S. Khrushchev** of the Soviet Union toured the United States and had private talks with President Eisenhower at Camp David. Another summit meeting was planned to take place in Paris in May 1960. But on May 5, 1960, Khrushchev announced that the Russians had brought down an American **U-2 reconnaissance** (**spy**) **plane** four days earlier, 1,200 miles inside the Soviet Union. Two days later Khrushchev announced that the pilot, Francis Gary Powers, was alive and had confessed to spying. Powers was tried in the Soviet Union for espionage and was sentenced to ten years imprisonment but was released less than two years later.

A State Department bulletin of May 1960 stated that unarmed reconnaissance flights were common practice by many nations and admitted that the United States had been engaged in this activity over the Soviet Union for four years. The bulletin claimed that these flights would have been unnecessary if the Soviet Union had not rejected President Eisenhower's "open skies" proposal made in 1955.

In a subsequent statement, issued May 25, 1960, President Eisenhower declared that he had ordered that the U-2 reconnaissance flights be stopped. He refused Khrushchev's demand for a public apology, whereupon the Soviet leader canceled the summit conference scheduled for May.

Sputnik: The Space Missile Race

Experiments with rockets that could project missiles into outer space had been carried on long before World War II. In the last year of the war, the German army launched V-2 rockets, each carrying a ton of explosives, into cities in England, bringing death and destruction in their wake. After the war, Russia and the United States raced to perfect this new device, which would make it possible to send vehicles into orbit around the earth, reach out into space, and even land on the moon.

On October 4, 1957, the Russians launched the first successful earth satellite, which circled the earth and was called *Sputnik*, meaning "fellow traveler" (of the earth). A month later they launched *Sputnik II* with a dog on board to find out if an earth creature could live in space beyond the earth's atmosphere. It could!

The United States, stunned by the seeming superiority of Soviet science, quickly reacted to the challenge. The implications were ominous. Rocket-launched vehicles could soon carry the new H-bomb to pinpointed targets anywhere in the world. The first successful U.S. satellite, *Explorer I*, was launched in February 1958. Shortly thereafter, Congress passed the National Defense Education Act, appropriating $1 billion for science education. The defense budget for research, was increased by $4 billion, and the National Aeronautics and Space Administration (NASA) was established to carry out a program of space exploration and related defense applications.

Exercise Set 6.3

1. The Suez Crisis of 1956 was settled by
   A. the United States acting unilaterally.
   B. Russia and the United States acting through the UN.
   C. British and French voluntary withdrawal.
   D. the defeat of Israeli military and naval forces.

2. The belief in the 1950s and 1960s that the fall of one nation to communism would lead to the fall of neighboring nations was known as
   A. the domino theory.
   B. massive retaliation.
   C. brinkmanship.
   D. economic nationalism.

3. A scheduled 1959 summit meeting between Eisenhower and Khrushchev was canceled because of
   A. the Soviet testing of an H-bomb.
   B. the U-2 incident.
   C. U.S. intervention in suppressing uprisings in Poland and Hungary.
   D. U.S. launching of *Explorer I*.

4. The 1957 Eisenhower Doctrine empowered the president to extend economic and military aid to nations of
   A. Africa.
   B. the Middle East.
   C. Southeast Asia.
   D. Central and Eastern Europe.

5. The Dulles policy of "massive retaliation" was dependent on the use of
   A. nuclear weapons.
   B. conventional forces.
   C. joint action with our allies.
   D. the overwhelming weight of public opinion.

Unit Six A WORLD IN UNCERTAIN TIMES

Exercise Set 6.4

1. In his farewell address, President Eisenhower warned against the growing power of the "military-industrial complex." He was referring to
   A. the arms race between the United States and the Soviet Union.
   B. the confrontation between the members of NATO and the Warsaw Pact nations.
   C. the alliance of the Pentagon and American arms manufacturers.
   D. the growing power of the scientific community in American defense planning.

2. Under President Eisenhower, social programs for health, education, and welfare were
   A. turned back from the federal government to state, local, and private control.
   B. maintained but not expanded.
   C. expanded by Congress at the request of the President.
   D. passed by Congress over the President's veto.

3. The Submerged Lands Act, advocated by President Eisenhower and signed into law by him in 1953, provided
   A. that control of the tideland (offshore) oil should pass to the states.
   B. for joint exploitation of the tideland oil by state and federal agencies.
   C. for sale of the offshore properties by the federal government to private interests.
   D. that the potential oil resources be reserved to be available in case of national emergency.

THE WARREN COURT AND CIVIL RIGHTS

It is the spirit and not the form of law that keeps justice alive.

Earl Warren, 1955

In 1953, President Eisenhower appointed **Earl Warren**, Republican three-term Governor of California, as Chief Justice of the United States. Warren held this high office until 1969. This 16-year period was to witness many changes, particularly in the area of civil rights.

Brown v. *Board of Education of Topeka* (1954)

In 1896, the Supreme Court, with only Justice **John Marshall Harlan** in dissent, ruled in the case of *Plessy* v. *Ferguson*, that segregation of the races was legal under the Fourteenth Amendment as long as the facilities provided the races were equal. This "separate but equal" doctrine was reversed by unanimous decision of the Warren Court in 1954 in the case of *Brown* v. *Board of Education of Topeka*. Writing for the Court, Chief Justice Warren said, "To separate them [African American children] from others of similar age and qualifications solely because of their race generates a feeling of inferiority as to their status in the community that may affect their hearts and minds in a way unlikely ever to be undone . . . . We conclude that in the field of public education the doctrine of 'separate but equal' has no place. Separate educational facilities are inherently unequal."

In a subsequent ruling on May 31, 1955 (*Brown* v. *Board of Education*), the Supreme Court instructed federal district courts to require local school authorities to move "with all deliberate speed" toward full compliance with this decision. But resistance to the Court's order was intense in the Southern states and in parts of the North as well. Delaware and the District of Columbia integrated their schools promptly. But a dozen years after the Brown decision thousands of public schools in the South still had 100 percent black student bodies.

Beginning of the Civil Rights Movement

Little Rock (1957): School Desegregation

An attempt was made at the beginning of the 1957 school year to integrate Little Rock's Central High School by enrolling nine African American students. Governor Orval Faubus, alleging that violence was about to erupt, sent units of the Arkansas National Guard to the school and ordered them to turn away the black students. When the guard was withdrawn on orders of a federal court, the black students entered the school through a back door, but a mob rushed the building and was barely restrained by the local police. Reporters and photographers on the scene were beaten.

• President Eisenhower Takes Action. At this point, President Eisenhower decided to act. In an address to the nation on September 24, 1957, he declared; "In that city [Little Rock, Arkansas] under the leadership of demagogic extremists, disorderly mobs have deliberately prevented the carrying out of proper orders from a federal court. . . . the President's responsibility is inescapable. In accordance with that responsibility, I have today issued an Executive Order directing the use of troops under federal authority to aid in the execution of federal law at Little Rock, Arkansas."

Rosa Parks and the Montgomery Bus Boycott

On December 1, 1955, Rosa Parks, an African American seamstress in Montgomery, Alabama, boarded a crowded public bus on her way home from work. She sat down in a seat in the front part of the bus reserved for white passengers. The bus driver told her to give up her seat to a white passenger and move to the back of the bus. She refused to do so and was arrested for violating a Montgomery ordinance.

At that time Dr. Martin Luther King, Jr., was a 26-year-old pastor in a Baptist church in Montgomery. The black community was outraged by the injustice of segregation and were ready to take violent action, but Dr. King urged **nonviolent resistance** and organized a **bus boycott**. Blacks refused to ride the buses of Montgomery until all riders were treated alike.

The boycott went on for 381 days. Many walked long distances to and from work, while others organized car pools. A number of white people in Montgomery cooperated in the boycott, which attracted national attention. The Montgomery boycott achieved its purpose peaceably when the bus company gave up its practice of segregated seating.

Segregation in Interstate Transportation Unconstitutional

In *NAACP* v. *St. Louis-San Francisco Railway Company* (1955), the Interstate Commerce Commission ruled that segregation in interstate transportation was unconstitutional and ordered desegregation on all interstate transportation facilities.

Sit-ins, Civil Disobedience

The next step was to challenge local laws throughout the South requiring separate restaurants, lunch counters, or other public food and drink establishments for whites and blacks. This also included drinking fountains and restrooms, which were marked either "white" or "colored." The non-violent method used by blacks (aided by some whites) was the **sit-in**. On February 1, 1960, four African American college students entered a Woolworth restaurant in Greensboro, North Carolina. This was the first of many sit-ins. There were many arrests for violation of local ordinances, which enforced segregation. In May 1963 the Supreme Court ruled that the arrests were illegal because the segregation laws on which they were based were in violation of the Fourteenth Amendment's "privileges or immunities" clause.

First Civil Rights Legislation

In 1957, in a bipartisan effort supported by the Eisenhower administration, Congress passed the first **Civil Rights Act** since the Civil War. It addressed the key issue of **voting rights**, since blacks in the South were systematically disenfranchised by "literacy tests," poll taxes, and intimidation. The act created a Civil Rights Commission composed of members of both the Democratic and Republican parties and authorized the Justice Department to bring suits against persons interfering with anyone's right to vote.

When voting rights continued to be denied to blacks, a second and much stronger Civil Rights Act was passed in 1960. The act provided for the appointment of federal referees with power to issue voting certificates. It declared obstruction of voting rights by "threats or force" a federal crime. The number of black voters increased slowly but there was still a long way to go.

Exercise Set 6.5

1. In the landmark 1954 decision, *Brown* v. *Board of Education of Topeka*, the United States Supreme Court
   A. confirmed the earlier decision of *Plessy* v. *Ferguson*.
   B. established the principle that "separate educational facilities are inherently unequal."
   C. ordered immediate integration of all public educational facilities.
   D. divided 5 to 4 in favor of the plaintiffs.

2. Implementation of the Supreme Court's school integration decision in Little Rock, Arkansas led to
   A. reluctant but prompt compliance by state authorities.
   B. a subsequent reversal of the Court's decision.
   C. an Executive Order by President Eisenhower directing the use of federal troops to enforce the Court's order.
   D. disclosure of corruption in the local educational establishment.

3. Throughout the year 1956, public attention in the nation was centered on Montgomery, Alabama, because
   A. the outcome of a nonviolent bus boycott could put an end to segregation on local public transportation facilities.
   B. violence had erupted in connection with the bus boycott.
   C. Rosa Parks had attempted to integrate the schools of Montgomery.
   D. Dr. Martin Luther King, Jr., was a minister in Montgomery.

4. The Warren Court is generally associated with
   A. a more liberal approach to the rights of minorities.
   B. adherence to conservative principles of criminal justice.
   C. split decisions representing divergent opinions of the justices on basic civil rights issues.
   D. overwhelming public support of the Court's decisions.

THE AFFLUENT SOCIETY

Postwar Consumption

Homes

The postwar economic boom, stimulated in part by the demand for housing, witnessed a vast building expansion, especially in the suburbs. The **Housing Act of 1955** provided for 45,000 new public housing units a year for four years. This obviously fell far short of the nation's needs.

By 1960, average real income in the United States had risen nearly 20 percent since the end of World War II, and 15 million new housing units had been constructed. By 1972, the Bureau of the Census reported that 45 million housing units (of a total of 70 million) were owned by their occupants.

Automobiles

The family car was a symbol of the affluent society. A few years after the end of World War II, when production of civilian goods had returned to high gear, 45 percent of American families owned an automobile. By 1970 it was 75 percent. The percentage increased to 80 in the next five years and, in addition, 30 percent of all American families now had at least two cars. Factory sales of passenger cars exceeded 8 million in 1985, with an additional 3.3 million trucks and buses. Over 255 million cars, trucks, and buses were registered in the United States in 2008.

Television

Television, with only a few thousand sets in use in the United States at the outbreak of World War II, became an important medium after the war. By 1960, nine of every ten American homes had television sets. A decade later TV had become the universal mass medium for communicating with the American public. People all over the world watched their TV screens in awe as the two American astronauts, Armstrong and Aldrin, walked on the moon in July 1969. As of 2010, the average American home had 2.93 TV sets per household.

Baby Boom

The post-World War II baby boom helped cause a marked increase in the population, which rose from 132 million in 1940 to 151 million in 1950. At the peak of the boom, the average number of children per family was 3.8. (It was below 2 in 1992.) The population boom continued in the 1950s with the total nearing 180 million by 1960. The number was swelled, in part, by the admission of 2.5 million refugees from war-torn regions. Although the boom slowed down during the 1960s and came to a halt in 1972, the population of the United States continues to increase. It was 226 million in 1980, 249 million in 1990, and 308,745,538 in 2010.

Year	Population	Year	Population	Year	Population
2010	308,746	1930	123,202	1860	31,443
1990	248,709	1920	106,021	1850	23,191
1980	226,545	1910	92,228	1840	17,069
1970	203,302	1900	76,212	1830	12,866
1960	179,323	1890	62,979	1820	9,638
1950	151,325	1880	50,198	1810	7,239
1940	132,164	1870	38,558	1800	5,308

Figure 6.3   U.S. Population (in thousands)

Migration and Immigration

Americans on the Move

About 3 percent of the population moves annually from one state to another. Special circumstances affect migration. For example, the figure was much higher during the Great Depression of the 1930s when people lost their jobs, their farms, and their savings, and many pulled up roots and went West looking for a new life.

The war years of the 1940s were another era of large-scale migration. This time the move tended to be from South to North and from rural to urban areas where there were better economic opportunities in the new war industries. An estimated 15 million people, or more than 10 percent of the population, were involved in this migration. Another 15 million or more in the military were moved from place to place before going overseas.

The momentum of westward migration was accelerated after World War II. The population of Arizona was half a million in 1940. By 1990 it was more than 7 times as great at 3.6 million. California grew from 7 million to 29 million in the same period. By 1964, California had surpassed New

York as the most populous state in the nation, and in 2010 had 37,691,912 people. In the 1960s the previous migration trend (chiefly blacks) from South to North was sharply reversed by the new trend (chiefly whites) from North to South. The population of Houston, now the fourth largest city in the United States, leaped from half a million to 1.75 million since 1950. Dallas, the eighth largest city, more than doubled in population (434,000 to over 1 million) in the same period, and San Antonio went from 408,000 to 900,000. The "sunbelt" states of the South and Southwest became the fastest growing section of the country.

Suburbanization

A major postwar trend was the exodus of the middle class from the cities to the suburbs. Long Island, New York, long famous for its potato farms, was suddenly transformed into a strip of bedroom communities reaching eastward 100 miles from Manhattan.

The ingenious builder, William J. Levitt, secured large tracts of land, laid out plans approved by local authorities, and rapidly constructed thousands of reasonably priced homes on small plots of land. **Levittowns** sprang up within commuting distance of New York and Philadelphia. Other builders soon adopted this pattern to meet the almost insatiable appetite of migrants from the cities. When President Eisenhower delivered his farewell address in January 1961, the population of the suburbs already exceeded that of the cities.

New Immigration Patterns

The pattern of immigration (legal and illegal) has been changing. The new immigration stems from Mexico and other lands south of the border, from the Caribbean, and from Asia.

In an attempt to solve the problem of the vast number of immigrants who entered the United States illegally and had to remain "underground," the Immigration and Naturalization Service, as provided in the Immigration and Control Act of 1986, offered amnesty to those who could prove they had resided in the United States since January 1, 1982. By the deadline date of May 4, 1988, the Service had received applications for amnesty from 1.4 million undocumented immigrants, 71 percent of whom had entered from Mexico and more than half of whom were living in California.

Immigration to the United States is limited to 270,000 annually, but additional provision is made under the **Refugee Act of 1980** for the admission of persons for humanitarian reasons who would be subjected to political persecution if they were returned to their country of last residence.

During the decade 1970–1980 a total of 1,588,200 immigrants were admitted from Asia, chiefly from the Philippines, Korea, and India. During the same period, nearly 2 million were admitted from countries south of the border—600,000 from Mexico, 271,000 from the West Indies, 265,000 from Cuba, and 170,000 from Colombia. In the 1980s the numbers increased.

Some 2 million were admitted from Asia by the end of 1990, and about 3.5 million from Latin America. The **Secure Fence Act** was passed in 2006 in an attempt to reduce illegal immigration across the Mexican border.

Exercise Set 6.6

1. During the decade following World War II, the United States experienced
   A. a recession similar to the one that followed World War I.
   B. an economic boom stimulated in part by a vast building expansion.
   C. a slow but steady rise in income keeping pace with inflation.
   D. rapid fluctuations in stock and bond prices.

2. In the post-World War II period, transportation trends were characterized by
   A. expansion in the use of canals, lakes, and rivers for moving heavy freight.
   B. a rapid development of the railroads.
   C. a leveling off of international air traffic.
   D. the extensive use of the family car.

3. In the affluent American society of the post-World War II period
   A. unemployment was virtually abolished.
   B. television had become a standard source of entertainment and information in 90 percent of homes.
   C. labor strife was a relatively rare occurrence.
   D. the national budget showed a surplus in most years.

4. Which has *not* been responsible for major migrations within the United States?
   A. Loss of economic security brought on by the Great Depression
   B. Dislocations resulting from World War II
   C. Attraction of the wide open spaces of the Great Plains
   D. A movement to the so-called Sunbelt

5. A major cause of the movement to the suburbs in the decades following World War II was
   A. the growth of the middle class during the post-World War II period.
   B. greater economic opportunities found in the suburbs.
   C. the availability of comfortable and efficient railroad transportation from suburban to urban centers.
   D. opportunities for minorities to find jobs and homes in the suburbs.

CHAPTER REVIEW QUESTIONS

1. In the case of *Brown* v. *Board of Education* (1954), the United States Supreme Court decided that
   A. busing children to overcome segregation is unconstitutional.
   B. closing public schools to avoid integration is unconstitutional.
   C. separate educational facilities are inherently unequal and unconstitutional.
   D. the use of civil disobedience to achieve legal rights is constitutional.

2. The development and operation of the Tennessee Valley Authority by the U.S. government is an example of
   A. a return to laissez-faire economics.
   B. government's attempt to earn maximum profits in business.
   C. experimentation with nuclear technology.
   D. federal intervention to meet regional needs.

3. An experience of the majority of immigrants to the United States was that they
   A. settled in rural areas where cheap land was available.
   B. frequently met resentment.
   C. joined radical political parties to bring about economic reform.
   D. were rapidly assimilated into the predominant lifestyle.

4. Which is a major difference between immigration to the United States during the period 1860–1920 and immigration since 1970?
   A. Immigrants today are not likely to experience discrimination.
   B. There is a greater need for unskilled labor today.
   C. The primary areas of origin have changed dramatically.
   D. Today's immigrants tend to be members of the middle class.

5. "A just society is one that treats fairly the most disadvantaged members of its society." Which government action would best illustrate this principle?
   A. Creating "separate but equal" schools for minority groups
   B. Shifting governmental funds from public schools to private schools
   C. Establishing programs to train unskilled workers
   D. Passing legislation making ownership of property a requirement for voting

THEMATIC ESSAY

Directions: Write a well-organized essay that includes an introduction, several paragraphs addressing the task below, and a conclusion.

Theme: Environment

The second half of the 20th century has proven to be a time of growing environmental concerns.

Task:

From your study of environmental concerns of the second half of the 20th century in the United States, identify *three* threats to the delicate environmental balance of the planet.

For each environmental threat:

- Identify the cause of the threat to the environment.
- Discuss the dangers the problem poses to the environment.
- Describe an action, either national or international, that has been taken to address the environmental problem.

You may use any dangers to the environment that have become an issue during the second half of the 20th century. Some suggestions you may wish to consider are depletion of the planet's ozone layer and resulting global warming (greenhouse effect), deforestation and increased release of carbon dioxide into the atmosphere, acid rain, water pollution, waste disposal (including nuclear), and air pollution.

You are *not* limited to these suggestions.

DOCUMENT-BASED QUESTION

The following questions (Part A and Part B) are based on the accompanying documents (1–6). Some of these documents have been edited for the purpose of this exercise. The question is designed to test your ability to work with historical documents and to demonstrate your knowledge of the subject matter being presented. As you analyze the documents, take into account both the source of the document and the author's point of view.

Historical Context:

The momentous school desegregation decision in 1954 started the Earl Warren Supreme Court (1953–1969) on a path that would undertake sweeping reforms in numerous areas. Many saw the Supreme Court's actions during the term of Chief Justice Earl Warren as encroachments on rights reserved to the States and to the People.

Task:

Using information from the documents and your knowledge of United States history, answer the questions that follow each document in Part A. Your answers to the questions will help you write the Part B essay, in which you will be asked:

The momentous school desegregation decision in 1954 by the Earl Warren Supreme Court (1953–1969) raised the debate concerning state versus federal powers. Was the Supreme Court's decision in *Brown* v. *Board of Education* (1954) an infringement upon state's rights, or was it the correct interpretation of the provisions of the Fourteenth Amendment?

Part A
Short-Answer Questions

The documents below refer to the era of the Warren Supreme Court. Examine each document carefully and then answer the questions that follow.

DOCUMENT 1

We come then to the question presented: Does segregation of children in public schools solely on the basis of race, even though the physical facilities and other "tangible" factors may be equal, deprive the children of the minority group of equal educational opportunities? We believe that it does. . . .

Separate educational facilities are inherently unequal. . . .

—*Brown* v. *Board of Education* (1954)

1*a*. According to the Supreme Court in the *Brown* decision, what was making the education facilities (schools) not equal?

_____

_____

_____

_____

1*b*. What type of educational facilities are being discussed in the decision?

_____

_____

_____

_____

DOCUMENT 2

Southern opposition to the Supreme Court's decision in the *Brown* v. *Board of Education* case was expressed in March, 1956 when 19 Southern Senators and 77 Southern Congressman expressed their concerns in a statement known as the "Southern Manifesto."

We regard the decision of the Supreme Court in the public school cases as a clear abuse of judicial power. It climaxes a trend of the Federal Judiciary undertaking to legislate, in derogation of the authority of Congress, and to encroach upon the reserved rights of the states.
    The original Constitution does not mention education. Neither does the 14th Amendment nor any other amendment. . . .

—*Southern Manifesto* (March 1956)

2. What argument regarding the division of powers between the federal government and state governments (federalism) is being made in the "Southern Manifesto?"

_____

_____

_____

_____

DOCUMENT 3

> I have a dream that one day this nation will rise up and live out the true meaning of its creed: "We hold these truths to be self-evident; that all men are created equal."

—"I Have a Dream" speech, Dr. Martin Luther King, Jr.,
Washington, D.C. (1963)

3. According to Dr. King, what was one reason why civil rights activists organized the march on Washington?

_____

_____

_____

DOCUMENT 4

> Then-Republican Presidential prospect Marion G. (Pat) Robertson was interviewed by the *Washington Post* on the subject of the Supreme Court and judicial review.
>
> A Supreme Court ruling is not the law of the land. The law of the United States is the Constitution, treaties made in accordance with the Constitution and laws duly enacted by the Congress and signed by the President. . . .
> I am bound by the laws of the United States and all 50 states. . . . I am not bound by any case or any court to which I myself am not a party. . . .
> I am concerned, as I think millions of others are, when those justices (Supreme Court) say "the Constitution is what we say it is."

—Marion G. (Pat) Robertson, *The Washington Post* (June 27, 1986)

4. Having read candidate Robertson's response regarding the limited jurisdictional power of a Supreme Court decision, create a possible argument supporting the position that the holding in *Brown* v. *Board of Education* did not have to be applied to the individual states.

_____

_____

_____

DOCUMENT 5

In each of the cases, minors of the Negro race, through their legal representatives, seek the aid of the courts in obtaining admission to the public schools of their community on a nonsegregated basis. In each instance, they had been denied admission to schools attended by white children under laws requiring or permitting segregation according to race. This segregation was alleged to deprive the plaintiffs of the equal protection of the laws under the Fourteenth Amendment.

—*Brown* v. *Board of Education* (1954)

5. What specific provision of the Fourteenth Amendment was being quoted by the Supreme Court in the *Brown* decision in support of their decision that public schools segregated on the basis of race was unconstitutional?

_____

_____

_____

_____

DOCUMENT 6

The constitutional status of racial classification had been addressed in the case of *Plessy* v. *Ferguson* in 1896. The following is a segment of the Court's decision.

The statute of Louisiana, acts of 1890, c. 111, requiring railway companies carrying passengers in their coaches in that State, to provide equal, but separate, accommodations for the white and colored races . . . are not in conflict with the provisions either of the Thirteenth Amendment or of the Fourteenth Amendment to the Constitution of the United States.

—*Plessy* v. *Ferguson* (1896)

6. How did the Supreme Court's decision in the *Plessy* case in 1896 differ from the later decision in *Brown* v. *Board of Education* in 1954?

_____

_____

_____

_____

Part B
Essay

Your essay should be well organized with an introductory paragraph that states your position on the question. Develop your position in the next paragraphs and then write a conclusion. In your essay, include specific historical details and refer to the specific documents you analyzed in Part A. You may include additional information from your knowledge of social studies.

Historical Context:

The momentous school desegregation decision in 1954 started the Earl Warren Supreme Court (1953–1969) on a path that would undertake sweeping reforms in numerous areas.

Task:

The school desegregation decision in 1954 by the Earl Warren Supreme Court (1953–1969) raised the debate concerning state versus federal powers. Using the documents provided and your knowledge of United States history, answer the following question: Was the Supreme Court's decision in *Brown* v. *Board of Education* (1954) an infringement upon state's rights, or was it a correct interpretation of the provisions of the Fourteenth Amendment?

Guidelines:

In your essay, be sure to
- Develop all aspects of the task.
- Incorporate information from *at least five* documents.
- Incorporate relevant outside information.
- Support the theme with many relevant facts, examples, and details.
- Use a logical and clear plan of organization, including an introduction and a conclusion that are beyond a restatement of the theme.

DECADE OF CHANGE (THE 1960s)

THE KENNEDY YEARS: THE NEW FRONTIER

> We stand today on the edge of a New Frontier—the frontier of the 1960s—a frontier of unknown opportunities and perils—a frontier of unfulfilled hopes and threats.
>
> John F. Kennedy accepting nomination for President
> at Democratic National Convention, 1960

The 1960 Election

The election of 1960 pitted **John F. Kennedy**, Senator from Massachusetts, against **Richard M. Nixon**, Vice President. In this election, television played a key role for the first time. The two candidates faced the nation in four one-hour televised debates. An estimated 70 million Americans viewed each debate. Kennedy, at 43, was the youngest candidate ever elected to the presidency. In addition, he was a Roman Catholic, and no one of his religion had ever been President. Kennedy faced the religious question head-on when he said, "I believe in an America where the separation of church and state is absolute . . ."

The 1960 election was one of the closest in American history. Of the total votes cast—68.8 million—Kennedy's margin over Nixon was 119,450 votes or 3/10ths of 1 percent. In the electoral college, Kennedy received 303 votes to 219 for Nixon.

Domestic Policies and Programs

> Let the word go forth from this time and place, to friend and foe alike, that the torch has been passed to a new generation of Americans— born in this century, tempered by war, disciplined by a hard and bitter peace, proud of our ancient heritage, and unwilling to witness or permit the slow undoing of those human rights to which this Nation has always been committed . . .
>
> And so, my fellow Americans—ask not what your country can do for you—ask what you can do for your country.
>
> John F. Kennedy, Inaugural Address, January 20, 1961

Domestic Gains

Kennedy did secure from Congress approval of a number of social pro-grams—the minimum wage was raised, Social Security benefits were extended, unemployment compensation was increased, additional funds were appropriated for housing, mental health, and public works, and a Federal Water Pollution Control Act was approved. The President responded to an increase in steel prices by calling the steel magnates to his office and forc-ing them to rescind the price increases. He initiated a multi-billion-dollar program to put a man on the moon, which eventually bore fruit in July 1969.

Kennedy and Civil Rights

Appointments

Kennedy appointed members of the black community to key positions in the federal government. His appointment of **Thurgood Marshall** to the U.S. Circuit Court of Appeals later led to the elevation of Marshall to the Supreme Court by President Johnson in 1967. Marshall had been general counsel of the National Association for the Advancement of Colored People (NAACP) when he argued the case of *Brown* v. *Board of Education of Topeka* before the Supreme Court in 1954. Kennedy also appointed a number of African Americans to the federal bench as U.S. district court judges.

Attorney General Robert F. Kennedy

President Kennedy appointed his brother, Robert F. Kennedy, to the sensi-tive post of Attorney General in a time of turmoil over civil rights and other constitutional issues. "Bobby" Kennedy proved to be a firm advocate of civil rights. While he held office, the Justice Department brought over 50 suits to secure voting rights for African Americans in states where they were virtu-ally disenfranchised. The suits were brought under the Civil Rights Act of 1960, which empowered the federal courts to appoint referees to investigate claims that citizens' voting rights had been violated by state voting regula-tions. The act authorized federal courts to levy heavy penalties on anyone who infringed on the civil rights of others.

James H. Meredith

In the fall of 1962 James H. Meredith, an African American Air Force vet-eran of the Korean War, attempted to enroll in the all-white University of Mississippi in his home state. The governor of the state took charge of the university and ordered that Meredith, who had met all necessary qualifica-tions, be denied admission because he was black. When federal marshals escorted him to the university, a white mob touched off violence in which two people were killed and many were seriously injured. President Kennedy dispatched 5,000 federal troops to Mississippi and Meredith was registered in the university.

Medgar Evers

On June 11, 1963, President Kennedy, who was trying to get Congress to pass stronger civil rights legislation, delivered a stirring appeal to the nation on television. He asked his audience, "Are we to say . . . that this is a land of the free except for Negroes . . . that we have no class or caste system, no ghettos, no master race, except with respect to Negroes?"

That night, Medgar Evers, head of the NAACP of Mississippi, and a war veteran, was murdered outside his home by a white racist. Despite President Kennedy's efforts, stronger civil rights legislation had to wait until the administration of Lyndon Johnson.

Martin Luther King, Jr.

I have a dream that one day on the red hills of Georgia the sons of former slaves and the sons of former slave owners will be able to sit down together at the table of brotherhood . . .

I have a dream that my four little children will one day live in a nation where they will not be judged by the color of their skin but by the content of their character.

Martin Luther King, Jr.
at the Lincoln Memorial on the occasion of the Civil Rights March
in Washington, D.C., August 28, 1963.

Dr. Martin Luther King, Jr., (1929–1968) led the civil rights movement in the 1950s and 1960s.

Rise to Leadership

Martin Luther King, Jr., was born in Atlanta, Georgia, January 15, 1929, and died in Memphis, Tennessee, April 4, 1968, the victim of an assassin's bullet. Like his father and his maternal grandfather, he was a Baptist minister in Alabama.

King's rise to leadership in the civil rights movement began when he led the bus boycott in Montgomery, which began on December 1, 1955. Although he was arrested in January 1956 and his parsonage was bombed, his leadership succeeded in integrating Montgomery's buses. In February

466

1957, he became president of a new antisegregation organization known as the **Southern Christian Leadership Conference (SCLC)**. The organization sponsored nonviolent sit-ins at lunch counters and other nonviolent protests.

Birmingham Protest

Like Gandhi in India, King preached that racism and social injustice should be fought by disobedience but not by violence. King urged **civil disobedience** of Birmingham's segregation laws as a means of bringing injustice out where all could see it. He and his followers persisted despite violence against them instigated by Birmingham's police commissioner. King was arrested and put in solitary confinement in the jail, where he wrote his famous "Letter from a Birmingham Jail," giving the rationale for nonviolent disobedience to unjust laws.

March on Washington and Later Activities

In 1963 King led the famous march on Washington where, on August 28, he delivered the classic "I Have a Dream" speech. He continued to campaign for civil rights and for equal treatment of African Americans. In 1964 he was awarded the **Nobel Prize** for peace. In 1966 he led a campaign for slum clearance in Chicago. In 1968 he was in Memphis helping to coordinate a strike of sanitation workers. He was making plans to lead a Poor People's Crusade on Washington and had taken a public stand against the Vietnam War. King's life was cut short in Memphis on April 4, 1968, by a bullet that struck him in the head as he stood on the balcony of his hotel room. He received recognition as one of America's great leaders when his birthday was designated a national holiday by an act of Congress in 1983.

Exercise Set 6.7

1. Which would be most in accord with the ideals of Dr. Martin Luther King, Jr.?
   A. Underpaid workers sabotage the machinery at their factory
   B. A minority worker assaults a bigot
   C. An 18-year-old pacifist accepts a jail term rather than register for military service
   D. Radical leaders advocate black separatism if their group's demands are not met

2. "Under a government which imprisons any unjustly, the true place for a just man is also a prison."

   Henry David Thoreau

   Which idea does this quotation most strongly support?
   A. Social control
   B. Conformity
   C. Suspension of civil liberties
   D. Civil disobedience

3. President Kennedy's inability to secure passage of many of his legislative recommendations was due to
   A. a combination of Republicans and Conservative Democrats.
   B. a lack of legislative experience on the part of the President.
   C. distractions of foreign problems.
   D. a Republican majority in one or both houses of Congress.

4. President Kennedy made use of federal troops to force the racial integration of
   A. public schools in Little Rock, Arkansas.
   B. the University of Mississippi.
   C. the lunch counters of Greensboro, North Carolina.
   D. the Montgomery, Alabama bus companies.

ACTION IN FOREIGN POLICIES

Latin American Policies

Review of Earlier Policies

> The American continents are henceforth not to be considered as subjects for future colonization by any European Power. We should consider any attempt on their part to extend their system to any portion of this Hemisphere as dangerous to our peace and safety.
>
> President James Monroe, 1823

The principles established by the Monroe Doctrine became basic to American foreign policy and were followed throughout the 1800s. Concern in the United States over the ruthless conduct of the Spanish government against internal Cuban opposition came to a head in 1898 when the U.S. battleship *Maine* was blown up in Havana harbor and the United States declared war against Spain.

The years between the Spanish-American War and the New Deal era beginning in 1933 have been described as a period of "**dollar diplomacy**" in American foreign policy. American business invested heavily in economic exploitation of resources in Latin America. When the safety of these investments was threatened by local violence, the American response generally was to send in detachments of U.S. Marines "to restore order" and protect the investments. Under this policy during the 35-year period after the Spanish-American War, troops were deployed at various times in Cuba, Haiti, the Dominican Republic, Nicaragua, Honduras, and Panama.

In 1933 President Franklin D. Roosevelt changed American policy toward Latin America and declared, "I would dedicate this nation to the policy of the good neighbor." With the outbreak of World War II, the republics of the Western Hemisphere held an Inter-American Conference in 1939 and issued the Declaration of Panama, warning the combatants to keep armed vessels clear of a 300-mile zone surrounding the United States and Latin America.

The Bay of Pigs

Shortly after President Kennedy took office, he was informed that under the previous (Eisenhower) administration the **Central Intelligence Agency** (**CIA**) had been training, arming, and financing thousands of Cuban refugees in Florida and Guatemala for an attempt to overthrow the anti-American Castro dictatorship in Cuba. Kennedy met with his advisers and reluctantly agreed to let the plans go forward on condition that no U.S. military or naval forces be used in the invasion of Cuba. He was assured that the anti-Castro Cubans could accomplish the task on their own, with strong internal support.

On the morning of April 17, 1961, about 1,400 Cuban exiles who had embarked from Florida and Guatemala landed at the **Bay of Pigs** on the southern coast of Cuba. They were met by a force of some 14,000 well-armed defenders who, in three days of fighting, killed or captured almost all of the anti-Castro invaders. With the invasion a total failure, President Kennedy admitted that it was a mistake and accepted full responsibility for the outcome.

The Cuban Missile Crisis

Following the Bay of Pigs fiasco, **Fidel Castro** invited the Soviets to install intermediate-range ballistic missiles on Cuban soil. Installation of these missiles was under way when they were discovered by a **U-2 plane** taking photographs from high altitude on October 14, 1962. Careful analysis of the photographs revealed that launching pads were being installed and that nuclear warheads would soon be capable of striking as far north as Hudson Bay in Canada and as far south as Lima, Peru.

Kennedy convened top advisers from the Defense and State Departments, the CIA, the Cabinet, and his personal staff. They met daily and considered all possible responses for turning back this grave threat. Two possible courses emerged—a lightning air strike to destroy the installations, or a **blockade** to prevent offensive weapons from being delivered to Cuba. The latter course was agreed upon. The gravity of the crisis was clearly understood. "The worst course of all," said the President, "would be for us to do nothing." In a television address to the nation on Monday evening, October 22, he explained the threat contained in the installations and said, "A strict quarantine of all offensive military equipment under shipment to Cuba is being initiated . . . Let no one doubt that this is a difficult and dangerous effort on which we have set out."

Meanwhile, contact with the Soviets was maintained and every effort was made to enable Khrushchev to retreat gracefully without loss of face. Kennedy accepted Khrushchev's offer to remove the missiles in return for his public promise not to invade Cuba. Kennedy also agreed privately to withdraw American missiles from Turkey. Soviet ships bound for Cuba turned back and the tension was relieved. The missiles were subsequently removed and the launching pads dismantled under the eyes of UN observers. The Cuban Missile Crisis was resolved.

The Vienna Summit (Berlin Wall)

On January 6, 1961, two weeks before Kennedy's inauguration, Soviet Premier Nikita Khrushchev made a threatening speech about the city of Berlin. Located in East Germany, the city was divided into East Berlin, the

Communist part, and West Berlin, the free part. Khrushchev threatened to end free access by the Western nations to West Berlin.

Khrushchev invited Kennedy to meet with him for a friendly talk in Vienna in June 1961. Khrushchev again threatened to close off West Berlin. Kennedy responded that our national security was involved in Berlin and that our abandoning it would mean abandoning our commitments not only to our allies but to all of Europe. Afterward, Kennedy made plans to defend Berlin, and he increased the military budget and the size of the armed forces.

In mid-August the Communists sealed off West Berlin by erecting the **Berlin Wall**, a wall of concrete and barbed wire between the two sectors. But access to Berlin from the West was not cut off and the crisis subsided.

In June 1963 Kennedy visited West Berlin and made the memorable statement: "All free men, wherever they may live, are citizens of Berlin, and therefore, as a free man, I take pride in the words 'Ich bin ein Berliner.' "

In November 1989 tremendous changes took place in East Germany as a result of demands and demonstrations by the people. The Berlin Wall was opened and East Germans were allowed to travel freely to West Berlin and all of West Germany for the first time in 28 years. In 1990 East and West Germany were reunited to form one nation.

The Peace Corps

In 1961, President Kennedy recommended to Congress the establishment of a permanent Peace Corps, which he had set in motion on an experimental basis by executive order. He described the Peace Corps as "an organization which will recruit and train American volunteers, sending them abroad to work with the people of other nations." Peace Corps members could help the people in the developing nations with their day-to-day problems. They could teach English in primary and secondary schools, help establish and operate public health and sanitation projects, aid in village development, and increase agricultural productivity by assisting local farmers to use modern implements and techniques.

The Peace Corps was approved by Congress on September 22, 1961 with an appropriation of $40 million. **Sargent Shriver**, who had proposed the idea, was appointed first director of the Peace Corps. At home, the Peace Corps was received with enthusiasm, and abroad, in the emerging nations of Asia, Africa and Latin America, it helped to replace the negative image of the "Ugly American" with one of American idealism and altruism.

The Race to the Moon

In April 1961 the Soviet astronaut **Yuri Gagarin** became the first human to orbit the earth. A month later, President Kennedy declared, "This nation should commit itself to achieving the goal, before this decade is out, of landing a man on the moon and returning him safely to earth." There was an immediate enthusiastic response from the nation and from Congress, and a $25 billion program was launched.

The Nuclear Test Ban Treaty

In August 1961, after the Berlin Wall was built, Khrushchev announced that the Soviet Union would again begin nuclear testing, in violation of a 1958 agreement between the United States, Great Britain, and the Soviet Union to suspend tests for three years. The Soviets began tests in the fall of 1961 and after they refused a test ban treaty, the United States agreed to set up a "hot line" telephone between Washington and Moscow, to be installed August 30, 1963. President Kennedy said the purpose of the line was "to avoid on each side the dangerous delays, misunderstandings, and misreadings of the other's actions which might occur at a time of crisis."

Finally, three-power talks between the United States, Great Britain, and the Soviet Union began in Moscow in July 1963. A treaty banning nuclear tests in the atmosphere, in outer space, and under water (but not under ground) was concluded on July 25. It was signed by the three powers in Moscow on August 5 and was ratified by the U.S. Senate on September 24. Two weeks later, President Kennedy approved the sale of $250 million of wheat to the Soviet Union. The nuclear test ban treaty was soon signed by more than 100 nations.

Assassination in Dallas

In November 1963 President Kennedy traveled to Texas to help heal a rift in the state Democratic party. On Friday, November 22, 1963, during the visit, President Kennedy was riding in an open car, sitting next to Governor **John B. Connally** of Texas, in a motorcade along the main street of Dallas, Texas. Suddenly he was hit in the head and neck by two rifle bullets. Governor Connally was wounded but recovered. The President died within an hour. The shots that killed the President were fired from a building adjoining the route of the motorcade. The suspected killer, **Lee Harvey Oswald**, was apprehended an hour and a half later.

Lyndon B. Johnson Sworn in as President

Vice President Lyndon B. Johnson, who was also riding in the motorcade, was unharmed. He was sworn in as President on a plane returning that day to Washington. Two days after the assassination, Oswald was being moved by police from the city jail to a more secure county jail when he was shot and killed by **Jack Ruby**, a Dallas nightclub operator.

472

The Warren Commission

President Johnson appointed a special commission to investigate the assassination of President Kennedy. The Commission was headed by **Earl Warren**, Chief Justice of the United States, and included leaders in the Senate and House of Representatives. The Commission conducted an exhaustive inquiry and presented its report on September 24, 1964. The report concluded that there was no conspiracy to assassinate the President and that "the shots which killed President Kennedy and wounded Governor Connally were fired by Lee Harvey Oswald." Warren asserted that "no one has produced any facts that are contrary to the commission's conclusion." But allegations continue to be made that the evidence is inconclusive and that there may have been a conspiracy to assassinate the President.

Exercise Set 6.8

1. The most serious crisis in foreign affairs under Kennedy before the mid-term elections in 1962 was
   A. in Berlin.
   B. in Cuba.
   C. in Vietnam.
   D. with Britain.

2. In space exploration the idea of placing astronauts on the moon and bringing them back safely to earth was
   A. first undertaken by the Soviet Union.
   B. at first rejected by the National Aeronautic and Space Administration.
   C. considered too costly by Congress.
   D. advocated by President Kennedy within a few months after his inauguration.

3. Most consider which of the following to be a foreign policy failure of President Kennedy?
   A. The Bay of Pigs affair
   B. Controversy over Berlin
   C. The Cuban Missile Crisis
   D. Peace Corps operations

4. The Warren Commission concluded that the assassination of President Kennedy
   A. had been planned for 1,000 days.
   B. was planned and executed by conspirators.
   C. was accomplished by Lee Harvey Oswald.
   D. had no precedent in American history.

5. The nuclear test ban treaty of 1963 was
   A. rejected by the U.S. Senate.
   B. negotiated by representatives of more than 100 nations.
   C. designed to prohibit testing of nuclear weapons in the atmosphere, in outer space, and under water, but not underground.
   D. approved at a time when the United States and the Soviet Union were engaged in frantic testing of nuclear weapons.

JOHNSON AND THE GREAT SOCIETY

> This nation, this generation, in this hour has man's first chance to build a Great Society, a place where the meaning of man's life matches the marvels of man's labors.
>
> Lyndon B. Johnson,
> Democratic National Convention, August 1964

Expanding the Kennedy Social Programs

Soon after he was sworn in as President on the day of Kennedy's assassination, November 22, 1963, **Lyndon B. Johnson** moved to implement and expand Kennedy's program of domestic civil rights and social legislation.

The War on Poverty

President Johnson prevailed on Congress to give him the key measure in his war on poverty, the billion-dollar Economic Opportunity Act (1964) creating the Office of Economic Opportunity (OEO). The act set up job- and work-training programs and provided for loans to college students and to small businesses for hiring the unemployed. The appropriation was doubled the following year with appropriations for rehabilitation in poverty-stricken Appalachia and for granting aid directly to needy elementary and secondary school students in public and nonpublic schools.

One agency in OEO was called Volunteers in Service to America (VISTA). It was organized in 1965 as the domestic counterpart to the Peace Corps. Volunteers receive training in working with children, the elderly, Native Americans, agricultural migrant workers, and the mentally ill. VISTA operated chiefly in pockets of poverty in rural areas.

Other programs of OEO included **Operation Head Start** for aid to preschoolers from underprivileged homes, a **Job Corps** for school dropouts, a **Neighborhood Youth Corps** for unemployed teenagers, and a Community Action Program whereby inner-city neighborhoods get financial aid for planning and executing programs of self-help.

Congress approved a rent-supplement program for poor families and established a **Department of Housing and Urban Development (HUD)** with Cabinet rank. The appointment of Robert C. Weaver as head of HUD made him the first Cabinet member from the African American Community.

Medicare and Medicaid

The Health Insurance Act for the Aged, passed in 1965 as an amendment to the Social Security Act, provided federally funded hospital insurance for people over 65. It also included limited nursing home care and home visits by nurses and health care workers other than physicians. Those covered by

475

Social Security could also secure medical care other than hospitalization by paying a small monthly fee. These fees were sharply increased during the 1980s. The plan called **Medicare** (for seniors) was accompanied by a plan called **Medicaid** for the needy of all ages. It required the states to administer financially aided programs of care for people below the poverty level as well as for needy families with dependent children, the blind, and the totally disabled.

Aid to Education

In a speech at the University of Michigan in May 1964, President Johnson declared, "The Great Society is a place where every child can find knowledge to enrich his mind and to enlarge his talents." This precept was advanced by the **Elementary and Secondary Education Act of 1965**. The act provided federal aid in the amount of $1.3 billion directly to pupils in school districts. To promote school integration as required by law the U.S. Office of Education now required proof as a condition of federal aid, that beginning with the 1966–1967 school year, desegregation had been undertaken in good faith.

The Moon Landing

Kennedy's prophetic vision to land a man on the moon was realized on July 20, 1969, when **Neil Armstrong** and Colonel **Edwin E. Aldrin, Jr.**, walked on the moon and returned safely to earth. Their spaceship, *Apollo 11*, carried a four-legged landing module, the *Eagle*, which placed them on the moon. When Armstrong descended from the *Eagle* and set foot on the moon he said, that's one small step for man, one giant leap for mankind." Colonel Aldrin joined him later while **Michael Collins**, the third astronaut on the mission, guided *Apollo 11's* command module, the *Columbia*, in orbit around the moon. The world watched this historic event on television.

A year later a Soviet spaceship left a robot on the moon to perform some of the same operations the astronauts had done.

The *Apollo 11* voyage was followed by six additional moon landings during which ten other American astronauts walked on the moon. The program was phased out after the last landing in December 1972.

The Struggle for Equal Rights

A Review: From Slavery to Equality Under the Law

A contingent of 20 blacks arrived in Jamestown, Virginia, in 1619, before the *Mayflower* landed at Plymouth Rock. These 20 Africans came as indentured servants, as did many thousands of whites prior to the American Revolution. However, by the 1640s, blacks were enslaved to work in the sugar, rice, and tobacco fields on Southern plantations as well as to serve as domestics in the homes of their masters. With the invention of the cotton gin in 1793, cotton became the basis of the economy of the South and slavery spread. Since slaves were considered property, they had no legal rights and could be bought and sold according to the owner's whim.

Meanwhile the evils inherent in slavery caused thoughtful people in both the North and the South to seek its end. Jefferson, contemplating slavery in 1784, wrote: "I tremble for my country when I reflect that God is just." By the mid 1800s, many Northerners came to believe that slavery was morally wrong. In the North, **William Lloyd Garrison**, a leading abolitionist, began publishing *The Liberator* in 1831. Anti-slavery societies with nearly a quarter of a million members sprang up in the North and the **underground railroad** was established to help slaves escape to freedom.

At the outbreak of the Civil War, there were more than 4 million slaves in the United States. In the free states of the North there were close to half a million free blacks, many of them former slaves or descendants of slaves. With emancipation and the passage of the Fourteenth Amendment it was thought that equality for blacks would be secure. But this was not to be the case. Blacks were disenfranchised through the use of the poll tax, Grandfather clause, and intimidation. **Jim Crow laws** were passed in the South to separate the races. In *Plessy* v. *Ferguson* (1896) the Supreme Court's doctrine of "**separate but equal**" institutionalized the inferior status of the African Americans in American society. The reversal of this doctrine in *Brown* v. *Board of Education* (1954) opened the way for equality. But its complete attainment remained elusive.

Black Protest, Pride, and Power

With the passage of Jim Crow laws and disenfranchisement in the late 1800s, African Americans sought various means to gain equality. Over the years, they formed various organizations to struggle for their civil rights.

• *The National Association for the Advancement of Colored People (NAACP).* This organization was founded in 1909 by a group of black and white leaders, including **W. E. B. Du Bois**, the black scholar and activist, **Jane Addams**, a white social reformer, and **John Dewey**, a white philosopher-educator. The NAACP provided leadership in the early 20th century in the struggle for civil rights and voting rights for African Americans. It was the NAACP chief counsel, **Thurgood Marshall**, who successfully argued for school integration in *Brown* v. *Board of Education* (1954). Under the leadership of Roy Wilkins, who joined the national staff of NAACP in 1931 and rose to the top position in 1955, the membership grew to over 400,000 by 1977. Its methods also became more militant, supplementing education, lobbying, and court action with demonstrations, sit-ins, and boycotts.

• *The National Urban League.* This organization was founded in 1910 and its efforts first concentrated on helping blacks who had migrated from the South to Northern cities find homes, jobs, and training programs in their new environment.

• *Congress of Racial Equality (CORE).* Another civil rights organization, the **Congress of Racial Equality**, founded in 1942, was committed to nonviolent, direct action to end racial discrimination. Many of its members were recruited on college campuses. Sit-ins and freedom rides were adopted as means to dramatize demands of equal treatment for blacks.

• *Southern Christian Leadership Conference (SCLC).* In 1957, **Dr. Martin Luther King, Jr.**, organized the Southern Christian Leadership Conference (SCLC). This organization provided the leadership for the 1963 **March on Washington**, where a quarter of a million people heard Dr. King deliver the memorable "I Have a Dream" speech at the Lincoln Memorial. The SCLC worked primarily in the South to attain "full citizenship rights, equality, and the integration of the Negro in all aspects of American life." The Reverend **Ralph David Abernathy** became the leader of SCLC after the assassination of Dr. King in 1968.

• *Student Nonviolent Coordinating Committee (SNCC).* Founded in 1960 to eliminate segregation through nonviolent means, it was later led by **Stokely Carmichael** and other more militant leaders who favored "black power." SNCC had a substantial following on college campuses. One technique used by SNCC was to have buses with black and white "freedom riders" tour the South, stopping in various cities to demonstrate against discrimination. Another technique used by SNCC was the sit-in. College students sat at segregated lunch counters until they were served or evicted. In 1964 over 500 SNCC volunteers, blacks and whites, went to Mississippi to work on voter registration.

By 1967, under leader **H. Rap Brown**, SNCC began to resort to violence and discourage white membership. The term "black power" was first used in a march into Jackson, Mississippi, led by **James Meredith**, the first member of the black community to be admitted to the University of Mississippi.

• *Black Muslims.* Elijah Muhammad's **Nation of Islam** (sometimes called the **Black Muslims**) rejected integration and sought to establish a separate African American government in one or more of the United States. Its best known member was **Malcolm X**, who later broke with the Black Muslims and formed his own organization. His followers used "X" as a surname to designate their rejection of names acquired under slavery. A gifted speaker and writer, Malcolm X conveyed a message of hatred against white injustice, which he describes in his widely read *Autobiography*. He had begun to change and speak of alliances with white radicals before he was assassinated in 1965.

• *Civil Unrest.* In August 1965, **Watts**, the black ghetto district of Los Angeles, erupted in a week of terrible rioting. Shooting, burning, and looting resulted in 34 deaths and over 100 wounded. Violence during the "long hot summer" of 1965 was followed by more racial violence the following summer. The unrest reached its peak in the summer of 1967. In Detroit, 38 people died and property damage exceeded $200 million. Newark, New Jersey, and other cities also experienced racial violence. More than 100 riots raged in American cities in the 1960s. The racial violence, following on the heels of the Civil Rights Act of 1964 and the Voting Rights Act of 1965, caused disillusionment and even a backlash. President Johnson, a strong advocate of civil rights, understood the frustration of the African American people and said, "God knows how little we've really moved on this issue despite all the fanfare. As I see it, I've moved the Negro from D+ to C–. He's still nowhere and he knows it. That's why he's out in the streets."

Assassinations of the 1960s

President Kennedy once said, "Those who make peaceful revolution impossible will make violent revolution inevitable." He was assassinated in Dallas in 1963; Dr. Martin Luther King, Jr., was shot to death in Memphis, Tennessee in 1968; and Robert F. Kennedy, whose campaign for the presidency was gaining momentum, was fatally wounded by an assassin's bullet at the Ambassador Hotel in Los Angeles on the night of June 5, 1968.

Exercise Set 6.9

1. Which was *not* included in the Equal Opportunity Act sponsored by President Johnson?
   A. Volunteers in Service to America (VISTA)
   B. A new Department of Housing and Urban Development (HUD)
   C. Loans to college students and to small business
   D. Job- and work-training programs

2. Which was *not* part of President Johnson's program for aid to underprivileged inner-city residents?
   A. Operation Head Start
   B. Medicare and Medicaid
   C. A rent-supplement program
   D. The Alliance for Progress

3. In *Plessy* v. *Ferguson* (1896) the Supreme Court decided that
   A. the Dred Scott Decision was unconstitutional.
   B. the "separate but equal" doctrine was not a violation of the Fourteenth Amendment.
   C. blacks were full-fledged citizens of the United States and of the state wherein they resided.
   D. the Court lacked jurisdiction in that case.

4. The chief counsel of NAACP who argued *Brown* v. *Board of Education* before the Supreme Court was
   A. W. E. B. Du Bois.
   B. Robert C. Weaver.
   C. Thurgood Marshall.
   D. Roy Wilkins.

THE MOVEMENT FOR EQUAL RIGHTS

> The fight must go on. The cause of civil liberty must not be surrendered at the end of one or even one hundred defeats.
> Abraham Lincoln, November 19, 1858

> The core of the civil rights problem is the matter of achieving equal opportunity for Negroes in the labor market. For it stands to reason that all our other civil rights depend on that one for fulfillment. We cannot afford better education for our children, better housing or medical care unless we have jobs.
> Whitney M. Young, Director of the National Urban League, 1968

Truman and Civil Rights

In 1946, President Harry Truman appointed a **President's Committee on Civil Rights**. The Committee issued its report in 1947 in a document entitled "To Secure These Rights" and, based on this report, Truman called on Congress to pass a Fair Employment Practices law, to establish a Civil Rights Commission, to prohibit poll taxes, and to protect the right to vote. This blueprint for civil rights paved the way for a comprehensive civil rights program. Truman did all he could in the face of congressional resistance. He moved toward integration of the armed forces and issued an executive order prohibiting discrimination in employment in federal agencies.

The leading Supreme Court segregation case, *Brown* v. *Board of Education of Topeka* (1954), along with similar cases from South Carolina, Virginia and Delaware, moved through the lower federal courts during the Truman administration. The Supreme Court took jurisdiction and heard arguments in 1952, the last year that Truman was in office, and rendered its unanimous decision two years later.

Civil Rights Legislation

Beginning in the 1950s, laws were passed to ensure equal civil rights for African Americans.

Civil Rights Act of 1957

In 1957, Congress passed the first civil rights law in the 20th century. It established a bipartisan **Civil Rights Commission** with authority to investigate denial of voting rights and/or denial of equal protection as provided in the Fourteenth Amendment. It authorized federal courts to issue injunctions to prevent interference with voting rights.

Civil Rights Act of 1960

The act authorized federal courts to appoint referees with power to evaluate state voting qualifications. Suits could be brought against states, and heavy penalties could be imposed for violations of civil rights.

Civil Rights Act of 1964

This comprehensive civil rights legislation (1) prohibited discrimination in places of public accommodation (hotels and motels); (2) established an **Equal Opportunity Commission** to end job discrimination; (3) strengthened voting rights statutes; and (4) allowed federal funds to be withheld from school districts that violated integration orders.

Voting Rights Act of 1965

This landmark law was designed to end the denial of voting rights to blacks in the South. The act authorized the "appointment of federal examiners . . . to enforce the guarantees of the Fifteenth Amendment." It outlawed literacy tests and other voter-qualification tests in states or counties where fewer than half of those of voting age had registered or voted in 1964. It authorized the use of federal examiners to register voters in counties that practiced voter discrimination.

The act substantially increased the number of African American voters, particularly in the deep South. More than 150,000 black voters were registered in the three years following its passage. In Mississippi, where fewer than 7 percent of voting-age blacks were registered prior to the 1965 law, close to 60 percent were on the voting rolls in 1968.

Civil Rights Act of 1968

The last of the civil rights legislation passed during the Johnson administration contained a strong open-housing provision that prohibited discrimination in the sale or rental of housing. It also provided penalties for persons who intimidated or injured civil rights workers and for those who traveled from one state to another to "incite, organize, promote, encourage, participate in, or carry on a riot."

Twenty-Fourth Amendment

The Twenty-Fourth Amendment to the Constitution, ratified in January 1964, abolished the poll tax in federal elections.

Court Decisions

Besides legislation to end discrimination and ensure equal civil rights, African Americans also received support for equal rights from the courts.

- *NAACP* v. *St. Louis-San Francisco Railway Company.* In this 1955 case the Interstate Commerce Commission ruled that segregation on interstate trains and buses was illegal.

- *Brown* v. *Board of Education of Topeka (1954).* This case struck down racial segregation in the public schools.

- *Baker* v. *Carr (1962).* This case involved the apportionment of legislative districts. Those who brought the case contended that failure by the state of Tennessee to redraw and reapportion districts for election to the state legislature for 60 years constituted a denial of "the equal protection of the laws accorded them by the Fourteenth Amendment by virtue of the debasement of their votes." The Court's ruling in this case, frequently referred to as "**one man, one vote**," was a major victory for equal representation in the state legislatures. This was particularly significant in crowded areas where blacks and poor people generally were underrepresented.

- *Heart of Atlanta Motel* v. *United States (1964).* In the area of civil rights the Court declared that Congress had the power under its authority to control interstate trade to forbid racial discrimination in motels and hotels serving interstate travelers.

The Drive for Equal Rights for Women

The colonial patriarchal tradition, derived from Europe, established the principle of the father's primary authority in the home, in the world of work, in politics, and in the church. Women in the 17th and 18th centuries had no political rights and were generally considered inferior.

- *The 19th Century.* During the period of reform between 1820 and the 1840s, the women's rights movement began. The first women's rights convention was held at **Seneca Falls**, New York, in 1848. The delegates adopted a Declaration of Sentiments that said, "All men and women are created equal" and listed demands for political, social, and economic equality with men. The earliest victories came in education as some schools were gradually opened to women, starting in the 1840s and 1850s.

Prominent 19th-century feminist leaders included **Susan B. Anthony**, a relentless advocate of women's suffrage; **Lucy Stone**, who was both a women's rights advocate and an abolitionist; **Elizabeth Cady Stanton**, the philosopher of the 19th century feminist movement; and **Lucretia Mott**, feminist, abolitionist, and a founder of Swarthmore College. **Harriet Tubman** and **Sojourner Truth**, better known for their efforts to free their people from slavery, were also ardent advocates of women's suffrage. **Carrie Chapman Catt**, in the early 20th century, carried forward the effort for women's suffrage.

The Modern Women's Movement

> We can no longer ignore that voice within women that says: "I want something more than my husband and my children and my home."
> Betty Friedan, in *The Feminine Mystique* (1963)

• *Kennedy Commission and the 1964 Civil Rights Act.* In 1963 President Kennedy appointed a Commission on the Status of Women headed by **Eleanor Roosevelt**. The Commission report disclosed that discrimination against women was rampant in virtually every aspect of American life. The following year, Congress passed the **Civil Rights Act** of 1964, designed to protect the civil rights of blacks. However, it also contained a provision pertaining to women's rights. The provision was introduced as an amendment to **Title VII** of the act banning discrimination on the basis of sex as well as race and made discrimination in employment on the basis of sex a violation of federal law.

• *NOW, 1966 to Present.* The **National Organization for Women** (**NOW**) was founded by **Betty Friedan** in 1966. NOW used strikes, boycotts, and demonstrations to attain equality with men in all aspects of life in the 1960s and 1970s.

As the **women's liberation** movement gained momentum, women sought equal pay for equal work, equal opportunity for promotion, the right to maternity leave without loss of job or seniority, advancement to positions of responsibility and authority in government, industry, and in the professions, recognition of the value of work in the home, participation of men in the duties and responsibilities traditionally performed by women, recognition in textbooks of women's role in history, and a more positive image in the media than the traditional one of sex symbol.

NOW has continued to agitate for women's rights, particularly for the adoption of the **Equal Rights Amendment**. The organization includes both women and men in its membership. Its agenda comprises a broad spectrum of social reforms, including affordable child care, LGBT rights, pay equity, keeping abortion and birth control legal, greater research on diseases such as breast cancer, and reducing military expenditures.

• *Shifting Roles and Images.* The roles and images of male and female in our society have undergone radical transformation in one generation. The idea of the wife as homemaker and the husband as breadwinner has given way to one of equal responsibility for home and work.

• *The Equal Rights Amendment (ERA).* The recognition that women often received the poorest paying jobs in the work force and that they were generally paid lower wages (sometimes as little as one-half those paid to men for the same work), led to a demand by the National Women's Party in 1923 for the adoption of an Equal Rights Amendment to the Constitution. This would force states and cities to change laws and end practices that discriminated against women.

An Equal Rights Amendment was introduced in Congress in 1923 and every year thereafter until 1948, but failed to pass. During the ensuing years the measure was bottled up in the Judiciary Committee of the House of Representatives. It was finally forced out of Committee in 1970 and passed with an overwhelming vote in the House. Two years later it was approved by the necessary two-thirds vote in the Senate and sent to the states for ratification by the state legislatures. Approval by three fourths of the states, as required by Article V of the Constitution for ratification of amendments, proved difficult to attain.

The original time limit for ratification was set at March 22, 1979 (seven years after it was submitted by Congress to the states). Although the deadline was extended to June 30, 1982, it nevertheless failed to be ratified since by that date only 35 of the necessary 38 states (three-fourths of the 50 states) had voted approval.

• *Roe v. Wade (1973).* In a 7 to 2 decision, written for the Court by Justice **Harry Blackmun**, the constitutional right of a woman to have an abortion was recognized. The Court held that this was part of the right to privacy implied by the **Bill of Rights**. The decision gave unqualified abortion rights to the pregnant woman during the first trimester (3 months), permitted the states to place limitations during the second trimester, and affirmed the right of the state to prohibit abortion during the final trimester except when the mother's life was in jeopardy.

With the appointment of three new justices by President Reagan and the elevation of Justice **William H. Rehnquist** to the position of Chief Justice, it was widely believed that the decision might be overturned. The Court agreed to hear challenges to the decision during its 1988–1989 term. On July 3, 1989, in *Webster* v. *Reproductive Health Services*, the Court upheld a restrictive Missouri abortion law, stopping just short of overturning *Roe* v. *Wade*. By a 5 to 4 vote, in an opinion written by Chief Justice William H. Rehnquist, the Court indicated that it no longer considered abortion to be a woman's fundamental right. The determination was left up to the individual states.

• *Equality in the Workplace.* During the 1970s and 1980s women entered the work force in ever-increasing numbers. Barriers fell as prestigious colleges became coeducational, women entered the professions on a par with men, and engaged in work such as mining, construction, heavy industry, transportation, police, and other arduous and dangerous jobs previously regarded as exclusively male occupations.

Admission of women to the service academies—West Point, Annapolis, and the Air Force Academy—began in 1976. By 1980 there were 19,000 women officers in the armed forces including a number of generals and admirals. In 2010 women made up 20 percent of the U.S. military forces. Women were governors of states, members of the Senate, and judges on both the federal and state benches. Thousands of women held legislative and judicial offices in the states. **Sandra Day O'Connor** became the first woman member of the Supreme Court in 1981 as the first Reagan appointee to the Court. Justice O'Connor has been followed by Ruth Bader Ginsburg (1993), Sonia Sotomayor (2009), and Elena Kagan (2010). In 1984 **Geraldine Ferraro** was the first woman vice-presidential candidate.

• *Affirmative Action.* In 1965 President Johnson signed an executive order requiring employers on federal contracts to take "affirmative action" to bring the number of women, African Americans, Hispanics, Native Americans, and Asians into better balance with the number of men and whites employed. The rationale was to correct past injustices done to these groups by giving preferences in employment, college admissions, and appointments to members of the disadvantaged categories who were equally qualified. The implementation of this directive aroused resentment and anger as some white men contended they were the victims of "reverse discrimination" based on past injustices to which they were not a party.

The Supreme Court faced this issue in two cases during the 1970s. In the case of *Regents of the University of California* v. *Bakke* (1978), the Court ruled 5 to 4 that the University of California at Davis, which was receiving federal funds, had acted unconstitutionally in setting up a 16 percent admission quota for minority students in its medical school, thus denying admission to **Allan Bakke**, a white applicant who was better qualified than some minority applicants admitted under their quota.

But in a 1979 case, *Kaiser Aluminum Co.* v. *Weber* (1979), Brian Weber sued the Kaiser Aluminum and Chemical Corporation when he was denied a place in a training program for advancement because less qualified black applicants were admitted under the 50 percent quota. The Court ruled 5 to 4 that this private company was within its constitutional right to adopt this quota system in an attempt to overcome past "patterns of social segregation and hierarchy."

Rising Consciousness of Hispanic Americans

Background

Spanish-speaking Americans (Hispanics or Latinos) have a cultural background reaching back to Columbus and before. Settlers from Spain have been in the Americas since 1492. Texas, New Mexico, Arizona, Utah, Nevada, California, and part of Colorado were part of Spanish-speaking Mexico until the middle of the 19th century. Puerto Ricans, whose culture is Hispanic, came under American rule about a century ago (1898), and became American citizens even more recently (1917). Cuba was part of the Spanish empire for four centuries before the Spanish-American War (1898).

Immigration

The term "**Chicanos**" designates Mexican-Americans, while the Mexicans refer to Americans as "Anglos." By the early 1990s there were more than 15 million Chicanos in the United States, though the actual number is certainly much larger because of illegal immigration. Many came during the Mexican Revolution, which caused turmoil in Mexico from 1910 until the end of World War I. Immigration was spurred by the demand for migrant labor to pick fruits and vegetables in California, Arizona, New Mexico, and Texas. Those who chose to remain, often without legal status, settled in the "barrios" (inner city neighborhoods—generally slums) of Los Angeles and other cities of the Southwest. As economic conditions worsened in Mexico, illegal immigration skyrocketed. These immigrants became the poorest-paid workers in the textile industry, in restaurants, as domestics, on farms, factories, ranches, and estates.

Migration from Puerto Rico to the United States on a permanent basis became legal after 1917, when Puerto Ricans became American citizens. By the early 1990s there were about 2 million Puerto Ricans living in the United States, chiefly in New York and other cities of the Northeast.

Immigration of Cubans to the United States dates from the overthrow of the **Batista** regime in Cuba in 1959 by revolutionary forces led by **Fidel Castro**. About 1 million Cubans fled to the United States, and most settled in the Miami, Florida, area.

After the attempt to overthrow the Castro regime failed at the Bay of Pigs (1961), the United States imposed an economic blockade. Despite the hardships suffered by the people of Cuba, Castro remained in power with considerable help from his communist ally, the Soviet Union. This aid vanished in 1989 with the demise of the Soviets. As economic conditions became intolerable, many Cubans attempted to escape to the United States. In 1994, the trickle became a deluge as Cubans began to arrive on rafts and by other hastily improvised means. Many were picked up at sea by the U.S. Coast Guard and taken to "temporary" quarters at the U.S. naval base at Guantanamo Bay in Cuba. By October 1994, there were over 15,000 Cubans at Guantanamo.

During the 1980s the Hispanic population of the United States grew four times as fast as the total population, reaching nearly 24 million or about 10 percent of the U.S. population. As of July 1, 2009, the estimated Hispanic population of the United States was 48.4 million; 16 percent of the U.S. population.

César Chavez

In 1963, César Chavez, a Chicano who had been a migrant farm worker, emerged as a leader of the exploited Mexican workers. He established the **United Farm Workers Organizing Committee** and led the union in a strike against the powerful grape growers of California. After a five-year struggle, during which he went on a 25-day fast to prevail upon his members to renounce violence, the union won contracts providing for an increase in pay and better working conditions.

Luis Muñoz Marin

Marin, a charismatic public figure, led Puerto Rico to "Commonwealth" status—partway between independence and statehood—within the United States. He was elected Governor of Puerto Rico in 1952. To raise the standard of living, he instituted a program called "Operation Bootstrap," whereby the resources of the Commonwealth—people, capital, and natural endowments—were marshaled to increase per capita income. The income level did rise, but it remained far below that of the United States, so many Puerto Ricans chose to come to or remain in the United States. The people of Puerto Rico are divided about their political relationship with the United States. The major-ity prefer Commonwealth status, which gives them U.S. citizenship without requiring them to pay federal taxes on money earned in Puerto Rico. As a self-governing Commonwealth, they do not vote in U.S. national elections for President and Vice President, nor do they elect members to the Senate or House of Representatives. They do have representation in Congress by a resident com-missioner, who can speak but does not have a vote.

Hispanic Power

With growing numbers in the United States and a rising ethnic conscious-ness, Hispanics have become more aggressive in seeking recognition in eco-nomic, political, and cultural aspects of American life.

The time when the use of Spanish in the public schools was forbidden, as it was for a time in Texas, is long gone. Indeed in a number of states, English is now taught as a second language to Spanish-speaking immigrant children, who are instructed in Spanish in public schools until they become proficient in English. In many cities, election laws mandate the printing of ballots and other election instructions in both English and Spanish. Spanish has become the number one language taught in the public schools of the United States. Fear that Spanish might force the United States to become a bilingual coun-try, as French did in Canada, has caused a severe backlash and a strong move-ment for legislation to establish English legally as the sole official language of the United States.

Equality for Native Americans: American Indian Movement (AIM)

The relationship between the U.S. government and Native Americans is, for the most part, shameful. In his book, *Custer Died for Your Sins*, **Vine Deloria, Jr.**, who is a Standing Rock Sioux and former Executive Director of the **National Congress of American Indians**, writes: "America has yet to keep one Indian treaty or agreement despite the fact that the United States government signed four hundred such treaties and agreements with Indian tribes."

When whites arrived in America, there were an estimated 850,000 Indians in what is now the lower 48 states. By 1890 that population had declined to 250,000. Since then, it has come back and surpassed the original number, but the economic status of Native Americans remains severely depressed. The 2010 census indicates that Native Americans comprise 0.9 percent of the U.S. population. An Indian is three times as likely to be unemployed as is a non-Indian living in the United States.

Alcatraz

In the 1960s Native Americans began to show a new militancy as they witnessed the developing counterculture of other disaffected Americans. In 1969, 78 Native Americans seized and held **Alcatraz Island**, a former federal prison, in San Francisco Bay. They were finally ousted by federal marshals, but not before nationwide publicity had brought their cause to the attention of the American public.

Wounded Knee (1973)

Indian Power manifested itself in surprising acts of defiance. In 1972, militant members of **AIM** (the **American Indian Movement**) occupied the Washington, D.C., offices of the Bureau of Indian Affairs, demanding that the Bureau be put in the hands of Indians and that treaty promises made to Indians be honored. They remained in control of the building for a week while talks were held with officials of the Department of the Interior.

A year later, about 200 armed members of AIM took control of the village of **Wounded Knee** on the Oglala Sioux Pine Ridge Reservation in South Dakota. They remained in the village for two months, during which violence broke out repeatedly in fighting with government agents. Major buildings were destroyed by the occupants and two Indians were killed in the fighting. The decision to occupy Wounded Knee was symbolic: it was near there that the last Indian resistance was broken when the U.S. 7th cavalry killed **Sitting Bull** and massacred 200 men, women, and children in 1890.

Example of Treaty Violation

The building of **Kinzua Dam** in western New York in the early 1960s inundated a large part of the Seneca reservation. Flooding the Indians out of their ancestral homeland was a violation of the **Pickering Treaty** of 1794, negotiated between the United States and the Seneca tribe of the Iroquois Nation and signed by George Washington as President of the United States.

Exercise Set 6.10

1. Of the five major civil rights acts passed during the period 1957–1968, the Voting Rights Act of 1965 is often regarded as the most far-reaching because
   A. prior to 1965 there was no legal guarantee of the right to vote for African Americans.
   B. protection of the right to vote was regarded as a means whereby other basic rights could be secured.
   C. voting rights would put an end to riots and racial violence.
   D. Martin Luther King, Jr., was a strong advocate of the Voting Rights Act of 1965.

2. The Supreme Court decision in *Baker* v. *Carr* (1962), involving reapportionment of state legislative districts, was a necessary complement to the 1965 Voting Rights Act because
   A. it protected voting rights in state elections.
   B. the decision established the supremacy of federal over state voting regulations.
   C. voting rights were reduced in practice by voting districts that were substantially unequal.
   D. the appeal came from Tennessee, a state not directly involved in voting rights.

3. The National Organization for Women (NOW)
   A. was founded in 1948 by Eleanor Roosevelt.
   B. took the lead in support of the Civil Rights Act of 1964.
   C. receives overt or tacit support from virtually all women.
   D. includes in its membership both women and men.

4. An Equal Rights Amendment to the Constitution
   A. was first proposed in 1970.
   B. was declared unconstitutional by the Supreme Court.
   C. failed to be approved by two-thirds of each house of Congress.
   D. failed to be ratified by the necessary three-fourths of state legislatures.

5. Women's organizations, for example—the National Organization of Women (NOW)—favored an Equal Rights Amendment (ERA) primarily because
   A. there is only one woman on the Supreme Court.
   B. women in many jobs still receive lower pay than men for the same work.
   C. educational opportunities for women are limited.
   D. recent gains may be lost without a constitutional amendment.

6. In the last decades of the 20th century, Native Americans
   A. ceased to be a recognizable ethnic group because of intermarriage.
   B. steadily declined in population since the arrival of Europeans.
   C. demanded a return of territory taken from them in violation of treaties with the American government.
   D. no longer lived on reservations.

CHAPTER REVIEW QUESTIONS

1. The Supreme Court decision that overturned a previous 19th-century civil rights case was
   A. *Pennsylvania Association for Retarded Children (PARC)* v. *Commonwealth of Pennsylvania.*
   B. *Baker* v. *Carr.*
   C. *Brown* v. *Board of Education.*
   D. *Regents of the University of California* v. *Bakke.*

2. African Americans realized they could not escape from the ghetto unless
   A. the right to vote was guaranteed.
   B. open housing was assured.
   C. children could be bused to integrated schools.
   D. Black Power succeeded in establishing businesses owned and operated by blacks.

3. The President responsible for beginning the program to land astronauts on the moon was
   A. Truman.
   B. Eisenhower.
   C. Kennedy.
   D. Johnson.

4. Which is a valid generalization about U.S. relationships with Latin America in the last 100 years?
   A. The success of democracy in Latin America is due largely to United States intervention.
   B. Latin American resentment of the United States is due to Communist influence.
   C. The United States has gradually realized that events in Latin America have little bearing on United States security.
   D. Economic interests have generally influenced United States policy toward Latin America.

5. Which of the following describes the program of the Kennedy Administration?
   A. Great Society
   B. New Deal
   C. New Freedom
   D. New Frontier

6. The Kerner Commission reported: "Our nation is moving toward two societies, one black, one white—separate and unequal." The major reason for the failure to solve the race problem is
   A. failure of the black community to agree on a proper course of action.
   B. preoccupation of administrations in Washington with foreign affairs.
   C. lack of concern coupled with racism in the white society.
   D. unfavorable Supreme Court decisions.

Directions: Write a well-organized essay that includes an introduction, several paragraphs addressing the task below, and a conclusion.

Theme: Civic Values and Citizenship

> Although the Reconstruction Period (1865–1870) saw the nationalization of civil rights with the addition of the Thirteenth, Fourteenth, and Fifteenth Amendments to the Constitution, it was not until nearly 100 years later that federal legislation and Supreme Court decisions started to enforce many of the rights granted in those amendments.

Task:

> From your study of the 1950s and 1960s, identify *three* actions by the federal government (legislation or Supreme Court decisions) that furthered the rights previously granted in the Thirteenth, Fourteenth, and Fifteenth Amendments.
>
> For each action:
>
> - Identify the action or Supreme Court decision.
> - Discuss the civil rights issue that necessitated the action.
> - Describe how the legislation or Supreme Court action helped address the civil rights issue.

You may use any examples of federal legislation or Supreme Court decisions that occurred in the 1950s and 1960s. Some suggestions you may wish to consider are *Brown* v. *Board of Education* (1954), *Baker* v. *Carr* (1962), Civil Rights Act of 1957, Civil Rights Act of 1960, Civil Rights Act of 1964, Voting Rights Act of 1965, and the Civil Rights Act of 1968.

You are *not* limited to these suggestions.

DOCUMENT-BASED QUESTION

The following questions (Part A and Part B) are based on the accompanying documents (1–6). Some of these documents have been edited for the purpose of this exercise. The question is designed to test your ability to work with historical documents and to demonstrate your knowledge of the subject matter being presented. As you analyze the documents, take into account both the source of the document and the author's point of view.

Historical Context:

> At different times in the history of the United States, poignant protest against the policies of government and practices of society have been expressed through song. Bob Dylan's lyrics during the 1960s and 1970s addressed numerous issues including civil rights and war.

Task:

> Using information from the documents and your knowledge of United States history, answer the questions that follow each document in Part A. Your answers to the questions will help you write the Part B essay, in which you will be asked:
>
> From the documents, discuss some of the issues that were addressed and discuss how the popular music of protest was able to bring widespread attention to the issues mentioned.

Part A
Short-Answer Questions

The documents provided are excerpts from various songs by Bob Dylan (hereinafter referred to as "the author"). Examine each document carefully and then answer the questions which follow.

DOCUMENT 1

Come you masters of war
You that build all the guns
You that build the death planes
You that build the big bombs
You that hide behind walls
You that hide behind desks
I just want you to know
I can see through your masks

You fasten the triggers
For others to fire
Then you sit back and watch
When the death count gets higher
You hide in your mansion
As young people's blood
Flows out of their bodies
And is buried in the mud

And I hope that you die
And your death'll come soon
I will follow your casket
In the pale afternoon
And I'll watch while you're lowered
Down to your deathbed
And I'll stand o'er your grave
'Til I'm sure that you're dead

—Bob Dylan, "Masters of War" (1963)

1. Who are the "Masters of War" referred to in the selected lyrics from the song?

_____

_____

_____

_____

2. What is the relationship portrayed in the song between the "Masters of War" and those who actually fight the wars?

_____

_____

_____

_____

DOCUMENT 2

Medgar Evers, head of the National Association for the Advancement of Colored People (NAACP) and a war veteran was murdered outside his home on June 11, 1963, the very evening that President Kennedy made a passionate plea to the American people for the passage of stronger civil rights legislation. Dylan's "Only a Pawn in Their Game" was written shortly thereafter.

A bullet from the back of a bush took Medgar Evers' blood. . . .

A South politician preaches to the poor white man,
"You got more than the blacks, don't complain.
You're better than them, you been born with white skin," they explain.
And the Negro's name
Is used it is plain
For the politician's gain
As he rises to fame
And the poor white remains
On the caboose of the train
But it ain't him to blame
He's only a pawn in their game.

The deputy sheriffs, the soldiers, the governors get paid,
And the marshalls and cops get the same.
But the poor white man's used in the hands of them all like a tool.
He's taught in his school
From the start by the rule
That the laws are with him
To protect his white skin
To keep up his hate
So he never thinks straight
'Bout the shape that he's in
But it ain't him to blame
He's only a pawn in their game.

—Bob Dylan, "Only a Pawn in Their Game" (1963)

3. How do the verses quoted above suggest that the politician is using the poor white population?

_____

_____

_____

_____

DOCUMENT 3

> How many roads must a man walk down
> Before you call him a man?
> Yes, 'n how many seas must a white dove sail
> Before she sleeps in the sand?
> Yes 'n how many times must the cannon balls fly
> Before they are forever banned?
> The answer, my friend, is blowin' in the wind,
> The answer is blowin' in the wind.
>
> How many years can a mountain exist
> Before it is washed to the sea?
> Yes, 'n how many years can some people exist
> Before they are allowed to be free?
> Yes, 'n how many times can a man turn his head,
> Pretending he just doesn't see?
> The answer, my friend, is blowin' in the wind,
> The answer is blowin' in the wind.

—Bob Dylan, "Blowin' in the Wind" (1962)

4. What two issues in particular does the author address in the two verses from "Blowin' in the Wind"?

_____

_____

_____

_____

DOCUMENT 4

Emmett Till was a 14-year-old black child from Chicago visiting a relative in Mississippi in 1955. After making a comment to a white woman in a local store, he was taken by a group of white men, beaten, tortured, murdered, and left in a nearby pond. Those charged with the murder were acquitted by an all-white Mississippi jury.

'Twas down in Mississippi not so long ago,
When a young boy from Chicago town stepped through a Southern
  door.
This boy's dreadful tragedy I can still remember well,
The color of his skin was black and his name was Emmett Till.

And then to stop the United States of yelling for a trial,
Two brothers they confessed that they had killed poor Emmett Till.
But on the jury there were men who helped the brothers commit
  this awful crime,
And so this trial was a mockery, but nobody seemed to mind.

I saw the morning papers but I could not bear to see
The smiling brothers walkin' down the courthouse stairs.
For the jury found them innocent and the brothers they went free,
While Emmett's body floats the foam of a Jim Crow southern sea.

—Bob Dylan, "The Death of Emmett Till" (1963)

5. How is the Mississippi trial presented in the lyrics by the author?

_____

_____

_____

_____

6. In your opinion, why has the reference to Jim Crow been made in the song "The Death of Emmett Till"?

_____

_____

_____

_____

DOCUMENT 5

. . . I've stumbled on the side of twelve misty mountains
I've walked and I've crawled on six crooked highways,
I've stepped in the middle of seven sad forests,
I've been out in front of a dozen dead oceans,
I've been ten thousand miles in the mouth of a graveyard,
And it's a hard, and it's a hard, it's a hard, and it's a hard,
And it's a hard rain's a-gonna fall.

. . . I saw a black branch with blood that kept drippin',
I saw a room full of men with their hammers a-bleedin' . . .
I saw guns and sharp swords in the hands of young children . . .

I'll walk to the depths of the deepest black forest,
Where the people are many and there hands are all empty,
Where the pellets of poison are flooding their waters,
Where the home in the valley meets the damp dirty prison,
Where the executioner's face is always well hidden . . .

—Bob Dylan, "A Hard Rain's A-Gonna Fall" (1963)

7. The author appears to be discussing a number of tragic issues in "A Hard Rain's A-Gonna Fall." Identify three of the issues mentioned in the lyrics above.

_____

_____

_____

_____

DOCUMENT 6

Bob Dylan wrote "Hurricane" in response to what he and many others felt was the wrongful conviction and imprisonment of middle-weight boxing contender Rubin Carter.

> Meanwhile, far away in another part of town
> Rubin Carter and a couple of friends are drivin' around.
> Number one contender for the middleweight crown
> Had no idea what kind shit was about to go down
> When a cop pulled him over to the side of the road
> Just like the time before and the time before that.
> In Paterson that's just the way things go.
> If you're black you might as well not show up on the street
> 'Less you wanna draw the heat.

—Bob Dylan, "Hurricane" (1975)

8. How does the author see the treatment of blacks in Paterson, New Jersey, compared to the treatment of others?

_____

_____

_____

_____

Part B
Essay

Your essay should be well organized with an introductory paragraph that states your position on the question. Develop your position in the next paragraphs and then write a conclusion. In your essay, include specific historical details and refer to the specific documents you analyzed in Part A. You may include additional information from your knowledge of social studies.

Historical Context:

> At different times in the history of the United States, poignant protest against the policies of government and practices of society have been expressed through song. Bob Dylan's lyrics during the 1960s and 1970s addressed numerous issues including civil rights and war.

Task:

> Using information from the documents and your knowledge of United States history, discuss some of the issues that were addressed and discuss how the popular music of protest was able to bring widespread attention to the issues mentioned.

Guidelines:

In your essay, be sure to
• Develop all aspects of the task.
• Incorporate information from *at least five* documents.
• Incorporate relevant outside information.
• Support the theme with many relevant facts, examples, and details.
• Use a logical and clear plan of organization, including an introduction and a conclusion that are beyond a restatement of the theme.

CHAPTER 4

THE LIMITS OF POWER: TURMOIL
AT HOME AND ABROAD (1965–1972)

INVOLVEMENT IN ASIA

Prior to the 19th Century

United States involvement in Asia is not a recent development.

• *The China Trade.* In 1787 the Boston ship *Columbia*, loaded with ginseng, made a historic voyage from Boston to Oregon, where it picked up furs, and sailed across the Pacific Ocean to China, where it traded its cargo for tea and silk. The *Columbia* returned home in 1790, beginning a regular and profitable trade between the United States and China. From the late 1790s on, the China trade increased, and by 1850 the swift American clipper ships carried on most of the trade. After the **Opium War** with Britain (1839–1842), China opened more of its ports to trade. Prior to this, only Canton had been open to trade. In 1844, the American diplomat **Caleb Cushing** traveled to China with four warships and received generous trade arrangements for the United States. In the 1840s the first Chinese immigrants began to arrive in San Francisco. Chinese laborers were brought to California to help build the transcontinental railroads.

The 19th Century

The 19th century saw increased United States involvement in Asia.

• *Opening of Japan.* President **Millard Fillmore**, seeking trade with Japan, sent a special mission headed by **Commodore Matthew C. Perry**, that arrived in Tokyo Bay in 1853. He returned the following year with a fleet of seven warships and negotiated the Treaty of Kanagawa, a treaty of peace, friendship, and commerce. The Japanese, confronted with superior American power, agreed to open several ports to United States trade.

• *19th-Century Imperialism in Asia.* The United States became an imperial power in Asia toward the end of the 19th century by acquiring the Hawaiian Islands and Samoa in 1898 and the Philippine Islands from Spain at the conclusion of the Spanish-American War. Events in China at the close of the 19th century prompted Secretary of State **John Hay** to propose in 1899 the "**Open Door Policy**" for trade with China. This policy declared that China should be open to all nations on an equal basis. Hay announced (March 20, 1900) that the acceptance of the Open Door Policy by the major powers (Germany, Russia, Britain, France, Italy, and Japan) was "final and definitive." The United States returned to China part of the money awarded for damages resulting from the **Boxer Rebellion** of the same year.

The 20th Century

By the 20th century, the United States had become a major power, and its contacts with all areas of the world, including Asia, increased.

• *Theodore Roosevelt and the Russo-Japanese War.* In 1905, President Theodore Roosevelt helped bring to an end the war in Asia between Japan and Russia when he met with the envoys of the warring powers at Portsmouth, New Hampshire. He was awarded the Nobel Peace Prize for this act.

• *World War I (1914–1918).* While the war was fought primarily in Europe, there were repercussions in Asia. Japan joined the war against Germany in 1914. At the peace negotiations at Versailles, Japan acquired several islands in the Pacific previously held by Germany and was made a permanent member of the Council of the League of Nations.

• *World War II (1939–1945).* Asia was a major battleground of World War II. At the conclusion of the war, the United States had become the leading world power and a great power in Asia. The challenge was now perceived to be from the Soviet Union, itself a major power in Asia, the Middle East, and Europe.

• *The Korean War (1950–1953).* By prompt action, the United States and the UN prevented all of Korea from becoming a Communist outpost in Asia.

The French-Indochina War

The French in Indochina

Vietnam was part of a French colonial empire in Indochina that also included **Cambodia** and **Laos**. During World War II the Japanese took control of Indochina from the French and made it part of their "greater East Asia co-prosperity sphere." When the war ended, France attempted to reestablish its control over Vietnam. However, in 1946 the **Viet Minh**, a group of revolutionary nationalists and Communists led by **Ho Chi Minh**, began a war to drive out the French and their anti-Communist allies led by **Bao Dai**. In 1950, after it was found that Communist China was aiding the Viet Minh, President Truman sent military equipment and economic aid to the Vietnamese and French armies. Although President Eisenhower believed that a French defeat might lead to the Communist domination of Southeast Asia, he did not send American troops to war. He did continue to send military equipment, and the United States paid for much of the cost of the war. The civil war went on for eight years until a decisive battle at Dien Bien Phu in May 1954 resulted in the defeat of the French. After the fall of Dien Bien Phu to the Communists, the French withdrew from Indochina and the Communist Viet Minh took over North Vietnam.

An international conference was held at Geneva, Switzerland, attended by representatives of both Vietnams, France, Great Britain, the Soviet Union, the People's Republic of China, and the United States. At the Geneva conference, the independence of Cambodia, Laos, and Vietnam was recognized. Vietnam was divided along the 17th parallel into North Vietnam and South Vietnam. North Vietnam became a Communist state under the leadership of Ho Chi Minh. South Vietnam became a republic and was led by Ngo Dinh Diem. Provision was made for elections to be held in 1956 to reunite Vietnam, but the elections were never held. Neither South Vietnam nor the United States signed these accords. When the time for the election to unify Vietnam arrived (July 1956), Ngo Dinh Diem, with approval of the United States, refused to participate in the election. He was convinced that he would lose to Communist North Vietnam, and American intelligence sources agreed with this conclusion.

The War in Vietnam

The Domino Theory

The American attempt to prevent a Communist victory in Vietnam was based primarily on the fear that such a victory would result in the spread of communism in Asia. According to President Eisenhower's domino theory, ". . . you knock over the first one [domino—in this case, Vietnam] and . . . the last one . . . will go over very quickly." Americans feared that the dominoes in Southeast Asia might include not only Indochina but also Thailand, Malaysia, Indonesia, the Philippines, and Burma, since each of these countries was also facing problems with Communist insurgencies.

Early American Involvement in Vietnam

• *Under Eisenhower.* President Eisenhower offered economic aid to South Vietnam soon after the Geneva Conference in 1954 and began sending **military advisors** there.

• *Under Kennedy and Johnson.* The war in South Vietnam carried on by the **Viet Cong**, Communist guerrilla forces aided by the North Vietnamese, was going badly for the South Vietnamese government. Consequently, President Kennedy, who also believed in the domino theory, increased the number of American military advisers.

In 1954 the United States had helped to install **Ngo Dinh Diem** in power in Saigon. In May 1963, Diem's troops killed nine Buddhists taking part in an anti-Diem demonstration in Hué. The demonstrators were protesting a government order barring the flying of flags and processions on Buddha's birthday. On June 11 the first of seven monks committed suicide by burning himself to death in Saigon to dramatize protest of government policies toward Buddhists. On November 1, 1963, a military coup deposed and assassinated Diem. The United States welcomed the coup but denied direct involvement.

When Lyndon Johnson became President (November 22, 1963) there were 15,000 American troops, including "Green Beret" special forces, in Vietnam. By January 1965, when Johnson began his full four-year term, there were 23,000 American troops in Vietnam.

Johnson and the Escalation of the War

In August 1964, two United States destroyers were reportedly fired upon by North Vietnamese patrol boats in the Gulf of Tonkin, off the coast of North Vietnam. At the time it was not known that these U.S. naval vessels, with President Johnson's approval, were cooperating with the South Vietnamese in raids on the North Vietnamese coastal areas. Johnson called these incidents "unprovoked attacks" and ordered retaliatory air raids on North Vietnam. He asked Congress for wider authority to take military action. On August 7, 1964, Congress overwhelmingly passed the **Gulf of Tonkin Resolution** authorizing the President to "take all necessary measures to repel any armed attack against the forces of the United States and to prevent further aggression."

The Gulf of Tonkin Resolution marked a turning point in the war and led to the beginning of large-scale American involvement. In February 1965 Johnson began the bombing of North Vietnam, which continued until 1968. More American troops were sent to Vietnam and committed to combat. Before this, Americans had served as military advisers. As American involvement increased, so too did North Vietnamese involvement. Supplies were sent from the north, and for the first time troops from North Vietnam went south to fight with the Viet Cong.

Prior to the November 1964 election Johnson said, "We will seek no wider war." He also told the voters, "We are not going to send American boys nine or ten thousand miles away from home to do what Asian boys ought to be doing for themselves." His Republican opponent, Barry Goldwater, called for more intensive bombing of North Vietnam. In the presidential election, the voters gave Johnson an overwhelming victory—more than 60 percent of the popular vote and a 486 to 52 triumph in the electoral college. It was clear that the people wanted no wider war in Asia, and Johnson was their "peace candidate." However, soon after the election Johnson proceeded to widen the war. In February 1965 after an attack on an American base in South Vietnam, Johnson ordered an escalation in the war. American planes began to bomb North Vietnam, and in June 1965 U.S. field commanders were authorized to send American troops into combat. By November 1966 the U.S.

had 358,000 troops in Vietnam. By the middle of 1968, the number exceeded half a million.

Opposition to the Vietnam War

Early Opposition

From the very beginning, a few well-placed voices spoke out against the war. Some senators opposed the war because Americans were being drafted and sent into combat without a declaration of war by Congress. Heavy casualties were being incurred. The bombardment and the overwhelming fire power of the American forces were proving ineffective in the jungle against the hit-and-run guerrilla tactics of the Viet Cong.

Draft Resistance

At home the war was brought into people's living rooms on television screens. As they watched the horrors of war, Americans began to oppose the war, because there was no consensus as to what we were fighting for in Vietnam. Many young men sought to avoid the draft by failing to register or by seeking exemptions. Some fled to Canada, Sweden, and other foreign sanctuaries. Quotas were filled quickly in the National Guard and Coast Guard, two branches of the service not generally assigned to overseas duty.

Intensified Opposition

By 1967 many leading senators were openly demanding U.S. withdrawal from Vietnam. In an effort to answer the opposition, President Johnson addressed the nation on September 29, 1967, and once again used the domino theory to support the war.

But the nation did not accept the President's explanation. **Peace marches** and **protest meetings** throughout the United States showed the deep disaffection. Others were frustrated over the way the war was being fought, and many Americans believed that "hold back" tactics were being used. By March 1968, polls showed that only 36 percent of the people approved of Johnson's presidency.

Reports from the front fueled the discontent with the war. The nation learned of a massacre by American troops at **My Lai** village in March 1968. Frustrated American troops under the command of Lieutenant **William Calley** entered the village and murdered its inhabitants (old men, women, and infants). Many villages were destroyed in indiscriminate bombing. **Agent Orange**, a powerful chemical with long-lasting, serious health effects on people, was used extensively as a defoliant. Land mines took life and limb from countless civilians. In a war against guerrillas, it was impossible to distinguish combatants from noncombatants. Despite assurances from General

William Westmoreland, Commander of American forces in Vietnam, that the war was being won, there was growing skepticism in Congress.

The Tet Offensive

In January 1968, during the Vietnamese New Year's holiday called "Tet," the Viet Cong and North Vietnamese launched a powerful offensive. Virtually all of South Vietnam, including the U.S. embassy in Saigon, was suddenly besieged. The attack was over in a few days and the North Vietnamese suffered tremendous losses. But the offensive demonstrated the Vietnamese will to continue to engage the U.S. military forces. Reports of the attack profoundly affected public opinion and the political situation in the United States. Opposition to the war intensified, and candidates in the Democratic party challenged President Johnson in the primaries for the November 1968 election.

On March 31, 1968, President Johnson delivered an address to the nation. He stated, "Tonight I renew the offer I made last August—to stop the bombardment of North Vietnam We ask that [peace] talks begin promptly . . ." He then startled the nation by declaring that he would not run for another term as President.

President Nixon and the Vietnam War

"Vietnamization" of the War

During the election campaign of 1968, **Richard Nixon** delared that he had a "secret plan" to end the war. Although President Johnson had tried to induce peace talks by halting bombing raids for short periods and offering economic aid, North Vietnam insisted that the United States leave Vietnam before talks could begin. In November 1969 Nixon unveiled his plan, which was later termed Vietnamization, of shifting the responsibility of fighting the war to South Vietnamese forces. He said, "We shall furnish military and economic assistance when requested in accordance with our treaty commitments. But we shall look to the nation directly threatened to assume the primary responsibility of providing the manpower for its defenses."

However, the fighting in Vietnam, including heavy bombing raids, continued. With the lack of success of peace negotiations being held in Paris, Nixon widened the war. In April 1970 he ordered American and South Vietnamese forces to invade **Cambodia**, a neutral nation neighboring Vietnam where the North Vietnamese and Viet Cong had bases. This action set off a chain of fierce protests, particularly on college campuses. To many, Nixon's credibility was minimal, and his assertion that the invasion was designed to facilitate the withdrawal of American troops from Vietnam was widely rejected. However, at the same time as the Cambodia invasion, Nixon began to withdraw American troops from the war. By the end of 1972, Nixon withdrew 500,000

American soldiers, leaving only about 24,000 in Vietnam Under the policy of Vietnamization, the United States armed and trained the South Vietnamese. Heavy bombing of Communist-controlled areas was undertaken.

Negotiations for a Cease-Fire

During this period the war continued while negotiations for a cease-fire, first begun under President Johnson in April 1968, were carried on in Paris by Nixon's foreign policy adviser (later Secretary of State) **Henry A. Kissinger**. On March 30, 1972, North Vietnamese forces launched a sustained offensive into South Vietnam. Heavy American bombing of North Vietnam was resumed, and on May 8, 1972, Nixon ordered the mining of North Vietnam's ports. Although United States participation in the ground war terminated in August 1972, aerial bombardment continued.

Shortly before the 1972 election, Kissinger announced from Paris that "peace is at hand." In November, Nixon was reelected in an overwhelming victory, defeating George McGovern, the Democratic anti-war candidate, by an electoral vote of 520 to 17. However, by December, no agreement had been reached and Nixon authorized the "carpet bombing" of North Vietnam declaring "I will show them no mercy." Hospitals, schools, and residences, were indiscriminately destroyed.

This attack caused peace talks to resume, and the long-awaited cease-fire agreement was finally reached on January 27, 1973, in the Paris negotiations between Henry Kissinger and Le Duc Tho, chief of the Vietnam mission. The United States agreed to respect the independence, unity, and territorial integrity of Vietnam and to withdraw all forces within 60 days. The Communist government of North Vietnam agreed to release all prisoners and to account for all soldiers missing in action. The final U.S. troops left Indochina on March 29, 1973. To achieve "peace with honor," the United States retained the right to recognize the government of **President Thieu** as the sole legitimate government of South Vietnam. But it was obvious to all that the Thieu government could not endure long against the forces of North Vietnam. The end came in April 1975, when North Vietnam mounted a major offensive and gained control of all of Vietnam. As Communist troops from the north besieged Saigon, President Thieu and his followers fled the country. Thousands of refugees fled to Thailand.

The Vietnam Veterans Memorial in Washington is engraved with the names of 58,156 Americans who died in Vietnam; 300,000 more were wounded. The monetary cost of the war was over $150 billion. The intangible costs are still being assessed and the lessons pondered. Nearly 5,000 American servicemen were missing in action (MIAs) at the end of the war.

The Pentagon Papers

Background

In June 1967 **Robert S. McNamara**, President Johnson's Secretary of Defense, authorized a comprehensive study to review the policy-making procedures whereby the United States became so deeply involved in Vietnam. After a year and a half of intensive study, a 47-volume report known as the **Pentagon Papers** was compiled. Only 15 copies were issued. They were classified as top secret and were given only to McNamara, former President Johnson, President Nixon, the State Department, and the Pentagon files. The *Papers* revealed new facts about the Tonkin Gulf incident of 1964, which President Johnson used to gain a free hand in Vietnam. It appeared that the North Vietnamese attack on American destroyers in the Tonkin Gulf (if indeed, it ever *had* occurred) had been deliberately provoked by attacks on North Vietnamese territory carried out by South Vietnam and supported by U.S. destroyers in order to gain Congressional approval for the free hand sought by the President.

Publication of the Papers

One of the authors who compiled the *Pentagon Papers* was Daniel Ellsberg. Ellsberg had volunteered for service in Vietnam and spent two years in combat with the marines. He felt strongly that the American people should be informed of the contents of the *Pentagon Papers*. Considering it to be an act of the highest patriotism, he decided to release the report to the press. On June 13, 1971, *The New York Times* startled the nation with its front-page installment of the secret government report. The Justice Department indicted Ellsberg for theft, conspiracy, and espionage.

While Ellsberg awaited trial, the Nixon administration, via **John D. Ehrlichman**, assistant to the President for domestic affairs, sounded out the presiding judge on becoming the new director of the FBI. He also authorized a special secret contingent called "the plumbers" (leak stoppers) to break into the California office of Ellsberg's psychiatrist and steal whatever data they could find (they found none) about Ellsberg's personal affairs or problems. They also carried out other illegal activities, including wiretaps. When it was revealed that an illegal FBI wiretap had been in operation on Ellsberg's telephone from late 1969 to early 1970, the judge in the case dismissed the charges against Ellsberg, stating, "The conduct of the government has placed the case in such a posture that it precludes the fair, dispassionate resolution of these issues by a jury."

The New York Times Co. v. United States

When *The New York Times* began publication of the *Pentagon Papers*, the Justice Department obtained a court order enjoining the newspaper from further publication of any material contained in the confidential report. *The New York Times* sought an order from the Supreme Court vacating the injunction, on the grounds that prior restraint was a violation of the free press guarantee of the First Amendment. The government contended that disclosure of the contents would work "irreparable injury" to the "national security." The Court was asked to order prior censorship against a newspaper for the first time in American history.

The Court, in a 6 to 3 decision, rejected the government's request and vacated the injunction. Nine opinions, totaling over 11,000 words, were issued. The arguments against prior restraint were strongly stated by Justice Black with whom Justice Douglas joined in concurrence:

> Now for the first time in 182 years since the founding of the Republic, the federal courts are asked to hold that the First Amendment does not mean what it says . . .
>
> In revealing the workings of government that led to the Vietnam War, the newspapers nobly did that which the Founding Fathers hoped and trusted they would do . . .
>
> To find that the President has "inherent power" to halt the publication of news by resort to the courts would wipe out the First Amendment and destroy the fundamental liberty and security of the very people the government hopes to make "secure."

Exercise Set 6.11

1. Which of the following did *not* involve U.S. relations with China prior to 1901?
   A. John Hay's "Open-Door Policy"
   B. Building of the transcontinental railroads
   C. Acquisition of the Philippine Islands
   D. The "Boxer Rebellion"

2. President Johnson's use of American troops to save the independence of South Vietnam was
   A. unpopular in Congress almost from the beginning.
   B. a logical development of the policies pursued by Presidents Truman, Eisenhower, and Kennedy.
   C. contrary to the advice of the Joint Chiefs of Staff of the Armed Forces.
   D. tacitly approved by China, Japan, and Russia.

3. The decision of the Supreme Court in *The New York Times Company* v. *United States* (1971) [the *Pentagon Papers* case] is important because
   A. it involved important officials in the U.S. government.
   B. it was widely reported in newspapers throughout the country.
   C. the government's attorneys lost the case in a 6 to 3 decision.
   D. the Court ruled that the First Amendment prevented "prior restraint" of publication, even against a charge that such publication would jeopardize national security.

4. U.S. actions in the Vietnam War demonstrated that
   A. the domino theory is an effective military tactic.
   B. military policy in a democracy is affected by popular opinion.
   C. advanced technology ensures victory.
   D. limited use of tactical nuclear weapons can be successful.

5. The executive branch of the U.S. government has traditionally gained power during periods when
   A. the presidency has been occupied by a high-ranking military officer.
   B. the Republican Party was in the majority in Congress and the President was a Democrat.
   C. there has been a serious domestic or international problem facing the United States.
   D. the Supreme Court and Congress have been in conflict over constitutional issues.

PROTEST AND THE COUNTERCULTURE

Sources of Discontent

The decade of the 1960s was a period of rapid social change in American life. The traditional family underwent radical transformation. The authority of parents, teachers, churches, leaders in business, industry, the professions, and government was questioned, challenged, and attacked. By 1967 half of America's 200 million people had been born after the Great Depression and had no memory of the economic problems of that period.

Young people, impatient to correct injustice, found two areas for discontent: the unequal treatment of minorities and the war in Vietnam. The Kerner Commission had found that the nation's two societies—one black and one white—were becoming increasingly "separate and unequal." Senator **Eugene McCarthy** of Minnesota described the war in Vietnam in his 1967 book *The Limits of Power*: "Vietnam is a military problem. Vietnam is a political problem; and as the war goes on it has become more clearly a moral problem."

Vexing social problems were associated with these sources of injustice—one was that a disproportionate share of fighting was being borne by young black Americans. For African Americans and other minorities and the poor, lack of opportunity, unequal education and health care, unemployment, hunger, and slum living produced a permanent underclass, alien to the tradition of the "American dream."

The Counterculture

The rejection of traditional American society, because of its many injustices, by many young Americans created a **counterculture**. Many young people rejected the norms and values of people "over 30."

The baby boom of the 1950s had produced a generation of 36 million Americans between the ages of 15 and 24 in 1970. In the 1960s many of these young people seriously questioned the injustice in American society and the unexplained war for which they were expected to risk their lives. They felt alienated from American society. The counterculture was one way of showing their rejection of their parents', teachers', and the older generation's values. Many wore long hair, beads, and bizarre clothing, and went barefoot. "Flower children" handed flowers to police officers. Many tried drugs, most commonly marijuana and LSD. Some followed gurus and went to live in communes. The "rock music" of groups such as the **Beatles** expressed their yearnings and feelings. In 1969, near **Woodstock**, New York, 400,000 gathered for an outdoor concert that became a symbol of the togetherness of this generation. Some young Americans rejected the quest for economic advancement, turning to part-time occupations or crafts such as making furniture, pottery, or jewelry. They rejected ideas of personal achievement, material gain, and, above all, conformity. Rebellious youths referred to themselves as "**hippies**." (They were "hip" or wise to what was going on.)

The counterculture mood of rejection and rebellion was strongly reflected in the behavior of the military in Vietnam.

The Election of 1968

In 1968 a sharply divided Democratic party faced a united Republican party that chose **Richard Nixon** as its candidate. Nixon picked Governor **Spiro T. Agnew** of Maryland as his running mate.

The contest for the Democratic presidential nomination began in the New Hampshire primary on March 12, 1968. Senator **Eugene McCarthy** of Minnesota, virtually unknown outside his own state, ran as an "end the war" candidate and challenged President Johnson. To everyone's surprise, he received 42 percent of the vote and showed how vulnerable the President was in his own party. Four days later, Senator **Robert F. Kennedy** of New York announced his candidacy for the presidential nomination. And on March 31, in an address to the nation, President Johnson announced, "I shall not seek, and I will not accept the nomination of my party for a second term as your President." The way was now clear for Vice President **Hubert Humphrey** to seek the Democratic party nomination. The assassination of Robert F. Kennedy in Los Angeles on June 5 made the selection of Humphrey a virtual certainty, and it was confirmed at the Democratic convention in Chicago in August.

A third candidate, **George C. Wallace**, Democratic Governor of Alabama, ran as the Independent party candidate espousing segregation, hoping to garner enough electoral votes in the South to throw the election into the House of Representatives.

The Democratic convention was marred by a bitter battle over the party platform on Vietnam. The followers of Eugene McCarthy (and the Kennedy delegates) sought a quick withdrawal from Vietnam. However, the Humphrey delegates wrote a platform calling for stopping the bombing of Vietnam only when "it would not endanger the lives of our troops." But the greatest damage to the Humphrey candidacy was caused by what the voters saw on television. Outside the Chicago convention, fierce fighting broke out in the streets between antiwar demonstrators and the police, who were under orders from Chicago Mayor **Richard J. Daley** to preserve order, if necessary with their clubs. Among the demonstrators were the "**Yippies**" (**Youth International party**), who ridiculed the convention and nominated a pig named "Pigasus" for President.

During the campaign, which hinged on the issue of our involvement in the Vietnam War, Nixon said he had a secret plan to bring the war to a successful end. In the weeks before the November election, Humphrey gained steadily but failed to overcome the Republican lead. Nixon won in a close race by half a million votes of 73 million cast. Wallace received nearly 10 million votes. In the electoral college Nixon took 301 votes against 191 for Humphrey and 46 for Wallace.

Rallies, Protests, and Demonstrations

Students on the Offensive

Many young Americans, especially college students, expressed their resentment against the Vietnam War and other institutions and practices. Even before the war, students had begun to show a new militancy. At the University of California in Berkeley they had organized **a Free Speech Movement** and attempted to disrupt a San Francisco hearing conducted by the **House Un-American Activities Committee**. Some 800 members of Berkeley's Free Speech Movement staged a violent sit-in at the administration building and heard their spokesman, Mario Savio, claim, "There's a time when the operations of the machine become so odious . . . you've got to put your bodies on the gears . . . and make it stop."

At Greensboro, North Carolina, African American students from the nearby state university staged a sit-in in February 1960 at a segregated lunch counter in Woolworth's and started the process that brought integration to the nation's restaurants.

In colleges and universities around the country, indeed around the world, students were occupying and barricading buildings, holding vigils, and disrupting university procedures. During the first six months of 1968 there were major demonstrations in 101 American colleges and universities. In *Tinker* v. *Des Moines School District* (1969) the Court found high school antiwar protests, including the wearing of black armbands, to be protected speech, holding that students do not shed their freedom of expression "at the schoolhouse gate."

In Washington in November 1969, a quarter of a million people converged on the nation's capital to demand an end to the Vietnam War. The following May, the nation was shocked at President Nixon's announcement of the "incursion" of United States troops into Cambodia. A rally opposing this action was quickly organized, bringing 100,000 people to the Capitol.

Kent State and Jackson State

Meanwhile at colleges and universities, demonstrations against the widening of the war in Indochina were common occurrences. In April 1971 an "end the war" demonstration resulted in the arrest and imprisonment of some 10,000 protesters and spectators, who were held without trial in the Washington Football Team's stadium. Participating in the demonstration were the VVAW (Vietnam Veterans Against the War), who took the dramatic action of throwing their medals over a fence at the Capitol.

The extension of the war into Cambodia brought on a massive student demonstration at **Kent State University**. The Governor of Ohio sent 600 armed National Guard troops to the University to suppress the violence. The guardsmen fired a volley into the crowd, killing four of the demonstrators and wounding nine others. At **Jackson State College** in Mississippi, an institution with a predominantly black student body, protests against the invasion of Cambodia were broken up when the state highway patrol fired into a dormitory, killing two students.

Opposition to the War in Congress

After the invasion of Cambodia (April 29, 1970) a measure was introduced in the U.S. Senate by **Mark Hatfield** of Oregon and **George McGovern** of South Dakota, that would have required all U.S. troops to be recalled from Vietnam by the end of 1971. It was defeated 55 to 39. In June 1969 the Senate had approved by a vote of 76 to 10 a "sense of the Senate" resolution requiring the President to refrain from committing men or funds to any country without the express approval of Congress. And on June 24, 1970, the Senate voted 81 to 10 to repeal the Tonkin Gulf Resolution of 1964. On April 2, 1970, Massachusetts passed a law attempting to exempt its citizens from serving in combat overseas "unless such hostilities were initially authorized or subsequently ratified by a congressional declaration of war according to the constitutionally established procedures in Article I, Section 8, of the Constitution of the United States." The act underscored the fact that Congress had not declared war. The Supreme Court refused to hear arguments on the constitutionality of this Massachusetts act. But the principle involved continued to surface.

The efforts of Congress to regain its constitutional war power, which was eroded during the Vietnam War era, culminated in November 1973 when Congress passed the **War Powers Act** over President Nixon's veto. The act provided that the President, within 48 hours of sending troops where they might be involved in combat in a foreign country, must fully explain his action to Congress. Unless Congress gave its approval, the troops were to be brought home within 60 days.

Unit Six **A WORLD IN UNCERTAIN TIMES**

Exercise Set 6.12

1. The candidate running against Richard Nixon on the Democratic ticket in the election of 1968 was
   A. Robert Kennedy.
   B. Adlai Stevenson.
   C. Edmund Muskie.
   D. Hubert Humphrey.

2. The most important protest movements during President Nixon's first term were against
   A. war in Vietnam.
   B. broken treaties with Native Americans.
   C. discrimination against Native Americans.
   D. pollution of the environment.

3. Since World War II, African Americans in the United States have made the greatest gains in the area of
   A. equal economic opportunity.
   B. major corporate leadership.
   C. voting rights.
   D. desegregation of social life.

4. Which was *not* true of the election of 1968?
   A. The Democrats were badly divided.
   B. Nixon won by a close vote in the electoral college.
   C. Democrats retained control of both houses of Congress.
   D. Humphrey lost overwhelmingly in the popular vote.

5. U.S. participation in the undeclared war in Vietnam during the 1960s and 1970s raised a serious question in the United States about the
   A. loyalty of U.S. military commanders.
   B. authority of the President to make war.
   C. intervention of the Supreme Court in matters of national security.
   D. ability of Congress to finance a war.

6. The War Powers Act of 1973 was passed in order to
   A. strengthen the hand of President Nixon in pursuing the elusive victory on the battlefields of Vietnam.
   B. modify the constitutional provisions pertaining to presidential power in wartime.
   C. reassert the constitutional war-making power of Congress.
   D. reassert the authority of the Supreme Court as an arbiter between the executive and legislative branches of government.

1. Which of the following is *not* true about support for the Vietnam War effort?
   A. It was maintained in Congress along partisan lines.
   B. It showed a steady buildup from the Eisenhower Administration well into the Johnson Administration.
   C. It was rejected by many of our traditional democratic allies abroad.
   D. It divided the American people into two groups generally described as "doves" and "hawks."

2. "We shall look to the nation directly threatened to assume the primary responsibility of providing the manpower for its defense." This statement represents
   A. President Johnson's strategy for successful prosecution of the war in Vietnam.
   B. Senator Goldwater's position as candidate for President in 1964.
   C. Senator McGovern's position as candidate for President in 1972.
   D. Richard Nixon's "secret plan" to win the war as revealed after his election in 1968.

3. Which of the following is not connected directly with the war in Vietnam?
   A. The Free Speech Movement at the University of California in Berkeley
   B. A rally in 1969 at which a quarter of a million people converged in Washington
   C. A demonstration that resulted in the arrest of some 10,000 people who were held without bail in the Washington Redskin's (Washington Football Team's) stadium
   D. The killing of two students at Jackson State College in Mississippi by members of the state highway patrol

4. The 1973 War Powers Act
   A. created an all-volunteer army.
   B. required the president to report to Congress any commitment of American troops.
   C. authorized the expansion of the war into Cambodia.
   D. gave the president the power to declare war.

THEMATIC ESSAY

Directions: Write a well-organized essay that includes an introduction, several paragraphs addressing the task below, and a conclusion.

Theme: Civic Values and Citizenship

Historical Context:

> The momentous school desegregation decision in 1954 started the Earl Warren Supreme Court (1953–1969) on a path that would undertake sweeping reforms in numerous areas of the electoral system, political representation, criminal justice within the states, race relations, freedom of speech, and the role of religion in public life.
>
> The Supreme Court during the term of Chief Justice Earl Warren (1953–1969) would hand down decisions resulting in sweeping reforms in the areas of the electoral system, political representation, criminal justice, race relations, and religion.

Task:

> From your study of the Warren Court years and decisions in the 1950s and 1960s, identify *three* issues that came to the Supreme Court.
>
> For each issue:
>
> * Name the Supreme Court case that addressed the issue.
> * Briefly describe the facts of the case.
> * Discuss the decision and its impact on American society.

You may use any appropriate decisions of the Warren Court (1953–1969). Some suggestions you may wish to consider are *Brown* v. *Board of Education* (1954), *Baker* v. *Carr* (1962), *Wesberry* v. *Sanders* (1964), *Mapp* v. *Ohio* (1961), *Gideon* v. *Wainwright* (1963), *Escobedo* v. *Illinois* (1964), *Miranda* v. *Arizona* (1966), *New York Times* v. *Sullivan* (1964), and *Engel* v. *Vitale* (1962).

You are *not* limited to these suggestions.

DOCUMENT-BASED QUESTION

This question is based on the accompanying documents. The question is designed to test your ability to work with historical documents. Some of these documents have been edited for the purposes of this exercise. As you analyze the documents, take into account the source of each document and any point of view that may be presented in the document. Keep in mind that the language used in a document may reflect the historical context of the time in which it was written.

Historical Context:

Throughout the latter half of the 20th century, protecting United States national interests was a major goal of United States foreign policy. This goal led the United States to fight wars in **Korea (1950–1953)**, **Vietnam (1955–1973)**, and the **Persian Gulf (1990–1991)**. These wars had a significant impact on the United States and on other countries.

Task:

Using the information from the documents and your knowledge of United States history, answer the questions that follow each document in Part A. Your answers to the questions will help you write the Part B essay in which you will be asked to

Choose *two* wars mentioned in the historical context and for *each*

- Describe the historical circumstances that led to United States involvement in that war.
- Discuss the impact of the war on the United States and/or on another country or region.

Unit Six A WORLD IN UNCERTAIN TIMES

519

Part A
Short-Answer Questions

Analyze the documents and answer the short-answer questions that follow each document in the space provided.

DOCUMENT 1a

President Harry Truman was in Independence, MO, when he learned that North Korea had invaded South Korea. He flew back to Washington, D.C.

. . . The plane left the Kansas City Municipal Airport at two o'clock, and it took just a little over three hours to make the trip to Washington. I had time to think aboard the plane. In my generation, this was not the first occasion when the strong had attacked the weak. I recalled some earlier instances: Manchuria, Ethiopia, Austria. I remembered how each time that the democracies failed to act it had encouraged the aggressors to keep going ahead. Communism was acting in Korea just as Hitler, Mussolini, and the Japanese had acted ten, fifteen, and twenty years earlier. I felt certain that if South Korea was allowed to fall Communist leaders would be emboldened [encouraged] to override nations closer to our own shores. If the Communists were permitted to force their way into the Republic of Korea without opposition from the free world, no small nation would have the courage to resist threats and aggression by stronger Communist neighbors. If this was allowed to go unchallenged it would mean a third world war, just as similar incidents had brought on the second world war. It was also clear to me that the foundations and the principles of the United Nations were at stake unless this unprovoked attack on Korea could be stopped. . . .

Source: President Harry Truman, *Memoirs, Volume Two: Years of Trial and Hope*,
Doubleday & Company, 1956

1*a.* According to President Harry Truman, how would United States national interests be threatened if South Korea were allowed to fall to the communists?

_____

_____

President Harry Truman met with congressional leaders on Tuesday, June 27, 1950, to discuss possible United States actions regarding the crisis in Korea. Secretary of State Dean Acheson gave a briefing at the meeting.

> . . . On Monday [June 26, 1950], Mr. Acheson continued, it became apparent in Washington that the United States should adopt a very firm stand in the Far East, for two reasons: (a) the Korean forces appeared to be weakening fast and their leadership was weak and indecisive; (b) the governments of many Western European nations appeared to be in a state of near-panic, as they watched to see whether the United States would act or not. Therefore, Mr. Acheson concluded, the President had called another meeting at Blair House on Monday evening at which he decided, after consultation with his State and Defense advisers, to take additional steps which the President would now describe....
>
> Sen. [Senator Thomas] Connally [Democrat, Texas] said that it was quite apparent that this was the clearest test case that the United Nations has ever faced. If the United Nations is ever going to do anything, this is the time, and if the United Nations cannot bring the crisis in Korea to an end, then we might just as well wash up the United Nations and forget it. There was general agreement around the table that this was the case and the President once again stated that he was going to make absolutely certain that everything we did in Korea would be in support of, and in conformity with, the decision by the Security Council of the United Nations. . . .

Source: President Harry S. Truman Library & Museum

1*b*. Based on this document, why was it important for the United States to aid South Korea?

_____

_____

DOCUMENT 2a

A changing front in Korea reflected military victories and losses until an armistice line near the 38th parallel was established.

Source: Thomas A. Bailey, *A Diplomatic History of the American People*, Prentice Hall, 1980

DOCUMENT 2b

During the "talking war" to reach an armistice, the fighting continued and casualties (dead and wounded) increased.

> . . . It had been a long and terrible war, the cost of which could never be accurately reckoned. The Pentagon estimated that military casualties on both sides came close to 2.4 million. Other sources estimated that North and South Korean civilian casualties were about 2 million. If these figures are approximately accurate, then about 4.4 million men, women, and children were killed, murdered, wounded, or otherwise incapacitated [injured] in the war. Both North Korea and South Korea were utterly ravaged. It would take decades for each nation to rise from the rubble.
>
> Americans paid a high price for President Truman's decision to "draw the line" in South Korea: 54,246 dead (33,629 killed on the battlefield; 20,617 military dead from other causes) and 103,284 wounded. The cost of the last two years of the talking war, in order to fix the DMZ [Demilitarized Zone] at Line Kansas [armistice line], to guarantee former enemies freedom of choice in repatriation [returning home], and to effect the release of 12,773 surviving UN POW's [prisoners of war] (including 3,597 Americans), was especially dear: 63,200 American casualties alone, 12,300 of whom were killed on the battlefield. . . .

Source: Clay Blair, *The Forgotten War: America in Korea 1950–1953*,
Times Books, 1987 (adapted)

2. Based on these documents, what were *two* results of the conflict in Korea?

(1) _____

_____

(2) _____

_____

DOCUMENT 3

ALTHOUGH the armistice has remained in effect since July 1953, in the absence of a formal peace treaty a state of war technically continues to exist between North and South Korea. Glaring at each other across the demilitarized zone, the two regimes have as yet not even made any progress toward mutual recognition, let alone toward cooperation. They have no diplomatic or economic relations whatsoever, not even postal or telephone links. Thus, although some 10 million of South Korea's 42 million people have close relatives living in the north, they are unable to communicate with them except, in a very limited number of cases, by means of an occasional supervised visit of an hour or two along the border. Fears of a new Communist attack remain so intense that on the fifteenth of every month the wail of sirens sends the entire population of Seoul scurrying for shelter in a full-dress air-raid drill . . . .

Source: Richard Whelan, *Drawing the Line: The Korean War, 1950–1953*,
Little, Brown and Company, 1990

3. According to Richard Whelan, what was *one* result of the Korean War?

_____

_____

DOCUMENT 4

1946
Indo-China War begins between
France and Vietnam

1955
U. S. takes over training of
South Vietnamese troops

1964
Congress approves
Gulf of Tonkin
Resolution

1945   1950   1955   1960   1965

1950
President Truman
sends $15 million in
military aid to France
to assist in Vietnam

1954
French defeated at Dien Bien Phu

Geneva Convention divides
Vietnam at 17th parallel

Creation of Southeast Asia Treaty
Organization (SEATO)

1962
President Kennedy
raises number of U. S.
advisors in Vietnam to
10,000

4. Based on this time line, state *one* way the United States was involved in Vietnam between 1946 and 1964.

_____

_____

DOCUMENT 5

This is an excerpt from a speech by Secretary of Defense Robert S. McNamara in which he argues that supporting South Vietnam is in the national interest of the United States.

> . . . We do so in their interest; and we do so in our own clear self-interest. For basic to the principles of freedom and self-determination which have sustained our country for almost two centuries is the right of peoples everywhere to live and develop in peace.
>
> Our own security is strengthened by the determination of others to remain free, and by our commitment to assist them. We will not let this member of our family down, regardless of its distance from our shores. . . .
>
> Second, Southeast Asia has great strategic significance in the forward defense of the United States. Its location across east-west air and sea lanes flanks the Indian subcontinent on one side and Australia, New Zealand and the Philippines on the other, and dominates the gateway between the Pacific and Indian Oceans.
>
> In Communist hands this area would pose a most serious threat to the security of the United States and to the family of free world nations to which we belong. To defend Southeast Asia we must meet the challenge in South Vietnam. . . .

Source: *New York Times*, March 27, 1964

5. According to Robert McNamara, what are *two* reasons Vietnam was important to the national interest of the United States?

(1) _____

_____

(2) _____

_____

DOCUMENT 6a

. . . Under five Presidents and 12 Congresses, the United States was engaged in Indochina. Millions of Americans served, thousands died, and many more were wounded, imprisoned, or lost. Over $150 billion have been appropriated for that war by the Congress of the United States. And after years of effort, we negotiated, under the most difficult circumstances, a settlement which made it possible for us to remove our military forces and bring home with pride our American prisoners. This settlement, if its terms had been adhered to [followed], would have permitted our South Vietnamese ally, with our material and moral support, to maintain its security and rebuild after two decades of war. . . .

Source: President Gerald R. Ford, Address to Joint Session of Congress, April 10, 1975

DOCUMENT 6b

Vietnam, 1965

Source: *The History Place* (adapted)

DOCUMENT 6c

Vietnam, 1975

Source: *The World Factbook* (adapted)

6. Based on these documents, what were *two* results of United States involvement in Vietnam?

(1) _____

_____

(2) _____

_____

DOCUMENT 7

. . . Less than a week ago, in the early morning hours of August 2d [1990], Iraqi Armed Forces, without provocation or warning, invaded a peaceful Kuwait. Facing negligible resistance from its much smaller neighbor, Iraq's tanks stormed in blitzkrieg fashion through Kuwait in a few short hours. With more than 100,000 troops, along with tanks, artillery, and surface-to-surface

President George H. W. Bush gives a press conference regarding Iraq's invasion of Kuwait, August 8, 1990.
Source: George Bush Presidential Library and Museum

missiles, Iraq now occupies Kuwait. This aggression came just hours after Saddam Hussein specifically assured numerous countries in the area that there would be no invasion. There is no justification whatsoever for this outrageous and brutal act of aggression.

A puppet regime imposed from the outside is unacceptable. The acquisition of territory by force is unacceptable. No one, friend or foe, should doubt our desire for peace; and no one should underestimate our determination to confront aggression.

Four simple principles guide our policy. First, we seek the immediate, unconditional, and complete withdrawal of all Iraqi forces from Kuwait. Second, Kuwait's legitimate government must be restored to replace the puppet regime. And third, my administration, as has been the case with every President from President [Franklin D.] Roosevelt to President [Ronald] Reagan, is committed to the security and stability of the Persian Gulf. And fourth, I am determined to protect the lives of American citizens abroad. . . .

Source: President George H. W. Bush, Address to the Nation, August 8, 1990

7. According to President George H. W. Bush, what were *two* reasons for United States involvement in the Persian Gulf region?

(1) _____

_____

(2) _____

_____

DOCUMENT 8

"They set out to confront an enemy abroad," President [George H. W.] Bush declared last week as he praised the men and women who won the most decisive American military victory since World War II. "And in the process, they transformed a nation at home."

To a president triumphant, to a nation relieved and to a military that almost seemed to be born anew, the victory over Iraq was only half the story: Desert Storm was also a victory over two decades of American self-doubt. On the wall of the briefing room at the Riyadh [Saudi Arabia] Hyatt Regency Hotel, a hand-drawn cartoon appeared: a rock in the empty Iraqi desert, bearing the epitaph "Here Lies Vietnam.". . .

Source: Stephen Budiansky, "A force reborn," *U.S. News & World Report*, March 18, 1991

8. According to Stephen Budiansky, what was *one* result of the 1991 Persian Gulf War?

_____

_____

DOCUMENT 9

. . . The military campaign had been successful in forcing Saddam Hussein's withdrawal from Kuwait, but the Iraqi leader remained in power.

A UN mandate for weapons inspections was established in a resolution passed in April 1991.

The first operation by the inspections body, Unscom [United Nations Special Commission], was carried out in June, setting in train [starting] seven years of monitoring.

Economic sanctions imposed after Iraq invaded Kuwait remained in place, with Iraq banned from importing or exporting anything but food and medicines.

These continued for 12 years, although Iraq agreed in 1996 to a UN offer to allow it to export a limited amount of oil to raise funds for humanitarian supplies.

Source: "Flashback: 1991 Gulf War," *BBC NEWS*, March 20, 2003

9. According to this article, what was *one* result of the 1991 Persian Gulf War?

_____

_____

Part B
Essay

Write a well-organized essay that includes an introduction, several para-graphs, and a conclusion. Use evidence from *at least four* documents in the body of the essay. Support your response with relevant facts, examples, and details. Include additional outside information.

Historical Context:

> Throughout the latter half of the 20th century, protecting United States national interests was a major goal of United States foreign policy. This goal led the United States to fight wars in **Korea (1950–1953)**, **Vietnam (1955–1973)**, and the **Persian Gulf (1990–1991)**. These wars had a sig-nificant impact on the United States and on other countries.

Task:

> Using information from the documents and your knowledge of United States history, write an essay in which you:
>
> Choose *two* wars mentioned in the historical context and for *each*
>
> - Describe the historical circumstances that led to United States involvement in that war.
> - Discuss the impact of the war on the United States and/or on another country or region.

Guidelines:

In your essay, be sure to
- Develop all aspects of the task.
- Incorporate information from *at least four* documents.
- Incorporate relevant outside information.
- Support the theme with relevant facts, examples, and details.
- Use a logical and clear plan of organization, including an introduction and a conclusion that are beyond a restatement of the theme.

THE TREND TOWARD CONSERVATISM (1972–1992)

NIXON AND THE IMPERIAL PRESIDENCY (1969–1974)

> The truth is America's most potent weapon. We cannot enlarge upon the truth. But we can and must intensify our efforts to make the truth more shining.
>
> Richard M. Nixon, *The Challenge We Face,* 1960

> Nixon is a shifty-eyed . . . liar . . . He's one of the few in the history of this country to run for high office talking out of both sides of his mouth at the same time and lying out of both sides.
>
> Harry S. Truman, from Leo Rosten, *Infinite Riches* (1978)

In the election campaign of 1968, Richard Nixon ran against Hubert Humphrey. The three main issues in the campaign were the Vietnam War, violence and disorder at home, and racial strife. Nixon promised to end the war and to restore "law and order" in the United States. The election was very close, with Nixon winning by 260,000 votes. When he became President, the Vietnam War was the most pressing problem facing the nation. President Nixon began "**Vietnamization**" and increased bombing. American troops were withdrawn gradually and finally, in 1973, a cease-fire agreement was reached.

During the Nixon presidency some Americans realized that the President had grown increasingly powerful in the American political system. This power was largely the result of World War II and the Cold War, as the President took control of foreign affairs in a world situation of ever-increasing danger. Some Americans, alarmed by presidential power, began to speak of an "**imperial presidency**."

Foreign Affairs

President Nixon took charge of foreign affairs himself and used **Henry Kissinger** as his adviser. Kissinger served first as a member of the National Security Council and in 1973 became Secretary of State. Nixon's foreign policies, except for the Vietnam War, were widely approved by the American people. Especially popular was the policy of **détente**, or easing tensions, between the United States and the Communist nations.

Détente with the Soviet Union

Closer relations between the United States and the two Communist super-powers—the Soviet Union and the People's Republic of China—during the Nixon presidency could hardly have been foreseen from his adamant anti-Communist record at home. Shortly after he became President, Nixon began exploratory talks with the Soviets on a number of issues that concerned both powers, particularly the reduction or limitation of nuclear arms. In May 1972 Nixon arrived in Moscow for talks with the leaders of the Soviet Union. He was the first President to visit Moscow. Discussions proceeded over a wide range of subjects. Most important were the **Strategic Arms Limitation Talks** (**SALT**). Agreements were reached on arms limitation, particularly antiballistic missile systems (subject to ratification by the U.S. Senate) and a treaty was signed May 26, 1972. Under the treaty each party agreed "not to develop, test, or deploy ABM systems or components which are sea-based, air-based, space-based, or mobile land-based." Interpretation of this provision later caused controversy over President Reagan's proposal to develop the Strategic Defense Initiative (SDI), often called "**Star Wars**," in the 1980s. The treaty also provided that "ABM systems in excess of those prohibited by this treaty shall be destroyed or dismantled within the shortest possible agreed period of time."

Shortly after the signing of the ABM treaty, the United States sold $750 million worth of wheat, corn, and other cereals to the Soviet Union. The huge surplus of grains produced by American farms went to help relieve food shortages in the Soviet Union.

Détente with the People's Republic of China

When Nixon took office in 1969, the Communist government had ruled China for almost 20 years. Yet diplomatic relations between China and the United States had never been established because the United States still recognized the **Nationalist** (**Chiang Kai-shek**) government in Taiwan as the legitimate government of China.

In a television address to the nation, delivered July 15, 1971, President Nixon made a startling declaration: "The announcement I shall now read is being issued simultaneously in Peking and in the United States . . . Premier Chou En-lai and Dr. Henry Kissinger [President Nixon's Assistant for National Security Affairs] held talks in Peking from July 9 to 11, 1971 . . . the government of the People's Republic of China has extended an invitation to President Nixon to visit China . . . President Nixon has accepted the invitation with pleasure."

On October 25, 1971, the People's Republic of China, with the acquiescence of the United States, was admitted to the United Nations. The UN General Assembly then recommended that the permanent seat on the Security Council held by the Nationalist government on Taiwan be turned over to the government of the People's Republic of China.

The historic visit of President Nixon and his wife to China took place in February 1972. Nixon met with Chairman Mao Zedong and Premier Zhou En-lai. The visit culminated in a joint communiqué issued at Shanghai February 27, 1972, stating: ". . . that Taiwan is a part of China. The U.S. government does not challenge that position . . . it affirms the ultimate objective of the withdrawal of all U.S. forces and military installations from Taiwan."

The Arab-Israeli War of October 1973

On the eve of Yom Kippur, the holiest day of the Jewish year, Israel was suddenly attacked by the armed forces of Egypt and Syria. At first the Israelis were driven back. The attackers had the initiative and were armed with Soviet military equipment. But, despite heavy losses, the Israelis, supplied with American equipment, drove the invaders back beyond their borders and occupied the Golan Heights previously held by Syria. Sporadic fighting continued until a cease-fire was urged on the Arabs and the Israelis by the United States and the Soviet Union and negotiated by May 31, 1974. But the uneasy peace was regarded on all sides as merely temporary.

The Arab nations were angered by the American support for Israel and several halted oil shipments to the United States. This **oil embargo** resulted in long lines at gas stations and calls for conservation measures.

Domestic Policies and Developments

Many pressing problems faced President Nixon when he took office. The Vietnam War divided American society as protests continued across the nation, while **inflation**, also largely a result of the war, caused problems at home.

Dismantling the Great Society

The Great Society of President Johnson was based on the idea that the federal government had a major responsibility to provide for the health, education, and welfare of the American people. Nixon rejected this idea and, instead, proceeded to shift the burden of responsibility to the states in what he called "**the new federalism.**" Through **revenue sharing**, the federal government would aid the states in providing minimum levels of social benefits. The idea was that each state could decide its own needs and how to meet them. However, over the years, the diminishing share of federal funds left the states in a position of reducing these services or raising taxes. In 1969, with inflation mounting, 10 million Americans were on welfare. Unemployment among young people, especially African American teenagers, was at a post-World War II high. Also, as American troops left Vietnam, Americans in war industries were becoming unemployed. A **recession** was in progress and new economic measures had to be undertaken.

Economic Initiatives

Although he had previously rejected a Democratic proposal to freeze wages and prices in order to stem inflation, in August 1971, Nixon yielded and ordered a 90-day wage-price freeze (the first in peacetime). A special pay board and a price commission were authorized to grant or deny wage and price increases when the freeze expired.

To improve America's position in world trade, Nixon freed the dollar from its tie to gold, permitting the dollar to decline in relation to the currency of other nations. This gave American-made goods an advantage in foreign markets, because foreigners could pay for the goods with cheaper American dollars. Nixon also imposed a 10 percent surcharge on foreign imports. Improvements in the economy helped set the stage for Nixon's re-election in 1972.

Moon Landings

On Sunday, July 20, 1969, while Michael Collins guided the command module of *Apollo 11,* **Neil Armstrong** and **Edwin (Buzz) Aldrin, Jr.**, landed on the moon. As the world watched on TV, the two astronauts walked on the surface of the moon, set up scientific apparatus, collected rocks, and planted the American flag. The mission, planned eight years earlier by the Kennedy administration, was a 20th-century miracle.

In all, six Apollo missions landed twelve American astronauts on the moon, the last one in 1972.

The Environment

Congress took a strong stand on the environment by passing the **Water Quality Improvement Act of 1970**. The act created the **Office of Environmental Quality** and made oil companies responsible for cleaning up oil spills. It limited the use of pesticides and water pollutants and restricted thermal pollution of waters by discharges from power plants.

An oil spill that caused severe damage to the Santa Barbara coastline resulted in an order from Nixon's Secretary of the Interior Walter J. Hickel stopping undersea oil drilling in the area. Hickel also delayed the construction of an 800-mile oil pipeline in Alaska because of the potential damage to the flora, fauna, and other natural elements in the area. However, Nixon ordered work on the pipeline to be completed.

The Supreme Court

The Supreme Court under Chief Justice **Earl Warren** (1953–1969), former Republican Governor of California, who had been appointed by President Eisenhower, often came under attack during the 1950s and 1960s as being too "activist." Its liberal approach to civil rights, criminal procedures, church and state, and other social issues, was opposed by conservative Americans. They were especially critical of the Court's decisions concerning criminal proce- dures. *Mapp* v. *Ohio* (1961) marked further incorporation of criminal proce- dure guarantees into the due process clause of the Fourteenth Amendment when the Court ruled that the federal exclusionary rule disallowing evidence wrongfully obtained would be applied to the states. In *Gideon* v. *Wainright* (1963) the Court set aside a state court verdict in a felony criminal case because the state had failed to furnish counsel for the defendant, an indigent person, at his request. In *Escobedo* v. *Illinois* (1964) and *Miranda* v. *Arizona* (1966) the Court set aside verdicts against the defendants because the police had failed to notify them of their right to remain silent and to be represented by counsel during questioning.

In 1962, in *Engle* v. *Vitale*, the Court ruled that a New York State decision permitting the reading of a "nonsectarian" prayer in the public schools was a violation of the First Amendment. The following year the Court prohibited Bible reading in public school assemblies or classrooms for the same reason.

In his 1968 campaign for election to the presidency, Nixon promised to reverse these trends by appointing "**strict constructionalist**" judges to the Supreme Court. Nixon's opportunity to reform the Court was not long in coming. In 1969 Chief Justice Earl Warren retired, and the President nominated **Warren E. Burger** of Minnesota to be Chief Justice. Burger, who was on the District of Columbia Federal Court of Appeals, was quickly confirmed by the Senate.

Twenty-Sixth Amendment

In 1971, during Nixon's first term as President, the Twenty-Sixth Amendment was added to the Constitution. Proposed by Congress in March 1971, it was ratified by the required 38 states by June 30, partly because it granted voting rights to many young Americans who served in Vietnam. The amendment provided: "The right of citizens of the United States, who are eighteen years of age or older, to vote shall not be denied or abridged by the United States or by any state on account of age."

The Election of 1972

Both parties held their national nominating conventions at the Miami Beach convention hall in Florida—the Democrats in July and the Republicans in August. The Republicans again nominated Nixon and Agnew. The chief contender for the Democratic nomination was Senator **George McGovern** of South Dakota, a liberal and an advocate of withdrawing American troops from Vietnam. Another contender was Governor **George Wallace** of Alabama, who had run as a third party candidate in 1968. His campaign was virtually ended when he was shot and paralyzed from the waist down while delivering a campaign speech at Laurel, Maryland. A third contender, **Edmund Muskie** of Maine, was the early Democratic front-runner.

During the election campaign, McGovern promised to end the war in Vietnam and to introduce basic economic and social reforms at home. Nixon was the "law and order" candidate and pointed to his impressive foreign affairs achievements in improving relations with the Soviet Union and the People's Republic of China. In October, shortly before the election, Nixon's campaign received a crucial boost when Henry Kissinger, who was then negotiating with the North Vietnamese, announced "peace is at hand."

The results of the 1972 election gave Nixon and Agnew an almost clean sweep in the electoral college. The vote was 521 to 17, with Nixon winning the entire country except for Massachusetts and the District of Columbia. The popular vote gave Nixon 46,631,189 votes to McGovern's 28,422,015.

The Resignation of Spiro Agnew

Vice President Agnew, a hard-line conservative, stood for "law and order." But after the 1972 election it was discovered that Agnew was himself a law-breaker. While serving as Governor of Maryland, he had taken bribes from contractors and was still receiving "kickbacks" while Vice President of the United States. He resigned as Vice President, was fined $10,000, and was placed on three years probation. He was also disbarred as a lawyer.

With the resignation of Vice President Agnew, the Twenty-Fifth Amendment to the Constitution, adopted in February 1967, came into effect. It provides: "Whenever there is a vacancy in the office of the Vice President, the President shall nominate a Vice President who shall take office upon confirmation by a majority vote of both houses of Congress." The choice in 1973 was of crucial importance because of the growing concern over the **Watergate** scandal. Nixon nominated **Gerald R. Ford** of Michigan, a twelve-term member and minority leader of the House of Representatives. Congress promptly confirmed the nomination, and Ford took the oath of office as Vice President on December 6, 1973.

Watergate: The Imperial Presidency in Trouble

> When the President does it, that means that it is not illegal.
> Richard M. Nixon, in a television interview, May 20, 1977

Nixon's second term was overshadowed by the Watergate affair, which included both the break-in at Democratic headquarters at Watergate and other political scandals in the Nixon administration, drawing up a list of enemies (those who opposed Nixon's policies) to be harassed by every means available to the administration, including the CIA, the FBI, and even the IRS. Many members of the press were on the enemies list, as were the leaders of the opposition to the Vietnam War. To discover who was "leaking" information to the press, Nixon also had illegal wiretaps placed on the telephones of suspects. He formed a special secret unit in the White House whose mission was to stop the leaks. The unit became known as **"the plumbers,"** and they carried out a number of illegal activities.

The Break-in

On June 17, 1972, at the Watergate apartment complex in Washington, a burglary in progress was discovered in the Democratic National Headquarters. The burglars, who were rummaging through files, taking photographs, and installing bugging equipment, were arrested and pleaded guilty. It was discovered that some of them were connected to Nixon's **"Committee to Reelect the President"** (**CREEP**), including **James W. McCord, Jr.**, a former CIA wiretap expert; **G. Gordon Liddy**, a former FBI agent and White House consultant; and **E. Howard Hunt, Jr.**, a former CIA agent and a White House aide.

The Cover-up

Five days after the break-in, President Nixon said the matter was "under investigation . . . by the proper legal authorities" and that "the White House had no involvement whatever in this particular incident." At a news conference on August 29, 1972, the President said that, under his direction, his counsel **John Dean** had "conducted a complete investigation which disclosed that no one on the White House staff, no one in this administration, presently employed, was involved in this bizarre incident." Dean later testified under oath that he had had a series of meetings about Watergate with the President, that he had warned him that Watergate was "a cancer growing on the presidency" and that the President had taken part in the cover-up for eight months.

At first the President's cover-up statements were successful. The press seemingly lost interest in the case. However, two investigative reporters on the *Washington Post*—**Robert Woodward** and **Carl Bernstein**—pursued every lead and kept the story alive in the press. It was not until May 31, 2005, that it became known that Woodward and Bernstein's source for their information, known only as "Deep Throat" for more than thirty-three years, was William Mark Felt, Deputy Director of the FBI.

The Watergate Hearings

With pressure for a thorough investigation mounting, the U.S. Senate, in February 1973, adopted a resolution establishing the Senate Select Committee on Presidential Campaign Activities, headed by Senator Sam J. Ervin, Jr. The committee was directed to conduct an investigation into the extent to which illegal, improper, or unethical activities were involved in the 1972 presidential election. Televised hearings began in May 1973, and interrogation of witnesses continued for seventeen months.

Along with the establishment of the investigating committee, **Archibald Cox** of the Harvard Law School and former Solicitor General of the United States, was appointed as special prosecutor (counsel) the day after the hearings began. He was to collect evidence that would eventually lead to the indictments, trial, and conviction of those who had committed crimes.

In April 1973, **H. R. Haldeman**, Nixon's Chief of Staff, and **John D. Ehrlichman**, his Chief Assistant for Domestic Affairs, resigned. Both were deeply involved in the matters under investigation. The same day, Nixon fired his counsel, John Dean, who had revealed damaging information in testimony before the Senate committee. On May 22, Nixon declared, "It is clear that unethical, as well as illegal surveillance activities took place in the course of the campaign. None of these took place with my specific approval or knowledge."

The Tapes

During testimony before the Senate committee, it was revealed that President Nixon had ordered the Secret Service to install listening devices in the White House Oval Office and other locations. Tapes of all conversations were made and stored "as a historical record."

When Nixon produced the tapes as ordered by the Federal District Court, it turned out that two of the key tapes were "missing" and that there was a "gap" of 18½ minutes in an important taped conversation that Nixon had with Haldeman, his Chief of Staff, three days after the Watergate break-in.

Special prosecutor Leon Jaworski demanded that the President release more of the relevant tapes. The Judiciary Committee of the House of Representatives also wanted the tapes to help them decide whether there were grounds for **impeachment**. In response, Nixon furnished edited tapes sprinkled with omissions and deletions. The President insisted that he had **"executive privilege"** to refuse Judge Sirica's subpoena to produce unedited tapes. Jaworski appealed to the Supreme Court, and in June 1974 the Supreme Court decided that the President was legally obligated to deliver the requested tapes to the Special Prosecutor. In *United States* v. *Nixon* (1974) the Court held that the importance of preserving confidentiality in White House conversations must be balanced against the need for evidence in a criminal trial. Nixon conceded that the tapes, which he was now required to release, were "at variance with my previous statements." In other words, he had lied in order to cover up illegal acts.

Impeachment Proceedings

Article I Section 2: The House of Representatives . . . shall have the Sole Power of Impeachment.

Article I Section 3: The Senate shall have the sole power to try all impeachments. When sitting for that purpose, they shall take an oath or affirmation. When the President of the United States is tried, the Chief Justice shall preside: and no person shall be convicted without the concurrence of two-thirds of the members present.

> Judgment in cases of impeachment shall not extend further than the removal from office, and disqualification to hold and enjoy any office of honor, trust, or profit under the United States: but the party convicted shall nevertheless be liable and subject to indictment, trial, judgment, and punishment, according to law.
>
> Article II Section 4: The President, Vice President and all civil officers of the United States shall be removed from office on impeachment for, and conviction of, treason, bribery, or other high crimes and misdemeanors.

The Judiciary Committee of the House of Representatives began conducting an inquiry and gathering data to prepare **Articles of Impeachment**. It had become clear that the President had engaged in "high crimes and misdemeanors" sufficient to warrant his impeachment.

On July 30, 1974, the Judiciary Committee of the House of Representatives voted for, and sent to the full House, three Articles of Impeachment: (1) the President was charged with obstruction of justice; (2) he was charged with abusing his authority and violating his oath of office; and (3) he was charged with subverting the Constitution by defying eight subpoenas for tapes in order to block impeachment. On August 5, the transcripts of Nixon and Haldeman's tape-recorded conversations from June 23, 1972, were made public. These tapes were considered a "smoking gun" because they showed that, contrary to Nixon's previous statements, he had attempted to cover up the Watergate burglary. There was little doubt that the House would vote to impeach him and the Senate would convict him. On August 8, 1974, President Nixon announced his resignation of the office of President of the United States to take effect the following day.

Indictments, Trials, and Convictions

Several important members of the Nixon administration were indicted for illegal activities. In March 1974, indictments were handed down against Mitchell, Haldeman, Ehrlichman, and four others connected with the Committee to Re-elect the President, for crimes including obstruction of justice, conspiring to obstruct justice, and perjury. Mitchell, Haldeman, and Ehrlichman were convicted and sentenced to prison terms of from twenty months to five years.

Watergate led to an erosion of public trust in government. On the positive side, it demonstrated the effectiveness of our democratic institutions. Freedom of the press and our two-party system worked in a crisis. The Constitution, with its carefully crafted procedures for checks and balances, provided the resilience necessary to meet the severe challenges presented by Watergate.

1. Which of the following is generally regarded as *the* major accomplishment of the Nixon administration?
   A. Economic reforms
   B. Environmental regulations
   C. Détente with the Soviet Union and China
   D. Supreme Court appointments

2. The Watergate crimes were undertaken in order to
   A. assure success in the 1972 election.
   B. secure approval for Nixon's domestic programs.
   C. support continued prosecution of the war in Vietnam.
   D. provide funds for "the plumbers."

3. Which of the following did *not* occur during Nixon's presidency?
   A. The Arab-Israeli War of 1973
   B. An attempt to cut back on the Great Society
   C. A 90-day freeze on wages and prices
   D. Conviction of President Nixon of "high crimes and misdemeanors" by the Senate

4. In the United States, informing suspects in custody of their legal rights before they are questioned by a government official is required as a result of
   A. customs adopted from English common law.
   B. state legislation.
   C. decisions of the U.S. Supreme Court.
   D. laws passed by Congress.

5. Which description best characterizes the decisions of the U.S. Supreme Court of the 1950s and 1960s under Chief Justice Earl Warren?
   A. Activist, with a liberal approach to interpreting the Constitution
   B. Cautious, with a philosophy of strict construction
   C. Traditional, with a stress on states' rights
   D. Conservative, with a strong emphasis on "cracking down" on war criminals

6. Since World War II, a major goal of U.S. foreign policy in the Middle East has been to bring about
   A. permanent United Nations control of disputed territories.
   B. a peaceful settlement of Arab-Israeli issues.
   C. ownership of oil resources by Western nations.
   D. an end to U.S. cooperation with Arab nations.

THE FORD AND CARTER PRESIDENCIES (AUGUST 1974–JANUARY 1981)

> I am a Ford, not a Lincoln.
>> Gerald R. Ford of Michigan upon being sworn in as Vice President,
>>> Dec. 6, 1973

> To me the presidency and the vice presidency were not prizes to be won but a duty to be done.
>> Gerald R. Ford in *A Time to Heal*, 1979

Gerald R. Ford served in the House of Representatives for 25 years (1949–1973), and was minority (Republican) leader from 1965 to 1973, when President Nixon appointed him Vice President to replace Spiro Agnew. Upon the resignation of Nixon, Ford became President on August 9, 1974. No other person has ever served in this high office without having been elected on a national ticket.

Domestic Developments Under President Ford

Vice President Rockefeller

To fill the vacancy in the vice presidency created by his elevation to the presidency, Ford followed the provisions of the Twenty-Fifth Amendment to the Constitution. He nominated **Nelson A. Rockefeller**, Governor of New York from 1958 to 1973. Congress confirmed the nomination in December 1974. For the first time in history, the United States had an appointed President and Vice President, neither having been elected to office. Ford retained Henry A. Kissinger as Secretary of State along with most of the remaining members of the Nixon cabinet. The nation felt relieved at the transition from the Nixon administration to the frank, open, and amiable administration of the new President.

The Pardon

In September 1974, a month after taking office, Ford declared, "By virtue of the authority vested in me by the Constitution of the United States, I hereby grant to Richard M. Nixon a full, free and absolute pardon . . . for all offenses against the United States which he . . . has committed or may have committed or taken part in" during his presidency. The pardon was designed "to end the nightmare" and avoid the rancor of a public trial of the ex-President with its unpleasant consequences. Many Americans protested the pardon, claiming it was unfair to grant immunity to Nixon while those who had carried out his orders had served prison terms. It also raised the question of whether there had been a "deal" between Nixon and Ford.

542

The pardon was followed by a presidential announcement of **clemency** (but not amnesty) for draft evaders and deserters during the Vietnam War. Only about 25,000 of the 125,000 eligible accepted the offer. The others were later pardoned by President Carter.

Economic Difficulties

Within a year of Ford's assuming the presidency, the nation faced the worst **economic recession** since the 1930s. Unemployment reached an alarming level of nearly 10 percent in 1975, while annual inflation reached a high of 12 percent. The combination gave rise to a new term "**stagflation**," an economic anomaly. The economic situation improved slowly, but hard times continued throughout Ford's presidency and worked against his election in 1976.

Rising oil prices played a large part in the inflation of the 1970s. As the nation cut back on coal (an air pollutant) and nuclear energy (a safety hazard) and as the number of motor vehicles on the highways steadily increased, the use of oil (for gasoline) began to exceed the national production. The United States, traditionally an oil exporter, began to import oil in the early 1970s.

Led by **Venezuela**, oil producers in the Middle East, Asia, Africa, and Latin America formed a **cartel** (monopoly) named **Organization of Petroleum Exporting Countries** (**OPEC**). American motorists began paying five times what they had paid for gasoline only a few months earlier. Gas that sold for 16 cents a gallon in 1972 was now priced at $1.00, and oil companies made "windfall" profits.

Political Aspects

• *Freedom of Information Acts; Privacy Act.* The Freedom of Information Act of 1966 was strengthened by Congress in 1974 as a reaction to secret illegal dossiers compiled by the Nixon administration against his "enemies" and those who openly opposed his policies. Government agencies were required to open their files (except for national defense and foreign policy matters) and permit photocopying of contents by interested persons. The **Privacy Act of 1974** gave citizens the right to examine files compiled about them by government agencies.

• *Federal Election Campaign Finance Reform Act.* The act, passed in 1974 and revised in 1976, gave the President power to appoint a six-member Federal Election Commission. Candidates for President and Vice President in primary and national elections are required to file detailed accounts of sources of moneys received for their campaigns. Limitations are imposed on the amounts that **Political Action Committees** (**PACs**) of unions, corporations, or other organizations may contribute. Individuals who contribute over $100 must certify that the contribution was made without communicating with the candidate or the campaign committee. Violators are subject to severe civil and criminal penalties. The main source of presidential campaign funds was designed to be the $1.00 checkoff allotted to election campaigns from income tax return forms. This $100 million source plus small individual contributions takes the presidential election, to some extent, out of the control of large corporations, unions, and special interest political organizations. Efforts to impose similar restrictions on the election campaigns of members of Congress have proved unsuccessful.

• *Budget and Impoundment Act of 1974.* The act created a **Congressional Budget Office**, whereby Congress could maintain its own records of federal income and expenditures in order to monitor presidential compliance with the law.

• *Space Explorations. Viking 1*, launched in August 1975, landed on Mars in July 1976, and relayed back to earth detailed scientific research including photographs of the planet. It was designed for 90 days of operations but continued to function for almost 6½ years, until it ceased operating in November 1982. *Viking 2*, launched in September 1975, landed on Mars in September 1976, and continued to report its findings for 3½ years. Other launching and explorations (*Voyagers 1* and *2* of September 1977) explored the planets Jupiter, Saturn, and Uranus. *Voyager 2* passed Neptune in 1989 and sent back important new information on this planet. The Hubble Space Telescope was placed in orbit by the space shuttle *Discovery* in 1990. Problems with faulty equipment were repaired by astronauts in 1993.

• *Conrail (1976) and Amtrak (1971).* The **Consolidated Rail Corporation** (**Conrail**) was established in 1976 by combining seven freight lines in the Northeast. Conrail was granted a $2.1 million government loan to maintain the railroads, which were all in financial difficulties. The railroads would then be able to continue operating without a government takeover. Conrail handles about one fourth of the nation's freight and serves a population of 100 million.

Amtrak, a national passenger traffic combine, was organized in 1971 with federal subsidies to help maintain a viable system of national passenger transportation as an alternative to automobiles, buses, and airline transportation. Government subsidies were cut back during the Reagan administration. Yet Amtrak, despite its enforced elimination of many trains, has shown steady growth in the number of passengers served, particularly in the Northeast corridor (Boston–Washington), the Chicago area, and the West Coast. Because of motor vehicle highway gluts, air pollution, and accidents, it is expected that rail transportation will continue to increase in proportion to total passenger traffic.

Foreign Relations Under President Ford

Gerald Ford kept Henry Kissinger as Secretary of State and continued the policy of détente.

President Ford in the Soviet Union and Asia

In November 1974, three months after he took the oath of office as President, Ford met with Premier **Leonid Brezhnev** of the Soviet Union at a health resort near Vladivostok, the chief Soviet port on the Pacific Ocean. They agreed to place a ceiling on the number of **ICBMs** (intercontinental ballistic missiles) launched from submarines, of **MIRVs** (multiple independently targeted re-entry vehicles), and bombers. The meeting, a signal that both sides sought détente, was a tacit recognition of the need to avoid a nuclear holocaust.

Angola

This former Portuguese colony in East Africa was one of the last colonies to gain its independence. A revolution in 1974 led Portugal to grant Angola its independence in 1975. American interest in Angola was based on the intervention by the Soviets, bolstered by Cuban troops. President Ford had Secretary of State Kissinger use his diplomatic skill to prevent a full-scale war or a Communist takeover. The problem was complicated by South Africa's control of **Namibia**, south of Angola. Namibia, the former German colony of Southwest Africa, became a trust territory of South Africa after World War I. Despite pressure from the UN, South Africa retained a dominant influence in Namibia, and was deeply involved in developments in Angola.

South Vietnam

With the collapse of the Thieu government of South Vietnam in April 1975, Congress appropriated $405 million to aid refugees fleeing from the North Vietnamese Communists. President Ford admitted 140,000 South Vietnamese refugees to the United States after Congress rejected his appeal for military aid. Most of the refugees later became American citizens.

Helsinki Accords

In July 1975 President Ford attended a conference of representatives of 35 nations in Helsinki, Finland. Boundaries drawn in Eastern Europe at the end of World War II were officially legitimized. In return, the Soviet Union and its satellites signed a "human rights" guarantee, which included a provision for the right to emigrate. The hopes raised by these agreements did not materialize when the Soviets failed to implement them.

President Jimmy Carter (1977–1981)

> As President I will not be able to provide everything that every one of
> you might like. I am sure to make many mistakes. But I can promise
> you that you will never have the feeling that your needs are being
> ignored, or that we have forgotten who put us in office.
>   Jimmy Carter, in a televised address to the nation, February 1, 1977

The Election of 1976

In the 1976 election, the incumbent President Ford (Republican) ran against
the little known challenger, **James Earl (Jimmy) Carter** (Democrat), former Governor of Georgia. To gain the nomination, each overcame strong
competition from contenders in their respective parties. Ford was challenged
by **Ronald Reagan**, the former Governor of California, who appealed to the
conservative wing of the Republican party. Ford won the nomination on the
first ballot by a close vote—1187 to 1070.

On the Democratic side there were a number of logical contenders for the
nomination but no clear favorite. Among them were former Vice President
Hubert Humphrey, Senator **Henry "Scoop" Jackson** of Washington,
Congressman **Morris Udall** of Arizona, and Governor **George C. Wallace**
of Alabama. However, it was Jimmy Carter who won the nomination by conducting a well-planned campaign. He entered his name in every primary and
appealed to grassroots partisans willing to support an "outsider" who could
bring a breath of fresh air to the stale politics-as-usual atmosphere.

In the November election, Carter and the Democratic party won a hard-
fought victory. It was the first time since 1932 that an incumbent President
was defeated in his bid for re-election. Only 53 percent of the eligible
vot-ers cast their ballots. The Democrats also retained control of the House
and Senate and won nearly three fourths of the state governorships.

Domestic Policies of President Carter

Carter relied on his former Georgia associates when he took command in
Washington. He and they had little experience with how the federal government worked. Moreover, Carter did not know many members of Congress,
and he did not consult with them on his legislative program. As a result,
Congress blocked many of Carter's programs.

President Carter did win the approval of Congress to add two new Cabinet-
level departments to the executive branch—a **Department of Energy** in 1977
and a **Department of Education** in 1979.

Soon after he took office, Carter sought to end the Vietnam trauma. President Ford had offered clemency to draft evaders and deserters. Carter went
further and pardoned some 100,000 Americans who were still subject to
punishment.

• *The Economy.* Inflation plagued the Carter administration as it had Ford's. Led by rising oil prices, inflation reached 13 percent in 1979, while the economy remained in a slump. Mounting unemployment and skyrocketing interest rates (which reached more than 20 percent by 1980) added to the national economic malaise, while a budget deficit of $60 billion in 1980 called for new measures to turn the economy around. The proposal to raise taxes was rejected in favor of the alternative of reducing taxes in order to stimulate the economy. By 1980 the economy was suffering a recession. The same year, the Carter administration moved to bail out the **Chrysler Corporation**, which was facing bankruptcy, by supporting loan assurances of $1.5 billion.

The nation's economic problems were exacerbated by an energy crisis in 1979. Another oil shortage causing long gas lines was largely the result of a revolution in Iran, a major oil producer. The **Shah**, ruler of Iran, was forced to flee and was replaced by a fundamentalist Muslim religious regime headed by the **Ayatollah Ruhollah Khomeini**. As the Iranian oil supply temporarily stopped flowing into world markets, oil shortages developed and gasoline prices rose rapidly. Carter proposed a program to deal with the energy crisis. His proposals for making the nation independent of the OPEC oil included the development of synthetic fuels and other sources of energy such as solar, thermal, and nuclear, and a concerted national program of **energy conservation**.

• *The Environment.* President Carter secured Congressional approval of the Alaska National Interest Lands Conservation Act of 1980. This act set aside 103 million acres (an area larger than California) of unspoiled wilderness in Alaska. It was part of a compromise whereby other undeveloped areas in Alaska were opened for exploitation by oil, mining, and timber interests.

• *Judicial appointments.* President Carter made 265 appointments to the federal judiciary. His choice of a number of minority persons and women for the federal bench was widely hailed. No vacancies on the Supreme Court occurred during his term.

Foreign Affairs

Concern for human rights throughout the world was a key aspect of President Carter's foreign policy. He criticized the Soviet Union for failing to live up to the 1975 Helsinki Accords and denying dissidents and Jews the right to emigrate. His crusade for human rights was also directed against dictatorial regimes in Latin America and Africa. He denounced South Africa's practice of apartheid and castigated Cuba and Uganda for oppression. He cut off foreign aid to dictatorships in Argentina, Brazil, Ethiopia, and Uruguay. But he approved massive arms sales to Iran's dictatorial Shah because his government was serving as "a bastion against communism."

• *Panama Canal Treaties (1978).* By the Hay-Bunau-Varilla Treaty of 1903, a 99-year renewable lease to the Canal Zone in the newly established Republic of Panama was granted by Panama to the United States for the payment of an annual fee. In 1978 the lease still had 25 years to run, but discussions over the future of the Canal had been going on with Panama since the Eisenhower administration.

Two treaties were drawn up in 1977. One provided for the return of the Canal Zone and its operation to Panama by December 31, 1999. The other treaty provided that: "If operations [of the canal] are interfered with, the United States of America shall have the right to the use of force in the Republic of Panama."

• *Camp David Accord.* When Carter became President in 1977, three wars had already been fought between Israel and the neighboring Arab nations, which were determined to destroy the Jewish state. In 1977, President **Anwar el-Sadat** of Egypt surprised the world by accepting an invitation to visit Israel. He delivered a long, emotional plea for peace in an address to the Israeli Knesset (Parliament). President Carter promptly invited Sadat and Israeli Prime Minister **Menachem Begin** to join him at his Camp David retreat in the mountains of Maryland. In the ensuing dialogue, Carter acted to bring the positions of the two leaders closer together.

Finally, on September 17, 1978, a tentative agreement between Egypt and Israel was reached. President Carter went to Egypt and Israel in 1979 to facilitate peace negotiations and the peace treaty was signed in March 1979. Israel returned the **Sinai** peninsula to Egypt in return for guarantees of normal relations between the two countries. Exchange of ambassadors and the establishment of travel and trade relations raised hopes for an expanding good-neighbor relationship.

Shortly after this diplomatic success, President Carter took another significant move in foreign affairs by establishing full diplomatic relations with the People's Republic of China.

• *SALT.* The **Strategic Arms Limitation Treaty of 1972 (SALT I)**, between the United States and the Soviet Union, was scheduled to expire in December 1977. However, both sides continued to observe the terms of the treaty and a **SALT II** agreement was signed by President Carter and Soviet Premier Leonid Brezhnev in Vienna in June 1979. If ratified by the U.S. Senate, it would have extended arms limitations until December 1985. But it ran into strong opposition in the Senate and was tabled when Soviet troops invaded Afghanistan in December 1979.

• *Nicaragua.* Nicaragua, the largest country in Central America, was governed by the Somoza family from the 1920s until rebel forces known as **Sandinistas** succeeded in overthrowing the dictatorship of Anastasio Somoza in July 1979. The United States quickly recognized the new government, hoping to assist in the establishment of a democratic republic. But the

Sandinistas proceeded to establish a Socialist regime modeled on Marxist economic principles.

- *Afghanistan.* In December 1979 the Soviet army launched a full-scale invasion of Afghanistan. This attempt to strengthen the faltering pro-Soviet government in Kabul met with unexpectedly strong resistance from guerrilla forces.

President Carter responded energetically to this challenge. He sent naval forces into the Persian Gulf, declaring that the area was "vital" to American interests. He ordered an embargo on the shipment of grain and high-technology machinery to the Soviet Union, called for a boycott of the 1980 Olympic Games in Moscow, and requested Congress to pass legislation requiring young men and women to register for a possible military draft.

Aid to Afghanistani rebel forces resisting the Soviet troops was stepped up throughout 1980 and reached a climax during the second term of the Reagan presidency. American military supplies flowed to the anti-Soviet forces. The Soviet air force was neutralized by sophisticated American Stinger missiles. The invasion turned out to be a disaster for the Soviets and in February 1986, the new Soviet leader, **Mikhail S. Gorbachev**, announced the withdrawal of Soviet forces "in the nearest future." Peace talks were held in Geneva under UN auspices, and accords providing for Soviet withdrawal were signed in April 1988. The last of 100,000 Soviet troops left Afghanistan in February 1989.

- *American Hostages in Iran.* The Shah of Iran was overthrown early in 1979 and replaced by a fanatical religious leader, the Ayatollah Ruhollah Khomeini. Fierce hatred of the United States by Muslim fanatics erupted in an unprecedented act of international terrorism. On November 4, 1979, a mob surrounded the American embassy in Teheran and seized its occupants, 52 members of the American diplomatic corps. Although President Carter worked to free the hostages, it wasn't until **Ronald Reagan** took the oath of office as 40th President of the United States that they were released—having served 444 days in captivity.

Exercise Set 6.14

1. Nelson Rockefeller became Vice President in the Ford administration as a result of
   A. his election to the office in 1974.
   B. the decision of the Republican National Committee.
   C. his nomination by President Ford and confirmation by both houses of Congress.
   D. a decision by the U.S. Supreme Court.

2. The Federal Election Campaign Finance Reform Act of 1974 as amended in 1976 provides for
   A. a limit on the amount that candidates for the Senate or House of Representatives may spend on their election campaigns.
   B. a mandatory contribution to presidential campaigns by a $1.00 checkoff on federal income tax returns.
   C. the end of limitations on the amount that political action committees may contribute to candidates for national office.
   D. candidates in primary elections and regular national elections must file detailed accounts with the Federal Election Commission specifying the amounts and sources of contributions to their campaigns.

3. Which action was a major foreign policy achievement of President Jimmy Carter?
   A. Settling the Suez crisis
   B. Withdrawing the United States from the Vietnam War
   C. Establishing improved relations with Iran
   D. Mediating the Camp David Accord between Egypt and Israel

4. The largest contributor to the high rate of inflation during the Ford and Carter administrations was
   A. imports of oil.
   B. high farm commodity prices.
   C. high building costs.
   D. budget deficits.

THE REAGAN ERA (1981–1989)

The Election of 1980

> The Republican party is sharply different under Reagan from what it was under Gerald Ford and Presidents all the way back to Eisenhower.
>
> Jimmy Carter, Sept. 2, 1980

> In this present crisis, government is not the solution to our problems. . . . It is time to check and reverse the growth of government. . . .
>
> Ronald Reagan, first inaugural address, Jan. 20, 1981

As the 1980 election approached, the nation was plagued by unemployment, inflation, high interest rates, and frustration over the captivity of 52 American hostages in Iran. The apparent inability of the Carter administration to resolve these problems caused Senator **Edward M. (Ted) Kennedy** to challenge President Carter for the Democratic presidential nomination. Many members of the Democratic party feared that Carter would not be reelected. A public opinion poll in the summer of 1980 revealed that only 21 percent of the American people approved of President Carter's performance in office. This was an all-time low. Carter turned back Kennedy's challenge and won the nomination. He was opposed in the election by **Ronald Reagan**, who was nominated by the Republican party. Some voters turned to a third party, the Independent party, led by Representative John Anderson from Illinois, who won more than 5.7 million votes.

In the popular vote, Reagan received 51.6 percent against Carter's 41.7 percent, with 6.7 percent going to Anderson. But Reagan won an overwhelming majority of votes in the electoral college, 489 to 49.

In addition to winning the presidency, the Republicans gained control of the Senate for the first time in 28 years and picked up 33 seats in the House of Representatives.

Reagan Policies

Ronald Reagan had long been a leader of the conservative movement in the United States. He favored limited federal government, lower taxes, and reduced federal regulation of business. Although Reagan favored a more limited role for the federal government, in social issues he supported constitutional amendments to ban abortion and to permit prayer in public schools. He also favored a return to traditional values and family roles.

Attempt to Assassinate the President

On March 30, 1981, President Reagan was shot by **John W. Hinckley, Jr**. A bullet caused the collapse of the President's left lung, but after twelve days in the hospital, he returned to work. By April 28 he was able to deliver an address to Congress. His resiliency won public admiration.

Domestic Programs

President Reagan felt that he had a mandate from the electorate to carry out his programs for the nation. He immediately turned his attention to the nation's economic crisis.

Supply-side Economics

To bring down inflation, President Reagan adopted a policy known as **"supply-side" economics**, based on the belief that cuts in income taxes, especially on higher incomes, would result in business investment and act as a stimulus to business. Cuts in corporation taxes would promote business expansion, resulting in greater production of goods and bringing about full employment. Reagan prevailed on Congress to cut taxes on high incomes, corporations, and investors, and in July 1981, Congress passed the largest tax cut in the nation's history. American taxpayers received tax benefits of $750 billion over a five-year period.

The Federal Budget; Cuts and Priorities

To help him carry out his budgetary program, Reagan chose David Stockman as his director of the Office of Management and Budget. The goal of a balanced budget was to be attained through sharp cuts in federal expenditures. The one exception was the defense budget, which was expanded. Although the Reagan administration believed supply-side economics and cuts in the budget would painlessly decrease inflation, the economy did not respond as expected. Inflation came down, but within a year the nation was in a severe **recession**. In November 1982, unemployment reached 10.8 percent, with 11 million unemployed. By 1983, the economy began to recover and the twin demons—inflation and high interest rates—were brought under control. But the national budget remained unbalanced. By 1986, budget deficits, mounting annually, exceeded $200 billion. By 1989 the national debt was $3 trillion ($3 thousand billion). To remedy this, President Reagan called for an amendment to the Constitution requiring a balanced budget. In December 1985, Congress passed the **Gramm-Rudman-Hollings Act**, designed to achieve a balanced budget by 1991. The law set annual targets for reducing the deficit by across-the-board cuts in federal spending.

The first Reagan budget called for drastic cuts in social programs. The budget proposed a cut of $1.1 billion in aid to education with no provision for aid to handicapped or gifted students. Direct financial aid to college and university students (programs in existence since 1965) was phased out.

As for the poor, President Reagan spoke of a national "safety net," but this budget called for a reduction of $1.6 billion in school lunch programs for needy children, extinction of the Legal Services Corporation, reduction in Medicaid by nearly $1 billion, sharp cuts in federal aid to low-income housing, and a $2.3 billion cut in the food stamp program.

The "new federalism" of the Reagan administration offered grants to the states to help them assume responsibility for funding these programs.

Social Issues

The Reagan administration supported the position of conservatives on social issues, favoring organized prayer in the schools, support for nonpublic education, and less emphasis on civil rights. It opposed the Equal Rights Amendment, abortion, and sex education in the schools. Students' Fourth Amendment rights were redefined in *New Jersey* v. *T.L.O.* (1985) when the Supreme Court ruled that school officials needed only "reasonable suspicion" rather than "probable cause" to search students suspected of unlawful conduct. A later Supreme Court in 1995 would extend search rights over students to allow drug testing of student athletes in *Vernonia* v. *Acton* (1995).

Supreme Court Appointments

With the retirement of Justice Potter Stewart from the Supreme Court in 1981, President Reagan nominated **Sandra Day O'Connor** of the Arizona Supreme Court. She was confirmed by the Senate and sworn in September 25, 1981, the first woman to serve on the Supreme Court. Five years later additional openings came. Chief Justice **Warren E. Burger** retired in 1986 and President Reagan's nominee for the chief justiceship, Justice **William H. Rehnquist**, was confirmed by the Senate. The vacancy brought about by Justice Rehnquist's move to the chief justiceship was filled when the Reagan nominee, Judge **Antonin Scalia** of Virginia, was confirmed.

After the retirement of Justice Lewis F. Powell, Jr., in 1987, President Reagan nominated Judge Robert Bork of the United States Court of Appeals for the District of Columbia to fill the vacancy. Judge Bork, a former law professor at Yale Law School and Solicitor General in the Nixon administration, was a conservative whom Reagan described as "a powerful advocate of judicial restraint." He was opposed by many groups, and after hearings on the nomination the Senate Committee on the Judiciary recommended to the Senate that the nomination be rejected. Reagan's next nominee, Douglas Ginsberg, met with opposition because he admitted having once used marijuana. He asked to have his name withdrawn. Judge Anthony M. Kennedy of California was then nominated and promptly confirmed.

Meanwhile President Reagan nominated judges to fill vacancies on the lower federal courts—District Courts and Circuit Courts of Appeals—throughout the country. In selecting appointees, he was advised by his Attorney General, **Edwin Meese**, who sought candidates that satisfied the ideological criteria of conservative Republicans. During his eight years in office, Reagan appointed nearly 50 percent of all the judges on the federal bench.

The Environment

The assault on the environment caused by budget cuts for enforcement agencies such as the Environmental Protection Agency (EPA), the Food and Drug Administration (FDA), and the Occupational Safety and Health Administration (OSHA), was a source of concern for conservationists, environmentalists, and public health agencies.

In November 1986 President Reagan vetoed a clean water bill passed by Congress. The bill called for expenditure of $20 billion for facilities to treat sewage and water poisoned by toxic dumps. The bill was resubmitted and passed over the President's veto by the (new) 100th Congress in February 1987.

• *Depletion of Ozone.* In March 1989 the 12 European Community countries agreed to eliminate, by the end of the century, the production and use of chemicals that destroy the earth's protective ozone shield. The action was endorsed by William K. Reilly, head of the Environmental Protection Agency in the Bush administration. Ozone, the natural shield that gives protection from the sun's direct ultraviolet radiation, is declining steadily due to chemicals released into the air.

• *Greenhouse Effect.* The earth's temperature is slowly rising because of the "**greenhouse effect**." The global mean surface temperature has increased 0.5°F to 1.0°F since the late 19th century. Gases in the air, especially carbon dioxide released in automobile exhausts and industrial smoke stacks, prevent heat from the sun from radiating back into space. The rising temperature will have serious adverse effects on humans. The glacial ice at the polar regions is melting, bringing about a disastrous rise in the ocean level.

The Election of 1984

As the election of 1984 approached, the nation was in an economic upswing. The recession of 1981–1982 was over, inflation and interest rates were down, and employment was up. In January 1984 President Reagan sounded his campaign theme, declaring "America is back, standing tall, looking to the '80s with courage, confidence and hope." Despite a doubling of the national debt during his first term, the President stood firm on his economic program of tax reduction. He was equally consistent on social issues: opposing abortion, the Equal Rights Amendment, affirmative action, and busing for school desegregation.

The front-runner for the Democratic nomination, former Vice President **Walter Mondale**, was strongly challenged by Senator **Gary Hart** of Colorado and Reverend **Jesse Jackson** of Chicago. However, Mondale secured enough delegates to clinch the nomination before the convention. For Vice President he chose Representative **Geraldine Ferraro** of New York, the first woman candidate for the vice presidency nominated by a major party. Of the 92 million votes cast, 53,354,037 (59 percent) went for Reagan and 36,884,260 (41 percent) for Mondale. In the electoral college, the Republicans won 525 to 13.

Foreign Affairs

Cold War Resumed

During the 1980 election campaign, Ronald Reagan denounced SALT II, the Strategic Arms Limitation Treaty negotiated with the Soviets in 1979 by the Carter administration. The treaty, which was to run until 1985, was never acted on by the Senate because of the Soviet invasion of Afghanistan, but both sides observed its terms. In a press conference soon after his inauguration, President Reagan censured the Soviets, saying they were "prepared to commit any crime, to lie, to cheat" in order to achieve world conquest. Reagan's insistence on a hard-line approach toward the Soviet Union, as well as increased military spending and the placement of nuclear weapons in Europe, alarmed many. Fear of a global nuclear war increased throughout Europe and America. In New York's Central Park in June 1982, a peaceful demonstration against nuclear arms brought out more than 500,000 people. Antinuclear demonstrations took place in the major cities of our NATO allies. In 1985, a new leader, **Mikhail Gorbachev**, came to power in the Soviet Union. Reagan agreed to meet with him in Geneva in November.

Lebanon

On October 23, 1983, a truck carrying explosives drove into the marine barracks in Beirut, Lebanon, and blew up, killing 241 marines. The following year pro-Iranian terrorists took three American hostages in Beirut, including the CIA station chief, William Buckley, who died while being held captive.

Grenada

In October 1983 President Reagan made a surprise announcement of an invasion of the tiny eastern Caribbean nation on the island of Grenada by

6,000 U.S. marines and paratroopers. The leftist government of Grenada, supported by Cuba and the Soviet Union, was overthrown and replaced by a pro-American government. Protection of the 700 American medical students in Grenada was a factor in the invasion.

Nicaragua

In Central America, the Reagan administration found a more serious challenge. The **Somoza** dictatorship, which had governed Nicaragua since 1933, was overthrown in 1979 by the pro-Marxist revolutionists, called **Sandinistas**. Leftist guerrillas were also attempting to overthrow the government of neighboring **El Salvador**. The Reagan administration decided to support the opponents of the Sandinistas, called **Contras**, who operated from bases in Honduras. The United States financed and supplied the Contras with arms. Economic pressure was applied to Nicaragua. To prevent Soviet arms and supplies from entering Nicaragua, that country's harbors were mined by the CIA in violation of international law. Congress was divided, as were the American people, almost 50-50 as to whether this policy or a policy of seeking a political solution was preferable. The countries of Latin America, as well as some Americans, feared that force could lead to a wider war.

Reagan-Gorbachev Summit Meetings

In March 1985 Mikhail Gorbachev became the new General Secretary of the Soviet Communist party. His ideas began a new phase in both domestic and foreign policy in the Soviet Union. On the home front he called for "**glasnost**" (openness) and "**perestroika**" (restructuring). In foreign policy, he called for détente with the United States.

• *Geneva: November 1985.* President Reagan and Gorbachev held their first summit meeting in Geneva, where they met face-to-face for five hours. A stumbling block was Reagan's insistence on proceeding with the Strategic Defense Initiative (SDI), commonly called "Star Wars," which the Soviets regarded as destabilizing. Though no formal agreement was reached, the two leaders approved plans for arms control talks to make 50 percent reductions in strategic weapons their longterm goals. Provisions for cultural and educational exchanges were a concrete result of the talks.

• *Reykjavik.* The second meeting between Reagan and Gorbachev took place in October 1986 in Reykjavik, Iceland. On the American side, there was little planning for the hastily arranged meeting. The President made the astonishing proposal that all ballistic missiles—airborne, landbased, and seaborne—be eliminated by 1996. It fell apart when Reagan refused to agree to an interpretation of the 1972 ABM treaty that would restrict the Strategic Defense Initiative to laboratory research.

• *Washington—the INF (Intermediate Nuclear Forces) Treaty.* President Reagan and Soviet leader Gorbachev held their third summit meeting in Washington in December 1987. They signed a major arms limitation treaty providing for the dismantling of all short-range and intermediate-range (300–3,400 miles) missiles. This applied specifically to 1,752 American missiles in Europe, and 859 Soviet missiles in Europe facing them. The removal of these Soviet missiles was hailed by America's NATO allies as a long step toward ultimate security. After a four-month debate, the Senate, by a vote of 93 to 5, ratified the INF treaty for eliminating medium- and shorter-range land-based nuclear missiles. It was perhaps the most historic accomplishment of the Reagan presidency. In 1988, Reagan visited Moscow. Discussions were held regarding Soviet dissidents and the promotion of human rights.

Middle East

Constant turmoil in the Middle East marked the region as one of the danger areas requiring the constant attention of the United States.

• *Israel.* The Reagan administration's support for America's ally, Israel, was matched by Soviet support for Syria. In June 1981, Israeli war planes demolished an Iraqi atomic installation near Baghdad, charging that the plant was nearing completion for the production of atomic weapons. In June 1982 Israeli armed forces invaded southern Lebanon and advanced to Beirut. The area harbored **PLO** terrorist brigades that repeatedly attempted to infiltrate Israel. The immediate mission was accomplished, but the Israelis suffered losses and withdrew from Lebanon in 1985 without achieving any lasting results. An uprising ("**intifada**") of the Palestinians in areas occupied by Israel resulted in violence and was met by harsh repressive measures on the part of Israeli armed forces. In late 1988, **Yassir Arafat**, leader of the major PLO faction, seemed to renounce terrorism when he addressed the UN.

• *Libya.* A center of Middle East terrorism was Libya under the leadership of Colonel **Muammar Qaddafi**. Qaddafi, in power since 1969 and violently anti-American, trained and supplied international terrorists, using the profits of his oil-rich land to finance terrorist operations. In August 1981 Soviet-built Libyan fighter planes attacked American navy planes on maneuvers in the Mediterranean. In 1982 the United States placed restrictions on trade with Libya and in January 1986 all Libyan assets in the United States were frozen. In April 1986 American planes bombed Libyan military bases in retaliation for terrorist acts. In January 1989 two U.S. Navy F-14 fighter planes shot down two MIG-23 fighters off the coast of Libya.

• *The Persian Gulf.* A border dispute between Iraq and Iran, major oil-producing countries, precipitated a war in 1980. Oil tankers in the Persian Gulf came under attack from both Iraq and Iran. U.S. naval vessels were deployed in the Gulf to protect American shipping. Kuwait, a major oil-producing country on the Gulf, was supporting Iraq in the war. In March 1987 Kuwait asked the United States to protect its oil tankers in the Persian Gulf. In May 1987, an Iraqi aircraft, mistaking the *U.S.S. Stark* for an Iranian merchant vessel, fired two missiles killing 37 sailors and wounding 21 on the *Stark*. On the same day the United States agreed to replace the Kuwaiti flag with the American flag (called reflagging) on eleven Kuwaiti oil tankers and to provide naval escort for these ships in the Gulf. By the end of 1987, twelve major American warships were deployed in the Gulf to insure an uninterrupted flow of oil to America and its allies. In October 1987 one of the reflagged tankers was successfully attacked in Kuwaiti waters by Iranian Silkworm (Chinese-built) missiles. Other nations also sent ships to protect their countries' oil tankers and to keep the Gulf shipping lanes open. In April 1988 the Iranian navy attacked the United States fleet in the Persian Gulf. In less than one day the United States military destroyed one-fifth of Iran's navy while losing only one helicopter. In July 1988, an Iranian civilian airliner was destroyed over the Persian Gulf by gunfire from the *U.S.S. Vincennes*, which mistook the plane for a fighter jet. All 290 persons on the plane died in the attack. The destruction by a terrorist of a Pan Am flight bound from London to New York on December 21, 1988, was believed to be in retaliation for the *Vincennes* action. All 259 people on board the plane died, as well as 11 people on the ground, as the plane went down over Lockerbie, Scotland.

Reagan's Second Term

Income Tax Reform

The 1986 Income Tax Reform Act, which the President signed on October 22, completed a long overdue process. The tax code had become unwieldy, with patchwork changes and revisions introduced over the years. The 1986 act simplified the code, exempted millions of low-income families from federal income taxes, reduced the highest bracket to 28 percent, and closed numerous loopholes.

The Election of 1986

Attention focused on the Senate, where the Republicans had held a majority since the election of 1980. President Reagan toured the country to help elect Republicans to the Senate, but the voters gave the Democrats a resounding victory. They picked up eight seats, giving them a majority of 55 to 45.

Wall Street Crash

On Monday, October 19, 1987, the New York Stock Exchange registered its largest point decline in history when the Dow-Jones industrial average plummeted 508.32 points in a day of frenetic trading, as 604 million shares (by far the greatest number ever) changed hands. The Dow made a quick recovery and regained almost 300 points in the next two days.

The Balance of Trade

A worrisome aspect of the American economy was the persistent negative balance of trade which, during the Reagan years, had seen the United States change from a creditor to a debtor nation in international trade. The annual negative balance was running at $170 billion. The dollar, which was worth 360 yen during the first quarter century following World War II, was now trading at about 120 yen—one third its previous value. Americans were buying automobiles, cameras, computers, radio and television sets, even steel from Japan, while the Japanese were buying only unprocessed raw materials such as timber, oil, metals, grains, and fiber from the United States. The imbalance was causing the closing of factories and the displacement of labor in American industry.

The Iran-Contra Affair

On November 3, 1986, the Lebanese newspaper *Al-Shiraa* reported that the United States had sold arms to Iran after a secret visit by National Security Adviser Robert McFarlane. Less than 24 hours earlier, the U.S. hostage, David P. Jacobsen, who was kidnapped in May 1985, was released. Six hostages remained in Beirut. It was apparent that an "arms for hostages" deal had been made.

In an effort to win the release of the hostages, the Reagan administration secretly sold arms to Iran. The money paid by Iran for these arms was then used to fund the Contra rebels in Nicaragua. This secret and illegal diversion of funds was carried out by Lt. Colonel **Oliver North** with the knowledge of his superiors (Robert McFarlane and John Poindexter) on the National Security Council. It was an attempt by the Reagan administration to bypass Congress, which had passed the **Boland Amendment** outlawing aid to the Contras. Revelation of these activities caused a furor in the nation.

Investigation of the Iran-Contra Affair

Both the House and the Senate established select committees to investigate the Iran-Contra scandal. It was decided that the committees would meet jointly and conduct televised hearings. The hearings before the joint congressional committee opened in May 1987 and terminated three months later in August 1987. The committee's final report was submitted in November 1987. Criminal prosecution was assigned to an independent counsel, Lawrence E. Walsh.

Conclusion

Testimony at the hearing disclosed that high U.S. government officials provided the Contras with private and international sources of funds for conducting military operations against the Nicaraguan government.

In its final report, the majority concluded: "It was the President's policy—not an isolated decision by (Oliver) North or Poindexter—to sell arms secretly to Iran and to maintain the Contras, 'body and soul,' the Boland amendment notwithstanding . . ."

Independent counsel **Lawrence Walsh** secured indictment of **Oliver North** on twelve counts. North, a Lt. Colonel in the U.S. Marines, played a key role in the illegal Contra aid operations when he served as Assistant Director of the National Security Council from 1981 to 1986. He was tried in Federal District Court presided over by Judge Gerhard Gesell. The trial ended in a verdict of not guilty on nine counts and guilty on three counts: (1) aiding and abetting obstruction of Congress; (2) destroying government documents; and (3) receiving an illegal gratuity in the form of a security system for his home. North was fined $150,000 and given a three-year suspended sentence, but his conviction was later overturned on technical grounds. In 1994, North ran unsuccessfully for the U.S. Senate in Virginia.

Decline of President Reagan's Popularity

A "Special Review Board" was appointed by President Reagan on December 1, 1986 to investigate the Iran-Contra affair. John Tower was named chairman and the other two members were Edmund Muskie and Brent Scowcroft.

The Tower Commission report of February 26, 1987 stated "The President did not seem to be aware of the way in which the operation (arms for hostages) was implemented and the full consequences of U.S. participation . . . At no time did he insist on accountability."

In a nationally televised speech on March 4, 1987, President Reagan said, "I told the American people I did not trade arms for hostages. My heart and my best intentions still tell me that's true. But the facts and the evidence tell me it's not. . . . what began as a strategic opening to Iran deteriorated in its implementation into trading arms for hostages. It was a mistake." Disclosure of the arms deals had a dramatic impact on Reagan's standing in the polls. In *The New York Times*-CBS News poll reported December 1, 1986, his approval rating dropped from 67 percent a month earlier to 46 percent.

The decline in Reagan's popularity was reflected in his difficulty in gaining congressional support for his agenda. Congress overrode his veto of a transportation bill for spending $87.5 billion on highway and mass transit and allowing states to increase the speed limit to 65 m.p.h. The Senate rejected his nomination of Judge Robert H. Bork for the Supreme Court. In February 1988, the House voted against military aid to the Contras and the Contra forces went into decline.

But Ronald Reagan was flexible enough to ride out the storm. Moreover, his success at the Moscow summit with the Soviet leader Mikhail Gorbachev that produced a nuclear arms agreement helped to restore his popularity. In Moscow the President and Gorbachev signed the historic **Intermediate Nuclear Forces (INF)** treaty.

Exercise Set 6.15

1. President Reagan's "supply-side" economic program was characterized by
   A. a budget brought into balance by income equal to expenditures.
   B. a budget evenly balanced between spending for defense and spending for social programs.
   C. an effort to maintain a favorable balance of trade.
   D. a tax program designed to bring about an increase in the supply of consumer goods.

2. Which of the following was *not* an aspect of the 1984 elections?
   A. Ronald Reagan scored a landslide victory.
   B. Television debates were held between the presidential and vice presidential candidates.
   C. Democrats failed to gain control of the U.S. Senate.
   D. There was a growing movement in favor of modifying the method of electing a President.

3. Which of the following was *not* a foreign policy objective of the Reagan administration?
   A. Cessation of violence and armed conflict between Arabs and Israelis in the Middle East
   B. Immediate end of the apartheid policy of the South African government
   C. Overthrow of the Marxist government of Nicaragua
   D. Economic and diplomatic cooperation with the government and people of Japan

4. Which of the following was *not* a sign of President Reagan's declining influence during his second term?
   A. Appointment of a congressional committee to investigate the Iran-Contra affair
   B. Democrats regain control of the Senate in the 1986 election
   C. Congress passes the 1986 Tax Reform Act
   D. Congress passes the Clean Water Act of 1987 over President Reagan's veto

5. President Ronald Reagan used the concept of supply-side economics when he proposed
   A. reducing income taxes to stimulate growth.
   B. providing direct payments to people living in poverty.
   C. creating government jobs to keep people working.
   D. increasing regulations on business to promote competition.

PRESIDENT GEORGE BUSH (1989–1993)

The Election of 1988

The Primaries

Major contestants for the Republican nomination were Vice President George Bush, Senator Robert Dole of Kansas, minority leader of the Senate, television evangelist Pat Robertson, and Representative Jack Kemp of New York.

On the Democratic side there were more contestants. Former Senator Gary Hart was an early casualty of the media when he was caught in a liaison with a woman other than his wife. Others actively seeking the nomination were Governor Michael Dukakis of Massachusetts, Reverend Jesse Jackson of Chicago, Senator Albert Gore of Tennessee, Representative Richard Gephardt of Missouri, Senator Paul Simon of Illinois, and Senator Joseph R. Biden, Jr., of Delaware.

In the first Republican primaries, Dole made a strong showing, but Bush fought back, gained the lead, and pulled ahead, clinching the nomination in April, four months before the Republican convention. The Democratic race narrowed down to a contest between Dukakis and Jackson, with the former steadily increasing his lead. Dukakis was nominated at the Democratic convention in July and chose Senator Lloyd Bentsen of Texas for Vice President.

In August, **Bush** won the nomination at the Republican convention. He made a controversial choice for a running mate, the young and relatively inexperienced Senator **Dan Quayle** of Indiana.

The Campaign and Election

Neither candidate evoked enthusiasm from the electorate, and the campaign seemed lackluster. It was fought chiefly on television and in the press. Bush was accused of using negative campaigning for calling Dukakis a "card-carrying liberal" and for running the controversial and racist "Willie Horton" TV ad campaign.

	Popular Vote	Percent	Electoral Vote
Bush	47,917,341	54	426
Dukakis	41,013,030	46	112

In Congress the Democrats gained strength in both houses while failing to win the presidency. The voters evidently determined to divide governmental power between the two parties. In the Senate, the Democrats gained one seat, giving them a majority of 55 to 45. In the House, they added 5 seats to give them a majority of 262 to 173.

The Bush Program and Promises

In a 20-minute inaugural address on January 20, 1989, President Bush singled out major problems that his administration would address. Referring to the national deficit he said, "We have more will than wallet; but will is what we need." He called the national epidemic of drug abuse a scourge and said, "Take my word for it: this scourge will stop." He called on the Democratic Congress, whom he referred to as his "friends" in the "loyal opposition," to join him in a bipartisan effort to solve the social problems of homelessness, poverty, and "the rough crime of the streets." Bush had earlier expressed the hope that he could lead "a kinder, gentler nation."

In a nationally televised address to Congress in February 1989, Bush outlined his budget proposals, encompassing broad outlines for the future. "We must make a very substantial cut in the federal budget deficit." In addition to the immediate goal of "meeting the targets set forth in the Gramm-Rudman-Hollings law," he asked for enactment of two-year budgets, a line-item veto provision, and the passing of a constitutional amendment requiring a balanced budget. He repeated his pledge of no new taxes.

Specific proposals included $2.2 billion for the National Science Foundation; a permanent tax credit law to promote basic research; a cut in the maximum tax rate on capital gains; and incentive awards for educational excellence. He said, "I'd like to be the Education President." President Bush asked for an increase of almost a billion dollars in budget outlays to escalate the war against drugs. Additional outlays were proposed for a new attack on organized crime; for education to prevent AIDS and research to find a cure; for upgrading and protecting the environment through a new Clean Air Act, and enforcement of laws against toxic wastes.

He called for a new child-care tax credit adjustment and guaranteed full funding of Social Security, including a full cost-of-living increase. He asserted his support for restoring the integrity of the failing savings and loan industry. He asked for a one-year freeze in the military budget, and overhauling of the defense procurement process.

On plans for world peace he would carefully assess the changes taking place in the Soviet Union and added, "I have personally assured General Secretary Gorbachev that . . . we will be ready to move forward."

Domestic Events

Savings and Loan Scandal

Savings and loan institutions (S&Ls or "thrifts") boomed following World War II, primarily by financing veterans' guaranteed home-mortgage loans at low interest rates. The S&Ls were legally restricted from matching the higher interest rates charged by other financial institutions, like commercial banks. In the early 1980s Congress and the Reagan administration **deregulated** the S&L industry, eliminated interest ceilings, and allowed the S&Ls to make commercial loans. Although the S&Ls were still regulated, and their deposits insured by the Federal Savings and Loan Insurance Corporation (FSLIC), a laissez-faire attitude prevailed, and following deregulation many of the S&Ls began to make high-risk loans and unsound investments, often in commercial real estate.

When the nation's economy faltered, many of the S&Ls' borrowers were unable to repay their loans, and the savings and loan institutions began to collapse. The FSLIC soon ran out of funds to back up the failing S&Ls, and the **Federal Deposit Insurance Corporation** (**FDIC**) assumed the responsibility. The eventual cost to taxpayers over the next 40 years is estimated at $500 billion.

Census of 1990

Article I, Section 2, of the Constitution provides that a census be taken every ten years to determine the number of representatives a state shall have in Congress. According to the 1990 census, the nation's population in 1990 was approximately 249,500,000, an increase of about 23 million over the 1980 count. Adjustments in Congress, where the total number of Representatives remains at 435, included losses in New York (3 seats), Pennsylvania, Michigan, Ohio, and Illinois (2 seats each), and the loss of one seat in each of eight other states. Gains in congressional representation came in California (7 seats), Florida (4 seats), Texas (3 seats), and gains of one seat in each of five other states.

Americans with Disabilities Act (1990)

Passed by Congress July 13, 1990, the Americans with Disabilities Act (ADA) has been considered the most significant antidiscrimination legislation since the Civil Rights Acts of the 1960s. The law bans discrimination against people with physical or mental impairments in employment, transportation, public accommodations, and communications services.

Supreme Court Decisions

In *Cruzan* v. *Director, Missouri Department of Health* (1990), the Supreme Court addressed the issue of termination of life support. In a 6–3 decision, the Court found that a person did have a liberty interest under the due process clause of the Fourteenth Amendment to refuse medical treatment if there was clear and convincing evidence that they were competent when making the decision.

The issue of abortion was reviewed in *Planned Parenthood of Southeastern Pennsylvania* v. *Casey* (1992), when the Court reaffirmed a woman's right to have an abortion pursuant to *Roe* v. *Wade* (1973), but upheld waiting periods and parental notification by minors prior to obtaining an abortion.

Nomination and Confirmation of Clarence Thomas to the Supreme Court

President Bush selected Judge **Clarence Thomas** of the District of Columbia Circuit Court, a conservative Republican African American, to replace the retiring Justice **Thurgood Marshall**, an African American liberal and long-time proponent of civil rights. This nomination created some of the most heated Senate confirmation proceedings in the history of the nation. Major points of debate during the early hearings of the Senate Judiciary Committee were Thomas's opposition to **affirmative action** for minorities and women and questions about his stance on the *Roe* v. *Wade* decision on abortion rights.

In the course of the hearings, Democratic committee members raised allegations of sexual harassment, supported by testimony from law professor Anita Hill of the University of Oklahoma, who had worked for Judge Thomas at the Equal Employment Opportunity Commission during the Reagan administration. Judge Thomas reappeared before the committee to deny Professor Hill's charges and called the hearings a "high-tech lynching." After heated and partisan debate, the Senate confirmed his appointment on October 15, 1991, in a very close 52 to 48 vote, with 11 Democrats crossing party lines to vote with the Republicans.

Foreign Affairs

Invasion of Panama (December 20, 1989–January 3, 1990)

In April 1989 a report of the narcotics subcommittee of the Senate Foreign Relations Committee charged that the head of the Panamanian Defense Forces (PDF), **General Manuel Noriega**, "controlled all elements of the Panamanian government essential to the protection of drug trafficking and money laundering." Federal grand juries in Miami and Tampa, Florida, indicted Noriega on charges of drug trafficking. President Bush appealed for his overthrow, but Noriega survived economic sanctions and several coup attempts and annulled a May 1989 election in which he had been defeated.

On December 16, 1989, an off-duty American marine was shot to death by members of the PDF. With fairly wide approval, both in the United States and Panama, President Bush sent 10,000 American troops into Panama on December 20, 1989, to protect American lives and interests and to capture General Noriega and bring him to the United States to stand trial. Noriega surrendered on January 3, 1990, and was taken to Miami, where he was tried and found guilty of cocaine trafficking, racketeering, and money laundering; he was sentenced to a 40-year jail term. On December 11, 2011, Noriega was returned to Panama to serve a 20-year prison term. The invasion was condemned by the United Nations, but President Bush found legal support for the military action in a clause of the **1977 Panama Canal Treaty**, which allowed the United States to take action to protect the Panama Canal.

Operation Desert Storm

After unsuccessful talks about oil production and debt repayment between Iraq and its neighbor Kuwait, Iraqi president **Saddam Hussein** invaded and annexed Kuwait on August 2, 1990, declaring it to be a province of Iraq. Fearing that Iraq's next target might be Saudi Arabia, President Bush ordered 430,000 U.S. troops to Saudi Arabia to protect the world's largest oil reserves. "Operation Desert Shield," as this first phase was known, began on August 6, 1990, and its purpose was to "draw a line in the sand" (between Kuwait and Iraq) behind which Iraq's large army would have to retreat. On November 8, 1990, a United Nations Security Council resolution set a January 15, 1991, deadline for Iraq to withdraw from Kuwait.

The Iraqi withdrawal from Kuwait did not take place, and President Bush ordered a devastating air assault against military targets in Iraq and Kuwait. The phase of bombing and ground offensive by the allied powers was known as "Operation Desert Storm." The U.S. and allied forces carried out a massive bombing campaign for five weeks. On February 24, 1991, they began a ground campaign, directed by **General Norman Schwartzkopf**, that smashed through Hussein's armies, retaking Kuwait and occupying most of southern Iraq in only four days of combat. The retreating Iraqi forces set fire to over 500 of Kuwait's oil wells, causing a widespread environmental disaster. There were widespread fears that the Iraqis would resort to chemical and biological warfare, as they had previously done in their war with Iran and in campaigns against the Kurdish minorities. There has been no evidence that the Iraqis used any such weapons, although traces of nerve gas and mustard gas were detected, possibly from stockpiles destroyed by U.S. bombings.

On February 27, 1991, 100 hours after the land battle began, President Bush ordered a unilateral cease-fire, and on March 3, 1991, Iraq agreed to abide by the UN resolutions. An official cease-fire agreement was signed April 6, 1991.

South Africa

Although more than 75 percent of the people living in South Africa were black, throughout the 20th century the nation was ruled by its white minority, and blacks were not permitted to vote. In addition, the government had adopted **apartheid** a system of segregation that enforced a firm separation of different races and denied many basic civil rights to blacks. In 1986 Congress overrode a veto by President Reagan and passed legislation that implemented mandatory economic sanctions against South Africa, in an attempt to put pressure on its government to end apartheid.

In 1990 the South African government under President F. W. deKlerk, began to modify its policies. It recognized the African National Congress party and freed its leader, **Nelson Mandela** after 27 years' imprisonment. Later that year deKlerk began negotiations with Mandela regarding a new constitution which was adopted in 1993. In April 1994 the first multiracial elections were held in South Africa, which resulted in Mandela becoming president in May.

The End of the Cold War

The Soviet Union struggled under Gorbachev. Its economy had been weakened by years of mismanagement, poor achievement, and burden of supporting expensive military spending. Ecological disasters further strained the economy. Additionally, the war in Afghanistan, begun in 1979, proved unwinnable and unpopular, and caused unrest inside the Soviet Union and discredit outside. In February 1989 the last Soviet troops withdrew. Under Gorbachev the Soviet Union began rapidly loosening its grip on Eastern Europe and the various Soviet Republics. In August 1991 hard-line Communists with the Soviet government attempted to gain power through a coup. With the assistance of **Boris Yeltsin**, who later became the first elected President of Russia, the coup was defeated

Poland, Hungary, Romania, Bulgaria, Czechoslovakia, and East Germany, under Soviet control since the end of World War II, were permitted to become independent of Russian influence at the end of the 1980s and they began to change their Communist governments and adopt capitalism and democracy. In 1989 the **Berlin Wall**, the symbol of the Cold War, was torn down. Subsequently and peaceably, East Germany reunited with West Germany in 1990. The Warsaw Pact was disbanded.

The various republics that comprised the Soviet Union itself likewise became independent nations. In Europe, The Baltic republics of Estonia, Latvia, and Lithuania, and the more central republics of Belarus, the Ukraine, and Moldova become independent nations. In Asia, the transcaucasian republics of Georgia, Armenia, and Azerbaijan become independent nations, as did the central Asian republics of Kazakhastan, Uzbekistan, Turkmenistan, Kyrgyzstan, and Tajikistan. Finally, the vast majority of land and people comprising the former Soviet Union became the nation of Russia. In December 1991 the Soviet Union officially ceased to exist. President Bush stated that a "new world order" had begun, and in February 1992 he met with Russian President Yeltsin and they formally declared that the Cold War was over.

Exercise Set 6.16

1. In the United States, most new jobs created during the 1980s were jobs that
   A. were classified as managerial.
   B. provided services rather than goods.
   C. depended on heavy manufacturing.
   D. were farm related.

2. Both the Bay of Pigs invasion of Cuba (1961) and the invasion of Panama (1989) are examples of the U.S. attempt to
   A. eliminate unfriendly governments geographically close to the United States.
   B. cultivate good relations with Latin American nations.
   C. stop the drug trade.
   D. end the Cold War.

3. Under current federal laws, Americans with disabilities must be
   A. placed in federally funded institutions near their homes.
   B. guaranteed access to public transportation and facilities.
   C. educated and supported by their families without governmental help.
   D. educated only until they complete the eighth grade.

4. Which demographic trend has occurred in the United States during the past ten years?
   A. The average age of the population has decreased.
   B. The birthrate has rapidly increased.
   C. Life expectancy has decreased.
   D. The proportion of the population over age 65 has grown.

5. Which of the following was the result of a congressional declaration of war?
   A. The 1989 invasion of Panama
   B. Operation Desert Storm
   C. World War II
   D. Vietnam War

6. Presidential nominations of the Supreme Court Justices can lead to controversy because
A. Congress consistently refuses to approve candidates who are not members of the majority parties.
B. Congress claims it has the sole right to nominate justices.
C. presidents most often nominate their friends rather than persons with judicial experience.
D. the President and Congress sometimes have different views on the judicial philosophy that a proposed justice should hold.

7. The results of the national census taken every ten years most directly affects which of the following?
A. Number of justices on the Supreme Court
B. Total electoral votes
C. Composition of the House of Representatives
D. President's Cabinet

CHAPTER REVIEW QUESTIONS

1. President Ronald Reagan's federal budget proposals came under sharp criticism because they
A. lowered interest rates and decreased inflation.
B. increased social welfare spending.
C. included very large deficits.
D. advocated raising the income tax.

2. In the United States in the 1980s, negotiations between labor and management frequently resulted in labor's acceptance of lower wages and greater automation in return for management's guarantees of job security for workers. This trend best indicates that
A. labor and management are responding to the threats posed by foreign competition.
B. management is becoming more interested in strengthening labor unions.
C. legislation has required changes in labor contracts.
D. labor unions are becoming more powerful.

Base your answer to question 3 on the cartoon below and on your knowledge of social studies.

3. The main idea of the cartoon is that
    A. regulation of the savings-and-loan industry is more important than campaign reform.
    B. some problems cannot be solved by congressional action.
    C. Congress cannot agree on spending priorities.
    D. members of Congress sometimes avoid legislative actions that might limit their political careers.

4. In the United States, large corporations would most likely support a congressional plan to
    A. require corporation-funded pension plans to workers.
    B. grant capital investment tax credits.
    C. mandate union shops in all corporations.
    D. increase the minimum wage.

5. In the 1980s, the reason that the federal government aided certain corporations that were on the verge of bankruptcy was that the government
   A. used the opportunity to break up monopolies.
   B. pursued a trend toward public ownership of key industries.
   C. sought to minimize the economic harm from collapse of these corporations.
   D. wished to have more influence on the kinds of products made for sale to American consumers.

6. A major reason for the ending of the Cold War Era was that
   A. the Soviet Union was seriously weakened by internal conflict and economic difficulties.
   B. the United States and the Soviet Union were unable to destroy one another.
   C. the Berlin Wall fell and Germany was reunited.
   D. a recession forced the United States to cut military spending.

THEMATIC ESSAY

Directions: Write a well-organized essay that includes an introduction, several paragraphs addressing the task below, and a conclusion.

Theme: Equality, Change, Equal Protection

Throughout U.S. history, women have slowly gained equal status with men in the areas of voting, marriage rights, jury service, political office holding, and educational and professional opportunities, among others.

Task:

From your study of the women's movement for equal rights throughout U.S. history, identify *three* occurrences (legislation, cases, organizations, etc.) that have furthered the equal status of women.

For each occurrence selected:

- Discuss the issue(s) addressed.
- Describe the action(s) taken and results.
- Explain how the legislation, case, organization, etc., has ultimately changed the position of women in U.S. society.

You may use governmental actions from any period in U.S. history. Some suggestions you might wish to consider are married women's property acts, Nineteenth Amendment (1920), Fair Labor Standards Act (1963), Civil Rights Act (1964), Title IX Equal Education Access (1971), *Roe* v. *Wade* (1973), National Organization of Women (1966–Present), and Affirmative Action.

You are *not* limited to these suggestions.

DOCUMENT-BASED QUESTION

The following questions (Part A and Part B) are based on the accompanying documents (1–5). Some of these documents have been edited for the purpose of this exercise. The question is designed to test your ability to work with historical documents and to demonstrate your knowledge of the subject matter being presented. As you analyze the documents, take into account both the source of the document and the author's point of view.

Historical Context:

From the Korean conflict (1950–1953) through Operation Desert Storm (1991) the question of the President of the United States being able to order U.S. troops to a warring area of the world without a declaration of war by Congress has been debated.

Task:

Using information from the documents and your knowledge of United States history, answer the questions that follow each document in Part A. Your answers to the questions will help you write the Part B essay, in which you will be asked:

Did the War Powers Resolution (1973) infringe upon the executive powers associated with the Commander in Chief's responsibilities enumerated in the Constitution?

Part A
Short-Answer Questions

The documents below refer to the era of the Warren Supreme Court. Examine each document carefully and then answer the questions that follow.

DOCUMENT 1

Sec. 1. This joint resolution may be cited as the "War Powers Resolution."

PURPOSE AND POLICY Sec. 2. (a) It is the purpose of this joint resolution to fulfill the intent of the framers of the Constitution of the United States and insure that the collective judgment of both the Congress and the President will apply to the introduction of the United States Armed Forces into hostilities, or into situations where imminent involvement in hostilities is clearly indicated by the circumstances, and to the continued use of such forces in hostilities or in such situations.

—War Powers Resolution (1973)

1. What two branches of the federal government are required by Sec. 2 (a) of the War Powers Act to participate in decisions involving deployment of United States Armed Forces into hostilities?

_____

_____

_____

_____

DOCUMENT 2

(b) Within sixty calendar days after a report is submitted or is required to be submitted pursuant to section 4(a)(1), whichever is earlier, the President shall terminate any use of the United States Armed Forces with respect to which such report was submitted (or required to be submitted), unless the Congress (1) has declared war or has enacted a specific authorization for such use of United States Armed Forces, (2) has extended by law such sixty-day period, or (3) is physically unable to meet as a result of an armed attack upon the United States. Such sixty-day period shall be extended for not more than an additional thirty days if the President determines and certifies to the Congress in writing that unavoidable military necessity respecting the safety of United States Armed Forces requires the continued use of such armed forces in the course of bringing about a prompt removal of such forces.

—War Powers Resolution (1973)

2. Under what three circumstances would Congress allow the continuation of the deployment of troops by the President?

_____

_____

_____

_____

DOCUMENT 3

> In his veto message (October 24, 1973), President Richard Nixon argued that the War Powers Bill infringed upon his constitutional powers as Commander in Chief.
>
> I hereby return without my approval House Joint Resolution 542—the War Powers Resolution. . . .
> I am particularly disturbed by the fact that certain of the President's constitutional powers as Commander in Chief of the Armed Forces would terminate automatically under this resolution sixty days after they were invoked. . . .

—President Richard Nixon, Veto of War Powers Bill (October 24, 1973)

3. What power (checks and balances) was President Nixon using in his message above?

_____

_____

_____

4. What particular executive power did President Nixon see being jeopardized by the War Powers Bill?

_____

_____

_____

On August 2–4, 1964, two United States destroyers in the Gulf of Tonkin were reportedly fired on by North Vietnamese torpedo boats. President Johnson used the incident to secure from Congress the following mandate for United States military intervention.

The Tonkin Gulf Resolution

Whereas naval units of the Communist regime in Vietnam, in violation of the principles of the Charter of the United Nations and of international law, have deliberately and repeatedly attacked United States naval vessels lawfully present in international waters, and have thereby created a serious threat to international peace;

 . . . Now, therefore, be it *Resolved by the Senate and House of Representatives of the United States of America in Congress assembled,* that the Congress approves and supports the determination of the President, as Commander in Chief, take all necessary measures to repel any armed attack against the forces of the United States and to prevent further aggression.

—Tonkin Gulf Resolution, House and Senate Joint Resolution
(August 7, 1964)

5. How does the Tonkin Gulf Resolution (1964) differ from the War Powers Resolution (1973) regarding presidential power to send United States troops into action?

_____

_____

_____

_____

DOCUMENT 5

Toward the end of the Vietnam War...Congress, seeking to limit the Presidential power that had been used so ruthlessly in Indochina, passed the War Powers Act. . . .

Almost immediately, President Gerald Ford violated the act when he ordered the invasion of a Cambodian island and the bombing of a Cambodian town in retaliation for the temporary detention of American merchant seamen on the ship *Mayaguez*. . . .

In the fall of 1982, President Reagan sent American marines into a dangerous situation in Lebanon...again ignoring the requirements of the War Powers Act. The following year, over 200 of those marines were killed when a bomb was exploded in their barracks by terrorists . . .

—Howard Zinn, *A People's History of the United States* (1995)

6. What specific incidents does Professor Zinn cite as violations of the 1973 War Powers Resolution?

_____

_____

_____

_____

Part B
Essay

Your essay should be well organized with an introductory paragraph that states your position on the question. Develop your position in the next paragraphs and then write a conclusion. In your essay, include specific historical details and refer to the specific documents you analyzed in Part A. You may include additional information from your knowledge of social studies.

Historical Context:

From the Korean conflict (1950–1953) through Operation Desert Storm (1991) the question of the President of the United States being able to order U.S. troops to a warring area of the world without a declaration of war by Congress has been debated.

Task:

Using the documents provided and your knowledge of United States history, answer the following question: Did the War Powers Resolution (1973) infringe upon the Executive powers associated with the Commander in Chief's responsibilities enumerated in the Constitution?

Guidelines:

In your essay, be sure to
• Develop all aspects of the task.
• Incorporate information from *at least five* documents.
• Incorporate relevant outside information.
• Support the theme with many relevant facts, examples, and details.
• Use a logical and clear plan of organization, including an introduction and a conclusion that are beyond a restatement of the theme.

CHAPTER 6

THE CLINTON ADMINISTRATIONS

THE ELECTION OF 1992

> Political campaigns are designedly made into emotional orgies which
> endeavor to distract attention from the real issues involved.
> James Harvey Robinson, *The Human Comedy* (1937)

The national elections, besides ending 12 years of Republican control of the executive branch, had several interesting features.

The Primaries

Democrats

The major contestants for the Democratic presidential nomination were Governor Bill Clinton of Arkansas, former Governor Jerry Brown of California, former Senator Paul Tsongas of Massachusetts, Senator Robert Kerry of Nebraska, and Senator Thomas Harkin of Iowa. Tsongas, Kerry, and Harkin left the field early after poor showings in the early primaries and caucuses, and the Democratic race came down to Governor Clinton and former Governor Brown.

By June, Clinton had gained the support of enough delegates to assure him the nomination. At the Democratic National Convention in New York City in July the party's delegates selected Clinton to be the Democratic nominee for President. The delegates also approved Clinton's choice of Senator Albert Gore of Tennessee as the vice presidential candidate.

Republicans

The two main candidates for the Republican nomination were the incumbent President George Bush and conservative newspaper and television commentator Pat Buchanan. At the Republican National Convention in Houston in August, the party's delegates renominated George Bush for President and Dan Quayle for Vice President. The convention and the campaign were influenced, however, by conservative and religious elements within the Republican party who wanted stronger efforts to ban abortion and permit school prayer. Bush's efforts to accommodate the right-wing Republicans may have hindered his ability to appeal to more middle-of-the-road voters.

Independent

Ross Perot, a self-made Texas billionaire, entered the presidential race, withdrew, and then reentered. Perot's platform consisted mainly of a businessman's approach to economic reform. With the help of his "Volunteers," Perot succeeded in getting his name on the ballot in all 50 states, and in the November elections he polled 19 percent (19,236,411) of the popular vote, an unusually high showing for a third-party candidate.

The Campaign and the Election

Bush's popularity, based on his successes in foreign affairs (the Persian Gulf War, the end of Communism in the Soviet Union and Eastern Europe), appeared to assure him of an easy victory, but the realities of economic problems at home soon increased the electorate's demand for change. The recession of 1990 lingered on through 1992, and the unemployment rate remained at about 7.5 percent. Further reflecting a weak economy, the government reported that the poverty rate had risen again for the second consecutive year, to 14.2 percent of the population.

Governor Clinton's campaign concentrated on the economic issues, using the slogan "It's the economy, stupid." His platform included raising taxes on the wealthy and trimming tax breaks for corporations. President Bush criticized the Democratic platform as a "tax and spend" program and blamed the nation's economic troubles on the Democrat-controlled Congress.

Clinton Becomes the Nation's 42nd President

The total turnout of voters (101,129,210) for the presidential election represented about 55 percent of all those eligible to vote, an increase of about 5 percent over the 1988 election. Perot's showing in the election was the strongest for a third-party candidate since Theodore Roosevelt ran on the progressive Bull Moose ticket in 1912. Democrats maintained control of Congress, and four women were elected to the Senate (bringing the number of women Senators to six), including Carol Mosely Braun of Illinois, the first African American woman ever elected. The Senate also gained its first Native American member when Ben Nighthorse Campbell was elected as a Democrat from Colorado.

	Popular Vote	Percent	Electoral Vote
Clinton	43,727,625	43	370
Bush	38,165,180	38	168
Perot	19,236,411	19	0

PRESIDENT BILL CLINTON (1993–2001)

All progress has resulted from people who took unpopular positions.
Adlai E. Stevenson, Speech at Princeton University, New Jersey,
March 22, 1954

Clinton Policies and Programs

President William Jefferson ("Bill") Clinton took the oath of office as the nation's 42nd President on January 20, 1993. Born in Hope, Arkansas, August 19, 1946, he was the first President born after World War II. In contrast to the laissez-faire policies of his immediate predecessors, Clinton immediately proposed a series of far-reaching domestic reforms. Focusing on the economy and health care, his agenda included a North American Free Trade Agreement (NAFTA), anticrime legislation—which he characterized by the phrase "three strikes and you're out"—welfare reform designed to put people to work, and a national service program whereby federal education loans could be repaid through community service.

Family Leave

One of President Clinton's first initiatives was the signing of a family leave bill, which had been vetoed by the previous Republican administrations. The law permits employees up to 12 weeks of unpaid leave without loss of seniority in order to respond to family needs, such as the birth of a child or the illness of a parent.

Economic Program

President Clinton had made economic recovery the centerpiece of his election campaign. He was not able to obtain passage of his economic stimulus package, designed to reduce unemployment, due to a Republican filibuster in the Senate. However, Clinton's main economic legislation was contained in his first federal budget bill, which included a sizable tax increase targeted to pay for new spending and to reduce the budget deficit. The bill squeaked through Congress by a vote of 218 to 216 in the House of Representatives and by Vice President Gore voting in favor to break a 50 to 50 tie in the Senate.

The U.S. economy rebounded very strongly under Clinton's presidency. Overall, more the 20 million new jobs were created between 1993 and 2000. Unemployment declined significantly, decreasing from 7.5 percent in 1992 to 4.3 percent in 1999. Inflation declined, generally being under 3 percent thorough Clinton's presidency, and concomitantly real wages rose 6 percent since 1993. The budget deficit declined, as the President and Congress presented balanced budgets. The stock market registered historic gains, with the Dow Jones average rising from the mid-3,000s in January 1993 to over 11,000 in 2000. One of the few remaining economic problems was the foreign trade deficit, which continued to grow, reaching a record $271.3 billion in 1999.

Anticrime Measures

Clinton made passage of the Brady Handgun Violence Prevention Act a priority. The bill was name for **James Brady**, President Reagan's press secretary, who was seriously wounded in the 1981 assassination attempt on Reagan. The bill, initially proposed seven years earlier, finally passed and was signed into law in 1993. The Brady Law took effect in February 1994 and mandated that anyone seeking to purchase a handgun had to wait five days while local law enforcement conducted a background check to ensure that no one forbidden from owning a gun was sold a handgun.

Crime Bill

In 1994 Clinton was able to secure passage of a major crime bill. One provision of the bill was designed to add 100,000 extra police officers to local police departments throughout the nation. The most controversial part of the bill banned semiautomatic assault weapons, guns that can fire up to six bullets a second and hold up to 50 rounds of ammunition. The National Rifle Association strongly opposed the measure as infringing on the Second Amendment. However, the provision was able to pass, and it forbade the manufacture of importation of semiautomatic assault weapons or guns holding more than ten bullets in a round.

Health Care

A prominent element of Clinton's agenda was health care reform. He supported the goal of trying to pass legislation to provide for universal health care for every American child and adult, which would have had the effect of extending health care to more than 37 million uninsured Americans. He appointed his wife, Hillary Rodham Clinton, to head a task force on health care reform. The comprehensive health care plan that the administration ultimately proposed was attacked by many for being too large and costly. Most Republican legislators opposed the plan as impinging too much on the private sector. Attempts to reach a compromise failed, resulting in a major setback for President Clinton. In 1996 Congress passed a much more limited measure, the Health Insurance Portability and Accountability Act, which limited health insurance exclusions for pre-existing conditions and provided that persons who had insurance and switched jobs had a right to maintain their health insurance.

North American Free Trade Agreement (NAFTA)

The NAFTA pact was negotiated by the United States, Canada, and Mexico to stimulate trade among them by removing trade barriers, most notably tariffs. The international agreement was signed by President Bush in December 1992, and had strong Republican support. President Clinton worked diligently for its passage, arguing that in the increasing internationalized business world, such policies would assist American companies and consumers. It was opposed by labor groups, including the AFL-CIO, which feared that American workers would lose jobs to Mexico, where workers received lower wages and there were fewer government-mandated environmental and workplace protections. Former presidential candidate **Ross Perot** also opposed the agreement, stating the if NAFTA were adopted, there would be a large "sucking sound" of American jobs being siphoned off to Mexico. The final agreement included provisions for tighter enforcement of labor laws and environmental standards. A coalition of Republican and Democratic congressional votes enabled NAFTA to become law in November 1993.

1994 Midterm Elections

The Republicans won in a landslide in the 1994 midterm elections, gaining an additional 52 seats in the House of Representatives and 9 seats in the Senate, which enabled them to retake control of both the House and the Senate. It marked the largest midterm election gain since 1958, and was the first time since the 1952 election that the Republicans controlled Congress. Newt Gingrich became the first Republican Speaker of the House since 1952, and Robert Dole became Majority Leader of the Senate.

The Republican Agenda

The House Republicans sought to have a group of ten conservative programs, which they had labeled their "Contract with America," become law, achieving only mixed success. Initially, they successfully enacted into law measures that mandated that federal labor laws apply to Congress itself, and that prohibited Congress from passing "unfunded mandates," laws the federal government imposed upon the states, unless the states were also given funds for their enforcement. However, other measures ran into opposition from the Senate, the President, or even the House itself.

Term Limits, Line Item Veto, and Free Speech

The Twenty-Second Amendment to the Constitution, adopted in 1951, prohibits the President from serving more than two terms. Since 1990, attempts were made to have term limits apply to the House and Senate. The House of Representatives voted on a number of bills, most of which would have limited members to 12 years in the House and 12 years in the Senate. No measure was able to pass with most Democrats and a significant number of Republicans voting in opposition.

In *Clinton* v. *City of New York*, the Supreme Court noted that the line item veto gave the President powers that "are not the product of the 'finely wrought' procedure that the Framers designed." The Court held that the procedures in the Line Item Veto Act violated Article I, Section 7 of the Constitution and the act was thus unconstitutional.

In *Reno* v. *A.C.L.U.* (June 1997), the Supreme Court held that the Communication Decency Act was too broad in its restrictions of Internet speech and therefore violated freedom of speech protected by the First Amendment.

The Government Shutdown

In the first year in which President Clinton faced budget negotiations with Republican-controlled Congress, there were significant disagreements over priorities. In November 1995 Clinton vetoed two temporary measures, including a continuing resolution bill (a stopgap measure designed to be in effect until a permanent bill was enacted). He claimed that these bills contained "extreme proposals" that would have endangered the environment and spending for education. The Republicans sought cuts in Medicare spending over 150 percent higher than those favored by the President. The Republican congressional leadership refused to compromise and allowed a government shutdown, in which all nonessential government employees, approximately 770,000 workers, were furloughed. The shutdown was temporarily ended on November 20, but another went into effect on December 16, before finally ending on January 6, 1996. Polls showed that there was significantly more support for the President than for Congress. A compromise was finally reached when Clinton agreed to submit a bill to balance the federal budget by 2002 and the Republicans modified their proposed Medicare decrease. In 1997 Clinton and the Republican-led Congress enacted a plan to balance the federal budget by 2002.

Welfare Reform

Clinton had supported a welfare reform plan in his campaign, but had not obtained one by 1994. The Republicans campaigned for their own plan in the midterm election. Clinton vetoed two earlier Republican welfare bills, but with additional modifications enacted he signed the welfare bill. The law imposed time limits that individuals would have before they were removed from welfare, and added more money for childcare spending so that individuals with children could return to work. It provided that block grants would be made to the states and that each state would be able to design its own welfare program.

Foreign Affairs—The Search for Peace and Stability in the Post-Cold War World

After the breakup of the Soviet Union, the United States became the sole superpower in the world. With the Cold War now over, there was no longer any need to engage in proxy wars such as in Korea and Vietnam, and the fear of a nuclear war was significantly decreased. However, new foreign problems, including how to combat the increased threat of terrorism and what circumstances justified the use of U.S. troops abroad, faced the United States.

NATO Expansion

When Germany unified in 1990, the former East Germany became part of NATO. In 1997 NATO signed an agreement with Russia to cooperate in furthering peace in Europe and engage in joint operations. In 1999 NATO expanded by admitting the Czech Republic, Hungary, and Poland.

Somalia

On December 9, 1992, a UN-sanctioned force entered Somalia, led by 1,800 American marines. The military was there on a humanitarian relief mission to ensure delivery of food supplies to a famine-plagued country where 250,000 people had died and central authority had broken down under the pressure from competing warlords. In October 1993 18 U.S. marines were killed in a street battle with heavily armed Somalian factions. In March 1994 the last American troops were withdrawn, and in March 1995 the final UN peacekeeping troops left. Throughout the mission significant relief work occurred; however, lawlessness and the absence of any central government persisted; 30 U.S. soldiers died in combat and more than 175 were wounded.

Bosnia-Herzegovina

Following the death of its longtime leader Josip Broz, known as Tito, and the demise of the Soviet Union, Yugoslavia began to break up as century-old ethnic and religious conflicts flared up in violence. In 1992 Serb forces began a campaign of territorial expansion against their Croatian and Muslim neighbors, forcing them from villages they had occupied for centuries in a campaign of **ethnic cleansing** that bore many aspects of genocide. President Clinton condemned the actions of the aggressors but resisted pressure for American military intervention that would run counter to the wishes of the majority of Americans. In August and October 1995, NATO planes bombed Serb military positions in retaliation for bombings of civilians. After engaging in U.S.-sponsored peace talks, in December 1995 the parties signed a peace treaty that divided Bosnia into two autonomous sections, a Muslim-Croat federation and a Serb republic. The agreement called for 60,000 NATO troops to be employed to maintain peace.

Kosovo

In early 1999 Serb military and police began a concerted effort to force the majority ethnic Albanian population to leave the Serb province of Kosovo. This new campaign of ethnic cleansing again included the use of force, rape, and murder. By March 24 approximately 250,000 ethnic Albanians had fled. With the killings in Bosnia fresh in world memory, Clinton stated that "ending this tragedy is a moral imperative," and after Serb President **Slobodan Milosevic** had rejected a compromise on this issue, on March 24 NATO forces, including those of the United States, began an air bombardment campaign against Serb forces in Kosovo and military and related targets in Serbia itself. This marked the first time NATO had ever conducted an offensive military campaign against a country. The heavy bombing led Serbia to agree to a peace accord with NATO on June 3, and seven days later the bombing campaign ended. On June 12 NATO peacekeepers began to enter Kosovo and the UN authorized a peacekeeping force of 50,000.

No American troops were killed during the bombing. However, faulty intelligence reports led a U.S. B-2 "stealth" plane to bomb the Chinese embassy in Belgrade, killing three Chinese and wounding another twenty, a major embarrassment to the United States. While the success of the campaign ended the Serb ethnic cleansing, doubts persisted as to whether the Serb and Albanian populations in Kosovo would ever be able to coexist without the presence of peacekeeping troops.

Other Troubled Areas

In several troubled areas of the world the United States provided no military assistance or peacekeeping forces, but nevertheless played an important role in encouraging the peaceful resolution of long-standing difficulties.

The Middle East

In 1993 a major breakthrough for peace in the Middle East occurred during secret talks held in Oslo, Norway, between Israel and the Palestine Liberation Organization (PLO). In September **Yasir Arafat**, the chairman of the PLO, publicly stated the PLO recognized Israel's right to exist, while **Yitzhak Rabin**, the Prime Minister of Israel, stated that Israel recognized the PLO as the representative of the Palestine people.

At the White House on September 13, 1993, before a large gathering of international dignitaries organized by President Clinton, Israel and the PLO signed an interim accord providing for Palestinian self-rule in the Gaza Strip and the West Bank town of Jericho. The accord was the initial step in the peaceful resolution of the long-standing Israeli-Palestinian confrontation.

Northern Ireland

Since 1922, when Great Britain granted the lower twenty-six Irish counties independence but retained the six northern Irish provinces, tensions have existed in Northern Ireland between the Protestant majority and the Catholic minority. This conflict intensified in recent decades, with the Catholic Irish Republican Army and various Protestant paramilitary groups carrying out terrorist acts against each other, the British police force, and the civilian population in Northern Ireland and England. In 1996 President Clinton appointed former Senate Majority leader George Mitchell as a special envoy to attempt to negotiate a resolution to this impasse. With the support of both British Prime Minister **Tony Blair** and Irish Prime Minister **Bertie Ahern**, the "Good Friday Agreement" was reached on April 10, 1998. The principal provisions of the compromise included decommissioning arms, establishing a regional government that included representation on a cross-community basis, and allowing the decision of whether to be aligned with Britain or Ireland to be decided by the majority vote of the people of Northern Ireland. The agreement was approved with a "Yes" vote of over 94 percent in Ireland and over 71 percent in Northern Ireland in May 1998. In December 1999 Britain officially relinquished power over Northern Ireland to a new provisional government, although difficulties remained in getting all parties to give up their weapons.

Haiti

After the election as President of Father Jean-Bertrand Aristide, a Catholic priest, in September 1991, Haitian military commanders took control of the government and forced him to flee. The new dictatorship caused more than 50,000 Haitians to seek refuge abroad, many losing their lives at sea in fragile boats that sank or capsized.

With some 3,500 Americans remaining in Haiti, there was considerable pressure on President Clinton to use American military forces to liberate Haiti and restore Father Aristide to power. The military junta in Haiti signed an agreement in 1992 promising to step down, but it did not carry it out. The United States then enforced an economic embargo sanctioned by the UN. In 1994, when the military still refused to cede power, President Clinton threatened military action. At that point an eleventh-hour compromise was reached. President Clinton then sent 20,000 U.S. troops to Haiti to oversee the transition to democracy.

Terrorist Attacks

World Trade Center Attack

On February 5, 1993, a large bomb exploded at the World Trade Center in New York City. The explosion blew a 100-foot crater in the bottom of the building, killed six people, and wounded more than 1,000 others. The bombing was planned and carried out by a number of Middle East Islamic terrorists, motivated by anti-America and anti-Israel hatred.

Oklahoma City Attack

On April 19, 1995, the Alfred P. Murrah Federal Building in Oklahoma City, Oklahoma, was destroyed by a powerful bomb, which killed 168 people and injured more than 500 others. The enormous wanton destruction and the location of the attack, in the country's heartland, brought home to all Americans the danger of domestic terrorist activity. Further troubling was the fact that this attack was not made by foreign terrorists, but was carried out by U.S. citizens, who possessed far-right antigovernment beliefs. Two Americans were convicted in separate trials.

United States Embassy Bombings in Kenya and Tanzania

On August 7, 1998, the United States embassies in the East African countries of Kenya and Tanzania were destroyed by powerful terrorist bombs that exploded within minutes of each other. The two bombs killed over 260 people, including 12 Americans, and wounded more than 5,000 others. Evidence indicated that the bombings were masterminded and funded by the Islamic fundamentalist terrorist **Osama bin Laden**, then living in Afghanistan. In retaliation for the attack, on August 20 President Clinton ordered the firing of 75 Tomahawk cruise missiles at suspected terrorist facilities in Sudan and Afghanistan. In 1999 the UN imposed economic sanctions on Afghanistan for refusing to turn over bin Laden.

Columbine High School Shooting

On April 20, 1999, two students at Columbine High School in Littleton, Colorado, assaulted the school with guns, including a semiautomatic handgun, and bombs. Their rampage lasted several hours, ending after they killed 13 people (12 students and a teacher), wounded more than 30 others, and then committed suicide. The Columbine attack was the deadliest school attack in U.S. history. The nation was stunned by the ferocity of the attack and disturbed because it marked the seventh time within two years that a student had committed a fatal shooting at a U.S. school.

THE ELECTION OF 1996

Tonight we proclaim that the vital American center is alive and well.
William Jefferson Clinton, November 5, 1996

The Primaries

Democrats

Throughout most of 1995 it appeared that President Clinton might face one or more primary opponents. However, by early 1996, with President Clinton stating that he was standing up to "extreme" Republican congressional policies, and with the strong economy continuing, his popularity had rebounded sufficiently so that he was to gain renomination without a primary challenge. At the Democratic National Convention in August the party's delegates renominated Bill Clinton for President and Al Gore for Vice President. In his acceptance speech Clinton stressed his economic program and promised to seek enactment of pro-education and family measures "to build a bridge to the 21st century."

Republicans

The principal candidates for the Republican nomination were Senator **Robert J. Dole** of Kansas, the Senate majority leader, **Lamar Alexander,** former Governor of Tennessee, **Steve Forbes**, independently wealthy president of *Forbes Magazine*, and **Patrick Buchanan**, conservative press commentator.

At the Republican National Convention in August the party's delegates nominated Robert Dole for President and his choice, **Jack F. Kemp**, for Vice President. The convention stressed tax reduction, strengthening national defense, and reducing government.

Independent

Ross Perot again ran for President as the nominee of the independent Reform party. Although Perot stressed similar themes as in 1992, in this election he never showed sufficient strength to be a serious contender.

The Campaign and the Election

President Clinton was buoyed by a strong economy, which he made his central campaign issue, stressing the creation of 10 million jobs while maintaining low inflation and unemployment. President Clinton also stated that he was maintaining the center of the political spectrum, often acting as a bulwark against "extreme" Republican congressional proposals on such issues as Medicare and the environment. Senator Dole emphasized his long public service record, criticized Clinton's personal character, and stated that he would enact tax cuts to further stimulate the economy.

Clinton Easily Re-elected; Republicans Maintain Congressional Control

The 1996 election essentially endorsed the status quo. President Clinton won, becoming the first Democrat to be re-elected since Franklin Roosevelt, achieving just under 50 percent of the popular vote and a comfortable electoral vote majority. Meanwhile, the Republicans gained a few seats in the Senate and lost only a slightly larger number of seats in the House of Representatives, thus maintaining control of Congress. In 1996 only 49 percent of eligible voters actually voted, marking the first time that the majority of eligible voters did not vote in a presidential election. Perot, the Reform party candidate, garnered 8.5 percent, normally a strong third-party achievement but a significant decrease from the 19 percent he received in 1992.

	Popular Vote	Percent	Electoral Vote
Clinton	45,628,667	49.2	379
Dole	37,869,435	40.8	159
Perot	7,874,283	8.5	0

Clinton's Second Administration

Clinton's Team

President Clinton made several new key appointments following his re-election. He appointed **Madeleine K. Albright**, the U.S. ambassador to the UN, to be Secretary of State. Albright became the first woman to hold this position. President Clinton also appointed Senator William S. Cohen of Maine, a moderate Republican, to be Secretary of Defense.

The Paula Jones Lawsuit

In May 1994 Paula Jones filed a lawsuit in federal court against President Clinton. In the suit Ms. Jones alleged that in May 1999, when Mr. Clinton was Governor of Arkansas and she was a secretary working for the state, he sexually harassed her by asking her to have sex. She also claimed that he had defamed her character, a charge she later dropped. President Clinton denied these allegations, and his attorneys made legal claim that the lawsuit should not be permitted to proceed while Clinton was President because a civil lawsuit would distract a President from his official responsibilities and thus would undermine the institution of the presidency. The Supreme Court addressed this issue in 1997 in *Jones* v. *Clinton*, unanimously ruling that a civil lawsuit could proceed against an incumbent President.

Legal discovery in the lawsuit then continued. In April 1998 Judge Susan Webber Wright granted the defense motion to dismiss the lawsuit before trial, holding that "the plaintiff's allegations fall far short of the rigorous standards for establishing a claim of outrage under Arkansas law." Jones appealed this ruling, and in 1999, before the appeal was decided, she settled the case in return for a payment from President Clinton of $850,000.

After the lawsuit was settled, Judge Wright held President Clinton in civil contempt of court for giving "false, misleading and evasive answers that were designed to obstruct the judicial process." She imposed sanctions of just over $90,000 against Clinton to compensate opposing attorneys and the court for costs incurred by his untruthful testimony.

The Monica Lewinsky Scandal

In January 1998 Independent Counsel **Kenneth Starr** received permission to inquire whether President Clinton obstructed justice in the Jones lawsuit. Later that month it became public news that Starr's office was investigating President Clinton's relationship with **Monica Lewinsky**, whom President Clinton had first met in November 1995 when she was a 22-year-old intern at the White House. President Clinton publicly stated in January that he "did not have sex with that woman, Miss Lewinsky," and thereafter, although the news continued to be dominated by the scandal, he refused to discuss the matter publicly until August.

In August 1998 President Clinton testified before a federal grand jury. He admitted that he had "inappropriate intimate conduct" with Lewinsky, but denied that he had committed perjury in saying that he had not engaged in sexual relations, contending that his conduct had been outside the definition of sexual relations employed in the Jones case. Shortly thereafter, Clinton gave a televised speech in which he admitted to an "inappropriate relationship" with Lewinsky and asked for forgiveness. In September, Starr submitted a report to the House that provided intimate details of Clinton's physical relationship with Lewinsky, and listed 11 grounds for impeaching the President.

The Impeachment Proceedings

The Judiciary Committee of the House of Representatives held hearings on whether President Clinton should be impeached. Those in favor of impeaching the President claimed that he had committed perjury by denying he had engaged in sexual relations with Lewinsky in his civil testimony (and some contended in his grand jury testimony as well). They also claimed that Clinton had obstructed justice by attempting to cover up his relationship with Lewinsky. Some of those against impeachment stated that Clinton may not have technically committed perjury (as Clinton and his lawyers maintained), while more of those supporting the President claimed that even if he had committed perjury in denying a sexual relationship, this did not constitute a "high crime or misdemeanor" that should result in his being impeached.

After lengthy hearings, the Judiciary Committee voted in favor of four separate counts of impeachment. Although two of the counts were defeated, Clinton was impeached on two counts. The first count alleged that Clinton had committed perjury in denying under oath that he had a sexual relationship with Lewinsky. The second count alleged that Clinton obstructed justice in attempting to cover up his relationship with Lewinsky. This marked the first time a President had been impeached since Andrew Johnson in 1868. (President Nixon had resigned in 1974 after the Judiciary Committee had voted in favor of three impeachment counts against him, but before the House of Representatives as a whole had voted on impeachment.)

Pursuant to the Constitution, the Senate held a trial on the impeachment charges, at the end of which the President would be removed from office if two-thirds of the Senators voted to convict him on either count. The Senate decided to hear only brief additional testimony, relying principally on the evidence compiled in the House of Representatives. The same basic arguments made in the House supporting and opposing impeachment were repeated in the Senate. In February 1999 the Senate voted against removing President Clinton from office by a vote of 45 in favor, 55 opposed on the first count, and 50 in favor, 50 opposed on the second count. President Clinton was officially acquitted. He stated that he was "profoundly sorry" for his actions and called for "a time of reconciliation and renewal."

In the end the impeachment proceedings remained highly partisan—no Democratic Senator voted to impeach the President, while 50 of the 55 Republican Senators voted to impeach the President on at least one count. Although the country was divided on this issue, throughout the impeachment proceedings President Clinton's public approval ratings remained high and a majority of those polled were not in favor of removing him from office.

Comprehensive Test Ban Treaty Rejected

In September 1996 President Clinton was the first leader to sign the Comprehensive Test Ban Treaty, which was subsequently signed by 153 nations, including all nuclear-capable countries except India, Pakistan, and North Korea. The explosion of test nuclear bombs by both India and Pakistan in 1998, while they were in a state of undeclared war over Kashmir, emphasized the continued need for nuclear control. President Clinton pushed for a vote on the treaty the following year. Significant opposition among Senate Republicans revolved around concerns regarding whether treaty compliance could be adequately verified, as well as a dislike of the President. In October 1999 the treaty, which required a two-thirds affirmative vote to be ratified, did not even receive a majority, with 48 votes in favor to 51 votes against. This marked the first time since 1920 that a major arms control treaty had been defeated by the Senate.

THE ELECTION OF 2000

The Primaries

Democrats

From the time he was reelected Vice President, Al Gore was the odds-on favorite to secure the nomination. Former New Jersey Senator Bill Bradley was his only Democratic challenger. In the initial stages of the primary campaign, Vice President Gore obtained the endorsements of most elected party leaders and labor organizations. Senator Bradley ran as a reformist liberal, while Vice President Gore stressed that he would maintain and expand upon the policies of President Clinton. Although initially pressed, Vice President Gore won every primary, and Senator Bradley withdrew after losing all the "Super Tuesday" primaries in March.

Republicans

The principal candidates for the republican nomination were governor **George W. Bush** of Texas, son of the former President, Arizona Senator and war hero **John McCain**, and Steve Forbes, independently wealthy president of *Forbes Magazine*. Bush, who ran as a "compassionate Conservative" and McCain, who ran as a reformist Conservative alternated victories throughout the first month of primary contests. However, in the "Super Tuesday" primaries in March Governor Bush won most of the twelve states at stake, including the three with the most delegates, leading Senator McCain to concede the contest by "suspending" his campaign.

Nominations and Appointments During Clinton's Administrations

Supreme Court Justices

The retirement of Supreme Court Justice Byron H. White made Clinton the first Democratic President in 25 years to make a nomination for the Supreme Court. After two tentative choices, he nominated **Ruth Bader Ginsburg** of the U.S. Court of Appeals for the District of Columbia. The nomination was easily confirmed by the Senate, making Ginsburg the second woman on the high court, after **Sandra Day O'Connor** of Arizona, who was appointed in 1981 under President Reagan. In 1994 President Clinton nominated **Stephen G. Breyer**, Chief Judge of the U.S. Court of Appeals for the First Circuit in Boston, who was then confirmed by the Senate to sit on the Supreme Court.

The Presidential Election

The election of 2000 saw the nomination of Vice President Al Gore by the Democrats, Texas Governor George W. Bush by the Republicans, and a third party candidate, longtime consumer advocate, Ralph Nader, by the Green Party.

It was quickly realized as the popular vote returns were being tallied on November 7th that the election of 2000 would be one of the closest in U.S. history. (Al Gore: 50,158,094, George W. Bush: 49,820,518, Others: 3,835,594) The vote in Florida became crucial as the awarding of Florida's 25 electoral votes would give either Vice President Gore or Governor Bush the necessary 270 electoral vote majority. The popular vote in the State of Florida was so close (Governor Bush led by only a few hundred) that a recount was ordered pursuant to state law.

A separation of powers question arose between the Florida Supreme Court which supported the continuation of handcounts and the Florida Secretary of State who moved to end the recount and award the electoral vote to Governor George Bush. On December 9, 2000 the Supreme Court of the United States halted all recounts in the State of Florida and on December 12, 2000 the U.S. Supreme Court ruled in the case of *Bush* v. *Gore* that the recount ordered by the Florida Supreme Court had presented an "equal protection of the law" problem and ordered the recount to stop. This marked the first time that the Supreme Court of the United States had intervened in a presidential election.

On December 13, 2000 Vice President Al Gore conceded and Governor George W. Bush claimed victory.

Exercise Set 6.17

1. The most successful example of the United States commitment to international trade under President Clinton was
   A. the World Trade Organization's 1999 meeting in Seattle.
   B. the addition of Poland, Hungary, and the Czech Republic to NATO.
   C. "fast track" approval of trade treaties.
   D. NAFTA.

2. Following President Clinton's signing of the Comprehensive Test Ban Treaty in September 1996, the treaty, which was eventually defeated, was submitted for ratification to which of the following governmental bodies?
   A. Supreme Court
   B. House of Representatives
   C. Cabinet
   D. Senate

3. The reason why President Clinton was acquitted after his trial on impeachment charges in the United States Senate is that
   A. the Senate did not have 12 more Republican members.
   B. no Democratic Senator voted to convict him.
   C. a majority of the Senate did not vote to convict him.
   D. two-thirds of the Senate did not vote to convict him.

4. Which of the following was the major trouble area for the United States economy under President Clinton?
   A. Lower unemployment
   B. Lower inflation
   C. Higher trade deficit
   D. Higher stock market prices

5. A major argument against granting the President the line item veto was that it
   A. violated the principle of checks and balances.
   B. reduced "pork barrel" spending.
   C. encouraged Congress to be wasteful.
   D. prevented balanced budgets.

6. One criticism of affirmative action programs is that these programs
   A. ignore the needs of women in business and education.
   B. lead to discrimination against more qualified people.
   C. have a negative effect on immigration.
   D. have not eliminated segregated housing patterns.

7. One way in which the Watergate scandal, the Iran-Contra affair, and the Paula Jones/Monica Lewinsky investigation are similar is that each led to
   A. the impeachment of a President.
   B. the censorship of Congressional leaders.
   C. the addition of new amendments to the Constitution.
   D. a loss of respect for government leaders by the American people.

8. Following the impeachment by the House of Representatives, President Clinton was tried and acquitted by the Senate in February 1999. Which individual presided at the Senate trial of President Clinton?
   A. Vice President Al Gore
   B. Independent Counsel Kenneth Starr
   C. Honorable Ryan K. Dugan
   D. Chief Justice William Rehnquist

9. Base your answer to question 9 on the cartoon below and on your knowledge of social studies.

The main idea of this cartoon is that
A. economic considerations dictate United States foreign policy.
B. a free-trade policy is largely responsible for the success of the American economy.
C. a President can benefit from a strong national economy.
D. the United States no longer has a trade deficit.

UNIT SEVEN

The New Millennium

KEY IDEAS Unit Seven introduces the new millennium (2001) following the 2000 election, a time of moving forward into the next 1,000 years. The new millennium is violated in its infancy, and the war on terror changes both foreign and domestic policies beyond what the most astute futurists would have ever predicted.

UNIT CONNECTIONS: By the end of the unit you should understand the following points.

- The complexities and oddities of our electoral process
- George W. Bush and the resurgence of neoconservatism
- The horror and significance of September 11, 2001
- International cooperation versus unilateral approach to foreign policy
- Fighting the global war on international terrorism
- The balancing of civil liberties and national security during times of war
- The interpretation of 20th-century international law in 21st-century conditions
- Constitutional issues of the 21st century
- The attempts to control nuclear proliferation as more countries possess nuclear capabilities
- Congressional elections and their reflection of administration policies
- The complexities of a volatile Middle East

ECONOMIC AND DEMOGRAPHIC SHIFTS AT THE DAWN OF THE NEW MILLENNIUM

The United States has had to adapt to a changing world in the late 20th and early 21st centuries. Globalization and free trade have altered the world economy, as well as the economy of the United States. While Americans continue to debate the impact of pursuing a free-trade strategy, economic changes in the United States and beyond its borders have led to demographic shifts and new patterns of migration.

ECONOMIC CHANGES IN THE UNITED STATES

The Deindustrialization of America— Outsourcing and Automation

From the 1960s onward, large numbers of factories have closed in northeastern cities such as New York and Philadelphia, as well as in Midwestern **Rust Belt** cities such as Pittsburgh, Cleveland, Detroit, and Chicago. Some firms have relocated to the South and other areas within the United States where they can take advantage of lower-wage expectations and a weak labor movement.

Since the 1980s, there has been a rapid shift of the manufacturing sector from developed countries, including the United States, into less developed parts of the world. Increasingly, many of the products Americans purchase, from automobiles to blue jeans, are produced abroad. This **outsourcing** of American jobs to foreign countries has several causes. Currently, workers in many developing countries in Asia, Africa, and Latin America earn considerably less money than workers in the United States, thus reducing production costs for manufacturers operating in these countries. **Free-trade** agreements have accelerated this trend (see page 584). The rise of the private manufacturing sector in communist China has also contributed to the decline of United States manufacturing. Because firms in China are able to produce goods at lower costs—a result of considerably lower labor costs and an exchange rate that is favorable to China—American imports from China grew dramatically in the late 20th and early 21st centuries. In 2012, the U.S. trade deficit with China was $315 billion.

Another factor in the decline of industrial jobs has been **automation**. Automated processes and robots can, in many instances, achieve desired levels of productivity with far fewer workers. A study in the *American Economic Review* from 2015 noted the American steel industry lost 400,000 jobs between 1962 and 2005 (75 percent of its workforce). However, shipments of American steel did not decline. Other studies note that automation and robots can complement human labor, and that investment in automation does not consistently correlate with the loss of manufacturing jobs. Politicians debate whether the government should attempt to protect American jobs or let the market take its course. The issue was an important factor in the victory of Donald Trump in the 2016 presidential election (see pages 640–642).

Free-Trade Agreements and Changes in the American Economy

The United States began to aggressively pursue free-trade policies in the 1990s, under President **Bill Clinton** (1993–2001). As discussed in Unit 6, the **North American Free Trade Agreement (NAFTA)** (1993) and the **General Agreement of Trade and Tariffs (GATT)** are international trade agreements that sought to encourage countries to participate in the global economy by reducing barriers to trade. NAFTA eliminated all trade barriers and tariffs between the United States, Canada, and Mexico. GATT has existed since 1948, but the 1994 agreement was far reaching in its commitment to free trade. The 1994 GATT agreement called into being the World Trade Organization (1995), which has served as a global trade referee committed to reducing barriers to trade. In the 21st century, both President **George W. Bush** (2001–2008) and President **Barack Obama** (2009–2017) pursued free-trade agreements. More recently, the Obama administration negotiated the Trans-Pacific Partnership (TPP) with eleven Pacific Rim nations. The treaty was signed in 2016, but in 2017, President Donald Trump withdrew the United States from the treaty, preventing it from being finalized.

Free-trade supporters promise global prosperity as more nations participate in the global economy. Critics of free trade worry that nations will no longer be able to implement environmental regulations, ensure workers' rights, or protect industries from foreign competition. Many economists see the push toward free-trade agreements as an important factor in contributing to the decline of manufacturing jobs in the United States (see pages 601–602). A study by the Economic Policy Institute asserted that by 2010, the rise in the trade deficit with Mexico since the implementation of NAFTA has led to the loss of almost 700,000 American jobs. It estimated that approximately 60 percent of these jobs were high-paying manufacturing jobs in states like Ohio and Michigan. Supporters of free trade argue that NAFTA and similar treaties generate overall economic growth and a more dynamic business sector, which ultimately leads to increases in job creation. The issues of globalization and free trade have inspired vociferous protests, most notably at the 1999 meeting of the **World Trade Organization** in Seattle. More recently, the issue figured prominently in the 2016 presidential campaign. Opposition to free-trade treaties was a significant issue for Senator **Bernie Sanders** and was an important factor in the success of Donald Trump's candidacy (see pages 640–642).

The United States in the Age of Globalization

The outsourcing of jobs and the rise of international trade are part of a trend referred to as **globalization**. There are several related elements that are often mentioned in discussions of globalization. The first element is "free trade," as discussed above. The second element is the perceived harm done to local cultures and customs by large corporate entities, such as McDonald's and Disney. The third element of globalization is the ease of worldwide communications brought about by the Internet. Globalization is defended by many as a positive development that will create greater understanding in the world and will raise living standards in developing countries. Others condemn globalization as reducing environmental protections and shifting manufacturing jobs to sweatshops in poor countries.

Decline of Union Membership

The decline of manufacturing jobs in the United States has contributed to a decline in union membership among American workers. In 1954, union membership (as a percentage of the total workforce) peaked in the United States at 35 percent; currently, it is about 12 percent. Another contributing factor in the decline of unionized workers was the ability of conservative politicians to press an agenda that values deregulation and free-market economics. A major turning point in government policy toward unionized workers came earlier under President Ronald Reagan (1981–1989). In 1981, when air traffic controllers went on strike, Reagan had them all fired, breaking their union, the **Professional Air Traffic Controllers' Organization (PATCO)**. The destruction of PATCO was a major blow to organized labor in the late 20th century.

More recently, several states, including Michigan (2012) and Wisconsin (2015), have passed **right-to-work laws** (bringing the total to 28 states). These laws, enabled by the 1947 **Taft-Hartley Act**, undermine the strength of the union movement. Such laws forbid union contracts from mandating that all the workers in a firm pay dues to the union. Unions argue that they negotiate on behalf of all the workers, and, therefore, all should be required to pay dues (even workers who decide that they do not want to join the union). In right-to-work states, workers can opt out of paying union dues, even while being represented by the union. In addition, unions representing public workers have come under attack in several states. In Wisconsin, for example, Governor **Scott Walker** introduced legislation in 2011 to cut the **collective bargaining** rights and benefits of public employees. Despite a series of large-scale protests, the bill was passed and upheld in court.

In such an environment and with a falling membership, there has been a marked decline in the militancy of the union movement. In 1970, there were more than 380 major strikes or lockouts in the United States; by 1980, that figure dropped to under 200. In 2010, there were 11 major strikes or lockouts.

The Growth of the Service Sector

As the manufacturing sector has shrunk in the United States, the **service sector** has grown significantly in the period of 1980 to the present. The service sector of the economy is also called the **tertiary sector**. The **primary sector** includes the extraction and production of raw materials, such as mining, lumber operations, agriculture, and fishing. The **secondary sector** is generally considered manufacturing, or the process involved in transforming raw materials into finished products available to the public. The tertiary, or service, sector involves the production of services, rather than end products. Such services enable and enhance other sectors of the economy. The service, sector includes shipping and trucking, banking services, information technology, waste disposal, education, government, health care, legal services, and a whole host of retail and food-service operations. Throughout the Western world, service-sector employment, as a percentage of overall employment, has grown over the last century, with the pace of growth accelerating since 1980. Currently, 70 percent of jobs in the United States are in the service sector. The growth of the service sector illustrates a profound shift in the American economy from the production of materials to the providing of services.

While the service sector includes a wide variety of jobs, the growth of low-wage jobs in the retail and fast-food fields has contributed to the stagnation of wages and a growing income gap (see below). The three largest employers in the United States are currently Wal-Mart, Yum! Brands (which includes Taco Bell, KFC, and other fast-food outlets), and McDonald's.

Efforts to unionize workers in these fields have almost all failed due to vigorous anti-union activities by the corporations and to structural difficulties in organizing a decentralized workforce. Unions and worker-advocacy groups have pushed state legislatures to raise the minimum hourly wage allowed by law. The goal of a $15 minimum hourly wage has been a rallying cry of this movement.

Economic Inequality and Corporate Corruption

In the first decade of the 21st century, several high-profile cases of corruption led to calls for greater oversight and control of large corporations. These issues were brought into stark relief during the **Great Recession** of 2008 (see pages 627–628). In addition, calls for a restructuring of the economy in order to challenge economic inequality formed the basis of the **Occupy Wall Street** movement in 2011 (see page 664).

As the 21st century began, the gap between the wealthy and the rest of the population widened in the United States. Workers experienced stagnation in terms of real wages. Since the 1970s, economists have noted that the income gap between the wealthy and the middle class has grown increasingly wide. The incomes for the top-earning one percent of households increased by about 275 percent between 1979 and 2007, while the middle 60 percent of wage-earners saw their incomes rise by just under 40 percent during the same period. The flattening of wages for the middle class and the poor has meant an increase in debt for many Americans and, for many population groups, a decrease in consumer spending. A variety of political and economic factors can help explain this growing gap. Many economists cite factors mentioned above—the disappearance of higher-paying manufacturing jobs and the growth of low-wage service-sector jobs. Other factors include the decline of the union movement and changes in the tax code, including the massive tax cuts initiated by President George W. Bush (implemented in 2001 and 2003) (see page 623).

The perception that the economy was skewed in favor of the wealthy and that corporations could play by a different set of rules than the general population seemed to be bolstered by a series of corporate scandals that came to light in the first decade of the 21st century. The most serious scandal involved the **Enron Corporation**, the largest energy corporation in the United States at the turn of the century. In 2001, Enron shocked its employees by filing for bankruptcy. It soon came to light that Enron's corporate officers had been rapidly selling their shares in the company, while at the same time portraying the corporation as financially healthy. Federal investigators found that Enron was "cooking the books"—presenting false reports of higher earnings while hiding the company's debt. In addition, investigators found that that the company had illegally driven up power prices during California's energy crisis. It did this by creating phantom congestion on electricity transmission lines and sending power outside the state and then reselling it back to California to avoid price limits on transactions within the state. While corporate officers sold their shares before the crisis went public, many employees, whose pension funds were tied to Enron stock, were not so lucky. The illegal acts caused the loss of much of its employees' retirement funds. By the end of 2001, Enron stock prices plunged to less than a dollar, from being valued at over $90 just a year earlier. Employees' pension funds were wiped out. In addition to Enron, its accounting firm, Arthur Anderson, was convicted of destroying documents to protect both Enron and itself. Early in 2002, **Kenneth Lay**, the founder, chairman, and CEO of Enron, resigned. By 2004, several Enron officials were indicted by federal grand juries and found guilty in court. Lay died in 2006 before he was sentenced. In 2006, Jeffrey Skilling, a former CEO of Enron, was given a 24-year prison sentence, which was later reduced to 14 years.

In 2002, **WorldCom**, a major telecommunications corporation, went bankrupt after admitting to illegally altering its earnings and debt reports. On the heels of the Enron and WorldCom scandals were scandals involving Qwest, Global Crossing, Tyco, and Adelphia. Corporate America came under intense scrutiny for illegal activities, incredible greed, and criminal disregard for its employees.

DEMOGRAPHIC SHIFTS

The Decline of the Rust Belt and the Rise of the Sunbelt

The United States experienced a shift in population that began in the last decades of the 20th century and has continued into the 21st century. As discussed in Unit 6, the industrial growth that drew African Americans to cities like Detroit and Chicago from the period around the two World Wars began to slow by the 1950s. By the 1960s, 1970s, and 1980s, thousands of factories shut down in the old industrial belt from New York to Illinois. At the same time, the states of the **Sunbelt**—Florida, Georgia, Texas, Arizona, California—experienced remarkable economic growth. Corporations began to relocate to the South and educational facilities expanded. The region became a magnet for capital, as investors enthusiastically supported economic growth. Managers, engineers, professors, technicians, and other skilled employees were needed to manage these new facilities and institutions, and to oversee an expansion of infrastructure. The old **Rust Belt** suffered a net loss of people as the Sunbelt grew by millions of new inhabitants. In California, for example, the population increased by 7.5 million people between 1990 and 2010.

The political clout of the Sunbelt has grown tremendously, often at the expense of the old industrial Northeast and Midwest. This has generally augured well for the Republican Party, as national politics have come to reflect the more conservative views of those in the West and South. As a result of the most recent census (2010), Arizona, Nevada, South Carolina, Georgia, and Utah each gained one member of Congress; Texas added four seats; and Florida added two. In contrast, some of the more traditionally Democratic-leaning states of the Midwest and Northeast lost power in Congress. Pennsylvania, Illinois, Michigan, Massachusetts, and New Jersey each lost a House seat; New York and Ohio each lost two seats. In addition to the growth of political power in the Sunbelt, observers also note a change in the perception of the region. It is no longer seen as a "backwater." Cities in the region, including Houston, Raleigh, Atlanta, and Charlotte, now compete with the urban centers to their North as magnets for young people. The expanding population of the region and its thriving economy continue to feed upon one another.

The "Graying of America"

Along with demographic shifts, the average age of the United States population has been increasing. In 1970, about 10 percent of the population was over 65. That figure reached about 13 percent of the population in 2009, and is expected to reach 20 percent of the population by 2050. One reason for the growing percentage of senior citizens is the large number of **baby boomers**, people born in the period after World War II (1946–1964), who are now reaching retirement age. In addition, people are living longer. Advances in medicine and dramatic decreases in the percentage of Americans who regularly smoke cigarettes have increased life expectancy for Americans.

With the percentage of Americans over the age of 65 growing, many people worry that programs extending benefits to the elderly, notably **Medicare** and **Social Security**, will be unable to stay financially solvent.

The Growth of Nontraditional Families

The last decades of the 20th century witnessed major changes in family structures in the United States. These changes, in turn, generated intense debate about the identity of the American family. An important trend was the growth of nontraditional families. In 1960, "traditional" families—those composed of a heterosexual couple with or without children—stood at 74 percent of all households; that figure fell to under 50 percent by 2007. This trend has divided liberals and conservatives, with liberals pushing for measures to extend rights and services to such households and conservatives calling for a return to traditional family values.

Immigration and the Changing Ethnic Makeup of the United States

The increasing numbers of immigrants into the United States discussed in Unit 6 has continued into the 21st century and had generated a great deal of debate. The passage of the **Immigration and Nationality Act** of 1965 allowed for significant increases in immigration—especially from Asia, Africa, and the Middle East (see page 322). Overall, the impact of the act and of illegal immigration into the United States from within the Western Hemisphere has dramatically altered the demographics of the United States. Before the act, immigration accounted for less than 10 percent of population growth into the United States. Currently it accounts for approximately a third of the population growth. In 1970, less than five percent of the population was foreign born (down from a high of almost 15 percent in 1910); today it has risen to approximately 13 percent. This has been important factor in the growth of the Southwestern states (see pages 606–607).

As the percentage of the American population composed of Asian, African, Middle Eastern, and Latin American immigrants and their children has grown, the percentage of the American population composed of non-Hispanic whites has declined from 75 percent of the overall U.S. population in 1990 to just over 63 percent in 2011. It is estimated that by the year 2042, non-Hispanic whites will no longer constitute a majority of the population of the United States.

Exercise Set 7.1

1. What is one effect on national politics of the population changes in the United States from the 1980s to the 2010s?
   A. Reducing the number of senators from the Great Lakes region
   B. Increasing the representation of the South and West in the House of Representatives
   C. Enhancing the chances for the election of presidential candidates from New England
   D. Strengthening the Democratic Party's hold on the South

2. The North American Free Trade Agreement (NAFTA) supports
   A. raising the levels of protective tariffs between trading countries.
   B. isolationistic trade policies.
   C. the reduction of trade barriers between member countries.
   D. the greater use of trade sanctions between member countries.

3. What is considered a major problem associated with the increasing numbers of "baby boomers" reaching retirement age?
   A. American universities and medical centers will suffer a "brain drain" from the lack of qualified candidates to fill jobs.
   B. The armed forces will suffer from a lack of younger Americans to fill positions in the military.
   C. The percentage of Americans voting in elections will continue to decline because fewer senior citizens make the effort to go out and vote.
   D. The Social Security system will not be able to remain solvent as more people begin to draw from the system and fewer pay in.

4. A scandal engulfed the Enron Corporation in 2004 when it was learned that Enron officials
   A. knowingly sold faulty military equipment to the U.S. government as the war in Iraq was beginning.
   B. provided sensitive industrial information to Russia in violation of United States sanctions against Russia.
   C. hid the financial ill-health of the company from the public which resulted in many employees' pension funds becoming virtually worthless.
   D. dumped toxic materials in a river that was used for drinking and agriculture by Native American settlements.

5. Between 1990 and the present, the American economy has seen the largest increase in jobs in
   A. the service sector.
   B. the manufacturing sector.
   C. the agricultural sector.
   D. the mining and processing sector.

THE TERRORIST ATTACKS
OF SEPTEMBER 11, 2001
AND THEIR AFTERMATH

"To Americans across the nation who mourn and who are angry, I call on you to focus your anger on the perpetrators of this unlawful act and not to cast anger on neighbors, on coworkers, simply because of their certain religion, race, or nationality."

Representative Darrell Issa (Republican, California),
September 11, 2001

While the terrorist attacks on the United States in 2001 were not the first terrorist incidents in the United States, the impact of the 2001 attack cannot be overstated. The attacks altered American foreign policy, as two wars occupied American forces for much of the coming decade. Further, Americans were forced to grapple with ethical implications of certain tactics in the war on terrorism, including "enhanced interrogation" and the indefinite detention of suspected enemy combatants. The issue of balancing security with civil liberties, raised in the excerpt from Representative Issa in the above excerpt, also re-emerged in the aftermath of the 2001 attacks.

THE TERRORIST ATTACKS OF 9/11
AND THE RISE OF AL-QAEDA

September 11, 2001

On the morning of September 11, 2001, 19 terrorists working with the al-Qaeda organization hijacked four domestic American airplanes. American Airlines Flight 11 out of Boston's Logan Airport crashed into the north tower of the **World Trade Center** in New York City, tearing a gaping hole in the building and setting it afire. As people watched the burning tower in horror, a second hijacked airliner, United Airlines Flight 175 from Boston, crashed into the south tower of the World Trade Center. Both buildings were now in flames. Soon after, American Airlines Flight 77 out of Washington exploded when it hit the Pentagon, killing all 64 people aboard. United Airlines Flight 93 out of Newark and bound for San Francisco, also hijacked, crashed in Somerset County, Pennsylvania, southeast of Pittsburgh, killing 38 passengers, crew, and hijackers. The damage inflicted on each of the World Trade

Center towers weakened the structures of each so that both buildings collapsed within two hours of being hit. Approximately 3,000 people died in the four incidents. Most realized that many things would no longer be the same.

It soon became apparent that terrorism was behind the attacks. On the morning of September 11, Secretary of State **Colin Powell** indicated that the U.S. government believed **Osama bin Laden** and the terrorist group **al-Qaeda** were probably responsible for the attack. Al-Qaeda and bin Laden were well known by the United States by 2001. In 1993, the first World Trade Center bombing killed six people, and in 1998 the bombing of two United States embassies in Africa killed 224 people.

Osama bin Laden and al-Qaeda

The history of Osama bin Laden and al-Qaeda stretches back to the 1970s. Al-Qaeda had its origins in the uprising against the 1979 Soviet occupation of Afghanistan. Osama bin Laden and the Mujahedeen (guerrilla fighters in Islamic countries, especially those who are fighting against non-Muslim forces) had been supported by the United States in 1979 during the Soviet invasion of Afghanistan. Bin Laden explained the origin of the term, in a videotaped interview with an al-Jazeera (Arabic television channel) journalist in October 2001, "The name 'al-Qaeda' was established a long time ago by mere chance. The late Abu Ebeida El-Banashiri established the training camps for our Mujahedeen against Russia's terrorism. We used to call the training camp al-Qaeda [meaning 'the base' in English]. And the name stayed."

After the Soviet Union withdrew from Afghanistan, bin Laden returned to his native Saudi Arabia and later set up bases in Sudan in Northeast Africa. In 1994, Sudan expelled bin Laden, who moved his base of operations to Afghanistan. Bin Laden was welcomed by the Taliban ("Students of Islamic Knowledge Movement"), which came to power during Afghanistan's long civil war and ruled Afghanistan from 1996 until 2001. The United States drove the Taliban from power in November 2001.

Osama bin Laden saw the United States as an enemy and declared war on it. Bin Laden cited America's participation in the first Gulf War, its military involvement in Somalia and Yemen, and the U.S. military presence in Saudi Arabia as reasons for his war declaration. Attacks against the United States and its allies have included the 1993 bombing of the World Trade Center, which killed 6; the bombing of U.S. embassies in Kenya and Tanzania (1998), resulting in over 250 dead; and the suicide bombing attacks in central London in 2005, resulting in 52 deaths.

RESPONSES OF THE UNITED STATES TO THE TERRORIST ATTACKS OF SEPTEMBER 11, 2001

Soon after the attacks in 2001, the United States began to take measures that were meant to prevent a future attack. On September 20, 2001, President George W. Bush addressed a joint session of Congress and the American people from the House of Representatives. He focused his address on al-Qaeda, Osama bin Laden, and the hosting government, the **Taliban** in **Afghanistan**. The Bush administration subsequently carried out a series of actions, both internationally and domestically, as part of the war on terrorism.

War in Afghanistan and the Fall of the Taliban

After the terrorist attacks of September 11, 2001, President Bush immediately focused attention on the Taliban in Afghanistan. In his September 20 address, he demanded that the Taliban "close immediately and permanently every terrorist training camp in Afghanistan, and hand over every terrorist, and every person in their support structure, to appropriate authorities." He demanded that the United States gain "full access to terrorist training camps, so we can make sure they are no longer operating." He concluded that these demands must be met immediately or the Taliban would face retaliatory actions by the United States.

On October 7, 2001, after the Taliban failed to respond to President Bush's demands, the United States, Great Britain, and coalition forces launched a bombing campaign on the Taliban government and on al-Qaeda terrorist camps in Afghanistan. Although the immediate goal was to destroy al-Qaeda and capture bin Laden, the President stated that the "battle was broader." Within two months, the Taliban government had fallen. Although Osama bin Laden was not caught, al-Qaeda forces in Afghanistan were seriously weakened. After nearly a month and a half, the Taliban had lost its seat of government in Kabul and by December 9, it had been completely overpowered. On December 22, 2001, **Hamid Karzai**, who attended college in India, was fluent in English, and enjoyed strong support from the West, was sworn in as interim chairman of the government in Kabul.

USA PATRIOT Act: Balancing Civil Liberties and National Security

Forty-five days after the September 11 attacks, in October 2001, Congress, with little if any debate, passed the 342-page **USA PATRIOT Act (Uniting and Strengthening America by Providing Appropriate Tools Required** to Intercept and Obstruct Terrorism Act). The vote in the House of Representatives was 357 to 66 and in the Senate 98 to 1 with Senator Russ Feingold of Wisconsin being the only Senator to vote against the Act. Included in the legislation were sections that provided:

• Domestic terrorism definitions and greater authority to subject political organizations to surveillance.

• Greater powers to law enforcement authorities to conduct secret searches of phone, Internet, medical, banking, and student records with minimal judicial oversight.

• Greater powers to law enforcement authorities to investigate American citizens without probable cause if it is for "intelligence purposes."

• Incarceration of noncitizens for indefinite periods on mere suspicion with no right of counsel, habeas corpus, or opportunities to appear before public tribunals.

After its passage, nearly 200 cities and towns, as well as three states, passed resolutions stating that the PATRIOT Act is not enforceable within their jurisdictions claiming that among other concerns, the First, Fourth, Fifth, Sixth, Eighth, and Fourteenth Amendments were being threatened. The PATRIOT Act has been sometimes compared to the **Sedition Act of 1918** (repealed 1921), which suppressed antigovernment sentiments during World War I. The PATRIOT Act highlighted the tension that exists during times of war between national security and civil liberties. Following successful constitutional challenges to some sections of the act, the PATRIOT Act was renewed in March 2006. Later, despite protests from opponents of the act, President Obama signed extensions of portions of the PATRIOT Act in May 2011, after certain provisions of the act were amended by Congress.

Airport Security and the Department of Homeland Security

The **Transportation Security Administration (TSA)** immediately increased security at airports in the aftermath of the 2001 terrorist attacks. Passengers boarding flights would now be subject to thorough searches. Some passengers have objected to enhanced screening procedures that have included full-body scanning and pat-downs.

The **Department of Homeland Security** was created in November 2002, absorbing the Immigration and Naturalization Service, the Federal Emergency Management Agency (FEMA), and other agencies. It is a cabinet-level department, with the responsibility of protecting the United States from terrorist attacks and natural disasters. President George W. Bush appointed **Tom Ridge**, the former governor of Pennsylvania, as Secretary of Homeland Security. The new department would employ 170,000 people and combine all or part of 22 other agencies to better protect the United States from terrorist attacks.

United States Focus Shifts to Iraq

In 2002, despite difficulties faced by United States forces in Afghanistan, the Bush administration became increasingly focused on **Iraq**. President Bush, in his State of the Union Address in January 2002, cited Iraqi leader Saddam Hussein as a threat to world peace. In his address he stated, "States like these [North Korea, Iran, and Iraq], and their terrorist allies, constitute an **axis of evil**, arming to threaten the peace of the world." Members of his administration, including Vice President **Dick Cheney**, National Security Advisor **Condoleezza Rice**, and Secretary of Defense **Donald Rumsfeld**, accused **Saddam Hussein** of aiding in the terrorist attacks of 2001 and of developing weapons of mass destruction, specifically nuclear, biological, and chemical weapons. Later, the **9/11 Commission**, an independent, bipartisan commission created in 2002, concluded that there was "no credible evidence that Iraq and al-Qaeda cooperated on attacks against the United States."

Neoconservatives and the Bush Doctrine

Iraq had long been in the sights of the group of Republican **neoconservative** thinkers who formed the core of President Bush's foreign policy team. In addition to Cheney, Rumsfeld, and Rice, Bush's choice of **Paul Wolfowitz** as deputy defense secretary, **John Bolton** as undersecretary of state, and **Elliot Abrams** as deputy assistant to the president, set the stage for a very proactive, anti-Saddam Hussein foreign policy. These neoconservatives generally rejected negotiations in terms of resolving conflicts. Throughout the **Cold War**, neoconservatives pushed for the United States to use its military superiority to challenge the Soviet Union. After the Cold War, they continued to advocate the use of force, including preemptive military action. Under international law, a nation may only initiate a military strike if it is facing an imminent threat. The Bush administration lowered this standard; the **Bush Doctrine** held that the United States could wage pre-emptive war in "anticipatory self-defense."

A Call for Regime Change in Iraq

In September 2002, President Bush addressed the United Nations and called for **regime change** in Iraq. The call for regime change in Iraq dated back to the Clinton administration. In 1998, Clinton signed the **Iraq Liberation**

Act, which stated that United States policy should be "to support efforts to remove the regime headed by Saddam Hussein from power in Iraq and to promote the emergence of a democratic government to replace that regime." Critics of the regime change policy claimed that it was a violation of international law, stating that regime change is not a permissible just cause of war. In October 2002, Congress passed the Joint Resolution to Authorize the Use of United States Armed Forces Against Iraq.

The United Nations, Iraq, and Weapons of Mass Destruction

To gain international support for military action, the Bush administration reluctantly went to the **United Nations Security Council** to demand a return of weapons inspectors to Iraq, who had been expelled four years earlier, in 1998. In November 2002, the United Nations Security Council passed a unanimous resolution calling on Iraq to comply with earlier resolutions and disarm or face "serious consequences." The resolution called for United Nations arms inspectors to return to Iraq. In December, Iraq handed over a 12,000-page report to the United Nations stating that there were no prohibited weapons (chemical, biological, and nuclear) in Iraq.

The Bush administration continued to insist that Iraq posed a threat and geared up for war. In January 2003, President Bush received a letter signed by 130 members of the House of Representatives, urging him to "let the inspectors work." By this time, nearly 200,000 U.S. troops were in the Middle East region. The president's State of the Union address in January stated that Iraq was attempting to buy uranium from Africa, even though he already had intelligence reports stating that Iraq had not done so. By February 2003, United Nations weapons inspector Hans Blix indicated that there was some progress with Iraq's compliance.

In February 2003, Secretary of State Colin Powell attempted to convince skeptical members of the UN Security Council that Iraq was actively working to deceive UN weapons inspectors. In later statements, Powell said that his UN speech making the case for the U.S.-led war on Iraq was "a blot" on his record.

Later in February 2003, the United States, Great Britain, and Spain submitted a proposed resolution to the UN Security Council stating that authorization for war was necessary. Germany, Russia, and France blocked the resolution. By March, the United States was only able to secure four out of the nine votes on the UN Security Council for an authorization for military action, which would have required unanimous support.

World Wide Antiwar Protests

As the United States moved toward war in Iraq, protests occurred throughout the world. In February 2003, **The World Says No to War** was the largest coordinated day of protest in world history, with massive peace demonstrations in more than 600 cities. In Rome, nearly three million people protested, which is noted in the *Guinness Book of Records* as the largest antiwar rally in history. In New York City, nearly 400,000 protestors had their First Amendment rights limited when they were not allowed to rally around the UN building, but instead were "corralled" up First Avenue. Anti-American demonstrations erupted in many of the Arab countries as well.

Operation Iraqi Freedom: "Shock and Awe"

Failing to secure United Nations support, President Bush declared war on Iraq in March 2003. This concerted effort, called **Operation Iraqi Freedom**, consisted of the largest special operations force since the Vietnam War. While the vast majority of special operations forces were American, the United Kingdom and the Australian militaries also provided significant forces. Secretary of Defense Donald Rumsfeld promised an unprecedented show of military might "of a force and a scope and a scale that has been beyond what we have seen before." The phrase **"shock and awe"** came to be associated with this show of military force.

"Mission Accomplished"

On May 1, 2003, President Bush announced from the deck of the aircraft carrier USS *Abraham Lincoln* that major combat operations in Iraq were over. With a banner proclaiming "**Mission Accomplished**" in the background, the President hailed a job well done. There was controversy over the "Mission Accomplished" banner on the aircraft carrier. Although the White House initially said that it was the Navy that put up the banner, later reports from the White House stated that it was the White House itself that ordered the banner to be made for the Navy to put up on the ship. In retrospect, all agree it was unfortunately very premature.

The Capture and Trial of Saddam Hussein

In November 2003, the Bush administration agreed to transfer power to an interim Iraqi government early in 2004. In December 2003, Saddam Hussein was captured by American troops. He was found hiding in a dirt hole at a farmhouse about 10 miles south of his hometown, Tikrit. Saddam Hussein had not been seen since Baghdad fell to coalition forces in April 2003. President Bush announced to the Iraqi people, "You will not have to fear the rule of Saddam Hussein ever again." Hussein was subsequently tried by a tribunal, consisting of five Iraqi judges, established by the **Iraqi Interim Government**, for crimes against humanity that occurred during his presidency (1979–2003). These crimes included a genocidal campaign against ethnic Kurds in the late 1980s, known as the **al-Anful campaign**. Many international observers saw the trials against Hussein as show trials. He was found guilty, sentenced to death, and executed in 2006. The trial echoed principles established at the **Nuremburg Trials** following World War II— namely, that leaders can be held accountable for crimes against humanity.

Final Report Concludes No Weapons of Mass Destruction Are in Iraq

Following a July 2004 Senate Intelligence Committee report, which stated that the intelligence on Iraq's weapons was inaccurate, overstated, and flawed, the **Iraq Survey Group**—a multination task force—issued its final report in September. The report concluded that it found no evidence that Iraq developed or possessed **weapons of mass destruction (WMDs)** since sanctions had been imposed in 1991. The report also concluded that the intelligence that suggested the importation of nuclear materials and the capabilities for developing nuclear weapons was seriously flawed.

Exercise Set 7.2

1. The Islamic fundamentalist group al-Qaeda had its origin in which of
the following areas of the world?
A. Kuwait during the Gulf War
B. Afghanistan during the 1979 Soviet occupation
C. United States following the 1993 World Trade Center bombing
D. Iran following the overthrow of the Shah in 1979

2. In later statements, both Secretary of State Colin Powell and the 9/11
Commission concluded that there had never been any credible evidence
that linked Iraq with
A. al-Qaeda's attack upon the United States.
B. Sunni Muslims.
C. chemical weapons used against their own people.
D. the 1990 invasion of Kuwait.

Base your answer to question 3 on the cartoon below and on your knowledge
of social studies.

3. The author of the cartoon is suggesting that
A. all Arabs should return to the Middle East.
B. the United States is a pluralistic society that includes people of Arab
background.
C. there is a significant illegal Arab population in the United States.
D. all Americans are prejudiced against people from the Middle East.

4. The Nuremburg Trials following World War II and the trial of Saddam
Hussein in 2004 both demonstrate the principle that
A. ethnic rivalries can prevent justice from being carried out.
B. national leaders are not subject to international law.
C. leaders can be held accountable for crimes against humanity.
D. only generals can be considered responsible for wartime actions.

5. The term "shock and awe" is most closely associated with
   A. the terrorist attacks on the United States on September 20, 2001.
   B. the treatment of detainees held by the U.S. military in the war on terrorism.
   C. the United States invasion of Iraq.
   D. Saddam Hussein's plan to use weapons of mass destruction against Western Europe.

6. The "Bush Doctrine," set forth by President George W. Bush in 2002,
   A. moved the United States away from its traditional reliance on containment and deterrence and toward a more aggressive pre-emptive approach to foreign affairs.
   B. affirmed that the United States would only extend foreign aid to nations that demonstrated improvements in human rights.
   C. approved the use of torture and other enhanced interrogation techniques in dealing with suspected terrorists.
   D. put forth a comprehensive plan to eliminate nuclear weapons from the arsenals of the world.

7. Which of the following was the rationale that President George W. Bush provided for the 2003 United States invasion of Iraq?
   A. Iraq served as the host of numerous al-Qaeda training camps in the lead-up to the terrorist attacks of September 11, 2001.
   B. The Iraq occupation of Kuwait was destabilizing the region and needed to be ended.
   C. Israel needed protection from the Hezbollah organization, which was headquartered in Iraq.
   D. Iraq possessed weapons of mass destruction that could be used against the United States and its allies.

8. Relations with France, Germany, and Russia during the presidency of George W. Bush became strained because these nations
   A. did not comply with their military obligations as members of NATO.
   B. challenged the United States rationale for invading Iraq.
   C. did not endorse the Roadmap for Peace between Israel and the Palestinians.
   D. blocked the admission of China to the United Nations.

9. Which development led to the other three?
   A. Passage of the USA PATRIOT Act
   B. Establishment of the Department of Homeland Security
   C. The United States-led toppling of the Taliban government in Afghanistan
   D. The terrorist attacks on the United States in September 2001

THE PRESIDENCY
OF GEORGE W. BUSH

> There are no atheists in foxholes and there are no libertarians in
> financial crises.
> Paul Krugman, in an interview with Bill Maher, Sept. 19, 2008

The presidency of George W. Bush was dominated by the terrorist attacks
of September 11, 2001 and the subsequent war on terrorism (see Chapter
2 in this unit). However, the Bush administration took action on a number
of fronts, from tax reform to education. His second term was dominated
by a series of crises at home—the response to the devastation caused by
Hurricane Katrina and the economic recession of 2008. Ongoing foreign
policy concerns will be discussed in Chapter 5 in this unit.

A VICTORY FOR CONSERVATISM

The growing conservative movement, known as the **New Right**, achieved a
major electoral victory in the 2000 presidential election with the election of
George W. Bush. As discussed in Unit 6, the movement had been growing
since the 1960s. The 1964 presidential campaign of Senator **Barry Goldwater**
from Arizona inspired many conservatives, even though Goldwater did not
achieve victory. The movement gained momentum with the successful campaigns of President **Richard Nixon** in 1968 and 1972. However, the New Right
won a more important victory with the election of **Ronald Reagan** in 1980,
ushering in 12 years of a Republican White House (see pages 551–569). Even
during the presidency of **Bill Clinton** (1993–2001), the movement was active,
pushing for the **Contract with America** in 1994 and winning control of both
houses of Congress that year (see page 584). In **George W. Bush**, son of the
forty-first president, **George H. W. Bush**, the movement found a close ally.

Bush and the Conservative Movement

President **George W. Bush** was able to give voice to three different strands
within the conservative movement. First, he quickly invited into his administration many foreign policy neoconservatives who thought that the United
States should have engaged in a more aggressive, militarist foreign policy
during the Cold War and afterward (see page 442). Second, he appealed to
many economic conservatives, who had been pushing for greater deregulation of business and lower taxes. Finally, Bush's evangelical Christianity and
desire to engage in the hot-button issues of the "**culture wars**" energized the
religious and cultural wing of the conservative movement.

One-Party Rule During the Bush Administration

Republicans maintained control of Congress for most of the first six years of Bush's administration. It is unusual for one party to control both houses of Congress as well as the White House. It occurred during the **Era of Good Feelings** in the early nineteenth century, with the Democratic-Republican Party dominating the political process and the Federalist Party ceasing to function. In the 20th century, Republicans controlled the levers of power during the 1900s and during the 1920s. The Democratic Party controlled both the White House and Congress from 1933 to 1947. Some political scientists and historians look favorably at periods of one-party rule, noting that divided governments can lead to gridlock and lethargy. Others argue that prolonged one-party rule can be dangerous to democracy, undermining the checks and balances built into the system of governance. Critics of one-party rule note that a divided government encourages more policing of those in power by the opposition, as well as a greater degree of compromise.

The Election of 2000

The election of 2000 was one of the closest in U.S. history and was not decided for over four weeks after the election. As discussed in Unit 6, neither Governor **George W. Bush** nor Vice President **Al Gore** could declare victory immediately after the election. Neither could initially get to the required number of electoral votes—270. As the results were tallied during the night, Bush had won a total of 246 electoral votes, while Gore had won 255 votes. The popular vote in Florida was so close that neither side could immediately be declared the winner of that state's 25 electoral votes. Recounting of votes and legal wrangling continued for several weeks. Finally, in the case of *Bush* v. *Gore*, in December 2000, the Supreme Court reversed the Florida Supreme Court decision ordering a manual recount of ballots, effectively ending the presidential election in favor of George W. Bush.

The election was also significant because it was the first time since 1888 that the winner of the electoral vote (George W. Bush) received less of the national popular vote than his opponent. Gore received over 500,000 more votes nationally than Bush (48.4 percent to Bush's 47.9 percent). This phenomenon would occur again in the 2016 election (see page 642). These elections, in which the winner of the presidency did not win the largest percentage of the national popular vote, have led to calls to rethink or reform the **Electoral College** system. However, major changes to the system do not seem to be on the horizon.

TAX CUTS

The top item on President George W. Bush's domestic agenda, and a major campaign promise—a $1.6 trillion tax cut—was the subject of bitter debate in Congress. While Bush and his supporters claimed that the tax cuts would promote new investment and economic growth, Democrats argued that the bill heavily favored the rich and would squander an unprecedented budget surplus. The Senate eventually trimmed the tax cut to $1.35 trillion over 11 years; Bush signed it into law in June 2001. Almost 60 percent of the tax cuts were limited to the wealthiest 10 percent of Americans, with the richest 1 percent of Americans receiving nearly 45 percent of the tax cuts. In the final two years of the Clinton administration, there were budget surpluses of $122.7 billion (1999) and $230 billion (2000). As a result of the surpluses, the $5.7 trillion national debt had been reduced by $360 billion in the previous three years. One of the more controversial aspects of the Bush tax law was a plan to send checks to 95 million people. Those advanced payments were referred to as **tax rebates**. The rebates ranged from $300 to $600 depending on whether the recipient was single, married, or the head of a household. The total cost of the rebates was approximately $38 billion. By the time Americans began receiving their tax rebate checks in August 2001, the country's budget surplus was beginning to disappear. The Congressional Budget Office attributed the change to a slowing economy and the Bush tax cut. By the end of Bush's presidency in 2009, the **national debt** had increased by 101 percent over what it had been when he assumed office, climbing to $11.6 trillion.

ENERGY POLICY UNDER BUSH AND CHENEY

Early in his administration, President George W. Bush and his advisors identified the oil supply as an essential element to the health and profitability of leading U.S. industries. This concern prompted Bush to establish the **National Energy Policy Development Group (NEPDG)** with Vice President **Dick Cheney** selected to lead the task force. The group was primarily composed of oil and gas executives, including Kenneth Lay, the head of Enron and a major contributor to the Republican Party (see pages 605–606). The workings of the committee were not made public. The General Accounting Office, the investigative arm of Congress, requested information in 2001 about the task force, but was rebuffed by Cheney. After years of legal wrangling, an appeals court in 2005 allowed the committee to keep its proceedings secret. *The Washington Post* was able to obtain some of the committee's documents, including a list of the committee's participants, which it published in 2007.

The Cheney Report proposed to boost domestic production of coal, oil, nuclear power, and natural gas. Toward this end, it called for the exploitation of untapped reserves in protected wilderness areas, including the **Arctic National Wildlife Refuge (ANWR)**, an immense, untouched wilderness area in northeastern Alaska. Ultimately the bill that was passed by Congress in 2005 included most of the pro-energy industry provisions of the report, though it rejected drilling in the ANWR and it offered incentives for research on renewable energy sources.

EDUCATION POLICY UNDER BUSH

"No Child Left Behind"

The centerpiece of President George W. Bush's education policy was embodied in the **No Child Left Behind Act**, signed into law in 2002. The law, designed to reform public education, extended the reach of the federal government into education—traditionally a state responsibility. The law required that states set learning standards, that students attain "proficiency" in reading and math by 2014, and that teachers be "highly qualified" in the subject area. The law allowed students to transfer to other schools if they were attending a school that fell short of meeting new guidelines. The law also allowed the state to take over schools and school districts that did not meet the new guidelines. The program was criticized by many states for its lack of funding to help schools reach these new goals. Also, many educators questioned the increased reliance on standardized tests in judging schools and school districts.

School Vouchers

The Bush administration's approach to education also reflected the Republican Party's preference for addressing pressing social issues with private sector solutions. The administration embraced **school vouchers**, which would allow families of children in poorly performing public schools to receive grants for children to attend private, often religious, schools. Advocates for public education argued that such vouchers would undermine public education by siphoning taxpayer money to private schools. Congressional Democrats ultimately rejected the call for federally funded vouchers. However, the Supreme Court upheld the constitutionality of school vouchers in the case of *Zelman* v. *Simmons-Harris* (2002). The Court, in a five to four decision, ruled that an Ohio school voucher plan did not violate the **First Amendment's Establishment Clause**.

CAMPAIGN FINANCE REFORM AND ELECTIONS DURING THE BUSH ADMINISTRATION

The McCain-Feingold Act

By the turn of the century, many Americans had grown increasingly concerned about the role that money was playing in the political process. Earlier, important steps were taken to rein in the influence of wealthy contributors to political campaigns. The 1972 **Federal Election Campaign** law required disclosure of campaign contributions. Two years later it was amended to limit campaign contributions. However, in the subsequent decades, corporations, organizations, and individuals had figured out ways to bypass this law. The **McCain-Feingold Act** (2002) was an important step toward limiting "soft money" from corporations and organizations in campaigns. This effort was largely undermined by the Supreme Court decision in *Citizens United v. Federal Election Commission* (2010) (see page 636).

Midterm Elections of 2002

The May 2001 decision by Senator **Jim Jeffords** of Vermont to leave the Republican Party to become an Independent gave the Democrats a short-lived majority in the Senate (50-49-1). The midterm congressional elections of 2002 saw the Republicans gain two seats and retake control of the U.S. Senate and also establish a sizable majority in the House of Representatives (229-205-1).

2004 Elections

Although the media focused its attention primarily on the presidential race, the 2004 congressional races were also highly contested and extremely important to both parties in regard to the control of Congress. Before the elections, Republicans held a 12-seat majority in the House of Representatives, while in the Senate they held only a slim majority of 51 to 49. As a result of the 2004 congressional elections, the Republicans picked up four additional seats in the Senate; they now maintained a 10-seat majority, and in the House of Representatives they added three more seats to their majority. Some of the seats gained by the Republicans came as a result of redistricting (gerrymandering) in Texas, led by Republican Representative **Tom Delay**.

The 2004 presidential election was the closest reelection campaign in American history. President Bush was challenged by Senator **John Kerry** of Massachusetts. Kerry chose as his running mate Senator **John Edwards** of North Carolina, who had also competed for the nomination in the Democratic primaries. The war on terrorism, and specifically the ongoing wars in Iraq and Afghanistan, garnered much of the attention during the campaign. The Kerry/Edwards campaign asserted that the Bush administration had mishandled the 2003 invasion of Iraq. The Kerry/Edwards campaign sought to focus attention on Kerry's exemplary record of service in the Vietnam War. He was wounded twice and was decorated for bravery, before returning home and becoming an important figure in the group, Vietnam Veterans Against the War. The campaign hoped that Kerry's history of military service would blunt concerns that he was incapable or uninterested in taking strong actions on behalf of national security. Kerry, however, was hurt in the polls by a series of ads, produced by a group called **Swift Boat Veterans for Truth**, that falsely accused Kerry of lying about his service in Vietnam in order to win medals. In the end it was a very tight victory for the incumbent administration of George W. Bush and Dick Cheney.

George W. Bush's victory in the presidential election came with the popular mandate that eluded him in the 2000 election and a stronger base in Congress. In addition, he was the first president since his father, George H. W. Bush, to win a majority of the popular votes cast.

Midterm Elections of 2006

The Democratic Party made a strong showing in the 2006 midterm elections. The Democrats regained the majority in both houses of Congress for the first time since 1994, picking up six seats in the Senate and 31 seats in the House. In the Senate, each party had 49 seats after the election, but two independent senators, **Joe Lieberman** of Connecticut and **Bernie Sanders** of Vermont, caucused with the Democratic Party, giving them control of the chamber.

HURRICANE KATRINA

On August 25, 2005, **Hurricane Katrina** brought catastrophic damage to the Gulf Coast region, resulting in more than 1,000 deaths and millions left homeless. The heaviest damage was sustained by the city of New Orleans. The hardest hit parts of the city were predominantly African American and impoverished. Americans were shaken not simply by the magnitude of the disaster but also by how ill prepared all levels of government were in its aftermath. Within the federal government, it appeared that the various agencies were not communicating with one another and did not grasp the magnitude of the situation. The head of the **Federal Emergency Management Agency (FEMA)** testified that he informed White House officials on August 29 that the levees had been breached and the city was flooding, but the Bush administration stated that they did not hear of the breach until August 30. In a radio interview, Homeland Security Secretary **Michael Chertoff** dismissed reports of the thousands of people seeking refuge at the Convention Center. Bush's pronouncement that the head of FEMA, **Michael Brown**, was doing a "heck of a job" seemed to be further evidence of his inability to grasp the gravity of the situation. The mishandling of the crisis damaged President Bush's approval ratings.

THE SUPREME COURT UNDER PRESIDENT GEORGE W. BUSH

President Bush was able to nominate two justices to the Supreme Court. In 2005, he nominated Judge **John Roberts** to be the chief justice of the Supreme Court after Chief Justice **William Rehnquist** died. Roberts had been a judge on the U.S. Court of Appeals for the District of Columbia Circuit. He is considered a conservative justice, as Rehnquist had been. Later in 2005, he nominated **Samuel Alito** to serve on the Supreme Court to replace Justice **Sandra Day O'Connor**, who retired. Alito had been a judge on the U.S. Court of Appeals for the Third Circuit. He was confirmed in early 2006. O'Connor was regarded as a moderate Republican; she usually voted with the conservative bloc of the Court, but occasionally had served as a swing vote. Alito, on the other hand, is considered one of the most conservative members of the Court. With Bush's two nominations, the Court was divided between four justices who generally voted in a more conservative direction, four justices who tended to vote in a more liberal direction, and a swing vote, Anthony Kennedy, who sometimes voted with the conservative wing of the Court, sometimes with the liberal wing.

THE GREAT RECESSION

Starting in late 2007, the country faced its most severe economic crisis since the Great Depression. The **Great Recession**, as the economic crisis of late 2007 to 2009 has been labeled, led to high unemployment, falling wages, and a housing crisis characterized by widespread foreclosures. By the fall of 2008, the **Dow Jones Industrial Average**—the major indicator of the health of the stock market—had lost half of its value. The crisis was devastating to millions of Americans. In addition, it began during the 2008 campaign for the presidency (see pages 631–632). Despite actions taken by the Bush administration in 2008, many voters came to see the financial crisis and decisions made during the Bush administration as additional reasons to give the Democratic Party the chance to take the helm.

The Housing Crisis

Many economists see the crisis in the housing market as an important cause of the Great Recession. In the 2000s, lending institutions had been devising new methods of making borrowing money cheaper and easier. Many of these practices became widespread when, in 1999, Congress repealed most of the provisions of the 1933 **Glass-Steagall Act**, removing regulatory constraints on the banking industry. Banks lured first-time home buyers to take out mortgages for home purchases that were beyond their means. Banks, for instance, offered adjustable rate mortgages in which initial low rates would later jump to higher rates. These risky loans, characterized by high interest rates and less than favorable terms,were referred to as "**subprime mortgages**" because they were extended to people whose ability to repay and whose credit rating was less than prime. By 2008, almost 30 percent of mortgages were rated as "subprime."

Frequently in the 2000s, lenders would sell these subprime mortgages to investment banks and other Wall Street financial institutions. In turn, Wall Street would bundle these mortgages into stock offerings. Finally, pension funds, mutual funds, foreign banks, and individuals invested in these offerings. Therefore, the risk entailed in the original mortgages was spread throughout the financial world and to many individuals whose financial health was, in some way, tied to the stock market.

In 2007, the housing bubble burst as the real estate market weakened and interest rates increased. Many subprime borrowers found themselves "**underwater**"—that is, the market value of their homes sank below the amount they owed on their mortgages. In many such situations, individuals could neither sell their homes nor afford to pay their monthly mortgage payments. Their only option was to walk away from their homes and default on their loans, leading to widespread foreclosures.

The Crisis Deepens

The collapse of the housing market and the high rate of foreclosures created ripples throughout the economy. Major financial institutions that had invested in risky mortgages found themselves in desperate straits when foreclosure rates reached crisis proportions. Wall Street and investors were left holding "**toxic assets**." In September 2008, the giant financial services firm, **Lehman Brothers**, collapsed, declaring bankruptcy. Major banks cut back on loaning money, business activity slowed, and consumer spending was drastically reduced. Businesses laid off workers in large numbers; 2.8 million workers lost their jobs in 2008, pushing unemployment to 9.8 percent by September 2009. The Dow Jones Industrial Average plummeted from 14,000 on the eve of the economic crisis in October 2007 to under 8,000 by March 2009.

Government Responses to the Great Recession

The Bush administration and the **Federal Reserve Bank (the Fed)** took a number of steps to address the economic crisis and to prevent a collapse of major economic institutions. The Fed outlined a $200 billion loan program that let the country's largest banks borrow Treasury securities at discounted rates. It also approved a $30 billion loan in March 2008 to **JP Morgan Chase** so that it could take over **Bear Stearns**, which was on the verge of collapse. President George W. Bush and Secretary of the United States Treasury **Henry Paulson** proposed legislation that would extend up to $700 billion for the government to purchase "troubled mortgage-related assets" from financial firms. The goal of **Troubled Asset Relief Program (TARP)** was to strengthen the financial sector and restore confidence in the securities market. Congress passed TARP in October 2008. Critics claimed that the government did not tie this money to new rules and guidelines to ensure that the money would be used for recovery and that irresponsible practices would be curtailed.

Bailout of the Automobile Industry

The automobile industry also went into financial crisis in 2008, partly as a result of reduced consumer spending associated with the overall financial crisis and partly as a result of rising fuel prices. As fuel prices rose, sales of sports utility vehicles, a mainstay of Detroit, declined. President Bush agreed in December 2008 to lend $17.4 billion to **General Motors** and **Chrysler** to keep them afloat (these funds came from the Troubled Asset Relief Program). These loans were continued and expanded by the Obama administration (see page 663).

Exercise Set 7.3

1. Which of the following is most closely associated with the Great Recession in 2008 and 2009?
   A. A dramatic increase in home foreclosures
   B. The elimination of the federal budget surplus
   C. A lack of skilled workers in the United States to fill jobs in factories
   D. The marked decline in agricultural commodity prices

2. In the aftermath of Hurricane Katrina in 2005,
   A. massive rioting in New Orleans led to the National Guard intervening to put down the rebellion.
   B. the Army Corps of Engineers won praise for predicting the impact of the hurricane on New Orleans and taking effective steps to minimize the effect of the storm.
   C. a coalition of European nations initiated a massive economic package for the rebuilding of New Orleans.
   D. the George W. Bush administration was perceived by many as out of touch and incapable of taking decisive action.

3. The "No Child Left Behind" program, put into law in 2002 by President George W. Bush,
   A. authorized local authorities to take aggressive steps against sex offenders, including notifying the public of the presence of convicted sex offenders living in the community.
   B. made the adoption of children easier by removing restrictions that had been applied to gay couples and to single people.
   C. extended the reach of the federal government into education by setting up a set of standards that local school districts were to achieve.
   D. created a program to help child soldiers in Africa escape their captors and become reintegrated into civilian society.

4. In the system of checks and balances established in the Constitution, which of the following is an example of a governmental check?
   A. President Bush approving a bailout package of the automobile industry in 2008
   B. Congress voting in favor of the No Child Left Behind Act in 2002
   C. President Bush vetoing the Cell Research Enhancement Act in 2005
   D. President George W. Bush declaring a state of emergency in Louisiana following Hurricane Katrina in 2005

5. President Ronald Reagan and President George W. Bush both pressured Congress to reduce taxes because they believed that tax cuts would lead to
   A. an increase in economic activity and a decrease in unemployment.
   B. a reduction in exports and a revival of American manufacturing.
   C. a slowdown in economic activity and a reduction in inflation.
   D. a reduction of military spending and foreign aid.

6. One energy resource which was considered by the Bush-Cheney Energy Task Force and has caused considerable partisan disagreement in Congress is
   A. the development of solar energy.
   B. tapping oil resources in northeastern Alaska.
   C. expansion of northwestern hydropower facilities.
   D. development of coastal wind farms.

DOMESTIC POLICY UNDER PRESIDENT BARACK OBAMA AND THE ELECTION OF DONALD TRUMP

> If an institution is too big to fail, it is too big to exist.
> Senator Bernie Sanders (Independent, Vermont), 2015

The election of 2008 resulted in a profound milestone in American history—the election of the first African American to the presidency. Such an event was virtually unthinkable a generation earlier. As late as the 1960s, Jim Crow segregation was still the law of the land throughout the South and informal *de facto* segregation existed throughout the nation. The Civil Rights Movement challenged and altered many of these practices, but racist attitudes persist among large segments of the population.

Once elected, **Barack Obama** only had the benefit of a Democratic Congress for the first two years of his administration. After 2010, Republicans controlled the House, and after 2014, they controlled both houses of Congress. He was able to pass his most significant piece of legislation in 2010—the Affordable Care Act. Afterward, it became increasingly difficult for him to persuade Congress to act on his legislative initiatives.

The unemployment rate dropped dramatically during his time in office. It was over nine percent during his first year in office; it dropped to 4.7 percent when he left office in 2017. The recovery, however, was uneven, especially in regard to higher-paying jobs. In 2016, Donald Trump was able to benefit from the perception that the economic recovery following the Great Recession hadn't lifted all boats.

THE ELECTION OF PRESIDENT BARACK OBAMA

Barack Obama's victory in the 2008 presidential race was the result of a series of factors. First, his campaign successfully held off a strong challenge to the Democratic nomination by Senator **Hillary Clinton**. Clinton's bid for the nomination, if successful, could have resulted in a different historic milestone—the first female president in the United States. The Obama campaign was able to harness the power of the Internet, as well as the candidate's abundant charisma, to build a large base. Clinton subsequently threw her support behind the Obama campaign in the general election. She was later named secretary of state.

In the general election, the Democratic Party was aided by an unpopular sitting Republican president, **George W. Bush**, and by an unfocused campaign by Republican Senator **John McCain**. The McCain campaign failed to articulate a consistent message. McCain's selection of the relatively unknown candidate, Governor **Sarah Palin** of Alaska, for vice president failed to propel the campaign forward. Palin energized the more conservative elements of the Republican Party, but failed to broaden the party's appeal.

Obama and his running mate, Senator **Joe Biden** of Delaware, were able to cement support in traditionally "blue" (Democratic leaning) states and successfully challenged McCain in traditionally "red" (Republican leaning) states, such as North Carolina, Virginia, and Indiana. Obama and Biden garnered 53 percent of the popular vote and won 365 electoral votes to McCain and Palin's 173.

OBAMA CONFRONTS A WEAK ECONOMY

President Barack Obama took office during a major downturn in economic activity, known as the Great Recession (see pages 627–629). Unemployment reached almost 10 percent in 2009. Obama initiated several actions to address the economic crisis.

The Stimulus Package

President Obama addressed the **Great Recession** with a major stimulus bill—the **American Recovery and Reinvestment Act** (2009). The act provided almost $800 billion to state and local governments to be used for infrastructure projects, schools, and hospitals. The act reflected the thinking of the economist **John Maynard Keynes**, who wrote the book *The General Theory of Employment, Interest and Money* (1936), during the depths of the Great Depression. He argued that during times of recession, the government should increase spending, taking up the slack caused by a decrease in private spending. His theory was influential in shaping President Franklin D. Roosevelt's **New Deal** (see pages 339–345). The impact of the stimulus package has been debated by economists. Unemployment went down during Obama's time in office—it was at 10 percent in October 2009 and 4.7 percent when he left office in 2017. However, it is not clear how much of that drop was due to the stimulus package and how much of it was due to a generally improving economy. Some liberal economists, such as Paul Krugman, argued that the stimulus was not nearly expansive enough to dramatically impact unemployment.

Intervention in the Automobile Industry

The automobile industry suffered enormous losses during the Great Recession. In 2008, President George W. Bush initiated a $17.4 bailout to **General Motors** and **Chrysler** (see page 629). The Obama administration continued to extend loan money to General Motors and Chrysler. Eventually these loans reached $82 billion. The loans contained the condition that the government receive shares in the companies and oversee their restructuring before reprivatizing them. The bailout was successful; the American automobile industry recovered and paid back $71 billion of the $82 billion that was used in the bailout.

The Dodd-Frank Wall Street Reform and Consumer Protection Act

The Obama administration pushed for measures to add regulations to the financial industry in order to rein in some of the risky practices that led to the recession of 2008. The **Dodd-Frank Wall Street Reform and Consumer Protection Act** (2010) was designed to regulate financial markets and protect consumers. It constituted the most comprehensive financial reform act since the **Glass-Steagall Act** of 1933, which established regulations for the banking industry (the Glass-Steagall Act was largely repealed in 1999).

The act was designed, in part, to end the idea of "**too big to fail**." To describe certain financial institutions as "too big to fail" is to note that the size and interconnectedness of these institutions make their failure unthinkable, because their failure would have such devastating consequences on the United States economy. Many economists are critical of a situation in which certain financial institutions are perceived as being too big to fail. These economists fear that "too big to fail" creates a "moral hazard"—that is, it sets up a situation in which institutions will engage in excessively risky behavior because they believe that a government bailout will occur if the risky behavior leads to major financial losses. This occurred, these economists argue, in the lead-up to the Great Recession. Critics argue that the Dodd-Frank Act is not strong enough to end the idea of "too big to fail."

OBAMA AND THE SUPREME COURT

President Obama nominated the first Latina to the Supreme Court, **Sonia Sotomayor**, to replace Justice **David H. Souter**, who retired. Sotomayor, who had served as a judge on the U.S. Court of Appeals for the Second Circuit, was approved by the Senate in 2009. The following year, Obama nominated **Elena Kagan** to replace Justice **John Paul Stevens**, who also retired. Kagan had previously served as the nation's first female solicitor general (2009–2010). The Court was divided politically between four justices, nominated by Republican presidents, who generally voted in a more conservative direction and four justices, nominated by Democratic presidents, who tended to vote in a more liberal direction. The ninth justice, **Anthony Kennedy**, appointed by President **Reagan**, was often seen as a swing vote, sometimes siding with the conservative wing of the Court, sometimes with the liberal wing. In February 2016, Justice **Antonin Scalia** died suddenly, leaving a vacancy on the Court. President Obama nominated **Merrick Garland**, chief judge of the United States Court of Appeals for the District of Columbia Circuit, to fill Scalia's seat. However, Republicans in the Senate indicated that they would not take action on the president's nomination. Senator **Mitch McConnell**, a Republican from Kentucky and the majority leader, said that the next president should be able to fill the vacancy on the Court, even though the election was still ten months away.

REFORMING HEALTH CARE

Like President Clinton, President Obama chose health-care reform as one of his first major domestic initiatives. The issues that motivated President Clinton in 1993—spiraling health-care costs and large numbers of uninsured Americans—had become more pronounced in the ensuing years. Some reformers called for a "**single-payer plan**." In a single-payer plan, the government would provide medical insurance; private-run, for-profit insurance companies would cease to exist. This national health insurance program would have been similar to health insurance systems in Canada and many European nations. Many congressional Democrats pushed for a "**public option**." The public option would have created a federal insurance program, similar to **Medicare**, but for people under 65 years of age. Such a program would compete with private insurance plans and, proponents argued, provide lower cost health insurance to people. Proposals for creating a "public option" generated enthusiasm among many Democrats, but also fierce opposition from the pharmaceutical and insurance industries, and from the Republican Party. Many Republicans likened such a proposal to "socialism."

Passage of the Affordable Care Act

In 2009, both houses of Congress passed versions of health-care reform. In early 2010, a special election to fill the late Senator **Edward Kennedy's** seat was won by a Republican, ending the Democrats' 60-seat filibuster-proof majority in the Senate. Democrats were able to pass a watered-down version of health-care reform in March 2010. The **Patient Protection and**

Affordable Care Act overhauled much of the health-care industry. Among other things, the bill allowed children to stay on their parents' health insurance plans until they were 26, prevented insurance companies from denying coverage based on an individual's **pre-existing conditions** subsidized private insurance for low- and middle-income individuals, and required all Americans to have some sort of health insurance (the **individual mandate**). Finally, the act also called for the establishment of **health insurance exchanges** or marketplaces in each of the fifty states. States could establish and regulate their own exchange; a federal exchange would also be established for individuals in states that declined to establish an exchange. These exchanges are government-run, but the actual insurers are private companies which meet the requirements and guidelines of the exchange. Such exchanges can be more cost-efficient because individuals pool their purchasing power into larger groups.

The Supreme Court and the Affordable Care Act

The Affordable Care Act, also known as Obamacare, was challenged on several fronts in the federal court system. The Supreme Court has upheld the act in two significant decisions. In 2012, in the case of *National Federation of Independent Business* v. *Sebelius*, the Court upheld the act's "individual mandate." Opponents repeatedly targeted the "individual mandate," asserting that it was an onerous burden on individuals and represented governmental overreach. Chief Justice John Roberts, writing for the majority, asserted that the mandate is a valid tax, and thus within Congress's taxing power. It would not, on the other hand, have fallen within Congress's power to "regulate commerce," because the commerce clause of the Constitution does not extend to the regulation of economic *inactivity* (such as *not* purchasing insurance). Later, in *King* v. *Burwell* (2015), the Court upheld the provision that tax subsidies be extended to those who purchased health insurance through the federal-run marketplace. Opponents argued that the act indicated these tax credits are only to be distributed for marketplaces "established by the *state*"—not by the federal government. The Court reasoned that the intent of the act, as Congress understood it when it passed, was to provide credits to both federal- and state-run marketplaces.

Impact of the Affordable Care Act

According to a March 2016 report by the Congressional Budget Office, the Affordable Care Act has provided health insurance to 24 million people. There are approximately 12 million people covered by the exchanges, 11 million were made eligible for **Medicaid** by the act, and 1 million were covered by the act's **Basic Health Program.** The uninsured rate in the United States went down from 16 percent of the population in 2010 to 8.9 percent in 2016. At the same time, premium costs for some individuals have increased, especially those middle- and upper-income individuals who do not receive federal subsidies for their insurance plans. In addition, there is less choice of insurance providers in some areas, because some insurers have pulled out of certain marketplaces. As of the beginning of 2017, the future of the Affordable Care Act is up in the air.

CAMPAIGN FINANCE, VOTING RIGHTS, AND ELECTIONS DURING THE OBAMA ADMINISTRATION

The three national elections that occurred after President Obama came into power—in 2010, 2012, and 2014—were significant in three ways. First, the rules for funding changed dramatically in the months before the 2010 election, as the Supreme Court weakened certain limits on political spending in the name of free speech. Second, many state voting rules changed. In 2013, the Supreme Court weakened the 1965 **Voting Right Act**, paving the way for more restrictive voting rules in many states. Third, Republicans made significant gains in Congress, despite Obama's winning reelection in 2012. In 2010, the Republicans gained control of the House, and in 2014, they gained control of the Senate.

The *Citizen's United* Case

The rules governing political campaigns changed dramatically in 2010, allowing corporations and other organizations to spend unlimited amounts of money on political campaigns. Previously, the 1972 Federal Election Campaign law and the 2003 McCain-Feingold Act set limits and regulations on campaign contributions, both direct, "hard money" contributions to campaigns, as well as contributions of "soft money" to political parties. In the case of *Citizens United* **v.** *Federal Election Commission* (January 2010) the Court ruled, in a 5 to 4 decision, that the government cannot restrict the spending of corporations, unions, and other groups on political campaigns. Politically oriented nonprofits can now raise and spend unlimited amounts of money without disclosing their finances to the **Federal Election Commission**. The Court argued that such restrictions violated the free speech provision of the First Amendment.

The Midterm Elections of 2010

The impact of the *Citizens United* decision was felt almost immediately. The decision opened the floodgates for corporate campaign contributions for the midterm election of 2010. Overall, the 2010 elections generated over $4 billion in contributions. It was the costliest midterm election in history, until the following midterm election in 2014. In each election since *Citizens United*, the amount of undisclosed and anonymous contributions has increased, with much of this money going toward independent, and often negative, advertising.

In the midterm elections themselves, the Republican Party made significant gains in Congress. In the House of Representatives, the Republican Party gained 63 seats, recapturing the majority. It was the largest seat change in the House since 1948. The Republicans gained six seats in the Senate. After the election, the Democrats still held the majority in the Senate with 51 seats (plus 2 seats of Independents who caucused with the Democrats), while Republicans held 47 seats. Usually the party not in control of the White House makes gains during the midterm elections. Republicans were also energized by opposition to the Affordable Care Act. In addition, unemployment was still high, at nine percent, at the time of the election. Finally, the **Tea Party Movement** was able to harness discontent and mobilize voters for Republican candidates (see page 664).

Re-election of President Obama in 2012

President Barack Obama and Vice President Joe Biden were elected to a second term in 2012. Obama's victory in the Electoral College was solid, 332 to 206, but his margin of victory was smaller than it had been in 2008. He won all the states he had carried in 2008 except for North Carolina, Indiana, and Nebraska's second congressional district.

The Republican Party nominated **Mitt Romney**, former governor of Massachusetts. Romney chose Representative **Paul Ryan** of Wisconsin to be his running mate. Romney, who was seen as the choice of the Republican establishment, had to defend himself throughout the primary cycle against charges that he was insufficiently conservative. At one point, he labeled himself as "severely conservative." Conservative activists, many who allied with the Tea Party Movement, noted Romney's earlier support for *Roe* v. *Wade* and his signing, as governor of Massachusetts, of a health-care reform act that was very similar to the Affordable Care Act signed into law by President Obama in 2010 (see pages 634–635).

In the general election, Romney pivoted to more centrist positions on several issues, including health care and foreign policy. However, several factors undermined Romney and aided Obama. Economic indicators pointed toward growth and recovery. The unemployment rate, which had been over nine percent earlier in 2012, was less than eight percent by September 2014. The president pointed to a rebound in the American automobile industry, following the bailout of the industry in 2009 (see page 633). In addition, Obama could cite the May 2011 raid that killed Osama bin Laden and the withdrawal of troops from Iraq as foreign policy gains (see pages 650 and 656). In addition to carrying the Electoral College in November, Obama also won a clear victory in the popular vote, 51.1 percent to Romney's 47.2 percent.

In congressional elections in 2012, the Democrats also made gains. They continued to control the Senate, picking up two additional seats, and they made a modest dent in the Republican majority in the House, picking up eight additional seats.

Voting Rights

The 1965 **Voting Rights Act** was weakened by the Supreme Court in its decision in *Shelby County* **v.** *Holder* (2013). Provisions of the act had required certain states with a history of discriminatory voting laws to obtain federal approval, or preclearance, before carrying out any future changes to their voting laws or practices. The provisions were designed to prevent these states from introducing new procedures that would make voting more difficult, especially for African Americans. The Court asserted that the formula used to determine which states were more likely to implement discriminatory voting laws was outdated. The impact of the decision was felt almost immediately. Several states that had been required to get preclearance for changes to their voting rules passed strict voter ID laws. For example, after Texas was freed from federal preclearance, it passed one of the strictest voter ID laws in the country (2013). Republican politicians argue that such laws are needed to prevent fraud. Election observers note that election fraud is extremely rare in the United States.

Midterm Elections of 2014

The Republicans made an extremely strong showing in the 2014 midterm elections. The Republican Party picked up nine seats in the Senate, giving them a majority in that body with 54 seats to the 44 seats held by the Democrats (plus two seats of Independents who caucused with the Democrats). The Republicans added to their majority in the House of Representatives by picking up 13 seats. The 59-seat edge they held in the House was their largest majority since 1928.

IMMIGRATION REFORM

In the late 20th and early 21st centuries, debates around immigration policy have divided Americans. In 2010, **Jan Brewer**, the governor of Arizona, signed into law the country's toughest immigration bill. The law was designed to identify and deport undocumented immigrants. It allowed law enforcement to stop people suspected of being undocumented and to ask to see required documents. The Obama administration challenged the law in court. The case went to the Supreme Court in 2012, which struck down three provisions of the law but uphold the portion of the law allowing Arizona state police to investigate the immigration status of an individual if there is reasonable suspicion that the individual is in the country illegally.

Obama and Deferred Action for Childhood Arrivals (DACA)

President Obama pushed for a more comprehensive reform of immigration policy that combined deportations of undocumented immigrants who were deemed dangerous with providing pathways to legal status and citizenship for most undocumented immigrants. In 2012, he announced the **Deferred Action for Childhood Arrivals (DACA)** program, which allowed certain undocumented immigrants who entered the United States as minors to receive a renewable two-year period of deferred action from deportation. The program also contained provisions for these individuals to obtain work permits. The idea of the program was that children should not be punished for their parents' illegal action of entering the United States without documentation.

Congressional Inaction on Immigration Reform

In 2013, congressional leaders attempted to address the issue of immigration reform with the **Border Security, Economic Opportunity, and Immigration Modernization Act**. A bipartisan group of senators, labeled the "**gang of eight**," negotiated the bill. They hoped to solidify immigration reform in legislation, rather than allow it to be shaped on a temporary basis by executive action. The act would have provided a pathway to permanent residence status and citizenship for many undocumented immigrants as well as provisions for greater border security. The bill was approved by the Senate 68 to 32. Despite its bipartisan origins, Republican opposition in the House of Representatives blocked the bill.

Expanded Deferred Action and the Courts

In 2014, President Obama, realizing that comprehensive legislative action on the immigration issue was virtually impossible, took further executive action on the issue of immigration reform. By executive order, he expanded the scope of DACA. The action would have allowed as many as five million illegal immigrants who are the parents of citizens or of lawful permanent residents to apply for a program that would spare them from deportation and would provide them with work permits. The action, known as **Deferred Action for Parents of Americans and Lawful Permanent Residents (DAPA)**, was blocked in the federal court system by a preliminary injunction. In *United States* **v.** *Texas* (2016), the Supreme Court let stand the preliminary injunction issued by the lower court in a four to four tie vote.

Deportations Under President Obama

While President Obama worked toward immigration reform, he also aggressively pursued a policy of **deportations**. During Obama's time in office, 2009–2017, there were more deportations (2.5 million) than under any other previous president. The Obama administration targeted undocumented immigrants who were criminals, those who were deemed a threat to public safety or national security, and those who illegally entered the country recently.

Immigration and Donald Trump

Immigration remains a contentious issue in the United States. The issue was at the centerpiece of **Donald Trump's** successful campaign for the presidency in 2016. He promised to a build a wall between the United States and Mexico to prevent people from illegally crossing the border and to temporarily block immigration from certain Muslim majority nations. His pointed comments about undocumented immigrants were greeted with dismay by many, but with enthusiastic support by others.

THE ELECTION OF 2016

The presidential election of 2016 was notable for a number of reasons. It was the first election that included a woman as the candidate of one of the major political parties. **Hillary Clinton**, who served as First Lady during the administration of her husband, President Bill Clinton (1993–2001), as senator from New York State (2001–2009), and as secretary of state under President

Obama (2009–2013), was chosen by the Democratic Party. Clinton had previously run a strong campaign for the democratic nomination in 2008 before she was defeated by Barack Obama (see page 631). In 2016, Clinton faced a surprisingly strong challenge from Senator **Bernie Sanders** of Vermont. Sanders portrayed Clinton as a product of the Democratic Party establishment, unwilling to challenge financial or corporate interests. He generated a great deal of enthusiasm among young people and those who wanted a more activist-oriented Democratic Party. Ultimately, he lost the nomination, but he raised issues not traditionally raised in presidential campaigns.

The Republican Party also had an unusual nominating process. Seventeen individuals announced their candidacy for the nomination, with five dropping out before the first primary. The debates among the Republican candidates were freewheeling events, with businessman **Donald Trump** garnering a great deal of attention and airtime. By the fall of 2015, he emerged as the leading candidate for the nomination. His blunt, unpolished, and aggressive style of speaking appealed to many voters. He was perceived as "speaking his mind," unencumbered by what he called "political correctness." Many voters—Democrats and Republicans—were stunned and even disgusted by many of his comments and actions. In July 2015, for example, he questioned the status of **John McCain** as a war hero. McCain had been held as a prisoner of war in North Vietnam for five and a half years during the Vietnam War in miserable conditions; he was repeatedly beaten and tortured during the ordeal. Trump said of McCain, "He's not a war hero. He's a war hero because he was captured. I like people that weren't captured." Such comments did not seem to diminish his support. He focused his campaign events on immigration, security, and trade deals. Further, several establishment-oriented Republican candidates stayed in the race well into the primary season. In many ways, they divided the anti-Trump vote within the Republican Party. Finally, by early May 2016, Trump emerged with enough pledged delegates to become the party's presumptive nominee.

For the general election, Hillary Clinton chose Senator **Tim Kaine** of Virginia as her running mate, while Donald Trump chose Governor **Mike Pence** of Indiana. Trump continued to stress immigration, trade deals, and security. He criticized Clinton for maintaining a private e-mail server during her time as secretary of state, asserting that it was a sign of bad judgment. Clinton stressed middle-class job creation, campaign finance reform, and improving the Affordable Care Act. She also promised to push for a pathway to citizenship for certain undocumented immigrants and universal preschool. Most polls showed Clinton with a clearer path to victory in the Electoral College than Trump. This perception was bolstered by the release of video and audio, from 2005, in which Trump is heard discussing women in an obscene manner and excusing sexual assault. Clinton also had setbacks on the campaign trail. In September, at a fundraising event, she said that many of Trump's supporters could be put in a "basket of deplorables," citing increased evidence of racism, homophobia, xenophobia, Islamophobia, and sexism among some supporters of Trump. Before the election, in late October, the director of the FBI, **James Comey**, said that the Bureau was investigating newly found e-mails associated with Clinton. On the weekend before the election, Comey announced that the FBI would stand by its earlier conclusion that it would not initiate charges against Clinton.

In the general election, Trump carried enough states to win 306 electoral votes; Clinton won 232. Two hundred seventy votes are needed for victory; the actual count differed because seven **"faithless" electors** did not cast their vote for the candidate for whom they were pledged. Trump won three states that had been reliably Democratic in recent elections—Pennsylvania, Michigan, and Wisconsin. He also won the key swing states of Ohio and Florida, as well as Iowa and North Carolina. For the second time in the past five elections, the winner of the Electoral College vote, Trump, failed to win the overall popular vote. Nearly three million more people voted for Clinton than for Trump. She won 48 percent of the vote, while Trump won 45.9 percent of the vote. This was the largest deficit in the popular vote for a winner of the electoral vote in terms of absolute numbers and the third largest in terms of percentages.

PRESIDENT TRUMP'S FIRST 100 DAYS IN OFFICE

The most significant accomplishment of President Donald Trump's first 100 days in office was replacing Justice Antonin Scalia on the Supreme Court. In January 2017, President Donald Trump nominated **Neil Gorsuch**, judge of the Tenth Circuit Court of Appeals, to fill the vacancy on the Court. He was confirmed by the Senate in April. The 49-year-old Gorsuch is a proponent of **originalism**—a conservative approach to Constitutional interpretation that seeks to understand the original intent of the framers of the document.

However, the beginning of President Donald Trump's tenure in office in 2017 was marked by several missteps and reversals. His unorthodox approach to governing was welcomed by many of his supporters who hoped he would shake up the political establishment of Washington, D.C. However, his impulsive and ad hoc approach to major issues also sowed doubts about his ability to effect meaningful change. His initial attempt to undo the **Affordable Care Act** failed to win approval from the House of Representatives. A second attempt passed the House, but faces an uncertain future in the Senate. Congress failed to earmark money for a wall between the United States and Mexico that he had promised during the campaign. Further, his attempts to issue a **temporary travel ban** on individuals coming into the United States from primarily Muslim countries were held up in the court system. The administration indicated that it would challenge moves by several states to legalize marijuana for medical, and in some cases recreational, use. It initially did not act on this threat.

Accusations persisted that the Russian government interfered with the 2016 election on behalf of Trump and that members of the Trump team collaborated with Russian officials. These accusations grew louder when President Trump fired **James Comey** as head of the FBI, perhaps to halt possible investigations into Trump's ties to Russia. During the first 100 days, he failed to articulate a clear approach to foreign policy issues, including trade issues, raising concerns among several American allies.

Although President Trump did not make significant headway with Congress on major legislation in his first 100 days, he issued several executive orders rolling back environmental regulations put in place during the Obama administration and undoing several measures designed to regulate the financial industry.

Exercise Set 7.4

1. One feature of the Affordable Care Act that generated a great deal of opposition from many voters was
   A. the elimination of private, for-profit insurance providers in many states.
   B. the elimination of the Medicare program for senior citizens.
   C. the exclusion of prescription drugs from health insurance plans.
   D. the "individual mandate," requiring all Americans to obtain some sort of health insurance.

2. One way in which the elections of President George W. Bush (2000) and President Donald Trump (2016) are similar is that in both instances the
   A. winner of the Electoral College vote failed to win the popular vote.
   B. third-party candidate won the electoral vote in multiple states.
   C. eventual winner was selected by the House of Representatives.
   D. elections were settled by the Supreme Court.

3. President Franklin D. Roosevelt and President Barack Obama both pursued financial and banking reforms in order to
   A. shift regulatory responsibility from the federal government to the states.
   B. create greater stability in the American economy.
   C. free major financial institutions from oversight and regulation.
   D. better integrate the United States economy into the global economy.

4. Deferred Action for Childhood Arrivals (DACA) was an Obama administration policy that was designed to
   A. address concerns about the status of children of undocumented immigrants who were raised in the United States.
   B. provide federal funding for schools to help recently arrived immigrant children learn English.
   C. create a separate immigration processing system for children who arrived in the United States as refugees from war-torn countries.
   D. give priority to families with young children in regard to being allowed to legally immigrate into the United States.

5. In the case of *Shelby County* v. *Holder* (2013), the Supreme Court affected voting rights by
   A. forbidding states from using poll taxes or literacy tests as requirements for voting.
   B. lowering the voting age from 21 to 18.
   C. allowing southern states to implement changes to voting laws without getting prior approval from the Justice Department.
   D. mandating that all states require voters to show picture ideas when they show up to cast their ballot.

6. The Supreme Court decision in *Citizens United* v. *Federal Election Commission* (2010) had the effect of
   A. eliminating limits on the amount of money that corporations and unions could spend in regard to elections.
   B. limiting the amount of money that an individual could contribute to a particular candidate running for office.
   C. ensuring that television networks provide equal air time to major candidates during an election.
   D. allowing states greater freedom to redraw election districts.

FOREIGN POLICY CHALLENGES IN THE POST-9/11 WORLD

To a large degree, the war on terrorism has been the backdrop to American interactions with the world in the 21st century, just as the Cold War was the backdrop to global affairs in the second half of the 20th century. Both Presidents George W. Bush and Barack Obama had to deal with wars and conflicts stemming from the terrorist attacks on the United States on September 11, 2001 (see pages 611–612). In addition, the United States has dealt with a number of other international challenges and conflicts in the 21st century, including ongoing tensions between Israel and the Palestinians, provocative actions by Russia, the aftermath of the "Arab Spring," and evolving relations with Cuba.

PRESIDENT BUSH AND THE WITHDRAWAL FROM THE INTERNATIONAL COMMUNITY

The administration of President **George W. Bush** worked with a coalition of nations on the invasion of Iraq, but it distrusted many of the multilateral entities that the United States had previously participated in. Bush withdrew the United States from the **Kyoto Protocol**, an international agreement on environmental goals (see page 673). Also, the administration violated international guidelines about the treatment of military prisoners.

Bush withdrew from the **Anti-Ballistic Missile Treaty** with **Russia**, in effect since 1972, so that the United States could develop a space-based missile-defense system. President **Nixon** and General Secretary **Leonid Brezhnev** of the Soviet Union had signed the Anti-Ballistic Missile Treaty in 1972, providing a check on each nation's ability to launch multiple nuclear warheads upon the other. After the dissolution of the Soviet Union in 1991, the status of the treaty became somewhat unclear. In December 2001, President Bush gave notice that the United States would be withdrawing from the Anti-Ballistic Missile Treaty the following year, marking the first time in recent history that the United States withdrew from a major international arms treaty.

In 2002, the United States withdrew from the treaty creating the United Nation's **International Criminal Court (ICC)**, which was ratified in 1998. The court began operating in 2002, once it had reached the required number of participants. The Court is based in The Hague, Netherlands and hears cases involving international law including allegations of genocide, crimes against humanity, and war crimes, among others. To date, the United States has not ratified the ICC, arguing that prosecutions might be brought against U.S. nationals for political reasons.

CONTINUED WARFARE IN IRAQ AND AFGHANISTAN

The United States took swift action in the aftermath of the terrorist attacks of September 11, 2001. Before the year was out, the United States began a war in **Afghanistan**, which had harbored training camps for **al-Qaeda**. In addition to addressing security measures in the United States, the Bush administration also initiated war in Iraq (staring in 2003), which did not have direct connections with al-Qaeda or other **jihadist** groups (see pages 615–616). Both conflicts occupied much of the attention of the remaining years of the Bush administration.

The War in Iraq

In May 2003, President George W. Bush declared victory in the war in **Iraq** with a banner reading "**Mission Accomplished**" behind him. Seven months later, in December, **Saddam Hussein** was captured, and later tried and executed (see pages 617–618). These events, however, did not represent an end to American engagement in Iraq. The war continued for another six years. Public support for the war waned in the United States after 2003 and was an important issue in the presidential elections of 2004 and 2008.

Enhanced Interrogation and Abu Ghraib

In 2004, photographs of U.S. Army personnel humiliating and abusing prisoners at Abu Ghraib were released. The photos from the prison in Iraq cast light on new tactics used by the United States in its handling of prisoners in the aftermath of the 2001 terrorist attacks. Army personnel at detention centers in Iraq, Afghanistan, and Guantanamo Bay, Cuba were given permission to use **enhanced interrogation** techniques. These techniques, which include **waterboarding**, amount to torture. The government also began to hold suspects at these facilities indefinitely, denying them due process rights. The Supreme Court, in *Hamdan* v. *Rumsfeld* (2006), ruled that the Bush administration could not hold detainees indefinitely, without due process and without the protection of the **Geneva Accords**.

Following continuing reports of the use of torture in the interrogation methods of the United States, Congress voted in 2006 to support a bill, drafted in part by Senator **John McCain**, which held the president to the guidelines of the Geneva Convention. The bill also banned the use of evidence gathered using cruel, unusual, and inhumane treatment.

Continued Violence in Iraq

Attacks by insurgents in Iraq continued to destabilize the country. These attacks occurred against U.S. troops and Iraqi security forces, as well as among rival factions in Iraq. By October 2004, the British publication, *The Lancet*, estimated that 100,000 Iraqis had died as a result of the Iraq War.

The United States worked to establish a governing structure in Iraq. In 2003, a **Governing Council** was established with members of the three main ethnic and religious groups in Iraq—**Shiites**, **Sunnis**, and **Kurds**. Iraq is overwhelmingly **Muslim** (approximately 99 percent). About 75 percent of the people are **Arab**, approximately 20 percent are Kurdish, and about 5 percent are other ethnicities. In regard to religion, about 65 percent of the Muslim population identifies as Shiite and 35 percent identify as Sunni. The vast majority of Kurds identify as Shiite.

An interim government took power in June 2004. In January 2005, Iraq held elections to select a 275-seat **National Assembly**. The Shiites won a majority of the seats, with the Kurdish community winning about a quarter of the seats. The Sunni community boycotted the election. In October 2005, Iraqi voters ratified a new constitution and voted again for seats in the National Assembly in December. In this election, the Sunni community participated and the resulting Assembly was more representative of the different Iraqi factions. About 70 percent of the country's registered voters participated in selecting their first permanent parliament since the overthrow of Saddam Hussein. Once again, Shiites won a majority of the seats.

The threat of civil war increased in 2006 with an escalation in sectarian violence. In January, hundreds died at the hands of suicide bombers. In June, an attack by coalition forces north of Baghdad was successful in killing **Abu Musab al-Zarqawi**, the leader of **al-Qaeda** in Iraq. July 2006 was the deadliest month of the war for Iraqi citizens, with 3,438 civilian deaths.

David Petraeus and "the Surge"

In 2007, President George W. Bush named **David Petraeus** as the top commander of American forces in Iraq. He also ordered a sharp increase in the number American troops in Iraq. The **"surge"** resulted in 30,000 additional troops being sent to Iraq to stem an increase in deadly attacks by insurgents and militias. By 2008, the results of the surge were evident, as military and civilian casualties began to drop. The Iraqi parliament approved an agreement with the United States in 2008 for the reduction of American troops in the country and the withdrawal of combat troops by the end of 2011.

President Obama and the Winding Down of the Iraq War

During the presidential campaign of 2008, Barack Obama repeatedly said that the war in Iraq was the "wrong war" and that the United States should focus on Afghanistan instead of Iraq. Once in office, he promised to wind down the war in Iraq, in compliance with the 2008 agreement signed by President George W. Bush. The Iraqi government rejected maintaining even a small American force of trainers and advisors in the country. By December 2011, the last troops were withdrawn from Iraq and the U.S.-led war in Iraq was officially over. Almost 4,500 American troops lost their lives in the conflict. Iraqi deaths range from 200,000 to 500,000. Iraq still suffers from sectarian violence and political turmoil.

War in Afghanistan

By the end of 2001, the **Taliban** was ousted from power in **Afghanistan** by United States forces, and al-Qaeda's presence in the country was greatly diminished (see page 613). However, violence continued in Afghanistan as fundamentalists, members of the Taliban, and regional warlords vied for control of different parts of the country. The United States maintained its military presence in the country. It was joined by troops from about 30 nations who participated in the conflict under the auspices of **NATO**. By 2008, the situation worsened in Afghanistan. More allied troops died that year than in any other year since the war had begun in 2001 (that number was exceeded in 2009; the number of allied troop deaths peaked in 2010 with 711 deaths). In 2009, **Hamid Karzai** was reelected as president in an election widely seen as fraudulent. In the United States, public opinion began to turn against continued involvement in Afghanistan. In 2010, President Obama announced that American troops would remain in Afghanistan until the end of 2014. In 2012 and 2013, the United States began reducing its troop strength in Afghanistan and turning over operations to Afghani military forces. Violence in the country has gone down, but has certainly not been eliminated. Most U.S. troops were withdrawn by the end of 2014 as planned. The governments of Afghanistan and the United States agreed that approximately 10,000 American troops would remain in the country. During the 13 years of warfare, more than 2,300 American troops were killed in Afghanistan.

CONTINUING CONFLICT BETWEEN ISRAEL AND THE PALESTINIANS

The United States has continued to push for a settlement of the conflict between **Israel** and the **Palestinians** in the 21st century. The conflict between the two sides has lasted for decades. Since the **Six-Day War** in 1967, Israel has occupied adjacent lands where large numbers of Palestinians live. These lands currently include the **West Bank** of the Jordan River and **Eastern Jerusalem**. The **Gaza Strip** was occupied by Israeli troops until 2005 (see below). Palestinians have insisted these lands should comprise a Palestinian state. Israel has resisted agreeing to the formation of a Palestinian state as long as Palestinians launch attacks on Israel. The continued growth of Jewish settlements in the West Bank complicates the situation.

The Roadmap for Peace

In April 2003, the United States, the United Nations, the European Union, and Russia introduced their **Roadmap for Peace** to bring an end to the Israeli-Palestinian conflict; it was endorsed by the **United Nations Security Council** in November. The Roadmap consists of three phases: the first is an end to terror and violence, normalizing Palestinian life and building Palestinian institutions, mutual recognition, and a freeze on Israeli settlements; the second is a period of transition, including negotiations around resources and refugees; and the third is the establishment of permanent borders and a Palestinian State. However, by the end of 2003, the process stalled as it became apparent that the requirements for phase one of the Roadmap were not being executed—the Palestinian authority was not taking steps to end Palestinian terrorism and Israel was not taking steps to freeze settlement building.

The Israeli Withdrawal from Gaza and the Growth of Hamas

In 2004, Israeli **Prime Minister Ariel Sharon** proposed taking unilateral action—withdrawing troops and removing settlements from the Gaza Strip. Later that year, the long-time leader of the Palestinian movement, **Yasser Arafat**, died. The following year, **Mahmoud Abbas** was elected as the Palestinian president. He and Sharon agreed to a cease-fire later in 2005. By the end of the year, Israel completed its withdrawal from Gaza.

Violence between the two sides broke out again in 2006. Elections in Gaza led to an unexpected victory by **Hamas** over the ruling **Fatah Party**. The militant Hamas faction called for the destruction of Israel and is classified as a terrorist organization by the United States. Israel conducted air raids and ground operations in Gaza after Hamas killed two Israeli soldiers and kidnapped a third. Hamas fired rockets into Israel for several weeks. Israel became militarily engaged on another front in 2006. **Hezbollah**— the militant Shiite organization based in **Lebanon**—captured two Israeli soldiers as they patrolled Lebanon's border. Israel sent tanks into southern

Lebanon; Hezbollah responded with a barrage of missile and rocket strikes. A UN-sponsored cease-fire went into effect on the 34th day of fighting. In 2008, fighting broke out again between Israel and Hamas after Hamas renewed airstrikes against Israel. Israel responded with a series of intense airstrikes against Hamas military positions and smuggling tunnels. These airstrikes were followed by a ground war against Hamas.

Obama, Netanyahu, and the Stalled Peace Process

President Obama continued to maintain strong ties between the United States and Israel. For example, he opposed the move by the United Nations to upgrade the status of the **Palestinian Authority** to "non-member observer state" and in 2016 he agreed to provide Israel a record $38 billion in new military aid over the following decade. He hoped he could restart negotiations between Israel and the Palestinians by pressuring Israel to freeze building settlements in the West Bank. Israel, however, continued to expand settlement construction in the West Bank.

In 2015, violence again broke out between Israel and Hamas in Gaza following the kidnapping and killing of three Israeli teenagers. Later, the body of a Palestinian teenager was found in Israel. For seven weeks, Hamas launched rockets into Israel and Israel retaliated with air strikes against Hamas targets in Gaza.

Over time, President Obama grew increasingly frustrated with Prime Minister **Benjamin Netanyahu** of Israel. In 2010, the Israeli government announced the construction of new housing units in East Jerusalem just as Vice President **Joe Biden** was visiting Israel. Later, in 2015, the Obama administration was displeased with Netanyahu's speech to Congress condemning the Iran nuclear deal (see pages 656–657). These frustrations became more evident at the end of Obama's term; he decided in December 2016 not to block a UN Security Council resolution condemning Israeli settlements.

THE ARAB SPRING

On December 17, 2010, a Tunisian street vendor named **Mohamed Bouazizi** set himself on fire in a city in **Tunisia** as a protest against a municipal official who had, he claimed, repeatedly harassed and humiliated him. On this day, his wares had been confiscated. His protest set off a wave of protests in Tunisia, and, in 2011, protests spread throughout the Middle East and Northern Africa. The protests, known collectively as the **Arab Spring**, toppled several governments, including those in Tunisia, **Yemen**, and **Egypt**. In other countries, such as **Algeria** and **Jordan**, protests led to concessions from the government. While the **Tunisian Revolution** led to a transition to democratic rule, most of the other protest movements resulted in repression and violence. The backlash against the Arab Spring is sometimes referred to as the **Arab Winter**. In Egypt, for example, massive demonstrations led to the toppling of the authoritarian regime of **Hosni Mubarak**. However, he was replaced by an autocratic government of the **Muslim Brotherhood**, which was then replaced by a repressive militarist government.

The Response of the Obama Administration to the Arab Spring

The Obama administration found itself in an awkward position in regard to many of the Arab Spring protests. On the one hand, President Obama welcomed the calls for greater democracy and openness in the region. On the other hand, the administration feared alienating regimes that had close ties to the United States. In Egypt for example, Mubarak ruled in a dictatorial manner, but he was a long-term ally of the United States. With the exception of Libya, the United States avoided getting directly involved with the events of the Arab Spring.

The United States, Libya, and the Overthrow of Qaddafi

The United States and **NATO** provided military support to help overthrow the dictator **Muammar al-Qaddafi** of **Libya**. This represented a shift in policy for the United States in regard to Libya. Earlier, in 2006, President George W. Bush restored diplomatic relations with Libya and took it off the list of terrorist nations after Qaddafi admitted guilt for Libya's role in the 1988 terrorist bombing of **Pan Am flight 103**. After Qaddafi's ouster in 2011, the country descended into chaos and violence. In 2012 the fighting in Libya resulted in the death of four American embassy officials in the Libyan city of **Benghazi**, including Ambassador **J. Christopher Stevens**. The killing of American officials at Benghazi had repercussions in the 2016 U.S. presidential race. Republicans accused Democratic candidate Hillary Clinton, who was secretary of state at the time of the Benghazi incident, of not providing the compound with adequate security.

CIVIL WAR IN SYRIA

By far the deadliest aftermath of the Arab Spring protests of 2011 occurred in **Syria**. Protests against the government of **President Bashar al-Assad** began in March in Damascus, demanding democratic reforms and the release of political prisoners. Assad has been in power since 2000. He was elected president of Syria after the death of his father, **Hafez al-Assad**, who had ruled Syria from 1971 to 2000. An opposition movement developed in Syria that was composed of a variety of factions, from secular reformers to radical Muslims. By April, protesters had shifted their focus from democratic reform to the ouster of Assad. Assad then ordered a military crackdown on the protesters, leading to over a thousand civilian deaths by May 2007. Initially, many in the West saw Assad as a potential reformer, but as his repression became more brutal, the United States, the European Union, and the **Arab League** all called for his ouster. The events of the spring of 2011 turned out to be the beginning of a long, bloody, destabilizing **civil war**. A variety of groups grew in opposition to Assad. Initially the fighting was led by the **Free Syrian Army**, which was formed by individuals who had defected from the Syrian military. As time went on, the opposition splintered. More extremist factions, such as **al-Nusra Front** and **ISIS**, have grown in strength. In the northern part of the country, **Kurdish** groups have joined with other ethnicities to form the **Syrian Democratic Forces**.

The Syrian Refugee Crisis

The impact of the Syrian war has been catastrophic. At the beginning of the **Syrian Civil War**, the population of Syria was approximately 23 million people. The United Nations estimates that between 400,000 and 500,000 people have died in the war. In addition, the United Nations estimates that approximately 11 million Syrians have been displaced by war, with over 6 million displaced within Syria and 5 million people fleeing the country. The vast majority of external **refugees** have remained in neighboring countries in the Middle East, with approximately 10 percent of these refugees seeking to gain entrance into Europe or other countries. European nations have debated policies in regard to accepting Syrian refugees. Under President Obama, the United States agreed to accept up to 10,000 refugees (a total reached in 2016). President Donald Trump has pledged to end the resettlement of Syrian refugees and possibly deport the ones that are already in the United States. He has said that possible terrorists could be among the refugees; he labeled the influx of refugees, the "ultimate Trojan horse."

PRESIDENT OBAMA AND U.S. TACTICS IN THE WAR ON TERRORISM

Some of the concerns about the way the war on terrorism was being carried out under the administration of President George W. Bush helped elevate Barack Obama to the White House in 2008 over Republican John McCain.

However, to the disappointment of many of Obama's supporters in 2008, the president continued many of the controversial antiterrorism policies begun during the Bush administration and pursued some new programs. For instance, many of the provisions of the **PATRIOT Act** were renewed by Obama. In 2011, and again in 2015, Obama allowed for the extension of controversial measures within the PATRIOT Act that were set to expire. During the 2008 election campaign, he called the reports of prisoner abuse at the **Guantanamo Bay** detention camp "a sad chapter in American history" and promised to close it down by 2009. By the time Obama left office in 2017, the number of prisoners at Guantanamo Bay was reduced to 41, but he had not closed the facility. President Donald Trump has indicated that he will keep the facility open.

Use of Drones

President Obama generated a great deal of debate over the increased use of **unmanned drone attacks** on suspected terrorist targets. The program, begun under President George W. Bush, was greatly expanded under the Obama administration, despite it being criticized by the United Nations as "**extrajudicial killings**" and "**summary justice**." The total number of drone strikes was ten times higher under President Obama than under President Bush. Many attacks occurred in Afghanistan, a country in which the United States was engaged militarily; others occurred in countries such as **Pakistan** and **Yemen**, with which the United States was not involved militarily. President Obama personally oversaw the program of drone strikes. The strikes were carried out by the **Central Intelligence Agency (CIA)**, with little oversight or accountability.

Surveillance, Privacy, and Security in the War on Terrorism

In 2012, President Barack Obama renewed a clandestine surveillance program known as **PRISM**, which allows the **National Security Agency (NSA)** to conduct mass data mining of phone, Internet, and other communications—including, under certain circumstances, those of United States citizens. PRISM was first enabled by President Bush when he signed the **Protect America Act** into law in 2007. In 2013, the clandestine program was exposed by computer specialist and former NSA contractor, **Edward Snowden**. While in Hong Kong, Snowden met with three journalists and revealed thousands of classified NSA documents. Subsequent articles in *The Guardian* and *The Washington Post* brought the program, and Snowden himself, to international attention. Soon after, the Justice Department issued warrants for Snowden's arrest, charging him with theft of government property and violations of the **Espionage Act** (1917). He soon flew to Russia, where he was granted temporary asylum. The revelations revived the ongoing debate among Americans around the protection of civil liberties in the age of global terrorism.

The Killing of Osama bin Laden

In 2011, the Obama administration reported that a **Navy SEAL Team Six** unit had killed **Osama bin Laden**. The unit struck bin Laden's compound in Abbottabad, Pakistan. The government of Pakistan protested because the United States had not obtained authorization to conduct the raid. However, American forces were determined to keep the raid secret until it was executed. The killing of bin Laden and Anwar al-Awlaki represented major blows against the leadership of al-Qaeda.

IRAN AND NUCLEAR DEVELOPMENT

The **Joint Comprehensive Plan of Action** (2015), negotiated by the United States, Iran, and six other nations, and signed by 90 nations, was the culmination of a long and contentious series of interactions between Iran and the world community.

President George W. Bush and Iran's Push Toward a Nuclear Program

Controversy around **Iran's nuclear capability** stretches back to 2002. In that year, intelligence reports stated that Iran had built a large uranium plant without informing the United Nations. In December 2002, satellite photographs confirmed that nuclear sites existed in Iran. After the United States accused Iran of developing weapons of mass destruction, Iran agreed to inspections by the **International Atomic Energy Authority (IAEA)**. In 2005, hardliner **Mahmoud Ahmadinejad** was installed as Iranian president, and Iran pledged an "irreversible" resumption of uranium enrichment. In January 2006, Iran announced it would restart its nuclear energy program. The United States and several European nations condemned the move. During April 2006, President Mahmoud Ahmadinejad declared that Iran had successfully enriched uranium and would continue to produce nuclear fuel. The **IAEA** announced that Iran had not cooperated with inspectors. In July 2006, the **UN Security Council (UNSC)** resolution called on Iran to stop enriching uranium by August 31 or face the threat of sanctions. In

December 2006, the UNSC imposed sanctions demanding the suspension of enrichment activities, the first of several resolutions imposing sanctions on Iran over the next few years.

The Iran Nuclear Deal

In 2012, President Obama renewed efforts to negotiate a deal with Iran on its nuclear program. The United States and the **European Union** agreed to impose harsher economic sanctions on Iran to push it to the negotiating table. In addition, **Hassan Rouhani**, a centrist, was elected president of Iran in 2013. These factors set the stage for renewed dialogue with the West. Negotiations between Iran and the **P5 + 1 nations** (the five permanent members of the Security Council plus Germany) began in 2013. After several setbacks, the negotiations resulted in a deal entitled the **Joint Comprehensive Plan of Action** (2015). The main components of the deal involve removing sanctions against Iran in exchange for measures to ensure that Iran would not produce a bomb. The deal was endorsed by 90 nations that applauded the move toward bringing Iran into the broader community of nations. Many saw the deal as an important step toward making the world safer and toward opening up economic opportunities with Iran. The deal was roundly condemned by Republican and conservative observers and by Prime Minister **Benjamin Netanyahu** of Israel. Many conservatives saw the deal as capitulation to a dangerous regime with ties to terrorist organizations.

THE GROWTH OF ISIS AND TERRORISM IN EUROPE

A terrorist organization called the **Islamic State in Iraq and Syria (ISIS)** has become a major force in the Middle East and beyond. (It is also known by the name ISIL—the Islamic State of Iraq and the Levant.) This extremist Sunni Muslim group was founded in 1999 under a different name by the Jordanian **Abu Musab al-Zarqawi**. It was active in the insurgency in Iraq between 2003 and 2011. Al-Zarqawi was killed in 2006 by a U.S. air strike. The next leader, **Abu Omar al-Baghdadi**, failed to establish ISIS as a major force at the time. Many Iraqi Sunnis were alienated by the brutality of the group and sided with the American occupation. Al-Baghdadi was killed in 2010 and was replaced by the current leader, **Abu Bakr al-Baghdadi** (no relation to the earlier ISIS leader). In 2011, ISIS saw a reversal of its fortunes. In the **Syrian Civil War**, it became active in the resistance to the regime of **Bashar al-Assad** (see pages 653–654). In Iraq, the group gained adherents when the United States withdrew from the country. Immediately following the withdrawal of American troops, prominent Sunnis in the government of Iraq, including the vice president, were removed. Earlier power-sharing promises were ignored. ISIS was able to take advantage of the frustrations of many Sunni Iraqis.

By the end of 2015, ISIS was able to gain control of large sections of western Iraq and eastern Syria, controlling the lives of millions of people. The group gained additional notoriety with graphic videos of beheadings and caged prisoners being burnt alive or drowned. The group has demonstrated a sophisticated use of both traditional and social media. ISIS gained a great deal of exposure in 2014 after it released a video of **James Foley**, an American freelance journalist, as he was about to be beheaded. The video, entitled "A Message to America," also contains a warning that more bloodshed will occur in retaliation for United States airstrikes.

Several high-profile attacks in Europe were connected to ISIS. In some attacks, ISIS claimed responsibility; in other instances, attackers claimed to be inspired by ISIS. In November 2015, a coordinated string of bombings and mass shooting attacks occurred at several locations across **Paris**, including a soccer stadium and the Bataclan, a live music venue. ISIS took responsibility for the attacks, which resulted in approximately 130 people being killed and many more injured.

Starting in 2015, the United States engaged in an air campaign against ISIS locations in Syria and Iraq. By December 2015, President Obama noted that over 9,000 airstrikes had taken place against ISIS locations.

TENSIONS WITH RUSSIA

The United States and **Russia** have had a tense relationship in the post-Cold War world. As discussed previously, the United States withdrew from the 1971 Anti-Ballistic Missile Treaty with Russia in 2002. In addition, Russian President **Vladimir Putin** was opposed to the 2003 U.S.-led Iraqi war. Putin was also opposed to the admission of seven former communist Eastern European nations to NATO in 2004. He saw both moves as an expansion of American and Western European power. During this period, the United States grew concerned over Putin's rejection of democratic reforms and the establishment of limits on free expression. Many people in the United States and Europe have grown increasingly concerned about a resurgence of homophobia in Russia. The Russian government has passed legislation discriminating against gay, lesbian, bisexual, and transgender people and has censored materials related to "nontraditional" relationships. Several athletes commented on and carried out protests before and during the **Winter Olympic Games** held in Sochi, Russia in 2014. Others called on sponsors to boycott the games.

Russia's actions, in regard to neighboring countries, have led to criticism by the U.S. government and have contributed to increased tensions between the two countries. In 2008, for example, Russia sent troops and carried out airstrikes in support of two regions of **Georgia** that had declared their intention to break away from Georgia. Later that year, Russia expressed opposition to a plan by President Bush to install an anti-missile defense system in Poland. The following year President Obama canceled the plan. There was somewhat of an improvement in relations between Russia and the United States with the signing of a new arms-control agreement in 2010 called the **New START Treaty**. The agreement called for a reduction of nuclear warheads and launchers, and for on-site inspections.

Putin and the Syrian Civil War

Relations between the United States and Russia again took a turn for the worse starting in 2012. It became increasingly apparent that Russia and the West had very different priorities in regard to the **Syrian Civil War**. Russia made clear its support for Syrian leader **Bashar al-Assad**, despite Assad's brutal treatment of opposition forces; the **Arab League**, the United States, and the European Union, on the other hand, called for the ouster of Assad. Russia and China blocked a 2012 UN Security Council resolution calling for Assad to abdicate. Further, Russia supplied the Assad regime with military and diplomatic assistance.

Russia, Ukraine, and Sanctions

In 2013, Putin pressured the Ukrainian President **Viktor Yanukovych**, to pull out of a trade agreement with the European Union. Russia's actions in regard to **Ukraine** alarmed and angered leaders in the West. This move also angered many Ukrainians, who had hoped for closer economic and political relations with the democracies of Europe. Protests in Kiev and across Ukraine in 2014 led to the ouster of Yanukovych and the establishment of a pro-Western interim government. This turn of events led to protests against the interim government in **Crimea**, a region in the southern part of Ukraine with a Russian-majority population. Putin intervened militarily in Crimea, occupying the region with Russian troops. A referendum in Crimea was hastily held in 2014, with the majority calling for annexation by Russia. These moves were seen as illegal by the United States and the United Nations General Assembly. President Obama imposed sanctions on several wealthy businessmen and advisors close to Putin. The conflict continued as separatists, again aided by Russia, engaged in fighting in eastern Ukraine. The United States imposed additional sanctions on Russian individuals and companies. Finally, in 2015, a cease-fire was agreed upon, granting regions in eastern Ukraine "special status."

Russia and the American Elections of 2016

The bitterness between Putin and Obama became apparent in Putin's embrace of **Donald Trump** in the 2016 presidential campaign. The Office of the Director of National Intelligence declassified a report in January 2017 describing actions taken by Russia to interfere in the 2016 election in ways that "denigrate" Democratic candidate Hillary Clinton and "show a clear preference" for Donald Trump. This interference included covert operations, including hacking into computers of the Clinton campaign and the Democratic National Committee and releasing sensitive information. The impact these actions will have on President Trump's relations with Russia remains to be seen.

NORMALIZING RELATIONS WITH CUBA

The United States has had a fraught relationship with **Cuba** over the years. After the **Cuban Revolution** (1959), Cuba became a communist country under the leadership of **Fidel Castro**. It was allied with the Soviet Union during the Cold War. Tensions increased following the U.S.-organized **Bay of Pigs invasion** of Cuba in 1961 and the **Cuban Missile Crisis** (1962) (see page 470). For years, the United States refused to recognize the government of Cuba and enforced an economic boycott of the country. Into the 21st century, neither Democratic nor Republican presidents had pushed for normalizing relations with Cuba. This stems from concerns about human rights violations in Cuba as well as the presence of large numbers of anti-Castro Cubans in **Florida**, a swing state. However, in 2014, the United States and Cuba began the process of normalizing relations. After Cuba released an American prisoner, President Obama announced that the United States and Cuba would resume diplomatic relations and that the United States would open an embassy in **Havana**. In 2015, the two countries resumed relations after a half century of hostility.

Exercise Set 7.5

1. "President Franklin D. Roosevelt Issues Order Calling for Internment of Japanese-Americans"
   "President Lincoln Suspends Writ of Habeas Corpus"
   "President Obama Reauthorizes PRISM Allowing for Mass Data Mining"

   Which conclusion is best supported by these headlines?
   A. Technology can be used for positive or negative purposes.
   B. Perceived threats to national security can sometimes lead to limits placed on civil liberties.
   C. Presidential power is frequently reduced during times of national crisis.
   D. Constitutional privileges do not necessarily apply to lands conquered by the United States.

2. The Supreme Court decision in *Hamdan* v. *Rumsfeld* (2006) declared that the government
   A. could not hold detainees in the war on terrorism indefinitely without due process.
   B. could restrict speech that presents a "clear and present danger."
   C. did not have to extend Constitutional rights to the residents of United States colonies.
   D. could not target American citizens with drone attacks.

3. The decision by the United States to initiate negotiations with Iran in 2012 demonstrated the Obama administration's goal of
   A. implementing a regional strategy to achieving peace between Israel and the Palestinians.
   B. defunding al-Qaeda operations in the Middle East.
   C. preventing Iran from developing a nuclear weapons program.
   D. removing tariffs on trade between the two countries.

4. Images from the Abu Ghraib prison, made public in 2004, led many Americans to
   A. call for the death penalty for Saddam Hussein.
   B. support increased expenditures for rebuilding Iraqi infrastructure.
   C. condemn violations of human rights committed by American military personnel.
   D. endorse President George W. Bush's plan to restore law and order in Iraq.

5. One foreign policy accomplishment of President Barack Obama was
   A. brokering a major peace deal between Israel and the Palestinians.
   B. normalizing relations between the United States and Cuba.
   C. toppling the regime of Bashar al-Assad in Syria.
   D. pressuring Russia to withdraw from the Crimea in Ukraine.

6. Many people urged President Barack Obama to close down the prison
   complex at Guantanamo Bay, Cuba because
   A. it would send a signal to Cuban dissidents that the United States
      would support "regime change" in Cuba.
   B. it is jointly administered by the United States and Cuba.
   C. it is a financial drain on the resources of the military.
   D. it has been the site of human rights abuses against suspects in the war
      on terrorism.

DIVISIVE ISSUES
IN THE 21ST CENTURY

> The pundits like to slice and dice our country into red states and blue states—red states for Republicans, blue states for Democrats. But I've got news for them, too. We worship an awesome God in the blue states, and we don't like federal agents poking around in our libraries in the red states. We coach Little League in the blue states and, yes, we've got some gay friends in the red states.
>
> Senator Barack Obama, Speech,
> Democratic National Convention, 2004

Barack Obama's hopeful words at the **Democratic National Convention** acknowledged that divisive issues did exist in America. He expressed hope that Americans could transcend these divisions and focus on what unites them, rather than what divides them. However, during both President George W. Bush's and President Obama's terms in the White House, a series of cultural, social, political, religious, and economic issues generated heated debate and acrimony in the United States. Some argue that, indeed, there are two Americas out there; others work toward finding unity amid division. This chapter focuses on some the divisive issues that Americans have debated in the 21st century, and some of the movements that have grown around these issues.

MOVEMENTS FOR CHANGE

Two significant movements for change developed in the last decade, but with very different agendas. The **Tea Party movement** developed in opposition to the agenda of President Obama and also in opposition to establishment Republicans, who the movement felt were insufficiently conservative. The **Occupy Wall Street Movement** grew out of frustrations that neither of the two major political parties were prepared to tackle issues of economic inequality and corporate power. Both movements shifted the debate in regard to significant public issues.

The Tea Party Movement

The election of Barack Obama to the presidency in 2008 generated a vocal opposition movement known as the **Tea Party**, harkening back to the American colonists' action against perceived British tyranny. To some extent the movement was a creation of the media—heavily promoted by the **Fox News** channel—and, to some extent, it represented a grassroots sense of discontent with big government. The movement organized a large-scale march in September 2009, the **Taxpayer March on Washington**. In addition to taxation, the movement has protested against illegal immigration, gun control, and government spending on social programs. The Tea Party Movement has supported several important political figures in the Republican Party, including Senator **Marco Rubio** of Florida who ran for president in 2016 and **Paul Ryan**, who was elected to be Speaker of the House of Representatives in 2015. The movement has had a marked influence within the Republican Party. Some commentators see continuities between the Tea Party Movement and the movement that grew around the candidacy of Donald Trump. Others see the movement as more policy-driven rather than focused on a particular candidate.

Occupy Wall Street

Occupy Wall Street grew out of protests that began in September 2011 in **Zuccotti Park**, located in New York City's Wall Street financial district. The movement focused on economic inequality in the United States and the influence of corporate power over the political process. The original action in Zuccotti Park was initiated by *Adbusters*, an anti-consumerist, environmental group and magazine. Earlier in 2011, the economist Joseph Stiglitz published an article in *Vanity Fair* magazine entitled, "Of the 1%, by the 1%, for the 1%." The article highlighted the damaging effects of economic inequality on society. Many of the Occupy Wall Street protesters embraced his analysis; the chant **"We are the 99 percent"** was heard frequently at Occupy Wall Street events. Protesters occupied Zuccotti Park for almost two months; the park served as a meeting point and clearinghouse for the movement. Some criticized the movement for not having a clearly articulated set of goals. Others embraced the decentralized nature of the movement, which allowed for a high degree of participatory decision-making and improvisation. The movement spread to other cities and addressed a variety of issues.

MASS SHOOTINGS AND GUN CONTROL

Several high-profile mass shootings took place in the United States in the most recent decade, including mass shootings at schools. The issues of gun violence and gun control have been the subject of much public discussion and have led to bitter debates about policy.

A Wave of Mass Shootings

Within several months in 2012 there were several horrific shootings. In July, a shooting at a movie theater in **Aurora, Colorado** left 12 dead and 58 injured; in December, the shooting at Sandy Hook Elementary School in **Newtown, Connecticut** left 27 dead and one injured, including 20 children between six and seven years old. In 2015, a mass shooting took place at the Mother Emanuel A.M.E. church in **Charleston, South Carolina**. Nine people were killed during a bible study group at the historic Black church.

Debates Around Gun Control

In the wake of these shootings, especially the shooting of children at the Sandy Hook Elementary School, many Americans called for **gun control** legislation. Many individuals signed petitions calling for greater gun control and made contributions to organizations such as the **Brady Campaign to Prevent Gun Violence**. Days after the shooting, President Obama indicated that he would make gun control a central issue during his second term. In January 2013, Obama signed 23 executive orders dealing with gun ownership. He also proposed 13 pieces of legislation regarding gun control. Congress ended up addressing two bills—one banning assault weapons and one calling for expanded background checks for gun purchasers. Neither bill passed. In the months after the Sandy Hook shooting, New York passed the **Secure Ammunition and Firearms Enforcement (SAFE) Act**, and Connecticut and Maryland both expanded existing gun laws. The **National Rifle Association** lobbied strenuously against any type of gun control legislation. The leader of the group, **Wayne LaPierre**, argued that gun-free schools were the problem, not the solution. He argued for the hiring of armed officers at schools who would be able to stop armed intruders.

Earlier, two significant Supreme Court decisions, *District of Columbia* **v.** *Heller* (2008) and *McDonald* **v.** *Chicago* (2010), narrowed and clarified the scope of potential gun control laws. The *Heller* case dealt with a law passed by the city council of the District of Columbia that banned handguns, automatic firearms, and high-capacity semi-automatic firearms (unless they were previously registered). The law also mandated that any firearms kept in the home be unloaded, disassembled, and trigger locked. This provision was to prevent the use of firearms for self-defense in the home. The *Heller* decision declared this statute to be unconstitutional, inconsistent with the **Second Amendment**. The Court ruled that the Second Amendment protects an individual's right to own a gun for private use. Previously, courts generally recognized a collective right to bear arms, but not an individual right. In *Heller*, the Court also gave examples of gun laws that would be consistent with the Second Amendment—restrictions on types of weapons, bans on possession of firearms by felons and the mentally ill, prohibitions on carrying weapons in sensitive places, such as schools or government buildings. The *McDonald* decision asserted that the interpretation of the Second Amendment in the *Heller* decision also applies to states and localities. Wording in the *Heller* case implied that it only applied to federal districts.

GREATER ACCEPTANCE OF MARIJUANA

Attitudes and laws in regard to the **legalization** and **decriminalization** of **marijuana** in the United States have changed dramatically in the 21st century. In 2016, a Quinnipiac poll showed that 89 percent of Americans supported the legalization of medicinal marijuana; 60 percent favor full legalization in a Gallup poll. A few states had legalized the use of marijuana for medicinal purposes in the 1990s (California was first in 1996). The movement picked up speed after the turn of the century, despite a Supreme Court decision that declared that state **medical marijuana** laws were at odds with federal law. In ***United States* v. *Oakland Cannabis Buyers' Cooperative*** (2001), the Court rejected the argument that an exception should be made to the Controlled Substances Act of 1970 based on medical necessity. By 2017, a total of 28 states plus the District of Columbia legalized the medicinal use of marijuana. Residents of these states constitute 60 percent of the American people.

In 2012, residents of **Colorado** and **Washington** voted to legalize marijuana for recreational use. By 2017, six more states plus the **District of Columbia** joined them. There are a variety of arguments put forth in favor of legalization—including that legal sales of marijuana could be taxed and that legalization would provide relief for an overburdened criminal justice system. Still, many argue that marijuana is a gateway drug to more serious drugs and that it adversely affects people's health. Marijuana is still an illegal, controlled substance under federal law. In 2009, President Obama, however, instructed the **Justice Department** to issue a memorandum indicating that users of medicinal marijuana should not be prosecuted under federal law as long as they are following state law. In February 2017, the Trump administration seemed to shift direction, indicating that it would push for more strict enforcement of federal law in regard to the use of marijuana.

RACE, POLICE SHOOTINGS, AND THE BLACK LIVES MATTER MOVEMENT

Police Shootings

In 2014, protests erupted in **Ferguson, Missouri** in the aftermath of the shooting of **Michael Brown**, an unarmed, 18-year-old African American male. Witnesses asserted that he had his hands in the air when he was shot. Police argued that he acted in a threatening manner. Protests occurred right after the shooting happened in August, and again in November, when a grand jury decided to not indict the police officer involved in the shooting. In both cases, some protesters engaged in acts of violence. The Ferguson incident occurred only weeks after **Eric Garner**, a 43-year-old African American male, died in **Staten Island, New York City**, while being arrested by police officers. An officer put Garner in what has been described as a chokehold while arresting him. New York Police Department policy prohibits the use of chokeholds. Over the next two years, several other shootings of African Americans by police officers made headlines. The ubiquity of cell phones with video capability led to several of these instances being recorded (at least in part) by civilians; some incidents were recorded by the police themselves. In April 2015 in **Baltimore**, **Freddie Gray**, a 25-year-old African American male, died after being arrested and transported in a police van (without having been secured in the van). Video seemed to show that Gray was injured and in pain before he was dragged into the van. This incident led to widespread protests in Baltimore in the days following the incident.

The Black Lives Matter Movement

These and other incidents led to the growth of the **Black Lives Matter Movement**. The phrase appeared in social media in 2013, following the acquittal of **George Zimmerman**, a neighborhood watch coordinator in Florida. He had been accused of shooting and killing **Trayvon Martin**, an African American teenager. During and after the protests in Ferguson, the phrase "Black Lives Matter" became associated with protests against police shootings. The movement grew to focus on issues of racial profiling, police brutality, and racial and economic inequality.

Critics of the movement have accused it of being excessively anti-police. Some supporters of police officers have adopted the phrase **Blue Lives Matter**, in response to the Black Lives Matter Movement. Under President Obama, the Justice Department often intervened in conflicts between local police departments and the community. In Ferguson, the Justice Department found a longtime pattern of discrimination against African American residents and violations of constitutional protections. Many police departments have revised policies and procedures in regard to the use of force. In addition, several police departments have begun to implement training programs that emphasize defusing interactions between police officers and civilians rather than escalating them. Even with these reforms, the issue persists.

ISSUES RELATED TO GAY, LESBIAN, BISEXUAL, AND TRANSGENDER PEOPLE

The **Gay Rights Movement** grew in intensity after the **Stonewall Riots** of 1969. The movement became more visible and militant in the 1980s in response to the **AIDS crisis**. The growth and development of the movement, coupled with a strong conservative backlash against gay rights and against public acceptance of homosexuality, has shaped debates around gay, lesbian, bisexual, and transgender identity acceptance and rights.

Privacy and Anti-Sodomy Legislation

In 2003, the Supreme Court struck down a Texas law that outlawed sexual acts between gay men and women. As late as 1960, each state in the union had "**anti-sodomy laws**" criminalizing sexual activities between consenting same-sex individuals. Over the years, most states repealed these laws. The Supreme Court carved out a private sphere, for married couples, in its decision in *Griswold* v. *Connecticut* (1965). Still, it had not established that the right to privacy applied to same-sex sexual activities. In 1986, for instance, in *Bowers* v. *Hardwick*, the Court upheld a Georgia anti-sodomy law, drawing a distinction between heterosexual activities designed for procreation and sodomy. However, in *Lawrence* v. *Texas* (2003), the Court reversed itself and affirmed the right to privacy for all individuals, based on the constitutional guarantee of due process. The decision struck down anti-sodomy laws in Texas and 13 other states.

Repeal of "Don't Ask, Don't Tell"

The armed forces of the United States have historically discriminated against LGBTQ people serving in the military. In 1982, the Department of Defense issued a policy that stated, "Homosexuality is incompatible with military service." In the following years, LGBTQ members of the military, and those excluded from the military, began a campaign to change the policy. The **Gay and Lesbian Military Freedom Project** was founded in 1988. In 1994, the military changed its policy, allowing LGBTQ members of the military to serve, as long as they remained "closeted," keeping their sexual identity hidden from public view. Advocates for LGBTQ rights insisted that the policy, called **Don't Ask, Don't Tell** was discriminatory and that it limited the freedom of speech and expression of LGBTQ service members. The policy was repealed by an act of Congress, signed by President Obama in 2011.

Same-Sex Marriage

Perhaps the clearest indicator of the rapid changes in societal attitudes toward homosexuality can be seen in the changing legal status of marriage between same-sex couples. Although gay rights proponents have long demanded that the right to legally marry be extended to same-sex couples, the issue became part of the national dialogue in 1993, when in the case of *Baehr v. Lewin*, the Hawaii Supreme Court ruled that the state ban on **same-sex marriage** was discriminatory under the state constitution. Although the court did not mandate that the state begin issuing marriage licenses to gay couples, it had the effect of galvanizing social conservatives to mobilize against same-sex marriage and to defend "traditional" marriage. Hawaii ratified an amendment to its constitution, allowing the state legislature to ban same-sex marriage. Many states followed in Hawaii's footsteps by amending their constitutions so as to prevent the legalization of same-sex marriage. These amendments usually limited the definition of marriage as an act between a man and a woman. Further, Congress passed the **Defense of Marriage Act (DOMA)** in 1996, which allowed states to not recognize same-sex marriages performed in other states and also defined, for federal purposes, marriage as an act between one man and one woman.

The tide against same-sex marriage began to turn in 2003, when the **Massachusetts** Supreme Judicial Court ruled that the state may not forbid same-sex couples from legally marrying; it asserted that "the Massachusetts Constitution affirms the dignity and equality of all individuals. It forbids the creation of second-class citizens." Several other state high courts followed suit in the 2000s. In 2009, **Vermont** became the first state in the United States to legalize same-sex marriage through legislative means rather than through the court system. In 2013, in *United States v. Windsor*, the Supreme Court struck down the section of DOMA that defined marriage, for federal purposes, as an act between a man and a woman. Public opinion moved rapidly on this issue. According to the Gallup organization, the aggregate of polls taken in 1996 showed 68 percent of Americans opposed extending legal recognition to same-sex couples, with only 27 percent supporting such a move. By 2015, the aggregate of polls showed that nearly 60 percent of Americans favored legalized same-sex marriage. The Supreme Court took heed. In 2015, in the case of *Obergefell v. Hodges*, the Court ruled that marriage is a fundamental right that must be guaranteed to same-sex couples. The decision cited the due-process clause and the equal-protection clause of the **Fourteenth Amendment** to the Constitution.

Transgender Rights

Since 2012, the issue of rights for members of the transgender community has become a prominent part of policy debates. Transgender people are those who don't identify with their birth sex. An important policy debate has revolved around the use of public bathrooms for transgender people. Starting in 2012, some municipalities, including Austin, Philadelphia, and Seattle, began issuing guidelines that individuals would be permitted to use the bathroom of the gender they identify with, rather than of their birth sex. The Obama administration sided with advocates for the transgender community. In 2014, Attorney General **Eric H. Holder Jr.** added gender identity to the categories of discrimination that are covered in **Title VII of the Civil Rights Act** of 1964. In response, some cities and states moved in the opposite direction, passing ordinances and laws banning transgender people from bathrooms and locker rooms that did not match their birth sex. In March 2016, **North Carolina** passed such a law, leading the National Basketball Association (NBA) to move its All-Star Game out of the state in protest. The National College Athletic Association (NCAA) also moved play-off games in several sports out of the state.

In May 2016, the **Justice and Education Departments** stepped into the controversy, issuing new guidelines stating that, under **Title IX of the Education Amendments** of 1972, schools receiving federal money may not discriminate based on a student's transgender status. The Obama administration subsequently sent a letter to each public school district in the country instructing them to allow transgender students to use the bathrooms that match their gender identity. The controversy continued into the administration of President **Trump**. In February 2017, he rescinded the policy established by the Obama administration and instructed schools that students may only use bathrooms that match their birth sex.

CONSERVATIVE CHRISTIANITY, THE "PRO-LIFE" MOVEMENT, AND PUBLIC POLICY

Abortion has remained a contentious issue in public life for decades. The Supreme Court decision in *Roe* v. *Wade* (1973) declared that states shall not prohibit women from having an abortion during the first two trimesters of pregnancy. This was one of the major successes of the **Women's Liberation Movement** of the 1960s and 1970s. Previously, the decision had been left to the states, and many states forbade abortions (see page 485). Opposition to the decision has been one of the major factors in the growth of a broad Christian conservative movement. The issue of abortion propelled evangelical Protestants to put aside their long held suspicions of Catholicism, and unite in their desire to overturn *Roe* v. *Wade*. Conservative Christians have brought energy and numbers to a number of public issues in the 21st century, including stem cell research, end of life issues, and contraception mandates in health coverage.

Stem Cell Research

During the George W. Bush administration, the issue of **stem cell research** became increasingly divisive. Many scientists pointed out the usefulness of stem cells, particularly embryonic stem cells, in research on diseases. Many in the pro-life religious community believe that embryonic stem cell research violates the sanctity of life and is tantamount to murder, as the human embryos used in research are subsequently discarded. In 2005, Bush vetoed a pair of bills that were together known as the **Stem Cell Research Enhancement Act**, which would have required funding for stem cell research. This was the first time that President Bush vetoed legislation. The bills did not have enough votes in Congress to override his vetoes.

Limiting Abortion Rights on the State Level

While conservative Christians have not been successful in overturning *Roe* v. *Wade*, they have had successes in limiting access to abortions on the state level. Many state-funded health programs, which many low-income women depend upon for health services, do not cover abortion procedures. In addition, states have passed laws calling for mandatory waiting periods, parental notification for minors, ultrasound imaging, and counseling. In 2013, Texas passed a law requiring doctors at clinics to have hospital admitting privileges within 30 miles of the clinics and requiring abortion clinics to have facilities equal to those of an outpatient surgical center. These onerous requirements would have forced nearly 75 percent of the state's abortion clinics to close. In *Whole Women's Health* v. *Hellerstedt* (2016), the Supreme Court held that the law constituted an undue burden on abortion access, and thus violated the Constitution (Fourteenth Amendment).

The Right to Life Movement and End of Life Decisions

In 2005, **Terry Schiavo**, a 41-year-old brain-damaged woman, died in Florida nearly two weeks after doctors removed a feeding tube that had been keeping her alive for more than a decade. Terry Schiavo became the focal point of an ugly and, in many people's opinions, highly inappropriate and self-serving political battle over right to life and right to die. On March 21, 2015, three days after Schiavo's husband instructed doctors to remove the feeding tube, Congress passed a bill transferring jurisdiction of the case from Florida state court to a U.S. district court for a federal judge to review. President George W. Bush signed it into law the next day. However, federal courts refused to overturn the state court's decision to allow her to die.

Contraception and Health Care Coverage

Following the passage of the **Affordable Care Act** (see pages 634–636), the difficulties of balancing religious practices and public policy were also evident, especially in regard to contraception. The arts and crafts chain **Hobby Lobby** argued that it should not be mandated to fund the use of contraceptives as part of its employer-provided health care insurance. The Affordable Care Act had mandated that contraceptives be covered through health care insurance. The Supreme Court, in *Burwell* **v.** *Hobby Lobby* (2014), ruled that a business such as Hobby Lobby may not be forced to pay for insurance that covers contraceptives, citing federal law protecting religious freedom. However, the Court restricted the decision to "closely held" corporations— those owned and run by an individual or a family.

RELIGION AND THE PUBLIC SPHERE

The presence of overt symbols of religion in public, government-run institutions has divided many Americans. Many conservatives see a "war on religion" being carried out by liberals. They cite the push to have schools hold "holiday" celebrations in December rather than "Christmas" celebrations as evidence of this war. Some liberals, on the other hand, have opposed the ubiquity of religious symbolism and mentions of God in the public realm. A lawsuit in California was initiated to remove the words "**under God**" from the **Pledge of Allegiance**; the words had been added to the 1892 pledge in 1954 at the height of the Cold War. A federal appeals court ruled that the words were unconstitutional, violating the separation of church and state. The Supreme Court, however, overturned that ruling, 8–0 in *Elk Grove* **v.** *Newdow* (2004). Three members of the Court defended the inclusion of "under God" on constitutional grounds. Chief Justice **William Rehnquist** argued that the words didn't endorse or establish religion. Rather, they simply acknowledged the nation's religious heritage. However, the other five justices who voted with Rehnquist did not rule on the merits of the case. Rather, they asserted that the plaintiff, **Michael Newdow**, did not have standing because he did not have legal custody of his daughter, on whose behalf the suit was filed.

GENDER DISCRIMINATION

Advocates for greater gender equity have focused on a variety of issues in the 21st century. Some activists have focused on portrayals of female characters in movies, television shows, and video games that are sexist or demeaning. Others have sought to reform the ways that college administrations deal with accusations of rape by students. Many activists have focused on issues related to the workplace. Though women have made advances in the workplace, many note that disparities still exist. In the 1970s, white women earned on average 59 cents for each dollar that men earned doing comparable work. That gap has closed somewhat, to approximately 70 cents for each dollar earned by men, but still exists. In addition, many women assert that they are often barred from higher positions in the corporate world. Reformers and activists have also pushed for government-funded day care and greater participation by men in childcare.

The Fair Pay Act

The movement for equal pay for women achieved a victory with the very first bill President Obama signed into law in January 2009, the **Lilly Ledbetter Fair Pay Act**. The Act amended the Civil Rights Act of 1964, which contained a provision that stated that equal pay suits must be initiated within 180 days "after the alleged unlawful employment practice occurred." The Supreme Court, in *Ledbetter* v. *Goodyear Tire & Rubber Co.* (2007), asserted that this time limit begins on the date that the employer makes the initial discriminatory wage decision. Ledbetter asserted that women might not even be aware of wage discrimination within 180 days of being hired (or of being denied a raise); they might be made aware of wage discrimination only later in their careers. The Ledbetter act states that the 180-day statute of limitations resets with *each new paycheck* affected by a discriminatory action.

PRIVATE PROPERTY AND EMINENT DOMAIN

Debates have occurred across the United States about the use of the government's power of **eminent domain**. The Fifth Amendment allows the government to take private property for "**public use**," as long as the owner is provided with "just compensation." In the 2000s, a controversy arose around what constitutes "public use." Traditionally, public use has meant that the government would use the land in question for public projects—highways, schools, parks, etc. However, in *Kelo v. City of New London* (2005), the Court addressed the issue of whether "public use" could be defined more broadly. Could a government take possession of private property against the owner's will and, in the name of economic development, transfer it to private developers? In **New London, Connecticut**, developers proposed just such an arrangement—that land held by several home owners be taken by the city and subsequently transferred to the New London Development Corporation. The Court ruled five to four in favor of the developer. In the majority opinion, Justice **John Paul Stevens** wrote "public use" also means "public purpose." "Promoting economic development is a traditional and long accepted function of government," he said.

PRIVACY IN THE DIGITAL AGE

Personal electronic devices, most notably smartphones, may contain a great deal of information about our lives—who we have been in contact with, where we have been, what we have purchased, what websites we have visited. Debates between law-enforcement officials and privacy advocates have centered around how accessible this treasure-trove of data should be to officials. This debate made front-page news in 2013 when a former contractor with the National Security Agency, **Edward Snowden**, exposed a clandestine program known as **PRISM**, which permitted the federal government to conduct warrantless mass data mining of phone, Internet, and other communications as part of counter-terrorism efforts (see pages 655–656). The issue of digital privacy in regard to local law-enforcement officials came to the forefront in a 2014 Supreme Court case, *Riley v. California*. The Court addressed the issue of whether police officers could search the contents of someone's cell phone without a warrant as that person was being arrested. Previously, the Court ruled that police could search an arrested person and their immediate surroundings in order to either preserve evidence or to protect the safety of an officer. In the *Riley* case, however, the Court ruled that such searches incident to an arrest could not generally include the digital contents of one's cell phone.

CLIMATE CHANGE AND ENVIRONMENTAL CONCERNS

Since the early 1980s, scientists have become aware of a trend toward warmer global temperatures. It became evident that this warming trend was caused by trapped greenhouse gasses, which, in turn were caused by human activities, primarily the burning of fossil fuels. In the 1990s and 2000s, a virtual consensus emerged in the scientific community around the connection between global warming and the emissions generated by the burning of fossil fuels. Calls were made to limit the human activities linked to **global warming**. The 1992 **"Earth Summit"** in Brazil led to the adoption by most of the countries in the world to the **United Nations Framework Convention on Climate Change (UNFCCC)**. The 1997 **Kyoto Protocols** sets binding obligations on industrialized countries to reduce the emission of greenhouse gasses.

Environmental Policy Under President Bush

President **George W. Bush** did much to undermine measures that had been taken or were under consideration in regard to protecting the environment. First, he would not implement the Kyoto global climate change treaty. The **Kyoto Protocol** was adopted by 165 countries in 2001, but without the participation of the United States and Australia. In rejecting the protocol, he also cast doubt on the science that demonstrated an urgent need to deal with climate change. In the subsequent years, this casting of doubt on the science related to climate change has been adopted by many Republicans as part of the rationale to resist steps toward a more sustainable future. In addition, the **Environmental Protection Agency (EPA)** under President Bush issued new guidelines in 2002 that removed some of the protections of the 1970 **Clean Air Act**. The changes proposed by the EPA would have weakened air pollution control requirements for thousands of coal-fired power plants, oil refineries, and factories. In response, 14 states and a variety of organizations sued the government. A federal appeals court later struck down some of the proposed changes (2005). Also, the administration gutted key sections of the **Clean Water Act**, dismantled several protections of the **Endangered Species Act**, and opened millions of acres of wilderness to mining, oil and gas drilling, and logging.

Environmental Concerns in the Obama Era

The Obama administration was more amenable to environmental regulation and reform. The United States played an important role in the negotiations that led to the **Paris Agreement** (2015), which was negotiated through the United Nations Framework Convention on Climate Change (UNFCCC) and calls for broad carbon dioxide reduction measures. Global climate change has generated debate in the United States between those who would like to see limits placed on greenhouse-gas emissions and those who emphasize economic growth. In 2017, President Trump sided with climate change deniers and withdrew the United States from the Paris Agreement.

To some degree, American society is making changes. California passed legislation in 2006 that would reduce greenhouse-gas emissions from all sources, including automobiles. Other communities are taking steps that include encouraging bicycling and using mass transit. Scientists and many observers wonder if the small steps being taken in the United States and elsewhere will be able to slow down the process of global warming.

Exercise Set 7.6

1. The issue of religion in the public schools reached the Supreme Court in 2004 in the *Newdow* case. At the heart of the case was
   A. the phrase "under God" in the Pledge of Allegiance.
   B. school prayer.
   C. after-school religious clubs.
   D. the display of a Christmas tree in the school.

2. The underlying issue being addressed by the Kyoto Protocol was
   A. proliferation of nuclear weapons.
   B. military balance of power in the Far East.
   C. global warming and reduction of greenhouse gases.
   D. development of free-trade agreements.

3. The legal issue which is at the core of the same-sex marriage debate is
   A. equal protection of the laws.
   B. cruel and unusual punishment.
   C. freedom of religion.
   D. freedom of speech.

4. The argument over the use of stem cells for medicinal purposes has raised the issues most closely associated with which of the following Supreme Court cases?
   A. *Miranda* v. *Arizona*
   B. *Brown* v. *Board of Education*
   C. *Dred Scott* v. *Sanford*
   D. *Roe* v. *Wade*

5. The development of the Tea Party Movement could best be seen as a
   A. Democratic Party initiative to challenge Republican control of Congress.
   B. Cold War era response to the domestic anticommunist movement.
   C. conservative attempt to challenge big government and reduce taxes.
   D. left-wing response to economic inequality in American society.

6. The chant "We are the 99 percent" is most closely identified with
   A. the Tea Party Movement.
   B. the Occupy Wall Street Movement.
   C. the Pro-Life Movement.
   D. the movement for gun control laws.

7. In the case of *Kelo* v. *City of New London* (2005), the Supreme Court upheld the government practice of transferring land from one private owner to another private owner if the transfer promoted economic development. The Supreme Court based its decision on
   A. the phrase "public use" in the Fifth Amendment.
   B. the scope of state powers described in the Constitution.
   C. early treaties between the United States and Native American Indian nations.
   D. the "interstate commerce clause" of Article 1, Section 8 of the Constitution.

THEMATIC ESSAY

Directions: Write a well-organized essay that includes an introduction, several paragraphs addressing the task below, and a conclusion.

Theme: Presidential Decisions

> During the late 20th and early 21st centuries (1992–2017), United States presidents have made important decisions in an effort to solve crucial problems.

Task:

> From your study of United States history, identify two important presidential decisions made during the late 20th and early 21st centuries (1992–2017).
>
> For each decision identified:
>
> - State one goal the president hoped to accomplish by making the decision.
> - Discuss the historical circumstances surrounding the presidential decision.
> - Describe the extent to which the decision achieved the president's original goal.

You may use any important presidential decision from your study of late 20th- and early 21st-century United States history (1992–2017). Some suggestions you might wish to consider include: President Bill Clinton's decision to support passage of the North American Free Trade Agreement (NAFTA) (1994); President Bill Clinton's decision to push for the Personal Responsibility and Work Opportunity Reconciliation Act (welfare reform) (1996); President George W. Bush's decision to sign the No Child Left Behind Act (2002); President George W. Bush's decision to veto the Stem Cell Research Enhancement Act (2005); President Barack Obama's decision to push for passage of the Dodd-Frank Wall Street Reform and Consumer Protection Act (2010); and President Barack Obama's decision to sign into law the Affordable Care Act (2010).

You are *not* limited to these suggestions.

The following questions (Part A and Part B) are based on the accompanying documents (1–5). Some of the documents have been edited for the purpose of this exercise. The questions are designed to test your ability to work with historical documents and to demonstrate your knowledge of the subject matter being presented. As you analyze the documents, take into account both the source of the document and the author's point of view.

Historical Context:

Following the attacks on the United States on September 11, 2001, the question pitting national security against civil liberties created a debate regarding the Constitution and the powers it bestowed on the federal government and the function of the Constitution in protecting citizens from abusive governmental power.

Task:

Using information from the documents and your knowledge of United States history, answer the questions that follow each document in Part A. Your answers to the questions will help you write the Part B essay in which you will be asked to:

Evaluate the following statement: "In creating greater domestic security from future attacks by terrorists, the United States government must not trample on American liberties in the name of preserving them."

Part A
Short-Answer Questions

The documents below relate to issues concerning the powers and function of the Constitution. Examine each document carefully and then answer the questions that follow.

DOCUMENT 1

> During those first few hours after the attacks, I kept remembering a sentence from a case I had studied in law school. Not surprisingly, I didn't remember which case it was, who wrote the opinion, or what it was about, but I did remember these words: "While the Constitution protects against invasions of individual rights, it is not a **suicide** pact." I took these words as a challenge to my concerns about civil liberties at such a momentous time in our history; that we must be careful to not take civil liberties so literally that we allow ourselves to be destroyed.

— Senator Russ Feingold, Statement on the Anti-Terrorism Bill
(October 25, 2001)

1. Who, or what, would be committing suicide?

_____

_____

_____

_____

2. What is the common name of the Anti-Terrorism Bill that Senator Feingold was speaking about on October 25, 2001?

_____

_____

_____

_____

3. What is the main idea of the political cartoon?

_____

_____

_____

_____

4. The man leaving with the arm occupied what Cabinet position during the first George W. Bush administration?

_____

_____

_____

_____

DOCUMENT 3

Those who would give up essential Liberty, to purchase a little temporary Safety, deserve neither Liberty nor Safety.

— Benjamin Franklin (1755)

5. Applying Benjamin Franklin's quote to the war on terror, give two examples of "Liberty" that some believe are being given up in order to protect the security of the United States.

_____

_____

_____

_____

DOCUMENT 4

USA PATRIOT ACT
SEC. 501. ACCESS TO CERTAIN BUSINESS RECORDS FOR FOREIGN INTELLIGENCE AND INTERNATIONAL TERRORISM INVESTIGATIONS.
(a)(1) The Director of the Federal Bureau of Investigation . . . may make an application for an order requiring the production of any tangible things (including books, records, papers, documents, and other items) for an investigation to protect against international terrorism or clandestine intelligence activities, provided that such investigation of a United States person is not conducted solely upon the basis of activities protected by the first amendment to the Constitution.

— Sec. 501 USA PATRIOT Act

6. The protections provided by which two amendments included in the Bill of Rights are applicable to this section of the USA PATRIOT Act?

_____

_____

_____

_____

7. Who is the individual taking the oath and who is the individual giving the oath? Specific names are preferred, but titles are acceptable.

_____

_____

_____

8. What passages might not be protected and defended by the individual taking the oath? Give two examples.

_____

_____

_____

Part B
Essay

Your essay should be well organized with an introductory paragraph that states your position on the question. Develop your position in the next paragraphs and then write a conclusion. In your essay, include specific historical details and refer to specific documents you analyzed in Part A. You may include additional information from your knowledge of social studies.

Historical Context:

Following the attacks on the United States on September 11, 2001, the question pitting national security against civil liberties created a debate regarding the Constitution and the powers it bestowed on the federal government and the function of the Constitution in protecting citizens from abusive governmental power.

Task:

Evaluate the following statement: "In creating greater domestic security from future attacks by terrorists, the United States government must not trample on American liberties in the name of preserving them." Be sure to use the documents provided in structuring your response.

Guidelines:

In your essay, be sure to
• Develop all aspects of the task.
• Incorporate information from *at least five* documents.
• Incorporate relevant outside information.
• Support the theme with many relevant facts, examples, and details.
• Use a logical and clear plan of organization, including an introduction and a conclusion that are beyond a restatement of the theme.

CHRONOLOGY OF MAJOR EVENTS IN AMERICAN HISTORY

1607	Founding of Jamestown in Virginia
1619	Virginia House of Burgesses formed. First Africans brought to Virginia as slaves.
1620	Mayflower Compact
1676	Bacon's Rebellion in Virginia
1688	Glorious Revolution in England
1754	Albany Congress proposes Plan of Union drafted by Benjamin Franklin for defense against Indians and French. Plan is rejected by the colonies.
1763	Treaty of Paris ending Seven Years War (French and Indian War) gives Canada to Great Britain and ends French threat to colonies.
1765	Stamp Act Congress (delegates from nine colonies) meets in New York to oppose Stamp Act and other British taxes.
1770	Boston Massacre
1773	Boston Tea Party
1774	Parliament passes Coercive Acts and Quebec Act. First Continental Congress meets in Philadelphia.
1775	Battles of Lexington and Concord (April 19). Second Continental Congress meets in Philadelphia.
1776	Thomas Paine publishes *Common Sense*. Congress adopts Declaration of Independence, July 4; begins drafting Articles of Confederation.
1778	Treaties with France bring important military supplies and naval support.
1781	Maryland is thirteenth and last state to ratify Articles of Confederation. British commander Cornwallis surrenders to Washington at Yorktown, Virginia, October 19, ending major fighting in the Revolutionary War.
1782	Preliminary peace treaty with Great Britain recognizes independent United States with borders of Great Lakes in the north, the Mississippi River on the west, and the 31st parallel to the south.
1783	British evacuate New York City November 25, but continue to hold forts in Northwest territories.
1786	Annapolis Convention discusses interstate cooperation and recommends a convention to revise the Articles of Confederation. Shays' Rebellion in Massachusetts suppressed.
1787	Constitutional Convention meets in Philadelphia, May–September Continental Congress adopts Northwest Ordinance. The Constitution submitted to Congress, September 20, and to the people in special state conventions, September 28.
1788	Eleven states (all but Rhode Island and North Carolina) ratify Constitution, putting new federal government into effect.
1789	New federal Congress convenes in New York City. George Washington receives all 69 electoral votes for President; nominates Thomas Jefferson as Secretary of State, Alexander Hamilton as Secretary of the Treasury, and John Jay as Chief Justice of the Supreme Court. Congress passes Judiciary Act creating federal court system. Proposed amendments to the Constitution approved by Congress and submitted to the states. North Carolina ratifies Constitution.

1790   Rhode Island ratifies Constitution. First American textile mill built in
        Pawtucket, R.I.
1791   Bank of the United States chartered. Vermont admitted to the Union.
1792   Washington re-elected President, receiving all 132 electoral votes; vetoes
        first bill and veto is sustained by House. First ten amendments ("The
        Bill of Rights") officially ratified, March 1. Kentucky admitted to the
        Union.
1793   Supreme Court decision in *Chisolm* v. *Georgia* permits citizen of South
        Carolina to sue state of Georgia in federal court. Washington issues
        Proclamation of Neutrality in war between the new French Republic
        and Great Britain. Cotton gin invented by Eli Whitney.
1794   Whiskey Rebellion in Pennsylvania suppressed.
1795   Jay Treaty with England and Pinckney Treaty with Spain approved by
        Senate. Eleventh Amendment ratified, barring citizens of one state
        from suing another state in federal court.
1796   Washington refuses to furnish House of Representatives with documents
        about negotiation of Jay Treaty, establishing precedent for executive
        privilege; announces he will not seek a third term and publishes
        "Farewell Address." Oliver Ellsworth becomes Chief Justice.
        Tennessee admitted. John Adams elected President with 71 electoral
        votes to 68 for Thomas Jefferson, who is elected Vice President.
1798   Congress passes Alien and Sedition Acts. Adams administration
        hampered by interference from Alexander Hamilton. Undeclared naval
        war with France; creation of Navy Department. Kentucky and Virginia
        Resolutions, passed by state legislatures, assert the Alien and Sedition
        Acts are unconstitutional and claim that states have the power to
        declare them void.
1800   Republican presidential and vice presidential candidates, Thomas
        Jefferson and Aaron Burr, receive 73 votes each in Electoral College
        (incumbent President John Adams receives 65), throwing election into
        House of Representatives. After 36 ballots over six days, Jefferson is
        elected President.
1801   Outgoing Secretary of State John Marshall becomes Chief Justice.
        Judiciary Act passed by lame-duck Congress. President Jefferson sends
        naval squadron to Mediterranean to protect American shipping from
        Barbary pirates in Tripoli.
1802   Congress repeals Judiciary Act of 1801.
1803   Louisiana Territory purchased from France for $15 million; treaty
        approved by Senate. Supreme Court decision in *Marbury* v. *Madison*
        declares the Judiciary Act of 1789 unconstitutional; decision establishes
        principle of judicial review of acts of Congress. Ohio admitted.
1804   Twelfth Amendment allows separate balloting for President and Vice
        President. Jefferson sends Meriwether Lewis and William Clark to
        explore and map Louisiana Territory. Vice President Aaron Burr kills
        Alexander Hamilton in a duel. Jefferson re-elected President; George
        Clinton elected Vice President.
1807   Embargo Act prohibits exports to foreign nations.
1808   James Madison elected President. Importation of slaves prohibited.

1809	Non-Intercourse Act reopens trade with all nations except France and England.
1810	Supreme Court decision in *Fletcher* v. *Peck* establishes Court's power to declare state laws unconstitutional.
1811	Macon's Bill No. 2 allows trade with France and forbids trade with England.
1812	Madison re-elected President. Louisiana admitted. War declared on Great Britain.
1814	British military expedition burns Washington, D.C. Hartford Convention of New England federalists declares states' right to oppose federal actions. Treaty of Ghent approved by Senate.
1816	Congress charters Second Bank of the United States; passes Tariff of 1816 and Bonus Bill for internal improvements (vetoed). Indiana admitted. Supreme Court decision in *Martin* v. *Hunters Lessee* sets appellate jurisdiction over state courts. James Monroe elected President.
1817	Mississippi admitted. Thomas Gallaudet founds first school for the deaf at Hartford, Ct.
1818	Illinois admitted.
1819	Supreme Court decision in *McCulloch* v. *Maryland* accepts broad implied powers of Congress, including power to create a bank, and asserts that states cannot tax federal agencies; in *Dartmouth College* v. *Woodward*, Court holds that states cannot interfere with contracts. Alabama admitted.
1820	Monroe re-elected President. Maine admitted. Missouri Compromise bars slavery north of 36° 30' in Louisiana Purchase.
1821	Missouri admitted.
1823	James Monroe sets forth Monroe Doctrine to Congress, barring intervention by European powers in Western Hemisphere.
1824	Supreme Court decision in *Gibbons* v. *Ogden* asserts federal power to control interstate commerce. John Quincy Adams elected President in House of Representatives.
1825	Erie Canal completed; first American steam locomotive built in Hoboken, N.J.
1828	Tariff of Abominations. Andrew Jackson elected President.
1829	David Walker publishes *Appeal to the Colored Citizens of The United States* in Wilmington, N.C.
1830	Indian Removal Act

Andrew Jackson (1767–1845), 7th President of the U.S., had the most popular and electoral votes for President in 1824, but was short of a majority. The House of Representatives decided the election in favor of John Quincy Adams.

1831   Nat Turner's Rebellion in Virginia. William Lloyd Garrison begins to publish *The Liberator*. Cyrus McCormick invents mechanical reaper. First regularly scheduled railroad service.

1832   Congress recharters Second Bank of the United States (vetoed). South Carolina nullifies Tariff of Abominations. Jackson reelected President.

1833   Congress passes Compromise Tariff. American Anti-Slavery Society founded.

1836   Roger B. Taney becomes Chief Justice. American settlers in Mexico revolt and declare Texas an independent nation. Martin Van Buren elected President.

1837   Michigan admitted. John Deere develops steel plow.

1838   Van Buren sends troops to force Cherokee removals to Oklahoma Territory, known as Trail of Tears. Frederick Douglass escapes from slavery in Maryland to Massachusetts.

1839   Vulcanized rubber developed by Charles Goodyear.

1840   William Henry Harrison ("Tippecanoe") elected President.

1841   Harrison dies; John Tyler becomes President.

1844   James K. Polk elected President. Telegraph developed by Samuel F.B. Morse.

1845   Florida and Texas admitted.

1846   Oregon Territory purchased from Great Britain. War declared on Mexico. Iowa admitted.

1848   Treaty ending Mexican War acquires territory from Texas to Pacific Ocean. Wisconsin admitted. Women's Rights Convention at Seneca Falls, N.Y., organized by Lucretia Mott and Elizabeth Cady Stanton. Zachary Taylor elected President.

1849   California Gold Rush

1850   Taylor dies; Millard Fillmore becomes President. Compromise of 1850, including Fugitive Slave Law, passed by Congress. First land grants for development of railroads. California admitted.

James K. Polk (1795–1849), 11th President of the U.S., used the Monroe Doctrine to justify annexing Texas and California.

1851   Indian Appropriations Act

1852   Harriet Beecher Stowe publishes *Uncle Tom's Cabin*. Franklin Pierce elected President.

1853   Gadsden Treaty purchases parts of Arizona and New Mexico from Mexico.

1854   Kansas-Nebraska Act

1856   Mass production of steel developed by Henry Bessemer and William
         Kelly. John Brown and followers kill five proslavery settlers at
         Pottawatomie Creek, Kansas. S.C. Representative Preston Brooks
         assaults Sen. Charles Sumner of Massachusetts with cane in Senate
         chamber. James Buchanan elected President.
1857   Supreme Court decision in *Dred Scott* v. *Sandford* denies slaves right
         to sue, declares Missouri Compromise unconstitutional, and opens
         territories to slavery.
1858   Minnesota admitted.
1859   Oregon admitted; John Brown leads attack on federal arsenal at Harper's
         Ferry, Va., hoping to begin popular insurrection.
1860   Abraham Lincoln elected President, winning 180 of 303 electoral votes in
         four-way race. South Carolina secedes.
1861   Virginia, North Carolina, Georgia, Florida, Alabama, Mississippi,
         Louisiana, Texas, Arkansas, and Tennessee secede. Lincoln attempts to
         resupply federal Fort Sumter in Charleston, S.C., harbor. Confederate
         forces attack fort April 12, and it surrenders April 15. Lincoln calls out
         75,000 militia, orders blockade of Southern ports, and suspends habeas
         corpus in some areas. Kansas admitted.
1862   Lincoln abolishes slavery in District of Columbia. Congress passes
         Homestead Act, Morrill Land Grant Act, and Confiscation Act,
         granting freedom to slaves escaped from persons in rebellion. Lincoln
         issues Emancipation Proclamation September 22, to take effect
         January 1, 1863.
1863   Confederate invasion of North halted at Gettysburg July 3; Grant takes
         Vicksburg, Miss., July 4, securing federal control of Southwest. West
         Virginia, created from Virginia counties loyal to Union, admitted.
1864   Salmon P. Chase becomes Chief Justice. Nevada admitted. Lincoln
         reelected, with 212 of 233 electoral votes; Sherman marches from
         Chattanooga, Tenn., through Atlanta, Georgia, to the sea.
1865   Confederate army surrenders to Grant. Lincoln assassinated April 14 by
         actor John Wilkes Booth; Andrew Johnson, a Tennessee Democrat,
         becomes President. Thirteenth Amendment abolishes slavery. John D.
         Rockefeller buys oil-refining company.
1866   National Labor Union founded. Ku Klux Klan founded. Congress passes
         Civil Rights Act of 1866 and Freedman's Bureau Act.
1867   Congress passes Military Reconstruction Act and Tenure of Office
         Act. Senate ratifies treaty with Russia acquiring Alaska. Nebraska
         admitted. National Grange of the Patrons of Husbandry founded.
         Andrew Carnegie adopts Bessemer steel-making process.
1868   Johnson impeached but avoids removal by single vote. Fourteenth
         Amendment assures citizenship, equal rights, and due process to
         freed slaves, repeals "three-fifths clause," and repudiates debts of
         Confederate states. Ulysses Grant elected President.
1869   Knights of Labor founded. First transcontinental railroad completed.
         Wyoming Territory grants voting rights to white women. First
         professional baseball team organized in Cincinnati. Black Friday
         financial panic on Wall Street, September 24.

1870   Fifteenth Amendment guarantees voting rights to African-American men. Congress passes Force Act (federal supervision of elections). Department of Justice established. Standard Oil Co. founded by John D. Rockefeller.

1871   Congress passes Ku Klux Klan Act. Tweed Ring in New York City exposed.

1872   Amnesty Act restores suffrage to former Confederates. Yellowstone Park established. Grant reelected.

1874   Morrison R. Waite becomes Chief Justice. Women's Christian Temperance Union founded. Invention of barbed wire.

1875   Congress passes Specie Resumption Act, returning dollar to gold standard. Whiskey Ring in St. Louis exposed.

Rutherford B. Hayes (1822–93), 19th President of the U.S., a Republican, narrowly won the disputed election of 1876 and then ended Reconstruction in the South.

1876   Colorado admitted. Alexander Graham Bell patents telephone. Gen. George A. Custer's forces wiped out by Sioux and Cheyenne at Little Big Horn, Montana. Disputed returns in close presidential race between Rutherford B. Hayes and Samuel Tilden are decided by Congress in favor of Hayes, leading to his election by single electoral vote.

1877   Hayes withdraws last federal troops from South, ending Reconstruction. National railroad strike; Nez Perce Indian uprising.

1878   Thomas Edison forms Edison Electric Light Co.

1880   James Garfield elected President.

1881   Garfield assassinated; Chester Arthur becomes President. American Federation of Labor founded. Normal and Industrial Institute at Tuskegee, Alabama, founded by Booker T. Washington. Helen Hunt Jackson publishes *A Century of Dishonor.*

1882   Congress passes Chinese Exclusion Act.

1883   Congress passes Pendleton Act establishing Civil Service. Supreme Court decision invalidates Civil Rights Act of 1875 and allows segregation in public facilities.

1884   First skyscraper built in Chicago. Linotype machine patented. Grover Cleveland elected President.

1886   Haymarket Riot in Chicago. American Federation of Labor formed.

1887   Congress passes Interstate Commerce Act and Dawes Act.

1888   Melville Fuller becomes Chief Justice. Benjamin Harrison elected President.

1889	South Dakota, North Dakota, Montana, and Washington admitted. Andrew Carnegie publishes *The Gospel of Wealth*.
1890	Congress passes Sherman Antitrust Act. Army troops massacre 300 Sioux at Wounded Knee, S.D. Populist party founded. Wyoming and Idaho admitted.
1892	Homestead Strike against Carnegie Steel Co. Grover Cleveland elected President.
1894	Pullman Strike in Chicago. Congress repeals Force Acts of 1870–1875.
1895	J.P. Morgan Co. founded.
1896	Supreme Court decision in *Plessy v. Ferguson* sets "separate but equal" standard for segregation. Utah admitted. William McKinley elected President.

Grover Cleveland (1837–1908), 22nd & 24th President of the U.S., sent troops to Chicago to "protect the mails" during the 1894 Pullman strike.

1898	Congress declares war on Spain, April 25. Senate approves treaty annexing Hawaii.
1899	Thorstein Veblen publishes *The Theory of the Leisure Class*. McKinley sends troops to Philippines to put down uprising. Open-Door Policy in China.
1900	McKinley sends troops to China to help suppress Boxer Rebellion. Congress passes Gold Standard Act. McKinley re-elected.
1901	Platt Amendment to Cuban constitution allows U.S. intervention. McKinley assassinated; Theodore Roosevelt becomes President. U.S. Steel Co. organized.
1902	Newlands Reclamation Act for Western irrigation.
1903	Elkins Anti-Rebate Act passed by Congress. Department of Labor and Commerce established. W. E. B. Du Bois publishes *The Souls of Black Folk*. First baseball World Series. Panama Revolt; Hay-Bunau-Varilla Treaty.
1904	Roosevelt re-elected.
1905	Niagara Movement demands suffrage and civil rights for blacks. Industrial Workers of the World (IWW) founded.
1906	Upton Sinclair publishes *The Jungle*. Congress passes Pure Food and Drug Act, Meat Inspection Act, and Hepburn Act controlling railroads.
1907	Inland Waterways Act. Oklahoma admitted.
1908	William H. Taft elected President.
1909	International Ladies Garment Workers Union founded. National Association for the Advancement of Colored People (NAACP) founded. Congress passes Payne-Aldrich Tariff Act.
1910	Congress passes Mann-Elkins Act, extending control over telephone and telegraph systems. Edward White becomes Chief Justice. Ford Motor Co. begins production of Model T. National Urban League founded.

1911   Triangle Shirtwaist Factory fire in New York City kills 146 workers. U.S. troops sent to Nicaragua.

1912   New Mexico and Arizona admitted. Lawrence Textile strike by IWW. Woodrow Wilson elected President, defeating Republican William H. Taft and Bull Moose Theodore Roosevelt.

1913   Jewish Anti-Defamation League organized. Underwood Tariff Act and Federal Reserve Act passed by Congress. Sixteenth Amendment allows federal income tax; Seventeenth Amendment provides for direct election of senators.

1914   Congress passes Clayton Antitrust Act and Federal Trade Commission Act.

1915   Wilson sends U.S. marines to Haiti.

1916   Marcus Garvey founds Universal Negro Improvement Association. Wilson reelected. Congress passes Keating-Owen Act limiting child labor (ruled unconstitutional in 1918).

1917   Congress passes Selective Service Act, Espionage Act, and Jones Act (citizenship for Puerto Ricans). Wilson sends marines to Dominican Republic. War declared on Germany.

1918   Overman Act (presidential war powers) and Sedition Act passed by Congress. Wilson announces Fourteen Points.

1919   Eighteenth Amendment prohibits manufacture, sale, and transport of alcoholic beverages (Prohibition). Supreme Court decision in *Schenck* v. *United States* establishes "clear and present danger" standard for limiting free speech. Senate rejects Treaty of Versailles. Volstead Act (Prohibition enforcement) passed.

1920   Nineteenth Amendment extends voting rights to white women. Republican Warren G. Harding elected President.

1921   Conviction of Sacco and Vanzetti in Massachusetts; Emergency Quota Immigration Act; William Howard Taft becomes Chief Justice.

1922   Dyer Anti-Lynching Bill defeated by Senate filibuster.

1923   President Harding dies; Calvin Coolidge becomes President.

1924   Congress passes Snyder Indian Citizenship Act and Immigration Act. Coolidge elected President.

1925   Trial of John Scopes in Tennessee. Supreme Court decision in *Gitlow* v. *New York* applies guarantees of Bill of Rights to the states.

1927   Congress passes Immigration Act of 1927. *The Jazz Singer* first talking movie. Charles Lindbergh first to fly across Atlantic.

1928   Herbert Hoover elected President.

1929   National Origins Act passed by Congress. Stock market crash on October 29 sets off Great Depression.

1930   Congress passes Hawley-Smoot Tariff Act. Charles Hughes becomes Chief Justice.

1932   Congress passes Norris-LaGuardia Act (labor). Drought turns much of Midwest into Dust Bowl. Hoover orders troops to disperse "Bonus Army" of WWI veterans in Washington. Franklin D. Roosevelt elected President defeating incumbent Hoover.

1933   Frances Perkins named Secretary of Labor, first woman to serve in Cabinet. Congress passes Emergency Banking Relief Act, Federal Emergency Relief Act, National Industrial Recovery Act, Glass-Steagall Banking Act, Tennessee Valley Authority, Civilian

Conservation Corps, and First Agricultural Adjustment Act. Twentieth Amendment reduces "lame-duck" period by moving inauguration of President and beginning of Congressional term to January. Twenty-First Amendment repeals Prohibition.

1934   Congress establishes Federal Housing Authority, Home Owners Loan Corporation, and Securities and Exchange Commission, and passes Indian Reorganization Act.

1935   Supreme Court decision in *Schecter* v. *United States* declares National Recovery Act of 1933 unconstitutional. Congress passes National Labor Relations Act (Wagner Act), Neutrality Act, Social Security Act, and Works Progress Administration.

1936   Neutrality Act and Soil Conservation and Domestic Allotment Act passed by Congress. Roosevelt reelected President.

1937   Congress establishes Farm Security Administration.

1938   Congress passes Second Agricultural Adjustment Act, Fair Labor Standards Act, and Foreign Agents Registration Act.

1939   Congress passes Neutrality Act. John Steinbeck publishes *The Grapes of Wrath*.

1940   Smith Alien Registration Act passed. Harlan Stone becomes Chief Justice. Roosevelt reelected to third term.

1941   Congress on Racial Equality founded. Congress passes Lend-Lease Act and declares war on Japan and Germany following attack on Pearl Harbor, Hawaii, December 7.

1942   Naval battle at Midway, June 3–6, halts Japanese advance in Pacific. Military relocates 125,000 Japanese-Americans from West Coast to interior for security reasons.

1944   Supreme Court decision in *Korematsu* v. *United States* upholds internment of American citizens of Japanese descent. Allied forces invade Europe on D-Day, June 6. Roosevelt reelected to fourth term.

1945   Roosevelt meets with Stalin and Churchill in Yalta. Harry Truman becomes President when Roosevelt dies April 12. Germany surrenders on V-E Day, May 8. United Nations chartered. Truman at Potsdam Conference with Stalin and new British Prime Minister Clement Atlee. First atomic bomb exploded on Hiroshima, Japan. Japan surrenders on V-J Day, August 14.

1946   Congress passes Regulation of Lobbying Act and G.I. Bill of Rights. Frederick Vinson becomes Chief Justice.

1947   Truman announces Truman Doctrine and proposes Marshall Plan. Congress passes Taft-Hartley Act and National Security Act. Brooklyn Dodgers integrate Major League baseball by signing Jackie Robinson.

1948   Berlin airlift. Former State Department official Alger Hiss convicted of perjury before House Committee to Investigate Un-American Activities. Congress passes Displaced Persons Act. W. E. B. Du Bois dismissed from NAACP staff for criticising American foreign policy. Truman reelected, defeating Republican Thomas Dewey.

1949   Congress passes National Housing Act. North Atlantic Treaty Organization (NATO) formed.

1950   North Korean armies invade South Korea; United Nations and American troops committed. Congress passes McCarran Internal Security Act.

1951   Truman relieves Gen. MacArthur of command in Korea for attempting to
        broaden the war and invade China. Twenty-Second Amendment sets
        two-term limit for President. Julius and Ethel Rosenberg convicted of
        espionage for passing atomic secrets to Soviet Union (executed 1953).
        W. E. B. Du Bois arrested, tried, and acquitted of being a foreign
        agent.

1952   Congress passes McCarran-Walter Act, allowing deportation of subversives.
        Dwight D. Eisenhower elected President, defeating Adlai Stevenson.

1953   Secretary of State John Foster Dulles practices brinkmanship and
        declares policy of massive retaliation against Soviets. Earl Warren
        becomes Chief Justice. Submerged Lands Act gives oil drilling rights
        to states. Department of Health, Education and Welfare established.

1954   J. Robert Oppenheimer deprived of security clearance by Atomic Energy
        Commission. Sen. Joseph McCarthy censured by Senate. Supreme
        Court decision in *Brown* v. *Board of Education of Topeka* holds
        "separate but equal" standard to be unconstitutional, ends legal racial
        segregation of education.

1955   Bus boycott organized in Montgomery, Alabama.

1956   Eisenhower reelected, defeating Adlai Stevenson for second time.

1957   Eisenhower sends federal marshals and troops to enforce school
        integration in Little Rock, Ark. Congress passes Civil Rights Act
        of 1957. Southern Christian Leadership Conference organized by
        Dr. Martin Luther King, Jr.

1958   Eisenhower sends U.S. marines to Lebanon.

1959   Alaska and Hawaii admitted.

1960   Congress passes Civil Rights Act of 1960. Student Nonviolent
        Coordinating Committee (SNCC) founded. U-2 spy plane shot down
        over Soviet Union, leading to cancellation of Paris summit meetings.
        Democrat John F. Kennedy elected President, defeating Vice President
        Richard M. Nixon.

1961   Freedom riders protest racial segregation in Southern bus systems. Kennedy
        permits invasion of Cuba by exile forces at Bay of Pigs. Twenty-Third
        Amendment allows District of Columbia to vote in presidential elections.

1962   Supreme Court decision in *Engel* v. *Vitale* bans prayer in public schools;
        decision in *Baker* v. *Carr* establishes "one person, one vote" standard
        for apportionment. Kennedy orders blockade of Cuba to force removal
        of Soviet nuclear missiles.

1963   Supreme Court decision in *Gideon* v. *Wainwright* declares accused
        persons must be furnished an attorney. United Farm Workers
        organized by César Chavez. Poor Peoples' March on Washington.
        NAACP leader Medgar Evers assassinated in Mississippi. President
        Kennedy assassinated in Dallas by Lee Harvey Oswald; Lyndon B.
        Johnson becomes President.

1964   Congress passes Civil Rights Act of 1964, Gulf of Tonkin Resolution,
        Voting Rights Act, Federal Clean Water Act, Immigration Act of 1965,
        and Medicare Act. Twenty-Fourth Amendment prohibits poll tax.
        Johnson re-elected, defeating Republican Barry Goldwater.

1965   Malcolm X assassinated. Summer riots in Watts district of Los Angeles.
        Escalation of Vietnam War.

1966   Congress passes Freedom of Information Act. Supreme Court decision in *Miranda* v. *Arizona* requires persons arrested to be informed of their rights. National Organization of Women founded by Betty Friedan. Black Panthers founded in Oakland, California.

1967   Twenty-Fifth Amendment allows for appointment of new Vice President to fill vacant office.

1968   Tet Offensive in Vietnam. Civil Rights Act of 1968 passed by Congress. Martin Luther King, Jr., assassinated in Memphis. American Indian Movement founded. Republican Richard M. Nixon elected President, defeating Vice President Hubert H. Humphrey.

1969   Warren Burger becomes Chief Justice. American astronauts Neil Armstrong and E. E. Aldrin walk on the moon. 250,000 march on Washington demanding end to Vietnam War.

1970   National Guard troops fire on students protesting invasion of Cambodia at Kent State University in Ohio, killing four. Congress passes Clean Air Act; Senate repeals Gulf of Tonkin Resolution. Earth Day celebrations held.

1971   Top-secret *Pentagon Papers* on Vietnam policy published in *The New York Times*, and right to publish them is upheld by Supreme Court. Amtrak, national passenger rail system, established with government subsidies. Twenty-Sixth Amendment extends voting rights to citizens who have reached age 18.

1972   Federal Water Pollution Control Act passed by Congress. Burglary attempt at Democratic National Headquarters in Watergate Tower foiled; burglars appear to have links to Nixon reelection campaign. Nixon visits China. Nixon re-elected, defeating Democrat George McGovern by 521 to 17 electoral votes.

1973   White House staff members H. R. Haldeman and John Ehrlichman resign, and John Dean is fired over involvement in Watergate coverup. Vice President Spiro Agnew resigns and pleads *nolo contendere* to charges of extortion and tax evasion, October 11. Nixon nominates Gerald Ford to be Vice President. Supreme Court decision in *Roe* v. *Wade* recognizes woman's right to an abortion. War Powers Act passed by Congress over Nixon's veto. U.S. troops leave Vietnam.

1974   Privacy Act and Federal Election Campaign Finance Reform Act passed by Congress. Nixon resigns August 8; Gerald R. Ford becomes President. Nelson Rockefeller appointed Vice President. Ford issues pardon to Nixon and offers amnesty to Vietnam draft evaders.

1975   Congress passes Education Act.

1976   Democrat Jimmy Carter elected President, defeating Gerald Ford.

1977   Carter pardons Vietnam deserters and draft resisters. Panama Canal Treaties negotiated. Department of Energy created.

1979   Strategic Arms Limitation Treaty (SALT II) signed in June, but not approved by Senate. Department of Education created. In November, Iranian extremists occupy American embassy in Teheran, holding 52 diplomats and others hostage. In December, Soviet troops occupy Afghanistan to support faltering Communist government.

1980   Congress passes Alaska National Interest Lands Conservation Act. Chrysler Corporation gets $1.5 billion in loan guarantees in government bailout. Republican Ronald Reagan elected President, defeating Carter by 489 to 49 electoral votes.

1981   Hostages in Iran freed the day Carter leaves office. President Reagan shot by John Hinckley, Jr., but recovers. Congress passes Economic Recovery Tax Act.

1983   U.S. forces invade Grenada to secure pro-American government. Forces committed to Beirut, Lebanon, to assist UN peacekeeping; 241 marines killed by terrorist bombing.

1984   Income Tax Reform Act passed by Congress. Reagan re-elected President, defeating Democrat Walter Mondale, 525 to 13 electoral votes.

1985   Congress passes Gramm-Rudman-Hollings Act, requiring balanced budget by 1991. Summit meeting between Reagan and Soviet leader Mikhail Gorbachev in Geneva.

1986   Reagan attends summit with Gorbachev in Reykjavik. National Security Council staff Oliver North, John Poindexter, and Robert McFarland secretly and illegally sell anti-aircraft missiles and parts to Iran to gain the release of hostages held in Lebanon, and they divert money from the sales to the Contra rebels opposing the socialist Sandinista government in Nicaragua. Congress passes Federal Clean Water Act (vetoed) and Income Tax Reform Act. Justice William Rehnquist becomes Chief Justice.

1987   Federal Clean Water Act passed by Congress over Reagan's veto. Summit with Gorbachev in Washington. Intermediate Nuclear Forces Treaty signed. Wall Street crash on October 19.

1988   Reagan visits Moscow. Vice President George Bush elected President, defeating Democrat Michael Dukakis with slogan "Read my lips: no new taxes."

1989   Congress creates Resolution Trust Corporation to handle S&L bailout. Bush sends U.S. forces to invade Panama and capture Gen. Manuel Noriega, who is wanted on federal drug charges.

1990   Congress passes Americans with Disabilities Act.

1991   UN forces, including American troops, expel Iraqi army from Kuwait in Operation Desert Storm.

1992   Twenty-Seventh Amendment bars Congressional pay raises from taking effect until after a new election. Democrat Bill Clinton elected President, defeating incumbent George Bush and independent Ross Perot.

1993   Congress passes Family and Medical Leave Act, Brady Bill on gun control, and economic package; ratifies North American Free Trade Agreement (NAFTA).

1994   Crime Bill passed by Congress. Military junta forced out of Haiti and elected president restored to power in a peaceful invasion by American troops. Republicans gain control of House and Senate in midterm elections.

1995   Domestic terrorists blow up federal building in Oklahoma City. Budget negotiation impasse leads Republican Congress to shut down federal government.

1996   Congress passes Welfare Reform Bill. Clinton re-elected President, defeating Republican Robert Dole and Reform party candidate Ross Perot. Republicans retain Congressional control.

1997   Congress enacts plan to balance federal budget by 2002.

1998   Clinton presidency overshadowed by year-long Monica Lewinsky scandal concerning sex, perjury, and obstruction of justice. Independent Prosecutor Starr issues detailed report recommending impeachment, and House of Representatives impeaches Clinton on two counts. U.S. embassies in Tanzania and Kenya destroyed by terrorist bombs.

1999   Senate holds trial and acquits Clinton. Bombing campaign by NATO forces, spearheaded by U.S. armed forces, force Serb troops to withdraw from Kosovo. Senate rejects ratification of Comprehensive Test Ban Treaty.

2000   Democratic Vice President Albert Gore and Republican Governor of Texas George W. Bush obtain party nominations for President. Following one of the closest elections in United States history, by a 5–4 vote, Supreme Court justices overturn Florida bench and rule there can be no further counting of disputed Florida ballots in presidential election. Vice President Al Gore concedes election to George W. Bush, governor of Texas.

2001   President Bush signs new tax-cut law, the largest in 20 years. Oklahoma City bomber Timothy McVeigh executed. Terrorist hijackers ram jetliners into New York City's World Trade Center and the Pentagon. A fourth hijacked plane crashes 80 miles outside of Pittsburgh. Toll of dead and injured in thousands. Islamic militant Osama bin Laden and the al Qaeda terrorist network are identified as the parties behind the attacks.

2002   Kenneth L. Lay, chairman of bankrupt energy trader Enron, resigns; company under federal investigation for hiding debt and misrepresenting earnings. U.S. withdraws from International Court treaty. U.S. abandons 31-year-old Anti-Ballistic Missile Treaty. Bush addresses United Nations, calling for a "regime change" in Iraq. President Bush signs legislation creating Cabinet Department of Homeland Security.

2003   Space shuttle *Columbia* explodes, killing all seven astronauts. President Bush signs ten-year, $350-billion tax-cut package, the third-largest tax cut in U.S. history. Supreme Court upholds the right of affirmative action in higher education. California Governor Gray Davis ousted in recall vote; actor Arnold Schwarzenegger elected in his place. President Bush signs $87.5 billion emergency package for postwar Iraq reconstruction; this supplements $79 billion approved in April.

2004   John Kerry secures Democratic nomination. U.S. media release graphic photos of American soldiers abusing and sexually humiliating Iraqi prisoners at Abu Ghraib prison. Senate Intelligence Committee reports that intelligence on Iraq's weapons programs was "overstated" and flawed. September 11 commission harshly criticizes government's handling of terrorist attacks. George W. Bush is re-elected president, defeating John Kerry.

2005   President Bush is officially sworn in for his second term as president. President Bush announces his plan to reform Social Security. The president signs the Central American Free Trade Agreement (CAFTA), which will remove trade barriers between the United States and Costa Rica, the Dominican Republic, El Salvador, Guatemala, Honduras, and Nicaragua. Hurricane Katrina wreaks catastrophic damage on the Gulf coast; more than 1,000 die, and millions are left homeless. Chief Justice William H. Rehnquist, who served on the U.S. Supreme Court for 33 years, dies and John Roberts becomes 17th chief justice.

2006   Surveillance debate over wiretapping of domestic phone calls and emails without obtaining legally required warrants. Republican lobbyist Jack Abramoff was convicted of fraud, tax evasion, and conspiracy to bribe public officials. The Iraq Study Group, led by former Secretary of State James Baker and former Democratic Congressman Lee Hamilton, concluded that "the situation in Iraq is grave and deteriorating" and "U.S. forces seem to be caught in a mission that has no foreseeable end." November midterm elections resulted in Democrats gaining control over the House of Representatives and the Senate for the first time in 12 years.

2007   President Gerald Ford, 38th president of the United States, dies. California Democrat Nancy Pelosi becomes first woman Speaker of the House of Representatives. Lewis "Scooter" Libby, former chief of staff to Vice President Dick Cheney, is found guilty of lying to FBI agents and to a grand jury in the investigation of who leaked to the press the name of a covert CIA agent. Attorney General Alberto Gonzales admits that the Justice Department made mistakes in firing eight federal prosecutors in late 2006.

2008   The federal government begins to intervene in the U.S. financial system to avoid a financial crisis. Democrat Senator Barack Obama wins the presidential election against Senator John McCain, taking 338 electoral votes to McCain's 161. President George W. Bush announces plans to lend General Motors and Chrysler $17.4 billion.

2009   The American Recovery and Reinvestment Act of 2009, commonly referred to as the Stimulus or The Recovery Act, is passed by Congress and signed by President Obama. President Obama announces his intention to withdraw most American troops from Iraq by August 31, 2010. The Senate approves the nomination of Sonia Sotomayor to the Supreme Court. Iraq's cabinet passes an agreement that will govern the U.S. presence in Iraq through 2011. The pact calls for the withdrawal of all U.S. combat troops by December 31, 2011.

2010   Supreme Court ruled that the government cannot restrict the spending of corporations for political campaigns, maintaining that it's their First Amendment right to support candidates as they choose. President Obama signed the health-care overhaul bill, called the *Patient Protection and Affordable Care Act*, into law. The governor of Arizona signed into law the country's toughest immigration bill. President Obama's most recent nominee to the U.S. Supreme Court, Elena Kagan, is confirmed by the Senate. The Republican Party gains control of the House of Representatives.

2011 "Don't Ask, Don't Tell" is repealed. Osama bin Laden is killed in Pakistan by U.S. troops. Standard & Poor's lowers the U.S. credit rating. Occupy Wall Street Movement continues to grow. Libyan civil war and death of Muammar Gaddafi. U.S. troops start to withdraw from Iraq.

2012 In *National Federation of Independent Business* v. *Sebelius*, the Supreme Court upholds the act's "individual mandate" of the Affordable Care Act. President Obama announces the Deferred Action for Childhood Arrivals (DACA) program to allow for deferred action from deportation for certain undocumented immigrants. Fighting in Libya results in the death of four American embassy officials in the city of Benghazi, including the ambassador, J. Christopher Stevens. Russia begins extending aid to the regime of Bashar al-Assad in the Syrian Civil War. Horrific mass shootings take place in Aurora, Colorado, and at Sandy Hook Elementary School in Newtown, Connecticut. Residents of Colorado and Washington vote to legalize marijuana for recreational use. President Obama and Vice President Joe Biden are elected to a second term, defeating the Republican nominee Mitt Romney, former governor of Massachusetts, and his running-mate, Representative Paul Ryan of Wisconsin.

2013 The Supreme Court weakens the 1965 Voting Rights Act in *Shelby County* v. *Holder* (2013). A bipartisan group of senators, labeled the "gang of eight," fails to enact comprehensive immigration reform. Edward Snowden releases information about the clandestine National Security Agency program known as PRISM. In *United States* v. *Windsor*, the Supreme Court strikes down the Defense of Marriage Act.

2014 Russian President Vladimir Putin intervenes militarily in Crimea, occupying the region with troops. President Obama attempts to expand immigration reform with the Deferred Action for Parents of Americans and Lawful Permanent Residents (DAPA) program (the program is halted in the courts). The shooting of Michael Brown by a police officer in Ferguson, Missouri, leads to protests and is a catalyst for the Black Lives Matter movement. Attorney General Eric H. Holder Jr. adds gender identity to the categories of discrimination that are covered in Title VII of the Civil Rights Act of 1964. The Supreme Court, in *Burwell* v. *Hobby Lobby* (2014), rules that a business may not be forced to pay for insurance that covers contraceptives. In midterm elections, the Republicans pick up nine seats and majority control in the Senate, and also add to their majority in the House.

2015 In *King* v. *Burwell* (2015), the Supreme Court upholds the Affordable Care Act's tax subsidies. A mass shooting at the Mother Emanuel A.M.E. church in Charleston, South Carolina, takes nine individuals' lives. Ninety nations sign the Joint Comprehensive Plan of Action (2015), in which Iran agrees to limit its nuclear program to peaceful purposes. ISIS is able to gain control of large sections of western Iraq and eastern Syria. U.S. forces engage in an air campaign against ISIS locations in Syria and Iraq. In *Obergefell* v. *Hodges*, the Court rules that marriage is a fundamental right that must be guaranteed to same-sex couples. The United Nations Framework Convention on Climate Change agrees to the Paris Agreement (2015). The United States and Cuba resume relations after a half century of hostility.

2016   The Obama administration negotiates the Trans-Pacific Partnership (TPP). Justice Antonin Scalia dies suddenly; President Obama nominates Merrick Garland, but the Senate refuses to deliberate on the nominee. Businessman Donald Trump and running-mate Governor Mike Pence of Indiana represent the Republican Party in the presidential election. They win the Electoral College vote over the Democratic candidate, Secretary Hillary Clinton and her running-mate, Senator Tim Kaine of Virginia. By the end of the year, the U.N. estimates that approximately 11 million Syrians have been displaced by the Syrian Civil War, out of a population of 23 million.

2017   Donald Trump is inaugurated as the 45th president. President Trump nominates Neil Gorsuch to replace Justice Antonin Scalia on the Supreme Court. President Trump withdraws the United States from the Trans-Pacific Partnership (TPP).

ANSWER KEY

UNIT 1

Chapter 1

Exercise Set 1.1
1. D   3. A   5. A   7. C   9. C   11. A   13. A   15. D
2. B   4. B   6. B   8. B   10. C   12. B   14. C

Exercise Set 1.2
1. C   3. C   5. B   7. A   9. A
2. D   4. C   6. B   8. C   10. C

Exercise Set 1.3
1. D   2. C   3. B   4. B   5. C   6. A   7. C   8. B

Exercise Set 1.4
1. C   2. B   3. C   4. C   5. D   6. C   7. B   8. B   9. D

Chapter Review Questions
1. D   4. C   7. A   10. D   13. B   16. A   19. D
2. B   5. B   8. C   11. C   14. B   17. C   20. A
3. C   6. C   9. A   12. B   15. B   18. B

Chapter 2

Exercise Set 1.5
1. C   2. C   3. A   4. D   5. C   6. C   7. D

Exercise Set 1.6
1. C   2. B   3. B   4. D   5. A   6. D   7. C

Chapter Review Questions
1. B   3. C   5. C   7. C   9. A
2. B   4. C   6. C   8. C   10. B

UNIT 2

Chapter 1

Exercise Set 2.1
1. D   2. B   3. A   4. C   5. D   6. B

Exercise Set 2.2
1. B   2. B   3. D   4. A   5. C

Exercise Set 2.3
1. D   2. C   3. C   4. D

Exercise Set 2.4
1. D   2. C   3. B   4. A

Chapter Review Questions
1. A   2. B   3. D   4. C   5. B   6. A

Chapter 2

Exercise Set 2.5
1. B   2. A   3. A   4. C   5. D

Exercise Set 2.6
1. A   2. B   3. D   4. D

Exercise Set 2.7
1. C   2. B   3. D

Exercise Set 2.8
1. A   2. C   3. B   4. A

Exercise Set 2.9
1. C   2. D   3. A   4. B

Chapter Review Questions
1. D   3. D   5. C   7. A   9. D
2. B   4. C   6. B   8. B   10. B

Chapter 3

Exercise Set 2.10
1. B   2. A   3. A

Exercise Set 2.11
1. B   2. B   3. C   4. D   5. C   6. A

Exercise Set 2.12
1. D   2. B   3. B   4. C

Chapter Review Questions
1. C   2. B   3. A   4. B   5. A   6. D   7. D   8. A

UNIT 3

Chapter 1

Exercise Set 3.1
1. B   2. D   3. C   4. D   5. B   6. D

Exercise Set 3.2
1. D   2. D   3. B   4. A

Chapter Review Questions
1. C   2. C   3. A   4. B   5. C   6. B

Chapter 2

Exercise Set 3.3
1. D   2. C   3. A   4. A

Exercise Set 3.4
1. C   2. A   3. D   4. B   5. D   6. C

Exercise Set 3.5
1. C   2. D   3. A   4. B

Exercise Set 3.6
1. D   2. C   3. A   4. C

Exercise Set 3.7
1. C   2. C   3. B   4. B

Chapter Review Questions
1. A   2. B   3. D   4. B   5. C   6. A   7. B

UNIT 4

Chapter 1

Exercise Set 4.1
1. D   2. C   3. A   4. C   5. D   6. A   7. C   8. B   9. D

Exercise Set 4.2
1. A   2. A   3. C   4. C   5. B

Exercise Set 4.3
1. B   3. B   5. C   7. B   9. C
2. D   4. B   6. B   8. D   10. D

Chapter Review Questions
1. D   2. A   3. C   4. B   5. C

Chapter 2

Exercise Set 4.4
1. C   2. A   3. B   4. A

Exercise Set 4.5
1. B   2. B   3. D   4. C   5. D

Exercise Set 4.6
1. B   2. A   3. A   4. C   5. D   6. A

Exercise Set 4.7
1. C   2. A   3. C   4. B

Chapter Review Questions
1. A   2. C   3. D   4. D   5. C   6. C   7. A   8. B

UNIT 5

Chapter 1

Exercise Set 5.1
1. A   2. D   3. B   4. D

Exercise Set 5.2
1. A   2. C   3. D   4. C   5. A

Exercise Set 5.3
1. A   2. C   3. B   4. B   5. D

Exercise Set 5.4
1. A   2. B   3. A   4. D   5. C

Exercise Set 5.5
1. D   2. B   3. D   4. A   5. C

Chapter Review Questions
1. D   2. C   3. A   4. C   5. C

Chapter 2

Exercise Set 5.6
1. B   2. C   3. D   4. D   5. A

Exercise Set 5.7
1. A   2. B   3. B   4. B   5. B   6. A

Exercise Set 5.8
1. C   2. A   3. C   4. C

Chapter Review Questions
1. B   2. A   3. A   4. D   5. C   6. B   7. D

UNIT 6

Chapter 1

Exercise Set 6.1
1. D   2. A   3. B

Exercise Set 6.2
1. B   2. A   3. D   4. B   5. B   6. A

Chapter 2

Exercise Set 6.3
1. B   2. A   3. B   4. B   5. A

Exercise Set 6.4
1. C   2. C   3. A

Exercise Set 6.5
1. B   2. C   3. A   4. A

Exercise Set 6.6
1. B   2. D   3. B   4. C   5. A

Chapter Review Questions
1. C   2. D   3. B   4. C   5. C

Chapter 3

Exercise Set 6.7
1. C   **2.** D   **3.** A   **4.** B

Exercise Set 6.8
1. B   **2.** D   **3.** A   **4.** C   **5.** C

Exercise Set 6.9
1. B   **2.** D   **3.** B   **4.** C

Exercise Set 6.10
1. B   **2.** C   **3.** D   **4.** D   **5.** B   **6.** C

Chapter Review Questions
1. C   **2.** B   **3.** C   **4.** D   **5.** D   **6.** C

Chapter 4

Exercise Set 6.11
1. C   **2.** B   **3.** D   **4.** B   **5.** C

Exercise Set 6.12
1. D   **2.** A   **3.** C   **4.** D   **5.** B   **6.** C

Chapter Review Questions
1. A   **2.** D   **3.** A   **4.** B

Chapter 5

Exercise Set 6.13
1. C   **2.** A   **3.** D   **4.** C   **5.** A   **6.** B

Exercise Set 6.14
1. C   **2.** D   **3.** D   **4.** A

Exercise Set 6.15
1. D   **2.** D   **3.** B   **4.** C   **5.** A

Exercise Set 6.16
1. B   **2.** A   **3.** B   **4.** D   **5.** C   **6.** D   **7.** C

Exercise Set 6.17
1. D   **2.** D   **3.** D   **4.** C   **5.** A   **6.** B   **7.** C   **8.** D   **9.** C

Chapter Review Questions
1. C   **2.** A   **3.** D   **4.** B   **5.** C   **6.** A

UNIT 7

Chapter 1

Exercise Set 7.1
1. B   2. C   3. D   4. C   5. A

Chapter 2

Exercise Set 7.2
1. B   2. A   3. B   4. C   5. C   6. A   7. D   8. B   9. D

Chapter 3

Exercise Set 7.3
1. A   2. D   3. C   4. C   5. A   6. B

Chapter 4

Exercise Set 7.4
1. D   2. A   3. B   4. A   5. C   6. A

Chapter 5

Exercise Set 7.5
1. B   2. A   3. C   4. C   5. B   6. B

Chapter 6

Exercise Set 7.6
1. A   2. C   3. A   4. D   5. C   6. B   7. A

GLOSSARY OF TERMS

Abolitionists those who supported ending the institution of slavery.

Acid rain rain, snow, or sleet containing nitric or sulphuric acid produced from the contamination of the atmosphere by smokestack and automobile emissions. It can damage plants and animals and erode stone and buildings.

Acculturation the modification of a people's culture through adaptation or borrowing from other cultures; the merging of cultures.

Affirmative action public policy of incorporating women and racial and ethnic minorities into economic, political, and social institutions; usually applied through legislation or court orders.

Albany Plan of Union 1754 plan of inter-colonial defense by Benjamin Franklin that provided a federal plan of governing later used as a model for the United States Constitution.

Amendment change or addition made in the Constitution; proposed by Congress or a national convention called by Congress and ratified by state legislatures or special state conventions.

American Federation of Labor Early labor union (1881) of craft unions founded by Samuel Gompers. The AFL merged with the Congress of Industrial Organizations (CIO) in 1955.

Amnesty a general pardon for political offenses.

Anarchist one who believes in the abolition of government or is opposed to organized government.

Anarchy the absence of government; a state of disorder or chaos.

Antifederalists opponents of ratification of the Constitution in 1787 and 1788; opponents of the extension of federal power.

Antitrust relating to the limitation or control of monopolies, trusts, or unfair business combinations.

Antitrust laws legislation designed to prevent the abuses of large business organizations (i.e., monopolies).

Apartheid racial segregation, specifically in South Africa.

Appalachia vast region of the Appalachian Mountains characterized in many parts by poverty and economic underdevelopment.

Appeasement attempts to conciliate an aggressor by making concessions. The policy of appeasement toward Hitler in the 1930s ultimately failed to avoid war.

Apportionment allotment of voting districts as required by law.

Arab Spring widespread wave of pro-democracy protests occurring in the Arab world that began at the end of 2010. The protests have resulted in despot rulers being removed in Tunisia, Egypt, Libya, and Yemen while uprisings continue in Bahrain and Syria.

Arbitration process of settling a dispute by referring it to a third party; both sides usually agree beforehand to abide by the arbitrator's decision.

Armistice a truce preliminary to a peace treaty.

Articles of Confederation the charter of the first national government of the United States; in effect from 1781 until replaced by the Constitution in 1789.

Assembly a gathering or body of representatives, usually of a state or locality.

Assembly line manufacturing process in which parts are added to a product to create a finished product. Perfected by Henry Ford in 1913 in his automobile production factories.

Atlantic Charter document issued in 1941 by President Franklin Roosevelt and Prime Minister Winston Churchill outlining the mutual wartime goals of the United States and England and their principles for assuring peace after the war.

Balance of power policy aimed at securing peace by maintaining approximate military equality among countries or blocs.

Balanced budget plan for government taxes and spending in which expenses do not exceed income.

Belligerent a participant in a war.

Berlin airlift in response to the 1948 blockade set up by the Soviets around Berlin, the United States, Great Britain, and France flew food and other necessities to the 2 million people there. The blockade was withdrawn in 1949.

Bicameral legislature lawmaking body made up of two houses or chambers.

Big stick policy willingness to use military power to influence foreign affairs. It derives from Theodore Roosevelt's saying, "Walk softly, but carry a big stick."

Bill of Rights first ten amendments to the Constitution, adopted in 1791.

Bipartisan involving the cooperation of two political parties.

Black codes a series of laws that sought to control and regulate the conduct of freed slaves during and after the Reconstruction period in the Southern states. Generally, they denied blacks their basic civil rights.

Bloc a group of countries or voters with similar political views.

Bolsheviks radical socialists and communists under the leadership of Lenin and Trotsky who came to power following the Russian Revolution in 1917.

Boston Massacre in 1770 five colonists were killed in Boston when British soldiers fired on a crowd throwing rocks and snowballs; the soldiers were tried and acquitted of murder.

Boston Tea Party incident in Boston, December 16, 1773, when colonists dressed as Indians forced their way aboard merchant ships in the harbor and threw overboard their cargoes of tea so that recently imposed British taxes on it could not be collected.

Bourgeoisie economic and social class between the aristocracy, or the very wealthy class, and the working class (the proletariat); the commercial or professional class; the middle class.

Boycott to join together in refusing to deal with or buy from a party in order to compel negotiation or concessions.

Brain trust experts without official positions who served as advisers to President Franklin Roosevelt.

Brinkmanship pushing a dangerous situation to the limit before stopping.

Budget deficit the amount by which expenses exceed revenue or income.

Bureaucracy administrative officials of government.

Cabinet the advisers to the President who also manage the principal executive departments of the U.S. government. The Cabinet is not mentioned in the Constitution, but has grown over time from custom and practice.

CAFTA (2003) United States–Central America Free Trade Agreement, which promotes lowering and doing away with tariffs between the United States and Costa Rica, El Salvador, Guatemala, Honduras, and Nicaragua. CAFTA is modeled after the North American Free Trade Agreement (1994).

Camp David Accords agreements reached in 1978 between President Sadat of Egypt and Prime Minister Begin of Israel, negotiated by President Carter at the presidential retreat in Camp David, MD. The accords evolved into a peace treaty between Israel and Egypt in 1979, providing for Egypt's official recognition of Israel and Israel's withdrawal from the Sinai Peninsula.

Capital (1) the seat or main location of a government; (2) money invested or used to return a profit.

Capitalism economic system in which the means of production and distribution are privately owned and operated for profit.

Capital punishment death sentence imposed by a court.

Capitol building in which state or federal legislature assembles.

Carpetbaggers Northerners who went to the South during the Reconstruction period to participate in and profit from its political reorganization.

Caucus a closed meeting of a political party.

Censorship preventing the publication of written material or the showing of a film, television program, or play because the government or a segment of society finds it objectionable.

Census a counting of the inhabitants of a region.

Central Powers In World War I, Germany, Austro-Hungary, and their allies.

Charter written document establishing the rules under which an organization will operate; an organization's constitution.

Checks and balances division of powers among the three branches of the federal government so that each branch may limit actions and power of the others. *See also* Separation of powers.

Chicanos Americans of Mexican origin or descent.

Citizen person entitled by birth or naturalization, to the rights and protection provided by the state or nation.

Civil disobedience refusal to obey a law in order to draw attention to its unfairness or undesirability.

Civil rights the liberties and privileges of citizens, especially those guaranteed in the Bill of Rights.

Civil Service system begun in 1880s for filling government jobs through impartial and nonpolitical means, such as standardized exams.

Civil war a war between factions or regions of one country (i.e., United States Civil War, Russian Revolution).

Clear and present danger standard established by the Supreme Court for determining when the right of free speech may be limited or denied—"when there is a clear and present danger that they will bring about the substantive evils that [the government] has a right to prevent."

Coalition temporary alliance of groups or factions.

Cold war a conflict between nations short of actual military conflict; the political, diplomatic, economic, and strategic competition between the United States and the Soviet Union from 1946 until 1991.

Collective bargaining method by which workers negotiate as a group with their employer through their union representatives.

Collective security agreement among a group of nations to help each other maintain their safety and territory; usually by agreeing that an attack by a foreign power upon one nation will be considered an attack upon all.

Colonialism national policy based on control over dependent areas or colonies.

Colony a territory ruled or administered by a distant nation, usually for the benefit of the ruling nation.

Commerce among the states business carried on across state lines, which Congress is given power to regulate by Article I, Section 8, of the Constitution.

Commodities common economic goods, such as agricultural products, that are bought and sold.

Common law body of law formed over time by accumulation of precedents and prior decisions, as opposed to laws enacted by legislative bodies.

Common Sense a pamphlet by Thomas Paine that helped rally public support for the Revolutionary War.

Commonwealth an organization of independent states; official designation (instead of state) of KY, MA, PA, and VA in the United States.

Communism political philosophy advocating collective ownership of property and the means of production and the abolition of the capitalist economic system.

Compact theory of union doctrine held by many states' rights supporters that the Union was a voluntary compact among the states and that states had the right to leave the Union in the same manner they had chosen to enter it.

Compromise of 1850 the results of debate and compromise by Henry Clay, Daniel Webster, Stephen Douglas, and John Calhoun; this set of laws temporarily resolved slavery/sectional balance questions raised by the Mexican War.

Confederate States the eleven Southern states that seceded or officially withdrew from the Union in 1860 and 1861 to form an independent nation called the Confederate States of America. They were defeated in the Civil War and reabsorbed into the Union.

Congress the legislative branch of the federal government; composed of the Senate and the House of Representatives.

Conscription compulsory enrollment into the armed forces; draft.

Consensus general agreement.

Conservative reluctant or resistant to change; favoring traditional views and values.

Constitution the basic charter of the U.S. government, effective since 1789; it was written by the Constitutional Convention in 1787, ratified by the states 1787–1788, and put into effect in 1789.

Constitutionalism belief that government is limited by legal and political restraints and accountable to the governed.

Constitutional Convention gathering of delegates from the thirteen states in 1787 in Philadelphia for the purpose of revising the Articles of Confederation; instead, they drafted an entirely new Constitution that was adopted in 1788 and put into effect in 1789.

Constitutional Republicanism elected government limited by legally defined guidelines.

Consumerism protection of the interests and rights of consumers against false advertising or faulty or dangerous products.

Containment policy adopted by the Western democracies after World War II to prevent the further expansion of communism and the Soviet Union.

Continental Congress (1) any of several assemblies of delegates from the American colonies before the Revolution to promote cooperation on various issues; (2) the national legislative body under the Articles of Confederation (1781–1788).

Cooperative a corporation owned collectively by members who share in the profits and benefits. Cooperatives were first developed by farmers in the late 19th century to avoid high prices charged by middlemen for grain storage, transportation, and farm supplies.

Corollary a proposition that follows a previous one, which it modifies or enlarges, such as the Roosevelt Corollary to the Monroe Doctrine.

Corporation an organization legally empowered to act as one person, including the ability to borrow and lend money, make contracts, own property, and engage in business.

Coup an overturning; a coup d'état is the overthrow of a government.

Court packing attempts by President Franklin Delano Roosevelt in 1937 to increase the number of justices on the Supreme Court in order to ensure passage of his New Deal legislation.

Craft union labor union made up of workers with the same skill or craft, such as carpenters or electricians.

Crédit Mobilier railroad construction company that cheated on government contracts and bribed Congressmen during the late 1860s.

Creditor nation a nation that exports more than it imports, so that it is owed money by other nations.

709

Cuban Missile Crisis October 1962 Cold War crisis that occurred when the Soviet Union placed nuclear missiles in Cuba. Resolved when the Soviets dismantled the missiles and the United States agreed to remove missiles from Turkey and end the Cuban blockade.

Cultural pluralism the acceptance of multiple ethnic, religious, and racial groups within one society; respect for ethnic diversity.

Darwinism (1) the theories of biologist Charles Darwin, who explained the evolution of species by natural selection; (2) social theories loosely based on Darwin's work and arguing that "the survival of the fittest" meant that government should not protect the weak from exploitation by the strong.

Debasement a reduction of value.

Debtor nation a nation that imports more than it exports and so owes money to other nations.

Declaration of Independence document passed and signed by the Continental Congress, effective July 4, 1776, declaring the United States an independent and sovereign nation.

Delegate a representative chosen to act for a group or another person.

Delegated power powers given to the national government by Article I, Section 8 of the United States Constitution.

Demilitarized zone area where no military equipment or personnel may be deployed.

Demobilize to discharge from military service.

Democratic Party political party that evolved out of the Democratic Republicans around 1820.

Democratic Republicans political party formed around 1800 by Jefferson, Madison, and others opposed to the Federalists.

Demographic relating to the statistical study of human populations.

Desegregation the ending of segregation, which is the separation of whites and blacks.

Despot a sovereign or authority without legal restraints; an absolute monarch; tyrant.

Détente relaxation of strained relations or tensions.

Diplomacy the practice of conducting relations between countries by negotiations rather than force.

Direct election election in which votes are cast by the people themselves rather than by their representatives.

Directive order issued by a high authority calling for specific action.

Disarmament giving up or reducing armed forces.

Discrimination partiality, prejudice, or distinctions in treatment; the denial of rights and advantages to minority groups.

Disenfranchise to take away the right to vote.

Dissenting opinion written statement by a member of a court disagreeing with the court's decision.

Distribution of wealth statistical measure of how the property or wealth of a nation is divided among its population.

Dollar diplomacy use of American political and military power abroad (usually in Latin America) to promote or advance the interests of American businesses.

Domino theory belief in the 1950s and 1960s that the fall of one nation to communism would lead to the fall of neighboring nations.

"Don't Ask, Don't Tell" official policy of the United States from 1993–2011 regarding LGBTQ members of the military. The policy prohibited discrimination as long as LGBTQ military personnel did not demonstrate their sexual identity openly.

Due process of law doctrine that government's power cannot be used against an individual except as prescribed by established law. Applied to the state governments by the 14th Amendment.

Dust Bowl an ecological disaster for Plains farmers during the 1930s, which was created in part by bad weather and bad land management.

Eisenhower Doctrine statement made in 1957 by President Eisenhower that the United States would provide military and economic aid—and direct military intervention, if necessary—to nations of the Middle East if they were threatened by communist aggression.

Elastic clause part of the Constitution (Article I, Section 8) that gives the federal government the right to make laws "necessary and proper" to carry out its specific powers and functions; it has sometimes been used to expand the powers of the federal government; also known as the "necessary and proper clause."

Electoral college means of electing President and Vice President established by the Constitution and subsequent amendments; voters in each state choose "electors" who later meet to elect the President and Vice President. Electors were originally free to vote for any candidate they chose, but they are currently pledged to vote for specific candidates. The number of electors from each state is equal to the number of Representatives and Senators from that state.

Emancipation Proclamation issued by President Lincoln in 1863, it declared free the slaves in the Southern states in rebellion but did not affect slaves held in states loyal to the Union, such as Maryland, Kentucky, or Missouri.

Embargo prohibition of commerce with a nation or region, usually to apply pressure or force concessions.

Emigrate to leave one country or region to settle in another.

Encroachment step-by-step interference with the rights or possessions of others.

Enjoin to legally forbid or prohibit, usually by court order or injunction.

Enlightenment era during the 17th and 18th centuries when reason replaced religion as guide to politics, philosophy, and government.

Equal protection principle that all people or classes of persons be treated the same under the law.

Espionage the act or practice of spying.

Ethnic belonging to a particular group identified by nationality or national origin and culture or customs.

Ethnocentric believing that one's own ethnic group is superior to others.

Evolution change over time; an adjustment in the existing order.

Executive person or office having administrative and managerial functions; in government, the branch responsible for carrying out the laws and for the conduct of national affairs; it includes the President and Cabinet and the departments under their jurisdiction.

Executive privilege principle that an executive (such as the President) should not divulge certain sensitive or protected information.

Expansionism policy of adding to a country's territory, usually by seizing land from other nations.

Extraterritoriality right of a resident of a foreign country to be tried in the judicial system of his or her home country.

Fascism political philosophy advocating totalitarian government power, intense nationalism, and military expansionism. Mussolini's Fascist party governed Italy from the 1920s through World War II.

Far East the nations on the Pacific coast of Asia.

Favorable balance of trade exporting or selling more goods than are imported or bought.

Federal relating to the central national government created by the Constitution.

Federal Housing Administration federal agency established in 1934 to

711

insure mortgages and set construction standards.

Federal Reserve Note Currency or paper money issued by the Federal Reserve System and representing a promissory obligation of the federal government.

Federal Reserve System federal agency created by Congress in 1913 to regulate the banking system. Federal Reserve banks in 12 districts supervise banking operations, lend money to banks, and issue currency; a Federal Reserve Commission sets and regulates interest rates.

Federalism system of government in which powers are divided between a central authority and local subdivisions.

Federalists advocates of adopting the Constitution in 1787–1788 and of more powerful central government during the period 1789–1820. Many Federalists later joined the Whig party.

Feminism movement advocating equal rights and privileges for women.

Filibuster use of delaying tactics, such as unlimited debate in one or both houses of Congress, to prevent action on a legislative proposal.

Fiscal having to do with government revenues, expenditures, and budgets.

Foreclosure the act of a lender's taking possession of mortgaged property from a borrower who is unable to make the required payments.

Foreign aid assistance in the form of money or goods supplied to a foreign country.

Foreign policy a nation's policy in dealing with other nations.

Fossil fuels buried combustible geologic deposits of organic materials, formed from decayed plants and animals. Fossil fuels include crude oil, coal, natural gas, etc.

Fourteen Points President Wilson's plan for international peace presented to Congress on January 22, 1918.

Franchise the right to vote; suffrage.

Free enterprise the freedom of private businesses to operate without undue government interference.

Free trade the freedom to exchange goods with other countries, especially without tariffs.

Freedman a freed slave, usually referring to a former slave freed by the Thirteenth Amendment.

Freedom of religion right of citizens to hold and practice religious beliefs without government interference.

Freedom of speech right of citizens to say or write their views without regulation or reprisal from government; restricted in some cases; *see* Clear and present danger.

Freedom of the press right of publishers to print material without prior approval by government; *see* Prior restraint.

Freedom riders civil rights advocates who traveled the South on buses to promote the desegregation of public facilities.

Free-Soil party political party before the Civil War opposed to the extension of slavery and the admission of slave states.

Frontier thesis the historical argument put forth by Professor Frederick Jackson Turner in 1893 that suggested that the spirit and success of the United States was directly tied to the country's westward expansion.

Fugitive Slave Law federal law passed in 1850 that required Northern states to return escaped slaves to their owners in the South. It was widely opposed by a variety of legal and extra-legal means.

Geneva Convention(s) four international treaties created and adopted in Geneva, Switzerland. The Geneva Conventions established much of the international law concerning humanitarian issues.

Genocide systematic annihilation of a particular group, usually racial, ethnic, or political in nature.

Gerrymandering drawing the boundaries of election districts to insure the victory of one party or faction by including or excluding neighborhoods of a particular ethnic or social class.

GI Bill of Rights (1944) congressional legislation granting monthly allowances to World War II veterans for education, loans to purchase farms, businesses, and homes.

Gilded Age in American history the "Gilded Age" refers to the post-Civil War and post-Reconstruction era, from 1865 to 1901, which saw economic, territorial, industrial, and population expansion.

Global warming warming of the planet Earth, which has been taking place throughout the last century. Scientists are more than 90 percent certain that most of it is caused by increasing concentrations of greenhouse gases produced by human activities such as deforestation and burning fossil fuels.

Good Neighbor Policy policy first announced by President Franklin Roosevelt to promote friendly relations with all Latin American nations.

Graduated income tax system of taxation that taxes those with a greater amount of disposable income, sometimes referred to as a progressive tax.

Great Compromise agreement in the Constitutional Convention of 1787 to have two houses of Congress, one (the Senate) to represent the states equally and the other (the House of Representatives) to represent the people proportionately. Also known as the Connecticut Compromise.

Great Depression period from the stock market crash of 1929 until the start of World War II during which industrial production declined and unemployment rose to over one fourth of the labor force.

Great Society collective name for various social programs of President Lyndon Johnson, including the so-called War on Poverty and programs for job-training, subsidized housing, and free medical care for the poor and aged.

Greenhouse effect a global rise in temperature due to the accumulation of certain gases in the atmosphere (carbon dioxide, methane, among others) which traps the Earth's heat.

Green revolution the increase in agricultural crop yields brought about by the use of machinery, fertilizers, pesticides, and improved seeds.

Guerilla an active participant in a war who is not a member of the regular armed forces; a kind of warfare characterized by sabotage, harassment, and hit-and-run tactics.

Habeas corpus a writ or legal order directed to an official holding a person in custody, commanding the official to produce the person in court, show cause why the person has been confined, and prove that the person has not been deprived of liberty without due process.

Harlem Renaissance a movement among black writers, artists, and musicians centered in Harlem, New York City, during the 1920s.

Haymarket Riot 1886 gathering of labor activists and anarchists in Haymarket Square, Chicago, to protest a lockout of Knights of Labor union members by McCormick Harvester Company.

Head Start educational aid to preschool children from disadvantaged homes.

Hessians hired soldiers from the district of Hesse in Germany, employed by the British before and during the Revolutionary War.

Heterogeneous composed of unlike parts; a society made up of different races, nationalities, or ethnic groups.

Holocaust since World War II, it refers to the genocidal murders of six million European Jews by the Nazis.

Homestead Act passed by Congress in 1862, it gave 160 acres of Western land to any head of a family who agreed to cultivate it for five years; it encouraged the rapid settlement of the West by giving immigrants and Easterners free land.

Homogeneous made up of similar elements; a society consisting primarily of the same race, nationality, or ethnic group.

House of Burgesses (1619) first elected legislative body in the English Colonies (Virginia).

House of Representatives the half of Congress composed of representatives allotted among the states according to their population.

Immigration moving into a country where one is not a native to become a permanent resident.

Impeach to bring formal charges against a public official for misconduct. The House of Representatives has the power to impeach federal officials, and the trial is held by the Senate.

Imperialism the practice of forming and maintaining an empire; possession of foreign territories or colonies for the benefit of the home country; the policy of seeking to dominate economically, politically, or militarily weaker areas of the world.

Import quota a limit on the amount of a commodity that can be brought into the country.

Inauguration a ceremonial beginning, especially the installing of an official at the beginning of a term.

Incumbent person currently serving in political office.

Indians European term for the native inhabitants of the Americas.

Industrialization economic transformation of society by the development of large industries, machine production, factories, and an urban work force.

Industrial Revolution the transformation from an agricultural society to one based upon large-scale mechanized production and factory organization. It began in Europe (especially England)

in the late 18th century and in America in the early 19th century.

Industrial Workers of the World Labor movement formed in 1905 under the leadership of Big Bill Haywood. Advocated militant agitation and damage to businesses if necessary to obtain demands. Also known as the Wobblies.

Infiltration gradual entrance or buildup with the intent of taking control.

Inflation general and continuing rise in the price of goods, often due to the relative increase of available money and credit.

Initiative process for the direct involvement of voters in the making of laws; by gathering enough signatures on a petition, a group can force a legislature to consider a proposal or require it to be placed on the ballot for public vote.

Injunction order issued by a court directing someone to do or refrain from doing some specific act.

Insurgency an uprising or revolt against an established authority, short of actual declared war.

Integration bringing together or making as one; unification; applied especially to blacks and whites.

Interdependent depending on one another, such as nations that rely on each other's trade.

Internal improvements roads, canals, and other means to assist transportation and commerce.

Internationalism policy of cooperation among nations.

Internment the detainment and isolation of ethnic groups for purposes of national security (such as Japanese Americans during World War II); this is now widely held to have been unconstitutional.

Interposition an argument that the states could legitimately object to acts of Congress if those acts exceeded Congress's legitimate authority. Interposition fell short of Nullification.

Interstate taking place across state lines; involving the citizens of more than one state.

Interstate Commerce Commission established by Congress in 1887 to regulate railroad rates and prevent abuses by railroads; it was later expanded to have jurisdiction over other forms of transportation.

Intervention interference in the affairs of another country, including the use of force.

Intolerable Acts series of acts of Parliament directed against the American colonies and intended to assert British authority and increase revenues from the colonies.

Invalidate to make null and void.

Iran-Contra Affair an illegal conspiracy by officials of the Reagan administration to provide funding for the anti-communist Contra rebels in Nicaragua by secretly selling missiles to Iran and diverting the money to the Nicaraguans.

Iron Curtain the series of fortified borders separating Western Europe from Soviet-dominated Eastern Europe; term made popular by Winston Churchill.

Isolationism policy of keeping a nation apart from alliances or other political relations with foreign nations.

Jacksonian Democracy the phrase "Jacksonian Democracy" has been the subject of much debate because, on one hand, it is the term that refers to the political platform of Andrew Jackson and his party, but the broader meaning, as described in Alexis de Tocqueville's classic *Democracy in America* (1835), suggests the blossoming of the democratic spirit in American life around the time of Jackson's presidency.

Jim Crow laws laws enforcing segregation or control of blacks in such a way as to make them unequal.

Joint resolution a legislative act that is the same in both houses of Congress.

Judicial activism developing social policy through court decisions instead of through legislative action, often in response to changing values and circumstances.

Judicial nationalism term used to describe the Supreme Court under the leadership of John Marshall, when its decisions consolidated the power of the federal government by centralizing responsibility for commerce, contracts, and finance.

Judicial restraint the preference of a court to avoid upsetting existing law or practice.

Judicial review power of the Supreme Court to void acts of Congress that are found to violate the Constitution.

Judiciary the branch of government that interprets the law and tries cases; the system of courts.

Jurisdiction authority of a court to interpret and apply the law; in general, the area of authority of a government.

Kansas-Nebraska Act (1854) Congressional legislation that provided for popular sovereignty to be applied to the Kansas Territory and the Nebraska Territory, assuming that Kansas would be slave and Nebraska would be free.

Kellogg-Briand Pact (1928) pact eventually signed by 62 nations "condemning recourse to war for the solution to international controversies."

Knights of Labor early labor union, formed in 1869.

Kremlin complex of government offices in Moscow; the center of government of Russia and the former Soviet Union.

Ku Klux Klan secret organization founded in 1866 to intimidate freed slaves and keep them in conditions of servitude through threats and acts of violence; it later developed into a nativist organization opposed to Jews, Catholics, and immigrants, as well as African Americans.

Laissez-faire doctrine opposing government regulation of economic matters beyond what is necessary to maintain property rights and enforce contracts. *Laissez-faire* is French for "let alone" or "let be."

Lame duck an official who has not been reelected and is serving out the remainder of a term.

League of Nations International organization of countries formed after World War I to promote world peace. It was supported by President Wilson, but the Senate refused to allow the United States to join. After World War II it was replaced by the United Nations.

Legislature a body of persons elected to make laws for a nation or state; a congress or parliament.

Lend-Lease Act (1941) congressional legislation that allowed the sale, transfer, exchange, or lease of war equipment to any nation for use in the interests of the United States.

Liberal advocating political or social views that emphasize civil rights, democratic reforms, and the use of government to promote social progress.

Line-item veto power of an executive to veto specific provisions of a bill without vetoing the entire bill that contains them. The President does not have line-item veto power.

Lobbying actions by private citizens or organizations seeking to influence (by legal means) the decisions of a legislature or executive department of government.

Loose construction, loose interpretation reading of the Constitution that allows broad use of the elastic clause and implied powers.

Louisiana Purchase the purchase from France by the United States in 1803 for $15 million of the Louisiana Territory, stretching from New Orleans west to the Rocky Mountains, more than doubling the size of the United States.

Loyalists American colonists who remained loyal to England during the American Revolution; also known as Tories.

Magna Carta agreement signed by King John I of England in 1215, granting certain rights (including trial by jury and habeas corpus) to the barons who had taken him prisoner.

Manifest Destiny belief, held by many Americans in the 19th century, that the United States was destined to control the continent between the Atlantic and Pacific Oceans.

March on Washington (1963) civil rights massive demonstration in Washington, D.C. Site of Martin Luther King's "I Have a Dream" speech. The march was attended by some 250,000 people; it was the largest demonstration ever seen in the nation's capital and one of the first to have extensive television coverage.

Market economy an economic system in which decisions about production and pricing are based on the actions of buyers and sellers in the marketplace; usually associated with capitalism.

Marshall Plan the program of U.S. aid to Europe following World War II to help those nations recover from the extensive damage to their cities, industries, and transportation.

Mayflower Compact an agreement made by Pilgrims and others aboard the Mayflower (1620) which established a civil government for "the general Good of the Plymouth Colony."

McCarthyism term that had its origin in the investigative methods of Senator Joseph McCarthy (1950s) and came to mean the practice of making accusations of disloyalty, especially of pro-Communist activity, in many instances unsupported by proof.

Mediator person who solves differences between two parties. Both sides do not usually agree beforehand to accept the decisions of the mediator, as they usually do with an arbitrator.

Mercantilism the economic policies of European nations from the 15th century until the Industrial Revolution, based on mercantile (commercial, trading) activities and characterized by the acquisition of colonies and the establishment of a favorable balance of trade. The American colonies were established under the mercantile system.

Mexican War military conflict fought between the United States and Mexico from 1846 to 1848 resulting in the U.S. gain of the Mexican Cession.

Middle class the members of a society having a socio-economic position between the very wealthy and the poor.

Militaristic characterized by military discipline and aggressiveness.

Military-industrial complex the combined power of the Defense Department and the industries that supply it with equipment. The phrase was popularized by Eisenhower, who claimed that it worked for unnecessary increases in armaments.

Militia part-time soldiers who do not belong to the regular armed forces.

Minimum wage federally established minimum hourly wage that can be paid to most workers. Adopted in the United States at the federal level in 1938. Currently $7.25/hour (July 2009). Many states have raised their own considerably higher than the federal government's rate.

Missouri Compromise an agreement in 1820 between Congressional advocates and opponents of the extension of slavery that preserved sectional balance. It included the simultaneous admission of the slave state Missouri and the free state Maine and the prohibition of slavery in the northern parts of the Louisiana Purchase.

Monopoly the exclusive control or ownership of an industry by a single person or company.

Monroe Doctrine policy announced in 1823, during the presidency of James Monroe, that the United States would oppose European attempts to extend their control of the Western Hemisphere. It became and remains a basic principle of American foreign policy.

Montgomery bus boycott (1954) in response to the arrest of Rosa Parks for violating city Jim Crow ordinances, a 381 day refusal by many in Montgomery, Alabama, to use public transportation. Led by Martin Luther King, Jr. The city and the bus companies removed the segregationist policies.

Moratorium agreement to postpone payment of a debt or other obligation.

Muckraker journalists in the late 19th and early 20th centuries who reported on political or commercial corruption.

Munitions armaments and ammunition used in warfare.

NAACP National Association for the Advancement of Colored People formed in 1909 by, among others, Jane Addams, W. E. B. DuBois, and John Dewey.

NAFTA North American Free Trade Agreement (1994). Agreement between the United States, Canada, and Mexico to encourage the reduction of trade duties and tariffs.

Nationalism (1) sense of pride in one's country; (2) extreme devotion to national interests.

National Labor Relations Board federal agency established in 1935 to enforce laws against unfair labor practices.

National Origins Act laws passed in 1921, 1924, and 1929 that limited immigration into the United States and established quotas for nations based on the number of persons from those nations living in the United States according to an earlier census. It was regarded as discriminatory because it favored immigrants from Western Europe.

Native one who is connected with a place by birth; an original inhabitant as distinguished from immigrants or visitors.

Native Americans original inhabitants of the Americas and their descendants.

Nativism in the United States, the policy of favoring native-born Americans and opposing immigrants.

Naturalization the process of conferring citizenship upon an immigrant.

Natural rights rights or liberties to which one is entitled as a human being, as distinguished from those that are created by laws or governments.

Necessary and proper clause portion of the Constitution granting Congress power to "make all Laws which shall be necessary and proper for carrying into Execution" its other powers.

Neutrality policy of not helping either side in a war.

Neutrality Acts laws passed in 1935 and 1937 to avoid U.S. involvement in a war in Europe; they placed an embargo on arms sales to any nation engaged in war.

New Deal name adopted by President Franklin Roosevelt for the reforms and social programs instituted by his administration, beginning in 1933.

New Freedom program of President Wilson to regulate banking and currency to influence the direction of the economy and to support stronger antitrust legislation.

New Nationalism program of President Theodore Roosevelt during his unsuccessful campaign for the presidency in 1912. It promised greater government supervision of the economy to balance the power of big business.

Nineteenth Amendment granted suffrage (the right to vote) to women; enacted in 1920.

Nonintervention policy of not becoming involved in the affairs of other nations.

Nonpartisan not based on party interests or bias.

Nonsectarian not affiliated with any religious group.

Normalcy the state of being normal; the term was applied to the era of the 1920s, following the disruptions of World War I.

North Atlantic Treaty Organization (NATO) collective security military alliance formed in 1949 by the United States, Canada, and nations of Western Europe to oppose the threat posed by the Soviet Union and Warsaw Pact nations to Europe.

Northwest Territory federal administrative district west of the Allegheny Mountains, north of the Ohio River, south of the Great Lakes, and east of the Mississippi River, including the present states of Ohio, Indiana, Michigan, Illinois, and Wisconsin, and part of Minnesota. The Territory was organized by the Continental Congress in 1787 from lands claimed by several eastern states.

Nullification argument or doctrine claiming that states could refuse to abide by acts of Congress if the states felt Congress had exceeded its enumerated powers. Used by states' rights advocates; championed by John C. Calhoun of South Carolina.

Nuremberg Tribunal international military court held in Nuremberg, Germany, in 1945–46; top Nazi leaders were tried and convicted of crimes against humanity and violations of international law.

Occupy Movement among the prime concerns of the movement begun in the summer, 2011, is the claim that big corporations and the global financial system control the world in an unstable way that benefits only few and is undermining democracy.

Open Door policy an attempt by the United States in 1899 to preserve trade interests in China by asking European nations to respect the territorial integrity of China and to permit free access to ports they held in Asia.

Ordinance a law or regulation, usually of a local municipality.

Organized labor workers represented by labor unions.

Original jurisdiction the first court with authority to consider and decide a case, as opposed to appellate jurisdiction.

Parity government support of prices for agricultural products to insure that farm income keeps pace with income in other economic sectors.

Parliament the legislative body of Great Britain, consisting of the House of Commons and the House of Lords.

Partition division of a country into two or more separate parts.

PATRIOT Act this anti-terrorism legislation was passed during the administration of George Bush in response to the attacks of September 11, 2001.

Peace Corps U.S. government agency formed by President Kennedy in 1961; it sought to assist developing countries by sending American volunteers to teach and provide technical assistance.

Pentagon headquarters of the U.S. armed forces, near Washington, D.C.

Persian Gulf War (1990–1991) war following Iraq's invasion of Kuwait. Mandated by United Nations and led by United States forces with a coalition of approximately 30 nations.

Plea bargaining pleading guilty to a lesser charge in order to avoid standing trial for a more serious one.

Pluralistic type of society in which diverse ethnic, racial, and national groups coexist while maintaining their own cultural heritage.

Plurality a number of votes greater than any other candidate but less than a majority of all the votes cast.

Pocket veto an automatic veto that occurs if the President does not sign a bill passed by Congress during the last ten days of its session.

Pogrom organized, officially encouraged persecution or massacre of a group.

Political machine combination of party and political officials who maintain themselves in office, sometimes through corrupt means.

Poll tax (1) a tax paid to register or vote in elections (prohibited under the Twenty-Fourth Amendment); (2) a per-person or per-capita tax, not based on income or employment.

Pools business agreements designed to fix prices and divide profits.

Popular sovereignty 1) doctrine in democratic forms of government that power ultimately derives from the people and that the consent of the governed is exercised through the vote; 2) in the years before the Civil War, a political position advocating that the legality of slavery in the western territories be decided by popular vote of the inhabitants; it was ridiculed by its opponents as "squatter sovereignty."

Populism movement that began in agricultural areas in the late 19th century seeking government regulation to curb excesses and exploitation by big business.

Power of the purse the power to authorize revenues and spending; in the federal government, Congress holds the power of the purse.

Pragmatism belief in a practical (rather than an ethical or theoretical) approach to problems and affairs.

Preamble introductory part, especially the opening of the Constitution, which begins "We the people . . ."

Precedence the right to be first or have more authority.

Precedent rule or decision that serves as a guide for future actions or decisions.

President the chief executive officer of the federal government.

Price supports government measures to maintain the price of a commodity at an artificially set level.

Prior restraint the prohibition of publication of an article, book, or story by a court order before the material is disclosed to the public. Permissible only in cases of obscenity or of "clear and present danger."

Primary election election in which members of a political party choose their candidates for the upcoming election.

Progressive Era the period roughly from 1900 to 1920, marked by political, economic, and social reform movements.

Progressive tax a tax that is higher for the wealthy than for the poor, such as income tax.

Progressivism a broad reform movement during the late 19th and early 20th centuries that sought to remedy the worst effects of industrialism and urbanization by imposing governmental controls on big business, improving social justice, and increasing direct democratic participation in politics.

Prohibition period from the enactment of the 18th Amendment in 1919 until its repeal by the 21st Amendment in 1933, during which the manufacture, sale, import, export, and transportation of alcoholic beverages was illegal.

Proletariat the industrial working class, who sell their labor and do not own the means of production.

Protective tariff tax on imported goods intended to protect the interests of internal or domestic industries by raising the price of imports.

Protectorate an area under the control and protection of a country that does not have full sovereignty over it.

Proviso clause in a document or statute making some condition or provision.

Pullman strike (1894) strike by Pullman Car Company workers under the leadership of American Railway Union president Eugene V. Debs. President Cleveland sent federal troops to end strike in the interest of "protecting the delivery of the mails."

Pure Food and Drug Act (1906) congressional legislation during the progressive administration of President Theodore Roosevelt requiring the contents of food and drug preparations be described on the labels of the product.

Quartering forcibly housing soldiers in private residences.

Quota a maximum limit; a share or portion assigned to a group.

Racism belief that some races are inherently superior to others.

Radical, Radicalism favoring extreme and fundamental changes.

Ratification formal legal approval and adoption.

Rearmament rebuilding of a nation's armed forces, often with new and better weapons.

Recall political reform procedure for removing a public official from office before the end of a term by popular vote; it is usually initiated by a petition.

Reconstruction period from 1865 through 1876, when Southern states were occupied by federal troops and under the control of the national government.

Red Scare fears about the danger of communist subversion or invasion; after World War II, "Red Scare" tactics were used by Senator Joseph McCarthy and others for political purposes.

Referendum a proposal submitted to a popular vote before putting it into effect.

Reform to improve or change, especially a social institution.

Regulatory enforcing the rules or laws.

Reparations payments imposed on nations defeated in war to help the victors recover the costs of war.

Representative (1) a delegate or agent of another person or group of people; (2) a federal legislator; (3) a type of government by persons chosen from among the governed, usually by election.

Republican Party political party formed in the 1840s, opposed to the extension of slavery; Lincoln was the first Republican elected President (in 1860).

Reserved powers powers not specifically granted to Congress or the federal government under the Constitution, and so held to be reserved to the states.

Restraint of trade language used in the Sherman Antitrust Act (1890) to describe combinations and activities of groups (businesses, labor unions) that were prohibited under the Act.

Return to normalcy Republican campaign slogan of Warren G. Harding in 1920 following World War I.

Revenue the income of governments from taxation, tariffs, and other fees.

Right to counsel entitlement of an accused person to have an attorney present during questioning or trial.

Rights individual liberties protected by the state or federal constitutions.

Rights of Englishmen an expression of the American colonists during their struggle with England; they claimed to want only the same liberties and privileges enjoyed by British subjects in England, as established by Magna Carta, common law, and the English Bill of Rights, including habeas corpus, trial by jury, and representation in Parliament.

Rights of the accused include the 5th Amendment guarantee against self-incrimination and the right to counsel, also known as "Miranda rights," after the Supreme Court decision in the case of *Miranda* v. *Arizona* (1966).

Roaring Twenties the decade between the end of World War I and the beginning of the Great Depression.

Robber barons business owners of the latter part of the 19th century who often used unscrupulous methods to make their fortunes.

Roosevelt Corollary supplement to the Monroe Doctrine asserted by President Theodore Roosevelt, who claimed the right of the United States to exercise international police power in the Western Hemisphere and to intervene in the affairs of Latin American nations.

Rosie the Riveter World War II icon demonstrating the domestic contributions of women in the war effort.

"Rule of Reason" term used by the Supreme Court in its decision in the case of *Standard Oil Co.* v. *United States* (1911), which held that only "bad" trusts were illegal.

Salutary neglect phrase describing the belief that the American colonies benefited from lack of interest in their affairs by the British government during the period before 1763.

Satellite state a nation controlled by a more powerful nation.

Scopes trial the trial of John T. Scopes in Dayton, Tennessee, in 1925 for violating a state law prohibiting the teaching of Darwinian evolution. William Jennings Bryan was the prosecutor and Clarence Darrow represented Scopes, who was found guilty and fined $100.

Search and seizure police power to look for and hold evidence in the investigation and prosecution of a crime; evidence from unreasonable searches or searches without probable cause may be excluded from a trial.

Secession withdrawal of a member from a political group; withdrawal of a state from the Union.

Sectarian a member of a sect, which is a group of people forming a distinct unit within a larger group.

Sectionalism development of internal divisions based on geographic and economic alliances; rivalry between different areas of the country.

Securities and Exchange Commission federal agency established in 1934 to regulate the stock market and to prevent the abuses practiced during the 1920s that led to the stock market crash of 1929.

Sedition the act of stirring up rebellion against a government.

Segregation the isolation or separation of one group from another, usually applied to keeping whites and blacks apart.

Senate   the part of the federal legislature made up of two members from each state.

Seneca Falls Convention   convention held in Seneca Falls, New York, on July 19–20, 1848. It was the first women's rights convention held in the United States.

Separate but equal   legal doctrine established by the Supreme Court in the case of *Plessy* v. *Ferguson* (1896) that separate accommodations for blacks and whites did not violate the Fourteenth Amendment if the accommodations were of equal quality. Overruled by the later Supreme Court decision in *Brown* v. *Board of Education* (1954).

Separation of church and state   doctrine that government may not restrict the free exercise of religious beliefs nor support any religious group or principle.

Separation of powers   doctrine that liberty of the people is best assured by the division of government into separate branches. *See also* Checks and balances.

Sexual harassment   policy or practice of compelling female employees to submit to the sexual advances of male superiors or to endure verbal or physical harassment, in violation of the Civil Rights Act of 1964.

Sharecroppers   tenant farmers who leased and cultivated pieces of land in exchange for a percentage of the crop.

Shays' Rebellion   armed insurrection in western Massachusetts in the fall of 1786 led by Captain Daniel Shays and others in protest against economic policies and foreclosures of farms for failure to pay taxes. It was suppressed by the state militia, but it had a significant effect on the framing of the Constitution the following summer.

Sherman Antitrust Act   passed in 1890 declaring combinations in restraint of trade to be illegal; it was passed to maintain competition in private industry and to correct abuses of companies that had gained monopoly power.

Sit-in   action of protesters in occupying a public place to force concessions; especially by civil rights advocates seeking desegregation of public facilities.

Social contract   the implied agreement among individuals in a community or between the people and their rulers.

Socialism   political philosophy advocating ownership and operation of the means of production (such as land, mines, factories) by society as a collective whole, with all members sharing in the work and benefits. Socialist economic systems usually include government ownership and operation of industries.

Social mobility   movement up or down the class scale within a society.

Social Security Act   passed in 1935 to provide an income for persons who are disabled or aged and for families without a wage earner; it has become the basic means of support for retired persons who lack private pensions from employers.

Social welfare   organized services for helping disadvantaged people.

Sovereign   holding supreme authority.

Sovereignty   the ultimate power and authority to make laws, either directly or through representatives; in a democracy, sovereignty lies in the people.

Special interest   group or industry that seeks to influence government for its own benefit.

Spoils system   system wherein government positions and offices are awarded to political supporters on the basis of party loyalty or service rather than qualification or merit; based on the saying "To the victor go the spoils"; the system was replaced to some extent by the Civil Service in the 1880s.

Stamp Act   enacted by Parliament in 1765, it required a tax stamp on all printed and legal documents. It was soon repealed after American resistance.

Star-Spangled Banner the name by which the flag of the United States is known.

States' rights group of doctrines holding that the states retained the power to overrule, oppose, or withdraw from the federal government if they chose.

Stock market crash a rapid fall in the price of stocks. The great crash of 1929 was caused by overspeculation that increased stock prices far above their true value; prices started to fall when knowledgeable investors began to sell their shares; that forced speculators, who had invested with borrowed money, to sell as well, and the combined rush to sell caused a panic, which drove prices even lower.

Strict construction doctrine that the Constitution limits governmental powers to those explicitly stated; contrast with Loose construction.

Subjugation the act of bringing under control.

Subpoena official written order commanding a person to appear in court or to produce specific items.

Subsidiary in business, a company that is controlled by another company.

Subversion the undermining, overthrowing, or destroying of an established institution, such as government.

Suffrage the right to vote.

Supremacy clause portion of the Constitution declaring it "the supreme law of the land" and overriding any state or local laws in conflict with it.

Supreme Court the highest court in the federal judicial branch.

Taliban Islamist militant and political group that ruled large parts of Afghanistan and its capital, Kabul, from September 1996 until October 2001. It gained diplomatic recognition from only three states: Pakistan, Saudi Arabia, and the United Arab Emirates. The main leader of the Taliban movement is Mullah Mohammed Omar. Today the Taliban continue to operate in Afghanistan and northwest Pakistan.

Tariff taxes on imports into a country to collect revenues or to protect domestic industries.

Tea Party an American populist political movement that is generally recognized as conservative and libertarian. The movement has supported political candidates since 2009.

Teapot Dome federal oil reserve in Wyoming that was secretly and illegally leased to a financial backer of President Harding.

Temperance moderation in the consumption of alcoholic beverages; a movement supporting governmental measures to curb alcohol consumption.

Tennessee Valley Authority federal public works project established in 1933 that constructed dams and reengineered waterways to control flooding and generate electricity in seven Southern states.

Tenure the act or right of holding an office.

Terrorism the use of violence as unconventional warfare to intimidate a population. Terrorists usually do not belong to any recognized national armed force.

Third parties political parties existing at various times in the United States other than the two predominant political parties.

Third World the group of nations, especially in Asia and Africa, that were not aligned with either the Communist bloc or the Western democracies.

Three-fifths clause clause in the Constitution saying that three-fifths of the number of persons held as slaves be included in calculating representation in Congress, even though those persons were not citizens and were not entitled to vote. Superceded by the Fourteenth Amendment.

"Too Big to Fail" term that implies certain financial institutions are so large and so interconnected that their failure will be disastrous to an economy, and therefore a government has a responsibility to support them when they face difficulty.

Tories supporters of British rule during the Revolutionary War; also known as Loyalists.

Totalitarian characterized by the government's having total control over the lives of citizens.

Town meeting meeting of the citizens of a town as a legislative body.

Trade deficit the amount by which imports exceed exports; how much is owed to other nations.

Trade gap difference in amount between imports and exports.

Trail of Tears the forced relocation in 1838 of, among others, the Cherokee Native American tribe to the Western United States, which resulted in the deaths of an estimated 4,000 Cherokees. The Cherokees were not the only Native Americans forced to emigrate as a result of the Indian Removal efforts of the United States.

Treason acts that intentionally endanger the security or sovereignty of one's own nation; waging war against one's country or giving aid to its enemies.

Triangular trade pattern of commerce pursued in the late 18th and early 19th centuries by New England merchants who carried sugar and molasses from the West Indies to New England, rum and manufactured goods from New England to Africa, and slaves from Africa to the West Indies.

Truman Doctrine policy announced by President Truman in 1947, stating that the United States would provide military and economic aid to nations threatened by subversion or invasion; it was established specifically to assist Greece and Turkey, which were threatened with communist takeover.

Trust a combination of companies or industries established to reduce competition and increase profits.

Tweed Ring Followers of William M. Tweed, 1860s and 1870s corrupt political boss of New York City's Democratic Party (Tammany Hall). Exposed by cartoonist Thomas Nast.

Tyranny absolute and arbitrary power without legal restraints.

Uncle Tom's Cabin inflammatory 1851 anti-slavery literary work by Harriet Beecher Stowe. Sold 300,000 copies in one year.

Unconditional surrender total surrender without exceptions or conditions; the phrase was made popular by Ulysses S. Grant.

Unconstitutional prohibited by or in opposition to the principles of the Constitution.

Underclass class of the permanently poor.

Underground railroad extensive system of escape routes for slaves coming to the north and many on to Canada. Harriet Tubman; underground railroad conductor.

Unicameral of a legislature, having only one house or chamber.

Union (1) the political combination of the states; (2) the northern and border states that opposed secession during the Civil War; (3) an organization of workers seeking collective bargaining with their employer.

United Nations an organization of over 150 nations formed in 1945 to deal with international disputes and threats to world peace.

Universal suffrage the right of all citizens to vote, regardless of sex, race, or economic status.

Unwritten Constitution governmental practices and institutions not specifically set down in the Constitution but based upon custom and practice.

Utopian advocating impossibly idealistic or impractical forms of government or society.

Versailles Treaty peace treaty signed in 1919 between Germany and the Allies; it required Germany to give up its colonies, pay substantial reparations, and surrender territory to France, Poland, and Czechoslovakia.

Veto action by an executive official preventing the enactment of a legislative act. A veto by the President can be overridden by a two-thirds majority of Congress. *See also* Pocket veto.

VISTA Volunteers in Service to America, a program of President Johnson's 1964 Economic Opportunity Act.

Wagner Act (1935) New Deal legislation that established the National Labor Relations Board to solve labor/management disputes and avoid strikes and job actions.

War on Poverty President Johnson's domestic programs for social renovation, including the VISTA, Job Corps, and Head Start programs and the establishing of the Department of Housing and Urban Development.

War Powers Act law passed in 1973 to limit the power of the President to use armed forces in combat without the authorization of Congress; it was adopted in response to the Vietnam War, in which millions of armed forces were sent to Vietnam without a declaration of war.

Warsaw Pact organization of Soviet-led countries in response to the 1949 creation of the North Atlantic Treaty Organization.

Watergate hotel in Washington, D.C., where the national Democratic Party headquarters were burglarized in 1972 by operatives of the Republican Committee to re-elect the President (Nixon). Attempts by the White House staff to cover up links to the burglars led to a widespread scandal and the resignation of President Nixon.

Weapons of mass destruction (WMD) arms that have the ability to kill massive numbers of people. Usually refers to nuclear, chemical, biological, and radiological weapons.

Whigs in the United States from around 1800 until the Civil War, a political party opposed to the Jeffersonian Republicans and Jacksonian Democrats. Many of its supporters later joined the Republican Party.

Whiskey Rebellion armed insurrection in 1792 by settlers in western Pennsylvania and Virginia protesting federal excise tax on distilled spirits (whiskey). Suppressed by federal troops under Washington, who pardoned most of the participants.

Yalta Agreements agreements reached between Roosevelt, Churchill, and Stalin at Yalta in February 1945, regarding the organization of postwar Europe in anticipation of the defeat of Germany. The agreements divided Germany and Berlin into temporary zones of occupation and established the basis for the United Nations.

Yellow journalism irresponsible, sensational, or misleading reporting of news.

Zimmermann note (1917) publication of German correspondence with Mexico in which Germany promised Mexico recovery of the Mexican Cession if Mexico would assist Germany in the world war. It inflamed anti-Germany feelings.

Examination
June 2019
United States History and Government

PART I: MULTIPLE CHOICE

Write in the space provided.

Directions (1–50): For each statement or question, write in the space provided the *number* of the word or expression that, of those given, best completes the statement or answers the question.

1 In colonial America, the Magna Carta, the English Bill of Rights, and the writings of John Locke contributed to the

  (1) diversity of religious beliefs among the colonists

  (2) political ideals and practices of the colonists

  (3) economic relationships between the colonists and the mother country

  (4) demands of colonists to end the slave trade and the practice of slavery   1 _____

2 Before 1763, most American colonists settled near the Atlantic Coast or rivers because

  (1) port cities could be more easily defended in times of war

  (2) valleys were less fertile

  (3) English colonists were only allowed to settle in these locations

  (4) navigable water offered easier access to trade and employment   2 _____

3 One way in which the Declaration of Independence and the original United States Constitution are similar is that both promote the idea of

(1) the consent of the governed
(2) equal rights for women
(3) voting rights for all adult citizens
(4) judicial review of unjust laws   3 _____

4 The main purpose of the Federalist Papers was to

(1) discourage the creation of political parties
(2) support the candidacy of George Washington
(3) urge ratification of the Constitution
(4) advocate independence from Great Britain   4 _____

5 ". . . Constitutions should consist only of general provisions: The reason is, that they must necessarily be permanent, and that they cannot calculate for the possible changes of things. . . ."

— Alexander Hamilton, 1788

Which provision of the United States Constitution best supports the idea expressed in this quotation?

(1) eminent domain
(2) electoral college
(3) separation of powers
(4) elastic clause   5 _____

6 The main objection to the adoption of the United States Constitution was based primarily on the belief that

(1) the number of new states admitted to the Union should be limited
(2) individual freedoms could be restricted by a strong central government
(3) a separate judiciary would make the government ineffective
(4) slave populations gave the South too much power   6 _____

7 Which viewpoint of the framers of the United States Constitution is demonstrated by the use of the electoral college to select the president?

(1) distrust of the average citizen's judgment
(2) belief that political parties strengthen the campaign process
(3) desire to end property qualifications for voting
(4) commitment to universal suffrage

7 _____

Base your answer to question 8 on the diagram below and on your knowledge of social studies.

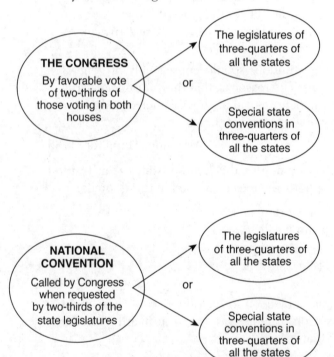

THE CONGRESS

By favorable vote of two-thirds of those voting in both houses

or

The legislatures of three-quarters of all the states

Special state conventions in three-quarters of all the states

NATIONAL CONVENTION

Called by Congress when requested by two-thirds of the state legislatures

or

The legislatures of three-quarters of all the states

Special state conventions in three-quarters of all the states

Source: National Archives (adapted)

8 What is the best title for this diagram?

(1) Methods of Amending the Constitution
(2) Procedures of the Executive Branch
(3) Process of Nominating Presidential Candidates
(4) Admission of New States to the Union

8 _____

9 The United States wanted to acquire New Orleans in 1803 in order to

(1) end British influence in North America
(2) promote the growth of manufacturing in the region
(3) establish a military base to defend against attacks from Mexico
(4) secure a port that would improve the transportation of agricultural goods

9 _____

10 The Supreme Court decision in *Gibbons v. Ogden* (1824) is important because it

(1) banned the importation of manufactured goods
(2) encouraged state investment in internal improvements
(3) expanded federal control over interstate commerce
(4) permitted taxes on exported goods

10 _____

11 Under Chief Justice John Marshall (1801–1835), Supreme Court decisions generally upheld Alexander Hamilton's belief that

(1) a national debt would violate the economic principles of the Constitution
(2) states should have more economic power than the federal government
(3) the power of Congress should be greater than the power of the president
(4) a loose interpretation of the Constitution could be used to increase federal power

11 _____

Base your answer to question 12 on the passage below and on your knowledge of social studies.

. . . I am not a Know-Nothing. That is certain. How could I be? How can any one who abhors the oppression of negroes [African Americans], be in favor of degrading classes of white people? Our progress in degeneracy appears to me to be pretty rapid. As a nation, we began by declaring that *"all men are created equal."* We now practically read it "all men are created equal, *except negroes."* When the Know-Nothings get control, it will read "all men are created equal, except negroes, *and foreigners, and catholics."* When it comes to this I should prefer emigrating to some country where they make no pretence of loving liberty—to Russia, for instance, where despotism can be taken pure, and without the base alloy of hypocracy. . . .

— Abraham Lincoln, letter to Joshua Speed,
August 24, 1855

12 In this 1855 letter, Abraham Lincoln opposed the Know-Nothing party because it

(1) supported the policy of imperialism
(2) favored unrestricted immigration
(3) promoted resentment against minority groups
(4) wanted equal rights for all people

12 _____

13 The Supreme Court's decision in *Dred Scott* v. *Sanford* was nullified by the passage of the

(1) Kansas-Nebraska Act
(2) 13th and 14th amendments
(3) Compromise of 1850
(4) Reconstruction Act

13 _____

14 The Civil War directly affected the Northern economy by

(1) causing a severe depression
(2) destroying much of its farmland
(3) greatly expanding the canal system
(4) stimulating the growth of factories

14 _____

15 Rapid industrialization during the late 1800s contributed to

   (1) a decline in the membership of the American Federation of Labor (AFL)
   (2) a reduction in government regulation of railroads
   (3) a rise in the number of family farms
   (4) an increase in immigration to the United States   15 _____

16 Which factor aided the building of transcontinental railroads?

   (1) The federal government provided free land to the railroad companies.
   (2) The railroads established fair rates for customers.
   (3) Congress repealed antitrust laws against the railroads.
   (4) The Supreme Court approved public ownership of the railroad industry.   16 _____

17 Which tactics were used by big business during the late 1800s to limit the power of labor unions?

   (1) strikebreakers and lockouts
   (2) picketing and walkouts
   (3) collective bargaining and mediation
   (4) wage increases and shorter hours   17 _____

18 Which constitutional right was the central focus in *Plessy* v. *Ferguson* (1896)?

   (1) freedom of assembly guaranteed by the first amendment
   (2) due process of the law in the fifth amendment
   (3) equal protection of the law under the 14th amendment
   (4) equal voting rights guaranteed by the 15th amendment   18 _____

Base your answer to question 19 on the cartoon below and on your knowledge of social studies.

The Monster Monopoly

Source: Frank Beard, *Judge,* July 19, 1884 (adapted)

19 What is being criticized in this cartoon?

    (1) environmental damage   (3) oil exploration

    (2) business consolidation   (4) federal tax laws   19 ____

20 Which event was a result of the Spanish-American War?

(1) Cuba was divided into spheres of influence.
(2) Puerto Rico became a possession of the United States.
(3) The Philippines became a Spanish colony.
(4) The United States lost control of the Panama Canal. 20 _____

21 • Chinese Exclusion Act (1882)

• Gentlemen's Agreement (1907)

• Emergency Quota Act (1921)

These federal actions demonstrate that Americans have

(1) supported the principle of open immigration
(2) provided immigrants equal access to jobs and social programs
(3) forced immigrants to settle in designated areas
(4) favored limiting immigration at different times in the nation's history 21 _____

22 In the early 20th century, muckraking authors Upton Sinclair and Ida Tarbell primarily criticized the federal government for

(1) wasting money on foreign wars
(2) ignoring abuses committed by big business
(3) excessive regulation of the steel industry
(4) overspending on social welfare programs 22 _____

23 During the Progressive Era, voters were given more opportunities to select political party candidates through

(1) direct primary elections
(2) term limits on elected officials
(3) initiative and recall
(4) public funding of elections 23 _____

24 Theodore Roosevelt's Square Deal and Woodrow Wilson's New Freedom shared the goal of

(1) achieving equal rights for minority groups
(2) protecting the interests of big business
(3) strengthening federal regulatory power over large corporations
(4) instituting laissez-faire policies   24 _____

25 The Federal Reserve System was created in 1913 to

(1) balance the budget
(2) control the money supply
(3) insure savings account deposits
(4) regulate the stock market   25 _____

Base your answer to question 26 on these statements by President Woodrow Wilson and on your knowledge of social studies.

". . . The United States must be neutral in fact as well as in name. . ."
— message to U.S. Senate, 1914

". . . America can not be an ostrich with its head in the sand. . . ."
— address in Des Moines, Iowa, 1916

". . . The world must be made safe for democracy. . . ."
— address to Congress asking for a declaration of war, April 2, 1917

26 What do these statements demonstrate about President Wilson during the three years before the United States entered World War I?

(1) He gradually changed his foreign policy goals.
(2) He eagerly became involved in a war.
(3) He abused the principle of separation of powers.
(4) He was consistent in his policy of strict neutrality.   26 _____

27 President Warren Harding's call for a "return to normalcy" meant the United States should

    (1) limit the number of exports
    (2) reduce its role in world affairs
    (3) expand efforts to end racial discrimination
    (4) support woman's suffrage   27 _____

28 Which heading best completes the partial outline below?

> I. _____
>
>   A. Overproduction
>   B. Underconsumption
>   C. Buying on margin
>   D. Unequal distribution of wealth

    (1) Causes of the Industrial Revolution
    (2) Causes of World War I
    (3) Causes of the Great Depression
    (4) Causes of World War II   28 _____

Base your answer to question 29 on the graph below and on your knowledge of social studies.

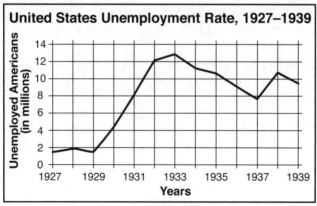

Source: *Historical Statistics of the United States, Colonial Times to 1970* (adapted)

29 Which conclusion is most clearly supported by the information provided on the graph?

   (1) Deficit spending ended unemployment.
   (2) World War II increased unemployment.
   (3) New Deal programs only partially relieved unemployment.
   (4) Unemployment after the New Deal was the same as before the stock market crash.

   29 _____

---

30 During the 1930s, poor land management and severe drought conditions across parts of the Midwest resulted in the

   (1) establishment of the United States Department of Agriculture
   (2) creation of wheat surpluses
   (3) decreased support for conservation
   (4) development of the Dust Bowl conditions on the Great Plains

   30 _____

31 During the 1930s, United States neutrality legislation was primarily designed to

   (1) provide military and economic aid to Italy and Japan
   (2) give the United States time to plan an attack against Germany
   (3) protect American lives and property in Latin America
   (4) avoid foreign policy mistakes that led to involvement in World War I

   31 _____

Base your answers to questions 32 and 33 on the song lyrics below and on your knowledge of social studies.

That's Why We're Voting For Roosevelt

Herbie Hoover promised us "Two chickens in each pot,"
Breadlines and Depression were the only things we got.
I lost my job, my bank blew up, and I was on the spot.
That's why I'm voting for Roosevelt.

Hooray! Hooray! Herb Hoover's gone away,
Hooray! Hooray! I hope he's gone to stay.
For now I'm back to work and get my three squares ev'ry day.
That's why I'm voting for Roosevelt. . . .

Wall Street sure is kicking for they know they're on the pan.
Franklin D. in Washington upset their little plan,
And now the one on top is that poor once forgotten man,
That's why we're voting for Roosevelt.

Hooray! Hooray! He banished all our fear.
Hooray! Hooray! Our banks are in the clear.
He brought us back prosperity, he gave us back our beer,
That's why I'm voting for Roosevelt.

— Thomas O'Dowd, 1936

32 Which group would most likely have agreed with the lyrics of this song?

   (1) Prohibition advocates   (3) New Deal supporters

   (2) Republican Party leaders   (4) Supply-side economists   32 _____

33 According to the song lyrics, people supported Franklin D. Roosevelt primarily because he

   (1) implemented economic relief and recovery programs

   (2) favored a national suffrage amendment

   (3) continued Herbert Hoover's economic policies

   (4) reduced federal income taxes   33 _____

Base your answer to question 34 on the cartoon below and on your knowledge of social studies.

NEVER SATISFIED

Source: Vaughn Shoemaker, *Chicago News,* April 27, 1937 (adapted)

34 This cartoon is critical of President Franklin D. Roosevelt's efforts to

(1) force Congress to reduce government waste
(2) convince the Supreme Court to pass a constitutional amendment to balance the budget
(3) reverse the effects of the Great Depression
(4) increase his power over the Supreme Court

34 _____

Base your answers to questions 35 and 36 on the poster below and on your knowledge of social studies.

Source: Office of Price Administration, 1943

35 The poster indicates that rationing during World War II was a

(1) policy to encourage small-business owners
(2) way of assuring that only the wealthy could buy certain products
(3) necessity caused by farm failures during the Great Depression
(4) program that was to be applied equally to all Americans

35 _____

36 What was a major reason for wartime rationing?

(1) ensuring that troops were adequately supplied
(2) restricting lower-priced food imports
(3) providing jobs for the unemployed
(4) preventing currency deflation

36 _____

37 What would be the most appropriate heading for the partial outline below?

I. _____

    A. Treatment of Japanese Americans
    B. Segregation of African Americans in the armed forces
    C. United States reactions to the Nazi Holocaust
    D. Use of the atomic bomb

(1) Issues of Morality during World War II
(2) Domestic Policies during World War II
(3) Economic Problems during World War II
(4) Reasons for the Success of the Allies during World War II

37 _____

Base your answer to question 38 on the graph below and on your knowledge of social studies.

Source: *The NYSTROM Atlas of United States History,* 2000
(adapted)

38 What is the best title for this graph for the years 1946–1964?

(1) The Graying of America
(2) The Growth of the Middle Class
(3) The Baby Boom Generation
(4) From Suburbs to Cities

38 _____

Base your answers to questions 39 and 40 on the map below and on your knowledge of social studies.

Cuban Missile Crisis, 1962

Source: Gary B. Nash and Carter Smith, *Atlas of American History,* Facts on File, 2007 (adapted)

39 What was the immediate cause of the action taken by the United States that is shown on the map?

(1) Cuban refugees lobbied President Dwight Eisenhower to overthrow Fidel Castro.

(2) The Soviet Union built nuclear missile launch sites within range of United States cities.

(3) United States military bases in the Caribbean were closed by Cuban armed forces.

(4) Puerto Rican citizens asked Congress to assist them in repelling communist advances.

39 _____

40 One positive outcome of the situation shown on the map was that the United States and Soviet Union increased

   (1) communication between the two nations to avert war

   (2) military control of their Latin American colonies

   (3) cooperative humanitarian efforts in Caribbean nations suffering from natural disasters

   (4) joint efforts to end the cruel practices of Cuba's leaders

40 _____

41 The main reason President John F. Kennedy proposed the establishment of the Peace Corps was to

   (1) promote trade with Africa

   (2) combat drug use in American cities

   (3) gain support from immigrant voters

   (4) improve conditions in developing nations

41 _____

42 What was an outcome of the Watergate affair during the administration of President Richard Nixon?

   (1) Presidential powers were expanded.

   (2) Respect for the office of the president declined.

   (3) The Supreme Court cleared President Nixon of all charges.

   (4) Congress refused to take action against President Nixon.

42 _____

43 The goal of the War Powers Act of 1973 was to

   (1) allow the president to declare war without congressional approval

   (2) give Congress the sole power to authorize the use of military force

   (3) limit the president's power to use military force without congressional approval

   (4) require a declaration of war for all uses of military forces

43 _____

44 "... The United States, together with the United Nations, exhausted every means at our disposal to bring this crisis to a peaceful end. However, Saddam [Hussein] clearly felt that by stalling and threatening and defying the United Nations, he could weaken the forces arrayed against him. ..."

— President George H. W. Bush, address to the nation, January 16, 1991

President George H. W. Bush used this statement to defend

(1) taking military action to liberate Kuwait from Iraqi aggression
(2) providing foreign aid to Israel
(3) supporting Egypt against attacks by terrorists
(4) using United States troops as peacekeepers in Bosnia

44 _____

Base your answer to question 45 on the cartoon below and on your knowledge of social studies.

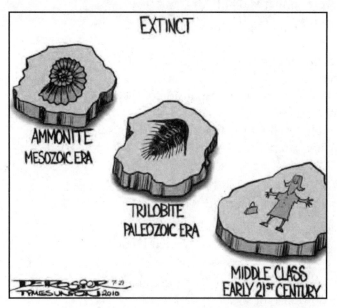

EXTINCT

AMMONITE
MESOZOIC ERA

TRILOBITE
PALEOZOIC ERA

MIDDLE CLASS
EARLY 21ˢᵀ CENTURY

Source: John de Rosier, *Albany Times Union,*
July 29, 2010

45 Which combination of factors has led to the problem shown in the cartoon?

(1) lower medical costs and high interest rates
(2) business monopolies and depletion of natural resources
(3) consumer debt and nearly stagnant wages
(4) population migration and the graying of America

45 _____

46 One way in which the goals of the Know-Nothing Party in the 1850s and the response to the Red Scare of 1919 were similar is that both

(1) called for equal rights for women and African Americans
(2) sought to limit immigration to the United States
(3) supported the overseas expansion of the United States
(4) attempted to limit the influence of big business on American politics   46 _____

47 Which term most accurately describes United States foreign policy during the Cold War?

(1) containment   (3) Big Stick
(2) nonalignment   (4) Open Door   47 _____

Base your answer to question 48 on the chart below and on your knowledge of social studies.

Action	Reaction
President Andrew Johnson disobeys the Tenure of Office Act.	Congress impeaches Johnson and he remains in office by one vote.
Congress passes the National Industrial Recovery Act (NIRA).	The Supreme Court declares the NIRA unconstitutional in *Schechter Poultry Corporation* v. *United States*.

48 Which aspect of governmental power is best illustrated by both examples in the chart?

(1) federalism   (3) States rights
(2) checks and balances   (4) judicial review   48 _____

49 Which economic policy argues that government should limit, as much as possible, any interference in the economy?

    (1) socialism   (3) mercantilism

    (2) laissez-faire   (4) protectionism   49 _____

50 W. E. B. Du Bois, Jackie Robinson, and James Meredith are considered pioneers in the area of

    (1) labor relations

    (2) educational reform

    (3) civil rights

    (4) environmental protection   50 _____

In developing your answer to Part II, be sure to keep these general definitions in mind:

(a) <u>describe</u> means "to illustrate something in words or tell about it"

(b) <u>discuss</u> means "to make observations about something using facts, reasoning, and argument; to present in some detail"

PART II: THEMATIC ESSAY

Directions: Write a well-organized essay that includes an introduction, several paragraphs addressing the task below, and a conclusion.

Theme: Westward Movement of the Frontier

> Throughout United States history, efforts to settle new land pushed the frontier further west. Several important events influenced this westward movement. These events often led to conflict with Native American Indians or with foreign governments.

Task:

> Select *two* events that significantly influenced the westward movement of the frontier and for *each*
>
> • Describe the historical circumstances surrounding the event
> • Discuss the positive *and/or* negative effects of the event on the settlement of the West

You may use any event that significantly influenced the westward movement of the frontier from your study of United States history. Some events you might wish to consider include:

Signing of the Treaty of Paris (1783)
Creation of the reservation system (1800s)
Purchase of the Louisiana Territory (1803)
Opening of the Erie Canal (1825)
War with Mexico (1846–1848)
Discovery of gold in California (1848)
Passage of the Homestead Act (1862)

Purchase of Alaska (1867)
Completion of the transcontinental railroad (1869)
You are *not* limited to these suggestions.

Guidelines:

In your essay, be sure to:

- Develop all aspects of the task
- Discuss *at least* **two** effects for each event
- Support the theme with relevant facts, examples, and details
- Use a logical and clear plan of organization, including an introduction and a conclusion that are beyond a restatement of the theme

In developing your answers to Part III, be sure to keep these general definitions in mind:
  (a) <u>describe</u> means "to illustrate something in words or tell about it"
  (b) <u>discuss</u> means "to make observations about something using facts, reasoning, and argument; to present in some detail"

PART III: DOCUMENT-BASED QUESTION

This question is based on the accompanying documents. The question is designed to test your ability to work with historical documents. Some of these documents have been edited for the purposes of this question. As you analyze the documents, take into account the source of each document and any point of view that may be presented in the document. Keep in mind that the language and images used in a document may reflect the historical context of the time in which it was created.

Historical Context:

> In the decades following World War II, significant domestic and foreign policy issues led to political and social tensions in the United States. These issues motivated individuals and groups to organize protest movements to bring about change. Protest movements such as the *civil rights movement*, the *anti–Vietnam War movement*, and the *environmental movement* met with varying degrees of success.

Task:

Using the information from the documents and your knowledge of United States history, answer the questions that follow each document in Part A. Your answers to the questions will help you write the Part B essay in which you will be asked to

Choose *two* protest movements mentioned in the historical context and for *each*
- Describe the historical circumstances surrounding the protest movement
- Discuss the extent to which the protest movement was successful

Part A: Short-Answer Questions

Directions: Analyze the documents and answer the short-answer questions that follow each document in the space provided.

Document 1a

"AND REMEMBER, NOTHING CAN BE ACCOMPLISHED BY TAKING TO THE STREETS"

Source: Herblock, *Washington Post*, September 6, 1963 (adapted)

Document 1b

If You Miss Me At the Back of the Bus

If you miss me at the back of the bus
you can't find me nowhere
come on over to the front of the bus
I'll be riding up there. . . .

If you miss me on the picket line
you can't find me nowhere
come on over to the city jail
I'll be rooming over there. . . .

If you miss me in the cotton fields
you can't find me nowhere
come on over to the courthouse
I'll be voting right there. . . .

Source: recorded by Pete Seeger, 1963,
written by Carver Neblett

1 Based on these documents, state **one** form of discrimination African Americans experienced in the 1960s. [1]

_____

_____

Document 2

> . . . In its regional breadth, the uprising resembled the sit-in movement of 1960. But the 1963 demonstrations [after Birmingham] were more widespread, involved much larger numbers, and drew in people of all ages and backgrounds. To list the places where black people engaged in nonviolent protests would be to name virtually every town and city in the South: about 115 communities experienced 930 demonstrations of one kind or another. The number of people arrested topped 20,000, four times as many as in 1960.
>
> The 1963 surge of nonviolent direct action made the maintenance of segregation in public accommodations untenable [unable to continue]. Black people knew that if segregation could be cracked in Birmingham, it could be cracked anywhere. Birmingham exposed the vulnerability of the South's political regime, and black people seized the opportunity to attack it. In city after city, under the relentless pressure of demonstrations, whites sat down to negotiate. During a single three-week period after Birmingham, the Justice Department noted that 143 cities had acceded [agreed] to some degree of integration. By year's end the number exceeded three hundred. Many cities set up biracial committees that enabled blacks to press for further desegregation. . . .

Source: Adam Fairclough, *Better Day Coming: Blacks and Equality, 1890–2000*, Viking Penguin, 2001

2 According to Adam Fairclough, what was *one* effect of the 1963 demonstrations in Birmingham, Alabama? [1]

_____

_____

Document 3

. . . In far too many ways American Negroes have been another nation: deprived of freedom, crippled by hatred, the doors of opportunity closed to hope.

In our time change has come to this Nation, too. The American Negro, acting with impressive restraint, has peacefully protested and marched, entered the courtrooms and the seats of government, demanding a justice that has long been denied. The voice of the Negro was the call to action. But it is a tribute to America that, once aroused, the courts and the Congress, the President and most of the people, have been the allies of progress.

Thus we have seen the high court of the country declare that discrimination based on race was repugnant [disagreeable] to the Constitution, and therefore void. We have seen in 1957, and 1960, and again in 1964, the first civil rights legislation in this Nation in almost an entire century. . . .

The voting rights bill will be* the latest, and among the most important, in a long series of victories. But this victory—as Winston Churchill said of another triumph for freedom—"is not the end. It is not even the beginning of the end. But it is, perhaps, the end of the beginning."

That beginning is freedom; and the barriers to that freedom are tumbling down. Freedom is the right to share, share fully and equally, in American society—to vote, to hold a job, to enter a public place, to go to school. It is the right to be treated in every part of our national life as a person equal in dignity and promise to all others.

But freedom is not enough. You do not wipe away the scars of centuries by saying: Now you are free to go where you want, and do as you desire, and choose the leaders you please. . . .

This is the next and the more profound stage of the battle for civil rights. We seek not just freedom but opportunity. We seek not just legal equity but human ability, not just equality as a right and a theory but equality as a fact and equality as a result.

*The Voting Rights Act was signed into law on August 6, 1965.

> For the task is to give 20 million Negroes the same chance as every other American to learn and grow, to work and share in society, to develop their abilities—physical, mental and spiritual, and to pursue their individual happiness. . . .

Source: Lyndon B. Johnson, Commencement Address at Howard University, June 4, 1965

3*a* According to President Lyndon B. Johnson, what is *one* achievement of the civil rights movement?   [1]

_____

_____

b According to President Lyndon B. Johnson, what is *one* remaining goal for the civil rights movement?   [1]

_____

_____

Document 4

. . . As the U.S. commitment increased, so did the number of bombs dropped on the North, the volume of North Vietnamese coming into the South, the fervor of the protest movement, the billion dollar military grants, and the number of casualties. Johnson's pledge to fight communism in Southeast Asia had degenerated into what anti-war folk singer Pete Seeger labeled "the Big Muddy." And yet, the refrain of that song said, "the old fool says to push on." Tempers on both sides flared as the body counts increased, and each night's TV broadcasts introduced American viewers to faraway hell holes where their sons, brothers, friends, and husbands were stepping on land mines, perishing in Vietcong mantraps, and being cut down in hand-to-hand combat. The week of September 18–24 brought with it a grim statistic: 142 U.S. soldiers killed, 825 wounded, 3 missing—the war's highest toll in 1966. . . .

Every time American troops won a small victory or held a strategic position, the President's advisers used the occasion to press for more troops and more money. These were vital, they repeatedly declared, to consolidate our gains and increase our advantages. The monthly draft was doubled several times, up to 46,000 a month in October 1966, as General Westmoreland constantly increased his call for troops. He had almost a half-million men in combat by April 1967. By the following year, he told the President, he would need almost 700,000. With that number, he said, we could win the war in two years. The "light at the end of the tunnel," which President Johnson optimistically referred to in his news broadcasts, had dimmed considerably since his earlier predictions. . . .

Source: Toby Goldstein, *Waking from the Dream: America in the Sixties,*
Julian Messner, 1988

4 According to Toby Goldstein, what were *two* reasons for the development of the anti–Vietnam War movement? [2]

(1) _____

_____

(2) _____

_____

Document 5

American protest against the war in Vietnam was begun and sustained by American citizens who believed that in a representative democracy, individuals can make themselves heard and, more, can affect public policy.

To us, the antiwar movement during the Vietnam era is important not because it stopped the war, which it may or may not have done; rather, it is important because it existed. It is a reminder to Americans that times come when citizens can and, indeed, must challenge their government's authority. . . .

Every war has had its opponents. There was a sizable antiwar sentiment in Great Britain during the South African War (1899–1902), and in America there has always been during every war a small protest movement—most notably, until Vietnam, during the Mexican War in 1846–48 and the Philippine Insurrection in 1899–1901. But the Vietnam War was different: increasingly unpopular, undeclared and therefore in the opinion of many citizens illegal and unconstitutional as well, it was the most frustrating war in American history, and the ugliest, and the longest. The movement opposing it had years in which to grow. . . .

Source: Nancy Zaroulis and Gerald Sullivan, *Who Spoke Up?: American Protest Against the War In Vietnam, 1963–1975,* Holt, Rinehart and Winston, 1984

5 According to Nancy Zaroulis and Gerald Sullivan, what was *one* reason for protest against the Vietnam War?   [1]

_____

_____

Document 6

... The impact of the antiwar protests remains one of the most controversial issues raised by the war. The obvious manifestations [displays] of dissent in the United States probably encouraged Hanoi's will to hold out for victory, although there is nothing to suggest that the North Vietnamese would have been more compromising in the absence of the movement. Antiwar protest did not turn the American people against the war, as some critics have argued. The effectiveness of the movement was limited by the divisions within its own ranks. Public opinion polls make abundantly clear, moreover, that a majority of Americans found the antiwar movement, particularly its radical and "hippie" elements, more obnoxious than the war itself. In a perverse sort of way, the protest may even have strengthened support for a war that was not in itself popular. The impact of the movement was much more limited and subtle. It forced Vietnam onto the public consciousness and challenged the rationale of the war and indeed of a generation of Cold War foreign policies. It limited Johnson's military options and may have headed off any tendency toward more drastic escalation. Perhaps most important, the disturbances and divisions set off by the antiwar movement caused fatigue and anxiety among the policymakers and the public, and thus eventually encouraged efforts to find a way out of the war. . . .

Source: George C. Herring, *America's Longest War: The United States and Vietnam, 1950–1975,* Alfred A. Knopf, 1986 (adapted)

6*a* According to George C. Herring, what was *one* way the anti–Vietnam War movement was *not* successful? [1]

_____

_____

b According to George C. Herring, what was *one* way the anti–Vietnam War movement was successful?   [1]

_____

_____

Document 7

. . . For the first time in the history of the world, every human being is now subjected to contact with dangerous chemicals, from the moment of conception until death. In the less than two decades of their use, the synthetic pesticides have been so thoroughly distributed throughout the animate and inanimate world that they occur virtually everywhere. They have been recovered from most of the major river systems and even from streams of groundwater flowing unseen through the earth. Residues of these chemicals linger in soil to which they may have been applied a dozen years before. They have entered and lodged in the bodies of fish, birds, reptiles, and domestic and wild animals so universally that scientists carrying on animal experiments find it almost impossible to locate subjects free from such contamination. They have been found in fish in remote mountain lakes, in earthworms burrowing in soil, in the eggs of birds—and in man himself. For these chemicals are now stored in the bodies of the vast majority of human beings, regardless of age. They occur in the mother's milk, and probably in the tissues of the unborn child. . . .

Source: Rachel Carson, *Silent Spring,* Houghton Mifflin, 1962

7 According to Rachel Carson, what is **one** issue that has led to concerns about the environment? [1]

_____

_____

Document 8a

Millions Join Earth Day Observances
Across the Nation

Throngs jamming Fifth Avenue yesterday in response to a call for the regeneration of a polluted environment.

Source: *New York Times,* April 23, 1970 (adapted)

Document 8b

Earth Day, the first mass consideration of the globe's environmental problems, preempted [commanded] the attention and energies of millions of Americans, young and old, across the country yesterday. . . .

Organizers of Earth Day said more than 2,000 colleges, 10,000 grammar and high schools, and citizen groups in 2,000 communities had indicated intentions of participating. . . .

The purpose of the observance was to heighten public awareness of pollution and other ecological problems, which many scientists say urgently require action if the earth is to remain habitable. . . .

Summarizing the implications of the day's activities, Senator Nelson said:

"The question now is whether we are willing to make the commitment for a sustained national drive to solve our environmental problems." . . .

Source: Gladwin Hill, "Activity Ranges From Oratory to Legislation," *New York Times,* April 23, 1970

8 Based on these documents, state *one* reason the observance of Earth Day is important to the environmental movement.   [1]

_____

_____

Document 9a

. . . Earth Day had consequences: it led to the Clean Air Act of 1970, the Clean Water Act of 1972, and the Endangered Species Act of 1973, and to the creation, just eight months after the event, of the Environmental Protection Agency. Throughout the nineteen-seventies, mostly during the Republican Administrations of Richard Nixon and Gerald Ford, Congress passed one environmental bill after another, establishing national controls on air and water pollution. And most of the familiar big green groups are, in their current form, offspring of Earth Day. Dozens of colleges and universities instituted environmental-studies programs, and even many small newspapers created full-time environmental beats. . . .

Source: Nicholas Lemann, "When the Earth Moved: What Happened to the Environmental Movement?" *The New Yorker,* April 15, 2013

9a According to Nicholas Lemann, what is *one* impact of Earth Day? [1]

_____

_____

Document 9b

Frances Beinecke served as president of the Natural Resources Defense Council [NRDC] from 2006–2014. The Council writes and lobbies for public policy to protect the environment.

My work at NRDC has brought me to the front lines of the climate crisis. I have flown over the massive tar sands strip mines in the boreal forest. I have visited the homes of people coping with frack pads [an area of land used in the fracking process] and wastewater ponds in their backyards. And I have helped my neighbors recover from the devastation of Superstorm Sandy. . . .

Never in my lifetime have the challenges been greater than those we face from climate change. Never have the solutions been more clearly at hand. We know how to defuse the climate threat. We just have to act now. . . .

It's time for us, as Americans, to state as a national goal that we'll hit fast-forward on efforts to clean up our carbon pollution, invest in energy efficiency and shift to renewable power so that we will become a carbon-neutral nation that no longer contributes to climate change. . . .

We have already begun slashing climate change pollution. More than 3.4 million Americans are on the job every day helping to clean up our dirty power plants, get more electricity from the wind and sun, manufacture more hybrid and electric cars, and cut energy waste in our homes, at work and on the road. . . .

The modern environmental movement exists for one purpose: we're here to change the world—to become a place where we care for the natural systems of the Earth as if our very lives depended on them, because they do. That is not yet the world we live in. It is the world we must create.

Source: Frances Beinecke, "The World We Create: My New Book and a Message of Hope for the Planet," *Switchboard: National Resources Defense Council Blog,* October 14, 2014

9*b* According to Frances Beinecke, state *one* reason the environmental movement continues to be important. [1]

_____

_____

Part B: Essay

Directions: Write a well-organized essay that includes an introduction, several paragraphs, and a conclusion. Use evidence from
at least *four* documents in the body of the essay. Support your
response with relevant facts, examples, and details. Include additional outside information.

Historical Context:

> In the decades following World War II, significant
> domestic and foreign policy issues led to political
> and social tensions in the United States. These issues
> motivated individuals and groups to organize protest
> movements to bring about change. Protest move-
> ments such as the *civil rights movement,* the *anti–
> Vietnam War movement,* and the *environmental
> movement* met with varying degrees of success.

Task:

> Using the information from the documents and
> your knowledge of United States history, write an
> essay in which you
>
> Choose *two* protest movements mentioned in the
> historical context and for *each*
>
> • Describe the historical circumstances surround-
>   ing the protest movement
> • Discuss the extent to which the protest move-
>   ment was successful

Guidelines:

In your essay, be sure to
• Develop all aspects of the task
• Incorporate information from *at least four* documents
• Incorporate relevant outside information
• Support the theme with relevant facts, examples, and details
• Use a logical and clear plan of organization, including an introduc-
  tion and a conclusion that are beyond a restatement of the theme

Answers
June 2019
United States History and Government

Answer Key

PART I

1. 2	14. 4	27. 2	40. 1
2. 4	15. 4	28. 3	41. 4
3. 1	16. 1	29. 3	42. 2
4. 3	17. 1	30. 4	43. 3
5. 4	18. 3	31. 4	44. 1
6. 2	19. 2	32. 3	45. 3
7. 1	20. 2	33. 1	46. 2
8. 1	21. 4	34. 4	47. 1
9. 4	22. 2	35. 4	48. 2
10. 3	23. 1	36. 1	49. 2
11. 4	24. 3	37. 1	50. 3
12. 3	25. 2	38. 3	
13. 2	26. 1	39. 2	

INDEX

BARRON'S

Regents Exams and Answers

United States History and Government

Revised Edition

EUGENE V. RESNICK, B.A., M.A.
Social Studies Teacher, Midwood High
School, Brooklyn, New York

JOHN MCGEEHAN, B.A., M.A., J.D.
Consultant and Writer, New York State
Education Department,
Bureau of Social Studies Education,
Educational Testing, and Curriculum
Development

MORRIS GALL, J.D., PH.D.
Former President, Association of Teachers
of Social Studies in the City of New York

WILLIAM STREITWIESER, B.A., M.A.
Former Social Studies Teacher, Northport
High School, Northport, New York

Test-Taking Tips by
MARK WILLNER, M.A.
Chairman of Social Studies Department,
Midwood High School, Brooklyn, New York

Published by Kaplan, Inc., d/b/a Barron's Educational Series
750 Third Avenue
New York, NY 10017
www.barronseduc.com

ISBN: 978-1-5062-6665-7

10 9 8 7 6 5 4 3 2 1

Kaplan, Inc., d/b/a Barron's Educational Series print books are available at special quantity discounts to use for sales promotions, employee premiums, or educational purposes. For more information or to purchase books, please call the Simon & Schuster special sales department at 866-506-1949.

Contents

What the Exam Is About

If you are reading this, you are probably at the end of 11th grade and preparing to take the Regents exam in Social Studies. You probably already know that New York State requires you to take the U.S. History and Government Regents exam. Almost every 11th-grade student in New York State will be taking the same exam at the same time you are.

U.S. History and Government is part of a sequence of social studies courses you are required to take from first grade through 12th grade. The purpose of social studies is to help you understand the events and developments that shape the nation and the world you live in. In ninth and tenth grade, you studied cultures on continents other than North America because you need to understand that we live in an interdependent world. In 11th grade, you returned to a study of the United States of America. Now that you are more mature and may be eligible to vote in a year or two, you should have a clear understanding of the nature of the Constitution and the workings of the United States government.

Students in 11th-grade social studies learn about the Constitutional foundations of American society before studying the history of the United States from after the Civil War to modern times.

WHAT IS THE U.S. HISTORY AND GOVERNMENT REGENTS EXAM LIKE?

If you took the Global Studies Regents last year, you already have some idea of what the exam is like. The U.S. History and Government Regents is divided into three parts. All parts have questions on the topics, themes, and skills covered in 11th grade.

The exam is constructed as follows:

- 50 Multiple-Choice Questions   50 minutes   55 percent of grade
- One Thematic Essay   45 minutes   15 percent of grade
- 8 Document-Based Questions
                                      60 minutes   30 percent of grade
- One Document-Based Essay

Many students lose points because they neglect to answer some parts of questions or misread the questions. Be sure to review the following sections: "How to Use This Book" (pages 3–5) and "Test-Taking Tips" (beginning on page 6).

How to Use This Book

This book is designed to help you get the most out of your review for the Regents exam in U.S. History and Government.

TEST-TAKING TIPS

The first section, Test-Taking Tips, will help you become a *better* test taker. Be sure to read this valuable material carefully. The brief rules, many hints, and practice questions will increase your understanding and confidence in answering short-answer and essay questions. The sample answers will enable you to distinguish between a complete and well-written essay and a poor one.

Reread the Test-Taking Tips after taking two or more of the exams, and feel your assurance grow.

PREVIOUS REGENTS EXAMS AND ANSWERS

The second section contains previous Regents exams and answer analyses. The exams will serve as a content review and as a study guide to indicate what is important. By answering the multiple-choice and essay questions, you will be able to discover your weak points. You will then be able to remedy your deficiencies by carefully studying the answers provided. They are more than just model answers; additional facts and explanations have been included for a more thorough understanding of the subjects on which the questions are based. Careful study of the answers will increase your skill in interpreting the questions and in applying the facts learned.

SELF-ANALYSIS CHARTS

The Self-Analysis Charts enable you to note the content areas tested on the exam and the number of questions in each content area. You can calculate your score in each of the content areas of a test to see in which content areas you show strengths or weaknesses.

Each chart has three columns:

1. Column 1 names each topic included in the exam.
2. Column 2 lists the number of each short-answer question on that topic asked in the given exam.
3. Column 3 shows the total point value of short-answer questions on each topic. Since each correct answer is worth about $1\frac{1}{7}$ points, totals are shown to the nearest full point in each content category.

You can calculate the number of points you earned for each content category by multiplying the number of questions you got right by the point value for each question noted at the bottom of the Self-Evaluation Chart. You can calculate the percentage of questions you got right in each content category by dividing the number of points you earned by the total number of points for each category given in Column 3.

If you score lower than 75 percent on any topic, first review your class notes and textbook material; then review the model answers in the book AND the explanations of all choices for each question on that topic. Studying the explanations of the wrong choices will greatly enhance your understanding of the subject matter and alert you to possible errors. It will also be helpful to you to review additional content.

SKILLS QUESTIONS

Please note that space has been provided in the Self-Analysis Charts for you to score and compare separately your achievement on the skills questions on each exam. The skills material includes interpretation of reading passages, cartoons, charts, diagrams, graphs, and maps.

SUMMARY

1. Read the first section, Test-Taking Tips.
2. Take the first exam under test conditions.
3. Answer as many essay questions as possible.
4. Mark Part I of the exam.
5. Complete the Self-Analysis Chart for that exam.
6. Record your weak spots.
7. Answer both the Part II and Part III questions.
8. Study the answers to ALL the questions you could not answer, or answered inadequately.
9. Review your notes and text material on those topics before taking the next exam. Reread the Test-Taking Tips.

Repeat this procedure, exam by exam, and watch that mark soar.

IMPORTANT TERMS TO KNOW

The Glossary of Terms is designed to show you which terms or concepts appeared most frequently on past tests. As you review the Glossary of Terms, you will notice one, two, or three asterisks (*) preceding some of the terms defined. While all the terms are important to know, those with asterisks should be considered most crucial. One asterisk (*) denotes a term that is frequently tested; two asterisks (**) denote a term that is **very** frequently tested; and three asterisks (***) denote a term that is **most** frequently tested.

Test-Taking Tips

TAKING THE REGENTS EXAM

Although teachers and students alike find an "all or nothing" exam at the completion of the course distasteful, the Regents exam in U.S. History and Government in some ways, unfortunately, falls into this category. Without passing the Regents exam, you cannot graduate.

Although this brief section does not claim to provide a comprehensive study guide for taking the Regents, it does contain several tips to help you achieve a good grade on the U.S. History and Government Regents. They are divided into GENERAL HELPFUL TIPS and SPECIFIC HELPFUL TIPS.

GENERAL HELPFUL TIPS

TIP 1
Be confident and prepared.

SUGGESTIONS

- Review short-answer sections from previous tests.
- Use a clock or watch, and take previous exams at home under exam conditions (i.e., don't have the radio or television on).
- Get a review book (The preferred book is Barron's *Let's Review: U.S. History and Government.*)
- Visit *www.barronseduc.com* for the latest information on the Regents exams.
- Talk over the answers to questions on these tests with someone else. Use Barron's website to communicate with subject specialists.
- Finish all your homework assignments.
- Look over classroom exams that your teacher gave during the term.

- Take class notes carefully.
- Practice good study habits.
- Know that there are answers for every question.
- Be aware that the people who made up the Regents want you to pass.
- Remember that thousands of students over the last few years have taken and passed the Regents. You can pass too!
- On the night prior to the exam, lay out all the things you will need, such as clothing, pens, and admission cards.
- Go to bed early; eat wisely.
- Bring at least two pens to the exam room.
- Once you are in the exam room, arrange your things, get comfortable, be relaxed, and attend to personal needs (the bathroom).
- Keep your eyes on your own paper; do not let them wander over to anyone else's.
- Be polite in making any reasonable demands of the proctor, such as changing your seat or having window shades raised or lowered.

TIP 2

Read test instructions and questions carefully.

SUGGESTIONS

- Be familiar with the test directions ahead of time.
- Decide upon the task(s) that you have to complete.
- Know how the test will be graded.
- Know which question or questions are worth the most points.
- Give only the information that is requested.
- Underline important words and phrases.
- Ask for assistance from the proctor if you do not understand the directions.

> ### TIP 3
>
> **Budget your test time in a balanced manner.**

SUGGESTIONS

- Bring a watch or clock to the test.
- Know how much time is allowed.
- Arrive on time; leave your home earlier than usual.
- Prepare a time schedule and try to stick to it. (The suggested times for each section are 50 minutes for the 50 multiple-choice questions, 45 minutes for the one thematic essay, and 60 minutes for the document-based questions.)
- Answer the easier questions first.
- Devote more time to the harder questions and to those worth more credit.
- Don't get "hung up" on a question that is proving to be difficult; go on to another question and return later to the difficult one.
- Ask the proctor for permission to go to the bathroom, if necessary, or if only to "take a break" from sitting in the room.
- Plan to stay in the room for the entire three hours. If you finish early, read over your work—there may be some things that you omitted or that you may wish to add. You also may wish to polish your grammar, spelling, and penmanship.

> ### TIP 4
>
> **Be "kind" to the exam grader/evaluator.**

SUGGESTIONS

- Assume that you are the teacher grading/evaluating your test paper.
- Answer questions in an orderly sequence.
- Write legibly.
- Use proper grammar, spelling, and sentence structure.
- Write essay answers in ink.
- Proofread your answers prior to submitting your exam paper. Have you answered all the short-answer questions and the required number of essays?

TIP 5
Use your reasoning skills.

SUGGESTIONS

- Answer *all* questions.
- Relate (connect) the question to anything that you studied, wrote in your notebook, or heard your teacher say in class.
- Relate (connect) the question to any film you saw in class, any project you did, or to anything you may have learned from newspapers, magazines, or television.
- Decide whether your answers would be approved by your teacher.
- Look over the entire test to see whether one part of it can help you answer another part.
- Write down as many of the **16 key concepts** and the **13 enduring constitutional issues** that you remember from your U.S. History and Government classes. (Among the **concepts** are culture, diversity, empathy, and interdependence.) Try to remember the meanings of these terms. Use them in answering questions, where relevant.

TIP 6
Don't be afraid to guess.

SUGGESTIONS

- In general, go with your first answer choice.
- Eliminate obvious incorrect choices.
- If still unsure of an answer, make an educated guess.
- There is no penalty for guessing; therefore, answer ALL questions. An omitted answer gets no credit.

Let's now review the six GENERAL HELPFUL TIPS for short-answer questions:

SUMMARY OF TIPS
1. Be confident and prepared.
2. Read test instructions and questions carefully.
3. Budget your test time in a balanced manner.
4. Be "kind" to the exam grader/evaluator.
5. Use your reasoning skills.
6. Don't be afraid to guess.

SPECIFIC HELPFUL TIPS FOR THE
SHORT-ANSWER (MULTIPLE-CHOICE) QUESTIONS

TIP 1
Answer the easy questions first.

The best reason for using this hint is that it can build up your confidence. It also enables you to use your time more efficiently. You should answer these questions first, while skipping over and circling the numbers of the more difficult questions. You can always return to these later during the exam. Easy questions usually contain short sentences and few words. The answer can often be arrived at quickly from the information presented.

Example

The authors of the United States Constitution believed that the voice of the people should be heard frequently. Which part of the Government was instituted to respond most directly to the will of the people?

1. Senate
2. House of Representatives
3. Supreme Court
4. Presidency

(from an actual Regents exam)

The correct answer, choice 2, is obvious. It is the only choice describing a component—in fact, the only component—in the original Constitution that was chosen directly by *the will of the people*. Senators were initially chosen by state legislatures (choice 1). Supreme Court judges have always been appointed (choice 3), while the President (choice 4) is chosen via an indirect vote by the people and at times has not been reflective of *the will of the people*.

TIP 2

Consider what the questioner wants you to do, and underline key words.

Remember that the people who made up the Regents questions had specific tasks they want you to accomplish. These tasks can be understood if you read instructions carefully, underline key words, and put yourself "in their shoes." Try to figure out what they would want a student to do with a given question. Determine for yourself exactly what is being tested. Underlining helps you focus on the key ideas in the question.

Example

At times, the United States Government has passed protective tariffs to

1. encourage foreign trade
2. help the nation's manufacturers
3. reduce the cost of consumer goods
4. improve the quality of goods

(from an actual Regents exam)

By underlining *protective tariffs*, you are on your way to focusing on the thrust of this question. You are being asked to identify something done that was presumed to be beneficial to the U.S. economy at specific times in history. The correct answer, choice 2, contains the only beneficial impact that a protective tariff would have. Choices 1 and 3, although beneficial, describe consequences likely to occur with the removal of tariffs. Choice 4 has little to do with whether or not tariffs exist. Now, in the next question, underline the key words.

The Republican presidents of the 1920s generally followed a foreign policy based on

1. collective security
2. brinkmanship
3. noninvolvement
4. militarism

(from an actual Regents exam)

The key words in the stem that needed to be underlined were *Republican* and *1920s*. You would thus be led to conclude that the only relevant choice would be 3, which describes the isolationist foreign policy of the United States in the post-World War I period. All the presidents in the 1920s were Republicans and generally wanted to reduce America's involvement with other nations.

TIP 3

Look for clues among choices in the question, as well as in other questions.

By reading questions and choices carefully, you may often find words and phrases that provide clues to an answer. This hint is important because it assists you in making links and connections between various questions.

Example

Which events best support the image of the 1920s as a decade of nativist sentiment?

1. the passage of the National Origins Act and the rise of the Ku Klux Klan
2. the Scopes trial and the passage of women's suffrage
3. the Washington Naval Conference and the Kellogg-Briand Pact
4. the growth of the auto industry and the Teapot Dome affair

(from an actual Regents exam)

Choice 1 is correct. It is the only choice naming events that were connected to harsh feelings toward foreigners. That harshness was part of the thinking of Americans who had *nativist sentiments*.

Let's examine another attempt to find a clue.

In the Colonial Era, developments such as the New England town meetings and the establishment of the Virginia House of Burgesses represented

1. colonial attempts to build a strong national government
2. efforts by the British to strengthen their control over the colonies
3. steps in the growth of representative democracy
4. early social reform movements

(from an actual Regents exam)

Can you determine the right answer? Both developments were political in purpose, and both were examples of democracy. The only choice that relates to these features is 3.

TIP 4

Examine all possibilities. Beware of tricky and tempting foils (decoys).

By remembering this tip you will be careful to survey all possible responses before making a selection. A given choice, or two, may initially appear to be the correct answer. This often happens when you are asked to make a generalization about a group of people or events.

Example

A similarity between the Red Scare of the 1920s and McCarthyism in the 1950s was that during each period

1. thousands of American citizens were expelled from the United States
2. the Communist Party gained many members in the United States
3. many government employees were convicted of giving secrets to the Soviet Union
4. the civil liberties of American citizens were threatened

(from an actual Regents exam)

Choice 4 is correct; however, all the other choices certainly "sound" correct. Indeed, the other choices represent true decoys. Choices 1 and 2 are tempting, as they do have a connection with the color *Red* in *Red Scare*. Choice 1 is certainly something "scary," even though no such event ever occurred in American history.

TIP 5

Always select the broader, more encompassing choice.

This tip is most helpful when two or more choices are correct, but you conclude that one choice is broader (or more encompassing) than the other. Indeed, one choice may actually include the other or others.

Example

"Up to our own day, American history is the history of the colonization of the Great West. The existence of an area of free land, . . . and the advance of American settlement westward explain American development."

This quotation of the 1890s suggests that the American frontier

1. should be preserved for free use by all the people
2. has mirrored European values and social patterns
3. will continue indefinitely as a region to be colonized
4. has had a positive effect on the growth of the United States

(from an actual Regents exam)

Choices 1, 2, and 3 have some validity, as they have been characteristic of varying attitudes toward the frontier. However, choice 4 is the best choice. It more fully and broadly answers the question. Examine the next question and see if you can figure out the answer.

Throughout United States history, the most important aim of the country's foreign policy has been

1. participation in international organizations
2. advancement of national self-interest
3. containment of communism
4. development of military alliances

(from an actual Regents exam)

Choices 1, 3, and 4 have all characterized U.S. foreign policy at varying times in the nation's history. However, each of these policies was put forth only when the United States of America decided it helped meet what it perceived to be its national self-interest at the time. Therefore, choice 2 is the best, all-encompassing answer for this question.

TIP 6

Use a process of elimination.

This tip provides a very good way of arriving at an answer. It is particularly useful when you face a difficult question and are unsure of the best response. Also, it increases your chances of coming up with the correct answer and (1) assists in discarding *unacceptable* choices and (2) narrows the possible *acceptable* choices. (You may wish to physically cross out on the question page the choices that you decide are incorrect.)

Example

How did the personal diplomacy conducted by President Franklin D. Roosevelt during World War II affect the presidency?

1. Subsequent presidents have refused to use this unsuccessful method.
2. The president's role in shaping United States foreign policy was strengthened.
3. The president's war powers as Commander in Chief were sharply reduced.
4. Congress increased its power over the executive branch.

(from an actual Regents exam)

In wartime, a president's ability to expand his powers as a result of his role as Commander in Chief is very great. This was certainly true of Franklin D. Roosevelt during World War II. Choice 3, therefore, is clearly wrong as it states an untrue situation. Choice 4 is wrong, as Congress during wartime will usually side with the president. Choice 1 can be eliminated, as it is simply untrue. Presidents since Roosevelt have sought to increase their diplomatic powers, well aware of his precedent-setting actions. Therefore, choice 2 is correct.

See if you can use a process of elimination to figure out the right answer to this next question.

Which statement is accurate about American culture during the Great Depression?

1. The federal government provided money to support the arts.
2. Most movies featured realistic themes and unhappy endings.
3. Rock-and-roll music became popular.
4. Interest in professional sports declined.

(from an actual Regents exam)

Did you pick choice 1? Good! Choice 2 can be eliminated, as it describes the opposite of what happened—most movies had happy themes, and sought to uplift peoples' spirits. The sadness of the times also spurred people to seek some enjoyment in entertainment forms such as sporting events (choice 4). Rock-and-roll music was not to become popular until the 1950s, many years after the Great Depression.

TIP 7

Detect differences among the choices presented.

You should be careful in picking out foils and decoys, something we mentioned in Tip #4. In a similar manner, this tip helps you in choosing among general and specific answers. This is especially important when you have reduced your selections to two choices.

Example

In the 1920s, the depressed situation of United States agriculture was chiefly caused by

1. overregulation by government
2. mechanization and overproduction
3. inefficient production techniques
4. stock-market speculation

(from an actual Regents exam)

The four choices all sound like factors that would lead to economic crises but, upon closer examination, choices 1 and 3 can be ruled out, as neither was characteristic of the United States in the 1920s. There was little regulation by government, as laissez-faire was a commonly held belief. Also, while production techniques were inefficient by today's standards, they were adequate in the 1920s as they resulted in a surplus of goods. Choices 2 and 4 were indeed factors leading to the Great Depression, yet stock-market speculation, choice 4, did not significantly affect *the depressed situation of United States agriculture*. Factors that did affect this situation are described in choice 2, the correct answer.

TIP 8

Don't choose an answer that is correct in itself but incorrect as it relates to the question.

It is crucial to keep this tip in mind when evaluating a question that has attractive choices. They will appear attractive because each has an element of truth; however, you must decide which one of these has the greatest relationship to the question itself. Let's look at a question we have seen elsewhere—Tip #7.

Example

In the 1920s, the depressed situation of United States agriculture was chiefly caused by

1. overregulation by government
2. mechanization and overproduction
3. inefficient production techniques
4. stock-market speculation

(from an actual Regents exam)

As you know, the correct answer is choice 2. Yet, although choices 2 and 4 were factors leading to the Great Depression, it is only choice 2 that best relates to the question. (See the discussion for Tip #7.) Now, try the following question.

Example

Which event of the early 1900s is evidence that Upton Sinclair's novel, *The Jungle*, had an important impact on the United States?

1. adoption of reforms in public education
2. passage of legislation limiting immigration
3. adoption of the 18th Amendment establishing Prohibition
4. passage of legislation requiring federal inspection of meat

(from an actual Regents exam)

Choice 4 is the correct answer, as it describes an event relating directly to Upton Sinclair's novel. The other three choices describe events that did occur in the first third of the 20th century, but had nothing to do with the novel.

TIP 9

Look for "giveaways" and "freebies."

There are times when a test question practically gives away the answer. You can determine such rare moments by focusing on obvious words, prefixes, grammatical construction, and other revealing tips.

Example

Which New Deal program was chiefly designed to correct abuses in the stock market?

1. Federal Emergency Relief Act
2. Civilian Conservation Corps
3. Works Progress Administration
4. Securities and Exchange Commission

(from an actual Regents exam)

Choice 4 stands out as the correct answer; *securities* is a word practically synonymous with *stock market*. The New Deal programs named in choices 1, 2, and 3 had nothing to do with correcting *abuses in the stock market.*

TIP 10

Think out the answer before looking at the possible choices.

This tip helps to stimulate memory recall. As you read a question, your "intellectual radar" may pick up something that will jog loose a key thought, concept, or fact in your mind.

Example

The Great Society of Lyndon Johnson is most similar to which other presidential program?

1. Warren Harding's Return to Normalcy
2. Franklin D. Roosevelt's New Deal
3. Ronald Reagan's New Federalism
4. George Bush's Thousand Points of Light

(from an actual Regents exam)

As you were reading the question, you should have thought about some well-known president and his domestic program that aimed to improve the nation's standard of living. Choice 2 meets these criteria. Along with the Great Society program, the New Deal sought to have the federal government take an active role in promoting peoples' health and welfare. The programs identified in choices 1, 3, and 4 did not have this goal.

This tip is also useful when interpreting cartoons. As you look at a cartoon, try to guess its meaning prior to looking at the choices. Most cartoon interpretation questions will require you to decide on a title for the cartoon or to indicate the message of the cartoonist.

Example

Which aspect of the United States Government is best illustrated by the cartoon?

1. system of checks and balances
2. veto power of the president
3. congressional committee system
4. civilian control of the military

(from an actual Regents exam)

The cartoon suggests something that the Senate can do and/or has already done. It also conveys a negative thought, to judge by the torn paper in a wastebasket labeled "rejections." The correct choice is 1. Choices 2, 3, and 4 do not deal with a specific power of the Senate, even though they do describe ways by which a governmental action can be restricted.

TIP 11

Make informed and educated guesses.

If you are not sure of an answer, don't be afraid to guess. Any answer is better than no answer—you have nothing to lose, as there is no penalty for guessing. Remember that the correct answer is there, somewhere, right on the exam page, waiting for you to find it. If you've eliminated one or more options, then your chances of picking the right answer increases from one out of four to one out of three, etc. A word of caution—guessing should be used only as a last resort. Do not go into the Regents expecting to pass by guessing your way through the questions. There is no substitute for careful, diligent exam preparation long before the exam date itself.

Example

Which New Deal reforms most directly targeted the basic problem of the victims of the Dust Bowl?

1. guaranteeing workers the right to organize and bargain collectively
2. regulating the sale of stocks and bonds
3. providing farmers low-cost loans and parity payments
4. raising individual and corporate income tax rates

(from an actual Regents exam)

Choice 3 is the correct answer. It contains the word *farmers*, a clear link to the phrase *Dust Bowl*. Even if you did not recognize this phrase right away, you could certainly eliminate choices 2 and 4; they do not refer to people (*victims*). While choice 1 does refer to people (*workers*), it does not name a group that would be associated with *dust*. Let's look at another question whose answer could be arrived at by making an informed and educated guess.

The widespread use of computers had led to a national concern over

1. increased pollution of the environment
2. guarding the right of privacy
3. protection of the right to petition
4. a decline in television viewing

(from an actual Regents exam)

At first reading, this question might appear strange because you might not expect to see a question about computers on a history exam. In addition, it is possible that your teacher did not cover the subject of computers in your social studies class. Nevertheless, even if these things were true and if you don't know how to use a computer, you can still guess at the answer. Careful rereading of the question would reveal that choices 3 and 4 are not really items causing *national concern*. Choices 1 and 2 do describe issues of such concern; however, using computers has little to do with causing pollution. Since they do have the capacity to store great amounts of information about people, abuse of this capacity could cause problems affecting the right to privacy—choice 2.

Let's now review the 11 SPECIFIC HELPFUL TIPS for short-answer questions:

SUMMARY OF TIPS

1. Answer the easy questions first.
2. Consider what the questioner wants you to do, and underline key words.
3. Look for clues among choices in the question, as well as in other questions.
4. Examine all possibilities. Beware of tricky and tempting foils (decoys).
5. Always select the broader, more encompassing choice.
6. Use a process of elimination.
7. Detect differences among the choices presented.
8. Don't choose an answer that is correct in itself but incorrect as it relates to the question.
9. Look for "giveaways" and "freebies."
10. Think out the answer before looking at the possible choices.
11. Make informed and educated guesses.

In addition to these SPECIFIC HELPFUL TIPS, here are five more bonus ones:

1. Read each question twice.
2. Generally, try to go with your first inclination.
3. Avoid looking for patterns.
4. Be aware that universals (i.e., *always, never, only*) should usually be disregarded as possible correct choices.
5. Bear in mind that sometimes the essays will provide answers to the short answers.

SPECIFIC HELPFUL TIPS FOR THE ESSAY QUESTIONS

TIP 1
Understand the essay format: thematic and document-based questions.

Part II of the Regents exam consists of one thematic essay for which you will have 45 minutes to write. The thematic essay will be worth 15 percent of your score. Write a well-organized essay that includes an introduction, several paragraphs that address the task, and a conclusion. Be aware of key terms in the question, for example, *show, discuss, compare*. The thematic essay does not ask only for a recollection of facts, but rather asks the student to focus on themes and to demonstrate critical thinking. Those scoring the essay will use the following Generic Scoring Rubric:

GENERIC SCORING RUBRIC
THEMATIC ESSAY

5

- Shows a thorough understanding of the theme
- Addresses all aspects of the task
- Shows an ability to analyze, evaluate, compare, and/or contrast issues and events
- Richly supports essay with relevant facts, examples, and details
- Writes a well-developed essay, consistently demonstrating a logical and clear plan of organization
- Includes a strong introduction and conclusion

4

- Shows a good understanding of the theme
- Addresses all aspects of the task
- Shows an ability to analyze, evaluate, compare, and/or contrast issues and events
- Includes relevant facts, examples, and details, but may not support all aspects of the task evenly
- Writes a well-developed essay, demonstrating a logical and clear plan of organization
- Includes a good introduction and conclusion

3

- Presents a satisfactory understanding of the theme
- Addresses most aspects of the task or addresses all aspects in a limited way
- Is able to analyze or evaluate issues and events, but not in any depth
- Writes a satisfactorily developed essay, demonstrating a general plan of organization
- Uses some facts, examples, and details
- Restates the theme in the introduction and concludes with a simple restatement of the theme

2

- Attempts to address the theme, but uses vague and/or inaccurate information
- Develops a faulty analysis or evaluation of theme
- Writes a poorly organized essay, lacking focus and using few facts, examples, and details
- Has vague or missing introduction and/or conclusion

1

- Shows limited understanding of the theme; omits concrete examples; details are weak or nonexistent
- Lacks an analysis or evalution of the issues and events beyond stating vague and/or inaccurate facts
- Attempts to complete the task, but essay demonstrates a major weakness in organization
- Uses little or no accurate or relevant facts, details, or examples
- Has no introduction or conclusion

0

- Fails to address the theme
- Is illegible
- Blank paper

Part III of the Regents exam consists of one document-based question for which you will have 60 minutes to write. The document-based essay will be worth 30 percent of your score. The document-based question will be divided into two parts; a Part A short-answer section (15 percent) and a Part B essay (15 percent). Following the questions, approximately eight short documents will be provided. Each Part A question will address a specific document. Answer the question using the document and the author's point of view and incorporate information about the time period from which the document has been selected. The Part B essay requires you to state your position (thesis) in an introductory paragraph, then develop your argument in the body of the essay using information from most of the documents to support your position. Using outside information from your knowledge of the time period will enhance the essay. You should include a brief conclusion restating your position. As with the multiple-choice section, budget your time. Those scoring the essay will use the following Generic Scoring Rubric:

GENERIC SCORING RUBRIC
DOCUMENT-BASED QUESTION

5

- Thoroughly addresses all aspects of the task by accurately analyzing and interpreting most of the documents
- Incorporates relevant outside information
- Richly supports essay with relevant facts, examples, and details
- Writes a well-developed essay, consistently demonstrating a logical and clear plan of organization
- Uses information from the documents in the body of the essay
- Includes a strong introduction and conclusion

4

- Addresses all aspects of the task by accurately analyzing and interpreting most of the documents
- Incorporates relevant outside information
- Includes relevant facts, examples, and details, but discussion may be more descriptive than analytical
- Writes a well-developed essay, demonstrating a logical and clear plan of organization
- Includes a good introduction and conclusion

3

- Addresses most aspects of the task or addresses all aspects in a limited way; uses some of the documents
- Incorporates limited or no relevant outside information
- Uses some facts, examples, and details, but discussion is more descriptive than analytical
- Writes a satisfactorily developed essay, demonstrating a general plan of organization
- States the theme in the introduction and concludes with a simple restatement of the theme or topic

2

- Attempts to address some aspects of the task, making limited use of the documents
- Presents no relevant outside information
- Uses few facts, examples, and details; discussion simply restates contents of the documents
- Writes a poorly organized essay, lacking focus
- Has vague or missing introduction and/or conclusion

1

- Shows limited understanding of the task with vague, unclear references to the documents
- Presents no relevant outside information
- Attempts to complete the task, but essay demonstrates a major weakness in organization
- Uses little or no accurate or relevant facts, details, or examples
- Has no introduction or conclusion

0

- Fails to address the task
- Is illegible
- Blank paper

TIP 2
Go over the thematic essay before writing any answers and draw initial impressions.

Write down some ideas that come to mind, while underlining key words and phrases. This tip is valuable as it helps you retain initial ideas and thoughts about the subject matter of the question. In addition, it could provide you with some outline notes that could ultimately be used for your answer.

TIP 3
Go over the document-based question and draw initial impressions.

Go over the Historical Context section and the Task sections of the document-based question. Write down any quick notes about the time period being addressed by the question. Once again, this could provide you with some outline notes that could ultimately be used for your answer.

TIP 4
Prepare a time schedule.

This tip enables you to organize your test-taking time and allows you to focus your attention on those essays that are easiest for you. Allow sufficient time for each essay part. If there are three parts to an essay, decide how much time to allocate for each part. Write as much as you know for each part. The more you write, using as many examples as possible to answer the question, the better your chances for obtaining maximum credit. However, make adjustments according to the number of parts and to the value of each one. If you allocate 30 minutes for a three-part essay in which each part has equal worth, and then devote 20 minutes to part *a*, you will probably get maximum credit for part *a* but very little credit for parts *b* and *c*. Apportion time and values accordingly.

> **TIP 5**
>
> **Look for key words, both in the directions and in the question itself.**

By understanding key words in the directions, you are on your way to answering the question in a proper manner. The key directive words for all Regents essay questions are listed in a set of general instructions on the exam itself, between the short-answer questions and the essay questions.

The key directive words in the instructions are *discuss*, *describe*, *explain*, and *evaluate*. They are defined and these definitions should be referred to as you answer the essay question.

PART II: THEMATIC ESSAY

Directions: Write a well-organized essay that includes an introduction, several paragraphs addressing the task below, and a conclusion.

Theme: Government—Power of the Judiciary

> Shortly after the formation of the new constitutional government, the Supreme Court established itself as an equal to the legislative and executive branches.

Task:

> From your study of the Supreme Court under the leadership of Chief Justice John Marshall, identify two cases that strengthened the power of the Supreme Court.
>
> For each case identified:
>
> - *Discuss* the facts of the case
> - *Describe* the court's decision
> - *Explain* how the decision strengthened the power of the Supreme Court and the federal government

You may use cases decided during the Marshall Court era. Some suggestions you might wish to consider are *Marbury* v. *Madison* (1803), *McCulloch* v. *Maryland* (1819), and *Gibbons* v. *Ogden* (1824).

You are *not* limited to these suggestions.

Guidelines: The key content words in the question are *judiciary, equal, strengthened, decision.* The focus of the thematic essay should be concentrating on how the Supreme Court strengthened itself with powers granted or assumed through the cases provided. It is critical that you limit your discussion after describing the facts and the decision to how the case strengthened the power of the Supreme Court.

TIP 6

Outline an answer before writing.

By following this tip, you will be able to begin organizing your essay answers in a definitive manner. You will also be able to put down important ideas quickly and clearly. Your outline can be structured in any format you wish—it will not be graded. It can be placed in your exam booklet.

Example

An example of a simple, usable outline is given on page 30. It is based on the Thematic Essay from a Regents exam.

Theme: Reform Movements in the United States

Reform movements are intended to improve different aspects of American life. Through the actions of individuals, organizations, or the government, the goals of these reform movements have been achieved, but with varying degrees of success.

Task:

Identify **two** reform movements that have had an impact on American life and for **each**

- *Discuss* **one** major goal of the movement
- *Describe* **one** action taken by an individual, an organization, or the government in an attempt to achieve this goal
- *Evaluate* the extent to which this goal was achieved

You may use any reform movement from your study of United States history. Some suggestions you might wish to consider include the abolitionist movement, women's suffrage movement, temperance movement, progressive movement, civil rights movement, women's rights movement, and environmental movement.

You are *not* limited to these suggestions.

I. Progressive Movement
    A. Major goal
           Use the power of the government to address problems associated with the rise of industry in the United States, such as unsafe and unsanitary conditions.
    B. Action taken
           In 1906, Upton Sinclair, one of several "muckrakers," wrote *The Jungle*, a novel that exposed the dangerous and unhealthy conditions in the meatpacking industry.
    C. Level of success
           The Progressive Movement was successful in achieving its goal. In 1906 the federal government passed the Meat Inspection Act and the Pure Food and Drug Act.

II. Civil Rights Movement
    A. Major goal
           Change policies in the United States that segregated African Americans from whites in public facilities, and that limited the ability of African Americans to vote.
    B. Action taken
           In 1955, the Rev. Martin Luther King, Jr., led the African American community in Montgomery, Alabama, to boycott the bus system following the arrest of Rosa Parks for not giving up her seat to a white rider.
    C. Level of success
           The bus boycott was successful in pressuring the city of Montgomery to end its discriminatory policies in regard to bus ridership. By the mid-1960s, the movement was successful in pushing for major legislation in regard to civil rights, such as the Civil Rights Act (1964) and the Voting Rights Act (1965).

This outline is like a skeleton. A good essay will add "muscle, flesh, ligaments," etc., in complete sentences.

TIP 7

Make use of the question to compose your introductory sentence.

Directions: Write a well-organized essay that includes an introduction, several paragraphs addressing the task below, and a conclusion.

Theme: Separation of Powers

> The balance of the three branches of the federal government has, historically, been in a constant state of flux.

Task:

> From your study of the Reconstruction Period (1863–1876), identify two examples of the operation of checks and balances within the federal government.
>
> For each example identified:
>
> - *Discuss* a specific proposed action by the particular branch of government (executive, legislative, or judicial).
> - *Describe* the reaction to the action by another branch of government.
> - *Explain* the settlement or outcome of the debated issue.

You may use any examples from the Reconstruction Period. Some suggestions you might wish to consider are Lincoln's Proclamation of Amnesty and Reconstruction (December 1863) and Congress's Wade-Davis Bill (July 1864), President Johnson's plan of Reconstruction (May 1865) and the reaction of Congress with the passage of the Military Reconstruction Act (March 1867) and the passage by Congress of the Tenure in Office Act (March 1867), President Johnson's veto of the Act (1867), and the subsequent impeachment of President Johnson (1868).

You are *not* limited to these suggestions.

Guidelines: Once you have read the question and decided on the two examples of checks and balances, you can begin to write your answer with a topic sentence that "borrows" words from the question. Consider the following:

Example

> The Reconstruction Period (1863–1876) provides a helpful time period in United States history to discuss examples of the system of checks and balances and how the system has contributed to the flexibility of government.

TIP 8

Be sure to include sufficient details and examples in your answer.

This tip is very important and will help you to do well on an answer by letting the grader know that *you know* your material. Following this tip will show that you have explained and given support to the main ideas you have expressed. You should use it after writing your topic sentence and any other introductory statements. For the general statements you make, along with the main ideas you express, you must present any necessary, requested supporting data. This could include events, names, dates, reason, results, or other facts. As you write your essay answers, make believe that the person who will grade them is *not* a social studies teacher. Therefore, it becomes your responsibility to state *all* necessary information in a clear, logical, and supportive manner. Below is an essay question and a sample, partial answer to each of three parts.

Directions: Write a well-organized essay that includes an introduction, several paragraphs addressing the task below, and a conclusion.

Theme: Government—Power of the Judiciary

> Shortly after the formation of the new constutitional government, the Supreme Court established itself as an equal to the legislative and executive branches.

Task:

> From your study of the Supreme Court under the leadership of Chief Justice John Marshall, identify two cases which strengthened the power of the Supreme Court.
>
> For each case identified:
> - *Discuss* the facts of the case
> - *Describe* the court's decision
> - *Explain* how the decision strengthened the power of the Supreme Court and the federal government

You are *not* limited to these suggestions.

Guidelines: You may use cases decided during the Marshall Court era. Some suggestions you might wish to consider are *Marbury* v. *Madison* (1803), *McCulloch* v. *Maryland* (1819), and *Gibbons* v. *Ogden* (1824).

Example

> *Gibbons* v. *Ogden* (1824) involved competing steamboat companies navigating the waters of the Hudson River between New Jersey and New York. Because of the fact that the Hudson River made the common boundary of New York and New Jersey, the issue became one involving interstate commerce, a power delegated in the Constitution to the Congress of the United States. The Supreme Court's decision clearly defined Congress's power to regulate interstate (and foreign) commerce.

TIP 9

Use connective and linking words in your answers.

The use of such words, also called transitional words, is important when writing your essay answers. These words make your answers clearer and more logical, while helping the reader to understand the development of your ideas. The words are also useful in providing supporting data for main ideas, as well as changing from one idea to another. Here is a list of words that are often used to make connections and linkages, along with the specific purposes they serve in constructing a meaningful essay answer.

Connective and Linking Words	Purpose
1. first, second, next, last	to show sequence and order
2. because, therefore, thus, consequently, ultimately	to show cause and effect
3. for example, in other words, indeed	to emphasize something, to clarify an idea
4. however, but, yet, on the other hand, instead, still, although	to show contrast or change
5. similarly, in like manner	to show no change
6. furthermore, moreover, in addition, also, another	to note added information
7. meanwhile, presently, previously, subsequently	to show time relationship
8. finally, in conclusion, to sum up	to present a summary, to tie things together

The above suggestions would be useful when doing any kind of expository writing, whether in social studies or any other subject. Try them out on your next U.S. History and Government classroom exam, as well as when practicing essay writing with previous Regents exam essay questions.

TIP 10

If you are short of time, give an answer in outline form.

A Regents exam is three hours long; however, for any number of reasons, you may find yourself running short of time. If this happens, you should briefly, but neatly, put your answer in an outline form. (*Some* answer is better than *no* answer.) You should do this *only* as an *emergency measure*—not something you planned to do initially. For that reason, be assured that this tip is not contradicting #6. The advice in that tip was simply a guideline for you, to help in putting forth the complete essay answer that would be graded. In regard to the advice in this tip, however, the outline *is* the answer; it is what will be graded. Consequently, you should devote much care to its construction. It should follow a specific, easy-to-read style, such as the Harvard outline standard. Roman numerals, followed by capital letters and Arabic numerals, should be used. Sentences and phrases, as both topics and sub-topics, should be written in the same form and in the same tense. This is called *parallel construction.*

TIP 11

If you are uncertain about what to write, make an informed and educated guess.

If you are not sure of what to write down for an answer, don't be afraid to guess. This is the advice we gave you in Tip #11 for the short-answer questions. With the essays, as with the short answers, you have nothing to lose by making an educated guess; there is no penalty for guessing. Indeed, with the essays, you may even be able to get some extra credit—part credit is certainly better than no credit at all! You cannot afford to leave blank a 15-point question. Present whatever information you can give about an item.

A word of caution, however, as we said in Tip #11 for short answers. Guessing should be used *only* as a last resort in answering a question. Do not go into the Regents expecting to pass by guessing your way through the questions. There is no substitute for careful, diligent exam preparation long before the exam date itself.

PART III: DOCUMENT-BASED ESSAY

The following questions (Part A and Part B) are based on the accompanying documents (1–6). Some of these documents have been edited for the purpose of this exercise. The question is designed to test your ability to work with historical documents and to demonstrate knowledge of the subject matter being presented. As you analyze the documents, take into account both the source of the document and the author's point of view.

Directions: Write a well-organized essay that includes your analysis of the documents. You should include specific historical details and you may discuss documents not provided in the question.

Historical Context:
The Bill of Rights was added to the Constitution in 1791 to protect individual liberties against government abuse.

PART A

The documents below relate to issues concerning the Fourth, Fifth, Sixth, and Eighth Amendments. Examine each document carefully and then answer the questions that follow.

Document 1

> I have little patience with people who take the Bill of Rights for granted. The Bill of Rights, contained in the first ten amendments to the Constitution, is every American's guarantee of freedom.
>
> President Harry Truman, Memoirs, Vol. II (1955)

1. What did President Truman mean by the statement "the first ten amendments . . . is every American's guarantee of freedom"?

Note: Eight documents form this segment of the actual exam. A single document is supplied as an example.

PART B

Essay Response:

Your essay should be well organized with an introductory paragraph that states your position on the question. Develop your position in the next paragraphs and then write a conclusion. In your essay, include specific historical details and refer to the specific documents you analyzed in Part A. You may include additional information from your knowledge of social studies.

Example

> The Bill of Rights was added to the Constitution in 1791 to protect individual liberties against government abuse. Assess the validity of this statement with particular attention to the areas of search, interrogation, and prosecution.

Even if you are not familiar with President Truman and the specific cases defining amendments in the areas of search, interrogation, and prosecution, you would most likely be able to respond to the question by describing protections in your own environment, perhaps the school setting. Can your locker be searched by the school principal? What steps have to be taken by the school before you can be suspended or expelled? You know more than you think!

TIP 12

Write a suitable summary statement.

A suitable summary statement shows that you have successfully developed your main ideas in your essay. In addition, composing your summary statement helps to conclude your essay in a logical manner. A summary statement can be a rephrasing of the major points asserted in the introduction to the essay. It can also present the conclusions of the essay, which contains an orderly development of ideas. Thus, the person grading your essay will be impressed with its ending.

Example

Write a well-organized essay that includes an introduction, several paragraphs addressing the task below, and a conclusion.

Theme: Science and Technology

Science and technology have brought about great changes in many areas of American life.

Task:

From your study of the 20th century, choose three major scientific/technological developments.

For each scientific/technological development chosen:

- *Identify* the scientific/technological development.
- *Describe* the effects of the scientific/technological development on American life.
- *Discuss* the extent to which the development had a positive or a negative effect on American life.

You may use any major scientific/technological developments from your study of 20th-century U.S. history. Some suggestions you may wish to consider are mass production of the automobile (1900–1930), invention of the airplane and eventual trans-Atlantic flight (1903–1927), television (1945–present), nuclear weapons (1945–present), and home use of the personal computer (1980–present).

You are *not* limited to these suggestions.

Guidelines: After selecting the examples you chose to use and presenting the required descriptions and discussions, finish with a summary statement that "returns" to the main point of the essay identified in the question. A suitable summary statement for this essay would be as follows:

Example

> Science and technology have brought about great changes in many areas of American life. The effects of the development of nuclear weapons and missile defense systems have had a negative effect on American life in the sense that they have contributed to society living in a perpetual state of fear of a nuclear holocaust. On the other hand, the home use of the personal computer has brought much of the world's information into people's homes through the Internet, therefore having a positive effect on American life.

TIP 13

Edit and proofread your writing.

You should make use of this tip after writing each essay answer to be sure that you have checked the following: legible penmanship, organization of the answer, sufficient content, and proper grammar and spelling. A sloppy and poorly written answer is not going to make a good impression on the grader. If you cannot read your own handwriting, you cannot expect a grader to be able to read it.

Below are some guidelines that will assist you in editing your answers to essay questions. Did you:

1. write an introductory topic sentence that states what the essay is about?
2. compose factual and detailed sentences that support the main ideas?
3. express a complete thought in each sentence?
4. use suitable transitional and connective words? (See Tip #9.)
5. indent the first word of each paragraph?
6. begin each sentence with a capital letter?
7. punctuate your sentences correctly?
8. spell all names and words correctly?
9. write legibly?

10. answer the question?

11. answer the question without extraneous and unwanted material?

12. write your answer in a clear manner, so that even a non-social studies teacher could understand it?

TIP 14

Refer to the sources, dates, and authors of the documents in the document-based question.

You should note important information about the document that is provided immediately following the document—specifically the author, title, publisher and date of the document. This information can give you a better understanding of the document and its reliability. Knowing the background of a document's author—such as his or her religion, gender, political affiliation, class position, race, or country of origin—might provide insight into the document's purpose or point of view. A careful analysis of sourcing information can strengthen an essay's argument.

Let's now review the 14 SPECIFIC HELPFUL TIPS for answering essay questions described above:

SUMMARY OF TIPS

1. Understand the essay format: thematic and document-based questions.

2. Go over the thematic essay before writing any answers and draw initial impressions.

3. Go over the document-based question and draw initial impressions.

4. Prepare a time schedule.

5. Look for key words, both in the directions and in the question itself.

6. Outline an answer before writing.

7. Make use of the question to compose your introductory sentence.

8. Be sure to include sufficient details and examples in your answer.

9. Use connective and linking words in your answers.

10. If you are short of time, give an answer in outline form.

11. If you are uncertain about what to write, make an informed and educated guess.
12. Write a suitable summary statement.
13. Edit and proofread your writing.
14. Refer to the sources, dates, and authors of the documents in the document-based question.

In addition to these tips, here are five more bonus ones:

1. Read each question twice.
2. Include everything in an answer that you wish to say. Don't cross-reference answers. (Don't make reference in one essay answer to something in another answer.) It is very possible that no teacher will grade more than one of your three essays.
3. Select the essays easiest for you, and not those that you feel will impress the graders.
4. Do not abbreviate. Write *and*, not &. Write *United States*, not *U.S.*
5. Write as much as you know that is relevant for the thematic essay. The more you write, the better your chances for obtaining maximum credit.

Glossary of Terms

* **Abolitionists** those who supported doing away with (abolishing) the institution of slavery.
* **abortion** the ending of a pregnancy before a live birth.
  acid rain rain, snow, or sleet containing nitric or sulphuric acid produced from the contamination of the atmosphere by smokestack and automobile emissions. It can damage plants and animals and erode stone and buildings.
* **acculturation** the modification of a people's **culture** through adaptation or borrowing from other cultures; the merging of cultures.
* **activism** belief in direct vigorous action.
  administration the management of government; the body of officials in the executive branch; the term of office of a **president**.
* **advocate** (1) to plead a case or support a particular issue; (2) one who pleads such a case or supports an issue.
* **affirmative action** public policy of incorporating women and racial and **ethnic** minorities into economic, political, and social institutions; usually applied through legislation or court orders.
* **affluent** wealthy, well-to-do.
* **aggression** unprovoked attack or act of violence.
** **agrarian** relating to agriculture or land.
* **airlift** supplying a city or region by airplane. In the Berlin Airlift of 1948–1949, the United States and allies flew food and other necessities into West Berlin because the Soviet Union had imposed a blockade on land routes.
** **ally** a person, party, or country joined with another for a common purpose.
*** **amendment** change or addition made in the **Constitution**; proposed by **Congress** or a national convention called by Congress and ratified by state legislatures or special state conventions.

---

* Denotes a term that has been frequently tested on past exams.
** Denotes a term that has been very frequently tested on past exams.
*** Denotes a term that has been most frequently tested on past exams.

amnesty a general pardon for political offenses, generally to a large group of individuals.

anarchist one who believes in the abolition of government or is opposed to organized government.

* **anarchy** the absence of government; a state of disorder or chaos.

* **Antifederalists** opponents of **ratification** of the **Constitution** in 1787 and 1788; opponents of the extension of federal power.

* **antitrust** relating to the limitation or control of monopolies, trusts, or unfair business combinations.

apartheid racial **segregation**, specifically in South Africa before 1991.

Appalachia region of the Appalachian Mountains from Alabama to New York and western New England characterized in many parts by poverty and economic underdevelopment.

* **appeasement** attempts to conciliate an aggressor by making concessions. The policy of appeasement toward Hitler in the 1930s ultimately failed to avoid war.

* **appoint** to name to an office. A president's major appointments must be confirmed by the **Senate**.

apportionment allotment of voting districts as required by law.

* **arbitration** process of settling a dispute by referring it to a third party; both sides usually agree beforehand to abide by the arbitrator's decision.

armageddon a vast, final, destructive conflict.

armistice a truce preliminary to a peace treaty.

* **Articles of Confederation** the charter of the first national government of the United States; in effect from 1781 until replaced by the **Constitution** in 1789.

assembly a gathering or body of representatives, usually of a state or locality.

* **assimilation** process of being absorbed into a group or culture.

Atlantic Charter document issued in 1941 by President Franklin Roosevelt and Prime Minister Winston Churchill outlining the mutual wartime goals of England and the United States and their principles for assuring peace after the war.

backlash strong negative reaction to a law or political event.

* **balance of power** policy aimed at securing peace by maintaining approximate military equality among countries or **blocs**.

* **balanced budget** plan for government taxes and spending in which expenses do not exceed income.

belligerent a participant in a war.

bicameral legislature law-making body made up of two houses or chambers.

** **big business** group of large profit-making corporations.

* **Big Stick policy** willingness to use military power to influence foreign affairs. It derives from Theodore Roosevelt's saying, "Walk softly, but carry a big stick."

** **Bill of Rights** first ten amendments to the **Constitution**, adopted in 1791.

bipartisan involving the cooperation of two political parties.

* **birth control** artificial or natural means of avoiding pregnancy.

** **black codes** a series of laws that sought to control and regulate the conduct of freed slaves during and after the **Reconstruction** period in the southern states. Generally, they denied blacks their basic civil rights.

* **bloc** a group of countries or voters.

Bolsheviks radical socialists and communists under the leadership of Lenin and Trotsky who came to power following the Russian Revolution in 1917.

bonus a government payment to war veterans usually based on length of service.

* **boom** period of economic expansion.

Boston Massacre incident in 1770 in which five colonists were killed in Boston when British soldiers fired on a crowd throwing rocks and snowballs; the soldiers were tried and acquitted of murder.

Boston Tea Party incident in Boston, December 16, 1773, when colonists dressed as Native Americans forced their way aboard merchant ships in the harbor and threw overboard their cargoes of tea so that recently imposed British taxes on it could not be collected.

bourgeoisie economic and social class between the aristocracy or the very wealthy class and the working class (the **proletariat**); the commercial or professional class; the middle class.

** **boycott** method used by unions and other political groups to force concessions from management or opponents. To boycott is to join together in refusing to deal with or buy from a party in order to influence them to negotiate or make concessions.

brain trust experts without official positions who served as advisors to President Franklin Roosevelt.

brinkmanship pushing a dangerous situation to the limit before stopping.

* **brown power** phrase describing attempts by Hispanic Americans to use their growing numbers to improve their political and economic standing.

* **budget** financial plan for income and expenses.

* **budget deficit** the amount by which a government's expenses exceed its revenue or income.

bureaucracy administrative officials of government.

* **cabinet** the advisors to the **president** who also manage the principal executive departments of the U.S. government. The **cabinet** is not mentioned in the **Constitution**, but has grown and developed over time from custom and practice.

* **Camp David Accords** agreements reached in 1978 between President Sadat of Egypt and Prime Minister Begin of Israel, negotiated by President Carter at the presidential retreat in Camp David, Maryland. The accords evolved into a peace treaty between Israel and Egypt in 1979, providing for Egypt's official recognition of Israel and Israel's withdrawal from the Sinai Peninsula.

* **capital** (1) the seat or main location of a government; (2) money invested or used to return a profit.

* **capital gains tax** a tax on profits made from the sale of property or securities.

** **capital punishment** death sentence imposed by a court.

* **capitalism** economic system in which the means of production and distribution are privately owned and operated for profit.

Carpetbaggers northerners who went to the South during the **Reconstruction** period to participate in and profit from its political reorganization.

caucus a closed meeting of a political party.

censorship preventing the publication of written material or the showing of a film, television program, or play because the government or a segment of society finds it objectionable.

* **census** a counting of the inhabitants of a region.

* **Central Powers** in World War I, Germany, Austro-Hungary, and their allies.

centralized with power or authority concentrated in a central organization.

charter written document establishing the rules under which an organization will operate; an organization's constitution.

** **checks and balances** division of powers among the three branches of the federal government so that each branch may limit actions and power of the others. *See also* **separation of powers**.

Chicanos Americans of Mexican origin or descent.

** **citizen** person entitled to the rights and protection provided by the state or nation.

civil relating to the state, politics, or government.

** **civil disobedience** refusal to obey a law in order to draw attention to its unfairness or undesirability.

* **civil liberties** *see* **civil rights**.

*** **civil rights** the liberties and privileges of citizens, especially those guaranteed in the **Bill of Rights**.

* **civil service** system for filling government jobs through impartial and nonpolitical means, such as standardized exams. Begun by the federal government in the 1880s.

* **civilian** a person who is not a member of the military or armed forces; pertaining to matters outside the military.

clandestine secret; performed secretly.

* **clear and present danger** standard established by the Supreme Court for determining when the right of free speech may be limited or denied—"when there is a clear and present danger that they will bring about the substantive evils that [the government] has a right to prevent."

* **coalition** temporary alliance of groups or factions.

* **coinage** money made of metal; sometimes called hard money.

* **cold war** a conflict between nations short of actual military conflict; the political, diplomatic, economic, and strategic competition between the United States and the Soviet Union from 1946 until 1991.

** **collective bargaining** method by which workers negotiate as a group with their employer through their union representatives.

** **collective security** agreement among a group of nations to help each other maintain their safety and territory; usually by agreeing that an attack by a foreign power upon one nation will be considered an attack upon all.

** **colonialism** international policy based on control over dependent areas or colonies.

** **colony** a territory ruled or administered by a distant nation, usually for the benefit of the ruling nation.

* **commerce** the exchange or buying and selling of goods; business.

* **commerce among the states** business carried on across state lines, which **Congress** is given power to regulate by Article I, Section 8, of the **Constitution**.

* **committee** a group of people appointed or delegated for a particular purpose.

* **commodities** common economic goods that are bought and sold, such as agricultural products.

common law body of law formed over time by accumulation of precedents and prior decisions, as opposed to laws enacted by legislative bodies.

Common Sense a pamphlet by Thomas Paine that helped rally public support for the Revolutionary War.

commonwealth an organization of independent states; form of government of several states in the United States.

communiqué official bulletin, statement, or other communication.

*** **communism** political philosophy advocating collective ownership of property and the means of production and the abolition of the capitalist economic system.

compact theory of union doctrine held by many states' rights supporters that the **union** was a voluntary compact among the states and that states had the right to leave the union in the same manner they had chosen to enter it.

compromise a settlement in which each side makes concessions.

concession something yielded or given up, often in exchange for something else.

Confederate States the 11 southern states that seceded or officially withdrew from the Union in 1860 and 1861 to form an independent nation called the Confederate States of America. Their withdrawal was not recognized by the federal government or the remaining states. They were defeated in the Civil War and reabsorbed into the Union.

* **confirm** to approve or agree with.

*** **Congress** the legislative branch of the federal government; composed of the **Senate** and the **House of Representatives**.

conscription compulsory enrollment into the armed forces; forced military service; draft.

consensus general agreement.

* **conservation** careful management and protection, especially of natural resources.

conservative reluctant or resistant to change; favoring traditional views and values; one belonging to a conservative party or political group.

constituents the citizens represented by an elected public official; group of supporters.

*** **Constitution** the basic charter of the United States government, effective since 1789; it was written by the **Constitutional Convention** in 1787, ratified by the states in 1787–1788, and put into effect in 1789.

constitutionalism belief that government is limited by legal and political restraints and accountable to the governed.

* **Constitutional Convention** gathering of delegates from the 13 states in 1787 in Philadelphia for the purpose of revising the **Articles of**

Confederation; instead, they drafted an entirely new **Constitution** that was adopted in 1788 and put into effect in 1789.

Constitutional Republicanism elected government limited by legally defined guidelines.

* **consumer** the final buyer and user of a product.

* **consumerism** protection of the interests and rights of consumers against false advertising or faulty or dangerous products.

** **containment** policy adopted by the Western democracies after World War II to prevent the further expansion of communism and the Soviet Union.

* **Continental Congress** (1) any of several assemblies of delegates from the American colonies before the Revolution to promote cooperation on various issues; (2) the national legislative body under the **Articles of Confederation** (1781–1788).

* **convention** a meeting of political delegates.

conventional traditional or ordinary; in military affairs, it refers to forces or measures other than nuclear weapons.

* **cooperative** a corporation owned collectively by members who share in the profits and benefits. **Cooperatives** were first developed by farmers in the late 19th century to avoid high prices charged by middlemen for grain storage, transportation, and farm supplies.

corollary a proposition that follows a previous one, which it modifies or enlarges, such as the **Roosevelt Corollary** to the **Monroe Doctrine**.

* **corporation** an organization legally empowered to act as one person, including the ability to borrow and lend money, make contracts, own property, and engage in business.

* **corruption** illegal or improper practices; abuses of authority, especially in connection with bribery or theft.

coup an overturning; a coup d'état is the overthrow of a government.

craft union labor union made up of workers with the same skill or craft, such as carpenters or electricians.

credibility grounds for being believed or trusted.

Crédit Mobilier railroad construction company that cheated on government contracts and bribed congressmen during the late 1860s.

* **creditor nation** a nation that exports more than it imports, so that it is owed money by other nations.

* **cultural pluralism** the acceptance and encouragement of multiple ethnic, religious, and racial groups within one society; respect for ethnic diversity.

** **culture** the beliefs, social forms, and accumulated knowledge of a group, race, or people.

* **currency** money in circulation, especially paper money.

* **Darwinism** (1) the theories of biologist Charles Darwin, who explained the evolution of species by natural selection; (2) social theories loosely based on Darwin's work and arguing that "the survival of the fittest" meant that government should not protect the weak from exploitation by the strong.

Dayton Accord agreement to end the war in Bosnia negotiated by the presidents of Bosnia, Croatia, and Yugoslavia at Dayton, Ohio, in November 1995 with the assistance of the United States; agreement that established two autonomous regions—a Serb republic and a Muslim-Croat federation—within the nation of Bosnia and Herzegovina and provided for a multinational **United Nations** force to supervise the agreement.

debasement a reduction of value.

* **debtor nation** a nation that imports more than it exports and so owes money to other nations.

* **Declaration of Independence** document passed and signed by the **Continental Congress**, effective July 4, 1776, declaring the United States an independent and sovereign nation.

** **defense spending** government spending for military armaments, equipment, and personnel.

degradation a decline into a lower or worse condition.

* **delegate** a representative chosen to act for a group or another person.

demilitarized zone area where no military equipment or personnel may be deployed.

demobilize to discharge from military service.

Democratic Party political party that evolved out of the **Democratic Republicans** around 1820.

Democratic Republicans political party formed around 1800 by Jefferson, Madison, and others opposed to the **Federalists**.

demographic relating to the statistical study of human populations.

** **depression** an economic downturn, especially one characterized by high unemployment.

* **desegregation** the ending of **segregation**, which is the separation of whites and blacks.

despot a **sovereign** or authority without legal restraints; an absolute monarch; tyrant.

* **détente** relaxation of strained relations or tensions.
* **diplomacy** the practice of conducting relations between countries by negotiations rather than force.
** **direct election** election in which votes are cast by the people themselves rather than by their representatives.
directive order issued by a high authority calling for specific action.
* **disarmament** giving up or reducing armed forces.
* **discrimination** partiality, **prejudice**, or distinctions in treatment; the denial of rights and advantages to minority groups.
disenfranchise to take away the right to vote.
dissenting opinion written statement by a member of a court disagreeing with the court's decision.
distribution of wealth statistical measure of how the property or wealth of a nation is divided among its population.
* **diversity** variety; being made up of unlike parts.
dollar diplomacy use of American political and military power abroad (usually in Latin America) to promote or advance the interests of American businesses.
* **domestic** having to do with the internal affairs of a country.
* **domino theory** belief in the 1950s and 1960s that the fall of one nation to communism would lead to the fall of neighboring nations.
** **due process of law** doctrine that government's power cannot be used against an individual except as prescribed by established law. Applied to the state governments by the 14th Amendment.

* **ecological** concerning the relationship between living things and the environment.
** **economy** the total system for business, production, consumption, and investment in a country.
* **Eisenhower Doctrine** statement made in 1957 by President Eisenhower that the United States would provide military and economic aid—and direct military intervention, if necessary—to nations of the Middle East if they were threatened by communist aggression.
* **elastic clause** part of the **Constitution** (Article I, Section 8) that gives the federal government the right to make laws "necessary and proper" to carry out its specific powers and functions; it has sometimes been used to expand the powers of the federal government; also known as the "necessary and proper clause."
** **election** process of choosing officers by vote.

* **electoral college** means of electing a **president** and vice president established by the **Constitution** and subsequent amendments; voters in each state choose "electors" who later meet to elect the **president** and vice president. Electors were originally free to vote for any candidate they chose, but they are currently pledged to vote for specific candidates. The number of electors from each state is equal to the number of **Representatives** and **Senators** from that state.

emancipation the act of setting free; freeing from restraint or, especially, slavery.

* **Emancipation Proclamation** issued by President Lincoln in 1863, it declared free the slaves in the southern states in rebellion but did not affect slaves held in states loyal to the Union, such as Maryland, Kentucky, or Missouri.

* **embargo** prohibition on commerce with a nation or region, usually to apply pressure or force concessions.

* **emigrate** to leave one country or region to settle in another.

encroachment step-by-step interference with the rights or possessions of others.

endorsement approval or recommendation.

* **enjoin** to legally forbid or prohibit, usually by court order or **injunction**.

Enlightenment era during the 17th and 18th centuries when reason replaced religion as a guide to politics, philosophy, and government.

* **environmentalists** persons concerned about the quality of air, water, and land and the protection of natural resources, "green" space, and plant and animal species.

envoy a messenger or **representative**.

** **equal protection** principle that all people be treated the same under the law.

* **equality** condition of having the same rights, privileges, and advantages as all other citizens.

* **escalate** to increase the extent, level, or volume.

espionage the act or practice of spying.

* **ethnic** belonging to a particular group identified by nationality or national origin and **culture** or customs.

* **ethnocentric** believing that one's own ethnic group is superior to others.

evacuate to remove to a safer area.

* **evolution** change over time; an adjustment in the existing order.

*** **executive** person or office having administrative and managerial functions; in government, the branch responsible for carrying out the laws and for the conduct of national affairs—it includes the **president** and **cabinet** and the departments under their jurisdiction.

* **executive privilege** principle that an **executive** (such as the **president**) should not divulge certain sensitive or protected information.

* **expansionism** policy of adding to a country's territory, usually by seizing land from other nations.

exploitation wrongful or unethical use of someone or something for one's own benefit.

extraterritoriality right of a resident of a foreign country to be tried in the judicial system of his or her home country.

fascism political philosophy advocating **totalitarian** government power, intense **nationalism**, and military **expansionism**. Mussolini's Fascist party governed Italy from the 1920s through World War II.

* **Far East** the nations on the Pacific coast of Asia.

* **favorable balance of trade** exporting or selling more goods than are imported or bought.

*** **federal** relating to the central national government created by the **Constitution**.

Federal Housing Administration federal agency established in 1934 to insure mortgages and set construction standards.

Federal Reserve Note currency or paper money issued by the **Federal Reserve System** and representing a promissory obligation of the federal government. **Federal Reserve Notes** replaced the older gold and silver certificates, which were backed by or based upon specific reserves of gold and silver.

* **Federal Reserve System** federal agency created by Congress in 1913 to regulate the banking system. Federal Reserve banks in 12 districts supervise banking operations, lend money to banks, and issue currency; a Federal Reserve Commission sets and regulates interest rates.

** **federalism** system of government in which powers are divided between a central authority and local subdivisions.

* **Federalists** advocates of adopting the **Constitution** in 1787–1788 and of more powerful central government during the period 1789–1820. Many **Federalists** later joined the **Whig** Party.

* **feminism** movement advocating equal rights and privileges for women, including economic, political, legal, and social status.

filibuster use of delaying tactics, such as unlimited debate in the Senate, to prevent action on a legislative proposal.

* **fiscal** having to do with government revenues, expenditures, and budgets.

fission splitting or breaking up; nuclear fission refers to the splitting of an atomic nucleus to release a vast quantity of energy.

fluctuation a series of movements up and down or back and forth.

foreclosure the act of a lender taking possession of mortgaged property from a borrower who is unable to make the required payments.

* **foreign aid** assistance in the form of money or goods supplied to a foreign country.

*** **foreign policy** a nation's policy in dealing with other nations.

* **Fourteen Points** President Wilson's plan for international peace presented to **Congress** on January 22, 1918.

franchise the right to vote; **suffrage**.

* **free enterprise** the freedom of private businesses to operate without undue government interference.

** **free trade** the freedom to exchange goods with other countries, especially without **tariffs**.

* **freedman** a freed slave, usually referring to a former slave freed by virtue of the 13th Amendment.

* **freedom of religion** right of citizens to hold and practice religious beliefs without interference from government.

** **freedom of speech** right of citizens to say or write their views without regulation or reprisal from government; restricted in some cases, *see* **clear and present danger**.

* **freedom of the press** right of publishers to print material without prior approval by government; *see* **prior restraint**.

Freedom Riders civil rights advocates who traveled the South on buses to promote the desegregation of public facilities.

Free-Soil party political party before the Civil War opposed to the extension of slavery and the admission of slave states.

* **frontier** border region between two distinct areas, especially (in America) between settled and unsettled territory. In European usage, a frontier is the border between two countries.

Fugitive Slave Law federal law passed in 1850 that required northern states to return escaped slaves to their owners in the South. It was widely opposed by a variety of legal and extra-legal means.

* **fundamental rights** *see* **natural rights**.

GATT General Agreement on Tariffs and Trade signed by 132 countries to lower trade barriers.

gerrymandering drawing the boundaries of election districts to ensure the victory of one party or faction by including or excluding neighborhoods of a particular ethnic or social class.

* **global** relating to the world as a whole; international; worldwide.

* **Good Neighbor policy** policy first announced by President Franklin Roosevelt to promote friendly relations with all Latin American nations.

*** **government** the institutions and people responsible for the conduct of public affairs.

Great Compromise agreement in the **Constitutional Convention** of 1787 to have two houses of **Congress**, one (the **Senate**) to represent the states equally and the other (the **House of Representatives**) to represent the people proportionately. Also known as the Connecticut Compromise.

** **Great Depression** period from the stock market crash of 1929 until the start of World War II during which industrial production declined and **unemployment** rose to over one fourth of the labor force.

* **Great Society** collective name for various social programs of President Lyndon Johnson, including the so-called War on Poverty and programs for job training, subsidized housing, and free medical care for the poor and aged.

green revolution the increase in agricultural crop yields brought about by the use of machinery, fertilizers, pesticides, and improved seeds.

greenhouse effect belief that excessive carbon dioxide in the atmosphere caused by burning fossil fuels will create a layer in the upper atmosphere that retains heat and will cause the Earth's temperature to rise.

guerilla an active participant in a war who is not a member of the regular armed forces; a kind of warfare characterized by sabotage, harassment, and hit-and-run tactics.

* **habeas corpus** a writ or legal order directed to an official holding a person in custody, commanding the official to produce the person in court, show cause why the person has been confined, and prove that the person has not been deprived of liberty without **due process of law**.

* **Harlem Renaissance** a movement among black writers, artists, and musicians centered in Harlem, New York City, during the 1920s.

Head Start educational aid to preschool children from disadvantaged homes.

health maintenance organization (HMO) organization that provides health services such as hospitalization and doctors' fees to members who make a fixed monthly payment.

Hessians hired soldiers from the district of Hesse in Germany, employed by the British before and during the Revolutionary War.

* **heterogenous** composed of unlike parts; a society made up of different races, nationalities, or ethnic groups.

Holocaust originally, a burnt sacrificial offering; since World War II, it refers to the genocidal murders of millions of European Jews by the Nazis.

home front during a war, the area of a nation's domestic and civilian affairs.

* **Homestead Act** act passed by **Congress** in 1862 that gave 160 acres of western land to any head of a family who agreed to cultivate it for five years; it encouraged the rapid settlement of the West by giving immigrants and Easterners free land.

* **homogenous** made up of similar elements; a society consisting primarily of the same race, nationality, or **ethnic** group.

hot line direct telephone link, especially between the White House and the Kremlin, always ready for instant communication.

** **House of Representatives** the half of **Congress** composed of representatives allotted among the states according to their population.

*** **immigration** act of moving into a country where one is not a native to become a permanent resident.

* **impeach** to bring formal charges against a public official for misconduct. The **House of Representatives** has the power to impeach federal officials, and the trial is held by the **Senate**.

** **imperialism** the practice of forming and maintaining an empire; possession of foreign territories or colonies for the benefit of the home country; the policy of seeking to dominate economically, politically, or militarily weaker areas of the world.

implementation the means of accomplishing or carrying out a plan or program.

* **import quota** a limit on the amount of a commodity that can be brought into the country.

* **inauguration** a ceremonial beginning, especially the installing of an official at the beginning of a term.

* **incumbent** person currently serving in political office, especially one seeking reelection.

* **Indians** European term for the native inhabitants of the Americas; it was based on the mistaken belief that the continents were part of Asia or India.

indictment a legal action to charge someone with a crime.

* **individualism** doctrine that the rights and interests of individual persons are the most important source of values.

*** **industrialization** economic transformation of society by the development of large industries, machine production, factories, and an urban workforce.

* **Industrial Revolution** the transformation from an agricultural society to one based upon large-scale mechanized production and factory organization. It began in Europe (especially England) in the late 18th century and in America in the early 19th century.

* **infiltration** gradual entrance or buildup with the intent of taking control.

* **inflation** general and continuing rise in the price of goods, often due to the relative increase of available money and credit.

* **initiative** process for the direct involvement of voters in the making of laws; by gathering enough signatures on a petition, a group can force a legislature to consider a proposal or require it to be placed on the ballot for public vote.

* **injunction** order issued by a court directing someone to do or refrain from doing some specific act.

* **installment buying** practice of buying a product through regular monthly or weekly payments; failure to pay gives the seller the right to repossess the product.

insurgency an uprising or revolt against a government, short of actual war.

* **integration** bringing together or making as one; unification; applied especially to blacks and whites.

* **interdependent** depending on one another, such as nations that rely on each other's trade.

* **internal improvements** roads, canals, and other means to assist transportation and commerce. In the first half of the 19th century, debate concerned who should fund internal improvements: the states or the federal government.

** **internationalism** policy of cooperation among nations.

* **internment** the detainment and isolation of **ethnic** groups for purposes of national security (such as Japanese Americans during World War II); this is now widely held to have been **unconstitutional**.

interposition an argument that the states could legitimately object to acts of **Congress** if those acts exceeded **Congress**'s legitimate authority. Interposition fell short of **nullification**.

* **interpret** to explain or determine the meaning.

* **interstate** taking place across state lines; involving the citizens of more than one state.

* **Interstate Commerce Commission** established by **Congress** in 1887 to regulate railroad rates and prevent abuses by railroads; it was later expanded to have **jurisdiction** over other forms of transportation.
* **intervention** interference in the affairs of another country, including the use of force.

Intolerable Acts series of acts of **Parliament** directed against the American colonies and intended to assert British authority and increase revenues from the colonies.

invalidate to make null and void; to destroy the existence or effectiveness of, as, for example, a law.

Iran-Contra Affair an illegal conspiracy by officials of the Reagan administration to provide funding for the anticommunist Contra rebels in Nicaragua by secretly selling missiles to Iran and diverting the money to the Nicaraguans.

Iron Curtain the series of fortified borders separating Western Europe from Soviet-dominated Eastern Europe; the term was made popular by Winston Churchill.

** **isolationism** policy of keeping a nation apart from alliances or other political relations with foreign nations.

* **Jim Crow laws** laws enforcing **segregation** or control of blacks in such a way as to make them unequal.
* **joint resolution** a legislative act that is the same in both houses of **Congress**.
* **judicial activism** developing social policy through court decisions instead of through legislative action, often in response to changing values and circumstances.
* **judicial nationalism** term used to describe the **Supreme Court** under the leadership of John Marshall, when its decisions consolidated the power of the federal government by centralizing responsibility for commerce, contracts, and finance.
* **judicial restraint** the preference of a court to avoid upsetting existing law or practice.
** **judicial review** power of the **Supreme Court** to void acts of **Congress** that are found to violate the **Constitution**.
* **judiciary** the branch of government that interprets the law and tries cases; the system of courts.

jurisdiction authority of a court to interpret and apply the law; in general, the area of authority of a government.

* **Knights of Labor** early labor union, formed in 1869.

Kremlin complex of government offices in Moscow; the center of government of Russia and the Soviet Union.

* **Ku Klux Klan** secret organization founded in 1866 to intimidate freed slaves and keep them in conditions of servitude through threats and acts of violence; it later developed into a nativist organization opposed to Jews, Catholics, and immigrants, as well as African Americans.

** **laissez-faire** doctrine opposing government interference or regulation of economic matters beyond what is necessary to maintain property rights and enforce contracts. *Laissez faire* is French for "let alone" or "let be."

lame duck an official who has not been reelected and is serving out the remainder of a term.

*** **League of Nations** international organization of countries formed after World War I to promote world peace. It was supported by President Wilson, but the **Senate** refused to allow the United States to join. After World War II it was replaced by the **United Nations**.

** **legislature** a body of persons elected to make laws for a nation or state; a congress or parliament.

* **levy** to place and collect a tax; to draft persons for military service.

liberal advocating political or social views that emphasize **civil rights**, democratic reforms, and the use of government to promote social progress.

* **liberty** freedom; the power to do as one pleases.

life expectancy statistical estimate of the average lifespan of a particular population.

* **limited government** *see* **constitutionalism.**

* **line-item veto** power of an **executive** to **veto** specific expenditures without vetoing the entire bill that contains them. Congress gave the **president** a limited line-item veto in 1996.

* **lobbying** actions by private citizens or organizations seeking to influence (by legal means) the decisions of a **legislature** or **executive** department of government.

* **loose construction, loose interpretation** reading of the **Constitution** that allows broad use of the **elastic clause** and **implied powers**.

* **Louisiana Purchase** the purchase from France by the United States in 1803 for $15 million of the Louisiana Territory, stretching from New Orleans west to the Rocky Mountains, more than doubling the size of the United States.

Loyalists American colonists who remained loyal to England during the American Revolution; also known as **Tories**.

* **Magna Carta** agreement signed by King John I of England in 1215, granting certain rights (including trial by jury and **habeas corpus**) to the barons who had taken him prisoner.

  majority number greater than one half of the votes cast (simple majority); a "two-thirds majority" requires at least two thirds of the votes cast.

  malaise vague sense of unhappiness or discomfort.

* **Manifest Destiny** belief, held by many Americans in the 19th century, that the United States was destined to control the continent between the Atlantic and Pacific Oceans.

* **market economy** an economic system in which decisions about production and pricing are based on the actions of buyers and sellers in the marketplace; usually associated with capitalism.

* **Marshall Plan** the program of U.S. aid to Europe following World War II to help those nations recover from the extensive damage to their cities, industries, and transportation.

  materialism valuing economic or material things more than spiritual or intellectual interests.

* **media** the industries of mass communication, such as television, radio, and newspapers.

  mediator person who solves differences between two parties. Both sides do not usually agree beforehand to accept the decisions of the mediator, as they usually do with an arbitrator.

* **Medicaid** federal government program to pay the hospital and medical costs for those on welfare or whose incomes are very low.

* **Medicare** federal government program to pay the hospital costs of those over age 65 who pay a premium for additional coverage.

* **mercantilism** the economic policies of European nations from the 15th century until the **Industrial Revolution**, based on mercantile (commercial, trading) activities and characterized by the acquisition of colonies and the establishment of a **favorable balance of trade**. The American colonies were established under the mercantile system.

* **middle class** the members of a society having a socioeconomic position between the very wealthy and the poor.

* **migration** the movement of people from one place to another.

  militancy aggressive opposition.

* **militaristic** characterized by military discipline and aggressiveness.

  military-industrial complex the combined power of the Defense Department and the industries that supply it with equipment. The phrase was popularized by Eisenhower, who claimed that it worked for unnecessary increases in armaments.

militia part-time soldiers who do not belong to the regular armed forces.

** **minority** the portion of a group less than one half; an **ethnic** or racial group that is smaller than the dominant group and may be subjected to **discrimination**.

* **Miranda rights** constitutionally guaranteed rights of those accused of crimes to be informed by the police that they have a right to remain silent, a right to an attorney, and a right to be supplied with legal counsel if they cannot afford a private attorney; established by *Miranda* v. *Arizona* (1966).

Missouri Compromise an agreement in 1820 between congressional advocates and opponents of the extension of **slavery** that preserved sectional balance. It included the simultaneous admission of the slave state Missouri and the free state Maine and the prohibition of slavery in the northern parts of the **Louisiana Purchase**.

** **monopoly** the exclusive control or ownership of an industry by a single person or company.

* **Monroe Doctrine** policy announced in 1823, during the presidency of James Monroe, that the United States would oppose European attempts to extend their control of the Western Hemisphere. It became and remains a basic principle of American foreign policy.

moratorium agreement to postpone payment of a debt or other obligation.

mortgage legal instrument specifying payments to be made on a loan for the purchase of property. Failure to make payments gives the mortgager the legal right to repossess the property.

* **muckraker** journalists in the late 19th and early 20th centuries who reported on political or commercial corruption.

* **multicultural** different cultural beliefs and practices followed by different ethnic groups living in harmony within the same community.

multinational involving more than two nations.

municipality a city or local political unit.

munitions armaments and ammunition used in warfare.

NAFTA North American Free Trade Agreement (1993). An agreement ratified during President Clinton's first administration to eliminate trade barriers between the United States, Canada, and Mexico.

* **nationalism** (1) sense of pride in one's country; (2) extreme devotion to national interests.

* **National Labor Relations Board** federal agency established in 1935 to enforce laws against unfair labor practices.

* **National Origins Act** laws passed in 1921, 1924, and 1929 that limited **immigration** into the United States and established **quotas** for nations based on the number of persons from those nations living in the United States according to an earlier **census**. It was regarded as **discriminatory** because it favored immigrants from Western Europe.

native one who is connected with a place by birth; an original inhabitant as distinguished from immigrants or visitors.

** **Native Americans** descendants of the original inhabitants of the Americas.

* **nativism** in the United States, the policy of favoring native-born Americans and opposing immigrants.

* **natural rights** rights or liberties to which one is entitled as a human being.

necessary and proper clause portion of the **Constitution** granting **Congress** power to "make all Laws which shall be necessary and proper for carrying into Execution" its other powers.

** **neutrality** policy of not helping either side in a war.

* **Neutrality Acts** laws passed in 1935 and 1937 to avoid U.S. involvement in a war in Europe; they placed an embargo on arms sales to any nation engaged in war.

*** **New Deal** name adopted by President Franklin Roosevelt for the reforms and social programs instituted by his administration, beginning in 1933.

* **New Freedom** program of President Wilson to regulate banking and **currency** to influence the direction of the economy and to support stronger **antitrust** legislation.

* **New Nationalism** program of President Theodore Roosevelt during his unsuccessful campaign for the presidency in 1912. It promised greater government supervision of the economy to balance the power of **big business**.

* **19th Amendment** granted **suffrage** (the right to vote) to women; enacted in 1920.

* **nomination** proposal of a candidate for an office.

nonintervention policy of not becoming involved in the affairs of other nations.

* **nonpartisan** not based on party interests or bias.

nonsectarian not affiliated with any religious group.

* **nonviolence** principle that all violence is to be avoided; the use of peaceful means for political ends.

* **normalcy** the state of being normal; the term was applied to the era of the 1920s, following the disruptions of World War I.

* **North Atlantic Treaty Organization (NATO)** collective security military alliance formed in 1949 by the United States, Canada, and nations of Western Europe to oppose the threat posed by the Soviet Union and Warsaw Pact nations to Europe.

Northwest Territory federal administrative district west of the Allegheny Mountains, north of the Ohio River, south of the Great Lakes, and east of the Mississippi River, including the present states of Ohio, Indiana, Michigan, Illinois, and Wisconsin, and part of Minnesota. The Territory was organized by the **Continental Congress** in 1787 from lands claimed by several eastern states.

nullification argument or doctrine claiming that states could refuse to abide by acts of **Congress** if the states felt **Congress** had exceeded its enumerated powers. Used by states' rights advocates; championed by John C. Calhoun of South Carolina.

* **Nuremberg Tribunal** international military court held in Nuremberg, Germany, in 1945–46; top Nazi leaders were tried and convicted of crimes against humanity and violations of international law.

* **Open Door policy** an attempt by the United States in 1899 to preserve trade interests in China by asking European nations to respect the territorial integrity of China and to permit free access to ports they held in Asia.

ordinance a law or regulation, usually of a local municipality.

*** **organized labor** workers represented by labor unions.

original jurisdiction the first court with authority to consider and decide a case, as opposed to appellate jurisdiction.

* **overproduction** production of a commodity in excess of the demand for it; it usually results in falling prices.

* **parity** government support of prices for agricultural products to ensure that farm income keeps pace with income in other economic sectors.

* **Parliament** the legislative body of Great Britain, consisting of the House of Commons and the House of Lords.

partition division of a country into two or more separate parts.

* **Peace Corps** U.S. government agency formed by President Kennedy in 1961; it sought to assist developing countries by sending American volunteers to teach and provide technical assistance.

penal having to do with punishment; liable to be punished.

Pentagon headquarters of the U.S. armed forces, near Washington, D.C.

* **per capita** the average per person for a particular population, as in per capita income.

perjury making a false statement under oath.

* **philanthropy** literally, the love of mankind; desire to help humankind, usually through gifts or endowments to charitable institutions.

* **picketing** method of demonstration by workers or political groups, usually taking place at the employer or the offices of the opposition; it includes notifying the public of the unfairness of the employer with signs and conversation.

plea bargaining pleading guilty to a lesser charge in order to avoid standing trial for a more serious one.

* **pluralistic** type of society in which diverse **ethnic**, racial, and national groups coexist while maintaining their own cultural heritage.

* **plurality** a number of votes greater than any other candidate but less than a majority of all the votes cast.

pocket veto an automatic veto that occurs if the **president** does not sign a bill passed by **Congress** during the last ten days of its session.

pogrom organized, officially encouraged persecution or massacre of a group.

political machine combination of party and political officials who maintain themselves in office, sometimes through corrupt means.

*** **politics** the practice of government; the art of winning control of public affairs.

* **poll tax** (1) a tax paid to register or vote in elections (prohibited under the 24th Amendment). (2) a per-person or per-capita tax, not based on income or employment.

* **pollution** the contamination of the atmosphere by burning of automobile and smokestack emissions or the contamination of water by chemicals dumped into streams by factories or by fertilizers washed into water sources by rainfall.

popular sovereignty (1) doctrine in democratic forms of government that power ultimately derives from the people and that the consent of the governed is exercised through the vote; (2) in the years before the Civil War, a political position advocating that the legality of **slavery** in the western territories be decided by popular vote of the inhabitants; it was ridiculed by its opponents as "squatter sovereignty."

* **populism** movement that began in agricultural areas in the late 19th century seeking government regulation to curb excesses and exploitation by big business.

pragmatism belief in a practical (rather than an ethical or theoretical) approach to problems and affairs.

* **Preamble** introductory part, especially the opening of the **Constitution**, which begins "We the people. . . ."

precedence the right to be first or have more authority.

precedent rule or decision that serves as a guide for future actions or decisions; attorneys look for precedents to support their arguments when presenting a case in court.

* **prejudice** a preconceived opinion or judgment, usually negative, not based on fact.

preside to act as chairman.

*** **president** the chief executive officer of the federal government.

* **press** the news-gathering and publishing industry, including television, radio, magazines, and newspapers.

* **price supports** government measures to maintain the price of a commodity at an artificially set level.

prior restraint the prohibition of publication of an article, book, or story by a court order before the material is disclosed to the public. Permissable only in cases of obscenity or of **"clear and present danger."**

* **primary election** election in which members of a political party choose their candidates for the coming general elections.

* **processing tax** a tax on industries that convert raw materials into finished goods, such as cotton into cloth.

* **Progressive Era** the period roughly from 1900 to 1920, marked by political, economic, and social reform movements.

* **progressive tax** a tax that is higher for the wealthy than for the poor, such as income tax.

* **progressivism** a broad reform movement during the late 19th and early 20th centuries that sought to remedy the worst effects of industrialism and **urbanization** by imposing governmental controls on **big business**, improving social justice, and increasing direct democratic participation in politics.

* **prohibition** period from the enactment of the 18th Amendment in 1919 until its repeal by the 21st Amendment in 1933, during which the manufacture, sale, import, export, and transportation of alcoholic beverages was declared illegal.

proletariat the industrial working class, who sell their labor and do not own the means of production.

propaganda promotion of particular ideas and doctrines.

* **protective tariff** tax on imported goods intended to protect the interests of internal or domestic industries by raising the price of imports.

protectorate an area under the control and protection of a country that does not have full **sovereignty** over it.

proviso clause in a document or statute making some condition or provision.

* **purse** the power to authorize revenues and spending; in the federal government, **Congress** holds the power of the purse.

quarantine isolation of a person or country, usually to prevent spread of communicable diseases.

quartering forcibly housing soldiers in private residences.

* **quota** a maximum limit; a share or portion assigned to a group.

** **racism** belief that some races are inherently superior to others.

* **radical, radicalism** favoring extreme and fundamental changes.

*** **ratification** formal legal approval and adoption.

* **raw materials** products or resources not yet manufactured into their final state, such as many agricultural products, lumber, or ores.

rearmament rebuilding of a nation's armed forces, often with new and better weapons.

* **recall** political reform procedure for removing a public official from office before the end of a term by popular vote; it is usually initiated by a petition.

** **Reconstruction** period from 1865 through 1876, when the southern states were occupied by federal troops and under the direct control of the national government.

* **Red Scare** fears about the danger of **communist** subversion or invasion; especially after World War II, "Red Scare" tactics were used by Senator Joseph McCarthy and others for political purposes.

* **referendum** a proposal submitted to a popular vote before putting it into effect.

refinance to change the terms of a **mortgage** or loan to make it easier for the borrower to make the payments.

*** **reform** to improve or change, especially a social institution.

** **regulatory** enforcing the rules or laws.

rehabilitation restoration to a former or better condition.

* **relocation** the movement (sometimes by force) of a group of people to a new place.

* **reparations** payments imposed on nations defeated in war to help the victors recover the costs of war.

repercussion a widespread or indirect effect of an act.

** **representative** (1) a **delegate** or agent of another person or group of people; (2) a federal legislator; (3) a type of government by persons chosen from among the governed, usually by election.

* **Republican Party** political party formed in the 1840s, opposed to the extension of **slavery**; Lincoln was the first Republican elected president (in 1860).

  repudiate to disown or disavow.

* **reserved powers** powers not specifically granted to **Congress** or the federal government under the **Constitution**, and so held to be reserved to the states.

* **restraint of trade** language used in the **Sherman Antitrust Act** (1890) to describe combinations and activities of groups (businesses, labor unions) that were prohibited under the Act.

* **retaliatory** done in response to an attack or **aggression**; strong enough to deter an attack.

* **revenue** the income of governments from taxation, **tariffs**, fees, and other activities.

* **reverse discrimination** discrimination against whites or males.

* **revolution** rapid change, often accompanied by violence.

* **right to counsel** entitlement of an accused person to have an attorney present during questioning.

* **rights** individual liberties protected by the state or federal constitutions.

  Rights of Englishmen an expression of the American colonists during their struggle with England; they claimed to want only the same liberties and privileges enjoyed by British subjects in England, as established by **Magna Carta**, common law, and the English Bill of Rights, including **habeas corpus**, trial by jury, and representation in **Parliament**.

** **rights of the accused** include the Fifth Amendment guarantee against self-incrimination and the **right to counsel**; also known as **"Miranda rights,"** after the **Supreme Court** decision in the case of *Miranda* v. *Arizona* (1966).

* **Roaring Twenties** the 1920s, during which the United States returned to "normalcy" after World War I, with rapid economic expansion, changed social values, high spending for consumer goods, and the popularization of the automobile, radio, and motion pictures.

* **Roosevelt Corollary** supplement to the **Monroe Doctrine** asserted by President Theodore Roosevelt, who claimed the right of the United States to exercise international police power in the Western Hemisphere and to intervene in the affairs of Latin American nations.

* **"Rule of Reason"** term used by the **Supreme Court** in its decision in the case of *Standard Oil Co.* v. *United States* (1911), which held that only "bad" trusts were illegal.

* **ruling** an official decision.

** **SALT II** Strategic Arms Limitation Treaty signed by the United States and the Soviet Union to limit the number of bombers capable of carrying nuclear weapons; signed in 1979 as a major step in reducing the danger of nuclear war; a follow up to SALT I, which was the first step taken to slow the increase in nuclear weapons.

salutary neglect phrase describing the belief that the American colonies benefitted from lack of interest in their affairs by the British government during the period before 1763.

sanctuary place of refuge or protection.

satellite state a nation controlled by a more powerful nation.

* **Scopes trial** the trial of John T. Scopes in Dayton, Tennessee, in 1925 for violating a state law prohibiting the teaching of Darwinian evolution. The highly publicized trial featured William Jennings Bryan as prosecutor and Clarence Darrow for the defense. Scopes was found guilty and fined $100.

* **search and seizure** police power to look for and hold evidence in the investigation and prosecution of a crime; evidence from unreasonable searches or searches without probable cause may be excluded from a trial.

* **secession** withdrawal of a member from a political group; withdrawal of a state from the Union.

* **second-class citizenship** condition of having fewer or inferior rights and privileges.

* **sectionalism** development of internal divisions based on geographic and economic alliances; rivalry between different areas of the country.

* **Securities and Exchange Commission** federal agency established in 1934 to regulate the stock market and to prevent the abuses practiced during the 1920s that led to the **stock market crash** of 1929.

security safety; freedom from danger.

sedition the act of stirring up rebellion against a government.

** **segregation** the isolation or separation of one group from another, usually applied to keeping whites and blacks apart.

*** **Senate** the half of the federal legislature made up of two members from each state.

** **separate but equal** legal doctrine established by the **Supreme Court** in the case of *Plessy* v. *Ferguson* (1896) that separate accommodations for blacks and whites did not violate the 14th Amendment if the accommodations were of equal quality. Overruled by the later **Supreme Court** decision in *Brown* v. *Board of Education* (1954).

* **separation of church and state** doctrine that government may not restrict the free exercise of religious beliefs nor support any religious group or principle.

** **separation of powers** doctrine that liberty of the people is best assured by the division of government into separate branches. *See also* **checks and balances**.

* **sexual harassment** policy or practice of compelling female employees to submit to the sexual advances of male superiors or to endure verbal or physical harassment, in violation of the Civil Rights Act of 1964.

* **sharecroppers** tenant farmers who leased and cultivated pieces of land in exchange for a percentage of the crop.

Shays' Rebellion armed insurrection in western Massachusetts in the fall of 1786 led by Captain Daniel Shays and others in protest against economic policies and foreclosures of farms for failure to pay taxes. It was suppressed by the state **militia**, but it had a significant effect on the framing of the **Constitution** the following summer.

* **Sherman Antitrust Act** passed in 1890 declaring combinations in restraint of trade to be illegal; it was passed to maintain competition in private industry and to correct abuses of companies that had gained **monopoly** power.

* **sit-in** action of protesters in occupying a public place to force concessions; especially by **civil rights** advocates seeking **desegregation** of public facilities.

** **slavery** system of holding persons against their will for involuntary servitude; in a system of "chattel slavery" the person held could be bought or sold as property. Slavery in the United States was abolished by the 13th Amendment.

smokestack industries heavy industries that burn large amounts of fossil fuels, such as steel-making or auto manufacturing.

social contract the implied agreement among individuals in a community or between the people and their rulers.

* **socialism** political philosophy advocating ownership and operation of the means of production (such as land, mines, factories) by society as a collective whole, with all members sharing in the work and benefits. Socialist economic systems usually include government ownership and operation of industries.

* **social mobility** movement up or down the class scale within a society.

* **Social Security Act** passed in 1935 to provide an income for persons who are disabled or aged and for families without a wage earner; it has become the basic means of support for retired persons who lack private pensions from employers.

** **social welfare** organized services for helping disadvantaged people.

* **sovereign** holding supreme authority.

* **sovereignty** the ultimate power and authority to make laws, either directly or through representatives; in a democracy, sovereignty lies in the people.

  space satellite an object in space that orbits a planet or other body on a regular path.

* **special interest** group or industry that seeks to influence government for its own benefit.

* **speculation** taking extreme risks in business or investing in hopes of earning large profits.

  spoils system system wherein government positions and offices are awarded to political supporters on the basis of party loyalty or service rather than qualification or merit; based on the saying "To the victor go the spoils"; the system was replaced to some extent by the **Civil Service**, beginning in the 1880s.

  stability the ability to remain unchanged or permanent.

* **Stamp Act** act enacted by **Parliament** in 1765 that required a tax stamp on all printed and legal documents. It was soon repealed due to American resistance.

* **START II** Strategic Arms Reduction Treaty signed in 1993 by the United States and Russia to reduce the number of nuclear warheads held by each nation by half; a follow-up to START I in 1991, which was the first agreement for each nation to scrap some of its nuclear weapons.

  statehood condition of being a state and a full member of the United States; for example, Hawaii achieved statehood in 1959.

*** **states' rights** group of doctrines holding that the states retained the power to overrule, oppose, or withdraw from the federal government if they chose.

* **stock market crash** a rapid fall in the price of **stocks**. The great crash of 1929 was caused by overspeculation that increased stock prices far above their true value; prices started to fall when knowledgeable investors began to sell their shares; that forced speculators, who had invested with borrowed money, to sell as well, and the combined rush to sell caused a panic, which drove prices even lower.

* **stocks** certificates showing shares of ownership in a **corporation**.

  strict construction doctrine that the **Constitution** limits governmental powers to those explicitly stated; *contrast with* **loose construction**.

** **strike** work stoppage by labor in an attempt to force the employer to make concessions.

* **subjugation** the act of bringing under control.

  subpoena official written order commanding a person to appear in court or to produce specific items.

subsidiary in business, a company that is controlled by another company.

subterranean below the surface of the earth.

subversion the undermining, overthrowing, or destroying of an established institution, such as government.

** **suffrage** the right to vote.

supremacy the highest power or authority.

supremacy clause portion of the **Constitution** declaring it "the supreme law of the land" and overriding any state or local laws in conflict with it.

*** **Supreme Court** the highest court in the federal judicial branch.

surcharge an extra charge.

synthetic artificially produced or man-made by combinations of chemicals.

* **tariff** taxes on imports into a country to collect revenues or to protect domestic industries.

* **Teapot Dome** federal oil reserve in Wyoming that was secretly and illegally leased to a financial backer of President Harding.

** **technology** applied science used in production.

temperance moderation in the consumption of alcoholic beverages; a movement supporting governmental measures to curb alcohol consumption.

Tennessee Valley Authority federal public works project established in 1933 that constructed dams and reengineered waterways to control flooding and generate electricity in seven southern states.

tenure the act or right of holding an office.

* **term limits** legislation that limits elected officials to a set number of years in office, usually eight to 12 years or two to three terms; a concept that has become popular in recent years and has been applied to elected officials in a number of states.

** **third parties** political parties existing at various times in the United States other than the two predominate political parties.

Third World the group of nations, especially in Asia and Africa, that were not aligned with either the communist **bloc** or the Western democracies.

* **three-fifths clause** clause in the **Constitution** saying that three fifths of the number of persons held as slaves be included in calculating representation in **Congress**, even though those persons were not citizens and were not entitled to vote. Superceded by the 14th Amendment.

Tories supporters of British rule during the Revolutionary War; also known as **Loyalists**. In England, the Tory party generally supported the king or conservative interests.

totalitarian characterized by the state or government having total control over the lives of citizens.

town meeting meeting of the citizens of a town as a legislative body.

* **trade deficit** the amount by which imports exceed exports; how much is owed to other nations.

* **trade gap** difference in amount between imports and exports.

treason acts that intentionally endanger the security or **sovereignty** of one's own nation; waging war against one's country or giving aid to its enemies.

triangular trade pattern of commerce pursued in the late 18th and early 19th centuries by New England merchants who carried sugar and molasses from the West Indies to New England, rum and manufactured goods from New England to Africa, and slaves from Africa to the West Indies.

* **Truman Doctrine** policy announced by President Truman in 1947, stating that the United States would provide military and economic aid to nations threatened by subversion or invasion; it was established specifically to assist Greece and Turkey, which were threatened with communist takeover.

** **trust** a combination of companies or industries established to reduce competition and increase profits.

* **turnout** the number of eligible voters who participate in an election.

tyranny absolute and arbitrary power without legal restraints.

unconditional surrender total surrender without exceptions or conditions; the phrase was made popular by Ulysses S. Grant.

* **unconstitutional** prohibited by or in opposition to the principles of the **Constitution**.

* **underclass** class of the permanently poor.

** **unemployment** being out of work; government compensation to people who have lost their jobs.

* **unicameral** of a legislature having only one house or chamber.

*** **union** (1) the political combination of the states; (2) the northern and border states that opposed **secession** during the Civil War; (3) an organization of workers seeking **collective bargaining** with their employer.

** **United Nations (UN)** international organization established in 1945 to preserve peace; currently has 185 members. Security Council made up of five permanent members (United States, Russia, China, Great Britain, and France) and ten nonpermanent members can cause military action, as it did during the Korean War and the Persian Gulf War, the deployment of peacekeeping forces to monitor cease-fire agreements, as it's done in the Middle East and Bosnia, and can impose economic sanctions, as it has done with Iraq, Yugoslavia, and South Africa.

* **universal suffrage** the right of all citizens to vote, regardless of sex, race, or economic status.

* **Unwritten Constitution** governmental practices and institutions not specifically set down in the **Constitution** but based upon custom and practice.

* **urbanization** the growth of cities and the increasing concentration of population in them.

utilities companies that furnish electric power, water, gas, or other services without competition and are regulated by law.

utopian advocating impossibly idealistic or impractical forms of government or society.

* **Versailles Treaty** peace treaty signed in 1919 between Germany and the Allies; it required Germany to give up its colonies, pay substantial reparations, and surrender territory to France, Poland, and Czechoslovakia.

* **veto** action by an executive official preventing the enactment of a legislative act. A veto by the **president** can be overridden by a two-thirds majority of **Congress**.

VISTA Volunteers in Service to America, a program of President Johnson's 1964 Economic Opportunity Act.

* **war crimes** crimes against humanity; actions commited by armed forces against civilian populations during military conflicts, including genocide, murder, rape, extermination, deportation, enslavement, and persecutions on religious, racial, or political grounds; actions under jurisdiction of war crimes tribunals established under international law.

* **War on Poverty** President Johnson's domestic programs for social renovation, including the **VISTA**, Job Corps, and **Head Start** programs and the establishing of the Department of Housing and Urban Development.

* **War Powers Act** law passed in 1973 to limit the power of the **president** to use armed forces in combat without the authorization of **Congress**; it was adopted in response to the Vietnam War, in which millions of armed forces were sent to Vietnam without a declaration of war.

* **Watergate** hotel in Washington, D.C., where the Democratic National Committee headquarters were burglarized in 1972 by operatives of the Republican Committee to Reelect the President (Nixon). Attempts by the staff of the White House to cover up their links to the burglars eventually led to a widespread scandal and the resignation of President Nixon.

* **welfare** a government social support program to provide a limited income to people who are unemployable because of age or physical or mental condition or who are unemployed because they lack skills or initiative or because the economy has not created enough jobs; a program that has become more restrictive in recent years by limiting the number of people eligible to receive benefits or the number of years a person may receive benefits.

Whigs in the United States from around 1800 until the Civil War, a political party opposed to the Jeffersonian Republicans and Jacksonian Democrats. Many of its supporters later joined the **Republican Party**. In England, the Whig Party generally opposed the extension of the king's power and supported the predominance of **Parliament**.

Whiskey Rebellion armed insurrection in 1792 by settlers in western Pennsylvania and Virginia protesting federal excise tax on distilled spirits (whiskey). Suppressed by federal troops under Washington, who pardoned most of the participants.

Whitewater (1994) name of an investigation in which legal questions arose regarding Arkansas land investments made by President and Mrs. Clinton. Attorney General Janet Reno appointed Kenneth Starr as independent counsel to investigate the charges. On Wednesday, September 20, 2000, Special Prosecutor Robert Ray concluded the investigation without charging the Clintons with wrongdoing, saying there was insufficient evidence to prove they "knowingly participated in any criminal conduct."

work ethic belief in the value and moral good of productive labor.

* **World Trade Organization (WTO)** a specialized agency of the United Nations that is the most important organization supervising international trade; administers trade agreements, monitors trade policies and practices of nations, tries to settle trade disputes, and keeps track of statistics on trade.

Yalta Agreements agreements reached between Roosevelt, Churchill, and Stalin at Yalta in February 1945, regarding the organization of post-war Europe in anticipation of the defeat of Germany. The agreements divided Germany and Berlin into temporary zones of occupation and established the basis for the **United Nations**.

yellow journalism irresponsible, sensational, or misleading reporting of news.

Regents Examinations, Answers, Self-Analysis Charts, and Regents Specification Grids

Examination
August 2017
United States History and Government

PART I: MULTIPLE CHOICE

Directions (1–50): For each statement or question, write in the space provided the *number* of the word or expression that, of those given, best completes the statement or answers the question.

1 Which geographic feature contributed most to the settlement of colonies along the Atlantic Coast?

(1) mountainous terrain
(2) extensive mineral deposits
(3) subtropical climate
(4) navigable rivers and harbors   1 _____

2 During the 1700s, the British government used mercantilism to

(1) profit from its colonies
(2) develop colonial manufacturing
(3) discourage colonial agriculture
(4) promote colonial trade with other nations   2 _____

3 The French and Indian War (1754–1763) was a turning point in the relationship between American colonists and the British government because the war

(1) increased French influence in North America
(2) ended Native American Indian attacks west of the Appalachian Mountains
(3) resulted in British debt and attempts to tax colonists
(4) created an alliance with Canada against the British   3 _____

4 The main reason Thomas Paine wrote *Common Sense* was to

  (1) urge adoption of the Albany Plan of Union
  (2) gain support for declaring independence from Great Britain
  (3) bring an end to the Revolutionary War
  (4) convince states to ratify the new Constitution   4 _____

Base your answer to question 5 on the passage below and on your knowledge of social studies.

... That your Sex are Naturally Tyrannical is a Truth so thoroughly established as to admit of no dispute, but such of you as wish to be happy willingly give up the harsh title of Master for the more tender and endearing one of Friend. Why then, not put it out of the power of the vicious and the Lawless to use us with cruelty and indignity with impunity [exemption]. Men of Sense in all Ages abhor [hate] those customs which treat us only as the vassals of your Sex. Regard us then as Beings placed by providence under your protection and in immitation of the Supreem Being make use of that power only for our happiness....

—Abigail Adams, Letter to John Adams, March 31, 1776

5 Which document most directly addressed the concerns expressed by Abigail Adams in this passage?

  (1) Federalist Papers
  (2) Monroe Doctrine
  (3) Declaration of Sentiments
  (4) Emancipation Proclamation   5 _____

6 The Northwest Ordinance of 1787 was important in United States history because it established a method for

  (1) admitting new states to the Union
  (2) promoting diplomatic relations with foreign nations
  (3) funding internal improvements
  (4) securing ports on the Pacific Coast   6 _____

7 Antifederalists insisted that a bill of rights be added to the Constitution in order to

(1) grant more power to Congress
(2) provide a method of settling disputes between states
(3) prevent states from denying individuals the right to vote
(4) protect individual rights from the power of the central government   7 _____

Base your answer to question 8 on the passage below and on your knowledge of social studies.

> ...An *elective despotism*, was not the government we fought for; but one which should not only be founded on free principles, but in which the powers of government should be so divided and balanced among several bodies of magistracy [governance], as that no one could transcend their legal limits, without being effectually checked and restrained by the others....
>
> —James Madison, *Federalist No. 48*, 1788

8 Which principle of the United States Constitution is supported by this passage?

(1) representative government
(2) writ of habeas corpus
(3) separation of powers
(4) due process of law   8 _____

9 The term *federalism* is best described as the

(1) division of power between the national government and state governments
(2) creation of a two-house legislature in the national government
(3) method of reviewing laws and executive actions
(4) establishment of three branches of government   9 _____

Base your answer to question 10 on the passage below and on your knowledge of social studies.

> The right of citizens of the United States, who are eighteen years of age or older, to vote shall not be denied or abridged by the United States or by any State on account of age.

> —United States Constitution, 26th Amendment, Section 1

10 Which factor contributed most directly to public support for this amendment?

  (1) high crime rates
  (2) the Vietnam War
  (3) the Watergate affair
  (4) increased life expectancy   10 _____

11 A presidential veto of a bill can be overridden by a

  (1) majority vote of registered voters
  (2) majority vote of the Supreme Court
  (3) two-thirds vote of the state legislatures
  (4) two-thirds vote of both houses of Congress   11 _____

12 The opening of the Erie Canal in 1825 was important to the development of the nation because it

  (1) linked the industrial centers of the North and the South
  (2) allowed the United States Navy to defend the Great Lakes
  (3) forced the Spanish to sell Florida to the United States
  (4) increased trade between the East Coast and the Midwest   12 _____

13 Before the Civil War, the collapse of the Whig Party and the formation of the Free Soil and the Republican parties showed that

  (1) opposing views on slavery affected national unity
  (2) Americans were united in their political views
  (3) major political parties received most of their support in the South
  (4) Americans were divided over the issue of unlimited coinage of silver   13 _____

14 Throughout the Civil War, an important advantage the North had
over the South was that the North

   (1) had superior military leaders
   (2) had greater manufacturing capabilities
   (3) received support from Great Britain and France
   (4) used a strategy for fighting a defensive war   14 _____

15 The Compromise of 1877 brought an end to Radical Reconstruction by providing for the

   (1) resignation of President Rutherford B. Hayes
   (2) removal of federal troops from Southern states
   (3) establishment of a system of sharecropping
   (4) strict enforcement of the 14th amendment   15 _____

Base your answers to questions 16 and 17 on the charts below and on your
knowledge of social studies.

Sources of Immigration to the United States

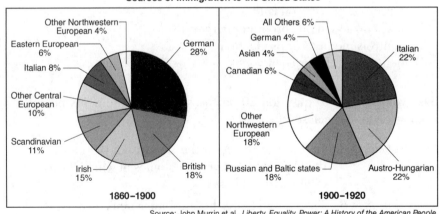

Source: John Murrin et al., *Liberty, Equality, Power: A History of the American People,*
Thomson Wadsworth, 2006 (adapted)

16 Which conclusion is best supported by the information in the charts?

   (1) Immigration from the Western Hemisphere declined after 1900.
   (2) The percentage of German immigrants increased between 1860
and 1920.
   (3) Northern Europeans were not permitted to enter the
United States from 1860 to 1920.
   (4) Southern and eastern Europeans made up a majority of
immigrants from 1900 to 1920.   16 _____

17 What was one result of the changes in immigration patterns shown on the charts?

(1) Restrictive immigration laws were passed.
(2) Business increased its demand for workers.
(3) Urban population declined.
(4) Requirements for citizenship were eased.   17 _____

18 During the late 1800s, political machines controlled the governments of many cities by

(1) denying voting rights to immigrants
(2) attracting dissatisfied voters from the two major political parties
(3) using corrupt practices and patronage
(4) favoring civil service reform   18 _____

19 The federal government follows the economic principle of laissez-faire when it

(1) places restrictions on land usage
(2) takes no action on corporate mergers
(3) controls methods of production
(4) determines the price of goods   19 _____

Base your answer to question 20 on the speakers' statements below and on your knowledge of social studies.

Speaker A: In order to maintain the security of the nation, the United States needs colonies in which it can establish naval bases.

Speaker B: The United States has problems of its own to be concerned about, so we must focus our attention here at home.

Speaker C: If the United States is to compete in a global economy, it needs to look beyond its borders for markets.

Speaker D: Supporting an overseas empire would become an enormous burden on the American people.

20 The focus of the speakers' debate is the controversy over the

    (1) purchase of Alaska
    (2) policy of imperialism
    (3) size of the United States military
    (4) closing of the frontier   20 _____

21 **"Carnegie Donates Millions to Build Libraries"**
"Rockefeller Creates Foundation for Medical Research"

These headlines reflect the actions of Andrew Carnegie and John D. Rockefeller as

    (1) muckrakers   (3) socialists
    (2) philanthropists   (4) conservationists   21 _____

22 The Progressive Era presidents were considered trustbusters because they

    (1) used government power to promote business competition
    (2) supported the elimination of trade barriers
    (3) encouraged more voter participation in government
    (4) canceled treaties with other nations   22 _____

23 The primary objective of the women's movement during the first two decades of the 20th century was to

    (1) gain property rights
    (2) promote higher education
    (3) secure full suffrage rights
    (4) win equal pay for equal work   23 _____

Base your answers to questions 24 and 25 on the cartoon below and on your knowledge of social studies.

"Touch Not a Single Bough [Branch]!"

Source: *Literary Digest,* August 9, 1919 (adapted)

24 The situation shown in this cartoon was mainly caused by the

    (1) cost of paying reparations after World War I

    (2) failure of President Woodrow Wilson to promote the Treaty of Versailles

    (3) overwhelming public rejection of the peace terms in the Treaty of Versailles

    (4) disagreement over United States participation in the League of Nations   24 _____

25 Which constitutional principle is shown in this cartoon?

    (1) due process

    (2) checks and balances

    (3) popular sovereignty

    (4) judicial review   25 _____

26 The 1920s are often called the Roaring Twenties because the decade was noted for

(1) political reform
(2) economic depression
(3) social and cultural changes
(4) ending Prohibition   26 _____

27 The Great Migration that took place between 1915 and 1930 refers to

(1) workers who left the northeast for the south
(2) Native American Indians who left their reservations
(3) middle-class whites who left cities to settle in the suburbs
(4) African Americans who left the rural south for northern cities   27 _____

28 Breadlines, Hoovervilles, and the Bonus Army were all direct results of

(1) housing shortages in the 1920s
(2) relief efforts of the New Deal
(3) mechanization of agriculture
(4) unemployment during the Great Depression   28 _____

29 The Fair Labor Standards Act (1938) helped American workers by

(1) establishing health plans
(2) legalizing strikes and boycotts
(3) establishing a minimum wage in many industries
(4) making labor unions accept women and African Americans as members   29 _____

30 Adoption of the "cash and carry" policy in 1939 and passage of the Lend-Lease Act in 1941 showed a growing commitment of the United States to

(1) provide aid to the Allied nations
(2) force the Japanese out of Korea
(3) increase trade with Italy
(4) end German violations of American territory   30 _____

31 A direct result of United States involvement in World War II was

    (1) an increase in the production of consumer goods
    (2) the entry of more women and minorities into the workplace
    (3) a decrease in industrial activity
    (4) a decrease in federal control over the economy   31 _____

32 Which event was a cause of the other three?

    (1) Congress declared war against Japan.
    (2) Japanese Americans were interned by the federal government.
    (3) The United States was attacked at Pearl Harbor.
    (4) The United States dropped an atomic bomb on both
         Hiroshima and Nagasaki.   32 _____

33 McCarthyism of the early 1950s resulted in

    (1) the end of the arms race
    (2) reduced spending on national defense
    (3) increased discrimination against returning veterans
    (4) damage to the reputations of many innocent people   33 _____

34 During the 1950s, United States foreign policy was shaped by

    (1) the principle of nonalignment
    (2) a return to pre–World War II isolationism
    (3) a willingness to compromise with communist nations
    (4) the emergence of two world superpowers   34 _____

35 The formation of the North Atlantic Treaty Organization (NATO) and the Southeast Asia Treaty Organization (SEATO) were attempts by the United States and other nations to

    (1) create mutual defense pacts
    (2) increase tariff rates between members
    (3) decrease the number of nuclear weapons
    (4) provide economic aid to poor nations   35 _____

36 In 1958, the United States government increased spending on science education and research in reaction to the

(1) creation of the Warsaw Pact
(2) launching of *Sputnik*
(3) installation of Soviet missiles in Cuba
(4) U-2 incident 36 _____

Base your answer to question 37 on the quotation below and on your knowledge of social studies.

... Believing this as I do, I have concluded that I should not permit the Presidency to become involved in the partisan divisions that are developing in this political year.

With America's sons in the fields far away, with America's future under challenge right here at home, with our hopes and the world's hopes for peace in the balance every day, I do not believe that I should devote an hour or a day of my time to any personal partisan causes or to any duties other than the awesome duties of this office—the Presidency of your country....

—President Lyndon B. Johnson, Address to the Nation,
March 31, 1968

37 What was one problem facing President Lyndon B. Johnson at the time this speech was delivered?

(1) Americans had experienced several judicial scandals.
(2) His participation in peace talks threatened the war effort.
(3) Opposition to the Vietnam War was becoming more widespread.
(4) Great Society programs forced a reduction in military spending. 37 _____

38 What was the primary method used by Dr. Martin Luther King Jr. to advance civil rights?

(1) nonviolent protest of segregation practices
(2) support for black separatism
(3) pursuit of elective public office
(4) practical education for economic gain 38 _____

Base your answers to questions 39 and 40 on the cartoon below and on your knowledge of social studies.

National-Security Blanket

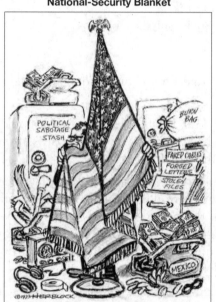

Source: Herblock, *Washington Post*, May 27, 1973
(adapted)

39 Which action by President Richard Nixon is the focus of this cartoon?

(1) recalling diplomats from Mexico
(2) supporting tax decreases and budget cuts
(3) attempting to hide evidence from investigators
(4) making concessions to the Soviet Union

39 _____

40 The outcome of the events illustrated in the cartoon resulted in the

(1) expansion of the Vietnam War into Cambodia
(2) resignation of President Richard Nixon
(3) growing support for environmental protection legislation
(4) visit to Communist China by President Richard Nixon

40 _____

Base your answer to question 41 on the cartoon below and on your knowledge of social studies.

Source: Tom Toles, *Washington Post*, April 25, 2007

41 Which statement best supports the cartoonist's view in 2007 about global warming?

(1) The federal government has been slow to take action on global warming.
(2) Most people support efforts to address global warming.
(3) Dealing with global warming is too expensive.
(4) Global warming is damaging the ozone layer.   41 _____

42 Since the presidency of Ronald Reagan, the Republican Party has generally tried to deal with economic problems by supporting

(1) lower taxes and reduced government spending
(2) the elimination of free trade and the free-market system
(3) deficit spending and decreased military spending
(4) increased social spending and strict regulation of the stock market   42 _____

43 Which statement about the Hurricane Katrina disaster (2005) is an opinion rather than a fact?

   (1) The levee system in New Orleans failed.
   (2) The federal government did not do enough to aid the victims.
   (3) The federal government was criticized for its initial response to the emergency.
   (4) The Federal Emergency Management Agency (FEMA) provided housing for victims.   43 _____

Base your answer to question 44 on the cartoon below and on your knowledge of social studies.

Source: Clay Bennett, *Chattanooga Times Free Press*,
November 5, 2008

44 According to the cartoonist, one important result of the election of President Barack Obama in 2008 was that

   (1) public facilities in the South were finally integrated
   (2) the executive branch of government gained power over the legislative branch
   (3) a racial barrier in government had been broken
   (4) racial discrimination was legally eliminated in the United States   44 _____

45 The practice of yellow journalism most influenced United States entry into which war?

   (1) War of 1812
   (2) Spanish-American War
   (3) World War II
   (4) Persian Gulf War   45 _____

46 The suspension of habeas corpus during the Civil War and the passage of the USA Patriot Act during the war on terror both illustrate the national government's willingness to

   (1) uphold the rights of minority citizens
   (2) tolerate criticism of its wartime policies
   (3) expand the power of the states to prosecute radical
        groups
   (4) limit civil liberties when the nation is facing immediate
        danger   46 _____

47 The Washington Naval Conference (1921), the Kellogg-Briand Pact (1928), and the Neutrality Acts of the 1930s were all attempts by the United States to

   (1) increase military spending
   (2) show support for the United Nations
   (3) assume a position of world leadership
   (4) avoid policies likely to lead to war   47 _____

48 The baby boom following World War II resulted in the

   (1) development of urban unrest in the 1950s
   (2) need to increase the number of schools in the 1960s
   (3) migration from cities to farms in the 1970s
   (4) need to decrease the number of nursing homes
        in the 1980s   48 _____

49 • *Tinker* v. *Des Moines School District* (1969)
   • *New Jersey* v. *T.L.O.* (1985)
   • *Vernonia School District* v. *Acton* (1995)

Which similar issue was addressed in these Supreme Court cases?

(1) balancing the rights of students with the need of schools to maintain order
(2) allowing principals to determine students' constitutional rights
(3) denying public school districts the authority to allow prayer in schools
(4) giving state legislatures the power to fund charter schools   49 _____

50 President John F. Kennedy and President Ronald Reagan both visited the Berlin Wall in order to

(1) assess the military strength of the Soviet Union
(2) prepare for an invasion of the Soviet Union
(3) demonstrate the commitment of the United States to maintain freedom in Western Europe
(4) challenge the North Atlantic Treaty Organization (NATO) nations that were supported by the Soviet Union   50 _____

In developing your answer to Part II, be sure to keep these general definitions in mind:

(a) <u>describe</u> means "to illustrate something in words or tell about it"

(b) <u>explain</u> means "to make plain or understandable; to give reasons for or causes of; to show the logical development or relationships of"

(c) <u>discuss</u> means "to make observations about something using facts, reasoning, and argument; to present in some detail"

PART II: THEMATIC ESSAY

Directions: Write a well-organized essay that includes an introduction, several paragraphs addressing the task below, and a conclusion.

Theme: Presidential Decisions and Actions

Throughout United States history, presidents have taken actions to address critical problems facing the nation. These actions have met with varying degrees of success.

Task:

Select *two* presidents who took actions to address a critical problem faced by the nation and for *each*

- Describe the historical circumstances that led to the problem
- Explain an action taken by the president to address the problem
- Discuss the extent to which this action resolved the problem

You may use any United States president who took an action to solve a critical problem facing the nation from your study of United States history. Some suggestions you might wish to consider include:

George Washington—Whiskey Rebellion
Andrew Jackson—nullification crisis
Abraham Lincoln—secession of Southern states
Franklin D. Roosevelt—Great Depression
Dwight D. Eisenhower—school integration
John F. Kennedy—Cuban missile crisis
Lyndon B. Johnson—discrimination faced by minorities
George H. W. Bush—invasion of Kuwait by Iraq
George W. Bush—attacks of September 11, 2001

You are *not* limited to these suggestions.

Guidelines:

In your essay, be sure to:

- Develop all aspects of the task
- Support the theme with relevant facts, examples, and details
- Use a logical and clear plan of organization, including an introduction and a conclusion that are beyond a restatement of the theme

In developing your answers to Part III, be sure to keep this general definition in mind:

> <u>discuss</u> means "to make observations about something using facts, reasoning, and argument; to present in some detail"

PART III: DOCUMENT-BASED QUESTION

This question is based on the accompanying documents. The question is designed to test your ability to work with historical documents. Some of these documents have been edited for the purposes of this question. As you analyze the documents, take into account the source of each document and any point of view that may be presented in the document. Keep in mind that the language used in a document may reflect the historical context of the time in which it was written.

Historical Context:

> During the 19th and early 20th centuries, the development of the West had political, economic, and social effects on various groups. These groups include ***Native American Indians***, ***women***, and ***Chinese immigrants***.

Task:

> Using the information from the documents and your knowledge of United States history, answer the questions that follow each document in Part A. Your answers to the questions will help you write the Part B essay in which you will be asked to
>
> Select ***two*** groups mentioned in the historical context and for ***each***
>
> - Discuss political, economic, ***and/or*** social effects of the development of the West on the group

Part A: Short-Answer Questions

Directions: Analyze the documents and answer the short-answer questions that follow each document in the space provided.

Document 1a

Buffalo hides stacked at Dodge City, Kansas, for shipment to the East, 1878

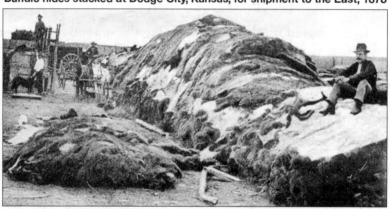

Source: National Archives (adapted)

Document 1b

"…White men had found gold in the mountains around the land of the Winding Water [in Oregon]. They stole a great many horses from us and we could not get them back because we were Indians. The white men told lies for each other. They drove off a great many of our cattle. Some white men branded our young cattle so they could claim them. We had no friends who would plead our cause before the law councils. It seemed to me that some of the white men in Wallowa [a valley in Oregon] were doing these things on purpose to get up a war. They knew we were not strong enough to fight them. I labored hard to avoid trouble and blood-shed.…"

Source: Chester Anders Fee, *Chief Joseph: The Biography of a Great Indian*, Wilson-Erickson

1 Based on these documents, what were *two* effects of the development of the West on Native American Indians? [2]

(1) _____

_____

(2) _____

_____

Document 2a

By the mid-1880s, the biggest single area in the West suitable for farming and still largely untouched by white settlement was Indian Territory. Representatives of some fifty-five tribes now called it home, but there were large tracts within it upon which no one lived.

One of these—2 million empty and unassigned acres—was called "the Oklahoma District," and the army was soon kept busy driving from it armed parties of squatters from Kansas who called themselves "Boomers." Furious lobbying eventually succeeded where invasion failed, and Congress finally voted to buy out all Indian claims to the Oklahoma District....

Source: Geoffrey C. Ward, *The West: An Illustrated History*,
Little, Brown and Company, 1996

Document 2b

Native American Indians in the West: Major Battles and Reservations

Source: Robert A. Divine et al., *America: Past and Present*, Addison Wesley Longman, 1999 (adapted)

2 Based on these documents, what was *one* impact of westward settlement on Native American Indians? [1]

_____

_____

Document 3a

After the Battle of Wounded Knee, Commissioner of Indian Affairs Thomas Jefferson Morgan made recommendations about how to avoid future conflicts with Native American Indians.

> ...*Fifth*—The only possible solution of our [Native American] Indian troubles lies in the suitable education of the rising generation. So long as the Indians remain among us aliens, speaking foreign languages, unable to communicate with us except through the uncertain and often misleading medium of interpreters, so long as they are ignorant of our ways, are superstitious and fanatical, they will remain handicapped in the struggle for existence, will be an easy prey to the medicine man and the false prophet, and will be easily induced, by reason of real or imaginary wrongs, to go upon the war-path. An education that will give them the mastery of the English language, train their hands to useful industries, awaken within them ambition for civilized ways, and develop a consciousness of power to achieve honorable places for themselves, and that arouses within them an earnest and abiding patriotism, will make of them American citizens, and render future conflicts between them and the Government impossible....

Source: T.J. Morgan, *The Present Phase of the Indian Question*, 1891

Document 3b

Lakota boys are pictured when they arrived at the Carlisle Indian Industrial School in Pennsylvania, left, and three years later, right.

Source: New York Public Digital Gallery (adapted)

3 Based on these documents, what are *two* ways Native American Indians were being affected by the development of the West? [2]

(1) _____

_____

(2) _____

_____

Document 4

...By 1800 the external aspect of the landscape was changing, with the extension of cleared fields, and the gradual rebuilding of cabins over the older areas. But inside the cabins the family life still embraced the whole range of domestic manufactures. The frontier graveyards show how hard the early life was on the women of the family. The patriarch laid to rest in his family tract, beside two, three, or four wives who had preceded him, is much more common than the hardy woman who outlived her husbands. The housewife came to her new home young and raw, and found for neighbors other girls as inexperienced. She bore the children; and buried a staggering number of them, for medicine and sanitation, inadequate everywhere, were out of reach for the cabin on the border. She fed her men and raised her children, cooked their food and laid it by [stored it] for winter. She was at once butcher, packer, and baker. The family clothes showed her craftsmanship, with skins playing a large part, and homespun or knitting revealing a luxury established. When one adds to the grinding and unavoidable labor, the anguish that came from sickness and danger, the frontier woman who survived becomes an heroic character, and the children who felt her touch become the proper material from which to choose the heroes of a nation....

Source: Frederic L. Paxson, *History of the American Frontier,*
1763–1893, Houghton Mifflin, 1924

4　According to Frederic L. Paxson, what was **one** effect of westward development on frontier women living in the West? [1]

_____

_____

Document 5

> It perhaps ought to be stated here, for the benefit of widows and single women over twenty-one years of age, that they are as much entitled to homesteads as men, and the women of Dakota generally avail themselves of the privilege. We can point you to young women in Dakota who carry on quite a stroke of farming now, who came here penniless a few years ago. One woman has now three hundred and twenty acres of land, paid for from her wages as servant girl, at $4.00 per week. It is the investment of what she has saved from her wages in the last two years. We, of Dakota, believe in Women's Rights, especially the right to take a homestead and manage it to their own liking....

Source: James S. Foster, Commissioner of Immigration for Dakota
Territory, *Outlines of History of the Territory of Dakota*, 1870

5 According to James S. Foster, what is *one* opportunity the development of the West offered to women? [1]

_____

_____

Document 6

This circular appeared in Kentucky's *Lexington Herald*, informing readers of the benefits of women voting in Wyoming.

WOMAN SUFFRAGE IN WYOMING.

Suffrage Circular

Women have voted in Wyoming for forty-one years on equal terms with men.

During the past thirty years there has been less divorce in Wyoming than in any state in the Union....

A smaller number of married women are working outside the home in Wyoming than in any other State in the Union.

Women teachers get equal pay for equal work in Wyoming.

There are fewer illiterate children in Wyoming than in any other State in the Union.

Young girls are better protected in Wyoming than in any State in the Union....

Source: *Lexington Herald*, May 19, 1910

6 According to this circular, what were *two* benefits of granting suffrage to women in Wyoming? [2]

(1) _____

_____

(2) _____

_____

Document 7

...A combination of push and pull factors thus triggered a wave of Chinese immigration to America. More than 20,000 Chinese arrived in the United States in 1852, quickly augmenting [increasing] the number of Chinese in California, which reached 34,933 on the eve of the Civil War. Of these Chinese, some three-fourths lived in counties where mining was the principal occupation. Most Chinese miners missed the initial rush, but they gradually took control of California placer mining. Within a decade they possessed most of the claims in the original strike region and together constituted the single largest national group of miners. Their slow start and quick dominance in California's mines formed a distinctive pattern that would be repeated throughout the mining West....

As a story of economic mobility and self-improvement, the Chinese experience on the western mining frontier was a success. To be sure, the Chinese had many disadvantages. They possessed little starting capital, they had staked no initial claims, they faced legal discrimination, and they encountered racial violence. But these disadvantages were often compensated for by advantages, including mining experience, cooperative culture, a healthy life-style, skill at aquatic management, and environmental adaptability, all of which ensured Chinese competitiveness in the American West. In 1870, several Chinese companies in Montana were listed among the territory's most profitable. For six months Chang-Ling Company with seven persons cleared $13,000 in gold. According to one 1871 account, Chinese miners took out $500,000 in gold from the Tuscarora region in Nevada. Between 1855 and 1870 more than 10 percent of the gold and silver exports through the Port of San Francisco went to China, an amount ($72,581,219) equivalent to more than $1 billion today....

Source: Liping Zhu, "No Need to Rush: The Chinese, Placer Mining, and the Western Environment," *Montana: The Magazine of Western History*, Autumn 1999 (adapted)

7 According to Liping Zhu, what were *two* ways living in the West affected Chinese immigrants? [2]

(1) _____

_____

(2) _____

_____

Document 8a

... Besides railroad work, Chinese found opportunities elsewhere. When they learned that $8 was the going rate for a basket of laundry in San Francisco, they did it for $5 and were swamped with business. Soon scores of laundries opened, often one group working daytime, another at night. Even in smaller towns the Chinese laundry became an institution—the lone laundryman wielding his iron long hours in an isolated existence, unable to communicate with Americans, dreaming only of his hoped-for return to China....

Source: David Lindsey, "Cathay Comes to El Dorado,"
American History Illustrated

Document 8b

... Meanwhile, in the rural regions, the Chinese were participating in the development of California's agriculture, which was turning from wheat to fruit acreage. "They were a vital factor," historian Carey McWilliams writes, "one is inclined to state *the* vital factor, in making the transition possible." Formerly farmers in the Pearl River Delta in Guangdong, the Chinese shared their agricultural experience and knowledge. They "taught their over-lords how to plant, cultivate, and harvest orchard and garden crops." Their contributions extended beyond California: Ah Bing in Oregon bred the famous Bing cherry, and Lue Gim Gong in Florida developed the frost-resistant orange that bore his name and that gave the state its citrus industry....

Source: Ronald Takaki, *Strangers from a Different Shore: A History of Asian Americans*, Little, Brown and Company, 1989 (adapted)

8 Based on these documents, what were **two** opportunities the development of the West offered to Chinese immigrants? [2]

(1) _____

_____

(2) _____

_____

Document 9

Opposition to Chinese immigration included the Workingmen's Party in the late 1870s.

> ...After being occupied during the 1850s, 1860s, and early 1870s in the placers [mines] and on major construction projects, many Chinese turned toward the cities and new industries. San Francisco was the mecca for most, for it was both the industrial capital of the Pacific Coast and the headquarters for the Chinese. The timing was unfortunate, for it brought the Chinese into conflict with the struggling labor movement that had been trying to organize itself in San Francisco during the preceding two decades, and it did so at a time when unemployment and threats to the traditionally high level of western wages made white workers angrily sensitive to the dangers of Chinese competition. A very high percentage of those workers were themselves immigrants, especially Irish and Germans—but they were white immigrants....

Source: Rodman W. Paul, *The Far West and the Great Plains in Transition, 1859–1900*, Harper & Row, 1988

9 According to Rodman W. Paul, state *one* reason for opposition to Chinese immigrants in San Francisco. [1]

_____

_____

Part B: Essay

Directions: Write a well-organized essay that includes an introduction, several paragraphs, and a conclusion. Use evidence from *at least* ***four*** documents in your essay. Support your response with relevant facts, examples, and details. Include additional outside information.

Historical Context:

> During the 19th and early 20th centuries, the development of the West had political, economic, and social effects on various groups. These groups include ***Native American Indians***, ***women***, and ***Chinese immigrants.***

Task:

> Using the information from the documents and your knowledge of United States history, write an essay in which you
>
> Select ***two*** groups mentioned in the historical context and for ***each***
>
> * Discuss political, economic, ***and/or*** social effects of the development of the West on the group

Guidelines:

In your essay, be sure to:
* Develop all aspects of the task
* Incorporate information from *at least* ***four*** documents
* Incorporate relevant outside information
* Support the theme with relevant facts, examples, and details
* Use a logical and clear plan of organization, including an introduction and a conclusion that are beyond a restatement of the theme

Answers
August 2017
United States History and Government

Answer Key

PART I

1. 4	11. 4	21. 3	31. 2	41. 1
2. 1	12. 4	22. 1	32. 3	42. 1
3. 3	13. 1	23. 3	33. 4	43. 2
4. 2	14. 2	24. 4	34. 4	44. 3
5. 3	15. 2	25. 2	35. 1	45. 2
6. 1	16. 4	26. 3	36. 2	46. 4
7. 4	17. 1	27. 4	37. 3	47. 4
8. 3	18. 3	28. 4	38. 1	48. 2
9. 1	19. 2	29. 3	39. 3	49. 1
10. 2	20. 2	30. 1	40. 2	50. 3

PART II: Thematic Essay   *See* **Answers Explained** section.

PART III: Document-Based Question   *See* **Answers Explained** section.

Answers Explained

PART I (1–50)

1. **4** The geographic feature that contributed most to the settlement of colonies along the Atlantic Coast was navigable rivers and harbors. Plymouth (1620), Massachusetts Bay Colony (1630), Providence (1636), Newport (1639), and New Amsterdam (1624) were all established on protected harbors at the mouths of rivers. Jamestown (1607) was founded on the James River some 40 miles upriver from the Atlantic Ocean. The Connecticut Colony (1636) was founded on the Connecticut River, about 40 miles upriver from the Long Island Sound. Such locations allowed for trade with European countries and with the West Indies and Africa. Rivers aided agricultural development through irrigation and transportation of goods. Within a generation, as the flow of English migrants into North America increased, settlements were established inland from these initial coastal and river settlements. The push of settlers into the interior of the continent increased tensions with Native American Indians.

WRONG CHOICES EXPLAINED:

(1) Mountainous terrain did not contribute to the settlement of colonies along the Atlantic Coast. The Appalachian Mountains rise inland from the Atlantic Coast. However, they served as more of an impediment to settlement rather than an aid.

(2) Mineral deposits did not contribute to the settlement of colonies along the Atlantic Coast. Mineral deposits in the Atlantic Coast were not valuable to colonists nor were they extensively mined. The gold and silver deposits exploited by the Spanish in New Spain were not present in British North America.

(3) A subtropical climate did not contribute to the settlement of colonies along the Atlantic Coast. Subtropical climate conditions, characterized by hot and humid summers and mild winters, are generally located between 25 and 35 degrees latitude. Jamestown, Virginia, is slightly above this range, and the colonies of New England are well above it.

2. **1** During the 1700s, the British government used mercantilism to profit from its colonies. Mercantilism is the economic theory that guided the British in establishing an empire. The theory holds that only a limited amount of wealth exists in the world. Nations increase their power by increasing their share of the world's wealth. One way of acquiring wealth is by maintaining a favorable

balance of trade, with the value of exports exceeding the value of imports. Mercantilist theory suggests that governments should advance these goals by maintaining colonies so as to have a steady and inexpensive source of raw materials. The theory also holds that the colonies should not develop manufacturing but, instead, should serve as markets for goods manufactured in the ruling country. Great Britain imposed several navigation laws on the North American colonies to make sure that colonial trade occurred within the British Empire and not with Great Britain's rivals. However, some of these laws were difficult to enforce. By the 17th century, the colonies began to develop an economy independent of Great Britain.

WRONG CHOICES EXPLAINED:

(2) The British government did not use mercantilism to develop colonial manufacturing. Mercantilist theory insists that manufacturing occur primarily in the mother country so that the mother country gains the profits from producing and selling manufactured items. The role of colonies is to supply raw materials and to serve as markets for manufactured items. Several acts—such as the Wool Act (1699), the Hat Act (1732), and the Iron Act (1750)—prohibited the colonies from manufacturing these items.

(3) The British government did not use mercantilism to discourage colonial agriculture. Mercantilist theory insists that colonies develop agriculture to provide raw materials to the mother country. In this way, the mother country has a reliable and inexpensive supply of necessary raw materials. Some of these raw materials are consumed (sugar and tobacco), while others are manufactured into finished products (lumber).

(4) The British government did not use mercantilism to encourage colonial trade with other countries. British mercantilist rules insisted that certain goods could be sold only to the mother country. Parliament developed a list of "enumerated goods"—goods from the colonies that could be shipped only to Britain. These included goods that were essential for ship building, such as tar, pitch, and trees for masts. Goods that were not enumerated could be sold to other countries, but the trade had to be carried out in British ships and through British ports.

3. **3** The French and Indian War (1754–1763) was a turning point in the relationship between American colonists and the British government because the war resulted in British debt and attempts to tax colonists. In many ways, the war was a catalyst for much of the tension that culminated in the American Revolution. The French and Indian War was caused, in part, by colonial expansion into the lands beyond the Appalachian Mountains. Before the war, a few settlers crossed over the Appalachian Mountains and established farms in the Ohio River Valley. This expansion led to conflicts with the French, who had

earlier established outposts in the area, and eventually led to war with the French and their Native-American allies. The British won the war, but the war led to a massive debt for the British government. The British asserted that the colonists, who benefited from the results of the war, should help repay some of this debt. Therefore, the British enacted several taxes—the Sugar Act (1764), the Stamp Act (1765), and the Townshend Acts (1767). Many colonists asserted that only representatives elected by the colonists themselves could enact taxes on the colonies. "No taxation without representation" became the rallying cry of the colonists as protests mounted in the years leading up to the ratification of the Declaration of Independence (1776).

WRONG CHOICES EXPLAINED:

(1) The French and Indian War (1754–1763) did not result in increased French influence in North America. The opposite was true. France lost its possessions in North America and gave up its claims to disputed territory.

(2) The French and Indian War (1754–1763) did not result in an end to Native-American Indian attacks west of the Appalachian Mountains. Immediately following the war, conflicts ensued as Native American Indians faced a crisis—their French allies were displaced and British troops and colonists were expanding into areas beyond the Appalachian Mountains. Chief Pontiac, of the Ottawa people, and other Indian leaders organized resistance to British troops stationed around the Great Lakes in forts that were previously held by the French. These attacks were followed by strikes on colonial settlements along a swath of land from upstate New York to the area south of Lake Michigan and along the Appalachian frontier.

(4) The French and Indian War (1754–1763) did not result in an alliance with Canada against the British. The American colonies were still under British control, so they could not have formed alliances with other countries. In addition, Canada came under British control as a result of the French and Indian War.

4. **2** The main reason Thomas Paine wrote *Common Sense* was to gain support for declaring independence from Great Britain. Relations between Great Britain and the colonies were strained at the time Paine wrote his pamphlet. In April 1775, fighting began between opponents of Great Britain and British troops in the Massachusetts towns of Lexington and Concord. During the remainder of 1775, relations between the colonies and Great Britain worsened. In June 1775, the Battle of Bunker Hill occurred in Boston and the British parliament declared that American ships were enemy vessels. The Second Continental Congress, a body of representatives from the 13 colonies, created an army, declared war against Great Britain, and began issuing its own currency. At the same time, some members of Congress still hoped for reconciliation.

Congress sent the Olive Branch Petition to the king of England, affirming loyalty to the monarch and blaming the current problems on Parliament. Paine argued against the logic of the petition, plainly and forcefully putting the blame on the king. Paine's arguments carried the day. On July 4, 1776, the delegates to the Second Continental Congress formally ratified the Declaration of Independence.

WRONG CHOICES EXPLAINED:

(1) Thomas Paine did not write *Common Sense* in order to urge adoption of the Albany Plan of Union. Paine's 1776 pamphlet was written well after the 1754 Albany Plan of Union. The Albany Plan of Union grew out of the Albany Congress, a meeting called by Benjamin Franklin. The goal of the plan was to unite the 13 colonies in order to provide for their common defense. Franklin wanted to organize support for British forces in the French and Indian War. The plan was rejected by the colonial assemblies as well as by British authorities.

(3) Thomas Paine did not write *Common Sense* (1776) in order to bring an end to the Revolutionary War, which had started in April 1775. Paine was not arguing that the war should end. He wanted to shape the intent of the struggle and to bring more colonists to the side of supporting the move toward independence.

(4) Thomas Paine did not write *Common Sense* in order to convince states to ratify the new Constitution. Debates over the Constitution occurred over a decade after Paine's pamphlet was published. During debates over the Constitution (1787–1790), Paine strongly argued against the conservative and elitist nature of the document.

5. **3** The concerns addressed by Abigail Adams were most directly addressed by the Declaration of Sentiments. In her letter to her husband John Adams, Abigail Adams expressed hope that as John and other leaders of the patriot cause formulated a new legal framework, they would include women on an equal footing with men. Abigail Adams was not alone in her assertion of gender equality. The experience of women participating in the struggle for independence, from organizing boycotts to aiding men on the battlefield, instilled a sense of egalitarianism among many women. In addition, the rhetoric of the revolutionary era railed against tyrannical rule. Many found analogies between the tyranny of king over subject and the tyranny of husband over wife. The concerns voiced by Abigail Adams and others were not incorporated into the state and federal constitutions that were framed in the post-revolutionary era. Later, in 1848, women and their male allies met in Seneca Falls, New York, to organize a women's rights convention. The Seneca Falls Convention, which is often considered the birth of the women's rights movement, formulated the Declaration of Sentiments. The convention was organized by Lucretia Mott and Elizabeth

Cady Stanton. They argued that the laws of the country relegated women to a second-class status. Women could not vote or sit on juries. Women were not entitled to protection against physical abuse by their husbands. When women married, any property they owned became the property of their husbands. Society defined women as intellectually inferior and insisted that the proper role for women was maintaining the house and caring for children. The Declaration of Sentiments was modeled after the Declaration of Independence. The document declared that "all men and women are created equal."

WRONG CHOICES EXPLAINED:

(1) The Federalist Papers do not address the issues of gender equality raised by Abigail Adams in the passage. The Federalist Papers, written by Alexander Hamilton, John Jay, and James Madison in 1787 and 1788, were intended to win support for ratification of the Constitution. These supporters of the Constitution, who became known as Federalists, argued that the existing structure of government was inadequate for the United States. Many Federalists were alarmed at the inability of the central government established under the Articles of Confederation to raise revenue or to put down rebellions.

(2) The Monroe Doctrine does not address the issues of gender equality raised by Abigail Adams in the passage. The Monroe Doctrine, issued by President James Monroe in 1823, warned European nations to avoid further colonization of the Americas. The United States did not have the military might to enforce this pronouncement at the time. However, the Monroe Doctrine was an important statement of intent. The Monroe Doctrine and Washington's farewell address (1797) became cornerstones of America's isolationist foreign policy.

(4) The Emancipation Proclamation does not address the issues of gender equality raised by Abigail Adams in the passage. The Emancipation Proclamation was issued during the Civil War in 1862. In it, Lincoln declared that all slaves in Confederate-held territory would be freed as of January 1, 1863. Although the Emancipation Proclamation did not immediately free any slaves, it was important because it made it clear that the Civil War had become a war to liberate the slaves.

6. **1** The Northwest Ordinance of 1787 was important in United States history because it established a method for admitting new states to the Union. The act dealt with the Northwest Territory, the vast stretch of land north of the Ohio River that is between the western border of Pennsylvania and the Mississippi River. Earlier, the government established by the Articles of Confederation persuaded the various states to give up their land claims in the region. Then it passed two significant pieces of legislation. The Land Ordinance provided for an orderly system of development for the Northwest Territory. It divided up the

land and provided a plot in every town for public schools. The Northwest Ordinance spelled out the steps that these areas would have to go through in order to become states. In addition, the Northwest Ordinance banned slavery in the Northwest Territory. Although these acts are considered to be successes of the government established by the Articles of Confederation, contemporaries and historians have tended to focus on the problems of the period, such as inflation and lack of government revenues. In fact, the period is often labeled the *critical period* in the sense of a patient being in critical condition.

WRONG CHOICES EXPLAINED:
(2) The Northwest Ordinance of 1787 did not establish a method for promoting diplomatic relations with foreign nations. Diplomatic relations are carried out by the president—either personally or through his or her designated representatives. Treaties must be approved by the Senate.

(3) The Northwest Ordinance of 1787 did not establish a method for funding internal improvements. The term *internal improvements* was used in the 19th century to describe infrastructure projects, such as canals, roads, and railroads. These projects did much to expand trade, especially between the Midwest (then known as the West) and eastern cities. Most significant was the Erie Canal (completed in 1825), which connected the Hudson River in upstate New York to the Great Lakes. Public funding of such projects generated a great deal of debate among politicians.

(4) The Northwest Ordinance of 1787 did not establish a method for securing ports on the Pacific Coast. With the acquisition of the Mexican Cession (1848) following the Mexican War (1846–1848), the United States secured ports on the Pacific, including Los Angeles and San Francisco.

7. **4** Antifederalists insisted that a bill of rights be added to the Constitution in order to protect individual rights from the power of the central government. Antifederalists feared the Constitution would create an omnipotent and unaccountable government. They had vivid memories of the intrusions of the royal British government into their lives and wanted assurances that the people would have basic protections from government abuses. Eventually, many leading Antifederalists agreed to support ratification of the Constitution, which had been written in 1787, if a list of individual rights was added. This agreement led to the writing and ratification of the first ten amendments to the Constitution, known as the Bill of Rights (1791). The First Amendment protects the people from government limitations on freedom of expression and of religion. It also affirms the right of people to protest against government actions. The First Amendment also established the separation of church and state. The Second Amendment established the right to bear arms. The Fourth Amendment holds that people are to be free

from unwarranted searches by government authorities. The Fifth and Sixth Amendments list a variety of protections that people have when they are accused of crimes, such as the right to a speedy and public trial. The Eighth Amendment states that the government shall not inflict cruel and unusual punishments on people.

WRONG CHOICES EXPLAINED:

(1) The Bill of Rights, which was ratified to address the concerns of the Antifederalists, limited the power of Congress by prohibiting it from abridging certain rights. It did not grant *more* power to Congress. Antifederalists were concerned about the federal government assuming too much power.

(2) The Bill of Rights, which was ratified to address the concerns of the Antifederalists, was intended to protect the basic rights of individuals from governmental overreach. It did not settle disputes between states. The Constitution states that the Supreme Court has the power to resolve disputes between states.

(3) The Bill of Rights, which was ratified to address the concerns of the Antifederalists, was intended to protect basic rights of individuals from governmental overreach. It did not prevent states from denying individuals the right to vote. The right to vote has been extended to different groups of people with three amendments to the Constitution. The 15th Amendment (1870) prevented states from denying a citizen the vote based on that citizen's race. The 19th Amendment (1920) extended the right to vote to women. The 26th Amendment (1971) prohibited using age as a reason to deny any citizen the right to vote who is at least 18 years old.

8. **3** The passage by James Madison supports the constitutional principle of separation of powers. In the passage, Madison expressed concern about too much power being exercised by any one of the branches of government. Madison and the other framers of the Constitution created three branches of government—legislative, executive, and judicial—each with powers separate from the other two. The legislative branch creates laws. The executive branch carries out laws. The judicial branch interprets laws. The Constitution spells out the powers of each branch. After living under the British monarchy, the framers of the Constitution came to believe that a powerful government without checks was dangerous to liberty. Therefore, they created a governmental system with three branches, each with the ability to check the powers of the other two. The goal was to keep the three branches in balance.

WRONG CHOICES EXPLAINED:

(1) The passage by James Madison does not address the constitutional principle of representative government. The Constitution does call for a representative government. Congress is made up of representatives of the people. Members of the House of Representatives were to be elected by the people, while Senators were to be appointed by popularly elected state legislatures.

(2) The passage by James Madison does not address the constitutional principle of the writ of habeas corpus. The Constitution does assert that the right to obtain a writ of habeas corpus shall not be denied (except during times of rebellion or invasion). This privilege was included in the Constitution to curtail the age-old practice of tyrannical rulers throwing people into jail without formal procedures or just cause.

(4) The passage by James Madison does not address the constitutional principle of due process of law. The Constitution does spell out the procedures, known as due process, that individuals must be subjected to before they are punished. The framers of the Constitution wanted to protect people from arbitrary authority. They did not want the authorities to be able to throw people into jail indefinitely at their will.

9. **1** The term *federalism* is best described as the division of power between the national government and state governments. The Constitution created a federal system, granting powers to both the national (federal) government and the state governments. This system of divided power is different from the government established by the Articles of Confederation (1781–1788). The Articles left most power on the state level and created merely a "firm league of friendship" among the sovereign states. The federalist system is also different from the unitary system of countries such as France. In France, the central government sets policies for the entire country with very little decision-making power at the local level.

WRONG CHOICES EXPLAINED:

(2) The term *federalism* does not refer to the creation of a two-house legislature in the national government. The Great Compromise at the Constitutional Convention (1787) settled the dispute over how the states would be represented in Congress and created a two-house legislature. The dispute pitted states with larger populations against those with smaller populations. The larger states wanted representation in Congress to be based on population; the smaller states wanted an equal number of representatives for each state. The Great Compromise created the basic structure of Congress as it now exists. The plan called for a House of Representatives, in which representation would be determined by the population of each state, and a Senate, in which each state would get two members.

(3) The term *federalism* does not refer to the method of reviewing laws and executive actions. It was the Supreme Court decision in *Marbury* v. *Madison* that established the method of reviewing laws and executive actions. The 1803 case, heard under Chief Justice John Marshall, was perhaps the most important decision in the history of the Supreme Court in that it established the Supreme Court's power of judicial review. This decision strengthened the judiciary by asserting that the Supreme Court has the power to review laws and executive actions to determine whether they are consistent with the Constitution. The power of judicial review has been the main function of the Supreme Court since then.

(4) The term *federalism* does not refer to the establishment of three branches of government. The Constitution created a government with three branches, each with powers separate from the other two. The legislative branch creates laws. The executive branch carries out laws. The judicial branch interprets laws. The Constitution spells out the powers of each branch. The framers were very conscious of the problems of a government with limitless powers. Therefore, they created a governmental system with three branches, each with the ability to check the powers of the other two. The goal was to keep the three branches in balance.

10. **2** The factor that contributed most directly to public support for passage of the 26th Amendment was the Vietnam War. The 26th Amendment (1971) prohibited using age as a reason to deny any citizen the right to vote who is at least 18 years old. The amendment was ratified as many men as young as 18 were being drafted into the war in Vietnam. Proponents of the change argued that if these young men were old enough to serve in the military, they were old enough to vote. In 1964, the United States became heavily involved in the Vietnam War after Congress gave President Lyndon Johnson a blank check with the Tonkin Gulf Resolution. As the war dragged on and as the United States suffered more casualties, many Americans began to question the wisdom of American policies in Vietnam. By 1968, Johnson decided that his war policies imperiled his reelection, so he decided to not run for a second term. The following president, Richard Nixon, did not have any more success in moving the United States closer to victory in Vietnam. Many young opponents of the war pushed for ratification of the 26th Amendment, arguing that the young should have a voice in the direction of American policies.

WRONG CHOICES EXPLAINED:

(1) High crime rates did not directly contribute to public support for the constitutional amendment lowering the voting age to 18. Crime rates did climb in the 1960s and 1970s in many areas of the United States, but this development was not directly related to the push for passage of the 26th Amendment.

(3) The Watergate affair did not directly contribute to public support for the constitutional amendment lowering the voting age to 18. The Watergate scandal began in June 1972, a year after ratification of the 26th Amendment. The scandal began when five men were caught breaking into the headquarters of the Democratic Party at the Watergate Hotel in Washington, D.C. Persistent reporting drew connections between the burglars and President Richard Nixon's reelection committee and, ultimately, the White House. As Nixon's complicity in attempts to cover up the scandal became known, pressure built on the president to resign, which occurred in 1974.

(4) Increased life expectancy did not directly contribute to public support for the constitutional amendment lowering the voting age to 18. Life expectancy for both men and women in the United States has risen steadily since 1940 and is projected to continue to rise through 2080.

11. **4** A presidential veto of a bill can be overridden by a two-thirds vote of both houses of Congress. The Constitution gives the president the power to veto, or reject, legislation that he or she finds objectionable. The president vetoes a bill by returning it to Congress within ten days of having received it. The president must also submit in writing his or her objections to the bill. If the president simply does not sign the bill within those ten days, it becomes law. However, a situation might occur in which the president does not sign a bill but Congress adjourns before the ten-day period is up. In such a scenario, the bill does not become law. In that scenario, the president has carried out a pocket veto (in effect, he has put the bill into his pocket rather than returning it to Congress). In either case—a regular veto or a pocket veto—Congress has the power to override the veto with a two-thirds majority vote in both houses. In the case of a Congressional override, the bill becomes law without the president's signature.

WRONG CHOICES EXPLAINED:

(1) A majority vote of registered voters cannot override a presidential veto. There is no mechanism on a national level for voters to express either support or opposition for federal statutes. The only recourse for voters is to support or oppose candidates in state-by-state elections.

(2) A majority vote of the Supreme Court cannot override a presidential veto. The Supreme Court can undo existing legislation by a majority vote through the

process of judicial review. It can hear a case that involves an existing law. If the Supreme Court finds that the law is unconstitutional, that law is stricken from the books.

(3) A two-thirds vote of the state legislatures cannot override a presidential veto. States do not have the power to nullify federal actions. The theory that states could nullify federal actions was put forth by Thomas Jefferson and James Madison in 1796 in the Virginia and Kentucky Resolutions, which were written in response to the Alien and Sedition Acts. The theory was again put forward by John C. Calhoun and other opponents of the Tariff Act of 1828, labeled the Tariff of Abominations.

12. **4** The opening of the Erie Canal in 1825 was important to the development of the nation because it increased trade between the East Coast and the Midwest. The United States was faced with a vexing problem during its first decades. On maps, the country extended to the Mississippi River following independence and then to the Rocky Mountains following the Louisiana Purchase (1803). However, most residents of the United States resided in communities close to the Atlantic Coast, east of the Appalachian Mountains. The Erie Canal helped open up the vast landmass of the country to trade and settlement. The Erie Canal connected the Hudson River in upstate New York to the Great Lakes. The canal created an all-water route from New York City to the Midwestern communities around the Great Lakes. This connection facilitated trade between the East Coast and the Midwest. A shipment of wheat, for example, could now be transported from Chicago to New York City by an all-water route at a tenth of the cost and a fraction of the time of an overland route.

WRONG CHOICES EXPLAINED:
(1) The Erie Canal did not link the industrial centers of the North and the South. The main linkages between the North and South in the period before the Civil War were water routes on the Atlantic Ocean.

(2) The Erie Canal did not result in the United States Navy defending the Great Lakes. The canal did open up a water route between the Atlantic Ocean and the Great Lakes. However, after the War of 1812, the Great Lakes were largely demilitarized. The Rush-Bagot Treaty (ratified in 1818), which was between the United States and Great Britain, limited the number of naval vessels on the Great Lakes.

(3) The Erie Canal did not force the Spanish to sell Florida to the United States. The United States acquired Florida from Spain with the Adams-Onis Treaty (1819). That treaty occurred before the completion of the canal and is largely unrelated to developments associated with the building of the canal.

13. **1** Before the Civil War, the collapse of the Whig Party and the formation of the Free Soil and the Republican Parties showed that opposing views on slavery affected national unity. The issue of slavery became increasingly contentious in the late 1840s and 1850s. In the 1840s, both the major political parties, the Whigs and the Democrats, avoided taking strong stands on the issue of slavery. In response to the conspicuous silence on the part of the major parties on the slavery question, antislavery men in both parties founded the Free Soil Party in 1848. That party ran candidates in the presidential elections of 1848 and 1852. Those candidates garnered only 10 percent of the vote in 1848 and only 5 percent in 1852. In 1854, the Kansas-Nebraska Act intensified existing sectional divisions. The act allowed for the possibility of slavery in the territories of Kansas and Nebraska if the residents of those territories voted for it. This principle, called *popular sovereignty*, angered antislavery northerners who were assured by the Missouri Compromise (1820) that slavery would forever be prohibited from the northern half of the Louisiana Territory, which included Kansas and Nebraska. The act divided Whigs into the proslavery Cotton Whigs and the antislavery Conscience Whigs. These divisions undermined the party, which ceased to function as a national party by 1856. Meanwhile, in 1854, the modern Republican Party was born. This party was composed of many different factions—former members of the Free Soil Party, Conscience Whigs, abolitionists, and former Democrats, to name a few. Although the party was critical of slavery, it did not advocate abolition. Rather, it adopted the position that slavery should not be allowed to spread to the new territories. As the Republican Party rapidly gained strength in the North, the Democratic Party became more proslavery, with its base of support in the South. The sectional and political tensions over the slavery issue intensified and degenerated into civil war by 1861.

WRONG CHOICES EXPLAINED:
(2) The developments described in the question did not show that Americans were united in their political views. The Whig Party collapsed because of divisions over the question of slavery. The formation of the Free Soil Party and the Republican Party, both antislavery parties, also reflected division among Americans.

(3) The developments described in the question did not show that major political parties received most of their support in the South. The Republican Party received most of its support in the North. Its candidate, Abraham Lincoln, won the presidency in 1860.

(4) The developments described in the question did not show that Americans were divided over the issue of unlimited coinage of silver. The issue that divided the political parties in the 1850s was slavery. Later, in the 1890s, the issue of unlimited coinage of silver divided the major political parties. Many farmers

wanted the United States to get off the gold standard and to issue money backed by silver as well. This would increase the amount of money in circulation and would lead to inflation. Farmers supported inflationary policies so that the prices they received for their produce would increase. The issue divided the Democratic and Republican presidential candidates in the 1896 election. The Democratic candidate, William Jennings Bryan, took up the call for the unlimited coinage of silver.

14. **2** Throughout the Civil War, an important advantage the North had over the South was that the North had greater manufacturing capabilities. The Civil War spurred rapid industrialization of the North. During the war, the Union government required an enormous amount of war materials, from guns and bullets to boots and uniforms. Manufacturers rose to the occasion by rapidly modernizing production. These changes in production sped up the process of industrialization that was in its beginning stages before the war. The manufacturing capabilities of the North were only one advantage the North had over the South during the Civil War. The North also had considerably more miles of railroad tracks. Of the 30,000 miles of railroad tracks in the United States in 1861, only 9,000 were in the states that formed the Confederacy. This gave the Union the ability to resupply its troops rapidly. In addition, the North had a far greater population than that of the rebellious southern states (22 million versus six million, excluding slaves), allowing the North to recruit reinforcements for fallen soldiers. All of these advantages became significant as the war dragged on.

WRONG CHOICES EXPLAINED:
(1) The South, not the North, tended to have superior military leaders. The South had a rich military tradition. The Confederacy, therefore, had able generals and a cohort of military men to draw from.

(3) The North did not receive support from Great Britain and France. President Abraham Lincoln feared that Great Britain would form an alliance with the Confederacy in order to guarantee a steady flow of raw cotton from the plantations of the South to the textile mills of England. Lincoln's issuing of the Emancipation Proclamation (1862) was partly motivated by the desire to keep Great Britain at bay during the war. The British might decide to aid the Confederacy for economic reasons, but the British population would not condone joining the South to perpetuate slavery.

(4) The South, not the North, used a strategy for fighting a defensive war. The Confederacy did not have to invade and conquer the North in order to declare victory. The Union, on the other hand, had to fight an offensive war in southern territory in order to win.

15. **2** The Compromise of 1877 brought an end to Radical Reconstruction by providing for the removal of federal troops from southern states. The period of Reconstruction, when the United States attempted to extend democratic rights to African Americans in the South, ended after only a dozen years. However, the end did not occur all at once. Throughout the 1870s, southern conservative Democrats, who called themselves "redeemers," aggressively sought to regain power state by state. The redeemers were aided by networks of white terrorist organizations that used violence to silence African Americans and to intimidate them from participating in public life. Also, northern whites simply lost their zeal for reforming the South. However, the formal end of Reconstruction followed the disputed election of 1876. The Democratic candidate, Samuel J. Tilden, won the majority of the popular vote. However, neither he nor his Republican opponent, Rutherford B. Hayes, were able to claim enough electoral votes to be declared the winner. In three states—South Carolina, Louisiana, and Florida—the Democrats and the Republicans both claimed victory. A special electoral commission, with a Republican majority, declared Hayes the winner in the three contested states. Democrats protested, with some threatening to block Hayes's inauguration. Party leaders on both sides reached an informal agreement, known as the Compromise of 1877, which allowed Hayes to win the presidency. In return, the Republicans agreed to remove the last federal troops from the South and end Reconstruction, paving the way for rule by the Democratic Party in the South.

WRONG CHOICES EXPLAINED:

(1) The Compromise of 1877 did not provide for the resignation of President Rutherford B. Hayes. The compromise settled the disputed election of 1877. It resulted in Hayes assuming the presidency and the Republicans agreeing to end Reconstruction by pulling out the last federal troops from the South.

(3) The Compromise of 1877 did not provide for the establishment of sharecropping. The system of sharecropping developed on its own during the Reconstruction period. After the Civil War, African Americans wanted to acquire land but did not have the financial resources to do so. In this context, the sharecropping system developed. In this system, African Americans (and poor whites) would farm a few acres of a large estate and give a share, often half, of the crops to the owner as rent. In this way, African Americans were not under the direct supervision of whites. However, the system created a cycle of debt, which prevented African Americans from acquiring money and owning land.

(4) The Compromise of 1877 did not provide for the strict enforcement of the 14th Amendment. It did the opposite. The compromise ended the government's Reconstruction efforts in the South, thus effectively ending enforcement

of the 14th Amendment. In the post-Reconstruction period, the southern states developed methods of working around the equal protection guarantees of the 14th Amendment, initiating a system of Jim Crow segregation laws.

16. **4** The information in the charts supports the conclusion that southern and eastern Europeans made up the majority of immigrants from 1900 to 1920. The graph on the right indicates that between 1900 and 1920, eastern and southern Europeans made up 62 percent of immigrants coming into the United States. Eastern Europeans include people from Russia and the Baltic states as well as people from within the Austro-Hungarian empire; southern Europeans include people from Italy. The wave of immigrants from eastern and southern Europe was labeled "new immigrants." The term "new" was used by some nativists of the late 1800s and early 1900s to draw a distinction between the old immigrants and the new immigrants. These nativists came to believe that the new immigrants were somehow incapable of being assimilated into the culture of the United States. The negative feelings toward the new immigrants contributed to the passage of the quota acts of the 1920s, limiting the number of immigrants allowed into the United States.

WRONG CHOICES EXPLAINED:
(1) The information in the charts does not support the conclusion that immigration from the Western Hemisphere declined after 1900. The second chart indicates that 6 percent of immigrants into the United States were from Canada. Most of these were French Canadians who immigrated from Quebec into the states of New England. Also, immigrants from several Latin American countries made their way into the United States during the periods shown in the two charts.
(2) The information in the charts does not support the conclusion that the percentage of German immigrants increased between 1860 and 1920. The percentage of German immigrants was actually higher in the period from 1860 to 1900 (28 percent) than in the period from 1900 to 1920 (4 percent).
(3) The information in the charts does not support the conclusion that northern European immigrants were prohibited from entering the United States from 1860 to 1920. The charts do not contain information about immigration laws. There were no such laws that prohibited northern European immigrants from entering the United States.

17. **1** The changes in immigration patterns shown on the charts resulted in the passage of restrictive immigration laws. The large number of "new immigrants" into the United States—from eastern and southern Europe—led to the growth of a strong nativist (anti-immigrant) movement. Some nativists focused

on the fact that most of the new immigrants were not Protestant. Poles and Italians tended to be Catholic; Russians and Greeks tended to be Eastern Orthodox; and Jewish immigrants came from several countries in eastern Europe. Some nativists objected to the cacophony of languages heard on the streets of New York or Chicago and to the variety of food smells that filled immigrant neighborhoods. Also, some nativists argued that the new immigrants, many of whom had darker features than their English and Germanic predecessors, were a different race. Nativism rose steeply in the years after World War I, leading to the passage of the Emergency Quota Act of 1921 and the Immigration Act of 1924. These acts greatly reduced the number of immigrants allowed into the United States by establishing quotas for different nations based on the numbers of each national group present in the United States decades earlier. The first act set the quota for each nationality at 3 percent of the total number of that nationality that was present in the United States in 1910. The second act reduced the percentage to 2 percent and moved the year back to 1890.

WRONG CHOICES EXPLAINED:
(2) The changes in immigration patterns shown in the charts did not result in the business community increasing its demand for workers. The immigrant patterns shown in the charts led to large numbers of potential laborers entering the United States.

(3) The changes in immigration patterns shown in the charts did not result in the decline of urban populations. The large numbers of immigrants who entered the United States in the late 1800s and early 1900s tended to settle in cities, thus increasing the population of urban areas.

(4) The changes in immigration patterns shown in the charts did not result in an easing in requirements for citizenship. The Naturalization Act of 1906 standardized procedures for becoming citizens, requiring applicants for citizenship to demonstrate competence in the English language.

18. **3** During the late 1800s, political machines controlled the governments of many cities by using corrupt practices and patronage. Corrupt and inefficient political operations—labeled political machines—became more common in this era. Political parties on the local level created organizations whose purpose was to achieve and maintain political power. Political ideology was barely a concern in these bare-knuckled electoral contests. New York City was dominated by the Democratic Party machine, headquartered at Tammany Hall. The most famous Tammany chief was William Marcy Tweed. "Boss" Tweed and other political leaders earned a reputation for corruption. Tweed's complicated schemes included the building of a courthouse that involved millions of dollars in

kickbacks to Tammany Hall. Patronage refers to the handing out of government jobs to the friends and relatives of political leaders, regardless of their level of competency. The muckraker journalist Lincoln Steffens exposed urban corruption in *The Shame of the Cities* (1902).

WRONG CHOICES EXPLAINED:
   (1) During the late 1800s, political machines did not attempt to deny voting rights to immigrants. Political machines tended to be popular with immigrant groups, particularly German and Irish immigrants.
   (2) During the late 1800s, political machines did not attempt to attract voters who were dissatisfied with the two-party system. The political machines of the late 1800s were the local operations of one of the two major political parties. In most cities, the dominant political machine was associated with the Democratic Party.
   (4) During the late 1800s, political machines did not favor civil service reform. Many reformers in the late 1800s and early 1900s attempted to end the corruption and patronage associated with the political machines. The political machines, therefore, were the target of these reform efforts, not the initiators of them.

   19. **2** The federal government follows the economic principle of laissez-faire when it takes no action on corporate mergers. The French phrase *laissez-faire* means "to let alone." It describes a hands-off approach in regard to the relationship between the government and the economy. During the Gilded Age of the late 1800s, mergers and trusts allowed corporations to gain monopoly control over entire industries. The men who controlled the major corporations in the United States came to be known as "robber barons," a scornful title meant to call attention to their cutthroat business practices. Corporate leaders and their allies in government argued that any attempt at government intervention into the economic and social worlds would hinder economic progress and growth. Many of these corporate leaders subscribed to the ideas of Social Darwinism— the attempt to apply Charles Darwin's ideas about the natural world to social relations. Social Darwinism was popularized in the United States by William Graham Sumner, who was attracted to Darwin's ideas about competition and survival of the fittest. Social Darwinism appealed to owners of large corporations because it justified their great wealth and power and also warned against any type of regulation or reform. Critics of corporate power pushed the government to take steps to rein in these massive corporations. The government passed the Sherman Antitrust Act (1890), for instance, but that had limited success.

WRONG CHOICES EXPLAINED:

(1), (3), and (4) These choices do not describe examples of the government following the economic principle of laissez-faire. The French phrase *laissez-faire* means "to let alone." It describes a government policy that takes a hands-off approach in regard to economic activities. These choices—placing restrictions on land usage (choice 1), controlling methods of production (choice 3), and determining the price of goods (choice 4)—all involve a high degree of government intervention in economic activities.

20. **2** The focus of the speakers' debate is the controversy over the policy of imperialism. *Speakers A* and *C* support the policy of imperialism. The United States began to play a more active role in the world, especially in the Western Hemisphere, after the Spanish-American War (1898). *Speaker A* is arguing that attaining colonies is an important step for the United States to take as it expands its power in the world. The passage reflects the thinking of historian Alfred Thayer Mahan, a retired admiral, who stressed the importance of naval power in achieving and maintaining influence on the world stage. In an 1890 book, he pushed for the United States to develop a strong navy, maintain military bases and coaling stations throughout the world, and administer an overseas empire. *Speaker C* is citing the economic aspects of imperialism. He notes that new colonies could provide the United States with additional markets for its products. New markets and new sources for raw materials became increasingly important as the United States expanded its industrial sector in the late 1800s and early 1900s. *Speakers B* and *D* are opposed to the United States pursuing a policy of imperialism. *Speaker B* is arguing that United States policy should focus on helping people in the United States rather than looking abroad. *Speaker B* is responding to pro-imperialists who believe it is the burden of the "civilized" nations to "uplift" the peoples of Asia, Africa, and Latin America. *Speaker D* is noting the economic costs to the United States of maintaining an overseas empire. The most prominent anti-imperialist was the author Mark Twain, who chaired the American Anti-Imperialist League.

WRONG CHOICES EXPLAINED:

(1) The focus of the speakers' debate is not the purchase of Alaska. The United States purchased Alaska from Russia in 1867. Many Americans thought that the purchase of Alaska was a waste of money. They labeled the purchase as Seward's Folly, named for Secretary of State William H. Seward, who negotiated the deal with Russia.

(3) The focus of the speakers' debate is not the size of the United States military. Debates around the size of the American military have existed throughout American history. The debate is often presented as guns versus butter, with

policy makers weighing the merits of increasing military spending versus spending more money on civilian needs.

(4) The focus of the speakers' debate is not the closing of the frontier. In the 19th century, the frontier was the unofficial boundary line between settled and sparsely settled or unsettled lands. The frontier line shifted farther and farther west as more of the United States became settled. The 19th-century historian Frederick Jackson Turner argued, in 1893, that the existence of this frontier had been a positive factor in the development of the American character. Some public thinkers saw the closing of the frontier as a call for the United States to look for new lands and new opportunities abroad.

21. **3** The headlines reflect the actions of Andrew Carnegie and John D. Rockefeller as philanthropists. The first headline refers to Carnegie's support for libraries. Carnegie gained his wealth in the steel industry. The second headline refers to Rockefeller's support for medical research. Rockefeller gained his wealth in the oil industry. Several wealthy businessmen partook in philanthropy. Carnegie asserted in an essay entitled "Wealth" (1899) that the wealthy have a duty to live responsible, modest lives and to give back to society. This "gospel of wealth" asserted that wealthy entrepreneurs should distribute their wealth so that it could be put to good use rather than be frivolously wasted. Carnegie ended up donating the majority of his fortune to charity and public-oriented projects. Carnegie believed in a laissez-faire approach to social problems. He did not want the government interfering in the social and economic spheres. That is, in part, why Carnegie urged his fellow millionaires to take action on behalf of the community. In this way, the government would not have to.

WRONG CHOICES EXPLAINED:

(1) The headlines do not reflect the actions of muckrakers. The term *muckraker* was applied to journalists who wrote magazine articles and books that exposed wrongdoing by government officials, showed the negative side of industrialization, and let the world see a variety of social ills. Important muckrakers include Upton Sinclair, who exposed the dangerous and unhygienic conditions of the meat-packing industry in his novel *The Jungle* (1906); Ida Tarbell, who wrote a scathing history of the Standard Oil Trust in 1904; and Lincoln Steffens, whose book *The Shame of Our Cities* (1902) showed the corruption of urban political machines.

(2) The headlines do not reflect the actions of socialists. Both Carnegie and Rockefeller were capitalists, not socialists. The term *socialism* refers to a range of economic and social systems as well as political ideologies, theories, movements, and parties that seek to establish such systems. Socialist systems are characterized by some form of social ownership of the means of production—either by the government or by the workers themselves—through collective or

cooperative ownership. Socialists generally believe in some form of democratic control of the economic sphere. Eugene V. Debs, who was a leader in the labor movement, was one of the founders of the Socialist Party of America in 1901.

(4) The headlines do not reflect the actions of conservationists. Conservationists were concerned about the rapid disappearance of natural areas in the United States. Logging and mining operations were taking a toll on forested areas starting in the late 1800s. President Theodore Roosevelt (1901–1909) embraced the cause of conservationism.

22. **1** The Progressive Era presidents were considered trustbusters because they used government to promote business competition. During the late 1800s, many of the leading figures in the business community—such as John D. Rockefeller, Andrew Carnegie, and J. P. Morgan—shared the view that economic competition was inefficient and wasteful. Business leaders often created trusts (combinations of companies) in order to eliminate competition and control a particular industry. Rockefeller established the first large trust in the oil-processing industry. He often drove competitors in an area out of business by drastically reducing his prices so that smaller companies could not compete. Eventually, Rockefeller would either buy out the competition or simply drive them out of business. Once the competition was eliminated, he would raise his prices. Progressive critics and reformers, who believed that competition was important for consumers, saw the concentration of economic power in a few hands as potentially dangerous to the economy as a whole. Though the Sherman Antitrust Act (1890) was passed to limit monopolistic practices, the act was not enforced with a great deal of enthusiasm. In the Progressive Era of the early 1900s, political leaders moved more aggressively against trusts. President Theodore Roosevelt (1901–1909) made a point of using the act to pursue "bad trusts." He defined these bad trusts as ones that interfered with commerce, but they were not necessarily the biggest trusts. One of Roosevelt's first targets was the Northern Securities Company, a railroad holding company. His efforts were challenged in court. In *Northern Securities Co. v. United States* (1904), the Supreme Court upheld the power of the government to break up Northern Securities under the Sherman Antitrust Act. The case was a victory for Roosevelt. President William Howard Taft (1909–1913) expanded Roosevelt's trust-busting efforts, initiating 70 antitrust suits in his four years as president. Under Taft, the government was successful in breaking up Rockefeller's Standard Oil Trust in 1911. Later, President Woodrow Wilson strengthened the antitrust powers of the federal government with the Clayton Antitrust Act (1914).

WRONG CHOICES EXPLAINED:

(2) Trust-busting did not involve support for the elimination of trade barriers. The most common barrier to international trade is higher tariff rates. The rate of tariffs on goods coming into the United States has generated a great deal of debate in United States history. Some have argued that higher tariff rates would protect American manufacturing, while others have argued that higher tariff rates would push up retail prices for consumer goods. Progressives generally supported lower tariff rates. President Woodrow Wilson pushed for the Underwood Tariff Act, which lowered tariff rates from an average of 40 percent to 25 percent.

(3) Trust-busting did not involve encouraging more voter participation in government. Many Progressive Era reformers did encourage greater voter participation. Reformers pushed for the recall, which would allow the populace to remove elected officials before their term ended; the referendum, which would allow people to vote directly on proposed legislation; and the initiative, which would enable citizens to introduce a bill to the local or state legislature by petition.

(4) Trust-busting did not involve canceling treaties with other nations. At times, the Senate has refused to approve a treaty that the president negotiated. This occurred in 1919 when supporters of the Treaty of Versailles failed to garner two-thirds of senators to approve the treaty. Wilson pushed for approval so that the United States would be a participant in the newly formed League of Nations. However, some senators wanted to isolate the United States from world affairs and opposed membership in the League.

23. **3** The primary objective of the women's movement during the first two decades of the 20th century was to secure full suffrage rights. The right to vote was central to the women's rights movement for nearly a century before the ratification of the 19th Amendment in 1920, which prohibited states from denying citizens the right to vote based on sex. In 1848, a group of women and their male allies held a convention in Seneca Falls, New York, to publicize their cause and to organize their movement. The main product of the convention was the issuing of the Seneca Falls *Declaration of Sentiments*, modeled after the Declaration of Independence. By the end of the 19th century, suffragists won voting rights for women in several of the states. However, women were still prohibited from participating in national elections. In 1913, women held an important suffrage parade in Washington, D.C., to publicize their cause. However, it was not until the World War I period that the movement fully got the ear of President Woodrow Wilson. The suffrage movement was successful in achieving its goal with the ratification of the 19th Amendment to the Constitution in 1920.

WRONG CHOICES EXPLAINED:

(1) The agenda of the women's rights movement included extending property rights to women, but that was not the central demand of the movement in the first two decades of the 20th century. During the colonial period and during the first decades of United States history, the legal doctrine of *femme covert* applied to women. The doctrine held that wives had no independent legal or political standing. Therefore, any property or belongings that a woman might have brought into the marriage became her husband's. In the 1830s and 1840s, many states passed Married Women's Property Acts, which allowed married women to own property independent of their husbands.

(2) The agenda of the women's rights movement included promoting higher education for women, but that was not the central demand of the movement in the first two decades of the 20th century. Women's rights advocates in the 19th century pushed for expanded higher-education opportunities for women. Several teaching seminaries for women opened in the 1700s and 1800s. Oberlin College was the first coeducational college in the United States. It began accepting women in 1837.

(4) The agenda of the women's rights movement included winning equal pay for equal work, but that was not the central demand of the movement in the first two decades of the 20th century. In the 1960s, this became an important goal of the women's rights movement. The Equal Pay Act of 1963 and the Civil Rights Act of 1964 include provisions that are intended to guarantee equal pay for equal work. However, these acts have had mixed results. Women were earning approximately 60 percent of men's salaries for comparable work in the 1970s. That figure has grown to approximately 78 percent today.

24. **4** The situation in the cartoon was mainly caused by disagreements over United States participation in the League of Nations. In the cartoon, President Woodrow Wilson is depicted as protecting a tree labeled League Covenants from the Senate's ax. The cartoon was published as the Senate debated approval of the Treaty of Versailles in 1919. By approving the Treaty of Versailles, the Senate would have also made the United States a member of the League of Nations. Earlier, in his Fourteen Points document, President Wilson championed the idea of an organization composed of the world's nations. The victorious powers in Europe after World War I largely ignored Wilson's idealistic vision for a postwar world, but they agreed to create the League of Nations. Wilson pushed for Senate approval of the Treaty of Versailles so that the United States would be a participant in this new organization. However, some senators wanted to isolate the United States from world affairs and opposed membership in the League. These isolationists announced that they would vote to reject the treaty. Another group of senators, alluded to in the cartoon, took a middle position.

They would agree to vote to approve the treaty if the Senate put certain conditions on U.S. participation in the League of Nations. Wilson refused to compromise with these senators and urged his Senate allies to reject any conditions for U.S. membership in the League. Without the support of these senators in the middle, the Treaty of Versailles was rejected by the Senate. As a result, the United States did not join the League of Nations.

WRONG CHOICES EXPLAINED:
(1) The situation in the cartoon was not caused by the cost of paying reparations after World War I. After World War I, the Treaty of Versailles (1919) demanded that Germany pay reparations for war-related damages. However, the debate in the United States over ratification of the treaty centered around participation in the League of Nations, not reparations.

(2) The situation in the cartoon was not caused by the failure of President Woodrow Wilson to promote the Treaty of Versailles. The opposite was true. Wilson was a staunch supporter of the League. Instead, isolationist Senators opposed United States membership in the League and voted against ratification of the Treaty of Versailles.

(3) The situation in the cartoon was not caused by the overwhelming public rejection of the peace terms in the Treaty of Versailles. It is extremely difficult to gauge public opinion accurately in the era before professional polling. Evidence points to a mixed reaction to the treaty, with a large degree of opposition. German Americans and Irish Americans were especially critical of the terms of the treaty. However, the showdown depicted in the cartoon is between the executive branch and the legislative branch, not between the government and the American people.

25. **2** The cartoon depicts the constitutional principle of checks and balances. The cartoon shows a conflict between two branches of the federal government—the executive branch that was represented by President Woodrow Wilson protecting the tree labeled League Covenants and the legislative branch that was threatening to chop down that tree with its ax. The Constitution gives the president the power to negotiate treaties with foreign nations. However, such treaties are approved only with the "advice and consent" of two-thirds of the Senate. This ability of the legislative branch to block an initiative of the executive branch is one of several checks built into the system of governance established by the Constitution. The framers of the Constitution were very conscious of the problems of a government with limitless powers. After living under the British monarchy, they came to believe that a powerful government without checks was dangerous to liberty. Therefore, they created a governmental system with three branches, each with the ability to check the powers of the other two.

The goal was to keep the three branches in balance. Other examples of this concept include the president's ability to veto bills and the Supreme Court's ability to use the power of judicial review to strike down laws it deems unconstitutional.

WRONG CHOICES EXPLAINED:

(1) The situation depicted in the cartoon does not illustrate the constitutional principle of due process. The term *due process* refers to the formal legal proceedings that are carried out, in conformity with established rules and principles, before an individual is punished by the state. Due process rules are contained in both the Fifth Amendment and the 14th Amendment to the Constitution. The cartoon does not allude to such procedures.

(3) The situation depicted in the cartoon does not illustrate the constitutional principle of popular sovereignty. The term *popular sovereignty* literally means the power of the people to decide something. In American history, the term was used in relation to the question of whether or not slavery would exist in new states. The people of a territory would vote on the issue before the territory applied for statehood. The Kansas-Nebraska Act allowed for the possibility of slavery, under the principle of popular sovereignty, in the territories of Kansas and Nebraska—areas that had been closed to slavery by the Missouri Compromise (1820).

(4) The situation depicted in the cartoon does not illustrate the constitutional principle of judicial review. The term *judicial review* refers to the power of the Supreme Court to determine whether laws are consistent with the Constitution. If the Court determines that a particular law is unconstitutional, that law is immediately voided. This power was established in the Supreme Court's decision in the *Marbury* v. *Madison* case (1803). The cartoon does not allude to this power.

26. **3** The 1920s are often called the Roaring Twenties because the decade was noted for social and cultural changes. The decade was characterized by changing ideas concerning gender. The "new woman" of the 1920s was more engaged in public issues than in previous decades. She might have participated in the political struggles of the progressive movement and gained a new sense of confidence in public issues, especially after women achieved the right to vote in 1920. The changing image of women during the 1920s was symbolized by the popularity of the flappers and their style of dress. Flappers were independent-minded young women of the 1920s who openly defied Victorian moral codes about "proper" ladylike behavior. The decade also witnessed the development of mass culture. Radio grew from being virtually nonexistent at the beginning of the decade to becoming an extremely popular medium by the end of it. By 1923, there were almost 600 licensed radio stations. Movie attendance achieved staggering levels in the 1920s. By the end of the decade, three-fourths

of the American people (roughly 90 million) were going to the movies every week. The first talkie, *The Jazz Singer*, came out in 1927. An important cultural development was the Harlem Renaissance, which was a literary, artistic, and intellectual movement centered in the African-American neighborhood of Harlem, in New York City. A key goal of the movement was to increase pride in African-American culture by celebrating African-American life and forging a new cultural identity among African-American people. Contributions included the poetry of Langston Hughes, Claude McKay, and Countee Cullen and the jazz music of Louis Armstrong, Duke Ellington, and Bessie Smith.

WRONG CHOICES EXPLAINED:
(1) The label "Roaring Twenties" did not refer to political reform in the 1920s. In fact, the decade is not noted for political reform. The Progressive Era of the 1900s and 1910s is noted for political reform. The Progressive reform movement was a response to the economic instability, social inequality, and political corruption that began during the Gilded Age and continued into the 20th century. Progressive reformers called for greater government intervention in the economy as well as increased democratization of the political process, social justice, and conservation of natural resources.

(2) The label "Roaring Twenties" did not refer to economic depression in the 1920s. In fact, the economy was healthy for most of the 1920s. The following decade, the 1930s, experienced the Great Depression. Not everyone shared equally in the economic growth of the 1920s. The gap between the wealthy and poor increased, and farmers struggled to get by. The Great Depression began with the stock market crash of October 1929.

(4) The label "Roaring Twenties" did not refer to ending Prohibition in the 1920s. Prohibition was in effect throughout the decade; it did not end until 1933. Prohibition went into effect with the ratification of the 18th Amendment, which banned the production, transport, and sale of alcohol as of January 1, 1920. Although per capita consumption of alcohol dropped dramatically in the early 1920s, it increased as the decade progressed, possibly approaching pre-Prohibition levels by 1925. Further, the amount of lawlessness in America went up as bootleggers, speakeasies, and organized crime filled the gap left by the death of the legitimate alcoholic beverage industry.

27. **4** The Great Migration that took place between 1915 and 1930 refers to African Americans who left the rural south for northern cities. There were several important reasons for the Great Migration. One factor was the mistreatment that African Americans received in the South. Jim Crow laws, which segregated public facilities, made African Americans second-class citizens. In addition, African Americans were excluded from the political system in the

South. A series of obstacles, such as literacy tests and poll taxes, limited their ability to vote. However, the main factor that drew African Americans north was jobs. By the turn of the 20th century, the industrial revolution was in full swing in northern cities such as New York and Chicago. Factories using new mass production techniques were able, at first, to fill the jobs with local people and European immigrants. However, World War I created a labor crisis for these factories. Factories were producing goods around the clock. Even before the United States entered the war in 1917, U.S. factories were producing war goods for Great Britain. After entering the war, demand for these goods increased. In addition, European immigration to the United States dropped significantly due to the war. Finally, millions of potential factory workers were pressed into the U.S. military. Factory agents from the North frequently made recruiting trips to the South, offering immediate employment and free passage to the North.

WRONG CHOICES EXPLAINED:

(1) The Great Migration that took place between 1915 and 1930 does not refer to workers who left the Northeast for the South. Later, in the post–World War II period, many Americans abandoned the states of the Northeast and the upper Midwest and moved to the Sun Belt states of the South and the West. This migration was caused, in part, by the decline of the industrial base of the Northeast and the upper Midwest. The states of the upper Midwest, from Ohio to Wisconsin, became known as the Rust Belt as factories closed in this region.

(2) The Great Migration that took place between 1915 and 1930 does not refer to Native American Indians who left their reservations. Native-American Indian reservations are parcels of land that are managed by Native-American Indian tribes under the auspices of the federal government's Bureau of Indian Affairs. Over time, many Native Americans have left reservations to seek opportunities elsewhere. Of the 2.5 million Native American Indians in the United States, approximately one million live on reservations.

(3) The Great Migration that took place between 1915 and 1930 does not refer to middle-class whites who left cities to settle in suburbs. In the post–World War II period, many middle-class whites did make the move from city to suburb. A key motive for the move was simply a housing shortage in urban centers. Not much new housing was built during the Great Depression or during World War II. The sudden return of millions of G.I.s after World War II created a crisis. In addition, some white veterans were not pleased to return from the war to find that their neighborhoods had changed as African Americans had moved in during the war. Whether motivated by racism or concern for property values, a "white flight" out of New York, Detroit, Philadelphia, Chicago, and other major cities occurred from the late 1940s to the 1970s.

28. **4** Breadlines, Hoovervilles, and the Bonus Army were all direct results of unemployment caused by the Great Depression. The Great Depression (1929–1939) was devastating for American workers. Between 1929 and 1933, wages fell by 60 percent and unemployment tripled to over 12 million people. Breadlines formed in many cities as many unemployed people sought basic foodstuffs from charitable organizations. Hoovervilles were shantytowns occupied by homeless people. There were hundreds of Hoovervilles across the United States, occupied by hundreds of thousands of homeless people. The name "Hoovervilles" was meant to mock President Herbert Hoover. Critics held that Hoover did not take sufficient action on behalf of the nation's neediest people. Hoover was a believer in supply-side economics. This approach to the economy stressed stimulating the supply side of the economy—manufacturers, banks, and insurance corporations. The theory is that if there is growth in the supply side, there will be a general economic revival. As a result, the theory continues, the benefits of a robust economy will trickle down to everyone. The Bonus Army was a protest movement of unemployed veterans of World War I. Its main goal was to pressure the Hoover administration to support the early payment of money promised to veterans (veterans were scheduled to receive bonuses in 1945). In June 1932, a group of World War I veterans who called themselves the Bonus Expeditionary Force, or Bonus Army, marched into Washington, D.C., to demand their bonuses immediately. About 15,000 men, mostly unemployed and poor, set up an encampment in the nation's capital to demand their money.

WRONG CHOICES EXPLAINED:
(1) Breadlines, Hoovervilles, and the Bonus Army were not the result of housing shortages in the 1920s. Significant housing shortages did not exist in the 1920s. Housing shortages in the United States occurred later, in the 1940s after World War II. Relatively few units were added to the existing housing stock during the years of the Great Depression and World War II. When hundreds of thousands of G.I.s returned from the war in 1945 and 1946, many were eager to start families in new homes, but few units were available. Eventually, the shortage was alleviated, most notably through the building of suburban developments.

(2) Breadlines, Hoovervilles, and the Bonus Army were not the result of relief efforts of the New Deal. In many ways, the New Deal was a response to the breadlines and Hoovervilles that appeared in many cities as the devastation of the Great Depression was felt by more people. The handling of the Bonus Army protest in Washington, D.C. (1932) damaged the reputation of President Herbert Hoover and helped pave the way for the election of Franklin D. Roosevelt. Roosevelt initiated a breathtaking number of relief programs upon taking office in 1933. His New Deal efforts did not end the Great Depression, but they did alleviate the suffering of millions of individuals.

(3) Breadlines, Hoovervilles, and the Bonus Army were not the result of mechanization of agriculture. The mechanization of agriculture did frequently have negative repercussions on farmers. While mechanization reduced the hours needed for agricultural tasks, it also undermined small-scale family farms. First, mechanization increased overall production. This lowered the prices that farmers received per bushel of corn or wheat. Second, many farmers could not afford the new equipment or went into debt purchasing new equipment. However, the negative impact of mechanization was more of a rural phenomenon. The developments in the question were more urban phenomena.

29. **3** The Fair Labor Standards Act (1938) helped American workers by establishing a minimum wage in many industries. President Franklin D. Roosevelt pushed a number of New Deal programs that benefited industrial workers in a variety of ways. An important aspect of his New Deal was increasing workers' wages and therefore their purchasing power. He saw that one of the causes of the Great Depression was that workers in the 1920s were not able to purchase enough consumer goods to keep the economy growing. The act established a minimum wage that employers would be required to pay workers. Certain classes of workers were exempted from the minimum wage requirements. Workers receiving tips are generally not subject to the minimum wage unless the amount of tips received does not bring the worker's earnings up to minimum wage requirements. Also, independent contractors are not subject to minimum wage requirements. The Department of Labor has taken action against employers who have illegally classified workers as independent contractors in order to evade minimum wage requirements. Finally, certain white collar employees—professional, administrative, and executive—are exempt from the act. The Fair Labor Standards Act also established the maximum number of hours a worker may be expected to work, establishing the 40-hour week as the standard for many industries. Roosevelt said that other than the Social Security Act, the Fair Labor Standards Act was "the most far-sighted program for the benefit of workers ever adopted here or in any other country."

WRONG CHOICES EXPLAINED:
(1) The Fair Labor Standards Act did not establish health plans for workers. Employment-based health plans, offered to employees and their families, cover approximately 150 million people in the United States. Unions have frequently negotiated such health plans as one of the benefits of employment. The Affordable Care Act (2010) includes provisions to extend several protections to the health plans of employees of large businesses.
(2) The Fair Labor Standards Act did legalize strikes and boycotts. An earlier New Deal act called the Wagner Act, or National Labor Relations Act (1935),

affected workers by protecting their rights to form unions and bargain collectively. The act strengthened unions by mandating that employers bargain with unions. It also established the National Labor Relations Board to conduct elections among workers to see if they wanted to be represented by a union. The act also banned certain unfair labor practices.

(4) The Fair Labor Standards Act did not make labor unions accept women and African Americans as members. Unions have been on both sides of the question of racial justice. In the 1800s, the Knights of Labor accepted African-American members. However, the American Federation of Labor maintained racist practices well into the 20th century, keeping African-American membership to a minimum. The Congress of Industrial Organizations, organized during the Great Depression, actively courted African-American workers. After World War II, most unions removed barriers to African-American membership, making the labor movement more integrated than American society as a whole. Women were part of the labor movement from its inception in the 1830s. Many of the first industrial workers in the United States, the women of the Lowell, Massachusetts, textile mills, went out on strike in 1834 and again in 1836. Women have continued to play a central role in the labor movement in the 20th century.

30. **1** Adoption of the "cash and carry" policy in 1939 and passage of the Lend-Lease Act in 1941 showed the growing commitment of the United States to provide aid to the Allied nations. The two actions took place in the context of World War II. The war started in 1939, when Nazi Germany attacked Poland and then Great Britain and France declared war on Germany. From the onset, the United States was officially neutral in regard to World War II. However, President Franklin D. Roosevelt's sympathies were with the countries fighting against fascism. Soon after the beginning of the war, Roosevelt pushed for legislation allowing the United States to send armaments to Britain with the condition that Britain pay for the weapons first and transport them in their own ships. This cash and carry policy allowed the United States to support Britain without the risk of U.S. ships being destroyed. By mid-1940, the American public began to shift toward a more interventionist stance. The situation in Europe grew dire. Americans were shaken by the defeat of France at the hands of the Nazis in 1940. Americans saw how one of the great democratic powers was easily defeated by the Nazi war machine. With this shift in public opinion and with his victory in the presidential election of 1940, Roosevelt was ready to take more direct action. In March 1941, Congress approved his Lend-Lease Act, which allowed the United States to send armaments to Britain in American ships. The Lend-Lease Act was extended to the Soviet Union after Hitler launched an invasion of the Soviet Union in June 1941. The United States entered the war in late

1941 after Japan attacked the American naval base at Pearl Harbor, Hawaii Territory.

WRONG CHOICES EXPLAINED:

(2) Adoption of the "cash and carry" policy in 1939 and passage of the Lend-Lease Act in 1941 were not intended to force the Japanese out of Korea. In 1945, Japanese forces in Korea surrendered to American and Soviet forces. Subsequently, Korea was divided at the 38th parallel.

(3) Adoption of the "cash and carry" policy in 1939 and passage of the Lend-Lease Act in 1941 were not intended to increase trade with Italy. The United States and Italy were on opposing sides in World War II. Trade did not occur between the countries during the war.

(4) Adoption of the "cash and carry" policy in 1939 and passage of the Lend-Lease Act in 1941 were not intended to end German violations of American territory. German forces did not land on American territory during World War II.

31. **2** A direct result of United States involvement in World War II was the entry of more women and minorities into the workplace. Women and minorities were needed because factories were working around the clock producing military goods and much of the male work force was in the military. The government produced many images, usually through the Office of War Information, that showed women in industrial settings. The fictional Rosie the Riveter was often featured in this public relations campaign. These female workers were presented in a positive light—helping the nation as well as the men in combat abroad. Such a campaign was needed because prewar societal mores discouraged women from doing industrial work. The campaign was successful. By 1945, one-third of the work force was female. In addition, African Americans joined millions of other Americans in moving toward industrial centers and finding work in war-related industries. Initially, many war industries were reluctant to hire African Americans. An important African-American labor leader, A. Phillip Randolph, the president of the Brotherhood of Sleeping Car Porters, planned a public demonstration in Washington, D.C., in 1941 to protest discrimination in war-related industries. When the Roosevelt administration heard of these plans, it worked out a bargain. Roosevelt issued Executive Order 8802, banning discrimination in war-related industries. Randolph called off the march.

WRONG CHOICES EXPLAINED:

(1) United States involvement in World War II did not result in an increase in the production of consumer goods. The opposite occurred. There was a shortage of consumer goods during the war as factories converted to war-related

production. For example, from early 1942 until the end of the war in 1945, American factories produced no new automobiles.

(3) United States involvement in World War II did not result in a decrease in industrial activity. The opposite is true. Factories were running around the clock to produce weaponry to aid the American military and its allies. The increase in industrial activity quickly brought the Great Depression of the 1930s to an end.

(4) United States involvement in World War II did not result in a decrease in federal control over the economy. The opposite is true. A variety of federal agencies regulated economic activity to ensure that the needs of the military were met. These agencies included the War Production Board, the National War Labor Board, and the Office of Economic Stabilization.

32. **3** The attack on the United States naval base at Pearl Harbor, Hawaii Territory, by Japanese forces caused the other three events in the question. In the days after the attack in December 1941, Congress declared war against Japan (mentioned in choice 1). In 1942, the federal government began the internment of Japanese Americans (mentioned in choice 2). The internment was initially authorized when President Franklin D. Roosevelt issued Executive Order 9066. The order allowed the government to remove 120,000 Japanese Americans, two-thirds of them citizens, from west coast states and relocate them to camps throughout the West. Most of their property was confiscated by the government. In the case of *Korematsu* v. *United States* (1944), the Supreme Court ruled that the relocation was acceptable on the grounds of national security. The *Korematsu* decision is one of several rulings by the Supreme Court that have curtailed civil liberties in times of war. In 1945, the United States dropped two atomic bombs on Japanese cities, one on Hiroshima and one on Nagasaki (mentioned in choice 4). Soon after, Japan surrendered, thus ending World War II. Earlier in 1945, the last two battles between the United States and Japan, at Iwo Jima and Okinawa, were extremely costly. After those battles, the United States was faced with the daunting task of forcing Japan to surrender. The American people and the American military were preparing for what seemed inevitable—a long and bloody attack on the Japanese home islands. In the meantime, scientists in the United States had recently completed and tested a devastating new weapon—the atomic bomb. It was in this context that President Truman decided to drop this powerful bomb. At the time, the decision to drop the atomic bomb did not generate much public debate. The atomic bombing swiftly ended a bloody conflict that consumed 50 million lives. However, in the decades since the war, some Americans have raised questions about Truman's decision. Critics argue that it was morally wrong for the United States to have targeted civilian populations and that the Japanese were ready to surrender anyway. Many stand by the decision to drop the bomb. It is not clear that the

Japanese were on the verge of surrendering. Some members of the Japanese military argued against surrendering even after the second bomb was dropped.

WRONG CHOICES EXPLAINED:
(1), (2), and (4) These choices were not the cause of the other developments mentioned in the question. All three of these choices describe developments that occurred after the United States was attacked at Pearl Harbor (mentioned in choice 3).

33. **4** McCarthyism of the early 1950s resulted in damage to the reputations of many innocent people. The anticommunist movement of the 1950s came to be known as McCarthyism. It was named for Senator Joseph McCarthy, who became the central figure in this movement. McCarthy gained prominence when he announced that he had a list of names of State Department employees who were members of the Communist Party (1950). This and similar claims, mostly base-less, created a name for McCarthy and set the stage for a host of measures to halt this perceived threat. An atmosphere reminiscent of the Salem witch trials of the 1690s pervaded America as wild accusations became more common. Fears of communist spying on the United States intensified when the Soviet Union first tested an atomic bomb (1949). The government accused two members of the Communist Party, Ethel and Julius Rosenberg, of passing secrets of the nuclear bomb to the Soviet Union. The Rosenbergs insisted on their innocence. However, they were found guilty and were sent to the electric chair (1953). Congress inves-tigated suspected communist sympathizers in different sectors of society. Congress especially targeted the entertainment industry, fearing that communists would subtly get their message out through television and movies. The Hollywood 10 was a group of ten prominent figures who refused to cooperate with the House Un-American Activities Committee (1947); they were jailed for contempt and subsequently blacklisted. The most intense period of McCarthyism was over by 1954. By that time, the Korean War had ended and McCarthy himself was dis-credited for making baseless accusations against members of the military. The hearings on these accusations, known as the Army-McCarthy hearings, were widely seen on the new medium of television (1954), demonstrating to the American public the reckless nature of McCarthy's accusations.

WRONG CHOICES EXPLAINED:
(1) McCarthyism of the early 1950s did not result in the end of the arms race. The arms race intensified in the 1950s as both the United States and the Soviet Union developed and expanded nuclear arms programs. McCarthyism served to heighten Cold War fears in the United States and created a political climate that was more amenable to sharp increases in the military budget.

(2) McCarthyism of the early 1950s did not result in reduced spending on national defense. The defense budget increased in the 1950s as both the United States and the Soviet Union expanded nuclear arms programs as well as conventional forces. McCarthyism served to heighten Cold War fears in the United States and created a political climate that was more amenable to sharp increases in the military budget.

(3) McCarthyism of the early 1950s did not result in increased discrimination against returning veterans. Veterans returning from World War II and the Korean War did not, for the most part, experience discrimination based on their prior military service. Later, in the 1960s and 1970s, some veterans of the Vietnam War experienced hostility from members of the public who were opposed to the war.

34. **4** During the 1950s, United States foreign policy was shaped by the emergence of two world superpowers. The two superpowers that emerged following World War II were the Soviet Union and the United States. The United States became increasingly concerned about the growing power of the Soviet Union after World War II and put forth a policy of attempting to prevent the expansion of communism, known as containment. President Harry S. Truman articulated this goal, which has come to be known as the Truman Doctrine, in a speech to Congress in 1947. The rivalry between the two superpowers became known as the Cold War. Truman put the idea of containment into practice in 1947 by providing $400 million in military aid to Greece and Turkey to prevent those countries from becoming communist. Another example of the containment policy was the Berlin Airlift. In 1948, before the status of Berlin was settled, the Soviet Union decided it would prevent any food or other supplies from entering the western sector of the city. The goal of this action was for the Soviet Union to block the influence of the United States and its western allies in Berlin. Ultimately, the Soviet Union hoped to make all of Berlin part of what would become East Germany. Truman decided to send thousands of planes filled with supplies into the western sector of Berlin in an action known as the Berlin Airlift. The Berlin Airlift prevented people living in the western sector of Berlin from starving and prevented the Soviet Union from taking over the city. The formation of the North Atlantic Treaty Organization (NATO) was also part of the Cold War strategy of containment. NATO was created in 1949 by the United States and its allies to challenge the growing power of the Soviet Union. The members of NATO pledged that they would view an attack on any one member as an attack on all members.

WRONG CHOICES EXPLAINED:

(1) United States foreign policy in the 1950s was not shaped by the principle of nonalignment. The nonaligned countries during the Cold War period (1945–1991) were those nations that did not ally themselves with either the United States or the Soviet Union. These countries formalized their status with the organization of the Non-Aligned Movement in 1956. The nations that initiated the movement were Yugoslavia, India, Indonesia, Egypt, and Ghana.

(2) United States foreign policy in the 1950s was not shaped by a return to pre–World War II isolationism. After World War I, the United States retreated to a policy of isolationism. However, after World War II, the United States became engaged in challenging the Soviet Union and participating in a Cold War between the two nations.

(3) United States foreign policy in the 1950s was not shaped by a willingness to compromise with communist nations. During the 1950s, the United States challenged the power of the Soviet Union and other communist nations. The United States engaged in the Korean War (1950–1953) and bolstered its military to challenge the Soviet Union. Later, under President Richard Nixon (1969–1974), the United States pursued a policy of *détente*, which involved a willingness to compromise with communist nations.

35. **1** The formation of the North Atlantic Treaty Organization (NATO) and the Southeast Asia Treaty Organization (SEATO) were attempts by the United States and other nations to create mutual defense pacts. The United States demonstrated its commitment to protect Western Europe when it participated in the founding of NATO in 1949. The members of NATO vowed to resist collectively any aggressive actions by the Soviet Union. This marked the first time that the United States joined a peacetime alliance. Five years later, SEATO was created (1954), during the administration of President Dwight D. Eisenhower, in order to challenge further communist advances in Southeast Asia. United States participation in NATO and SEATO were designed to check the power of the Soviet Union. The United States and the Soviet Union emerged at the end of World War II as rival superpowers in the Cold War. The Soviet Union occupied the nations of Eastern Europe after the war. The United States was worried that the Soviet Union would try to push into Western Europe and later into Asia. In order to block any further aggression by the Soviet Union, Truman issued the Truman Doctrine, in which he said that the goal of the United States would be to contain communism. Toward this end, the United States extended military aid to Greece and Turkey (1947) and economic aid to the war-ravaged nations of Western Europe in the form of the Marshall Plan (1948). These moves, along with participation in NATO and SEATO, represented a clear break

with the pre–World War II position of the United States. The United States made it clear even in peacetime that the country would be involved in world affairs.

WRONG CHOICES EXPLAINED:

(2) The goals of the North Atlantic Treaty Organization (NATO) and the Southeast Asia Treaty Organization (SEATO) did not include increasing tariff rates among members. These organizations were focused on mutual defense, not trade. Later, the United States participated in the North American Free Trade Agreement (1993) and the World Trade Organization (1995), which were focused on trade. The goal of both of these entities was to reduce tariff rates among participants.

(3) The goals of the North Atlantic Treaty Organization (NATO) and the Southeast Asia Treaty Organization (SEATO) did not include decreasing the number of nuclear weapons. These organizations were focused on mutual defense, not arms reduction. Later, the United States and the Soviet Union participated in the Strategic Arms Limitation Talks (SALT), which led to two arms control agreements in 1972.

(4) The goals of the North Atlantic Treaty Organization (NATO) and the Southeast Asia Treaty Organization (SEATO) did not include providing economic aid to poor nations. The United States has consistently extended economic aid to many developing nations over the years. Under President John F. Kennedy (1961–1963), the United States expanded foreign aid with the creation of the Peace Corps to assist underdeveloped countries in Africa, Latin America, and Asia. Kennedy also created the Agency for International Development to coordinate aid to foreign countries and the Alliance for Progress, which was a series of development projects in Latin America.

36. **2** In 1958, the United States government increased spending on science education and research in reaction to the launching of *Sputnik*. When the Soviet Union launched the unmanned satellite *Sputnik* into space in 1957, many Americans were caught off guard. Before the launch, America had assumed that it was technologically superior to the Soviet Union. In addition, the launching of *Sputnik* was troubling for the United States because government officials realized that the same type of rocket that launched the satellite could also be used to deliver atomic weapons quickly to any place on Earth. The launching of *Sputnik* led the American government to devote more resources to teaching science and math to young people. Local school districts made greater efforts to identify gifted students and create accelerated programs for them. In addition, districts began receiving matching funds for math, science, and foreign language instruction from

the federal government. The launching of *Sputnik* also initiated a space race with the Soviet Union. In 1969, the United States was the first nation to land a man on the moon.

WRONG CHOICES EXPLAINED:

(1) The increase in United States government spending on science education and research in 1958 was not a reaction to the creation of the Warsaw Pact. The Warsaw Pact was a military alliance that the Soviet Union created in 1955 with the communist nations of eastern and central Europe. The creation of the Warsaw Pact did not point to a gap in science education and research between the Soviet Union and the United States, as many believed that the launch of *Sputnik* did.

(3) The increase in United States government spending on science education and research in 1958 was not a reaction to the installation of Soviet missiles in Cuba. The attempt by the Soviet Union to install nuclear missiles in Cuba was discovered in 1962, four years after the initiatives referred to in the question. President John F. Kennedy saw these missiles, which were in close proximity to the United States, as an unacceptable provocation and ordered Soviet Premier Nikita Khrushchev to halt the operation and dismantle the bases. Khrushchev insisted on the right of the Soviet Union to install the missiles. For about a week, the world stood on the brink of nuclear war. Finally, a deal was reached in which the Soviet Union would abandon its Cuban missile program and the United States would quietly remove its missiles from Turkey.

(4) The increase in United States government spending on science education and research in 1958 was not a reaction to the U-2 incident. That event occurred in 1960, two years after the initiatives referred to in the question. The incident involved a U-2 American spy plane being shot down over Soviet air space. At first, the United States insisted that the plane was a weather aircraft. However, this story did not hold up to scrutiny after the Soviet Union produced the pilot of the plane, alive, along with photographs taken of Soviet military installations.

37. **3** A problem facing President Lyndon B. Johnson at the time he delivered the speech excerpted in the question (1968) was that opposition to the Vietnam War was becoming more widespread. In the speech, Johnson is announcing that he would not seek reelection. He asserts that he would focus on "America's sons in the fields far away," not on "personal partisan causes." The war in Vietnam had become increasingly contentious by 1968. The United States became heavily involved in Vietnam after Congress gave President Lyndon Johnson a blank check with the Tonkin Gulf Resolution in 1964. The United States feared that South Vietnam would become a communist nation as North Vietnam had. Over

the next several years, Johnson sent hundreds of thousands of troops to Vietnam, reinstituted the draft, and began aerial bombardment of Vietnam. Despite the presence of over half a million United States troops and the firepower of the U.S. military, President Johnson was not able to declare victory over the communist rebels in South Vietnam. As the war dragged on and as the United States suffered more casualties, many Americans began to question the wisdom of American policies in Vietnam. Some thought the war was more of a civil war that the United States should not be part of. Many young men began to oppose the war because they feared they might be drafted. Finally, many Americans grew to oppose the war after seeing unsettling images on television news programs. Families saw American soldiers burn down Vietnamese villages. They saw body bags coming back to the United States. They saw Vietnamese children burned by napalm. All of these images contributed to the growing antiwar movement in the United States. By 1968, Johnson decided that his war policies imperiled his reelection, so he decided to not run for a second term.

WRONG CHOICES EXPLAINED:

(1) President Lyndon Johnson's decision to not run for reelection was related to widespread opposition to the Vietnam War, not to judicial scandals. During Johnson's administration, the most prominent scandal involving the judiciary involved Abe Fortas, a justice on the Supreme Court. Accusations of ethics violations forced Fortas to resign from the Court in 1969.

(2) President Lyndon Johnson's decision to not run for reelection was related to widespread opposition to the Vietnam War, not to his participation in peace talks. Johnson initiated peace talks in 1968. In the following decades, evidence has emerged indicating that the Republican candidate for the presidency in 1968, Richard Nixon, used surrogates to pressure the government of South Vietnam to stall the peace talks. Nixon feared that successful peace talks in 1968 could bolster the campaign of the Democratic candidate for president, Hubert Humphrey. These efforts, and other factors, were successful in scuttling Johnson's efforts at a substantive agreement to end the fighting in Vietnam.

(4) President Lyndon Johnson's decision to not run for reelection was related to widespread opposition to the Vietnam War, not to a shifting of money from the Vietnam War to Great Society programs. The opposite was closer to the truth. Increased spending on the Vietnam War took resources away from Great Society programs, undermining their effectiveness. Dr. Martin Luther King, Jr., said at a conference in 1967, "The promises of the Great Society have been shot down on the battlefields of Vietnam."

38. **1** The primary method used by Dr. Martin Luther King, Jr., to advance civil rights was nonviolent protest of segregation practices. King drew on several religious, philosophical, and political traditions in developing his approach to social change. King's insistence on nonviolence had deep roots. Many Christians cite the biblical injunction to turn the other cheek if struck. Pacifism is especially strong in the Quaker tradition. King also gained inspiration from Mahatma Gandhi's campaign to resist British authority in India in the first half of the 20th century. Gandhi taught that to resort to violence was to stoop to the moral level of the oppressor. King also emphasized civil disobedience—the philosophical principle that asserts it is one's right, indeed one's responsibility, to resist unjust laws. Earlier in American history, that principle was articulated by the transcendentalist thinker Henry David Thoreau in his essay *Resistance to Civil Government (Civil Disobedience)* (1849). King was a central figure in the civil rights movement of the 1950s and 1960s. The high point of the movement might have been the march on Washington in 1963, where King gave his "I Have a Dream" speech. The movement culminated in the Civil Rights Act of 1964, which banned segregation in public facilities, and the Voting Rights Act of 1965, which removed barriers to African Americans voting.

WRONG CHOICES EXPLAINED:

(2) While working to advance civil rights, Dr. Martin Luther King, Jr., did not support black separatism. A central demand of the civil rights movement was that Jim Crow segregation laws be eliminated. King envisioned an integrated society, where people are judged "by the content of their character," not by "the color of their skin." Some activists who addressed the issue of social justice for African Americans did not emphasize separatism. Malcolm X, for example, advocated that African Americans organize among themselves, separate from whites. After making a pilgrimage to Mecca in 1964 and seeing Muslims of different races interacting as equals, Malcolm X revised his views about black separatism.

(3) While working to advance civil rights, Dr. Martin Luther King, Jr., did not pursue elective public office. King was generally nonpartisan. At different times, he was critical of both of the two main political parties. By 1964, when President Lyndon Johnson pushed strongly for the passage of the Civil Rights Act, King worked closely with Johnson and let the public know that he supported Johnson's reelection. However, King never ran for public office.

(4) While working to advance civil rights, Dr. Martin Luther King, Jr., did not advocate practical education for economic gain. Earlier, Booker T. Washington founded the Tuskegee Institute (1881) to teach vocational skills to African

Americans. Washington emphasized educational and economic progress for African Americans, rather than political equality and civil rights.

39. **3** The focus of this cartoon is President Richard Nixon attempting to hide evidence from investigators. In the cartoon, Nixon is depicted as hiding behind an American flag, implying that his pronouncements about national security should not be taken at face value. Instead, they are designed to distract the American public from the real issue at hand—rampant corruption within the Nixon administration. Nixon is attempting to use the flag as a "national security blanket" to cover up illegal activities, including "faked cables," "stolen files," the use of a cash slush fund, and eavesdropping on opponents. The most prominent scandal of the Nixon administration was the Watergate affair, which involved spies breaking into the headquarters of the Democratic National Committee at the Watergate Hotel in Washington, D.C. These spies were caught by local police. Their arrest led to investigations, hearings, and legal proceedings that ultimately led to the resignation of President Nixon.

WRONG CHOICES EXPLAINED:

(1) The focus of the cartoon is not President Richard Nixon recalling diplomats from Mexico. Nixon did not take such an action. The money bag labeled "Mexico" refers to a large private contribution to Nixon's Committee to Reelect the President (CRP). The money was part of a fundraising blitz in the spring of 1972, right before the implementation of a new campaign finance disclosure law. The contribution being referred to was funneled through a bank in Mexico to hide the source of the money. The source of the money was later discovered after some of the money was found in the account of one of the Watergate burglars.

(2) The focus of the cartoon is not President Richard Nixon supporting tax decreases and budget cuts. Nixon did not take such actions. The federal budget grew during each year of Nixon's presidency, and there were no significant decreases in tax rates under President Nixon. Later, President Ronald Reagan (1981–1989) signed legislation cutting taxes, although the federal budget grew for most of the years of his presidency.

(4) The focus of the cartoon is not President Richard Nixon making concessions to the Soviet Union. Nixon took steps to improve relations with the Soviet Union. In 1972, Nixon held meetings with Soviet leaders in Moscow. Improved relations with the Soviet Union spurred ongoing talks between the superpowers about their nuclear arsenals. This easing of tensions in the Cold War is known as *détente*, the French word for loosening or relaxing.

40. **2** The outcome of the events illustrated in the cartoon resulted in the resignation of President Richard Nixon. Nixon's web of illegal acts began to unwind in June 1972 when five men were caught breaking into the headquarters of the Democratic National Committee at the Watergate Hotel in Washington, D.C. Persistent reporting by Carl Bernstein and Bob Woodward of the *Washington Post* drew connections between the burglars, Nixon's reelection committee, and ultimately the White House. When it became known that Nixon taped conversations in the White House Oval Office, investigators demanded that the tapes be turned over. Nixon argued that executive privilege allowed him to keep the tapes. In *United States* v. *Nixon* (1974), the Supreme Court ordered Nixon to turn over the tapes. Nixon told a press conference in November 1973, "I am not a crook." However, less than a month after the Supreme Court decision in 1974, Nixon resigned. The next president, Gerald Ford, issued a blanket pardon of Nixon in 1974 so that Nixon would not be brought before the justice system.

WRONG CHOICES EXPLAINED:

(1) The events illustrated in the cartoon did not result in the expansion of the Vietnam War into Cambodia. By the time this cartoon was drawn (1973), Nixon had already expanded the war into Cambodia. In 1969, Nixon began a secret bombing campaign in Cambodia. In 1970, he ordered an invasion of that country. Widening the war to Cambodia led to a renewed intensity of the American antiwar movement in the spring of 1970.

(3) The events illustrated in the cartoon did not result in growing support for environmental legislation. Public support for environmental legislation had been building for a decade before the events illustrated in the cartoon. The movement was inspired partly by Rachel Carson's book *Silent Spring* (1962), which detailed the harmful effects of toxic chemicals. Earth Day, which started in 1970, also created awareness about environmental concerns. President Nixon signed legislation to create the Environmental Protection Agency (EPA) in 1970. He approved amendments to the 1963 Clean Air Act (also in 1970) that established regulatory and enforcement mechanisms.

(4) The events illustrated in the cartoon did not result in the visit to Communist China by President Richard Nixon. By the time this cartoon was drawn (1973), Nixon had already visited China. His trip to Beijing in 1972 was part of President Nixon's policy of *détente*, a policy of reducing Cold War tensions and establishing warmer relations between the communist world and the United States. Nixon's strong anticommunist credentials enabled him to open relations with communist nations without being accused of being soft on communism. Nixon became the first American president to visit Communist China. Later in 1972, he held meetings with Soviet leaders in Moscow.

41. **1** The cartoonist's view about global warming is that the federal government has been slow to take action on global warming. The cartoon creates a satirical version of the instructions listed on a fire alarm. Typical instructions on a fire alarm read, "In case of fire, break glass, pull fire alarm." These straightforward instructions are reimagined to describe the government's approach to dealing with global warming. The government's approach to global warming is depicted as indecisive, overly cautious, and unproductive. The instructions require that "everyone…agrees" that a crisis exists and that skeptics be brought in to cast doubt on the gravity of the situation. The upshot of the instructions is that political leaders have hindered taking significant steps to address global warming, citing a host of excuses that, in the cartoonist's view, are misguided and petty ("think about who is going to clean up the broken glass"). Since the early 1980s, scientists have become aware of a trend toward warmer global temperatures. Many became convinced that this warming trend was caused by trapped greenhouse gases, which, in turn, were caused by human activities, primarily the burning of fossil fuels. In the 1990s and 2000s, a virtual consensus emerged in the scientific community around the connection between global warming and the emissions generated by the burning of fossil fuels. Calls were made to limit the human activities linked to global warming. The 1992 Earth Summit in Brazil led to the adoption by most of the countries in the world of the United Nations Framework Convention on Climate Change. The 1997 Kyoto Protocols set binding obligations on industrialized countries to reduce the emission of greenhouse gases. President George W. Bush (2001–2009), who was in office at the time the cartoon was published (2007), did much to undermine measures that had been taken or were under consideration in regard to protecting the environment. First, he would not implement the Kyoto global climate change treaty. The Kyoto Protocol was adopted by 165 countries in 2001 but did not have the participation of the United States and Australia. In rejecting the protocol, Bush also cast doubt on the science that demonstrated an urgent need to deal with climate change. In the subsequent years, this casting of doubt on the science related to global warming has been adopted by many Republicans as part of their rationale to resist steps toward a more sustainable future.

WRONG CHOICES EXPLAINED:
(2) The cartoonist is not making the point that most people support efforts to address global warming. The cartoon is commenting on the response of the government to global warming, not on public opinion in regard to global warming. In polls since the 1990s, a growing majority of Americans indicate that they are "worried" or "concerned" about global warming. (This figure was approximately 65 percent in Pew and Gallup polls in 2016.) Polls also indicate that a majority of Americans support policies that address global warming.

(3) The cartoonist is not making the point that dealing with global warming is too expensive. One of the items in the instructions reads, "Realize that calling the fire dept. isn't free, you know." However, this line is meant to mock government officials who come up with a variety of excuses to avoid taking action on global warming. The cartoonist is not arguing that such actions are too expensive.

(4) The cartoonist is not making the point that global warming is damaging the ozone layer. There is no mention of damage to the ozone layer in the cartoon. The ozone layer is a region of Earth's stratosphere with a relatively high concentration of the gas ozone. The ozone layer shields Earth by absorbing most of the sun's ultraviolet radiation. Damage has been done to the ozone layer in two ways. First, the overall percentage of ozone in the ozone layer has declined. Second, holes in the ozone layer have opened around Earth's poles. The main cause of these two phenomena is man-made chemicals, such as chlorofluorocarbons (CFCs), being released into the atmosphere.

42. **1** Since the presidency of Ronald Reagan, the Republican Party has generally tried to deal with economic problems by supporting lower taxes and reduced government spending. President Reagan advanced a series of economic initiatives that bear the name Reaganomics. Reagan supported economic policies that favored big business. He based this on a belief in the effectiveness of supply-side economics. This approach to the economy stressed stimulating the supply side of the economy, such as manufacturers, banks, and insurance corporations. The idea is that if there is growth in the supply side, there will be general economic growth and the benefits of that growth will reach everyone. The alternative approach is to stimulate the demand side, which are consumers. Demand-side economics emphasizes government policies designed to increase workers' wages and expands social programs such as welfare and unemployment benefits. As a believer in supply-side economics, Reagan implemented policies that he thought would stimulate business. Reagan cut taxes for corporations and greatly reduced regulations on industry. He also cut spending on social programs to reduce government spending. By cutting corporate taxes and taxes on wealthy individuals, he cut government revenues. However, at the same time, Reagan increased spending on armaments. This combination of increased spending and decreased revenues led to a doubling of the national debt from around $900 billion in 1980 to over $2 trillion in 1986. Reagan's pro-business economic policies had mixed results. A large debt is a problem because it requires large interest payments. By 1988, the interest on the national debt reached 14 percent of total annual government expenditures. This huge debt has hindered economic growth to some degree since and forced future administrations to make difficult decisions in regard to keeping the debt under control.

WRONG CHOICES EXPLAINED:

(2) The elimination of free trade and the free-market system have not been part of the Republican Party's agenda since the Reagan administration (1981–1989). Leaders in both political parties have supported policies to bolster free trade by endorsing international agreements to lower or eliminate tariffs. Neither political party endorses eliminating the free-market system. Socialists and communists embrace the idea of replacing free-market capitalism with an alternative system.

(3) Deficit spending and decreased military spending have not been part of the Republican Party's agenda since the Reagan administration (1981–1989). Republicans have pushed for a fiscally conservative approach to spending and working toward a balanced budget. They have also supported increasing the size of the military budget. Occasionally, these two goals have come into conflict with one another.

(4) Increased social spending and stricter regulation of the stock market have not been part of the Republican Party's agenda since the Reagan administration (1981–1989). Republicans have pushed for decreases in spending on social programs and have worked to reduce regulations on the stock market and the banking industry.

43. **2** The statement, "The federal government did not do enough to aid the victims [of Hurricane Katrina]," is an opinion rather than a fact. In August 2005, Hurricane Katrina brought catastrophic damage to the Gulf Coast, resulting in more than 1800 deaths and millions left homeless, mostly in the city of New Orleans. The hardest-hit parts of the city were African American and impoverished. Many Americans were critical of the government for being ill-prepared to handle such a crisis and for not doing enough to help the people of New Orleans (as noted in choice 2). Within the federal government, it appeared that the various agencies were not communicating with one another and did not grasp the magnitude of the situation. The head of the Federal Emergency Management Agency (FEMA), Michael Brown, testified that he informed White House officials on August 29 that the levees had breached and the city was flooding (as noted in choice 1). However, the Bush administration stated that they did not hear of the breach until August 30. In a radio interview, Homeland Security Secretary Michael Chertoff dismissed reports that thousands of individuals had taken refuge in the New Orleans Convention Center. President George W. Bush's pronouncement that FEMA Chief Michael Brown was doing a "heck of a job" seemed to be further evidence of the president's inability to grasp the gravity of the situation. Eventually, FEMA was able to provide housing to approximately 114,000 households in trailers (as noted in choice 4). The mishandling of the crisis damaged President Bush's approval ratings.

WRONG CHOICES EXPLAINED:
(1), (3), and (4) These are all incorrect choices because they are all indisputable facts. The correct choice (2), by contrast, presents an evaluation of the federal government's response to Hurricane Katrina and therefore is an opinion.

44. **3** According to the cartoonist, one important result of the election of President Barack Obama in 2008 was that a racial barrier in government had been broken. The cartoon alludes to photographs of water fountains in the South before passage of the 1964 Civil Rights Act. Water fountains often had signs above them saying "Whites Only" or "White Only." Sometimes water fountains would sit near one another, one labeled "White" and the other labeled "Colored." The practice of having separate water fountains was part of the system of Jim Crow segregation. This system developed after the Reconstruction period (1865–1877) in the southern states of the United States, creating separate facilities for African Americans and white people. These included separate waiting rooms at train stations, separate entrances to public buildings, and separate schools. In many cases, African Americans were simply barred from certain public facilities. The legal foundation of separate facilities was called into question in the *Brown* v. *Board of Education of Topeka* case (1954) when the Supreme Court asserted that segregation in public schools was inherently unfair and detrimental to African-American students. Later, the Civil Rights Act (1964) barred discrimination in all public facilities. Even with the dismantling of segregation, the idea of an African American successfully running for the presidency seemed unlikely to many Americans. However, the symbolic "Whites Only" sign on the presidency came down in 2008. Barack Obama first fended off a strong challenge to the Democratic nomination by Senator Hillary Clinton. Clinton's bid for the nomination, if successful, could have resulted in a different historic milestone—the first female president in the United States. In the general election, the Democratic Party was aided by an unpopular sitting Republican president, George W. Bush, and by an unfocused campaign by Republican Senator John McCain. The McCain campaign failed to articulate a consistent message. Obama and his running mate, Senator Joe Biden of Delaware, were able to cement support in traditionally blue (Democratic-leaning) states and successfully challenged McCain in traditionally red (Republican-leaning) states such as North Carolina, Virginia, and Indiana. Obama garnered 53 percent of the popular vote and won 365 electoral votes to McCain's 173.

WRONG CHOICES EXPLAINED:

(1) The cartoonist is not asserting that the election of President Barack Obama in 2008 resulted in the integration of public facilities in the South. The Civil Rights Act of 1964 prohibited segregation in public facilities. The allusion to "Whites Only" water fountains is meant to illustrate the fall of one last historically all-white institution—the presidency.

(2) The cartoonist is not asserting that the election of President Barack Obama in 2008 resulted in the executive branch of government gaining power over the legislative branch. The cartoonist is not commenting on the distribution of power within the government. The basic system of checks and balances remained in place following the 2008 presidential elections.

(4) The cartoonist is not asserting that the election of President Barack Obama in 2008 resulted in the legal elimination of racial discrimination in the United States. The Civil Rights Act of 1964 banned racial discrimination in public facilities. Laws that existed before the 2008 election also prohibited racial discrimination in housing and employment. It is very difficult, however, to eliminate all forms of racial discrimination in society completely.

45. **2** The practice of yellow journalism most influenced United States entry into the Spanish-American War. Yellow journalism refers to the sensationalistic, irresponsible coverage of events in the media. Yellow journalists created support for the Spanish-American War by writing articles about the sinking of the United States battleship *Maine*. In 1898, the *Maine* exploded and sunk in the harbor of Havana, Cuba. Many in the United States thought that the destruction of the ship was the work of Spain, especially after American newspapers bluntly accused Spain of the crime despite the scarcity of evidence. The coverage of the sinking of the *Maine* was one of several causes of the war. Spain controlled Cuba at the time, but a Cuban independence movement was trying to break its ties to Spain. Many Americans wanted the United States to intervene on Cuba's side in this struggle. Some Americans saw parallels between the Cuban struggle for independence from Spain and America's struggle for independence from Great Britain. Also, some American businessmen were angered by the interruption of the sugar harvest by the fighting between Cuban rebels and Spanish forces. American newspapers breathlessly followed events in Cuba, with lurid accounts of Spanish wrongdoing. The Spanish-American War was brief. American forces landed in Cuba on June 22, 1898, and Spain surrendered on July 17. Fighting in the Philippines, which was also a Spanish possession, lasted just days. The United States and Spain negotiated the Treaty of Paris (1898) following the war. In the treaty, Spain agreed to cede the Philippines, Puerto Rico, and Guam to the United States; the United States agreed to pay Spain $20 million for these possessions.

WRONG CHOICES EXPLAINED:

(1) Yellow journalism did not play a significant role in the United States entry into the War of 1812. Newspapers carried news of the events leading up to the war. However, these accounts are not seen as important factors in the U.S. declaration of war against Great Britain. The War of 1812 had many causes, including the British impressment of American sailors and British assistance to Native American Indian tribes in the Great Lakes region.

(3) Yellow journalism did not play a significant role in the United States entry into World War II. Newspapers, magazines, radio stations, and theatrical newsreels all carried news of events leading up to the United States entrance into World War II. However, these accounts are not seen as important factors in the U.S. declaration of war against the Axis powers in 1941. Many Americans hoped that the United States would intervene in the war earlier. The event that brought the United States into the war was the Japanese attack on the United States naval base at Pearl Harbor, Hawaii Territory.

(4) Yellow journalism did not play a significant role in the United States entry into the Persian Gulf War. Traditional forms of media, as well as cable news and the Internet, all carried news of events leading up to the United States declaration of war against Iraq. However, these accounts are not seen as important factors in the beginning of the Persian Gulf War in 1991. Tensions developed in 1990 when Iraqi leader Saddam Hussein sent the Iraqi military into Kuwait to occupy that country. Operation Desert Storm initiated by President George H. W. Bush was the name given to the efforts of the United States–led coalition in the Persian Gulf War in 1991. The goal of Operation Desert Storm was to remove Iraqi forces from Kuwait. The operation was successful. Hussein was quickly forced to withdraw his troops.

46. **4** The suspension of habeas corpus during the Civil War and the passage of the USA Patriot Act during the war on terror both illustrate the national government's willingness to limit civil liberties when the nation is facing immediate danger. The writ of habeas corpus was suspended by President Abraham Lincoln during the Civil War. In 1863, he authorized the arrest without due process of people he thought were aiding the Southern cause. By the end of the war, over 14,000 people had been arrested under Lincoln's wartime provisions. Most of those arrested, however, were people actively aiding the Southern side in the Civil War. The Democratic Party, the party of the Southern slaveholders, still operated openly in the North during the war, running a vigorous campaign for president against Lincoln in 1864. The USA Patriot Act was passed by Congress less than two months after the September 2001 terrorist attacks. It greatly expanded the government's authority in the fight against terrorism. The law gave federal authorities greater authority to subject political organizations to

surveillance and to conduct secret searches of phone, Internet, medical, banking, and student records with minimal judicial oversight. Also, the act gives greater powers to law authorities to investigate American citizens *without* probable cause; authorities can assert that such investigations are for "intelligence purposes." Finally, the USA Patriot Act allows for the incarceration of noncitizens for indefinite periods on mere suspicion with no right of counsel, habeas corpus, or opportunities to appear before public tribunals. Some critics have argued that it gives the government too much power to circumvent the Constitution.

WRONG CHOICES EXPLAINED:
(1) The suspension of habeas corpus during the Civil War and the passage of the USA Patriot Act during the war on terror do not illustrate the national government's willingness to uphold the rights of minority citizens. The national government has taken actions to protect the rights of minority citizens, such as the Civil Rights Act of 1964 and the Americans with Disabilities Act of 1990. However, the two actions mentioned in the question limited the rights of people.
(2) The suspension of habeas corpus during the Civil War and the passage of the USA Patriot Act during the war on terror do not illustrate the national government's willingness to tolerate criticism of wartime policies. The national government has frequently tolerated criticism of wartime policies, as it did during the Vietnam War. However, the two actions mentioned in the question limited certain rights during wartime.
(3) The suspension of habeas corpus during the Civil War and the passage of the USA Patriot Act during the war on terror do not illustrate the national government's willingness to expand the power of the states to prosecute radical groups. Both acts expanded the powers of the national government, not state governments.

47. **4** The Washington Naval Conference (1921), the Kellogg-Briand Pact (1928), and the Neutrality Acts of the 1930s were all attempts by the United States to avoid policies likely to lead to war. The presidents of the 1920s attempted to isolate the United States from world affairs and to reduce spending on war munitions. President Warren Harding successfully pressed for a reduction of naval power among Britain, France, Japan, Italy, and the United States at the Washington Naval Conference in 1921. Later, President Calvin Coolidge continued to pursue an isolationist foreign policy and helped to negotiate the Kellogg-Briand Pact (1928). The United States was one of 63 nations to sign the pact, which renounced war in principle. Because the pact was negotiated outside of the League of Nations, it was unenforceable, rendering it meaningless. Isolationism continued to hold sway into the 1930s, even as the world was becoming increasingly dangerous with the rise of fascism in Europe and a

militarist government in Japan. In the Neutrality Acts of 1935–1937, Congress made it clear that neither the United States government nor private U.S. firms were to trade with belligerent nations. President Franklin Roosevelt grew frustrated with these acts because they did not make a distinction between aggressors and victims in the conflicts of the 1930s. A later Neutrality Act (1939) allowed the United States to supply the opponents of fascism with materials on a cash and carry basis.

WRONG CHOICES EXPLAINED:

(1) The Washington Naval Conference (1921), the Kellogg-Briand Pact (1928), and the Neutrality Acts of the 1930s were not attempts by the United States to increase military spending. The opposite is true. The three items were designed to avoid the possibility of war and to reduce military expenditures.

(2) The Washington Naval Conference (1921), the Kellogg-Briand Pact (1928), and the Neutrality Acts of the 1930s were not attempts by the United States to show support for the United Nations. The three items all occurred before the founding of the United Nations (1945).

(3) The Washington Naval Conference (1921), the Kellogg-Briand Pact (1928), and the Neutrality Acts of the 1930s were not attempts by the United States to assume a position of world leadership. The three items were all expressions of isolationism, reflecting a desire among U.S. political leaders to withdraw from world affairs.

48. **2** The baby boom following World War II resulted in the need to increase the number of schools in the 1960s. For several years before 1946, birth rates in the United States remained relatively low. Couples tended to have fewer children during the lean years of the Great Depression. The dislocation and physical separation caused by World War II kept the birth rate even lower. However, when the war ended, returning veterans quickly got down to the business of starting families. The spike in birth rates from 1946 through the early 1960s produced a baby boom that has had lasting repercussions in American society. The baby boom required states to spend more money on constructing and operating new schools in the 1950s and 1960s. In addition, these young families needed housing. The baby boom contributed to the growth of suburban communities outside of major cities in the 1950s and 1960s. The Servicemen's Readjustment Act (1944), more commonly known as the G.I. Bill, provided low-interest loans for veterans to purchase homes. Developers often bought large tracts of land to build hundreds of houses. To save time and money, these developments included many houses that each had identical plans. The most famous suburban developer was William Levitt. Levittown, on Long Island, New York, became synonymous with these mass-produced communities.

WRONG CHOICES EXPLAINED:

(1) The baby boom following World War II did not result in the development of urban unrest in the 1950s. Urban unrest is more associated with the 1960s as major riots occurred in African-American neighborhoods in several cities in the United States (Watts, Los Angeles in 1965; Detroit and Newark in 1967; Washington, D.C., Baltimore, and Chicago in 1968). Some urban unrest occurred in the 1950s and was often associated with clashes over civil rights, but this was not the result of the baby boom.

(3) The baby boom following World War II did not result in the migration from cities to farms in the 1970s. There was not a major migration from cities to farms in the 1970s. Some members of the counterculture formed rural communes in the 1960s and 1970s, but this trend was counterbalanced by the decline of the family farm.

(4) The baby boom following World War II did not result in the need to decrease the number of nursing homes in the 1980s. As the baby boomers, born between 1946 and 1964, approach old age in the coming years, the need for nursing homes will increase.

49. **1** The Supreme Court cases of *Tinker* v. *Des Moines* (1969), *New Jersey* v. *T.L.O.* (1985), and *Vernonia School District* v. *Acton* (1995) addressed the issue of balancing the rights of students with the need of schools to maintain order. In the case of *Tinker* v. *Des Moines* (1969), the Court ruled that a school board prohibition against students wearing black armbands in protest of the war in Vietnam was unconstitutional. The Court ruled that students in school had the right to free speech, including symbolic speech, as long as their actions did not interfere with the educational process. The Court said, "Students do not shed their constitutional rights at the schoolhouse gate." The Supreme Court moved in a different direction in *New Jersey* v. *T.L.O.* (1985) and *Vernonia School District* v. *Acton* (1995). Both cases established limits on a student's right to privacy and demonstrated that students in school do not always enjoy the same constitutional liberties that adults do. The case of *New Jersey* v. *T.L.O.* deals with the legality of searching students without search warrants. T.L.O. is the initials of a female student in a New Jersey high school whose bag was searched by school officials. In the search, evidence was found implicating her in both taking and selling marijuana. T.L.O. was convicted of delinquency charges. She appealed to the Supreme Court, arguing that the school's search of her bag was illegal because the school did not have a warrant and therefore violated the Fourth Amendment. The Supreme Court ruled that the search was permissible, noting that school officials may balance a student's expectation of privacy with the school's need to maintain discipline and security. The case of *Vernonia School*

District v. *Acton* upheld the random drug testing of students. Opponents challenged random drug testing on the grounds that it amounted to a search without a warrant. The Supreme Court acknowledged that the drug tests amounted to a search but ruled that a school could conduct them. The Court ruled that school districts have a legitimate interest in preventing teenage drug use.

WRONG CHOICES EXPLAINED:

(2) The three cases listed in the question do not address the issue of allowing principals to determine students' constitutional rights. It is the Constitution itself as well as Supreme Court decisions that determine individuals' constitutional rights. It is the job of principals and other school officials to establish policies that are consistent with the Constitution and Supreme Court decisions. States, districts, and schools may afford students additional rights, but they may not abridge established constitutional rights.

(3) The three cases listed in the question do not address the issue of denying public school districts the authority to allow prayer in school. Schools districts do not have the authority to mandate prayer in school. In the case of *Engel* v. *Vitale* (1962), the Supreme Court ruled that the Regents' Prayer, a state-mandated prayer that was recited by public school children in New York State, was unconstitutional because it violated the doctrine of separation of church and state. Schools districts may set aside spaces within a school for students to engage in private prayer.

(4) The three cases listed in the question do not address the issue of giving state legislatures the power to fund charter schools. State legislatures have the power to fund charter schools. In the future, the Supreme Court may examine whether states may allow religious institutions to establish publicly funded charter schools.

50. **3** President John F. Kennedy and President Ronald Reagan both visited the Berlin Wall in order to demonstrate the commitment of the United States to maintain freedom in Western Europe. The communist government of East Germany built the Berlin Wall in 1961 to encircle West Berlin completely and to separate it from East Germany. Berlin was divided when Germany was divided into East Germany and West Germany in 1949. Berlin was located completely within East German territory, so West Berlin was physically separate from the rest of West Germany. Before construction of the wall, many residents of East Germany escaped to the west through West Berlin. Two years later, in 1963, President John F. Kennedy visited West Berlin to express solidarity with the city's residents. He visited Checkpoint Charlie, one of the eight crossings in the wall. During the visit, Kennedy delivered a famous speech at a square that was later renamed John-F.-Kennedy-Platz. Kennedy critiqued the communist system and delivered the line *"Ich bin ein Berliner,"* which means in English, "I too am a

Berliner." Later, in the 1980s, President Reagan visited West Berlin several times. His most noted speech made in West Berlin occurred in June 1987 when he encouraged Soviet leader Mikhail Gorbachev to allow more openness in the communist world. Specifically, Reagan implored the Soviet leader, "Mr. Gorbachev, tear down this wall!" The speech was given at the historic Brandenburg Gate, which became part of the Berlin Wall when the wall was erected. The gate was another one of the eight crossings in the Berlin Wall. In 1989, communist governments began to collapse in Eastern Europe. It was clear that Soviet leader Mikhail Gorbachev would not try to halt this development as previous Soviet leaders had. The iconic image of this movement was the collapse of the Berlin Wall in November 1989. The wall had become a symbol of the rift between the communist bloc countries and the western democratic countries. By 1991, the Soviet Union itself collapsed, ending communism in Europe.

WRONG CHOICES EXPLAINED:
(1) The visits to the Berlin Wall by President John F. Kennedy and President Ronald Reagan were not meant to assess the military strength of the Soviet Union. Specialists in the Pentagon, the State Department, the Central Intelligence Agency, and other agencies worked diligently at assessing the Soviet Union's military capabilities.

(2) The visits to the Berlin Wall by President John F. Kennedy and President Ronald Reagan were not meant to prepare for an invasion of the Soviet Union. Such an invasion never occurred. It would have led to a third world war.

(4) The visits to the Berlin Wall by President John F. Kennedy and President Ronald Reagan were not meant to challenge the North Atlantic Treaty Organization (NATO) nations that were supported by the Soviet Union. In fact, no such nations existed. During the Cold War, NATO stood united in opposition to the Soviet Union and the Warsaw Pact nations.

PART II: THEMATIC ESSAY

Presidential Decisions and Actions

Over time, various United States presidents have been confronted with crucial issues and problems that demanded immediate attention. Presidents have frequently had to make important decisions to act in these circumstances. Some of these presidential actions have been more successful than others. Two successful presidential actions were President George Washington's response to the Whiskey Rebellion and President Dwight D. Eisenhower's response to the crisis in Little Rock, Arkansas, over school desegregation.

In 1794, farmers in western Pennsylvania rose in protest over a federal excise tax on whiskey. The historical circumstances that led to the protest can be traced back several years. In 1791, Secretary of the Treasury Alexander Hamilton proposed a broad, ambitious financial program to establish the United States on sound financial ground. First, he pushed for the creation of a national bank, which would hold the government's tax revenues and act as a stabilizing force on the economy. President Washington signed the bank into law in 1791. Hamilton also proposed an elaborate and controversial plan to deal with the new nation's substantial debt. He insisted that debts carried over from the war years be paid back, or funded, at full value. In addition, Hamilton insisted that the government assume, or agree to pay back, state debts incurred during the war. To provide revenue for these measures, Hamilton also proposed new taxes.

The most prominent, and controversial, of these taxes was an excise tax, or sales tax, on whiskey. This tax hit grain farmers especially hard. These hardscrabble farmers in remote rural areas were barely making ends meet. Distilling grain into whiskey allowed these farmers to increase their meager profits. Transporting bushels of grain over primitive roads to population centers was prohibitively expensive; distilling it down to whiskey made it easier to transport. The grain farmers of western Pennsylvania felt that they could not shoulder this substantial tax. In 1794, farmers took action. Fifty men gathered and marched to the home of the local tax collector. From there, the gathering swelled to 7000 men who then marched to Pittsburgh. At this point, the federal government took action. Washington nationalized nearly 13,000 militiamen into the army and marched them himself to Pennsylvania to suppress the rebellion and ensure that the laws of the land were followed.

The action was successful in that it both put down the rebellion and established federal authority. Alexander Hamilton and George Washington had vivid memories of Shays' Rebellion, which occurred less than a decade earlier. They were determined that the current rebellion would not get out of control, as had Shays' Rebellion. Washington made it clear that a strong national government would not tolerate unlawful challenges to its authority.

In the 1950s, another challenge to federal authority prompted a president to take a strong stand. In 1957 in Little Rock, Arkansas, President Dwight D. Eisenhower called in army paratroopers to enforce federal desegregation mandates in the face of resistance by Arkansas state authorities as well as by protesters who were resisting integration. The historical circumstances that led to Eisenhower's action include the landmark *Brown v. Board of Education of Topeka* decision in 1954. This decision declared segregated schools inherently unfair and ordered states and communities to take measures to undo this system. Segregation of public facilities had long been the rule in the South. White southerners created the system of Jim Crow segregation to put African Americans into a second-class status. In the 1950s, activists challenged segregation, winning a major victory in the *Brown* decision.

The school board in Little Rock, Arkansas, decided to begin the desegregation of Central High School at the start of the 1957 school year by admitting nine African-American students. The plan developed without much controversy. However, just before the beginning of the school year, Arkansas governor Orville Faubus decided to send the National Guard to block the school and not permit the nine African-American students to enter the building. The news of Faubus's action prompted a large crowd of pro-segregation whites to come to the school. Faubus instigated a mob to enforce white supremacy in Little Rock.

At this point, the federal government acted. President Dwight D. Eisenhower was not a strong supporter of the civil rights movement, but he was alarmed to see the Arkansas governor directly challenge federal authority. At first, Eisenhower urged the governor to comply with the segregation plan. Governor Faubus gave Eisenhower his word that he would withdraw the National Guard troops from the school. However, Faubus made no provisions for the safety of the nine African-American students. The students had to confront an angry mob of white people with only a small contingent of local police to protect the students. At that point, President Eisenhower decided to send in federal troops to guarantee the safety of the students and to ensure that Little Rock High School would comply with the *Brown* decision. Some of the troops remained at the school for the entire school year. Eisenhower's decision led to a backlash among white Arkansans. The school board ended up closing Central High School for the entire next year. However, the action was ultimately successful. Central High School reopened in 1959 and by the 1960s became increasingly more integrated. In a larger sense, the action was successful in demonstrating the resolve of the federal government to enforce African-American civil rights in the face of massive resistance by opponents of desegregation.

Both President Washington and President Eisenhower took decisive actions in regard to crises. President Washington was eager to assert the power of the federal government in maintaining law and order. President Eisenhower was reluctant to use the power of the federal government to intervene in a state issue. However, both decided to use the military to subdue challenges to the rule of law and to ensure that similar challenges did not happen in the future.

PART III: DOCUMENT-BASED QUESTION

Part A: Short Answer

Document 1a and Document 1b

1(1) Based on the two documents, one effect of the development of the West on Native American Indians was the destruction of the buffalo, which many Native American Indians depended upon.

1(2) Based on the two documents, another effect of the development of the West on Native American Indians was that many of their horses and cattle were often stolen by white settlers.

These answers receive full credit because they state two effects of the development of the West on Native American Indians.

Document 2a and Document 2b

2 One impact of westward settlement on Native American Indians was that they lost lands that had been set aside for them.

This answer receives full credit because it states one impact of westward settlement on Native American Indians.

Document 3a and Document 3b

3(1) Based on these documents, one way Native American Indians were being affected by the development of the West was that their culture was demeaned by white society as "superstitious and fanatical."

3(2) Based on these documents, another way Native American Indians were being affected by the development of the West was that Native American Indian children attending the Carlisle Indian Industrial School were forced to stop wearing traditional clothes and began to dress like whites.

These answers receive full credit because they state two ways Native American Indians were being affected by the development of the West.

Document 4

4 According to Frederic L. Paxson, one effect of westward development on frontier women living in the West was that they had to work very hard in difficult conditions to provide for the varied necessities of life for their families.

This answer receives full credit because it states one effect of westward development on frontier women living in the West.

Document 5

5 According to James S. Foster, one opportunity the development of the West offered to women was that it made land available for single women to obtain a homestead and to engage in farming.

This answer receives full credit because it states one opportunity the development of the West offered to women.

Document 6

6(1) According to the circular, one benefit of granting suffrage to women in Wyoming was that women teachers were getting paid at the same rate as male teachers.

6(2) According to the circular, another benefit of granting suffrage to women in Wyoming was that young girls were safer in Wyoming than they were in any of the other states in the United States.

These answers receive full credit because they state two benefits of granting suffrage to women in Wyoming.

Document 7

7(1) According to Liping Zhu, one way living in the West affected Chinese immigrants was that they were very successful in mining operations, establishing several very profitable mining operations.

7(2) According to Liping Zhu, another way living in the West affected Chinese immigrants was that they experienced legal discrimination and ethnic violence.

These answers receive full credit because they state two ways living in the West affected Chinese immigrants.

Document 8a and Document 8b

8(1) Based on the two documents, one opportunity the development of the West offered to Chinese immigrants was starting successful laundry businesses.

8(2) Based on the two documents, another opportunity the development of the West offered to Chinese immigrants was purchasing land and developing successful agricultural enterprises.

These answers receive full credit because they state two opportunities the development of the West offered to Chinese immigrants.

Document 9

9 According to Rodman W. Paul, one reason for opposition to Chinese immigration in San Francisco was that Chinese immigrants competed for jobs with white immigrant groups that had previously moved to the region.

This answer receives full credit because it states one reason for opposition to Chinese immigration in San Francisco.

Part B: Document-Based Essay

The development of the West in the late 19th and early 20th centuries was profoundly important for the United States as a whole. Two particular groups that were affected by the development of the West were women and Chinese immigrants. Both groups experienced political, economic, and social changes in the growing region of the West. For both groups, the West provided challenges as well as opportunities. Women worked extremely hard on the western frontier but were also able to achieve economic and political progress. Chinese immigrants suffered discrimination and violence in the West but were also able to achieve a great deal of economic success.

In the late 19th and early 20th centuries, hundreds of thousands of settlers made their way to the West. A variety of economic opportunities drew people to the West, including building railroads, mining, logging, farming, and ranching. Migrants to the West hoped to achieve a degree of self-sufficiency and independence. The Homestead Act of 1862 also drew settlers to the West. The act granted people up to 160 acres as an enticement for moving west. The populations of Minnesota, the Dakotas, Kansas, and Nebraska all grew dramatically between the end of the Civil War and 1900: from 300,000 to five million.

Life on the frontier demanded great physical efforts by both men and women. In more settled communities back east, middle-class women of the 19th century were expected to play a secondary, domestic role. Men were expected to compete in the rough-and-tumble public realm of business and politics. Women, though, were expected to tend to the children and create a moral, Christian setting in the home to aid the children's development. In the West, women had far greater responsibilities. They were expected to grow, store, and prepare food. Women were expected to be the "butcher, packer, and baker." Further, they were expected to create all of the family's clothing—to knit, to sew, and to treat animal pelts. Women, of course, bore children. The demands of frontier life and of childbirth, in conditions that were rudimentary and often unsanitary, took their toll on women. Women often died much earlier in life than men did. Grave markers from the frontier era often indicate that the adult male in a family was often buried with a second, third, or fourth wife. (Document 4)

The West in the late 19th century was physically demanding and often dangerous to the health of women, but it also offered opportunities for them. Under the Homestead Act, widowed and unmarried women over the age of 21 could apply for homesteads. An 1870 account of life in the Dakota Territory by the territory's Commissioner of Immigration notes approvingly the large number of women who acquired their own homesteads. The account points to women who came to the territory penniless and eventually became successful farmers. (Document 5)

The importance of women's contributions to the success of homesteads in the West—either as part of a family unit or on their own—bolstered arguments for greater political equality for women. "We, of Dakota, believe in Women's Rights," the Commissioner of Immigration for the Dakota Territory asserted in 1870. (Document 5) A 1910 description of the benefits of women voting in Wyoming noted that 41 years earlier, in 1869, Wyoming had granted women full voting rights. (Document 6) Other states in the West followed suit—Colorado in 1893 and both Utah and Idaho in 1896. Women not only attained the vote in western states, but they shaped politics in those states as well. In Wyoming, for instance, female voters helped assure that the principle of "equal pay for equal work" was applied to female and male teachers in the state. Wyoming also had a lower rate of illiteracy than other states and less divorce than other states. (Document 6) The spread of woman's suffrage in the West paved the way for the ratification of the 19th Amendment in 1920, preventing any state from denying the vote to women.

Chinese immigrants also settled in the West. Chinese immigrants were initially drawn to North America by the gold rush in California in 1849. By 1852, more than 20,000 Chinese immigrants had moved to the United States. By 1860, over 34,000 lived in California alone. The initial rush of gold seekers partook in placer mining—looking for pieces of gold in streambeds and near the surface, as opposed to hard rock mining, which extracts veins of precious minerals from solid rock well beneath the surface. Placer mining generally requires little initial capital. By 1860, Chinese immigrants had most of the placer mining claims in California. They continued to have success and by the 1870s, owned several prominent mining companies throughout the West. (Document 7)

In addition to mining, Chinese immigrants experienced success in several other fields. Thousands of Chinese workers helped complete the first transcontinental railroad in 1869, representing 90 percent of the workforce. In addition to railroad work, Chinese immigrants gravitated to the laundry business. The Chinese laundry became an "institution" in San Francisco and in small towns throughout the West. Chinese laundries were able to offer services at lower prices than were standard at the time, charging $5 instead of $8 to do a basket of laundry. (Document 8a) Chinese immigrants also excelled at agriculture. Many Chinese immigrants had worked in agriculture in the Pearl River Delta in China. They brought knowledge of agricultural techniques with them to America. They were a "vital factor" in shifting the agricultural base of California from wheat to fruit. (Document 8b)

Chinese immigrants faced a great deal of discrimination and outright hostility. Many Chinese abandoned placer mining as the industry became more large scale and industrial. They moved to cities to seek work there. The timing of this move was "unfortunate." When the economy suffered a major downturn in the 1870s following the Panic of 1873, many Californians singled out the Chinese population as the cause of the crisis. Many labeled Chinese residents as coolie labor and insisted that their presence in California depressed wages. The Workingmen's Party was formed in 1876 to argue for legislation excluding Chinese immigrants from the United States. (Document 9) This activism, coming as Reconstruction was ending in the South, proved to be successful. Federal naturalization laws, which were altered after the Civil War to accommodate African Americans, denied citizenship to Asian immigrants. The 1882 Chinese Exclusion Act excluded most Chinese from entrance into the United States. It represents the only instance in which legislation has explicitly denied a particular national group entrance into the United States.

The development of the western portion of the United States affected different groups in dramatically different ways. Mexicans who had lived in the area of the Mexican Cession (1848) were often dispossessed of their land by white settlers. In addition, Native-American Indian lands were greatly reduced. In 1867, Congress passed legislation to force Native American Indians onto reservations and make them wards of the government until they learned "to walk on the white man's road." Native Americans resisted this effort, and a series of bloody battles ensued between Native American Indians and U.S. troops. By 1890, the last resistance was subdued when the military defeated the Sioux at Wounded Knee Creek, South Dakota. Women and Chinese immigrants both faced hardships, but they also found opportunities in the West. Both married and single women were able to assume a greater degree of independence and political power than they had in the East. Chinese immigrants to the West faced hostility and discrimination, but they also found economic opportunity in a number of pursuits. The development of the West greatly altered the political, social, and economic lives of a wide variety of people.

Topic	Question Numbers	Number of Points
American political history	6, 13, 14, 15, 18, 36, 39, 40 44, 46	12
Political theory	5, 9	2
Economic theory/policy	2, 19, 21, 22, 29, 42	7
Constitutional principles	7, 8, 10, 11, 25, 49	7
American foreign policy	3, 20, 24, 30, 31, 32, 34, 35, 37, 45, 47, 50	14
American studies— the American people	4, 16, 17, 23, 28, 33, 38, 43, 48	12
Social/cultural developments	26	1
Geography	1, 12, 41	4
Skills questions included in the above content areas		
Reading comprehension	5, 8, 10, 20, 21, 37, 49	
Graph/table interpretation	16, 17	
Cartoon/image interpretation	24, 25, 39, 40, 41, 44	
Cause-effect relationship	32	
Distinguishing fact from opinion	43	

PART I

Multiple-Choice Questions by Standard

Standard	Question Numbers
1—United States and New York History	3, 4, 10, 13, 14, 15, 17, 18, 20, 24, 26, 28, 31, 32, 33, 36, 37, 39, 41, 43, 45, 47
2—World History	30, 34, 35, 50
3—Geography	1, 12, 16, 27, 48
4—Economics	2, 19, 21, 22, 29, 42
5—Civics, Citizenship, and Government	5, 6, 7, 8, 9, 11, 23, 25, 38, 40, 44, 46, 49

Parts II and III by Theme and Standard

	Theme	Standards
Thematic Essay	Presidential Decisions and Actions; Constitutional Principles; Government; Foreign Policy; Diversity; Citizenship	Standards 1, 2, 3, 4, and 5: US and NY History; World History; Geography; Economics; Civics, Citizenship, and Government
Document-based Essay	Places and Regions; Immigration and Migration; Environment; Citizenship; Government; Foreign Policy; Diversity	Standards 1, 3, 4, and 5: US and NY History; Geography; Economics; Civics, Citizenship, and Government

Examination
June 2018
United States History and Government

PART I: MULTIPLE CHOICE

Directions (1–50): For each statement or question, write in the space provided the *number* of the word or expression that, of those given, best completes the statement or answers the question.

1 What was a main reason large plantations developed in the South during the colonial period?

(1) British laws promoted the growth of slavery in the South.
(2) Cotton could only be grown in wetlands.
(3) Southern mountains led to the development of isolated, self-sufficient farms.
(4) The climate in the South provided longer growing seasons.   1 ____

2 In the 1780s, the national government under the Articles of Confederation established its authority in the Northwest Territory by

(1) providing a system for the formation of new states
(2) settling the border dispute with Mexico
(3) extending the nation's border to the Rocky Mountains
(4) rejecting Native American Indian claims of sovereignty   2 ____

3 A fundamental principle of a republican form of government is that

(1) hereditary rulers are the legitimate possessors of political power
(2) legislation must be passed by the elected representatives of the people
(3) laws should be created directly by the citizens
(4) governments are not responsible for protecting individual rights　3 ＿＿＿

4 What was a major argument used by the Antifederalists to oppose ratifying the Constitution?

(1) Congress was given the power to tax exports.
(2) The executive branch lacked the power to maintain order.
(3) The proposed Constitution contained no bill of rights.
(4) Only the national government could coin money.　　4 ＿＿＿

5 The judicial branch of government can check the legislative branch of government by

(1) vetoing bills passed by Congress
(2) declaring laws unconstitutional
(3) calling special sessions of Congress
(4) reducing congressional budgets　　5 ＿＿＿

6 "...Because finally, 'the equal right of every citizen to the free exercise of his Religion according to the dictates of conscience' is held by the same tenure with all our other rights. If we recur to [go to] its origin, it is equally the gift of nature; ..."

— James Madison

The belief expressed in this statement was put into law by the

(1) signing of the Mayflower Compact
(2) creation of the Articles of Confederation
(3) establishment of a federal system of government
(4) addition of the first amendment to the United States Constitution　　6 ＿＿＿

7 "…To make all Laws which shall be necessary and proper for carrying into Execution the foregoing Powers, and all other Powers
vested by this Constitution in the Government of the United
States, or in any Department or Officer thereof."

— Article I, Section 8,
United States Constitution

This clause was used by Secretary of the Treasury Alexander
Hamilton to justify

(1) establishing the Bank of the United States
(2) creating a federal postal system
(3) sending troops to end the Whiskey Rebellion
(4) imposing an embargo on trade with Great Britain   7 ____

Base your answers to questions 8 and 9 on the map below and on
your knowledge of social studies.

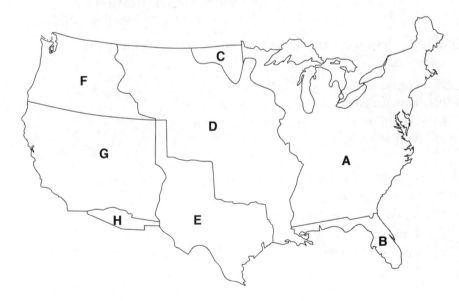

8 Which two areas of the map made up the United States in 1803 as
a result of the Louisiana Purchase?

(1) *A* and *B*
(2) *A* and *D*
(3) *B* and *D*
(4) *E* and *G*   8 ____

9 Which of these areas was acquired as a result of the Mexican-American War?

(1) *A*

(2) *B*

(3) *F*

(4) *G*   9 _____

Base your answer to question 10 on the quotation below and on your knowledge of social studies.

"...As a bond of union between the Atlantic and the western states, it may prevent the dismemberment of the American empire. As an organ of communication between the Hudson, the Mississippi, the St. Lawrence, the great lakes of the north and west, and their tributary rivers, it will create the greatest inland trade ever witnessed...."

— New York Governor DeWitt Clinton,
April 26, 1824

10 Which development in transportation is Governor Clinton describing?

(1) National Road

(2) Erie Canal

(3) steamboats

(4) railroads   10 _____

11 An example of the use of the unwritten constitution is the

(1) president's cabinet

(2) amendment process

(3) bicameral legislature

(4) electoral college   11 _____

Base your answer to question 12 on the chart below and on your knowledge of social studies.

Resources of the North and South, 1861

Resources	North		South	
	Number (approximate)	Percent of National Total	Number (approximate)	Percent of National Total
Farmland	105,817,694 acres	65%	56,832,154 acres	35%
Railroad Track	21,847 miles	71%	8,947 miles	29%
Value of Manufactured Goods	$1,794,417,000	92%	$155,531,281	8%
Factories	119,500	85%	20,631	15%
Workers in Industry	1,198,000	92%	110,721	8%
Population	22,340,000 (includes 432,720 enslaved persons)	63%	9,103,332 (includes 3,521,043 enslaved persons)	37%

Source: James West Davidson et al., *The American Nation,* Prentice Hall, 2000; 1860 Census, U.S. Census Bureau (adapted)

12 Which generalization is supported by the information in the chart?

(1) The South exported more manufactured goods than the North.

(2) The North would have more difficulty supplying an army than the South.

(3) The North had greater economic strength than the South.

(4) The South would be better able to transport an army than the North.

12 _____

Base your answer to question 13 on the poster below and on your knowledge of social studies.

Source: National Archives

13 Which government action most directly prompted the publication of this poster?

(1) issuance of the Emancipation Proclamation
(2) passage of the Kansas-Nebraska Act
(3) rejection of the Wilmot Proviso
(4) adoption of the Missouri Compromise

13 _____

14 At the start of the Civil War, President Abraham Lincoln stated that the major reason for fighting the war was to

(1) break the South's economic ties to Great Britain
(2) uphold the Constitution by preserving the Union
(3) enforce the terms of the Compromise of 1850
(4) punish the Confederate states for leaving the Union

14 _____

15 Passage of the Homestead Act in 1862 encouraged settlement of the Great Plains by

(1) providing free land to farmers
(2) removing barriers to Asian immigration
(3) supplying land to build transcontinental railroads
(4) placing Native American Indians on reservations

15 _____

16 Which heading best completes the partial outline below?

I. _____

  A. Freedmen's Bureau
  B. Passage of the 14th amendment
  C. Military occupation of the South

(1) Development of States Rights
(2) Results of Manifest Destiny
(3) Elements of Reconstruction
(4) Limits on Civil Rights   16 _____

17 Between 1865 and 1900, how did the growth of industry affect American society?

(1) Trade with other nations declined.
(2) Business leaders called for lower tariffs.
(3) The urban population increased.
(4) Corporations supported the growth of labor unions.   17 _____

18 The federal government reacted to the Supreme Court's ruling in *Wabash, St. Louis & Pacific Railway Co.* v. *Illinois* (1886) by

(1) passing the Interstate Commerce Act
(2) weakening the influence of banks over big business
(3) abandoning the government's attempts to break up monopolies
(4) encouraging railroad employees to form unions   18 _____

19 In the late 1800s, the corporation became an important form of business organization primarily because it

(1) had closer ties with its employees
(2) could raise large amounts of investment capital
(3) made better quality products
(4) called for conservation of natural resources   19 _____

Base your answer to question 20 on the passage below and on your knowledge of social studies.

...The object of the amendment was undoubtedly to enforce the absolute equality of the two races before the law, but, in the nature of things, it could not have been intended to abolish distinctions based upon color, or to enforce social, as distinguished from political, equality, or a commingling of the two races upon terms unsatisfactory to either. Laws permitting, and even requiring, their separation in places where they are liable to be brought into contact do not necessarily imply the inferiority of either race to the other, and have been generally, if not universally, recognized as within the competency of the state legislatures in the exercise of their police power. The most common instance of this is connected with the establishment of separate schools for white and colored [African American] children, which has been held to be a valid exercise of the legislative power even by courts of States where the political rights of the colored race have been longest and most earnestly enforced....

— United States Supreme Court, 1896

20 In this 1896 decision, the Supreme Court upheld the constitutionality of

(1) the Three-fifths Compromise
(2) Jim Crow laws
(3) affirmative action programs
(4) racial integration   20 _____

Base your answer to question 21 on the cartoon below and on your knowledge of social studies.

The News Reaches Bogota

Source: W. A. Rogers, *New York Herald*, December 1903

21 The foreign policy illustrated in this cartoon was used by the United States to

(1) punish Mexico for siding with Germany in World War I

(2) enforce the Monroe Doctrine against Great Britain

(3) secure control of land for the Panama Canal Zone

(4) announce the Open Door policy   21 _____

Base your answer to question 22 on the poster below and on your knowledge of social studies.

Source: J. H. Donahey, Smithsonian National Museum of American History, 1917 (adapted)

22 This 1917 poster indicates that one important educational goal for new immigrants during this time period was

   (1) teaching them to read and write in their native language
   (2) promoting religious tolerance
   (3) ensuring the preservation of their native cultures
   (4) promoting the English language as a method of assimilation   22 _____

23 The United States became directly involved in World War I as a result of Germany's

  (1) negotiation of an alliance with Russia
  (2) threat to spread the war to the Middle East
  (3) resumption of unrestricted submarine warfare
  (4) acquisition of new African colonies   23 _____

24 Progressivism was an early 20th-century movement that promoted

  (1) limited war to spread social justice to other countries
  (2) increased immigration to diversify the nation's population
  (3) colonialism to increase United States power throughout the world
  (4) government actions to correct political, economic, and social problems   24 _____

25 Which government action is directly related to the "clear and present danger" doctrine established in *Schenck* v. *United States* (1919)?

  (1) limiting the first amendment rights of antiwar protesters
  (2) rejecting membership in the League of Nations
  (3) banning immigration from western Europe
  (4) passage of the Prohibition amendment   25 _____

26 Hosting the Washington Naval Disarmament Conference (1921) and signing the Kellogg-Briand Pact (1928) were efforts by the United States to

  (1) form new military alliances
  (2) increase its military preparedness
  (3) avoid future wars
  (4) collect payment for war debts   26 _____

27 The Harlem Renaissance of the 1920s is best known for

  (1) ending racial segregation in public facilities
  (2) promoting the cultural creativity of African Americans
  (3) encouraging passage of new voting rights legislation
  (4) supporting legislation to eliminate the Ku Klux Klan   27 _____

28 Which factor best accounts for the affordability of Ford Model T automobiles in the 1920s?

(1) the efficiencies created by the assembly line
(2) the expertise of individual craftsmanship
(3) strong support from labor unions
(4) low taxes and government subsidies

28 _____

Base your answers to questions 29 and 30 on the statements below and on your knowledge of social studies.

...The ever-growing complexity of modern life, with its train of evermore perplexing and difficult problems, is a challenge to our individual characters and to our devotion to our ideals. The resourcefulness of America when challenged has never failed. Success is not gained by leaning upon government to solve all the problems before us. That way leads to enervation [lessening] of will and destruction of character. Victory over this depression and over our other difficulties will be won by the resolution of our people to fight their own battles in their own communities, by stimulating their ingenuity to solve their own problems, by taking new courage to be masters of their own destiny in the struggle of life....

— President Herbert Hoover,
February 12, 1931

...I am prepared under my constitutional duty to recommend the measures that a stricken Nation in the midst of a stricken world may require. These measures, or such other measures as the Congress may build out of its experience and wisdom, I shall seek, within my constitutional authority, to bring to speedy adoption....

— President Franklin D. Roosevelt,
March 4, 1933

29 Which idea would best be supported by President Hoover's statement?

(1) rugged individualism
(2) unemployment insurance
(3) deficit spending
(4) collective bargaining

29 _____

30 These statements illustrate a difference in opinion between the two presidents over

(1) granting subsidies to big business
(2) promoting free-trade policies in the Western Hemisphere
(3) regulating supply and demand
(4) expanding the federal government's role in the economy   30 _____

31 Which problem did Franklin D. Roosevelt address *first* in his presidency?

(1) ending the Red Scare
(2) standing up to dictators in Europe
(3) bringing stability to the banking system
(4) approving bonus payments to World War I veterans   31 _____

32 **"National Defense at Any Expense, but Keep Our Boys at Home."**

This 1941 slogan of the America First Committee promoted

(1) globalism
(2) protective tariffs
(3) isolationism
(4) reduced military spending   32 _____

Base your answers to questions 33 and 34 on the cartoon below and on your knowledge of social studies.

And He Doesn't Mean Maybe!

Source: Jim Berryman, *Washington Evening Star*, January 1943 (adapted)

33 What is the main idea of the cartoon?

(1) United States factories will not be able to manufacture military supplies in sufficient quantities.

(2) The federal government will most likely need to seize ownership of manufacturing plants.

(3) President Franklin D. Roosevelt expects other nations to supply the same amount of armaments as the United States.

(4) President Franklin D. Roosevelt is determined to supply the United States military and its allies with whatever it takes to defeat the Axis powers.

33 _____

34 One major result of the production efforts described in the cartoon was that

- (1) the high unemployment of the Great Depression was greatly reduced
- (2) most companies that produced military supplies went out of business after the war
- (3) critics claimed that President Franklin D. Roosevelt was abusing his treaty-making power
- (4) the military had difficulty enlisting soldiers because the men were working in the munitions factories   34 _____

Base your answer to question 35 on the newspaper headlines below and on your knowledge of social studies.

Source: *Pittsburgh Courier*, April 19, 1947 (adapted)

35 Which conclusion can be drawn from an examination of these 1947 newspaper headlines concerning Jackie Robinson?

(1) Robinson's integration of major league baseball was an important event in the history of civil rights.

(2) Robinson went on to organize the civil rights movement.

(3) Sports fans overwhelmingly encouraged the desegregation of public accommodations.

(4) Robinson's major league debut had no impact on race relations in the United States.

35 _____

"...From Stettin in the Baltic to Trieste in the Adriatic, an iron curtain has descended across the Continent...."

— Winston Churchill, March 5, 1946

36 With this observation, Winston Churchill warned the United States that Europe was threatened by

(1) an embargo of its Middle East oil supplies
(2) the growth of fascism in Great Britain
(3) the expansion of communism in Eastern Europe
(4) a nuclear attack by the Soviet Union   36 _____

37 The North Atlantic Treaty Organization (NATO) and the Warsaw Pact are examples of

(1) dollar diplomacy
(2) Lend-Lease
(3) mutual defense
(4) Manifest Destiny   37 _____

38 Belief in the domino theory by presidents Dwight D. Eisenhower, John F. Kennedy, and Lyndon B. Johnson directly influenced their decisions to

(1) reject the policy of collective security
(2) support a return to neutrality
(3) end the Berlin airlift
(4) increase United States military involvement in Vietnam   38 _____

39 The War on Poverty was an attempt by President Lyndon B. Johnson to

(1) send medical aid to African nations
(2) strengthen the Peace Corps
(3) decrease the number of immigrants from Latin America
(4) raise the standard of living for many Americans   39 _____

Base your answer to question 40 on the passage below and on your knowledge of social studies.

...You express a great deal of anxiety over our willingness to break laws. This is certainly a legitimate concern. Since we so diligently urge people to obey the Supreme Court's decision of 1954 outlawing segregation in the public schools, it is rather strange and paradoxical to find us consciously breaking laws. One may well ask, "how can you advocate breaking some laws and obeying others?" The answer is found in the fact that there are two types of laws: There are *just* and there are *unjust* laws. I would agree with Saint Augustine that "An unjust law is no law at all." ...

— Martin Luther King Jr.
"Letter from Birmingham Jail," April 16, 1963

40 Which approach best represents the argument made in the passage?

   (1) civil disobedience
   (2) armed resistance
   (3) Black Power
   (4) containment

40 _____

41 A main goal of President Richard Nixon's policy of détente was to

   (1) sponsor free elections in North Korea
   (2) negotiate an end to the Arab-Israeli conflict
   (3) end diplomatic relations with China
   (4) reduce tensions between the United States and the Soviet Union

41 _____

42 Which charges led to President Bill Clinton's impeachment?

   (1) excessive use of the pardon power
   (2) perjury and obstruction of justice
   (3) illegal use of campaign funds
   (4) misuse of war powers and deficit spending

42 _____

43 One way in which Social Security, Medicare, and Medicaid are similar is that they are all

(1) programs that provide aid to education
(2) examples of social welfare programs
(3) attempts to balance the federal budget
(4) aspects of public works projects   43 _____

Base your answer to question 44 on the cartoon below and on your knowledge of social studies.

Source: Jim Morin, *Miami Herald*, July 21, 2006

44 This cartoonist is critical of the leadership of President George W. Bush and Vice President Richard B. Cheney for

(1) supporting the clear-cutting of forests
(2) overusing the presidential veto power
(3) weakening the system of checks and balances
(4) waging the war in Iraq   44 _____

45 Which presidential action was most consistent with the ideas presented by President George Washington in his Farewell Address?

  (1) President James Monroe's proclamation of the Monroe Doctrine in 1823
  (2) President James Polk's policy toward Mexico in 1846
  (3) President William McKinley's request for a declaration of war against Spain in 1898
  (4) President George H. W. Bush's decision to engage in the Persian Gulf War in 1990   45 _____

46 The Populist movement of the 1890s and the civil rights movement of the 1950s and 1960s are similar in that both movements were attempts to

  (1) restrict the power of the executive branch
  (2) solve the problems brought about by industrialization
  (3) improve the lives of groups who were oppressed
  (4) require state governments to promote racial equality   46 _____

Base your answer to question 47 on the cartoon below and on your knowledge of social studies.

"You Read Books, Eh?"

Source: Herblock, *Washington Post* (adapted)

47 The tactics illustrated in the cartoon were most closely associated with

(1) isolationists supporting neutrality policies during the 1930s
(2) government leaders investigating communist activities after World War II
(3) increased federal spending for education during the 1960s
(4) Congress promoting increased security after the September 11, 2001 attacks

47 _____

48 "Flappers" in the 1920s, "beatniks" in the 1950s, and "hippies" in the 1960s are all examples of

   (1) political groups who wanted to limit individual civil rights
   (2) citizens who wanted to return to simpler lifestyles
   (3) writers who supported United States foreign policy goals
   (4) individuals who disagreed with traditional societal values   48 _____

49 The Great Depression and the economic crisis known as the Great Recession (December 2007– June 2009) were similar in that both led to

   (1) a surplus in the federal budget
   (2) a decrease in federal support for unemployment insurance
   (3) a limit on the power of the Federal Reserve System
   (4) an expansion of the federal government's role in stabilizing the economy   49 _____

Base your answer to question 50 on the map below and on your knowledge of social studies.

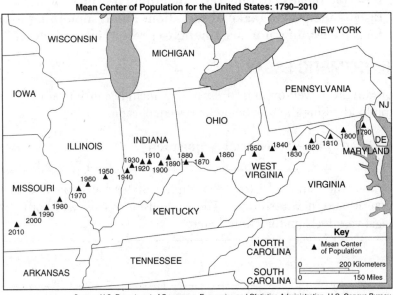

Mean Center of Population for the United States: 1790–2010

Source: U.S. Department of Commerce, Economics and Statistics Administration, U.S. Census Bureau
(adapted)

50 What has been the principal cause of the population changes shown on the map?

   (1) employment opportunities in northeastern states
   (2) continued westward migration
   (3) enactment of immigration quotas
   (4) movement from farms to cities   50 _____

In developing your answer to Part II, be sure to keep these general definitions in mind:

(a) <u>describe</u> means "to illustrate something in words or tell about it"
(b) <u>discuss</u> means "to make observations about something using facts, reasoning, and argument; to present in some detail"

PART II: THEMATIC ESSAY

Directions: Write a well-organized essay that includes an introduction, several paragraphs addressing the task below, and a conclusion.

Theme: Geography—Territorial Acquisition

Throughout the nation's history, the United States has expanded through the acquisition of new territories. These acquisitions have had both positive and negative effects on the United States.

Task:

Select *two* territories acquired by the United States and for *each*

- Describe the historical circumstances that led the United States to acquire the territory
- Discuss *positive and/or negative* effects of the acquisition of the territory on the United States

You may use any territory acquired by the United States since 1776 from your study of United States history. Some suggestions you might wish to consider include the Ohio River valley (1783), the Louisiana Territory (1803), Florida (1819), Texas (1845), the Oregon Territory (1846), California (1848), Alaska (1867), Hawaii (1898), Puerto Rico (1899), and the Philippines (1899).

You are *not* limited to these suggestions.

Guidelines:

In your essay, be sure to:
- Develop all aspects of the task
- Support the theme with relevant facts, examples, and details
- Use a logical and clear plan of organization, including an introduction and a conclusion that are beyond a restatement of the theme

In developing your answers to Part III, be sure to keep these general definitions in mind:

- (c) <u>describe</u> means "to illustrate something in words or tell about it"
- (d) <u>discuss</u> means "to make observations about something using facts, reasoning, and argument; to present in some detail"

PART III: DOCUMENT-BASED QUESTION

This question is based on the accompanying documents. The question is designed to test your ability to work with historical documents. Some of these documents have been edited for the purposes of this question. As you analyze the documents, take into account the source of each document and any point of view that may be presented in the document. Keep in mind that the language used in a document may reflect the historical context of the time in which it was written.

Historical Context:

> Throughout United States history, individuals have used written works as a way to focus attention on issues facing American society. These written works have had a significant influence on the United States and American society. These written works include **Common Sense** by **Thomas Paine**, **Uncle Tom's Cabin** by **Harriet Beecher Stowe**, and **The Jungle** by **Upton Sinclair**.

Task:

> Using the information from the documents and your knowledge of United States history, answer the questions that follow each document in Part A. Your answers to the questions will help you write the Part B essay in which you will be asked to
>
> Choose **two** written works mentioned in the historical context and for **each**
>
> - Describe the historical circumstances surrounding the issue addressed by the author
> - Discuss the influence of the written work on the United States and/or on American society

Part A: Short-Answer Questions

Directions: Analyze the documents and answer the short-answer questions that follow each document in the space provided.

Document 1

In 1768 John Dickinson of Pennsylvania argued for a new colonial theory which limited the power of Parliament over the colonies.

> ...Then events in due course pushed the colonial theory [of limited Parliamentary power] to a final stage. Thomas Paine's *Common Sense*, appearing in January 1776, tore every shred of authority from both King and Parliament. The two years or so preceding had piled crisis upon crisis. The Bostonians had sunk the tea; Parliament had retorted with the Intolerable Acts; the First Continental Congress had instituted a program of intercolonial economic resistance; war had erupted on Lexington Green; and an American army under the Second Congress had shut up [surrounded] General Gage and his regulars in Boston. In stirring and violent rhetoric the English-born Paine, who had recently settled in Philadelphia with a heart full of rancor for his native land, addressed the emotions as well as the minds of his readers. The "period of debate is closed," he concluded, "'TIS TIME TO PART." Although a half year was to elapse before Congress complied, Paine's trumpet call was a mighty factor in influencing the public as well as the delegates themselves to adopt the fateful step. No other work written in America, save perhaps *Uncle Tom's Cabin*, has ever had such crucial repercussions....

Source: Arthur M. Schlesinger, *The Birth of the Nation*, Houghton Mifflin, 1968

1 According to Arthur M. Schlesinger, what were **two** events that motivated Thomas Paine to write *Common Sense*? [2]

(1) _____

(2) _____

Document 2

... Paine published *Common Sense* in Philadelphia, and his Forester essays* first appeared in that city's newspapers. His friends also chose Philadelphia newspapers, and so did his political enemies. But since the controversy involved the "continent," *Common Sense* was reprinted in all the major American cities and the minor ones as well. Of course the debate spread, drawing in big men, John Adams, for example, and small ones as well. Within a few months over 100,000 copies of *Common Sense* had appeared, and the debates between independence and reconciliation dominated the newspapers.

A part of the common sense offered by Thomas Paine was the observation that Britain's old enemies in Europe would be more likely to provide support to the colonies if they declared their independence. No European power wanted to meddle in an internal dispute which might be settled by Britain and her colonies joining forces, as they had in the past, against an external enemy. Declaring independence would reassure Europe, reassure in particular France, the nation that some in Congress looked to for money and arms....

Source: Robert Middlekauff, *The Glorious Cause: The American Revolution, 1763–1789*, Oxford University Press, 2005 (adapted)

2 According to Robert Middlekauff, what is **one** way Thomas Paine's *Common Sense* promoted support for independence? [1]

_____

_____

Document 3

...There is an exaltation, an excitement, about *Common Sense* that conveys the very uncommon sense of adventure Americans felt as they moved toward independence. With it would come new perils, but also new opportunities, new freedoms. They knew they were on the threshold of a great experience not only for themselves but perhaps for the whole world. "The cause of America," Paine told them, "is in a great measure the cause of all mankind." And they believed him.

On May 15, 1776, the Virginia House of Burgesses voted to instruct its delegates in Congress to propose independence, and on the same day the Congress adopted a resolution sponsored by John Adams, advising the various colonies to assume complete powers of government within themselves. On June 7 Richard Henry Lee, following the instructions of his Virginia constituents, moved a resolution formally declaring the colonies independent. On July 2 this resolution was adopted and two days later the famous declaration to the world, drafted by Thomas Jefferson....

Source: Edmund S. Morgan, *The Birth of the Republic, 1763–89*,
Fourth Edition, The University of Chicago Press, 2013

3 According to Edmund S. Morgan, what was *one* effect of Thomas
  Paine's *Common Sense*? [1]

_____

_____

Document 4

...Among the provisions of the Compromise of 1850 were the end of the slave trade, but not slavery, in Washington D.C., and the creation of a new, stricter, Fugitive Slave Law. Helping runaways had been illegal since 1793, but the 1850 law required that everyone, law enforcers and ordinary citizens, help catch fugitives. Those who refused to assist slave-catchers, or aided fugitives, could be fined up to $1,000 and jailed for six months.

It also eliminated what little legal protection fugitives once had. Before 1850, some northern states had required slave-catchers to appear before an elected judge and be tried by a jury which would determine the validity of a claim. After the 1850 Fugitive Slave Law, anyone could be taken from the street, accused of being a fugitive from slavery, and taken before a federally appointed commissioner who received $5 for every fugitive released and $10 for every one sent south. Free blacks and anti-slavery groups argued the system bribed commissioners to send kidnapped people into slavery, and obliged citizens to participate in the slavery system.

[Harriet Beecher] Stowe was furious. She believed the country was requiring her complicity in a system she thought was unjust and immoral. Living in Brunswick, ME [Maine] while Calvin Stowe taught at Bowdoin College, Stowe disobeyed the law by hiding runaways. When she shared her frustrations and feelings of powerlessness with her family, her sister-in-law Isabella Porter Beecher suggested she do more: "...if I could use a pen as you can, Hatty, I would write something that would make this whole nation feel what an accursed thing slavery is."

Moved by the letter, Stowe swore she would "if [she] lived."...

Source: Harriet Beecher Stowe Center, 2011

4 Based on this document, why was Harriet Beecher Stowe concerned about the new Fugitive Slave Law? [1]

_____

_____

Document 5a

This poster was an advertisement for Harriet Beecher Stowe's *Uncle Tom's Cabin*.

Source: The Authentic History Center

Document 5b

...Stowe is often credited with influencing the country to think differently about slavery. But what do we know about how Stowe influenced Lincoln?

A decade earlier, *Uncle Tom's Cabin* (1852) had been a publishing and propaganda phenomenon. Using stories to illustrate the human impact of slavery, Stowe's blistering pen lit the world on fire. The statistics remain record-breaking: 10,000 copies sold in the first week; a million and a half British copies in a year. The book was so successful it was immediately dramatized for the stage, where it became a theatrical icon. Massachusetts Senator Charles Sumner, leader of the radical Republicans, said, "Had there been no *Uncle Tom's Cabin*, there would have been no Lincoln in the White House."...

But pro-slavery critics charged that Stowe had made it all up and that slavery was a humane system. So Stowe wrote a nonfiction retort, *The Key to Uncle Tom's Cabin* (1853), compiling the real-life evidence that had informed her fictional stories....

Source: Katherine Kane,
"Lincoln and *The Key to Uncle Tom's Cabin*,"
Connecticut Explored, Winter 2012/2013

5 Based on these documents, what is **one** reason Southern slave owners were concerned about the publication of *Uncle Tom's Cabin*? [1]

_____

_____

Document 6

...It is not possible to measure precisely the political influence of *Uncle Tom's Cabin*. One can quantify its sales but cannot point to votes that it changed or laws that it inspired. Yet few contemporaries doubted its power. "Never was there such a literary *coup-de-main* [sudden attack] as this," said Henry Wadsworth Longfellow. In England, Lord Palmerston, who as prime minister a decade later would face a decision whether to intervene on behalf of the South in the Civil War, read *Uncle Tom's Cabin* three times and admired it not so much for the story as "for the statesmanship of it." As Abraham Lincoln was grappling with the problem of slavery in the summer of 1862, he borrowed from the Library of Congress *A Key to Uncle Tom's Cabin*, a subsequent volume by Stowe containing documentation on which she had based the novel. When Lincoln met the author later that year, he reportedly greeted her with the words: "So you're the little woman who wrote the book that made this great war."

Uncle Tom's Cabin struck a raw nerve in the South. Despite efforts to ban it, copies sold so fast in Charleston and elsewhere that booksellers could not keep up with the demand. The vehemence of southern denunciations of Mrs. Stowe's "falsehoods" and "distortions" was perhaps the best gauge of how close they hit home. "There never before was anything so detestable or so monstrous among women as this," declared the *New Orleans Crescent*. The editor of the *Southern Literary Messenger* instructed his book reviewer: "I would have the review as hot as hellfire, blasting and searing the reputation of the vile wretch in petticoats who could write such a volume." Within two years proslavery writers had answered *Uncle Tom's Cabin* with at least fifteen novels whose thesis that slaves were better off than free workers in the North was capsulized by the title of one of them: *Uncle Robin in His Cabin in Virginia and Tom Without One in Boston*. A decade later during the Civil War a South Carolina diarist with doubts of her own about slavery reflected the obsession of southerners with *Uncle Tom's Cabin* by using it as a constant benchmark to measure the realities of life in the South....

Source: James M. McPherson, *Battle Cry of Freedom: The Civil War Era*, Oxford University Press, 1988 (adapted)

6 According to James M. McPherson, what were **two** effects of the publication of *Uncle Tom's Cabin*? [2]

(1) _____

(2) _____

Document 7

...The freedom of big business seemed limitless. Drug companies sold patent medicines containing heroin, morphine, and cocaine that promised to cure all sorts of diseases, but actually cured none of them. Food companies sold children's candy colored with toxic heavy metals. Cheap margarine was routinely marketed as butter. Crude mixtures of apple scraps, glucose, timothy seeds, and food coloring made from coal tar were sold as strawberry jam. In the age of the great trusts, the gulf between the wealthy and the poor became enormous. Robber barons built their homes in imitation of European palaces, while millions of American workers lived in urban slums.

Upton Sinclair was moved by these injustices. During the fall of 1904 he left his home in New Jersey and traveled to Chicago, intending to write a novel about the plight of the city's meatpacking workers. The beef trust controlled the industry with an iron fist. It had recently crushed a strike by union members who were seeking a pay raise of less than three cents an hour. The meatpacking industry seemed to embody everything that was wrong with American society, operating largely in secret, wielding unchecked power, threatening the health of workers and consumers. As Sinclair later argued in *The Jungle*, the beef trust was "the incarnation [representation] of blind and insensate [insensitive] greed...the Great Butcher.... the spirit of capitalism made flesh."...

Source: Eric Schlosser, Foreword to Upton Sinclair's *The Jungle*, Penguin Books, 2006

7 According to Eric Schlosser, what were **two** issues that concerned Upton Sinclair? [2]

(1) _____

(2) _____

Document 8a

... Upton Sinclair wrote "The Jungle" as a labor exposé. He hoped that the book, which was billed as "the 'Uncle Tom's Cabin' of wage slavery," would lead to improvements for the people to whom he dedicated it, "the workingmen of America." But readers of "The Jungle" were less appalled by Sinclair's accounts of horrific working conditions than by what they learned about their food. "I aimed at the public's heart," he famously declared, "and by accident I hit it in the stomach.".. .

When "The Jungle" was published, the public reaction was instantaneous. Outraged readers deluged President Theodore Roosevelt with letters. Roosevelt was ambivalent, but he invited Sinclair to the White House for lunch, and promised to send his labor commissioner and assistant Treasury secretary to Chicago to investigate... .

Source: Adam Cohen, "100 Years Later, the Food Industry Is Still 'The Jungle'," New York Times, January 2, 2007

Document 8b

...By the spring of 1906, both meat inspection and pure food and drugs legislation had many supporters. This was not a simple, black-and-white fight between the public on one side and big business on the other. But the pure food and drugs issue encouraged a broad range of Americans to think of their identities as consumers, as people who were imperiled by rotten meat or adulterated drugs. Physicians, federal experts, and women's groups supported legislation. State officials, assiduously [persistently] courted by Harvey Wiley [a pioneer consumer activist], agreed that federal supervision was necessary. So did Westerners, angry at the "foreign" corporations from the East and Midwest. So, too, did more than a few of those corporations. Pabst, H. J. Heinz, and other producers, setting individualism aside, recognized the benefits of federal regulation: Washington's supervision could bring order and stability to the business; it could protect the big companies from state supervision; it could make the business too expensive for potential competitors. At the least, regulation could rescue the corporations from their public predicament in 1906. Roosevelt's investigators had largely confirmed the essentials of *The Jungle*; the meatpackers were unable to discredit Sinclair's account. Under the circumstances, a crucial group of food and drug producers accepted the inevitability of regulation and tried to shape the legislation to protect their interests as much as possible....

Source: Michael McGerr, *A Fierce Discontent: The Rise and Fall of the Progressive Movement in America, 1870–1920*, Oxford University Press, 2005

8 Based on these documents, what were **two** effects of the publication of *The Jungle*? [2]

(1) _____

(2) _____

Document 9

Upton Sinclair was present when President Lyndon B. Johnson signed legislation amending the Meat Inspection Act.

> ..."A man was wrapping pork shoulders. He dropped one in the sawdust, picked it up and wiped it off with a dirty, sour rag.... Beef was being broken on an open dock, by a dirt road, in 95-degree weather. There were flies in the meat. Drums of bones and meat scraps were covered with maggots."
>
> What I just read to you was not from "The Jungle." It did not happen 60 years ago when Upton Sinclair was writing his book. It happened in July 1967. It was written by a United States Federal Government inspector after a visit to one of our great, modern packing plants....
>
> This is an intolerable condition in the 20th century in a modern nation that prides itself on reputed leadership of the world. I have been urging and I have been asking for a strong meat inspection bill since 1964.
>
> The Wholesome Meat Act of 1967—which has been brought to me by the good work of the Congress—will give something priceless, I think, to American housewives. It will give them assurance that the meat that they put on the dinner table for their husbands and their children is pure; that it has been packed and it has been processed in a sanitary plant....
>
> This Wholesome Meat Act is a landmark, we think, in consumer protection. It helps every American—by assuring him that the meat his family consumes has been inspected with their health and their safety in mind....
>
> Mr. Sinclair, we are so glad to have you here in the East Room with many of the distinguished Members of the Congress and people who are interested in this wholesome meat legislation.
>
> This bill really crowns the crusade that you, yourself, began some 60 years ago.
>
> We salute you, sir, and we thank you....

Source: President Lyndon B. Johnson, Remarks Upon
Signing Bill Amending the Meat Inspection Act, December 15, 1967

9 According to President Lyndon B. Johnson, what is the continuing influence of Upton Sinclair's *The Jungle*? [1]

_____

_____

Part B: Essay

Directions: Write a well-organized essay that includes an introduction, several paragraphs, and a conclusion. Use evidence from *at least four* documents in your essay. Support your response with relevant facts, examples, and details. Include additional outside information.

Historical Context:

> Throughout United States history, individuals have used written works as a way to focus attention on issues facing American society. These written works have had a significant influence on the United States and American society. These written works include **Common Sense by Thomas Paine**, *Uncle Tom's Cabin* **by Harriet Beecher Stowe**, and *The Jungle* **by Upton Sinclair**.

Task:

> Using the information from the documents and your knowledge of United States history, write an essay in which you
>
> Choose *two* written works mentioned in the historical context and for *each*
>
> - Describe the historical circumstances surrounding the issue addressed by the author
> - Discuss the influence of the written work on the United States and/or on American society

Guidelines:

In your essay, be sure to:

- Develop all aspects of the task
- Incorporate information from *at least four* documents
- Incorporate relevant outside information
- Support the theme with relevant facts, examples, and details
- Use a logical and clear plan of organization, including an introduction and a conclusion that are beyond a restatement of the theme

Answers
June 2018
United States History and Government

Answer Key

PART I

1. 4	11. 1	21. 3	31. 3	41. 4
2. 1	12. 3	22. 4	32. 3	42. 2
3. 2	13. 1	23. 3	33. 4	43. 2
4. 3	14. 2	24. 4	34. 1	44. 3
5. 2	15. 1	25. 1	35. 1	45. 1
6. 4	16. 3	26. 3	36. 3	46. 3
7. 1	17. 3	27. 2	37. 3	47. 2
8. 2	18. 1	28. 1	38. 4	48. 4
9. 4	19. 2	29. 1	39. 4	49. 4
10. 2	20. 2	30. 4	40. 1	50. 2

PART II: Thematic Essay   *See* **Answers Explained** section.

PART III: Document-Based Question   *See* **Answers Explained** section.

Answers Explained

PART I (1–50)

1. **4** A main reason large plantations developed in the South during the colonial period was that the climate of the South provided longer growing seasons. The growing season is the part of the year during which local weather conditions, such as rainfall and temperature, permit normal plant growth. Although each plant or crop has a specific growing season, the growing season of a region is usually defined as the number of days between the last frost in the spring and the first frost in the fall. The fertile soul, relatively flat land, and long growing season of the coastal regions of the South made the area ideal for large tobacco, rice, and indigo plantations. (Cotton did not become a major crop in the United States until the 1790s.) These large plantations lent themselves to the slave system of labor. In contrast, the hilly, rocky soil and shorter growing season of the northern colonies proved more suitable for smaller-scale agriculture and a more mixed economy. The smaller farms of the northern colonies were generally worked by the owner of the property and his family, with, perhaps, more people hired for planting and harvesting.

WRONG CHOICES EXPLAINED:

(1) British laws in the colonial period permitted slavery throughout the colonies. However, local geographic factors—fertile soul, relatively flat land, and a long growing season—favored the development of large plantations and slavery in the South rather than in the North.

(2) Wetlands, which are land areas saturated with water for at least part of the year, are not conducive to agriculture. Wetlands do play important roles in regard to water purification and the prevention of coastal flooding. They exist through the coastal areas of the United States.

(3) Large plantations developed in the areas of the South that were near the coast, not in the mountainous interior sections of the South. The strip of relatively flat, well-irrigated land adjacent to the coast was more favorable to large-scale agriculture. The more hilly, interior region of the South saw the development of smaller-scale farms and focused more on meeting the food needs of the local population rather than on producing staple crops.

2. **1** In the 1780s, the national government under the Articles of Confederation established its authority in the Northwest Territory by providing a system for the formation of new states. The Northwest Ordinance of 1787

provided a method for the creation of new states. It stipulated that when a territory reached 60,000 free inhabitants, it would be eligible for statehood. The law
was passed during the Articles of Confederation period (1781–1788). Dealing
with the land of the Northwest Territory was one of the major successes of the
government under the Articles. The method for creating new states continued to
be used after the Articles were replaced by the Constitution in 1789. The national
government under the Articles of Confederation is often cited for its inability to
resolve difficult issues. However, its actions in regard to western lands are generally seen as effective measures.

WRONG CHOICES EXPLAINED:
(2) The national government under the Articles of Confederation did not
address a border dispute with Mexico. At the time that the Articles of
Confederation were replaced by the Constitution (1789), the United States
extended to the Mississippi River. There was no border between the United
States and Mexico at that time. Later, a border dispute between the United
States and Mexico contributed to the Mexican-American War (1846–1848).

(3) The national government under the Articles of Confederation did not
extend the nation's border to the Rocky Mountains. At the time that the Articles
of Confederation were in place (1781–1789), the United States extended to the
Mississippi River. Only after the acquisition of the Louisiana Territory (1803)
and the Mexican Cession (1848) did the Rocky Mountains become part of the
United States.

(4) The national government under the Articles of Confederation did not
directly address the issue of Native American Indian claims of sovereignty in the
Northwest Territory. Settlers and Native American Indians clashed in the
Northwest Territory during the 1780s, but there was no final resolution of land
claims by Native American Indians.

3. **2** A fundamental principal of a republican form of government is that legislation must be passed by elected representatives of the people. In a republican
form of government, the act of governing is a public affair. The Latin phrase *res
publica*, from which the word "republic" is derived, means "public affair" or
"public matter." Throughout history, most governments have been seen as the
private concern of the rulers. In a monarchy, for example, power is often passed
to an heir within the family of the monarch. A common characteristic of many
republics is that elected representatives, who are supposed to reflect the will of
the public, have the power to pass legislation. From its founding, the United
States has adopted a republican form of government, as have the states within
the United States.

WRONG CHOICES EXPLAINED:

(1) A republican form of government does not include the principle that hereditary rulers are the legitimate possessors of political power. Monarchies, on the other hand, are typically based on hereditary rulers. The United Kingdom has a constitutional monarchy. The oldest continuing hereditary monarchy is the Japanese monarchy.

(3) A republican form of government does not include the principle that laws should be created directly by the citizens. Direct democracy—in which citizens meet face-to-face to make decisions about their communities—is not widespread in the United States. The town meetings of colonial New England embodied the concept of direct democracy. Republican forms of government generally include elected representatives who have the power to pass legislation.

(4) A republican form of government does not include the principle that governments have no responsibility for protecting individual rights. Republican forms of government are generally built around a social contract in which the people agree to follow the rules of the government and the government is obligated to protect people's individual rights. This idea was put forth by John Locke in his *Two Treatises on Government*, written in the early 1690s, and in the Declaration of Independence (1776).

4. **3** A major argument used by the Antifederalists to oppose ratifying the Constitution was that the proposed Constitution contained no bill of rights. When the newly written Constitution was submitted to the states for ratification in 1787, many Americans were concerned that it would create a powerful central government that would take away the rights and liberties of the people. The Constitution itself does not devote much attention to individual rights. The opponents of the Constitution, labeled *Antifederalists*, demanded a list of individual rights that the government would not be allowed to take away. Many Antifederalists in the various states refused to support ratification of the Constitution unless such a list was added. Supporters of the Constitution, known as *Federalists*, promised to add such a list if the Antifederalists agreed to support ratification. This agreement led to the writing and ratification of the first ten amendments to the Constitution, known as the Bill of Rights.

WRONG CHOICES EXPLAINED:

(1) The Antifederalists did not express concern that Congress was given the power to tax exports. In fact, the Constitution specifically forbids Congress from taxing exports. This provision was especially important to southern states, which relied heavily on the export of various staple crops.

(2) The Antifederalists did not argue that the executive branch lacked the power to maintain order. In fact, they argued the opposite. They were concerned with the expanded powers of the executive branch in the proposed Constitution.

(4) The Antifederalists did not take issue with the fact that the Constitution stipulated that only the national government could coin money. Although Antifederalists argued that state governments should retain significant powers, they did not argue against the national government having the power to coin money.

5. **2** The judicial branch of government can check the legislative branch of government by declaring laws unconstitutional. This power, called judicial review, is one of many checks built into the system of governance in the United States. The framers of the Constitution were very conscious of the problems of a government with limitless powers. After living under the British monarchy, they came to believe that a powerful government without checks was dangerous to liberty. Therefore, the framers created a governmental system with three branches, each with the ability to check the powers of the other two. The goal was to keep the three branches in balance. Examples of this concept of checks and balances are the president's ability to veto (or reject) bills passed by Congress, the Senate's power to approve or reject presidential nominees for Supreme Court justices and ambassadors, and the Senate's power to reject or approve treaties. The primary power of the judicial branch in this system of checks and balances is judicial review. This power was established by the Supreme Court in the case of *Marbury* v. *Madison* (1803). The decision, arguably the Supreme Court's most important, established the Court's power to review laws and determine if they are consistent with the Constitution. Laws declared unconstitutional by the Court are immediately disallowed.

WRONG CHOICES EXPLAINED:
(1) The judicial branch does not have the power to veto bills passed by Congress. The vetoing of bills passed by Congress is an example of a governmental check—but it is a power of the president, not of the judiciary.

(3) The judicial branch does not have the power to call special sessions of Congress. The calling of special sessions of Congress, which occurs during periods when Congress is adjourned, is an example of a governmental check—but it is a power of the president, not of the judiciary.

(4) The judicial branch does not have the power to reduce congressional budgets. Congress has the power to establish the annual budget of the government. The president initially submits a budget request to Congress. The two branches of Congress then work out the details of the budget and write appropriations bills. Next, the two branches vote on the bills and then reconcile differences

that may exist between the House and Senate bills. Finally, these bills are presented to the president for approval.

6. **4** The belief expressed in the statement in the question was put into law by the addition of the First Amendment to the Constitution. The statement by James Madison asserts the importance of citizens having the "free exercise" of religion. Madison states that this right is no less important than any other right. The First Amendment addresses religion in two ways. First, the establishment clause prohibits the creation of an official religion in the United States. This is the basis of the separation of church and state. The First Amendment also asserts that Congress shall not prohibit the "free exercise" of religion. In other words, Congress cannot pass laws that impinge upon people's religious beliefs. In practice, it is difficult to pin down the exact meaning of this constitutional principle. The Supreme Court has been called upon over the years to attempt to interpret the principle. In *Reynolds* v. *United States* (1878), for example, the Court upheld a federal law banning polygamy, a practice common among some Mormons at the time. The Court asserted that it was permissible to ban practices, such as polygamy and human sacrifice, but that it was impermissible for the government to interfere with mere religious beliefs and opinions. Later, in *West Virginia State Board of Education* v. *Barnette* (1943), the Court upheld the rights of Jehovah's Witnesses not to salute the flag. In the 1960s, the Warren Court continued the trend toward a more expansive view of the free exercise clause. In *Sherbert* v. *Verner* (1963), the Court held that states must have a "compelling interest" to refuse to accommodate religiously motivated conduct. The case involved a Seventh-day Adventist who was denied unemployment benefits after having been fired for refusing to work on Saturdays.

WRONG CHOICES EXPLAINED:
(1) The principle of free religious exercise, advocated by James Madison in the statement in the question, was not put into law by the signing of the Mayflower Compact. The Mayflower Compact (1620) was signed over a century before Madison's birth and did not call for free religious exercise. Its references to God and Christianity presume a strict adherence to Puritan separatism, not to the free exercise of religion. The document was written and signed by the Pilgrims on board the *Mayflower* before it touched land at Plymouth, Massachusetts, in 1620. To give themselves a sense of legitimacy in an area in which they had no legal status, the Pilgrims agreed in this document to set up a government and obey its laws.

(2) The principle of free religious exercise, advocated by James Madison in the statement in the question, was not put into law by the creation of the Articles of Confederation. The Articles essentially put into writing the governing

structure that had evolved during the American Revolution. An important principle of the Articles was to preserve the independence and sovereignty of the states. The Articles did not make any provisions for the protection of religious freedom.

(3) The principle of free religious exercise, advocated by James Madison in the statement in the question, was not put into law by the establishment of a federal system of government. The term *federalism* describes the relationship among the state governments and the national government. In the governing system developed in the Constitution, powers are shared by the national government and the states. The goal is that excessive power is not concentrated in either level of government. The establishment of this system did not include provisions for the protection of religious freedom.

7. **1** Secretary of the Treasury Alexander Hamilton used the clause of the Constitution excerpted in the question to justify establishing the Bank of the United States. The clause, known as the necessary and proper clause, or the elastic clause, expands the powers of Congress. During the constitutional convention, the delegates were aware of the importance of creating a document that could meet the needs of a changing society. To meet this goal, they included the elastic clause, which stretched the powers of Congress by allowing it to "make all laws necessary and proper...." However, the definition of "necessary and proper" soon became a matter of much debate. Alexander Hamilton pushed for the creation of a national bank. This national bank would be 20 percent publicly controlled and 80 percent privately controlled. Hamilton thought it was important to have wealthy investors financially and psychologically invested in the new government. Though the power to create a national bank was not granted to Congress in the Constitution, Hamilton argued that it was permissible under the elastic clause. Thomas Jefferson argued that the creation of a national bank was not "necessary and proper." Hamilton won this debate, and a national bank was created in 1791. It existed until 1811.

WRONG CHOICES EXPLAINED:

(2) Alexander Hamilton did not use the elastic clause to justify creating the federal postal system. Congressional legislation created the postal system. The Constitution explicitly grants Congress the power to create a postal system; the elastic clause was not invoked in this situation.

(3) Alexander Hamilton did not use the elastic clause to justify sending troops to end the Whiskey Rebellion. The Constitution explicitly grants the president the power to suppress armed insurrections; the elastic clause was not invoked in this situation. President George Washington first obtained certification from a Supreme Court justice that local authorities were incapable of suppressing the

rebellion. Historians have debated the appropriateness of the federal government's response to the Whiskey Rebellion, but the actions were within the powers of the executive.

(4) Alexander Hamilton did not use the elastic clause to justify imposing an embargo on trade with Great Britain. Such an embargo was enacted under the administration of President Thomas Jefferson with the Embargo Act (1807) and the Non-Intercourse Act (1809). The Commerce Clause of the Constitution explicitly grants Congress the power to regulate trade with foreign countries.

8. **2** The two areas of the map that made up the United States as a result of the Louisiana Purchase were *A* and *D*. Area A is the original territory of the United States as established by the Treaty of Paris in 1783. The treaty established the Mississippi River as the western boundary of the United States. In 1803, the purchase of the Louisiana Territory, area *D*, enlarged the territory of the United States and pushed the western boundary beyond the Mississippi River. During the administration of President Thomas Jefferson, the United States purchased the Louisiana Territory from France for $15 million. The purchase nearly doubled the size of the United States and gave the United States control of the Mississippi River and the port city of New Orleans. New Orleans became increasingly important as pioneers in the late 1700s and early 1800s crossed over the Appalachian Mountains, settled in the Mississippi and Ohio River Valleys, and established farms there.

WRONG CHOICES EXPLAINED:
(1), (3), and (4) Only choice 2 consists of two areas that comprised the United States in 1803. The other three choices contain one or two areas that were acquired later. Area *B*, which is included in choices 1 and 3, consists of Florida and parts of modern-day Louisiana, Mississippi, and Alabama. It was acquired after 1803. The United States acquired the land from Spain in 1819 with the Adams-Onis Treaty. Area *E*, which is included in choice 3, is Texas. It was acquired after 1803. Texas had become independent from Mexico in 1836 and was annexed by the United States in 1845, soon after the victory of the expansionist James K. Polk in the presidential election of 1844. Area *G*, which is included in choice 4, is the Mexican Cession. It was acquired after 1803. This area was acquired as a result of the Mexican-American War. After the annexation of Texas by the United States in 1845, the United States and Mexico disagreed over the southern border of Texas. Skirmishes in the disputed area led to war between Mexico and the United States. The United States won the war, which lasted from 1846 to 1848, and acquired the Mexican Cession.

9. **4** Area *G* was acquired as a result of the Mexican-American War. The push toward the Pacific Ocean generated a desire among many Americans to obtain Mexican territory. Americans had been settling in the Mexican territory of Texas as far back as the 1820s. In 1836, Texans fought for and won independence from Mexico. Texas then became the Lone Star Republic. Many Texans were eager for their Lone Star Republic to join the United States. However, concern about the expansion of slavery put the issue of Texas annexation on the back burner until the election of the expansionist President James Polk in 1844. Even before he took office, the outgoing President John Tyler saw Polk's victory as a mandate for Texas annexation and pushed annexation through Congress. Texas joined the United States as the 15th slave state in 1845. Conflict between the United States and Mexico soon ensued. The two countries disagreed over the southern border of Texas. Mexico said it was at the Nueces River. The United States insisted it was at the Rio Grande, 150 miles to the south. In 1846, Polk sent troops into this disputed territory. Skirmishes in the disputed area led to war between Mexico and the United States. The United States won the war, which lasted from 1846 to 1848, and acquired the huge territory that comprised the northern provinces of Mexico, known as the Mexican Cession. These lands included the gold deposits discovered in California in 1849 and the lush agricultural land along the west coast.

WRONG CHOICES EXPLAINED:

(1) Area *A* is the original territory of the United States as established by the Treaty of Paris in 1783. The treaty established the Mississippi River as the western boundary of the United States.

(2) Area *B* consists of Florida and parts of modern-day Louisiana, Mississippi, and Alabama. It was granted by Spain to the United States in the Adams-Onis Treaty of 1819. The western portion of the Florida panhandle had been acquired earlier, with the Louisiana Purchase. This portion was later incorporated into the states of Alabama, Mississippi, and Louisiana.

(3) Area *F* is the Oregon Territory, which was incorporated into the United States in 1848 following the resolution of a border dispute with Great Britain. The two nations agreed that the border would be along the 49th parallel. The Oregon Territory included the entire future states of Oregon, Washington, and Idaho as well as parts of Montana and Wyoming.

10. **2** Governor DeWitt Clinton is describing the Erie Canal. Governor Clinton championed the project and successfully pushed the legislature of New York State to provide financial support. The Erie Canal (completed in 1825) provided an important link between the Atlantic Ocean and the Great Lakes. The United States was faced with a vexing problem during its first decades. On paper, the country extended to the Mississippi River following the American

Revolutionary War (1775–1783) and then to the Rocky Mountains following the Louisiana Purchase (1803). However, most residents of the United States resided in communities close to the Atlantic Coast, east of the Appalachian Mountains. The Erie Canal helped open up the vast landmass of the country to settlement by United States residents. The canal created an all-water route from New York City to the midwestern communities around the Great Lakes. This connection facilitated settlement and trade between the Atlantic Coast and the Midwest, creating, in the words of Governor Clinton, the "greatest inland trade ever witnessed." A shipment of wheat, for example, could now be transported from Chicago to New York City by an all-water route at a tenth of the cost and in a fraction of the time than when using an overland route.

WRONG CHOICES EXPLAINED:

(1) Governor DeWitt Clinton is not describing the National Road. The National Road, also known as the Cumberland Road, stretched from Maryland into the Ohio River Valley. Construction took place from 1811 to 1853. Clinton's description notes connecting the Hudson River with the St. Lawrence River and the Great Lakes—and, ultimately, with the Mississippi River. These points were not connected by the National Road.

(3) Governor DeWitt Clinton is not describing steamboats. Steamboats— developed by several people, including Robert Fulton (1807)—were used on the Erie Canal. However, Clinton is describing a specific transportation project, not a mode of transportation.

(4) Governor DeWitt Clinton is not describing railroads. In many ways, railroads rendered canals, such as the Erie Canal, far less efficient for transporting goods. The first railroad tracks in the United States were laid in 1829 by the Baltimore and Ohio Railroad. By 1860, railroads connected the far reaches of the country east of the Mississippi River and beyond. Clinton is describing a specific transportation project, not a mode of transportation.

11. **1** An example of the unwritten constitution is the president's cabinet. The unwritten constitution refers to those traditions and practices that have become part of the American political system but are not mentioned in the Constitution. Many of these practices date back to the administration of President George Washington. President Washington regularly convened a cabinet, comprised of the heads of government departments, to advise him. Additional elements of the unwritten constitution include the development of political parties, a practice unforeseen by most of the founding fathers and not mentioned in the Constitution. Congressional committees are not mentioned in the Constitution, yet the committee system has become instrumental in the functioning of Congress. Occasionally, a practice goes from being part of the unwritten

constitution to being part of the written Constitution. President Washington set a precedent of serving for no more than two terms. This tradition, however, became law with the ratification of the 22nd Amendment (1951), ratified after President Franklin D. Roosevelt broke tradition and won the presidency four times.

WRONG CHOICES EXPLAINED:

(2) The amendment process is not an example of the use of the unwritten constitution. It is spelled out in the written Constitution. First, a constitutional amendment can be proposed, either by Congress (by two-third majorities in both houses) or by a national convention. Then three-fourths of the states must approve an amendment for it to be ratified. The state-by-state approval process can occur by the consent of the state legislatures or by state ratifying conventions. Twenty-seven amendments have been added to the Constitution.

(3) The bicameral legislature is not an example of the use of the unwritten constitution. It is spelled out in the written Constitution. A two-house, or bicameral, legislature was the result of the Great Compromise at the Constitutional Convention of 1787. The compromise settled a dispute between the large states and the small states over how the states would be represented in Congress. The Great Compromise called for a House of Representatives, in which representation would be determined by the population of each state, and a Senate, in which each state would get two members.

(4) The electoral college is not an example of the use of the unwritten constitution. It is spelled out in the written Constitution. The president is officially chosen by the electoral college. The number of electors for each state is equal to the number of members of Congress from that state. The Constitution allows each state to establish a method for appointing electors. Currently, all states use the popular vote to appoint electors. In all the states except for Maine and Nebraska, whichever candidate wins the popular vote in a particular state gets all the electoral votes for that state. Maine and Nebraska voters select one elector within each congressional district; two additional electors are awarded based on the statewide popular vote. Presently, there are 538 electoral votes. A candidate must win the majority, or 270 votes, to be declared the "president elect."

12. **3** The information in the chart supports the generalization that the North had greater economic strength than the South. The chart compares acres of farmland, miles of railroad track, industrial capacity, and population of the North and the South as the Civil War was beginning in 1861. The contrast in industrial capacity—the value of manufactured goods, the number of factories, and the number of industrial workers—is striking. The North dominates each category by 85 percent or more. The greater industrial capacity of the North allowed the

United States government to procure far more weapons and ammunition than the breakaway southern states. Furthermore, the advantage that the northern states had in regard to miles of railroad tracks—71 percent compared to 29 percent—allowed the Union to move goods and people more quickly and efficiently. The difference in farmland between the two regions is less extreme—the North had 65 percent of farmland to the South's 35 percent. However, these numbers obscure the fact that a large percentage of southern farmland was devoted to cotton production. All told, the North was far better prepared to feed its soldiers than was the South. Finally, the difference in population proved to give the Union side a major advantage. If slaves are excluded from the totals of each region, the North had about 22 million free people compared to less than six million free people in the South. These figures became increasingly important as the Civil War dragged on for nearly four years. The northern states were better able to reinforce the ranks of the United States army than the southern states were able to sustain the Confederate army. All the factors in the chart help explain the victory of the Union army over Confederate forces.

WRONG CHOICES EXPLAINED:
(1) The information in the chart does not support the generalization that the South exported more manufactured goods than the North. The chart does not include statistics about exports. The chart does indicate that the overall manufacturing capacity of the South was far less than that of the North. Further, the Union was successfully in blockading South ports, thereby greatly reducing Southern exports (mainly cotton).

(2) The information in the chart does not support the generalization that the North would have had more difficulty supplying an army than the South. The information in the chart indicates the opposite. The North had more acres under cultivation, allowing for greater food production. Also, the North had greater industrial production, allowing for greater production of weaponry and ammunition. Finally, the extensive railroad network of the North would allow these goods to reach the army more easily.

(4) The information in the chart does not support the generalization that the South would be better able to transport an army than the North. The information in the chart suggests the opposite. Of the national total, 71 percent of railroad tracks were in the North, suggesting that the North would be better able to transport an army than the South.

13. **1** The publication of the poster was most directly prompted by the issuance of the Emancipation Proclamation. Perhaps President Abraham Lincoln's greatest achievement during the Civil War was playing a key role in the liberation of the slaves. Lincoln was partly motivated by the desire to keep Great Britain at bay

during the Civil War. Great Britain might have aided the Confederacy to ensure the steady flow of southern cotton, but it would not have joined the South to continue slavery. However, Lincoln did not achieve this historic goal on his own. Abolitionists, Radical Republicans, and, of course, the slaves themselves all contributed to the effort to put the issue of liberation on the wartime agenda. Lincoln was able to convince a reluctant country that ending slavery was consistent with the most basic American values. By the summer of 1862, Lincoln had come to believe that the time was right for moving forward in regard to emancipation. He waited until the Union had achieved a victory on the battlefield. The Battle of Antietam in September 1862 was enough of a Union victory to prompt the president to issue the Emancipation Proclamation. The edict ordered the freeing of all slaves in rebel-held territory as of January 1, 1863. The order exempted slaves in the loyal border states and even in Union-held areas of Confederate states. Of course, orders from the United States government did not hold any weight for Confederate leaders. So the Emancipation Proclamation did not actually free any slaves. However, the order clearly changed the goals and tenor of the war. It made clear that this was as much a war for the liberation of the slaves as it was a war to preserve the Union. The proclamation also authorized the recruiting of African Americans for service in the army. Secretary of War Edwin M. Stanton began to take action to recruit African-American troops. In January 1863, he instructed the governor of Massachusetts to begin raising an African-American regiment. The 54th Regiment Massachusetts Volunteer Infantry, led by Colonel Robert Gould Shaw, was the first African-American regiment. By the end of the Civil War in April 1865, the United States Army had organized approximately 175 African-American units; these troops constituted about one-tenth of the manpower of the army.

WRONG CHOICES EXPLAINED:

(2) The publication of the poster was not prompted by the passage of the Kansas-Nebraska Act. This 1854 act allowed for the possibility of slavery, under the principle of popular sovereignty, in the territories of Kansas and Nebraska—areas that had been closed to slavery by the Missouri Compromise (1820). Violence erupted in Bleeding Kansas as pro-slavery and antislavery men fought for control of the territory. The call to "military duty" in the poster was not extended to African-American men during the violence in Kansas.

(3) The publication of the poster was not prompted by the rejection of the Wilmot Proviso. Following the beginning of the Mexican-American War (1846–1848), Congressman David Wilmot and other northern politicians tried, unsuccessfully, to ban slavery in territories that might be gained in the war by putting forth the Wilmot Proviso (1846). The Mexican-American War was already in progress when the proviso was proposed and rejected. Its rejection did not lead to calls for African-American men to participate in military duty.

(4) The publication of the poster was not prompted by the adoption of the Missouri Compromise. The Missouri Compromise (1820) maintained the balance between free and slave states. Controversy arose between the slave-holding states and the free states in 1820 when Missouri applied for statehood as a slave state. The admission of Missouri would have upset the balance between free and slave states. A compromise was reached that allowed for the admission of two new states—Missouri as a slave state and Maine as a free state. It also divided the remaining area of the Louisiana Territory at 36° 30′ north latitude. North of that line, slavery was not permitted (except in Missouri). South of that line, it was permitted. The compromise did not lead to military action not to call for African-American men to participate in "military duty."

14. **2** At the start of the Civil War, President Abraham Lincoln stated that the major reason for fighting the Civil War was to uphold the Constitution by preserving the Union. Lincoln had been opposed to the institution of slavery his entire life. As he ran for president in 1860, he promised to block the expansion of slavery to new territories in the West. However, he said that the Constitution prohibited him from interfering with slavery where it already existed. As the war progressed, Lincoln slowly began to change his views in regard to the relationship between the federal government and slavery. He began to see that the institution of slavery was a major strength of the Southern economy. Further, abolitionists, Radical Republicans, and, of course, the slaves themselves all contributed to the effort to put the issue of liberation on the wartime agenda. At first, Lincoln was reluctant to take action against slavery for fear of pushing the border states toward secession. When Congress passed the Confiscation Acts in 1861 and 1862, Lincoln was opposed to them. However, he did not veto them. These acts were framed as military measures. The first declared that any slaves pressed into working for the Confederacy could be taken as "contraband of war," meaning "confiscated property." The second act allowed for the seizure of the slaves owned by Confederate officials. In the summer of 1862, Lincoln wrote a letter to Horace Greeley, editor of the *New-York Tribune*, that shows his evolving views. Lincoln reiterated that his "paramount object" in the Civil War was "to save the Union." However, he also stated that if "I could save the Union without freeing any slave I would do it, and if I could save it by freeing all the slaves I would do it." Here he acknowledged that "freeing all the slaves" was a possible course of action. Soon after, in September 1862, he issued the Emancipation Proclamation, which went into effect on January 1, 1863. This document changed the direction and objective of the war. It also made clear that the future existence of slavery would be determined by the outcome of the war.

WRONG CHOICES EXPLAINED:

(1) Lincoln did not state that the major reason for fighting the Civil War was to break the South's economic ties to Great Britain. He implemented a naval blockade during the war to prevent trade between the Confederacy and Great Britain. However, this was part of the strategy to defeat the Confederacy and to maintain the Union.

(3) Lincoln did not state that the major reason for fighting the Civil War was to enforce the terms of the Compromise of 1850. The compromise grew out of the controversy around California's application for statehood as a free state. When Southern senators objected to the admission of an additional free state, Senate negotiators worked out a series of measures that became known as the Compromise of 1850. The most important elements of the compromise were the admittance of California as a free state, which pleased northern politicians, and a more stringent Fugitive Slave Law, which pleased southern politicians. Enforcing the Fugitive Slave Law was controversial. However, it was not Lincoln's primary objective in fighting the Civil War; maintaining the Union was.

(4) Lincoln did not state that the major reason for fighting the Civil War was to punish the Confederate states for leaving the Union. Lincoln insisted that the Confederate states had not actually left the Union. He held the position that the states were in rebellion and that his goal, as president, was to suppress the rebellion and maintain the Union. Toward the end of the war, he pushed for more lenient terms for Reconstruction. In his Second Inaugural Address, Lincoln said that "[w]ith malice toward none, with charity for all," he hoped to "bind up the nation's wounds." This generous attitude toward the rebellious South did not reflect a desire to punish those states.

15. **1** Passage of the Homestead Act in 1862 encouraged settlement of the Great Plains by providing free land to farmers. By the time of the Civil War, the government wanted to encourage settlement in the huge area of relatively flat land between the Mississippi River and the Rocky Mountains known as the Great Plains. Much of this area has rich soil and a long growing season. With the absence of Democrats from Congress during the Civil War, the Republicans were able to pass several pieces of legislation that reflected their vision of America. Hundreds of thousands of people applied for and were granted homesteads. Many of these homesteaders did not have extensive farming skills and went bankrupt. Increasingly by the late 1800s, it became difficult for small farmers, even competent ones, to compete with large-scale agricultural operations.

WRONG CHOICES EXPLAINED:

(2) The Homestead Act did not remove barriers to Asian immigrants. Later, in 1882, Congress passed the Chinese Exclusion Act, which excluded most Chinese from entering the United States. This act represents the only instance in which legislation has explicitly denied a particular national group entrance into the United States.

(3) The Homestead Act did not supply land to build transcontinental railroads. The Pacific [Transcontinental] Railroad Act (1862) supplied land to railroad companies. The act encouraged expansion of the railroad network by giving railroad companies wide swaths of land. These generous land grants totaled more than 180 million acres, an area equal to the size of Texas. Completion of the first transcontinental railroad at Promontory Summit, Utah, in 1869 was a milestone in the development of a network of railroad lines that connected the far reaches of the country.

(4) The Homestead Act did not place Native American Indians on reservations. After the Civil War, starting in 1867, the government attempted to solve the "Indian problem" through peaceful means, rather than through more warfare. The center of this policy was pushing Native American Indians onto reservations—confined areas that were set aside by the government. This policy made Native American Indians wards of the government until they learned "to walk on the white man's road." Often the lands set aside for reservations were incapable of sustaining crops, reducing the inhabitants to utter poverty. Many tribal groups resisted being put onto reservations.

16. **3** The heading, "Elements of Reconstruction" best completes the partial outline. Reconstruction occurred from 1865 to 1877, following the Civil War. It was the period in which attempts were made to address the political, social, and economic legacies of slavery and to solve the problems arising from the readmission of the 11 secessionist states to the Union. Reconstruction began even before the Civil War ended, when President Abraham Lincoln announced his Proclamation of Amnesty and Reconstruction (1863). Lincoln and his successor, President Andrew Johnson, controlled the first phase of Reconstruction. Their goal was to reunite the country quickly and easily and to establish functioning governments in the southern states. During this first phase of Reconstruction, Congress created the Freedman's Bureau (outline entry A) in 1865 to help freedmen and freedwomen adjust to life after slavery. The bureau provided freedmen and freedwomen with job training, emergency food, and help finding housing. President Johnson tried to abolish the bureau in 1866 but was blocked by Congress. The bureau was finally abolished in 1872. Starting in 1867, the Radical Republicans in Congress took over control of Reconstruction. This second phase of Reconstruction involved more sweeping changes in the South, including the military occupation of the rebellious southern

states (outline entry C) and assurances that African Americans in the South would finally get some basic rights. This phase of Reconstruction also witnessed the ratification of the 14th Amendment (outline entry B). The modest gains for African Americans were short-lived. Reconstruction came to an end as part of a compromise to settle the disputed presidential election of 1876.

WRONG CHOICES EXPLAINED:

(1) The heading "Development of States Rights" does not complete the partial outline in the question. An outline with that heading would include subheadings such as "The Virginia and Kentucky Resolutions (1798)" and "The South Carolina Exposition and Protest (1828)."

(2) The heading "Results of Manifest Destiny" does not complete the partial outline in the question. An outline with that heading would include subheadings such as "Texas annexation (1845)" and "the Mexican Cession (1848)."

(4) The heading "Limits on Civil Rights" does not complete the partial outline in the question. An outline with that heading would include subheadings such as "Enactment of Jim Crow laws in the 1880s and 1890s" and "The Supreme Court decision in *Plessy* v. *Ferguson* (1896)."

17. **3** Between 1865 and 1900, one effect of the growth of industry in the United States was an increase in the urban population. Cities grew rapidly in the second half of the 1800s due to large-scale immigration as well as rapid industrialization. Between 1865 and 1900, the number of Americans who lived in cities jumped from 6.2 million to over 30 million, which amounted to a shift in the urban population from 20 percent of the total population to 40 percent. This rapid urbanization offered people many opportunities but also brought several problems. Corrupt and inefficient political operations—labeled political machines—became more common in this era. New York City was dominated by the Democratic Party machine, headquartered at Tammany Hall. The most famous Tammany chief was "Boss" William Marcy Tweed. The muckraker journalist Lincoln Steffens exposed urban corruption in *The Shame of the Cities* (1902). Another problem in this era was the proliferation of substandard tenement housing. The wretched living conditions that workers often experienced in tenements were documented in Jacob Riis's book *How the Other Half Lives* (1890).

WRONG CHOICES EXPLAINED:

(1) The growth of industry between 1865 and 1900 did not lead to a decline in trade with other nations. The opposite occurred. Trade with other nations increased as American industrial firms imported greater amounts of raw materials and exported finished products.

(2) The growth of industry between 1865 and 1900 did not lead to a call for lower tariff rates by business leaders. The opposite occurred. American business leaders in the late 19th century called for higher tariff rates on imported goods. This raised prices on imported goods and made American-made products comparably more affordable.

(4) The growth of industry between 1865 and 1900 did not lead corporations to support the growth of labor unions. The opposite occurred. Corporations took steps to limit the influence of unions. These steps included locking out unionized workers, hiring replacement workers (known as "scabs"), forcing workers to sign "yellow dog" contracts (in which the worker agreed to not join a union), and using armed guards to break strikes.

18. **1** The federal government reacted to the Supreme Court's ruling in *Wabash, St. Louis & Pacific Railroad* v. *Illinois* (1886) by passing the Interstate Commerce Act. The Wabash case arose as a result of efforts to regulate railroad rates. Starting in the 1870s, groups organized to promote the interests of farmers, such as the Grange, became concerned about the power and the abuses of large railroad companies. Railroads often overcharged small-scale farmers. The Grange successfully pushed for laws in several states in the 1870s and 1880s to limit abusive practices by railroads. However in the 1886 *Wabash* case, the Supreme Court ruled that Illinois could not regulate railroad rates on rail lines that crossed state boundaries, citing the interstate commerce clause of the Constitution. In response, the federal government created the Interstate Commerce Commission (ICC), the first federal regulatory agency. However, the ICC was chronically underfunded and was, therefore, largely ineffective.

WRONG CHOICES EXPLAINED:
(2) The federal government did not react to the Supreme Court's ruling in *Wabash, St. Louis & Pacific Railroad* v. *Illinois* (1886) by weakening the influence of banks over big business. During the late 1800s, the federal government made no attempts to regulate the banking industry. Later, during the Great Depression of the 1930s, the federal government passed legislation to regulate the banking industry. The Glass-Steagall Act (1933), which was part of President Franklin D. Roosevelt's New Deal, limited how banks could invest their assets and also created the Federal Deposit Insurance Corporation.

(3) The federal government did not react to the Supreme Court's ruling in *Wabash, St. Louis & Pacific Railroad* v. *Illinois* (1886) by abandoning attempts to break up monopolies. During the late 1800s, the federal government first enacted antitrust legislation. In 1890, the federal government passed the Sherman Antitrust Act to break up monopolies. However, the act was used with

limited success. Later, President Woodrow Wilson strengthened the antitrust powers of the federal government with the Clayton Antitrust Act (1914).

(4) The federal government did not react to the Supreme Court's ruling in *Wabash, St. Louis & Pacific Railroad* v. *Illinois* (1886) by encouraging railroad employees to form unions. During the late 1800s, federal government policies and actions tended to side with management over employees in regard to workplace conflicts. In the aftermath of the Pullman Strike (1894), for example, the Supreme Court upheld an injunction issued by the federal government against the strike. The Court ruled in the case *In re Debs* that the government had the right to ensure that interstate commerce not be interrupted and that the United States mail be delivered.

19. **2** In the late 1800s, the corporation became an important form of business organization primarily because it could raise large amounts of investment capital. Individuals must obtain a corporate charter from the state in order to function as a corporation. A corporate model of ownership is different from when a company is owned by a single proprietor or by a small group of proprietors. In the corporate model, individuals may invest in shares in the company that are traded on the open market. These shareholders are, in effect, partial owners of the corporation. In the late 1700s and early 1800s, corporate charters were granted to individuals but mainly on a temporary basis and mainly for a public-oriented purpose, such as building a bridge or a road. After 1810, states began rewriting incorporation laws, allowing for the chartering of businesses. Incorporation encouraged investment into the company and protected the individual investors from liability laws.

WRONG CHOICES EXPLAINED:

(1) Corporations do not necessarily have closer ties with their employees than do companies owned by a sole proprietor. The opposite is often true. Employees tend to have closer ties with the proprietor of a firm than with the members of a board of trustees. Corporate charters allow for the rapid growth of companies and a more impersonal form of management.

(3) Corporations do not necessarily make better quality products than do companies owned by a sole proprietor. The opposite is often true. Quality is determined by a variety of factors. The rise of corporations went hand in hand with the spread of mass-production techniques. Frequently, the products made in large mass-production facilities were inferior to the handmade products made by smaller firms.

(4) Corporations do not necessarily issue calls for conservation of natural resources. The opposite is often true. The growth of large production operations, facilitated by the spread of the corporate model, used increasingly large amounts of natural resources and often caused damage to the natural environment.

20. **2** In the 1896 decision cited in the question, the Supreme Court upheld the constitutionality of Jim Crow laws. The excerpt is from the decision in *Plessy* v. *Ferguson*. The decision stated that segregation was acceptable as long as the facilities for both races were of equal quality—hence "separate, but equal." In the case, the Supreme Court decided that racial segregation did not violate the equal protection provision of the 14th Amendment. It stated, "Laws permitting ... separation" of the races "do not necessarily imply the inferiority" of either race. The decision was a setback for those who sought an end to the Jim Crow system of racial segregation in the South. Jim Crow laws were state and local ordinances that first appeared after Reconstruction ended (1877). Typical laws called for separate schools or separate train cars for African Americans. Opponents of racial segregation argued that Jim Crow laws violated the 14th Amendment (1868), which was alluded to in the first sentence of the excerpt. These opponents stated that Jim Crow laws relegated African Americans to inferior public accommodations and had the effect of making African Americans second-class citizens. The 14th Amendment, ratified during Reconstruction, stated that no person shall be denied "equal protection of the laws." However, the Court disagreed. The "separate but equal" doctrine allowed for the continuation of the Jim Crow system until the 1950s and 1960s. The beginning of the end to the system came with the *Brown* v. *the Board of Education of Topeka* decision of 1954.

WRONG CHOICES EXPLAINED:

(1) In the 1896 decision cited in the question, the Supreme Court was not upholding the constitutionality of the Three-fifths Compromise. The compromise, arrived at during the Constitutional Convention (1787), settled the issue of how slaves would be counted when figuring out a state's representation in the House of Representatives. The Three-fifths Compromise stipulated that slaves, labeled "other persons" in the Constitution, would be counted as three-fifths of a person in the census. This compromise, however, was a moot point by 1896 because slavery had ended with the ratification of the 13th Amendment (1865).

(3) In the 1896 decision cited in the question, the Supreme Court was not upholding the constitutionality of the affirmative action programs. Affirmative action programs were not proposed until well after 1896. They began in the mid-1960s primarily as a way to increase economic and educational opportunities for minorities. The movement for affirmative action occurred after the civil rights movement successfully pushed for an end to legal segregation. In many ways, affirmative action was the next step in the struggle for civil rights. The impact of the *Plessy* decision was to uphold racial discrimination, not to rectify it.

(4) In the 1896 decision cited in the question, the Supreme Court was not upholding the constitutionality of racial integration. The decision did the

opposite; it upheld the constitutionality of racial segregation. Later, the Supreme Court did rule that segregation was unconstitutional. The landmark *Brown* v. Board of Education of Topeka decision (1954) declared segregated schools to be inherently unfair and ordered states and communities to take measures to undo this system.

21. **3** The foreign policy illustrated in the cartoon was used by the United States to secure control of land for the Panama Canal Zone. The building of the Panama Canal was a major goal of President Theodore Roosevelt, who is featured in the cartoon. The United States had recently obtained Puerto Rico, the Philippines, and other colonies after the Spanish-American War (1898). Traveling from the east coast of the United States or the Caribbean Sea to the Philippines or other Pacific Ocean possessions took a great deal of time and effort. Merchant ships and naval ships had to travel around the southern tip of South America to reach the Pacific Ocean. Roosevelt used unorthodox means to obtain land for the canal. Before 1903, Panama was a region of Colombia. When Colombia refused the U.S. offer of $10 million to build a canal, American investors, with the backing of President Roosevelt and the U.S. military, instigated a "rebellion" in Panama against Colombia. Panama became an independent country and immediately reached a deal with the United States to build a canal. This deal is alluded to in the cartoon by the "New Treaty" flag. The cartoon depicts President Roosevelt as tossing dirt onto Bogota, the Colombian capital. The cartoonist approvingly describes the dirt tossed by the president as being symbolic of "The News Reaches Bogota." The president himself was equally unapologetic about American actions in regard to Colombia; he later boasted that he "took Panama."

WRONG CHOICES EXPLAINED:
(1) The foreign policy illustrated in the cartoon did not result in the United States punishing Mexico for siding with Germany in World War I. There was some concern about Mexico joining Germany in World War I after the United States became aware of the Zimmerman note (1917), in which German foreign secretary Arthur Zimmerman indicated that Germany would help Mexico regain territory it had lost to the United States if Mexico joined the war on Germany's side. However, Mexico stayed out of World War I. The references to Bogota, rather than to Mexico City, indicate the subject of the cartoon is the Panama Canal, not Mexican foreign policy.

(2) The foreign policy illustrated in the cartoon did not result in the United States enforcing the Monroe Doctrine against Great Britain. The major purpose of the Monroe Doctrine (1823) was to limit European influence in the Western

Hemisphere. President Monroe was alarmed at threats by the Holy Alliance of Russia, Prussia, and Austria to restore Spain's lost American colonies. He also opposed a decree by the Russian czar that claimed all the Pacific northwest above the 51st parallel. By 1903, the United States did not have reason to be concerned about British actions in the Western Hemisphere.

(4) The foreign policy illustrated in the cartoon did not result in the United States announcing the Open Door policy. The Open Door policy was put forth by President William McKinley's Secretary of State John Hay (1899) in regard to China. Earlier, the major European powers had established spheres of influence in China. Each European power declared that it had exclusive trading privileges in its sphere of influence. Since the United States did not have a sphere of influence in China, the United States asserted that all of China should be open to trade with all nations. The European nations begrudgingly accepted this concept. The references to Bogota, rather than to Beijing (or Peking, as it was spelled in English at the time), indicate that the cartoon refers to the Panama Canal, not the Open Door Policy.

22. **4** The 1917 poster indicates that one important educational goal for new immigrants during that time period was promoting the English language as a method of assimilation. The poster was published by the Cleveland Americanization Committee. Such committees were part of a large-scale, nationwide Americanization movement in the 1910s. The movement was successful in pressuring over 30 states to pass laws requiring programs to assimilate immigrants. The movement focused on the learning of English and on exposure to particular American cultural values. In addition, the movement frequently condemned expressions of "foreign" cultural practices. Although some participants in the movement were motivated by a desire to help newly arrived immigrants, the movement was widely seen as xenophobic. Many supporters of Americanization also pushed for laws restricting the flow of immigrants into the United States, leading to the passage of the Emergency Quota Act of 1921 and the Immigration Act of 1924. Immigrants themselves were of different minds in regard to attempts at assimilation. Many embraced the cultural ways of their new land, but many also sought to retain elements of their native cultures and a sense of ethnic solidarity. In New York, Chicago, and other large cities, foreign language papers emerged, such as the Yiddish-language *Jewish Daily Forward* and the Italian-language *Il Progresso Italo-Americano*. Neighborhoods in New York became increasingly defined by ethnicity, such as Little Italy and the Jewish Lower East Side. Immigrant groups established savings institutions, insurance programs, choruses, political organizations, and summer camps.

WRONG CHOICES EXPLAINED:

(1) The 1917 poster does not indicate that an important educational goal for new immigrants during that time period was teaching them to read and write in their native language. The Americanization movement focused on the opposite—teaching immigrants to read and write in English. The movement often called for the suppression of foreign languages in schools.

(2) The 1917 poster does not indicate that an important educational goal for new immigrants during that time period was promoting religious tolerance. The poster does not allude to religion. Some individuals in the Americanization movement promoted Protestantism and denigrated Catholicism, Judaism, and other religions.

(3) The 1917 poster does not indicate that an important educational goal for new immigrants during that time period was ensuring the preservation of their native cultures. The Americanization movement encouraged immigrants to abandon their native cultures. Many immigrants preserved elements of their native culture despite the prodding of the Americanization movement.

23. **3** The United States became directly involved in World War I as a result of Germany's resumption of unrestricted submarine warfare. When World War I began in 1914, President Woodrow Wilson initially assumed that the United States could stay neutral and maintain commercial ties with nations on both sides of the conflict. However, Great Britain successfully blocked American ships from reaching Germany. Out of necessity, American trade shifted to Great Britain exclusively. Germany responded by warning that American ships in the waters off of Great Britain would be subject to attack by U-boats, or submarines. The sinking of the British ocean liner *Lusitania* infuriated many Americans (128 Americans were among the dead). Germany, however, wanted to keep the United States out of the war and agreed in the Sussex Pledge (1916) to make no surprise submarine attacks on American ships. The United States took advantage of this pledge and traded extensively with Great Britain. In 1917, Germany rescinded the Sussex Pledge and declared that it would resume unrestricted submarine warfare. Soon after, the United States declared war on Germany.

WRONG CHOICES EXPLAINED:

(1) The entrance of the United States into World War I in 1917 was not prompted by Germany's negotiation of an alliance with Russia. Such an alliance did not occur. Russia and Germany fought on opposite sides in the war until Russia withdrew from the war. Russian forces, fighting under the provisional government, were defeated in July 1917. After the Bolsheviks took power in November 1917, Vladimir Lenin withdrew Russia from the war. Russia and Germany signed the

Treaty of Brest-Litovsk in March 1918, but they did not form an alliance. These events occurred after the United States had entered the war (April 1917).

(2) The entrance of the United States into World War I in 1917 was not prompted by Germany's threat to spread the war to the Middle East. Fighting did occur in the Middle East as early as 1914. The main combatant in the Middle East on the side of the Central Powers was the Ottoman Empire. The British, Russians, and French were the main combatants on the side of the Allied Powers.

(4) The entrance of the United States into World War I in 1917 was not prompted by Germany's acquisition of new African colonies. Germany had established colonies in Africa before World War I, mostly in the 1880s. It did not acquire new colonies during World War I.

24. **4** Progressivism was an early 20th-century movement that promoted government actions to correct political, economic, and social problems. Progressivism existed at the grassroots level as well as in the corridors of power. The movement claimed many legislative victories and ultimately influenced both the New Deal and 20th-century liberalism. In the political realm, Progressives hoped to expand democratic participation and limit the power of corrupt and inefficient political machines. They pushed for states to adopt the initiative, referendum, and recall to increase the power of voters over the political process. The initiative would enable citizens to introduce a bill to the local or state legislature by petition. The referendum would allow people to vote directly on proposed legislation. The recall would allow the populace to remove elected officials before their term ended. In the economic realm, Progressives challenged the abuses of unbridled capitalism. Reformers were successful in pushing Congress to pass the Keating-Owens Act (1916), which regulated child labor, but the act was struck down by the Supreme Court two years later. Progressive reformers also challenged the practices and shear power of large monopolies and trusts in various industries. The Clayton Antitrust Act (1914) was part of the agenda of Progressive reformers. In the social realm, Progressives pushed for legislation on the state and local level to regulate housing conditions. Also, many Progressives addressed what they perceived as the problem of excessive drinking of alcoholic beverages. They were successful in pushing for the 18th Amendment (1919), which banned the production, transport, and sale of alcohol as of January 1, 1920.

WRONG CHOICES EXPLAINED:

(1) Progressivism did not promote limited war to spread social justice to other countries. Progressives were divided on whether or not to support American intervention in World War I. Some did believe that America could use the war to spread democracy. However, World War I was not a limited war, nor was military engagement central to the Progressive agenda.

(2) Progressivism did not promote increased immigration to diversify the nation's population. Some Progressives formed alliances with working-class immigrant communities. However, many were active in the Nativist movement, which sought to limit immigration into the United States. This movement was successful in pushing for passage of the Emergency Quota Act of 1921 and the Immigration Act of 1924.

(3) Progressivism did not promote colonialism to increase American power in the world. Progressives were divided on whether or not to support American colonialism. Some saw it as a way to bring "civilization" and "uplift" to the peoples of the world. Others saw it as an expression of power and domination over other peoples.

25. **1** The Supreme Court gave its approval to limiting the First Amendment rights of antiwar protestors by establishing the "clear and present danger" doctrine in *Schenck v. United States* (1919). The decision in the *Schenck* case upheld the Espionage and Sedition Acts passed during World War I to put limits on public expressions of antiwar sentiment. Charles Schenck and other members of the Socialist Party were arrested for printing and distributing flyers opposing the war and for urging young men to resist the draft. The Supreme Court argued that freedom of speech is not absolute and that the government is justified in limiting certain forms of speech during wartime. The Court argued that certain utterances pose a "clear and present danger." By analogy, the Court asserted that one is not allowed to shout "Fire!" falsely in a crowded theater.

WRONG CHOICES EXPLAINED:

(2) The "clear and present danger" doctrine, established by the Supreme Court in *Schenck* v. *United States* (1919), is not related to rejecting membership in the League of Nations. The United States did reject membership in the League of Nations when the Senate failed to ratify the Treaty of Versailles in 1920. President Woodrow Wilson pushed for the United States to approve the treaty. However, some senators wanted to isolate the United States from world affairs and opposed membership in the League. These isolationists were numerous enough to prevent the Senate from reaching the two-thirds vote necessary to ratify treaties.

(3) The "clear and present danger" doctrine, established by the Supreme Court in *Schenck* v. *United States* (1919), is not related to banning immigration from western Europe. In the 1920s, the United States did pass legislation greatly reducing the number of immigrants allowed into the country. The Emergency Quota Act (1921) and the National Origins Act (1924) established immigration quotas for different nations based on the number of each national group present in the United States decades earlier.

(4) The "clear and present danger" doctrine, established by the Supreme Court in *Schenck* v. *United States* (1919), is not related to passage of the Prohibition amendment. Prohibition, which was the outlawing of the production, sale, and consumption of alcoholic beverages, became the law of the land with the ratification of the 18th Amendment to the Constitution in 1919. It ended when the 21st Amendment (1933) repealed Prohibition.

26. **3** Hosting the Washington Naval Disarmament Conference (1921) and signing the Kellogg-Briand Pact (1928) were efforts by the United States to avoid future wars. The presidents of the 1920s attempted to isolate the United States from world affairs and to reduce spending on war munitions. President Warren Harding successfully pressed for a reduction of naval power among Britain, France, Japan, Italy, and the United States at the Washington Naval Conference in 1921. Later, President Calvin Coolidge continued to pursue an isolationist foreign policy and helped to negotiate the Kellogg-Briand Pact (1928). The United States was one of 63 nations to sign the pact, which renounced war in principle. Because the pact was negotiated outside of the League of Nations, it was unenforceable, rendering it meaningless.

WRONG CHOICES EXPLAINED:
(1) Hosting the Washington Naval Disarmament Conference (1921) and signing the Kellogg-Briand Pact (1928) were not efforts by the United States to form new military alliances. Both actions required cooperation among nations, but neither resulted in the formation of a new military alliance. The actions were expressions of isolationism; forming a military alliance would have been an expression of engagement in world affairs.
(2) Hosting the Washington Naval Disarmament Conference (1921) and signing the Kellogg-Briand Pact (1928) were not efforts by the United States to increase its military preparedness. Both actions were driven by a desire to reduce military budgets by reducing the risk of war.
(4) Hosting the Washington Naval Disarmament Conference (1921) and signing the Kellogg-Briand Pact (1928) were not efforts by the United States to collect payment for war debts. The Dawes Plan of 1924 was an effort by the United States to collect payment for war debts. The Treaty of Versailles (1919) stipulated that Germany be punished by having to pay war reparations to the victorious European powers. Under the Dawes Plan, the United States extended loans to Germany so that Germany could pay war reparations to Great Britain and France. Great Britain and France would then have funds to retire wartime debts to the United States.

27. **2** The Harlem Renaissance of the 1920s is best known for promoting the cultural creativity of African Americans. The Harlem Renaissance was a literary, artistic, and intellectual movement that celebrated African-American life and forged a new cultural identity among African-American people. The movement was centered in the African-American neighborhood of Harlem, in New York City. Contributions included the poetry of Langston Hughes, Claude McKay, and Countee Cullen and the jazz music of Louis Armstrong, Duke Ellington, and Bessie Smith. Some of Hughes' important poems include "Harlem," "The Negro Speaks of Rivers," and "I, Too, Sing America." Duke Ellington was a composer, pianist and bandleader who was perhaps the most important figure in 20th-century jazz. Some of his most important compositions are "Mood Indigo," "Don't Get Around Much Anymore," and "Take the A Train."

WRONG CHOICES EXPLAINED:

(1) The Harlem Renaissance was not focused on ending racial segregation in public facilities. Much of Harlem Renaissance art was political in nature, but the movement was more creative than political. The civil rights movement, which reached its peak in the 1950s and 1960s, challenged the Jim Crow system of racial segregation. The events in the movement include the Supreme Court decision in *Brown* v. *Board of Education of Topeka* (1954), the Montgomery bus boycott in 1956, the lunch counter sit-ins in 1960, the Freedom Rides in 1962, and the March on Washington in 1963.

(3) The Harlem Renaissance was not focused on encouraging passage of new voting rights legislation. Much of Harlem Renaissance art was political in nature, but the movement was more creative than political. The civil rights movement, which reached its peak in the 1950s and 1960s, pushed for voting rights for African Americans. A major march to raise awareness of the issue of voting rights was scheduled for March 1965. The participants began in Selma, Alabama, and marched 54 miles to Montgomery, Alabama. Unfortunately, the police acted violently against the marchers. The incident, known as "Bloody Sunday," was broadcast on national television and aroused indignation among many Americans. It was in this context that President Lyndon Johnson pushed Congress to pass the Voting Rights Act of 1965.

(4) The Harlem Renaissance was not focused on supporting legislation to eliminate the Ku Klux Klan. Much of the Harlem Renaissance art was political in nature, but the movement was more creative than political. Earlier, in 1870 and 1871, Congress passed three Enforcement Acts that protected the basic rights of African Americans. These acts, also known as the Ku Klux Klan Acts, specifically targeted the Klan for using violence and terrorism to prevent African Americans from exercising their rights as citizens. By 1872, the Klan had largely been defeated. The actions of the federal government reduced racial violence throughout the South.

In the 20th century, racial violence increased. A new Ku Klux Klan was born (1915) and, by the 1920s, was a genuine mass movement. However, the federal government did not take action against the organization this time.

28. **1** The efficiencies created by the assembly line best account for the affordability of Ford Model T automobiles in the 1920s. In 1913, Henry Ford opened a plant with a continuous conveyor belt. The belt moved the chassis of the car from worker to worker so that each did a small task in the process of assembling the final product. This mass production technique reduced the price of Ford's Model T car and also dealt a blow to the skilled mechanics who previously built automobiles. Unskilled assembly line workers gradually replaced skilled craft workers in American industry. The production and consumption of mass-produced goods stoked the American economy for much of the 1920s. New products captured the public's imagination, and new production techniques increased industrial output. If the quality of work deteriorated for factory workers in the 1920s, the availability of consumer goods to average workers greatly increased. Cars, radios, toasters, health and beauty aids, and other consumer goods filled the shelves of stores. Eventually, consumption of mass-produced goods just could not keep up with production. Manufacturers made the logical decision of beginning layoffs. Of course, unemployed workers had even less ability to purchase goods. Thus, a spiral of economic problems began that resulted in the Great Depression of the 1930s.

WRONG CHOICES EXPLAINED:

(2) The affordability of Model T Fords in the 1920s is unrelated to the expertise of individual craftsmanship. The main factor in the reduction in price of Ford automobiles—the use of the assembly line and mass production techniques—undermined individual craftsmanship and rendered trained mechanics obsolete.

(3) The affordability of Model T Fords in the 1920s is unrelated to strong support from labor unions. Henry Ford was strongly antiunion. Ford used unskilled workers in the assembly line process rather than trained mechanics. These unskilled workers were easier to replace and, therefore, more difficult to organize into a union. Ford was the last major car manufacturer to sign a contract with the United Auto Workers (1941).

(4) The affordability of Model T Fords in the 1920s is unrelated to low taxes and government subsidies. Taxes for corporations were reduced in the 1920s, but this was not the primary reason for the affordability of the Model T. The tax rate was uniform throughout the automobile industry. Instead, it was Ford's mass-produced cars that initiated the trend toward lower prices. The government did not advance subsidies to the Ford Corporation in the 1920s.

29. **1** The idea of rugged individualism would best be supported by President Hoover's statement. Hoover was arguing against expanding the role of government in the economy. He asserted that government intervention would result in the "destruction of character." Rather, he urged people to rely on themselves and on their communities to triumph over economic difficulties and to become "masters of their own destiny." Hoover reflected a laissez-faire approach to the economy, which asserts that government interference in the economy should be as limited as possible. The French phrase *laissez-faire* means "to let alone." Throughout much of the history of the United States, Americans were suspicious of government intervention into the economy. However, by the 20th century, the country began to face serious economic problems that called into question the laissez-faire doctrine. In the early decades of the 20th century, progressive reformers pushed for greater government involvement in the economy to reign in capitalism—to break up monopolies, to regulate the food production industry, to help the poor, and to create peace between owners and workers. Hoover, and the other Republican presidents of the 1920s, sought to return to a laissez-faire approach. When the economy spiraled out of control starting in 1929 and millions of American were afflicted by poverty, hunger, and unemployment, Hoover still argued for "rugged individualism." Hoover did implement the far-reaching Reconstruction Finance Corporation (1932), which provided needed funds to key components of the economy. By the election of 1932, many Americans came to believe that Hoover did not do enough to help ordinary Americans. He lost the election to the Democratic candidate, Franklin D. Roosevelt.

WRONG CHOICES EXPLAINED:

(2) President Hoover's statement did not support the idea of unemployment insurance. Hoover was arguing against such government programs—against "leaning upon government to solve all the problems before us." Unemployment insurance is a government program that provides temporary cash payments to people who become unemployed through no fault of their own. During the Great Depression, Wisconsin created such a program (1932) before President Franklin D. Roosevelt enacted the first federal unemployment insurance program as part of the Social Security Act (1935).

(3) President Hoover's statement did not support the idea of deficit spending. Hoover was arguing against expanding the role of the federal government. Limiting government spending would decrease, not increase, the federal deficit. On the other hand, President Franklin D. Roosevelt's set of government programs, known as the New Deal, increased the federal deficit. Roosevelt, who took office in 1933, was influenced by the thinking of economist John Maynard Keynes. Keynes argued

that deficit spending by the government was acceptable, and even desirable, as a means of increasing overall demand and stimulating economic activity.

(4) President Hoover's statement did not support the idea of collective bargaining. Collective bargaining refers to the act of all the workers in a shop negotiating together, through a union, for better wages, better conditions, and shorter hours. The Republican presidents of the 1920s generally supported anti-union policies. Later, President Franklin D. Roosevelt (1933–1945) pushed for passage of the Wagner Act (1935), which defined "collective bargaining" as a legal right of workers in the United States. Roosevelt encouraged workers to join unions so that their wages and "purchasing power" would rise.

30. **4** The two statements illustrate a difference of opinion between the two presidents over expanding the federal government's roles in the economy. The context of both statements is the Great Depression. The Great Depression was the most devastating economic downturn in American history. Between 1929 and 1933, wages fell by 60 percent and unemployment tripled to over 12 million people. With no safety net in place, families were forced out of their homes. President Herbert Hoover (1929–1933) expressed skepticism about the usefulness of government intervention during this economic crisis. He urged people to "fight their own battles" and to be "masters of their own destiny." He was arguing for a laissez-faire, or a hands-off, approach in regard to economic policy. President Franklin D. Roosevelt (1933–1945), on the other hand, was arguing for an expansion of the role of the government in the economy. He proposed a set of programs, known as the New Deal, to address the economic crisis of the 1930s. The Roosevelt administration provided direct relief, or what would be known as Temporary Assistance for Needy Families (TANF) today, to millions of families. In addition, the New Deal included jobs programs such as the Civilian Conservation Corps (1933), which focused on young men, and the vast Works Progress Administration (1935) or WPA, which consisted of a myriad of public projects. The WPA built schools, installed sewer lines, wrote guidebooks, and produced theatrical productions. Also, the New Deal addressed the welfare of retired people and people with disabilities by creating the Social Security system in 1935.

WRONG CHOICES EXPLAINED:
(1) The two statements do not discuss granting subsidies to big business. Throughout history, the government has extended subsidies to big business in a variety of ways. Such subsidies included land grants to railroad companies in the late 1800s. More recently, subsidies included tax breaks, tax loopholes, bailouts, regulatory decisions, and direct cash subsidies. Supporters of such measures argued that these subsidies promoted economic growth; opponents argued that they were wasteful and amounted to "corporate welfare."

(2) The two statements do not discuss promoting free-trade policies in the Western Hemisphere. Later, President Bill Clinton promoted free-trade policies in the Western Hemisphere. The North America Free Trade Agreement (NAFTA), which was ratified by Congress in 1993, eliminated all trade barriers and tariffs among the United States, Canada, and Mexico. NAFTA was the subject of much controversy when it was promoted by Clinton. Free trade supporters promised global prosperity as more nations participated in the global economy. Opponents worried that nations would no longer be able to implement environmental regulations, ensure workers' rights, or protect fledging industries from foreign competition.

(3) The two statements do not discuss regulating supply and demand. President Hoover's business-friendly economic policies are often labeled supply-side economics. The theory is that if there is growth in the supply side—in regard to manufacturers, banks, and insurance companies—there will be a general economic revival and the benefits of a robust economy will trickle down to everyone. The alternative approach is to stimulate the demand side—consumers. Demand-side economics emphasize government policies designed to increase workers' wages and benefits, such as welfare and unemployment benefits. President Roosevelt tended to favor demand-side policies.

31. **3** One of the first problems President Franklin D. Roosevelt addressed was bringing stability to the banking system. When Roosevelt took office in 1933, many people had lost confidence in the banking system and had withdrawn their money in fears that their bank might fold. With thousands of people withdrawing their money at the same time, many banks actually did fold, turning their fear into a self-fulfilling prophecy. The Emergency Banking Act (1933), which was passed during Roosevelt's first week in office, closed down the banking system in the United States for four days. During this "bank holiday," the Federal Reserve Bank guaranteed that it would supply banks with currency when they reopened. This action restored people's faith in the banking system and stopped the runs on banks that were destabilizing the system. Later in 1933, Roosevelt signed the Glass-Steagall Act, which created the Federal Deposit Insurance Corporation (FDIC). The FDIC insures deposits so that if a bank does fold, people will not lose their savings.

WRONG CHOICES EXPLAINED:

(1) Ending the Red Scare was not a problem addressed by President Franklin D. Roosevelt. The Red Scare of the post–World War I era was a crusade against suspected communists, anarchists, labor leaders, and other radicals. The Bolshevik Revolution in Russia in 1917, the backlash against the large strike wave of 1919, and the virulent strain of patriotism unleashed by World War I all

set the groundwork for the Red Scare. Anticommunist sentiment continued to exist in the United States during Roosevelt's time in office (and beyond), but the most intense phase of the Red Scare was over by 1920.

(2) Standing up to dictators in Europe was not a problem addressed by President Franklin D. Roosevelt in his fist months in office in 1933. Throughout much of the 1930s, Roosevelt focused his administration's energy on the Great Depression. In addition, isolationist sentiment remained strong in the United States despite the rise of aggressive, dictatorial regimes in Germany and Italy. In the Neutrality Acts of 1935 to 1937, Congress made clear that neither the United States government nor private U.S. firms were to trade with belligerent nations. Roosevelt grew frustrated with these acts because they did not make a distinction between aggressors and victims in the conflicts of the 1930s. A later Neutrality Act (1939) allowed the United States to supply the opponents of fascism with materials on a cash-and-carry basis.

(4) Approving bonus payments to World War I veterans was not a problem addressed by President Franklin D. Roosevelt in his first months in office in 1933. The payment of bonuses was a contentious issue during the administration of Herbert Hoover (1929–1933). In June 1932, during the depths of the Great Depression, a group of World War I veterans, who called themselves the Bonus Expeditionary Force (BEF), or Bonus Army, marched into Washington, D.C. to demand a bonus that they had been promised for their service in the military. About 50,000 men, mostly unemployed and poor, set up an encampment in the nation's capital to demand their money. The handling of the Bonus Marchers—which included aggressively dismantling the encampment—seemed to reinforce many people's perception of President Hoover that he did not have the interests of ordinary Americans at heart. In 1935, Congress overrode President Roosevelt's veto and paid the veterans their bonus nine years early.

32. **3** The 1941 slogan by the America First Committee, "National Defense at Any Expense, but Keep Our Boys at Home," promoted isolationism. Throughout the 1930s, isolationists pushed for American neutrality in regard to the aggressive actions of Germany, Italy, and Japan. Many Americans remembered the horrors of World War I. In addition, the Senate's Nye committee (1934–1937) uncovered evidence that certain American corporations greatly profited from World War I. Americans wondered if the so-called merchants of death had pushed the country into World War I. Once World War II began, many Americans came to understand the gravity of the situation and began to side with the nations fighting against fascism. With this shift in public opinion and with his victory in the presidential election of 1940, President Franklin D. Roosevelt was ready to take more direct action. In March 1941, Congress approved his Lend-Lease Act, which allowed the United States to ship armaments to Britain in American ships. Although officially neutral,

the United States was moving steadily toward intervening on the side of Great Britain. The public, however, was not unified in its support of intervention. Isolationists, such as the renowned aviator Charles Lindbergh, continued to argue against any U.S. steps toward helping Britain. He was a leader of the America First Committee and, historians argue, a Nazi sympathizer. Even as late as 1941, many Americans still clearly had major reservations about America entering World War II. Debates about intervention ended abruptly on December 7, 1941. Japanese planes attacked the U.S. base at Pearl Harbor, Hawaii. Almost immediately, the United States entered World War II. With American involvement in World War II, the isolationist position was largely silenced.

WRONG CHOICES EXPLAINED:

(1) The America First Committee slogan, "National Defense at Any Expense, but Keep Our Boys at Home," did not promote globalism. As World War II began, the committee urged the United States to pursue an isolationist policy and stay out of the war. Globalism involves the opposite sentiment—greater involvement in global issues.

(2) The America First Committee slogan, "National Defense at Any Expense, but Keep Our Boys at Home," did not promote protective tariffs. Isolationists often support higher tariff rates, but the slogan does not refer to trade or tariffs.

(4) The America First Committee slogan, "National Defense at Any Expense, but Keep Our Boys at Home," did not promote reduced military spending. Although the committee was isolationist, it did endorse military expenditures. The slogan argues for "national defense at any expense."

33. **4** The main idea of the cartoon is that President Franklin D. Roosevelt is determined to supply the United States military and its allies with whatever it takes to defeat the Axis powers. In a 1940 speech, Roosevelt pledged that the United States would become the "arsenal for democracy" in the fight against fascism and militarism. To meet this pledge and reiterated by Roosevelt in the cartoon, the United States would have to step up its production of war-related materials dramatically and rapidly. In 1942, Roosevelt created the War Production Board, and later the Office of War Mobilization, to oversee the conversion from civilian industry to war production. Almost overnight, the persistent unemployment of the 1930s ended. After the United States entered the war in December 1941, the country faced the opposite problem—labor shortages. With millions of men and hundreds of thousands of women in the armed forces, the Roosevelt administration took several important steps to ensure a sufficient supply of factory workers. The government made a concerted effort to recruit women to participate in the war effort. Many recruiting posters were produced by the government, usually through the Office of War Information, showing women in industrial settings. The fictional

Rosie the Riveter character was often featured in this public relations campaign. Female workers were presented in a positive light—helping the nation as well as the men in combat abroad. Such a campaign was needed because prewar societal mores discouraged women from doing industrial work. During the Great Depression of the 1930s, women were encouraged to leave the job market so that there would be enough jobs available for male "breadwinners." The World War II recruiting campaign was successful. By 1945, one-third of the work force was female.

WRONG CHOICES EXPLAINED:

(1) The cartoon is not asserting that United States factories will not be able to manufacture military supplies in sufficient quantities. President Roosevelt says, "They're going to get it," in regard to military equipment for the United States military and its allies. The cartoon echoes Roosevelt's resolve; it says, "And he doesn't mean maybe!"

(2) The cartoon is not asserting that the federal government will most likely need to seize ownership of manufacturing plants. The cartoon doesn't allude to government seizures of factories. The government organized the conversion from civilian industry to war production with the War Production Board, and later the Office of War Mobilization. However, manufacturing plants stayed in private hands.

(3) The cartoon is not asserting that President Franklin D. Roosevelt expects other nations to supply the same amount of armaments as the United States. The cartoon focuses on Roosevelt's vow to supply the allies with armaments; it does not allude to the contributions of other nations.

34. **1** One major result of the production efforts described in the cartoon was that the high unemployment of the Great Depression was greatly reduced. In many ways, World War II, rather than the New Deal, ended the Great Depression. Unemployment fell from over 14 percent in 1940 to less than 2 percent for the last three years of the war—1943 to 1945. The United States began producing military equipment and ammunition when World War II started in 1939. War production spiked after the United States became involved in the war in late 1941. America's gross national product (GNP), which measures the total value of all goods produced and services provided by a country during a given year, rose steadily during the war years.

WRONG CHOICES EXPLAINED:

(2) The production efforts described in the cartoon did not result in producers of war-related materials going out of business after World War II. The United States successfully made the transition from a wartime economy to

a peacetime economy. Factories efficiently converted to the production of consumer goods, fueling robust economic growth in the 1950s and 1960s.

(3) The production efforts described in the cartoon did not result in critics claiming that president Franklin D. Roosevelt was abusing his treaty-making power. The production of war-related materials did not require the signing of a treaty. Further, the steps that Roosevelt took in regard to World War II, including the cash-and-carry policy, the Lend-Lease Act (1941), and the declaration of war all took place with the endorsement of Congress.

(4) The production efforts described in the cartoon did not result in the military having difficulty enlisting soldiers because the men were working in the munitions factories. A substantial number of men and women volunteered to participate in World War II. Over six million men and women enlisted in the armed services during the war. This accounts for almost 40 percent of the personnel in the armed services; the other 60 percent were drafted.

35. **1** The 1947 newspaper headlines concerning Jackie Robinson indicate that Robinson's integration of major league baseball was an important event in the history of civil rights. Robinson was the first African American to play major league baseball in the modern era. He began his major league career with the Brooklyn Dodgers in 1947. The headlines are generally positive in regard to Robinson's debut in major league baseball. One headline notes that the crowd of 26,000 cheered for Robinson when he scored a run. Another called the event "historic." Robinson met with a great deal of racist anger during his first year in major league baseball. Players on the St. Louis Cardinals threatened to go on strike if Robinson took the field for the Dodgers. In a famous incident during the 1948 season, fans in Cincinnati booed Robinson and shouted racist epithets at him before a game. In the face of this abuse, Robinson's teammate Pee Wee Reese put his arm around Robinson on the field in an act of solidarity. In the 1950s, Robinson publicly supported the civil rights movement and urged President Dwight D. Eisenhower to take action to resolve the crisis around the desegregation of public schools in Little Rock, Arkansas, in 1957.

WRONG CHOICES EXPLAINED:

(2) The 1947 headlines do not indicate that Jackie Robinson went on to organize the civil rights movement. Robinson supported the civil rights movement. He wrote a letter to President Dwight D. Eisenhower during the crisis over the integration of public schools in Little Rock, Arkansas, in 1957, urging the president to take action in defense of integration. However, Robinson was not an organizer of the movement.

(3) The 1947 headlines do not indicate that sports fans overwhelmingly encouraged the desegregation of public facilities. The headlines show that many

fans supported Robinson. However, they do not indicate either support or opposition to the broader issue of the desegregation of public facilities.

(4) The 1947 headlines do not indicate that Robinson's major league debut had no impact on race relations in the United States. One headline describes Robinson's debut as "historic." The extensive coverage of the event on the front page of the paper reflects the significance the paper placed on Robinson's debut in the major leagues.

36. **3** Winston Churchill's observation that an "iron curtain" had fallen across Europe warned the United States that Europe was threatened by the expansion of communism in Eastern Europe. This 1946 speech was one of several events that indicated that a Cold War had begun between the United States and the Soviet Union. In the following year, 1947, President Harry Truman announced that the United States would commit itself to containing communist expansion in Europe. Following World War II, the United States became increasingly alarmed with the expansionistic actions of the Soviet Union. The Soviet Red Army had pushed German troops out of Eastern Europe during the war, but Soviet troops did not evacuate this region once Germany surrendered. The Soviet Red Army stayed in Hungary, Romania, Bulgaria, Czechoslovakia, Poland, and the newly created East Germany. The Soviet Union installed communist regimes in those countries. The United States was alarmed at these moves but was unwilling to begin a third world war to push out the Soviets. However, the United States was determined not to tolerate the establishment of communist regimes beyond the "iron curtain." The term "containment" was coined after World War II to describe this policy. Truman put the idea of containment into practice in 1947 by providing $400 million in military aid to Greece and Turkey to prevent those countries from becoming communist. Other elements in the containment strategy were the Marshall Plan (1948), the Berlin Airlift (1948–1949), and the Korean War (1950–1953).

WRONG CHOICES EXPLAINED:

(1) The "iron curtain" speech by Winston Churchill was not intended to warn the United States that Europe was threatened by an embargo of its Middle East oil supplies. Much later, in 1973, the Organization of Petroleum Exporting Countries (OPEC), comprised of the Arab oil-producing nations, cut off oil exports to the United States and increased the price of oil. These moves were in retaliation for the United States' support for Israel in the 1973 Yom Kippur War between Israel and its Arab neighbors.

(2) The "iron curtain" speech by Winston Churchill was not intended to warn the United States that Europe was threatened by the growth of fascism in Great Britain. Fascist movements existed in the 1930s and 1940s in Great Britain, but

these movements represented a minority of the British population. Such fringe movements continued to exist after the war, as they did in many of the democracies of Western Europe as well as in the United States.

(4) The "iron curtain" speech by Winston Churchill was not intended to warn the United States that Europe was threatened by a nuclear attack by the Soviet Union. The United States had a monopoly on nuclear weapons at the time of Churchill's speech (1946). The Soviet Union did not successfully test a nuclear weapon until 1951.

37. **3** The North Atlantic Treaty Organization (NATO) and the Warsaw Pact are examples of mutual defense. The United States and the Soviet Union emerged at the end of World War II as rival superpowers in the Cold War. The Soviet Union occupied the nations of Eastern Europe after the war. The United Stated was worried that the Soviet Union would try to push into Western Europe. The leader of the Soviet Union, Joseph Stalin, insisted that he wanted to have only friendly nations on the border of the Soviet Union. In order to block any further aggression by the Soviet Union, Truman issued the Truman Doctrine, in which he said that the goal of the United States would be to contain communism. Toward this end, the United States extended military aid to Greece and Turkey (1947) and economic aid to the war-ravaged nations of Western Europe in the form of the Marshall Plan (1948). In 1948, the United States decided to challenge the Soviet blockade of West Berlin. In addition, the United States was one of the founding members of NATO in 1949. This marked the first time that the United States joined a peacetime alliance. The idea of mutual defense means that members of NATO view an attack on any one member as an attack on all members. In response, the Soviet Union organized the Warsaw Pact in 1955, a mutual defense alliance between the Soviet Union and the communist nations of Eastern and Central Europe.

WRONG CHOICES EXPLAINED:
(1) The North Atlantic Treaty Organization and the Warsaw Pact are not examples of dollar diplomacy. Dollar diplomacy describes the policy, put forth by President William Howard Taft (1909–1913), of protecting the United States' commercial interests in the Caribbean rather than pursuing strategic military goals.

(2) The North Atlantic Treaty Organization and the Warsaw Pact are not examples of Lend-Lease. The Lend-Lease Act (March 1941) was a measure initiated by President Franklin D. Roosevelt to extend military aid to Great Britain during World War II before the United States entered the conflict. Later in 1941, the United States entered the conflict following the Japanese attack on American territory—the naval base at Pearl Harbor, Hawaii (December 1941).

(4) The North Atlantic Treaty Organization and the Warsaw Pact are not examples of manifest destiny. The term *manifest destiny* was coined in an 1845 newspaper article. It captured the fervor of the westward expansion movement, implying that it was God's plan that the United States take over and settle the entire continent. Americans who did settle out West were probably driven more by economic factors, such as cheap land or precious metals, than by a desire to fulfill God's plan.

38. **4** Belief in the domino theory by presidents Dwight D. Eisenhower, John F. Kennedy, and Lyndon B. Johnson directly influenced their decisions to increase United States military involvement in Vietnam. The domino theory asserts that when a nation becomes communist, its neighbors will be more likely to become communist. The name of the theory alludes to the game of lining up dominos in a row so that when the first one is pushed over, the next ones in the row will each be knocked over as well. The theory presumes that communism is imposed on a country from the outside—that communism does not develop as a result of internal conditions. The United States' interest in Vietnam began under President Eisenhower in the 1950s when it sent military advisors and assistance to the government of South Vietnam after Vietnam was divided in 1954. The United States feared that South Vietnam would become a communist nation, as had North Vietnam. President Kennedy continued supporting the government of South Vietnam. The United States became heavily involved in the Vietnam War after Congress gave President Johnson a blank check with the Tonkin Gulf Resolution (1964). Despite the presence of over half a million United States troops and the firepower of the U.S. military, President Johnson was not able to declare victory over the communist rebels in South Vietnam. As the war dragged on and as the United States suffered more casualties, many Americans began to question the wisdom of American policies in Vietnam. United States involvement in Vietnam continued until 1973 when President Richard Nixon withdrew the last American troops. In 1975, the government of South Vietnam became communist.

WRONG CHOICES EXPLAINED:
(1), (2), and (3) According to the domino theory, communist movements do not emerge as responses to conditions within a country. Rather, communism is forced upon a country by a neighboring country. If this is the case, as U.S. policy makers believed during the Cold War, the United States had a responsibility to act as a countervailing force and to block communist aggression. That approach meant that the United States would be more active in global affairs. During the entirety of the Cold War, the United States led the charge against the expansion of communism. It would not, therefore, have abandoned the North Atlantic Treaty Organization (NATO) and not rejected the ideas of collective security, as

in choice 1. The United States would not have supported a return to neutrality, as in choice 2. Finally, the United States would not have abandoned Berlin to communist aggression by ending the Berlin airlift, as in choice 3.

39. **4** The War on Poverty was an attempt by President Lyndon B. Johnson to raise the standard of living for many Americans. The War on Poverty, which was part of Johnson's Great Society agenda, refers to a series of domestic programs that Johnson pushed through Congress in 1964 and 1965. The War on Poverty included the creation of Medicare to provide health insurance for the elderly and of Medicaid to provide health insurance for welfare recipients. Johnson sought to improve education for poor students with the Head Start program, which created preschool programs, and with the Elementary and Secondary Education Act. Other initiatives included creating welfare programs, expanding civil rights for African Americans, and building public housing projects. The programs had limited success. The cycle of poverty proved to be too difficult to break in a short period of time. In addition, the Vietnam War became increasingly costly, diverting billions of dollars that could have been used for antipoverty programs.

WRONG CHOICES EXPLAINED:
(1) President Lyndon Johnson's War on Poverty was not an attempt to send medical aid to African nations. The United States provided extensive foreign aid to the developing world during the Cold War. Much of United States foreign aid came under the umbrella of the newly created United States Agency for International Development (USAID), which started in 1961. The War on Poverty, however, focused on poverty in the United States.
(2) President Lyndon Johnson's War on Poverty was not an attempt to strengthen the Peace Corps. The Peace Corps was created in 1961 by President John F. Kennedy (1961–1963) in order to give support to developing nations in fields such as education, agriculture, and health care. The program depended on volunteers, often recent college graduates, to work on development projects in poor countries. The War on Poverty, however, focused on poverty in the United States.
(3) President Lyndon Johnson's War on Poverty was not an attempt to decrease the number of immigrants from Latin America. Johnson expanded opportunities for immigrants to enter the United States with the passage of the Immigration and Nationality Act of 1965 (also known as the Hart-Celler Act), which was part of the Great Society agenda. The act changed American immigration policy that had been in place since the 1920s. It abolished the national quota system and replaced that system with overall limits on immigration into the United States. The War on Poverty, however, focused on poverty in the United States.

40. **1** In the "Letter from Birmingham Jail," Martin Luther King, Jr., was arguing for civil disobedience. King drew on several religious, philosophical, and political traditions in developing his approach to social change. Civil disobedience is a philosophical principle that asserts that it is one's right, indeed, one's responsibility to resist unjust laws. Earlier in American history, the principle was articulated by the transcendentalist thinker Henry David Thoreau in his 1849 essay *Resistance to Civil Government (Civil Disobedience)*. King also stressed the importance of nonviolence and pacifism, which have deep roots. Many Christians cite the biblical injunction to "turn the other cheek" if struck. Pacifism is especially strong in the Quaker tradition. King also gained inspiration from Mahatma Gandhi's campaign to resist British authority in India in the first half of the 20th century. Gandhi taught that to resort to violence was to stoop to the moral level of the oppressor. King was a central figure in the civil rights movement of the 1950s and 1960s. In 1963, his organization, the Southern Christian Leadership Conference, decided to launch a major campaign in Birmingham, Alabama, to protest racial segregation. The public safety commissioner of Birmingham, Eugene "Bull" Connor, would not tolerate public demonstrations. He used fire hoses, police dogs, and brutal force to put down the campaign. During the Birmingham campaign, King was arrested and wrote his famous "Letter from Birmingham Jail," a response to a call by white clergy members to allow the legal system to address the issue of racial injustice. King insisted that the black community had waited long enough for change to happen. The campaign proved to be a turning point in the push for federal legislation, including the Civil Rights Act (1964).

WRONG CHOICES EXPLAINED:

(2) In the "Letter from Birmingham Jail," Martin Luther King, Jr., was not arguing for armed resistance. The passage makes no reference to either violence or weaponry. Rather, King discussed the reason that civil rights activists were violating unjust laws.

(3) In the "Letter from Birmingham Jail," Martin Luther King, Jr., was not arguing for Black Power. Later in the 1960s, some advocates for civil rights adopted the call for Black Power. The Black Panther Party, which formed in 1966, grew out of the Black Power movement and embraced self-defense and militant rhetoric. Initially, the Back Panthers focused on community organizing. However, their activities grew increasingly confrontational.

(4) In the "Letter from Birmingham Jail," Martin Luther King, Jr., was not arguing for containment. Containment refers to the goal of preventing the expansion of communism during the Cold War (approximately 1945–1991). President Harry S. Truman articulated this goal, also known as the Truman Doctrine, in a speech to Congress in 1947.

41. **4** A main goal of President Richard Nixon's policy of détente was to reduce tensions between the United States and the Soviet Union. *Détente* is the French word for "loosening." It refers to an easing of tensions in the Cold War and to a warming of relations between the United States and the Soviet Union. It may seem ironic that Richard Nixon, a man who made a name for himself as a strong anticommunist, was responsible for the policy of détente. After all, as a congressman, Nixon pursued suspected Soviet spy Alger Hiss (1950). However, Nixon's anticommunist credentials enabled him to open relations with communist nations without being accused of being "soft on communism." In 1972, Nixon became the first United States president to visit Communist China. Later in 1972, he held meetings with Soviet leaders in Moscow. The meetings produced several agreements, including an agreement to limit antiballistic missile systems (ABMs).

WRONG CHOICES EXPLAINED:

(1) Sponsoring free elections in North Korea was not a goal of President Richard Nixon's détente policy. Currently, the Korean peninsula is divided into North Korea and South Korea at the 38th parallel. Korea was divided into two occupation zones after World War II, one controlled by the United States and one controlled by the Soviet Union. The two sides were unable to agree on a unification plan. By 1948, two separate nations were established with a border at the 38th parallel. North Korea has always been run in an authoritarian manner by the communist Workers' Party of Korea. It does not hold free elections, nor has this been a demand of the United States.

(2) Negotiating an end to the Arab-Israeli conflict was not a goal of President Richard Nixon's détente policy. The United States has made attempts to ease Arab-Israeli tensions. Since the founding of Israel in 1948, tensions have existed in the Middle East. In 1977, Egyptian President Anwar Sadat and Israeli Prime Minister Menachem Begin met with President Jimmy Carter at the Camp David presidential retreat in Maryland for 13 days and emerged with the basis for a peace treaty. The treaty resulted in an end to hostilities between Israel and Egypt, but tensions continued to exist between Israel and its other neighbors. The most serious tension since the Camp David Accords has been between Israel and Palestinians.

(3) Ending diplomatic relations with China was not a goal of President Richard Nixon's détente policy. Nixon began the process of restoring diplomatic relations between the two countries. The United States ended relations with China after China had become a communist country in 1949. With his trip to Beijing in 1972, Nixon became the first American president to visit Communist China. In 1973, both nations established liaison offices in the other country. This was a first step toward establishing formal diplomatic relations, which occurred in 1979.

42. **2** Charges of perjury and obstruction of justice led to President Bill Clinton's impeachment. The impeachment of President Clinton represents an important turning point in the deterioration of relations between the two main political parties. The proceedings also demonstrate the growing strength of the more conservative elements within the Republican Party. Republicans doggedly pursued evidence of scandal relating to President Clinton. During President Clinton's first term, Kenneth Starr was appointed as an independent counsel to investigate the participation of Bill and Hillary Clinton in a failed and fraudulent real estate project in Arkansas that dated back to 1978, when Bill Clinton was governor. Starr pursued this Whitewater case relentlessly but never tied the Clintons to the fraud. President Clinton, however, was not able to avoid implication in a more salacious scandal. Clinton was publicly accused of having a sexual affair with a White House intern named Monica Lewinsky. Clinton denied the accusations publicly and also before a federal grand jury. When Clinton was later forced to admit the affair, Congressional Republicans felt they had evidence of impeachable crimes—committing perjury to a grand jury and obstructing justice. Clinton was impeached by the House of Representatives in 1998. Impeachment is the act of bringing charges against a federal official; it is parallel to indictment in the criminal court system. After impeachment by the House, the Senate conducts a trial based on the charges listed in the "articles of impeachment." Clinton was found "not guilty" by the Senate (two-thirds are needed for conviction). Many Americans disapproved of his personal misconduct but also resented the attempt by Republicans to remove the president from office.

WRONG CHOICES EXPLAINED:
(1) The impeachment of President Bill Clinton did not stem from charges of excessive use of the pardon power. The Constitution gives the president the power to pardon individuals found guilty in federal criminal proceedings. The Constitution does not place a limit on the number of pardons a president may issue, so "excessive" use of the pardon power would not be considered an impeachable offense.

(3) The impeachment of President Bill Clinton did not stem from charges of illegal use of campaign funds. Federal campaign regulations stipulate that a candidate or an elected official cannot use campaign funds for personal purposes, unrelated to getting elected. Campaign funds cannot be treated as a personal piggy bank. Clinton was not accused of improperly using campaign funds.

(4) The impeachment of President Bill Clinton did not stem from charges of the misuse of war powers and deficit spending. During the Vietnam War, members of Congress accused President Richard Nixon of the misuse of war powers by conducting secret bombing campaigns in Cambodia (1969–1973).

The president may seek congressional approval for military actions and may take actions unilaterally in times of emergency. The degree of latitude given the president is open to interpretation and debate. In the aftermath of the bombing of Cambodia, Congress passed the War Powers Resolution (1973), which placed checks on the president's ability to use military force without congressional approval. Deficit spending is defined as the amount by which government spending exceeds revenue over a particular period of time. Although deficit spending is subject to disagreement among economists and politicians, it is not a crime.

43. **2** One way in which Social Security, Medicare, and Medicaid are similar is that they are all examples of social welfare programs. The Social Security system was one of several programs that comprised the New Deal, which was President Franklin D. Roosevelt's (1933–1945) agenda to address the poverty and dislocation caused by the Great Depression of the 1930s. The Social Security system addressed the welfare of retired people and people with disabilities. Working people pay into the system during their working years and then receive monthly payments once they reach the age of 65. Medicare and Medicaid were part of President Lyndon B. Johnson's War on Poverty, which was a series of domestic programs that Johnson pushed through Congress in 1964 and 1965. The War on Poverty was a key component of President Johnson's Great Society agenda. Medicare provides health insurance for the elderly, and Medicaid provides health insurance to low-income people. Other initiatives included creating additional welfare programs, expanding civil rights for African Americans, and building public housing projects. The programs had mixed results. Medicare and Medicaid have proved to be highly successful, but the cycle of poverty proved to be too difficult to break in a short period of time. Both the New Deal and the War on Poverty expanded social welfare programs.

WRONG CHOICES EXPLAINED:
(1) Social Security, Medicare, and Medicaid are not programs that provide aid to education. As part of the Great Society, President Lyndon Johnson sought to improve education for poor students with the Head Start program (1965), which created preschool programs, and with the Elementary and Secondary Education Act (1965).

(3) Social Security, Medicare, and Medicaid are not programs that attempt to balance the federal budget. The Social Security system is funded primarily through payroll taxes. People pay into the system when they are working, and they draw from the system when they retire. Social Security does not, for the most part, draw from the general fund. Therefore, it does not have an impact on the budget. Medicare is funded by the Social Security system; Medicaid draws its funds from the general fund.

(4) Social Security, Medicare, and Medicaid are not programs that create public works projects. President Franklin D. Roosevelt's New Deal did create several public works programs to put the unemployed to work. Most notable were the Civilian Conservation Corps (1933), which targeted young men to improve parks and to do conservation work, and the Works Progress Administration (1935), which created millions of jobs in a variety of fields, including building roads and painting murals.

44. **3** The cartoonist is critical of the leadership of President George W. Bush and Vice President Dick Cheney for weakening the system of checks and balances. In the system of checks and balances, each of the three branches of government—the executive, the legislative, and the judicial—has the ability to limit, or check, the powers of the other two. The goal is to create balance among the three branches, with no branch able to dominate the other two. Examples include the president's ability to veto bills passed by Congress and the Senate's ability to approve or reject Supreme Court nominees. The cartoon depicts the three branches of government as three actual branches on a tree. Bush, dressed as a king, and Cheney sit on one branch—the executive branch. The other two branches are missing in the cartoon; they have been cut by Cheney. The implication is that Bush and Cheney have amassed greater power in the executive branch and have severely undermined the powers of the other two branches.

WRONG CHOICES EXPLAINED:
(1) The cartoon does not allude to the clear-cutting of forests. The cutting of tree branches in the cartoon is meant metaphorically; the branches symbolize the branches of government. Logging companies have often cut every tree in an area, causing erosion and ecological disruption. The practice has been roundly condemned by environmental groups. Currently, logging companies are encouraged to manage forests by cutting only certain trees and leaving others for future years.

(2) The cartoon alludes to the relationship among the three branches of government. It does not specifically refer to presidential vetoes. The Constitution grants the president the power to issue vetoes. President Bush did not overuse the power. He issued his very first veto, after five years in office, just two days before the cartoon was published, in July 2006. Bush vetoed the Stem Cell Research Enhancement Act, which would have provided federal funding for embryonic stem cell research. That veto might have prompted the cartoon, but the cartoon focused on the system of checks and balances.

(4) The cartoon does not allude to the war in Iraq. President George W. Bush did initiate war in Iraq. Operation Iraqi Freedom (2003–2011) was the attempt by the United States to remove Saddam Hussein from office and create a less belligerent and more democratic government in Iraq. President George W. Bush insisted that Hussein was developing weapons of mass destruction that

could be used against the United States and its allies. U.S. forces failed to find evidence of such weapons. Defeating the Iraqi army and removing Saddam Hussein from office was relatively easy. However, creating stability in Iraq proved to be an elusive goal. Attacks by insurgents continued, both against U.S. forces and between different factions within Iraq, until most American forces had withdrawn from Iraq by 2011.

45. **1** President James Monroe's proclamation of the Monroe Doctrine was most consistent with the ideas presented by George Washington in his Farewell Address. President Washington is closely identified with the idea of neutrality. He issued the 1793 Neutrality Act. In his Farewell Address, Washington urged the United States to avoid "permanent alliances" with foreign powers. He did not want the newly independent nation, which was on precarious footing, to be drawn into the seemingly endless conflicts of Europe. The particular circumstances of the 1793 Neutrality Act grew out of the French Revolution, which began in 1789. Americans were divided over France's revolution. The debates took on greater significance after France and Great Britain went to war in 1793. Many Americans felt that the United States had an obligation to help France because France had helped the United States in the American Revolution. A treaty between the two countries (1778) committed the United States to help France if it were under attack. Others argued that the United States should stay out. After all, the treaty was made with a French government that no longer existed, and the French Revolution had devolved from a democratic movement into a bloodbath. The latter position won Washington's support. His calls for neutrality have been invoked by isolationists throughout American history. In 1823, President James Monroe issued the Monroe Doctrine with the intent of preventing European powers from taking over Latin-American nations. Monroe was alarmed by the threats made by the Holy Alliance of Russia, Prussia, and Austria to restore Spain's lost American colonies. He also opposed a decree by the Russian czar that claimed all the Pacific Northwest north of the 51st parallel. Although both problems worked themselves out, Monroe issued a statement warning European nations not to attempt to set up colonies in the Americas. Both Washington and Monroe took steps to avoid conflicts with European nations. The Monroe Doctrine and Washington's Farewell Address became cornerstones of America's isolationist foreign policy.

WRONG CHOICES EXPLAINED:
(2) President James Polk's policy toward Mexico in 1846 was not consistent with the ideas presented by President George Washington in his Farewell Address. President Washington argued for neutrality. President Polk, on the other hand, pushed for United States to declare war on a foreign power.

The Mexican-American War (1846–1848) grew out of the annexation of Texas (1845). The United States and Mexico disagreed over the southern border of Texas. Skirmishes in the disputed area led to war between the two countries. The United States won the war and acquired the huge territory that comprised the northern provinces of Mexico, known as the Mexican Cession.

(3) President William McKinley's request for a declaration of war against Spain in 1898 was not consistent with the ideas presented by President George Washington in his Farewell Address. President Washington argued for neutrality and avoidance of "entanglements" with Europe. President McKinley, on the other hand, pushed for the United States to declare war on a European power. The Spanish-American War had several causes—concern over American sugar investments in Cuba, sympathy for the Cuban people in their struggle for independence from Spain, the sinking of the American ship the USS *Maine* in the Havana harbor, and sensationalistic "yellow journalism." In the Treaty of Paris, which ended the Spanish-American War, Spain ceded Puerto Rico, Guam, and the Philippines to the United States.

(4) President George H.W. Bush's decision to engage in the Persian Gulf War in 1990 was not consistent with the ideas presented by President George Washington in his Farewell Address. President Washington argued for neutrality and avoidance of alliances. President Bush pushed for war against Iraq and organized a coalition of nations to join the United States. In 1990, Iraqi leader Saddam Hussein sent the Iraqi military into Kuwait to occupy that country. The goal of Operation Desert Storm was to remove Iraqi forces from Kuwait. The operation was successful. Hussein was quickly forced to withdraw his troops. The United States suffered relatively few casualties.

46. **3** The Populist movement of the 1890s and the civil rights movement of the 1950s and 1960s are similar in that both were attempts to improve the lives of groups who were oppressed. The Populist movement was a political insurgency by small-scale farmers in the late 1800s. The Populists grew angry at the concentration of wealth and power by eastern industrialists. By the late 1800s, it became increasingly difficult for small farmers to compete with large-scale agricultural operations. Expensive machinery replaced handheld tools. Although mechanization reduced the man-hours needed for agricultural tasks, it worked to undermine small-scale, family farms. Populists followed in the footsteps of the Granger movement (founded in 1867) by pushing for regulation of railroad companies, which often overcharged small-scale farmers. They also supported a national income tax so that those with higher incomes would pay more than the poor. Populists also supported increasing the amount of money in circulation. Farmers supported inflationary policies so that the prices they received for their

produce would increase. The civil rights movement focused on the oppression of African Americans. By the 1950s and 1960s, a massive movement had developed in the United States to challenge the Jim Crow system. The civil rights movement gained strength after the Supreme Court, in the case of *Brown* v. *Board of Education of Topeka* (1954), declared that segregation in schools had no place in America. In the years following the *Brown* decision occurred the Montgomery bus boycott in 1955 and 1956, the lunch counter sit-ins in 1960, the Freedom Rides in 1962, and a whole host of other civil rights activities. The high point of the movement might have been the March on Washington in 1963, where Martin Luther King, Jr., gave his "I Have a Dream" speech. It was in this context that the movement achieved significant victories. The Civil Rights Act of 1964 banned segregation in public facilities, and the Voting Rights Act of 1965 removed barriers to African Americans voting.

WRONG CHOICES EXPLAINED:

(1) Neither the Populist movement of the 1890s nor the civil rights movement of the 1950s and 1960s sought to restrict the power of the executive branch. On several occasions, the civil rights movement called on the president to take executive action to ensure that civil rights court decisions and orders were enforced. For example in 1957, when violence erupted in Little Rock, Arkansas, in response to the desegregation of Central High School, President Eisenhower sent in federal troops to guarantee the safety of the students and to ensure that Little Rock would comply with the Supreme Court decision in *Brown* v. *Board of Education of Topeka* (1954).

(2) Neither the Populist movement of the 1890s nor the civil rights movement of the 1950s and 1960s focused exclusively on solving the problems brought about by industrialization. The Populist movement did seek to check the power of industrial corporations. However, the focus of the movement was more on problems faced by farmers than by factory workers. The focus of the civil rights movement was more on political reform than on solving problems brought about by industrialization.

(4) The civil rights movement of the 1950s and 1960s focused on racial equality. The movement did not focus exclusively on pressuring states to change their policies. Much of the focus was on pressuring the three branches of the federal government to promote racial equality. Earlier, the Populist movement did not embrace racial equality. Many of its members reflected prevailing white supremacist ideas. Some white southern Populists saw that they would have more power as a biracial movement, but racist attitudes in the South prevented the formation of such a movement. In response, African-American tenant farmers and sharecroppers in the South formed the Colored Farmers Alliance in 1886. The organization had 1.2 million members at its height.

47. **2** The tactics illustrated in the cartoon were most closely associated with government leaders investigating communist activities after World War II. The cartoon is mocking the government's tactics of investigating individuals during the late 1940s and 1950s. The cartoon is depicting a teacher who appears to be guilty of nothing more than having a world map on the wall that includes the Soviet Union and displaying an image of Thomas Jefferson. The investigators are about to alter the world map by simply cutting out the Soviet Union. Perhaps the investigators in the cartoon perceived Jefferson's words from the Declaration of Independence—that "all men are created equal"—to be subversive during the Jim Crow era. A central figure in the anticommunist movement was Senator Joseph McCarthy. In 1950, he announced that he had a list of "known communists" who had infiltrated the State Department. This and similar claims, which were mostly baseless, created a name for McCarthy and set the stage for a host of measures to halt this perceived threat. Congress established committees to investigate Communist Party infiltration in different sectors of society. Congress especially targeted the entertainment industry, fearing that communists would subtly get their message out through television and movies. Loyalty oaths became commonplace for public sector employees, such as teachers. The movement drew on a long history of anti-intellectualism in the United States; the cartoon notes that one of the teacher's "crimes" is that she "reads books." The movement began to lessen in intensity by the mid-1950s. McCarthy himself went too far, accusing members of the military establishment of being communists. The Senate voted to censure him in 1954, thus ending the worst excesses of what many people referred to as a witch hunt.

WRONG CHOICES EXPLAINED:
(1) The cartoon is not associated with isolationists supporting neutrality during the 1930s. The references to the Soviet Union and "anti-subversive" committees indicate that the cartoon is commenting on anticommunism in the 1950s. Isolationism—entailing a retreat from world affairs—was strong in the 1920s and 1930s. The policy of isolationism led to the Senate rejecting the Treaty of Versailles. Approval of the treaty by the Senate would have made the United States a member of the League of Nations. Isolationist sentiment in the 1920s also led to the enactment of legislation that dramatically restricted immigration into the United States.
(3) The cartoon is not associated with increased federal spending for education in the 1960s. The purpose of the cartoon is to depict overzealous anticommunist investigators, who were searching for nonexistent evidence in garbage cans and among school supplies. Schools did struggle to gain sufficient funds in the 1950s and 1960s as the baby boom generation began to enter public schools. Schools receive the vast majority of their funds from local government, not from

the federal government. However, Great Society initiatives such as the Head Start (1965) program, which created preschool programs, and the Elementary and Secondary Education Act (1965), expanded the role of the federal government in public education.

(4) The cartoon is not associated with Congress promoting increased security after the September 11, 2001, attacks. The references to the Soviet Union and "anti-subversive" committees indicate that the cartoon is commenting on anti-communism in the 1950s. The United States did take measures to promote increased security after the 2001 terrorist attacks. The Transportation Security Administration (TSA) was created after the attacks and immediately increased security at airports. In 2003, the TSA was folded into the Department of Homeland Security. The department also absorbed the Immigration and Naturalization Service. The TSA is a cabinet level department, with the responsibility of protecting the United States from terrorist attacks and natural disasters.

48. **4** "Flappers" in the 1920s, "beatniks" in the 1950s, and "hippies" in the 1960s are all examples of individuals who disagreed with traditional societal values. All three groups challenged mainstream cultural norms. The decade of the 1920s saw many women challenging traditional gender norms. The "new woman" of the 1920s was more engaged in public issues. She might have participated in the political struggles of the progressive movement and gained a new sense of confidence in public issues, especially after women achieved the right to vote in 1920. The changing image of women during the 1920s was symbolized by the popularity of the flappers and their style of dress. Flappers openly defied Victorian moral codes about "proper" ladylike behavior. In the 1950s, beatniks challenged an increasingly homogenous mass culture. They rejected some of the central pillars of postwar culture—conformity, the suburban lifestyle, the consumer society, and patriotism. The values and norms of the beatniks are evident in the beat literary movement. The most important text of the beat movement is *On the Road*, by Jack Kerouac (1957). Initially written on a scroll—a stream of consciousness screed—the book depicts a life of spontaneity and freedom. Also important is Allen Ginsberg's book of poems, *Howl* (1956), which ripped apart the foundations of Cold War American society. The beatniks of the 1950s influenced the hippie movement. This countercultural movement became visible in the late 1960s in neighborhoods such as San Francisco's Haight-Ashbury and New York's Lower East Side. A variety of activities came to be associated with the hippie movement—urban and rural communal living, a do-it-yourself approach to the varied tasks of life, mystic spiritual experiences, drug use, experimental music, and avant-garde art. Taking inspiration from sit-ins of the civil rights movement, the counterculture organized be-ins—gatherings of young people in San Francisco's Golden Gate Park or New York's Central Park.

WRONG CHOICES EXPLAINED:

(1) "Flappers" in the 1920s, "beatniks" in the 1950s, and "hippies" in the 1960s are not examples of political groups that wanted to limit individual rights. The opposite is closer to the truth. Although none of the three cultural movements was explicitly political, many flappers supported the cause of women's rights, and many beatniks and hippies supported the civil rights movement and other movements for change.

(2) "Flappers" in the 1920s and "beatniks" in the 1950s are not examples of citizens who wanted to return to simpler lifestyles. Some hippies in the 1960s did attempt to simplify their lives. Many moved to rural communes, grew their own food, created their own art and music, and produced various products (bread, soap, ceramics) by hand.

(3) "Flappers" in the 1920s, "beatniks" in the 1950s, and "hippies" in the 1960s are not examples of writers who supported United States foreign policy goals. The opposite is closer to the truth. Many beatniks in the 1950s were critical of the nuclear arms race. In the 1960s, many hippies participated in the large-scale anti–Vietnam War movement.

49. **4** The Great Depression and the economic crisis known as the Great Recession (December 2007–June 2009) were similar in that both led to an expansion of the federal government's role in stabilizing the economy. The Great Depression was the most severe economic downturn in American history. President Franklin D. Roosevelt (1933–1945) greatly expanded the role of the federal government with the New Deal, which was the set of programs proposed by the administration to address the poverty and dislocation caused by the Great Depression. Roosevelt's initiatives were unprecedented in their scope and direction. The Roosevelt administration provided direct relief, or what would be known as welfare today, to millions of impoverished families. In addition, the New Deal created jobs programs such as Civilian Conservation Corps (1933), which focused on young men, and the vast Works Progress Administration (1935), which consisted of a myriad of public projects. In addition, the New Deal addressed the welfare of the aged by creating the Social Security system in 1935. The Great Recession of December 2007–June 2009, which resulted from the bursting of the housing bubble, from problems in the automobile industry, and from the collapse of major financial institutions, was the worst economic crisis since the Great Depression. Presidents George W. Bush and Barack Obama again expended the role of the federal government to respond to the economic crisis. In 2008, President George W. Bush initiated a $17.4 bailout of Generals Motors and Chrysler; the Obama administration continued this program. The bailout was successful. The American automobile industry recovered and paid back most of the money that was used in the bailout. President Obama also enacted a major

stimulus bill—the American Recovery and Reinvestment Act (2009). The act provided almost $800 billion to state and local governments to be used for infrastructure projects, schools, and hospitals. Finally, the Obama administration pushed for measures to add regulations to the financial industry in order to rein in some of the risky practices that led to the recession of 2008. The Dodd-Frank Wall Street Reform and Consumer Protection Act was designed to regulate financial markets and to protect consumers.

WRONG CHOICES EXPLAINED:

(1) The Great Depression and the economic crisis known as the Great Recession (December 2007–June 2009) did not lead to a surplus in the federal budget. Economic crises tend to lead to budget deficits. If unemployment is high, fewer people are paying income tax, thus reducing government revenue. Further, the government often creates programs to soften the blow of the economic downturn—as it did during both the Great Depression and the Great Recession. Such programs draw money from the federal budget. Declining revenues and rising expenditures lead to budget deficits.

(2) The Great Depression and the economic crisis known as the Great Recession (December 2007–June 2009) did not lead to a decrease in support for unemployment insurance. High unemployment during both periods led to an increase in support for unemployment insurance. Unemployment insurance was created during the Great Depression. The establishment of federal unemployment insurance was part of the Social Security Act of 1935. Unemployment insurance is a joint federal-state venture. Employers pay payroll taxes to the government, which can then extend unemployment benefits to workers if they lose their job through no fault of their own.

(3) The Great Depression and the economic crisis known as the Great Recession (December 2007–June 2009) did not lead to a limit on the power of the Federal Reserve System. In both cases, the Federal Reserve Bank (the Fed) implemented policies intended to stem the crises. If the economy is sluggish the Fed will attempt to stimulate economic growth by increasing the money supply. An important mechanism for regulating the money supply is raising or lowering the interest rates at which the Fed loans money to other banks. Other banks follow suit, raising or lowering the interest rates at which they loan money to the public. By lowering interest rates, the Fed stimulates economic activity, making it more attractive for people to borrow money to make major purchases and thus putting more money into circulation.

50. **2** The principal cause of the population changes shown on the map is continued westward expansion. The small triangles on the map depict the mean center of population at different points in United States history. To understand the

concept of the mean center of population, first imagine the United States as represented by a rigid and flat surface. Next, imagine identical weights being placed onto this plane, with each weight representing a person living in the U.S. If each and every person living in the United States was represented by a weight, the mean center of population would be the point that would keep the plane in perfect balance. Therefore if people moved farther west, the mean center of population would have to move west as well to keep the plane in balance. The mean center of the United States has done just that over the nation's history. In 1790, it was in the far eastern section of the United States (Maryland). This indicates that the eastern portion of the country contained the vast majority of the population. The mean center moved to the Midwest (Missouri) by 2010, indicating the continued westward movement of people. Several factors have contributed to the western migration of people. In the 19th century, many Americans thought of westward expansion as a divinely sanctioned march, that it was the manifest destiny of the United States to take over the entire continent. The government encouraged westward expansion with the Homestead Act (1862), which provided free land in the West to settlers who were willing to farm it. Hundreds of thousands of people applied for and were granted homesteads. The expansion of railroads into the west, leading to the completion of a transcontinental railroad in 1869, also encouraged white settlement in the Great Plains region. This movement was especially damaging for the Native American Indians of the West who were driven off their lands and relegated to several western reservations. The westward march continued in the 20th century. Americans have been drawn by the climate and economic opportunities offered by Sun Belt states, such as Arizona, Nevada, and California.

WRONG CHOICES EXPLAINED:
(1) The population changes shown on the map were not caused by employment opportunities in the northeastern states. The map shows the continued trend of westward migration. If employment opportunities in the northeastern states led to a reversal of that trend, the mean center of population would have moved east.

(3) The population changes shown on the map were not caused by the enactment of immigration quotas. The immigration quota acts of the 1920s—the Emergency Quota Act (1921) and the National Origins Act (1924)—greatly reduced immigration into the United States. However, these acts did not have an impact on migration patterns within the United States.

(4) The population changes shown on the map were not caused by movement from farms to cities. The trend of Americans moving from rural communities to urban communities was strong during the late 1800s. Between 1860 and 1900, the number of Americans who lived in cities jumped from 6.2 million to over 30

million, which amounted to a shift in the urban population from 20 percent of the total population to 40 percent. By 1920, census data indicated that, for the first time, more Americans lived in cities than in the countryside. However, the movement of people from rural areas in states such as Iowa or Kansas to urban centers such as New York or Philadelphia was offset by a general movement of the population in a western direction, including to cities in California.

PART II: THEMATIC ESSAY

Geography—Territorial Acquisitions

The physical size of the United States has grown dramatically over the course of its history. Colonists initially lived on or near the Atlantic Coast. Slowly, they moved into the interior of the continent, crossing the Appalachian Mountains and moving westward toward the Mississippi River. When the United States officially received its independence from Great Britain in 1783, its western boundary extended to the Mississippi River. In less than a century, the nation extended all the way to the Pacific Ocean. By the end of the 19th century, the United States had acquired possessions in the Caribbean, the Pacific, and Asia. The United States acquired new territory by a variety of methods. These acquisitions have had both positive and negative effects on the United States. This essay focuses on two territorial acquisitions, California (1848) and Puerto Rico (1899).

The United States acquired California as a result of the Mexican-American War. The war took place in the context of the American quest to spread over the North American continent. Many Americans came to believe that it was the nation's manifest destiny to extend all the way to the Pacific. The term captured the fervor of the westward expansion movement, implying that it was God's plan for the United States to take over and settle the entire continent. Americans who did settle out West were probably driven more by economic factors, such as cheap land or precious metals, than by a desire to fulfill a divine plan.

The push toward the Pacific Ocean generated interest in Mexican territory among many Americans. Americans had been settling in the Mexican territory of Texas as far back as the 1820s. In 1836, Texans fought for and won independence from Mexico, becoming the Lone Star Republic. Many Texans were eager for their Lone Star Republic to join the United States. However, concern about the expansion of slavery put the issue of Texas annexation on the back burner until the election of the expansionist President James Polk in 1844. Texas joined the United States as the 15th slave state in 1844. Conflict between the United States and Mexico soon ensued. The two countries disagreed over the southern border of Texas. Mexico said it was at the Nueces River. Polk insisted it was at the Rio Grande, 150 miles to the south. In 1846, Polk sent troops into this disputed territory. Skirmishes in the disputed area led to war between Mexico and the United States. Ultimately, the United States prevailed and acquired the huge territory that comprised the northern provinces of Mexico, which is known as the Mexican Cession. The war strengthened the United States, greatly increasing its territorial holdings. These lands included the territory that would soon become the state of California.

The acquisition of California immediately had both positive and negative effects on the United States. On the positive side, gold was discovered in California soon after it was acquired by the United States. As word spread, thousands of people came to California to try to strike it rich. A large percentage of the 300,000 people who migrated to California came in 1849, thus their nickname "forty-niners." The gold rush drew immigrants from all over—from eastern cities, from Canada, from Europe, from Latin America, and from China. By 1852, 20,000 Chinese immigrants had moved to the United States. By 1860, over 34,000 lived in California alone. California quickly became a thriving, multiethnic territory. California also became a center for American trade. In 1852, President Millard Fillmore, who was determined to open Japan to American trade, sent two naval expeditions to Japan. They were each led by Commodore Matthew C. Perry. By 1854, Perry was able to secure a trade treaty with Japan. The lucrative trade with Asia went through California ports. Soon after the American Civil War, completion of the first transcontinental railroad connected California with the population centers in the East and the Midwest. California continued to grow and continued to generate wealth for the United States.

On the negative side, California's application for statehood into the United States intensified sectional tensions in the United States. By 1850, California had enough people to form a state. Californians wrote up a constitution to submit to Congress in which slavery would be illegal. Southern senators objected to the admission of an additional free state. Senate negotiators worked out a series of measures to resolve this extremely contentious problem. These measures became known as the Compromise of 1850. The most important elements of the compromise were the admittance of California as a free state, which pleased northern politicians, and a more stringent Fugitive Slave Law, which pleased southern politicians. Many northerners grew alarmed at the enforcement of the Fugitive Slave Law. Previously, the majority of northerners could ignore the brutality of the slave system. Following 1850, though, slave catchers brought the system to the streets of northern cities. In response, many northern states passed "personal liberty laws" that offered protection to fugitives. Many whites and free African Americans in northern cities even formed vigilance committees to prevent the slave catchers from carrying out their orders. The tensions that intensified following the Compromise of 1850 continued throughout the decade and contributed to the Civil War.

Fifty years after the acquisition of California, the United States acquired Puerto Rico. The context for the acquisition of Puerto Rico was the rise of imperialism among the wealthy nations of the world. The scramble to imperialize Africa and Asia began among the European powers—Great Britain, France, Belgium, and Germany. By the 1890s, many American policy makers were pushing the United States to adopt an imperialist foreign policy. Imperialist ventures were motivated by a particular cultural set of ideas that created a racial hierarchy. Mainstream thinking in the United States in the late 1800s posited the superiority of the descendants of the Anglo-Saxon people and the inferiority of the nonwhite peoples of the world. This racist notion led some white Americans to feel it was the duty of the "civilized" peoples of the world to uplift the less fortunate. The push to uplift the peoples of the world was made clear in Rudyard Kipling's famous poem "The White Man's Burden" (1899). Josiah Strong, a Protestant clergyman, echoed Kipling's sentiment. Strong argued that the Anglo-Saxon race had a responsibility to "civilize and Christianize" the world.

The ideology of "The White Man's Burden" and developments in Cuba in the 1890s set the stage for the Spanish-American War and for the acquisition of Puerto Rico. A Cuban independence movement was trying to break Cuba's ties to Spain. The Spanish governor of Cuba used brutal tactics to suppress the rebellion. Many Americans wanted the United States to intervene on Cuba's side in its struggle against Spanish rule. Some Americans saw parallels between the Cuban struggle for independence from Spain and America's struggle for independence from Great Britain. Also, some American businessmen were angered by the interruption of the sugar harvest by the fighting between Cuban rebels and Spanish forces. Events in Cuba were brought to the attention of ordinary Americans through sensationalistic accounts in mass-produced and mass-distributed newspapers (nicknamed yellow journalism). Finally, the destruction of a United States warship, the USS *Maine*, in the harbor of Havana, Cuba, led to calls for war. Many in the United States thought that the destruction of the ship was the work of Spain. All of these factors combined to propel the U.S. into war with Spain in 1898.

The United States won the Spanish-American War and, as a result, acquired an empire. The United States and Spain negotiated the Treaty of Paris (signed in 1898 and ratified in 1899) following the war. In the treaty, Spain agreed to cede the Philippines, Puerto Rico, and Guam to the United States. The United States agreed to pay Spain $20 million for these possessions. The acquisition of Puerto Rico had both positive and negative effects for the United States.

On the negative side, the United States struggled to maintain its democratic ideals while simultaneously maintaining an empire. The United States was born in an anticolonial war, defeating the British to gain its independence. For much of its history, Americans stood in solidarity with other nations challenging European rule. Many Americans felt a kinship with Simón Bolívar as he led independence movements in the Spanish-held colonies of South America in the first decades of the 19th century. Bolívar himself was grateful to the United States for issuing the Monroe Doctrine in 1823, warning the European powers to keep their hands off the Americas. Many Americans, therefore, felt betrayed when the United States joined the European powers in pursuing an empire. In 1898, as the Treaty of Paris was debated in the Senate, a group of these critics of American imperialism formed the American Anti-Imperialist League. The league included American author Mark Twain, who was the vice president of the league from 1901 to 1910 and who wrote some of the league's more scathing condemnations of imperialism. Further, it became increasingly clear that the native people who lived in Puerto Rico and other American possessions would not enjoy the same constitutional rights as American citizens. The Supreme Court declared in a series of cases in 1901 that the United States was not obligated to grant its colonial subjects constitutional rights. The decisions for these Insular Cases were based on the racist assumptions that the colonial subjects were of an inferior race and that the colonial power had the responsibility to uplift these peoples before granting them autonomy.

On the positive side, American economic interests grew as a result of the acquisition of Puerto Rico. Puerto Rico became a major producer of American sugar in the first decades of the 20th century. Puerto Rico gained a greater degree of autonomy after the United States passed the Jones-Shafroth Act in 1917. The act also granted citizenship to Puerto Ricans born in 1898 or after. Since Puerto Ricans have become United States citizens, waves of migrants have moved from Puerto Rico to the United States. Puerto Ricans created vital neighborhoods in American cities such as New York City, filling entry-level jobs as generations of immigrants had done before them. Puerto Ricans have also made major contributions to the culture of the United States, from Puerto Rican astronaut Joseph Michael Acaba to baseball player Roberto Clemente to singer and actress Rita Moreno.

Territorial acquisitions have had both positive and negative effects on the United States. On the one hand, they have contributed to the wealth and power of the United States. The vast lands of the United States have provided ample living space for a growing population to reside in and have been a source of abundant natural resources. At the same time, these acquisitions have sometimes challenged basic American ideals of democracy and self-rule.

PART III: DOCUMENT-BASED QUESTION

Part A: Short Answer

Document 1

1 (1) According to Arthur M. Schlesinger, one event that motivated Thomas Paine to write *Common Sense* was that the British Parliament had passed the Intolerable Acts.

1 (2) According to Arthur M. Schlesinger, another event that motivated Thomas Paine to write "Common Sense" was that fighting had erupted in Lexington, Massachusetts.

> *These answers receive full credit because they state two events that motivated Thomas Paine to write Common Sense.*

Document 2

2 According to Robert Middlekauff, one way that Thomas Paine's *Common Sense* promoted support for independence was that it was widely reprinted throughout the colonies and generated a great deal of debate.

> *This answer receives full credit because it states one way that Thomas Paine's Common Sense promoted support for independence.*

Document 3

3 According to Edmund S. Morgan, one effect of Thomas Paine's *Common Sense* was that more and more delegates to the Second Continental Congress came to support independence. By July 1776, independence-minded delegates were in the majority and voted for declaring independence.

> *This answer receives full credit because it states one effect of Thomas Paine's Common Sense.*

Document 4

4 Based on the document, Harriet Beecher Stowe was concerned about the new Fugitive Slave Law because she believed it forced all Americans, including northerners, to be complicit in the slave system.

> *This answer receives full credit because it states one reason Harriet Beecher Stowe was concerned about the new Fugitive Slave Law.*

Document 5a and Document 5b

5 Based on the documents, Southern slave owners were concerned about the publication of *Uncle Tom's Cabin* because its antislavery massage was read by a large number of Americans. It had become a publishing "phenomenon."

This answer receives full credit because it states one reason Southern slave owners were concerned about the publication of Uncle Tom's Cabin.

Document 6

6 (1) According to James McPherson, one effect of the publication of *Uncle Tom's Cabin* was that it encouraged important leaders, including the British Prime Minister and President Abraham Lincoln, to think more deeply about the "problem of slavery."

6 (2) According to James McPherson, another effect of the publication of *Uncle Tom's Cabin* was that it set off a vehement campaign among southern defenders of slavery to both defend the institution of slavery and to denounce the book's "falsehoods" and "distortions."

These answers receive full credit because they state two effects of the publication of Uncle Tom's Cabin.

Document 7

7 (1) According to Eric Schlosser, one issue that concerned Upton Sinclair was that the food and drug industries were unregulated and regularly sold unhealthy and fraudulent products to the public.

7 (2) According to Eric Schlosser, another issue that concerned Upton Sinclair was that a small number of millionaire "robber barons" lived like European aristocrats while their workers could afford to live only in wretched slums.

These answers receive full credit because they state two issues that concerned Upton Sinclair.

Document 8a and Document 8b

8 (1) Based on the documents, one effect of the publication of *The Jungle* was that readers became concerned about the unhygienic conditions of the meat-packing industry and demanded that President Theodore Roosevelt take action.

8 (2) Based on the documents, another effect of the publication of *The Jungle* was that the federal government passed the Meat Inspection Act and the Pure Food and Drug Act to regulate the meat processing industry.

These answers receive full credit because they state two effects of the publication of The Jungle.

Document 9

9 According to President Lyndon B. Johnson, one continuing influence of Upton Sinclair's *The Jungle* was that the government continued its role in regulating the meat-processing industry; Congress had just passed the Wholesome Meat Act of 1967.

This answer receives full credit because it states one continuing influence that President Lyndon B. Johnson thinks Upton Sinclair's The Jungle *has had.*

Part B: Document-Based Essay

At different points in United States history, the publication of a particular book has dramatically altered the direction of society. The written word can have a powerful effect on history. Two significant written works that dramatically impacted society were *Common Sense* by Thomas Paine and *The Jungle* by Upton Sinclair. The first challenged American colonists to rethink their relationship with Great Britain; the second encouraged Americans to think about the way food is processed in the United States.

Thomas Paine's pamphlet *Common Sense*, written in January 1776, played an important role in convincing many Americans that the 13 North American colonies should declare independence from Great Britain. Relations between the colonies and Great Britain had been deteriorating for several years leading up to the publication of the pamphlet. The beginning of the tensions can be traced to the aftermath of the French and Indian War. After that war, which lasted from 1754 to 1763, the British government enacted a series of measures that many colonists found objectionable, including new taxes to defray the costs of the war. The Stamp Act of 1765 provoked the most intense opposition. Many colonists asserted that only representatives elected by them could enact taxes on the colonies. "No taxation without representation" became the rallying cry of the colonists. A series of taxes by the British and protests by the colonists continued over the next several years. Relations reached a boiling point after a violent standoff that led to British troops firing on a crowd of colonists (1770). The Boston Massacre intensified colonial resentment of the British presence.

In 1773, the British passed the Tea Act, which eliminated British tariffs from tea sold in the colonies by the British East India Company. This act actually lowered tea prices in Boston. However, it angered many colonists, who accused the British of doing special favors for a large company. The colonists responded by dumping cases of tea into Boston Harbor. The British responded to the Boston Tea Party by imposing a series of punitive measures known as the Intolerable Acts (1774). In April 1775, fighting began between patriots and British troops on "Lexington Green." During the rest of 1775, relations between the colonies and Great Britain worsened. The Second Continental Congress, a body of representatives from the 13 colonies, created an army and "shut up General Gage" in the Battle of Bunker Hill in Boston. (Document 1) At the same time, some members of the congress still hoped for reconciliation. Congress sent the Olive Branch Petition to the king of Great Britain, affirming loyalty to the monarch and blaming the current problems on Parliament. (King George III rejected the petition.)

It was in this context that Paine wrote *Common Sense*. He wrote about the logic of the Olive Branch Petition. Paine plainly and forcefully concluded that the period of negotiations and debate was over; "'Tis Time to Part," he concluded. The work, according to historian Arthur Schlesinger, had "crucial repercussions." (Document 1) The pamphlet was soon reproduced in newspapers throughout the colonies. Soon after publication, "over 100,000 copies" of the pamphlet were distributed in major cities and minor towns. (Document 2) He put the blame on the king, not on missteps by parliament. Paine argued that the 13 colonies would thrive if they were free of their ties to Great Britain. Paine not only argued that declaring independence made logical and moral sense, but he also argued that the colonies would more likely get support from Great Britain's rivals in Europe if they declared independence. A foreign power would not likely get involved in the internal struggles of another nation. However, they might aid an independent nation in a war against Great Britain. (Document 2)

Paine's arguments carried the day. The excitement of his prose and the forcefulness of his arguments captured the "sense of adventure" many Americans felt at the time, according to historian Edmund S. Morgan. Paine convinced Americans that their struggle for independence was "the cause of all mankind." (Document 3) Things moved quickly in the spring and summer of 1776. The Virginia House of Burgesses voted to instruct their delegates to the Second Continental Congress to support an independence resolution. By June, Richard Henry Lee of Virginia put forth a resolution to declare independence in Congress. On July 2, the delegates formally declared independence. (Document 3) On July 4, the delegates ratified the wording of the final draft of the Declaration of Independence, began signing the document (a treasonous act), and started distributing it throughout the colonies.

In the early 20th century, another publication, *The Jungle* by Upton Sinclair, also shook up the public and challenged the prevailing order. The 1906 book shined a spotlight on the unsanitary and dangerous conditions in the meatpacking industry. The book was written in the context of the rapid expansion of industry in the late 19th century. At that time, many substandard products were made available to the public. In the mad dash to maximize profits in a growing economy, producers cut corners, adulterated food, did not test their products, and routinely ignored even the most basic health and safety precautions. Food was tainted with chemicals. Drug companies sold unproved concoctions that "promised to cure all sorts of diseases" but were largely ineffective. (Document 7) Government officials either looked the other way or did not think it was within their purview to address these issues. As corporations amassed great profits for their owners, the public suffered. These shoddy production practices were brought to light by crusading journalists who worked to expose the underside of industrial production. These crusaders, known as muckrakers, used photography, mass circulation magazines, and indignant language to let the world know of these practices.

Upton Sinclair fell within this tradition of muckraking journalists. After reading about the practices of the meatpacking industry, he became "moved by these injustices." He traveled to Chicago to investigate the condition of the meatpackers. He saw firsthand the power of the beef trust over its workers, how the industry was easily able to defeat a strike by the union. The power dynamics of the meat industry represented, for Sinclair, "everything that was wrong" with industrial capitalism. (Document 7) Sinclair's research led to the publication of a stirring novel in 1906 called *The Jungle*. The book follows a Lithuanian immigrant family through the stockyards of Chicago and exposes the conditions in the meatpacking industry. Though the book is a novel, it was thoroughly researched and well written. We see the horrible conditions that existed in this industry. Meat that spoiled was brought back to the plant, doused in bleach, and flavored with spices. Workers were not provided facilities to wash their hands. Rat droppings were swept into the hopper and mixed into the sausage meat. The conditions of the meatpacking industry were thoroughly unsanitary and dangerous. Though he hoped to draw attention to the workers in the meatpacking industry, the public was more moved by the disgusting processes involved in meat processing. As Sinclair said, "I aimed at the public's heart and by accident I hit it in the stomach." (Document 8a)

President Theodore Roosevelt, after he was "deluged" with letters from the public, was moved to take action. His first action was to create an investigative commission to examine the practices of the meatpacking industry. (Document 8a) Calls for action came from many sectors of American society. Certainly, consumers were concerned. Consumer advocate Harvey Wiley lobbied for the federal government to take a more supervisory role in the meatpacking industry. Even members of the business community realized that federal action was necessary. Some owners of big businesses hoped that federal inspection would "bring order and stability" to what had become a disreputable industry. (Document 8b) In the wake of the investigative work of the federal government, Roosevelt was able to persuade Congress to take action. In 1906, Congress passed the Meat Inspection Act and the Pure Food and Drug Act, which established the Food and Drug Administration.

The impact of these actions was immediate and sweeping. By the end of 1906, meat processors were announcing that their products were in strict compliance with the provisions of the Pure Food and Drug Act. The push for safe food was not fleeting. Sixty years later, during the administration of Lyndon B. Johnson, additional food safety laws were passed to strengthen the earlier laws. The Wholesome Meat Act of 1967 continued the push of the 1906 Meat Inspection Act. President Johnson, upon signing the bill, said that consumers could rest assured that their meat was "pure" and "processed in a sanitary plant." Johnson invited an elderly Upton Sinclair to the signing ceremony to stress the impact of *The Jungle* decades after its publication. (Document 9)

Both Paine and Sinclair used the power of the written word to bring attention to matters of public concern, to convince people to rethink long-held convictions, and to move officials to take decisive action.

Topic	Question Numbers	Number of Points
American political history	2, 14, 16, 33, 39, 42, 43, 47	10
Political theory	3	1
Economic theory/policy	12, 17, 18, 19, 28, 29, 30, 31, 34, 49	12
Constitutional principles	4, 5, 6, 7, 11, 20, 25, 44	10
American foreign policy	21, 23, 26, 32, 36, 37, 38, 41, 45	11
American studies—the American people	13, 15, 22, 24, 35, 40, 46, 48, 50	11
Social/cultural developments	27	1
Geography	1, 8, 9, 10	5
Skills questions included in the above content area		
Reading comprehension	6, 7, 10, 20, 29, 30, 32, 36, 40	
Cartoon/image interpretation	13, 21, 22, 33, 34, 35, 44, 47	
Graph/table interpretation	12	
Map interpretation	8, 9, 50	
Outlining skills	16	

PART I

Multiple-Choice Questions by Standard

Standard	Question Numbers
1—United States and New York History	7, 10, 11, 14, 15, 16, 21, 22, 24, 26, 27, 29, 30, 32, 33, 35, 38, 39, 42, 45, 48
2—World History	23, 36, 37, 41
3—Geography	1, 8, 9, 50
4—Economics	12, 17, 18, 19, 28, 31, 34, 43, 49
5—Civics, Citizenship, and Government	2, 3, 4, 5, 6, 13, 20, 25, 40, 44, 46, 47

Parts II and III by Theme and Standard

	Theme	Standards
Thematic Essay	Places and Regions; Presidential Decisions and Actions; Diversity; Foreign Policy	Standards 1, 2, 3, 4, and 5: United States and New York History; World History; Geography; Economics; Civics, Citizenship, and Government
Document-Based Essay	Constitutional Principles; Civic Values; Citizenship; Government; Reform Movements; Presidential Decisions and Actions; Change; Culture and Intellectual Life	Standards 1, 2, 3, 4, and 5: United States and New York History; World History; Geography; Economics; Civics, Citizenship, and Government

Examination
August 2018
United States History
and Government

PART I: MULTIPLE CHOICE

Directions (1–50): For each statement or question, write in the space provided the *number* of the word or expression that, of those given, best completes the statement or answers the question.

1 The geography of the Atlantic Coastal Plain most influenced the southern economy during the period from 1620 to 1865 because it

(1) promoted a plantation system of agriculture
(2) led to diversified manufacturing
(3) encouraged development of the railroad industry
(4) resulted in widespread mining of coal   1 _____

2 Which event during the Colonial Era most influenced the concept of freedom of the press?

(1) passage of the Navigation Acts
(2) trial of John Peter Zenger
(3) creation of the Albany Plan of Union
(4) establishment of the House of Burgesses   2 _____

3 The social contract theory as applied to the Declaration of Independence most directly reflects the ideas of

(1) John Locke   (3) Baron de Montesquieu
(2) Thomas Hobbes   (4) Adam Smith   3 _____

4 A principal reason for calling the Constitutional Convention of 1787 was to

(1) strengthen the central government
(2) settle land disputes with Canada
(3) increase the power of the states
(4) weaken the system of checks and balances   4 _____

5 One reason Antifederalist governors of New York and Virginia opposed ratification of the United States Constitution was because it would

(1) force them to abandon western land claims
(2) weaken the powers of state governments
(3) strengthen slavery
(4) make the amendment process more difficult   5 _____

6 Political parties, the president's cabinet, and national nominating conventions are considered examples of

(1) delegated powers   (3) the elastic clause
(2) separation of powers   (4) the unwritten constitution   6 _____

7 Thomas Jefferson used a loose interpretation of the United States Constitution when he

(1) negotiated the purchase of the Louisiana Territory from France in 1803
(2) asked Congress to increase the size of the United States Navy
(3) ran for a second term as president
(4) opposed the reelection of John Adams in 1800   7 _____

8 Between 1820 and 1850, Southern lawmakers consistently opposed protective tariffs because these tariffs

(1) decreased trade between the states
(2) harmed American shipping
(3) increased the cost of imports
(4) weakened national security   8 _____

9 In the 1840s, westward expansion was justified by a belief in

(1) laissez-faire   (3) cultural pluralism
(2) popular sovereignty   (4) Manifest Destiny   9 _____

10 Which reform movement is most closely associated with William Lloyd Garrison, Frederick Douglass, and Harriet Beecher Stowe?

(1) abolitionist   (3) Populist
(2) labor   (4) Progressive   10 _____

Base your answers to questions 11 and 12 on the statements below and on your knowledge of social studies.

Speaker A: The political union created by the Constitution of the United States is not a temporary compact of the states but rather an unbreakable bond created by the people of the nation.

Speaker B: The reserved powers are clearly indicated and protected in both the original Constitution and in the 10th amendment of the Bill of Rights.

Speaker C: Liberty is best preserved in the hands of the government closest to the people. Union is desirable only if it preserves our liberty.

Speaker D: Nullification! Secession! What miserable words—words that threaten the continuance of both our liberty and our Union.

11 Which two speakers express the greatest support for the concept of States rights?

(1) *A* and *B*   (3) *B* and *C*
(2) *A* and *D*   (4) *C* and *D*   11 _____

12 The political opinions expressed in these statements relate most directly to the start of which war?

(1) Revolutionary War   (3) Mexican-American War
(2) War of 1812   (4) Civil War   12 _____

13 Passage of the Kansas-Nebraska Act (1854) was criticized by Northern newspapers because it

(1) limited settlement in those territories
(2) repealed the 36°30' line of the Missouri Compromise
(3) upheld the Supreme Court decision in *Gibbons v. Ogden*
(4) admitted Maine to the Union as a free state   13 _____

14 After the Civil War, the most common occupations for freedmen were

(1) sharecroppers and tenant farmers
(2) factory owners and teachers
(3) skilled artisans and mechanics
(4) miners and soldiers   14 _____

15 Which geographic factor presented a major problem for settlers on the Great Plains?

(1) limited rainfall   (3) mountainous terrain
(2) dense forests   (4) frequent flooding   15 _____

Base your answer to question 16 on the graphic organizer below and on your knowledge of social studies.

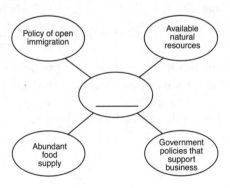

16 Which title is most appropriate for this graphic organizer?

(1) Rise of Labor Unions
(2) Innovations and Technology
(3) Vertical Integration of Business
(4) Factors Contributing to Industrialization   16 _____

17 In the United States, third parties have been influential because they have often

(1) outspent their political opponents
(2) provided the presidential candidate of the major parties
(3) suggested reforms later adopted by the two major parties
(4) elected majorities in both Congress and state legislatures

17 _____

18 One purpose of the Chinese Exclusion Act (1882) was to

(1) speed construction of the western railroads
(2) encourage settlement of the Pacific Coast
(3) expand the civil rights of immigrants
(4) protect the jobs of American workers

18 _____

19 The Interstate Commerce Act of 1887 and the Sherman Antitrust Act of 1890 were passed by Congress to

(1) help regulate the money supply
(2) promote investment in manufacturing
(3) control business practices that limited competition
(4) limit the hours of working women

19 _____

20 Which demographic change resulted from the economic developments of the late 1800s?

(1) an increase in African American migration from the North to the South
(2) an increase in the number of people living in urban areas
(3) a decrease in the number of immigrants coming to the United States
(4) a decrease in the number of factory workers in the Northeast

20 _____

21 Between 1900 and 1930, United States relations with Latin America were characterized by repeated United States efforts to

(1) encourage the redistribution of land to the poor
(2) deny economic aid to developing nations
(3) limit the influence of communist dictators
(4) control the internal affairs of many nations in the region   21 _____

22 President Theodore Roosevelt earned a reputation as a trustbuster because he

(1) favored the conservation of natural resources
(2) used court actions to break up business monopolies
(3) sided with labor unions against big business
(4) opposed the efforts of consumer advocates   22 _____

23 One way in which Ida Tarbell, Upton Sinclair, and Jacob Riis were similar is that each sought to

(1) end racial discrimination
(2) control illegal immigration
(3) limit government regulations
(4) expose economic and social abuses   23 _____

24 The purpose of the initiative, referendum, and recall was to

(1) eliminate the two-party system
(2) limit participation in state elections
(3) increase citizen influence in government
(4) strengthen the power of political machines   24 _____

Base your answer to question 25 on the photograph below and on your knowledge of social studies.

Bibb Mill No. 1, Macon, Ga.

Source: Lewis Hine, January 19,1909

25 Which conclusion is most clearly supported by this photograph?

(1) Textile manufacturing was not important to the national economy.
(2) State and federal governments did not adequately regulate child labor.
(3) American factories were less productive than factories in other countries.
(4) Strict federal safety standards were enforced in factories across the nation.

25 _____

26 During the 1920s, Congress established a quota system for immigration in order to

  (1) ensure that the United States would have enough factory workers
  (2) keep migrant workers out of the country
  (3) reduce immigration from southern and eastern Europe
  (4) assist refugees from war-torn countries　　　　26 _____

27 Which event is an example of nativism in the 1920s?

  (1) the trial of Sacco and Vanzetti
  (2) the verdict in the Scopes trial
  (3) the Teapot Dome scandal
  (4) the stock market crash　　　　27 _____

28 • They are suffering because they have little control over the prices for what they produce.

  • They have worldwide competition.
  • They have difficulty organizing to protect themselves.
  • They pay high prices for capital goods.

  Which group's economic situation in the 1920s is most accurately described in these statements?

  (1) farmers　　　　　　　　(3) manufacturers
  (2) railroad companies　　　(4) factory workers　　　28 _____

Base your answers to questions 29 and 30 on the cartoon below and on your knowledge of social studies.

"Yes, You Remembered Me"

Source: C. D. Batchelor, *New York Daily News*, October 11, 1936

29 The main idea of this political cartoon from the 1930s is that President Franklin D. Roosevelt

   (1) continued the laissez-faire policies of earlier presidents
   (2) supported business over labor
   (3) favored government ownership of major industries
   (4) extended help to those in need   29 ____

30 The New Deal attempted to carry out the theme of the cartoon by

   (1) restricting labor union membership
   (2) loaning money to foreign countries
   (3) funding many public works projects
   (4) banning the sale of stocks and bonds   30 ____

31 The defeat of President Franklin D. Roosevelt's "court packing" plan by Congress is an example of

(1) federalism
(2) checks and balances
(3) due process
(4) the amendment process

31 _____

Base your answer to question 32 on the excerpt from the letter below and on your knowledge of social studies.

. . . This new phenomenon [nuclear chain reaction] would also lead to the construction of bombs, and it is conceivable—though much less certain—that extremely powerful bombs of a new type may thus be constructed. . . .

Yours very truly,
Albert Einstein

— Letter to President Franklin D. Roosevelt from Albert Einstein, August 2, 1939

32 The administration of President Franklin D. Roosevelt reacted to the information contained in this letter by

(1) declaring war on the Axis powers
(2) creating the Manhattan Project
(3) proposing the Lend-Lease plan
(4) initiating the D-Day invasion of Europe

32 _____

33 The internment of Japanese Americans during World War II primarily affected those Japanese Americans who lived

(1) in the Ohio River valley
(2) along the Gulf Coast
(3) on the West Coast
(4) near the Rio Grande border with Mexico

33 _____

34 After World War II, one important outcome of the passage of the Servicemen's Readjustment Act of 1944 (GI Bill) was that it

 (1) allowed women to serve in combat positions
 (2) limited suburban growth
 (3) provided funds for new military bases
 (4) created educational and housing assistance
     for veterans   34 _____

35 What was the primary reason for the creation of both the Truman Doctrine and the Marshall Plan?

 (1) to reward the Chinese for their role in the Allied victory over Japan
 (2) the fear of Soviet communist expansion throughout Europe
 (3) the need to support colonial independence movements in the developing world
 (4) the protection of vital United States interests in Middle East oil fields   35 _____

36 The United States responded to the Berlin blockade in 1948 by

 (1) boycotting German-made imports
 (2) building the Berlin Wall
 (3) stopping all traffic leaving Berlin
 (4) airlifting food and supplies into Berlin   36 _____

37 A major significance of the Korean War (1950–1953) is that for the first time

 (1) an atomic bomb was used in warfare
 (2) Asian and United States troops fought against each other
 (3) the United Nations used military force to oppose aggression
 (4) the Soviet Union and the United States supported the same side   37 _____

38 **"All Federal Employees Required to Take Loyalty Oath"**
"Army-McCarthy Hearings Begin" "Rosenbergs Convicted"

These newspaper headlines from the decade following World
War II are all connected to the

(1) war crimes trials in Japan
(2) passage of civil rights legislation in the United States
(3) fear of communism in the United States
(4) debate over economic aid to Europe   38 _____

39 In 1962, President John F. Kennedy responded to the discovery of
nuclear missiles in Cuba by

(1) ordering a naval quarantine of Cuba
(2) capturing strategic locations in Cuba
(3) threatening to invade the Soviet Union
(4) prohibiting travel to the southeastern United States   39 _____

40 During the 1960s, the actions of Cesar Chavez led to improved
conditions for

(1) coal miners
(2) migrant farm workers
(3) autoworkers
(4) health care workers   40 _____

41 Which phrase best completes the heading of the partial outline
below?

> I. Native American Indian _____
>
>   A. Occupation of Alcatraz
>   B. Wounded Knee (1973)
>   C. Formation of American Indian
>   Movement (AIM)

(1) Protests Against the Vietnam War
(2) Demands for Equality
(3) Attempts to Culturally Assimilate
(4) Support for the War on Poverty   41 _____

42 Which document is the result of President Jimmy Carter's efforts to increase stability in the Middle East?

(1) Camp David Accords   (3) Panama Canal Treaty

(2) Nuclear Test Ban Treaty   (4) Paris Peace Accords   42 _____

43 What was the reason the Equal Rights Amendment did not become part of the United States Constitution?

(1) President Ronald Reagan vetoed it.

(2) Three-fourths of the states did not ratify it.

(3) The National Organization for Women (NOW) did not support it.

(4) The Supreme Court ruled it was unconstitutional.   43 _____

44 Which combination of factors contributed most directly to the severe recession in the United States economy in 2008?

(1) immigration restrictions and lack of skilled workers

(2) cuts in defense spending and social welfare programs

(3) excessive use of credit and bank speculation in the mortgage market

(4) tight monetary policy and overregulation of banks   44 _____

Base your answer to question 45 on the cartoon below and on your knowledge of social studies.

Source: Walt Handelsman, *Newsday*, April 26, 2006

45 The main idea of this cartoon is that public approval of the president in 2006 was directly linked to the

(1) cost of gasoline in the United States
(2) success in stopping human rights abuses abroad
(3) ability to restrict the flow of illegal drugs
(4) amount of the budget surplus

45 _____

Base your answer to question 46 on the cartoon below and on your knowledge of social studies.

Source: Jim Morin, *Miami Herald*, May 10, 2015

46 The main idea of this cartoon is that telephone surveillance by the National Security Administration (NSA)

(1) has been troubled by technical difficulties

(2) violates some of the protections of the United States Constitution

(3) is legal because it protects the privacy of Internet users

(4) increases hacking of top-secret government information

46 _____

47 The Alien and Sedition Acts of 1798 were similar to the Espionage and Sedition Acts passed during World War I because they both

(1) provided for the draft of men into the military
(2) gave the government greater control over the production of goods
(3) tried to restrict criticism of and opposition to government policies
(4) attempted to justify United States involvement in a foreign war

47 _____

48 Which set of events in United States history is most closely associated with westward expansion?

(1) passage of the Indian Removal Act of 1830 and the Compromise of 1877
(2) issuing the Emancipation Proclamation of 1863 and creation of the Federal Reserve System in 1913
(3) passage of the Agricultural Adjustment Act of 1933 and creation of the Tennesee Valley Authority in 1933
(4) passage of the Homestead Act of 1862 and opening of the transcontinental railroad in 1869

48 _____

49 The National Association for the Advancement of Colored People (NAACP), the Congress of Racial Equality (CORE), and the Southern Christian Leadership Conference (SCLC) are all associated with which movement?

(1) temperance
(2) abolition
(3) civil rights
(4) environmentalism

49 _____

Base your answer to question 50 on the cartoon below and on your knowledge of social studies.

Trying to Close the Gap

Source: Art Bimrose, *Portland Oregonian* (adapted)

50 Which action was an attempt to close the "gap" referred to in the cartoon?

(1) signing the Yalta Agreement
(2) passing the Gulf of Tonkin Resolution
(3) proposing the Strategic Defense Initiative (SDI)
(4) agreeing to the Strategic Arms Limitation Treaty (SALT)   50 _____

In developing your answer to Part II, be sure to keep these general definitions in mind:
   (a) <u>describe</u> means "to illustrate something in words or tell about it"
   (b) <u>explain</u> means "to make plain or understandable; to give reasons for or causes of; to show the logical development or relationships of "
   (c) <u>discuss</u> means "to make observations about something using facts, reasoning, and argument; to present in some detail"

PART II: THEMATIC ESSAY

Directions: Write a well-organized essay that includes an introduction, several paragraphs addressing the task below, and a conclusion.

Theme: Supreme Court Decisions

> The United States Supreme Court has issued decisions that have defined the constitutional rights of individuals and groups of people. These decisions by the Court have had a great impact on the nation.

Task:

> Select *two* United States Supreme Court cases and for *each*
>
> • Describe the historical circumstances surrounding the case
> • Explain the Court's decision
> • Discuss the impact of the Court's decision on the United States or on American society

You may use any appropriate Supreme Court case from your study of United States history. Some suggestions you might wish to consider include *Worcester v. Georgia* (1832), *Dred Scott v. Sanford* (1857), *Plessy v. Ferguson* (1896), *Korematsu v. United States* (1944), *Brown v. Board of Education of Topeka* (1954), *Engel v. Vitale* (1962), *Miranda v. Arizona* (1966), *Roe v. Wade* (1973), and *New Jersey v. T.L.O.* (1985).

You are *not* limited to these suggestions.

Guidelines:

In your essay, be sure to:

- Develop all aspects of the task
- Support the theme with relevant facts, examples, and details
- Use a logical and clear plan of organization, including an introduction and a conclusion that are beyond a restatement of the theme

In developing your answers to Part III, be sure to keep these general definitions in mind:
  (a) <u>describe</u> means "to illustrate something in words or tell about it"
  (b) <u>explain</u> means "to make plain or understandable; to give reasons for or causes of; to show the logical development or relationships of "
  (c) <u>discuss</u> means "to make observations about something using facts, reasoning, and argument; to present in some detail"

PART III: DOCUMENT-BASED QUESTION

This question is based on the accompanying documents. The question is designed to test your ability to work with historical documents. Some of these documents have been edited for the purposes of this question. As you analyze the documents, take into account the source of each document and any point of view that may be presented in the document. Keep in mind that the language used in a document may reflect the historical context of the time in which it was written.

Historical Context:

Under the Constitution, Congress has the power to support the armed forces and to declare war, but only the president is authorized to act as commander in chief. Throughout United States history, the president has used his power as commander in chief to respond to many foreign crises. These crises include the ***Mexican-American War (1846–1848)*** during the presidency of James K. Polk, the ***Vietnam War (1964–1975)*** during the presidency of Lyndon B. Johnson, and the ***Persian Gulf War (1990–1991)*** during the presidency of George H. W. Bush.

Task:

Using the information from the documents and your knowledge of United States history, answer the questions that follow each document in Part A. Your answers to the questions will help you write the Part B essay in which you will be asked to

Select ***two*** foreign crises listed in the historical context and for ***each***

  • Describe the historical circumstances that led to the crisis
  • Explain an action taken by the president to respond to the crisis
  • Discuss an effect of the president's action on the United States and/or on American society

Part A: Short-Answer Questions

Directions: Analyze the documents and answer the short-answer questions that follow each document in the space provided.

Document 1

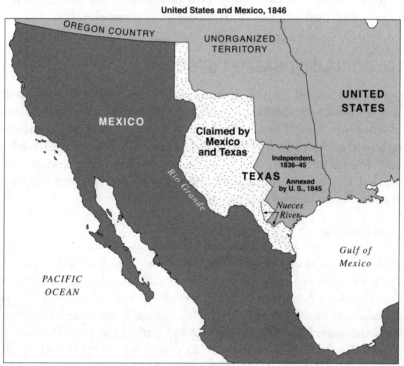

United States and Mexico, 1846

Source: Thomas A. Bailey et al., *The American Pageant*, Houghton Mifflin (adapted)

1 Based on the information provided by this map, state **one** cause of the conflict between the United States and Mexico in 1846. [1]

_____

_____

Document 2

. . . In my message at the commencement of the present session I informed you that upon the earnest appeal both of the Congress and convention of Texas I had ordered an efficient military force to take a position "between the Nueces and the Del Norte [Rio Grande]." This had become necessary to meet a threatened invasion of Texas by the Mexican forces, for which extensive military preparations had been made. The invasion was threatened solely because Texas had determined, in accordance with a solemn resolution of the Congress of the United States [March 1, 1845], to annex herself to our Union, and under these circumstances it was plainly our duty to extend our protection over her citizens and soil. . . .

Source: President James K. Polk, *War Message*, May 11, 1846 (adapted)

2 Based on this document, what action did President James K. Polk take in 1846 regarding Texas? [1]

_____

_____

Document 3a

> . . . It was a peculiarity of nineteenth-century politics that more than a year elapsed between the election of a Congress and its initial meeting. The Thirtieth Congress, elected in 1846, assembled in December 1847 to confront the complex questions arising from the Mexican War. Although Democrats in the Senate outnumbered their opponents by almost two to one, the Whig party enjoyed a narrow margin in the House—the only time in his entire legislative career that Lincoln found himself in the majority. Both parties, however, were internally divided, especially on the question of the future expansion of slavery. In August 1846, just as the previous Congress drew to a close, Congressman David Wilmot of Pennsylvania had proposed an amendment to an appropriation bill requiring that slavery be prohibited in any territory acquired from Mexico. The Wilmot Proviso, which passed the House but failed in the Senate, split both parties along sectional lines and ushered in a new era in which the slavery issue moved to the center stage of American politics. . . .

Source: Eric Foner, The Fiery Trial: Abraham Lincoln and American Slavery,
W. W. Norton & Company, 2010

3a According to Eric Foner, what issue did the Wilmot Proviso attempt to address?   [1]

_____

_____

Document 3b

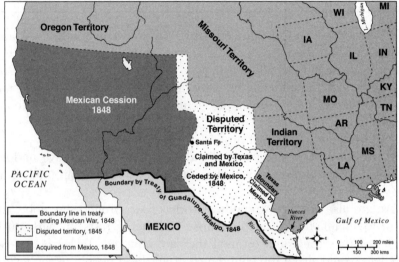

United States Acquisitions from Mexico, 1848

Source: *Historical Maps on File*, Facts on File, 2002 (adapted)

3b Based on the information provided by this map, what was *one* effect of the Mexican-American War on the United States in 1848? [1]

_____

_____

Document 4

WHY ARE WE IN VIET-NAM?

. . . Why are these realities our concern? Why are we in South Viet-Nam?

We are there because we have a promise to keep. Since 1954 every American President has offered support to the people of South Viet-Nam. We have helped to build, and we have helped to defend. Thus, over many years, we have made a national pledge to help South Viet-Nam defend its independence.

And I intend to keep that promise.

To dishonor that pledge, to abandon this small and brave nation to its enemies, and to the terror that must follow, would be an unforgivable wrong.

We are also there to strengthen world order. Around the globe, from Berlin to Thailand, are people whose well-being rests, in part, on the belief that they can count on us if they are attacked. To leave Viet-Nam to its fate would shake the confidence of all these people in the value of an American commitment and in the value of America's word. The result would be increased unrest and instability, and even wider war. . . .

Source: "Peace Without Conquest," President Lyndon B. Johnson,
Address at Johns Hopkins University, April 7, 1965

4 Based on this document, state *one* reason President Lyndon B. Johnson believed the United States should continue to assist South Vietnam.   [1]

_____

_____

Document 5a

. . . What are our goals in that war-strained land?

First, we intend to convince the Communists that we cannot be defeated by force of arms or by superior power. They are not easily convinced. In recent months they have greatly increased their fighting forces and their attacks and the number of incidents.

I have asked the Commanding General, General Westmoreland, what more he needs to meet this mounting aggression. He has told me. We will meet his needs.

I have today ordered to Viet-Nam the Air Mobile Division and certain other forces which will raise our fighting strength from 75,000 to 125,000 men almost immediately. Additional forces will be needed later, and they will be sent as requested.

This will make it necessary to increase our active fighting forces by raising the monthly draft call from 17,000 over a period of time to 35,000 per month, and for us to step up our campaign for voluntary enlistments. . . .

Source: President Lyndon B. Johnson, "Why We Are in Viet-Nam,"
News Conference, July 28, 1965 (adapted)

5a Based on this document, what was *one* action President Lyndon B. Johnson took in 1965 regarding Vietnam?   [1]

_____

_____

Document 5b

Allied Troop Levels in Vietnam, 1959–1969

Year	United States	South Vietnam	Australia	Korea	New Zealand	Philippines	Thailand
1959	760	243,000	--	--	--	--	--
1960	900	243,000	--	--	--	--	--
1961	3,205	243,000	--	--	--	--	--
1962	11,300	243,000	--	--	--	--	--
1963	16,300	243,000	--	--	--	--	--
1964	23,300	514,000	198	200	30	20	--
1965	184,300	642,500	1,560	20,620	120	70	20
1966	385,300	735,900	4,530	25,570	160	2,060	240
1967	485,600	798,700	6,820	47,830	530	2,020	2,200
1968	536,100	820,000	7,660	50,000	520	1,580	6,000
1969	475,200	897,000	7,670	48,870	550	190	11,570

Source: Church Committee Report on Diem Coup–1963, Vietnam,
War Statistics and Facts 1, 25thaviation.org (adapted)

5*b* Based on the information in this chart, what was *one* effect of the
actions taken by President Lyndon B. Johnson in 1965?   [1]

_____

_____

Document 6a

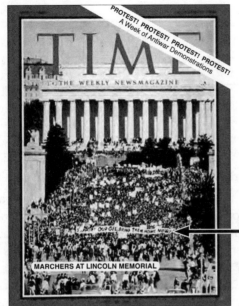

"Support Our GIs, Bring Them Home Now!"

MARCHERS AT LINCOLN MEMORIAL

Source: *Time*, October 27, 1967 (adapted)

Document 6b

. . . With America's sons in the fields far away, with America's future under challenge right here at home, with our hopes and the world's hopes for peace in the balance every day, I do not believe that I should devote an hour or a day of my time to any personal partisan causes or to any duties other than the awesome duties of this office—the Presidency of your country.

Accordingly, I shall not seek, and I will not accept, the nomination of my party for another term as your President. . . .

Source: President Lyndon B. Johnson, Address to the Nation Announcing Steps to Limit the War in Vietnam and Reporting His Decision Not to Seek Reelection, March 31, 1968

6 Based on these documents, state *two* effects of the Vietnam War on the United States.   [2]

(1) _____

   _____

(2) _____

   _____

Document 7a

Iraq Deploys Troops Near Kuwait Border Amid Dispute on Oil

WASHINGTON, July 23—American military officials are closely watching a new deployment of thousands of troops by Iraq along its border with Kuwait, where recent tensions appear to be escalating into a flaunting of strength by the two Persian Gulf countries, Pentagon officials said tonight. . . .

Source: *New York Times*, July 24, 1990

Document 7b

**IRAQ ARMY INVADES CAPITAL OF KUWAIT
IN FIERCE FIGHTING
EMERGENCY U.N. SESSION**

**Casualties Are Called Heavy—Emir's Palace Besieged as
Explosions Jolt City**

WASHINGTON, Thursday, August 2—Iraqi troops crossed the Kuwait border today and penetrated deeply into the country and into Kuwait's capital city, senior Administration officials said late Wednesday. . . .

Source: *New York Times*, August 2, 1990

Document 7c

> ### Iraq's Naked Aggression
>
> Without warrant or warning, Iraq has struck brutally at tiny Kuwait, a brazen [bold] challenge to world law. Iraq stands condemned by a unanimous U.N. Security Council and major Western oil purchasers. President [George H. W.] Bush's taste for bluntness stands him in good stead: "Naked aggression" is the correct term for President Saddam Hussein's grab at a vulnerable, oil-rich neighbor. . . .

Source: *New York Times*, August 3, 1990

7 Based on these documents, what was **one** cause of the Persian Gulf War? [1]

_____

_____

Document 8

Just 2 hours ago, allied air forces began an attack on military targets in Iraq and Kuwait. These attacks continue as I speak. Ground forces are not engaged.

This conflict started August 2d [1990] when the dictator of Iraq invaded a small and helpless neighbor. Kuwait—a member of the Arab League and a member of the United Nations—was crushed; its people, brutalized. Five months ago, Saddam Hussein started this cruel war against Kuwait. Tonight, the battle has been joined.

This military action, taken in accord with United Nations resolutions and with the consent of the United States Congress, follows months of constant

President George H. W. Bush

and virtually endless diplomatic activity on the part of the United Nations, the United States, and many, many other countries. Arab leaders sought what became known as an Arab solution, only to conclude that Saddam Hussein was unwilling to leave Kuwait. Others traveled to Baghdad in a variety of efforts to restore peace and justice. Our Secretary of State, James Baker, held an historic meeting in Geneva, only to be totally rebuffed. This past weekend, in a last-ditch effort, the Secretary-General of the United Nations went to the Middle East with peace in his heart—his second such mission. And he came back from Baghdad with no progress at all in getting Saddam Hussein to withdraw from Kuwait.

Now the 28 countries with forces in the Gulf area have exhausted all reasonable efforts to reach a peaceful resolution—have no choice but to drive Saddam from Kuwait by force. We will not fail. . . .

Source: President George H. W. Bush, Address to the Nation Announcing Allied
Military Action in the Persian Gulf, January 16, 1991

8 Based on this document, what was *one* action taken by President George H. W. Bush in response to Iraq's 1990 invasion of Kuwait?   [1]

_____

_____

Document 9a

NEWS of success in the ground war has sent America's hardcore peace activists into retreat and prompted citizens from coast to coast to proclaim that, after two decades, the country is finally purging the "Vietnam syndrome".

While families of servicemen waited anxiously, a sense of pride sometimes approaching glee infused the talk on the streets and on the air waves all day on Sunday and early yesterday. Again and again, people voiced the same view: after all the sneering and humiliation of recent years, America has proved it has the will and the might to fight and win a war. . . .

Spot opinion polls yesterday showed that well over 80 per cent of the population supported President Bush's decision to launch the ground war, and 75 per cent believed they should keep fighting until President Saddam Hussein is removed.

Commentators and historians are pointing out that Iraq is reaping all the anger pent up through years of humiliation since the debacle and retreat from Vietnam in the early 1970s. USA Today, the popular national newspaper, said the ground war "held the promise of completion, a chance to get past the anguish of Vietnam, and this time to do it right". . . .

Source: *The Times*, London, February 26, 1991

Document 9b

. . . Tonight the Kuwaiti flag once again flies above the capital of a free and sovereign nation. And the American flag flies above our Embassy.

Seven months ago, America and the world drew a line in the sand. We declared that the aggression against Kuwait would not stand. And tonight, America and the world have kept their word.

This is not a time of euphoria, certainly not a time to gloat. But it is a time of pride: pride in our troops; pride in the friends who stood with us in the crisis; pride in our nation and the people whose strength and resolve made victory quick, decisive, and just. And soon we will open wide our arms to welcome back home to America our magnificent fighting forces. . . .

Source: President George H. W. Bush, Address to the Nation on the Suspension of Allied Offensive Combat Operations in the Persian Gulf, February 27, 1991

9 Based on these documents, what were **two** effects of the Persian Gulf War on the United States?   [2]

(1) _____

_____

(2) _____

_____

Part B: Essay

Directions: Write a well-organized essay that includes an introduction, several paragraphs, and a conclusion. Use evidence from *at least* **four** documents in the body of the essay. Support your response with relevant facts, examples, and details. Include additional outside information.

Historical Context:

> Under the Constitution, Congress has the power to support the armed forces and to declare war, but only the president is authorized to act as commander in chief. Throughout United States history, the president has used his power as commander in chief to respond to many foreign crises. These crises include the **Mexican-American War (1846–1848)** during the presidency of James K. Polk, the **Vietnam War (1964–1975)** during the presidency of Lyndon B. Johnson, and the **Persian Gulf War (1990–1991)** during the presidency of George H. W. Bush.

Task:

> Using information from the documents and your knowledge of United States history, write an essay in which you
>
> Select **two** foreign crises listed in the historical context and for **each**
>
> - Describe the historical circumstances that led to the crisis
> - Explain an action taken by the president to respond to the crisis
> - Discuss an effect of the president's action on the United States and/or on American society

Guidelines:

In your essay, be sure to
- Develop all aspects of the task
- Incorporate information from *at least* **four** documents
- Incorporate relevant outside information
- Support the theme with relevant facts, examples, and details
- Use a logical and clear plan of organization, including an introduction and a conclusion that are beyond a restatement of the theme

Answers
August 2018
United States History and Government

Answer Key

PART I

1. 1	**11.** 3	**21.** 4	**31.** 2	**41.** 2
2. 2	**12.** 4	**22.** 2	**32.** 2	**42.** 1
3. 1	**13.** 2	**23.** 4	**33.** 3	**43.** 2
4. 1	**14.** 1	**24.** 3	**34.** 4	**44.** 3
5. 2	**15.** 1	**25.** 2	**35.** 2	**45.** 1
6. 4	**16.** 4	**26.** 3	**36.** 4	**46.** 2
7. 1	**17.** 3	**27.** 1	**37.** 3	**47.** 3
8. 3	**18.** 4	**28.** 1	**38.** 3	**48.** 4
9. 4	**19.** 3	**29.** 4	**39.** 1	**49.** 3
10. 1	**20.** 2	**30.** 3	**40.** 2	**50.** 4

PART II: Thematic Essay   *See* **Answers Explained** section.

PART III: Document-Based Question   *See* **Answers Explained** section.

Answers Explained

PART I (1–50)

1. **1** The geography of the Atlantic Coastal Plain most influenced the southern economy during the period from 1620 to 1865 because it promoted a plantation system of agriculture. The fertile soil, relatively flat land, and long growing season of the coastal regions of the South made the area ideal for large tobacco, rice, and indigo plantations. (Cotton did not become a major crop in the United States until the 1790s). While each plant or crop has a specific growing season, the growing season of a region is usually defined as the number of days between the last frost in the spring and the first frost in the fall. These large plantations lent themselves to the slave system of labor. In contrast, the hilly, rocky soil and shorter growing season of the northern colonies proved more suitable for smaller-scale agriculture and a more mixed economy. The smaller farms of the northern colonies were generally worked by the owner of the property and his family, with, perhaps, more people hired for planting and harvesting.

WRONG CHOICES EXPLAINED:

(2) The southern economy during the period from 1620 to 1865 was not known for developing a diversified manufacturing sector. Manufacturing operations began in the United States in the first half of the 19th century. An early factory complex—textile mills in Lowell, Massachusetts—opened in 1814. However, these early factories were concentrated in the northern states. A strong northern manufacturing sector aided Union forces in the Civil War. Even after the Civil War, the South was slow to industrialize.

(3) The southern economy during the period from 1620 to 1865 was not known for developing a strong railroad industry. The first section of railroad line, built and operated by the Baltimore and Ohio Railroad, opened in 1830. Railroad lines rapidly expanded in the following decades, but most of this development occurred in the northern states. By the time of the Civil War, the states of the Union had 22,000 miles of railroad tracks, compared to 9,500 miles in the states of the Confederacy.

(4) The southern economy during the period from 1620 to 1865 was not known for widespread coal mining. Coal mining increased in the United States every decade of the 1800s. However, most of this mining occurred in the northern states, most notably Pennsylvania. A smattering of coal mining operations existed in the South during the Civil War, but these were inland, not in the Atlantic Coastal Plain.

2. **2** The trial of John Peter Zenger was the event that most influenced the concept of freedom of the press during the colonial period. In 1734, Zenger, a New York City newspaper publisher, was arrested and charged with seditious libel for printing articles critical of the royal governor. His lawyer argued that he had the right to print such articles because they were truthful. The jury acquitted Zenger. In the wake of the case, more newspaper publishers were willing to print articles critical of royal authorities. The concept of freedom of the press is one of several protections enshrined in the First Amendment of the Constitution.

WRONG CHOICES EXPLAINED:

(1) The passage of the Navigation Acts is not associated with the concept of freedom of speech. The Navigation Acts were part of Great Britain's mercantilist approach to its North American colonies. The goal of the acts was to define the colonies as suppliers of raw materials to Britain and as markets for British manufactured items. Toward this end, Parliament developed a list of "enumerated goods"—goods from the colonies that could only be shipped to Britain. The enumeration of these goods was a double-edged sword; the colonies could not always get the highest price for their goods, but they had a consistent market for them. Several of the acts—such as the Wool Act (1699), the Hat Act (1732), and the Iron Act (1750)—set restrictions on colonial production of these manufactured items. In this way, Parliament gave an advantage to manufacturers in Britain.

(3) The creation of the Albany Plan of Union is not associated with the concept of freedom of speech. The Albany Plan of Union grew out of the Albany Congress, a 1754 meeting called by Benjamin Franklin. The goal of the plan was to unite the 13 colonies in order to provide for common defense and support for British forces in the French and Indian War. The plan was rejected by the colonial assemblies, as well as by British authorities, but it established the precedent of intercolonial cooperation.

(4) The establishment of the House of Burgesses is not associated with the concept of freedom of speech. The House of Burgesses was created by the Virginia Company in 1619. The company had founded the colony of Virginia in 1607 as a profit-generating venture. The company saw the need for some sort of body to govern the inhabitants of the colony and created this representative assembly. All free adult men could vote for representatives. Later, this was limited to wealthy men. After Virginia came under the jurisdiction of the crown instead of the Virginia Company (1624), the king allowed the House of Burgesses to continue. It is seen as an early example of representative government.

3. **1** The social contract theory as applied to the Declaration of Independence most directly reflects the ideas of John Locke. Locke was one of the main intellectual influences in the writing of the Declaration of Independence. He wrote *Two Treatises on Government* in the early 1690s to defend England's Glorious Revolution (1688) and to challenge Thomas Hobbes's defense of an absolutist monarchy. The body of the Declaration of Independence is a list of grievances against the king of Great Britain, but the eloquent preamble contains key elements of Locke's social contract theory. The basic idea of the theory is that people surrender some of their freedoms to the rules established by the government and the government is obligated to protect people's natural rights. Conversely, if a government violates people's natural rights, the people have the right "to alter or abolish it."

WRONG CHOICES EXPLAINED:

(2) The social contract theory as applied to the Declaration of Independence does not reflect the ideas of Thomas Hobbes. Hobbes defended an absolutist monarchy. He believed that humans were driven by selfish motives and that the natural state of humanity was a state of war. Therefore, he believed an absolute ruler was necessary in order to maintain peace and security.

(3) The social contract theory as applied to the Declaration of Independence does not reflect the ideas of Baron de Montesquieu. Montesquieu promoted the idea of separation of powers in government. He praised the English system for preventing the king from exercising absolute power. Power was separated with the king having certain powers and Parliament having certain powers. This principle was adopted by the framers of the United States Constitution. The Constitution separates power into three branches—the executive, the legislative, and the judicial. All three branches are given certain powers and each has the ability to limit, or check, the powers of the other two. The goal is to create balance among the three branches, with no branch able to dominate the other two. This principle is known as *checks and balances*.

(4) The social contract theory as applied to the Declaration of Independence does not reflect the ideas of Adam Smith (1723–1790). Smith's ideas provide the basis of classical free market economic theory. He argued that self-interest and competitiveness stimulated economic growth and prosperity.

4. **1** A principal reason for calling the Constitutional Convention of 1787 was to strengthen the central government. At the time, the United States government was based on the Articles of Confederation (1781–1788). The national government under the Articles of Confederation lacked many powers; most power remained with the state governments. The framers of this first American government created a "firm league of friendship" among the states, rather than a strong, centralized

government. Before 1776, they had lived under a powerful, distant authority and did not want to repeat that experience. Also, many of these early leaders were fiercely loyal to their states and did not want to see state power superseded. Funding the government proved to be a major problem. As written, the Articles did not give the national government the power to levy taxes. A proposal to alter the document and allow the national government to collect import duties was blocked by Rhode Island and New York, states with major ports. Concerns about the weaknesses of the government under the Articles of Confederation seemed to be borne out by Shays' Rebellion (1786–1787). This revolt of Massachusetts farmers who felt cheated by the state's economic policies was eventually put down by state armed forces. The delegates at the Constitutional Convention in Philadelphia (1787) believed that a stronger national government was needed to quickly put down any future disturbances.

WRONG CHOICES EXPLAINED:

(2) The Constitutional Convention was not called in order to settle land disputes with Canada. The United States had several conflicts with Great Britain over the border between the U.S. and British-ruled Canada. In the Webster-Ashburton Treaty (1842), the United States settled a dispute with Great Britain over the border between Maine and Canada. The treaty split the disputed territory and also settled a dispute over the border between the Minnesota territory and Canada. In 1846, the Polk administration reached a compromise with Great Britain over control of Oregon, establishing the border at the 49th parallel. That line is the current boundary between the western United States and Canada.

(3) The Constitutional Convention was not called in order to increase the power of the states. A major goal of the Constitutional Convention was to do the opposite—to decrease the power of the states and to increase the power of the central government. The government under the Articles of Confederation (1781–1788) was envisioned as a "firm league of friendship" among the states, rather than a strong, centralized government. The experience of living under the British government led to a distrust of a powerful, distant authority. Eventually, many political leaders saw the limits of this type of government and pushed for a Constitutional Convention to create a stronger central government.

(4) The Constitutional Convention was not called in order to weaken the system of checks and balances. The Constitutional Convention voted to create a central government with three branches—the legislative, the executive, and the judicial. In the Constitution, all three branches are given certain powers and each has the ability to limit, or check, the powers of the other two. The goal is to create balance among the three branches, with no branch able to dominate the other two. Thus, the principle known as *checks and balances* is central to the structure of the Constitution.

5. **2** One reason Antifederalist governors of New York and Virginia opposed ratification of the United States Constitution was because it would weaken the powers of state governments. Antifederalists feared the Constitution would create an omnipotent and unaccountable national government. Under the Articles of Confederation, which governed the United States in the 1780s before the ratification of the Constitution, the states retained major powers and the national government was given very limited powers. A central goal of the Constitution was to change this situation by giving the national government far more power and declaring it the "supreme law of the land." The Antifederalists were distrustful of distant authority. The 13 colonies had just emerged from under the thumb of the British Empire, so many colonists were eager to see power exercised locally. Eventually, many leading Antifederalists agreed to support ratification of the Constitution if a list of individual rights was added. This agreement led to the writing and ratification of the first ten amendments to the Constitution, known as the Bill of Rights.

WRONG CHOICES EXPLAINED:

(1) Antifederalist reasons for opposing the Constitution did not include forcing states to abandon western land claims. In fact, the issue of competing claims to the lands west of the established states had already been settled. Earlier, the Second Continental Congress had convinced states to give up their land claims as a condition for ratifying the Articles of Confederation. Maryland was the last state to agree to give up its western land claims (1781). These western lands then fell under the auspices of the national government until residents petitioned for territorial status and then statehood.

(3) Antifederalist reasons for opposing the Constitution did not include strengthening slavery. The Constitution recognized the institution of slavery and created regulations around the implementation of slavery. The Three-Fifths Compromise, for example, settled the issue of how slaves would be counted in the census (which would determine representation in the House of Representatives). The Fugitive Slave Clause required that slaves who escaped to another state be returned to their owners in the state from which they escaped. On the other hand, the Constitution did not include the words *slaves* or *slavery*, reflecting the unease of many of the framers of the Constitution with the institution of slavery. However, the issue of slavery was not central to the concerns of the Antifederalists.

(4) Antifederalist reasons for opposing the Constitution did not include making the amendment process more difficult. The process for amending the Constitution is not easy. First, an amendment can be proposed by Congress (by two-third majorities in both houses) or by a national convention.

Then, three-fourths of the states must approve an amendment for it to be ratified. The state-by-state approval process can occur by the consent of the state legislatures or by state ratifying conventions. However, the process for amending the Articles of Confederation—requiring unanimity among all the states—had also been difficult. In any case, the issue of the amendment process was not central to the concerns of the Antifederalists.

6. **4** Political parties, the president's cabinet, and national nominating conventions are considered examples of the unwritten constitution. The unwritten constitution refers to those traditions and practices that have become part of the American political system, but were not mentioned in the Constitution. Many of these practices date back to the administration of George Washington. Washington's administration witnessed the development of political parties, a practice unforeseen by most of the founding fathers. For most of the nation's history, two major rival parties have existed. The political parties serve to focus debate in Congress, as members of Congress tend to support their party's position. The president is, by virtue of his office, the most prominent public voice of his party, and therefore acts as its leader (although each party has a formal leader). President Washington also first regularly convened a cabinet, a group of advisors to the president that is comprised of the heads of major government departments. There are currently 15 cabinet-level departments, including the Department of Defense, the State Department, and the Department of the Interior. There are additional cabinet members who are not department heads. Cabinet members are nominated by the president and confirmed by the Senate. Political parties began holding national nominating conventions in the 1830s. Before that, members of Congress met as party caucuses to select presidential nominees for each party.

WRONG CHOICES EXPLAINED:
(1) Political parties, the president's cabinet, and national nominating conventions are not examples of delegated powers. Delegated powers are those powers given (or delegated) to the national government by the Constitution. State powers, on the other hand, are called reserved powers, in that they are held on to (or reserved) by the states. Powers held by both the federal and the state governments are called concurrent powers. Delegated powers include declaring war, entering treaties, coining money, establishing import duties and tariffs, and regulating commerce between states.
(2) Political parties, the president's cabinet, and national nominating conventions are not examples of separation of powers. Separation of powers describes a basic feature of the governing structure created by the Constitution. The framers of the Constitution created three branches of government, each with powers

separate from the other two. The legislative branch creates laws, the executive branch carries out laws, and the judicial branch interprets laws. The Constitution spells out the powers of each branch. The framers were very conscious of the problems of a government with limitless powers. After living under the British monarchy, they came to believe that a powerful government without checks was dangerous to liberty. Therefore, they created a governmental system with three branches, each with the ability to check the powers of the other two. The goal was to keep the three branches in balance.

(3) Political parties, the president's cabinet, and national nominating conventions are not examples of the elastic clause. The elastic clause to the Constitution, also known as the *necessary and proper clause*, addressed the concerns of some of the framers of the Constitution that Congress would not have the latitude to effectively carry out its powers. They feared that by listing specific powers, the Constitution might be seen as denying Congress additional powers to address unforeseen circumstances. They, therefore, pushed for the elastic clause, which stretched the powers of Congress by allowing it to "make all laws necessary and proper" in regard to carrying out its functions. Antifederalists were especially critical of the elastic clause, fearing that it would grant Congress limitless powers.

7. **1** Thomas Jefferson used a loose interpretation of the United States Constitution when he negotiated the purchase of the Louisiana Territory from France in 1803. The Louisiana Purchase initially presented a dilemma for President Jefferson. Previously, he had held a strict constructionist view of the Constitution. This view, also referred to as a strict interpretation of the Constitution, held that governmental officials should follow exactly what was stated and allowed for in the document. For example, in the 1790s he opposed the creation of a national bank, arguing that Congress was not granted the power to create such an institution. Secretary of the Treasury Alexander Hamilton countered this argument by invoking the elastic clause, asserting that the creation of a national bank was permissible under the Constitution. Later, Jefferson set aside his strict constructionist view of the Constitution when the Louisiana Territory became available to the United States. The territory was long held by France until France ceded it to Spain in 1763 following the French and Indian War. France then regained the territory in 1801. The ambitious French leader Napoleon Bonaparte quickly decided that it was in France's best interest to sell the Louisiana Territory at a reasonable price in order to attain cash to fund war with Great Britain. In 1803, American negotiators quickly agreed to a price of $15 million. Jefferson realized that the purchase of such land was not allowed for in the Constitution, but if he waited for a constitutional amendment specifically allowing Congress to acquire new

lands, Napoleon could rescind his offer. So Jefferson violated his long-held strict constructionist view and quickly presented the offer to Congress, which appropriated the money. For $15 million, the United States bought this vast expanse of land and nearly doubled its size. This flat area west of the Mississippi would become the most important agricultural region in the United States. In addition, the United States gained full control of the port of New Orleans and the Mississippi River.

WRONG CHOICES EXPLAINED:

(2) A president would not have to use a loose interpretation of the Constitution in order to ask Congress to increase the size of the United States Navy. The Constitution explicitly gives the president the power to suggest to Congress "such measures as he shall judge necessary." The powers of Congress include the power "to provide and maintain a Navy." Further, President Jefferson did not move to increase the size of the Navy. He took steps to reduce the size of both the navy and army. He argued that both could be reduced during times of peace.

(3) A president would not have to use a loose interpretation of the Constitution in order to run for a second term as president. The Constitution does not prohibit a president from running for a second term. President Jefferson ran for and was elected to a second term, just as President George Washington had done earlier.

(4) A president, or any individual, would not have to use a loose interpretation of the Constitution in order to oppose the election of another individual to office. The First Amendment to the Constitution protects freedom of speech, and the Constitution allows for an individual to oppose a sitting president and to run for the office of the presidency. Jefferson did just that in 1800. He opposed President John Adams in the election and was elected to be the third president of the United States.

8. **3** Between 1820 and 1850, southern lawmakers consistently opposed protective tariffs because these tariffs increased the cost of imports. Tariff rates divided northerners and southerners in the first half of the 19th century. Northern manufacturing interests supported the higher tariff rates, which would increase the price of imported goods and, therefore, make American-made goods more desirable for consumers. Such tariffs were labeled "protective" because they would protect American manufacturers from foreign competition. Southern cotton farmers, who supplied much of Great Britain's cotton, feared that high tariffs would cause a drop in international trade and would make imported items more expensive. The conflict over tariffs came to a head

following the passage of the Tariff Act of 1828. Labeled the "Tariff of Abominations" by its critics, the act set extraordinarily high tariffs on imported goods. John C. Calhoun and a group of South Carolina politicians took a strong stand against the Tariff Act and insisted on the states' right to nullify an unjust law. Ultimately, a compromise was reached, resulting in lower tariff rates.

WRONG CHOICES EXPLAINED:

(1) Southern lawmakers did not oppose protective tariffs on the grounds that they would decrease trade between the states. Protective tariffs targeted imports from foreign countries, not trade within the states. If anything, protective tariffs would encourage trade between the states.

(2) Southern lawmakers did not oppose protective tariffs on the grounds that they would harm American shipping. Shipping operations were more concentrated in northern port cities, such as Boston and New York. The southern economy was more focused on agriculture.

(4) Southern lawmakers did not oppose protective tariffs on the grounds that they would weaken national security. The revenue from tariffs went to the federal government. Increasing federal revenues would not result in a weakening of national security. If anything, more money would be available for national security.

9. **4** In the 1840s, westward expansion was justified by a belief in Manifest Destiny. The term *Manifest Destiny* was coined in an 1845 newspaper article. It captured the fervor of the westward expansion movement, implying that it was God's plan that the United States take over and settle the entire continent. Americans who did settle out West were probably driven more by economic factors, such as cheap land or precious metals, than they were by a desire to fulfill God's plan. The history of the settlement of West includes many noteworthy episodes: Texas independence from Mexico (1836), the opening of the Oregon Trail (1841), the Mexican War (1846–1848), the Mormon exodus to Utah (1847), and the California gold rush (1849). This movement was especially damaging for the Native Americans of the West who were driven off their land and relegated to several western reservations.

WRONG CHOICES EXPLAINED:

(1) Westward expansion was not justified by a belief in laissez-faire. The French phrase *laissez-faire* means "to leave alone." It describes a government policy that would take a hands-off approach in regard to economic activities. Territorial expansion occurred as a result of actions taken by the federal government—such as carrying out military engagements and negotiating treaties.

(2) Westward expansion was not justified by a belief in popular sovereignty. Popular sovereignty referred to letting the people of a particular territory decide whether or not to allow slavery in that territory. The principle was applied to the newly created Kansas and Nebraska Territories under the Kansas-Nebraska Act (1854). Violence soon erupted in "Bleeding Kansas" as proslavery and antislavery men fought for control of the state. The principle was intended to settle disputes over slavery in new territories, but it was not used to justify westward expansion.

(3) Westward expansion was not justified by a belief in cultural pluralism. *Cultural pluralism* is a term used to describe a social order in which smaller ethnic and racial groups participate in the dominant mainstream society, but still maintain their unique cultural identities. The concept implies acceptance by the broader society of the values and practices of the smaller groups. The idea of cultural pluralism came into wide usage in the early decades of the 20th century, both as a description of contemporary society and as a societal goal. The idea stood in contrast to the conception of the United States as a "melting pot," in which different ethnic groups lose their unique cultural traits as they assimilate into mainstream culture. Westward expansion was often accompanied by a belief in the superiority of mainstream American culture and institutions.

10. **1** William Lloyd Garrison, Frederick Douglass, and Harriet Beecher Stowe are closely associated with the abolitionist movement. Antislavery sentiment has existed in American society as long as slavery has existed. Most obviously, African Americans—both free and enslaved—opposed the existence of slavery. Small numbers of white Americans, from the 1600s onward, opposed slavery. Many believers in Enlightenment thought condemned slavery on humanistic grounds, while Quakers and some Evangelical Christians argued that slavery was inconsistent with Christian teachings. During the era of the American Revolution, more white Americans, including some slave-holders, began to see slavery as inconsistent with the democratic values of the revolution. Starting in the 1830s, in the wake of the Second Great Awakening, a broader movement for the abolition of slavery began to form. William Lloyd Garrison was a key figure in the movement. He called for the immediate abolition of slavery, in contrast to many other white activists who advocated a more gradual approach to ending slavery. He also asserted that there should be no compensation to slave owners and that freed slaves were entitled to the same rights as white people. He started a newspaper called *The Liberator* in 1831 to prod the public into challenging the institution of slavery. Starting in the 1840s, the towering figure in the abolitionist movement was Frederick Douglass. Douglass was born into slavery (1818) and escaped to the North in 1838. He had learned to read and write and soon

became a powerful speaker in the antislavery movement. Douglass's autobiography, *Narrative of the Life of Frederick Douglass*, written in 1845, became a best-seller. One of the most well-known and important antislavery speeches is Douglass's July 5, 1852, address to the Rochester Anti-Slavery Sewing Society, "What to the slave is the 4th of July?" The speech is critical of the United States for not abiding by its founding principles. He asserts that it is preposterous to expect enslaved African Americans to celebrate the birth of American freedom when they themselves are still oppressed. Douglass remained an important figure before, during, and after the Civil War, until his death in 1895. Harriet Beecher Stowe brought antislavery sentiment into the homes of many northerners with the publication of her best-selling novel, *Uncle Tom's Cabin*. The novel depicted, in graphic detail, the brutality of slavery. For many northerners, slavery now had a human face. The novel outraged southern supporters of slavery, who attempted to ban it.

WRONG CHOICES EXPLAINED:

(2) William Lloyd Garrison, Frederick Douglass, and Harriet Beecher Stowe are not associated with the labor movement. A large-scale union movement developed in the gilded age of the post–Civil War period. A significant early union was the Knights of Labor, founded in 1869. This union welcomed all members, regardless of race, sex, or level of skill. The Knights had a broad agenda that included not only improvements in wages and hours for their workers, but also social reforms such as an end to child labor and better safety rules. A second early union was the American Federation of Labor (1886). One of its founders and its first leader was a cigar-maker named Samuel Gompers. The AFL differed from the Knights of Labor in that it included only skilled workers, the "aristocracy of labor." Further, the AFL did not engage in any sort of political activities for broader social reform.

(3) William Lloyd Garrison, Frederick Douglass, and Harriet Beecher Stowe are not associated with the Populist movement. The Populist movement became a formidable force in the 1890s. The Populists grew angry at the concentration of wealth and power by eastern industrialists. They supported a national income tax so that those with higher incomes would pay more than the poor. The Populist Party, organized in 1892, wanted the United States to get off the gold standard and to issue money backed by silver as well. This would increase the amount of money in circulation and would lead to inflation. Farmers supported inflationary policies so that the prices they received for their produce would increase.

(4) William Lloyd Garrison, Frederick Douglass, and Harriet Beecher Stowe are not associated with the Progressive movement. The Progressive movement was a response to the economic instability, social inequality, and political

corruption that had begun during the gilded age of the post–Civil War period and continued into the 20th century. Progressive reformers, who were most active in the 1900s and 1910s, called for greater government intervention in the economy, as well as social justice measures, increased democratization of the political process, and conservation of natural resources.

11. **3** Speakers B and C express the greatest support for the concept of states' rights. The concept of states' rights describes the idea that states would retain certain rights even though the national government was supreme. The issue of states' rights became closely identified with the defense of slavery. Defenders of slavery in the South felt that the institution had sufficiently broad support among white southerners, but they feared that northern political leaders might use the power of the federal government to limit or abolish slavery. Hence, they firmly embraced the right of states to resist or nullify federal edicts. Speaker B is arguing that states' rights are clearly protected in the Constitution. The original Constitution acknowledges that states will still retain certain rights. The Tenth Amendment makes the concept of states' rights more explicit. It states that the federal government has certain powers. These powers include powers expressly stated, as well those that are implied. All remaining powers, the Tenth Amendment states, are "reserved to the States respectively, or to the people" (unless the Constitution specifically prohibits them). Speaker C goes further, opening up the possibility of secession. The speaker argues that "liberty" can only be ensured if power is maintained on the state level—"closest to the people." When the federal government attempts to limit this liberty, then "union" is no longer desirable and secession is called for. The extent of these states' rights, known as reserved powers, became the subject of much debate between the time of the ratification of the Constitution and the Civil War.

WRONG CHOICES EXPLAINED:
(1), (2), and (4) All three of these choices are incorrect because they contain either Speaker A or Speaker D, or both. Speaker A and Speaker D both express support for federal power, not states' rights. Speaker A argues that the Constitution is not a temporary measure created by the states. If it were, then states would have the right to leave the union if they so desired. Rather, the Constitution was created by the people and cannot be undone by individual states. The preamble states, "We the people . . . do ordain and establish this Constitution," not "We the states. . ." Speaker D roundly rejects both nullification and secession. Nullification is the theory that a state could declare an objectionable federal law or action null and void within that state. The speaker is arguing that nullification and secession would threaten liberty and the very existence of the United States.

12. **4** The political opinions expressed in the statements relate most directly to the start of the Civil War. On the eve of the Civil War, southern political leaders asserted the most drastic of states' rights—the right to secede. Seven southern states announced their intent to secede in the three months after the 1860 presidential election because they believed that President-elect Abraham Lincoln would undermine or abolish slavery. Four more southern states followed suit and announced their intent to secede after Lincoln was inaugurated. Lincoln made clear that he believed secession was unconstitutional and that it was not among the rights of the states. In his First Inaugural Address, he stated that, according to the Constitution, "the Union of these States is perpetual." Therefore, he added, "no State, upon its own mere motion, can lawfully get out of the Union." The southern states announced the formation of the Confederate States of America. Lincoln continued to insist that secession was illegal. The question of secession—and, indeed, of slavery—was settled by the victory of the Union army over the rebellious states of the South. Since then, it is clear that states' right do not include the right to secede.

WRONG CHOICES EXPLAINED:
    (1) The political opinions expressed in the statements, relating to the issue of states' rights, are not related to the start of the Revolutionary War. The Revolutionary War grew out of tensions between Great Britain and 13 of its North American colonies. These 13 colonies grew increasingly frustrated with British colonial policies in the aftermath of the French and Indian War (1754–1763). As Great Britain attempted to assert greater control over its empire, the colonies began to protest and resist. Fighting broke out in the Massachusetts towns of Lexington and Concord in 1775. The colonies formally declared their independence from Great Britain in July 1776. Fighting continued in North America into 1781; the Treaty of Paris formally ended the war in 1783.
    (2) The political opinions expressed in the statements, relating to the issue of states' rights, are not related to the start of the War of 1812. This war grew out of tensions between the United States and Great Britain. The United States grew increasingly resentful of British impressment of American sailors and of British assistance to Native American tribes in the Great Lakes region. The Treaty of Ghent (1815) ended the War of 1812 roughly where it had begun. The United States and Great Britain agreed to stop fighting, give back any territory seized in the war, and recognize the boundary between the United States and Canada that had been established before the war.
    (3) The political opinions expressed in the statements, relating to the issue of states' rights, are not related to the start of the Mexican-American War. This war grew out of the desire of the United States to expand its territory. Americans had

been settling in the Mexican territory of Texas as far back as the 1820s. In 1836, Texans fought for and won independence from Mexico; Texas joined the United States in 1845. Conflict between the United States and Mexico soon ensued. The two countries disagreed over the southern border of Texas. President James K. Polk sent troops into this disputed territory. Skirmishes in the disputed area led to war between Mexico and the United States. The United States won the war, which lasted from 1846 to 1848, and acquired the huge territory that comprised the northern provinces of Mexico, which is known as the Mexican Cession.

13. **2** Passage of the Kansas-Nebraska Act (1854) was criticized by northern newspapers because it repealed the 36°30′ line of the Missouri Compromise. The Kansas-Nebraska Act allowed for the possibility of slavery in the territories of Kansas and Nebraska—areas that had been closed to slavery by the Missouri Compromise (1820). The act mandated that the question of slavery in these territories be decided by popular sovereignty. Popular sovereignty called for settlers in new territories to vote on the issue of slavery. Many northerners were angry at the act and at the sponsor of the act, Senator Stephen A. Douglas, for making additional territory open to the possibility of slavery. The act divided Whigs—between proslavery "Cotton Whigs" and antislavery "Conscience Whigs." These divisions undermined the party, which ceased to function as a national party by 1856. In addition, violence erupted in Kansas as proslavery and antislavery men fought for control of the state. "Bleeding Kansas" can be seen as a dress rehearsal for the Civil War. The question of slavery in Kansas was unresolved when the Civil War began. After southern secession, Kansas quickly joined the Union as a free state in 1861.

WRONG CHOICES EXPLAINED:
(1) The Kansas-Nebraska Act did not limit settlement in those territories. The act was designed to encourage settlement by creating a pathway for these areas to attain territorial status and then to become states. In practice, the act resulted in a flood of proslavery and antislavery men into the territory who both hoped to influence the status of slavery in the territories.
(3) The Kansas-Nebraska Act did not uphold the Supreme Court decision in *Gibbons v. Ogden*. The case of *Gibbons v. Ogden* (1824) took place earlier and did not deal with the issue of slavery. In this case, the Supreme Court invalidated a monopoly on ferry transportation between New York and New Jersey that had been issued by New York, and asserted that only the federal government could regulate interstate trade.
(4) The Kansas-Nebraska Act did not admit Maine to the Union as a free state. Maine was admitted as part of the Missouri Compromise (1820). The compromise settled a controversy that arose between the slave-holding states

and the free states in 1820 when Missouri applied for statehood as a slave state. The admission of Missouri would have upset that balance between slave-holding states and free states. The compromise allowed for the admission of two new states—Missouri as a slave state and Maine as a free state. It also divided the remaining area of the Louisiana Territory at 36°30' north latitude. Above that line, slavery was not permitted (except for in Missouri); below the line, it was permitted. The compromise was repealed by the Kansas-Nebraska Act.

14. **1** After the Civil War, the most common occupations for freedmen were sharecroppers and tenant farmers. The Civil War disrupted the agricultural system in the South by ending slavery. It was not immediately clear what would replace it. White landowners needed African American laborers to work the cotton fields. The landowners wanted to hire groups of African American laborers, to be directed by white overseers. African Americans were resistant to this setup because it reminded them too much of the slave system. However, African Americans could not become landowners themselves, because they lacked the financial resources. Out of this impasse grew the sharecropping system. In the sharecropping system, African Americans (and poor whites) would farm a few acres of a large estate and give a share, often half, of the crops to the owner as rent. In this way, African Americans were not under the direct supervision of whites. After paying back loans for seed money and the use of tools, sharecroppers were left with very little, if anything. The system created a cycle of debt, which prevented African Americans from acquiring money and owning land. Tenant farming was considered a step up on the agricultural ladder (with actual ownership of land being the highest rung). Tenant farmers often had their own tools, animals, and a small amount of capital. They rented land to farm from a landowner, but usually paid with cash instead of a share of the crop.

WRONG CHOICES EXPLAINED:
    (2) After the Civil War, factory owners and teachers were not common occupations for freedmen. Some African Americans became teachers in schools that served the African American population, but the vast majority of freedmen continued to work in agriculture. Very few former slaves would have accumulated enough capital in the post–Civil War period to own a factory.
    (3) After the Civil War, skilled artisans and mechanics were not common occupations for freedmen. Some African Americans performed skilled craft work, but the vast majority of freedmen continued to work in agriculture.
    (4) After the Civil War, miners and soldiers were not common occupations for freedmen. Some African Americans, including freedmen, ventured west and became miners. In addition, several regiments of African American troops were formed after the Civil War. These soldiers, known as Buffalo Soldiers, participated in wars against Native Americans and in the Spanish American War

(1898), and they continued to exist into the 20th century. The regiments included freedmen, as well as African Americans who had not been enslaved. However, the vast majority of freedmen continued to work in agriculture.

15. **1** A major problem for settlers on the Great Plains was limited rainfall. The Great Plains is the vast area that lies west of the Mississippi River and east of the Rocky Mountains. It includes the present-day states of Kansas, Nebraska, North Dakota, and South Dakota, as well as parts of the states of Colorado, Iowa, Minnesota, Montana, New Mexico, Oklahoma, Texas, and Wyoming. Today, the region produces a large portion of the country's agricultural products. Before being converted to farmland, the Great Plains was known for its extensive grasslands. The rainfall of the region is generally limited. The western section (roughly west of the 100th meridian) receives less than 20 inches of rainfall per year, while the eastern area receives more than 20 inches per year. Despite limited rainfall, the region has a long growing season and rich soil. The government encouraged development of the region by passing the Homestead Act (1862), which provided free land in the region to settlers who were willing to farm it. Hundreds of thousands of people applied for and were granted homesteads. The expansion of railroads into the West, leading to the completion of a transcontinental railroad in 1869, also encouraged white settlement in the Great Plains. The railroads provided an economic lifeline for these new settlers. Freight trains brought crops and cattle from the Great Plains states to cities such as Chicago. This increased economic activity led to Native Americans being pushed off their land. The railroads also brought sportsmen out west who shot at buffalo herds from their passing train cars. While these buffalo were sport for white travelers, they were a means of sustenance for many Plains Indians. These factors all led to the decline of the Plains Indians.

WRONG CHOICES EXPLAINED:

(2) The Great Plains region is not characterized by dense forests. Dense forests are common in much of the interior of the East Coast region, the area around the Great Lakes, and the Pacific Northwest.

(3) The Great Plains region is not characterized by mountainous terrain. The Great Plains are relatively flat, with the exception of the Ozark Mountain range. Major ranges in the United States include the Appalachian Mountains, in the interior of the East Coast region, and the Rocky Mountains, west of the Great Plains. A series of mountain ranges, including the Sierra Nevada Mountains, stretch along the West Coast.

(4) The Great Plains region is not characterized by frequent flooding. Areas adjacent to rivers, such as the Mississippi River and its tributaries, are prone to flooding. The city of New Orleans, along the banks of the Mississippi River, is prone to flooding. Severe flooding occurred in the city, much of which sits below sea level, in the wake of Hurricane Katrina in 2005, leading to over 1,400 deaths.

16. **4** The most appropriate title for the graphic organizer is "Factors Leading to Industrialization." The graphic organizer contains four important factors that contributed to the rapid industrialization of the United States in the decades after the Civil War. A policy of open immigration helped provide the workforce for this industrial era. The large wave of immigrants who came to the United States between 1880 and 1920 was essential to the industrialization of the United States. An estimated 20 million people—from Russia, Italy, Poland, the Balkan region, China, and elsewhere—immigrated to the United States, most settling in industrial cities such as New York, Pittsburgh, and Chicago. The label "new immigrants" was applied to these groups. In addition, the United States has an abundance of natural resources that contributed to industrial growth. Anthracite and bituminous coal, important fuel for industrial processes, was readily available in western Pennsylvania and West Virginia. The first oil well was established in 1859 by Edwin Drake in Pennsylvania. Later in the century, the demand for oil increased as it came to be refined into gasoline, a fuel for automobiles. Another factor that contributed to industrial growth was an abundant food supply. The farms of the Great Plains were able to supply wheat and corn to the growing urban population in the late 1800s. Dairy and vegetable farms, in areas adjacent to the industrial centers, also were important in supplying the industrial workforce. Finally, government policies supported industrial growth. For instance, the government encouraged the building of railroads by passing the Pacific (Transcontinental) Railroad Act (1862). The act encouraged the expansion of the railroad network by giving railroad companies wide swaths of federally owned land. These generous land grants totaled more than 180 million acres, an area equal to the size of Texas. Further, Supreme Court decisions favored big business. In *Santa Clara County v. Union Pacific Railway* (1886), for example, the Court established the concept of "corporate personhood" and shielded corporations from onerous regulation.

WRONG CHOICES EXPLAINED:
(1) "Rise of Labor Unions" would not be an appropriate title for the graphic organizer. A graphic organizer with that title might include items such as "the birth of the Knights of Labor," "the creation of the American Federation of Labor," and "workers resist long hours and low wages."

(2) "Innovations and Technology" would not be an appropriate title for the graphic organizer. A graphic organizer with that title might include items such as "Bessemer process," "vulcanization of rubber," and "generating electrical current."

(3) "Vertical Integration of Business" would not be an appropriate title for the graphic organizer. A graphic organizer with that title might include items such as "control of the supply chain," "Andrew Carnegie buys railroad and iron mine to enhance steel production," and "establishment of distribution network."

17. **3** In the United States, third parties have been influential because they have often suggested reforms later adopted by the two major parties. In the United States, third parties have had a difficult time attracting votes. For example, in the electoral college system, used to elect the president, the winner of each state takes *all* the electoral votes of that state. Therefore, people tend to vote for one of the major candidates; they fear that a vote for a third-party candidate will aid the candidate they find least desirable. If the United States had a proportional representation system, in which parties received seats in government in proportion to the percentage of the national vote they received, people might be more likely to vote for third-party candidates. That said, several third parties have been influential in terms of pushing the two major parties to adopt certain reforms. For example, in the late 1840s, the Free Soil Party was established to oppose the expansion of slavery. Though the party was not successful, its approach to slavery helped shape the formation of the Republican Party in 1856. In the 1890s, the People's (Populist) Party put forth a comprehensive platform of reforms that were seen as radical at the time. The Populist Party grew out of anger that many farmers had at the concentration of wealth and power by eastern industrialists. Some of their ideas were not adopted—such as government ownership of banks. However, their proposal to create a national income tax—one in which those with higher incomes would pay more than the poor—was adopted with the ratification of the 16th Amendment (1913). In addition, the Populists supported the direct election of senators to make officials more accountable to the public. This became reality with the ratification of the 17th Amendment (1913).

WRONG CHOICES EXPLAINED:

(1) In the history of U.S. elections, third parties have been influential, but not by outspending their political opponents. Third parties have generally had only a fraction of the financial resources of the two major political parties.

(2) In the history of U.S. elections, third parties have been influential, but not by providing the presidential candidates of the major parties. Generally, the candidates of the major parties are individuals who have been active in those parties, not people from third parties.

(4) In the history of U.S. elections, third parties have been influential, but not by electing majorities in both Congress and state legislatures. Third parties have at different times been successful in electing members of Congress, but they have never come close to electing majorities in Congress or in state legislatures. In their most successful electoral year (1892), the Populist Party sent to Congress 11 (out of 356) representatives and 3 (out of 88) senators.

18. **4** One purpose of the Chinese Exclusion Act (1882) was to protect the jobs of American workers. The act was mainly a response to economic- and race-based opposition to immigrants in the western United States. In the 1800s, many Chinese people immigrated to the United States. The California gold rush (1848–1855) and the building of transcontinental railroad lines attracted many Chinese immigrants to the West. Nativist, or anti-immigrant, sentiment developed in the United States alongside the growing number of immigrants. Chinese and Japanese immigrants were especially targeted by nativists. Racist assumptions of the time held that Asian immigrants would never fully assimilate into the United States and that they would take jobs away from Americans. The Chinese Exclusion Act was the only instance of legislation that prohibited a particular nationality from entering the country.

WRONG CHOICES EXPLAINED:
(1) The purpose of the Chinese Exclusion Act (1882) was not to speed the construction of western railroads. The act had the opposite effect. Many Chinese immigrants worked on western railroad construction. The Chinese Exclusion Act, which cut off immigration from China, made it more difficult to find new workers for construction of the railroads.

(2) The purpose of the Chinese Exclusion Act (1882) was not to encourage settlement of the Pacific Coast. Before passage of the act, many Chinese individuals and families moved to the United States and settled along the Pacific Coast. The Chinese Exclusion Act cut off immigration from China, reducing a source of settlers to the Pacific Coast.

(3) The purpose of the Chinese Exclusion Act (1882) was not to expand the civil rights of immigrants. The act grew out of nativist resentment of immigrants. This nativist movement sought to restrict the civil rights of Chinese immigrants, as well as cut off the flow of new immigrants from China.

19. **3** The Interstate Commerce Act of 1887 and the Sherman Antitrust Act of 1890 were passed by Congress to control business practices that limited competition. During the gilded age of the late 1800s, corporations and trusts came to dominate entire industries. The men who controlled the major industries in

the United States came to be known as *robber barons*, a scornful title meant to call attention to their cutthroat business activities and their attempts to control the government. These robber barons often created trusts (combinations of companies) in order to eliminate competition and control a particular industry. The formation of trusts in several industries was seen as harmful to the interests of consumers. John D. Rockefeller established the first large trust in the oil processing industry. Critics of corporate power pushed the government to take steps to reign in these massive corporations. However, their efforts often did not end up having the desired effect. After the Supreme Court ruled in the *Wabash v. Illinois* case (1886) that states could not regulate railroads because they cross state lines, the federal government created the Interstate Commerce Commission to regulate railroads. But the ICC was chronically underfunded and was, therefore, ineffective. The Sherman Antitrust Act was designed to break up trusts. The act had limited success. At first, only a few trusts were challenged. Ironically, the act was used with equal vigor against unions, on the grounds that they were illegal formations that interfered with free trade. In the case of *United States v. E.C. Knight Company* (1895), the Supreme Court greatly limited the scope of the act by making a distinction between trade (which would be subject to the act) and manufacturing (which would not).

WRONG CHOICES EXPLAINED:

(1) The intent of the Interstate Commerce Act (1887) and the Sherman Antitrust Act (1890) was to control business practices that limited competition, not to regulate the money supply. The Federal Reserve Bank was created in 1913 in order to regulate the money supply. If the economy is sluggish, the Fed will attempt to stimulate economic growth by taking steps to increase the amount of money in circulation. If inflation occurs, the Fed will attempt to slow down economic activity by taking steps to restrict the amount of money in circulation. The most important mechanism for regulating the money supply is raising or lowering the interest rate at which the Fed loans money to other banks.

(2) The intent of the Interstate Commerce Act (1887) and the Sherman Antitrust Act (1890) was to control business practices that limited competition, not to promote investment in manufacturing. At a different time in American history, the federal government has encouraged domestic manufacturing by raising tariff rates on imported manufactured items.

(4) The intent of the Interstate Commerce Act (1887) and the Sherman Antitrust Act (1890) was to control business practices that limited competition, not to limit the hours of working women. Several states passed laws during the Progressive Era to limit the hours of working women. An Oregon law limiting the number of hours that women could work was challenged in the courts and upheld by the Supreme Court. In *Muller v. Oregon* (1908), the Court cited the

supposed physical limitations of women and the threat to their health that long workdays posed. The case specifically cited women's role as child bearers.

20. **2** The economic developments of the late 1800s resulted in an increase in the number of people living in urban areas. In the last decades of the 1800s, the United States experienced rapid industrialization. New large-scale factories, no longer dependent on rapid-flowing rivers for power, were built in urban areas. The need for new workers in cities drew immigrants from abroad and migrants from rural areas of the United States. Between 1860 and 1900, the number of Americans who lived in cities jumped from 6.2 million to over 30 million, which amounted to a shift in the urban population from 20 percent of the total population to 40 percent. This rapid urbanization offered people many opportunities, but also brought several problems. Corrupt and inefficient political operations— labeled political machines—became more common in this era. New York City was dominated by the Democratic Party machine, headquartered at Tammany Hall. The most famous Tammany chief was "Boss" William Marcy Tweed. The muckraker journalist Lincoln Steffens exposed urban corruption in *The Shame of the Cities* (1902). Another problem in this era was the proliferation of substandard tenement housing. The wretched conditions that workers often experienced in tenements were documented in Jacob Riis's book of photography and writing, *How the Other Half Lives* (1890). A third problem faced by cities in the late 1800s was an increase in crime. Gang activities, ethnic rivalries, pickpockets, barroom fights, and other criminal activities contributed to this increase in crime.

WRONG CHOICES EXPLAINED:
(1) Economic developments of the late 1800s did not result in an increase in African American migration from the North to the South. The rapid industrialization of the United States drew migrants to the North; it did not lead to an exodus from the North. Later, in the 1910s and 1920s, the United States witnessed the Great Migration of African Americans from the rural South to the urban North.

(3) Economic developments of the late 1800s did not result in a decrease in the number of immigrants coming into the United States. The rapid industrialization of the United States led to an increase in immigration from abroad. An estimated 20 million people immigrated to the United States, most settling in industrial cities such as New York, Pittsburgh, and Chicago.

(4) Economic developments of the late 1800s did not result in a decrease in the number of factory workers in the Northeast. The rapid industrialization of the United States led to an increase in the number of factory workers in the Northeast. Northeastern cities such as Philadelphia, Newark, New York, Rochester, New Haven, and Boston were all centers of industry during this period.

21. **4** Between 1900 and 1930, U.S. relations with Latin America were characterized by repeated efforts by the United States to control the affairs of many nations in the region. President Theodore Roosevelt (1901–1909) is often associated with the efforts by the United States to play a more aggressive role in Latin America. His foreign-policy approach is neatly summed up in his famous adage that the United States should "speak softly, but carry a big stick" when dealing with other nations (Roosevelt borrowed the phrase from an African proverb). The "big stick" implied the threat of military force. He envisioned the United States acting as the world's policeman, punishing wrongdoers. He asserted that the "civilized nations" had a duty to police the "backward" countries of the world. This assertion of American might is known as the Roosevelt Corollary to the Monroe Doctrine. President William Howard Taft (1909–1913) continued to pursue an aggressive foreign policy, but he put more emphasis on expanding and securing American commercial interests than on pursuing the global strategic goals that Roosevelt had championed. Taft's foreign policy has come to be known as "dollar diplomacy." Roosevelt, Taft, and their successors repeatedly interfered in the internal affairs of countries in Latin America throughout the period 1900 to 1930. For example, United States military interventions in Cuba occurred four times (1898–1902, 1906–1909, 1912, and 1917–1922), in Nicaragua three times (1909–1910, 1912–1925, and 1926–1933), in the Dominican Republic four times (1903, 1904, 1914, and 1916–1924), and in Honduras seven times (1903, 1907, 1911, 1912, 1919, 1924, and 1925).

WRONG CHOICES EXPLAINED:
   (1) Between 1900 and 1930, U.S. relations with Latin America were not characterized by efforts to encourage the redistribution of land to the poor. In fact, the United States frequently intervened in Latin America to block efforts by Latin American leaders to redistribute land. The United States wanted land to stay in the hands of large-scale wealthy landowners, such as the United States–based United Fruit Company.
   (2) Between 1900 and 1930, U.S. relations with Latin America were not characterized by efforts to deny economic aid to developing nations. The United States was willing to extend foreign aid to developing nations if the governments of those nations worked to secure American economic and strategic goals.
   (3) Between 1900 and 1930, U.S. relations with Latin America were not characterized by efforts to limit the influence of communist dictators. U.S. opposition to communist governments is associated with the Cold War, a period of hostility between the United States and the Soviet Union that lasted from the end of World War II (1945) to the collapse of the Soviet Union (1991).

22. **2** President Theodore Roosevelt earned a reputation as a trustbuster because he used court actions to break up business monopolies. With the American economy growing by leaps and bounds in the 19th century, the presidents of the late 19th century did not challenge the doctrine of laissez-faire. The French phrase *laissez-faire* means "to let alone"; it describes a government policy that would take a hands-off approach in regard to economic activities. However, by the 20th century, the country began to face serious economic problems that called into question laissez-faire principles. President Roosevelt (1901–1909) saw the concentration of economic power in a few hands as potentially dangerous to the economy as a whole. Though the Sherman Antitrust Act (1890) was passed to limit monopolistic practices, the act was not enforced with a great deal of enthusiasm. Roosevelt made a point of using the act to pursue "bad trusts"—ones that interfered with commerce—not necessarily the biggest trusts. One of his first targets was the Northern Securities Company, a railroad holding company. His efforts were challenged in court. In *Northern Securities Co. v. United States* (1904), the Supreme Court upheld the power of the government to break up Northern Securities under the Sherman Antitrust Act. The case was a victory for Roosevelt. His efforts at challenging monopolies earned him his reputation as a trustbuster.

WRONG CHOICES EXPLAINED:

(1) President Theodore Roosevelt earned his reputation as a trustbuster by challenging monopolies, not because he favored conservation of natural resources. He did, in fact, pursue policies to conserve natural resources. Roosevelt, an avid outdoorsman, set aside millions of acres as protected areas. These areas include six national parks.

(3) President Theodore Roosevelt earned his reputation as a trustbuster by challenging monopolies, not because he sided with labor unions against big business. Roosevelt saw himself as a neutral arbitrator in regard to disputes between labor and big business, not as an advocate for labor unions. His most prominent action in regard to labor unions was helping to end the anthracite coal strike in 1902. He pressured the owners of the coal operations to accept arbitration by a government committee. The arbitration resulted in an end to the strike. The striking workers won a wage increase, but not union recognition.

(4) President Theodore Roosevelt earned his reputation as a trustbuster by challenging monopolies, not because he opposed the efforts of consumer advocates. In fact, Roosevelt pushed for legislation to protect consumers. Following publication of Upton Sinclair's novel, *The Jungle* (1906), which exposed the underside of meatpacking industry, Roosevelt signed the Meat Inspection Act (1906) and the Pure Food and Drug Act (also 1906), which established the Food and Drug Administration.

23. **4** One way in which Ida Tarbell, Upton Sinclair, and Jacob Riis were similar is that each sought to expose economic and social abuses. All three are considered *muckrakers*—journalists who wrote magazine articles and books that exposed wrongdoing by government officials, showed the negative side of industrialization, and let the world see a variety of social ills. Ida Tarbell's book, *The History of the Standard Oil Company* (1904), exposed the ruthlessness of John D. Rockefeller's oil company. Her book contributed to the government breaking up the Standard Oil Trust in 1911. Upton Sinclair exposed the underside of the meat-packing industry in the novel *The Jungle* (1906). The story follows a Lithuanian immigrant family through the stockyards of Chicago. The public uproar that followed the publication of the book led Congress to pass the Meat Inspection Act (1906) and the Pure Food and Drug Act (also 1906), which established the Food and Drug Administration. The photographs of Jacob Riis chronicled the living conditions of the urban poor. Riis was born in Denmark and immigrated to the United States in 1870. He worked as a police reporter but became interested in photographing the conditions of the urban poor. He turned his photographs of the poor in New York into the book *How the Other Half Lives* (1890). The book became influential in making middle-class people aware of the poverty that existed in the United States. These muckraking books inspired a generation of progressive reformers to push the government to intervene in these problems. A whole host of reforms were implemented by progressive reformers and their allies in the 1900s and 1910s.

WRONG CHOICES EXPLAINED:
(1) Ida Tarbell, Upton Sinclair, and Jacob Riis did not seek to end racial discrimination. Most white Progressive Era reformers turned a blind eye to the problems of race in the United States. However, African American reformers took the lead in challenging racial discrimination. For instance, Ida B. Wells, an African American muckraking journalist, challenged the mistreatment of African Americans in the country and exposed the horrors of lynching.
(2) Ida Tarbell, Upton Sinclair, and Jacob Riis did not seek to control illegal immigration. During the Progressive Era, there were few legal restrictions on immigration, so the issue of "illegal immigration" was not publicly debated. Nativists were successful in blocking immigration from China (with the Chinese Exclusion Act of 1882) and Japan (with the Gentlemen's Agreement of 1907). However, it was not until the 1920s, with the passage of the Emergency Quota Act (1921) and the National Origins Act (1924), that immigration was greatly restricted.

(3) Ida Tarbell, Upton Sinclair, and Jacob Riis did not seek to limit government regulations. They did the opposite. By exposing the negative side of industrialization and urbanization, muckraking journalists joined the call for greater government intervention into the economy.

24. **3** The purpose of the initiative, referendum, and recall was to increase citizen influence in government. All three items attempted to expand democracy and increase the power of citizens in state and local government. Progressive reformers in the first two decades of the 20th century were concerned that government was being taken over by corrupt and inefficient political machines. The muckraker journalist Lincoln Steffens exposed the underside of American municipal politics and the influence of wealthy businessmen in *The Shame of the Cities* (1902). Reformers hoped that by expanding democracy, the power of these political machines would be lessened. The initiative would enable citizens to introduce a bill to the local or state legislature by petition. The referendum would allow people to vote directly on proposed legislation. The recall would allow the populace to remove elected officials before their term ended.

WRONG CHOICES EXPLAINED:
(1) The purpose of the initiative, referendum, and recall was not to eliminate the two-party system. The three items were all designed to increase citizen participation in the political process. They did not address the number of political parties that participated in elections.
(2) The purpose of the initiative, referendum, and recall was not to limit participation in state elections. The three items were all designed to increase citizen participation in the political process, not to limit it.
(4) The purpose of the initiative, referendum, and recall was not to strengthen the power of political machines. Reformers hoped to limit the power of the corrupt, entrenched, inefficient political operations—labeled political machines—which controlled many municipal governments. They thought that one way to challenge the power of these political machines was to increase citizen participation through measures such as the initiative, referendum, and recall.

25. **2** The photograph supports the conclusion that state and federal governments did not adequately regulate child labor. Lewis Hine and other Progressive Era photographers sought to raise awareness of the prevalence of child labor in the United States. Because wages for working-class men remained relatively low, families often had to supplement their incomes with wages of children and women. In turn, the influx of women and children into the labor

force depressed overall wages. From the 1870s until World War I, child labor grew each decade. By 1900, children aged 10 to 15 years old made up 18 percent of the industrial workforce. In 1916, Congress addressed the issue of child labor and passed the Keating-Owen Child Labor Act. Using its power to regulate interstate commerce, Congress prohibited the sale across state lines of goods produced by factories that employed children under the age of 14. Less than a year later, in the case of *Hammer v. Dagenhart* (1917), the Supreme Court shot down the act. The Court asserted that the goods being regulated were not inherently "immoral," as prostitution or liquor might be. Therefore, what was being addressed by the law was manufacturing practices, and manufacturing practices were subject to state, not federal, law. Later, the Fair Labor Standards Act (1938), passed as part of President Franklin D. Roosevelt's New Deal, included strict limits on child labor.

WRONG CHOICES EXPLAINED:

(1) The photograph, of two children working in an industrial setting, would not support the conclusion that textile manufacturing was not important to the national economy. Documents containing statistics for the various categories of industrial production in the United States might shed light on the relative importance of textile manufacturing in the national economy. Such statistics could include profitability, income, or number of workers employed in different types of industrial production.

(3) The photograph, of two children working in an industrial setting, would not support the conclusion that American factories were less productive than factories in other countries. Documents containing statistics on the productivity of the industrial sector in the United States and in other countries might shed light on the relative productivity of American factories.

(4) The photograph, of two children working in an industrial setting, would not support the conclusion that strict federal safety standards were enforced in factories across the nation. In the photograph, there are not any obvious indications of safety standards being enforced. The fact that one of the children is barefoot indicates a lack of safety measures. At the time, the federal government had not yet passed safety standards for industrial operations. Such federal guidelines would not be passed until the 1930s, when New Deal legislation addressed conditions in factories.

26. **3** During the 1920s, Congress established a quota system for immigration in order to reduce immigration from southern and eastern Europe. Anti-immigrant sentiment ran very high in the 1920s. The United States had experienced a large wave of immigration in the decades leading up to World War I.

Between 1880 and 1920, an estimated 20 million people, from Russia, Italy, Poland, the Balkan region, and elsewhere, immigrated to the United States. Nativists feared that white Anglo-Saxon Americans were committing "race suicide" by allowing "inferior" races to enter America in large numbers. This anti-immigrant sentiment led to the passage of legislation that greatly reduced the number of immigrants allowed into the United States. The Emergency Quota Act (1921) and the National Origins Act (1924) set quotas for new immigrants based on nationality. The first act set the quota for each nationality at 3 percent of the total number of that nationality that was present in the United States in 1910. The second act reduced the quota to 2 percent and moved the year back to 1890. This had the effect of setting very low quotas for many of the "new immigrants"—from eastern and southern Europe. The acts did not set any limits on immigrants from within the Western Hemisphere.

WRONG CHOICES EXPLAINED:

(1) Congress's reason for establishing the quota system in the 1920s was to reduce immigration from southern and eastern Europe, not to ensure that the United States would have enough factory workers. In fact, the quota system reduced the number of potential factory workers in the United States by greatly reducing the number of immigrants allowed into the country.

(2) Congress's reason for establishing the quota system in the 1920s was to reduce immigration from southern and eastern Europe, not to keep migrant workers out of the country. Migrant farmers are seasonal farm workers who move from place to place, as crops in different locations are ready for harvest. Many migrant farmers in the 1920s, and since then, were foreign-born workers—from Mexico and other countries in Central America and the Caribbean. The quota system did not set limits on immigrants from within the Western Hemisphere so that migrant farmers from Mexico and other countries in the Western Hemisphere would not be affected by the quota laws.

(4) Congress's reason for establishing the quota system in the 1920s was to reduce immigration from southern and eastern Europe, not to assist refugees from war-torn countries. In the post–World War II period, the United States has played an important role in accepting refugees fleeing persecution or war. The U.S. took in hundreds of thousands of Europeans displaced by World War II and resettled refugees escaping from Communist regimes in Europe and Asia during the Cold War. More recently, the United States has greatly reduced the number of refugees it has allowed into the country from war-torn countries, most notably from Syria.

27. **1** The trial of Sacco and Vanzetti is an example of nativism in the 1920s. Nicola Sacco and Bartolomeo Vanzetti were accused of robbing and killing a payroll clerk in Massachusetts in 1920. The evidence against them was sketchy and the judge was openly hostile to the two men, who were not only immigrants but also anarchists. The trial illustrated the intolerance that many Americans had toward immigrants in the 1920s. After they were found guilty, many Americans protested the verdict and wondered if an immigrant, especially with radical ideas, could get a fair trial in the United States. Despite widespread protests, the two men were executed in 1927. Anti-immigrant sentiment ran very high in the 1920s. The United States passed the Emergency Quota Act (1921) and the National Origins Act (1924), both of which greatly reduced the number of new immigrants allowed into the United States. These acts set quotas for new immigrants based on nationality.

WRONG CHOICES EXPLAINED:

(2) The verdict in the Scopes trial is not an example of nativism. The trial did not involve immigrants or anti-immigrant sentiment. The 1925 Scopes trial involved the teaching of evolution in public schools. John Scopes, a Tennessee biology teacher, was arrested for violating a state law forbidding the teaching of evolution. The case turned into a national spectacle, with the famous lawyers Clarence Darrow representing Scopes and William Jennings Bryan representing the state. The trial pitted rural, traditional, and religious values against science. It is one of several important events that highlighted cultural divisions in the 1920s.

(3) The Teapot Dome scandal is not an example of nativism. The scandal did not involve immigrants or anti-immigrant sentiment. The 1922 Teapot Dome scandal occurred during the presidency of Warren Harding. Harding's Secretary of the Interior accepted bribes from oil companies in exchange for leasing them the rights to drill for oil on publicly held land in Teapot Dome, Wyoming. Although Harding was not directly implicated in the scandal, it was emblematic of a culture of corruption that existed in his administration and of the pro-business attitude of the Republican presidents of the 1920s.

(4) The stock market crash is not an example of nativism. The crash did not involve immigrants or anti-immigrant sentiment. The 1929 stock market crash led to the start of the Great Depression. In late October 1929, stock prices plummeted as investors lost confidence in the market and went on a selling frenzy. When the market finally bottomed out, the Dow Jones Industrial Average, the major indicator of stock market trends, had fallen 89 percent from its peak. The crash of the stock market is attributed to excessive speculation on the part of the public.

28. **1** The statements describe the economic situation faced by farmers in the 1920s. Throughout the 1920s, the agricultural sector lagged behind the rest of the economy. Prices farmers received for major commodities (wheat, corn, soy beans, milk) fell steeply in the 1920s. Farmers were increasingly at the mercy of middlemen and commodity brokers who set prices for farm goods (as noted in the first statement). The problems in the agriculture sector went back to the previous decade. Farmers had put more acres under cultivation during World War I to meet increased demand for agricultural products. By the 1920s, Europe was back on its feet, yet American farmers did not cut back on production. In addition, American farmers now had to compete with European producers on the global market (as noted in the second statement). Because of the decentralized nature of farming, it was difficult for farmers to organize associations or cooperatives to protect their interests (as noted in the third statement). In addition, farmers felt pressure to put a great deal of money in implements to mechanize production (as noted in the fourth statement). This push toward mechanization and expansion left the farmers of the 1920s in a cycle of debt, overproduction, and falling commodity prices. Increased tariff rates and an isolationist foreign policy further reduced the international market for American agricultural goods.

WRONG CHOICES EXPLAINED:
(2) The statements describe the economic situation of farmers in the 1920s, not of railroad companies. Railroad companies generally did well in the 1920s (at least until the late 1920s), as production and consumption of goods expanded, along with the necessity of transporting them. After the 1920s, railroad companies would begin to feel intense competition from trucks and automobiles. During the 1930s, many smaller railroad companies went out of business, and by the 1940s, the remaining ones had to consolidate their lines or face bankruptcy.

(3) The statements describe the economic situation of farmers in the 1920s, not of manufacturers. The manufacturing sector generally did well in the 1920s (at least until the late 1920s), as production and consumption of goods expanded. Manufacturers used mass-production techniques to produce an abundance of goods. New methods of advertising and distributing goods spurred a growth in consumption as well. However, the manufacturing sector began to slow down by the late 1920s, as consumption failed to keep up with production.

(4) The statements describe the economic situation of farmers in the 1920s, not of factory workers. The economic situation of factory workers was a mixed bag in the 1920s. On the one hand, jobs were plentiful in the manufacturing sector for most of the decade. Factories expanded production and needed unskilled and semi-skilled workers to operate machines. However, wages were stagnant in the 1920s. A weak union movement and pro-business government

policies contributed to keeping wages low. By the end of the decade, low wages contributed to sagging sales of manufactured goods, as consumption could not keep pace with production.

29. **4** The main idea of the political cartoon from the 1930s is that President Franklin D. Roosevelt extended help to those in need. By the time that Roosevelt was elected president in 1932, the Great Depression had been going on for three years. The limited response of President Herbert Hoover (1929–1933) to the Great Depression, coupled with his handling of the Bonus March protest in 1932 (which resulted in the deaths of two World War I veterans who were demanding early payment of their government bonuses), set the stage for the election of Roosevelt. Though Roosevelt was from an affluent background, he was able to convey to the public a sense of empathy and personal warmth. In a speech during the 1932 campaign for president, Roosevelt stated that he would promote government plans that are intended to help the "forgotten man." The 1936 cartoon asserts that Roosevelt had followed through with his promise. Upon taking office, Roosevelt moved the federal government in a new direction by asserting that it should take some responsibility for the welfare of the people. The Roosevelt administration developed a series of programs known collectively as the New Deal. Previously, people received assistance in times of need from churches, settlement houses, and other private charities. However, the levels of poverty and unemployment during the Great Depression were unprecedented. Roosevelt believed that the government needed to take action. The New Deal provided relief to individuals through a variety of agencies.

WRONG CHOICES EXPLAINED:
    (1) The cartoon is not asserting that President Franklin D. Roosevelt continued the laissez-faire policies of earlier presidents. The French phrase *laissez-faire* means "to leave alone." It describes a government policy that would take a hands-off approach in regard to economic activities. When the Great Depression struck the United States in the 1930s, Franklin D. Roosevelt argued more forcefully that the government must abandon a laissez-faire approach and play an activist role in the economy. Upon taking office, he initiated a sweeping array of programs known as the New Deal.
    (2) The cartoon is not asserting that President Franklin D. Roosevelt supported business over labor. Roosevelt favored policies that encouraged the formation of labor unions. Previously, government policies had generally favored business over labor. Roosevelt, however, believed that a major problem facing the economy was low wages for workers. He argued that if workers' wages increased, they would be able to purchase consumer goods. If more consumer

goods were purchased, then manufacturers would need to produce more and would hire more workers. He pushed for the Wagner Act (1935) to strengthen unions by mandating that employers bargain with their unions. This act established the National Labor Relations Board to conduct elections among workers to see if they wanted to be represented by a union. It also banned certain unfair labor practices.

(3) The cartoon is not asserting that President Franklin D. Roosevelt favored government ownership of major industries. While many of Roosevelt's critics labeled his policies "creeping socialism," Roosevelt did not challenge the basic tenets of the capitalist system, including private ownership of the means of production. Roosevelt's policies included the regulation of banks, industrial practices, and the stock market, but he did not advocate government ownership of industry.

30. **3** The New Deal attempted to carry out the theme of the cartoon— remembering "the forgotten man"—by funding many public works projects. During the depths of the Great Depression in the 1930s, President Franklin D. Roosevelt pushed for a series of reforms to address both the causes and effects of the economic crisis. Roosevelt and his advisors drew on progressive ideas in the creation of the New Deal. The administration created a series of public works agencies to address the problem of high unemployment, which hovered between 10 and 25 percent of working-age Americans. The Civilian Conservation Corps (1933), for example, provided outdoor jobs for young men. Later, Roosevelt created the Works Progress Administration (1935), one of the largest New Deal program. The WPA was a vast program of government projects that hired millions of unemployed workers. Individuals hired by the agency, for example, built schools, maintained highways, installed sewer lines, wrote guidebooks, and produced theatrical productions. At its peak in 1938, over three million people worked for the WPA; over eight million people in total worked for it by the time it was shuttered in 1943.

WRONG CHOICES EXPLAINED:

(1) The New Deal did not attempt to help "the forgotten man" by restricting labor union membership. The approach of the New Deal was the opposite; it sought to increase union membership. President Franklin D. Roosevelt believed that if workers were in unions, they would have greater purchasing power, which would, in turn, improve the overall economic situation. He pushed for the Wagner Act (1935) to strengthen unions by mandating that employers bargain with their unions. This act established the National Labor Relations Board to conduct elections among workers to see if they wanted to be represented by a union. It also banned certain unfair labor practices.

(2) The New Deal did not attempt to help "the forgotten man" by loaning money to foreign countries. The costs of the New Deal prevented the New Deal from expanding loan programs to other nations. In addition, expanding loans to foreign nations would not be seen as remembering "the forgotten man."

(4) The New Deal did not attempt to help "the forgotten man" by banning the sale of stocks and bonds. While it is true that reckless investment behavior led to the stock market crash of October 1929 (which signaled the beginning of the Great Depression), President Franklin D. Roosevelt did not attempt to ban the sale of stocks and bonds. Rather, Roosevelt sought to establish regulatory oversight of the stock market by signing legislation creating the Securities and Exchange Commission in 1934.

31. **2** The defeat of President Franklin D. Roosevelt's "court packing" plan by Congress is an example of checks and balances. By 1937, Roosevelt had grown increasingly frustrated with the conservative approach of the Supreme Court. It shot down the National Recovery Act in *Schechter v. United States* (1935) and the Agricultural Adjustment Act in *Butler v. United States* (1936). In 1937, he announced a plan to increase the number of justices on the Supreme Court to as many as 15. He said that some of the older justices had difficulty keeping up with the heavy workload. However, it was clear that the intent of his "court packing" plan was to create a Supreme Court friendlier to his New Deal programs. The Senate rejected Roosevelt's "court packing" plan in 1937 because the plan would have threatened the principle of checks and balances by making the Supreme Court a rubber stamp for New Deal legislation. Soon, however, openings on the Court allowed Roosevelt to appoint new justices and influence the direction of the Court.

WRONG CHOICES EXPLAINED:
(1) The defeat of President Franklin D. Roosevelt's "court packing" plan by Congress is not an example of federalism. Federalism describes the relationship between the national government and state governments. While the word itself implies a loose league of states, in the American context federalism gives the strong national government supremacy over the state governments. This system of divided power is different from the unitary system of countries such as France. In France, the central government sets policies for the entire country with very little decision-making power on the local level.

(3) The defeat of President Franklin D. Roosevelt's "court packing" plan by Congress is not an example of due process. *Due process* refers to procedures that people go through after they are arrested for committing a crime. These procedures must be consistent with the Constitution and apply equally to all citizens. Many of the due process guidelines are contained in several of the amendments

to the Constitution. The framers of the Constitution wanted to protect people from arbitrary authority.

(4) The defeat of President Franklin D. Roosevelt's "court packing" plan by Congress is not an example of the amendment process. The process for amending the Constitution is cumbersome. First, a constitutional amendment can be proposed, either by Congress (by two-third majorities in both houses) or by a national convention. Then, three-fourths of the states must approve an amendment for it to be ratified. The state-by-state approval process can occur by the consent of the state legislatures or by state ratifying conventions. Twenty-seven amendments have been added to the Constitution.

32. **2** The administration of President Franklin D. Roosevelt reacted to the information contained in the letter by creating the Manhattan Project. In the letter, Albert Einstein is warning Roosevelt of the potential for nuclear chain reactions to be harnessed and used in an "extremely powerful" bomb. In the context of World War II, Roosevelt decided that harnessing atomic power could be crucial to winning the war. He was especially concerned that scientists in Nazi Germany would beat the United States in developing an atomic bomb. He, therefore, allocated funding for the Manhattan Project, the secret project to develop the atomic bomb. The project, which began in 1941 in an office building in New York City, involved several sites around the country, but the final assembly of the atomic bomb occurred in Los Alamos, New Mexico. The bomb was ready by July 1945, as the United States was preparing for a final attack on Japan. After issuing an ultimatum to Japan, the United States dropped the atomic bomb on the Japanese city of Hiroshima on August 6, 1945. After the United States dropped a second atomic bomb on the city of Nagasaki, Japan surrendered, ending World War II.

WRONG CHOICES EXPLAINED:
(1) The information in the letter from Albert Einstein—about the possibility of harnessing atomic power for an "extremely powerful bomb"—did not lead President Franklin D. Roosevelt to declare war on the Axis powers. The president did declare war on the Axis powers, in December 1941, but that was in response to the Japanese sneak attack on the U.S. naval base at Pearl Harbor, Hawaii.

(3) The information in the letter from Albert Einstein—about the possibility of harnessing atomic power for an "extremely powerful bomb"—did not lead President Franklin D. Roosevelt to propose the Lend-Lease Act. The president did propose the Lend-Lease Act, in March 1941, but that was in response to the desperate situation that Great Britain faced in battling Nazi Germany. In 1940,

France had fallen to the Nazis, leaving Great Britain the only major power to fight against Hitler's war machine in Western Europe. The Lend-Lease Act allowed the United States to ship armaments to Great Britain in American ships. Though officially neutral in World War II at that point, the United States was moving steadily toward intervening on the side of Great Britain.

(4) The information in the letter from Albert Einstein—about the possibility of harnessing atomic power for an "extremely powerful bomb"—did not lead President Franklin D. Roosevelt to initiate the D-Day invasion of Europe. The president did initiate the D-Day invasion of Europe, in June 1944, but that was in response to the difficulties the Allies had in defeating the Nazis in Western Europe. The goal of the D-Day invasion was for British and American troops to break through German coastal defenses and begin pushing Nazi forces out of occupied Western Europe and bring an end to the war in Europe. Soviet forces were, at the same time, waging war on German forces in Eastern Europe. Germany finally surrendered in May 1945.

33. **3** The internment of Japanese Americans during World War II primarily affected those Japanese Americans who lived on the West Coast. In 1942, President Roosevelt issued Executive Order 9066, authorizing the government to remove 120,000 Japanese Americans, two-thirds of them citizens, from West Coast states and relocate them to camps in the interior of the country. The order allowed the military to designate certain areas "military areas" from which "any or all persons may be excluded." The West Coast, which contained the vast majority of Japanese Americans, was designated a military area. (Hawaii, which was not yet a state, contained 150,000 people of Japanese descent, but only a small number of them were interned.) Most of their property was confiscated by the government. In the case of *Korematsu v. United States* (1944), the Supreme Court ruled that the relocation was acceptable on the grounds of national security. Much later, in 1988, the United States government publicly apologized to the surviving victims and extended $20,000 in reparations to each one. The *Korematsu* decision is one of several rulings by the Supreme Court that have curtailed civil liberties in times of war.

WRONG CHOICES EXPLAINED:
(1), (2), and (4) Executive Order 9066, authorizing the internment of Japanese Americans during World War II, did not affect Japanese Americans who lived in the Ohio River valley (choice 1), along the Gulf Coast (choice 2), or near the Rio Grande border with Mexico (choice 4). It was the West Coast that was designated a "military area," with certain residents subject to exclusion. At the time, the vast majority of Japanese Americans lived on the West Coast.

34. **4** After World War II, one important outcome of the passage of the Serviceman's Readjustment Act of 1944 (GI Bill) was that it created educational and housing assistance for veterans. The GI Bill provided cash payments for tuition and living expenses to attend college. In addition, the bill provided low-interest loans for veterans to purchase homes, as well as to start businesses. The intent of the GI Bill was to help the veterans of World War II adjust to life during peacetime. The program was very successful. It helped millions of veterans advance economically. A college education and home ownership have been seen as key components of entrance into the middle class. The generous benefits extended to World War II veterans can be seen in contrast to the sparse benefits extended to World War I veterans. World War I veterans staged a major protest in 1932, the Bonus March, to pressure the government to provide them with bonuses that had been promised them.

WRONG CHOICES EXPLAINED:

(1) The GI Bill was not intended to allow women to serve in combat positions. Women were not allowed to be used in combat roles during World War II. It was not until the Persian Gulf War in 1991 that significant numbers of women served in combat roles.

(2) The GI Bill was not intended to limit suburban growth. The GI Bill had the opposite effect. Much of the housing assistance to veterans was used to purchase houses in the suburbs.

(3) The GI Bill was not intended to fund new military bases. The United States did expand its military presence in the world after World War II, but this was not the function of the GI Bill. As the Cold War intensified after World War II, the United States established military bases throughout the world.

35. **2** The primary reason for the creation of both the Truman Doctrine and the Marshall Plan was the fear of Soviet communist expansion throughout Europe. The two items are important events in the history of the Cold War. After World War II, the wartime ally of the United States, the Soviet Union, became its rival. The Cold War lasted from the end of World War II (1945) to the collapse of the Soviet Union (1991). At times, the conflict was nothing more than a rivalry; at other times, the two nations were at the brink of war. Tensions intensified immediately following World War II when the Soviet Union left its troops in the nations of Eastern Europe, turning these nations into Soviet satellites. The United States was worried that the Soviet Union would try to push into Western Europe. The leader of the Soviet Union, Joseph Stalin, insisted that he only wanted to have allied nations on the border of the Soviet Union. In order to block any further aggression by the Soviet Union, Truman issued the Truman Doctrine (1947), in which he said that the goal of the United States

would be to contain communism. Toward this end, the United States extended military aid to Greece and Turkey. The United States created the Marshall Plan in order to help Europe's economic recovery. The Marshall Plan (1948) extended billions of dollars to war-torn Western Europe after the war. It was designed to strengthen the western democracies so that they would not turn to communism.

WRONG CHOICES EXPLAINED:

(1) The reason for the creation of the Truman Doctrine and the Marshall Plan was not to reward the Chinese for their role in the Allied victory over Japan. The United States and China fought together as allies during the war. After World War II, ongoing hostilities between the Chinese government and the Chinese Communist Party exploded into open civil war. The United States supported the government, which was run by the Kuomintang (Nationalist Party). The Communist Party, led by Mao Zedong, emerged victorious in 1949.

(3) The reason for the creation of the Truman Doctrine and the Marshall Plan was not to support the development of colonial independence movements. The United States frequently opposed independence movements in the developing world during the Cold War if it thought that an independent government might side with the Soviet Union. For example, in 1960, the United States approved of, and may have played a role in, the ouster of the first democratically elected leader of the Republic of the Congo, Patrice Lumumba. Lumumba had played an important role in the transformation of the Congo from a colony of Belgium into an independent republic, and he served as the first prime minister of the Republic of the Congo.

(4) The reason for the creation of the Truman Doctrine and the Marshall Plan was not to protect vital United States interests in Middle East oil fields, though the United States did seek to protect these interests. Following a conflict in Egypt over control of the Suez Canal (1956–1957), President Dwight D. Eisenhower took a more active role in protecting the oil interests of the United States. In a 1957 speech, he pledged that the United States would support any Middle Eastern countries threatened by "any nation controlled by international communism." The Eisenhower Doctrine was invoked in 1958 when a rebel movement emerged in Lebanon; U.S. Marines were quickly dispatched to support the Lebanese president.

36. **4** The United States responded to the Berlin Blockade in 1948 by airlifting food and supplies into Berlin. After World War II, Germany was divided by the Allied powers—the United States, France, Great Britain, and the Soviet Union. The city of Berlin, which was deep in the Soviet-occupied sector of Germany, was divided as well, with the western portion of the city occupied by the Western Allies

and the eastern portion occupied by the Soviet Union. In 1948, before the future status of Berlin was settled, the Soviet Union decided it would prevent any food or other supplies from entering the western portion of the city. The goal was for the Soviet Union to block the United States and its Western Allies from maintaining their presence in Berlin. Ultimately, the Soviet Union hoped to make all of Berlin part of what would become East Germany. The United States did not stand by idly when it learned of the Berlin blockade. President Harry Truman decided to send thousands of planes, filled with supplies, into the western sector of Berlin, in an action known as the Berlin Airlift. The Berlin Airlift prevented the western sector of Berlin from starving and prevented the Soviet Union from taking over the city. In 1949, the countries of West Germany and East Germany were formally established, and the city of West Berlin was officially established as part of West Germany. The Berlin airlift was one of the early American interventions in the Cold War.

WRONG CHOICES EXPLAINED:

(1) The United States did not respond to the Berlin Blockade in 1948 by boycotting German-made products. The United States continued to trade with the sectors of Germany occupied by the Western Allies during the Berlin Blockade, although the German economy was just getting on its feet following the destruction of World War II. The United States did not trade with the Soviet Union and its allies in Eastern Europe.

(2) The United States did not respond to the Berlin Blockade in 1948 by building the Berlin Wall. The communist government of East Germany built the Berlin Wall in 1961 to completely encircle West Berlin and separate it from East Germany. Berlin had been divided when Germany was divided into East Germany and West Germany in 1949. Berlin was located completely within East German territory, so West Berlin was physically separate from the rest of West Germany. Before construction of the wall, many residents of East Germany escaped to the west through West Berlin.

(3) The United States did not respond to the Berlin Blockade in 1948 by stopping all traffic leaving Berlin. Making such a move would not help solve the crisis created by the Berlin Blockade. The people of the western section of Berlin would starve if supplies were not airlifted into the city.

37. **3** A major significance of the Korean War (1950–1953) is that for the first time the United Nations used military force to oppose aggression. Although the United States played the leading role in military operations, the U.S. and its allies acted under the auspices of the United Nations. The United Nations was created mainly to work for international peace, following the carnage of World War II. Many world leaders, as well as ordinary citizens, pushed for an international

organization that could resolve conflicts and maintain peace. The United Nations formed in 1945, complete with a Security Council and peacekeeping troops. It continues to function as an international organization. The origins of the Korean War date back to the immediate aftermath of World War II. Korea had been divided into two occupation zones after World War II, one controlled by the United States and one controlled by the Soviet Union. The two sides were unable to agree on a unification plan, and by 1948 two separate nations were established with a border at the 38th parallel. In June 1950, North Korean troops invaded South Korea. President Harry S. Truman decided to commit troops to support South Korea, and he managed to secure United Nations sponsorship. United Nations forces, led by U.S. General Douglas MacArthur, pushed the North Korean troops back to the 38th parallel and then marched into North Korea. When UN troops got to within 40 miles of the border of North Korea and China, China sent 150,000 troops over the Yalu River to push back the UN forces. After intense fighting, the two sides settled into positions on either side of the 38th parallel. By 1953, an armistice was reached accepting a divided Korea.

WRONG CHOICES EXPLAINED:
(1) The events of the Korean War (1950–1953) did not include the use of an atomic bomb. Atomic bombs had been used earlier, in 1945, at the end of World War II. The United States dropped an atomic bomb on the Japanese city of Hiroshima in August 1945. After the United States dropped a second atomic bomb on the city of Nagasaki, Japan surrendered, ending World War II.
(2) During the Korean War (1950–1953), Asian and U.S. troops fought against each other, but not for the first time. During World War II (1941–1945), troops from Japan and from the United States fought against each other.
(4) During the Korean War (1950–1953), the Soviet Union and the United States did not support the same side. Earlier, during World War II (1939–1945), the two countries were on the same side, but during the Korean War, the United States supported South Korea and UN forces, while the Soviet Union supported North Korea and China.

38. **3** The three newspaper headlines from the decade following World War II are all connected to the fear of communism in the United States. The fear of communism in the late 1940s and 1950s occurred in the context of the Cold War—a period of hostility between the United States and the Soviet Union that lasted from the end of World War II (1945) to the collapse of the Soviet Union (1991). In 1947, President Harry S. Truman felt compelled to take action against the perceived threat of domestic communism by signing Executive Order 9835, designed to root out communist influence in the federal government. The order mandated that federal employees take a loyalty oath (alluded to in the first headline). Despite

Truman's actions in regard to fears of domestic communism, Republicans consistently accused him and the Democratic Party of being "soft on communism." This accusation was aggressively taken up by Senator Joseph McCarthy, who became the central figure in the movement that became known as *McCarthyism*. McCarthy gained prominence when he announced that he had a list of names of State Department employees who were members of the Communist Party (1950). An atmosphere reminiscent of the Salem witch trials of the 1690s pervaded America, as wild accusations became more common. Fears of communist spying intensified when the Soviet Union first tested an atomic bomb (1949). The government accused two members of the Communist Party, Ethel and Julius Rosenberg, of passing secrets of the nuclear bomb to the Soviet Union. The Rosenbergs insisted on their innocence, but were found guilty and were sent to the electric chair (1953) (alluded to in the third headline). The most intense period of the anti-communist movement ended by 1954. The Korean War had ended and McCarthy himself was discredited for making baseless accusations against members of the military. The hearings on these accusations, known as the Army-McCarthy hearings (1954), were widely seen on the new medium of television (alluded to in the second headline). A key moment in these hearings occurred when a lawyer for the Army, Joseph Welch, directly challenged McCarthy's tactics. McCarthy had publicly condemned a young lawyer who worked under Welch for previously working with the National Lawyers Guild, an organization that the government claimed was a front organization for the Communist Party. Welch came to the defense of the young lawyer, saying to McCarthy, "Have you no sense of decency, sir?" The hearings demonstrated to the American public the reckless nature of McCarthy's accusations.

WRONG CHOICES EXPLAINED:

(1) The three headlines are not connected to war crimes trials in Japan. The Allies did conduct war crimes trials against Japanese officials and members of the military after World War II. The war crimes committed by Japan occurred during World War II (1937–1945) and in fighting between Japan and China that predated the beginning of World War II. The war crimes included massacres, human experimentation, starvation, and forced labor. Historians estimate that these war crimes were responsible for the deaths of between three and 14 million civilians and prisoners of war. Ultimately, almost 6,000 Japanese officials and military personnel were tried, with over 900 executed.

(2) The three headlines are not connected with passage of civil rights legislation in the United States. The United States did pass important civil rights legislation in the 1960s. The Civil Rights Acts of 1964, banning racial discrimination in public places, and the Voting Rights Act of 1965 were important milestones in the struggle for African American equality.

(4) The three headlines are not connected with debate over economic aid to Europe. In the period after World War II, the United States implemented the Marshall Plan (1948) to extend billions of dollars to war-torn Western Europe after World War II. It was, in part, designed to strengthen the western democracies so that they would not turn to communism. The Marshall Plan was part of the United States policy of containment.

39. **1** In 1962, President John F. Kennedy responded to the discovery of nuclear missiles in Cuba by ordering a naval quarantine of Cuba. The discovery of missile sites in Cuba, by a U.S. U-2 plane, began a tense episode in the history of the Cold War called the Cuban Missile Crisis. President Kennedy felt that the missiles, in such close proximity to the United States, amounted to an unacceptable provocation and ordered Soviet Premier Nikita Khrushchev to halt the operation and dismantle the bases. Khrushchev insisted on the right of the Soviet Union to install the missiles. For about a week, the world stood on the brink of nuclear war. Finally, a deal was reached in which the Soviet Union would abandon its Cuban missile program. In exchange, the United States publicly promised to not attack Cuba; privately, it agreed to remove missiles from Turkey.

WRONG CHOICES EXPLAINED:
(2) President John F. Kennedy did not capture strategic locations in Cuba in response to the discovery of nuclear missiles in Cuba. Earlier, the United States did attempt to organize an invasion of Cuba, but this was unrelated to the discovery of nuclear missiles. The Bay of Pigs invasion was planned under the Eisenhower administration and implemented by President Kennedy. The plan called for the United States to train, arm, and aid a group of Cuban exiles opposed to the Communist government of Fidel Castro. The exiles landed at the Bay of Pigs in Cuba in April 1961, but were quickly captured by Cuban forces.

(3) President John F. Kennedy did not threaten to invade the Soviet Union in response to the discovery of nuclear missiles in Cuba. No such invasion was contemplated during the Cold War. American political leaders realized that such an invasion would bring about a third world war and massive devastation on both sides.

(4) President John F. Kennedy did not prohibit travel to the southeastern United States in response to the discovery of nuclear missiles in Cuba. The United States did implement an embargo and a travel ban to Cuba starting in 1963. In 2014, President Barack Obama rolled back restrictions on traveling to Cuba. More recently, President Donald Trump has undone some of the Obama-era rules, making it more difficult to travel on one's own in Cuba.

40. **2** During the 1960s, the actions of Cesar Chavez led to improved conditions for migrant farm workers. In the 1960s, Chavez was one of the organizers of United Farm Workers (UFW). The UFW organized strikes and boycotts of farm products to advance the cause of migrant farm workers' rights. The organization had mixed results. It brought the plight of farm workers into the public eye. In the 1960s, a strike in Texas organized by the UFW demanded the establishment of a minimum wage of $1.25 for migrant farm laborers. The strike was ultimately unsuccessful, but the UWF campaign in Texas led to Senate hearings on the conditions migrant farmers labored in. In the 1970s, Chavez initiated a series of high-profile actions focused on the grape and lettuce fields of California, tended to primarily by Chicano (Mexican-American) laborers. The UFW won union recognition for many of these workers and organized a nationwide boycott of grapes.

WRONG CHOICES EXPLAINED:
(1) The actions of Cesar Chavez did not address conditions for coal miners. Unionized coal miners are represented by the United Mine Workers, founded in 1890. In the late 1890s, the union won recognition in the soft-coal (bituminous coal) mines of the Midwest. It organized a large strike in 1902 against the hard-coal (anthracite coal) operations in Pennsylvania. After the intervention of President Theodore Roosevelt, the strike resulted in a pay increase for the miners but not in union recognition. By the 1930s, the UMW grew to over 800,000 members. Today, it is a shadow of its former self, with around 70,000 members.

(3) The actions of Cesar Chavez did not address conditions of autoworkers. Unionized autoworkers are represented by the United Automobile Workers, founded in 1935 as part of the newly formed Congress of Industrial Organizations. In the late 1930s and early 1940s, it was successful in gaining union recognition for workers at the "big three" automobile makers—General Motors, Chrysler, and Ford. Its high-profile sit-down strikes in 1936 and 1937 at the General Motors plant in Flint, Michigan, were milestones in its successful unionization of the automobile industry. By the 1970s, membership was over 1.5 million. The union has declined in the decades since, as American car makers have shifted operations abroad and foreign-based automobile production facilities in the United States have resisted unionization. In addition, automation of production facilities has reduced the number of workers in the auto industry.

(4) The actions of Cesar Chavez did not address conditions of health care workers. Unionized health care workers are represented by several unions. The largest health care workers' union is the Service Employees International Union.

41. **2** The heading for the partial outline should read, "Native American Indian Demands for Equality." The three items in the outline are all important events in struggle for civil rights for Native Americans. In the 1960s, Native American activists, inspired by the example set by the civil rights movement, protested for greater equality and justice. The American Indian Movement was founded in 1968 (alluded to in item C in the outline). The movement insisted on greater autonomy on reservation lands and the return of lands that it claimed had been illegally seized. The movement had a strong presence among urban Native Americans as well as among Native Americans who lived on reservations. The following year, the movement made headlines when several dozen activists seized control of Alcatraz Island, in San Francisco Bay, claiming the land that housed the former prison belonged to the first inhabitants of the area—Native American Indians (alluded to in item A in the outline). The occupation of Alcatraz Island lasted 19 months, until 1971.

In response to protests by the American Indian Movement, the administration of President Richard Nixon promised to extend greater self-determination to tribal councils and greater federal aid. However, the movement continued to press for more fundamental change. A major event occurred in 1973 when members of AIM occupied the town of Wounded Knee, South Dakota (alluded to in item B in the outline), the site of a massacre of the Sioux by federal troops in 1890. The occupation grew partially out of political conflicts within the Oglala Sioux tribe. The main impetus of the action was to pressure the federal government to honor treaties with Native Americans and to renegotiate certain treaties. The occupation, which involved the exchange of gunfire on both sides and garnered a great deal of publicity, lasted nearly three months.

WRONG CHOICES EXPLAINED:

(1) The partial outline does not deal with protests by Native Americans against the Vietnam War. Protests against the war in Vietnam occurred around the same time, in the late 1960s and early 1970s. However, the focus of the protests in the outline was demands for equality for Native American Indians.

(3) The partial outline does not deal with attempts by Native Americans to culturally assimilate. In fact, the American Indian Movement resisted the push toward assimilation. It encouraged a revitalization of traditional Native American cultural practices.

(4) The partial outline does not deal with attempts by Native Americans to support the War on Poverty. The War on Poverty, which was part of President Lyndon Johnson's Great Society agenda, refers to a series of domestic programs passed by Congress in 1964 and 1965. The enactment of the War on Poverty measures occurred before the items in the outline. Further, although the

American Indian Movement addressed poverty on reservations, it argued that federal anti-poverty programs did not address the needs of Native Americans.

42. **1** President Jimmy Carter's efforts to increase stability in the Middle East resulted in the Camp David Accords. The Camp David Accords are considered one of the few triumphs for President Carter's troubled presidency. Since the founding of Israel in 1948, tensions have existed in the Middle East. The Arab nations refused to recognize Israel's right to exist. Four wars occurred between Israel and its neighbors between 1948 and 1973. In 1977, Egyptian President Anwar Sadat broke with the other leaders of the Arab world and flew to Israel to meet with Israeli Prime Minister Menachem Begin. Negotiations ensued between the two leaders, but they were unable to come up with a peace treaty. Carter invited the two leaders to the presidential retreat at Camp David in Maryland. The three men met for 13 days and emerged with the basis for a peace treaty. The treaty resulted in an end to hostilities between Israel and Egypt, but tensions continued to exist between Israel and its other neighbors. The most serious tensions since the Camp David Accords have been between Israelis and Palestinians. Palestinians in the West Bank have been resentful of Israel's occupation and settlement of that area after the 1967 Six-Day War.

WRONG CHOICES EXPLAINED:

(2) The Nuclear Test Ban Treaty does not address efforts to increase stability in the Middle East. In the early 1960s, President John F. Kennedy made attempts to ease tensions between the Soviet Union and the United States. The calls for greater cooperation grew more intense in the aftermath of the Cuban Missile Crisis (1962). The following year, the United States, the Soviet Union, and Great Britain signed the Nuclear Test Ban Treaty (1963). The ban on testing nuclear weapons exempted underground tests.

(3) The Panama Canal Treaty does not address efforts to increase stability in the Middle East. The Panama Canal Treaty is one of two treaties negotiated by President Jimmy Carter and signed by the United States and Panama in 1977. The treaties were ratified by the United States Senate in 1978. In the Panama Canal Treaty, the United States agreed to turn over the Canal Zone to Panama by the end of 1999 (which occurred as agreed upon).

(4) The Paris Peace Accords do not address efforts to increase stability in the Middle East. The Paris Peace Accords (1973) established an end to the Vietnam War. The treaty included the governments of North Vietnam, South Vietnam, and the United States, as well as South Vietnamese rebels. The negotiations led to a withdrawal of American forces from Vietnam, but the accords were never ratified by the United States Senate. Soon after American forces withdrew,

fighting broke out again. By 1975, the government of South Vietnam collapsed, and Vietnam was reunited as a communist-run country.

43. **2** The reason the Equal Rights Amendment did not become part of the United States Constitution was that three-fourths of the states did not ratify it. The process for an amendment to become part of the Constitution is arduous. First, an amendment can be proposed by Congress (by two-third majorities in both houses) or by a national convention. Then, three-fourths of the states must approve an amendment for it to be ratified. The state-by-state approval process can occur by the consent of the state legislatures or by state ratifying conventions. The Equal Rights Amendment, proposed in 1972, would have prohibited the abridgement of "equality of rights under the law . . . on account of sex" either by the federal government or by the state governments. The push to ratify the amendment grew out of the efforts of the women's liberation movement, which developed in the 1960s to challenge inequities in the job market, representations of women in the media, violence against women, and an ingrained set of social values. The push led to a conservative backlash against the proposal. Conservatives argued that passage of the amendment would destroy the American family. The movement against the proposal was led by conservative activist Phyllis Schlafly. She organized a strong coalition, urging "positive women" to embrace femininity. The amendment was approved by both the House and the Senate but failed to get the required 38 states to ratify it, even after the deadline for ratification had been moved forward to 1982. It, therefore, did not become part of the Constitution.

WRONG CHOICES EXPLAINED:
(1) The reason that the Equal Rights Amendment did not become part of the Constitution was not that President Ronald Reagan vetoed it. The president is not directly involved in amending the Constitution. The president may argue in favor of or against a particular amendment, but he or she cannot introduce, ratify, or veto an amendment. The Constitution leaves that role to Congress and the states.

(3) The reason that the Equal Rights Amendment did not become part of the Constitution was not opposition from the National Organization of Women (NOW). The organization, founded in 1966, was strongly in favor of the amendment.

(4) The reason that the Equal Rights Amendment did not become part of the Constitution was not that the Supreme Court ruled that it was unconstitutional. The Supreme Court does not have the power to rule that an amendment is unconstitutional. Rather it reviews governmental acts to determine if they are consistent with the Constitution. This power is called judicial review.

44. **3** Excessive use of credit and bank speculation in the mortgage market were important contributing factors to the severe recession in the U.S. economy in 2008. Many economists cite the crisis in the housing market as an important cause of the Great Recession of 2008–2009. In the 2000s, lending institutions had been devising new methods of making money borrowing cheaper and easier, leading to the excessive use of credit. Many of these practices became widespread after Congress repealed most of the provisions of the 1933 Glass-Steagall Act in 1999, removing regulatory constraints on the banking industry. Banks lured first-time home buyers to take out mortgages for home purchases that were beyond their means. Banks, for instance, offered adjustable rate mortgages in which initial low rates would later jump to higher rates. These risky loans—characterized by high interest rates and less than favorable terms—were referred to as *subprime mortgages* because they were extended to people whose ability to repay and whose credit rating was less than prime. By 2008, almost 30 percent of mortgages were rated as subprime. To make this situation worse, banks would speculate in this shaky mortgage market. Lenders would sell these subprime mortgages to investment banks and other Wall Street financial institutions. In turn, Wall Street would bundle these mortgages into stock offerings. Finally, pension funds, mutual funds, foreign banks, and individuals invested in these offerings. Therefore, the risk entailed in the original mortgages was spread throughout the financial world and to many individuals whose financial health was, in some way, tied to the stock market. In 2007, the housing bubble burst as the real estate market weakened and interest rates increased. Many subprime borrowers found themselves "underwater"—that is, the market value of their home sank below the amount they owed on their mortgage. In many such situations, individuals could neither sell their homes nor afford to pay their monthly mortgage payments. Their only option was to walk away from their home and default on their loan, leading to widespread foreclosures.

WRONG CHOICES EXPLAINED:

(1) The severe recession in the United States of 2008 was not caused by immigration restrictions and lack of skilled workers. Immigration laws had not changed significantly in the lead-up to the Great Recession. Further, newly arrived immigrants tend to fill jobs as unskilled workers, rather than skilled workers.

(2) The severe recession in the United States of 2008 was not caused by cuts in defense spending and social welfare spending. Under President George W. Bush (2001–2009), spending on both domestic programs and on the military increased, with military spending increasing at a more rapid rate.

(4) The severe recession in the United States of 2008 was not caused by tight monetary policy and overregulation of banks. The opposite was true. Lending institutions made credit readily available, and the government rolled

back regulations on the banking industry that had been in place since the 1930s. Both of these factors—easy access to credit and unregulated, risky banking practices—are seen as important causes of the Great Recession.

45. **1** The main idea of the cartoon is that approval of the president in 2006 was directly linked to the cost of gasoline in the United States. The sign in front of the White House, labeled "Approval Rating," resembles a sign at a gas station indicating the price of a gallon of gasoline. When stations advertise their prices, they include nine-tenths of a cent at the end of the price, presumably so consumers will think the price is a penny cheaper than it actually is. The implication of the sign is that President George W. Bush had a low approval rating, and that an important reason for that was that gasoline prices had increased. Approval ratings for President George W. Bush steadily dropped from a high of over 90 percent following the terrorist attacks of 2001 to lows that hovered between around 30 and 40 percent from 2006 to 2008. At the time of publication of the cartoon, Bush's approval rating had dipped to around 31 percent and gasoline prices had risen to over three dollars in many areas. Changes in the price of a gallon of gasoline are determined by a number of factors—the price of a barrel of crude oil (which is subject to speculation and price swings), demand, changes in taxes and regulations, and relations with oil-producing countries. Some of these factors are within the president's control; many are not.

WRONG CHOICES EXPLAINED:
(2) The main idea of the cartoon is not that public approval of the president in 2006 was directly linked to success in stopping human rights abuses abroad. The cartoon is focused on the importance of the price of gasoline in determining presidential popularity. At different times, presidents have focused on policies designed to reduce human rights abuses abroad. President Jimmy Carter (1977–1981), for example, made this a priority of his administration. He took steps to tie foreign aid to the human rights records of recipient countries.

(3) The main idea of the cartoon is not that public approval of the president in 2006 was directly linked to ability to restrict the flow of illegal drugs. The cartoon is focused on the importance of the price of gasoline in determining presidential popularity. President Ronald Reagan (1981–1989) is often associated with the "war on drugs." In regard to the illegal flow of drugs into the United States, the Reagan administration grew increasingly frustrated with Panamanian President Manuel Noriega for a variety of reason, including his involvement with international drug trafficking. Reagan's successor, George H.W. Bush, initiated an invasion of Panama, which removed Noriega from office.

(4) The main idea of the cartoon is not that public approval of the president in 2006 was directly linked to the amount of the budget surplus. The cartoon is

focused on the importance of the price of gasoline in determining presidential popularity. Under President George W. Bush, there was a budget surplus in his first year in office (2001). This was the fourth year in a row of surpluses. After tax cuts and spending increases, there were budget deficits for the remaining years of his presidency.

46. **2** The main idea of the cartoon is that telephone surveillance by the National Security Agency violates some of the protections of the United States Constitution. The NSA employee in the cartoon is depicted saying to a colleague that he is having trouble listening in on a particular telephone conversation because of background noise. He attributes the background noise to static caused by a technical glitch. The viewer sees that the background noise is actually the framers of the Constitution complaining loudly that the whole program violates the Constitution. Debates between law-enforcement officials and privacy advocates have focused on how accessible data—culled from individuals' telecommunications activities—should be to officials.

This debate made front-page news in 2013 when a former contractor with the NSA, Edward Snowden, exposed a clandestine program known as PRISM, which permitted the agency to conduct warrantless mass data mining of phone, Internet, and other communications—including, under certain circumstances, those of United States citizens—as part of counterterrorism efforts. PRISM was first enabled by President Bush when he signed the Protect America Act into law in 2007; in 2012, President Barack Obama renewed PRISM. While in Hong Kong, Snowden met with three journalists and made available to them thousands of classified NSA documents. Subsequent articles in *The Guardian* and *The Washington Post* brought the program, and Snowden himself, to international attention. In May 2015, immediately prior to the publication of the cartoon, an appeals court ruled that the Patriot Act did not authorize the NSA to collect Americans' calling records in bulk. In June 2015, President Obama reauthorized provisions of the Patriot Act, putting some restrictions on the NSA's ability to collect bulk telecommunication data on U.S. citizens.

WRONG CHOICES EXPLAINED:
(1) The cartoon is not arguing that telephone surveillance by the National Security Agency has been troubled by technical difficulties. The men in the background are the framers of the Constitution challenging the constitutionality of the agency's PRISM program of warrantless surveillance of telecommunications data. They are not technicians or repair workers raising concerns about technical difficulties of the program.

(3) The cartoon is not arguing that telephone surveillance by the National Security Agency is legal because it protects the privacy of Internet users. The men in the background, the framers of the Constitution, are raising concerns about the constitutionality of the agency's PRISM program of warrantless surveillance of telecommunications data. They are not asserting that the program is legal. Indeed, the program did not protect the privacy of Internet users.

(4) The cartoon is not arguing that telephone surveillance by the National Security Agency increases hacking of top-secret government information. A goal of the agency's surveillance program was to identify attempts at cyberterrorism, including hacking of government information. Whether that goal was achieved is unknown, but one would not argue that the program *increased* hacking.

47. **3** The Alien and Sedition Acts of 1798 were similar to the Espionage and Sedition Acts passed during World War I because they both tried to restrict criticism of and opposition to government policies. Debates and conflicts over the proper balance between individual liberty and order have occurred throughout American history. The Alien and Sedition Acts (1798), comprised of four acts, were passed by a Federalist-dominated Congress in order to limit criticism from the opposition Republican Party during the undeclared Quasi-War with France (1798–1800). The Sedition Act made it a crime to defame the president or Congress. The broad wording of the Sedition Act seemed to challenge the free speech guarantees of the recently ratified First Amendment. The Espionage Act (1917) and Sedition Act (1918) made it a crime to interfere with the World War I draft or with the sales of war bonds, as well as to say anything "disloyal" in regard to the war effort. The Supreme Court decision in *Schenck v. United States* (1919) upheld the Espionage Act. Charles Schenck and other members of the Socialist Party had been arrested for printing and distributing flyers opposing the war and urging young men to resist the draft. The Supreme Court argued that freedom of speech is not absolute and that the government is justified in limiting certain forms of speech during wartime and other national emergencies. The Court argued that certain utterances pose a "clear and present danger." By analogy, the Court reasoned that one is not allowed to falsely shout "Fire!" in a crowded theater.

WRONG CHOICES EXPLAINED:
(1) Neither the Alien and Sedition Acts of 1798 nor the Espionage and Sedition Acts passed during World War I provided for the draft of men into the military. Drafting individuals into the military has a long history in the United States. A draft law was passed during the Civil War, but only a small percentage of men in the Union army were drafted. The Selective Service Act (1917) was passed to fill the ranks of the army during World War I. The Selective Training

and Service Act (1940) was passed in 1940, even before the United States officially entered World War II. The Selective Service Act of 1948 created the Selective Service System, which has been in operation until the present day. It was used to draft soldiers for the Korean War (1950–1953) and for the Vietnam War (1955–1975).

(2) Neither the Alien and Sedition Acts of 1798 nor the Espionage and Sedition Acts passed during World War I gave the government greater control over the production of goods. During World War I, the federal government played a greater role in regulating and guiding economic activity, through agencies such as the War Industries Board and the National War Labor Board. During World War II, agencies such as the War Production Board and the Office of Economic Stabilization gave the government greater control over production.

(4) Neither the Alien and Sedition Acts of 1798 nor the Espionage and Sedition Acts passed during World War I attempted to justify United States involvement in a foreign war. During World War I, the Committee on Public Information organized pro-war propaganda; the United States also embarked on a major propaganda campaign during World War II. The Office of War Information (1942–1945) put out a steady stream of posters and radio broadcasts, along with news releases.

48. **4** The events most closely associated with westward expansion are the passage of the Homestead Act of 1862 and the opening of the transcontinental railroad in 1869. The Homestead Act attempted to promote westward expansion by providing free land to settlers. By the time of the Civil War, the government wanted to encourage settlement in the huge area of relatively flat land between the Mississippi River and the Rocky Mountains known as the Great Plains. Much of this area has rich soil and a long growing season. Hundreds of thousands of people applied for and were granted homesteads. The Homestead Act reflected the "free labor" ideal of the Republicans. With the absence of Democrats from Congress during the Civil War, the Republican Party was able to pass several pieces of legislation that reflected their vision of America. This legislation included the Pacific Railroad Act (1862), which extended government bonds and tracts of land to companies engaged in building transcontinental railroads. The government ended up granting 130 million acres of federally held land to railroad companies. Individual states sweetened the pot for railroad construction by extending another 50 million acres to railroad companies. These generous land grants totaled more than 180 million acres, an area equal to the size of Texas. The first transcontinental railroad was completed in 1869. By the end of the 19th century, four additional transcontinental lines were completed.

WRONG CHOICES EXPLAINED:

(1) The passage of the Indian Removal Act of 1830 is associated with westward expansion, but the Compromise of 1877 is not. The Indian Removal Act authorized the president to negotiate with Native American tribes, including the Chickasaw, Choctaw, Creek, Seminole, and original Cherokee people, who lived in several southern states. Those who refused to leave their land were forced off. The forced removal of Native Americans in the 1830s and 1840s is known as the Trail of Tears. The motivation for the act was to open up land for white farmers to expand westward into the interior of the South.

(2) Neither the issuing of the Emancipation Proclamation (1863) nor the creation of the Federal Reserve System (1913) is associated with westward expansion. The Emancipation Proclamation was issued by President Abraham Lincoln during the Civil War. The document declared that as of January 1, 1863, slaves in Confederate-held territory would be free. Of course, United States laws were not enforceable in Confederate-held territory, but the Emancipation Proclamation had the important effect of turning the Civil War into a war for the liberation of the enslaved population of the South. The Federal Reserve System was created to control the money supply. The Federal Reserve Bank, which is part privately controlled and part publicly controlled, was created by legislation in 1913 during the administration of President Woodrow Wilson. One of its main functions is to regulate economic growth by regulating the supply of money.

(3) Neither the passage of the Agricultural Adjustment Act (1933) nor the creation of the Tennessee Valley Authority (1933) is associated with westward expansion. Both are part of the New Deal, President Franklin D. Roosevelt's legislative agenda designed to address the economic problems associated with the Great Depression. The Agricultural Adjustment Act extended subsidies to farmers. In effect, it paid farmers to not grow certain crops, so as to reduce surpluses and push up prices for farm commodities. In this way, farm incomes, which had taken a battering during the Great Depression, would rise. The Tennessee Valley Authority (TVA) was a set of development projects in the Tennessee River area of the South. The region was especially hard hit by the Great Depression. Even before the depression, poverty was pervasive; most homes in the region were without electricity. The TVA included major infrastructure projects, including electricity-generating dams along the Tennessee River.

49. **3** The National Association for the Advancement of Colored People (NAACP), the Congress of Racial Equality (CORE), and the Southern Christian Leadership Conference (SCLC) are all associated with the civil rights movement. The movement was perhaps the most important reform movement of the 20th century. The goal of the movement was to challenge racist practices and

create a more just society. Although its origins date to the early years of the century, if not earlier, the movement was most active between 1954 and 1968. The civil rights movement gained strength after the Supreme Court, in the case of *Brown v. Board of Education of Topeka* (1954), declared that segregation in schools had no place in America. In the years following the Brown decision, there was the Montgomery bus boycott in 1956, the lunch counter sit-ins in 1960, the Freedom Rides in 1962, and a whole host of other activities. The high point of the movement might have been the March on Washington in 1963, where Martin Luther King Jr. gave his "I Have A Dream" speech. The Civil Rights Act (1964) and the Voting Rights Act (1965) represent the crowning achievements of the movement.

The NAACP was formed in 1909. The leadership for the organization had first met in 1905 on the Canadian side of Niagara Falls, where they formed the Niagara movement. The Niagara movement and the NAACP were both led by W.E.B. Du Bois. Du Bois's call for full political equality and civil rights for African Americans was in marked contrast to the more accommodating approach of Booker T. Washington. CORE was founded in Chicago, Illinois, in 1942. The group was inspired, in part, by Mahatma Gandhi's teachings on nonviolent resistance; Gandhi was active at the time in the struggle against British rule of India. CORE was pacifist and believed that nonviolent civil disobedience could successfully be used by African Americans to challenge the Jim Crow system of segregation in the United States. In 1961, CORE organized a series of Freedom Rides through the South—bus rides with African American, as well as white passengers that challenged local codes against integrated buses. The SCLC, a key organization in the civil rights movement, was founded by Martin Luther King Jr. and approximately 60 other African American ministers and religious leaders in 1957. The SCLC consisted of a central board, which set the agenda of the organization, and local groups—churches and community groups—that affiliated with the national group.

WRONG CHOICES EXPLAINED:

(1) The NAACP, CORE, and the SCLC are not associated with the temperance movement. The temperance movement, against the consumption of alcoholic beverages, was the largest reform movement throughout the 19th century and into the 20th century. Some activists encouraged abstinence from drinking alcoholic beverages. Others pushed for laws limiting or prohibiting the sale of alcoholic beverages. The movement achieved major success with the passage of the 18th Amendment (1919), which prohibited the production, importation, transportation, and sale of alcoholic beverages. The prohibition period lasted from 1920 to 1933.

(2) The NAACP, CORE, and the SCLC are not associated with the abolition movement. The abolition movement challenged one of the most profound injustices in American history—slavery. Starting in the 1830s, William Lloyd Garrison was a key figure in the movement for the immediate and uncompensated abolition of slavery. Antislavery sentiment existed before that, but most antislavery groups advocated a more gradual approach to ending slavery. Starting in the 1840s, the towering figure in the abolitionist movement was Frederick Douglass.

(4) The NAACP, CORE, and the SCLC are not associated with the environmental movement. The environmental movement of the 1960s and 1970s pushed ecological concerns into public consciousness. The first Earth Day occurred in 1970. Also in 1970, President Richard Nixon created the Environmental Protection Agency. That same year, Nixon signed the Clean Air Act. The movement still exists, encouraging conservation of resources and raising awareness about the perils of global warming.

50. **4** The action that tried to close the "gap" referred to in the cartoon was agreeing to the Strategic Arms Limitation Treaty (SALT). In the cartoon, there is a gap between "disarmament efforts" and the "arms race." In other words, efforts by the Soviet Union and the United States to negotiate a reduction in nuclear arsenals were faltering as the race to build increasingly powerful nuclear weapons was advancing. By the 1960s, many Americans had become increasingly fearful of the massive nuclear arsenals that both the United States and the Soviet Union had developed. These weapons programs were also a drain on the resources of both countries. Starting in 1969, the two nations began negotiations to limit future weapons production. The United States and the Soviet Union signed the Strategic Arms Limitation Treaty (SALT) in 1972. This treaty called for a slight curb in the production of nuclear weapons. The treaty was part of the broader policy of détente—a warming of relations between the Soviet Union and the United States. The policy was initiated by Nixon. His strong anti-communist credentials enabled him to open relations with communist nations without being accused of being "soft on communism." In 1972, Nixon became the first American president to visit Communist China, and later that year he held meetings with Soviet leaders in Moscow.

WRONG CHOICES EXPLAINED:
(1) The Yalta Agreement did not deal with disarmament efforts or the nuclear arms race. The Yalta Conference (1945), held as World War II was coming to an end, was the most significant, and last, meeting of Prime Minister Winston Churchill of the United Kingdom, Soviet leader Joseph Stalin, and President

Franklin D. Roosevelt. In the Yalta Agreement, the "big three" agreed to divide Germany into four military zones of occupation (the fourth zone would be occupied by France). In 1949, two countries were formed out of Germany. West Germany, allied with the United States, was formed from the military zones occupied by the United States, the United Kingdom, and France. East Germany, a communist country, was formed from the military zone occupied by the Soviet Union.

(2) The Gulf of Tonkin Resolution (1964) did not deal with disarmament efforts or the nuclear arms race. The resolution provided congressional support for escalating military action in Vietnam. The United States became heavily involved in the Vietnam War after Congress gave President Lyndon Johnson a blank check with the resolution. In August 1964, Johnson announced that American destroyers had been fired upon in the Gulf of Tonkin, off the coast of North Vietnam. Later, reports questioned the accuracy of the announcement, but the incident led Congress to give Johnson the ability to escalate American military involvement in Vietnam. The Gulf of Tonkin Resolution can be considered the beginning of the war in Vietnam.

(3) The Strategic Defense Initiative (proposed in 1984) can be seen as part of the nuclear arms race, but it would not be considered a disarmament effort. The Strategic Defense Initiative, dubbed Star Wars by critics, was a proposal to create a missile defense system to protect the United States from attack by nuclear weapons. Such a system was never put into effect, but aspects of it are still being researched.

PART II: THEMATIC ESSAY

Supreme Court Decisions

Throughout American history, key Supreme Court decisions have greatly impacted individuals and groups of people. The Court has the ability to define constitutional rights. Some decisions have expanded constitutional rights, while others have restricted them. Two significant decisions, both from the second half of the 20th century, *Korematsu v. United States* (1944) and *Roe v. Wade* (1973) greatly impacted the definition of constitutional rights for Americans—with the first decision restricting them and the second decision expanding them.

In the case of *Korematsu v. United States*, the Supreme Court upheld Executive Order 9066, issued by President Franklin D. Roosevelt in 1942, just weeks after the attack by Japan on Pearl Harbor, which brought the United States into World War II. The order authorized the government to remove 120,000 Japanese American people, two-thirds of them citizens, from their homes in West

Coast states and relocate them to camps far from to the coastal cities. The order cited the possibility of "espionage" or "sabotage." It asserted that the relocation was necessary for the "successful prosecution" of the war against Japan.

The main circumstance surrounding the decision was American involvement in World War II. The United States again did not enter the conflict immediately. After German leader Adolf Hitler attacked Poland in 1939 and began World War II, the United States remained neutral. Though President Franklin D. Roosevelt sympathized with the opponents of Fascism and Nazism, isolationists argued strongly against United States intervention. The debate ended abruptly in December 1941 when Japan attacked the U.S. naval base at Pearl Harbor, Hawaii. This attack stunned many Americans and made them bitter toward Japan. Because the United States was attacked by Japan and because of American strategic interests in Asia, the primary focus of the U.S. military was Japan. The conflict between the two nations had ramifications on the home front. Japanese immigrants—*Issei* in Japanese—and native-born Americans of Japanese ancestry—*Nisei*—were increasingly looked at with anger and suspicion. It was in the context of this heightened suspicion of Japanese Americans that President Franklin D. Roosevelt issued Executive Order 9066.

Another important circumstance surrounding the decision was a history of racism in the United States toward Asians. Racist assumptions at the time held that Asian immigrants would never fully assimilate into the United States. The gold rush in California and the building of the transcontinental railroad attracted many Chinese immigrants to the West. The Chinese Exclusion Act (1882) was the only instance of legislation prohibiting a particular nationality from entering the country. In the late 1800s, many Japanese people immigrated to the West Coast of the United States. In California, these Japanese immigrants often suffered discrimination. Many white Californians harbored resentment toward their new neighbors. In the early years of the 20th century, California passed legislation ordering "orientals" to be segregated from white students in the public-school system. When Japan protested, President Theodore Roosevelt and Japanese leaders negotiated the Gentlemen's Agreement, in which Roosevelt agreed to reverse this legislation and Japan agreed to limit the number of emigrants coming into the United States. However, on the eve of World War II, anti-Japanese sentiment still existed in California and elsewhere in the United States. This anti-Asian racism predisposed white Californians to suspect their Japanese neighbors of espionage and sabotage as World War II began.

The circumstance surrounding the Korematsu case was the arrest of Fred Korematsu, a Japanese American who had refused to cooperate with the relocation order and had gone into hiding in the Oakland area. He went so far as to undergo plastic surgery on his eyelids in an unsuccessful attempt to appear less like a Japanese person. He changed his name to Clyde Sarah and claimed to be of Spanish and Hawaiian heritage. His attempts to "pass," however, came to naught. He was arrested in May 1942. Soon after, the local chapter of the American Civil Liberties Union heard about the case and asked him if they could use his case as a test of the constitutionality of Executive Order 9066. The case, *Korematsu v. United States*, made its way to the Supreme Court by 1944. The Supreme Court upheld his arrest and the relocation order. The majority decision held that the relocation was acceptable on the grounds of national security. However, the decision was not unanimous. Justice Robert Jackson asserted that the order was unconstitutional. Korematsu was a citizen of the United States, born in California; he was singled out only because he was "born of different racial stock" than white Americans. Jackson argued that that fact was not enough to incarcerate an American citizen.

The impact of the Court's decision on American society was widely felt. The internment of Japanese Americans continued throughout World War II. Much later, in 1988, the United States government publicly apologized to the surviving victims and extended $20,000 in reparations to each one. However, an important precedent of the case continues to reverberate in American society—that the government has the right to set aside constitutional protections and curtail civil liberties in times of war. This was evident with the passage of the Patriot Act in 2001, following the terrorist attacks of September 11. The Patriot Act allows for the use of National Security Letters, or NSLs, by the FBI. These NSLs allow the FBI to search telephone, email, and financial records without a court order, raising constitutional concerns for many people.

While the Court limited individual and group rights in the Korematsu case, it expanded them in the case of *Roe v. Wade* in 1973. The case dealt with the issue of a woman's right to an abortion. The act of inducing the termination of a pregnancy has occurred throughout recorded human history. In early U.S. history, abortions were generally illegal after the moment of "quickening"—when the mother could feel movement of the fetus. By 1900, most states had passed laws making abortion illegal altogether, except in cases of rape or if the health of the mother was at stake. However, abortions continued and, starting in the 1930s, safer techniques were developed.

The historical circumstances of the *Roe v. Wade* case can be traced back to the 1960s. In that decade, women's rights activists and health professionals began to push for states to decriminalize or legalize abortion. Some supporters of legalized abortion stressed the issue of safety. Pushing abortions to "back alley" clinics, they argued, encouraged the use of unsafe and unregulated procedures. Others argued that the decision should be made by the woman, not by politicians. By 1973, 20 states had made abortion legal under certain circumstances (which varied from state to state). The immediate circumstance surrounding the case involved a Texas woman, known at the time by the alias Jane Roe, who sued the state of Texas for prohibiting abortions in all cases, except in cases where the life of the woman was threatened.

The case, *Roe v. Wade*, went to the Supreme Court in 1973. The Court's decision struck down state statues that prohibited or severely limited abortions. The Court declared that states shall not prohibit women from having an abortion during the first two trimesters of pregnancy. The Supreme Court reasoned that the Constitution guaranteed people the right to privacy. Abortion, they argued, was a decision that should be left to the woman with the advice of her physician. This decision echoed the reasoning of an earlier decision, *Griswold v. Connecticut* (1965), in which the Court ruled that laws forbidding the use of birth control devices were unconstitutional.

The *Roe v. Wade* decision has profoundly affected the United States. It is estimated that 50 million abortions have been performed in the United States since 1973. Opponents of the decision argue that abortion is equivalent to terminating a human life. More broadly, they argue that the prevalence of abortion undermines people's appreciation of life—that many Americans have lost sight of the sacredness of every human life. Proponents of the decision argue that women now have greater control over their reproductive lives and have the ability to make the very personal decision about whether to carry a pregnancy to term or not. Politically, the legalization of abortion in the United States has been central to the rise of the New Right. The issue propelled cultural conservatives from the margins to the mainstream of the American political arena. The issue propelled evangelical Protestants to put aside their long-held suspicions of Catholicism and to create a broad Christian conservative movement. Abortion remains one of the most contentious issues in American politics.

PART III: DOCUMENT-BASED QUESTION

Part A: Short Answer

Document 1

1 Based on the information provided in the map, one cause of the conflict between the United States and Mexico was a dispute over the border between the two countries; the United States asserted it was at the Rio Grande, while Mexico asserted it was at the Nueces River.

> *This answer receives full credit because it states one cause of the conflict between the United States and Mexico.*

Document 2

2 Based on the document, one action President James K. Polk took in regard to Texas was to send troops to the area between the Nueces River and the Del Norte (Rio Grande).

This answer receives full credit because it states one action President James K. Polk took in regard to Texas.

Document 3a

3a According to Eric Foner, the issue that the Wilmot Proviso attempted to address was whether territory acquired from Mexico would allow slavery or not.

This answer receives full credit because it states the issue that the Wilmot Proviso attempted to address.

Document 3b

3b Based on the information provided by the map, one effect of the Mexican-American War on the United States in 1848 was that it acquired a large piece of territory from Mexico. This was known as the Mexican Cession.

This answer receives full credit because it states one effect of the Mexican-American War on the United States in 1848.

Document 4

4 Based on the document, one reason President Lyndon B. Johnson believed the United States should continue to assist Vietnam was to strengthen world order by letting countries of the world see that they could count on the United States to support them if attacked.

This answer receives full credit because it states one reason President Lyndon B. Johnson believed the United States should continue to assist Vietnam.

Document 5a

5a Based on the document, one action President Lyndon B. Johnson took in 1965 regarding Vietnam was increasing the monthly draft call from 17,000 men to 35,000 men.

This answer receives full credit because it states one action President Lyndon B. Johnson took in 1965 regarding Vietnam.

Document 5b

5b Based on the information in the charts, one effect of the actions taken by President Lyndon B. Johnson in 1965 was an increase in United States troops from 23,300 in 1964 to 184,000 in 1965.

This answer receives full credit because it states one effect of the actions taken by President Lyndon B. Johnson in 1965.

Document 6a and Document 6b

6(1) Based on the documents, one effect of the Vietnam War on the United States was the development of a large-scale protest movement against American involvement in Vietnam.

6(2) Based on the documents, another effect of the Vietnam War on the United States was that President Lyndon B. Johnson decided not to run for an additional term as president.

These answers receive full credit because they state two effects of the Vietnam War on the United States.

Document 7a, Document 7b, and Document 7c

7 Based on the documents, one cause of the Persian Gulf War was that Iraqi troops engaged in "naked aggression," crossing the border and invading the neighboring country of Kuwait.

This answer receives full credit because it states one cause of the Persian Gulf War.

Document 8

8 Based on the document, one action taken by President George H.W. Bush in response to Iraq's 1990 invasion of Kuwait was to create a coalition of 28 countries, including the United States, and to use the military force of these countries to drive Iraqi troops out of Kuwait.

This answer receives full credit because it states one action taken by President George H.W. Bush in response to Iraq's 1990 invasion of Kuwait.

Document 9a and Document 9b

9(1) Based on the documents, one effect of the Persian Gulf War on the United States was to send peace activists "into retreat" and to rid the general public of its aversion to American overseas military involvements, conquering the so-called "Vietnam Syndrome."

9(2) Based on the documents, another effect of the Persian Gulf War on the United States was to instill in the country a sense of pride because the military accomplished its goal and demonstrated to the world that the United States keeps its promises.

These answers receive full credit because they state two effects of the Persian Gulf War on the United States.

Part B: Document-Based Essay

The Constitution bestows upon the president the title commander in chief. This title gives the president a great deal of latitude in dealing with international crises. While it is true that Congress has the power to declare war and to allocate money for military actions, presidents have frequently taken actions unilaterally. It is understandable that presidents would take actions on their own. An attack on the United States would very likely require an immediate and decisive response; there would not be time to wait for Congress to convene and to debate the proper response to such a crisis. However, on different occasions, critics have accused presidents of abusing their powers and taking actions in an arbitrary and misguided manner. Presidential actions in the Mexican-American War (1846–1848) and in the Vietnam War (1964–1975) generated a great deal of debate and contention, and ultimately had major impacts on the United States.

The Mexican War occurred during the years 1846 to 1848. The historical circumstances that led to the conflict date back to Americans moving into the Mexican province of Texas. As early as the 1820s, white Americans began moving into the Mexican territory of Texas. Many of these settlers were southern whites who hoped to duplicate the plantation model from the Old South. Initially, Mexico was eager to attract settlers to its northern frontier. Led by Stephen Austin, settlers were attracted to Texas because there was an abundance of affordable land that could be used for cotton cultivation. By the 1820s, tensions began to develop between the Texas settlers and the Mexican government. Texans routinely flouted Mexican law—most notably in practicing slavery, which was banned in Mexico. In 1835, the Texans rebelled against Mexico. At first, they suffered a major setback at the Alamo in San Antonio, a former mission where they had taken refuge. Weeks later, the rebels regrouped and emerged victorious. Texans won independence from Mexico, establishing the independent Lone Star Republic in 1836. Most Texans were eager for their Lone Star Republic to join the United States. However, many Whig Party politicians opposed Texas annexation because they feared that it would create new tensions around the issue of slavery. Texas was finally annexed in 1845, soon after the victory of the expansionist James K. Polk in the presidential election of 1844.

When Polk took office, he set his sights beyond Texas—he wanted to acquire the remainder of Mexico's northern provinces, including California, on the Pacific coast. Toward this end, he antagonized Mexico by claiming land that the Mexican government (and many Americans) believed was actually part of Mexico. He said that the border between Texas and Mexico was at the Rio Grande rather than at the Nueces River. (Document 1) He further antagonized Mexico by sending "an efficient military force" into the disputed territory. He claimed that this action was necessary to repel a planned invasion by Mexico. He asserted that Mexico was determined to get revenge on the United States for annexing Texas. (Document 2)

The conflict with Mexico generated a great deal of debate in the United States. Many Americans, such as the Whig congressman Abraham Lincoln, argued that Polk's rationale for sending troops to the disputed territory was bogus. He wrote that Congress should not allow Polk to wage war simply because Polk felt that another nation was about to wage war on the United States. To do so, Lincoln argued, would be giving Polk limitless power to wage war. Other Americans were concerned that the acquisition of new territory would open the possibility of expanding slavery. In Congress, Representative David Wilmot of Pennsylvania put forth an amendment to an appropriations bill that would have prohibited the expansion of slavery to territories acquired from Mexico. The Wilmot Proviso passed the House (where the populous northern states were able to exert greater power), but it failed in the Senate (where each state has equal representation). (Document 3a)

The effects of the Mexican War on the United States were profound. As Polk had hoped, the United States acquired Mexico's northern provinces, as part of the Treaty of Guadalupe Hidalgo (1848) following the American victory in the Mexican War. The Mexican Cession includes the present-day states of California, Nevada, and Utah, as well as portions of present-day Arizona, New Mexico, Wyoming, and Colorado. (Document 3b) More importantly, the acquisition of new territory brought the question of slavery to the forefront of political debates. Soon after the acquisition of the Mexican Cession, gold was discovered in California (1848). As word spread, thousands of people came to California to try to strike it rich. By 1850, California had enough people to form a state. Californians wrote up a constitution, in which slavery would be illegal, to submit to Congress. Southern senators objected to the admission of an additional free state. Senate negotiators worked out a series of measures that became known as the Compromise of 1850. The most important elements of the compromise were the admittance of California as a free state, which pleased northern politicians, and a more stringent Fugitive Slave Law, which pleased southern politicians. The compromise proved to be a temporary solution to a deeply troubling issue. The two-party system of Democrats and Whigs collapsed, to be replaced by sectional parties. (Document 3a) By the end of the 1850s, the question of slavery so dominated public debates that the country seemed ready to break apart. It did exactly that in the months following the election of Abraham Lincoln in 1860. The secession of most of the slave-holding states led to Civil War in 1861.

A century after the conclusion of the Civil War, the United States began a large-scale intervention in a conflict on the other side of the globe. The Vietnam War, which lasted from 1955 to 1975, greatly impacted the United States and ultimately undid the presidency of Lyndon Johnson.

The roots of conflict in Vietnam stretch back to the period of French imperialism in Indochina. From the mid-19th century to the mid-20th century, Vietnam was a colony of France. It was then occupied by Japan during World War II. After the war, many Vietnamese hoped to finally be free of foreign control, but France reoccupied it. A war for independence, led by Ho Chi Minh, began in 1946. In 1954, French forces were defeated and withdrew from the region, leaving Vietnam divided at the 17th parallel between a communist-controlled North Vietnam, and a western-allied South Vietnam. A rebel movement, known as the Vietcong, continued to press its cause in South Vietnam. It was at this point that the United States became involved in the conflict. President Dwight Eisenhower cited the domino theory as a rationale for American involvement in Vietnam. The theory asserts that when a nation becomes communist, its neighbors will be more likely to become communist. Years later (in 1965), President Johnson cited this long history of support for South Vietnam as a reason for continuing involvement in Vietnam. He saw continued involvement as a key to maintaining "world order." (Document 4)

President Johnson took decisive action in regard to Vietnam in 1965. In August 1964, Johnson announced that American destroyers had been fired upon in the Gulf of Tonkin, off the coast of North Vietnam. Later, reports questioned the accuracy of the announcement, but the incident led Congress to give Johnson the ability to escalate American military involvement in Vietnam. The Gulf of Tonkin Resolution can be considered the beginning of the war in Vietnam. Soon after, Johnson increased the number of troops in Vietnam to 125,000, and he increased the monthly draft call to 35,000. (Document 5a) In the following years, Johnson continued to increase American troop strength in Vietnam—to 385,300 in 1966, 485,600 in 1967, and 536,100 in 1968. (Document 5b)

The effects of President Johnson's actions in regard to Vietnam were felt deeply in American society. The war divided Americans as no previous war had. President Johnson was not able to impose military censorship on the media. As such, it became known as a "living room war" because images from Vietnam were regularly broadcast on the evening news. Families saw American soldiers burn down Vietnamese villages. They saw body bags coming back to the United States. They saw children burned by napalm. All of these images contributed to the growing antiwar movement in the United States. Also, after President Lyndon Johnson had reinstated the military draft in order to meet the personnel needs of the Vietnam War (Document 5a), the possibility of being drafted led many young people to oppose the war. Protests against the war grew large and more intense. A massive demonstration at the Lincoln Memorial in October 1967 capped a year of major protests organized by the National Mobilization Committee to End the War in Vietnam (Document 6a). The demonstrations against the Vietnam War deeply shook the political establishment, dividing Democrats into pro-hawk and pro-dove factions. It also intensified divisions within American society around ideology, culture, politics, age, race, and gender. Ultimately, the war undid the Johnson presidency; in March 1968, he announced that he would not seek reelection. (Document 6b)

Presidential actions initiated both the Mexican-American War and the Vietnam War. In both cases, the actions taken by the president generated a great deal of debate. Critics wondered aloud if the circumstances around each conflict justified the actions taken by the U.S. president. Ultimately, both conflicts led to profound changes in American society. The Mexican-American War led to a reopening of the debate over the expansion of slavery—a debate that ended in the Civil War. The Vietnam War led to major divisions in American society that continued to be felt well beyond the end of the war.

Topic	Question Numbers	*Number of Points
American political history	11, 12, 13, 17, 18, 22, 24, 31, 38, 45, 47, 48	14
Political theory	3	1
Economic theory/policy	8, 16, 19, 28, 29, 30, 44	8
Constitutional principles	2, 4, 5, 6, 7, 43, 46	8
American foreign policy	21, 32, 35, 36, 37, 39, 42, 50	10
American studies—the American people	9, 10, 14, 20, 23, 25, 26, 27, 33, 34, 40, 41, 49	16
Geography	1,15	2
Skills questions included in the above content area		
Reading comprehension	11, 12, 28, 32, 38	
Cartoon/image interpretation	25, 29, 30, 45, 46, 50	
Outlining skills	16, 41	

*Note: The 50 questions in Part I are worth a total of 60 percent of the exam. Since each correct answer is worth 60/50 or 1.2 points, totals are shown to the nearest full point in each content category.

PART I

Multiple-Choice Questions by Standard

Standard	Question Numbers
1—United States and New York History	7, 9, 10, 12, 13, 14, 17, 18, 21, 23, 25, 26, 27, 29, 32, 33, 38, 40, 43, 45, 50
2—World History	35, 36, 37, 39, 42
3—Geography	1, 15, 20, 48
4—Economics	8, 16, 19, 22, 28, 30, 34, 44
5—Civics, Citizenship, and Government	2, 3, 4, 5, 6, 11, 24, 31, 41, 46, 47, 49

Parts II and III by Theme and Standard

	Theme	Standards
Thematic Essay	Supreme Court Decisions; Constitutional Principles; Civic Values; Citizenship; Individuals, Groups, Institutions	Standards 1 and 5: United States and New York History; Civics, Citizenship, and Government
Document-Based Essay	Presidential Decisions and Actions; Foreign Policy; Places and Regions; Constitutional Principles; Interdependence	Standards 1, 2, 3, and 5: United States and New York History; World History; Geography; Civics, Citizenship, and Government

Examination June 2019

United States History and Government

PART I: MULTIPLE CHOICE

Directions (1–50): For each statement or question, write in the space provided the *number* of the word or expression that, of those given, best completes the statement or answers the question.

1 In colonial America, the Magna Carta, the English Bill of Rights, and the writings of John Locke contributed to the

   (1) diversity of religious beliefs among the colonists
   (2) political ideals and practices of the colonists
   (3) economic relationships between the colonists and the mother country
   (4) demands of colonists to end the slave trade and the practice of slavery   1 _____

2 Before 1763, most American colonists settled near the Atlantic Coast or rivers because

   (1) port cities could be more easily defended in times of war
   (2) valleys were less fertile
   (3) English colonists were only allowed to settle in these locations
   (4) navigable water offered easier access to trade and employment   2 _____

3 One way in which the Declaration of Independence and the original United States Constitution are similar is that both promote the idea of

   (1) the consent of the governed
   (2) equal rights for women
   (3) voting rights for all adult citizens
   (4) judicial review of unjust laws   3 _____

4 The main purpose of the *Federalist Papers* was to

  (1) discourage the creation of political parties
  (2) support the candidacy of George Washington
  (3) urge ratification of the Constitution
  (4) advocate independence from Great Britain   4 _____

5 ". . . Constitutions should consist only of general provisions: The reason is, that they must necessarily be permanent, and that they cannot calculate for the possible changes of things. . . ."

                            — Alexander Hamilton, 1788

Which provision of the United States Constitution best supports the idea expressed in this quotation?

  (1) eminent domain
  (2) electoral college
  (3) separation of powers
  (4) elastic clause   5 _____

6 The main objection to the adoption of the United States Constitution was based primarily on the belief that

  (1) the number of new states admitted to the Union should be limited
  (2) individual freedoms could be restricted by a strong central government
  (3) a separate judiciary would make the government ineffective
  (4) slave populations gave the South too much power   6 _____

7 Which viewpoint of the framers of the United States Constitution is demonstrated by the use of the electoral college to select the president?

  (1) distrust of the average citizen's judgment
  (2) belief that political parties strengthen the campaign process
  (3) desire to end property qualifications for voting
  (4) commitment to universal suffrage   7 _____

Base your answer to question 8 on the diagram below and on your knowledge of social studies.

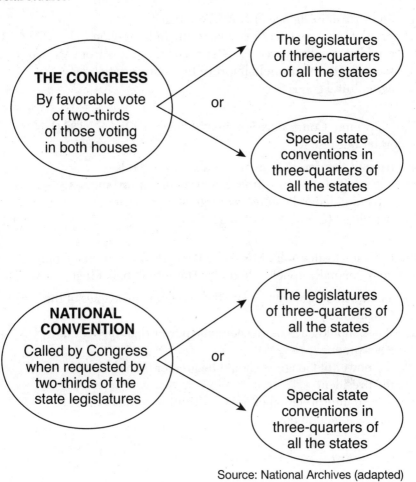

Source: National Archives (adapted)

8 What is the best title for this diagram?

  (1) Methods of Amending the Constitution
  (2) Procedures of the Executive Branch
  (3) Process of Nominating Presidential Candidates
  (4) Admission of New States to the Union   8 _____

9 The United States wanted to acquire New Orleans in 1803 in order to

(1) end British influence in North America
(2) promote the growth of manufacturing in the region
(3) establish a military base to defend against attacks from Mexico
(4) secure a port that would improve the transportation of agricultural goods

9 _____

10 The Supreme Court decision in *Gibbons* v. *Ogden* (1824) is important because it

(1) banned the importation of manufactured goods
(2) encouraged state investment in internal improvements
(3) expanded federal control over interstate commerce
(4) permitted taxes on exported goods

10 _____

11 Under Chief Justice John Marshall (1801–1835), Supreme Court decisions generally upheld Alexander Hamilton's belief that

(1) a national debt would violate the economic principles of the Constitution
(2) states should have more economic power than the federal government
(3) the power of Congress should be greater than the power of the president
(4) a loose interpretation of the Constitution could be used to increase federal power

11 _____

Base your answer to question 12 on the passage below and on your knowledge of social studies.

> . . . I am not a Know-Nothing. That is certain. How could I be? How can any one who abhors the oppression of negroes [African Americans], be in favor of degrading classes of white people? Our progress in degeneracy appears to me to be pretty rapid. As a nation, we began by declaring that *"all men are created equal."* We now practically read it "all men are created equal, *except negroes."* When the Know-Nothings get control, it will read "all men are created equal, except negroes, *and foreigners, and catholics."* When it comes to this I should prefer emigrating to some country where they make no pretence of loving liberty—to Russia, for instance, where despotism can be taken pure, and without the base alloy of hypocracy. . . .
>
> — Abraham Lincoln, letter to Joshua Speed,
> August 24, 1855

12 In this 1855 letter, Abraham Lincoln opposed the Know-Nothing party because it

(1) supported the policy of imperialism
(2) favored unrestricted immigration
(3) promoted resentment against minority groups
(4) wanted equal rights for all people

12 _____

13 The Supreme Court's decision in *Dred Scott* v. *Sandford* was nullified by the passage of the

(1) Kansas-Nebraska Act
(2) 13th and 14th amendments
(3) Compromise of 1850
(4) Reconstruction Act

13 _____

14 The Civil War directly affected the Northern economy by

    (1) causing a severe depression
    (2) destroying much of its farmland
    (3) greatly expanding the canal system
    (4) stimulating the growth of factories   14 _____

15 Rapid industrialization during the late 1800s contributed to

    (1) a decline in the membership of the American Federation of Labor (AFL)
    (2) a reduction in government regulation of railroads
    (3) a rise in the number of family farms
    (4) an increase in immigration to the United States   15 _____

16 Which factor aided the building of transcontinental railroads?

    (1) The federal government provided free land to the railroad companies.
    (2) The railroads established fair rates for customers.
    (3) Congress repealed antitrust laws against the railroads.
    (4) The Supreme Court approved public ownership of the railroad industry.   16 _____

17 Which tactics were used by big business during the late 1800s to limit the power of labor unions?

    (1) strikebreakers and lockouts
    (2) picketing and walkouts
    (3) collective bargaining and mediation
    (4) wage increases and shorter hours   17 _____

18 Which constitutional right was the central focus in *Plessy* v. *Ferguson* (1896)?

    (1) freedom of assembly guaranteed by the first amendment
    (2) due process of the law in the fifth amendment
    (3) equal protection of the law under the 14th amendment
    (4) equal voting rights guaranteed by the 15th amendment   18 _____

Base your answer to question 19 on the cartoon below and on your knowledge of social studies.

The Monster Monopoly

Source: Frank Beard, *Judge,* July 19, 1884 (adapted)

19 What is being criticized in this cartoon?

    (1) environmental damage   (3) oil exploration

    (2) business consolidation   (4) federal tax laws   19 _____

20 Which event was a result of the Spanish-American War?

(1) Cuba was divided into spheres of influence.
(2) Puerto Rico became a possession of the United States.
(3) The Philippines became a Spanish colony.
(4) The United States lost control of the Panama Canal.   20 _____

21 • Chinese Exclusion Act (1882)

• Gentlemen's Agreement (1907)

• Emergency Quota Act (1921)

These federal actions demonstrate that Americans have

(1) supported the principle of open immigration
(2) provided immigrants equal access to jobs and social programs
(3) forced immigrants to settle in designated areas
(4) favored limiting immigration at different times in the
    nation's history   21 _____

22 In the early 20th century, muckraking authors Upton Sinclair and
Ida Tarbell primarily criticized the federal government for

(1) wasting money on foreign wars
(2) ignoring abuses committed by big business
(3) excessive regulation of the steel industry
(4) overspending on social welfare programs   22 _____

23 During the Progressive Era, voters were given more opportunities
to select political party candidates through

(1) direct primary elections
(2) term limits on elected officials
(3) initiative and recall
(4) public funding of elections   23 _____

24 Theodore Roosevelt's Square Deal and Woodrow Wilson's New
Freedom shared the goal of

(1) achieving equal rights for minority groups
(2) protecting the interests of big business
(3) strengthening federal regulatory power over large
    corporations
(4) instituting laissez-faire policies   24 _____

25 The Federal Reserve System was created in 1913 to

   (1) balance the budget
   (2) control the money supply
   (3) insure savings account deposits
   (4) regulate the stock market   25 _____

Base your answer to question 26 on these statements by President Woodrow Wilson and on your knowledge of social studies.

"... The United States must be neutral in fact as well as in name. . ."

— message to U.S. Senate, 1914

"... America can not be an ostrich with its head in the sand. . . ."

— address in Des Moines, Iowa, 1916

"... The world must be made safe for democracy. . . ."

— address to Congress asking for a declaration of war, April 2, 1917

26 What do these statements demonstrate about President Wilson during the three years before the United States entered World War I?

   (1) He gradually changed his foreign policy goals.
   (2) He eagerly became involved in a war.
   (3) He abused the principle of separation of powers.
   (4) He was consistent in his policy of strict neutrality.   26 _____

27 President Warren Harding's call for a "return to normalcy" meant the United States should

(1) limit the number of exports
(2) reduce its role in world affairs
(3) expand efforts to end racial discrimination
(4) support woman's suffrage

27 _____

28 Which heading best completes the partial outline below?

I. _____

    A. Overproduction
    B. Underconsumption
    C. Buying on margin
    D. Unequal distribution of wealth

(1) Causes of the Industrial Revolution
(2) Causes of World War I
(3) Causes of the Great Depression
(4) Causes of World War II

28 _____

Base your answer to question 29 on the graph below and on your knowledge of social studies.

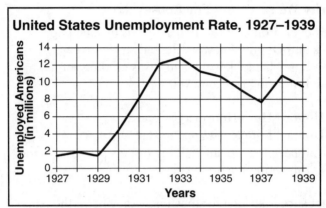

United States Unemployment Rate, 1927–1939

Source: *Historical Statistics of the United States, Colonial Times to 1970* (adapted)

29 Which conclusion is most clearly supported by the information provided on the graph?

(1) Deficit spending ended unemployment.
(2) World War II increased unemployment.
(3) New Deal programs only partially relieved unemployment.
(4) Unemployment after the New Deal was the same as before the stock market crash.   29 _____

30 During the 1930s, poor land management and severe drought conditions across parts of the Midwest resulted in the

(1) establishment of the United States Department of Agriculture
(2) creation of wheat surpluses
(3) decreased support for conservation
(4) development of the Dust Bowl conditions on the Great Plains   30 _____

31 During the 1930s, United States neutrality legislation was primarily designed to

(1) provide military and economic aid to Italy and Japan
(2) give the United States time to plan an attack against Germany
(3) protect American lives and property in Latin America
(4) avoid foreign policy mistakes that led to involvement in World War I   31 _____

Base your answers to questions 32 and 33 on the song lyrics below and on your knowledge of social studies.

That's Why We're Voting For Roosevelt

Herbie Hoover promised us "Two chickens in each pot,"
Breadlines and Depression were the only things we got.
I lost my job, my bank blew up, and I was on the spot.
That's why I'm voting for Roosevelt.

Hooray! Hooray! Herb Hoover's gone away,
Hooray! Hooray! I hope he's gone to stay.
For now I'm back to work and get my three squares ev'ry day.
That's why I'm voting for Roosevelt. . . .

Wall Street sure is kicking for they know they're on the pan.
Franklin D. in Washington upset their little plan,
And now the one on top is that poor once forgotten man,
That's why we're voting for Roosevelt.

Hooray! Hooray! He banished all our fear.
Hooray! Hooray! Our banks are in the clear.
He brought us back prosperity, he gave us back our beer,
That's why I'm voting for Roosevelt.

— Thomas O'Dowd, 1936

32 Which group would most likely have agreed with the lyrics of this song?

(1) Prohibition advocates   (3) New Deal supporters
(2) Republican Party leaders   (4) Supply-side economists   32 _____

33 According to the song lyrics, people supported Franklin D. Roosevelt primarily because he

(1) implemented economic relief and recovery programs
(2) favored a national suffrage amendment
(3) continued Herbert Hoover's economic policies
(4) reduced federal income taxes   33 _____

Base your answer to question 34 on the cartoon below and on your knowledge of social studies.

NEVER SATISFIED

Source: Vaughn Shoemaker, *Chicago News,* April 27, 1937 (adapted)

34 This cartoon is critical of President Franklin D. Roosevelt's efforts to

  (1) force Congress to reduce government waste

  (2) convince the Supreme Court to pass a constitutional amendment to balance the budget

  (3) reverse the effects of the Great Depression

  (4) increase his power over the Supreme Court   34 _____

Base your answers to questions 35 and 36 on the poster below and on your knowledge of social studies.

Source: Office of Price Administration, 1943

35 The poster indicates that rationing during World War II was a

(1) policy to encourage small-business owners
(2) way of assuring that only the wealthy could buy certain products
(3) necessity caused by farm failures during the Great Depression
(4) program that was to be applied equally to all Americans   35 _____

36 What was a major reason for wartime rationing?

(1) ensuring that troops were adequately supplied
(2) restricting lower-priced food imports
(3) providing jobs for the unemployed
(4) preventing currency deflation   36 _____

37 What would be the most appropriate heading for the partial outline below?

I. _____

    A. Treatment of Japanese Americans
    B. Segregation of African Americans in the armed forces
    C. United States reactions to the Nazi Holocaust
    D. Use of the atomic bomb

(1) Issues of Morality during World War II
(2) Domestic Policies during World War II
(3) Economic Problems during World War II
(4) Reasons for the Success of the Allies during World War II   37 _____

Base your answer to question 38 on the graph below and on your knowledge of social studies.

Source: *The NYSTROM Atlas of United States History*, 2000 (adapted)

38 What is the best title for this graph for the years 1946–1964?

(1) The Graying of America
(2) The Growth of the Middle Class
(3) The Baby Boom Generation
(4) From Suburbs to Cities   38 _____

Base your answers to questions 39 and 40 on the map below and on your knowledge of social studies.

Cuban Missile Crisis, 1962

Source: Gary B. Nash and Carter Smith, *Atlas of American History*, Facts on File, 2007 (adapted)

39 What was the immediate cause of the action taken by the United States that is shown on the map?

(1) Cuban refugees lobbied President Dwight Eisenhower to overthrow Fidel Castro.

(2) The Soviet Union built nuclear missile launch sites within range of United States cities.

(3) United States military bases in the Caribbean were closed by Cuban armed forces.

(4) Puerto Rican citizens asked Congress to assist them in repelling communist advances.

39 _____

40 One positive outcome of the situation shown on the map was that the United States and Soviet Union increased

(1) communication between the two nations to avert war
(2) military control of their Latin American colonies
(3) cooperative humanitarian efforts in Caribbean nations suffering from natural disasters
(4) joint efforts to end the cruel practices of Cuba's leaders

40 _____

41 The main reason President John F. Kennedy proposed the establishment of the Peace Corps was to

(1) promote trade with Africa
(2) combat drug use in American cities
(3) gain support from immigrant voters
(4) improve conditions in developing nations

41 _____

42 What was an outcome of the Watergate affair during the administration of President Richard Nixon?

(1) Presidential powers were expanded.
(2) Respect for the office of the president declined.
(3) The Supreme Court cleared President Nixon of all charges.
(4) Congress refused to take action against President Nixon.

42 _____

43 The goal of the War Powers Act of 1973 was to

(1) allow the president to declare war without congressional approval
(2) give Congress the sole power to authorize the use of military force
(3) limit the president's power to use military force without congressional approval
(4) require a declaration of war for all uses of military forces

43 _____

44 ". . . The United States, together with the United Nations, exhausted every means at our disposal to bring this crisis to a peaceful end. However, Saddam [Hussein] clearly felt that by stalling and threatening and defying the United Nations, he could weaken the forces arrayed against him. . . ."

— President George H. W. Bush, address to the nation,
January 16, 1991

President George H. W. Bush used this statement to defend

(1) taking military action to liberate Kuwait from Iraqi aggression
(2) providing foreign aid to Israel
(3) supporting Egypt against attacks by terrorists
(4) using United States troops as peacekeepers in Bosnia   44 _____

Base your answer to question 45 on the cartoon below and on your knowledge of social studies.

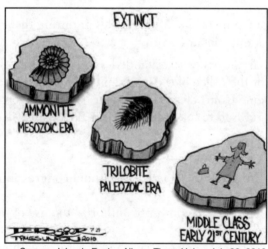

Source: John de Rosier, *Albany Times Union*, July 29, 2010

45 Which combination of factors has led to the problem shown in the cartoon?

(1) lower medical costs and high interest rates
(2) business monopolies and depletion of natural resources
(3) consumer debt and nearly stagnant wages
(4) population migration and the graying of America   45 _____

46 One way in which the goals of the Know-Nothing Party in the 1850s and the response to the Red Scare of 1919 were similar is that both

(1) called for equal rights for women and African Americans
(2) sought to limit immigration to the United States
(3) supported the overseas expansion of the United States
(4) attempted to limit the influence of big business on American politics   46 _____

47 Which term most accurately describes United States foreign policy during the Cold War?

(1) containment   (3) Big Stick
(2) nonalignment   (4) Open Door   47 _____

Base your answer to question 48 on the chart below and on your knowledge of social studies.

Action	Reaction
President Andrew Johnson disobeys the Tenure of Office Act. →	Congress impeaches Johnson and he remains in office by one vote.
Congress passes the National Industrial Recovery Act (NIRA). →	The Supreme Court declares the NIRA unconstitutional in *Schechter Poultry Corporation* v. *United States*.

48 Which aspect of governmental power is best illustrated by both examples in the chart?

(1) federalism   (3) States rights
(2) checks and balances   (4) judicial review   48 _____

49 Which economic policy argues that government should limit, as much as possible, any interference in the economy?

    (1) socialism   (3) mercantilism

    (2) laissez-faire   (4) protectionism   49 _____

50 W. E. B. Du Bois, Jackie Robinson, and James Meredith are considered pioneers in the area of

    (1) labor relations

    (2) educational reform

    (3) civil rights

    (4) environmental protection   50 _____

In developing your answer to Part II, be sure to keep these general definitions in mind:

(a) <u>describe</u> means "to illustrate something in words or tell about it"

(b) <u>discuss</u> means "to make observations about something using facts, reasoning, and argument; to present in some detail"

PART II: THEMATIC ESSAY

Directions: Write a well-organized essay that includes an introduction, several paragraphs addressing the task below, and a conclusion.

Theme: Westward Movement of the Frontier

> Throughout the nation's history, the United States has expanded through the acquisition of new territories. These acquisitions have had both positive and negative effects on the United States.

Task:

> Select **two** events that significantly influenced the westward movement of the frontier and for **each**
>
> - Describe the historical circumstances surrounding the event
> - Discuss the *positive **and/or** negative* effects of the event on the settlement of the West

You may use any event that significantly influenced the westward movement of the frontier from your study of United States history. Some events you might wish to consider include:

Signing of the Treaty of Paris (1783)

Discovery of gold in California (1848)

Creation of the reservation system (1800s)

Passage of the Homestead Act (1862)

Purchase of the Louisiana Territory (1803)

Purchase of Alaska (1867)

Opening of the Erie Canal (1825)

Completion of the transcontinental railroad (1869)

War with Mexico (1846–1848)

You are not limited to these suggestions.

Guidelines:

In your essay, be sure to:

- Develop all aspects of the task
- Discuss *at least* **two** effects for each event
- Support the theme with relevant facts, examples, and details
- Use a logical and clear plan of organization, including an introduction and a conclusion that are beyond a restatement of the theme

In developing your answers to Part III, be sure to keep these general definitions in mind:

(a) <u>describe</u> means "to illustrate something in words or tell about it"

(b) <u>discuss</u> means "to make observations about something using facts, reasoning, and argument; to present in some detail"

PART III: DOCUMENT-BASED QUESTION

This question is based on the accompanying documents. The question is designed to test your ability to work with historical documents. Some of these documents have been edited for the purposes of this question. As you analyze the documents, take into account the source of each document and any point of view that may be presented in the document. Keep in mind that the language and images used in a document may reflect the historical context of the time in which it was created.

Historical Context:

In the decades following World War II, significant domestic and foreign policy issues led to political and social tensions in the United States. These issues motivated individuals and groups to organize protest movements to bring about change. Protest movements such as the *civil rights movement,* the *anti–Vietnam War movement,* and the *environmental movement* met with varying degrees of success.

Task:

Using the information from the documents and your knowledge of United States history, answer the questions that follow each document in Part A. Your answers to the questions will help you write the Part B essay in which you will be asked to

Choose *two* protest movements mentioned in the historical context and for *each*

- Describe the historical circumstances surrounding the protest movement
- Discuss the extent to which the protest movement was successful

Part A: Short-Answer Questions

Directions: Analyze the documents and answer the short-answer questions that follow each document in the space provided.

Document 1a

"AND REMEMBER, NOTHING CAN BE ACCOMPLISHED BY TAKING TO THE STREETS"

Source: Herblock, *Washington Post,* September 6, 1963 (adapted)

Document 1b

If You Miss Me At the Back of the Bus

> If you miss me at the back of the bus you can't find me nowhere come on over to the front of the bus I'll be riding up there. . . .
>
> If you miss me on the picket line you can't find me nowhere come on over to the city jail I'll be rooming over there. . . .
>
> If you miss me in the cotton fields you can't find me nowhere come on over to the courthouse I'll be voting right there. . . .

Source: recorded by Pete Seeger, 1963,written by Carver Neblett

1 Based on these documents, state *one* form of discrimination African Americans experienced in the 1960s. [1]

_____

_____

Document 2

. . . In its regional breadth, the uprising resembled the sit-in movement of 1960. But the 1963 demonstrations [after Birmingham] were more widespread, involved much larger numbers, and drew in people of all ages and backgrounds. To list the places where black people engaged in nonviolent protests would be to name virtually every town and city in the South: about 115 communities experienced 930 demonstrations of one kind or another. The number of people arrested topped 20,000, four times as many as in 1960.

The 1963 surge of nonviolent direct action made the maintenance of segregation in public accommodations untenable [unable to continue]. Black people knew that if segregation could be cracked in Birmingham, it could be cracked anywhere. Birmingham exposed the vulnerability of the South's political regime, and black people seized the opportunity to attack it. In city after city, under the relentless pressure of demonstrations, whites sat down to negotiate. During a single three-week period after Birmingham, the Justice Department noted that 143 cities had acceded [agreed] to some degree of integration. By year's end the number exceeded three hundred. Many cities set up biracial committees that enabled blacks to press for further desegregation. . . .

Source: Adam Fairclough, *Better Day Coming: Blacks and Equality, 1890–2000*, Viking Penguin, 2001

2 According to Adam Fairclough, what was *one* effect of the 1963 demonstrations in Birmingham, Alabama? [1]

_____

_____

Document 3

. . . In far too many ways American Negroes have been another nation: deprived of freedom, crippled by hatred, the doors of opportunity closed to hope.

In our time change has come to this Nation, too. The American Negro, acting with impressive restraint, has peacefully protested and marched, entered the courtrooms and the seats of government, demanding a justice that has long been denied. The voice of the Negro was the call to action. But it is a tribute to America that, once aroused, the courts and the Congress, the President and most of the people, have been the allies of progress.

Thus we have seen the high court of the country declare that discrimination based on race was repugnant [disagreeable] to the Constitution, and therefore void. We have seen in 1957, and 1960, and again in 1964, the first civil rights legislation in this Nation in almost an entire century. . . .

The voting rights bill will be* the latest, and among the most important, in a long series of victories. But this victory—as Winston Churchill said of another triumph for freedom—"is not the end. It is not even the beginning of the end. But it is, perhaps, the end of the beginning."

That beginning is freedom; and the barriers to that freedom are tumbling down. Freedom is the right to share, share fully and equally, in American society—to vote, to hold a job, to enter a public place, to go to school. It is the right to be treated in every part of our national life as a person equal in dignity and promise to all others.

But freedom is not enough. You do not wipe away the scars of centuries by saying: Now you are free to go where you want, and do as you desire, and choose the leaders you please. . . .

This is the next and the more profound stage of the battle for civil rights. We seek not just freedom but opportunity. We seek not just legal equity but human ability, not just equality as a right and a theory but equality as a fact and equality as a result.

For the task is to give 20 million Negroes the same chance as every other American to learn and grow, to work and share in society, to develop their abilities—physical, mental and spiritual, and to pursue their individual happiness. . . .

Source: Lyndon B. Johnson, Commencement Address at Howard University, June 4, 1965

*The Voting Rights Act was signed into law on August 6, 1965.

3a According to President Lyndon B. Johnson, what is **one** achievement of the civil rights movement?   [1]

_____

_____

b According to President Lyndon B. Johnson, what is **one** remaining goal for the civil rights movement?   [1]

_____

_____

Document 4

. . . As the U.S. commitment increased, so did the number of bombs dropped on the North, the volume of North Vietnamese coming into the South, the fervor of the protest movement, the billion dollar military grants, and the number of casualties. Johnson's pledge to fight communism in Southeast Asia had degenerated into what anti-war folk singer Pete Seeger labeled "the Big Muddy." And yet, the refrain of that song said, "the old fool says to push on." Tempers on both sides flared as the body counts increased, and each night's TV broadcasts introduced American viewers to faraway hell holes where their sons, brothers, friends, and husbands were stepping on land mines, perishing in Vietcong mantraps, and being cut down in hand-to-hand combat. The week of September 18–24 brought with it a grim statistic: 142 U.S. soldiers killed, 825 wounded, 3 missing—the war's highest toll in 1966. . . .

Every time American troops won a small victory or held a strategic position, the President's advisers used the occasion to press for more troops and more money. These were vital, they repeatedly declared, to consolidate our gains and increase our advantages. The monthly draft was doubled several times, up to 46,000 a month in October 1966, as General Westmoreland constantly increased his call for troops. He had almost a half-million men in combat by April 1967. By the following year, he told the President, he would need almost 700,000. With that number, he said, we could win the war in two years. The "light at the end of the tunnel," which President Johnson optimistically referred to in his news broadcasts, had dimmed considerably since his earlier predictions. . . .

Source: Toby Goldstein, *Waking from the Dream: America in the Sixties,* Julian Messner, 1988

4 According to Toby Goldstein, what were ***two*** reasons for the development of the anti–Vietnam War movement?   [2]

(1) _____

_____

(2) _____

_____

Document 5

American protest against the war in Vietnam was begun and sustained by American citizens who believed that in a representative democracy, individuals can make themselves heard and, more, can affect public policy.

To us, the antiwar movement during the Vietnam era is important not because it stopped the war, which it may or may not have done; rather, it is important because it existed. It is a reminder to Americans that times come when citizens can and, indeed, must challenge their government's authority. . . .

Every war has had its opponents. There was a sizable antiwar sentiment in Great Britain during the South African War (1899–1902), and in America there has always been during every war a small protest movement—most notably, until Vietnam, during the Mexican War in 1846–48 and the Philippine Insurrection in 1899–1901. But the Vietnam War was different: increasingly unpopular, undeclared and therefore in the opinion of many citizens illegal and unconstitutional as well, it was the most frustrating war in American history, and the ugliest, and the longest. The movement opposing it had years in which to grow. . . .

Source: Nancy Zaroulis and Gerald Sullivan, *Who Spoke Up?: American Protest Against the War In Vietnam, 1963–1975*, Holt, Rinehart and Winston, 1984

5 According to Nancy Zaroulis and Gerald Sullivan, what was **one** reason for protest against the Vietnam War? [1]

_____

_____

Document 6

... The impact of the antiwar protests remains one of the most controversial issues raised by the war. The obvious manifestations [displays] of dissent in the United States probably encouraged Hanoi's will to hold out for victory, although there is nothing to suggest that the North Vietnamese would have been more compromising in the absence of the movement. Antiwar protest did not turn the American people against the war, as some critics have argued. The effectiveness of the movement was limited by the divisions within its own ranks. Public opinion polls make abundantly clear, moreover, that a majority of Americans found the antiwar movement, particularly its radical and "hippie" elements, more obnoxious than the war itself. In a perverse sort of way, the protest may even have strengthened support for a war that was not in itself popular. The impact of the movement was much more limited and subtle. It forced Vietnam onto the public consciousness and challenged the rationale of the war and indeed of a generation of Cold War foreign policies. It limited Johnson's military options and may have headed off any tendency toward more drastic escalation. Perhaps most important, the disturbances and divisions set off by the antiwar movement caused fatigue and anxiety among the policymakers and the public, and thus eventually encouraged efforts to find a way out of the war. ...

Source: George C. Herring, *America's Longest War:
The United States and Vietnam, 1950–1975,* Alfred A. Knopf, 1986 (adapted)

6a According to George C. Herring, what was *one* way the anti–Vietnam War movement was *not* successful?   [1]

_____

_____

b According to George C. Herring, what was *one* way the anti–Vietnam War movement was successful?   [1]

_____

_____

Document 7

. . . For the first time in the history of the world, every human being is now subjected to contact with dangerous chemicals, from the moment of conception until death. In the less than two decades of their use, the synthetic pesticides have been so thoroughly distributed throughout the animate and inanimate world that they occur virtually everywhere. They have been recovered from most of the major river systems and even from streams of groundwater flowing unseen through the earth. Residues of these chemicals linger in soil to which they may have been applied a dozen years before. They have entered and lodged in the bodies of fish, birds, reptiles, and domestic and wild animals so universally that scientists carrying on animal experiments find it almost impossible to locate subjects free from such contamination. They have been found in fish in remote mountain lakes, in earthworms burrowing in soil, in the eggs of birds—and in man himself. For these chemicals are now stored in the bodies of the vast majority of human beings, regardless of age. They occur in the mother's milk, and probably in the tissues of the unborn child. . . .

Source: Rachel Carson, *Silent Spring*, Houghton Mifflin, 1962

7 According to Rachel Carson, what is **one** issue that has led to concerns about the environment? [1]

_____

_____

Document 8a

Millions Join Earth Day Observances Across the Nation

Throngs jamming Fifth Avenue yesterday in response to a call for the regeneration of a polluted environment.

Source: *New York Times,* April 23, 1970 (adapted)

Document 8b

Earth Day, the first mass consideration of the globe's environmental problems, preempted [commanded] the attention and energies of millions of Americans, young and old, across the country yesterday. . . .

Organizers of Earth Day said more than 2,000 colleges, 10,000 grammar and high schools, and citizen groups in 2,000 communities had indicated intentions of participating. . . .

The purpose of the observance was to heighten public awareness of pollution and other ecological problems, which many scientists say urgently require action if the earth is to remain habitable. . . .

Summarizing the implications of the day's activities, Senator Nelson said:

"The question now is whether we are willing to make the commitment for a sustained national drive to solve our environmental problems." . . .

Source: Gladwin Hill, "Activity Ranges From Oratory to Legislation," *New York Times,* April 23, 1970

8 Based on these documents, state *one* reason the observance of Earth Day is important to the environmental movement.   [1]

_____

_____

Document 9a

> . . . Earth Day had consequences: it led to the Clean Air Act of 1970, the Clean Water Act of 1972, and the Endangered Species Act of 1973, and to the creation, just eight months after the event, of the Environmental Protection Agency. Throughout the nineteen-seventies, mostly during the Republican Administrations of Richard Nixon and Gerald Ford, Congress passed one environmental bill after another, establishing national controls on air and water pollution. And most of the familiar big green groups are, in their current form, offspring of Earth Day. Dozens of colleges and universities instituted environmental-studies programs, and even many small newspapers created full-time environmental beats. . . .

Source: Nicholas Lemann, "When the Earth Moved: What Happened to the Environmental Movement?"
The New Yorker, April 15, 2013

9a According to Nicholas Lemann, what is *one* impact of Earth Day? [1]

_____

_____

Document 9b

Frances Beinecke served as president of the Natural Resources Defense Council [NRDC] from 2006–2014. The Council writes and lobbies for public policy to protect the environment.

My work at NRDC has brought me to the front lines of the climate crisis. I have flown over the massive tar sands strip mines in the boreal forest. I have visited the homes of people coping with frack pads [an area of land used in the fracking process] and wastewater ponds in their back-yards. And I have helped my neighbors recover from the devastation of Superstorm Sandy. . . .

Never in my lifetime have the challenges been greater than those we face from climate change. Never have the solutions been more clearly at hand. We know how to defuse the climate threat. We just have to act now. . . .

It's time for us, as Americans, to state as a national goal that we'll hit fast-forward on efforts to clean up our carbon pollution, invest in energy efficiency and shift to renewable power so that we will become a carbon-neutral nation that no longer contributes to climate change. . . .

We have already begun slashing climate change pollution. More than 3.4 million Americans are on the job every day helping to clean up our dirty power plants, get more electricity from the wind and sun, manufacture more hybrid and electric cars, and cut energy waste in our homes, at work and on the road. . . .

The modern environmental movement exists for one purpose: we're here to change the world—to become a place where we care for the natural systems of the Earth as if our very lives depended on them, because they do. That is not yet the world we live in. It is the world we must create.

Source: Frances Beinecke, "The World We Create: My New Book and a Message of Hope for the Planet," *Switchboard: National Resources Defense Council Blog*, October 14, 2014

9*b* According to Frances Beinecke, state *one* reason the environmental movement continues to be important. [1]

_____

_____

Part B: Essay

Directions: Write a well-organized essay that includes an introduction, several paragraphs, and a conclusion. Use evidence from at least *four* documents in the body of the essay. Support your response with relevant facts, examples, and details. Include additional outside information.

Historical Context:

> In the decades following World War II, significant domestic and foreign policy issues led to political and social tensions in the United States. These issues motivated individuals and groups to organize protest movements to bring about change. Protest movements such as the **civil rights movement,** the **anti–Vietnam War movement,** and the **environmental movement** met with varying degrees of success.

Task:

> Using the information from the documents and your knowledge of United States history, write an essay in which you
> Choose *two* protest movements mentioned in the historical context and for *each*
>
> - Describe the historical circumstances surrounding the protest movement
> - Discuss the extent to which the protest movement was successful

Guidelines:

In your essay, be sure to
- Develop all aspects of the task
- Incorporate information from *at least four* documents
- Incorporate relevant outside information
- Support the theme with relevant facts, examples, and details
- Use a logical and clear plan of organization, including an introduction and a conclusion that are beyond a restatement of the theme

Answers
June 2019
United States History and Government

Answer Key

PART I

1. 2	11. 4	21. 4	31. 4	41. 4
2. 4	12. 3	22. 2	32. 3	42. 2
3. 1	13. 2	23. 1	33. 1	43. 3
4. 3	14. 4	24. 3	34. 4	44. 1
5. 4	15. 4	25. 2	35. 4	45. 3
6. 2	16. 1	26. 1	36. 1	46. 2
7. 1	17. 1	27. 2	37. 1	47. 1
8. 1	18. 3	28. 3	38. 3	48. 2
9. 4	19. 2	29. 3	39. 2	49. 2
10. 3	20. 2	30. 4	40. 1	50. 3

PART II: Thematic Essay   *See* **Answers Explained** section.

PART III: Document-Based Question   *See* **Answers Explained** section.

Answers Explained

PART I (1–50)

1. **2** In colonial America, the Magna Carta, the English Bill of Rights, and the writings of John Locke contributed to the political ideals and practices of the colonists. All three texts encouraged colonists to challenge the absolute power of the British monarchy. The Magna Carta was a document written by English barons in 1215 to limit the power of the king. The document puts forth the idea that the will of the monarch can be bound by law and by legal procedures; in other words, his power is limited. The English Bill of Rights grew out of a series of events in England in the late 17th century. A crisis had developed involving religion and succession to the throne. Many Protestants were troubled by the possibility that the successors of the Catholic king, James II, would also be Catholic, and that England could become officially Catholic again. Protestant parliamentarians would not stand for this. They rose up in the Glorious Revolution (1688), which empowered Parliament and ended absolute monarchy in England. It also led to the establishment of the English Bill of Rights. The document establishes limits on the powers of the monarch and asserts certain basic rights of Parliament, including having regular meetings, free elections, and freedom of speech in sessions of Parliament. The English Bill of Rights also puts into writing certain individual rights, including the prohibition of cruel and unusual punishment and the right not to be taxed without Parliament's agreement. John Locke's writings were extremely influential on colonial political thought. His work was one of the main intellectual influences in the writing of the Declaration of Independence. He wrote *Two Treatises on Government* in the early 1690s to defend England's Glorious Revolution (1688) and to challenge Thomas Hobbes's defense of an absolutist monarchy. The eloquent preamble of the Declaration of Independence contains key elements of Locke's social contract theory. The theory is based on the idea that people are born with certain basic rights. Governments come into existence to protect these rights. The social contract calls for the people to surrender some of their freedoms to the rules of the government and for the government to protect people's natural rights. Conversely, Locke asserted, if a government violates people's natural rights, the people have the right to abolish it.

WRONG CHOICES EXPLAINED:

(1) The three texts did not contribute to the diversity of religious beliefs among the colonists. Religious diversity existed in colonial America due to the backgrounds of the various groups who immigrated to the colonies. Migrants to

the New World included British men and women from a variety of Protestant sects, such as Anglicans, Puritans, Separatists, and Quakers. Also, French Huguenots (Calvinist Protestants), Jews, and Catholics made their way to the colonies. Enslaved Africans also brought with them a variety of religious beliefs, including Islam and a wide variety of traditional polytheistic belief systems. The concepts of religious toleration and religious freedom developed over time in the colonies due to the diverse nature of colonial society, as well as to the influence of Enlightenment thinkers.

(3) The three texts did not contribute to the economic relationships between the colonists and the mother country. Such economic relationships were shaped by mercantilist principles. There are several important elements of mercantilism. Mercantilism holds that nations increase their power by increasing their share of the world's wealth. A primary means to increasing wealth is for a nation to maintain a favorable balance of trade, with the value of exports exceeding the value of imports. Mercantilist theory suggests that governments should advance these goals by maintaining colonies so as to have a steady and inexpensive source for raw materials. The theory also holds that the colonies should not develop manufacturing but should purchase manufactured goods from the ruling country. Great Britain imposed several navigation laws on the American colonies to make sure the colonies fulfilled their role in the economic relationship.

(4) The three texts did not contribute to the demands of colonists to end the slave trade and the practice of slavery. Most white colonists did not question or challenge the practice of slavery. Colonists who did hold anti-slavery views were influenced by different religious and political traditions.

2. **4** Before 1763, most American colonists settled near the Atlantic Coast or rivers because navigable water offered easier access to trade and employment. Early coastal settlements included Plymouth (1620), Massachusetts Bay Colony (present-day Boston) (1630), Providence (1636), Newport (Rhode Island) (1639), and New Amsterdam (present-day New York) (1624). These settlements were all established on protected harbors at the mouths of rivers. Jamestown (1607) was founded on the James River some 40 miles upriver from the Atlantic Ocean. Connecticut Colony (1636), present-day Hartford, was founded on the Connecticut River, about 40 miles upriver from the Long Island Sound. Such locations allowed for trade with European countries and with the West Indies and Africa. Rivers aided agricultural development through irrigation and transportation of goods. Within a generation, as the flow of English migrants into North America increased, settlements were established inland from these initial coastal and river settlements. The push of settlers into the interior of the continent increased tensions with Native American Indians.

WRONG CHOICES EXPLAINED:

(1) The reason that most American colonists settled near the Atlantic Coast or rivers in the period before 1763 was not that port cities could be more easily defended in times of war. In fact, port cities might be more vulnerable to attack by foreign naval forces. Early colonists were more concerned with conflicts with Native American Indians.

(2) The reason that most American colonists settled near the Atlantic Coast or rivers in the period before 1763 was not that valleys were less fertile. In fact, river valleys are more fertile. Periodic flooding of rivers results in the deposit of nutrient-rich silt on floodplains, producing extremely fertile soil.

(3) The reason that most American colonists settled near the Atlantic Coast or rivers in the period before 1763 was not that English colonists were only allowed to settle in these locations. In 1763, following the French and Indian War, the British did pass an act forbidding colonists from venturing beyond the Appalachian Mountains—the Proclamation Act. The act was intended to reduce tensions between colonists and American Indians, but it resulted in increasing colonial resentment of British policies.

3. **1** One way in which the Declaration of Independence and the original United States Constitution were similar is that both promote the idea of the consent of the governed. The phrase "consent of the governed" refers to the source of the government's power. The Declaration of Independence puts forth the idea that governments derive their "just powers from the consent of the governed." The idea drew inspiration from Enlightenment thinkers, such as John Locke. Its implementation in the newly formed United States represented a radical break with the political arrangements of the day. Most government structures in the 18th century world were based on monarchical power. Many of these monarchs contended that their mandate to rule was granted by "divine right," not the consent of the governed. The Constitution enshrined the concept of the consent of the governed into the legal governing structure of the United States by creating a House of Representatives that is elected by the people. Senators were initially selected by state legislatures, rather than voted on directly by the people. However, it is the people of each state that elect state legislatures, so even the Senate could be said to reflect the consent of the governed.

WRONG CHOICES EXPLAINED:

(2) Neither the Declaration of Independence nor the original United States Constitution promoted the idea of equal rights for women. While neither document explicitly excludes women from political equality, both documents accepted prevailing ideas around male domination in the political realm. The original

Constitution did not prohibit states from excluding women from voting. It was not until ratification of the 19th amendment, in 1920, that the right of women to vote in the United States was enshrined in the Constitution.

(3) Neither the Declaration of Independence nor the original United States Constitution promoted the idea of voting rights for all adult citizens. The declaration does not specifically address the issue of voting rights. The Constitution left voting rules to each state, allowing states to establish property qualifications for voting and to exclude adult citizens from voting because of their race or gender. Property requirements for voting were eliminated by most states by the 1830s. Amendments to the Constitution further broadened the electorate. The 15th amendment (1870) prevented states from denying a citizen the right to vote based on that citizen's race. The 19th amendment (1920) extended the right to vote to women. The 26th amendment (1971) prohibited using age as a reason to deny any citizen the right to vote who are at least 18 years old.

(4) Neither the Declaration of Independence nor the original United States Constitution promoted the idea of judicial review of unjust laws. The declaration does not focus on the specifics of the legal system that would be created in an independent United States. The Constitution established that federal judiciary power shall be vested in a "supreme Court" as well as additional "inferior" courts. The Constitution does not explicitly grant the Supreme Court the power of judicial review. That power—to review laws and determine whether they were constitutional—was explicitly established by the Court in the case of *Marbury* v. *Madison* (1803).

4. **3** The main purpose of the *Federalist Papers* was to urge ratification of the Constitution. The supporters of the Constitution labeled themselves Federalists. Three leading Federalists, Alexander Hamilton, John Jay, and James Madison, wrote a series of articles as the New York convention was debating ratification of the Constitution in 1787 and 1788. The articles were later published in book form—*The Federalist* (in the 20th century, the collection was published as the *Federalist Papers*). This highly influential political tract outlined the failures of the Articles of Confederation and the benefits of a powerful government, with checks and balances. In Federalist Number 10, Madison argued that a complex government, governing a large and diverse population, was the best guarantee of liberty. With such a complex government, no single group could gain control and dominate others. This argument challenged the traditional republican notion that republics must be small in order to be democratic. In Federalist Number 51, he argued for a separation of powers within the government and a system of checks and balances. In that essay, Madison asserted that "ambition must be made to counteract ambition."

WRONG CHOICES EXPLAINED:

(1) The main purpose of the *Federalist Papers* was not to discourage the creation of political parties; the articles were written in support of ratification of the Constitution. The writers saw the development of political parties, or factions, as inevitable. In Federalist Number 10, Madison argues that in a large republic, the effect of factions will be less than it would be in a small republic. In a small republic, one faction could dominate and restrain the liberty of the minority. This would be less likely, he argues, in a large republic.

(2) The main purpose of the *Federalist Papers* was not to support the candidacy of George Washington; the articles were written in support of ratification of the Constitution. Washington did not affiliate with a political party, although his policies and preferences were closer to those of the emerging Federalist Party than those of the Democratic-Republican Party. Washington was the unanimous choice for president of the 69 electors who cast votes in 1788–1789. At the time, electors cast two votes for two different candidates. John Adams received 34 of the second votes cast by electors and became vice-president (other candidates split the remaining second votes).

(4) The main purpose of the *Federalist Papers* was not to advocate independence from Great Britain; the articles were written in support of ratification of the Constitution. The articles were written in 1787 and 1788, over a decade after the United States had declared independence (1776). Great Britain recognized the independence of the United States by signing the Treaty of Paris in 1783.

5. **4** The inclusion of the elastic clause in the Constitution best supports the idea expressed in the quotation. Hamilton is arguing for a flexible document that could meet the needs of a changing society. Many people call the Constitution a living document because it can change—both through the use of the elastic clause and through the amendment clause. The elastic clause stretches the powers of Congress by allowing it to "make all laws necessary and proper" in regard to carrying out its functions. However, the definition of "necessary and proper" soon became a matter of much debate. In 1791, Alexander Hamilton pushed for the creation of a national bank. This national bank would be 20 percent publicly controlled and 80 percent privately controlled. Hamilton thought it was important to have wealthy investors financially and psychologically invested in the new government. Though the power to create a national bank was not granted to Congress in the Constitution, he argued that it was permissible under the elastic clause. Thomas Jefferson argued that the creation of a national bank was not "necessary and proper." Hamilton won this debate, and a national bank was created in 1791. It existed until 1811.

WRONG CHOICES EXPLAINED:

(1) The inclusion of eminent domain in the Constitution does not directly support the idea expressed in the quotation. The quotation focuses on the idea of a changeable Constitution. Eminent domain refers to a specific constitutional principle—that the government may, for a just price, force property owners to sell their property if the government deems that the property will be used for a public purpose. This power is in the fifth amendment of the Constitution.

(2) The inclusion of the electoral college in the Constitution does not directly support the idea expressed in the quotation. The quotation focuses on the idea of a changeable Constitution. The electoral college was established in Article Two of the Constitution as the basic process for how the president would be elected. Today, after the popular vote for president on Election Day, election boards determine which candidate won in each of the states. Whichever candidate wins the popular vote in a particular state, that candidate receives the electoral votes for that state. (However, in two states, Maine and Nebraska, electoral votes can be divided between candidates.) The number of electors for each state is equal to the number of members of Congress from that state. Bigger states, therefore, get more electors.

(3) The inclusion of separation of powers in the Constitution does not directly support the idea expressed in the quotation. The quotation focuses on the idea of a changeable Constitution. Separation of powers refers to an unchanging, defining feature of the Constitution. Separation of powers describes the basic structure of the government. The framers of the Constitution created a governmental system with three separate branches—the legislative, the executive, and the judicial—each with the ability to check the powers of the other two. The goal was to keep the three branches in balance. The framers were very conscious of the problems of a government with limitless powers. After living under the British monarchy, they came to believe that a powerful government without checks was dangerous to liberty.

6. **2** The main objection to the adoption of the Constitution was based primarily on the belief that individual freedoms could be restricted by a strong central government. Such objections were voiced by a group of opponents—who came to be known as "Antifederalists"—during the debate over ratification of the United States Constitution, which occurred between 1787 and 1789. Antifederalists feared the Constitution would create an omnipotent and unaccountable government. They had vivid memories of the intrusions of the royal British government into their lives, and wanted to have assurances that the people would have basic protections from government abuses. Many Antifederalists agreed to support ratification of the Constitution only after the framers assured them that a bill of

rights would be immediately added to the Constitution. The Bill of Rights, the first ten amendments to the Constitution, was ratified in 1791. The first amendment protects the people from government limitations on freedom of expression and of religion. It also affirms the right of people to protest against government actions. In addition, it also established separation of church and state. The second amendment established the right to "bear arms." The fourth amendment holds that people are to be free from unwarranted searches by government authorities. The fifth and sixth amendments list a variety of protections that people have when they are accused of crimes, such as the right to a "speedy and public trial." The eighth amendment states that the government shall not inflict "cruel and unusual" punishments on people.

WRONG CHOICES EXPLAINED:

(1) Limiting the number of new states that could be admitted to the Union was not a concern of opponents of adopting the Constitution. The Constitution spelled out the process for admitting new states. The Admissions Clause, in Article Four, gives Congress the authority to admit new states. Over time, the Supreme Court has asserted that the Constitution requires all states to be admitted on an equal footing, though this is not specifically spelled out in the Admissions Clause. There is no limit on the number of states admitted.

(3) The impact of a separate judiciary on the effectiveness of the government was not a concern of those opposing the adoption of the Constitution. The Constitution, in Article Three, calls for the establishment of a separate federal judiciary comprised of a Supreme Court and additional "inferior courts," created by Congress.

(4) The enhanced power of the South, stemming from its slave population, was not a concern of opponents of adopting the Constitution. The number of slaves in a particular state did increase that state's representation in the House of Representatives. The Three-fifths Compromise, arrived at during the Constitutional Convention (1787), stipulated that slaves, labeled "other persons" in the Constitution, would be counted as three-fifths of a person in the census. This issue, however, was not a primary concern of those opposed to the Constitution.

7. **1** The use of the electoral college reflects a distrust, among many of the framers of the Constitution, of the average citizen's judgment. Many of the supporters of the Constitution, known as Federalists, voiced their fears of democracy and of the judgment of ordinary people. In a speech to the Constitutional Convention in June 1787, Alexander Hamilton was quoted as saying that within all communities, there are "the few and the many." The first, he said, were the

"rich and the well-born"; the second group was comprised of the "mass of the people." He said that the second group should not be fully trusted with the levers of government, because they "seldom judge or determine right." His solution was to give the wealthy a more prominent voice in the government—"a distinct, permanent share in the Government." The creation of the electoral college demonstrates this concern. It was created as a check on the popular will of the people. It is the electoral college, not the popular vote of the people, that ultimately determines who will be president. Initially, the plan was for electors to be chosen, in a nonpartisan fashion, either by nominating committees or by popular vote. It was expected that these independent-minded men would then choose the most qualified men to be the president. Over time the system become more partisan, driven by voter preference. Today, after the popular vote for president on Election Day, election boards determine which candidate won in each of the states. Whichever candidate wins in a particular state, that candidate gets the electoral votes for that state. (However, in two states, Maine and Nebraska, electoral votes can be divided between candidates.)

WRONG CHOICES EXPLAINED:
    (2) The use of the electoral college does not reflect a belief that political parties strengthen the campaign process. The Constitution does not assert that political parties should be part of the electoral college process. It was initially thought that electors would choose a president based on qualifications rather than on party affiliation. Formal political parties developed over time, after the Constitution had been ratified.
    (3) The use of the electoral college does not reflect a desire to end property qualifications for voting. The opposite is closer to the truth. The electoral college was intended to put more power in the hands of wealthier men. Property qualifications, which existed in many states when the Constitution was ratified, stipulate that citizens must own a certain amount of property in order to vote. By the end of the 1820s, most states reduced or removed property qualifications for voting so that most free males had the right to vote.
    (4) The use of the electoral college does not reflect a commitment to universal suffrage. When the Constitution was ratified, most states limited voting rights to free, white, male property owners. The electoral college, by granting the power to elect the president to a select group of men, did not challenge existing voting restrictions. Over time, the electorate has broadened. By the end of the 1820s, most states had eliminated property qualifications for voting. The Constitution was amended three times to expand voting rights. The 15th amendment (1870) barred discrimination based on race in voting, the 19th amendment (1920) extended the vote to women, and the 26th amendment (1971) lowered the minimum age requirement for voting to 18.

8. **1** The best title for the diagram is "Methods of Amending the Constitution." The diagram shows that either Congress (by two-third majorities in both houses) or a national convention, called by Congress, can propose a constitutional amendment. Then, three-fourths of the states must approve an amendment for it to be ratified. The state-by-state approval process can occur by the consent of the state legislatures or by special state ratifying conventions. The process is difficult, but not insurmountable. Twenty-seven amendments have been added to the Constitution. The amendment process has led to the ending of slavery (13th amendment, 1865), the federal income tax (16th amendment, 1913), women's suffrage (19th amendment, 1920), and an establishment of term limits for the presidency (22nd amendment, 1951).

WRONG CHOICES EXPLAINED:

(2) The title "Procedures of the Executive Branch" would not be appropriate for the diagram. Such a diagram might include the following items: "Nominating department heads and Supreme Court justices," "Signing legislation," and "Carrying out duties as commander-in-chief."

(3) The title "Process of Nominating Presidential Candidates" would not be appropriate for the diagram. Such a diagram might include the following items: "Running in state primary elections," "Having debates among candidates," and "Participating in national nominating conventions."

(4) The title "Admission of New States to the Union" would not be appropriate for the diagram. Such a diagram might include the following items: "The proposed state officially petitioning Congress for statehood," "Both the Senate and the House voting to accept the state," and "The president signing a bill to accept the state."

9. **4** The United States wanted to acquire New Orleans in 1803 in order to secure a port that would improve the transportation of agricultural goods. In the late 1700s and early 1800s, pioneers crossed over the Appalachian Mountains and settled in the Mississippi and Ohio River Valleys and established farms. It was impractical to transport agricultural goods such as wheat and corn by overland routes to the population centers along the Eastern Seaboard. Roads were primitive and railroads had not yet been developed. Therefore, water routes down the Ohio and Mississippi Rivers to New Orleans and beyond became very important for the farmers. However, the United States did not possess New Orleans. Spain controlled it until 1800 and France did after that. The United States got control of it in 1803 as part of the Louisiana Purchase. President Thomas Jefferson overcame any doubts about the constitutionality of a territorial purchase and gave his approval to the purchase of the territory from France for a mere $15 million.

WRONG CHOICES EXPLAINED:

(1) The United States' desire to acquire New Orleans in 1803 was not connected with ending British influence in North America. New Orleans and the entire Louisiana Territory were controlled by France at the time, not by Great Britain.

(2) The United States' desire to acquire New Orleans in 1803 was not connected with promoting the growth of manufacturing in the region. Manufacturing was just in its infancy in the United States in 1803. Further, manufacturing developed in the northeast. The first factory in the United States was built in 1790 in Rhode Island. The Lowell, Massachusetts, textile mills opened in 1823. The region around New Orleans was primarily agricultural.

(3) The United States' desire to acquire New Orleans in 1803 was not connected with establishing a military base to defend against attacks from Mexico. Mexico did not become an independent nation until 1821. Even after independence, Mexico was not seen as a threat to the United States. Later, in the Mexican-American War (1846–1848), the United States proved to be more of a threat to Mexico than Mexico was to the United States.

10. **3** The Supreme Court decision in *Gibbons* v. *Ogden* (1824) is important because it expanded federal control over interstate trade. The Supreme Court affirmed that only the federal government could regulate trade between states. The Court invalidated a monopoly given by the legislature of New York to a ferryboat company to navigate the Hudson River between New York and New Jersey. The Court declared that since the river goes through or between two or more states, it is subject to the interstate commerce clause of the Constitution. Under the leadership of Chief Justice John Marshall (1801–1835), the Supreme Court issued several decisions that established the supremacy of federal laws over state laws. These decisions also included *Fletcher* v. *Peck* (1810), *Dartmouth College* v. *Woodward* (1819), and *McCulloch* v. *Maryland* (1819).

WRONG CHOICES EXPLAINED:

(1) The Supreme Court decision in *Gibbons* v. *Ogden* (1824) did not address the importation of manufactured goods. The Court has never banned the importation of manufactured goods. Earlier, Congress passed the Embargo Act (1807) as a response to the harassment of U.S. shipping by England and France. The act cut off all U.S. trade with any nation. Jefferson thought that this would pressure the belligerent nations to agree to leave U.S. ships alone. However, the main effect of the embargo was to cripple America's mercantile sector. The embargo was meant to avoid warfare, but the United States eventually did go to war with England in 1812. At different points the United States has discouraged the importation of manufactured goods by raising import duties on certain items.

(2) The Supreme Court decision in *Gibbons* v. *Ogden* (1824) did not address state investment in internal improvements. Many states, at the time, did invest money into internal improvements. In 1825, for example, New York completed the Erie Canal, which created an all-water route from New York City to the Midwestern communities around the Great Lakes. This connection facilitated settlement and trade between the Atlantic Coast and the Midwest.

(4) The Supreme Court decision in *Gibbons* v. *Ogden* (1824) did not address taxes on exported goods. The United States does not tax exports. Every country, including the United States, wants to maximize exports; taxes on American exports would make American products less desirable to other countries.

11. **4** Under Chief Justice John Marshall (1801–1835), Supreme Court decisions generally upheld Alexander Hamilton's belief that a loose interpretation of the Constitution could be used to increase federal power. By contrast, believers in a strict interpretation of the Constitution, such as Thomas Jefferson, sought to limit federal power. Hamilton and other believers in a loose interpretation of the Constitution relied on the elastic clause of the Constitution to support their views. The elastic clause is included in Article I, Section 8 of the Constitution. That section lists the specific powers of Congress. Some delegates feared that by listing specific powers, Congress would not be able to exercise additional powers, nor could it address changing circumstances. They therefore pushed for the elastic clause, which stretched the powers of Congress by allowing it to "make all laws necessary and proper" in carrying out its duties. Marshall shared Hamilton's view of a federal government with expansive powers. The decision in *Marbury* v. *Madison*, for example, strengthened the federal judiciary by asserting that the Supreme Court has the power to review laws and determine whether they are consistent with the Constitution. This power of judicial review has been the main function of the Supreme Court since then. In the case of *McCulloch* v. *Maryland*, the Court sided with the Bank of the United States, a federal institution, over the state of Maryland. Maryland had imposed heavy taxes on the local branch of the bank, hoping to tax it out of existence. The Court declared this act unconstitutional. *Gibbons* v. *Ogden* invalidated a monopoly on ferry transportation between New York and New Jersey that had been issued by New York, and asserted that only the federal government could regulate interstate trade.

WRONG CHOICES EXPLAINED:
(1) Alexander Hamilton did not uphold the belief that a national debt would violate the economic principles of the Constitution. Hamilton believed that a national debt, "if it is not excessive, will be to us a national blessing." He believed that if a government took on debt and paid it off in a timely fashion,

then wealthy individuals and institutions would be more likely to invest in the government in the future. As part of his economic program, he argued for increasing the national debt in order to pay off debts carried over from the Revolutionary War (including debts owed by the various states) at full value.

(2) Alexander Hamilton did not uphold the belief that states should have more economic power than the federal government. He believed the opposite. He wanted a strong federal government to guide economic activity. His economic plan called for the creation of a national bank, high federal tariffs on imported manufactured goods, and a federal excise tax on whiskey.

(3) Alexander Hamilton did not uphold the power of Congress should be greater than the power of the president. He promoted the idea of a strong executive. In some ways, Hamilton was enamored by Great Britain's monarchical system. In the end, he accepted the idea of three equal branches, each with the power to check the other two.

12. **3** In the 1855 letter, Abraham Lincoln opposed the Know-Nothing Party because it promoted resentment against minority groups. The Know-Nothing Party (formally known as the American Party) emerged in the 1840s and, by the 1850s, achieved electoral success in several states, especially in the Northeast. The defining issue of the Know-Nothing party was opposition to immigration. The party was the political wing of a growing anti-Catholic, anti-Irish nativist movement that gained traction in the wake of the large-scale Irish immigration of the late 1840s and 1850s. In the letter, Lincoln asserts that followers of the Know-Nothing Party were betraying basic American values. He reminds the recipient of the letter that the United States began by declaring that "all men are created equal." Lincoln wonders whether Americans will still adhere to this assertion. In the future, he predicts that followers of the Know-Nothing Party will try to rewrite the Declaration of Independence so that it reads, "all men are created equal, except negroes, and foreigners, and catholics." When that happens, Lincoln posits that he might want to emigrate to another country.

WRONG CHOICES EXPLAINED:
(1) The Know-Nothing Party did not take a position on imperialism. Imperialism did not become a contentious issue in the United States until the late 1890s. The U.S. engaged in imperialist acts following its victory in the Spanish-American War in 1898. Lincoln's opposition to the Know-Nothing Party was based on its promoting resentment against minority groups, not on foreign policy positions.

(2) The Know-Nothing Party did not favor unrestricted immigration. It wanted to restrict immigration, especially from Ireland. Lincoln's opposition to

the Know-Nothing Party was based on its promoting resentment against minority groups, including recent immigrants.

(4) The Know-Nothing Party did not want equal rights for all people. It promoted nativist and anti-Catholic sentiments. Lincoln's opposition to the Know-Nothing Party was based on its promoting resentment against minority groups.

13. **2** The Supreme Court's decision in *Dred Scott* v. *Sandford* was nullified by the passage of the 13th and 14th amendments. The 1857 case intensified the rift between pro-slavery and anti-slavery Americans and, in many ways, pushed the nation a bit closer to civil war. The case involved the fate of a slave named Dred Scott. Scott was owned by a doctor serving in the United States army. Scott and his wife, along with their owner, lived for a time in the state of Illinois and in the Wisconsin Territories, areas in which slavery had been banned by the Northwest Ordinance. Years after returning to Missouri, Scott sued for his and his wife's freedom on the grounds that they had lived for a time in free areas and that that made them free. The Supreme Court did not find Dred Scott's arguments persuasive. First, the Court ruled that Scott was still a slave and did not even have the right to initiate a lawsuit. That could have been the end of the decision. However, the Court went further. In regard to the issue of free territories, the Supreme Court ruled that Congress had overstepped its bounds in declaring the northern portion of the Louisiana Purchase territory off-limits to slavery. It therefore invalidated the Missouri Compromise of 1820. The Court went even further than that. Not only did Dred Scott not have standing to file suit, the Court declared that no African Americans, not even free men and women, were entitled to citizenship in the United States because they were, according to the Court, "beings of an inferior order." Later, the 13th amendment (1865) ended slavery in the United States, rendering any references to slavery in the Dred Scott decision moot. The 14th amendment (1868) nullified the Court's assertion that African Americans were not entitled to citizenship in the United States. The amendment asserted that all persons born on United States soil were citizens of the United States. It also stated that no person shall be denied "equal protection of the laws."

WRONG CHOICES EXPLAINED:

(1) The Kansas-Nebraska Act did not nullify the Supreme Court's decision in *Dred Scott* v. *Sandford*. The Kansas-Nebraska Act was passed in 1854, three years before the Dred Scott decision. Furthermore, an act of Congress cannot nullify a Supreme Court decision; only the Court or a constitutional amendment can do that. The Kansas-Nebraska Act allowed for the possibility of slavery, under the principle of popular sovereignty, in the territories of Kansas and Nebraska—areas that had been closed to slavery by the Missouri Compromise (1820).

Following passage of the act, violence erupted in "Bleeding Kansas" as pro-slavery and anti-slavery men fought for control of the territory.

(3) The Compromise of 1850 did not nullify the Supreme Court's decision in *Dred Scott* v. *Sandford*. The compromise was reached nine years before the Dred Scott decision. Furthermore, an act of Congress cannot nullify a Supreme Court decision; only the Court or a constitutional amendment can do that. The compromise grew out of the controversy around California's application for statehood as a free state. When Southern senators objected to the admission of an additional free state, Senate negotiators worked out a series of measures that became known as the Compromise of 1850. The most important elements of the compromise were the admittance of California as a free state, which pleased Northern politicians, and a more stringent Fugitive Slave Law, which pleased Southern politicians.

(4) The Reconstruction Act did not nullify the Supreme Court's decision in *Dred Scott* v. *Sandford*. An act of Congress cannot nullify a Supreme Court decision; only the Court or a constitutional amendment can do that. Congress passed the Military Reconstruction Act and three other acts in 1867 in order to reorganize the South (except for Tennessee) as conquered territories. The act divided the South into five military zones. In order to be readmitted, the Southern states had to provide basic rights to African Americans and had to ratify the 14th amendment.

14. **4** The Civil War directly affected the Northern economy by stimulating the growth of factories. The Civil War spurred rapid industrialization of the North. During the Civil War, the Union government required an enormous amount of war materials, from guns and bullets to boots and uniforms. Manufacturers rose to the occasion by rapidly modernizing production. These changes in production sped up the process of industrialization that was in its beginning stages before the war. Key elements of this industrial growth were the development of the railway industry, the use of steam power in factories, the growth of the steel industry, the development of mass production, and the consolidation of big business. Two important changes that occurred as a result of this industrial growth were increased urbanization and the growth of labor unions.

WRONG CHOICES EXPLAINED:

(1) Severe depression was not an impact of the Civil War on the Northern economy. The spending involved in carrying out the Civil War expanded the Northern economy. There was an economic downturn in the decade following the Civil War—the Panic of 1873, which set off an economic depression that lasted from 1873 to 1877. Economic historians attribute the downturn to events

in Europe, speculative investments, inflation, and the demonetization of silver, but not to the Civil War itself. It is one of several economic downturns that have occurred throughout American history.

(2) The destruction of large areas of farmland was not an impact of the Civil War on the Northern economy. The vast majority of fighting in the Civil War took place in the South. The one major battle that took place in the North was the Battle of Gettysburg in Pennsylvania (1863).

(3) The expansion of the canal system was not an impact of the Civil War on the Northern economy. The era of canal building was largely over by the time of the Civil War. After 1830, railroads began to replace canals as a more efficient means of moving goods within the United States.

15. **4** Rapid industrialization during the late 1800s contributed to an increase in immigration to the United States. In response to the demand for labor caused by industrialization, the United States became a major destination for immigrants. During the 1860s, a little over two million new residents entered the United States. That figure jumped to nearly nine million for the first decade of the 20th century. Between 1880 and 1920, an estimated 20 million people, from Russia, Italy, Poland, the Balkan region, and elsewhere, immigrated to the United States. These "new immigrants" settled primarily in the growing industrial cities of the Northeast and the Midwest, such as New York, Philadelphia, Cleveland, and Chicago. Rapid industrialization and immigration led to another important social change— urbanization. Between 1860 and 1900, the number of Americans who lived in cities jumped from 6.2 million to over 30 million, which amounted to a shift in the urban population from 20 percent of the total population to 40 percent.

WRONG CHOICES EXPLAINED:
(1) Rapid industrialization during the late 1800s did not contribute to a decline in the membership of the American Federation of Labor (AFL). The opposite occurred. The AFL was one of several unions that formed and grew after the Civil War to increase the bargaining power of industrial workers as they dealt with owners. Many workers thought they had a better chance to gain concessions from owners if they banded together in unions. The AFL, which included only skilled workers, was born in 1886.

(2) Rapid industrialization during the late 1800s did not contribute to a reduction in government regulation of railroads. The opposite occurred. Several states passed regulatory measures in response to popular pressure. Farmers protested the power, abuses, and rate structures of the major railroad companies. After the Supreme Court ruled in *Wabash* v. *Illinois* (1886) that individual states could not regulate railroads because they crossed state lines, the federal

government created the Interstate Commerce Commission (1887) to regulate railroads. However, the commission was chronically underfunded and was, therefore, ineffective.

(3) Rapid industrialization during the late 1800s did not contribute to a rise in the number of family farms. The opposite occurred. Mechanization and mass-production techniques affected agriculture as much as it affected industry. Expensive, motorized machinery, such as the mechanical reaper and the combine harvester, replaced hand-held tools. Mechanization had both positive and negative effects for American farmers. Mechanization increased overall agricultural production and reduced the man-hours needed for agricultural tasks. At the same time, it worked to undermine small-scale family farms.

16. **1** An important factor that aided the building of the transcontinental railroad was the federal government providing free land to the railroad companies. The completion of the transcontinental railroad at Promontory Summit, Utah, in 1862 was a milestone in the development of a network of railroad lines that connected the far reaches of the country. Railroads sped up the movement of goods and expanded markets. The government encouraged this expansion of the railroad network by giving railroad companies wide swaths of land. These generous land grants totaled more than 180 million acres, an area equal to the size of Texas. The railroad companies built rail lines on this land and also sold land adjacent to the tracks.

WRONG CHOICES EXPLAINED:
(2) Railroads did not establish fair rates for their customers. They were consistently accused of establishing unfair rate structures. Starting in the 1870s, groups that organized to promote the interests of farmers, such as the Grange, became concerned about the power and abuses of large railroad companies. Railroads often overcharged small-scale farmers. The Grange successfully pushed for laws in several states in the 1870s and 1880s to limit abusive practices by railroads.

(3) Congress did not repeal antitrust laws against the railroads. The Sherman Antitrust Act of 1890 was designed to break up trusts. The act had limited success. At first, only a few trusts were challenged. Ironically, the act was used with equal vigor against unions, on the grounds that they were illegal formations that interfered with free trade. In the case of *United States* v. *E.C. Knight Company* (1895), the Supreme Court greatly limited the scope of the act by making a distinction between trade (which would be subject to the act) and manufacturing (which would not).

(4) The Supreme Court did not approve public ownership of the railroad industry; the issue was never brought before the Court. In the United States,

there has been great reluctance to bring any type of economic activity under government ownership. Such moves strike many as steps toward socialism, though many European countries have much greater government involvement in economic activities, including railroads.

17. **1** Big business used strikebreakers and lockouts to limit the power of labor unions. Owners of industrial firms, often labeled "robber barons," could employ a variety of tactics to gain the upper hand in conflicts with labor unions during the late 1800s. One common tactic used by employers was hiring replacement workers, called "scabs" by the union movement, during strikes. Another tactic was locking out workers—preventing them from working and from getting paid. An employer might threaten a lockout to force unionized workers to accept new conditions (such as a pay cut). If the union refused to capitulate, the owner might carry out the threat and lock out the workers. This occurred at the Homestead steel mill in Homestead, Pennsylvania, in 1892. After several wage cuts and disputes with the owners, the union called for a strike. Andrew Carnegie and his plant manager, in an attempt to break the union, shut down the plant and locked out all the workers. The workers responded by declaring a strike. A pitched battle over control of the plant ensued, involving the workers and the community against armed Pinkerton guards and, later, National Guard troops. Ultimately, the union suffered a major defeat, setting back efforts to unionize steelworkers. Employers in the late 1800s also maintained lists of workers who were seen as "troublemakers." These lists would include workers who participated in union activities or who publicly supported political organizations sympathetic to workers. Such blacklists would be distributed among employers, allowing them to deny employment to individuals on the list. Most of the pitched workplace battles of the late 1800s ended in defeat for the workers. Workers saw their position and status erode during this period.

WRONG CHOICES EXPLAINED:
(2) Neither picketing nor walkouts were tactics used by big business in the late 1800s to limit the power of labor unions. Both terms are associated with labor strikes. Striking workers frequently engage in picketing—gathering and marching outside the entrance of their place of employment. The goals of a picket line are both to publicize the cause and to dissuade replacement workers and customers from entering the establishment. A walkout is a spontaneous strike. Normally, strikes are voted on ahead of time by the union; walkouts can occur with little to no advance warning.
(3) Neither collective bargaining nor mediation were tactics used by big business in the late 1800s to limit the power of labor unions. Collective bargaining is the process of a union negotiating on behalf of all the workers in the union.

Instead of each worker bargaining individually with management, unionized workers bargain collectively through their union. Mediation describes efforts by a third party to resolve a labor dispute. The role of the mediator is to listen to the positions of both parties, to make suggestions for a resolution, and to help them reach an agreement satisfactory to both parties. Generally, the results of mediation are not binding. A conflict might end up in arbitration, where the results of the arbitrator are binding on both parties.

(4) Neither wage increase nor shorter hours were tactics used by big business in the late 1800s to limit the power of labor unions. Both are goals of labor unions. A labor strike that resulted in significant wage increases as well as a shorter workday would, almost certainly, represent a victory for the union.

18. **3** The constitutional right that was the central focus in *Plessy* v. *Ferguson* (1896) was equal protection of the law under the 14th amendment. In that case, the Supreme Court ruled that separate rail cars for African Americans were permissible, as long as the facilities for both races were of equal quality. In the case, the Supreme Court decided that racial segregation did not violate the equal protection provision of the 14th amendment. The decision was a setback for those who sought an end to the Jim Crow system of racial segregation in the South. Jim Crow laws were state and local ordinances that first appeared after Reconstruction ended (1877). Typical laws called for separate schools or separate train cars for African Americans. Opponents of racial segregation argued that Jim Crow laws violated the 14th amendment (1868). The amendment, ratified during Reconstruction, states that no person shall be denied "equal protection of the laws." Jim Crow laws, opponents argued, violated the 14th amendment because the laws relegated African Americans to inferior public accommodations and had the effect of making African Americans second-class citizens. However, the Court disagreed. The "separate but equal" doctrine allowed for the continuation of the Jim Crow system until the 1950s and 1960s. The beginning of the end to the system came with the *Brown* v. *Board of Education* decision of 1954.

WRONG CHOICES EXPLAINED:
(1) The constitutional issue of freedom of assembly, as stipulated in the first amendment (1791), was not the focus of *Plessy* v. *Ferguson* (1896). The Supreme Court has generally struck down attempts to limit freedom of assembly. In *Edwards* v. *South Carolina* (1963), for example, the Court overturned the convictions of students arrested for peaceful demonstrations against segregation. The decision stated that the state could not "make criminal the peaceful expression of unpopular views." In *Village of Skokie* v. *National Socialist Party* (1978), the Court ruled that Nazis could not be prohibited from marching peacefully because of the content of their message.

(2) The constitutional issue of due process of the law, as stipulated in the fifth amendment (1791), was not the focus of *Plessy* v. *Ferguson* (1896). The due process clause of the fifth amendment—stating that no one shall "be deprived of life, liberty, or property, without due process of law"—deals with the legal procedures the state must follow in administering justice. The idea of due process is to balance the power of the legal system with the rights of individuals. Supreme Court decisions have interpreted the due process clause in a variety of ways. For example, in the case of *Dred Scott* v. *Sandford* (1857), the Court ruled that prohibiting slavery in U.S. territories would violate the due process clause of the fifth amendment. Other cases, including *Santa Clara County* v. *Southern Pacific Railroad* (1886), have extended due process protections to corporations, based on the theory that they are "legal persons" (establishing "corporate personhood").

(4) The constitutional issue of equal voting rights, as stipulated in the 15th amendment (1870), was not the focus of *Plessy* v. *Ferguson* (1896). In the 19th century the Court narrowed the scope of the 15th amendment. In *United States* v. *Reese* (1876), the Court upheld voting restrictions that were, on the surface, race neutral, but were clearly intended to prevent African Americans from voting. These restrictions included poll taxes, literacy tests, and a grandfather clause. In the 20th century, the Court has interpreted the 15th amendment more broadly. In 1966, the Court ruled, in *Harper* v. *Virginia State Board of Elections*, that state poll taxes violated the fourteenth amendment's equal protection clause.

19. **2** The cartoon is criticizing business consolidation. The specific business being criticized is the Standard Oil Company created by John D. Rockefeller. The cartoonist is depicting the extent of the power Standard Oil exerted in the United States. Standard Oil is represented as an octopus with its tentacles wrapped around the banking and insurance industries, railroads and shipping firms, smaller oil and gas companies, and even a town. The men who established these giant corporate entities were given the nickname "robber barons," implying that they had the power of a medieval baron and the scruples of a common criminal. Giant corporations, such as Standard Oil, are a post–Civil War phenomenon. In the last three decades of the 19th century, corporations came to play a very large role in society. Several of these corporations were able to exercise near-monopoly control of a particular industry. The formation of trusts was seen as harmful to the interests of consumers. Consequently, the government passed the Sherman Antitrust Act. The act had limited success. In the case of *United States* v. *E.C. Knight Company* (1895), the Supreme Court greatly limited the scope of the act by making a distinction between trade (which would be subject to the act) and manufacturing (which would not).

WRONG CHOICES EXPLAINED:

(1) The cartoon is not criticizing environmental degradation. Unregulated industrial growth in the late 19th century took a major toll on the environment. Slowly, reformers pushed for government action. An early champion of preserving wilderness was John Muir. He was one of the founders of the Sierra Club (1892), an organization dedicated to preserving wilderness and to monitoring the federal government's oversight of protected lands. President Theodore Roosevelt (1901–1909) championed the cause of environmental conservation. In pursuit of his conservationist agenda, Roosevelt set aside millions of acres as protected areas. These included six national parks.

(3) The cartoon is not criticizing oil exploration. The cartoon depicts oil wells, but that is in order to show Standard Oil's ruthless crusade to dominate the entire oil processing industry, not to criticize oil exploration. In the 21st century, environmentalists have been critical of government efforts to open protected areas and off-shore sites to oil exploration.

(4) The cartoon is not criticizing federal tax laws. The cartoon does not make any allusions to tax laws. Federal taxes consisted of import duties at the time.

20. **2** One result of the Spanish-American War (1898) was that Puerto Rico became a possession of the United States. The Spanish-American War lasted only several months, but profoundly impacted the direction of the United States. The historical circumstances that led to the war are varied. Many Americans became sympathetic to Cubans who were fighting for independence from Spain. By the 1890s, the conflict became intense with Spanish authorities taking extreme and brutal measures to suppress those seeking independence. Also, some American businessmen were angered by the interruption of the sugar harvest by the fighting between Cuban rebels and Spanish forces. Finally, a United States battleship, the U.S.S. *Maine*, exploded and sunk in the harbor of Havana, Cuba. Many in the United States thought that the destruction of the ship was the work of Spain, especially after American newspapers bluntly accused Spain of the crime, despite the scarcity of evidence. The Spanish-American War was brief. The U.S. declared war on Spain in April; an armistice was signed in August. The United States and Spain negotiated the Treaty of Paris (1898) following the war. In the treaty, Spain agreed to cede Puerto Rico, as well as the Philippines and Guam, to the United States; the United States agreed to pay Spain $20 million for these possessions.

WRONG CHOICES EXPLAINED:

(1) Cuba was not divided into spheres of influence following the Spanish-American War. Cuba, which had been a Spanish possession before the war, became independent following the war, but, in many ways, Cuba became

independent in name only. The United States took steps to ensure that American economic interests would not be challenged by a future Cuban administration. The term "spheres of influence" was applied to China in the late 1800s. By the 1890s, the major European powers had established spheres of influence in China. These nations each declared that they had exclusive trading privileges in their sphere of influence. The Open Door Policy, put forth by the administration of President William McKinley in 1900, asserted that all of China should be open to trade with all nations. The European nations begrudgingly accepted this concept.

(3) The Philippines did not become a Spanish colony following the Spanish-American War. It had been a Spanish colony before the war. The Treaty of Paris transferred possession of the Philippines to the United States. A resistance movement against American control developed in the Philippines and a bloody war, known as the Philippine-American War, ensued. Filipino forces were led by Emilio Aguinaldo. The war cost the American forces 4,000 lives; over 20,000 members of the Filipino resistance died in the conflict, and up to another 100,000 civilians died.

(4) The United States did not lose control of Panama following the Spanish-American War. The United States gained control of the Panama Canal Zone in 1903, five years after the Spanish-American War. Before 1903, Panama was a region of Colombia. American investors had picked the narrow piece of land as an ideal location for a canal. When Colombia refused the United States' offer of $10 million to build a canal, American investors, with the backing of President Theodore Roosevelt and the U.S. military, instigated a "rebellion" in Panama against Colombia. Panama became an independent country and immediately allowed the United States to build and administer a canal. Much later, the United States did agree to give up control of the Panama Canal. President Jimmy Carter negotiated two treaties with Panama in 1977 in which the United States agreed to turn over the Canal Zone to Panama by the end of 1999 (which occurred as agreed upon).

21. **4** The federal actions mentioned in the question—the Chinese Exclusion Act (1882), the Gentlemen's Agreement (1907), and the Emergency Quota Act (1921)—all demonstrate that Americans have favored limiting immigration at different times in the nation's history. Immigration has been a contentious issue throughout American history. The first two items mentioned reflect the strong anti-Asian racism at the time. Racist assumptions held that Asian immigrants would never fully assimilate into the United States. The Gold Rush in California (1848–1855) and the building of the transcontinental railroad attracted many Chinese immigrants to the West. The Chinese Exclusion Act, passed by Congress in 1882, prevented Chinese workers from entering the country. These workers were

generally employed in unskilled positions. It was the only instance of legislation prohibiting a particular nationality from entering the country. In the late 1800s, many Japanese people immigrated to the West Coast of the United States. In California, these Japanese immigrants often suffered discrimination. In the early years of the 20th century, California passed legislation ordering "Orientals" to be segregated from white students in the public school system. When Japan protested, President Theodore Roosevelt and Japanese leaders negotiated a "Gentlemen's Agreement" in which Roosevelt agreed to pressure California to reverse this legislation and Japan agreed to limit the number of emigrants coming into the United States. Later, in the period immediately following World War I, anti-immigrant sentiment, known as nativism, rose steeply. A large wave of immigrants from southern and eastern Europe had arrived in the United States between 1880 and 1920. There are several reasons nativists resented this new wave of immigration. Some nativists focused on the fact that most of the new immigrants were not Protestant, while others objected to the cacophony of languages heard on the streets of New York or Chicago. Some nativists associated the immigrants with either radical movements or drunkenness. Finally, working class people feared that low wage immigrant laborers would take jobs from native-born American workers. This sentiment led to passage of the Emergency Quota Act of 1921. This act greatly reduced the number of immigrants allowed into the United States by establishing quotas for different nations based on the numbers of each national group present in the United States decades earlier. A later act, the National Origins Act (1924), reduced the quotas of different nationalities even further.

WRONG CHOICES EXPLAINED:

(1) The federal actions mentioned in the question—the Chinese Exclusion Act (1882), the Gentlemen's Agreement (1907), and the Emergency Quota Act (1921)—do not demonstrate that Americans have supported the principle of open immigration. Throughout history, many Americans have held a welcoming attitude toward immigrants. Many Americans see the United States as a refuge from oppressive regimes in different parts of the world. In addition, since many Americans are descended from immigrants, they want to give others the same opportunities in the United States that their parents or grandparents were afforded. Also, many Americans have seen immigration as a strong engine for economic growth; immigrants bring their labor power, as well as their purchasing power, to the United States. However, the three items reflect anti-immigrant sentiment.

(2) The federal actions mentioned in the question—the Chinese Exclusion Act (1882), the Gentlemen's Agreement (1907), and the Emergency Quota Act (1921)—do not demonstrate that Americans provided immigrants equal access

to jobs and social programs. Many immigrants have benefited from employment opportunities and social programs in the United States. However, the implementation of the actions in the question reflect moves in the opposite direction. Nativists were determined to deny foreign-born workers better-paying jobs and access to social programs.

(3) The federal actions mentioned in the question—the Chinese Exclusion Act (1882), the Gentlemen's Agreement (1907), and the Emergency Quota Act (1921)—do not demonstrate that Americans forced immigrants to settle in designated areas. This has never been a serious proposal in American history. Immigrants have been denied certain housing opportunities and have gravitated toward certain ethnic enclaves, but there have not been proposals to force immigrants to settle in certain areas of the country. During World War II, President Franklin D. Roosevelt issued Executive Order 9066 (1942), authorizing the government to remove 120,000 Japanese Americans, two-thirds of them citizens, from West Coast states and relocate them to camps throughout the West. In the case of *Korematsu* v. *United States* (1944), the Supreme Court ruled that the relocation was acceptable on the grounds of national security. However, this relocation only lasted for the duration of the war; it was not permanent.

22. **2** In the early 20th century, muckraking authors Upton Sinclair and Ida Tarbell primarily criticized the federal government for ignoring abuses by big government. The term *muckrakers* refers to the crusading journalists and writers of the Progressive Era who exposed wrongdoing by government officials, showed the negative side of industrialization, and let the world see a variety of social ills. Upton Sinclair, for example, wrote a stirring book, *The Jungle* (1906), that exposed conditions in the meatpacking industry at the turn of the 20th century. Though the book is a novel, it was thoroughly researched. The conditions of the meatpacking industry were extremely unsanitary and dangerous. The public uproar that followed publication of the book led Congress to pass two laws in 1906—the Meat Inspection Act and the Pure Food and Drug Act, which established the Food and Drug Administration. Ida M. Tarbell's book, *The History of the Standard Oil Company* (1904), exposed the ruthlessness of John D. Rockefeller's oil company. Her book contributed to the government breakup of the Standard Oil Company in 1911. The push toward increased regulation represented a break with nineteenth-century laissez-faire economic policies. The policy of laissez-faire asserts that government should limit, as much as possible, any interference in the economy. The French phrase *laissez-faire* means "to let alone."

WRONG CHOICES EXPLAINED:

(1) In the early 19th century, neither Upton Sinclair nor Ida Tarbell criticized the government for wasting money on foreign wars. Several authors were critical of American foreign policy in the early 20th century. For example, the author Mark Twain was vice president of the American Anti-Imperialist League from 1901 to the time of his death. In addition, some Progressive reformers were critical of United States' involvement in World War I.

(3) In the early 20th century, neither Upton Sinclair nor Ida Tarbell criticized the government for excessive regulation of the steel industry. In general, muckraking journalists such as Sinclair and Tarbell urged the government to expand its regulatory powers, not reduce them.

(4) In the early 20th century, neither Upton Sinclair nor Ida Tarbell criticized the government for overspending on social welfare programs. Many muckraking journalists and Progressive Era reformers urged the government to create social welfare programs. However, it was not until the New Deal of the 1930s that the government began to play a major role in ensuring the social welfare of vulnerable individuals.

23. **1** During the Progressive Era, voters were given more opportunities to select political party candidates through direct primary elections. Today, primary elections are held by political parties to determine what candidate the party will select to run in the general election. Before direct primary elections, party leaders picked the candidates that would run in the general election. Wisconsin was the first state to adopt a direct primary in 1903. Most other states adopted direct primaries by 1916. Progressive reformers pushed for several reforms that would make the American political system more democratic. For example, they pushed for the 17th amendment (1913), which called for the direct election of senators. Previously, senators were chosen by state legislatures.

WRONG CHOICES EXPLAINED:

(2) The purpose of term limits has been to limit the power of elected officials, not to give voters a greater say in selecting their party's candidates. Some reformers have pushed for term limits for elected officials over the years. Advocates of term limits argue that incumbent candidates have a built-in advantage over challengers; they can use the platform of their office to push for reelection. In addition, these reformers argue that term limits will bring more individuals into public office. Opponents of term limits argue that experienced office holders, such as state legislators or city counselors, might be better able to hold strong executives accountable and create a better sense of balance in government. The Supreme Court ruled in 1995 that states could not impose term

limits on their federal representatives. The 22nd amendment (1951) limited presidential power by allowing the president to serve only two terms.

(3) The purpose of the initiative and the recall has been to give voters more of a voice in the political process, but not to specifically give them a greater say in selecting their party's candidates. The recall would allow the populace to remove unpopular or corrupt elected officials from office before their terms ended. Voters would have to gather a certain number of signatures, and then a special election would be announced. At least nineteen states allow for the recall of state officials. The initiative would enable citizens to introduce a bill to the local or state legislature by petition.

(4) The purpose of public funding of elections has been to remove excessive monetary influence on politicians, not to give voters a greater say in selecting their party's candidates. Publicly funded elections, it is argued, would reduce corruption by funding elections with federal tax dollars. Candidates would not depend on campaign contributions from corporations or wealthy individuals.

24. **3** Theodore Roosevelt's Square Deal and Woodrow Wilson's New Freedom shared the goal of strengthening federal power over large corporations. Both Roosevelt (1901–1909) and Wilson (1913–1921) are considered Progressive presidents. These Progressive Era presidents moved federal policy away from the laissez-faire approach—or hands-off economic matters—that characterized federal policy in the 19th century. Roosevelt saw the concentration of economic power in a few hands as potentially dangerous to the economy as a whole. Using the Sherman Antitrust Act (1890), he made a point of pursuing "bad trusts"— ones that interfered with commerce—but not necessarily the biggest trusts. One of his first targets was the Northern Securities Company, a railroad holding company. His efforts at challenging monopolies earned him the nickname "trust buster." Roosevelt also pushed for important consumer protections in the wake of the publication of *The Jungle*, and stronger measures to protect the environment. Also, Roosevelt pushed for stronger regulation of the powerful railroad industry. Roosevelt strengthened the Interstate Commerce Commission (created in 1887) with the Elkins Act (1903), which targeted the railroad practice of granting rebates to favored customers, and the Hepburn Act (1906), which gave the commission greater latitude to set railroad rates. President Wilson was a strong supporter of small business and took a dim view of the growing power of large corporations. Wilson strengthened the antitrust powers of the federal government with the Clayton Antitrust Act (1914). President Wilson also pushed for the creation of the Federal Trade Commission (1914) to regulate business practices. One of the many regulatory responsibilities of the commission is reducing the power of trusts and guarding against "unfair trade practices."

WRONG CHOICES EXPLAINED:

(1) Neither Theodore Roosevelt's Square Deal nor Woodrow Wilson's New Freedom had the goal of achieving equal rights for minorities. The era of Progressive reform in the first two decades of the 20th century was also a low point in race relations in the United States, as a strong Ku Klux Klan organization, a pervasive Jim Crow system, and increased incidents of lynching characterized American society. Most white Progressive Era reformers, as well as the two Progressive-minded presidents in question, turned a blind eye to the problems of race in the United States. However, African American reformers took the lead in challenging racial discrimination. For instance, Ida B. Wells, an African-American muckraking journalist, challenged the mistreatment of African Americans in the country and exposed the horrors of lynching.

(2) Neither Theodore Roosevelt's Square Deal nor Woodrow Wilson's New Freedom had the goal of protecting the interests of big business. Both reform agendas sought to limit the power of big business by strengthening federal regulatory powers. By contrast, the Republican presidents of the 1920s generally sought to protect the interests of big business. President Calvin Coolidge famously said in 1925, "the chief business of the American people is business."

(4) Neither Theodore Roosevelt's Square Deal nor Woodrow Wilson's New Freedom had the goal of instituting laissez-faire policies. The French phrase *laissez-faire* means "to let alone." It describes a government policy that would take a hands-off approach in regard to economic activities. The Progressive Era presidents in question pursued policies to expand government intervention in economic activities.

25. **2** The Federal Reserve System was created in 1913 to control the money supply. The Federal Reserve Bank, which is part privately controlled and part publicly controlled, was created by legislation in 1913 during the administration of President Woodrow Wilson. One of its main functions is to regulate economic growth by regulating the supply of money. If the economy is sluggish, the Fed will attempt to stimulate economic growth by increasing the money supply; if inflation occurs, the Fed will attempt to slow down economic activity by reducing the money supply. An important mechanism for regulating the money supply is raising or lowering the interest rates at which the Fed loans money to other banks. Other banks follow suit, raising or lowering the interest rates at which they loan money to the public. By lowering interest rates, the Fed stimulates economic activity, making it more attractive for people to borrow money to make major purchases, thus putting more money into circulation.

WRONG CHOICES EXPLAINED:

(1) The Federal Reserve System (1913) was not created to balance the budget. A balanced budget would mean that governmental spending would not surpass its income. Balancing the budget has been a goal of conservative policymakers since the 1980s. Reformers have pushed for an amendment to the Constitution that would require a balanced federal budget. As of 2017, 29 states have submitted requests for a national amendment-proposing convention. Two-thirds, or 34, of the states are required for such a convention to occur.

(3) The Federal Reserve System (1913) was not created to insure savings account deposits. Later, President Franklin D. Roosevelt instituted federal regulation of the banking industry. As part of the New Deal, he pushed for passage of the Glass-Steagall Act (1933), which created the Federal Deposit Insurance Corporation (FDIC). The FDIC insures deposits, so that if a bank does fold, people would not lose their savings.

(4) The Federal Reserve System (1913) was not created to regulate the stock market. Later, President Franklin D. Roosevelt instituted federal regulation of the stock market. As part of the New Deal, he pushed for passage of the Securities and Exchange Commission (1934), which oversees stock market operations by monitoring transactions, licensing brokers, limiting buying on margin, and prohibiting insider trading.

26. **1** The three statements by President Woodrow Wilson demonstrate that during the three years before the United States entered World War I, he gradually changed his foreign policy goals. Wilson initially assumed that the United States could stay neutral in World War I and maintain commercial ties to nations on both sides of the conflict. However, England successfully blockaded U.S. ships from reaching Germany. Out of necessity, U.S. trade shifted to England exclusively. Germany responded by warning that U.S. ships in the waters off of Great Britain would be subject to attack by U-boats, or submarines. The sinking of the British ocean liner *Lusitania* infuriated many Americans (128 Americans were among the dead). Germany, however, wanted to keep the United States out of the war and agreed in the Sussex Pledge (1916) to make no surprise submarine attacks on U.S. ships. The United States took advantage of this pledge and traded extensively with Great Britain. In 1917, Germany rescinded the Sussex Pledge and declared that it would resume unrestricted submarine warfare. When Wilson ran for reelection in 1916, he still maintained an anti-war position, but after reelection, Wilson became increasingly convinced that United States participation in World War I was necessary to make the world "safe for democracy." The United States finally entered the war in 1917.

WRONG CHOICES EXPLAINED:

(2) The three statements by President Woodrow Wilson do not indicate that he eagerly became involved in a war. Initially, Wilson expressed a desire to remain neutral in regard to World War I. It was only over time, and in response to new circumstances, that Wilson changed his foreign policy goals, and urged Congress to issue a declaration of war.

(3) The three statements by President Woodrow Wilson do not indicate that he abused the principle of separation of powers. Wilson followed the procedures outlined in the Constitution in regard to the United States entering a war. He asked Congress for a declaration of war, and Congress voted affirmatively. If he had carried out military actions without congressional approval, this might be seen as an abuse of the principle of separation of powers. During the Vietnam War, Congress became increasingly concerned that President Richard Nixon had abused his power to deploy troops. After the United States withdrew from Vietnam, Congress passed the War Powers Act (1973) as an attempt to check presidential power and strengthen the legislative branch in matters of war.

(4) The three statements by President Woodrow Wilson do not indicate that he was consistent in his policy of strict neutrality. The first statement demonstrates Wilson's desire to stay neutral in regard to World War II. However, the second and third statements indicate that he had changed his foreign policy goals and was ready to intervene in World War I.

27. **2** President Warren Harding's call for a "return to normalcy" meant that the United States should reduce its role in world affairs. The phrase was used by Harding during his presidential campaign of 1920. His call for a "return to normalcy" implied a rejection of the internationalist impulses that propelled the United States into World War I, as well as a rejection of the reformist impulses of the Progressive Era. An important part of this conservative push was isolationism, or retreating from world affairs. Isolationist political leaders were vehemently opposed to United States participation in the League of Nations. Ultimately, in a blow to President Woodrow Wilson, the Senate rejected the Treaty of Versailles, which meant a rejection of United States membership in the league. The League of Nations was dear to Wilson. He included the concept in his Fourteen Points program for the post-war world, and he campaigned vigorously for it in Europe and the United States. Isolationist senators feared that membership in the league might obligate the United States to participate in future wars.

WRONG CHOICES EXPLAINED:

(1) President Warren Harding's call for a "return to normalcy" did not mean that the United States should reduce the number of exports. Policymakers have rarely argued that the United States should limit the number of exports.

When American goods are sold overseas, it benefits the American economy and expands opportunities for American workers. Often, leaders have called for limits on goods imported into the country. Many isolationists in the 1920s argued for higher tariff rates in order to keep imported goods out of the United States.

(3) President Warren Harding's call for a "return to normalcy" did not mean that the United States should expand efforts to end racial segregation. In the first three decades of the 20th century, no president called for an end to racial segregation. Politicians in both major political parties accepted policies that relegated African Americans to a second-class status in the United States.

(4) President Warren Harding's call for a "return to normalcy" did not mean that the United States should support women's suffrage. Harding made his call for a "return to normalcy" the same year that the 19th amendment, which extended the vote to women, was ratified (1920). However, Harding is not voicing support for it. Harding's call for a "return to normalcy" meant a return to traditional values, including a return to traditional ideas around gender.

28. **3** The heading "Causes of the Great Depression" best completes the partial outline. The Great Depression began with the crash of the stock market in 1929. However, the underlying causes of the Great Depression are varied. The first two items in the partial outline, "Overproduction" and "Underconsumption," are two terms describing different aspects of the same phenomenon. In both the industrial sector and the agricultural sector, producers were turning out more and more goods, while consumers were not able to absorb such high levels of production. Mechanization and mass-production techniques boosted production—in both factories and on farms. For much of the 1920s, the public, induced by easy credit and seductive advertising, was able to purchase large quantities of mass produced industrial products. However, consumers, after overspending for several years, could not keep up on paying off their debts. By 1927, consumption slackened, inventories ballooned, and many manufacturing firms began laying off workers. Farmers suffered a similar fate. Farmers had put more acres under cultivation during World War I to meet increased demand for agricultural goods. By the twenties, Europe was back on its feet, yet American farmers did not cut back on production. Overproduction and underconsumption were worsened by the fourth item in the partial outline, "Unequal distribution of wealth." While the wealthiest people saw their fortunes grow even larger in the 1920s, workers saw their wages stagnate. If workers had received higher wages in the 1920s, they might have been able to absorb more of the consumer goods that were piling up in warehouses from 1927 onward. The third item in the partial outline, "Buying on margin," refers to the stock market. Buying stock on margin is the practice of paying only a small portion of the purchase price upfront, with the promise of paying the remainder in the future. This practice worked as long as stock prices

rose, which they did throughout most of the 1920s. By the late 1920s, however, serious investors began to see that stock prices were reaching new heights as the actual earnings of major corporations were declining. This discrepancy between the price per share and the actual earnings of a corporation led investors to begin selling stocks, which stimulated a panic. In October 1929, the stock market crashed, destroying individuals' investments and signaling the beginning of the Great Depression.

WRONG CHOICES EXPLAINED:

(1) The heading "Causes of the Industrial Revolution" would not complete the partial outline in the question. An outline with that heading might include items such as "Abundant natural resources," "Ample labor supply," and "Sufficient amount of investment capital."

(2) The heading "Causes of World War I" would not complete the partial outline in the question. An outline with that heading might include items such as "Rise of nationalism in Europe," "Conflicts over imperialist ambitions," and "The assassination of the heir presumptive of the Austro-Hungarian Empire."

(4) The heading "Causes of World War II" would not complete the partial outline in the question. An outline with that heading might include items such as "The failure of appeasement," "The formation of the Axis Powers," and "The German invasion of Poland."

29. **3** The information provided in the graph supports the conclusion that New Deal programs only partially relieved unemployment. The graph shows that the number of unemployed Americans did go down after President Franklin D. Roosevelt came into office in 1933. After reaching a high of over twelve million in 1933, the number of unemployed hovered between eight and twelve million until 1939. Roosevelt instituted the New Deal to deal with the Great Depression. The administration created a series of public works agencies to address the problem of high unemployment. The Civilian Conservation Corps (1933), for example, provided outdoor jobs for young men. Later, Roosevelt created the Works Progress Administration (1935), one of the largest New Deal programs. The WPA was a vast program of government projects that hired millions of unemployed workers. Individuals hired by the agency, for example, built schools, maintained highways, installed sewer lines, wrote guidebooks, and produced theatrical productions. At its peak in 1938, over three million people worked for the WPA; over 8 million people in total worked for it by the time it was shuttered in 1943. In many ways, it was World War II that ended the Great Depression. The United States began producing military equipment and ammunition when World War II started in 1939. War production spiked after the United States became involved in the war in late 1941.

WRONG CHOICES EXPLAINED:

(1) The information provided in the graph does not support the conclusion that deficit spending ended unemployment. The New Deal did entail deficit spending, when spending outpaces government income. Roosevelt was influenced by the thinking of the economist John Maynard Keynes. Keynes argued that deficit spending by the government was acceptable, and even desirable, as a means of increasing overall demand and stimulating economic activity. However, the graph does not indicate that deficit spending ended unemployment.

(2) The information provided in the graph does not support the conclusion that World War II increased unemployment. The graph ends, in 1939, just as World War II was beginning. If the graph continued throughout the years of World War II (1939–1945), it would show that the number of unemployed Americans dropped to almost zero. Many factories had trouble filling all their slots because war production greatly expanded employment opportunities.

(4) The information provided in the graph does not support the conclusion that unemployment after the New Deal began (1939) was the same as it was before the stock market crash (1929). Before the stock market crash, the number of unemployed Americans was low—less than two million. After the New Deal began, the number of unemployed Americans did not drop below eight million.

30. **4** During the 1930s, poor land management and severe drought conditions across parts of the Midwest resulted in the development of Dust Bowl conditions on the Great Plains. The natural grass cover of the region, which includes parts of Oklahoma and Texas, as well as smaller parts of neighboring states, had been removed in the years leading up to the Dust Bowl, as wheat farmers increased the number of acres under cultivation. With this natural root system gone, the fertile topsoil simply blew away when drought struck from 1934 to 1937. The government, through the Soil Conservation Service, encouraged farmers to replant trees and grass and purchased land to be kept out of cultivation. The Dust Bowl caused the largest migration in American history within a short period of time. During the 1930s, approximately 3.5 million people moved out of the Great Plains states. A major destination for Dust Bowl refugees, often referred to as "Okies" and "Arkies," was California. The Dust Bowl exodus prompted some significant cultural responses, such as the album *Dust Bowl Ballads* by the folk singer Woody Guthrie (1940), which included the songs "I Ain't Got No Home in This World Anymore" and "Blowin' Down This Road." The novel *The Grapes of Wrath* (1939), by John Steinbeck, chronicled the plight of a family of Dust Bowl refugees.

WRONG CHOICES EXPLAINED:

(1) During the 1930s, poor land management and severe drought conditions across parts of the Midwest did not result in the establishment of the United States Department of Agriculture. The Department of Agriculture grew out of the Agricultural Division of the Patent Office, which was established in 1839. Later, in 1849, the office was transferred to the newly formed Department of the Interior. President Abraham Lincoln signed legislation making it an independent agency in 1862. The department was elevated to a Cabinet-level department in 1889.

(2) During the 1930s, poor land management and severe drought conditions across parts of the Midwest did not result in the creation of wheat surpluses. The opposite occurred. Crops were devastated in parts of the Midwest as Dust Bowl conditions led to the fertile topsoil blowing away. Fields lay barren in the 1930s in the areas affected by these conditions.

(3) During the 1930s, poor land management and severe drought conditions across parts of the Midwest did not result in decreased support for conservation. The opposite occurred. The government encouraged conservation through the Soil Conservation Service. This New Deal agency encouraged farmers to replant trees and grass and purchased land to be kept out of cultivation.

31. **4** During the 1930s, United States neutrality legislation was primarily designed to avoid foreign policy mistakes that led to involvement in World War I. Isolationism, which gained strength in the 1920s, continued to hold sway into the 1930s, even as the world was becoming increasingly dangerous with the rise of fascism in Europe and a militaristic government in Japan. In the Neutrality Acts of 1935–1937, Congress made clear that neither the United States government nor private U.S. firms were to trade with belligerent nations. A later Neutrality Act, passed in 1939 as World War II was beginning, allowed the United States to supply the opponents of fascism with materials on a cash-and-carry basis. The cash-and-carry approach allowed the United States to send armaments to Great Britain with the condition that Great Britain pay for the weapons first and transport them in their own ships. The stipulations were intended to avoid American ships being put in the line of fire. The sinking of American merchant ships during the first years of World War I was one of the main factors that convinced many Americans to take action against Germany. As the war progressed, President Franklin Roosevelt pushed for greater American support for the Allied powers. In early 1941, Roosevelt was able to make military supplies more readily available to the Allies with the Lend-Lease Act. This act demonstrated the commitment of the United States to the Allies, but it was not until the attack on Pearl Harbor on December 7, 1941, that the United States formally entered the war.

WRONG CHOICES EXPLAINED:

(1) United States neutrality legislation in the 1930s was not designed to provide military and economic aid to Italy and Japan. Neutrality legislation was designed to keep the United States out of foreign conflicts; providing economic aid to one of the sides would push the United States toward greater involvement. It is true that some advocates of neutrality were sympathetic to fascism. The aviator Charles Lindbergh, for example, and other leading members of the America First Committee were sympathetic to fascism. They called for neutrality, knowing that it was out of the question for the United States to actively support the Axis side in World War II.

(2) United States neutrality legislation in the 1930s was not designed to give the United States time to plan an attack against Germany. The United States was not planning an attack against Germany. It was readying its military for combat, but its main foe for most of World War II was Japan. It was not until D-Day, in June 1944, that the United States launched a major offensive against Germany.

(3) United States neutrality legislation in the 1930s was not designed to protect American lives and property in Latin America. The conflicts of the 1930s, leading toward World War II (1939–1945), occurred in Europe and in Asia, not in Latin America.

32. **3** New Deal supporters would most likely have supported the lyrics of the song. The song is unequivocally pro–New Deal and pro–President Franklin D. Roosevelt. The title of the song, "That's Why We're Voting For Roosevelt," makes clear the lyricist's point of view. The song praises Roosevelt for prioritizing the plight of the "once forgotten man" by getting individuals "back to work" and bringing "prosperity back" to America. The song also praises Roosevelt for challenging the power of the banking industry and of the financial industry. It approves of Roosevelt putting "Wall Street… on the pan"—that is, reining in its power through agencies such as the Securities and Exchange Commission (1934). The line, "Our banks are in the clear," refers to actions Roosevelt took to regulate the banking industry and restore public faith in banks. In 1933, he pushed for passage of the Glass-Steagall Act, which created the Federal Deposit Insurance Corporation (FDIC). The FDIC insures deposits so that if a bank folds, people would not lose their savings. Previously, as rumors swirled about the precariousness of the banking system, thousands of people began withdrawing their money. Such actions often turned rumors into self-fulfilling prophecies. These and other New Deal measures did not end the Great Depression, but they gave many Americans a sense of hope and proved to be very popular with voters. Roosevelt was overwhelmingly reelected in 1936, winning over 60 percent of the vote and carrying all but two states.

WRONG CHOICES EXPLAINED:

(1) Prohibition advocates would not have supported the lyrics of the song, "That's Why We're Voting For Roosevelt." Roosevelt was critical of America's experiment in prohibiting the manufacture, sale, and transportation of "intoxicating beverages." Prohibition began with ratification of the 18th amendment in 1919. Roosevelt had been ambivalent throughout his career about Prohibition. However, by the time he ran for president in 1932, he agreed with most Americans that the experiment was not working. He signed legislation in 1933 allowing for the sale of low-alcohol beer and wine, thought to be nonintoxicating. Later that same year, the 21st amendment, ending Prohibition, was ratified with Roosevelt's support.

(2) Republican Party leaders would not have supported the lyrics of the song, "That's Why We're Voting For Roosevelt." President Franklin D. Roosevelt was a Democrat. His opponent in the 1936 election was Republican Alf Landon. Republican Party leaders would have sung his praises, not Roosevelt's.

(4) Supply-side economists would not have supported the lyrics of the song, "That's Why We're Voting For Roosevelt." Supporters of supply-side economics would have opposed President Franklin D. Roosevelt and the New Deal. Supply-side economics stresses stimulating the supply side of the economy—manufacturers, banks, and insurance corporations. The theory is that if there is growth in the supply side, there will be a general economic revival and the benefits of economic expansion will trickle down to everyone. The presidents of the 1920s, including Herbert Hoover, subscribed to this approach to the economy in the decade before the Great Depression. Roosevelt, on the other hand, supported a demand-side approach, which would emphasize government policies designed to increase workers' wages and benefits, such as welfare and unemployment benefits.

33. **1** According to the song lyrics, people supported Franklin D. Roosevelt primarily because he implemented economic relief and recovery programs. The character in the song had been out of work, but "for now I'm back to work and get my three squares ev'ry day." (The "three squares" refer to three square meals each day.) Roosevelt's New Deal included many relief and recovery programs to help the "forgotten man" get back on his feet. Relief programs, such as the Federal Emergency Relief Agency (1933), provided welfare payments to millions of unemployed Americans. In addition, the New Deal included several public works programs. The Civilian Conservation Corps focused on providing work for young men and the Works Progress Administration created hundreds of public projects. The WPA built schools, installed sewer lines, wrote guidebooks, and produced theatrical productions. Also, the New Deal addressed the welfare of retired

people and people with disabilities by creating the Social Security system in 1935. While this array of programs did not end the Great Depression, Roosevelt was able to convey to the American people that the government was on their side. The New Deal and Roosevelt's assuring tone lessened the fears of many Americans during the Great Depression.

WRONG CHOICES EXPLAINED:

(2) The song lyrics do not imply that Roosevelt's support came from his favoring a national suffrage amendment. Such an amendment was not proposed during Roosevelt's time in office. The 15th amendment (1870) prevented states from denying a citizen the right to vote based on that citizen's race. The 19th amendment (1920) extended the right to vote to women. Later, the 26th amendment (1971) mandated that states lower the minimum voting age to 18 years.

(3) The song lyrics do not imply that Roosevelt's support came from his continuation of Herbert Hoover's economic policies. In fact, Roosevelt broke with Hoover's economic approach to the Great Depression. The song lyrics contrast Hoover's lack of action with the activist approach of the New Deal. President Herbert Hoover (1929–1933) encouraged people affected by the Great Depression to rely on their "rugged individualism," believing that direct relief would make people dependent on the government. Roosevelt's approach was to create programs that were designed to benefit unemployed and poor Americans.

(4) The song lyrics do not imply that Roosevelt's support came from a reduction in federal income taxes. In fact, Roosevelt did not reduce federal taxes. Roosevelt pushed for several increases in tax rates in the 1930s. He hoped to increase revenues in order to fund New Deal programs.

34. **4** The cartoon is critical of President Franklin D. Roosevelt's efforts to increase his power over the Supreme Court. In the cartoon, Roosevelt is depicted as putting his hands in several jars; the jars look like jars of jam, but they are labeled with different sectors of the economy and different branches of the government. The implication is that Roosevelt is overstepping his authority, and that he is "never satisfied" in his drive for power. His next target is labeled "Full control of the Supreme Court." The cartoon is alluding to Roosevelt's "court packing" plan. By 1937, Roosevelt had grown increasingly frustrated with the conservative approach of the Supreme Court. It shot down the National Recovery Act in *Schechter* v. *United States* (1935) and the Agricultural Adjustment Act in *Butler* v. *United States* (1936). In 1937, he announced a plan to increase the number of justices on the Supreme Court to as many as fifteen. He said that some of the older justices had difficulty keeping up with the heavy workload. However, it was

clear that the intent of his "court packing" plan was to create a Supreme Court friendlier to his New Deal programs. The Senate rejected Roosevelt's "court packing" plan in 1937 because the plan would have threatened the principle of checks and balances by making the Supreme Court a rubber stamp for New Deal legislation. Soon, however, openings on the Court allowed Roosevelt to appoint new justices and influence the direction of the Court.

WRONG CHOICES EXPLAINED:
(1) The cartoon is not commenting on President Franklin D. Roosevelt's efforts to force Congress to reduce government waste. Roosevelt appears to be wasting jam in the cartoon, but that is meant to serve as a metaphor for his hunger for power. His desire to get his hands in all the jars is meant to symbolize his attempts to gain greater control over the economy and the government.

(2) The cartoon is not commenting on President Franklin D. Roosevelt's efforts to convince the Supreme Court to pass a constitutional amendment to balance the budget. In fact, the idea of an amendment to balance the budget was not proposed in the 1930s. If it had, Roosevelt would have opposed it. New Deal programs contributed to a deficit in the federal budget, not to a balanced budget. Roosevelt was influenced by the thinking of the economist John Maynard Keynes. Keynes argued that deficit spending by the government was acceptable, and even desirable, as a means of increasing overall demand and stimulating economic activity. Later, Republicans put forth the idea of a balanced budget amendment in the 1980s.

(3) The cartoon is not commenting on President Franklin D. Roosevelt's efforts to reverse the effects of the Great Depression. The cartoon is not depicting the enactment of New Deal programs, which were designed to provide economic relief for individuals, help the economy recover, and reform basic sectors of the economy so that future economic downturns would not be so severe. Rather, the jars in the cartoon represent different sectors of the economy and different branches of government that Roosevelt is attempting to gain control over.

35. **4** The poster indicates that rationing during World War II was a program that applied equally to all Americans. In the first frame of the cartoon, labeled "Without Rationing," a wealthy woman buys a large amount of meat from the butcher, while there is nothing left for the next customer, apparently of more modest means, to purchase. During World War II, a wide variety of goods were diverted to military use—from steel and oil to food products. Consequently, fewer products were available for domestic consumption. The Office of Price Adjustment set up a rationing system in which people could obtain goods needed by the

military only if they had rationing coupons. These goods included butter, meat, shoes, and sugar. The system was designed not only to conserve materials for the military, but also to keep inflation down. During times of war, inflation is a constant threat due to the lack of consumer goods and the additional money that people have in their pockets from all the work available in defense-related industries. Government efforts to control inflation were moderately successful; inflation was about half as much as it was during World War I.

WRONG CHOICES EXPLAINED:

(1) The poster does not indicate that rationing during World War II was a policy to encourage small business owners. Rationing programs applied to large businesses as well as small businesses.

(2) The poster does not indicate that rationing during World War II was a way of assuring that only the wealthy could buy certain products. The poster asserts the opposite—that rationing would be applied equally to all Americans.

(3) The poster does not indicate that rationing during World War II was caused by farm failures during the Great Depression. The poster makes no reference to the causes of shortages during World War II. Most Americans realized that the war effort required a great amount of material goods and that less would be available for civilian use. While it is true that many farms failed during the Great Depression, one of the key problems facing the agricultural sector in the 1920s and 1930s was overproduction and low prices—not underproduction and shortages.

36. **1** A major reason for wartime rationing was ensuring that troops were adequately supplied. During World War II, there were shortages of key items because of the needs of the military. Nearly 18 million men and women served in the United States military during the war. Starting in 1942, the Office of Price Administration began rationing key commodities to civilians, such as gasoline and tires. Next, the government began rationing food—sugar, meat, coffee, lard, butter, and many other items. Families were given ration books and would use ration stamps, along with cash, when they purchased the affected items. In many ways, World War II required the participation of the entire American public, not simply members of the military. These efforts created a sense of unity and common cause in the country.

WRONG CHOICES EXPLAINED:

(2) Restricting lower-priced food imports was not a reason for food rationing during World War II. There were no restrictions imposed on imports during the war, but trade did decline due to the fighting of World War II. Enemy ships routinely sunk merchant ships, making trade difficult.

(3) Providing jobs for the unemployed was not a reason for food rationing during World War II. Unemployment virtually disappeared as the United States began producing armaments for World War II.

(4) Preventing currency deflation was not a reason for food rationing during World War II. The opposite was true. During times of war, inflation often occurs due to the scarcity of consumer items as well as an increase in incomes for workers. Rationing was instituted, in part, to reduce the threat of inflation.

37. **1** The most appropriate heading for the partial outline would be "Issues of Morality during World War II." All the items in the outline refer to controversies during World War II in which Americans took different positions based on their sense of morality. "Treatment of Japanese Americans" (item A) refers the effects of Executive Order 9066 (1942) issued by President Franklin D. Roosevelt during World War II. The order authorized the government to remove 120,000 Japanese Americans, two-thirds of them citizens, from West Coast states and relocate them to camps throughout the West. Most of their property was confiscated by the government. In the case of *Korematsu* v. *United States* (1944), the Supreme Court ruled that the relocation was acceptable on the grounds of national security. "Segregation of African Americans in the armed forces" (item B) refers to the continued practice of maintaining separate units in the military based on race. Despite this, during World War II, African Americans participated in the war effort in unprecedented numbers. Ultimately, around one million African Americans served overseas during World War II. The most famous segregated African-American units were the Tuskegee Airmen and the 761st Tank Battalion. African-American effectiveness on the battlefield encouraged President Truman to later (1948) desegregate the armed services with Executive Order 9981, although he failed to implement it until the Korean War, when the military needed additional personnel. "United States reactions to the Nazi Holocaust" (item C) refers to long debate over whether the United States could have done more to prevent the Holocaust. The Holocaust was the systematic murder of six million European Jews and other "undesirables" by the Nazis. Many have criticized President Roosevelt for refusing to let nearly one thousand Jewish refugees disembark from the German ocean liner *St. Louis* on the eve of World War II. These refugees eventually had to go back to Europe, where most of them died in the Holocaust. Some historians have argued that American planes could have destroyed some of the death camps, such as Auschwitz. The politics, ethics, effectiveness, and logistics of such actions are still being debated. "The Use of the Atomic Bomb" (item D) refers to debates around the decision by the United States to drop the atomic bomb on the Japanese cities of Hiroshima and Nagasaki at the end of World War II in 1945. At the time, the decision to drop the atomic

bomb did not generate much public debate. However, in the decades since the war, some Americans have raised questions about the decision. Critics argue that it was morally wrong for the United States to have targeted civilian populations and that the Japanese were ready to surrender anyway. Many stand by the decision to drop the bomb. The atomic bombing swiftly ended a bloody conflict that consumed 50 million lives. It is not clear that the Japanese were on the verge of surrendering. Some members of the Japanese military argued against surrendering even after the second bomb dropped.

WRONG CHOICES EXPLAINED:

(2) "Domestic policies during World War II" would not be an appropriate heading for the partial outline in the question. Although the first item in the outline, "Treatment of Japanese Americans," would be considered a domestic policy, the others are more clearly military and foreign policy issues. Other domestic policies during World War II include the enactment of wartime rationing, the enforcement of price controls on certain items, and the recruitment of women to work in the defense industry.

(3) "Economic Problems during World War II" would not be an appropriate heading for the partial outline in the question. An outline with that heading might include items such as shortages of certain consumer items and increases in income taxes. Overall, however, World War II proved to provide a boost to the American economy. It was World War II, rather than the New Deal, that ended the Great Depression. Unemployment fell from over 14 percent in 1940 to less than two percent for the last three years of the war—1943 to 1945.

(4) "Reasons for the Success of the Allies during World War II" would not be an appropriate heading for the partial outline in the question. An outline with that heading might include items such as planning and coordination among the "big three" (President Roosevelt, Prime Minister Winston Churchill of the United Kingdom, and Soviet leader Joseph Stalin) and successful mobilization of troops and materials.

38. **3** The best title for the graph for the years 1946 to 1964 is "The Baby Boom Generation." The spike in birthrates from 1946 through the early 1960s produced a baby boom that would have lasting repercussions in American society. The baby boom required states to spend more money on constructing and operating new schools in the 1950s and 1960s. In addition, these young families needed housing. The baby boom contributed to the growth of suburban communities outside of major cities in the 1950s and 1960s. The federal government's Servicemen's Readjustment Act (1944), more commonly known as the GI Bill, provided low interest loans for veterans to purchase homes. Developers often bought large

tracts of land to build hundreds of houses. To save time and money, these developments included many houses that had identical plans. The most famous suburban developer was William Levitt. Levittown, on Long Island, New York, became synonymous with these mass-produced communities.

WRONG CHOICES EXPLAINED:

(1) "The Graying of America" would not be an appropriate title for the graph in the question. A graph with that title would show an increase in the number of people getting to retirement age. This phenomenon is occurring today as the percentage of Americans over the age of sixty-five grows. One reason for the growing percentage of senior citizens is the large number of "baby boomers," born in the period after World War II, reaching retirement age. When such a large percentage of the American public is retired, many people worry that programs extending benefits to the elderly, notably Medicare and Social Security, will be unable to stay financially solvent.

(2) "The Growth of the Middle Class" would not be an appropriate title for the graph in the question. A graph with that title would indicate percentages of Americans at different income levels over time. There was, in fact, a growth in the middle class during the years 1946 to 1964, but this is not indicated in the graph. A number of factors contributed to the rise of the middle class after World War II. The GI Bill (1944), formally known as the Servicemen's Readjustment Act, provided low interest loans for veterans to purchase homes as well as funds for college. The intent of the GI Bill was to help the veterans of World War II adjust to life during peacetime. The program was very successful. It helped millions of veterans advance economically. A college education and home ownership are key components of entrance into the middle class.

(4) "From Suburbs to Cities" would not be an appropriate title for the graph in the question. A graph with that title would indicate the change over time in percentages of Americans living in suburbs and living in cities. Such a graph for the years 1946 to 1964, however, would indicate the opposite trend. Many families left cities and moved to suburbs. Suburbs were built outside of major cities in the years after World War II. Huge numbers of veterans returned from war, quickly married, had children—collectively known as the "baby boom" generation—and looked for affordable housing. The federal government's Servicemen's Readjustment Act (1944), more commonly known as the GI Bill, provided low interest loans for veterans to purchase homes.

39. **2** The immediate cause of the action taken by the United States that is shown in the map was the building of nuclear missile launch sites within range of the United States by the Soviet Union. The action by the United States depicted

in the map was a blockading of Soviet ships, a key move in the Cuban Missile Crisis (1962). The crisis began when an American U-2 spy plane discovered that Cuba was preparing bases for Soviet nuclear missiles to be installed. President Kennedy felt that these missiles, in such close proximity to the United States, amounted to an unacceptable provocation and ordered Soviet Premier Nikita Khrushchev to halt the operation and dismantle the bases. Khrushchev insisted on the right of the Soviet Union to install the missiles. For about a week, the world stood on the brink of nuclear war.

WRONG CHOICES EXPLAINED:

(1) The immediate cause of the Cuban Missile Crisis, which is the subject of the map in the question, was not Cuban refugees lobbying President Dwight Eisenhower to overthrow Fidel Castro. Such lobbying did occur earlier and led to Eisenhower giving the green light to the Bay of Pigs invasion. The administration of President John F. Kennedy implemented the plan to overthrow the Communist government of Castro in 1961. Over one thousand Cubans landed at the Bay of Pigs, but their invasion failed after three days. Though the invasion failed, it heightened Cold War tensions between the United States and the Soviet Union.

(3) The immediate cause of the Cuban Missile Crisis, which is the subject of the map in the question, was not Cuban armed forces closing down United States military bases in the Caribbean. The strength of the Cuban military was dwarfed by the firepower of the United States military. Cuba did not contemplate attempting to close down American bases, nor would such an attempt have been successful. An American naval base, at Guantanamo Bay, was established in Cuba in 1903, and continued to operate after the Cuban Revolution of 1959. It is still in operation despite protests by the Cuban government, which insists that the lease agreement for the base was forced upon Cuba.

(4) The immediate cause of the Cuban Missile Crisis, which is the subject of the map in the question, was not Puerto Rican citizens asking Congress to assist them in repelling Communist advances. Puerto Rico is outside of the blockade area indicated on the map. There was never an attempt by outside Communist forces to "advance" upon Puerto Rico. There is a pro-independence Communist Party within Puerto Rico, but it has a small following.

40. **1** One positive outcome of the situation shown on the map was that the United States and Soviet Union increased communications between the two nations to avoid war. After an American U-2 spy plane discovered that Cuba was preparing bases for Soviet nuclear missiles to be installed, on an island in close proximity to the United States, President John F. Kennedy took several different

actions. Publicly, he ordered a naval blockade of Cuba to prevent Soviet ships from landing at Cuba. Behind the scenes, American and Soviet officials began intense negotiations to avoid World War III. The United States began with the position that the Soviet Union must halt the operation of installing missiles in Cuba and dismantle the bases. Khrushchev insisted on the right of the Soviet Union to install the missiles. Finally, a deal was reached to diffuse the Cuban Missile Crisis. The Soviet Union agreed to abandon its Cuban missile program, and the United States agreed to not invade Cuba without provocation. The United States also quietly agreed to remove missiles from Turkey, which the Soviets argued were as close to the Soviet Union as missiles in Cuba would be to the United States.

WRONG CHOICES EXPLAINED:
(2) An outcome of the Cuban Missile Crisis, which is the subject of the map, was not increased military control by the United States and the Soviet Union over their Latin American colonies. One outcome of the crisis was that the United States agreed to recognize the autonomy of Cuba. The crisis did not lead to any other military engagements in the Americas.

(3) An outcome of the Cuban Missile Crisis, which is the subject of the map, was not cooperative humanitarian efforts in Caribbean nations suffering from natural disasters. There have been cooperative humanitarian efforts to aid Caribbean nations suffering from disasters, but these are unrelated to the Cuban Missile Crisis. Many nations, including the United States, aided Haiti in the aftermath of a powerful earthquake in 2010 that left at least 100,000 people dead. This incident occurred almost two decades after the collapse of the Soviet Union.

(4) An outcome of the Cuban Missile Crisis, which is the subject of the map, was not joint efforts to the end the cruel practices of Cuba's leaders. United States leaders repeatedly called attention to human rights abuses by the Cuban government and organized an embargo against Cuba. However, the Soviet Union denied that such abuses took place, and fully supported the Cuban government from soon after the 1959 Cuban revolution until the collapse of the Soviet Union in 1991.

41. **4** The main reason President John F. Kennedy proposed the establishment of the Peace Corps was to improve conditions in developing nations. In his Inaugural Address in 1961, he implored Americans to be more public-minded and generous with their time and resources—to ask themselves what they could do for their country and for the cause of freedom throughout the world. Toward this end, Kennedy pushed for the creation of the Peace Corps (1961) in order to give support to developing nations in fields such as education, agriculture, and health

care. The program depends on volunteers, often recent college graduates, to work on development projects in poor countries. The Peace Corps reflected a sense of optimism that many saw in the Kennedy administration and in the era of the 1960s. It was also an attempt by the United States, in the midst of a Cold War with the Soviet Union, to shed negative perceptions of its role in foreign countries. The Peace Corps still exists.

WRONG CHOICES EXPLAINED:

(1) President John F. Kennedy's goal in proposing the establishment of the Peace Corps was not to promote trade with Asia. The Peace Corps promotes projects that help communities move to greater self-sufficiency, not greater reliance on goods from the United States.

(2) President John F. Kennedy's goal in proposing the establishment of the Peace Corps was not to combat drug use in American cities. Over the years, officials from all levels of government have taken steps to reduce drug use in American cities, from punitive measures based on strict enforcement of drug possession and dealing laws to expanding the scope of treatment centers for drug addicts. However, these efforts are unrelated to the Peace Corps, which is focused on development projects in other countries.

(3) President John F. Kennedy's goal in proposing the establishment of the Peace Corps was not to gain support from immigrant voters. Immigrant voters are not homogeneous in their voting patterns. Some might support initiatives such as the Peace Corps; others might support programs aimed at helping urban communities in the United States.

42. **2** An outcome of the Watergate affair during the administration of President Richard Nixon was that respect for the office of the president declined. The Watergate affair was one of the most serious presidential scandals in American history. The scandal began in June 1972, when five men were caught breaking into the headquarters of the Democratic Party at the Watergate Hotel in Washington, D.C. Persistent reporting by Carl Bernstein and Bob Woodward of the *Washington Post* drew connections between the burglars and Nixon's reelection committee and ultimately the White House. When it became known that Nixon taped conversations in the White House Oval Office, investigators demanded that the tapes be turned over. Nixon argued that executive privilege allowed him to keep the tapes. In *United States* v. *Nixon* (1974), the Supreme Court ordered Nixon to turn over the tapes. Nixon told a press conference in November 1973, "I am not a crook." However, less than a month after the Supreme Court decision in 1974, Nixon resigned. The scandal damaged people's respect for the presidency and led to an erosion in trust of the government.

WRONG CHOICES EXPLAINED:

(1) The Watergate affair during the administration of President Richard Nixon did not lead to an expansion of presidential power. After the scandal began, Congress took action in regard to the president's war-making powers that reduced presidential power. In 1973, it passed the War Powers Act (1973) over President Nixon's veto. The act was passed after the United States had withdrawn from Vietnam. Many congressmen thought the president had abused his power to deploy troops during the Vietnam War. The War Powers Act was an attempt to check presidential power and strengthen the legislative branch in matters of war.

(3) The Watergate affair during the administration of President Richard Nixon did not lead to the Supreme Court clearing President Nixon of charges. In a key case related to the Watergate affair, the Court ruled against Nixon. In *United States* v. *Nixon* (1974), the Supreme Court ordered Nixon to turn over secret tapes that he had made of White House conversations. Less than a month after the Supreme Court decision, Nixon resigned.

(4) The Watergate affair during the administration of President Richard Nixon did not lead Congress to refuse to take action against President Nixon. The opposite occurred. In 1974, the House Judiciary Committee voted in favor of articles of impeachment against President Nixon. Before the question of impeachment could be addressed by the entire House of Representatives, Nixon resigned.

43. **3** The goal of the War Powers Act of 1973 was to limit the president's power to use military force without congressional approval. The act was passed, over President Richard Nixon's veto, soon after the United States withdrew from Vietnam. Many congressmen thought the president had abused his power to deploy troops during the Vietnam War. While it is Congress that has the power to declare war and to allocate money for military actions, presidents have frequently taken military actions unilaterally. It is understandable that presidents would take actions on their own. An attack on the United States would very likely require an immediate and decisive response; there would not be time to wait for Congress to convene and to debate the proper response to such a crisis. However, on different occasions, critics have accused presidents of abusing their power and taking military actions in an arbitrary and misguided manner. The War Powers Act was an attempt to check presidential power and strengthen the legislative branch in matters of war. The act requires the president to report any troop deployments to Congress within 48 hours and thus give Congress the ability to force the withdrawal of U.S. troops after 60 days.

WRONG CHOICES EXPLAINED:

(1) The goal of the War Powers Act of 1973 was not to allow the president to declare war without congressional approval. Congress's power to declare war is enshrined in the Constitution. It would take a constitutional amendment, not an act of Congress, to change that.

(2) The goal of the War Powers Act of 1973 was not to give Congress the sole power to authorize the use of military force. While Congress has the power to formally issue a declaration of war, it is a long accepted practice for the president to order military actions. In many situations, an immediate response is called for. The president would not always have sufficient time to wait for Congress to convene and come to a decision about an appropriate response.

(4) The goal of the War Powers Act of 1973 was not to require a declaration of war for all uses of military force. Situations may arise in which an immediate military response is warranted. If an American base is attacked, for example, the president may call for an immediate counterstrike. Subsequently, Congress would have the option of issuing a formal declaration of war. The act limits the president's power to use military force, but it does not take it away.

44. **1** President George H.W. Bush used the statement in the question to defend taking military action to liberate Kuwait from Iraqi aggression. The United States gets a great deal of its oil from the Middle East, and it has sought to maintain alliances and to prevent any Middle Eastern country from assuming a dominant role in the region. President George H.W. Bush, therefore, became alarmed in 1990 when Iraqi leader Saddam Hussein ordered an Iraqi invasion of Kuwait, another oil-rich Middle Eastern country. In the statement, he expresses a desire to end the crisis peacefully, but states that the United States had exhausted peaceful means of removing Iraqi troops from Kuwait. He described Kuwait, in a different statement, as "small and helpless." President Bush carried out his pledge to defend Kuwaiti autonomy. He organized the Persian Gulf War in 1991. The war accomplished its immediate goal of ousting Iraqi forces from Kuwait. Some criticized President Bush for not attempting to oust Hussein. However, when the United States did topple Hussein as part of Operation Iraqi Freedom (2003), Iraq descended into violence and disorder that led to a longtime United States military presence in that country.

WRONG CHOICES EXPLAINED:

(2) President George H.W. Bush's statement was not meant to defend providing foreign aid to Israel. Israel has been one of the top recipients of foreign aid (including military assistance) since its founding in 1948. This has been true

during Democratic as well as Republican presidential administrations. In 2016, the Obama administration pledged over $38 billion in military aid to Israel over the following decade—the biggest deal of its kind in United States history.

(3) President George H.W. Bush's statement was not meant to defend supporting Egypt against terrorist attacks. Egypt has been an important ally of the United States and one of the largest recipients of foreign aid. In 2017, the United States suspended military aid to Egypt over human rights concerns, but released almost $200 million in 2018 in an effort to strengthen bilateral relations and counterterrorism efforts.

(4) President George H.W. Bush's statement was not meant to defend using United States troops as peacekeepers in Bosnia. The United States did become involved in Bosnia later in the 1990s, as ethnic violence developed in Bosnia after the breakup of Yugoslavia. In 1990, Yugoslavia divided into several smaller nations and a brutal war ensued. Serbian forces clashed with Bosnian Muslims. The United States and other countries decided to take action as reports of Serbian brutality became known. President Bill Clinton brought leaders from Bosnia, Serbia, and Croatia together in 1995 in Ohio. A peace treaty was signed and 20,000 NATO troops were dispatched to enforce it.

45. **3** The cartoon suggests that the middle class is disappearing in the United States. Two factors that have contributed to this problem are consumer debt and nearly stagnant wages. The cartoon depicts the middle class as another extinct species—like ancient ammonites (an extinct marine mollusk) or trilobites (an extinct marine arthropod). Future scientists, the cartoonist imagines, would only find evidence of these extinct species by examining fossilized remains. A variety of political and economic factors can help explain the stagnation of wages for many Americans. From the 1960s onward, the United States has experienced the disappearance of higher-paying manufacturing jobs and the growth of low-wage service-sector jobs. Large numbers of factories have closed in northeastern cities such as New York and Philadelphia, as well as in Midwestern Rust Belt cities such as Pittsburgh, Cleveland, Detroit, and Chicago. Many jobs have been outsourced to countries such as India and China with lower wage scales. Another factor in keeping wages down is the decline of the union movement. As wages have stagnated, consumer debt has mushroomed. Banks and credit card companies have lured people into taking on more debt than they could handle. The most vivid example of this occurred in the early 2000s in regard to the housing market. Banks offered adjustable rate mortgages in which initial low rates would later jump to higher rates. These risky loans were referred to as "subprime mortgages" because they were extended to people whose ability to repay and whose credit rating was less than prime. By 2008, almost 30 percent of mortgages were rated

as "subprime." In 2007 and 2008, the housing bubble burst as housing prices plummeted. Many subprime borrowers found themselves "underwater"—that is, the market value of their homes sank below the amount they owed on their mortgages. In many such situations, individuals could neither sell their homes nor afford to pay their monthly mortgage payments. Their only option was to walk away from their homes and default on their loans, leading to widespread foreclosures.

WRONG CHOICES EXPLAINED:
(1) The problem shown in the cartoon—the disappearance of the middle class—was not caused by lower medical costs and high interest rates. Lower medical costs would help the middle class. Variable-rate loans proved to be problematic for many middle-class people, but high interest rates were not, in and of themselves, a major contributing factor in the decline of the middle class.

(2) The problem shown in the cartoon—the disappearance of the middle class—was not caused by business monopolies and the depletion of natural resources. These two developments are more closely associated with economic problems of the late 1800s. As American industry expanded in the post–Civil War era, powerful monopolies came to dominate several industries. During this era, reformers began to take note of the damage done to natural resources by unregulated industrial growth.

(4) The problem shown in the cartoon—the disappearance of the middle class—was not caused by population migration and the graying of America. There have been major shifts in population in recent decades. The population of the old "Rust Belt" states of the upper Midwest has stagnated as the population of the "Sun Belt" states of the South and the West has grown. In addition, the population of the United States is getting older, or "graying," as the baby boom generation has reached retirement age. However, neither of these two developments are direct causes of the disappearance of the middle class.

46. **2** One way in which the goals of the Know-Nothing Party in the 1850s and the response to the Red Scare of 1919 were similar is that both sought to limit immigration into the United States. The Know-Nothing Party emerged in the wake of large-scale immigration from Ireland in the 1840s and 1850s. The collapse of the potato crop in Ireland had devastating effects on the Irish people. It is estimated that a million Irish starved to death between 1845 and 1850, while another million left for America. Many Americans thought that the new immigrants, who were mostly non-Protestant, lacked the self-control of "proper," middle-class Protestant Americans. For nativists, this lack of self-control was evident in the drinking habits of immigrants. It was in this context that the anti-immigrant and

anti-Catholic Know-Nothing Party emerged. The Know-Nothing Party (formally known as the American Party) was born in 1844 and, by the 1850s, had achieved electoral success in several states, especially in the Northeast. In the 20th century, anti-immigrant sentiment again emerged. In the aftermath of World War I, many Americans were swept up in a crusade against suspected communists, anarchists, labor leaders, and other radicals. This Red Scare contributed to a strong anti-immigrant movement in the 1920s. This movement achieved legislative success with the passage of the Emergency Quota Act (1921) and the National Origins Act (1924), which greatly reduced the number of immigrants allowed into the United States.

WRONG CHOICES EXPLAINED:
(1) Neither the goals of the Know-Nothing Party in the 1850s nor the response to the Red Scare of 1919 called for equal rights for women and African Americans. Anti-immigrant movements frequently have racist undertones. Many nativists base their opposition to immigration on a desire to have a racially "pure" country. In addition, there is often an overlap between nativists and those who call for a return to traditional gender roles. Therefore, these movements are not likely to embrace equal rights for African Americans and women.

(3) Neither the goals of the Know-Nothing Party in the 1850s nor the response to the Red Scare of 1919 supported overseas expansion of the United States. The issue of overseas expansion was not yet part of public debates in the 1850s; it became a contentious issue in the 1890s and 1900s in the wake of the Spanish-American War (1898). In the 1920s, there was an overlap between nativists and isolationists. Therefore, these movements are not likely to support overseas expansion.

(4) Neither the goals of the Know-Nothing Party in the 1850s nor the response to the Red Scare of 1919 attempted to limit the influence of big business on American politics. Some nativists espoused anti-big business politics, asserting that corporations were importing cheap labor into the United States. Others were more pro-business, sharing conservative, laissez-faire views about the role of the government in the economy.

47. **1** The term *containment* best describes United States foreign policy during the Cold War. The United States became increasingly concerned about the growing power of the Soviet Union after World War II and put forth a policy of attempting to prevent the expansion of communism, known as containment. President Harry S. Truman articulated this goal, which has come to be known as the Truman Doctrine, in a speech to Congress in 1947. Truman put the idea of

containment into practice in 1947 by providing $400 million in military aid to Greece and Turkey to prevent those countries from becoming communist. Another example of the containment policy was the Berlin Airlift of 1948. In 1948, before the status of Berlin was settled, the Soviet Union decided it would prevent any food or other supplies from entering the western sector of the city. The goal was for the Soviet Union to block the influence of the United States and its western allies from maintaining its presence in Berlin. Ultimately, the Soviet Union hoped to make all of Berlin part of what would become East Germany. The United States did not stand by idly when it learned of the Berlin blockade. Truman decided to send thousands of planes, filled with supplies, into the western sector of Berlin, in an action known as the Berlin Airlift. The Berlin Airlift prevented the western sector of Berlin from starving and prevented the Soviet Union from taking over the city. The formation of the North Atlantic Treaty Organization (NATO) was also part of the Cold War strategy of containment. NATO was created in 1949 by the United States and its allies to challenge the growing power of the Soviet Union. The members of NATO pledged that they would view an attack on any one member as an attack on all members.

WRONG CHOICES EXPLAINED:

(2) The term *nonalignment* does not accurately describe United States foreign policy during the Cold War. The nonaligned countries during the Cold War period (1945–1991) were those nations that did not ally themselves with either the United States or the Soviet Union. These countries formalized their status with the organization of the Non-Aligned Movement in 1956. The nations who initiated the movement were Yugoslavia, India, Indonesia, Egypt, and Ghana.

(3) The term *Big Stick* does not accurately describe United States foreign policy during the Cold War. The Big Stick Policy is associated with the efforts of President Theodore Roosevelt (1901–1909) for the United States to play a more aggressive role in Latin America. His foreign-policy approach is neatly summed up in his famous adage that the United States should "speak softly, but carry a big stick" when dealing with other nations (Roosevelt borrowed the phrase from an African proverb). The "big stick" implied the threat of military force. He asserted that the "civilized nations" had a duty to police the "backward" countries of the world. This assertion of American might is known as the Roosevelt Corollary to the Monroe Doctrine.

(4) The term *Open Door* does not accurately describe United States foreign policy during the Cold War. The Open Door Policy was put forth by the administration of President William McKinley in 1900 in order to open up China to American trade. In the 1890s, the major European powers had established spheres of influence in China. These nations each declared that they had

exclusive trading privileges in their sphere of influence. The United States asserted that all of China should be open to trade with all nations. The European nations begrudgingly accepted this Open Door concept.

48. **2** The examples in the chart illustrate checks and balances. The chart lists, on the left side, particular actions by different branches of government, and on the right side, reactions taken by another branch of government to limit the power of the first branch. The top pair of entries deals with events during the Reconstruction period, following the Civil War. The action taken by President Andrew Johnson was firing his secretary of war Edwin Stanton (1867), in violation of the Tenure of Office Act. Stanton was the government official in charge of carrying out the government's Reconstruction agenda in the South. Congressional Republicans passed the act in order to protect Stanton, their one ally in the Johnson administration. Johnson proceeded to fire Stanton despite the law, setting off the process that led to his impeachment. The lower two entries deal with events during the Great Depression of the 1930s. The National Industrial Recovery Act (1933) was one of many initiatives, collectively known as the New Deal, that were put forth by the administration of President Franklin D. Roosevelt to address the economic crisis of the 1930s. NIRA called for representatives from labor and competing corporations to draw up a set of codes. These codes were designed to shorten hours for workers, guarantee trade union rights, establish minimum wage levels, regulate the price of certain petroleum products, and promote fair business practices. The idea was that cutthroat competition hurt the economy, pushed workers' wages down, and limited their ability to purchase goods. In the *Schechter* v. *United States* decision (1935), the Court shot down NIRA on the grounds that the president had assumed legislative powers in creating NIRA regulations. It was one of several decisions limiting the powers of the executive branch. Both reactions—Congress's impeachment of Johnson and the Supreme Court's striking down of NIRA—are checks that one branch of government made on another branch. The desired end result of such checking is that all three branches will be in balance. The framers of the Constitution were very conscious of the problems of a government with limitless powers. After living under the British monarchy, they came to believe that a powerful government without checks and balances was dangerous to liberty.

WRONG CHOICES EXPLAINED:
(1) The examples in the chart do not illustrate federalism. Federalism refers to the relationship between the state governments and the national government. In the governing system developed in the Constitution, powers are shared by the national government and the state governments. The goal is that excessive power is not concentrated in either level of government.

(3) The examples in the chart do not illustrate states' rights. The concept of states' rights describes the idea that states would retain certain rights even though the national government was supreme. The issue of states' rights became closely identified with the defense of slavery. Defenders of slavery in the South felt that the institution had sufficiently broad support among white Southerners, but they feared that Northern political leaders might use the power of the federal government to limit or abolish slavery. Hence, they firmly embraced the right of states to resist or nullify federal edicts.

(4) The examples in the chart do not illustrate judicial review. Judicial review is the Supreme Court's ability to review laws and determine whether they are consistent with the Constitution. It is not specifically mentioned in the Constitution. It was first exercised by the Supreme Court in the case of *Marbury* v. *Madison* (1803), and has been the main function of the Supreme Court since then.

49. **2** The economic policy that argues that government should limit, as much as possible, any interference in the economy is laissez-faire. The French phrase *laissez-faire* means "to let alone." It describes a government policy that would take a hands-off approach in regard to economic activities. Throughout much of the history of the United States, Americans have been suspicious of government intervention into the economy. The founders of the United States had vivid memories of the overbearing mercantilist policies of Great Britain. With the American economy growing by leaps and bounds in the 19th century, few challenged this doctrine. However, by the 20th century, the country began to face serious economic problems that called into question the laissez-faire doctrine. In the first decades of the 20th century, Progressive reformers called on the government to break up monopolies, regulate the food production industry, help the poor, and create peace between owners and workers. When the Great Depression struck the United States in the 1930s, Franklin D. Roosevelt argued more forcefully that the government must play an activist role. After Roosevelt won the presidential election in 1932, he initiated a sweeping array of programs known as the New Deal. Since the Great Depression, politicians have argued about the nature and degree of government economic intervention in the economy, but few today argue for a complete laissez-faire policy.

WRONG CHOICES EXPLAINED:

(1) Socialism is an economic policy that argues for government ownership of key sectors of the economy. It is the opposite of a laissez-faire approach of nonintervention by the government in the economy.

(3) Mercantilism is an economic policy that argues that the government should play an active role in the economy. A laissez-faire approach, by contrast, argues that the government should play no role in the economy. Mercantilist theory holds that governments should try to increase the wealth of a nation by maintaining colonies so as to have a steady and inexpensive source of raw materials. The theory guided Great Britain in maintaining its American colonies before the American Revolution.

(4) Protectionism is an economic policy that argues that the government should impose tariffs on goods imported into the United States. These tariffs would raise the prices of foreign-made goods and would make American goods comparatively more affordable. The tariffs would, in theory, protect American industry from foreign competition. Protectionism involves government intervention in the economy; laissez-faire implies no government intervention in the economy.

50. **3** W. E. B. Du Bois, Jackie Robinson, and James Meredith are considered pioneers in the area of civil rights. W. E. B. Du Bois was a militant civil rights activist who wrote about the injustices carried out against African Americans in the South. He was one of the founders of the National Association for the Advancement of Colored People (NAACP) in 1909. Du Bois's call for full political equality and civil rights for African Americans was in marked contrast to the more conciliatory approach of Booker T. Washington. Jackie Robinson was the first African American to play major league baseball in the modern era. He began his career with the Brooklyn Dodgers in 1947. Robinson met a great deal of racist anger during his first year in major league baseball. Players on the St. Louis Cardinals threatened to go on strike if Robinson took the field for the Dodgers. In the 1950s, Robinson publicly supported the civil rights movement and urged President Dwight D. Eisenhower to take action to resolve the crisis around the desegregation of public schools in Little Rock, Arkansas, in 1957. James Meredith was the first African American to be admitted to the University of Mississippi in 1962. His admission was met with violent opposition. Riots in the town of Oxford, Mississippi, resulted in the death of two people. All three individuals contributed to the ongoing struggle for civil rights in the United States. The high point for the civil rights movement occurred in the 1950s and 1960s. The civil rights movement gained strength after the Supreme Court, in the case of *Brown* v. *Board of Education of Topeka* (1954), declared that segregation in schools had no place in America. In the years following the *Brown* decision, we see the Montgomery bus boycott in 1955 and 1956, the lunch counter sit-ins in 1960, the Freedom Rides in 1962, and a whole host of other activities. It was in this context that the movement achieved significant victories. The Civil Rights Act of 1964 banned segregation in public facilities and the Voting Rights Act of 1965 removed barriers to African Americans voting.

WRONG CHOICES EXPLAINED:

(1) Neither W. E. B. Du Bois, Jackie Robinson, nor James Meredith are considered pioneers in the area of labor relations. Important figures in the labor movement include Samuel Gompers, one of the founders and the first leader of the American Federation of Labor (AFL) in 1886; Eugene V. Debs, a founder of the American Railway Union (ARU) in 1893 and leader of the Pullman strike of 1894; and John L. Lewis, one of the founders of the Committee for Industrial Organizations (1935) within the AFL.

(2) Neither W. E. B. Du Bois, Jackie Robinson, nor James Meredith are considered pioneers in the area of educational reform. Important figures in the field of educational reform include Horace Mann, who campaigned for free public education from the 1830s to the 1850s and served as a member of the House of Representatives as a Whig (1848–1853), and John Dewey, who critiqued the focus on rote learning rather than critical engagement with the world around the student and founded the experimental Laboratory Schools in Chicago in 1896.

(4) Neither W. E. B. Du Bois, Jackie Robinson, nor James Meredith are considered pioneers in the area of environmental protection. Important figures in the field of environmental protection include John Muir, the preservationist and founder of the Sierra Club (1892), and Rachel Carson, the author of the ground-breaking book, *Silent Spring*, which vividly described the impact of the agricultural chemical DDT on the environment and how modern society was poisoning the Earth.

PART II: THEMATIC ESSAY

Westward Movement of the Frontier

The frontier was, in the 19th century, the unofficial boundary line between settled and unsettled lands. The frontier line shifted farther and farther west as more and more of the United States became settled. The 19th century historian Frederick Jackson Turner argued, in 1893, that the existence of this frontier had been a positive factor in the development of the American character. The experience of living in a frontier situation instilled in the settlers—and their descendants—a sense of egalitarianism, individualism, and freedom. These values, Turner argued, helped create an American identity separate from the more aristocratic and rigid European culture. There are several events in United States history that propelled this westward movement of people. Two significant events were the signing of the Treaty of Paris (1783), ending the American Revolution, and the discovery of gold in California (1848), setting off a frantic Gold Rush. Both of these events had positive and negative effects, both for American settlers and for American Indians.

The Treaty of Paris (1783) opened up the land beyond the Appalachian Mountains to settlement by Americans. Following the American Revolution, thousands of settlers pushed beyond the Appalachian Mountains into the lands along the Ohio River Valley. This was land that the British had tried to close to settlement following the French and Indian War. Great Britain had put forth the Proclamation Act (1763) in an attempt to halt colonists who wanted to settle beyond the mountain range and to prevent future clashes between the colonists and American Indians. With the Treaty of Paris, Great Britain acknowledged the independence of the United States and accepted as its western boundary the Mississippi River, not the Appalachian Mountains. The entire area between the Appalachians and the Mississippi was now under the control of the newly independent United States. No provisions in the treaty recognized the sovereignty of the American Indian nations that lived there and that had been recognized by the British. Of course, the American Indians of this region had not been consulted.

The movement of Americans beyond the Appalachian Mountains following the Treaty of Paris had many positive effects for Americans. Farming thrived in the flat, fertile soil of the Ohio River Valley. The Ohio River and the Mississippi River became busy conduits for trade. The government passed the Harrison Land Law, facilitating the sale of smaller plots of land to settlers. Soon, settlers established the Ohio Territory, and then the Indiana Territory. The opening of this region prompted a series of internal improvements in the early 1800s, including new roads, such as the National Road (also known as the Cumberland Road) from Maryland into the Ohio River Valley, and new canals, most notably the Erie Canal, from the Hudson River in upstate New York to the Great Lakes.

As more Americans began to migrate into the interior of the continent, beyond the Appalachian Mountains, conflicts inevitably ensued with American Indians, especially those in the more northern part of the region—between the Ohio River and the Great Lakes. The government tried to solve the problem by working out the Treaty of Fort Stanwix in 1784. In the treaty, American Indians ceded much of the land in question to the United States. However, this treaty was negotiated with members of the Iroquois Confederacy—a group of American Indian nations that did not, for the most part, occupy the land in question, and whose claims to the land were dubious at best. The main occupants of the region, the Shawnee, the Delaware, and the Miami, were not part of these negotiations and protested bitterly that their land had been ceded without their consent. Subsequently, a series of military conflicts ensued in the 1790s in the region. American troops led by General Arthur St. Clair suffered a massive defeat at the mouth of the Wabash River in 1791. Later, at the Battle of Fallen Timbers (1794), American Indians were soundly defeated by superior American firepower. In the following year, 1795, American Indians gave up claim to most of Ohio in the Treaty of Greenville. The treaty brought only a temporary peace. Within a generation, settlers would push farther into the Ohio and Indiana territories; these incursions would soon create additional conflicts that would not be resolved until the War of 1812.

Later in the 19th century, another historical development—the discovery of gold in California in 1848—led to additional opportunities for Americans and additional conflicts with American Indians. The discovery, and the subsequent Gold Rush, took place within the context of the United States pursuing its "manifest destiny" of expansion across the continent to the Pacific Ocean. This vision of continental domination became a reality with the victory of the United States in the Mexican-American War. Americans had been settling in the Mexican territory of Texas as far back as the 1820s. In 1836, Texans fought for and won independence from Mexico. Texas finally joined the United States as the fifteenth slave state in 1845. Conflict between the United States and Mexico soon ensued. The two countries disagreed over the southern border of Texas. It was at this point, in 1846, that President James K. Polk sent troops into this disputed territory. Skirmishes in the disputed area led to war between Mexico and the United States. The United States won the war, which lasted from 1846 to 1848, and acquired the huge territory that comprised the northern provinces of Mexico, which is known as the Mexican Cession.

An astounding discovery was made in the Mexican Cession territory, just about a week before the Treaty of Guadalupe Hidalgo between the United States and Mexico was signed—gold was found in California at Sutter's Mill in Coloma in January 1848. In March, a month after the United States formally acquired California, word spread far and wide about the existence of gold there. On the positive side, California was quickly settled with thousands of newcomers. A large percentage of the 300,000 people who migrated to California came in 1849—thus their nickname "forty-niners." The Gold Rush drew immigrants from all over—from eastern cities, from Canada, from Europe, from Latin America, and from China. By 1852, 20,000 Chinese immigrants had moved to the United States; by 1860, over 34,000 lived in California alone. California quickly became a thriving, multi-ethnic territory. Most migrants to California did not strike it rich in gold mining, but many thrived by farming in the region's lush valleys. Boomtowns and eventually cities sprouted up, providing additional opportunities for men and women to earn a living.

On the negative side, the rapid settlement of California following the Gold Rush intensified sectional tensions in the United States and pushed the nation closer to civil war. By 1850, California had enough people to form a state. Californians wrote up a constitution to submit to Congress in which slavery would be illegal. Southern senators objected to the admission of an additional free state. Senate negotiators, led by the aging Henry Clay, worked out a series of measures to resolve this extremely contentious problem. These measures became known as the Compromise of 1850. The most important elements of the compromise were the admittance of California as a free state, which pleased Northern politicians, and a more stringent Fugitive Slave Law, which pleased Southern politicians. Ultimately, the Senate "unbundled" the elements of the compromise, so that they were voted on individually. The measures all passed and were signed into law. Many Northerners grew alarmed at the enforcement of the Fugitive Slave Law. Previously, the majority of Northerners could ignore the brutality of the slave system, but following 1850, slave catchers brought the system to the streets of Northern cities. In response, many Northern states passed "personal liberty laws" offering protection to fugitives. Many whites and free African Americans in Northern cities even formed vigilance committees to prevent the slave catchers from carrying out their orders.

Meanwhile, the rapid settlement of California had a devastating impact on American Indians who lived there. Prospectors saw American Indians as impediments to their search for gold, leading to massacres, enslavement, and removal. It is estimated that the Indian population of California dropped from about 150,000 in 1848, on the eve of the Gold Rush, to less than 30,000 by 1860. Disease took the lives of thousands of Indians, but systematic campaigns of extermination by white settlers against the native peoples of California contributed to what many historians label a genocide. White Californians organized paramilitary death squads, with the support of the state government, to kill American Indians. A brutal massacre occurred at Bridge Gulch in 1852, when a group of settlers attacked a band of Wintu Indians in response to the killing of a white settler. The state's first governor, Peter Burnett, saw the massacre of Indians as regrettable but inevitable. In addition, many farmers were eager to exploit the labor of Indians. When the framers of the California constitution prohibited slavery, they had African American slavery in mind, not Indian slavery. Farmers frequently pressed Indians into forced agricultural work. By the 1860s, several Indian groups simply ceased to exist, with their people either killed or dispersed.

The pushing of the frontier farther, and the opening up of new lands to settlement, has profoundly affected the United States. On the one hand, it has provided space for Americans to acquire land, to start over again, and to carve new lives and new communities out of a rugged frontier. On the other hand, the settlement of the West created conflict and suffering. The opening up of new lands intensified sectional conflicts over slavery and contributed to the onset of the Civil War. In addition, the movement of settlers to the West decimated American Indians who were in the path of settlement.

PART III: DOCUMENT-BASED QUESTION

Part A: Short Answer

Document 1a and Document 1b

1 Based on the documents, one form of discrimination that African Americans experienced in the 1960s was segregation in regard to education, housing, and job opportunities.

This answer receives full credit because it states one form of discrimination that African Americans experienced in the 1960s.

Document 2

2 According to Adam Fairclough, one effect of the 1963 demonstrations in Birmingham, Alabama, was that they inspired African Americans in other communities to take action because they saw that if segregation could be successfully challenged in Birmingham, then it was vulnerable throughout the South.

This answer receives full credit because it states one effect of the 1963 demonstrations in Birmingham, Alabama.

Document 3

3a According to President Lyndon B. Johnson, one achievement of the civil rights movement was that it pressured the federal government to pass the Civil Rights Act of 1964.

This answer receives full credit because it states one achievement of the civil rights movement.

3b According to President Lyndon B. Johnson, one remaining goal of the civil rights movement was expanding opportunities so that all Americans can live full and meaningful lives.

This answer receives full credit because it states one remaining goal of the civil rights movement.

Document 4

4(1) According to Toby Goldstein, one reason for the development of the anti–Vietnam War movement was the ever-increasing body count of the war, as more and more American families had to deal with loved ones dying in the war. Another reason for the development of the anti–Vietnam War movement, according to Toby Goldstein, was the dishonest assessment of the war by President Lyndon B. Johnson, who asserted that America could see "light at the end of the tunnel," when in actuality the situation in Vietnam was becoming increasingly grim for American forces.

This answer receives full credit because it states two reasons for the development of the anti–Vietnam War movement.

Document 5

5 According to Nancy Zaroulis and Gerald Sullivan, one reason for protest against the Vietnam War was that many Americans perceived the war to be unconstitutional and illegal because it was an undeclared war.

This answer receives full credit because it states one reason for protest against the Vietnam War.

Document 6

6a According to George C. Herring, one way the anti–Vietnam War movement was not successful was that it did not actually turn large segments of Americans against the war; many Americans became more resentful of the anti-war movement than of the war itself.

This answer receives full credit because it states one way the anti–Vietnam War movement was not successful.

6b According to George C. Herring, one way the anti–Vietnam War movement was successful was that it forced the Johnson administration to act in a more constrained manner and may have prevented Johnson from taking more extreme actions in Vietnam and elsewhere.

This answer receives full credit because it states one way the anti–Vietnam War movement was successful.

Document 7

7 According to Rachel Carson, one issue that has led to concerns about the environment has been the increased exposure to synthetic chemicals that virtually every human being has been subjected to.

This answer receives full credit because it states one issue that has led to concerns about the environment.

Document 8a and Document 8b

8 Based on the documents, one reason the observance of Earth Day is important to the environmental movement is that Earth Day demonstrations captured the attention of millions of ordinary Americans who heard about them in the media or saw the numerous demonstrations in person.

This answer receives full credit because it states one reason the observance of Earth Day is important to the environmental movement.

Document 9a

9a According to Nelson Lemann, one impact of Earth Day is that several key environmental laws were passed, including the Clean Air Act of 1970, the Clean Water Act of 1972, and Endangered Species Act of 1973.

This answer receives full credit because it states one impact of Earth Day.

Document 9b

9b According to Frances Beinecke, one reason the environmental movement continues to be important is that Americans need to be constantly pushed to take immediate action to reduce the causes of climate change before the Earth reaches a tipping point of sustainability.

This answer receives full credit because it states one reason the environmental movement continues to be important.

Part B: Document-Based Essay

In France, during a period of tumultuous protests against the government in 1968, someone wrote on a wall, "Be realistic, demand the impossible." In the decades following World War II, many individuals and groups in America have done just that—they have taken action to change situations that seemed impossible to change. Starting with individuals and small groups, substantial protest movements developed that led to momentous change. Though protest movements didn't accomplish everything they set out to accomplish, they have been remarkable in reforming the United States. One movement for change is the civil rights movement, which challenged systematic racial discrimination and the social assumptions that buttressed that system. Another is the environmental movement, which raised awareness around threats to the planet's ecological balance and today continues to push America to take action on the issue of climate change.

The civil rights movement developed in the context of systematic discrimination, known as the Jim Crow system. After the Civil War, Southern whites created a system of separate facilities for African Americans and white people. Public accommodations—waiting rooms at train stations, water fountains, lunch counters, public schools—had restrictions on African Americans, who either were outright banned or were relegated to separate sections. (Document 1a) African Americans were made to sit toward the back of busses and had to give up their seats as more white passengers boarded. In addition, African Americans were effectively excluded from the political process by a series of carefully tailored voting laws that excluded African Americans without outright stating that African Americans could not vote. (Document 1b) These measures including poll taxes, literacy tests, and grandfather clauses. Without the ability to vote, there was no formal way for African Americans to change the Jim Crow system. This system was the public manifestation of white supremacy—a daily reminder of the second-class status that African Americans were kept in.

The more immediate context of the civil rights movement was World War II. After the war, many African Americans felt a sense of empowerment after having served in the armed forces and were ready to fight for democracy at home. Many veterans had participated in the "Double V" campaign during the war; they wore buttons promoting victory against fascism abroad and victory against racism at home. These veterans, mostly men, as well as organizations of African American women, became increasingly vocal in the late 1940s and early 1950s. Their activism pushed President Harry Truman to integrate the armed forces in 1948 and pushed the Supreme Court, in *Brown* v. *Board of Education* (1954), to abolish "whites only" schools and to order the creation of integrated public schools. Still, the Jim Crow system existed in everyday life for millions of African Americans in the South.

In community after community in the South, African Americans challenged the Jim Crow system. In 1963 activists picked a difficult target—Birmingham, Alabama, a conservative city in the deep South with an entrenched system of segregation. (Document 2) The public safety commissioner of Birmingham, Eugene "Bull" Connor, would not tolerate public demonstrations. He used fire hoses, police dogs, and brutal force to put down the campaign. During the Birmingham campaign, Dr. Martin Luther King Jr. was arrested and wrote his famous "Letter from Birmingham Jail." Connor might not have realized it at the time, but by taking extreme measures against the civil rights movement, he actually helped it. Even if Americans were not so concerned about segregation in the South before, images of police brutality in the media conveyed to Americans that the movement was justified and the authorities were unjust. After several weeks, authorities in Birmingham sat down with activists and negotiated a transition away from the Jim Crow system. Activists throughout the South were heartened; if segregation could be successfully challenged in Birmingham, then it could be brought down anywhere. The actions "exposed the vulnerability" of the entire Jim Crow system, according to historian Adam Fairclough. In the aftermath of the Birmingham campaign, the movement targeted 115 communities with 930 actions. By the end of 1963, over 300 cities agreed to some degree of integration. (Document 2)

The Birmingham campaign and the actions following it in 1963 proved to be a turning point in regard to federal civil rights legislation. In June 1963, the same month that civil rights leader Medgar Evers was murdered in front of his house in Jackson, Mississippi, President John F. Kennedy made a national address in which he called civil rights a "moral issue" and pledged to support civil rights legislation. After Kennedy's assassination in November 1963, President Lyndon Johnson took up the cause of civil rights legislation with vigor, pressuring reluctant Democrats to support the cause. As Johnson said, "the voice of the Negro was the call to action." (Document 3) His efforts helped ensure passage of the 1964 Civil Rights Act, which guaranteed equal access for all Americans to public accommodations. Another section banned discrimination in employment based on race or sex. The following year, Johnson, with equal vigor, pushed for passage of the Voting Rights Act, which outlawed many of the practices that Southern states used to prevent African Americans from voting. It also gave the Justice Department the power to review any new changes to voting rules in Southern states. (Document 3)

Passage of the Civil Rights Act in 1964 and the Voting Rights Act in 1965 were major milestones, but the work of the civil rights movement was not over. As President Johnson said, "freedom is not enough." Persistent patterns of discrimination continue to exist in the United States. The legacy of racism affects the job market and housing patterns. In many ways, African Americans did not have "the same chance as every other American," as President Johnson said in 1965. (Document 3) Equality under the law had been accomplished, but equality of opportunity had not been fully realized. Activists and reformers have continued to push for a more egalitarian society in the decades since the 1960s. In recent years, the Black Lives Matter movement emerged. The phrase "Black lives matter" began to appear in social media in 2013, following the acquittal of George Zimmerman, a neighborhood watch coordinator in Florida who had been accused of shooting and killing Trayvon Martin, an African American teenager. The movement grew to focus on issues of racial profiling, police brutality, and racial and economic inequality.

Another important protest movement that has pressed for change is the environmental movement. The environmental movement developed in the context of nearly a century of industrial growth in the United States. The expansion of industry, accompanied by the extraction of raw materials, the harnessing of fossil fuels, the creation of items that are quickly discarded, and the discharge of pollutants, all took their toll on the environment. Reformers and political leaders around the turn of the 20th century, such as John Muir and Theodore Roosevelt, called attention to the destruction done to natural areas by large-scale mining and logging. Their efforts led to the expansion of the National Park system and the establishment of thousands of acres of protected national forests. However, it is only after World War II that writers and scientists began to note the more systematic damage done to the Earth's ecosystem by various industrial processes. In 1962, Murray Bookchin (writing under the pseudonym Lewis Herber) wrote a groundbreaking book, *Our Synthetic Environment*, warning of the dangers of pesticide use. Later that same year, Rachel Carson published the best-selling book, *Silent Spring*, a detailed description of the harmful effects of toxic chemicals on the environment. She vividly described how synthetic chemicals can be found throughout the environment, even in fish in remote lakes. Most troubling for many readers was the fact that these chemicals were found in humans, even in mothers' milk. She said that the big chemical companies spread false information about their products. The book was especially critical of chemical pesticides such as DDT. (Document 7) Her book shocked many people and was a catalyst for the environmental movement of the 1960s and 1970s.

The environmental protest movement went from consisting of many local efforts to being a national movement in 1970 with the development of Earth Day. Thousands of people, for example, marched down Fifth Avenue in New York City. (Document 8a) In all, demonstrations and other public events occurred at over 2000 colleges and 10,000 schools and in over 2000 communities. (Document 8b) The environmental protest movement became front page news. Earth Day brought people together to protest environmental destruction and inspired others to make a commitment to push for change.

The movement could soon claim some major legislative victories. The administration of President Richard M. Nixon and Congress created the Environmental Protection Agency in 1970 and approved amendments to the 1963 Clean Air Act (also in 1970) that established regulatory and enforcement mechanisms. These amendments first set limits on factory emissions. President Nixon also signed the Clean Water Act of 1972 and the Endangered Species Act to provide the EPA with additional mechanisms to protect the environment. (Document 9a) In addition, many communities across the nation began recycling programs to reduce the amount of garbage and to reuse resources such as aluminum and glass. In the 1970s, many Americans bought smaller, more fuel-efficient cars and were conscious about turning lights off when not in use.

Despite substantial victories, the environmental movement has had only limited success in addressing an even more pressing challenge—climate change. The environmental activist Frances Beinecke has written that, "Never in my lifetime have the challenges been greater" than those posed by climate change. (Document 9b) Since the early 1980s, scientists have become aware of a trend toward warmer global temperatures. Some became convinced that this warming trend was caused by trapped greenhouse gasses, which, in turn, were caused by human activities, primarily the burning of fossil fuels. In the 1990s and 2000s, a virtual consensus emerged in the scientific community around the connection between climate change and the emissions generated by the burning of fossil fuels. Calls were made to limit the human activities linked to climate change. Beinecke praises the movement for raising the issue of climate change and for beginning the work to make the shift toward renewable sources of power. However, she notes, the goal of becoming a "carbon-neutral nation" is still far away. She laments that this is "not yet the world we live in," but asserts that it is the world "we must" create if we hope to avoid the disastrous effects of climate change.

Both the civil rights movement and the environmental movement have played important roles in raising awareness of issues that seemed impossible to tackle. Both movements also contributed to major interim victories. The civil rights movement pushed the government to pass the Civil Rights Act and the Voting Rights Act to end discriminatory government policies. The environmental movement pushed the government to create the Environmental Protection Agency and to pass important protective legislation. However, the work of both protest movements continues. Entrenched patterns of everyday discrimination and white supremacist attitudes continue to exist. Likewise, the industrial production system, as well as everyday practices of millions of Americans, continue to generate the conditions that are worsening climate change. It remains to be seen whether the movements will be able to remake the world in a way where these problems are successfully addressed.

Topic	Question Numbers	*Number of Points
American political history	12, 16, 22, 23, 24, 34, 42, 43, 46	11
Political theory	1, 3	2
Economic theory/policy	14, 19, 25, 28, 29, 45, 49	8
Constitutional principles	4, 5, 6, 7, 8, 10, 11, 13, 18, 48	12
American foreign policy	9, 20, 26, 27, 31, 39, 40, 41, 44, 47	12
American studies—the American people	15, 17, 21, 30, 32, 33, 35, 36, 37, 38, 50	13
Geography	2	1
Skills questions included in the above content areas		
Reading comprehension	5, 12, 21, 26, 32, 33, 44	
Graph/table/diagram interpretation	8, 29, 38, 48	
Cartoon/image interpretation	19, 34, 35, 36, 45	
Map interpretation	39, 40	
Outlining skills	28, 37	

*Note: The 50 questions in Part I are worth a total of 60 percent of the exam. Since each correct answer is worth 60/50 or 1.2 points, totals are shown to the nearest full point in each content category.

PART I

Multiple-Choice Questions by Standard

Standard	Question Numbers
1—United States and New York History	1, 4, 9, 11, 12, 13, 16, 20, 22, 24, 26, 27, 31, 32, 35, 41, 42, 45, 46, 47, 50
2—World History	37, 39, 40, 44
3—Geography	2, 21, 30, 38
4—Economics	14, 15, 17, 19, 25, 28, 29, 33, 36, 49
5—Civics, Citizenship, and Government	3, 5, 6, 7, 8, 10, 18, 23, 34, 43, 48

Parts II and III by Theme and Standard

	Theme	Standards
Thematic Essay	Change; Citizenship; Diversity; Foreign Policy; Government; Immigration and Migration; Technology; Presidential Decisions and Actions	Standards 1, 2, 3, 4, and 5: United States and New York History; World History; Geography; Economics; Civics, Citizenship, and Government
Document-Based Essay	Citizenship; Civic Values; Diversity; Environment; Government; Individuals, Groups, Institutions; Presidential Decisions and Actions; Technology	Standards 1, 2, 3, and 5: United States and New York History; World History; Geography; Civics, Citizenship, and Government

Examination
August 2019
United States History and Government

PART I: MULTIPLE CHOICE

Answer all questions in this part

Directions (1–50): For each statement or question, write in the space provided the *number* of the word or expression that, of those given, best completes the statement or answers the question.

1 Which geographic features contributed to the economic development of the plantation system in the South?

(1) rocky soil and deep harbors
(2) short rivers and many waterfalls
(3) rich soil and warm climate
(4) high mountains and numerous rivers

1 _____

2 The slogan "no taxation without representation" was first used by Americans to protest Britain's
(1) policy of salutary neglect
(2) issuance of the Proclamation of 1763
(3) passage of the Coercive Acts
(4) attempts to raise revenue through the Stamp Act

2 _____

3 Weaknesses in the central government under the Articles of Confederation exposed by Shays' Rebellion contributed directly to the

(1) signing of the Declaration of Independence
(2) creation of the United States Constitution
(3) development of a policy of neutrality
(4) passage of the Northwest Ordinance

3 _____

4 A central issue in the debate between Federalists and Antifederalists over the ratification of the United States Constitution was the

  (1) power of judicial review being granted to the judicial branch

  (2) threat posed by a strong central government to the rights of citizens

  (3) role of the president as commander in chief of the armed forces

  (4) danger of unrestricted interstate commerce   4 _____

5 During the 1790s, which factor best explains why the United States was able to stay out of foreign conflicts?

  (1) Europe depended on farm products from the United States.

  (2) The United States had announced the Monroe Doctrine.

  (3) France and Great Britain agreed to end colonialism.

  (4) The Atlantic Ocean helped the United States remain isolated from foreign threats.   5 _____

6 Which statement describes an effect of the Louisiana Purchase (1803)?

  (1) The size of the United States was doubled.

  (2) The boundary with Mexico was finally established.

  (3) The Northwest Territory became part of the United States.

  (4) The Mississippi River became the western boundary of the United States.   6 _____

7 Many New England citizens opposed United States participation in the War of 1812 because they

  (1) feared a Russian invasion in the Northwest

  (2) worried that France might try to regain Canada

  (3) resented disruption of their trade with England

  (4) resisted the extension of slavery into western territories   7 _____

8 The protection against double jeopardy and the right to a speedy trial are evidence that the United States Constitution supports the principle of

   (1) eminent domain
   (2) due process of law
   (3) representative democracy
   (4) reserved powers   8 _____

9 During the early 1800s, advances in democratic government included

   (1) eliminating property ownership as a voting requirement
   (2) ending the role of the electoral college
   (3) increasing education and religious requirements for voting
   (4) giving states the right to secede from the Union   9 _____

10 One reason abolitionists were unpopular with many Northerners from the 1830s to 1860 was because the abolitionists

   (1) favored the growth of slavery
   (2) encouraged the annexation of Texas
   (3) advocated views that increased tensions with the South
   (4) supported the Fugitive Slave Law   10 _____

11 The Compromise of 1850 was an attempt to resolve issues related to

   (1) the protection and spread of slavery
   (2) boundary disputes between the United States and Britain over the Oregon Country
   (3) relations with the Native American Indians of the Great Plains
   (4) the role of the federal government in industrial development   11 _____

12 One reason the decision in *Dred Scott* v. *Sandford* (1857) was so controversial is that it

   (1) strengthened the idea of popular sovereignty
   (2) gave enslaved persons full citizenship
   (3) ruled that Congress had no power to limit slavery in the territories
   (4) supported Harriet Beecher Stowe's point of view in *Uncle Tom's Cabin*   12 _____

13 When Andrew Carnegie stated, "The man who dies rich, dies disgraced," he was supporting

(1) consumer credit

(3) Social Darwinism

(2) charitable giving

(4) antitrust legislation

13 _____

Base your answer to question 14 on the chart below and on your knowledge of social studies.

Buffalo Population: 1800 to 1895

Date	Population
1800	40,000,000
1850	20,000,000
1865	15,000,000
1870	14,000,000
1875	1,000,000
1880	395,000
1885	20,000
1889	1,091
1895	Less than 1,000

Source: U.S. Department of Interior
(adapted)

14 A major impact of the trend shown on the chart was that

(1) frontier trading posts became more prosperous
(2) Plains Indians lost their main source of food, shelter, and clothing
(3) reservations were relocated closer to buffalo migration routes
(4) white settlers became dependent on buffalo products

14 _____

15 "A government's primary role is to provide a favorable atmosphere for business, including a stable currency, hands-off regulation, and domestic order."

A supporter of this idea would most likely favor

(1) establishing consumer protection laws
(2) securing collective-bargaining rights
(3) levying high taxes on business
(4) following laissez-faire economics   15 _____

Base your answer to question 16 on the photograph below and on your knowledge of social studies.

Source: Solomon Butcher, 1886

16 Which act of Congress most directly contributed to the situation shown in this photo?

(1) the Homestead Act   (3) the purchase of Alaska
(2) the Sherman Antitrust Act   (4) the Interstate Commerce Act 16 _____

Base your answer to question 17 on the passage below and on your knowledge of social studies.

> . . . We think the enforced separation of the races, as applied to the internal commerce of the State, neither abridges the privileges or immunities of the colored man, deprives him of his property without due process of law, nor denies him the equal protection of the laws within the meaning of the 14th Amendment . . .

17 Which Supreme Court decision is reflected in this passage?

(1) *Wabash, St. Louis & Pacific R.R.* v. *Illinois* (1886)
(2) *United States* v. *E. C. Knight Co.* (1895)
(3) *In Re Debs* (1895)
(4) *Plessy* v. *Ferguson* (1896)   17 _____

18 In the late 1800s, one reason labor unions struggled to gain support was because

(1) employers could easily replace striking employees
(2) the wages of industrial laborers were high
(3) government-funded public-works jobs were readily available
(4) corporations ended the use of court injunctions   18 _____

19 Which term is most closely associated with the start of the Spanish-American War?

(1) socialism   (3) yellow journalism
(2) populism   (4) isolationism   19 _____

Base your answer to question 20 on the cartoon below and on your knowledge of social studies.

The Appearance of the New Party in the Political Field

Source: W. A. Carson, *Utica Saturday Globe*, 1912 (adapted)

20 What is the main idea of this 1912 cartoon?

(1) The Democratic Party is losing support.

(2) Republicans outnumber Democrats in the United States.

(3) The political process has no room for more than two parties.

(4) A third political party can threaten the two major parties.   20 _____

21 In the late 1800s, the major goal of United States policy in both the annexation of Hawaii and the acquisition of the Philippines was to

(1) obtain coaling stations and seaports for United States ships
(2) expand United States fishing rights in international waters
(3) limit the spread of Japanese influence
(4) protect the area around the Panama Canal   21 _____

22 **"Income Tax Amendment Passes"**
"Congress Enacts Federal Reserve Act"
"Pure Food and Drug Act Passed by Congress"

Which reform movement supported the actions described by these headlines?

(1) Progressive   (3) labor
(2) Prohibition   (4) conservation   22 _____

23 In his war message to Congress, President Woodrow Wilson urged the United States to enter World War I in order to

(1) protect the empires of European countries
(2) create a new world government
(3) make the world safe for democracy
(4) stop a British attack on the United States   23 _____

Base your answer to question 24 on the cartoon below and on your knowledge of social studies.

Step by Step

Source: Sid Greene, *New York Evening Telegram*, 1919
(adapted)

24 What is the cartoonist's point of view in this 1919 cartoon?

(1) Immigrants will easily assimilate into American society.
(2) Industrial production will expand and create more jobs.
(3) Civil liberties will be restricted and ordinary American citizens will be hurt.
(4) The actions of labor unions threaten the American way of life. 24 _____

Base your answer to question 25 on the photograph below and on your knowledge of social studies.

Source: Photo taken in Dayton, Tennessee, 1925;
University of Missouri-Kansas City, School of Law (adapted)

25 This photograph shows one side of the 1920s conflict between

  (1) union men and factory owners

  (2) science and religion

  (3) nativists and immigrants

  (4) censorship and free press   25 _____

Base your answer to question 26 on the poem below and on your knowledge of social studies.

I, TOO

I, too, sing America.

I am the darker brother.
They send me to eat in the kitchen
When company comes,
But I laugh,
And eat well,
And grow strong.

Tomorrow,
I'll be at the table
When company comes.
Nobody'll dare
Say to me,
"Eat in the kitchen,"
Then.

Besides,
They'll see how beautiful I am
And be ashamed—

I, too, am America.

—Langston Hughes, "I, Too," 1926

26 During the 1920s, which development was most closely associated with this poem?

(1) growth of the motion-picture industry
(2) emergence of an antiwar party
(3) blossoming of African American culture
(4) expansion of mass consumption   26 _____

27 In the 1920s, authors such as F. Scott Fitzgerald, Ernest Hemingway, and Sinclair Lewis wrote primarily about

(1) the intolerance of the Ku Klux Klan
(2) post–World War I disillusionment and materialism
(3) the failure of cultural pluralism
(4) the lack of educational opportunities for younger Americans   27 _____

28 The Federal Deposit Insurance Corporation (FDIC) and the Securities and Exchange Commission (SEC) were part of President Franklin D. Roosevelt's efforts to

(1) reduce the power of business monopolies during the Great Depression
(2) give organized labor a stronger voice in politics
(3) reform economic problems that contributed to the Great Depression
(4) bring electricity to rural areas   28 _____

29 President Franklin D. Roosevelt proposed a plan in 1937 to add justices to the Supreme Court primarily because the Court

(1) lacked representation from minority groups
(2) had declared major New Deal laws unconstitutional
(3) had little judicial experience
(4) supported a loose interpretation of the Constitution   29 _____

Base your answers to questions 30 and 31 on the graph below and on your knowledge of social studies.

Unemployment, 1929–1945

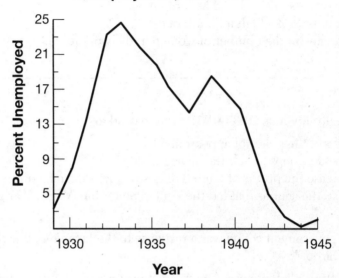

Source: *Historical Statistics of the United States: Colonial Times to 1970*, U.S. Census Bureau, 1975 (adapted)

30 What was the major reason for the change in unemployment shown on the graph between 1933 and 1937?

  (1) Banks increased their lending to new businesses, who hired more workers.

  (2) The profits of corporations were heavily taxed by the states.

  (3) Job opportunities were created by New Deal public-works projects.

  (4) The federal government nationalized the transportation and utility industries.   30 _____

31 What was the main cause of the trend in employment shown on the graph between 1942 and 1945?

(1) increased manufacturing to meet the needs of World War II
(2) the success of the Social Security Act
(3) the impact of a high inflation rate
(4) a decline in the number of women in the work force   31 _____

32 The Neutrality Acts (1935–1937) were passed to

(1) support the policy of appeasement
(2) provide troops to halt Italian aggression
(3) increase the profits of United States weapons manufacturers
(4) avoid the actions that led the United States into World War I   32 _____

33 Which government action was a response to the Japanese attack on Pearl Harbor?

(1) drafting all Japanese American men into the United States Army
(2) passing labor laws banning the employment of immigrants
(3) ending all oil sales to Japan
(4) forcing the relocation and internment of Japanese Americans   33 _____

Base your answer to question 34 on the posters below and on your knowledge of social studies.

Source: New York State Works Progress Administration Art Project

Source: Office for Emergency Management

34 Which United States government action was most similar to the goal shown in these World War II posters?

(1) institution of the draft by the Selective Service Act (1940)
(2) aid to Russia under the Lend-Lease Act (1941)
(3) rationing by the Office of Price Administration (1941)
(4) development of the Manhattan Project (1942)

34 _____

35 The Servicemen's Readjustment Act of 1944 (GI Bill) made a significant impact on post–World War II America because it provided for

  (1) aid to veterans for housing and college costs
  (2) the rapid demobilization of soldiers
  (3) pensions for soldiers from World War I
  (4) the establishment of a draft for all males over 18 years of age   35 _____

36 Following World War II, the United States adopted the foreign policy of containment primarily to

  (1) return to pre-war isolationism
  (2) limit the spread of communism
  (3) force European nations to end colonialism
  (4) support the work of the World Court   36 _____

37 One important effect of President Eisenhower's proposal for interstate highways was a significant increase in

  (1) health-care spending
  (2) suburban communities
  (3) educational opportunities
  (4) sectional differences   37 _____

Base your answer to question 38 on the passage below and on your knowledge of social studies.

> The people of the United States share with the people of the Soviet Union their satisfaction for the safe flight of the astronaut in man's first venture into space. We congratulate you and the Soviet scientists and engineers who made this feat possible. It is my sincere desire that in the continuing quest for knowledge of outer space our nations can work together to obtain the greatest benefit to mankind.
>
> —President John F. Kennedy, Telegram to Nikita Khrushchev,
> April 12, 1961

38 One way President Kennedy responded to the Soviet action referred to in the telegram was to support

(1) a decrease in the budget for space exploration
(2) an expansion of the Peace Corps to aid impoverished nations
(3) the removal of Soviet troops from East Berlin
(4) the commitment to a Moon landing by the end of the decade   38 _____

39 • Establishing a direct telephone line between Washington and Moscow
   • Negotiating a limited nuclear test-ban treaty
   • Selling surplus wheat to the Soviet Union

These actions by presidents John F. Kennedy and Richard Nixon are examples of their attempts to

(1) meet the Soviet Union's Cold War demands
(2) establish peaceful coexistence with the Soviet Union
(3) support Soviet troops fighting in Afghanistan
(4) weaken the military power of the Soviet Union   39 _____

40 During the 1960s, the escalation of United States involvement in the Vietnam War was based on the belief that

(1) restoring French colonial power was necessary for political stability in Southeast Asia
(2) a strong military presence would limit Japanese trade with Vietnam
(3) a North Vietnamese victory would lead to further losses as predicted by the domino theory
(4) a cease-fire agreement would increase college protests

40 _____

41 What was the major effect of the Civil Rights Act of 1964?

(1) Racial discrimination in public facilities was banned.
(2) Citizenship and voting rights were extended to Native American Indians.
(3) The use of poll taxes and literacy tests for voting were outlawed.
(4) Busing to integrate schools was authorized.

41 _____

42 Which pair of Supreme Court cases upheld the right to counsel for defendants in state criminal cases?

(1) *Mapp* v. *Ohio* (1961) and *Heart of Atlanta Motel* v. *United States* (1964)
(2) *Baker* v. *Carr* (1962) and *Engel* v. *Vitale* (1962)
(3) *Gideon* v. *Wainwright* (1963) and *Miranda* v. *Arizona* (1966)
(4) *Tinker* v. *Des Moines* (1969) and *Roe* v. *Wade* (1973)

42 _____

Base your answer to question 43 on the graph below and on your knowledge of social studies.

Percent of Men and Women in Labor Force: 1950 to 1990

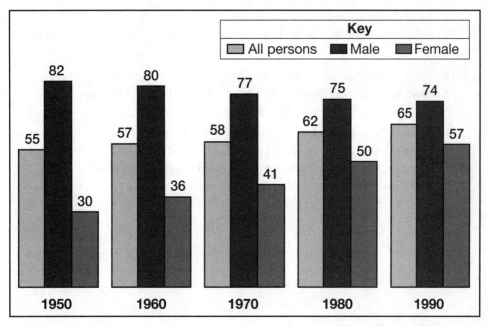

Source: U.S. Census Bureau, 1990 (adapted)

43 Which conclusion is most clearly supported by information in the graph?

(1) Older Americans remained in the labor force longer in 1990 than in 1950.

(2) All Americans born during the baby boom after World War II joined the labor force.

(3) Half as many men were in the labor force in 1990 as compared to 1950.

(4) In every decade shown, the percentage of women in the labor force grew while the percentage of men in the labor force declined.

43 _____

44 During the Persian Gulf War (1991), the primary aim of the United States was to force Iraq to

(1) withdraw its troops from Kuwait
(2) hold democratic elections
(3) increase the price of its oil exports
(4) submit to weapons inspections by the United Nations   44 _____

45 In 1993, many labor union leaders opposed United States membership in the North American Free Trade Agreement (NAFTA) because they feared it would

(1) cause Americans to lose jobs to foreign nations
(2) reduce the number of immigrants to the United States
(3) result in higher exports from the United States to Mexico and Canada
(4) outlaw wage increases for workers in the United States   45 _____

Base your answer to question 46 on the cartoon below and on your knowledge of social studies.

Source: Steve Breen, *San Diego Union-Tribune*, 2004 (adapted)

46 According to the cartoonist, the investigation of intelligence failures related to the 9/11 terrorist attacks resulted in

(1) praise for government efforts to stop intelligence leaks

(2) open immigration from all regions of the world

(3) recommendations to limit dependence on foreign intelligence

(4) various federal agencies attempting to avoid criticism by shifting responsibility

46 _____

47 Between 1881 and 1921, one major cause of the increasing number of immigrants to the United States was the

(1) availability of free land in the Southeast

(2) increased job opportunities in industry

(3) increased need for military personnel

(4) federal aid to pay the housing costs of new arrivals

47 _____

48 Prior to its military involvement in both the War of 1812 and World War I, the United States attempted to maintain a policy of

(1) neutrality   (3) collective security
(2) internationalism   (4) détente   48 _____

49 ". . . We conclude that, in the field of public education, the doctrine of 'separate but equal' has no place. Separate educational facilities are inherently unequal." . . .

These statements were included in which Supreme Court decision?

(1) *Schenck* v. *United States* (1919)
(2) *Korematsu* v. *United States* (1944)
(3) *Brown* v. *Board of Education of Topeka* (1954)
(4) *Vernonia School District* v. *Acton* (1995)   49 _____

50 • Alien and Sedition Acts of 1798
   • Espionage Act of 1917
   • USA Patriot Act of 2001

One common effect of these wartime laws has been to

(1) expand government regulation of the economy
(2) increase the nation's military defenses
(3) promote immigration from neighboring nations
(4) protect national security at the expense of civil liberties   50 _____

In developing your answer to Part II, be sure to keep these general definitions in mind:
- (a) <u>describe</u> means "to illustrate something in words or tell about it"
- (b) <u>discuss</u> means "to make observations about something using facts, reasoning, and argument; to present in some detail"

PART II: THEMATIC ESSAY QUESTION

Directions: Write a well-organized essay that includes an introduction, several paragraphs addressing the task below, and a conclusion.

Theme: Amendments

> The writers of the United States Constitution included an amending process to respond to changing times and unforeseen circumstances. Since the Civil War, important amendments have had an impact on the United States and/or on American society.

Task:

> Select **two** amendments to the United States Constitution *since* the Civil War and for **each**
> - Describe the historical circumstances surrounding the adoption of the amendment
> - Discuss the impact of this amendment on the United States and/or on American society

You may use any constitutional amendment that has been added since the Civil War. Some suggestions you might wish to consider include:

13th amendment—abolition of slavery (1865)
15th amendment—African American male suffrage (1870)
16th amendment—graduated income tax (1913)
17th amendment—direct election of United States senators (1913)
18th amendment—Prohibition (1919)
19th amendment—woman's suffrage (1920)
26th amendment—18-year-old vote (1971)

You are *not* limited to these suggestions.

Guidelines:

In your essay, be sure to:
- Develop all aspects of the task
- Support the theme with relevant facts, examples, and details
- Use a logical and clear plan of organization, including an introduction and a conclusion that are beyond a restatement of the theme

In developing your answers to Part III, be sure to keep these general definitions in mind:
  (a) <u>describe</u> means "to illustrate something in words or tell about it"
  (b) <u>discuss</u> means "to make observations about something using facts, reasoning, and argument; to present in some detail"

PART III: DOCUMENT-BASED QUESTION

This question is based on the accompanying documents. The question is designed to test your ability to work with historical documents. Some of these documents have been edited for the purposes of this question. As you analyze the documents, take into account the source of each document and any point of view that may be presented in the document. Keep in mind that the language and images used in a document may reflect the historical context of the time in which it was created.

Historical Context:

> The president of the United States has been granted power as the commander in chief by the Constitution. Although the president has used his military powers to commit troops overseas, he has also used this power to respond to domestic challenges. These challenges have included *President Grover Cleveland and the Pullman strike, President Herbert Hoover and the Bonus Army,* and *President Harry Truman and segregation in the armed forces.*

Task:

> Using the information from the documents and your knowledge of United States history, answer the questions that follow each document in Part A. Your answers to the questions will help you write the Part B essay in which you will be asked to
>
> Select *two* domestic challenges mentioned in the historical context and for *each*
>
> • Describe the historical circumstances that led to the president's action
> • Discuss how the president's action influenced the United States and/or American society

Part A: Short-Answer Questions

Directions: Analyze the documents and answer the short-answer questions that follow each document in the space provided.

Document 1

The nation's worst depression of the 19th century began in 1893. In 1894, the worst year of the depression, workers at the Pullman Company went on strike in Chicago.

> . . . The rents Pullman charged were excessive, running about 25 percent higher than in neighboring towns. He sold at ten cents per thousand gallons water that he bought from Chicago at four cents. He forced his tenants to buy their food and other necessities from company stores, where prices far exceeded those of regular outlets. The simmering cauldron of protest boiled over when in 1894 the company cut wages an average of 25 percent, without a comparable cut in rent or in the cost of necessities. Pullman refused to listen to complaints and dismissed from their jobs those who persisted in the outcry. He then closed the plant.
>
> At this juncture [time], the American Railway Union, which had a membership of 150,000, including several thousand Pullman employees, joined the struggle, ordering its members not to handle trains with Pullman cars attached. The strike was quickly turned into a national disruption. Within a month, railroad traffic, particularly in the western states, was almost at a standstill. The beset [besieged] railroad owners hit on the scheme of coupling Pullman cars to trains that carried mail, confident that any interference with the mail was a federal crime. When the strikers still refused to man the trains, the railroads persuaded Attorney General Olney to swear in an army of special deputies—actually in the pay of the railroads—in order to help keep the trains moving.
>
> The leader of the union was Eugene V. Debs, a gentle but dynamic person who had made the interests of workingmen the consuming enthusiasm of his life. He had instructed his members to avoid violence. But it broke out now anyhow between the deputies and the strikers. The railroads in their frustration asked President Cleveland to send federal troops to keep order and to guarantee the safe handling of the mails. . . .

Source: Henry F. Graff, *Grover Cleveland*, Henry Holt and Company, 2002

1a According to Henry F. Graff, what was *one* reason Pullman workers went on strike? [1]

_____

_____

b According to Henry F. Graff, what was *one* reason President Grover Cleveland was asked to send federal troops to Chicago? [1]

_____

_____

Document 2a

President Grover Cleveland responded to the strike and to the riots that followed by sending federal troops to Chicago.

. . . Cleveland also feared the worst, and responded accordingly. Federal troops arrived to quell [stop] the riots, ironically, on July 4. While patriotic citizens set off fireworks, in the city of Chicago they set fires. Thousands of angry protestors lay waste to the city. At the Chicago rail yards more freight trains were flipped over and cars set ablaze. A huge fire that night destroyed the expositions on the grounds of the World's Fair. Chicago degenerated into lawlessness and chaos.

It continued for four days. On July 6, a rail deputy shot two men, inciting the largest riot of all—6,000 rail workers destroyed over $340,000 worth of railroad property on a single day as over 700 railroad cars were torched. The next day, a mob attacked the state militia. The soldiers fired back, killing 4 rioters and wounding 20 others. Reinforcements for the federal troops were called up from surrounding states. No American city had ever experienced such anarchy in peacetime. . . .

Source: Chris Wallace, *Character: Profiles in Presidential Courage*, Rugged Land, 2004

Document 2b

Burning of Six Hundred Freight-Cars on the Panhandle Railroad, South of Fiftieth Street, on the Evening of July 6th.

Source: G. A. Coffin and Charles Mente, *Harper's Weekly*, July 21, 1894

2 Based on these documents, what was **one** effect of President Cleveland's decision to send federal troops to end the Pullman strike? [1]

_____

_____

Document 3

The Pullman Strike of 1894 was the first national strike in United States history. Before coming to an end, it involved over 150,000 persons and twenty-seven states and territories and would paralyze the nation's railway system. The entire rail labor force of the nation would walk away from their jobs. In supporting the capital side [railroad owners] of this strike President Cleveland for the first time in the Nation's history would send in federal troops, who would fire on and kill United States Citizens, against the wishes of the states. The federal courts of the nation would outlaw striking by the passing of the Omnibus indictment [federal charges against the leaders of the American Railway Union]. This blow to unionized labor would not be struck down until the passing of the Wagner act in 1935. This all began in the little town of Pullman, Illinois, just south of Chicago. . . .

Source: Keith Ladd and Greg Rickman, "The Pullman Strike," kansasheritage.org, 1998 (adapted)

3 According to Keith Ladd and Greg Rickman, what was *one* effect of President Cleveland's decision to support railroad owners during the Pullman strike? [1]

_____

_____

Document 4a

**Veterans' sheds, tents, and shanties sprawled across the
Anacostia Flats in Washington, D.C., in 1932.**

Source: National Archives (adapted)

Document 4b

Violent clash between police and veterans on the morning of July 28, 1932.

Source: General Douglas MacArthur Foundation

Document 4c

. . . No "civil commotion" attracted as much attention as the march of the "bonus army." Demanding immediate and full payment of bonuses for their service in World War I, 15,000 to 20,000 unemployed veterans moved on Washington in the spring of 1932. The House passed the bonus bill, but when the Senate voted it down by an overwhelming margin, half the men stayed on; they had no jobs, no homes, no place else to go. Most of them lived in mean shanties on the muddy Anacostia flats, some camped in unused government buildings. General Glassford, the head of the District police, treated the men decently and with discretion, but, as the men stayed on day after day, federal officials panicked. On July 28, 1932, the government decided precipitately [suddenly] to evict bonus marchers from vacant buildings on Pennsylvania Avenue. Two veterans were killed and several District police were injured in a scuffle that followed. President Hoover summoned the U.S. Army to take over. . . .

Source: William E. Leuchtenburg, *The Perils of Prosperity, 1914–1932*, University of Chicago Press, 1993

4a Based on these documents, state *one* reason World War I veterans marched on Washington, D.C., in 1932. [1]

_____

_____

b Based on these documents, state *one* reason President Hoover sent the United States Army to remove the Bonus Marchers. [1]

_____

_____

Document 5a

Source: *Washington Post*, Friday, July 29, 1932

Document 5b

... A storm of protest followed. Americans who viewed the photographs and read the reports over the next few days found the actions of their government inexcusable. Any remaining faith they still had in Washington was now called into question, especially when Hoover and MacArthur attempted to justify their orders by saying that the marchers were criminals and communists. Far from a revolutionary crowd, the veterans seemed to most people to be little different than the rest of the nation: they had no work and they wanted to feed their families. Squeezed from all directions, the people needed an ally—desperately—and in the Democratic candidate for president in 1932, they finally found one. ...

Source: Peter Jennings and Todd Brewster, *The Century*, Doubleday, 1998

5 According to these documents, what were *two* reasons many Americans thought the government's action against the veterans was wrong? [2]

(1) _____

_____

(2) _____

_____

Document 6

. . . American history is punctuated by moments and incidents that become prisms through which larger events are better understood—the Boston Tea Party, Nat Turner's Rebellion, the Alamo, John Brown's Raid. The march of the Bonus Army belongs in such company. But its significance has been obscured [dimmed] by time, even to its direct beneficiaries—the millions of later veterans whose bonus would be the GI Bill and the benefits that have followed to the present day. And, its legacy is everlasting. The First Amendment of the Constitution grants Americans the right "to petition the government for redress of grievances." Millions of Americans have since peacefully marched on Washington in support of various causes, their way paved by the veterans of 1932.

Source: Paul Dickson and Thomas B. Allen, *The Bonus Army: An American Epic*, Walker and Company, 2004

6 According to Paul Dickson and Thomas B. Allen, what was *one* impact of the Bonus Army? [1]

_____

_____

Document 7a

In 1941, civil rights activist A. Philip Randolph demanded an end to racial segregation in the Armed Forces.

> . . . Roosevelt ignored Randolph's call for a desegregated army. By that time, all branches of the military separated black soldiers into their own units, deployed them on segregated trains, and housed them in old, dilapidated barracks. Most black soldiers served as stewards and cooks or performed menial labor such as maintaining latrines [bathrooms]. As late as 1940, the U.S. armed services included only five black commissioned officers, including Benjamin O. Davis, Sr., the first African-American to reach the rank of general, and Benjamin O. Davis, Jr., the 20th century's first black graduate of West Point. Military leaders routinely denied black soldiers entry into many training classes that would have enabled them to advance in rank. . . .

Source: Mark Bauerlein et al., *Civil Rights Chronicle: The African American Struggle for Freedom*, Legacy, 2003

Document 7b

> . . . Not surprisingly, black organizations pressed hard for equality within the armed services. They viewed the military as a key institution in American life. A direct arm of the government, and a direct expression of the people, it personified the democratic values for which the United States fought. Ending racial discrimination in the armed forces would have a powerful effect on civil society. Moreover, if blacks made an equal contribution to the war effort, their claim to full citizenship would be much stronger. . . .

Source: Adam Fairclough, *Better Day Coming: Blacks and Equality, 1890–2000*, Viking, 2001

7 Based on these documents, what were **two** reasons African American civil rights leaders called for an end to racial segregation in the Armed Forces? [2]

(1) _____

_____

(2) _____

_____

Document 8a

Following World War II, on orders from President Truman, the Army, Navy, and Air Force abolished their traditional Jim Crow units and with very little fanfare integrated themselves. On a recent [September 1963] 3,200-mile tour of the South, we viewed the impressive results.

We saw Negro and white servicemen eating at the same mess-hall tables, drinking at the same on-base bars, playing ball on the same teams. They sleep in the same barracks, share lavatories and showers, borrow money from one another until pay day.

In on-base homes assigned without regard for race, white and Negro families live next door to one another, baby-sit for one another, watch TV together, share backyard barbecues. They swim together in on-base pools, worship together in military chapels. Their children play and squabble happily together on the lawns, attend on-base schools and Sunday schools together. All this has for years been accepted practice on military bases, including many in the Deep South. . . .

Source: Ruth and Edward Brecher, "The Military's Limited War Against Segregation,"
Reporting Civil Rights, The Library of America

Document 8b

Soldiers from the U.S. Army's Integrated Second Infantry Division in Korea

Source: Defense Media Network (adapted)

8 Based on these documents, what were *two* results of President Harry Truman's executive order abolishing segregated "Jim Crow units" in the military? [2]

(1) _____

_____

(2) _____

_____

Document 9

> . . . The military's last all-black unit disbanded in 1954, and the services, with the exception of the navy, which lagged somewhat behind, recruited African Americans for all specialties. Acceptance in the ranks did not, however, mean acceptance in communities adjacent to military installations. While black service personnel had equal access to integrated military family quarters on bases, they faced the same discrimination in housing in local civilian communities that had always existed. . . .
>
> Black military personnel also faced discrimination in furthering their own education. Universities near military installations, especially in the South, refused to accept black students.
>
> Outside the gates of their bases, black military personnel found that civilian communities treated them in the same manner as they did their local minority population. Jim Crow laws, again mostly in the South but to some degree throughout the country, separated black from white in shopping, eating, housing, transportation, and recreational facilities. Frequently these public areas exhibited Whites Only signs, and the towns had police more than willing to enforce these policies. . . .
>
> The arrival of the 1960s brought increased impatience in the black military and civilian communities. Protests continued, with sit-ins the dominant form of nonviolent action as blacks and their supporters challenged local Jim Crow laws restricting their access to eating establishments and other public facilities. . . .

Source: Lt. Colonel (Ret.) Michael Lee Lanning,
The African-American Soldier: From Crispus Attucks to Colin Powell,
Citadel Press, 2004 (adapted)

9 According to Michael Lee Lanning, what was ***one*** way discrimination against African Americans continued after President Truman's executive order?   [1]

_____

_____

Part B: Essay

Directions: Write a well-organized essay that includes an introduction, several paragraphs, and a conclusion. Use evidence from *at least* **four** documents in your essay. Support your response with relevant facts, examples, and details. Include additional outside information.

Historical Context:

> The president of the United States has been granted power as the commander in chief by the Constitution. Although the president has used his military powers to commit troops overseas, he has also used this power to respond to domestic challenges. These challenges have included **President Grover Cleveland and the Pullman strike, President Herbert Hoover and the Bonus Army,** and **President Harry Truman and segregation in the armed forces.**

Task:

> Using the information from the documents and your knowledge of United States history, write an essay in which you
>
> Select **two** domestic challenges mentioned in the historical context and for **each**
>
> - Describe the historical circumstances that led to the president's action
> - Discuss how the president's action influenced the United States and/or American society

Guidelines:

In your essay, be sure to
- Develop all aspects of the task
- Incorporate information from *at least* **four** documents
- Incorporate relevant outside information
- Support the theme with relevant facts, examples, and details
- Use a logical and clear plan of organization, including an introduction and a conclusion that are beyond a restatement of the theme

Answers
August 2019
United States History and Government

Answer Key

PART I

1. 3	11. 1	21. 1	31. 1	41. 1
2. 4	12. 3	22. 1	32. 4	42. 3
3. 2	13. 2	23. 3	33. 4	43. 4
4. 2	14. 2	24. 4	34. 3	44. 1
5. 4	15. 4	25. 2	35. 1	45. 1
6. 1	16. 1	26. 3	36. 2	46. 4
7. 3	17. 4	27. 2	37. 2	47. 2
8. 2	18. 1	28. 3	38. 4	48. 1
9. 1	19. 3	29. 2	39. 2	49. 3
10. 3	20. 4	30. 3	40. 3	50. 4

PART II: Thematic Essay   *See* **Answers Explained** section.

PART III: Document-Based Question   *See* **Answers Explained** section.

Answers Explained

PART I (1–50)

1. **3** The presence of rich soil and a warm climate in the South most directly contributed to the economic development of the plantation system. Many colonists from England were drawn to this region in the 1600s and 1700s—first to the colonies around Chesapeake Bay (Virginia and Maryland), and then farther south (the Carolinas and Georgia). The coastal areas of the South are characterized by rich soil and relatively flat land. In addition, the area has a warm climate, with ample rainfall and a long growing season. These qualities made the coastal areas of the South ideal for large-scale tobacco, rice, and indigo plantations. (Cotton did not become a major crop in the United States until the 1790s.) In contrast, the hilly, rocky soil and shorter growing season in the northern colonies proved more suitable for small-scale agriculture and a more mixed economy. The smaller farms of the northern colonies were generally worked by the owner of the property and his family, with, perhaps, more people hired for planting and harvesting. The plantation system of the South, by contrast, was largely worked by slave labor. The first Africans arrived in Virginia in 1619, just twelve years after the arrival of the first English settlers at Jamestown. Slavery became more prominent in colonial America, especially in the southern colonies, as the 17th century progressed.

WRONG CHOICES EXPLAINED:
(1) Rocky soil and deep harbors would not have contributed to the plantation system. These features are more characteristic of New England than of the South. The rocky soil and hilly terrain of New England help explain the persistence of small-scale, single-family farms. Deep harbors lent themselves to the fishing industry, especially cod fishing, which became a key sector of the New England economy. Deep harbors, such as those in Boston, Newport, and New York, also became focal points in the transatlantic trade.

(2) Short rivers and many waterfalls would not have contributed to the plantation system. The abundance of waterfalls in New England contributed to the growth of the factory system in the first half of the 19th century. These factories, mainly textile mills, depended on water power to operate.

(4) High mountains and numerous rivers would not have contributed to the plantation system. While agriculture thrives in areas adjacent to rivers, high mountains inhibit agricultural production. Large-scale farming depends on low-lying flat land.

2. **4** The slogan "no taxation without representation" was first used by Americans to protest Britain's attempts to raise revenue through the Stamp Act. The conflict over the Stamp Act can be traced to the aftermath of the French and Indian War. After that war, which lasted from 1754 to 1763, the British government enacted a series of measures that many colonists found objectionable. These measures included a series of revenue or tax acts that the British imposed, in part to defray the costs of the war. The British believed their victory in the French and Indian War had been especially beneficial to the colonists. In return, the British reasoned it was fair for the colonists to assume some of the costs of the war and of continued protection. The Stamp Act (1765), which imposed a tax on the paper used for various documents in the colonies, provoked the most intense opposition. Many colonists asserted that only representatives elected by them could enact taxes on the colonies. "No taxation without representation" became their rallying cry. The Stamp Act itself was rescinded, but a series of British moves and colonial responses in the coming years worsened the situation.

WRONG CHOICES EXPLAINED:

(1) The slogan "no taxation without representation" was not used by Americans to protest Britain's policy of "salutary neglect." The policy of "salutary neglect" grew out of the difficulty that Britain had in enforcing laws it had enacted to regulate colonial trade. The distance between the North American colonies and Britain made rigid enforcement of British navigation acts impractical. British policymakers saw that the colonies thrived under this "salutary neglect" approach. The policy benefited both the colonies and Great Britain. Great Britain abandoned this policy after the French and Indian War, which ended in 1763. Great Britain wanted the colonies to help pay off the debt from the war and to contribute to colonial defense.

(2) The slogan "no taxation without representation" was not used by Americans to protest Britain's issuance of the Proclamation of 1763. The Proclamation of 1763 established a line along the crest of the Appalachian Mountains. Colonists were forbidden from settling beyond the line. The line was established just after the conclusion of the French and Indian War (1754–1763), which was caused, in part, by colonial expansion into lands beyond the Appalachians. Many colonists protested the Proclamation, but it was not a tax.

(3) The slogan "no taxation without representation" was not used by Americans to protest Britain's passage of the Coercive Acts. Following the Boston Tea Party (1773), the British imposed a series of punitive measures known as the Coercive Acts (1774). These included the Massachusetts Government Act, which brought the governance of Massachusetts under direct British control, and the Administration of Justice Act, which allowed British

authorities to move trials from Massachusetts to Great Britain. Many colonists protested the Coercive Acts, which they labeled the "Intolerable Acts," but the acts did not include new taxes.

3. **2** Weaknesses in the central government under the Articles of Confederation exposed by Shays' Rebellion contributed most directly to the creation of the United States Constitution. The Articles of Confederation, which established governing procedures for the United States during the period 1781–1788, left major powers with the state governments. The framers of this first American government created a "firm league of friendship" among the states, rather than a strong, centralized government. Before 1776 they had lived under a powerful, distant authority and did not want to repeat that experience. Also, many of these early leaders were fiercely loyal to their states and did not want to see state power superseded. Several problems arose during this period, which some historians have labeled the "critical period" (in the sense of a patient being in critical condition). Funding the government proved to be a major problem. As written, the Articles did not give the national government the power to levy taxes. A proposal to alter the document and allow the national government to collect import duties was blocked by Rhode Island and New York—two states with major ports. The event that convinced many Americans that change was needed was Shays' Rebellion (1786–1787). This revolt of Massachusetts farmers who felt cheated by the state's economic policies was eventually put down by state armed forces, but many political leaders came to the conclusion that a stronger national government was necessary. Earlier in 1786, a group of reformers received approval from Congress to meet in Annapolis, Maryland, to discuss possible changes in the Articles of Confederation. A follow-up meeting was scheduled in Philadelphia for May 1787. By the time of the Philadelphia meeting, the delegates, with the news of Shays' Rebellion on their minds, were ready to scrap the entire Articles of Confederation and write something new. The delegates at the Constitutional Convention believed that a strong national government was needed to quickly put down any future disturbances.

WRONG CHOICES EXPLAINED:
(1) Weaknesses in the central government under the Articles of Confederation exposed by Shays' Rebellion did not contribute to the signing of the Declaration of Independence. Shays' Rebellion occurred in 1786 through 1787; the Declaration of Independence was signed a decade earlier, in 1776. The Declaration of Independence grew out of resistance to British rule, not out of frustrations with a limited central government.

(3) Weaknesses in the central government under the Articles of Confederation exposed by Shays' Rebellion did not contribute to the development of a policy of neutrality. Shays' Rebellion was a domestic disturbance, not an international affair. In the 1790s, President George Washington established a policy of neutrality in regard to fighting between Great Britain and the revolutionary government of France. He enunciated this position in the Neutrality Act (1793) and in his Farewell Address (1796), in which he urged the United States to avoid "permanent alliances" with foreign powers. His calls for neutrality have been invoked by isolationists throughout American history, especially preceding the U.S. entrance into both world wars.

(4) Weaknesses in the central government under the Articles of Confederation exposed by Shays' Rebellion did not contribute to passage of the Northwest Ordinance. The Northwest Ordinance (1787) was enacted just a few weeks after Shays' Rebellion was finally put down, but the ordinance does not address questions raised by the rebellion. The Northwest Ordinance spelled out the steps that the old Northwest Territory would have to go through in order to become states. In addition, the Northwest Ordinance banned slavery in the Northwest Territory.

4. **2** A central issue in the debate between Federalists and Antifederalists over the ratification of the Constitution was the threat posed by a strong central government to the rights of citizens. Antifederalists feared the Constitution would create an omnipotent and unaccountable government. They had vivid memories of the intrusions of the royal British government into their lives, and wanted to have assurances that the people would have basic protections from government abuses. Federalists, on the other hand, believed that the Articles of Confederation did not provide the United States with a sufficiently strong central government to meet a series of challenges—including internal rebellion, foreign policy conflicts, and revenue issues. Leading Federalists assured Antifederalists that a bill of rights would be added to the original document if the Antifederalists agreed to support ratification. The Bill of Rights, the first ten amendments to the Constitution, was ratified in 1791. The first amendment protects the people from government limitations on freedom of expression and of religion. In addition, it also established separation of church and state. The second amendment established the right to "bear arms." The fourth amendment holds that people are to be free from unwarranted searches by government authorities. The fifth and sixth amendments list a variety of protections that people have when they are accused of crimes, such as the right to a "speedy and public trial." The eighth amendment states that the government shall not inflict "cruel and unusual" punishments on people.

WRONG CHOICES EXPLAINED:

(1) The granting of the power of judicial review to the judicial branch was not a central issue in the debate between Federalists and Antifederalists over the ratification of the Constitution. In fact, the Constitution does not grant the power of judicial review to the judiciary. This power—to review laws and determine whether they are consistent with the Constitution—developed with the Supreme Court decision in *Marbury* v. *Madison* (1803). The details of the case have to do with the seating of judges that had been appointed during the last days of the John Adams administration. However, the case is important because it established the power of judicial review, which has been the main function of the Supreme Court since then.

(3) The role of the president as commander in chief of the armed forces was not a central issue in the debate between Federalists and Antifederalists over the ratification of the Constitution. Both factions saw the importance of the military being under civilian control. In the period leading up to the American Revolution, many Americans had become concerned that the British military was acting independently of civilian authority. Among the grievances against the king in the Declaration of Independence was that his government had rendered "the military independent of, and superior to, the civil power."

(4) The danger of unrestricted interstate commerce was not a central issue in the debate between Federalists and Antifederalists over the ratification of the Constitution. Commercial activity among the states was not seen as a threat; there was no talk of trying to restrict such trade. However, the power to regulate such trade was a matter of disagreement. The Commerce Clause of the Constitution explicitly grants Congress the power to regulate trade with foreign countries and "among the several States." This clause was an example of the expanded powers of the central government that concerned many Antifederalists.

5. **4** During the 1790s, an important factor as to why the United States was able to stay out of foreign conflicts was that the Atlantic Ocean helped the United States remain isolated from foreign threats. The Atlantic Ocean created distance between the United States and the major world powers—in the 1790s and beyond. This distance allowed the United States to develop independently and to avoid the conflicts that involved European powers. The foreign policy of neutrality is also associated with President George Washington. He issued the 1793 Neutrality Act, and in his Farewell Address (1796) he urged the United States to avoid "permanent alliances" with foreign powers. The context for the development of a neutrality stance in the 1790s was war between the revolutionary governments of France and Great Britain in 1793. Many Americans felt that the

United States had an obligation to help France because France had helped the United States in the Revolutionary War. A treaty between the two countries (1778) committed the United States to help France if it were under attack. Others argued that the United States should stay out. After all, the treaty was made with a French government that no longer existed, and the French Revolution had devolved from a democratic movement into a bloodbath. The latter position won Washington's support. His calls for neutrality have been invoked by isolationists throughout American history, especially preceding the United States entrance into both world wars.

WRONG CHOICES EXPLAINED:
(1) America's avoidance of foreign conflicts in the 1790s cannot be attributed to European dependence on farm products from the United States. At the time, Europe met most of its own food needs. The sale of American export crops to European nations, such as tobacco, declined during the American Revolution and was slow to recover. Cotton did not become a major export crop until the 19th century.

(2) America's avoidance of foreign conflicts in the 1790s cannot be attributed to the Monroe Doctrine. That statement was not issued until 1823. President James Monroe issued the Monroe Doctrine to warn European nations to keep their hands off of the Americas. The European powers honored the Monroe Doctrine, in part, because of the great physical distance between the United States and the European powers.

(3) America's avoidance of foreign conflicts in the 1790s cannot be attributed to France and Great Britain agreeing to end colonialism. In fact, no such agreement was made. Colonialism and imperialism continued well into the 20th century. The era of imperialism finally came to an end because of resistance movements in the nations that were imperialized. The British, for example, were driven out of India in 1947; the French were driven out of Vietnam in 1954 and out of Algeria in 1962.

6. **1** One effect of the Louisiana Purchase (1803) was that it doubled the size of the United States. The territory was long held by France until France ceded it to Spain in 1763 following the French and Indian War. France then regained the territory in 1801. The ambitious French leader Napoleon Bonaparte quickly decided that it was in France's best interest to sell the Louisiana Territory at a reasonable price in order to attain cash to fund war with Great Britain. In 1803, American negotiators agreed to a price of $15 million. President Thomas Jefferson realized that the purchase of such land was not allowed for in the Constitution, but if he waited for a constitutional amendment specifically allowing Congress to

acquire new lands, Napoleon could rescind his offer. So, Jefferson violated his long-held strict constructionist view and quickly presented the offer to Congress, which appropriated the money. The purchase doubled the size of the United States; it added the fertile Great Plains to the United States. This flat area west of the Mississippi would become the most important agricultural region in the United States. Second, the United States gained full control of the port of New Orleans. New Orleans is the outlet of the mighty Mississippi River, which stretches from Minnesota down the spine of the United States. The impact of the Louisiana Purchase on economic growth was remarkable. Between the 1810s and the 1850s, the value of produce from the interior of the United States received at the port of New Orleans increased over tenfold.

WRONG CHOICES EXPLAINED:

(2) The Louisiana Purchase did not establish a boundary with Mexico. Mexico did not gain its independence from Spain until 1821, nearly two decades after the Louisiana Purchase. It was the Treaty of Guadalupe Hidalgo, at the end of the Mexican-American War (1846–1848), and the Gadsden Purchase (1853) that established the boundary between Mexico and the United States.

(3) The Louisiana Purchase did not result in the acquisition of the Northwest Territory. The Northwest Territory was included in the territory of the newly established United States, as stipulated by the Treaty of Paris between Great Britain and the United States in 1783.

(4) The Louisiana Purchase did not establish the Mississippi River as the western boundary of the United States. The Mississippi River was the western boundary of the United States from the moment of its founding, under the Treaty of Paris between Great Britain and the United States in 1783. The purchase of the Louisiana Territory, which included the western banks of the Mississippi River, did give the United States full control of the river, allowing for unfettered navigation of it.

7. **3** Many New England citizens opposed United States participation in the War of 1812 because they resented disruption of their trade with England. The origins of the war can be traced back to ongoing conflicts between Great Britain and France. War between the two nations erupted again in 1803. At first, the United States benefited from trading with both warring partners. Soon, however, both countries tried to block American trade with the other. Great Britain was more aggressive in its efforts to stop American ships. British ships routinely stopped and boarded American ships, often seizing cargo and pressing American seamen into service in the British navy. This practice of impressment affected 6000 American seamen between 1803 and 1812. In 1811, the United States cut off

all trade with Great Britain. At the same time, conflicts with Native American Indians in the interior of the United States worsened tensions between the United States and Great Britain. Some congressmen became convinced that Great Britain was aiding Native American Indian resistance and called for war. The War of 1812 was unpopular among some Americans, especially among New England merchants, who saw their trade with Great Britain disappear. As diplomats were negotiating an end to the war, Federalists from New England convened in Hartford, Connecticut, in December 1814 to express their displeasure with the conflict. Some of the more radical delegates suggested that New England secede from the Union, but this proposal was rejected at the convention. The Hartford Convention did pass a resolution calling for a two-thirds vote in Congress for future declarations of war. The war itself was largely a standoff, with neither side able to achieve a decisive victory. The Treaty of Ghent ended the war where it had begun. The United States and Great Britain agreed to stop fighting and to give back any territory seized in the war. Great Britain agreed to recognize the boundary between the United States and Canada that had been established before the war.

WRONG CHOICES EXPLAINED:

(1) Opposition to the War of 1812 did not involve concerns of a Russian invasion in the Northwest. Russia had made claims to the lands of the Pacific Northwest in the 1700s. However, these claims were tenuous and not supported by settlements. There was never any concern of a Russian invasion. In 1818, the United States and Great Britain established joint ownership of what the United States called the Oregon Country. Later, the boundary between United States and British territories became a source of contention. The Oregon Treaty (1846) partitioned the region along the 49th parallel.

(2) Opposition to the War of 1812 did not involve worries that France might try to regain Canada. France had lost its North American colonial holdings, including the province of Quebec, to the British in 1763, following the French and Indian War. The War of 1812 did not include France, nor did it entail fears of French involvement.

(4) Opposition to the War of 1812 did not involve the question of extending slavery into western territories. A few years later, in 1819, disagreements over the expansion of slavery arose with Missouri's application for statehood. The controversy was temporarily settled with the Missouri Compromise (1820), which allowed for the admission of two new states—Maine as a free state and Missouri as a slave state. It also divided the remaining area of the Louisiana Territory at 36° 30′ north latitude. Above that line, slavery was not permitted (except for in Missouri); below the line, it was permitted.

8. **2** The protection against double jeopardy and the right to a speedy trial are evidence that the United States Constitution supports the principle of due process of law. Both of these elements of due process are found in the Bill of Rights—the first ten amendments to the Constitution. The guarantee against double jeopardy is spelled out in the fifth amendment. The government is given one chance to convict someone of a crime. If the government fails in its case, the defendant does not have to worry about being prosecuted for the same crime again in the future, even if new evidence emerges. Of course, this amendment does not bar a defendant from appealing a guilty verdict to a higher court. The right to a "speedy and public trial" judged by an "impartial jury" is in the sixth amendment. The phrase *due process of law* simply refers to procedures that one goes through after he or she is arrested for committing a crime. These legal procedures, contained in several of the amendments to the Constitution, are intended to protect people's interests and liberties from arbitrary authority and are supposed to be applied equally to all citizens.

WRONG CHOICES EXPLAINED:
(1) The protection against double jeopardy and the right to a speedy trial are not related to the principle of eminent domain. Eminent domain refers to the constitutional principle that the government may, for a just price, force property owners to sell their property if the government deems that the property will be used for a public purpose. This power is in the fifth amendment of the Constitution.

(3) The protection against double jeopardy and the right to a speedy trial are not related to the principle of representative democracy. A representative democracy is a governing system in which citizens vote for representatives to create legislation and to govern on their behalf. It can be differentiated from direct democracy, in which citizens meet face-to-face to make decisions about their communities, as well as from the various forms on undemocratic governments, such as absolute monarchies and dictatorships.

(4) The protection against double jeopardy and the right to a speedy trial are not related to the principle of reserved powers. In the governing system in the United States established by the Constitution, certain powers are given (or delegated) to the national government and certain powers are held onto (or reserved) by the states. Delegated powers include the power to declare war and to issue currency. Reserved powers include the power to establish public education systems and to establish procedures for conducting local elections. Powers held by both the federal and the state governments are called concurrent powers.

9. **1** During the early 1800s, advances in democratic government included eliminating property qualifications as a requirement for voting. In the 1820s, most states reduced or removed property qualifications for voting so that most free males had the right to vote. Previously, voting was frequently restricted to property owners, effectively excluding poor and working-class men from the political process. The election of 1828 is considered by many historians to be the first modern election. First, the electorate was much broader than in previous elections. Consequently, candidates had to campaign more aggressively and tailor their appeal to reach a broader audience. Related to the democratization of the voting process was an increased focus on character and personality.

WRONG CHOICES EXPLAINED:

(2) The development described in this choice—ending the role of the electoral college—has not occurred in United States history. Some argue that ending the role of the electoral college in selecting the president would advance democratic government. However, such a move would require a change to the Constitution, which would require approval of three-fourths of the states. Many smaller and medium-sized states, especially those that are considered swing states, fear that they would be ignored if the electoral college were eliminated.

(3) The development described in this choice—increasing education and religious requirements for voting—has not occurred in United States history. Such a development would not advance democratic government. It would eliminate people from voting rolls. Several states had religious tests for voting in the early decades of the United States. Maryland was the last state to remove such restrictions in 1828.

(4) The development described in this choice—giving states the right to secede—has not occurred in United States history. Such a development might be considered a step toward greater democracy, but that right was never given by the federal government. The United States fought the Civil War (1861–1865) to prevent several states from seceding over the issue of slavery.

10. **3** One reason abolitionists were unpopular with many Northerners from the 1830s to 1860 was because abolitionists advocated views that increased tensions with the South. Some of these anti-abolitionist Northerners might have supported the institution of slavery, some might have been ambivalent, and some might have been uncomfortable with slavery, but they all saw maintaining sectional harmony as more important than challenging slavery. Public opinion in the North became increasingly split on the question of slavery. Anti-slavery sentiment has existed in the North as long as slavery has existed. Most obviously, African Americans—both free and enslaved—opposed the existence of slavery.

Small numbers of white Americans, from the 1600s onward, opposed slavery. Many believers in Enlightenment thought condemned slavery on humanistic grounds, while Quakers and some Evangelical Christians argued that slavery was inconsistent with Christian teachings. During the era of the American Revolution, more white Americans, including some slave holders, began to see slavery as inconsistent with the democratic values of the revolution. Starting in the 1830s, in the wake of the Second Great Awakening, a broader movement for the abolition of slavery began to form. William Lloyd Garrison was a key figure in the movement. He called for the immediate abolition of slavery, in contrast to many other white activists who advocated a more gradual approach to ending slavery. He also asserted that there should be no compensation to slave owners, and that freed slaves were entitled to the same rights as white people. He started a newspaper called *The Liberator* in 1831 to prod the public into challenging the institution of slavery. Starting in the 1840s, the towering figure in the abolitionist movement was Frederick Douglass. Douglass was born into slavery (1818) and escaped to the North in 1838. He had learned to read and write and soon became a powerful speaker in the anti-slavery movement. Douglass remained an important figure before, during, and after the Civil War, until his death in 1895. Harriet Beecher Stowe brought anti-slavery sentiment into the homes of many Northerners with the publication of her best-selling novel, *Uncle Tom's Cabin* (1852). The novel depicted in graphic detail the brutality of slavery. For many Northerners, slavery now had a human face. The novel outraged Southern supporters of slavery, who attempted to ban it.

WRONG CHOICES EXPLAINED:
(1) Abolitionists did not favor the growth of slavery. They took the opposite position; they favored the ending of slavery. Many Southern slaveholders, on the other hand, favored the growth of slavery. Some Northerners took a middle position—they argued that slavery was constitutionally protected in the states where it already existed, but they were opposed to the growth of slavery into new territories and states. This became the position of the newly formed Republican Party, starting in 1854. However, as the Civil War progressed, many Republicans became convinced that slavery needed to come to an end.

(2) Abolitionists did not encourage the annexation of Texas. They took the opposite position; they were opposed to the annexation of Texas. As early as the 1820s, white Americans began moving into the Mexican territory of Texas. In 1835, these Texans rebelled against Mexico. Texans won independence from Mexico, establishing the independent Lone Star Republic in 1836. Most Texans were eager for their Lone Star Republic to join the United States. However, many Northern politicians opposed Texas annexation because they feared that it

would create new tensions around the issue of slavery. Texas was finally annexed in 1845, soon after the victory of the expansionist James K. Polk in the presidential election of 1844.

(4) Abolitionists did not support the Fugitive Slave Act. They took the opposite position; they were opposed to the act. The Fugitive Slave Act mandated that federal and local authorities and individuals cooperate with slave catchers in search of escaped slaves. The United States government passed this stringent Fugitive Slave Act as part of the Compromise of 1850. This compromise evolved following California's application for statehood in 1850. The most important elements of the Compromise of 1850 were the admittance of California as a free state, which pleased Northern politicians, and a more stringent Fugitive Slave Act, which pleased Southern politicians. The act was especially galling to abolitionists in the North; it brought the violence and coercion of Southern slavery to the cities and towns of the North.

11. **1** The Compromise of 1850 was an attempt to resolve issues related to the protection and spread of slavery. The compromise emerged from debates following the Mexican-American War (1846–1848). The United States was victorious in that war. Under the terms of the Treaty of Guadalupe Hidalgo, the United States acquired the Mexican Cession—the huge territory that includes the present-day states of California, Nevada, and Utah, as well as portions of present-day Arizona, New Mexico, Wyoming, and Colorado. The acquisition of new territory brought the question of slavery to the forefront of political debates. Soon after the acquisition of the Mexican Cession, gold was discovered in California (1848). As word spread, thousands of people came to California to try to strike it rich. By 1850, California had enough people to form a state. Californians wrote up a constitution to submit to Congress in which slavery would be illegal. Southern senators objected to the admission of an additional free state. Senate negotiators worked out a series of measures that became known as the Compromise of 1850. The most important elements of the compromise were the admittance of California as a free state, which pleased Northern politicians, and a more stringent Fugitive Slave Law, which pleased Southern politicians. The compromise proved to be a temporary solution to a deeply troubling issue. By the end of the 1850s, the question of slavery so dominated public debates that the country seemed ready to break apart. It did exactly that in the months following the election of Abraham Lincoln in 1860. The secession of most of the slaveholding states led to the Civil War in 1861.

WRONG CHOICES EXPLAINED:
(2) The Compromise of 1850 was not related to boundary disputes between the United States and Great Britain over the Oregon Country. In 1818, the United States and Great Britain established joint ownership of what the

United States called the Oregon Country. Later, the boundary between United States and British territories became a source of contention. In 1846, the administration of President James K. Polk reached a compromise with Great Britain over control of the Oregon Country. The Oregon Treaty (1846) partitioned the region, establishing the border at the 49th parallel. That line is the current boundary between the western United States and Canada.

(3) The Compromise of 1850 was not related to relations with Native American Indians of the Great Plains. The Great Plains is the huge area of relatively flat land between the Mississippi River and the Rocky Mountains. The area was inhabited by the Plains Indians, including the Cheyenne, Comanche, and Sioux nations. The Homestead Act, the mass killing of buffalo, and the completion of the transcontinental railroad contributed to the decline of the Plains Indians. The Plains Indians resisted white encroachment of their lands. The Treaty of Fort Laramie (1868) was an attempt to end the violence, but the treaty soon collapsed. Fighting continued on the Great Plains until the last American Indian resistance was subdued when the military defeated the Sioux at Wounded Knee Creek, South Dakota (1890).

(4) The Compromise of 1850 was not related to the role of the federal government in industrial development. In the 19th century, government policies favored industrial development. For instance, the government encouraged the building of railroads by passing the Pacific [Transcontinental] Railroad Act (1862). The act encouraged the expansion of the railroad network by giving railroad companies wide swaths of federally owned land. Further, Supreme Court decisions favored big business. In *Santa Clara County* v. *Union Pacific Railway* (1886), for example, the Court established the concept of "corporate personhood" and shielded corporations from onerous regulation.

12. **3** One reason the decision in *Dred Scott* v. *Sandford* (1857) was so controversial is that it ruled that Congress had no power to limit slavery in the territories. The decision was a blow to the Republican Party, which sought to use the power of the federal government to prevent the spread of slavery into America's new territories. As part of the decision, the Supreme Court struck down the Missouri Compromise of 1820, which had banned slavery from the northern portion of the Louisiana Purchase territory. The case revolved around Dred Scott, a slave who sued to obtain his freedom on the grounds that he had lived for a time in territories where slavery was banned. The Court ruled that Scott was still a slave and did not even have the right to initiate a lawsuit. The *Dred Scott* decision declared that no African Americans, not even free men and women, were entitled to citizenship in the United States because they were, according to the Court, "beings of an inferior order." The case alarmed African Americans and many white Northerners and is seen as one of the factors that led to the Civil War.

WRONG CHOICES EXPLAINED:

(1) The *Dred Scott* decision did not strengthen the idea of popular sovereignty. The decision did the opposite; it negated the idea of popular sovereignty. The Court affirmed the right of slave owners to take their slaves into the Western territories, thereby undoing the doctrine of popular sovereignty and undermining the platform of the newly created Republican Party.

(2) The *Dred Scott* decision did not give enslaved persons full citizenship. It did the opposite; it negated African-American claims to citizenship. The decision declared that African Americans, even free men and women, were not entitled to citizenship in the United States because they were, according to the Court, "beings of an inferior order."

(4) The *Dred Scott* decision did not support Harriet Beecher Stowe's point of view in *Uncle Tom's Cabin*. It did the opposite; the decision upheld the institution of slavery while the book was critical of it. The best-selling novel, published in 1852, depicted in graphic detail the brutality of slavery. For many Northern readers, slavery now had a human face. The novel outraged Southern supporters of slavery, who attempted to ban it.

13. **2** When Andrew Carnegie stated, "The man who dies rich, dies disgraced," he was supporting charitable giving. Carnegie was encouraging wealthy people to distribute their money to charitable organizations rather than hoarding it until their death. Andrew Carnegie asserted, in an essay entitled "Wealth" (1899), that the wealthy have a duty to live responsible, modest lives and to give back to society. This "gospel of wealth" asserted that wealthy entrepreneurs should distribute their wealth so that it could be put to good use, rather than be frivolously wasted. Carnegie ended up donating the majority of his fortune to charity and public-oriented projects. Carnegie believed in a *laissez-faire* approach to social problems. He did not want the government interfering in the social and economic spheres. That is, in part, why he urged his fellow millionaires to take action on behalf of the community. In this way, the government would not have to.

WRONG CHOICES EXPLAINED:

(1) The quote by Andrew Carnegie does not support consumer credit. Starting in the 1920s, consumers had easier access to credit, enabling them to purchase items that were often beyond their means. This trend led to an increase in consumer debt and is often seen as one of the causes of the Great Depression on the 1920s. Carnegie did not advocate reckless spending; he encouraged people to live within their means.

(3) The quote by Andrew Carnegie does not support Social Darwinism. Social Darwinism was an attempt to apply Charles Darwin's ideas about the natural world to social relations. Social Darwinism was popularized in the United

States by William Graham Sumner. Sumner was attracted to Darwin's ideas about competition and "survival of the fittest." He argued against any attempt at government intervention into the economic and social spheres. Interference, he argued, would hinder the evolution of the human species. This hands-off approach to economic activities is known by the French phrase *laissez-faire*. Social Darwinism appealed to owners of large corporations because it both justified their wealth and power and warned against any type of regulation or reform. While these ideas would appeal to Carnegie, the quote is about charitable giving, not competition in the economic sphere.

(4) The quote by Andrew Carnegie does not support antitrust legislation. Antitrust legislation, such as the Sherman Antitrust Act (1890), was designed to break up trusts. Trusts are combinations of companies established to reduce competition. John D. Rockefeller established the first large trust in the oil processing industry. The formation of trusts in several industries was seen as harmful to the interests of consumers. Consequently, the government passed the Sherman Act. Carnegie was opposed to such legislation.

14. **2** A major impact of the trend shown in the chart was that Plains Indians lost their main source of food, shelter, and clothing. The Plains Indians are the Native American Indian nations, including the Cheyenne, Comanche, and Sioux nations, that lived in the Great Plains region of the United States. The Great Plains is the huge area of relatively flat land between the Mississippi River and the Rocky Mountains. Much of this area has rich soil and a long growing season, making it desirable for white settlers. The government encouraged development of the region by passing the Homestead Act (1862), which provided free land in the region to settlers who were willing to farm it. Hundreds of thousands of people applied for and were granted homesteads. The expansion of railroads into the West, leading to the completion of a transcontinental railroad in 1869, also encouraged white settlement in the Great Plains. The railroads provided an economic lifeline for these new settlers. Freight trains brought crops and cattle from the Great Plains states to cities such as Chicago. This increased economic activity led to Native American Indians being pushed off their land. The railroads also brought sportsmen out west who shot at buffalo herds from their passing train cars. While these buffalo (formally known as American bison) were sport for white travelers, they were a means of sustenance for many Plains Indians. The chart indicates that the buffalo population decreased from approximately 40 million at the turn of the 19th century to less than one thousand by the end of the century. These factors all led to the decline of the Plains Indians. The buffalo, which were threatened with extinction a century ago, have made somewhat of a recovery due to federal protective measures. Currently there are over 30,000 buffalo in North America.

WRONG CHOICES EXPLAINED:

(1) The decline of the buffalo, as indicated on the chart, did not result in frontier trading posts becoming more prosperous. As white settlers became more established in communities in the West, the need for trading posts decreased. Furthermore, the decline of the buffalo was accompanied by a decline in the population of Native American Indians and the virtual destruction of their way of life.

(3) The decline of the buffalo, as indicated on the chart, did not result in reservations being located closer to buffalo migration routes. Federal authorities did not take into consideration the migration patterns of the buffalo when relocating, and often reducing, Native American Indian reservations. In addition, the buffalo were virtually eliminated from the Great Plains.

(4) The decline of the buffalo, as indicated on the chart, did not result in white settlers becoming dependent on buffalo products. The buffalo were killed for sport or were simply massacred. They were not used by white settlers.

15.   **4** A supporter of the idea in the quotation would most likely favor following laissez-faire economics. The quotation notes several pro-business government policies, including maintaining a stable currency and domestic order. These are measures designed to create an environment that is more conducive to business investment. It also advocates a "hands-off" policy in regard to regulating business. The speaker would likely be against government actions that regulate minimum wages paid to employees, environmental impacts of industrial processes, or monopolistic practices by large corporations. The policy of laissez-faire asserts that government should limit, as much as possible, any interference in the economy. The French phrase *laissez-faire* means "to let alone." It describes a government policy that would take a hands-off approach in regard to economic activities. Throughout much of the history of the United States, Americans have been suspicious of government intervention into the economy. The founders of the United States had vivid memories of the overbearing mercantilist policies of Great Britain. With the American economy growing by leaps and bounds in the 19th century, the presidents of the late 19th century did not challenge the doctrine of laissez-faire. However, by the 20th century, the country began to face serious economic problems that called into question the laissez-faire doctrine. In the first decades of the 20th century, Progressive reformers called on the government to break up monopolies, regulate the food production industry, help the poor, and create peace between owners and workers. During the Progressive Era of the early 20th century, Presidents Theodore Roosevelt and Woodrow Wilson both took up the call to regulate the economy, to varying degrees.

WRONG CHOICES EXPLAINED:

(1) A supporter of the idea in the quotation would not favor establishing consumer protection laws. Such laws would amount to regulations on business regulations, and the quotation specifically calls for a "hands-off" approach in regard to regulation. In the aftermath of the publication of *The Jungle* (1906), the muckraking novel that exposed conditions in the meatpacking industry, Congress passed the Meat Inspection Act and the Pure Food and Drug Act (both in 1906).

(2) A supporter of the idea in the quotation would not favor securing collective-bargaining rights. Collective bargaining is the process of negotiations between employers and groups of employees, usually through unions. The quotation supports pro-business policies; extending collective-bargaining rights to workers would be seen by business owners as a challenge to their prerogatives and profits. The National Labor Relations Act of 1935 (Wagner Act) guaranteed that workers would have collective-bargaining rights.

(3) A supporter of the idea in the quotation would not favor levying high taxes on business. The quotation reflects a pro-business approach. A supporter of the quotation would probably push for maintaining lower taxes on business, not raising taxes.

16. **1** The passage of the Homestead Act most directly contributed to the situation shown in the photo. The photo depicts a group of people (presumably a family) standing in front of a "soddy"—a rough house built using blocks of sod dug up by homesteaders. Draft horses in the foreground and a cow in the background indicate that this is an agricultural venture. The first-generation pioneers drawn to the Great Plains were nicknamed "sodbusters" because they had to cut through the thick layer of sod to get to the topsoil needed for farming. The Homestead Act (1862) granted people up to 160 acres as an enticement for moving west. The act, along with the completion of the transcontinental railroad (1869), facilitated the movement of settlers and speculators. In the last three decades of the 19th century, millions of native-born whites, immigrants, and African Americans settled on farms west of the Mississippi River. From the last years of the Civil War until the turn of the 20th century, nine new states joined the United States—starting with Nevada (1864) and Nebraska (1867) and ending with Wyoming (1890) and Utah (1896). About a fifth of the farmers who established farms in this era obtained land directly from the government through the Homestead Act and similar federal legislation. Most of the land was purchased either from railroads, which had substantial holdings as a result of land grants from the government, or from speculators who obtained land from unsuccessful homesteaders. As the century progressed, the dream of land ownership proved to

be beyond the means of many people. The family farms of the prairie gave way to large-scale agribusinesses.

WRONG CHOICES EXPLAINED:

(2) The situation shown in the photo—homesteaders living in a "soddy" house on the Great Plains—was not brought about by the passage of the Sherman Antitrust Act. In the late 1800s, critics of corporate power pushed the government to take steps to rein in these massive corporations. The government passed the Sherman Antitrust Act (1890), but it had limited success. In the case of *United States* v. *E.C. Knight Company* (1895), the Supreme Court greatly limited the scope of the act by making a distinction between trade (which would be subject to the act) and manufacturing (which would not). The act had nothing to do with homesteaders moving west.

(3) The situation shown in the photo—homesteaders living in a "soddy" house on the Great Plains—was not brought about by the purchase of Alaska. The purchase of Alaska did lead to more Americans moving there. However, photos of settlers to Alaska might depict them in mining camps or fishing operations; farming was not prevalent among Alaskan settlers due to the short growing season of the region.

(4) The situation shown in the photo—homesteaders living in a "soddy" house on the Great Plains—was not brought about by the Interstate Commerce Act. In the late 1800s, reformers and farmers' organizations took action to check the massive power of railroads to dictate terms of service. Many states passed laws regulating railroad rates and practices. After the Supreme Court ruled in the *Wabash, St. Louis and Pacific Railroad* v. *Illinois* case (1886) that states could not regulate railroads because train service crossed state lines, the federal government created the Interstate Commerce Commission to regulate railroads. The ICC was chronically underfunded and was, therefore, ineffective. The act had nothing to do with homesteaders moving west.

17. **4** The passage is an excerpt from the Supreme Court decision in *Plessy* v. *Ferguson* (1896). The decision was a setback for those who sought an end to the Jim Crow system of racial segregation in the South. Jim Crow laws were state and local ordinances that first appeared after Reconstruction ended (1877). Typical laws called for separate schools or separate train cars for African Americans. Opponents of racial segregation argued that Jim Crow laws violated the 14th amendment (1868). This amendment, ratified during Reconstruction, stated that no person shall be denied "equal protection of the laws." Jim Crow laws, opponents argued, violated the 14th amendment because the laws relegated African Americans to inferior public accommodations and had the effect of making

African Americans second-class citizens. However, the Court disagreed. The decision stated that segregation was acceptable as long as the facilities for both races were of equal quality. This "separate but equal" doctrine allowed for the continuation of the Jim Crow system until the 1950s and 1960s. The beginning of the end to the system came with the *Brown* v. *Board of Education* decision of 1954.

WRONG CHOICES EXPLAINED:

(1) The passage does not reflect the Supreme Court decision in *Wabash, St. Louis and Pacific Railroad* v. *Illinois* (1886). That case arose as a result of efforts to regulate railroad rates. Starting in the 1870s, groups to promote the interests of farmers such as the Grange became concerned about the power and abuses of large railroad companies. Railroads often overcharged small-scale farmers. The Grange successfully pushed for laws in several states in the 1870s and 1880s to limit abusive practices by railroads. However, in the *Wabash* case, the Court ruled that Illinois could not regulate railroad rates on rail lines that crossed state boundaries, citing the interstate commerce clause of the Constitution. In response, the federal government created the Interstate Commerce Commission.

(2) The passage does not reflect the Supreme Court decision in *United States* v. *E.C. Knight Company* (1895). That case arose in the aftermath of the passage of the Sherman Antitrust Act (1890), which made illegal certain business practices that reduced competition. The act was invoked in court, when the government sued the E.C. Knight Company, a key entity in the Sugar Trust that controlled 98 percent of sugar processing in the United States. In the decision, the Court greatly limited the scope of the Sherman Antitrust Act by making a distinction between trade, which would be subject to the act, and manufacturing, which would not.

(3) The passage does not reflect the Supreme Court decision in *In re Debs* (1895). That case arose in the aftermath of the Pullman strike (1894). The Court upheld an injunction issued by the federal government against the strike. The Court ruled, in *In re Debs*, that the government has the right to ensure that interstate commerce is not interrupted and that United States mail is delivered.

18. **1** In the late 1800s, one reason labor unions struggled to gain support was because employers could easily replace striking employees. Owners of industrial firms could employ a variety of tactics to gain the upper hand in conflicts with labor unions during the late 1800s. Without legal protections from the government, striking workers generally were at a marked disadvantage in their struggles against powerful corporations. Employers used replacement workers, called "scabs" by the union movement, during strikes and hired armed guards to prevent

strikers from attempting to block the replacement workers from entering the premises. There was a large pool of potential replacement workers because the United States had become a major destination for immigrants. During the 1860s, a little over two million new residents entered the United States. That figure jumped to nearly nine million for the first decade of the 20th century. In 1886, a strike at the McCormick Reaper Works in Chicago turned violent when unskilled workers at the McCormick works went on strike and their jobs were quickly given to replacement workers. Most of the pitched workplace battles of the late 1800s, such as the Homestead strike of 1892 and the Pullman strike of 1894, ended in defeat for the workers. Workers saw their position and status erode during this period.

WRONG CHOICES EXPLAINED:

(2) In the late 1800s, the failures of the labor movement would not be attributed to high wages for industrial laborers. Wages were not, generally speaking, high. In fact, a major motivation for workers to strike during this period was a desire on the part of the workers for higher wages.

(3) In the late 1800s, the failures of the labor movement would not be attributed to the ready availability of government-funded public-works projects. Local and state governments did initiate and partially fund projects that provided jobs to individuals. In New York City, such projects included the building of Central Park (1857–1876) and of the Brooklyn Bridge (1869–1883). However, it was not until the creation of the New Deal, by President Franklin D. Roosevelt, during the Great Depression of the 1930s that the federal government enacted major public-works projects.

(4) In the late 1800s, the failures of the labor movement would not be attributed to the ending of the use of court injunctions by corporations. The opposite occurred. Corporations requested court injunctions to prevent workers from striking. This occurred during the Pullman strike (1894). The Pullman Company requested and received a federal court injunction against the strike. Subsequently, in *In re Debs*, the Supreme Court upheld the injunction, asserting that the government has the right to ensure that interstate commerce is not interrupted and that United States mail is delivered.

19. **3** The term *yellow journalism* is associated with the start of the Spanish-American War (1898). Yellow journalism refers to the sensationalistic, irresponsible coverage of events in the media. Yellow journalists created support for the Spanish-American War by writing articles about the sinking of the United States battleship *Maine*. In 1898, the *Maine* exploded and sunk in the harbor of Havana, Cuba (which was a colony of Spain). Many in the United States thought that the

destruction of the ship was the work of Spain, especially after American newspapers bluntly accused Spain of the crime, despite the scarcity of evidence. The coverage of the sinking of the *Maine* was one of several causes of the war. An independence movement was trying to break Cuba's ties to Spain. Many Americans wanted the United States to intervene on Cuba's side in this struggle. Some Americans saw parallels between the Cuban struggle for independence from Spain and America's struggle for independence from Great Britain. Also, some American businessmen were angered by the interruption of the sugar harvest by the fighting between Cuban rebels and Spanish forces. American newspapers breathlessly followed events in Cuba, with lurid accounts of Spanish wrongdoing. The Spanish-American War was brief. The U.S. declared war in April; an armistice was signed in August. The United States and Spain negotiated the Treaty of Paris (1898) following the war. In the treaty, Spain agreed to cede the Philippines, Puerto Rico, and Guam to the United States; the United States agreed to pay Spain $20 million for these possessions.

WRONG CHOICES EXPLAINED:

(1) The term *socialism* is not usually associated with the start of the Spanish-American War. The term *socialism* refers to a range of economic and social systems, as well as political ideologies, theories, movements, and parties that seek to establish such systems. Socialist systems are characterized by some form of social ownership of the means of production—either by the government or by the workers themselves, through collective or cooperative ownership. Socialists generally believe in some form of democratic control of the economic sphere. Eugene V. Debs, who had been a leader in the labor movement, was one of the founders of the Socialist Party of America in 1901.

(2) The term *populism* is not usually associated with the start of the Spanish-American War. The term *populism* is associated with the political insurgency by small-scale farmers in the late 1800s. The populists grew angry at the concentration of wealth and power by eastern industrialists. They supported a national income tax so that those with higher incomes would pay more than the poor. They also supported increasing the amount of currency in circulation; farmers supported inflationary policies so that the prices they received for their produce would increase. In common usage, the term *populism* can refer to any political candidate or movement that tries to appeal to ordinary people who feel that their concerns are ignored by established political parties.

(4) The term *isolationism* is not usually associated with the start of the Spanish-American War. The term *isolationism* refers to a policy of neutrality or noninterference in world affairs. Isolationism has been an impulse in U.S. foreign policy for much of its history. President George Washington's farewell

address (1796) urged the United States to avoid "permanent alliances" with European nations. Later, the Monroe Doctrine (1823) urged European nations to stay out of the affairs of the Western Hemisphere and promised that the United States would not involve itself in European affairs. In 1920, the Senate voted to reject U.S. membership in the League of Nations.

20. **4** The main idea of the 1912 cartoon is that a third political party can threaten the two major parties. The cartoon depicts a moose, with the label "Bull Moose" attached to its ear and with eyeglasses suggestive of Theodore Roosevelt, striking fear into an elephant and a donkey—the symbols of the Republican and Democratic Parties. The letters "GOP" on the elephant refer to the nickname of the Republican Party—the Grand Old Party. The cartoon refers to the presidential election of 1912. The Bull Moose Party, formally known as the Progressive Party, was formed to support the independent candidacy of Theodore Roosevelt in 1912. The party formed after a rift had developed between Roosevelt and President William Howard Taft, a fellow Republican who had succeeded him. Roosevelt and his supporters walked out of the Republican Party nominating convention in 1912 after the party nominated Taft to run for reelection. Roosevelt and his loyalists founded the Bull Moose Party. Roosevelt won 4.1 million votes (27 percent) in the 1912 election. As it turned out, it was the Republican Party that had more to fear going into the election than the Democratic Party. Roosevelt divided the vote of the traditional Republican electorate and opened the way for a rare victory for a Democratic presidential candidate—Woodrow Wilson. The party existed until 1916. Third-party candidates—not in one of the two major political parties—have consistently garnered a small percentage of the vote in elections. Elections in the United States are on a "winner takes all" basis. If the United States had a proportional representation system, in which parties received seats in government in proportion to the percentage of the national vote they received, people might be more likely to vote for third-party candidates. But in a "winner takes all" system, people tend to vote for one of the two major political parties.

WRONG CHOICES EXPLAINED:

(1) The cartoon does not suggest that the Democratic Party is losing support. Both parties—the Democratic donkey and the Republican elephant—appear worried about the Bull Moose Party going into the presidential election of 1912. In the end, the Democratic Party benefited from the participation of the Bull Moose Party. The Bull Moose candidate, Theodore Roosevelt, drew support away from his former party, the Republican Party, paving the way for a victory by the Democratic candidate, Woodrow Wilson.

(2) The cartoon does not suggest that Republicans outnumber Democrats in the United States. The cartoon depicts both major parties as worried about the participation of the Bull Moose Party in the election of 1912. It does not suggest that one of the major parties is stronger or weaker than the other.

(3) The cartoon does not suggest that the political system has no room for more than two parties. The cartoon depicts the two major parties—the Democratic donkey and the Republican elephant—as worried about the third-party participation of the Bull Moose Party, but it does not portray this development in a negative way. It seems to suggest that the appearance of a new party is a positive development, shaking up a stagnant political order.

21. **1** In the late 1800s, the major goal of United States policy in both the annexation of Hawaii and the acquisition of the Philippines was to obtain coaling stations and seaports for United States ships. Both actions took place in the context of the United States becoming an imperialist power. Many Americans had long looked to bring Hawaii within the orbit of the United States. American missionaries arrived in Hawaii as early as the 1820s. Later in the century, American businessmen established massive sugar plantations, undermining the local economy. Discord between the American businessmen and the ruler of the island, Queen Liliuokalani, emerged after 1891. The American pineapple grower Sanford Dole urged the United States military to intervene. The American businessmen staged a coup in 1893, deposing Queen Liliuokalani. U.S. forces immediately protected the new provisional government led by Dole. The provisional government hoped for U.S. annexation of the islands, but that did not occur until 1898. The United States acquired the Philippines in the aftermath of the Spanish-American War. In the Treaty of Paris, which ended the war, Spain ceded Puerto Rico, Guam, and the Philippines to the United States. Many Filipino people were not happy to see one imperial power (Spain) replaced by another one (the United States). It took the United States seven years and thousands of casualties to gain control of the Philippines. The idea of establishing coaling stations can be traced to Alfred Thayer Mahan, a retired admiral, who stressed the importance of naval power in achieving and maintaining influence on the world stage. In an 1890 book, he pushed for the United States to develop a strong navy, maintain military bases and coaling stations throughout the world, and administer an overseas empire.

WRONG CHOICES EXPLAINED:

(2) In the late 1800s, the major goal of United States policy in both the annexation of Hawaii and the acquisition of the Philippines was not expanding United States fishing rights in international waters. Fishing rights in international waters has not been the subject of major disputes. International waters,

also known as the high seas, are parts of the oceans that are not under any country's jurisdiction. In these waters, countries have the rights to fishing, navigation, and overflight, as well as conducting scientific research.

(3) In the late 1800s, the major goal of United States policy in both the annexation of Hawaii and the acquisition of the Philippines was not limiting the spread of Japanese influence. The United States did become concerned about the rise of Japanese influence in Asia, but not until the 20th century, especially after Japan's victory in the Russo-Japanese War (1904–1905). The events in the question occurred in the 19th century.

(4) In the late 1800s, the major goal of United States policy in both the annexation of Hawaii and the acquisition of the Philippines was not protecting the area around the Panama Canal. The territories in the question are not in close proximity to the Panama Canal. Furthermore, the Panama Canal was not begun until 1904; it was not completed until 1914. The events in the question occurred in the 19th century.

22. **1** The actions referred to in the three headlines were supported by the Progressive reform movement. Progressivism was an early 20th-century reform movement that promoted government actions to address political, economic, and social problems. Progressivism existed at the grass-roots level as well as in the corridors of power. Two influential presidents, Theodore Roosevelt and Woodrow Wilson, took on the Progressive mantle. The movement claimed many legislative victories, and ultimately influenced both the New Deal and 20th-century liberalism. The three items in the headline reflect the breadth of the movement's concerns. The income tax did not exist in the United States until the 16th amendment was ratified in 1913. This amendment gave the federal government the authority to tax people's incomes. Previously the government gained its revenues almost entirely from import tariffs. A graduated, or progressive, income tax taxes the wealthy at a higher rate than it taxes the poor. The idea is that the wealthy have proportionally more disposable income and are better able to part with a sizable portion of their income. Progressive Era activists believed that such a tax would create a fairer society, especially in light of the disparities of wealth that developed during the Gilded Age of the late 19th century. The Federal Reserve System was created to regulate the money supply. The Federal Reserve Bank, which is in part privately controlled and in part publicly controlled, was created by legislation in 1913 during the administration of President Woodrow Wilson. One of its main functions is to regulate economic growth by regulating the supply of money. If the economy is sluggish, the Fed will attempt to stimulate economic growth by increasing the money supply; if inflation occurs, the Fed will attempt to slow down economic activity

by reducing the money supply. Congress passed the Pure Food and Drug Act, along with the Meat Inspection Act, in 1906, in the aftermath of the publication of the novel *The Jungle* (1906) by Upton Sinclair. Sinclair's novel exposed the underside of the meatpacking industry. The novel follows a Lithuanian immigrant family through the stockyards of Chicago. The novel created a public uproar about the safety of meat, leading Congress to pass the legislation in question.

WRONG CHOICES EXPLAINED:

(2) The actions referred to in the three headlines did not grow out of the concerns of the Prohibition movement. The goal of the Prohibition movement was to ban alcohol from American society. The movement against alcohol consumption was one of the largest movements in United States history, from the early 1800s, until it achieved success with the ratification of the 18th amendment (1919). The amendment, which prohibited the production, sale, and consumption of alcoholic beverages, was repealed in 1933 by the 21st amendment.

(3) The actions referred to in the three headlines did not grow out of the concerns of the labor movement. The goal of the labor movement was to organize workers into unions in order to advance their interests through collective bargaining. A significant early union was the Knights of Labor, founded in 1869. This union welcomed all members, regardless of race, sex, or level of skill. The Knights had a broad agenda that included not only improvements in wages and hours for their workers, but also social reforms such as an end to child labor and better safety rules. A second early union was the American Federation of Labor (1886). The AFL differed from the Knights of Labor in that it included only skilled workers, the "aristocracy of labor."

(4) The actions referred to in the three headlines did not grow out of the concerns of the conservation movement. The conservation movement was concerned with the rapid destruction and disappearance of natural areas in the United States. Logging and mining operations were taking a toll on forested areas starting in the late 1800s. President Theodore Roosevelt (1901–1909) embraced the cause of conservationism. Roosevelt, an avid outdoorsman, set aside millions of acres as protected areas. These included six national parks. Later, the environmental movement of the 1960s and 1970s pushed ecological concerns into public consciousness. The movement was inspired partly by Rachel Carson's book *Silent Spring* (1962), which detailed the harmful effects of toxic chemicals.

23. **3** In his war message to Congress, President Woodrow Wilson urged the United States to enter World War I in order to make the world safe for democracy. When World War I began in 1914, Wilson was opposed to United States participation in it. He initially assumed that the United States could stay neutral in World War I and maintain commercial ties to nations on both sides of the conflict. However, quickly into the war, Britain successfully blockaded American ships from reaching Germany. Out of necessity, United States trade shifted to Britain exclusively. Germany became increasingly belligerent toward the United States as the war progressed. Germany, however, wanted to keep the United States out of the war and agreed in the Sussex Pledge (1916) to make no surprise submarine attacks on U.S. ships. In 1917, Germany rescinded the Sussex Pledge and declared that it would resume unrestricted submarine warfare. Also in 1917, many Americans were angered by an intercepted telegram from German foreign secretary Arthur Zimmerman indicating that Germany would help Mexico regain territory it had lost to the United States in the Mexican-American War (1846–1848) if Mexico joined the war on Germany's side. These factors pushed Wilson toward an interventionist position. He framed American intervention in the altruistic language of fostering democratic practices in the world—that American participation was necessary to make the world "safe for democracy." The United States finally entered the war in 1917.

WRONG CHOICES EXPLAINED:

(1) In his war message to Congress, President Woodrow Wilson's rationale for the United States entrance into World War I was not to protect the empires of European countries. He argued for the opposite. In his Fourteen Points document (1918), he emphasized self-determination for European people—not imperial rule. The document also called for international cooperation, freedom of the seas, removal of barriers to trade, and an international organization to resolve conflicts.

(2) In his war message to Congress, President Woodrow Wilson's rationale for the United States entrance into World War I was not to create a new world government. Later, in his Fourteen Points document (1918), Wilson put forth the idea of a world government. Wilson's idealistic vision for a post-war world included the formation of the League of Nations. Most of the ideas in the Fourteen Points document were rejected by the victorious European powers except for the creation of the League of Nations. Isolationists in the Senate blocked the United States from joining the League.

(4) In his war message to Congress, President Woodrow Wilson's rationale for the United States entrance into World War I was not to stop a British attack on the United States. Though Britain and the United States have had a history of conflict, by the 20th century, the two nations were allies. There was no thought

that Britain would attack the United States. The United States was trading extensively with Britain during the war, much to the consternation of Germany.

24. **4** The cartoonist's point of view is that the actions of labor unions threaten the American way of life. The context of the publication of the cartoon was a massive strike wave by workers and the Red Scare. The cartoon is depicting "Labor" descending down a staircase. The steps in labor's descent are labeled "Strikes—Walkouts," "Disorder—Riots," "Bolshevism—Murder," and "Chaos." After the "Chaos" step, the cartoonist drew a question mark, inviting the viewer to speculate what comes next—perhaps a violent revolution. Organized labor was indeed engaging in a large number of strikes and walkouts in 1919. After World War I, the government disbanded the agencies that were created to control prices and to maintain workplace peace. As wages fell and prices rose, workers across America organized and fought to protect wartime gains. The year 1919 saw the biggest strike wave in American history. There were more than 4500 strikes involving 4 million workers. The biggest strike was the Seattle General Strike in February. In September, more than 340,000 steelworkers went on strike. Late in 1919 and into 1920, the police force in Boston went on strike. Partly in response to this labor militancy, the Red Scare, a crusade against suspected communists, anarchists, labor leaders, and other radicals, emerged. Other factors also contributed to the Red Scare, including the successful Bolshevik revolution in Russia in 1917 and the virulent strain of patriotism unleashed by World War I. The Red Scare was also set in motion by a series of bombs that were detonated in several cities in 1919 and 1920 by radical groups. In January 1920, Attorney General A. Mitchell Palmer began a broad hunt for suspected radicals. Palmer's Justice Department carried out unwarranted raids, known as "Palmer raids," of suspected radicals' homes. While Palmer did not uncover the makings of an uprising, he did end up deporting over 500 noncitizens including the Russian-born anarchist activist Emma Goldman (1919). The cartoon reflects the heightened fears of the era, equating labor strikes with violent revolution.

WRONG CHOICES EXPLAINED:
(1) The cartoon is not suggesting that immigrants assimilate easily into American society. The cartoon does not allude to immigrants, nor to their ability to assimilate. Many of the people who shared the point of view of the cartoonist—that labor strikes were tied to violent revolutionary movements—also held anti-immigrant views. Nativism rose steeply in the years after World War I, leading to the passage of the Emergency Quota Act of 1921 and the National Origins Act of 1924. These acts greatly reduced the number of immigrants allowed into the United States.

(2) The cartoon is not suggesting that industrial production will expand and create more jobs. It is suggesting that striking workers will undermine industrial stability and will lead to economic chaos and violent revolution.

(3) The cartoon is not suggesting that civil liberties will be restricted and ordinary American citizens will be hurt. In fact, the fears that this cartoon is reflecting (and stoking) led to a restriction on civil liberties. The Red Scare, which developed in the context of fears of labor militancy, included a broad hunt for suspected radicals. This hunt included raids of suspected radicals' homes, in violation of the fourth amendment's protection against "unreasonable" searches of people and their "houses, papers, and effects."

25. **2** The photograph shows one side of the 1920s conflict between science and religion. The photograph shows a table organized by the Anti-Evolution League in Dayton, Ohio, during the 1925 trial of John Thomas Scopes. The table is promoting copies of the organization's publication, *The Conflict*, as well as copies of a best-selling book by T.T. Martin, *Hell and the High School*. Martin's book, in vivid language, railed against teachers, "paid by our taxes, who feed our children's minds with the deadly, soul-destroying poison of Evolution." The Scopes trial involved the teaching of evolution in public schools. Scopes, a Tennessee biology teacher, was arrested for violating a state law forbidding the teaching of evolution. The case turned into a national spectacle, with the famous lawyers Clarence Darrow representing Scopes and William Jennings Bryan representing the state. The trial pitted rural, traditional, religious values against science. Though the trial was a local state trial, rather than a Supreme Court case, it garnered headlines across the country. It is one of several important events that highlighted the profound cultural divisions in the 1920s.

WRONG CHOICES EXPLAINED:
(1) The photograph does not show sides in the conflict between union men and factory owners. Such conflicts occurred in large numbers in 1919 and 1920. In 1919, there were more than 4500 strikes involving 4 million workers. Major strikes included the Seattle General Strike, a widespread steelworkers' strike, and a strike by the Boston police.

(3) The photograph does not show sides in the conflict between nativists and immigrants. Such a conflict did occur in the 1920s. Nativism rose steeply in the years after World War I, leading to the passage of the Emergency Quota Act of 1921 and the Immigration Act of 1924. These acts greatly reduced the number of immigrants allowed into the United States.

(4) The photograph does not show sides in the conflict between censorship and the free press. Such a conflict did occur during the Red Scare of 1919 and

1920. The government used World War I–era statutes—the Alien and Espionage Acts (1917 and 1918)—to target publishers of materials that were seen as sympathetic to radical causes.

26. **3** The poem, "I, Too," by Langston Hughes is associated with the blossoming of African-American culture in the 1920s. This cultural movement, known as the Harlem Renaissance, was a literary, artistic, and intellectual movement that celebrated African-American life and forged a new cultural identity among African-American people. The movement was centered in the African-American neighborhood of Harlem in New York City. Langston Hughes was a central figure in the movement. His poems include "Harlem" and "The Negro Speaks of Rivers," as well as "I, Too." "I, Too" notes the exclusion and segregation of African Americans from mainstream institutions in the United States—"They send me to eat in the kitchen," rather than with guests at the dining room table. However, the poem also asserts that in the future such exclusion will be ended—"Tomorrow, I'll be at the table." The poem is an affirmation of strength, determination, and beauty. It also notes the shame that white Americans will feel in the future for creating and benefiting from the system of discrimination they had created. The Harlem Renaissance also included many other influential cultural figures. Duke Ellington, a composer, pianist, and bandleader, was perhaps the most important figure in 20th-century jazz. Some of his most important compositions are "Mood Indigo," "Don't Get Around Much Anymore," and "Take the A Train." Bessie Smith was the most well-known blues and jazz singer of the 1920s. Other contributions to the Harlem Renaissance include the poetry of Claude McKay and Countee Cullen and the jazz music of Louis Armstrong.

WRONG CHOICES EXPLAINED:
(1) The poem is not associated with the growth of the motion-picture industry. The motion-picture industry was growing in prominence in the 1920s. Movie attendance achieved staggering levels. By the end of the decade, three-fourths of the American people (roughly 90 million) were going to the movies every week. The first "talkie," *The Jazz Singer*, came out in 1927. However, the poem does not reference motion pictures.

(2) The poem is not associated with the emergence of an anti-war party. The poem does not refer to war or political parties. During World War I, the Socialist Party (formed in 1901) opposed American participation in the war. Its leader, Eugene V. Debs, ran for president in 1920 from prison, having been convicted of violating the 1917 Espionage Act by speaking out against World War I.

(4) The poem is not associated with the expansion of mass consumption. The poem does not refer to consumer products. The decade of the 1920s is

often noted for the expansion of mass consumption. Mass-production tech-niques led to greater availability of consumer goods to average families. Cars, radios, toasters, health and beauty aids, and other consumer goods filled show-rooms and stores. Easy credit and layaway plans helped move merchandise. The advertising industry expanded to draw more people into the world of mass consumption.

27. **2** In the 1920s, authors such as F. Scott Fitzgerald, Ernest Hemingway, and Sinclair Lewis wrote primarily about post–World War I disillusionment and materialism. The three authors were part of the "Lost Generation" of writers fol-lowing World War I. Lost Generation writers tended to focus on the materialism and crassness of American society in the 1920s. Lost Generation writers also cast a critical eye at the glorification of war that characterized the World War I era. Hemingway's novel, *A Farewell to Arms* (1929), depicted the cynicism and brutal-ity of World War I. Fitzgerald's novel, *The Great Gatsby* (1925), depicted the carelessness and destructiveness of the very wealthy. Sinclair Lewis wrote a series of novels, including *Main Street* (1920), *Babbitt* (1922), and *Arrowsmith* (1925), satirizing the limited outlook and emptiness of small-town American life.

WRONG CHOICES EXPLAINED:

(1) The authors mentioned in the question did not write about the intoler-ance of the Ku Klux Klan. The writers of the Lost Generation tended to shy away from issues of race in the United States. African-American writers who were part of the Harlem Renaissance tackled issues of racism and Ku Klux Klan violence head-on. The poetry of Langston Hughes often focused on racism and white supremacy in American society.

(3) The authors mentioned in the question did not write about the failure of cultural pluralism. *Cultural pluralism* is a term used to describe a social order in which smaller ethnic and racial groups participate in the dominant, mainstream society, but still maintain their unique cultural identities. The concept implies acceptance by the broader society of the values and practices of the smaller groups. The idea of cultural pluralism came into widespread usage in the early decades of the 20th century, both as a description of contemporary society and as a societal goal. The idea stood in contrast to the conception of the United States as a "melting pot," in which different ethnic groups lose their unique cultural traits as they assimilate into mainstream culture.

(4) The authors mentioned in the question did not write about the lack of educational opportunities for young Americans. Debates over education policy occurred frequently in the 1920s. In general, educational facilities expanded to accommodate the large numbers of immigrant families that had come into the

United States in the period 1880 to 1920. Many saw public education as a way to assimilate young immigrants into American culture. Conservative reformers in several states attempted to pass laws mandating public education, a move designed to undermine Catholic and other parochial schools. Progressive educators attempted to incorporate the ideas of John Dewey into education by moving away from rote memorization and putting more emphasis on the process of learning and on student participation.

28. **3** The Federal Deposit Insurance Corporation (FDIC) and the Securities and Exchange Commission (SEC) were part of President Franklin D. Roosevelt's efforts to reform economic problems that contributed to the Great Depression. Roosevelt's New Deal agenda included a variety of reforms that were intended to restore people's confidence in the economy. Many people had lost confidence in the banking system and withdrew their money, fearing that their banks might fold. With thousands of people withdrawing their money at the same time, many banks actually did fold, turning their fears into a self-fulfilling prophecy. The Federal Deposit Insurance Corporation, created by the Glass-Steagall Act (1933), insures deposits so that if a bank does fold, people would not lose their savings. Many had also lost confidence in the stock market after the 1929 crash, which was partly caused by unsound practices. The Securities and Exchange Commission was created in 1934 to regulate the stock market and prevent the reckless investment behavior that led to the crash of October 1929. The Securities and Exchange Commission oversees stock market operations by monitoring transactions, licensing brokers, limiting buying on margin, and prohibiting insider trading.

WRONG CHOICES EXPLAINED:
(1) The Federal Deposit Insurance Corporation (FDIC) and the Securities and Exchange Commission (SEC) are not related to efforts to reduce the power of business monopolies during the Great Depression. The power of business monopolies was not seen as a major cause of the Great Depression. Earlier, Roosevelt's distant cousin, President Theodore Roosevelt (1901–1909), was more closely associated with efforts to reduce the power of business monopolies.
(2) The Federal Deposit Insurance Corporation (FDIC) and the Securities and Exchange Commission (SEC) are not related to efforts to give organized labor a stronger voice in politics. Other New Deal initiatives were designed to strengthen organized labor. Notably, the Wagner Act, also known as the National Labor Relations Act, mandated that employers bargain with their unions. It also established the National Labor Relations Board to conduct elections among workers to see if they wanted to be represented by a union. The act also banned certain unfair labor practices.

(4) The Federal Deposit Insurance Corporation (FDIC) and the Securities and Exchange Commission (SEC) are not related to efforts to bring electricity to rural areas. Another New Deal agency, the Tennessee Valley Authority, did that. The TVA was a set of development projects in the Tennessee River area, which includes the states of Kentucky, Virginia, North Carolina, Tennessee, Georgia, Alabama, and Mississippi. The region was especially hard hit by the Great Depression. Even before the depression, poverty was pervasive; most homes in the region were without electricity. The TVA included major infra-structure projects, including electricity-generating dams along the Tennessee River. The strategy was to provide jobs and electricity to people in the region.

29. **2** President Franklin D. Roosevelt proposed a plan in 1937 to add justices to the Supreme Court primarily because the Court had declared major New Deal laws unconstitutional. By 1937, Roosevelt had grown frustrated with the conser-vative approach of the Supreme Court. It shot down the National Industrial Recovery Act in *Schechter* v. *United States* (1935) and the Agricultural Adjustment Act in *Butler* v. *United States* (1936). In 1937, he announced a plan to increase the number of justices on the Supreme Court to as many as fifteen. He said that some of the older justices had difficulty keeping up with the heavy workload. However, it was clear that he was trying to create a Supreme Court friendlier to his New Deal programs. Congress opposed his "court packing" scheme, and, after much criticism, Roosevelt eventually backed away from it. Soon, however, openings on the Court allowed Roosevelt to appoint new justices and influence the direction of the Court.

WRONG CHOICES EXPLAINED:
(1) President Franklin D. Roosevelt's proposed plan in 1937 to add justices to the Supreme Court was not motivated by the Court lacking representation from minority groups. The Court was all white and male, but Roosevelt was not espe-cially concerned with creating a Supreme Court that reflected the diversity of the United States. He did nominate a Jewish justice—Felix Frankfurter, who replaced another Jewish justice, Benjamin Cardozo (1939). However, the first African-American justice (Thurgood Marshall, 1967), the first female justice (Sandra Day O'Connor, 1981), and the first Latina justice (Sonia Sotomayor, 2009) were all appointed well after Roosevelt's time.

(3) President Franklin D. Roosevelt's proposed plan in 1937 to add justices to the Supreme Court was not motivated by the lack of judicial experience on the Court. Several of the justices had served since the 1910s. In fact, Roosevelt argued the opposite; he argued that several of the judges were too old to keep up with the increased workload. Therefore, he argued, additional justices would

expedite the work of the Court. However, his real motivation was to change the ideological makeup of the Court.

(4) President Franklin D. Roosevelt's proposed plan in 1937 to add justices to the Supreme Court was not motivated by the Court supporting a loose interpretation of the Constitution. The debates between those who favored a loose interpretation of the Constitution and those who favored a strict interpretation date back to the early years of the republic. Thomas Jefferson and Alexander Hamilton disagreed over whether the Constitution allowed for the creation of a national bank. In the 1930s, when the Court struck down key New Deal acts, it was demonstrating a strict interpretation of the Constitution. A loose interpretation might have upheld the agencies in question by invoking the elastic clause, which lets Congress do what it considers "necessary and proper" to carry out its functions.

30. **3** A major reason for the change in unemployment shown on the graph between 1933 and 1937 was that job opportunities were created by New Deal public-works projects. The graph indicates that unemployment dropped during Franklin D. Roosevelt's first term in office from nearly 25 percent in 1933 to just over 14 percent in 1937. Roosevelt won the presidential election in 1932, promising a "new deal" to the American public. Roosevelt promised to take the federal government in a new direction by asserting that it should take some responsibility for the welfare of the people during the economic emergency. His immediate goal was relief for the unemployed through jobs programs. He promised "direct recruitment" of unemployed people to work on public works that would benefit the nation as a whole. The New Deal included jobs programs such as the Civilian Conservation Corps (1933), which focused on young men, and the vast Works Progress Administration (1935), which consisted of a myriad of public projects. The WPA, for example, built schools, installed sewer lines, wrote guidebooks, and produced theatrical productions. Roosevelt's initiatives were unprecedented in their scope and direction. In addition to creating public-works projects, the Roosevelt administration (1933–1945) provided direct relief, or what would be known as welfare today, to millions of families. Also, the New Deal addressed the welfare of retired people and people with disabilities by creating the Social Security system in 1935.

WRONG CHOICES EXPLAINED:

(1) The change in unemployment between 1933 to 1937—a drop from almost 25 percent of the working-age population to just over 14 percent—would not be attributed to banks increasing their lending to new businesses, who then hired additional workers. The banking industry was in crisis during the years in

question and few new businesses were opening in the midst of the worst economic downturn in the nation's history.

(2) The change in unemployment between 1933 to 1937—a drop from almost 25 percent of the working-age population to just over 14 percent—would not be attributed to states heavily taxing corporate profits. Such a move might lead corporations to laying off workers. The public-works projects that did reduce unemployment were funded through federal taxes, as well as deficit spending.

(4) The change in unemployment between 1933 to 1937—a drop from almost 25 percent of the working-age population to just over 14 percent—would not be attributed to the federal government nationalizing the transportation and utility industries. Such a move did not occur. The belief in government ownership of large-scale industry is consistent with socialist ideologies.

31. **1** The main cause of the change in unemployment shown on the graph between 1942 and 1945 was increased manufacturing to meet the needs of World War II. Though the New Deal stabilized the economy, it was really World War II that brought the United States out of the Great Depression. As early as 1939, unemployment in the United States plummeted as factories began the conversion to a wartime economy. The vitality of the wartime economy led to population shifts as people moved to industrial centers. The chart indicated the dramatic drop in the unemployment rate from 1939 until the end of World War II (1945). In 1944, the unemployment rate dropped to close to zero. The government made a concerted effort to recruit people who had not been part of the industrial workforce, including women. Women were needed because factories were working around the clock producing military goods, and much of the male workforce was in the military. Recruiting posters were produced by the government, usually through the Office of War Information, showing women, including the fictional "Rosie the Riveter," in industrial settings. Further, President Franklin D. Roosevelt signed Executive Order 8022 (1941), banning racial discrimination in defense industries. This had the dual effect of helping African Americans emerge from the Great Depression and helping the defense industry meet its wartime needs.

WRONG CHOICES EXPLAINED:

(2) The trend in unemployment between 1942 and 1945—a reduction in the unemployment rate to well below five percent of the workforce—would not be attributed to the success of the Social Security Act. The 1935 act, which created the Social Security system, addressed the welfare of retired people and people with disabilities. It did not create jobs and did not have a direct effect on the unemployment rate.

(3) The trend in unemployment between 1942 and 1945—a reduction in the unemployment rate to well below five percent of the workforce—would not be attributed to the impact of a high inflation rate. During times of war, inflation is a constant threat due to the lack of consumer goods and the additional money that people have in their pockets from defense-related industrial work. However, during World War II, the Office of Price Adjustment (created in 1941) kept inflation in check by imposing price ceilings on most consumer items. Between April 1942 and June 1946, the agency managed to keep the annual rate of inflation rate at around 3.5 percent.

(4) The trend in unemployment between 1942 and 1945—a reduction in the unemployment rate to well below five percent of the workforce—would not be attributed to a decline in the number of women in the workforce. The opposite occurred. The employment needs of the defense industry were so acute that the government made a concerted effort to recruit women to work in the defense industry. The fictional "Rosie the Riveter" character was often featured in this public relations campaign. The World War II recruiting campaign was successful. By 1945, one-third of the workforce was female.

32. **4** The Neutrality Acts (1935–1937) were passed to avoid the actions that led the United States into World War I. For the first three years of World War I, which began in 1914, the United States insisted on its right to trade with belligerent nations while remaining neutral. This insistence on trading with belligerent nations during wartime ultimately contributed to the decision by the United States to enter World War I. German attacks on American ships angered many Americans and pushed President Woodrow Wilson toward a pro-war position. In the Neutrality Acts of 1935–1937, Congress made clear that neither the United States government nor private U.S. firms were to trade with belligerent nations. The acts were an expression of isolationism. President Franklin Roosevelt grew frustrated with these acts because they did not make a distinction between aggressors and victims in the conflicts of the 1930s. A later Neutrality Act (1939) allowed the United States to supply the opponents of fascism with materials on a cash-and-carry basis.

WRONG CHOICES EXPLAINED:
(1) The Neutrality Acts of 1935–1937 were not designed to support the policy of appeasement. Appeasement is the policy of not challenging a rival's moves in order to avoid a direct conflict. This policy was pursued by Great Britain and France toward Germany in the 1930s. The United States was not part of the appeasement policy in the 1930s.

(2) The Neutrality Acts of 1935–1937 were not designed to provide troops to halt Italian aggression. Fascist Italy conquered Ethiopia in 1936. The United States, pursuing a policy of neutrality at the time, did not provide troops to halt Italy.

(3) The Neutrality Acts of 1935–1937 were not designed to increase the profits of weapons manufacturers. Pursuing a policy of neutrality would reduce the need for military preparedness and for additional weaponry. The policy would not, therefore, lead to increased profits for weapons manufacturers. By the 1930s, many Americans became critical of the profits made by weapons manufacturers during World War I. The Senate's Nye committee (1934–1937) uncovered evidence that certain American corporations greatly profited from World War I. Americans wondered if the so-called "merchants of death" had pushed the country into World War I. It was in this atmosphere that the first Neutrality Act was passed (1935).

33. **4** One government action that was taken in response to the Japanese attack on Pearl Harbor was forcing the relocation and internment of Japanese Americans. Emotions ran high following the attack by Japan on Pearl Harbor in 1941. This attack stunned many Americans and made them bitter toward Japan. Many Americans directed their anger at all Japanese people—even ones who had decided to immigrate to the United States. In 1942, President Roosevelt issued Executive Order 9066, authorizing the government to remove 120,000 people, two-thirds of them citizens, from West Coast states and relocate them to camps throughout the West. The order cited the possibility of "espionage" or "sabotage." It asserted that the relocation was necessary for the "successful prosecution" of the war against Japan. Most of their property was confiscated by the government. In the case of *Korematsu* v. *United States* (1944), the Supreme Court ruled that the relocation was acceptable on the grounds of national security. The *Korematsu* decision is one of several rulings by the Supreme Court that have curtailed civil liberties in times of war. Much later, in 1988, the United States government publicly apologized to the surviving victims of the internment and extended $20,000 in reparations to each one.

WRONG CHOICES EXPLAINED:
(1) In responding to the Japanese attack on Pearl Harbor (1941), the government did not draft all Japanese-American men. Some Nisei, American-born children of Japanese immigrants, were drafted over the course of World War II. However, significant numbers of Japanese Americans enlisted to serve. Approximately 33,000 Japanese Americans served in World War II, the vast majority of whom were being kept in internment camps before entering the military.

(2) In responding to the Japanese attack on Pearl Harbor (1941), the government did not pass labor laws banning the employment of immigrants. The defense industry was short of workers during World War II. The government encouraged all Americans—including immigrants, African Americans, and women—to make themselves available for work in the defense industry.

(3) In responding to the Japanese attack on Pearl Harbor (1941), the government did not end all oil sales to Japan. The United States ended oil sales to Japan before the attack on Pearl Harbor. In 1940, the United States, working with its allies, passed the Export Control Act to limit the exportation of important war-related materials, including oil, to Japan. The following year, months before the attack on Pearl Harbor, the United States initiated a complete oil embargo against Japan.

34. **3** The goal shown in the posters—conserving and collecting scrap materials that could be used by the military during World War II—was similar to rationing by the Office of Price Administration. In both cases, the government was attempting to ensure that the military had the materials it needed during World War II. During the war, there were shortages of key items because of the needs of the military. Starting in 1942, the Office of Price Administration began rationing key commodities to civilians, such as gasoline and tires. Next, the government began rationing food—sugar, meat, coffee, lard, butter, and many other items. Families were given ration books and would use ration stamps, along with cash, when they purchased the affected items. The two posters were encouraging Americans to participate in salvaging materials that could be used by the military—metals of various sorts, as well as rubber, rags, paper, and burlap. In many ways, World War II required the participation of the entire American public, not simply members of the military. These efforts created a sense of unity and common cause in the country.

WRONG CHOICES EXPLAINED:
(1) The goal shown in the posters—conserving and collecting scrap materials that could be used by the military during World War II—was not most similar to the institution of the draft by the Selective Service Act (1940). Both initiatives had the overall goal of achieving victory in World War II. However, the goal of the posters was to conserve and collect needed materials, while the purpose of the draft was to ensure that there were enough soldiers to serve in the military. Starting in October 1940, the Selective Service Administration began drafting men into military service by lottery. The Selective Service System ended up providing over 16 million men to the military.

(2) The goal shown in the posters—conserving and collecting scrap materials that could be used by the military during World War II—was not most similar to aid to Russia under the Lend-Lease Act (1941). Both initiatives had the overall goal of achieving victory in World War II. However, the goal of the posters was to conserve and collect needed materials, while the purpose of the Lend-Lease Act was for the United States to extend aid to nations fighting Nazi aggression at the beginning of World War II. The United States ended up supplying the Soviet Union with $11.3 billion worth of war materials.

(4) The goal shown in the posters—conserving and collecting scrap materials that could be used by the military during World War II—was not most similar to the development of the Manhattan Project (1942). Both initiatives had the overall goal of achieving victory in World War II. However, the goal of the posters was to conserve and collect needed materials, while the purpose of the Manhattan Project was to develop the atomic bomb. This secret project, launched in an office building in New York City, involved several sites, but the final assembly of the atomic bomb occurred in Los Alamos, New Mexico. The bomb was ready by July 1945, as the United States was preparing for a final attack on Japan. The United States dropped the atomic bomb on the Japanese city of Hiroshima on August 6, 1945. After the United States dropped a second atomic bomb on the city of Nagasaki, Japan surrendered, ending World War II.

35. **1** The Servicemen's Readjustment Act of 1944 (GI Bill) made a significant impact on post–World War II America because it provided for aid to veterans for housing and college costs. The GI Bill, as the act is more commonly known, provided cash payments for tuition and living expenses to attend college. In addition, the bill provided low-interest loans for veterans to purchase homes as well as to start businesses. The intent of the GI Bill was to help the veterans of World War II adjust to life during peacetime. The program was very successful. It helped millions of veterans advance economically. A college education and home ownership have been seen as key components of entrance into the middle class. The generous benefits extended to World War II veterans can be seen in contrast to the sparse benefits extended to World War I veterans. World War I veterans staged a major protest in 1932, the "Bonus March," to pressure the government to provide them with bonuses that had been promised them.

WRONG CHOICES EXPLAINED:
(2) The Servicemen's Readjustment Act of 1944 (GI Bill) did not provide for the rapid demobilization of soldiers after World War II. The demobilization of over 12 million men and women in the armed forces at the end of World War II was a major logistical challenge. These men and women had to be brought back

to the United States and had to be out-processed at military bases. The process was carried out by the military. The GI Bill was intended to provide aid to veterans once they returned to civilian life.

(3) The Servicemen's Readjustment Act of 1944 (GI Bill) did not provide for pensions for soldiers from World War I. Earlier, in the 1930s, a controversy arose over bonuses promised to World War I veterans. Though the bonuses were not scheduled to be distributed until 1945, a group of unemployed and poor men argued that, because of the Great Depression, they were in a desperate situation and needed their money immediately. In June 1932, a group of World War I veterans, who called themselves the Bonus Expeditionary Force, or Bonus Army, marched into Washington, D.C., to demand that the administration of President Herbert Hoover extend them their bonus—a bonus that they had been promised for their service in the military. About forty thousand people (mostly veterans and their families) set up an encampment in the nation's capital to demand their money. The handling of the Bonus Marchers—which included aggressively dismantling the encampment—seemed to reinforce many people's perception of President Hoover that he did not have the interests of ordinary Americans at heart.

(4) The Servicemen's Readjustment Act of 1944 (GI Bill) did not provide for the establishment of a draft for all males over the age of 18. When World War II began, the draft applied only to men between the ages of 21 and 36. After the United States entered World War II in December 1941, the age range was expanded to cover men between the ages of 18 and 45. Currently, all males, from age 18 through age 25, must be registered with the Selective Service System. Selective Service is waiting for guidance in regard to registering women following a 2019 Supreme Court ruling that declared that an all-male draft registry was unconstitutional.

36. **2** Following World War II, the United States adopted the foreign policy of containment primarily to limit the spread of communism. After the war, the Soviet Union and the United States became rivals in the Cold War. The United States became increasingly concerned about the growing power of the Soviet Union and put forth a policy of attempting to prevent the expansion of communism, known as containment. President Harry S. Truman articulated this goal, which has come to be known as the Truman Doctrine, in a speech to Congress in 1947. Truman put the idea of containment into practice in 1947 by providing $400 million in military aid to Greece and Turkey to prevent those countries from becoming communist. Another example of the containment policy was the Berlin Airlift of 1948. Before the status of Berlin was settled, the Soviet Union decided it would prevent any food or other supplies from entering the western sector of

the city. The goal was for the Soviet Union to block the United States and its western allies from maintaining their presence in Berlin. Ultimately, the Soviet Union hoped to make all of Berlin part of what would become East Germany. The United States did not stand by idly when it learned of the Berlin blockade. President Harry Truman decided to send thousands of planes, filled with supplies, into the western sector of Berlin, in an action known as the Berlin Airlift. The Berlin Airlift prevented the western sector of Berlin from starving and prevented the Soviet Union from taking over the city. The formation of the North Atlantic Treaty Organization (NATO) was also part of the Cold War strategy of containment. NATO was created in 1949 by the United States and its allies to challenge the growing power of the Soviet Union. The members of NATO pledged that they would view an attack on any one member as an attack on all members.

WRONG CHOICES EXPLAINED:

(1) The foreign policy of containment, adopted by the United States following World War II, was not designed to return to pre-war isolationism. The containment policy—working with allies to prevent the spread of communism—involves American engagement in world affairs. Isolationism, on the other hand, entails American withdrawal from world affairs.

(3) The foreign policy of containment, adopted by the United States following World War II, was not designed to force European nations to end colonialism. The United States did not pressure its European allies to withdraw from colonialism after World War II. In many colonies, anti-colonial movements developed after World War II, leading to a broad move away from colonialism. India, for example, gained independence from Great Britain in 1947, and Algeria gained independence from France in 1962. In the second half of the 20th century, the United States itself has sought to withdraw from direct colonial control over other nations. Rather, it has sought to install and cultivate leaders that are generally supportive of United States interests.

(4) The foreign policy of containment, adopted by the United States following World War II, was not designed to support the work of the World Court. The World Court, formally known as the International Court of Justice, was founded in 1945 as the principal judicial organ of the United Nations (which was founded the same year). It continues to exist, and arbitrates international disputes and hears legal issues brought by different UN bodies.

37. **2** One important effect of President Dwight Eisenhower's proposal for interstate highways was a significant increase in suburban communities. The Interstate Highway Act initiated the biggest public-works project in United States

history—a nationwide network of superhighways. The federal government paid 90 percent of the costs of construction, with the states paying the other 10 percent. Between 1956 and 1966, the federal government spent $25 billion to build 40,000 miles of highways. Initiated during the Cold War, the government also saw the act as a defense measure. The highways would allow for quick movement of troops and heavy military equipment. The act was one of a series of developments that made suburbia a viable and desirable option. Housing became affordable in the suburbs. Innovative developers such as William Levitt took large tracts of land outside of major cities and built huge developments of nearly identical, modest houses. He applied the techniques of mass production to these houses, building them rapidly and cheaply. In addition, the government made low-interest loans available to veterans through the GI Bill. Finally, the deterioration of American cities made the suburbs seem more desirable. As older American cities, especially in the Northeast and the upper Midwest, experienced a decline in industrial jobs starting in the 1950s, unemployment, poverty, and crime increased.

WRONG CHOICES EXPLAINED:

(1) President Dwight Eisenhower's proposal for interstate highways did not result in an increase in health care spending. Later, in 1965, the Medicare program was created to provide health care for every American once they reached the age of 65; Medicaid was created that same year to provide health coverage to impoverished Americans. The Patient Protection and Affordable Care Act, passed under President Barack Obama in 2010, overhauled much of the health care industry.

(3) President Dwight Eisenhower's proposal for interstate highways did not result in an increase in educational opportunities. Many new schools opened in the United States in the 1950s. However, this development was primarily a result of the large number of "baby boom" children reaching school age in the 1950s, not a result of the Interstate Highway Act.

(4) President Dwight Eisenhower's proposal for interstate highways did not result in sectional differences. The term *sectional differences* describes the development of regions in the United States with distinct economic and political interests, and even distinct cultural practices. The most important sectional divide in American history has been between the North and the South. In the first half of the 1800s, the practice of slavery persisted and even grew in the South, while it shrank and was eventually eliminated in the North. If anything, the interstate highway system brought the different sections of the country together.

38. **4** One way President John F. Kennedy responded to the action referred to in the telegram was to support the commitment to a Moon landing by the end of the decade. In the telegram, Kennedy is extending his congratulations to the Soviet leader, Premier Nikita Khrushchev, for the Soviet Union sending the first human into outer space. In 1961, Yuri Gagarin, in his capsule Vostok 1, completed one full orbit of Earth. For several years, the Soviet Union had been outpacing the United States in regard to space exploration. In 1957, the Soviet Union launched the unmanned satellite, Sputnik 1, into orbit. The early accomplishments of the Soviet space program were humiliating to the United States. American officials vowed to catch up to and surpass their rival in the Cold War in regard to exploring space. In 1958, Congress created the National Aeronautics and Space Administration (NASA), initiating its space program. In May 1961, a month after Gagarin's mission, Kennedy announced the goal of landing a man on the Moon before the close of the 1960s. This goal was accomplished, as the United States was the first nation to successfully land men on the Moon in 1969.

WRONG CHOICES EXPLAINED:
(1) President John F. Kennedy's response to news that the Soviets had sent a man into orbit was not to decrease the budget for space exploration. The United States saw itself in a bitter rivalry with the Soviet Union. After news of the Soviets sending a man into orbit, the United States put more money into its space program and President Kennedy vowed to land a man on the Moon by the end of the 1960s.

(2) President John F. Kennedy's response to news that the Soviets had sent a man into orbit was not to expand the Peace Corps. The Peace Corps had just been established by Kennedy weeks before Gagarin's mission in 1961. Though both can be understood in the context of the Cold War, the Peace Corps was not a response to the space race. The Peace Corps gives support to developing nations in fields such as education, agriculture, and health care. The program depends on volunteers, often recent college graduates, to work on development projects in poor countries.

(3) President John F. Kennedy's response to news that the Soviets had sent a man into orbit was not to push for the removal of Soviet troops from East Berlin. Kennedy did not make such a push. Throughout the Cold War, the United States maintained troops in West Germany, and the Soviet Union maintained troops in East Germany.

39. **2** The actions listed in the question by presidents John F. Kennedy and Richard Nixon are examples of their attempts to establish peaceful coexistence with the Soviet Union. The United States and the Soviet Union became engaged

in a bitter Cold War after they had been allies in World War II. The Cold War was the period of tensions between the United States and the Soviet Union that lasted from the end of World War II (1945) to the collapse of the Soviet Union (1991). By the 1950s, many Americans had become increasingly fearful of the massive nuclear arsenals that both the United States and the Soviet Union had developed. In the early 1960s, President John F. Kennedy made attempts to ease tensions between the Soviet Union and the United States. The first action, establishing a direct telephone line between the governments of the United States and the Soviet Union, occurred in 1963, several months after the Cuban Missile Crisis brought the two nations to the brink of nuclear war. A "Memorandum of Understanding" was signed by representatives of the United States and the Soviet Union, to create a communications link between the Pentagon and the Kremlin. This hotline was never an actual telephone. The memorandum called for a text-based system. It was originally a teletype machine; later a fax machine (1986); and, finally, a dedicated computer link (2008). The hotline was implemented to forestall crises in the future. The second action, also in 1963, was the negotiating of the Nuclear Test Ban Treaty by the United States, the Soviet Union, and Great Britain (1963). The limited ban on testing nuclear weapons exempted under-ground tests. The third action, carried out by President Richard Nixon in 1972, was the sale of wheat to the Soviet Union. The Soviet Union had generally been producing considerably more wheat than the United States (up to three times as much). However, difficult weather conditions in 1971 and 1972 led to a serious wheat shortfall in the Soviet Union. The agreement Nixon made with the Soviets led to the sale of 10 million tons of wheat. The sale was later criticized because Nixon agreed to sell the wheat at subsidized pricing, costing the United States government $300 million. Further, the sale of such a large quantity of grain contributed to a sharp increase in grain prices in the United States. The initiation of surplus wheat sales to the Soviet Union was part of the broader policy of détente—a policy of reducing Cold War tensions and establishing warmer relations between the Soviet Union and the United States. The policy was initiated by President Richard Nixon, who became the first American president to visit Communist China and who held meetings with Soviet leaders in Moscow (both in 1972).

WRONG CHOICES EXPLAINED:

(1) The actions by presidents John F. Kennedy and Richard Nixon described in the question are not attempts to meet the Soviet Union's Cold War demands. The actions represent attempts at coexisting and negotiating with the Soviet Union, not giving in to its demands.

(3) The actions by presidents John F. Kennedy and Richard Nixon described in the question are not attempts to support Soviet troops fighting in Afghanistan. The United States was opposed to Soviet actions in Afghanistan; it

would not have supported Soviet troops. The Soviet Union invaded Afghanistan in 1979. President Jimmy Carter protested this act by suspending grain sales to the Soviet Union and boycotting the 1980 Summer Olympics in Moscow.

(4) The actions by presidents John F. Kennedy and Richard Nixon described in the question are not attempts to weaken the military power of the Soviet Union. The United States had an interest in reducing the military power of the Soviet Union, but the actions in the question involve negotiations and coexistence, not challenging Soviet military power.

40. **3** During the 1960s, the escalation of United States involvement in the Vietnam War was based on a belief that a North Vietnamese victory would lead to further losses as predicted by the domino theory. The domino theory asserts that when a nation become communist, its neighbors will be more likely to become communist. The name of the theory alludes to the game of lining up dominos in a row, so that when the first one is pushed over, the next ones in the row will each in turn be knocked over as well. The theory presumes that communism is imposed on a country from the outside—that it does not develop as a result of internal conditions. United States interest in Vietnam began in the 1950s when it sent military advisors and assistance to the government of South Vietnam after Vietnam was divided in 1954. The United States feared that South Vietnam would become a communist nation as North Vietnam had. The United States became heavily involved in the Vietnam War after Congress gave President Johnson a blank check with the Tonkin Gulf Resolution (1964). Despite the presence of over half a million United States troops and the firepower of the U.S. military, President Lyndon Johnson was not able to declare victory over the communist rebels in South Vietnam. As the war dragged on, and as the United States suffered more casualties, many Americans began to question the wisdom of American policies in Vietnam. United States involvement in Vietnam continued until 1973, when President Richard Nixon withdrew the last American troops. In 1975, the government of South Vietnam became communist.

WRONG CHOICES EXPLAINED:
(1) During the 1960s, the escalation of United States involvement in the Vietnam War was not based on a belief that restoring French colonial power was necessary for political stability in Southeast Asia. The French had been defeated in Vietnam in 1954. France's imperial aspirations had greatly diminished by the 1950s and 1960s as one French colony after another gained independence.

(2) During the 1960s, the escalation of United States involvement in the Vietnam War was not based on a belief that a strong military presence would limit Japanese trade with Vietnam. The United States was allied with Japan in the 1960s. It would not have tried to limit Japanese trade with Vietnam. Earlier, during the lead-up to American involvement in World War II, the United States organized an oil embargo against Japan (1941).

(4) During the 1960s, the escalation of United States involvement in the Vietnam War was not based on a belief that a cease-fire agreement would increase college protests. Protests occurred on college campuses in the 1960s *against* American involvement in Vietnam. Many of the protesters would have welcomed a cease-fire in Vietnam.

41. **1** The major effect of the Civil Rights Act of 1964 was that racial discrimination in public facilities was banned. The passage of the bill was one of the crowning achievements of the civil rights movement of the 1950s and 1960s. Before the passage of the act, a rigid system of segregation of the races, known as the Jim Crow system, dominated Southern life. Jim Crow laws segregated public facilities, such as railroad cars, bathrooms, and schools. These laws, which first appeared in the South after Reconstruction ended (1877), relegated African Americans to a second-class status in the South. Jim Crow laws became more prevalent after 1896 when the Supreme Court, in the case of *Plessy* v. *Ferguson*, accepted segregation as constitutional as long as the facilities for both whites and African Americans were of equal quality. This "separate but equal" rule was the law of the land until the Supreme Court found segregated schools inherently unfair in the *Brown* v. *Board of Education* decision (1954). The Civil Rights Act, signed by President Lyndon Johnson, extended this edict to all public facilities. In addition to ending the segregation of public facilities, the law also put additional powers into the hands of the attorney general to ensure that schools took steps to desegregate. In addition, the law also took measures to ensure that women, as well as African Americans, enjoyed equal treatment in the United States.

WRONG CHOICES EXPLAINED:

(2) The Civil Rights Act of 1964 did not extend citizenship and voting rights to Native American Indians. Earlier, the Indian Citizenship Act (1924) granted citizenship to about 125,000 indigenous peoples of the United States (out of approximately 300,000). By 1948, after some states withdrew the resistance to extending state voting rights, Native American Indians had voting rights throughout the United States.

(3) The Civil Rights Act of 1964 did not outlaw the use of poll taxes and literacy tests for voting. The following year, President Lyndon Johnson signed the Voting Rights Act, which ended these practices. Barriers that had been erected to prevent African Americans from voting were removed by the act. Voting practices on the state level were now subject to the scrutiny of the Department of Justice. African Americans began voting in large numbers; between 1965 and 1977, the number of African Americans elected in Southern states rose from seventy to more than two thousand.

(4) The Civil Rights Act of 1964 did not authorize busing to integrate schools. School busing became a controversial issue in the 1970s. In the years following the Supreme Court decision in *Brown* v. *Board of Education* (1954), which declared racial segregation in public schools to be unconstitutional, many American schools continued to remain largely segregated due to housing patterns. In *Swann* v. *Charlotte-Mecklenburg Board of Education* (1971), the Supreme Court addressed this form of *de facto* segregation and ruled that the federal courts could use busing as a means of desegregating schools.

42. **3** The Supreme Court decisions in *Gideon* v. *Wainwright* (1963) and *Miranda* v. *Arizona* (1966) both upheld the right to counsel for defendants in state criminal cases. The right to have a lawyer in criminal prosecutions is enshrined in the sixth amendment. However, the Constitution does not address how to handle situations in which defendants cannot afford a lawyer or are unaware that they have the right to a lawyer. The Supreme Court addressed the first situation in *Gideon* v. *Wainwright* (1963). Clarence Earl Gideon had been accused of breaking into a poolroom and stealing money from the cash register. The state court rejected his demand for a state-appointed lawyer. After defending himself and being found guilty, he appealed, eventually bringing the case to the Supreme Court. The Court ruled that the states must provide court-appointed lawyers to impoverished defendants. The Court addressed the second situation, in which defendants are unaware that they have the right to a lawyer, in *Miranda* v. *Arizona* (1966). Ernesto Miranda was arrested in 1963 for kidnapping and rape. When police questioned him, he confessed to the crime. He did not know that he had the right to have a lawyer present when he was being questioned, nor that he had the right to remain silent. In this decision, the Court ruled that arrested people must be read basic rights, now known as "Miranda rights," including the right to remain silent and the right to have a lawyer.

WRONG CHOICES EXPLAINED:

(1) Neither *Mapp* v. *Ohio* (1961) nor *Heart of Atlanta Motel* v. *United States* (1964) addressed the issue of the right to counsel for defendants in state criminal cases. In the case of *Mapp* v. *Ohio*, the Supreme Court ruled that evidence

obtained in violation of the fourth amendment protection against "unreasonable searches and seizures" must be excluded from criminal prosecutions in state and federal courts. In the case of *Heart of Atlanta Motel* v. *United States* (1964), the Supreme Court upheld the 1964 Civil Rights Act and asserted that private businesses such as the Heart of Atlanta Motel cannot ban African-American customers.

(2) Neither *Baker* v. *Carr* (1962) nor *Engel* v. *Vitale* (1962) addressed the issue of the right to counsel for defendants in state criminal cases. In the case of *Baker* v. *Carr*, the Supreme Court ruled that states must periodically redraw legislative districts so they have roughly equal numbers of people. In *Engel* v. *Vitale* (1962), the Supreme Court ruled that the Regents' Prayer, a state mandated prayer that was recited by public school children in New York State, was unconstitutional because it violated the doctrine of separation of church and state.

(4) Neither *Tinker* v. *Des Moines* (1969) nor *Roe* v. *Wade* (1973) addressed the issue of the right to counsel for defendants in state criminal cases. In the case of *Tinker* v. *Des Moines*, the Supreme Court ruled that a school board prohibition against students wearing black armbands in protest of the war in Vietnam was unconstitutional. The Court asserted that students in school had the right to free speech, including symbolic speech, as long as their actions did not interfere with the educational process. In *Roe* v. *Wade*, the Supreme Court ruled that states shall not prohibit women from having an abortion during the first two trimesters of pregnancy. Previously the decision had been left to the states, and many states forbade abortions. The Supreme Court reasoned that the Constitution guaranteed people the right to privacy. Abortion, they argued, was a decision that should be left to the woman with the advice of her physician.

43. **4** The graph supports the conclusion that, in every decade shown, the percentage of women in the labor force grew while the percentage of men in the labor force declined. The graph shows that only 30 percent of women in the United States were part of the labor force in 1950. By 1990, the figure rose to 57 percent. In 1950, 82 percent of men were part of the labor force; that figure dropped to 74 percent by 1990. The increase in the percentage of women participating in the labor force is often called the "quiet revolution." There are several reasons for this development. The economy experienced sustained growth in the post–World War II period. As the economy grew in the 1950s and 1960s, the job market expanded, drawing large numbers of women who had previously worked in the home. The number of jobs in fields that were seen as "women's work"—such as secretarial work and teaching—increased dramatically during this period. In addition, in the 1960s the women's liberation movement challenged

traditional gender expectations. Many women felt less pressure to marry at a young age, have children, and work at home. Also, the availability of the birth control pill and of abortions allowed women to have greater control over their reproductive lives. Many women made the decision to focus on a career first, thereby putting off decisions about whether to have children until later.

WRONG CHOICES EXPLAINED:

(1) The graph does not support the conclusion that older Americans remained in the labor force longer in 1990 than in 1950. The graph does not include information about the ages of people in the workforce; it includes information about the percentage of men and women in the labor force—collectively and broken down by gender.

(2) The graph does not support the conclusion that all Americans born during the baby boom after World War II joined the labor force. The graph indicates that in the decades after World War II, participation in the labor force for all men and women ranged between 55 percent and 65 percent. The percentages would be considerably higher if all baby boomers (born between 1945 and 1964) entered the labor force.

(3) The graph does not support the conclusion that half as many men were in the labor force in 1990 as compared to 1950. The graph does not provide absolute numbers; it only provides percentages. The percentage of the total number of men who were in the labor force did fall between 1950 and 1990. In 1950, 82 percent of men were in the labor force; in 1990, that figure was 74 percent. However, the overall number of men in the United States increased between 1950 and 1990, as the overall population increased from 160 million to 258 million. Therefore, the number of men in the labor force increased from 1950 to 1990.

44. **1** During the Persian Gulf War (1991), the primary aim of the United States was to force Iraq to withdraw its troops from Kuwait. The Middle East has loomed large in American foreign policy for decades. The United States has gotten a great deal of its oil from the region, and it has sought to maintain alliances and to prevent any Middle Eastern country from assuming a dominant role in the region. Therefore, President George H.W. Bush became alarmed in 1990 when Iraqi leader Saddam Hussein ordered an Iraqi invasion of Kuwait, another oil-rich Middle Eastern country. He insisted that the United States, with backing from allies and the United Nations, would take action to ensure Kuwaiti independence. President Bush carried out his pledge to defend Kuwaiti autonomy by organizing the Persian Gulf War in 1991. The American military operation in the Persian Gulf War, named "Operation Desert Storm," was successful. Hussein was

quickly forced to withdraw his troops from Kuwait, while the United States suffered relatively few casualties. Some criticized President Bush for not attempting to remove the dictator Saddam Hussein and supporting a transition to a democratic government in the country. However, when President George W. Bush did exactly that a decade later (2003), following the terrorist attacks of 2001, the United States failed to restore stability to Iraq after nearly a decade of military engagement.

WRONG CHOICES EXPLAINED:

(2) During the Persian Gulf War (1991), the primary aim of the United States was not to force Iraq to hold democratic elections; rather, it was to force Iraq to withdraw its troops from Kuwait. Later, in 2003, President George W. Bush attempted to support a transition to a democratic government in Iraq, following the terrorist attacks of 2001. That effort faltered as the United States failed to restore stability to Iraq after nearly a decade of military engagement.

(3) During the Persian Gulf War (1991), the primary aim of the United States was not to force Iraq to increase the price of its oil exports; rather, it was to force Iraq to withdraw its troops from Kuwait. The United States would want Iraqi oil exports to be lower in price, since the U.S. is one of Iraq's customers. Therefore, it would not want to force Iraq to increase the price of its oil exports.

(4) During the Persian Gulf War (1991), the primary aim of the United States was not to force Iraq to submit to weapons inspections by the United Nations; rather, it was to force Iraq to withdraw its troops from Kuwait. Following the war, the United Nations located and destroyed chemical weapons that Iraqi leader Saddam Hussein had developed and used in the 1980s. Iraq was then pressured to agree to United Nations inspectors. The United Nations Special Commission on Iraq (UNSCOM) was established to carry out these inspections. UNSCOM did not find any evidence of the production of weapons of mass destruction. However, in 2001, President George W. Bush insisted that Hussein was developing weapons of mass destruction that could be used against the United States and its allies. The Bush administration used this assertion to justify an invasion of Iraq in 2003. In the aftermath of this invasion, American forces failed to find evidence of such weapons.

45. **1** In 1993, many labor union leaders opposed United States membership in the North American Free Trade Agreement (NAFTA) because they feared it would cause Americans to lose jobs to foreign nations. NAFTA is an international trade agreement that has sought to encourage countries to participate in the global economy by reducing barriers to trade. NAFTA, ratified by Congress in 1993, eliminated all trade barriers and tariffs among the United States, Canada, and Mexico.

NAFTA was the subject of much controversy when it was promoted by President Bill Clinton. Free trade supporters promised global prosperity as more nations participated in the global economy. Opponents worried that nations would no longer be able to implement environmental regulations, ensure workers' rights, or protect fledging industries from foreign competition. Many economists see the push toward free trade agreements as an important factor in the decline of manufacturing jobs in the United States. A study by the Economic Policy Institute asserts that by 2010, the rise in the trade deficit with Mexico since the implementation of NAFTA led to the loss of almost 700,000 American jobs. It estimates that about 60 percent of these jobs were high-paying manufacturing jobs in states like Ohio and Michigan. Supporters of free trade argue that it generates overall economic growth and a more dynamic business sector, which ultimately leads to increases in job creation. Clinton's championing of NAFTA represents a conscious decision by Clinton to try to move the Democratic Party away from its liberal traditions and toward a more centrist approach.

WRONG CHOICES EXPLAINED:

(2) Union leaders did not base their opposition to the North American Free Trade Agreement (1993) on concerns about a reduction in the number of immigrants to the United States. First, NAFTA did not contain provisions related to immigration. Second, labor unions have frequently supported measures that would limit the number of immigrants allowed into the United States in order to protect American jobs from immigrants who might accept work at lower wages.

(3) Union leaders did not base their opposition to the North American Free Trade Agreement (1993) on concerns about increased exports from the United States to Mexico and Canada. The idea of NAFTA was to reduce tariffs and to increase trade among the United States, Mexico, and Canada—with an increase in both imports and exports. Labor unions would not oppose an increase in exports from the United States. An increase in exports would probably entail an increase in manufacturing and an uptick in hiring in the United States for manufacturing jobs.

(4) Union leaders did not base their opposition to the North American Free Trade Agreement (1993) on concerns about the outlawing of wage increases for workers in the United States. NAFTA did not contain provisions that would outlaw wage increases for American workers.

46. **4** According to the cartoonist, the investigation of intelligence failures related to the 9/11 terrorist attacks resulted in various federal agencies attempting to avoid criticism by shifting responsibility. The cartoon is adapting the seal of the United States for satirical purposes. The actual seal depicts a bald eagle with

its two wings jutting out to the left and the right. In the cartoon, the wings are replaced by two hands, with the index finger of each pointed in opposite directions. In the actual seal, the bald eagle is holding a banner containing the nation's traditional motto, "*E pluribus unum.*" In the cartoon, the motto is replaced with the word "Blame." The finger-pointing in the cartoon is meant to symbolize different agencies of the government pointing to other agencies in terms of assessing blame for the intelligence failures that occurred before the terrorist attacks on September 11, 2001. On that day, nineteen terrorists working with the al-Qaeda organization hijacked four domestic American airplanes. The idea was to turn the airplanes into missiles that would destroy symbols of American power and wealth. One plane was flown into the Pentagon, inflicting heavy damage, and one plane crashed in a field after the hijackers were overtaken by passengers. The other two airplanes did the most damage, crashing into the two towers of the World Trade Center in New York City. The damage inflicted on each building weakened the structures of each so that both buildings collapsed within two hours. Approximately three thousand people died from the four incidents, with the vast majority of the deaths occurring at the World Trade Center. In 2002, the government established the National Commission on Terrorist Attacks Upon the United States, also known as the 9/11 Commission, to examine the circumstances around the attacks, to assess intelligence lapses that might have occurred, and to make recommendations about steps that could be taken in the future to prevent similar attacks. The commission's final report, issued in July 2004, cited major lapses by both the Central Intelligence Agency and the Federal Bureau of Investigation. The chair of the commission, Thomas Kean, stated that both presidents Bill Clinton and George W. Bush were "not well served" by the nation's intelligence apparatus.

WRONG CHOICES EXPLAINED:

(1) The cartoonist is not asserting that the intelligence failures related to the 9/11 terrorist attacks resulted in praise for government efforts to stop intelligence leaks. The 9/11 Commission report focused on intelligence failures, not on intelligence leaks. The cartoon is not alluding to intelligence leaks.

(2) The cartoonist is not asserting that the intelligence failures related to the 9/11 terrorist attacks resulted in open immigration from all regions of the world. The cartoon is not alluding to immigration policies. Anti-immigrant sentiment increased in the United States in the years after the 9/11 terrorist attacks.

(3) The cartoonist is not asserting that the intelligence failures related to the 9/11 terrorist attacks resulted in recommendations to limit dependence on foreign intelligence. Neither the 9/11 Commission report nor the cartoon alludes to dependence on foreign intelligence. The report calls for greater collaboration between the United States and other countries in regard to intelligence gathering and sharing.

47. **2** Between 1881 and 1921, one major cause of the increasing number of immigrants to the United States was the increased job opportunities in industry. Between 1880 and 1920, an estimated 20 million people, from Russia, Italy, Poland, the Balkan region, and elsewhere, immigrated to the United States, most settling in industrial cities such as New York, Pittsburgh, and Chicago. In the late 1800s, workers were needed as America experienced rapid industrial growth. A variety of factors contributed to a dramatic increase in the industrial production of goods after the Civil War. Technological innovations, greater access to raw materials, new business and financial models, advances in marketing, and a growing labor force all contributed to the development of mass production. During the late 1800s, the era of small, locally oriented businesses began to give way to large corporations and trusts that came to dominate entire industries. The three most important industries of the era were railroads, the steel industry, and the oil industry. As the number of immigrants into the United States increased in the late 1800s and early 1900s, an anti-immigrant, nativist movement gained strength. Some members of the movement expressed prejudice against people who seemed "different." Others did not want immigrant workers to compete with Americans for jobs. Nativists were successful in the 1920s in pushing Congress to restrict immigration. The United States passed the Emergency Quota Act (1921) and the National Origins Act (1924), both of which greatly reduced the number of new immigrants allowed into the United States. These acts set quotas for new immigrants based on nationality. The quotas were in place until the Immigration and Nationality Act of 1965 ended the quota system.

WRONG CHOICES EXPLAINED:

(1) Between 1881 and 1921, the availability of free land in the Southeast was not a cause of the increasing number of immigrants to the United States. Earlier, the Homestead Act (1862) offered free land to people who were willing to settle it, but this applied to sparsely populated lands in the West, not to land in the more populated Southeast.

(3) Between 1881 and 1921, an increased need for military personnel was not a cause of the increasing number of immigrants to the United States. There was a need for military personnel in the United States after it entered World War I in 1917. However, immigration greatly declined during the years of the war. Further, the need for military personnel in a country would not be a positive incentive for people to immigrate to that country.

(4) Between 1881 and 1921, federal aid to pay the housing costs of new arrivals was not a cause of the increasing number of immigrants to the United States. The United States has not implemented such a policy. Earlier, in the mid-19th century, the federal government made free land in the West available to settlers, including immigrants, through the Homestead Act (1862). Later, the federal government

began creating housing projects for low-income families, including immigrant families, through programs such as Title II of the Housing Act of 1949. Furthermore, Section 8 of the Housing Act of 1937 authorizes rental assistance to be paid on behalf of low-income families, including immigrant families.

48. **1** Prior to its military involvement in both the War of 1812 and World War I, the United States attempted to maintain a policy of neutrality. The impulse to maintain neutrality in regard to European conflicts has been strong in United States history. President George Washington is closely identified with the idea of neutrality. In addition to issuing the 1794 Neutrality Act, he urged the United States to avoid "permanent alliances" with foreign powers in his Farewell Address. He did not want the newly independent nation, on precarious footing, to be drawn into the seemingly endless conflicts of Europe. President Thomas Jefferson (1801–1809) attempted to maintain a policy of neutrality in regard to the ongoing conflict between Great Britain and France. He passed the Embargo Act (1807) as a response to the harassment of U.S. shipping by Great Britain and France. Jefferson's act cut off all U.S. trade with any nation. Jefferson thought that this would pressure the belligerent nations to agree to leave U.S. ships alone. However, the main effect of the embargo was to cripple American trade. The embargo was meant to avoid warfare, but the United States eventually did go to war with Great Britain in 1812. A century later, the United States initially assumed that it could stay neutral in World War I (1914–1918) and maintain commercial ties to nations on both sides of the conflict. However, Great Britain successfully blockaded American ships from reaching Germany. Out of necessity, United States trade shifted to Great Britain exclusively. Germany responded by warning the United States that ships in the waters off of England would be subject to attack by U-boats, or submarines. The sinking of the British ocean liner *Lusitania* infuriated many Americans (128 Americans were among the dead). Germany, however, wanted to keep the United States out of the war and agreed in the Sussex Pledge (1916) to make no surprise submarine attacks on American ships. The United States took advantage of this pledge and traded extensively with Great Britain. In 1917, Germany rescinded the Sussex Pledge and declared that it would resume unrestricted submarine warfare; soon after, the United States abandoned its policy of neutrality and declared war on Germany.

WRONG CHOICES EXPLAINED:
(2) Prior to its military involvement in both the War of 1812 and World War I, the United States did not attempt to maintain a policy of internationalism. Internationalism describes an approach to foreign policy that emphasizes increased political or economic cooperation among nations. For most of its history, the United States avoided such involvement. Since World War II, it has

participated in internationalist organizations, including the United Nations, the World Bank, and the International Monetary Fund. Participation in such organizations has generated debate in the United States. Some argue that United States interests would be better served by scaling back its participation in multilateral agreements. In 2017, for example, President Donald Trump announced his intention to withdraw the United States from the Paris Climate Agreement.

(3) Prior to its military involvement in both the War of 1812 and World War I, the United States did not attempt to maintain a policy of collective security. For most of its history, the United States avoided the alliances and treaty organizations that would constitute collective security. This changed after World War II, when the United States attempted to build a system of alliances in carrying out the Cold War against the Soviet Union and its allies. In 1949, it participated in the formation of the North Atlantic Treaty Organization (NATO).

(4) Prior to its military involvement in both the War of 1812 and World War I, the United States did not attempt to maintain a policy of détente. *Détente* is the French word for loosening and refers to an easing of tensions in the Cold War and a warming of relations between the United States and the Soviet Union. The policy was carried out by President Nixon. In 1972, Nixon became the first United States president to visit Communist China and later that year he held meetings with Soviet leaders in Moscow.

49. **3** The statements in the question were included in the Supreme Court decision in *Brown* v. *Board of Education of Topeka* (1954). This 1954 decision concerned segregated schools. After the Civil War, a rigid Jim Crow system in the Southern states of the United States established separate facilities for African Americans and white people. These included separate waiting rooms at train stations, separate drinking fountains, and separate schools. In many cases, African Americans were simply barred from certain public facilities. This Jim Crow system was challenged in the Supreme Court case *Plessy* v. *Ferguson* (1896), but the Supreme Court ruled that separate facilities were allowable, as long as the facilities for both races were of equal quality. Even though the facilities for African Americans were routinely of inferior quality, this "separate but equal" doctrine was the law of the land until the middle of the 20th century. In the *Brown* case, the Court asserted that segregation in public schools was inherently unfair and detrimental to African-American students.

WRONG CHOICES EXPLAINED:
(1) The statements were not included in the Supreme Court decision in *Schenck* v. *United States* (1919). The decision in *Schenck* v. *United States* upheld the Espionage and Sedition Acts, which were passed during World War I to put limits on public expressions of anti-war sentiment. Charles Schenck and Elizabeth

Baer of the Socialist Party had been arrested for printing and distributing flyers opposing the war and urging young men to resist the draft. The Supreme Court argued that freedom of speech is not absolute and that the government is justified in limiting certain forms of speech during wartime. The Court argued that certain utterances pose a "clear and present danger." By analogy, the Court reasoned that one is not allowed to falsely shout "Fire!" in a crowded theater.

(2) The statements were not included in the Supreme Court decision in *Korematsu* v. *United States* (1944). The decision in *Korematsu* v. *United States* upheld Executive Order 9066 (1942), which had authorized the government to remove over 100,000 Japanese Americans from West Coast states and relocate them to camps in the interior of the United States. The order applied to both *Issei* (Japanese Americans who had emigrated from Japan) and *Nisei* (native-born Japanese Americans). Most of their property was confiscated by the government. In the *Korematsu* case, the Supreme Court ruled that the relocation was acceptable on the grounds of national security.

(4) The statements were not included in the Supreme Court decision in *Vernonia School District* v. *Acton* (1995). The decision in *Vernonia School District* v. *Acton* upheld the random drug testing of students. Opponents challenged random drug testing on the grounds that it amounted to a search without a warrant. The Supreme Court acknowledged that the drug tests amounted to a search, but ruled that a school could conduct them. The Court ruled that school districts have a legitimate interest in preventing teenage drug use.

50. **4** One common effect of the laws listed in the question has been to protect national security at the expense of civil liberties. Debates and conflicts over the proper balance between individual liberty and order have occurred throughout American history. The Alien and Sedition Acts (1798) were passed by a Federalist-dominated Congress in order to limit criticism from the opposition Republican Party during the undeclared Quasi-War with France (1798–1800). The acts were actually comprised of four acts. The Sedition Act made it a crime to defame the president or Congress. The broad wording of the Sedition Act seemed to challenge the free speech guarantees of the recently ratified first amendment. The Espionage Act (1917) was passed soon after the United States entered World War I. This act, along with the Sedition Act (1918), made it a crime to interfere with the draft or with the sales of war bonds, as well as to say anything "disloyal" in regard to the war effort. Charles Schenck and other members of the Socialist Party were arrested in 1918 for printing and distributing flyers opposing the war and urging young men to resist the draft. The case made its way to the Supreme Court after Schenck and fellow Socialist Elizabeth Baer were found guilty in a federal jury trial. The Supreme Court, in *Schenck* v. *United States* (1919), supported the position that during national emergencies, civil liberties may be

limited. The Court argued that freedom of speech is not absolute and that the government is justified in limiting certain forms of speech during wartime and other national emergencies. The Court argued that certain utterances pose a "clear and present danger." By analogy, the Court reasoned that one is not allowed to falsely shout "Fire!" in a crowded theater. The passage of the USA Patriot Act of 2001 occurred in the aftermath of the September 11, 2001 terrorist attacks on the United States. On that day, nineteen terrorists working with the al-Qaeda organization hijacked four domestic American airplanes. One plane was flown into the Pentagon, inflicting heavy damage, and one plane crashed in a field after the hijackers were overtaken by passengers. The other two airplanes did the most damage, crashing into the two towers of the World Trade Center in New York City. Approximately three thousand people died from the four incidents, with the vast majority of the deaths occurring at the World Trade Center. In October 2001, the government passed the USA Patriot Act, giving the government additional powers to carry out surveillance of American citizens. Many argue that the government is using a crisis to circumvent constitutional protections that were intended to be in effect in good times as well as bad. Others contend that the Patriot Act and other such measures have been important in preventing another major terrorist attack.

WRONG CHOICES EXPLAINED:

(1) The wartime laws mentioned in the question did not expand government regulation of the economy. During both world wars, the government created agencies to expand government regulation of the economy. The government sought to ensure a steady flow of materials needed for the war and to prevent inflation from spiraling out of control. During World War I, agencies such as the War Industries Board and the National War Labor Board were created. During World War II, President Franklin D. Roosevelt created the War Production Board, and later the Office of War Mobilization, to oversee the conversion from civilian industry to war production.

(2) The wartime laws mentioned in the question did not increase the nation's military defenses. During times of war, Congress routinely allocates sufficient funds to carry out military operations. During World War II, for example, the government increased income tax rates, sold savings bonds, and borrowed money to meet the enormous monetary requirements of the war.

(3) The wartime laws mentioned in the question did not promote immigration from neighboring nations. During World War II, the administration of Franklin Roosevelt initiated the *bracero* program in 1942 to bring into the United States temporary contract workers from Mexico. The Mexican government pushed the United States to guarantee that these temporary workers

would not be drafted. More than 200,000 Mexicans participated in the program, and it is estimated that at least that number came into the United States as undocumented workers.

PART II: THEMATIC ESSAY

Amendments

The United States Constitution was written to be a living document—that is, the framers wanted the Constitution be a document that could be adapted by future generations to address changing circumstances. This can be seen clearly in the procedure for adopting constitutional amendments. Though the process for amending the Constitution is cumbersome, the document has been amended twenty-seven times, including fifteen times since the end of the Civil War. Two of the post–Civil War amendments address voting. Though the rules around voting are generally left to the states, federal Constitutional amendments have addressed suffrage several times, including with the 15th amendment, barring discrimination in voting based on race, and the 26th amendment, ensuring that all citizens as young as 18 years old could vote. Both of these amendments have profoundly impacted American society.

The immediate circumstances surrounding the adoption of the 15th amendment, which prohibits race-based discrimination in voting, were the tumultuous events of the Civil War and Reconstruction. However, the reasons that the 15th amendment, along with the 13th and 14th amendments, was needed stretch back to the founding of the United States. From its inception, African Americans were thought of as inferior to whites, and were treated as such. The most obvious manifestation of white supremacy was slavery—a system that denied African Americans the most basic of rights. Slaves were denied autonomy over themselves and were excluded from participation in the American democratic system. Even free African Americans were often denied the right to vote.

The more immediate historical circumstances of the 15th amendment grew out of the Civil War. The war ended slavery and the adoption of the 13th amendment (1865) assured that it would not come back, but the future political status of African Americans following the war was unclear. In the immediate aftermath of the war, many members of the old slave-owning class were now back in power in the South. These men tried to replicate the conditions of the old South, including passing a series of restrictive laws known as the Black Codes. Post-war conditions were so similar to pre-war conditions that many Northerners wondered if they had "won the war, but lost the peace." In this atmosphere, a group of Radical Republicans in Congress initiated a more sweeping Reconstruction program, implementing much of it by overriding

President Andrew Johnson's vetoes. Their program included passage of the 14th amendment (1868) to guarantee African Americans citizenship and equal treatment under the law. After passage of the 14th amendment, the Radical Republicans came to see that lasting change could not occur in the South unless African Americans were guaranteed the franchise. This led them to push for adoption of the 15th amendment (1870), which prevented discrimination in voting based on race.

African-American men had, in theory, achieved the right to vote with the ratification of the 15th amendment. During the Reconstruction period, African Americans were able to exercise their right to vote and elected political officials throughout the South. In the 1870s, two African Americans were elected to the United States Senate—Hiram Revels and Blanche K. Bruce—and more than a dozen representatives were elected to the House of Representatives.

After Reconstruction ended, the South figured out ways to limit the impact of the 15th amendment by creating many obstacles to voting for African Americans. Many Southern states had in place literacy tests for voting. Often, local registrars would give African Americans especially difficult passages to read in order to prevent them from registering to vote. In addition, many African Americans in the rural South had limited literacy. Another obstacle to voting was the poll tax. People had to pay a fee to vote. This fee might have been beyond the reach of many African Americans. Finally, white Southerners frequently resorted to violence against those who insisted on their right to vote. Secret societies in the South—notably the Ku Klux Klan—used terror tactics, including lynching, to make African Americans feel insecure about their safety if they ventured to the registrar's office.

Though the amendment was systematically sidestepped for nearly a century, it laid the constitutional framework for a robust defense of voting rights in the 1960s. Following protests by the civil rights movement, the government passed the sweeping Voting Rights Act (1965), which outlawed many of the schemes used by Southern states to violate the intent of the 15th amendment. In addition, the 24th amendment to the Constitution (ratified in 1964) made illegal the use of poll taxes as a condition to vote in federal elections.

Just over a century after the ratification of the 15th amendment, the 26th amendment, which extends voting rights to citizens who are at least 18 years old, was ratified. Several important historical circumstances surround the adoption of the 26th amendment. The tumultuous decade of the 1960s had just ended. This was the decade in which "baby boom" children came of age and took center-stage in the era's dramatic cultural and political developments. On the cultural front, young people developed a vibrant counterculture that questioned the values of their parents' generation. The "hippie" movement became visible in the late 1960s in neighborhoods such as San Francisco's Haight-Ashbury and New York's Greenwich Village. In many ways, this counterculture represented a complete rejection of the materialistic conformity that many young people grew up with in the 1950s.

In regard to politics, it was young people who first questioned the purpose of the armed advisors who were sent to Vietnam in the early 1960s. The United States became heavily involved in the Vietnam War after Congress gave President Lyndon Johnson a blank check with the Gulf of Tonkin Resolution. In August 1964, Johnson announced that American destroyers had been fired upon in the Gulf of Tonkin, off the coast of North Vietnam. The Gulf of Tonkin Resolution can be considered the beginning of the war in Vietnam. Over the next several years, President Johnson escalated American involvement in the Vietnam War. Johnson sent hundreds of thousands of troops to Vietnam, reinstituted the draft, and began aerial bombardment of Vietnam. As the war dragged on, and as the United States suffered more casualties, many young Americans began to protest against American policies in Vietnam. Some thought the war was more of a civil war that the United States should not be part of. In addition, many Americans grew to oppose the war after seeing many unsettling images on television news programs. Families saw American soldiers burn down Vietnamese villages. They saw body bags coming back to the United States. They saw children burned by napalm. Finally, many young men began to oppose the war because they feared they might be drafted. Many of these young men began to see a cruel and unjust irony in United States policies. On the one hand, 18-, 19-, and 20-year-old men could be drafted into the Vietnam War, but on the other hand, these same men could not enter a voting booth to change the political leaders that were carrying out the war.

The call for lowering the voting age intensified as the war continued to drag on despite vocal protests by young people against it. By 1968, Johnson decided that his war policies imperiled his reelection, so he decided to not run for a second term. The following president, Richard Nixon, did not have any more success in moving the United States closer to victory in Vietnam. Congress heeded the call for lowering the voting age by passing the Voting Rights Act amendments of 1970 that mandated that states allow voters as young as 18 to vote. However, later that year, the Supreme Court ruled, in *Oregon* v. *Mitchell*, that Congress cannot mandate that states lower the voting age for state elections. In 1971, Congress introduced and passed the 26th amendment. Within four months of congressional approval, the amendment was ratified by the requisite number of states (thirty-eight), and became part of the Constitution.

The immediate impact of the 26th amendment has been mixed. In the first presidential election after its ratification, young opponents of the Vietnam War did not seem to have a significant impact on the presidential election. President Richard Nixon soundly defeated George McGovern, an outspoken opponent of the war. In the following decades, youth turnout in presidential elections has fluctuated. In the 1972 election, youth turnout was over 50 percent. It declined in the coming decades, but rose to just under 50 percent in the 2008 presidential election, when Barack Obama was elected. (By comparison, overall voter turnout has generally been in the range of 50 to 58 percent in recent decades.) More broadly, the official inclusion of young people into the body politic of the United States has encouraged young people to become more involved in political activism. Young people were prominent in the movement to divest from businesses involved with the apartheid government of South Africa in the 1980s. Since then, college campuses have been centers of activism around issues such as gun violence, climate change, and justice for the lesbian, gay, bisexual, transgender, and queer community.

The ratification of the 15th amendment in the 19th century and of the 26th amendment in the twentieth illustrate the flexibility of the United States Constitution to adapt to changing circumstances. Both amendments changed basic elements of the American political process by broadening the electorate and influenced American society in profound ways. The two amendments demonstrate the ongoing struggle to make America a more democratic nation and a "more perfect Union."

PART III: DOCUMENT-BASED QUESTION

Part A: Short Answer

Document 1

1a According to Henry F. Graff, one reason Pullman workers went on strike was that the Pullman Company announced wage cuts that averaged 25 percent, but it did not make any reductions in rents in its company-owned housing.

This answer receives full credit because it states one reason Pullman workers went on strike.

1b According to Henry F. Graff, one reason President Grover Cleveland was asked to send federal troops to Chicago was that violence had broken out between striking workers and deputies that were being paid by the Pullman Company.

This answer receives full credit because it states one reason President Grover Cleveland was asked to send federal troops to Chicago.

Document 2a and Document 2b

2 Based on the documents, one effect of President Cleveland's decision to send federal troops to end the Pullman strike was that Chicago was beset by violence and chaos as troops and striking workers engaged in violence that resulted in property destruction and at least four deaths.

This answer receives full credit because it states one effect of President Cleveland's decision to send federal troops to end the Pullman strike.

Document 3

3 According to Keith Lass and Greg Rickman, one effect of President Cleveland's decision to support railroad owners during the Pullman strike was that federal courts issued indictments against the leaders of the strike that dealt a major blow to organized labor that would not be reversed for forty years.

This answer receives full credit because it states one effect of President Cleveland's decision to support railroad owners during the Pullman strike.

Document 4a, Document 4b, and Document 4c

4a Based on the documents, one reason World War I veterans marched on Washington, D.C., in 1932 was to demand the immediate and full payment of bonuses that they had been promised for having served in World War I.

This answer receives full credit because it states one reason World War I veterans marched on Washington, D.C., in 1932.

4b Based on the documents, one reason President Herbert Hoover sent the United States Army to remove the Bonus Marchers was that violence had erupted between the marchers and the local Washington, D.C. police.

This answer receives full credit because it states one reason President Herbert Hoover sent the United States Army to remove the Bonus Marchers.

Document 5a and Document 5b

5(1) Based on the documents, one reason many Americans thought the government's action against the veterans was wrong was that the government used gas bombs and flames, which resulted in at least one death and injuries to at least 60 veterans.

5(2) Based on the documents, another reason many Americans thought the government's action against the veterans was wrong was that the veterans did not seem like a revolutionary mob; rather, they appeared to be like most Americans—out of work, poor, and in need of relief.

These answers receive full credit because they state two reasons many Americans thought the government's action against the veterans was wrong.

Document 6

6 According to Paul Dickson and Thomas B. Allen, one impact of the Bonus March was that it raised the issue of fair treatment of veterans and paved the way for the Serviceman's Readjustment Act (GI Bill) for veterans of World War II.

This answer receives full credit because it states one impact of the Bonus March.

Document 7a and Document 7b

7(1) Based on the documents, one reason African-American civil rights leaders called for an end to racial segregation in the armed forces was that African Americans in the military were primarily relegated to menial jobs and were rarely elevated to officer status.

7(2) Based on the documents, another reason African-American civil rights leaders called for an end to racial segregation in the armed forces was that the military was seen as an expression of the democratic values of the United States and that equal participation in such an institution would constitute a powerful argument for full and fair inclusion in civil society.

These answers receive full credit because they state two reasons African-American civil rights leaders called for an end to racial segregation in the armed forces.

Document 8a and Document 8b

8(1) Based on the documents, one result of President Harry Truman's order abolishing segregated "Jim Crow units" in the military was that African-American and white servicemen lived side-by-side at military bases, eating at the same mess-hall tables, socializing at the same bars, and participating in recreational activities together.

8(2) Based on the documents, another result of President Harry Truman's order abolishing segregated "Jim Crow units" in the military was that African-American and white servicemen fought side-by-side in the Korean War.

These answers receive full credit because they state two results of President Harry Truman's order abolishing segregated "Jim Crow units" in the military.

Document 9

9 According to Michael Lee Lanning, one way discrimination against African Americans continued after President Truman's executive order was

that communities adjacent to army bases frequently continued enforcing Jim Crow segregationist practices in regard to housing and education.

This answer receives full credit because it states one way discrimination against African Americans continued after President Truman's executive order.

Part B: Document-Based Essay

The president of the United States can invoke his powers as commander-in-chief of the armed forces to deploy troops to faraway places—such as Korea, Vietnam, and Afghanistan. However, the president can also use his military powers to respond to challenges closer to home. On several occasions the president has deployed troops to quell disturbances in the United States. Such deployments have often generated controversy, as many Americans have the expectation that the military would be used to deal with foreign threats and that local police and national guard troops (under the control of the nation's governors) would respond to domestic situations. Two dramatic and controversial instances of U.S. troops being used at home were President Grover Cleveland's use of troops during the Pullman strike (1892) and President Herbert Hoover's use of troops during the Bonus Army protests (1932).

The long-term historical circumstances that led to President Cleveland's use of federal troops in the Pullman strike include rapid industrialization in the United States and the rise of the union movement in the late 1800s. After the Civil War, entrepreneurs and innovators developed and adapted techniques to mass produce goods. Using interchangeable parts, steam power, the assembly line, scientific management techniques, and other innovations, American companies transformed the production process. Between 1860 and 1910, the value of products manufactured in the United States went up an astonishing ten times. Also, the number of people employed in industrial processes went up dramatically. However, the benefits of this economic growth were not evenly distributed. While the owners of big industrial firms, often referred to as "robber barons" by their critics, grew wealthy, the typical factory operative struggled to make ends meet. To rectify this situation, workers formed unions to collectively press for higher wages and better working conditions. Many workers thought they had a better chance of gaining concessions from owners if they banded together in unions. Unions made demands for better wages, improved conditions, or shorter hours. They could call a strike if their demands were not met by management. Workers did just that—call a strike—at the Pullman Company in 1894.

The Pullman strike was the immediate historical circumstance surrounding President Cleveland's decision to call out federal troops. The Pullman Company, which built railroad cars, cut wages several times in 1893 and 1894 for a total of approximately 25 percent. (Document 1) These wage cuts occurred during the hard times following the Panic of 1893. The country descended into the worst economic depression up to that point, with 1894 being the worst year of the downturn. (Document 1) The wage cuts were not accompanied by any cuts in rent for the workers. Many of the workers lived in the town of Pullman, built by the Pullman Company in 1880 as a model company town. The housing was better than most working-class housing, but was also approximately 25 percent costlier than housing in neighboring towns. (Document 1) Rents, as well as expenses for supplies from the company store, were taken directly out of the workers' wages.

When workers protested the wage cuts, the Pullman Company closed the plant. (Document 1) Under these circumstances, the workers appealed to the American Railway Union (ARU), led by Eugene V. Debs, to come to their aid. The Pullman strike went from being a local conflict to a national conflict when ARU members across the nation voted to support the strike by refusing to handle trains that contained Pullman cars. Railroad traffic was brought to a standstill. The company then had the idea of coupling each train with at least one car carrying the U.S. mail. In this way, the company could accuse the union of interfering with the delivery of the mail (a federal crime) and could count on the federal government to intervene. (Document 1)

At first, President Cleveland was reluctant to send in troops, but the company pressed the issue by convincing the attorney general to send in special deputies (paid for by the company). Violence ensued between the deputies and the strikers. At this point, the company successfully pushed Cleveland to send troops. (Document 1) The presence of troops worsened an already tense situation. The troops were greeted with four days of rioting. Seven hundred railroad cars were burned, the grounds of the recently closed Chicago's World's Fair were destroyed, several strikers were shot, and chaos ensued. (Documents 2a and 2b) Eventually, twenty-five strikers would be killed in the violence surrounding the Pullman strike.

President Cleveland's actions influenced events in the short term and in the long term. In the short term, the presence of the troops ended the strike in a bitter defeat for the union. The Supreme Court declared Cleveland's actions legal and justified in its decision in *In re Debs* (1895). In the long term, Cleveland's actions influenced American society by dealing a major blow to organized labor. It became clear that, when push came to shove, the federal government would come down firmly on "the capital side," even when it meant

U.S. troops firing upon and killing U.S. citizens. Furthermore, the courts took the lead of the president. Federal courts issued a sweeping indictment against the ARU and the leaders of the strike. (Document 3) The case went to the Supreme Court, which declared Cleveland's actions legal and justified in its decision in *In re Debs* (1895). The setback suffered by the labor movement in the aftermath of Cleveland's actions would be felt for another four decades. It would not be until the New Deal, according to historians Keith Ladd and Greg Rickman, that the labor movement would recover from the events around the Pullman strike. In 1935, President Franklin D. Roosevelt signed the Wagner Act, which strengthened unions by mandating that employers bargain with their unions. (Document 3) The act also established the National Labor Relations Board to conduct elections among workers to see if they wanted to be represented by a union. The act also banned certain unfair labor practices.

During the Great Depression, which lasted from 1929 to the beginning of World War II, the military was again called upon to deal with a domestic situation. President Herbert Hoover called on U.S. troops to disperse the Bonus March protestors who had set up an encampment in the nation's capital. The long-term historical circumstance of the actions in Washington, D.C., was the Great Depression. Starting in 1929, the economy began a descent into the worst economic crisis of the nation's history, surpassing the downturn following the Panic of 1892. Between 1929 and 1933, wages fell by 60 percent and unemployment tripled to over 12 million. With no safety net in place, families were forced out of their homes. Most cities had makeshift communities of shacks known derisively as "Hoovervilles." People picked through garbage cans for food and formed long lines at soup kitchens. People who had managed to save some money in the 1920s frequently lost their savings when banks failed.

The Great Depression was the backdrop to the more immediate circumstance surrounding the Bonus March—the demands of a group of veterans from World War I for promised bonuses following their military service. (Document 4c) Though the bonuses were not to be distributed until 1945, these men were in a desperate situation and wanted their money immediately. The House of Representatives was supportive of their demands. It voted to take up a bill to allow for the immediate payment of the veterans' bonuses, and it was all set to pass such a bill. However, the marchers had fewer friends in the Senate, which rejected the measure. (Document 4c) The president indicated that he would veto such a bill if it came before him. The press was also hostile to the Bonus Marchers.

The Bonus Marchers set up an encampment on the Anacostia Flats in Washington, D.C., and were allowed to maintain their encampment for several weeks. (Document 4a) But, by the end of July, President Hoover had had enough, especially after violence occurred between the protesters and the local police. (Document 4b) He informed the secretary of war that he wanted the encampment "evicted." The *Washington Post* reported that the army moved in on the Bonus Army using tear gas and force. Very quickly, one marcher was killed and sixty were injured as the army "routed" the Bonus Army and burned their shacks. (Document 5a) The secretary of war ordered General Douglas MacArthur to carry out the evacuation of the Bonus Marchers' camp. (Document 5b)

The immediate influence of Hoover's actions against the Bonus Marchers was that it damaged his reputation. The image of current members of the military taking up arms against former members of the military angered many Americans. Hoover was held responsible for the violence against the Bonus Marchers. The handling of the Bonus Marchers seemed to reinforce many people's perception of President Hoover that he did not have the interests of ordinary Americans at heart. The American people "needed an ally," according to historians Peter Jennings and Todd Brewster, and Hoover was not that person. Hoover's handling of the Bonus Marchers was one of the key factors that led to his losing the election of 1932 to Franklin D. Roosevelt. (Document 5b)

In the long run, the outcome of the Bonus March incident influenced the way American society treated its veterans. After seeing the veterans of World War I treated in a shabby manner, many Americans were resolved to not make the same error in regard to the veterans of World War II. In 1944, Congress passed the GI Bill, formally known as the Servicemen's Readjustment Act, to provide low-interest loans for veterans to purchase homes as well as funds to attend college. The intent of the GI Bill was to help the veterans of World War II adjust to life during peacetime. The program was very successful. Over the decades, it has helped millions of veterans advance economically. (Document 6)

Hoover's handling of the Bonus March was a setback for the veterans involved, but the episode established a pattern of people descending on Washington, D.C., to make their voices heard and to demand change. Historians Paul Dickson and Thomas B. Allen note that "millions of Americans" have followed in the footsteps of the Bonus March. (Document 6) In many ways, the same is true of the Pullman strike. Though the handling of it by President Cleveland dealt a setback to the cause of workers' rights, the strike would inspire other workers in the 20th century to take similar actions. By the 1930s, workers won the right to organize a union and to collectively bargain with their employers.

In both episodes—federal troops suppressing the Pullman strike and federal troops ousting the Bonus Marchers—ideas that were initially dismissed by government officials and much of the public as radical or impractical were later embraced by American society as the fair and decent thing to do. The Pullman strikers' insistence that workers be allowed to engage in collective bargaining and the Bonus Marchers' demand that the government provide veterans with funds to readjust to civilian life were violently rejected at first by the actions of federal troops, but in the ensuing decades came to be seen as commonplace provisions.

Topic	Question Numbers	*Number of Points
American political history	9, 11, 20, 22, 29, 34, 46, 50	10
Economic theory/policy	2, 13, 15, 28, 30, 31	7
Constitutional principles	3, 4, 8, 12, 17, 42, 49	8
American foreign policy	5, 7, 19, 21, 23, 32, 33, 36, 38, 39, 40, 44, 45, 48	17
American studies—the American people	10, 14, 16, 18, 24, 25, 35, 37, 41, 43, 47	13
Social/cultural developments	26, 27	2
Geography	1, 6	2
Skills questions included in the above content areas		
Reading comprehension	15, 17, 22, 26, 38, 39, 49, 50	
Graph/chart/table interpretation	14, 30, 31, 43	
Cartoon/image interpretation	16, 20, 24, 25, 34, 46	

*Note: The 50 questions in Part I are worth a total of 60 percent of the exam. Since each correct answer is worth 60/50 or 1.2 points, totals are shown to the nearest full point in each content category.

PART I

Multiple-Choice Questions by Standard

Standard	Question Numbers
1—United States and New York History	3, 5, 7, 10, 11, 13, 16, 19, 21, 22, 23, 25, 26, 27, 31, 32, 33, 40, 41, 46, 48
2—World History	36, 38, 39, 44
3—Geography	1, 6, 37, 47
4—Economics	14, 15, 18, 24, 28, 30, 34, 35, 43, 45
5—Civics, Citizenship, and Government	2, 4, 8, 9, 12, 17, 20, 29, 42, 49, 50

Parts II and III by Theme and Standard

	Theme	Standards
Thematic Essay	Change; Citizenship; Civic Values; Constitutional Principles; Diversity; Government; Individuals, Groups, Institutions; Reform Movements	Standards 1, 4, and 5: United States and New York History; Economics; Civics, Citizenship, and Government
Document-Based Essay	Citizenship; Civic Values; Constitutional Principles; Diversity; Government; Individuals, Groups, Institutions; Presidential Decisions and Actions	Standards 1, 4, and 5: United States and New York History; Economics; Civics, Citizenship, and Government

NOTES

NOTES